DK
WORLD
HISTORY
ATLAS

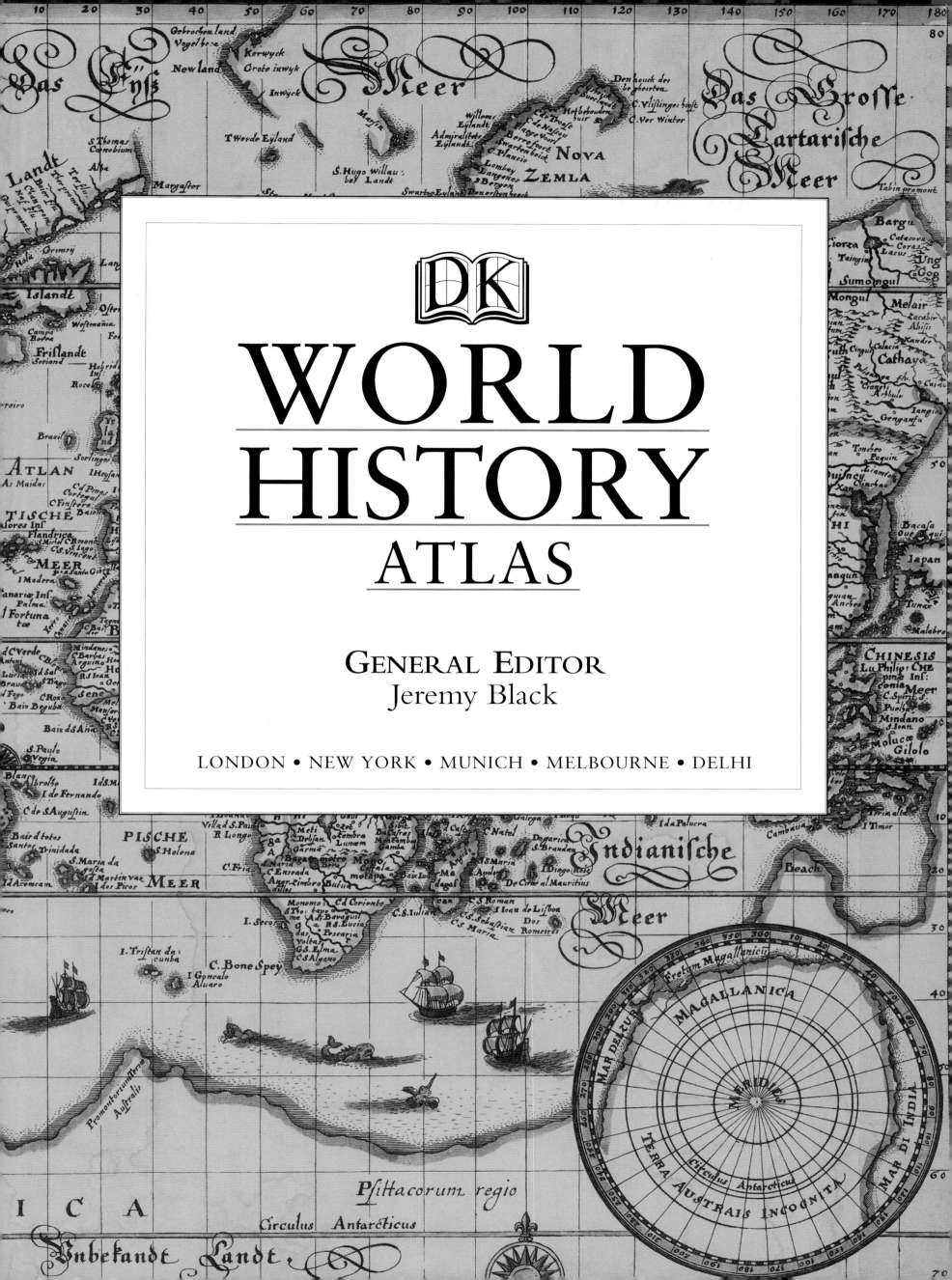

DK
WORLD
HISTORY
ATLAS

GENERAL EDITOR
Jeremy Black

LONDON • NEW YORK • MUNICH • MELBOURNE • DELHI

A DORLING KINDERSLEY BOOK
www.dk.com

CONSULTANTS

GENERAL EDITOR Professor Jeremy Black, Department of History, University of Exeter, UK

WORLD HISTORY
Professor Jerry Bentley, Department of History, University of Hawaii, USA
Professor James Chambers, Department of History, Texas Christian University, USA
Dr John France, Department of History, University of Swansea, UK
Dr Guy Halsall, Department of History, Birkbeck College, London, UK
Dr Chris Scarre, Department of Archaeology, Cambridge University, UK
H. P. Willmott, Royal Military Academy, Sandhurst, UK

NORTH AMERICA
Professor Donald S. Frazier, Department of History, McMurray University, Texas, USA
Professor Ross Hassig, Department of Anthropology, Oklahoma State University, USA
Dr Kendrick Oliver, Department of History, University of Southampton, UK
Professor George Raudzens, Department of History, Macquarie University, Sydney, Australia
Dr Brian Ward, Department of History, University of Florida, USA

SOUTH AMERICA
Dr Edwin F. Early, Department of Economics, University of Plymouth, UK
Dr Anthony McFarlane, Department of History, University of Warwick, UK
Dr Nicholas James, Cambridge, UK
Professor Neil Whitehead, Department of Anthropology, University of Wisconsin, USA

AFRICA
Professor John Thornton, Department of History, Millersville University, USA

EUROPE
Professor Richard Britnell, Department of History, University of Durham, UK
Dr Michael Broers, School of History, University of Leeds, UK
Professor Brian Davies, Department of History, University of Texas, San Antonio USA

EUROPE (continued)
Professor Michael Jones, Department of History, University of Nottingham, UK
Dr Don McRaild, Department of History, University of Sunderland
Dr Susan Rose, Department of History, Roehampton Institute, London, UK
Professor Peter Waldron, Department of History, University of Sunderland, UK
Dr Peter Wilson, Department of History, University of Sunderland, UK
Professor Spencer Tucker, Department of History, Virginia Military Institute, USA
Professor Edward M. Yates, Department of Geography, King's College, London, UK

WEST ASIA
Dr Ahron Bregman, Webster University, Regent's College, London, UK
Professor Ian Netton, School of Arabic Studies, University of Leeds, UK
Sajjid Rizvi, Department of Oriental Studies, Cambridge University, UK

SOUTH AND SOUTHEAST ASIA
Professor Joseph E. Schwartzberg, Department of Geography, University of Minnesota, USA
Dr Sunil Kumar, Department of Medieval History, University of New Delhi, India

NORTH AND EAST ASIA
Professor Gina Barnes, Department of East Asian Studies, University of Durham, UK

AUSTRALASIA AND OCEANIA
Dr Steven Roger Fischer, Institute of Polynesian Languages and Literatures, Auckland, New Zealand

The publishers would like to acknowledge additional contributions and advice from the following people: Professor Richard Overy, Professor Geoffrey Parker, Gordon Marsden, Professor Kenneth Kiple, Paul Keeler.

FOR THE SECOND EDITION

EDITORIAL DIRECTION Ailsa Heritage

Dr Paul Cornish, Centre for Defence Studies. King's College, London, UK
Dr Jane McIntosh
CIRCA Research and Reference Information, Cambridge, UK
Calum Macleod, Director, Great Britain - China Centre, London, UK

DORLING KINDERSLEY CARTOGRAPHY

EDITOR-IN-CHIEF Andrew Heritage

MANAGING EDITOR Lisa Thomas

SENIOR EDITOR Ferdie McDonald

PROJECT EDITORS Margaret Hynes, Elizabeth Wyse, Ailsa Heritage, Caroline Chapman, Debra Clapson, Wim Jenkins

ADDITIONAL EDITORIAL ASSISTANCE Louise Keane, Adele Rackley

SENIOR MANAGING ART EDITOR Philip Lord

PRINCIPAL DESIGNER Nicola Liddiard

PROJECT ART EDITORS Rhonda Fisher, Carol Ann Davis, Karen Gregory

CARTOGRAPHIC MANAGER David Roberts

SENIOR CARTOGRAPHIC EDITOR Roger Bullen

CARTOGRAPHIC DESIGN John Plumer

DIGITAL MAPS CREATED BY Rob Stokes

PROJECT CARTOGRAPHERS Pamela Alford, James Anderson, Dale Buckton, Tony Chambers, Jan Clark, Tom Coulson, Martin Darlison, Jeremy Hepworth, Chris Jackson, Julia Lunn, John Plumer, Alka Ranger, Ann Stephenson, Julie Turner, Peter Winfield

ADDITIONAL CARTOGRAPHY Advanced Illustration Ltd., Arcadia Ltd., Lovell Johns Ltd.

HISTORICAL CARTOGRAPHIC CONSULTANT András Bereznay

PICTURE RESEARCH Deborah Pownall, Louise Thomas, Anna Bedewell

JACKET DESIGNER Bob Warner

JACKET COPYWRITER Adam Powley

JACKET EDITOR Mariza O'Keeffe

INDEXING Julia Lynch, Janet Smy, Jo Russ, Sophie Park, Ruth Duxbury, Zoë Ellinson

DATABASE CONSULTANT Simon Lewis

SYSTEMS MANAGER Philip Rowles

PRODUCTION Stuart Masheter

First published in the United States as Atlas of World History by Dorling Kindersley Publishing Inc., 375 Hudson Street, New York, New York 10014
Copyright © Dorling Kindersley Limited, London 2000. Reprinted with Revisions 2001. Second Edition 2005
A Penguin Company

Library of Congress Catalog Card Number: 99-057342

Printed and bound by Star Standard, Singapore

Picture information: p.1 Andreas Cellarius, rector of the Latin school at Hoorn in northern Holland, produced this map of the eastern hemisphere in 1708 as part of his exquisite atlas of the heavens, *Atlas Coelestis; seu Harmonia Macrocosmica*. The map illustrates the seasons of the year and the various climate zones from pole to pole. pp.2-3 Produced in 1646, by Matthaüs Merian, a Swiss engraver. The geography in the map is based on world maps using the influential Mercator projection, produced by the Dutch Blaeu family, a dynasty of master cartographers. p.5 This 1598 Dutch engraving shows a cartographer at work, probably Rogerius Bullenius.

INTRODUCTION

SINCE THIS ATLAS was first published in 1999, the world has become a very different place. The process of globalization, already well under way by the end of the last century, has met with violent reaction and resistance, which has changed the international geo-political landscape in an unprecedented manner.

This new edition of the DK *World History Atlas* offers a history of the world relevant to the new Millennium, as we look back to see where we have come from and how we have created our world. Unlike other works of this type, we have produced an atlas that will make sense for all parts of the world. To achieve this, we have combined a comprehensive global overview of world history in Part One, with more detailed narratives of the development of each of the world's regions in Part Two.

This is not the only unique feature of this atlas. Again, unlike most historical atlases, this is a work that puts maps first, not simply a book with maps. The maps have been created using the most modern techniques and accurate digital data, drawing on the established state-of-the-art skills of DK as innovative map publishers. In addition, the atlas includes numerous examples of historical maps, setting past views on the world in contrast with modern knowledge.

The atlas is structured so that readers can look at history from a number of different angles: global, thematic, regional, and chronological. This offers a rich variety of approaches which allows the reader to form a comprehensive picture of the past.

The inclusion of past maps, both European and non-European, is valuable, as it reminds us that there are, and have been, many different ways of describing the world. Ours is not the only way to consider space, place, and the world.

A range of devices has been used to relate the past world to our own: the distribution of sites and cultures, political borders and structures, areas of cultural influence and political control, with arrows indicating the movements of peoples and the spread of technologies and ideas. Frequently, explanatory annotations have been added to the maps. Beyond the maps themselves, each page offers texts, chronological timelines, and carefully chosen pictures to build up as complete an impression of each period or historical episode as possible.

Change through time is multifaceted: political and economic, demographic and social, cultural and ecological. The DK *World History Atlas* attempts to cover all these features and, benefiting from a wide range of talent, it pushes forward the geography of the past as never before. It includes maps of familiar episodes from history and many more never previously described in cartographic form.

Mapping episodes through time demands dynamic narrative tools. The digital mapmaking techniques used in this atlas make it possible to offer exciting and informative perspectives and projections. The Earth can be seen from any viewpoint, creating explanatory yet accurate formats for the visualization of historical stories. The rigid orthodoxy of the north-oriented map is, after all, a relatively recent – and European – invention.

This atlas is produced with an awareness of the relationship between geography and history. It is up-to-date and of its time, not an atlas for all time, but the best possible for the new Millennium.

Since its first publication, foreign language editions of this atlas have appeared in Germany, Italy, Norway, Iceland, and Japan, and more are in preparation, significantly in many east and southeast European countries. We have received countless suggestions for adjustments and improvements from our co-publishers and from members of the public; all of these have been considered and, where possible, incorporated in this second edition. The publishers would like to thank all those responsible for such suggestions and contributions.

Jeremy Black,   November 2004

CONTENTS

PART ONE

ERAS OF WORLD HISTORY

GLOBAL CITIZENS at the beginning of the 3rd millennium are uniquely able to regard their world both as a totality and as a sum of its constituent parts. The first section of this Atlas presents history on a global basis, comprising a series of chronological overviews of the world across the last twenty millennia. These maps portray the changing map of the world and its cultures from ancient times down to the present day, accompanied by summaries of regional developments. Features highlighting the main technological advances of the period are complemented by maps or views of the world produced at the time. Each overview is followed by pages which examine aspects of the changing global scene – political, economic, religious, or demographic – which had a global impact during that period.

The Greek polymath Ptolemy wrote his famous *Guide to Geography* in the 2nd century CE, and his conclusions about the map of the world held sway until the 16th century. This woodcut map of the Ptolemaic world – incorporating Africa, Europe, and Asia – was published in 1486.

THE EARLY HISTORY OF HUMANITY

THE AUSTRALOPITHECINES, OR SOUTHERN APES, which emerged in Africa c.4.5 million years ago, possessed many apelike characteristics, but crucially had evolved the ability to walk upright. The best known of these species, *Australopithecus afarensis*, which is represented by the find of a skeleton of a small adult female, known as "Lucy," from the Hadar region of Ethiopia, may be ancestral to the earliest species of *Homo* (man), which emerged some 2.5 million years ago. The increased brain capacity of *Homo* was matched by the ability to make tools and control fire, vital cultural developments which enabled human ancestors to exploit a wide range of foods and colonize marginal environments. Fully modern humans, distinguished by their refined tool-making skills, resourcefulness, and ingenuity, were able to withstand the fluctuating and harsh climates of the last Ice Age and reach the most remote corners of the globe.

Human ancestors

The genus *Australopithecus* inhabited eastern and southern Africa between 4.5 and 1.7 million years ago. Australopithecines were small and sturdy, with apelike bodies, but they had mastered bipedalism, as finds of fossilized footprints, 3.6 million years old, from Laetolil in Tanzania testify. Four major Australopithecine species, classified by variations in their skulls and teeth, have been identified. The earliest known fossils of the *Homo* genus date to 2.5 million years ago. They are distinguished by larger brain size, rounded skulls, and a distinctively human formation to the hips and pelvis.

The virtually complete skeleton of a fully mature adult female, known as "Lucy," found at Hadar in Ethiopia, is c.3.4 million years old and belongs to the *Australopithecus afarensis* species.

Neanderthals

The Neanderthals, a separate and distinct branch of the *Homo* genus, evolved in Europe and West Asia about 120,000 years ago, surviving until up to 28,000 years ago. They had powerful heavy skeletons, with a projecting jaw, and broad nose and brow ridge, and their brains were the same size as those of fully modern humans. They adapted to a wide range of habitats and harsh climates. Neanderthal burials are clear evidence that they had developed cultural rituals.

The Neanderthal burial at Kebara in Israel is c.60,000 years old. The discovery of burials, often with items intended to equip the deceased for the afterlife, led to a revision of the view that Neanderthals were both brutal and primitive.

Prehistoric technology

A crucial development in the history of early technology was the appearance, about 1.3 million years ago, of stone handaxes, used for butchering hides, cutting wood, and preparing plant foods. Around 100,000 years ago, stone tools, shaped by striking flakes from the core, started to be made. Composite tools, where points, blades and scrapers were mounted in wooden or bone hafts, developed c.45,000 years ago.

Recent discoveries of a new australopithecine (*A.bahrelghazali*) stretch the geographical range 2,350 miles west of Great Rift Valley

Nearly complete remains of first hominid *Ardipithecus ramidus* dating to c. 4.4 million years ago, possibly ancestral to all the Australopithecines

Find site of "Lucy," skeleton of an adult female *Australopithecus afarensis*, dated to c.3.4 million years ago

Limited remains of first hominid *Australopithecus anamensis* dating to c.4.2 million years ago

Remains of hominid *Australopithecus anamensis* dating to c. 4.2 million years ago, possibly ancestral to *Australopithecus afarensis*

First finds of *Australopithecus boisei* c.2.7–1.7 million years ago

① Hominid ancestors

◆ *Ardipithecus ramidus*
Australopithecus remains
◇ anamensis
◇ afarensis
◇ africanus
◇ boisei
◇ robustus
◇ other

The skull of the "Taung child," is c.2.5 million years old. It was discovered in 1924 and revolutionized theories about human evolution.

Stone handaxes, such as these examples from Hoxne in eastern England dating to at least 100,000 years ago, were made by chipping away flakes to create a sharp, bifacial cutting edge. They became standard implements throughout Africa, Asia, and Europe.

The evolution of hominids

Hominid evolution is still a matter of dispute. The australopithecines, the earliest hominids, evolved some 4.5 million years ago. *Australophithecus anamensis* may be ancestral to the earliest species of *Homo*, the precursors of modern humans, which evolved some 2.5 million years ago. Alternatively, *Homo* may have evolved separately.

By around 30,000 years ago, tools and weapons had become infinitely more sophisticated, adapted both to the environment and methods of hunting, as demonstrated by the detailed carving and attention to function on these bone spearheads.

Human evolution

c.4.2 million years ago: *Australopithecus anamensis:* limited remains of bipedal hominid found on shores of Lake Rudolf	**c.3 million years ago:** *Australopithecus africanus:* notable for powerful build of upper body	**c.2.5 million years ago:** *Homo habilis:* large brain in relation to body size; thought to be maker of first stone tools; average male height, 1.32 m	**c.1.6 million years ago:** Earliest evidence of hominids in Asia	**c.1.3 million years ago:** First stone handaxes made	**c.800,000 years ago:** Archaic *Homo sapiens;* average male height, 1.75 m	**c.120,000 years ago:** Neanderthals: short-limbed, thick-bodied; average male height, 1.65 m. They disappear from Europe c.28,000 years ago	**c.45,000 years ago:** First fully modern humans in Europe

4,000,000 BP	3,000,000 BP	2,000,000 BP	1,000,000 BP	present

c.4.4 million years ago: *Ardipithecus ramidus:* nearly complete skeleton found at Aramis, Ethiopia	**c.3.8 million years ago:** *Australopithecus afarensis:* based on find of "Lucy" skeleton at Hadar, Ethiopia. Average male height, 1.5 m	**c.2.6 million years ago:** *Australopithecus boisei* with massive chewing muscles	**c.1.8 million years ago:** *Homo ergaster:* distinguished by long limbs; average male height, 1.77 m	**c.850,000 years ago:** Hominids reach Europe from Africa	**c.500,000 years ago:** Earliest well-attested evidence of use of fire	**c.150,000 years ago:** *Homo sapiens* (anatomically modern humans): earliest evidence in Africa

The emergence and spread of early humans

The first representative of the *Homo* genus, *Homo habilis* ("handy man"), emerged about 2.5 million years ago and was distinguished by the ability to make and use tools. *Homo ergaster*, which appeared about 1.8 million years ago, had a still larger brain capacity, tall, long-legged physique and ability to walk fully upright, and adapted successfully to a wide range of environments, rapidly spreading as far as East Asia, where it evolved into *Homo erectus*. The earliest fossil remains of fully modern humans, *Homo sapiens sapiens*, found in Africa, date to c.150,000 years ago. Resourceful and inventive, modern humans colonized the most marginal regions, and became the sole surviving human species.

Fossils of *Homo habilis* were discovered in the Olduvai Gorge in the 1960s, and are dated to 2.5 million years ago.

The fossils found at Koobi Fora in Kenya, dating to 1.7 million years ago, are amongst the earliest finds of *Homo ergaster*, and clearly demonstrate a marked increase in brain size.

Modern humans reached Europe from Africa c.45,000 years ago and replaced the Neanderthal population by 28,000 years ago. This skull was found at the site of Predmostí in eastern Europe.

SEE ALSO:

North America: pp.120–121

South America: pp.142–143

Africa: pp.160–161

Europe: pp.174–175

West Asia: pp.220–221

South and Southeast Asia: pp.240–241

North and East Asia: pp.258–259

Australasia and Oceania: pp.278–279

Evidence of *Homo erectus* community dating to c.450,000 years ago

Yuanmou Earliest evidence of hominids in East Asia, 1.7 million years ago

Sangiran Earliest evidence of hominids in maritime Southeast Asia, 1.3 million years ago

Teshik Tash Easternmost known expansion of Neanderthals; burial of child with a deposit of ibex horns

It is thought that early humanoids arrived in Europe from Africa c.1 million years ago

Bilzingsleben Evidence of big-game hunting and butchery at lakeside site

Neanderthal bones show that they suffered from diseases including arthritis and blindness

Modern-type humans were present here c.100,000 years ago, and seem to have coincided with Neanderthals – still present 60,000 years ago

Nariokotome The "Turkana Boy" is the most complete skeleton of a human ancestor, dating to 1.8 million years ago

Anatomically modern humans emerge in the south of continent 100,000 years ago

Klasies River Mouth Site of some of the earliest known of anatomically modern humans, c.100,000 years ago

Scale varies with perspective

13,340 km (8290 miles)

20,040 km (12,450 miles)

2 The emergence and spread of early humans

◆ finds of *Homo habilis*
◆ finds of *Homo ergaster*
◇ finds of *Homo erectus*
◆ finds of *Homo heidelbergensis*
◇ finds of Neanderthals
◇ finds of modern *Homo sapiens* (over 50,000 years old)

THE WORLD FROM PREHISTORY TO 10,000 BCE

FULLY MODERN HUMANS evolved in Africa between 200,000 and 100,000 years ago. With their tool-making skills and abilities to communicate and organize themselves into groups, these early hunter-gatherers were uniquely well-equipped to explore and settle new environments. By 30,000 years ago, they had colonized much of the globe. When the last Ice Age reached its peak 20,000 years ago, they were able to adapt; they refined their tool technology, enabling them to fully exploit the depleted resources, and used sturdy shelters and warm clothing to survive the harsh conditions. As the temperatures rose and the ice sheets retreated, plants and animals became more abundant and new areas were settled. By 9000 BCE larger populations and intense hunting had contributed to the near-extinction of large mammals, such as mastodons and mammoths. By 8000 BCE, in the Near East, groups of hunter-gatherers were living in permanent settlements, harvesting wild cereals and experimenting with the domestication of local animals. The transition to agriculture was under way.

HUNTER-GATHERERS AND THE ENVIRONMENT

Hunter-gatherers, whether semi-settled in one location or constantly on the move in search of food, would have carried a detailed mental map of important local landmarks. Precious water or food sources may have become centers of cultic activity, as in the rock painting below. Though its meaning is far from clear, the wavy vertical lines seem to represent cascades of water. The painting may even be a representation of a specific sacred site.

This painting, discovered at Kalhotia in Central India, seems to show a lizard or crocodile, cascades, a stream, and people carrying bundles of stone-tipped arrows.

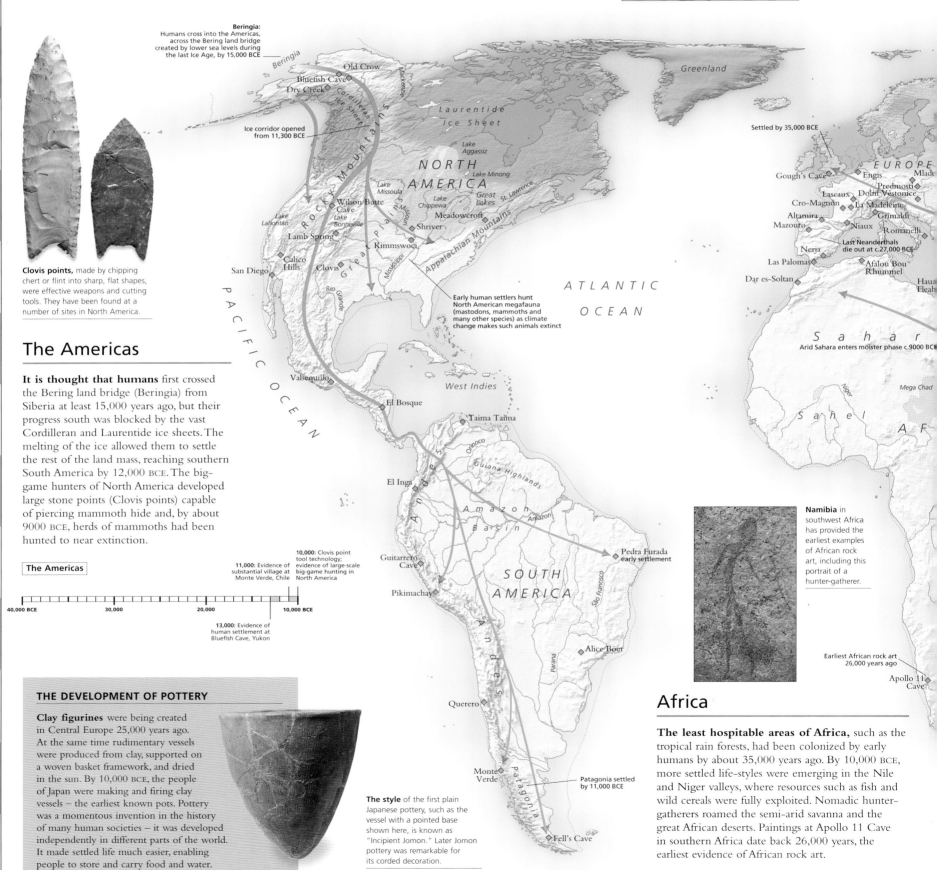

Clovis points, made by chipping chert or flint into sharp, flat shapes, were effective weapons and cutting tools. They have been found at a number of sites in North America.

The Americas

It is thought that humans first crossed the Bering land bridge (Beringia) from Siberia at least 15,000 years ago, but their progress south was blocked by the vast Cordilleran and Laurentide ice sheets. The melting of the ice allowed them to settle the rest of the land mass, reaching southern South America by 12,000 BCE. The big-game hunters of North America developed large stone points (Clovis points) capable of piercing mammoth hide and, by about 9000 BCE, herds of mammoths had been hunted to near extinction.

The Americas

40,000 BCE	30,000	20,000	10,000 BCE

11,000: Evidence of substantial village at Monte Verde, Chile

10,000: Clovis point tool technology; evidence of large-scale big-game hunting in North America

13,000: Evidence of human settlement at Bluefish Cave, Yukon

THE DEVELOPMENT OF POTTERY

Clay figurines were being created in Central Europe 25,000 years ago. At the same time rudimentary vessels were produced from clay, supported on a woven basket framework, and dried in the sun. By 10,000 BCE, the people of Japan were making and firing clay vessels – the earliest known pots. Pottery was a momentous invention in the history of many human societies – it was developed independently in different parts of the world. It made settled life much easier, enabling people to store and carry food and water.

The style of the first plain Japanese pottery, such as the vessel with a pointed base shown here, is known as "Incipient Jomon." Later Jomon pottery was remarkable for its corded decoration.

Namibia in southwest Africa has provided the earliest examples of African rock art, including this portrait of a hunter-gatherer.

Earliest African rock art 26,000 years ago

Africa

The least hospitable areas of Africa, such as the tropical rain forests, had been colonized by early humans by about 35,000 years ago. By 10,000 BCE, more settled life-styles were emerging in the Nile and Niger valleys, where resources such as fish and wild cereals were fully exploited. Nomadic hunter-gatherers roamed the semi-arid savanna and the great African deserts. Paintings at Apollo 11 Cave in southern Africa date back 26,000 years, the earliest evidence of African rock art.

Europe

Settled by modern humans by about 45,000 BCE, Ice Age conditions over much of Europe tested their ingenuity; wood, bone, hide, and antler were all used to build a range of shelters, and new tools – bows and arrows, spear-throwers, and harpoons – were used to hunt big game. As the climate stabilized, some sites were occupied year round, while others were used by seasonal hunters.

Portable art objects – sculptures and engravings of animals, like these chamois, on bone and antler, or small stone slabs or plaques – were being produced in Europe by 25,000 years ago.

West Asia

The world's earliest known burial, at Qafzeh Cave in Israel, dates back 100,000 years and is evidence of human self-awareness and ritual activity. By 13,000 BCE people from Wadi en-Natuf, also in Israel, were intensively harvesting, grinding, and storing the abundant wild grains which grew there. The same people also hunted gazelle herds, using drive lanes leading to traps.

This bone and shell necklace was one of the personal items found at a burial in Mugharet el-Kebara in Israel.

SEE ALSO:

North America: pp.118–119

South America: pp.144–145

Africa: pp.158–159

Europe: pp.174–175

West Asia: pp.220–221

South and Southeast Asia: pp.240–241

North and East Asia: pp.258–259

Australasia and Oceania: pp.280–281

Europe

c.45,000: Fully modern humans settle continent; new tool technology

10,000: Retreat of glaciers; temperate deciduous woodland spreads northward. Rich array of marine and land resources

26,000: Extinction of Neanderthals

120,000: Neanderthals present from western Europe to Central Asia

c.10,000: Large mammals, such as woolly rhinoceros, giant deer, and mammoth gradually become extinct

110,000 BCE   90,000   70,000   50,000   30,000   10,000 BCE

West and South Asia

100,000: World's first known burial at Qafzeh Cave, Israel

40,000: Neanderthals still present alongside modern humans in southwest Asia

13,000: Intensive harvesting of wild cereals by Natufian people, Israel

11,000: Dogs domesticated in Middle East; the world's first domesticated animals

45,000: Aurignacian flint tool technology developed in Israel and spreads across southern Europe

17,000: Evidence of wild cereal gathering in the Middle East

12,000: First use of grindstones in Middle East

110,000 BCE   90,000   70,000   50,000   30,000   10,000 BCE

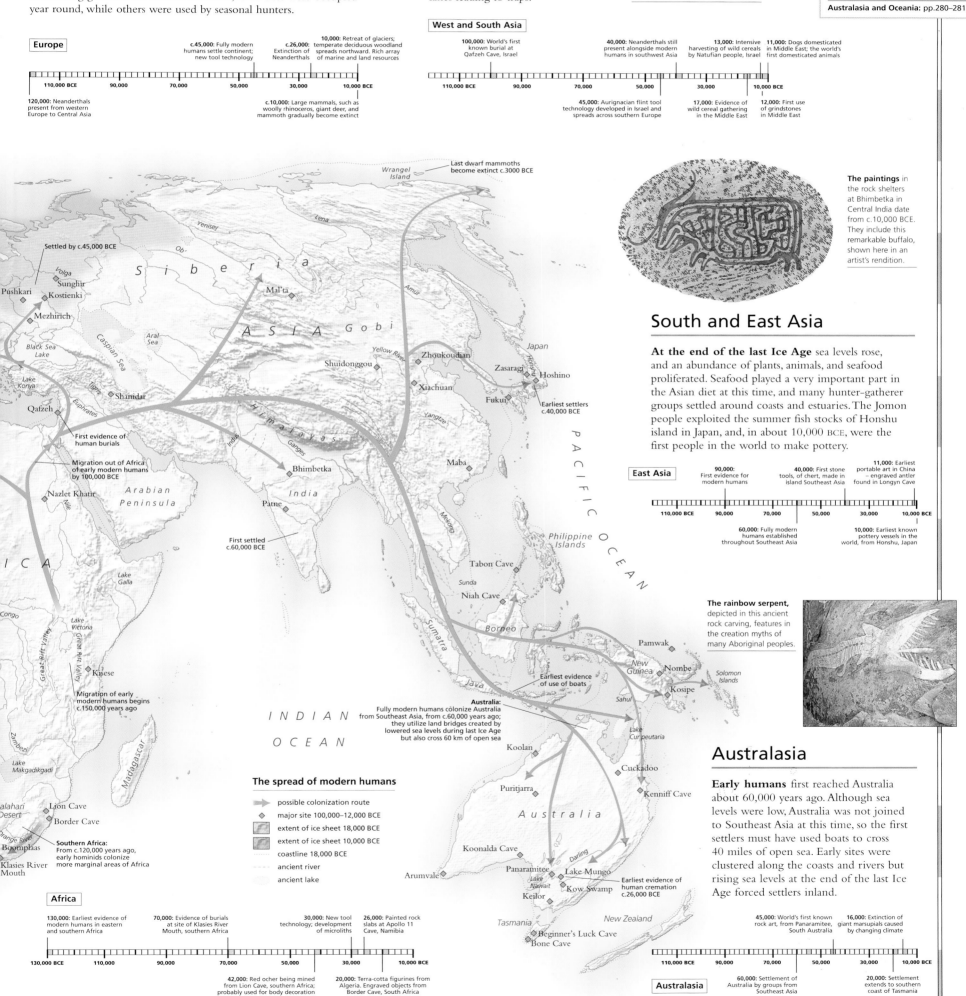

The paintings in the rock shelters at Bhimbetka in Central India date from c.10,000 BCE. They include this remarkable buffalo, shown here in an artist's rendition.

South and East Asia

At the end of the last Ice Age sea levels rose, and an abundance of plants, animals, and seafood proliferated. Seafood played a very important part in the Asian diet at this time, and many hunter-gatherer groups settled around coasts and estuaries. The Jomon people exploited the summer fish stocks of Honshu island in Japan, and, in about 10,000 BCE, were the first people in the world to make pottery.

East Asia

90,000: First evidence for modern humans

40,000: First stone tools, of chert, made in island Southeast Asia

11,000: Earliest portable art in China – engraved antler found in Longyn Cave

60,000: Fully modern humans established throughout Southeast Asia

10,000: Earliest known pottery vessels in the world, from Honshu, Japan

110,000 BCE   90,000   70,000   50,000   30,000   10,000 BCE

The rainbow serpent, depicted in this ancient rock carving, features in the creation myths of many Aboriginal peoples.

Australasia

Early humans first reached Australia about 60,000 years ago. Although sea levels were low, Australia was not joined to Southeast Asia at this time, so the first settlers must have used boats to cross 40 miles of open sea. Early sites were clustered along the coasts and rivers but rising sea levels at the end of the last Ice Age forced settlers inland.

### Map labels

Last dwarf mammoths become extinct c.3000 BCE

Wrangel Island

Settled by c.45,000 BCE

Pushkari
Kostienki
Sunghir
Volga
Mezhirich
Black Sea Lake
Caspian Sea
Aral Sea
Lake Konya
Tigris
Euphrates
Shanidar
Qafzeh
First evidence of human burials
Nazlet Khatir
Nile
Arabian Peninsula

Siberia
Ob
Yenisei
Lena
Mal'ta
ASIA
Gobi
Amur
Shuidonggou
Yellow River
Zhoukoudian
Xiachuan
Yangtze
Maba
Himalayas
Indus
Ganges
Bhimbetka
India
Patne
First settled c.60,000 BCE
Mekong

Japan
Zasaragi
Hoshino
Fukui
Earliest settlers c.40,000 BCE

PACIFIC OCEAN

Tabon Cave
Sunda
Niah Cave
Borneo
Sumatra
Java
Philippine Islands

Migration out of Africa of early modern humans by 100,000 BCE

Congo
Lake Victoria
Great Rift Valley
Green Rift Valley
Kisese
Lake Galla
Migration of early modern humans begins c.150,000 years ago

Lake Makgadikgadi
Madagascar
Zambezi
Lake Makgadikgadi

INDIAN OCEAN

Earliest evidence of use of boats

Australia:
Fully modern humans colonize Australia from Southeast Asia, from c.60,000 years ago; they utilize land bridges created by lowered sea levels during last Ice Age but also cross 60 km of open sea

Pamwak
New Guinea
Nombe
Kosipe
Solomon Islands
Sahul

Lake Carpentaria
Koolan
Puritjarra
Cuckadoo
Kenniff Cave
Australia
Koonalda Cave
Darling
Panaramitee
Lake Mungo
Earliest evidence of human cremation c.26,000 BCE
Arumvale
Keilor
Kow Swamp
Tasmania
New Zealand
Beginner's Luck Cave
Bone Cave

Kalahari Desert
Lion Cave
Border Cave
Orange River
Boomplaas
Klasies River Mouth

Southern Africa:
From c.120,000 years ago, early hominids colonize more marginal areas of Africa

The spread of modern humans

→ possible colonization route
◆ major site 100,000–12,000 BCE
▨ extent of ice sheet 18,000 BCE
▨ extent of ice sheet 10,000 BCE
— coastline 18,000 BCE
- - - ancient river
---- ancient lake

Africa

130,000: Earliest evidence of modern humans in eastern and southern Africa

70,000: Evidence of burials at site of Klasies River Mouth, southern Africa

30,000: New tool technology; development of microliths

26,000: Painted rock slabs at Apollo 11 Cave, Namibia

42,000: Red ocher being mined from Lion Cave, southern Africa; probably used for body decoration

20,000: Terra-cotta figurines from Algeria. Engraved objects from Border Cave, South Africa

130,000 BCE   110,000   90,000   70,000   50,000   30,000   10,000 BCE

Australasia

45,000: World's first known rock art, from Panaramitee, South Australia

16,000: Extinction of giant marsupials caused by changing climate

60,000: Settlement of Australia by groups from Southeast Asia

20,000: Settlement extends to southern coast of Tasmania

110,000 BCE   90,000   70,000   50,000   30,000   10,000 BCE

THE SETTLING OF THE GLOBE

This figure of a mammoth, carved from an animal's shoulder bone, dates from the last Ice Age.

MANY INNOVATIONS, such as sewn clothing, efficient housing, and a range of well-designed tools, enabled modern humans to adapt to a diversity of environments and colonize new areas. The melting of the glaciers at the end of the last Ice Age radically transformed the global environment; as the climate changed, with warmer temperatures and increased rainfall, food sources became more abundant and diverse, and populations increased.

In many regions, people began to live together in larger, more sedentary communities, working cooperatively and evolving more specialized roles within the group. Rituals and symbols were used to reinforce group identity – the beginnings of truly modern behavior.

Survival strategies

The challenging environments of the Ice Age and the rapidly changing conditions of the early postglacial world required a wide range of adaptations. In some regions, such as eastern Europe and North America, plentiful supplies of big game meant that hunters could depend on a specialized diet of mammoth, mastodon, or bison. In other regions, such as the fertile river valleys of the Middle East and East Asia, wild cereals – the ancestors of cultivated grains – were harvested. In Europe, a varied diet encompassed game, edible plants, and fish and shellfish, evidenced by deposits of discarded shells, or middens. The building of shelters was influenced by climate and local resources. Some shelters were portable, used by hunters following migrating herds; in other areas plentiful food supplies allowed year-round occupation.

Early peoples

27,000: Coldest phase of last Ice Age begins

19,000: Wild cereals harvested from shores of Lake Galilee

12,000: Grindstones in Fertile Crescent, to crush harvested seeds for flour

40,000 BP — 30,000 — 20,000 — 10,000 BP

35,000: Microliths developed as weapons in Africa

26,000: First known cremation, at Lake Mungo, Australia

20,000: Peak of last Ice Age

16,000: Climate starts to improve

12,000: Mammoth and woolly rhinoceros extinct in Eurasia

France

At Pincevent, in the Seine Valley, hunters following migrating reindeer herds around 14,000 BCE camped from midsummer to midwinter in portable tents, made of wooden poles covered by animal skins.

Israel

The El Wad cave on the eastern Mediterranean coast was used as a shelter by hunters stalking fallow deer in the nearby hills. The site may have been used during the summer months. The cave has been occupied many times in the past 100,000 years.

Ukraine

On the treeless, windswept steppes of the Ukraine, Ice Age mammoth-hunters, lacking wood, used the remains of their prey to build shelters. They constructed the walls from mammoth bones, which were then covered with animal hides, anchored down in high winds by heavy mammoth jawbones.

▼ **①** Different ways of life c.10,000 BCE

uninhabited and/or marginally inhabited areas

Coasts of Northern Europe: Shell middens indicate the importance of marine resources, as coastal lowlands are flooded by rising sea levels

Northern Eurasia: Mass extinctions of mammoth and woolly rhinoceros, probably caused by habitat changes. Deciduous forest, rich in deer, boar and aurochs, now spreads northward

Europe: Deciduous forests are rich in game, such as deer, aurochs, and wild boar

North America: Herds of big game, such as bison and mammoth, roam the Great Plains

Japan: Hunter-fishers and gatherers; shell middens reflect importance of shellfish in the diet

Sahara: Wetter conditions at the end of the last Ice Age turn desert to grassland; improved conditions attracted animals including elephants, lions, rhinoceroses, and hippopotami

Mainland Southeast Asia: Some sites located in upland caves and rock shelters

Middle East: Intensive harvesting of wild cereals c.12,000 BCE

Maritime Southeast Asia: Rising sea levels result in abundant marine resources. Evidence of hunter-gatherers is found along coasts and estuaries

Forest of west and central Africa: Groups of hunter-gatherers exploit small, tree-living game, such as monkeys

Amazonia: Early people ate fish and aquatic creatures such as turtles and manatee, as well as root crops

Kalahari Desert: Nomadic hunter-gatherers hunt and forage for seasonal plants

Australia: Arid conditions in the interior mean that early humans settle along coasts, estuaries and river valleys

Southern South America: Settled communities of hunter-gatherers exploit the forest resources c.10,000 BCE

Chile

In central Chile a village of timber buildings, roofed with animal hides, was built by early settlers at Monte Verde around 10,000 BCE. A small hearth was used to heat each hut; communal hearths were used for cooking.

Africa

In the more fertile conditions of the period, hunters foraging for seasonal plants in the Kalahari Desert built temporary shelters from brushwood branches.

Paleolithic art

The art of the last Ice Age and its aftermath, ranging from painted caves to engraved and finely carved objects and clay sculptures, is found in many parts of the world. Since much of this art is probably associated with religious rituals concerned with hunting, fertility, and the initiation of the young, it is a testament to the increasing complexity and sophistication of human society. One of the greatest flowerings of paleolithic art is undoubtedly the extraordinary painted caves of southwestern Europe, but there is evidence of a wide range of different regional artistic traditions, from the ocher-decorated rock shelters of Kisesse in East Africa to the rock art of Bhimbetka in South Asia, which dates to the coldest phase of the last Ice Age.

In the caves of southwest Europe, animals such as bison are depicted with grace and fluidity.

Hand stencils often dominate the part of the cave in which they are found. The red pigments could be made from either iron oxide or red ocher.

Hand paintings

Stencils of hands, made by blowing a spray of powdered pigment over the outstretched hand, are found on cave walls in both western Europe and Australia. The stencils may be associated with initiation rites – children's footprints have also been found in the European caves.

SEE ALSO:

North America: pp.116–117

South America: pp.140–141

Africa: pp.154–155

Europe: pp.170–171

West Asia: pp.216–217

South and Southeast Asia: pp.236–237

North and East Asia: pp.254–255

Australasia and Oceania: pp.276–277

◀ ❷ **Paleolithic art**

◦ early art site

European cave paintings

The caves of southwestern Europe, with their vibrant paintings and engravings of bison, deer, oxen, and horses, are unique. These images, often found in the darkest and most inaccessible parts of the caves, may have acted as forms of hunting magic or illustrated myths and traditions.

▼ ❸ **Painted caves and rock art**

◇ important rock art site

Portable art

Small plaques of engraved antler and bone, decorated ornaments of amber and ivory – including pendants and beads – and carved figurines of both animals and humans are found throughout Europe. Highly stylized female figurines *(right)* are possibly representations of the mother goddess, and may have been associated with fertility rituals.

The stone figure of the Venus of Willendorf *(left)* dates to c.20,000 BCE.

The pregnant female figure *(right),* from Lespugue, France, is thought to be 25,000 years old. It is carved from mammoth ivory.

❹ **Venus figurines in Europe** ▼

◇ important find of Venus figurines

Australia

The oldest rock engravings in the world, from Panaramittee, date to 45,000 BCE. Australian rock paintings and engravings are widespread; most designs are abstract, using lines, dots, crescents, and spirals. Some are thought to represent kangaroo and bird tracks.

Some of the earliest examples of Aboriginal rock carvings or petroglyphs – here in the form of circles and stars – are found at Wilpena Sacred Canyon in southern Australia.

▲ ❺ **Australian rock art**

◇ Panaramittee style rock engraving

▢ major rock art region

Early examples of human art

75,000: Geometric designs engraved on prepared pieces of ocher at Blombos Cave, South Africa

40,000: Ostrich eggshells, engraved with abstract patterns, from central India

29,000: Caves at Kisesse, East Africa decorated with ocher-stained palettes

26,000: Oldest rock paintings in Africa, from Apollo II Cave, Namibia

17,000: Cave paintings produced at Lascaux

45,000: Oldest rock engravings from Panaramittee, South Australia

32,000: Carved ivory statuette from Hohlenstein-Stadel Cave, Germany, is one of world's earliest figurines

25,000: Stylized female figurines found throughout Europe

20,000: Limestone pebble with human head from Aq Kupruk in central Asia

15,000: Hand stencils found in Wargata Mina Cave, Tasmania

THE WORLD 10,000–5000 BCE

IN THE MORE HOSPITABLE CLIMATE and terrain of the post-glacial world, groups of hunter-gatherers began to experiment with the domestication of wild cereals and animals. By 7000 BCE, farming was the main means of subsistence in West Asia, although hunter-gathering remained the most common form of subsistence elsewhere. Over the next 5000 years farming became established independently in other areas. The impact of the agricultural revolution on early societies was immense. Farming could support much larger populations, so settlement sizes increased significantly. Larger communities generated new demands and possibilities, and a class of specialized craftsmen evolved. Trade in raw materials and manufactured goods increased contact between farming communities. Communal ventures, such as irrigation, encouraged cooperation. All these developments paved the way for the much larger cities and states which were soon to follow.

THE FIRST USE OF METAL

The discovery that metals can be isolated from ore-bearing rocks by heating appears to have been made independently in West Asia and southeastern Europe between 7000–5000 BCE. Copper, gold, and lead, all soft metals that melt at relatively low temperatures, were the first metals in use. In early copper-using societies, most copper objects were decorative items that denoted the status of the owner: tools made from the new material could not compete with those of flint and stone.

This horned bull, fashioned from sheet gold is one of a pair from a rich set of grave goods unearthed at a cemetery in Varna, southeast Europe.

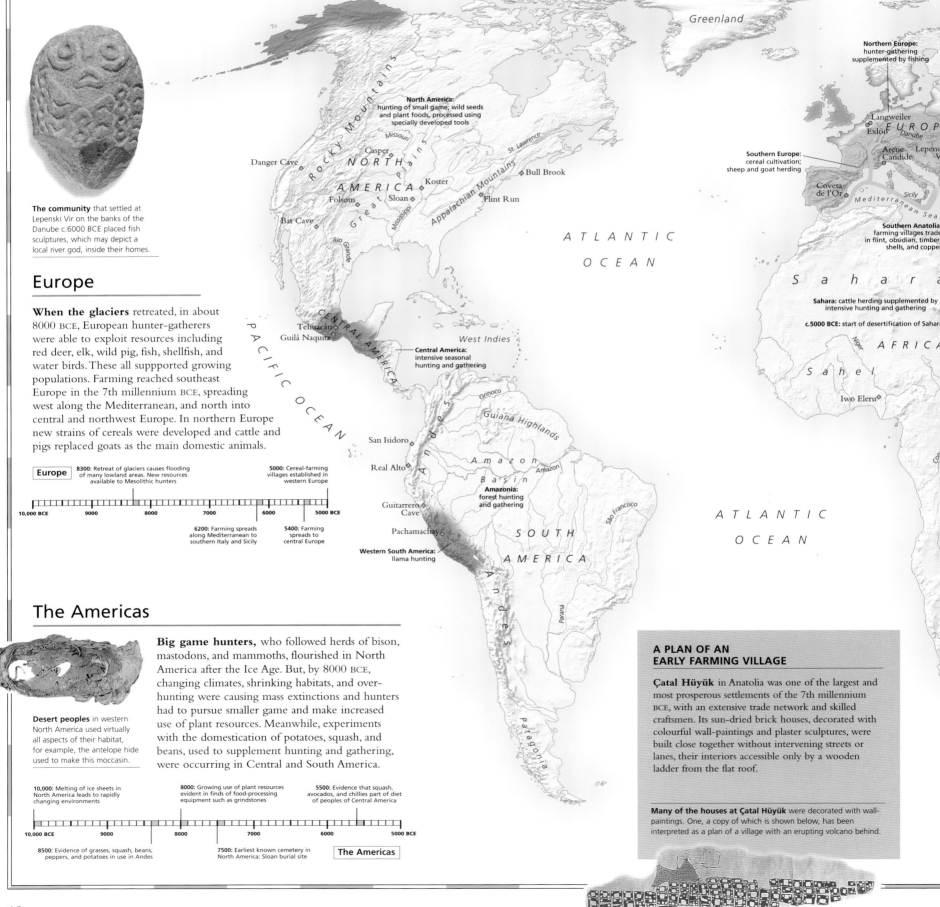

The community that settled at Lepenski Vir on the banks of the Danube c.6000 BCE placed fish sculptures, which may depict a local river god, inside their homes.

Europe

When the glaciers retreated, in about 8000 BCE, European hunter-gatherers were able to exploit resources including red deer, elk, wild pig, fish, shellfish, and water birds. These all supported growing populations. Farming reached southeast Europe in the 7th millennium BCE, spreading west along the Mediterranean, and north into central and northwest Europe. In northern Europe new strains of cereals were developed and cattle and pigs replaced goats as the main domestic animals.

Europe	
8300: Retreat of glaciers causes flooding of many lowland areas. New resources available to Mesolithic hunters	**5000:** Cereal-farming villages established in western Europe

10,000 BCE — 9000 — 8000 — 7000 — 6000 — 5000 BCE

6200: Farming spreads along Mediterranean to southern Italy and Sicily

5400: Farming spreads to central Europe

The Americas

Desert peoples in western North America used virtually all aspects of their habitat, for example, the antelope hide used to make this moccasin.

Big game hunters, who followed herds of bison, mastodons, and mammoths, flourished in North America after the Ice Age. But, by 8000 BCE, changing climates, shrinking habitats, and over-hunting were causing mass extinctions and hunters had to pursue smaller game and make increased use of plant resources. Meanwhile, experiments with the domestication of potatoes, squash, and beans, used to supplement hunting and gathering, were occurring in Central and South America.

10,000: Melting of ice sheets in North America leads to rapidly changing environments

8000: Growing use of plant resources evident in finds of food-processing equipment such as grindstones

5500: Evidence that squash, avocados, and chillies part of diet of peoples of Central America

10,000 BCE — 9000 — 8000 — 7000 — 6000 — 5000 BCE

8500: Evidence of grasses, squash, beans, peppers, and potatoes in use in Andes

7500: Earliest known cemetery in North America: Sloan burial site

The Americas

### Map labels

Greenland

Northern Europe: hunter-gathering supplemented by fishing

North America: hunting of small game; wild seeds and plant foods, processed using specially developed tools

Rocky Mountains
Missouri
Casper
NORTH AMERICA
Great Plains
Danger Cave
Folsom
Sloan
Koster
Mississippi
St. Lawrence
Appalachian Mountains
Bull Brook
Flint Run
Bat Cave
Rio Grande

Langweiler
Exloo
EUROPE
Danube
Arene Candide
Lepenski Vir
Coveta de l'Or
Mediterranean Sea
Sicily

Southern Europe: cereal cultivation; sheep and goat herding

Southern Anatolia: farming villages trade in flint, obsidian, timber, shells, and copper

ATLANTIC OCEAN

Sahara

Sahara: cattle herding supplemented by intensive hunting and gathering

c.5000 BCE: start of desertification of Sahara

AFRICA
Sahel
Niger
Iwo Eleru

PACIFIC OCEAN

CENTRAL AMERICA
Tehuacán
Guilá Naquitz

Central America: intensive seasonal hunting and gathering

West Indies

Orinoco
Guiana Highlands
Amazon Basin
Amazon

Amazonia: forest hunting and gathering

San Isidoro
Real Alto
Andes
Guitarrero Cave
Pachamachay

Western South America: llama hunting

SOUTH AMERICA
São Francisco
Paraná
Patagonia

ATLANTIC OCEAN

Congo

A PLAN OF AN EARLY FARMING VILLAGE

Çatal Hüyük in Anatolia was one of the largest and most prosperous settlements of the 7th millennium BCE, with an extensive trade network and skilled craftsmen. Its sun-dried brick houses, decorated with colourful wall-paintings and plaster sculptures, were built close together without intervening streets or lanes, their interiors accessible only by a wooden ladder from the flat roof.

Many of the houses at Çatal Hüyük were decorated with wall-paintings. One, a copy of which is shown below, has been interpreted as a plan of a village with an erupting volcano behind.

West Asia

The world's earliest farmers settled in the fertile arc of land stretching from the Persian Gulf to the eastern Mediterranean. Large-seeded grains were domesticated in Jericho by 8000 BCE. Villages of mud-brick houses appeared in Anatolia, and in central Mesopotamia by the 7th millennium BCE and craftsmen were smelting copper and lead by 6000 BCE. By 5500 BCE the farmers of southern Mesopotamia were irrigating arid land to improve crop yields.

Terra-cotta figurines of goddesses with swollen abdomens were found at Çatal Hüyük, suggesting a fertility cult.

West Asia

9000: Wheat (einkorn) harvested in Mesopotamia

8000: First fully domesticated cereals harvested in Jericho

7000: Goat becomes main domesticated animal throughout region. Foundation of settlement of Çatal Hüyük, Anatolia

6000: At Hassuna in northern Mesopotamia; painted pottery and copper and lead smelting

6500: Earliest known Old World textiles (linen) from Çatal Hüyük

5500: Ubaid culture of southern Mesopotamia harnesses spring floods of Euphrates for irrigation

10,000 BCE — 9000 — 8000 — 7000 — 6000 — 5000 BCE

East Asia

In northern China, agriculture dates back to c.7000 BCE. At farming villages such as Banpo, millet was cultivated and kept in grain storage pits, and there is evidence that pigs and dogs were domesticated. In a separate development, rice cultivation was initiated in the lowlands of the Yangtze delta, probably by 6000 BCE. In Japan, the Jomon people lived by hunting, fishing, and gathering in the well-stocked mountains and coastal waters. Although the Japanese were making pottery by 10,500 BCE, their way of life would remain based on hunting and gathering for several thousand years.

The people of Banpo were producing and firing pottery such as this cord-scored amphora by the 5th millennium BCE.

East Asia

9000: Limestone caves in central China give evidence of hunting, fishing, and gathering way of life

c.6000: Hunting and fishing villages in Yangtze river delta begin cultivating rice

5000: Jade imported into northern Manchuria from Central Asia or Siberia

6500: 'Jomon' pottery spreads throughout southern Japanese archipelago

10,000 BCE — 9000 — 8000 — 7000 — 6000 — 5000 BCE

SEE ALSO:

North America: pp.120–121

South America: pp.144–145

Africa: pp.158–159

Europe: pp.174–175

West Asia: pp.220–221

South and Southeast Asia: pp.240–241

North and East Asia: pp.258–259

Australasia and Oceania: pp.280–281

South and Southeast Asia

The first South Asian farmers were cultivating wheat and barley in the fertile highlands of northern India by the 5th millennium BCE. At the same time there was a gradual transition from hunting to farming, primarily rice, to the south of the Ganges valley. In Southeast Asia, post-glacial rises in sea levels created many new islands and estuaries with a marked increase in maritime resources. By c.2000 BCE farming had gradually become established in this region.

South and Southeast Asia

7000: Evidence of drainage and cultivation in the highlands of New Guinea

6000: Pottery in grave goods from Mehrgarh indicates trade with Central Asia

6000: First pottery production in mainland Southeast Asia

10,000 BCE — 9000 — 8000 — 7000 — 6000 — 5000 BCE

At Mehrgarh in the Baluchi highlands, burials took place in open spaces within the settlement; the dead were often accompanied by personal ornaments including bone, shell, and limestone beads.

The World in 5000 BCE

- intensive hunting and gathering
- centres of agricultural development
- secondary areas of settled agriculture
- → spread of farming
- ● early agricultural settlements and pre-urban sites 6000–5000 BCE
- ◆ hunter-gatherer sites

In Saharan rock art after c.5000 BCE hunting scenes such as these began to be supplanted by portrayals of domestic cattle, reflecting the transition towards pastoralism.

Africa

As the glaciers melted and rainfall increased, arid areas became habitable. Hunter-gatherers moved into the Sahara in about 9000 BCE. The semiarid grasslands of the desert and its southern fringes supported a variety of wildlife, including gazelles, giraffes, and elephants, while lakes and rivers were rich in fish. Many varieties of wild cereals grew in the Saharan region and in the fertile Nile valley. In about 3000 BCE, conditions in the Sahara became arid once again, forcing early settlers to move to more hospitable environments.

Africa

7500: Wavy-line pottery, made by dragging a catfish spine across the wet clay, introduced into Sahara and its southern fringes

8500: Saharan rock art depicts wide array of animals: elephants, giraffes, hippopotamus, rhinoceros

6500: Cattle successfully domesticated in North Africa

6000: Wheat and barley cultivation spreads to Nile Valley from Middle East

10,000 BCE — 9000 — 8000 — 7000 — 6000 — 5000 BCE

THE ADVENT OF AGRICULTURE

Fragments of Egyptian wavy line pottery, decorated with a fish spine from c.7000 BCE

THE APPEARANCE OF FARMING transformed the face of the Earth. It was not merely a change in subsistence – perhaps in some regions a necessity caused by over-hunting, limited natural resources, and population growth – it also transformed the way in which our ancestors lived. Agriculture, and the vastly greater crop yields it produced, enabled large groups of people to live in permanent villages, surrounded by material goods and equipment. Specialized craftsmen produced these goods, supported by the community as a whole – the beginnings of social differentiation. These developments led ultimately to the emergence of the first cities, but in 5000 BCE only a limited number of regions were fully dependent on agriculture. In many parts of the globe, small-scale farming was being used to supplement hunting and gathering – the first steps in the gradual transition to the sedentary agricultural way of life.

The agricultural revolution

The advent of farming brought large groups of people together into settled communities. Not only could food production be made more efficient, but animals could be tended communally, and food surpluses used to support villagers through the winter months. Some members of the community were therefore able to develop craft skills, engage in long-distance trade, and experiment with technology, such as pottery kilns, gold, and copper metallurgy and, by c.5500 BCE, irrigation. But sedentary coexistence also exposed people to infectious disease; the settlement of Çatal Hüyük, for example, was plagued by malaria.

Stone querns, dating to about 6000 years ago, were used by farmers for grinding grain into flour, which could then be kept in storage pits.

Ways of life

The exceptional productivity of the major cultivated species, in particular cereals, was vital to the viability of early farming villages. Cereals can be kept as a year-round resource, providing a staple supplement to more seasonal foods, thus creating a total dependence on farming. An inevitable, and necessary, by-product of this settled way of life was pottery – pottery containers could be used for both storing and cooking the harvested food. The technique of hand-modeling and firing clay pots evolved independently in many regions. Molds, wheels, and kilns were later innovations, and became the province of specialized craftsmen.

The earliest pottery had a round-based shape (right), and was sometimes decorated with incisions or impressions. A characteristic later vessel from western Europe was the flat-based beaker (left), again decorated with incisions. In other regions of Europe, notably the southeast, painted decoration was also used.

▼ **❶ The development of pottery**

Earliest era of widespread pottery production

- 11th millennium BCE
- 9th millennium BCE
- 8th millennium BCE
- 7th millennium BCE
- 6th millennium BCE
- 3rd millennium BCE
- ◇ first known pottery-making sites

Settlement and innovation

c.10,5000: Earliest pottery in the world, from southern Japan

9000: Earliest Chinese pottery

7000: First pottery in the Near East
7000: Foundation of Çatal Hüyük, Anatolia, the largest neolithic site in the Near East

6500: Small-scale copper smelting at Çatal Hüyük

5500: World's earliest irrigation system, at Choga Mami, Mesopotamia

5000: Gold and copper metallurgy in the Balkans

10,000 BCE — 9000 — 8000 — 7000 — 6000 — 5000 BCE

c.8500: Saharan rock art depicts wild animals, long since extinct in the region

c.7500: Characteristic "wavy line" pottery of the Sahara is produced

6500: Linen from Çatal Hüyük is earliest known textile in the world

6000: Pottery produced at Mehrgarh, Central Asia; First pottery in mainland Southeast Asia

5200: Bandkeramik pottery produced by farmers of central Europe

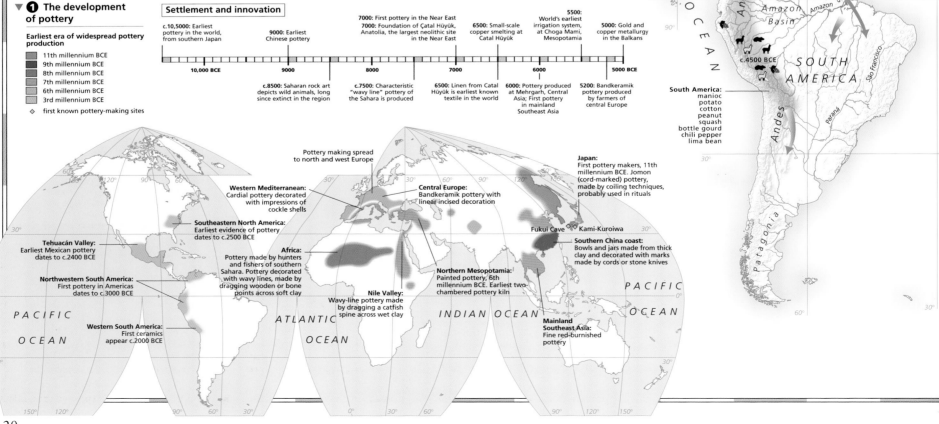

Pottery making spread to north and west Europe

Western Mediterranean: Cardial pottery decorated with impressions of cockle shells

Central Europe: Bandkeramik pottery with linear incised decoration

Japan: First pottery makers, 11th millennium BCE. Jomon (cord-marked) pottery, made by coiling techniques, probably used in rituals

Southeastern North America: Earliest evidence of pottery dates to c.2500 BCE

Tehuacán Valley: Earliest Mexican pottery dates to c.2400 BCE

Africa: Pottery made by hunters and fishers of southern Sahara. Pottery decorated with wavy lines, made by dragging wooden or bone points across soft clay

Nile Valley: Wavy-line pottery made by dragging a catfish spine across wet clay

Northern Mesopotamia: Painted pottery, 6th millennium BCE. Earliest two-chambered pottery kiln

Southern China coast: Bowls and jars made from thick clay and decorated with marks made by cords or stone knives

Northwestern South America: First pottery in Americas dates to c.3000 BCE

Western South America: First ceramics appear c.2000 BCE

Mainland Southeast Asia: Fine red-burnished pottery

Fukui Cave   Kami-Kuroiwa

### Map labels

Greenland

NORTH AMERICA

Rocky Mountains

Great Plains

Great Lakes

St. Lawrence

Appalachian Mountains

Missouri

Mississippi

Rio Grande

Gulf of Mexico

Eastern North America: sunflower sumpweed tepary bean

c.4500 BCE

c.4750 BCE

Central America: corn sweet potato manioc squash bottle gourd tomato avocado cotton

ATLANTIC OCEAN

Caribbean Sea

PACIFIC OCEAN

Equator

Orinoco

Guiana Highlands

Amazon Basin

Amazon

Andes

c.4500 BCE

1000 BCE

c.3000 BCE

SOUTH AMERICA

South America: manioc potato cotton peanut squash bottle gourd chili pepper lima bean

São Francisco

Paraná

Patagonia

PACIFIC OCEAN

ATLANTIC OCEAN

INDIAN OCEAN

PACIFIC OCEAN

Domestication

Domestication, a process of selecting and propagating beneficial traits in wild crops, occurred independently in a number of areas at different times, principally in the subtropical zone. Each region developed a dependence on different staple crops: wheat and barley in the Middle East and South Asia; millet and rice in China and Southeast Asia; corn in the Americas. Animals were also domesticated, and a process of selective breeding gradually enhanced useful traits. Sheep and goats, native to West and Central Asia, were domesticated for their meat, milk, hides and wool. Cattle were domesticated all over Eurasia, and eventually used to pull plows, thus increasing plant yields.

The early pastoral farmers of the Sahara made a number of paintings on rocks and in caves, depicting the animals they herded. Cattle are an important feature of these early paintings, some dating from 6000 BCE.

Wild einkorn has brittle stalks, which make it difficult to harvest.

Domestic einkorn has larger seeds and a tougher stalk than its wild form. It needs to be threshed in order for the seeds to disperse.

SEE ALSO:

North America: pp.120–121

South America: pp.144–145

Africa: pp.158–159

Europe: pp.174–175

West Asia: pp.220–221

South and Southeast Asia: pp.240–241

North and East Asia: pp.258–259

Australasia and Oceania: pp.280–281

Shelter

Since farming could support communities throughout the year, more time could be invested in the construction of permanent shelters, in building techniques and in the full exploitation of natural resources, from the timber, wattle and daub of northern Europe to the sun-baked mud brick of West Asia.

The farmers of Banpo, northern China, lived in thatched wattle-and-daub houses with a central hearth.

This lime plaster statue, dating to c.6800 BCE, from Ain Ghazal, Jordan was found in a burial pit. They were probably employed in public rituals or ceremonies.

Ritual

As people gathered together in large communities, there is evidence, in elaborate burials, shrines, and art objects, that ritual played a central role in their lives. The female deities of Çatal Hüyük were associated with the land's fertility, while in Jericho, ancestors were venerated.

21

THE WORLD 5000 – 2500 BCE

THE FERTILE VALLEYS of the Nile, Tigris, Euphrates, Indus, and Yellow rivers were able to support very large populations, and it was here that the great urban civilizations of the ancient world emerged. Although cities developed independently in several regions, they shared certain characteristics. Urban societies were hierarchical, with complex labor divisions. They were administered, economically and spiritually, by an elite literate class, and in some cases, were subject to a divine monarch. Monuments came to symbolize and represent the powers of the ruling elite. Elsewhere, farming communities came together to create ritual centers or burial sites, while craftsmen experimented with new materials and techniques, such as copper and bronze casting, and glazed pottery. All these developments indicate that urban and non-urban societies were attaining a high degree of social organization.

EARLY PERCEPTIONS OF THE COSMOS

The stone circles and alignments of northwestern Europe are extraordinary prehistoric monuments which have mystified successive generations. Astronomical observations are central to the ritual purpose of these structures; many have chambers or stone settings arranged to be illuminated by the Sun only on certain days, such as the winter or summer solstice.

central axis

Stonehenge became the preeminent ritual center of southern Britain c.2500 BCE. The rising sun on midsummer's day shines along the central axis of the site, but little is known of the ritual enacted there.

WHEELED VEHICLES

The origin of the wheel is uncertain; humans probably first made use of rotary motion in log rollers, and then in the potter's wheel. Wheeled vehicles were known in southwest Asia by 3500 BCE – a Sumerian pictograph from this period depicts a sledge equipped with wheels – and their use had spread to Europe and India by 3000 BCE. Early vehicles were probably ox-drawn, two-wheeled carts, on wheels formed from planks of wood secured with crosspieces.

This ceramic model of a two-wheeled bullock cart is from a grave at Harappa in the Indus Valley.

Greenland

Eastern Europe: Agriculture well established. Advanced copper technology

Scandinavia: Seasonal fishing communities

CORDED WARE BURIALS

Stonehenge · *Britain* · Carnac · *BEAKER BURIALS* · *Rhine* · *Danube*

Western Europe: Agriculture well established. Burial in megalithic tombs

Hunter-gatherers

Rocky Mountains

Great Lakes · *St. Lawrence*

Great Plains

MISSISSIPPI VALLEY

Appalachian Mountains

Southwest North America: Nomadic hunter-gatherers mainly dependent on wild plant foods

Rio Grande · *Mississippi*

Mississippi Valley: Sedentary hunter-gatherers dependent on year-round supply of wild food resources and occasional cultivation

CENTRAL AMERICA

Central America: Permanent settlements; slow transition from hunting and gathering to farming

ATLANTIC OCEAN

West Indies

Mediterranean Sea

S a h a r a

Sahara: Gradual desiccation. Inhabitants move to the periphery

Sudan

Niger

River Orinoco and River Amazon basin: Slow transition from hunting and gathering to horticultural villages

Orinoco · *Guiana Highlands*

Tropical Africa: Intensive use of forest resources

Sudan: Intensive use of wild finger millet and sorghum

A m a z o n   B a s i n · *Amazon*

PACIFIC OCEAN

Hunter-gatherers

São Francisco

Andes

Andes: Coastal groups live in large fishing camps

Congo

Kalahari Desert

Orange River

South America

The transition from hunting to farming was slow, but by 2500 BCE improvements in plant yields meant that farming could support larger communities. Permanent settlements on the western coast, and along river valleys, were living on rich marine resources and farming beans and squash. These communities built earthwork platforms up to 10 m high, surmounted by stone temples containing human burials and offerings. By 2600 BCE, large complexes of platforms, temples, and sunken courtyards, clearly regional ritual centers, were appearing.

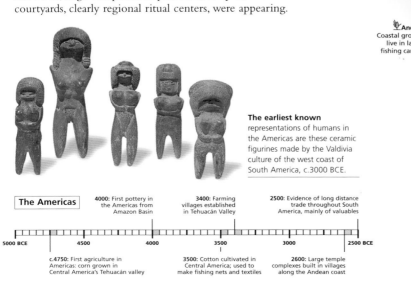

The earliest known representations of humans in the Americas are these ceramic figurines made by the Valdivia culture of the west coast of South America, c.3000 BCE.

Paraná · *Patagonia* · *Hunter-gatherers*

The pyramids at Giza were erected between 2530 and 2470 BCE. The first, the 147 m-high Great Pyramid of Khufu, was built during the annual Nile floods, when work on the land came to a halt. It took some 23 years to complete.

Africa

Pharaonic Egypt evolved from a series of fortified towns on the Nile into a formidable state, unified c.3000 BCE under its first divine ruler, King Narmer. A belief in life after death was a fundamental feature of this centralized state, and elaborate and well-equipped tombs were thought necessary for the afterlife. From about 2650 BCE the pyramids, a revolutionary new type of royal tomb, were built near the desert edge close to the capital city, Memphis. They represent a vast expenditure of resources and labor, illustrating the control the pharaoh exercised over his subjects.

The Americas	4000: First pottery in the Americas from Amazon Basin	3400: Farming villages established in Tehuacán Valley	2500: Evidence of long distance trade throughout South America, mainly of valuables

| 5000 BCE | 4500 | 4000 | 3500 | 3000 | 2500 BCE |

c.4750: First agriculture in Americas: corn grown in Central America's Tehuacán valley

3500: Cotton cultivated in Central America; used to make fishing nets and textiles

2600: Large temple complexes built in villages along the Andean coast

Europe

Elaborate burials, from the megalithic tombs of northern Europe to the large cemeteries of central and eastern Europe, indicate an increasing level of social organization among the scattered farming communities of the European continent. By the 3rd millennium BCE small farming communities were gathering to build defensive enclosures and to create regional centers. Stone circles, such as Stonehenge, or stone avenues, such as Carnac, were major communal undertakings which acted as social, economic, and ritual centers.

Skara Brae is a magnificently preserved prehistoric village on the Orkneys. The village consists of one-room houses of undressed stone, with paved walkways between them and a drainage system.

Europe

4500: Large cemeteries, for example on the western coast of the Black Sea, contain rich burials with elaborate gold jewelry	**3800:** Ditched enclosures around settlements in Central Europe create defended villages	**3200:** Stone circles and rows of standing stones built throughout northern and western Europe	

| 5000 BCE | 4500 | 4000 | 3500 | 3000 | 2500 BCE |

c.5000: Metallurgy discovered in southeastern Europe

c.4500: In western Europe, megalithic (large stone) chamber tombs, built as communal burial places

2900: Earliest burials containing Corded Ware pottery in northern and Central Europe

East Asia

As the early farming villages of China became more prosperous, new skills emerged. Farmers of the Longshan culture of eastern China invented the potter's wheel and were making eggshell-thin vessels by 3000 BCE; 250 years later they were raising silkworms and weaving silk. By 3000 BCE there was a marked difference between rich and poor burials, and walled settlements were appearing. The more complex social organization that these developments indicate was soon to lead to China's first urban civilization, the Shang.

This Kui (a pitcher with three hollow legs) is typical of Longshan pottery from the late 3rd millennium BCE.

East Asia

c.4000: Planned villages in northern China, with distinct residential, workshop, and burial areas

3000: First evidence of farming (millet cultivation) in Korea

2500: Banshan culture of western China produces boldly painted burial urns

| 5000 BCE | 4500 | 4000 | 3500 | 3000 | 2500 BCE |

c.3000: Potter's wheel invented during formative phase of Longshan culture of eastern China

South Asia

By 2500 BCE, an urban civilization had developed in the Indus Valley, dominated by Harappa and Mohenjo-Daro. At its height, the latter had a population of about 40,000. A network of residential streets, houses made with standardized bricks and sophisticated drains running into main sewers, overlooked by the "citadel," the religious and ceremonial focus of the city. Merchandise was traded as far afield as Mesopotamia.

The Harappans developed a pictographic form of writing which they used mainly on sealstones.

South Asia

5000: Evidence of use of pottery vessels at Mehrgarh and other Indus Valley settlements

2500: True cities emerge in Indus Valley. Cultural uniformity throughout Indus plain. Evidence of trade links with Central Asia and Mesopotamia

| 5000 BCE | 4500 | 4000 | 3500 | 3000 | 2500 BCE |

4500: Introduction of irrigation techniques in Indus Valley increases size and prosperity of farming settlements

3500: Indus Valley lowlands settled by farmers; walled towns develop

The royal standard of Ur depicts the Sumerian ruler at war and in peacetime. The panels are crafted in lapis lazuli and shell from as far away as Afghanistan.

West Asia

Mesopotamia's fertile floodplains were the crucible of the urban revolution. Uruk, one of the first city-states, developed c.3500 BCE. The early cities of Mesopotamia were built around the raised mud-brick temple complex. The temple administered much of the city's land and livestock and a priestly elite was responsible for recording and storing produce. The temple accounting system led to pictographic writing by c.3250 BCE.

*Map labels:*

Hunter-gatherers
Hunter-gatherers
Siberia
Gobi
Hunter-gatherers

Lena
Ob'
Yenisey
Amur

River Yenisey: Cereal cultivation

Pontic Steppes: Cereal cultivation

livestock herding

-GRAVE CULTURE

Aral Sea
Caspian Sea
Black Sea

Hattushash

Tell Brak

Yellow River Valley: Barley and millet cultivation

Iranian Plateau: scattered trading cities

Tigris
Euphrates
Mesopotamia

Susa
Uruk SUMER
Ur

Memphis

OLD KINGDOM OF EGYPT

Kachhi: Wheat and barley cultivation

Mehrgarh
Mohenjo-Daro
Harappa
INDUS VALLEY

Himalayas

Indus
Ganges

Ganges Valley: Wet rice cultivation

China

Yangshao LONGSHAN CULTURE

Korea

Yellow River
Yangtze

Japan: Hunter-gathering and fishing

Japan

Yangtze Delta: Wet rice cultivation

Arabian Peninsula

Nile

Upper Nile Valley: Wheat and barley cultivation

Deccan: Cattle pastoralists

Coastal Vietnam: Rice-farming villages, domesticated animals, bronze tools and ornaments

Mekong

Philippine Islands

PACIFIC OCEAN

Sumatra
Borneo
Java
New Guinea

Maritime Southeast Asia: Slow transition from hunting and gathering to farming

Hunter-gatherers

INDIAN OCEAN

Madagascar

Zambezi

Hunter-gatherers Australia

Darling

New Zealand

The world in 2500 BCE

- transition from hunting and gathering to agriculture
- agricultural areas
- urban areas
- urban hinterland

Africa

3400: First walled towns appear in Egypt

3000: Narmer unifies Upper and Lower Egypt and becomes first pharaoh. City of Memphis founded

2530: Construction of Great Pyramid of Khufu, the largest of the Egyptian pyramids, at Giza

| 5000 BCE | 4500 | 4000 | 3500 | 3000 | 2500 BCE |

3200: Earliest evidence of hieroglyphic writing system in Egypt

2650: The step pyramid of Zoser, the first Egyptian pyramid, is built at Saqqara

West Asia

c.3250: Pictographic clay tablets from Tell Brak: earliest evidence of writing

2500: City-states present throughout Mesopotamia and Levant

| 5000 BCE | 4500 | 4000 | 3500 | 3000 | 2500 BCE |

3500: Emergence of Uruk, the first city-state

2500: Rich array of grave goods at Royal Graves at Ur indicate extensive trade links

TRADE AND THE FIRST CITIES

This Egyptian ivory label is inscribed with the name of King Djet (c.3000 BCE).

BY 2500 BCE, CITIES WERE ESTABLISHED in three major centers: the Nile Valley, Mesopotamia, and the Indus Valley, with a scattering of other cities across the intervening terrain. The culmination of a long process of settlement and expansion – some early cities had populations tens of thousands strong – the first urban civilizations all relied on rich agricultural lands to support their growth. In each case, lack of the most important natural resources – timber, metal, and stone – forced these urban civilizations to establish trading networks which ultimately extended from the Hindu Kush to the Mediterranean. They imported a diverse range of goods: metals and precious stones, such as lapis lazuli, gold, and turquoise, met the demands of the growing social elites for luxury goods; diorite, limestone, and timber were needed for the monumental construction programs which were an integral part of urban life. Where trading contacts led, cultural influence followed, and cities soon began to develop in the trading hinterlands of the Iranian Plateau and Anatolia.

Ur: a trading city

The ancient city of Ur, was the capital of a south Mesopotamian empire toward the end of the 3rd millennium. It was a major economic center, with extensive trade links extending as far as Dilmun (Bahrain) and the cities of the Indus. Ships laden with gold, copper, timber, ivory, and precious stones had access to the Persian Gulf via canals which linked the city to the Euphrates. Archives of clay tablets record, in minute detail, transactions and ships' cargoes. The wealth this trade generated is reflected in the grandiose buildings which adorned the city, most notably the ziggurat dedicated to the city's deity, Ur-Nammu, and in the lavishly furnished burials of Ur's so-called "Royal Graves."

Cities and trade

c.3500: Rise of city-state of Uruk

c.3100: Sumerian trading post at Habuba Kabira, Syria. Sumerian merchants have their own quarters in Persian city of Godin Tepe

c.2500: City of Ur in southern Mesopotamia is a major center of trade and manufacture

c.2500: Indus Valley trading colony of Shortughai, 1000 km from Harappa, supplies gold and lapis lazuli

3500 BCE   3000   2500 BCE

c.3300: First walled towns in Egypt: Hieraconpolis and Naqada

c.3100: City of Byblos is founded on the Levantine coast

c.2500: The city of Ebla in western Mesopotamia begins to trade with Mediterranean peoples

1 Ur

- sacred enclosure
- royal palace
- other building
- ···· inner walls
- ▓▓ outer walls

[Map of Ur: city walls, Fortress, Northern Harbor, Palace, Temple, Royal Mausolea, houses c.1800 BCE, Temple of Enki, Canal, Temple of E-Nun-Mah, E-Dub-Lal-Mah, Palace of E-Khursag, Court of Nanna, Late Babylonian quarter, Shrine of Nanna, Giparu of Amar-Sin, Ziggurat, E-Temen-ni-Gur of Ur-Nammu, houses, Western Harbor, city walls, Canal, Euphrates]

200 meters
200 yards

Transportation

The long-distance trading networks of the ancient world required revolutionary developments in transportation. Much of the trade was maritime; the cities of Mesopotamia all had access, via rivers and canals, to the Persian Gulf and Indus Valley, and there is ample evidence for trade along the Gulf coast and Arabian Sea to the mouth of the Indus. The timber boats of the Nile, depicted carrying great columns of granite and alabaster, are known from tomb reliefs, models, and burials. Overland trade was dependent on newly-domesticated beasts of burden, such as donkeys and camels. Wheeled carts, pulled by oxen and bullocks, were also used.

A high-prowed reed boat can be seen on this impression from a cylinder seal from Uruk, dating to the 4th millennium BCE. The boat is being used to transport a priest or ruler, probably as part of a religious procession.

Egyptian culture was based on and around the Nile River, which offered the most effective means of transport. Some of the earliest vessels with sails were developed in Egypt.

This copper model from Tell Agrab, Mesopotamia, shows a two-wheeled chariot drawn by onagers, a type of wild donkey. Wheeled vehicles were used for both trade and warfare.

Levant: Coastal trade between Egypt and Mesopotamia

Egypt: The Nile enabled cargoes of precious metals and building materials to be shipped downriver from Nubia

[Map showing EUROPE, Black Sea, Caucasus, GREECE, Anatolia, Kızıl Irmak, Lake Van, Lake Urmia, Kültepe, Tarsus, Habuba Kabira, Ebla, Tell Brak, Hasanlu, Nineveh, Crete, Cyprus, Nuzi, Ashur, Kermanshah, Eshnunna, Syrian Desert, Mari, MESOPOTAMIA, Mediterranean Sea, Byblos, Sippar, PALESTINE, Kish, Nippur, Uruk, Ur, Heliopolis, Memphis, Saqqara, Sinai, Arabian Peninsula, EGYPT, Abydos, Naqada, Hieraconpolis, El Kab, Edfu, Elephantine, Tropic of Cancer, Sahara, Red Sea, NUBIA, AFRICA]

Inventions and innovations

c.5000: Copper first used in Mesopotamia

c.4500: First use of sail, Mesopotamia

c.4000: Use of plow in Mesopotamia

c.3250: Pictographic tablets from Uruk, southern Mesopotamia; earliest evidence of writing

c.3200: Wheeled carts buried in tombs of rulers of Ur and Kish

5000 BCE   4500   4000   3500   3000 BCE

c.3100: Development of cuneiform script in Mesopotamia. Experiments with bronze-working

SEE ALSO:

Africa: pp.158–159

West Asia: pp.174–175

South and Southeast Asia:
pp.240–241

❸ Archaeological sites and evidence of trade

◇ site location

Finds of:

🔲 chlorite vessel

▣ Gulf stamp seal

⬡ Indus carnelian beads

▤ Indus inscriptions

Trade in the 3rd millennium BCE

The active trade between Mesopotamia, the Iranian Plateau, and the Indus Valley can be traced through finds of traded goods. Indus Valley carnelian beads and inscribed seals, possibly recording the names of merchants, are found throughout southern Mesopotamia. Vessels made of chlorite schist, a soft mineral rock from southern Persia, are also found throughout the region. Dilmun (Bahrain) was an important Gulf entrepôt and trading post for copper from Oman, trading with both the main Mesopotamian ports of Ur and Lagash and the Indus Valley. Finds of Gulf stamp seals reflect the extent of Gulf trading contacts.

The Iranian Plateau was rich in chlorite schist, lapis lazuli, carnelian, gold, and silver. Imported chlorite, used to make this bowl from southern Persia, can be found throughout the region from Mari in the west to Mohenjo-Daro in the east.

Indus seals, used to stamp clay sealings securing bales of merchandise, have been found in Mesopotamia. The short inscriptions may record merchants' names.

This figure of a ram eating a bush is perhaps a table support from the Royal Graves at Ur. It is made of gold, silver, shell, and lapis lazuli – evidence of Ur's thriving long distance trade links.

❷ Urban centers and trade routes 3500–2000 BCE

▨ zone of urban civilization

▧ trading hinterland

○ urban centers

— major trade route

--- modern coast where different

--- modern river where different

Traded raw materials

🔲 alabaster

🔲 dolerite

🔲 flint

🔲 granite

🔲 limestone

🔲 steatite

🔲 copper

🔲 gold

🔲 silver

🔲 tin

⬭ carnelian

⬭ turquoise

⬭ lapis lazuli

🌲 timber

Iranian Plateau: Trading cities engaged in long distance trade with Mesopotamia and the Indus Valley

Oman: Coastal cities trade with both Mesopotamia and the Indus Valley

Dilmun major entrepôt

The ritual placing of a ceremonial peg beneath the foundations of a temple was a tradition of Mesopotamian civilizations. Some foundation pegs took the form of bronze statuettes; others, like this example from Ur, were made of baked clay and bore a written inscription.

Only scribes were literate, and they became a privileged class in ancient cities. The Egyptian scribe Imhotep, for example, designed the pyramid at Saqqara.

Writing

Perhaps the single greatest innovation of urban civilization, writing evolved to record trading transactions. The first texts, from Mesopotamia and dating to the 4th millennium BCE, are receipts, showing symbols and numbers only; soon a pictographic script, where pictures represent words, developed and, in time, symbols came to be used for sounds (cuneiform). Specialized scribes became keepers of temple archives, responsible for libraries of clay tablets which recorded the detail of state-run temple economies. Writing soon transcended its business roots, and was used to codify laws, record myths, and preserve religious transactions. Writing equally old is now known from the royal tombs at Abydos in Upper Egypt.

Sumerian cuneiform writing is named after the wedge-shaped marks or incisions made with a stylus on soft clay tablets. *Cuneus* is Latin for a wedge.

THE WORLD 2500–1250 BCE

AS THE FIRST CITIES expanded and proliferated, states developed, populations grew, and economic pressures increased. Rivalry for territory and power made the early states increasingly militaristic, and warfare, weapons, and diplomacy are conspicuous in the archaeology of this period. As these early societies became more stratified, distinct classes – warriors, priests, scribes, craftspeople, laborers – began to emerge. The great wealth of rulers and the social elite is reflected in the rich array of grave goods found in their burials. Urban civilizations still covered only a tiny fraction of the Earth's surface; in Europe, scattered agricultural communities were becoming more sophisticated, developing metallurgy and trade, and beginning to compete for land and resources. Hunter-gatherer groups still thrived in many areas, and many islands in the Pacific were yet to be settled at this time.

SUN SYMBOLISM

Symbolic representations of the Sun, suggestive of life, fertility, and creation, are found in almost all cultures. During this period in Egypt, the sun god Ra was the dominant figure among the high gods, his enhanced status culminating in the brief solar monotheism under Pharaoh Akhenaten c.1350 BCE. In Scandinavia, ritual finds such as the sun chariot found in a bog at Trundholm (*below*) attest to monotheistic sun worship and fertility rites in the region during the Bronze Age.

This bronze wheeled model of a horse drawing a disc, which dates to c.1650 BCE, may depict the sun's progress across the heavens.

The World in 1250 BCE

- New Kingdom Egypt
- Hittites
- Mitanni
- Elam
- Shang China
- Mycenaean civilization
- areas of transition from hunting and gathering to agriculture
- other urbanized regions

Major bronze-using regions c.1250 BCE

- Andronovo steppe cultures
- Bronze Age Europe
- Mainland Southeast Asia
- → colonization of Pacific from c.1500 BCE

Duck decoys, made from marsh bulrush, from Lovelock Cave in Nevada (c.1500 BCE), show the importance of the nearby lake and its resources to the occupants of the cave.

Great Lakes region: Evidence of trading contacts with Central America

Mississippi Valley: Large complexes of mounds and earthworks serve as ceremonial centers for agricultural villages

Central America: Settled agricultural economy well established

Orinoco and Amazon estuaries: Horticultural villages and early ceramics

Peruvian Andes: Nuclear area of Andean civilization; monumental architecture and ceremonial centers

Northern fringes of Europe: Hunting, fishing, and gathering way of life still persists

Europe: Extensive trade networks, fortified settlements, cremations in large urnfield cemeteries

Egypt: New Kingdom reaching height of its power

Sub-Saharan periphery: Increased population and gradual adoption of agriculture

Tropical woodlands: Yams and palm nuts cultivated

The Americas

The precursors of urban civilizations were emerging in both South and Central America during this period. The construction of the monumental ceremonial center of La Florida in Peru (c.1800 BCE) would have required the cooperation of several communities. On the Gulf coast of Central America, the Olmec centre of San Lorenzo was developing. In eastern North America the cultivation of sunflowers and gourds indicates that farming was becoming established; by 1500 BCE small settled communities had grown up along the river valleys of the Mississippi system.

2000: Earliest ceramics and large-scale cultivation of corn in Peru

c.1800: Ceremonial center of La Florida built in Peru

1500: Evidence of first metalworking in Peru

2500 BCE 2250 2000 1750 1500 1250 BCE

1800: Cultivation of sunflowers and gourds in eastern North America. Long-distance trade networks established

The Americas

THE DEVELOPMENT OF METALLURGY

During the 3rd millennium BCE the manufacture of tools, weapons, and vessels was transformed by the adoption of a new material: bronze. Made by alloying copper with tin, bronze was stronger and more durable than pure copper and could be beaten into different shapes or cast by pouring it into stone or clay moulds. Copper and tin were uncommon, but the search for new ores led to the creation of extensive trade networks for raw materials and finished products.

The Eygptians employed their most skilled craftsmen for working in gold. The metal was lavishly used to ornament vessels, furniture, and funerary equipment (*above*).

At Mycenae, the elite were buried with an opulent array of metal goods. This dagger blade (*left*) (1600–1550 BCE) of bronze inlaid with silver portrays a lion hunt.

Africa

Egyptian civilization reached its apogee during the New Kingdom (1530–1070 BCE). The power of the monarch was unrivaled and the wealth of the kingdom, based on control of the rich gold deposits of Nubia and the domination of Palestine and southern Syria. Conflict with the Hittites to safeguard this control was a major concern of the period. The New Kingdom's downfall came as a result of corruption and the decline of royal power, coupled with unrest in Palestine, and foreign attacks on Egypt.

Europe

European settlements, ranging from hillforts to lake dwellings, indicate that increased pressures on land were causing conflict. New types of bronze weapons show the emergence of a warrior elite. The palace of Knossos on Crete marked the appearance of the first Mediterranean state, and on the mainland, the small, palace-based cities of Mycenaean Greece grew wealthy on east Mediterranean trade, but were all sacked or abandoned by the 12th century BCE.

Many aspects of Minoan life are depicted in the colorful frescoes at Knossos, a recurring theme being the acrobatic bull-leaping game on which a religious cult was possibly centered.

Europe

- 2300: Bronze technology reaches Europe
- 2000: Fortified settlements appear in Central and Eastern Europe
- 1550: Mycenaeans become dominant power on Greek mainland

2500 BCE — 2250 — 2000 — 1750 — 1500 — 1250 BCE

- 2000: Minoan civilization becomes established on island of Crete; palace of Knossos is built
- 1650: Linear A script comes into use on Crete

West Asia

Northern Mesopotamia was dominated by a number of city-states, such as Ashur and Mari, which centered on palaces and religious complexes. The palace administered each city's long-distance trade and tribute, and recorded these transactions on archives of clay tablets. In the 18th century BCE, the city-state of Babylon gained temporary control of the region. In central Anatolia, the Hittites ruled a powerful kingdom from their fortified citadel at Hattushash. Their attempts to gain contol over the wealthy trading cities of the Levant brought them into conflict with Egypt.

This gold figurine of a Hittite king dates to c.1400 BCE.

West Asia

- 2300: City-states of southern Mesopotamia temporarily united under Sargon of Agade
- 1775: Construction of palace of Zimri-Lim at Mari. Palace archive contained 17,500 clay tablets
- 1650: Emergence of Hittite kingdom, with capital at Hattushash
- 1500: Period of endemic warfare between Hittites, Egyptians, and Mitanni of northern Mesopotamia

2500 BCE — 2250 — 2000 — 1750 — 1500 — 1250 BCE

- 1760: City-state of Babylon gains political hegemony over northern Mesopotamia
- 1600: Phoenicians start to use Canaanite script – the first alphabetic script
- 1290: Battle of Kadesh: Egypt versus the Hittites

SEE ALSO:

North America: pp.120–121

South America: pp.144–145

Africa: pp.158–159

Europe: pp.174–175

West Asia: pp.220–221

South and Southeast Asia: pp.240–241

North and East Asia: pp.258–259

Australasia and Oceania: pp.280–281

East Asia

The urban civilization of Shang China developed in about 1800 BCE in the middle valley of the Yellow River. The Shang dynasty exercised an absolute power reflected in their incredibly rich burials. Yet this absolute power was based on the labor of farmers who cultivated beans and millet with tools of wood and stone. Elsewhere, in Southeast Asia, the transition to farming was slow, although agricultural villages in Thailand were producing bronze vessels using similar techniques to the Chinese.

Chinese mastery of bronze casting is evident in the exquisite vessels, created primarily for ceremonial use, that often accompanied the wealthy elite into the grave.

East Asia

- 1800: Emergence of Shang dynasty in middle valley of Yellow River
- 1500: Evidence of bronze-working in mainland Southeast Asia
- 1400: Anyang succeeds Zhengzhou as the Shang capital

2500 BCE — 2250 — 2000 — 1750 — 1500 — 1250 BCE

- 2500: First domesticated animals and pottery in island Southeast Asia
- 1900 BCE: First Chinese city founded at Erlitou on the Yellow River
- 1800: First bronze vessels cast from ceramic molds
- 1400: First written inscriptions appear on oracle bones, which were used in a process of divination

When the Lapita people arrived in the western Pacific islands they were carrying a variety of food plants, the pig, and their distinctive style of pottery, the decoration of which was applied with short-toothed implements.

Map labels: Arctic hunter-gatherers, Siberia, Steppes, Yenisey, Ob', Lena, Amur, Lake Baikal, Volga, Aral Sea, Lake Balkhash, Gobi, Japan, **China:** Longshan groups form basis of Shang state c.1800 BCE, Anyang, Erlitou, Zhengzhou, Yellow River, **Japan:** Jomon hunter-gatherers living in villages, Black Sea, Caspian Sea, Troy, Anatolia, Hattushash, Nineveh, Mesopotamia, Ashur, Kadesh, Byblos, Tyre, Jerusalem, Jericho, Babylon, Tigris, Euphrates, **Iranian Plateau:** Scattered trading cities, El-Amarna, El-Lisht, Thebes, Nile, Nubia, Arabian Peninsula, **Levant:** City states repeatedly absorbed by neighboring empires; Hittite Empire, Elam and Kingdom of Mitanni vying with Egypt for control of region, Indus, Ganges, Himalayas, Deccan, Yangtze, **Indus Valley:** Disappearance of urban civilization; northwest India occupied by Aryan settlers, **Ganges Valley:** Rice-farming villages, **Red River valley:** Sophisticated bronze working; Dong Son drums, Mekong, **East Africa:** Teff and ensete cultivation, **Mainland Southeast Asia:** Rice-farming villages, bronze tools and ornaments, Sumatra, Borneo, Java, Philippine Islands, East Indies, **Maritime Southeast Asia:** Slow transition from hunting and gathering to agriculture, Bismarck Archipelago, New Guinea, **Polynesian dispersal:** Lapita population colonize the islands of Melanesia, PACIFIC OCEAN, INDIAN OCEAN, Madagascar, Lake Victoria, Zambezi, Kalahari Desert, pastoralists, hunter-gatherers, Hunter-gatherers Australia, Darling, New Zealand, Andronovo steppe cultures: Cattle herders and seasonal nomads

Egyptian agriculture centered on the cultivation of cereals, primarily emmer wheat and barley. The fertile soils of the Nile floodplain produced high annual yields and large surpluses were a major source of the state's wealth.

Africa

2500 BCE — 2250 — 2000 — 1750 — 1500 — 1250 BCE

- 1633: Much of Egypt ruled by the Hyksos, an Asiatic people
- c.1375: Egyptian prosperity, power and prestige reach high point under Amenophis III
- 2134: Egypt reunited under Middle Kingdom pharaohs after perod of dominance by nobles
- 1530: Rise of New Kingdom. New capital founded at Thebes
- 1350: Pharaoh Akhenaten introduces sun worship in Egypt

Oceania

One of the great population dispersals of the ancient world began c.1500 BCE, when the Lapita people, originally settlers from the East Indies, set off from New Guinea and the Solomons to explore and colonize the islands of the Pacific Ocean. The Lapita culture spread rapidly, reaching Tonga and Samoa, by 1000 BCE.

- c.2500: Dingo introduced to Australia, probably from Southeast Asia
- 1500: Lapita colonists start to colonize Pacific Ocean, reaching Tonga and Samoa by c.1000 BCE

2500 BCE — 2250 — 2000 — 1750 — 1500 — 1250 BCE

- c.1600: Earliest examples of Lapita pottery in Bismarck Archipelago

Oceania

THE GROWTH OF THE CITY

Pharaoh Akhenaten (1353–1336 BCE) was the founder of the new city of El-Amarna.

OVER THE COURSE OF 2000 YEARS from c.3500 BCE, cities evolved in many different ways, reflecting the culture from which they emerged, outside pressures, and the preoccupations of their rulers. Yet, in a period of increasing social stratification, all cities represented the gulf between the ruler and the ruled, the sacred and the secular. They were physically, and symbolically, dominated by the palaces of the ruling elite, and by temples and religious precincts. The elaborate monuments of these early centers, clearly segregated from the houses and workshops of the laboring classes, symbolized the absolute power wielded by royal dynasties, priests, and the aristocracy. But the *status quo* was underpinned by a relentless quest for new territory and greater wealth; ultimately, this urge to expand was to evolve into imperialism.

The urban heartland

By 1250 BCE, zones of urbanism extended from the Mediterranean to China. The early expansion of urban civilization in southern Mesopotamia had created a swathe of cities, from Ur to Mycenae, which thrived on trade and contact, supplemented by the levying of taxes, tolls, and tribute. Rivalry for control of key cities was endemic. While Egypt was also vying for political and economic control of the region, the cities of the Nile were stately religious and dynastic centers, adorned by magnificent temples, palaces, and cities of the dead. The distant cities of Shang China were strictly segregated – symbolic of a stratified society where the great wealth and luxury of the few rested on a simple farming base.

Nippur

Center of the worship of Enlil, the chief deity of the Sumerian pantheon, Nippur retained its importance over three millennia. Located on the Shatt al Nil, an ancient course of the Euphrates, the city was first occupied in c.4000 BCE. In c.2100 BCE, Ur-Nammu, ruler of the city-state of Ur, legitimized his role as Enlil's earthly representative by building the first temple and ziggurat to the deity. The temple was subsequently destroyed and rebuilt at least three times. The remains of the extensive religious quarter encompass a large scribal district as well as a temple to Inanna, queen of heaven.

A ruler's power was legitimized by the foundation of cities and temples, as this sculpture of a Babylonian king carrying building materials shows.

A map of the city of Nippur – probably the oldest plan in the world – was found on a clay tablet from the site dating to c.1500 BCE. The two lines on the far left denote the Euphrates River; adjoining lines show one wall of the city.

Sculpted lions flank the "Lion Gate," a major entrance into the city of Hattushash. In the 14th century BCE the fortifications of Hattushash were extended and strengthened, as befitted its status as an important imperial capital.

Hattushash

The Hittite kingdom, which emerged from the conquest of a number of Anatolian city states in the 17th century BCE, adopted the site of Hattushash (Boğazköy) as its capital. Situated at the head of a fertile river valley, the citadel, Büyükkale, was the core of the old city. By c.1400 BCE the walls had been extended to encompass the "Upper City," and Hattushash had been adorned with a series of grandiose monuments – five temples and a palace within the citadel with a large pillared audience hall and a royal archive of 3000 clay tablets. The city walls, which stood on stone-faced ramparts, with projecting towers and twin-towered gateways, made Hattushash one of the most strongly fortified cities in the Middle East.

② Nippur

- probable extent of inner city
- business and official quarter
- North Temple
- storehouses
- religious quarter
- first Great Temple wall
- ziggurat
- Inanna Temple
- Temple of Enlil
- original town
- first great temple wall
- scribal quarter (containing remains of many thousands of clay tablets)
- Outer Temple Wall
- moat
- canal
- underground course
- Shatt al Nil
- city wall
- probable extent of city wall

200 meters / 200 yards

① Urbanism 1250 BCE
- urban area of the Old World, c.1250 BCE
- area of secondary urbanization, with date
- extent of Indus civilization c.5000–2500 BCE
- major city

EUROPE

Europe: Urbanism spreads in early centuries CE with Roman imperialism

Danube · Black Sea · Caucasus · Caspian Sea · Volga · Elburz Mountains

c.750 BCE · Hattushash · Alaca Hüyük

Northern Greece c.750 BCE · Troy · Acemhüyük · Kanesh · Persia c.500 BCE

Italy c.750 BCE · Aegean Sea · Beycesultan · Anatolia · Karchemish · Tell Brak · Eshnunna

Mycenae · Athens · Karahüyük · Taurus Mountains · Aleppo · MESOPOTAMIA · Tigris · Zagros

Pylos · Tiryns · Miletus · Ugarit · Mari · Euphrates · Susa

Knossos · Malia · Qadesh · Syrian Desert · Babylon · Kish · Nippur · Lagash · Larsa · Ur

Phaistos · Zakro · Hazor · Megiddo · Uruk · Dagash

Mediterranean Sea · Lachish

Buto · Pi-Ramesse · Bubastis · Heliopolis

Sais · Memphis · El-Lisht

Phoenicia c.750 BCE · EGYPT

El-Amarna

Thebes · Luxor · Nile · Edfu · Red Sea

Tropic of Cancer

Arabian Peninsula: Harsh desert terrain is sparsely populated by desert pastoralists

Arabian Peninsula

Southern Arabia c.500 BCE

③ Hattushash

To Yazilikaya, Hittite religious centre · King's Gate · Citadel (Büyükkale) · Temple V · UPPER CITY · Büyük Kaya · Temple II · LOWER CITY · Temple III · Sphinx Gate · Nisantepe (inscription) · Temple IV · Assyrian colony · Yellow Castle (Sarikale) · Great Temple · New Castle (Yenicekale) · Lion Gate · Halys

Elevation (meters)
- 1200
- 1150
- 1100
- 1050
- 1000
- 950
- building
- city walls
- reconstructed wall
- city gate

500 meters / 500 yards

The development of cities

c.3100 BCE: Early urban communities emerge in the Nile Delta. Memphis is founded as the capital city of the new, unified Egyptian state

c.2500 BCE: Cities begin to appear in the Indus valley. Mohenjo-Daro and Harappa may have had populations of c.40,000

c.2000 BCE: First cities established in Anatolia

c.1990 BCE: New Egyptian capital at El-Lisht

c.1650 BCE: Anatolian city-states unite as Hittite Empire, with capital at Hattushash

c.1560 BCE: Thebes becomes center of New Kingdom Egyptian empire

c.1350 BCE: Short-lived Egyptian capital founded at El-Amarna

3600 · 3200 · 2800 · 2400 · 2000 · 1600 · 1200

c.3500 BCE: Uruk period; emergence of first city-states in southern Mesopotamia. Uruk may have been the first city in the world

c.2500 BCE: Emergence of cities in Levant and northern Mesopotamia, each focused on a palace complex

c.2400 BCE: Foundation of Akkadian dynasty in southern Mesopotamia

c.2000 BCE: Collapse of Indus valley civilization; cities abandoned

c.1900 BCE: First known Shang city at Erlitou on Yellow River

c.1600 BCE: Mycenae becomes center of Aegean civilization

c.1400 BCE: Zhengzhou becomes Shang capital

c.1245 BCE: Ramesses II moves Egyptian capital to new city Pi-Ramesse

Zhengzhou

The Shang dynasty ruled in the middle valley of the Yellow River from c.1800 BCE. Remains of Shang cities, rich tombs and luxury artifacts all indicate the presence of a highly sophisticated urban elite. Zhengzhou, one of successive Shang capitals, was founded c.1700 BCE. It consists of a roughly square enclosure, surrounded by 4 mile-long, 11 yd-high rammed earth walls. Within these walls stood the palace and ritual altar, dwelling places, storage pits for grain, pottery, and oracle bones (a means of divination, used by the Shang to consult their ancestors) and pits for human sacrifices. Outside the walls stood the residential areas, and specialist workshops producing fine artifacts in bone, bronze, and pottery.

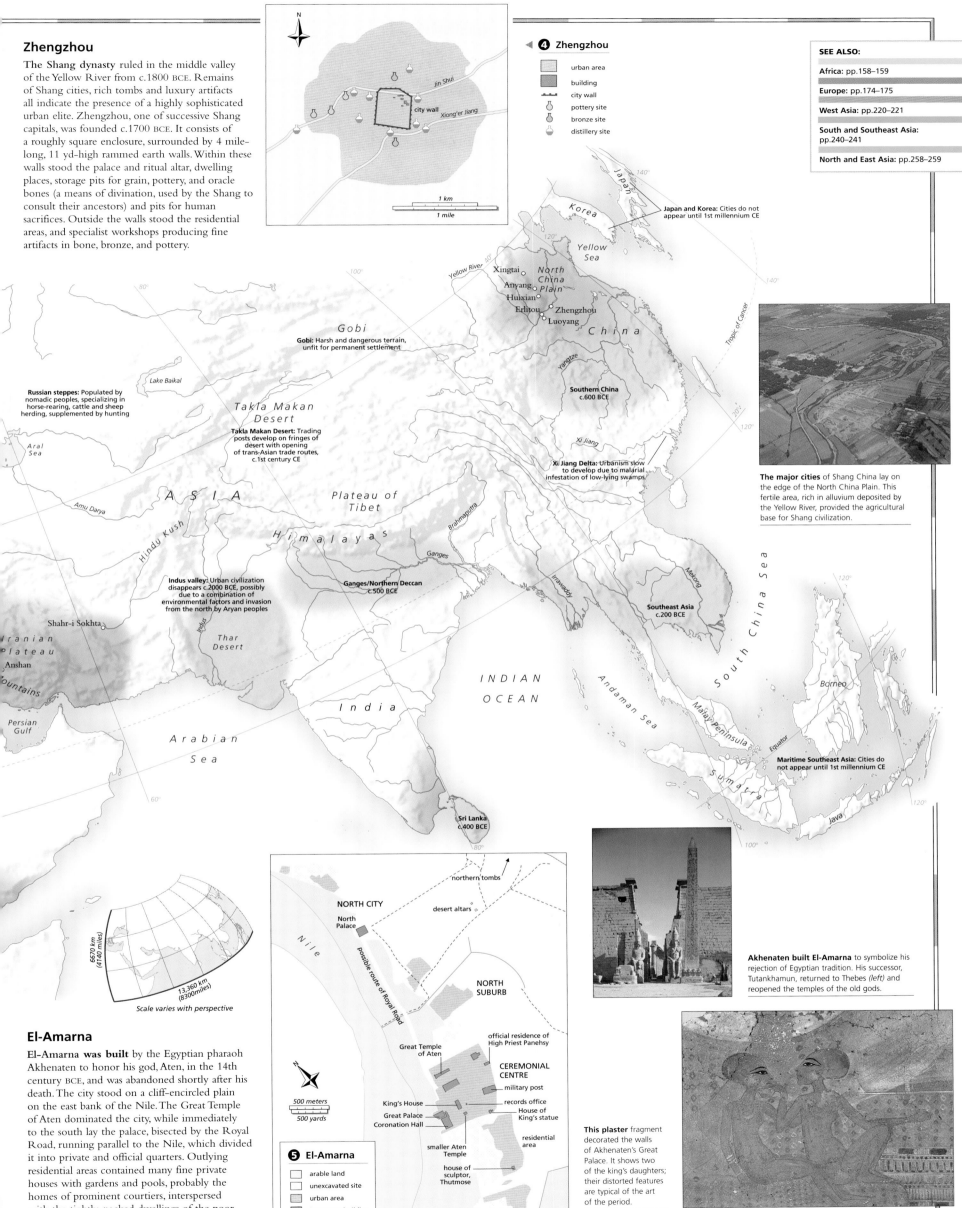

④ Zhengzhou

- urban area
- building
- city wall
- pottery site
- bronze site
- distillery site

Jin Shui

Xiong'er Jiang

city wall

1 km
1 mile

SEE ALSO:

Africa: pp.158–159

Europe: pp.174–175

West Asia: pp.220–221

South and Southeast Asia: pp.240–241

North and East Asia: pp.258–259

Japan and Korea: Cities do not appear until 1st millennium CE

Japan

Korea

Yellow Sea

Xingtai

North China Plain

Anyang
Huixian
Erlitou   Zhengzhou
Luoyang

China

Gobi: Harsh and dangerous terrain, unfit for permanent settlement

Gobi

Yellow River

Yangtze

Southern China c.600 BCE

Xi Jiang

Xi Jiang Delta: Urbanism slow to develop due to malarial infestation of low-lying swamps

Russian steppes: Populated by nomadic peoples, specializing in horse-rearing, cattle and sheep herding, supplemented by hunting

Lake Baikal

Takla Makan Desert: Trading posts develop on fringes of desert with opening of trans-Asian trade routes, c.1st century CE

Takla Makan Desert

A S I A

Plateau of Tibet

Himalayas

Brahmaputra

Amu Darya

Hindu Kush

Indus valley: Urban civilization disappears c.2000 BCE, possibly due to a combination of environmental factors and invasion from the north by Aryan peoples

Ganges

Ganges/Northern Deccan c.500 BCE

Irrawaddy

Mekong

Southeast Asia c.200 BCE

South China Sea

Borneo

Aral Sea

Shahr-i Sokhta

Iranian Plateau

Anshan

...ountains

Indus

Thar Desert

India

INDIAN OCEAN

Andaman Sea

Malay Peninsula

Equator

Maritime Southeast Asia: Cities do not appear until 1st millennium CE

Sumatra

Java

Persian Gulf

Arabian Sea

Sri Lanka c.400 BCE

The major cities of Shang China lay on the edge of the North China Plain. This fertile area, rich in alluvium deposited by the Yellow River, provided the agricultural base for Shang civilization.

6670 km (4140 miles)

13,360 km (8300 miles)

Scale varies with perspective

El-Amarna

El-Amarna was built by the Egyptian pharaoh Akhenaten to honor his god, Aten, in the 14th century BCE, and was abandoned shortly after his death. The city stood on a cliff-encircled plain on the east bank of the Nile. The Great Temple of Aten dominated the city, while immediately to the south lay the palace, bisected by the Royal Road, running parallel to the Nile, which divided it into private and official quarters. Outlying residential areas contained many fine private houses with gardens and pools, probably the homes of prominent courtiers, interspersed with the tightly-packed dwellings of the poor.

northern tombs

NORTH CITY

North Palace

desert altars

Nile

possible route of Royal Road

NORTH SUBURB

official residence of High Priest Panehsy

Great Temple of Aten

CEREMONIAL CENTRE

military post

King's House

records office
House of King's statue

Great Palace
Coronation Hall

smaller Aten Temple

residential area

house of sculptor, Thutmose

SOUTH SUBURB

500 meters
500 yards

⑤ El-Amarna

- arable land
- unexcavated site
- urban area
- important building
- irrigation channel
- path

Akhenaten built El-Amarna to symbolize his rejection of Egyptian tradition. His successor, Tutankhamun, returned to Thebes *(left)* and reopened the temples of the old gods.

This plaster fragment decorated the walls of Akhenaten's Great Palace. It shows two of the king's daughters; their distorted features are typical of the art of the period.

THE WORLD 1250–750 BCE

THE INEXORABLE RIVALRIES between the cities and states of the Old World and incursions by nomadic tribes created a shifting pattern of allegiance and control within West Asia. The Assyrians formed the world's first large empire, and ruled their territory with ruthless efficiency, utilizing cavalry and new iron technology to fashion more effective weapons and armor. In both Europe and Asia iron revolutionized weapons, tools, and agricultural implements. More efficient farming produced higher crop yields and supported larger populations. Long-distance trade networks disseminated political and cultural influences across Europe and along the Mediterranean shores, but many areas remained unaffected. The first major centers of the Americas, the Chavín in Peru and the Olmec in Central America, developed in isolation, evolving the art styles, religious motifs, and ceremonies which were to imbue the civilizations that succeeded them.

North America

The first great Mexican civilization, the Olmec, emerged in the coastal lowlands southwest of Yucatán in about 1200 BCE. The Olmec founded a number of ceremonial centers, notably at San Lorenzo and La Venta. They also established trade networks in commodities such as obsidian, jade, and basalt which extended far to the north and west. To the northeast, the peoples of the Adena culture, based along the Ohio River from about 1000–300 BCE, constructed burial chambers beneath earthen mounds.

At San Lorenzo, the Olmec sculpted remarkable stone monuments, including colossal basalt heads with characteristic flat faces, thickened lips, and protective helmets.

North America

1200: Olmec civilization, based at San Lorenzo, is flourishing

1000: Adena culture develops in middle Ohio River valley in eastern North America

1250 BCE | 1150 | 1050 | 950 | 850 | 750 BCE

1200: Town of Tlatilco is well established in the central Valley of Mexico

900: San Lorenzo is destroyed. Its leading role is taken over by La Venta

The World in 750 BCE

○ Greek cities and territories
○ Phoenician cities and territories
small Chinese states under the Eastern Zhou dynasty

The principal motifs of the Chavín decorative style were mythical and real animals, especially jaguars, caymans, and eagles, and fanged, snarling human faces.

South America

The earliest civilization of the Andes was the Chavín, which flourished between about 900 and 200 BCE. The temple at Chavín de Huantar was probably the center of a widespread religious cult and designs showing Chavín influence are found all over Peru. Trading networks were also well established; Chavín pottery, shell, and wood artifacts and painted textiles have been found throughout the region.

South America

1200: Chavín civilization emerges in the Andes

850: Chavin cult, based on the worship of part-human, part-animal supernatural beings, reaches its height in Peru

1250 BCE | 1150 | 1050 | 950 | 850 | 750 BCE

c.900: Chorrera-style pottery vessels are found widely distributed in northern South America

PAPYRUS MANUFACTURE

Papyrus is a grasslike aquatic plant that was long cultivated along the banks of the Nile. The Egyptians used its stems to make sails, cloth, twine, baskets, and mats, but its most prominent use was in the manufacture of a type of paper. The fibrous inner stems of the plant were removed, cut into strips and laid at right angles on top of each other to form a sheet before pressing and drying to produce a thin, smooth writing surface.

The Egyptian Book of the Dead was a collection of spells, hymns, and prayers placed in tombs to assist the soul on its journey to the afterlife. The text was copied onto papyrus rolls and sold for burial use.

Africa

In Egypt the end of the 20th Dynasty (1085 BCE) heralded the end of stable pharaonic rule. Rival kings ruled from several different cities, and short periods of stability alternated with protracted periods of civil war. By 750 BCE the Nubian kingdom of Kush was extending its power northwards. The Phoenicians, a Semitic people from the eastern Mediterranean, established trading colonies along the North African coast, most famously Carthage. Knowledge of iron metallurgy was probably transmitted along the trans-Saharan trade routes to settled agricultural communities to the south, but hunting and gathering were still the main means of subsistence for large areas of sub-Saharan Africa.

Europe

Independent city-states were founded throughout Greece and western Asia Minor. The establishment of trade links with Italy and the Levant increased prosperity and population and colonists began to build Greek trading cities along the shores of the Mediterranean. In Italy, the Etruscans built fortified hilltop cities and established trade links with Africa and Europe. Iron metallurgy, established in Central Europe by 1000 BCE, had reached Britain and Ireland by the 8th century. Iron was used to make sophisticated weapons and tools.

Mastery of the seas was vitally important to the Greeks as they began to establish overseas colonies. By 700 BCE advances in shipbuilding technology had produced swift, maneuverable galleys driven by three banks of oarsmen (triremes), as depicted on this pot.

BABYLONIAN ASTRONOMY

The Babylonians were one of the earliest peoples to make a systematic, scientific study of the skies. Their records go back to c.1800 BCE and accumulated over centuries. By 1000 BCE they were able to predict lunar eclipses and within two or three hundred years, the path of the Sun and some of the planets had been plotted with considerable accuracy. These astronomical records contributed to the later flowering of western astronomy.

This bronze model of the solar system is from Lake Sevan in Armenia. It dates from 10th–9th century BCE.

SEE ALSO:

North America: pp.120–121

South America: pp.144–145

Africa: pp.160–161

Europe: pp.176–177

West Asia: pp.222–223

South and Southeast Asia: pp.240–243

North and East Asia: pp.258–259

Australasia and Oceania: pp.280–281

Europe (timeline)

1150: Collapse of Mycenean Greece
1000: Colonists from mainland Greece settle coast of Asia Minor and islands of eastern Aegean
900: End of dark ages in Greece
800: Rise of Etruscan city-states in Central Italy
776: First Pan-Hellenic athletics festival held at the Sanctuary of Zeus, Olympia

1250 BCE — 1150 — 1050 — 950 — 850 — 750 BCE

1200: New Urnfield culture emerges in Danube area. Named after tradition of placing cremated ashes in urns in large communal burial fields
c.1000: Iron-working reaches Central Europe from the Near East
850: Earliest village on Rome's Palatine Hill
800: First phase of Celtic Iron Age named after cemetery at Hallstatt in Austria

Assyrian kings plowed the proceeds of their military conquests into the building of vast temples and palaces at Nimrud and Nineveh. Booty acquired during the campaigns, like this ivory panel of a sphinx, enriched many palace furnishings.

West Asia

Power struggles between the established empires of West Asia created opportunities for infiltration by barbarian tribes, such as the Medes, Chaldeans, Philistines, Hebrews, and Phrygians, who attempted to seize power. In the 9th century BCE Ahab, son of Omri, founder of the Kingdom of Israel, consolidated the power of his state by marrying Jezebel, princess of Sidon. However, from the 9th century BCE, the dominant power in the region was Assyria, originally based in the Tigris valley. By the 8th century BCE the Assyrian Empire extended from the Levant to the Persian Gulf. Subject peoples were ruled by provincial governors and resistance was ruthlessly suppressed. Only the Armenian kingdom of Urartu remained beyond Assyrian control.

West Asia (timeline)

1200: Collapse of the Hittite Empire
c.1100: Syria and Palestine settled by nomadic tribes
900: Kingdom of Urartu established in Armenia resists Assyrian expansion

1250 BCE — 1150 — 1050 — 950 — 850 — 750 BCE

c.1200: Jewish exodus from Egypt and settlement in Palestine
c.1000: Phoenicians dominate trade of Levant and develop an alphabetic script
950: Foundation of the Assyrian Empire
c.882: Omri founds the Kingdom of Israel

The need to preserve the body from decay through mummification was an integral part of the Egyptian belief in a life after death. This anthropomorphic case belonged to Shepenmut, Priestess of Thebes, who was buried around 800 BCE.

Zhou rulers maintained Shang cultural traditions, including ancestor worship. Food and drink were offered in bronze ritual vessels, often shaped into bizarre combinations of animal forms.

East Asia

In China the Zhou dynasty succeeded the Shang in the 11th century BCE, heralding a period of stability until the 8th century when central authority collapsed, former fiefs rose up against the Zhou, and China split into separate kingdoms. Bronze technology for weapons and ornaments reached the Korean peninsula from Manchuria in about 1000 BCE.

Africa (timeline)

1166: Death of Rameses III, Egypt's last great pharaoh.
945: Civil war in Egypt. By mid-8th century, Egypt divided into several small states
c.750: Kingdom of Kush extends power and influence northward

1250 BCE — 1150 — 1050 — 950 — 850 — 750 BCE

1085: End of 20th Dynasty and Egyptian New Kingdom
c.900: Foundation of Nubian kingdom of Kush
814: Foundation of Phoenician colony of Carthage

East Asia (timeline)

1027: Zhou dynasty replaces Shang in China
1000: Chinese bronze casting reaches level of craftsmanship unrivaled elsewhere at this period

1250 BCE — 1150 — 1050 — 950 — 850 — 750 BCE

c.1000: Wet rice cultivation introduced to Korea from China
c.770: Western Zhou period ends with collapse of centralized power

WRITING, COUNTING, AND CALENDARS

The Greek inscription *(above)* is an offering of thanks to Asclepius, the god of healing.

THE INTERTWINED DEVELOPMENT of writing and counting was closely related to the advent of agriculture and the need to record and tally stored goods, livestock, and commercial transactions. The precursors of the first known writing and numerical systems were clay counting tokens, used in Sumer from c.3400 BCE to record quantities of stored goods. They were eventually sealed in clay envelopes, and marked on the outside with signs indicating their contents – the first written symbols. Within a thousand years, writing and numerical systems had spread throughout West Asia (they evolved separately in China and Central America), bringing a revolutionary change in human consciousness. The ability to count in abstract enabled humans to measure, assess, record, and evaluate their world – calendrical systems, weights and measures, coinage, astronomical calculations, and geometry all followed. Writing became a powerful tool of government, a means of communicating over increasing distances, codifying laws, and recording myths and history.

The evolution and spread of major scripts

This inscription in Egyptian hieratic is a record of a trading transaction. Hieratic was a form of cursive script, written with ink and a reed brush.

The earliest symbolic records, of economic transactions, were used in Sumer from c.3400 BCE, and gradually evolved into a pictographic script, where pictures represented words. Cuneiform writing was used to record a variety of languages, and spread throughout West Asia. The system eventually became more complex, and written symbols also came to stand for concepts or sounds. Egyptian hieroglyphics probably developed under Sumerian influence, though the system was unique. Chinese pictographic writing developed independently, as did the Zapotec and Maya systems in Central America. The Proto-Canaanite alphabet, based on a selection of Egyptian hieroglyphs (developed by 1200 BCE), was the probable precursor of the Phoenician alphabet, adapted by the Greeks in the 8th century BCE.

Writing in Ancient Egypt was the preserve of trained scribes, whose high status was reflected in their exemption from taxes.

This glyph from Central America, represents the word "grass."

Oracle bones, the earliest examples of writing from Shang dynasty China, record predictions made by interpreting cracks in the bones.

The inscriptions on this black basalt pillar are the most complete example of the law code of Hammurabi, king of Babylonia (c.1790–1750 BCE), who is depicted on the top of the pillar.

▲ **1** The evolution and spread of major scripts

- Sumerian cuneiform
- spread of cuneiform
- Egyptian hieroglyphic
- spread of hieroglyphic
- Phoenician alphabet
- spread of alphabet
- Chinese script
- spread of Chinese script
- Mesoamerican script
- Runic script
- Indus script

Roman lapidary inscriptions used only capital letters. The letters were traced in chalk and brushwork and carved using an iron chisel.

This perfume jar from Corinth in Greece is inscribed in the alphabetic script which was adapted from the Phoenician, and used in Greece from the 8th century BCE.

Major developments in writing, counting, and calendrical systems

c.3400: Sumerians use clay counting tokens and first written symbols

c.3000: Development of Egyptian hieroglyphic writing system

c.2500: Egyptian calendar pioneers division of day into 24 units

c.1400: First written inscriptions in China, on Shang oracle bones

c.1100: Introduction of Phoenician alphabet

46: Julian calendrical reforms; "Year of Confusion" is 445 days long

| 3500 BCE | 3000 BCE | 2500 BCE | 2000 BCE | 1500 BCE | 1000 BCE | 500 BCE | 1 CE |

c.3250: Earliest writing in the world; clay pictographic tablets from Tell Brak, Syria

c.2000: Appearance of Cretan hieroglyphic writing

c.600: First Greek coins
c.600: First Central American script (Zapotec)

c.500: Hebrews evolve use of 7-day weeks
c.500: First coins used in China

The evolution of numerical systems

The Rhind mathematical papyrus dates to c.1575 BCE. It demonstrates that the Egyptians had some understanding of the properties of right-angled triangles.

Wooden tally sticks were used over 30,000 years ago, probably to record numbers of animals killed. From c.3400 BCE the Sumerians used clay counting tokens to represent order of magnitude, and evolved the first written numbering system. As humans count using their fingers and toes, most systems use base 10, while the Maya, Aztecs, and Celts chose base 20. The Sumerian and Babylonian use of base 60 (still evident in our use of 60 minutes and seconds, and 360 degrees) remains mysterious. Alphabetic counting systems, used by Greeks, Hebrews, and Arabs, wrote numbers by using letters. The concept of zero and the positional numbering system were independent Indian and Maya inventions.

This Babylonian mathematical text with cuneiform numbers dates to c.500 BCE. The use of the sexagesimal system was an important factor in the development of Babylonian astronomy.

SEE ALSO:

North America: pp.122–123

South America: pp.146–147

West Asia: pp.222–223

North and East Asia: pp.258–259

❷ The evolution of numerical systems

Earliest known date of counting system

Numerical system
- ⊕ additive
- ⊠ multiplicative
- ○ positional

Regions
- Mesopotamian
- Maya
- Roman
- Hittite
- Egyptian
- Greek
- Hebraic
- Gupta India
- Chinese

Base
- ● Base 10
- ● Base 20
- ○ Base 60

Heracles is shown stringing a bow on this Theban coin (c.446–426 BCE).

Weights and measures

The parts of the body, such as the fingers, palms, and toes, were used by all ancient civilizations for shorter units of measurement. Greater distances reflect the nature of the civilization; the Roman *passus* (1.6 m) reflects the Romans' road system and marching armies, the Greek stadion originates in the length of an athletic race track.

Bronze scales, using a simple balance system, were used extensively in Ancient Rome. Weights were verified by officials.

Mesopotamian weights were calculated according to the sexagesimal system. This 1st-millennium BCE relief from Nimrud, Iraq, shows tribute being weighed.

Coinage

As trade networks expanded, barter, which depended on long negotiations, became increasingly inconvenient. The need for an agreed system of equivalences of value led to the invention of coins, metal objects with a constant weight, marked with the official stamp of a public authority. The Greeks of Lydia developed the system in the 7th century BCE, and it was rapidly adopted elsewhere.

This Athenian coin is known as a tetradrachm (479 BCE). The owl was a symbol of Athena.

This early Egyptian counting stick was found with pieces of metal, used as money.

The evolution of calendrical systems

Fragments of a bronze Celtic lunisolar calendar have been found at Coligny, France. Pegs may have been inserted into holes to mark the passage of the days.

The development of calendars was linked to religion and the need to predict days of ritual significance, such as the summer solstice. Calendrical systems developed through astronomical observation and record-keeping, and were dependent on both writing and numeracy. All calendars had to resolve the incommensurate cycles of days, lunations and solar years, usually by intercalating extra days or months at regular intervals. Eras were assessed by different means, most commonly from the regnal years of monarchy, or from the year of birth of significant individuals, such as Buddha or Christ.

Light penetrates the neolithic tomb at Newgrange in Ireland at sunrise on 21 December, an example of the astronomical significance of many stone settings.

The Babylonians made systematic observations of the setting and rising of the planet Venus at the city of Kish, recorded on the Venus tablet (c.1700 BCE).

❸ The evolution and spread of calendrical systems

- ● lunar (months are kept in step with lunar cycle by intercalating days)
- ○ solar (lunar cycle is ignored; years are kept in step with the Sun by intercalating days)
- ◑ lunisolar (month are geared to lunar cycle; extra days are intercalated to key year synchronized with sun)
- ☐ wandering year (fixed number of days; lunar and solar cycles abandoned)
- ······· extent of Roman Empire in 2nd century CE

Core regions for the development of calendrical systems
- Roman
- Celtic
- Egyptian
- Greek
- Hebraic
- Early Historic India
- Mesopotamia
- Chinese
- Central America
- → spread of Egyptian calendar
- → spread of Julian calendar
- → spread of Chinese calendar

33

THE WORLD 750–500 BCE

THE CIVILIZATIONS OF EURASIA, although they only occupied a small portion of the Earth's surface, now lay in a more or less continuous belt from the Mediterranean to China. Both trade and cultural contact were well-established; understanding of iron metallurgy had spread from the Middle East as far as China, and by the 6th century BCE Chinese silk was beginning to appear in Europe, marking the beginning of 1,500 years of trans-Asian trade. All these civilizations, however, were increasingly subjected to incursions by tribes of nomadic pastoralists who were rapidly spreading across Central Asia, eastern Europe, and Siberia – a result of the invention of horse-riding. By 500 BCE, the Classical Age in Greece – a high point in the history of western civilization – was beginning. It was to have a profound impact on European political institutions, art, architecture, drama, and philosophy. In 505 BCE, the *polis* of Athens initiated radical political reforms and became the birthplace of democracy.

Europe

As the city-states of Greece became more prosperous, their civic pride was expressed through magnificent buildings. Greek colonies,

which stretched from the Black Sea to the Iberian Peninsula, were major trading centers, importing raw materials and food supplies in exchange for manufactures, such as pottery. The expanding European population moved into more marginal areas, using iron tools for land clearance and agriculture. Northern Europe was occupied by Celtic and Germanic peoples, whose tribal societies centered on princely graves and hill-top fortresses.

Revelry is a common theme in the tomb frescoes of the Etruscans, whose urban civilization reached its height in 6th-century BCE Italy.

Europe

700: Scythians from Central Asia begin to settle in eastern Europe and Black Sea area
600: Foundation of Greek colony of Massalia. Trade between Greeks and Celts
505: Establishment of democracy in Athens

750: First evidence of use of Greek alphabet
c.600: Defensive hill-top fortresses built throughout southern Germany and eastern France
510: Romans expel Etruscan overlords and establish a republic

750 BCE — 700 — 650 — 600 — 550 — 500 BCE

BABYLONIAN MAP

The earliest known graphic representations of parts of the Earth are the maps engraved by the Babylonians on clay tablets. On this tablet from around 600 BCE the Earth is depicted as a disc surrounded by water. The Euphrates River is shown as two curved lines and small circles carry the names of cities and adjacent countries in cuneiform script.

The Babylonians oriented their maps with Babylon at the center.

Among the monuments at Monte Albán is a series of stone slabs onto which male figures in contorted poses have been carved. Known as *Los Danzantes* (The Dancers), they may represent the vanquished enemies of the Zapotec.

The Americas

As the Olmec civilization continued to flourish around La Venta, other cultures emerged in Central America. The Zapotec civilization was centered on the site of Monte Albán. Hieroglyphic inscriptions of calendrical notations found in the city are the earliest example of writing in the Americas. Adena burials in the eastern woodlands of northern America were furnished with grave goods such as polished stone tools, tobacco pipes, beads, and bracelets. These indicate that a stratified, politically organized society was beginning to emerge.

The Americas

c.700: Growth of permanent horticulture villages in southeastern North America
c.600: Olmec jade artifacts, often used as offerings in ritual "cache" deposits, traded as far afield as southern Central America
500: Cultural influence of Chavín begins to weaken in western South America. Beginnings of Paracas culture

750 BCE — 700 — 650 — 600 — 550 — 500 BCE

c.600: Ball courts, used in ritual ball game of Central American civilizations, found in Olmec centers
500: Early hieroglyphic inscriptions from the Zapotec center of Monte Albán

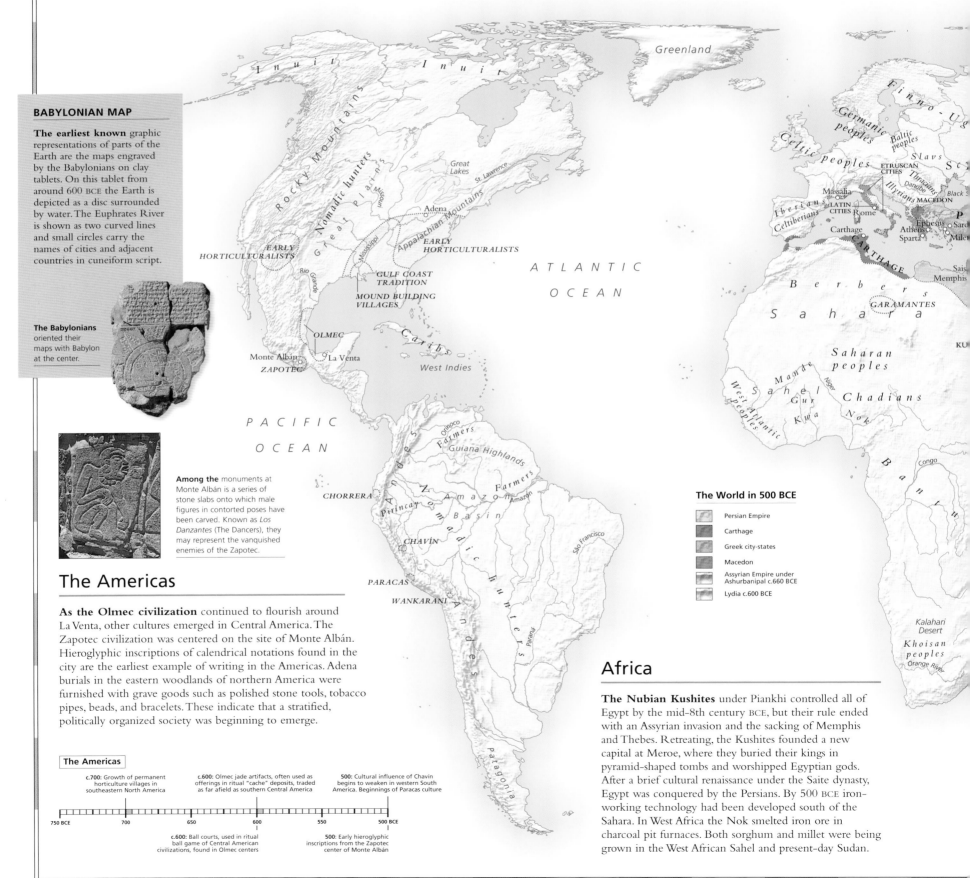

The World in 500 BCE

- Persian Empire
- Carthage
- Greek city-states
- Macedon
- Assyrian Empire under Ashurbanipal c.660 BCE
- Lydia c.600 BCE

Africa

The Nubian Kushites under Piankhi controlled all of Egypt by the mid-8th century BCE, but their rule ended with an Assyrian invasion and the sacking of Memphis and Thebes. Retreating, the Kushites founded a new capital at Meroe, where they buried their kings in pyramid-shaped tombs and worshipped Egyptian gods. After a brief cultural renaissance under the Saite dynasty, Egypt was conquered by the Persians. By 500 BCE iron-working technology had been developed south of the Sahara. In West Africa the Nok smelted iron ore in charcoal pit furnaces. Both sorghum and millet were being grown in the West African Sahel and present-day Sudan.

THE FIRST COINS

The use of metals to make payments can be traced back more than 4000 years, but standardization and certification in the form of coinage did not arrive until the 7th century BCE. The first coins were issued by the Lydians of western Anatolia. They consisted of bean-sized pieces of electrum – a natural alloy of gold and silver – with punchmarks testifying to their weight and therefore their value in payments. By 570 BCE coinage had spread west to Greece and east to Persia. It was invented independently in China and India c.500 BCE.

The first Chinese coins, introduced c.500 BCE, were miniature bronze hoes or spades (*left*), copies of the tools that previously had been used for barter. Early Greek coins carried stamped designs, many derived from the animal world (*right*).

West Asia

Assyria's enemies united to overthrow the empire in 612 BCE, and for a brief period Babylon again enjoyed ascendancy in Mesopotamia. This changed with the arrival of the Medes and Persians, Indo-Europeans from Central Asia. In 550 BCE the Persian king, Cyrus the Great, defeated the Medes and united the two peoples, founding the Achaemenid Empire, which became the largest state the world had yet seen, stretching from the Nile to the Indus. A later Persian ruler, Darius I, consolidated imperial rule: subject peoples were divided into provinces, or satrapies; taxes were levied and the construction of the Royal Road from Sardis to Susa facilitated fast, efficient communications.

The king is the focus of the decoration of the palace at Persepolis, ceremonial capital of the Achaemenid Persians. Reliefs depict his court and processions of tribute-bearers from his empire.

SEE ALSO:

North America: pp.120–121

South America: pp.144–145

Africa: pp.158–159

Europe: pp.176–179

West Asia: pp.222–223

South and Southeast Asia: pp.240–243

North and East Asia: pp.258–259

Australasia and Oceania: pp.280–281

West Asia

700: Nomadic Scythians begin to establish permanent settlements on western steppes

c.663: Assyrian Empire reaches greatest extent with sack of Thebes in Egypt

604: Nebuchadnezzar II rebuilds Babylon and captures Jerusalem

539: Cyrus takes Babylon, and Babylonian Empire, without bloodshed

750 BCE — 700 — 650 — 600 — 550 — 500 BCE

612: Nineveh and Nimrud are sacked by Babylonians and Medes; end of Assyrian Empire

c.550: Cyrus the Great of Persia defeats Medes and founds Achaemenid Empire

521: Persian Empire reaches greatest extent, under Darius I

East Asia

With the beginning of the Eastern Zhou period in 770 BCE, China experienced several centuries of conflict as many former vassals of the Zhou competed for supremacy. This was a period of technological and cultural change. The widespread use of iron tools improved the productivity of the land and led to a marked population increase. At the same time new ideas stimulated feverish intellectual debate. The teaching of Confucius was a practical, ethical guide to good government and social behavior, while Taoism was a philosophy based on a mystical faith in natural forces.

During this period Chinese chariots were elaborately decorated to enhance their appearance in battle. This bronze bull's head chariot fitting is inlaid with gold.

East Asia

c.650: Introduction of iron technology to China. Silk painting, lacquerwork, and ceramics become highly skilled

605: Birth of Lao-tzu, founder of Taoism

551: Birth of Confucius

c.500: Bronze coinage introduced in China

750 BCE — 700 — 650 — 600 — 550 — 500 BCE

c.500: Iron-casting used to manufacture huge quantities of tools and weapons in China

P A C I F I C   O C E A N

Philippine Islands

In India, early traditions, dating back before 2000 BCE, evolved into Hinduism. This stone statue portrays an early deity, Surya, the sun god.

South Asia

From about 1500 BCE the peoples of central north India began to adopt a sedentary life and expanded eastward to settle the Ganges plain. By the 7th century BCE, a patchwork of small states had emerged in northern India. Some were tribal republics, others absolute monarchies, but their common roots – apparent in the Hindu religion and the caste system – underpinned their religious and social organization. The Afghan region of Gandhara and the Indus Valley were absorbed into the Persian Empire in the late 6th century BCE.

From Meroe, the Cushites were able to maintain their rule over the middle Nile until the 4th century CE, while Egypt suffered a series of invasions. This stone ram lies among the ruins of a Meroitic temple at Naqa.

Africa

747: Rule of Egypt by Nubians

671: Assyrian king, Esarhaddon, captures Egyptian capital, Memphis

600: Nubian capital moves to Meroe

c.500: Darius I of Persia completes construction of a canal linking Nile and Red Sea

750 BCE — 700 — 650 — 600 — 550 — 500 BCE

663: Egypt regains independence under 26th Dynasty, which rules from Sais in the Nile Delta until 525 BCE

550: Cyrus the Great founds Persian Empire

525: Egypt becomes part of Persian Empire

South Asia

c.600: 16 Aryan kingdoms are spread across northern India

c.540: Birth of Mahavira, founder of Jain religion

750 BCE — 700 — 650 — 600 — 550 — 500 BCE

c.566: Birth of Buddha, who forsakes life of a nobleman to seek enlightenment through asceticism and good conduct

533: Kingdom of Gandhara becomes satrapy of Persia

THE ORIGINS OF ORGANIZED RELIGION

THE 6TH CENTURY BCE has been called the "axial age" in the development of religion. Judaism, Hinduism, and Taoism were well established. Reformers such as Deutero-Isaiah, Mahavira, Siddhartha Gautama, and Confucius were at work. Around the Mediterranean, a melting-pot of local cults was forming the roots of European Classical civilization, while in the Americas the first urban cultures brought with them organized religion. And frequently, it was the adoption by political rulers of a particular religion which would ensure its longevity and evolution – as in Buddhism, Confucianism, and, later, Christianity – into a world religion.

The development of a priestly class, as here at Sumer, was central in the organization of religious practice as a core social activity.

The development of organized religion

Zoroastrian worship focused on a supreme being, Ahura Mazda, who was widely worshiped at fire altars.

The development of organized religions was linked to the emergence of urban civilization. The earliest known state religion was that of Sumer in the 3rd millennium BCE, and the oldest coherent written mythology was that of Egypt, from the 2nd millennium BCE. By the 1st millennium a range of common characteristics and practices had emerged from local cults to acquire the trappings of organized religion: shamans became priests; myth became doctrine; sacrifice became ceremony; ancestor worship was celebrated in increasingly rich and elaborate burial practices and grandiose monumental architecture.

1 The emergence of organized religion

Cultural regions c.1500–500 BCE

Mesopotamia	Phoenicia	Olmec
Egypt	Greece	Maya
India	Etruscans	Oaxaca
China	Adena	Chavin
Persia	Hopewell	

Religious characteristics

- ancestor worship
- evidence of human sacrifice
- ceremonial burial
- deification of ruler
- monumental architecture
- monotheism

The development of religious architecture

2530: "True" pyramid of Khufu, Giza — 2100: Ziggurat at Ur in Sumer — 510: Temple of Jupiter Optimus Maximus, Rome — 400: Temple complex, Chavin de Huantar

2650: Zoser's stepped pyramid at Saqqara — c. 2000: Stonehenge erected — c. 700: First peristyle Greek temples — 432: Completion of Parthenon, Athens

3000 BCE — 2000 BCE — 1000 BCE — 1 CE

**Map labels:**

NORTH AMERICA

Widespread animistic cults and ancestor worship

Hopewell, Adena, Serpent Mound, Cahokia

Marksville, Mandeville, Mississippi

Olmec c.1200–300 BCE: Monumental sculpture; ceremonial centers; votive burials

Oaxaca c.500–150 BCE: Zapotec temples

Monte Albán, La Venta, San Lorenzo, Chichén Itzá

CENTRAL AMERICA

Maya c.300 BCE–900 CE: Ceremonial centers with pyramids

Adena before 1000 BCE–c.100 CE: Earth temple mounds; burials with grave goods

Mississippian c.1000–1500 CE: Earthwork ceremonial centers; rich grave goods

PACIFIC OCEAN

Chavin c.850–200 BCE: Temple complex; anthropomorphic pantheon

Chavin de Huantar

SOUTH AMERICA

ATLANTIC OCEAN

Northwest Europe: Bog bodies reveal human sacrifice

Northern Europe: Celtic ceremonial centers; burials with rich grave goods

Etruscans c.800–400 BCE: Rich burials and sarcophagi

Rome c.550 BCE–410 CE: 510 BCE: Dedication of temple of Jupiter Optimus Maximus; increasing adoption of Greek pantheon

Phoenician colonies c.800–146 BCE: Cult center at Carthage

Stonehenge, EUROPE

Caere, Rome, Delphi, Athens, Mt. Olympus

Carthage, Mediterranean Sea

Egypt c.3000–30 BCE: c.3100–2795 BCE: Archaic period c.2795–2180 BCE: Old Kingdom, monumental architecture and elaborate (pyramid) tombs c.2134–1640 BCE: Middle Kingdom c.1530–1070 BCE: New Kingdom 1352–1333 BCE: Akhenaten establishes monotheistic Aten (Sun God) cult at El-Armarna

Giza, Saqqara, Jerusalem, Ur, Sumer

Judah to 132 CE Monotheism; c.930 BCE: Temple of Solomon, destroyed 586; second temple built 538 From 132 CE: Jewish diaspora

Widespread animistic cults and ancestor worship

AFRICA

Nile, Niger, Congo

Greece c.900–350 BCE: c.900–500: Spread of city states with local deities and emergence of major cult centers 334–329: Alexander's campaigns spread Hellenistic culture and religion through Southwest Asia

Scythia 1st millennium BCE: Elaborate burials (often with horses) with grave goods

Kostromskaya, Pazyryk

Persia c.550 BCE–226 CE: 550 BCE: Zoroastrianism proclaimed monotheistic state cult of Achaemenid Persia; monumental temples; fire altars From c.116 CE: Zoroastrian cult of Mithraism spreads through Roman Empire

Mesopotamia from 3rd millennium BCE: Royal burials, including attendants, and rich grave goods; monumental (ziggurat) temples

Pasargadae

China from c.1800 BCE: c.1800–1027 BCE: Shang China; ancestor worship, use of oracle bones and bronze inscriptions for divination 1027 BCE–5th century CE: Zhou dynasty; emergence of Taoism, Confucianism 221–206: Qin Dynasty; elaborate royal graves with mass grave goods and terra-cotta armies

ASIA

Luoyang, Rajagriha

India from c.1800 BCE: c.1450 BCE: Composition of Vedas, recording Indian mythology begins c.800 BCE: Rise of cities on central Ganges; Upanishads recorded in Sanskrit

INDIAN OCEAN

Early religion in South Asia

A trimurti at the Temple of Shiva at Elephanta depicts the three principal Hindu divinities, Shiva, Vishnu, and Brahma.

The religion of the ancient Aryan tribes is known largely from the hymns of the *Rig Veda*, and the *Vedas, Brahmanas,* and *Upanishads*. It focused on sacrifices to a pantheon of deities and semigods. Vedic Hinduism spread over much of India before the rise of Buddhism and Jainism, which developed in reaction to the excesses of Aryan religious practices. These faiths emphasized *ahimsa* (nonviolence), meditation, and the suppression of desire for worldly possessions; these and other elements of Hinduism may derive from the religion of the Indus civilization (c.2600–1800 BCE).

2 Religions of South Asia

UDICHYA — broad cultural region recognised by ancient Aryans
MAGADHA — other regions
Yamuna — sacred river
■ core area of Buddhism and Jainism
⊥ Ashokan rock and pillar edicts

Map labels (South Asia):

Taxila, UDICHYA, SAPTA SINDHAVA, BHARATA VARSHA, KURU-KSHETRA, Hastinapura, PRATICHYA, MADHYA-DISH, Mathura, Ayodhya, Kashi, Kosala, Prayaga, Pataliputra, MAGADHA, PRACHYA, Rajagriha, DAKSINA-PATHA, Ujjayini, Tamralipti

Initial core Aryan region
Field of battle in epic Mahabharata war
Home city of Rama, hero of Ramayana epic
Area visited by Gautama Buddha and Mahavira
see inset
Later core Aryan region
Core region of Mauryan Empire

Thar Desert, Indus, Ganges, Yamuna, Narmada, Godavari, Deccan, Western Ghats, Eastern Ghats, Krishna, Kaveri, Brahmaputra, Arabian Sea, Bay of Bengal, Lanka (Simhala), Anuradhapura

Ashoka's bloody conquest of this region leads him to foreswear war and adopt Buddhism

Early religion in South Asia

c.1550: Aryans settle northern India — 6th century: Life of Mahavira, founder of Jainism — 566: Birth of Siddhartha Gautama, founder of Buddhism — 322: Chandragupta founds Mauryan dynasty

1400 BCE — 1000 — 600 — 200 BCE

c.800: Rise of urban culture in Ganges valley — c.600: Rise to dominance of Magadha — 272–232: Reign of Ashoka, who promulgates Buddhism as state religion

**Inset map labels:**

Legendary descent of the Buddha from heaven
566: Birthplace
537: Great Renunciation
483: Attainment of Nirvana
528: Attainment of Enlightenment
528: Sermon in the Deer Park

Kampilya, Samkashya, Kanauj, KOSHALA, Shravasti, Ayodhya, Lumbini, Kapilavatthu, Kusinagara, Prayaga, Kaushambi, Sarnath, Benares, Vaishali, Pataliputra, MAGADHA, Nalanda, Champa, ANGA, Bodh Gaya, Gaya, Rajgir, Sermon

200 km
200 miles

Religions of the Mediterranean

The Mediterranean world in the 1st millennium BCE was the home of a range of discrete cultures, each supporting its own religious beliefs. However, many of these shared striking similarities in mythology, in the character and nature of their pantheons, and in religious practice and observance. Rivalry, warfare, and trade created an interaction of influences and cross-fertilizations, and with the rise of Classical Greece, Hellenistic culture, and then Rome, certain local beliefs and practices became widespread.

Greece

The Greek mythological pantheon, developed during the Mycenaean period, was described by writers such as Homer and became, during the Classic Greek period, a central force in Greek life. Each city-state practiced favored cults, but the emergence of oracles and other cult centers (such as Mount Olympus) codified a pan-Hellenic religious tradition which was spread widely by colonization and the campaigns of Alexander the Great *(see pp. 40–41).*

Zeus (Jupiter for the Romans) was the supreme Greek deity.

SEE ALSO:

Africa: pp.160–161

Europe: pp.174–179

West Asia: pp.220–221

South and Southeast Asia: pp.242–243

North and East Asia: pp.258–259

❸ The Mediterranean cults ▶

Cult centers
- ◉ Egyptian
- ◉ Greek
- ○ other

Ares main divinity worshipped
- → spread of the cult of Cybele
- → spread of the Greek Pantheon
- → spread of Mithraism

Judaism

The traditional religion of Israel and Judah was unusual in having a single deity, Jahweh. The Babylonian exile (587–538 BCE) strengthened Judaism and encouraged the crystallization of its core beliefs by Deutero-Isaiah and other prophets. The religion survived persecution to become the seedbed of Christianity.

The Jewish candelabra *(menorah)* symbolizes the eternal light *(ner tamid)* which burned in the first Temple of Solomon.

The demigod Heracles (Hercules in Latin) formed part of the Greek mythological pantheon adopted by the Romans.

Rome

Rome's pantheon was largely adopted from that of Greece, although certain local cults gained popularity as the empire grew. One of the most widespread was that of Mithras, which spread from Persia to Syria, then throughout the empire; eventually the most influential was Christianity.

A dead man kneels before Anubis, god of mummification. Life after death was central to Egyptian theology, celebrated through a series of elaborate rituals.

Egypt

A detailed mythology and pantheon permeated Ancient Egyptian life and thought, and is recorded abundantly in votive statuary and hieroglyphic tomb paintings. The hierarchy and character of Egyptian cosmology probably influenced the development of the Mycenaean and Greek pantheon.

This Mycenaean ritual sprinkler takes the form of a bull's head.

Bull cults

Bull worshiping was widespread in the Mediterranean region, from Çatal Hüyük (c.7000 BCE) to the famous Minotaur cult in Crete (from c.2000 BCE); bulls also played a significant role in Egyptian, Mesopotamian, and Greek mythology.

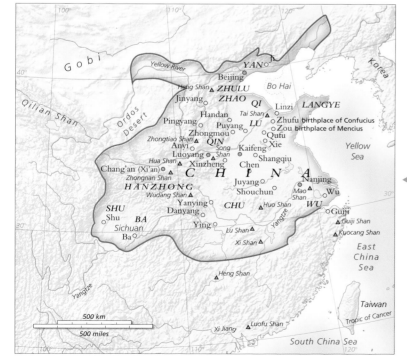

Taoism and Confucianism

Taoism developed during the Zhou dynasty as the most widespread of Chinese religions. Based on the worship of ancestors, nature spirits, and sacred places, it was codified by Lao-tzu (605–520 BCE). The philosopher Confucius (551–479 BCE) promulgated a system of filial observance, learning, obedience, and selflessness which became central to Chinese imperial policy and governance. Followers such as Mencius (c.370–300 BCE) ensured that his teachings survived the Warring States period (403–221 BCE).

❹ Taoism and Confucianism

- Chinese cultural area c.220 BCE
- *YAN* region associated with development of Taoism
- ▲ mountain sacred to Taoism

Centers of Confucianism
- ○ Imperial capital
- ◉ Qin state capital by c.220 BCE

The teachings of Confucius ensured that even the most lowly could, by ability, correct behavior, and hard work, aspire to high office.

Taoism and Confucianism in China

1027: Beginnings of Zhou dynastic rule

771: Decline of Zhou central administration

551–479: Confucius, author of the *Analects,* provides central philosophy for Chinese way of life

605–520: Lao-tzu, traditional founder of Taoism

403–221: Warring States period

c. 370–300: Mencius continues Confucian teaching

| 1050 BCE | 950 | 850 | 750 | 650 | 550 | 450 | 350 | 250 BCE |

THE WORLD 500–250 BCE

THE 5TH CENTURY BCE was an age of enlightened and innovative thought. It was the climax of the Classical Age in Greece, a period that was remarkable for its art, philosophy, drama, architecture, and political theory. At the same time the Buddhist religion, based on the precepts of renouncing all material desires as practiced by Siddhartha Gautama (c.566–486 BCE), was spreading throughout the Indian subcontinent. In China, the teachings of Confucius (551–479 BCE) were concerned with ethical conduct and propriety in human relations. Yet the ensuing centuries were a time of conflict and conquest. From 331–323 BCE Alexander the Great's military conquests created an empire which stretched from Macedon to the Indus. From c.272 BCE the emperor Ashoka absorbed most of the Indian subcontinent into his empire, while in China the Warring States period was a time of violent turmoil.

The shrine of Delphi was the site of the Pythian Games, one of four great athletic festivals that brought Greeks together at set intervals of years.

Europe

In the 5th century BCE, Greece reached the pinnacle of the Classical Age. Athens' conflict with Sparta in the Peloponnesian Wars weakened the Greek city-states, which in the 4th century fell to Philip of Macedon. Under his son, Alexander the Great, who conquered the Persian Empire, Macedon became a great imperial power. In Italy, by 264 BCE, Rome was poised to become a world power.

Europe

500 BCE	450	400	350	300	250 BCE

490: Greeks defeat Persians at Marathon
443–429: Athens flourishes under rule of Pericles
390: Celts sack Rome
336: Alexander embarks on conquest of Persian Empire
323: Death of Alexander the Great
264: Rome leads single Italian confederacy

c.450: Celts expand into British Isles and to east and south
431–404: Peloponnesian Wars between Athens and Sparta
338: Philip II of Macedon defeats Greek states
260: Start of Roman conflict with Carthage

THE ARCHIMEDEAN SCREW

Named after Archimedes, the Greek mathematician (287–212 BCE), the Archimedean screw is one of the earliest devices for raising water. It was probably invented in the 7th or 8th century BCE in Mesopotamia. Consisting of a spiral screw revolving inside a close-fitting cylinder, it has been widely used over the centuries for the irrigation and land drainage.

This Egyptian terra-cotta figurine from c.30 BCE shows a slave driving an Archimedean screw by means of a treadmill.

Textiles are one of the earliest and greatest art forms in the Andean region. This strikingly embroidered alpaca-wool piece shows the complex imagery of the Paracas culture.

The Americas

As the influence of Chavín culture waned, distinct local cultures began to emerge in South America. At Paracas in southern Peru cemeteries have been found containing thousands of mummified bodies, wrapped in colored woven textiles, decorated with mythical beasts and deities which bear a strong Chavín imprint. In North America the Hopewell culture of the eastern woodlands succeeded the Adena, continuing earlier traditions of building elaborate burial mounds and large earthworks.

The Americas

500 BCE	450	400	350	300	250 BCE

c.500: Paracas culture of southern Peru, famed for brightly colored textiles, emerges
c.350: Beginnings of Nazca culture in southern Peru

c.400: Early Zapotec culture flourishing around city of Monte Albán
c.300: Hopewell culture in eastern North America develops traditions of earlier Adena culture

The Nok produced clay portrait sculptures with elaborate hairstyles and naturalistic representations of facial peculiarities.

Africa

The western Mediterranean was dominated by the Phoenician city of Carthage, which also controlled trans-Saharan trade with West Africa. Iron-working was well established there by 500 BCE. The Nok of the Niger Delta was the most famous culture of this early Iron Age. The Persian satrapy of Egypt was conquered by Alexander the Great in 332 BCE. On Alexander's death, Egypt fell to his successor, Ptolemy, who founded the Ptolemaic dynasty.

MAPPING THE FIXED STARS

Ancient astronomers had noticed that the Sun, Moon, and planets did not remain stationary relative to the "fixed" stars. Instead, over the course of a year, they seemed to pass through a region in the sky occupied by twelve specific constellations that we now call the zodiac, from a Greek term meaning "circle of animals." The zodiacal signs appear to have been a Babylonian invention: their first appearance is on a cuneiform horoscope from c.410 BCE.

The twelve signs of the zodiac border a procession of horses and musicians on this 4th-century BCE fresco from a Thracian tomb.

West Asia

In 490 BCE Darius I of Persia sent a punitive expedition against Athens and other cities that had helped Greek cities in Asia Minor to rebel, but it was defeated at Marathon. Over the next century, the Persian empire was weakened by strife and rebellion. In 331 BCE Alexander the Great of Macedon defeated Darius III and brought the Persian Empire to an end. In 323 BCE, Alexander's vast empire was divided among three successors. Most of West Asia became part of the Seleucid Empire. Small local kingdoms were ruled by ethnic or mixed Greek dynasties.

Following his untimely death at the age of 32, Alexander the Great remained a legendary figure in the ancient world. This detail of a 1st-century BCE mosaic from Pompeii shows the young king in battle against the Persians at Issus in 333 BCE.

SEE ALSO:

North America: pp.120–121

South America: pp.144–147

Africa: pp.158–161

Europe: pp.176–179

West Asia: pp.222–223

South and Southeast Asia: pp.240–243

North and East Asia: pp.258–259

Australasia and Oceania: pp.280–281

West Asia

490: Persian expedition to Greece is defeated at Marathon

331: Alexander the Great's victory at the battle of Gaugamela brings Achaemenid Persian Empire to an end

276–272: Ptolemaic Empire expands into Syria during war with Seleucids

500 BCE — 450 — 400 — 350 — 300 — 250 BCE

480: Darius I is succeeded by his son Xerxes, who invades Greece and is defeated at Salamis, Plataea, and Mycale

312: Seleucus gains control of Persia, Syria, and much of Asia Minor; founds the Seleucid dynasty

East Asia

From about 1000 BCE, nomads reared cattle, goats, and sheep, supplemented by farming and hunting, on the Russian steppe. Contemporary burial sites in the Altai Mountains contain leather, wood, fur, textiles, a wooden wagon, and tattooed bodies. Steppe chieftains may have acted as middlemen in trade between China and Europe. From 403–221 BCE, China was locked in internal conflict, with seven major states competing for supremacy. By the 4th century BCE the Qin were starting to assert control over the whole region.

Mythical combat was a favored theme in the art of the hunting and herding peoples of the Altai region. On this wooden carving, a stag is gripped in the jaws of a griffin.

East Asia

c.450: Burials at Pazyryk and Noin Ula in Siberia give insight into life of steppe nomads

403: Beginning of Warring States period in China

c.350: The crossbow invented in China

256: Qin takes Luoyang area

500 BCE — 450 — 400 — 350 — 300 — 250 BCE

c.480: Death of Confucius, who developed humanistic ethical system

400: Iron-working introduced to Korea

c.350: Qin state develops new political and economic system based on strict system of rewards and punishments

Ashoka recorded his understanding of the moral teachings of Buddhism by inscribing edicts on pillars and stones at suitable sites throughout India. One pillar is crowned with four beautifully carved lions. These were chosen as the emblem of the modern state of India.

South Asia

During the 5th century BCE the states of the Ganges plain were eventually absorbed into the kingdom of Magadha. Shortly after Alexander's invasion of northwest India in 327 BCE, Chandragupta Maurya seized the throne and began to expand the empire. By the time of Ashoka (297–232 BCE), the Mauryans ruled most of the subcontinent. Ashoka became repelled by warfare and converted to Buddhism, which, under his patronage, became a major force in India, and beyond.

The World in 250 BCE

- Qin Empire
- Carthage
- Massalia
- Greek city-states
- Macedon
- Mauryan Empire
- Seleucid Empire
- ◇ Ptolemaic Empire
- Empire of Alexander the Great 323 BCE

Africa

c.500: First iron-working in sub-Saharan Africa. Beginning of period of Nok culture in Niger Delta

332: Alexander the Great conquers Egypt. He lays the foundations of Alexandria

302: Ptolemy I declares himself king of Egypt. The Ptolemies took pharaonic titles and worshipped Egyptian deities

500 BCE — 450 — 400 — 350 — 300 — 250 BCE

c.500: Iron-using Bantu begin to spread from Niger to East African lakes region and down west coast of Africa

c.250: Settlement of Jenne-jeno is founded on inland Niger Delta

South Asia

327: Alexander the Great occupies northwest India

260: Ashoka converts to Buddhism

500 BCE — 450 — 400 — 350 — 300 — 250 BCE

320: Chandragupta Maurya controls Magadha kingdom and advances towards Indus and Central India

272: Ashoka seizes throne and embarks on further imperial conquests

THE EMPIRE OF ALEXANDER

Alexander the Great, (356–323 BCE), was king of Macedonia and conqueror of a great Afro-Eurasian empire.

THE CONQUESTS OF ALEXANDER took Greek armies to Egypt, Mesopotamia, the Hindu Kush, and India's western borders, and forced Achaemenid Persia, the most powerful empire in the world, into submission. This extraordinary and audacious military feat, accomplished in just ten years, was to create a truly cosmopolitan civilization. Hellenism permeated the cultures of West Asia: some Hellenistic kingdoms survived into the 1st century CE, while Greek remained the official language in many parts of West Asia until the 8th and 9th centuries CE; cities founded in the aftermath of Alexander's conquests, perpetuated the ideals of Greek civilization – some, such as Alexandria, Kandahar, and Tashkent, survive to this day. Ultimately, Alexander opened up new horizons; his followers encountered different peoples and cultures and established trade routes which linked the Mediterranean with East Africa, India, and Asia.

The battle between the Greeks and Persians is depicted with vigorous, high-relief realism on this sarcophagus, found at Sidon.

The conquests of Alexander

Alexander succeeded to the Macedonian throne after the assassination of his father, Philip, in 336 BCE. He crossed into Asia in 334 BCE, defeated the Persian provincial army at Granicus and liberated the old Greek cities of Asia Minor. After a brief sojourn in Egypt, he won a spectacular victory over the Persian emperor, Darius III, at Issus and pursued him into Persia, taking the cities of Babylon, Susa, and Persepolis. He pressed on to Bactria and Sogdiana, the eastern outposts of the Persian Empire, and crossed the Hindu Kush. At the Hyphasis River (Beas) his army refused to go farther. He died in Babylon in 323 BCE, aged 32.

① The Empire of Alexander ▶

- ▨ Empire of Alexander
- ▨ dependent regions
- ▨ independent states
- → route of Alexander the Great
- → route of Nearchus
- → return route of Craterus
- ⚔ major battle
- ── Persian Royal Road

This 1st-century Roman mosaic (based possibly on a Macedonian original) shows Darius III, the Persian emperor, at the battle of Issus (333 BCE). His crushing defeat allowed Alexander to conquer the western half of the Persian Empire.

Hellenistic cities of West Asia

The most magnificent West Asian Hellenistic foundation was Pergamum, capital of the Attalid dynasty (282 to 133 BCE). Adorned by a new school of baroque architecture, characterized by its ornate and heavy style, the city had a spectacular theater and an impressive library, second only to Alexandria.

"The Dying Gaul" is a copy of one of the statues erected in Pergamum to commemorate the turning back of a Gaulish invasion in 241 BCE.

Scale varies with perspective

3330 km (2070 miles)

8900 km (5530 miles)

Spring 333 BCE: Over 30 cities in Lycia surrender to Alexander; he reaches Gordium, where he cuts Gordian Knot, said to be sign he will rule all Asia

May 334 BCE: Alexander visits Troy, where he appropriates so-called sword of Achilles

1 Oct 331 BCE: Alexander's second battle with Darius III, whose army includes elephants and scythe-wheeled chariots. Victory for Alexander signals effective end of Persian Empire

Feb 324 BCE: Returns to St Mass marriage of Gre soldiers to Persian bri

Nov 333 BCE: Alexander's first meeting in battle with Darius III. Persian army taken by surprise, suffer heavy losses, and Darius flees

Nov 331 BCE: Following surrender of Babylon, Alexander enters city in triumph
10 Jun 323 BCE: Alexander dies in Babylon

Sep–Nov 332 BCE: Siege of key Persian fortress of Gaza. Alexander wounded by catapult bolt

Midwinter 331 BCE: Alexander visits oracle of Ammon at Siwa; kinship with Ammon-Zeus proclaimed

The growth of Macedonian power

359: Philip starts rise to power, and begins to extend Macedonian territory	**342:** Philip master of Thrace; one of conquered cities renamed Philippopolis	**336:** Philip is succeeded by his son Alexander	**333:** Persian king Darius III is defeated at Issus	**326:** Alexander reaches Taxila; prevented from advancing into India by revolt of his troops	

360 BCE	350	340	330	320 BCE

| **356:** Philip II takes title of king; birth of his son Alexander | **346:** War in Central Greece ends in uneasy peace between Philip and Athens | **338:** Battle of Chaeronea; Philip II defeats Greek states | **332:** Alexander founds the city of Alexandria in northern Egypt | **331:** Decisive defeat of the Persians at battle of Gaugamela | **323:** Death of Alexander |

SEE ALSO:

Africa: pp.160–161

Europe: pp.176–179

West Asia pp.222–225

South and Southeast Asia: pp.240–241

CULTURAL EXCHANGE BETWEEN GREECE AND ASIA

The diffusion of Greek civilization resulted in a rich interplay of influences. The impact of Greek culture was extensive. Greek was spoken over a vast area; in Egypt it started to replace the native language, and inscriptions in Greek are found as far east as northern India. Greek styles of portraiture can be traced in the coins from the remote Greco-Bactrian kingdom of Central Asia, and in the massive sculptured heads of Nemrut Dag in Asia Minor. But Greek culture also absorbed West Asian influences, most notably in the appropriation of Egyptian deities into the Ptolemaic pantheon.

During the rule of the Ptolemies, Egyptian deities were Hellenized and absorbed into the Greek pantheon. This Greco-Roman statue depicts Anubis, the jackal-headed god of mummification.

War elephants, depicted here on an Italian plate, were brought back to the Mediterranean by Greeks who had fought against them in India. The fighting tower on the elephant's back was possibly a Greek invention.

Hellenism in the East

One of the most remote outposts of Hellenism was the city of Ai Khanoum (probably known in its day as Alexandria ad Oxum), on the borders of modern Russia and Afghanistan. It had all the characteristic features of a Greek city: agora, acropolis, temples, gymnasium, and library. The ruined temple of Cybele, however, suggests that oriental rites were used in the worship of the goddess. A Greek inscription found in the city records one of the maxims of the famous oracle at Delphi, some 3,700 miles away.

A silver disc from the temple of Cybele at Ai Khanoum shows a Hellenized version of the goddess riding in a chariot with a Persian priest standing at a fire altar.

This Hellenistic statue of a lion stands in the ruins of Buthara in present-day Pakistan.

The Alexandrian legacy

Alexander's death precipitated destructive wars between his Macedonian generals. Eventually, his empire was divided between three main dynasties. The Ptolemies ruled in Egypt until 30 BCE, and established a stable kingdom with its capital at Alexandria. The Antigonids, based in Macedonia, dominated the affairs of Greece. The Seleucids, who ruled over Syria and Babylon, lost much of their original territory in the east to independent Hellenistic kingdoms such as Bactria, while Pergamum came to dominate Asia Minor.

On this Bactrian coin, King Demetrios is portrayed wearing the symbolic elephant scalp that appeared on similar coins of Alexander after his eastern conquests.

Hellenistic empires and kingdoms

323: On Alexander's death, his empire disintegrates among warring factions	278: Three main Hellenistic kingdoms established; the Ptolemies in Egypt, the Seleucids in Babylonia and Syria, and the Antigonids in Macedonia	c.250: Bactrian kingdom becomes independent from Seleucid Empire	221: Accession of Philip V of Macedon	
325 BCE	300	275	250	225	200 BCE
312: Seleucus takes Babylon; foundation of Seleucid dynasty	304: Ptolemy I declares himself king of Egypt	240: Kingdom of Pergamum founded in Asia Minor. It lasts till annexation by Rome in 133 BCE	212: Rome becomes involved in Greece in First Macedonian War	

### Map labels

Gobi
Atlai Mountains
Yellow River
Tien Shan
Lake Balkhash
Takla Makan Desert
Plateau of Tibet
Himalayas
Brahmaputra
Jaxartes
Tashkent
Alexandria Eschate (Kokand)

Autumn 329 BCE: Greeks use Maracanda as forward base for raids into surrounding regions. Revolt by conquered peoples harshly repressed

Spring 328 BCE: Capture of Sogdian Rock

Spring 327 BCE: Alexander marries Roxanne, daughter of Sogdian baron, Oxyartes

Maracanda (Samarkand)
Sogdian Rock
Oxus
Bukhara
Nautaca
SOGDIANA
Aornos 327
Drapsaca
Taxila
Alexandria ad Oxum (Ai Khanoum)
PARAPAMISUS
Bactra
Bucephala
Hydaspes 326
Kara Kum
BACTRIA
Hindu Kush
Alexandria (Merv)
Spring 329 BCE: Alexander crosses Hindu Kush
Sangela
Hydaspes
Zeratros
330

Winter 327 BCE: Campaigns in Swat valley

Spring 326 BCE: Leading army of some 80,000 troops and 30,000 camp-followers, Alexander crosses Indus and marches on Taxila

Sep 326 BCE: At Hyphasis River, Greek troops refuse to go any further. Army turns back

May 326 BCE: Death of Alexander's horse, Bucephalus. City founded in his memory

MALAVA
ARIA
326
Meshed
Susia
Artacoana
Bojnurd
Alexandria Areion (Herat)
Alexandria Arachoton (Kandahar)
ARACHOSIA
Opiana
HYRCANIA
Hecatompylos
DRANGIANA
Quetta
Thar Desert
INDIA
PARTHIA
Nad-i-Ali

Nov 326 BCE: Army passes through Punjab and Sind, ruthlessly crushing all resistance

Summer 330 BCE: In pursuit of retreating Darius, Alexander passes through Caspian Gates (rocky defile guarded by Persian fortress). Discovers Darius dying, murdered by conspiring Persian commanders

Caspian Gates
Great Salt Desert
RAETACENE
Iranian Plateau
Gabae
CARMANIA
GEDROSIA
Pattala
Kokala
Pasargadae
325
Pura
PERSIS
330
Persepolis
Alexandria (Gulashkird)
324
Harmozia
Gwadar
Persian Gates
Zagros Mountains
331
SIANA
Arabian Sea
Gulf of Oman

Autumn 325 BCE: Alexander leads troops through Makran desert, where heat and thirst cause terrible loss of life. Rest of the army makes wide detour around the desert, under the leadership of Craterus

30 Jan 330 BCE: Alexander reaches Persepolis; army sacks city. Royal palace later put to torch by Alexander and troops

Jan 330 BCE: Alexander attempts to go through Persian Gates (a pass through Zagros Mountains). When ambushed by Persians, Alexander leads army up steep, narrow track to surprise enemy from the rear

Persian Gulf

325 BCE: Alexander's fleet, built to descend the Indus, is brought back to the Persian Gulf by Nearchus

Arabian Peninsula

Inset map: Hellenistic kingdoms 240 BCE

Philippopolis (Plovdiv)
Black Sea
Pella
MACEDONIA
Thessalonica
Nicomedia
Nicaea
Demetrias
Pergamum
Apollonis
Laodicea
Seleucia Sidera
Nysa
Attalia
Cnidus
Seleucia Pieria
Apamea
Laodicea
Edessa
Nisibis
Zeugma
Antioch
SYRIA
Euphrates
Tigris
Dura Europos
Artemita
Laodicea in Media (Nehavend)
Seleucia
BABYLONIA
Charax
Mediterranean Sea
Alexandria
Philadelphia
Babylon
EGYPT
AFRICA
Nile
Red Sea
Arabian Pensinula
Persian Gulf
Caspian Sea
Oxus
Jaxartes
Alexandria Margiana (Merv)
PARTHIA
Alexandria Areion
Begram
Taxila
Charsadda

500 km
500 miles

❷ Hellenistic kingdoms 240 BCE

- independent Greek states
- Ptolemaic Empire and dependencies
- Antigonid kingdom and dependencies
- Seleucid Empire and dependencies
- Hellenized non-Greek kingdoms
- Kingdom of Pergamum
- Graeco-Bactria
- ○ Hellenistic cities (founded 350–100 BCE)

THE WORLD 250 BCE – 1 CE

BY 1 CE HALF THE GLOBAL population, which had reached about 250 million, lived within three major empires – Rome, Parthia, and Han China. With the addition of the developing kingdoms of northern India and Southeast Asia, urban civilization now existed in a wide swathe across the Old World, from the Iberian Peninsula in the west to Korea in the east, surrounded by nomadic pastoralists, farmers, and increasingly marginalized hunter-gatherers. The opening up of the Silk Road in the 1st century BCE and the discovery of monsoon trade routes across the Indian Ocean led to an unprecedented degree of contact between empires, disseminating both religious and cultural influences. In the New World the increasingly sophisticated Nazca and Moche cultures were developing in Peru, while Teotihuacán in Mexico was poised to become one of the world's most populous cities.

Europe

The Ara Pacis (Altar of Peace) was set up in Rome in 9 BCE to commemorate the pacification of Gaul and Iberia by the Emperor Augustus.

Following the defeat of Carthage in the 2nd century BCE, Rome embarked on a program of expansion, which extended control to Greek territories in the east and Gaul to the north. In the 1st century BCE, a period of civil wars and rule by military dictators threatened the unity of the growing empire. In 27 BCE Octavian assumed imperial power (and the title Augustus), reuniting the Roman world and ushering in two centuries of stability and prosperity.

Europe

218–201: Second Punic War. Hannibal crosses Alps and invades Italy
146: With the sack of Corinth, Greece comes under Roman rule. Third Punic War ends with sack of Carthage by Rome
58–51: Gallic conquests of Julius Caesar
46: Julius Caesar appointed dictator. He is assassinated two years later

250 BCE — 200 — 150 — 100 — 50 — 1 CE

241: End of First Punic War between Rome and Carthage
168: Roman expansion into eastern Mediterranean begins
89: Roman citizenship extended to all Italians
31: Octavian defeats Antony and Cleopatra at Actium

This striking Nazca pottery figure shows a woman chewing coca leaves, an important cultural and ritual activity in the civilizations of the Andes.

The Americas

The Nazca people continued local traditions of fine textiles and pottery decorated with animals, birds, fish, plants, and human trophy heads. But the culture is best known for the Nazca Lines, long straight tracks and outlines of animals and mythical figures traced on the surface of the desert. Possibly created as offerings to the gods, their scale is so vast they can only be distinguished from the air. At the same time, the Moche culture of northern Peru, which has left a legacy of substantial urban and religious centers, fine pottery and goldwork, was beginning to emerge.

The Americas

c.200: Nazca Lines carved into the surface of the southern Peruvian desert
c.100: Adena culture of North America at its height
c.1 CE: The Moche, famous for their gold and pottery, dominate northern Peru

250 BCE — 200 — 150 — 100 — 50 — 1 CE

c.250: Many small coastal cultures, such as the Guangala, flourishing in present-day Ecuador
c.50: Teotihuacán in Valley of Mexico is largest city in the Americas, with population of 40,000

The Rosetta stone records events relating to the coronation of Ptolemy V of Egypt in 196 BCE in three languages: Egyptian hieroglyphic, Egyptian demotic *(both shown below)*, and Greek.

ROMAN SURVEYING

The Romans surveyed the terrain of their empire from Scotland to Egypt in order to build roads. The purpose of the roads was primarily military – to enable Roman legions to move quickly to trouble spots within the empire – but they also carried local commercial traffic. Distances were measured in thousands of paces *(milia passuum)* – hence the word mile – and milestones were placed at regular intervals. The Roman mile was about 1,680 yards (1,540 meters).

This Roman milestone stood on the Via Aemilia, which ran in a straight line across northern Italy. The inscription records road repairs undertaken in the reign of Augustus (27 BCE–14 CE).

Africa

Rome's defeat of Carthage in 146 BCE brought North Africa into the sphere of its growing Mediterranean empire. Throughout most of this period, Egypt was ruled by the Ptolemies, whose introduction of Greek language and writing hastened the decline of Egyptian civilization. In 31 BCE, when Octavian defeated Antony and Cleopatra at the battle of Actium, Egypt became a Roman province destined to serve as Rome's granary. To the south the kingdom of Meroe prospered, exporting frankincense to Rome along the Red Sea. The Bantu continued their progress into southern Africa, introducing agriculture and iron-working.

West Asia

Following the secession of Bactria, Sogdiana, and Parthia from Seleucid rule in the mid-3rd century BCE, the nomadic Parthians took advantage of the upheaval to extend their territory. By the early 1st century BCE, their empire included Mesopotamia and stretched from Syria to Bactria. With their light, maneuverable mounted bowmen, the Parthians withstood the might of Rome at the battle of Carrhae (53 BCE), halting Rome's eastern expansion. The Parthian Empire lasted 500 years, growing wealthy from its control of the Silk Road linking China and Rome.

This ivory rhyton (horn-shaped drinking cup) was found at Nisa, the early capital of the Parthians after they expanded south from their homelands east of the Caspian Sea.

West Asia

247: Arsaces founds the Arsacid, or Parthian, dynasty

171: Mithridates II founds Parthian Empire

141: Parthians control Mesopotamia following capture of the old Seleucid capital, Seleucia-on-the-Tigris

53: Defeat of Roman infantry at the battle of Carrhae in northern Syria

124 : Accession of Mithridates II. Parthian Empire reaches greatest extent

90: Ctesiphon established as Parthian capital

40: Rome recognizes Herod the Great as ruler of Judaea

250 BCE — 200 — 150 — 100 — 50 — 1 CE

East Asia

The Qin unified China in 221 BCE, their leader taking the title "First Emperor" and introducing a harsh, centralized, bureaucratic regime. His death in 210 was followed by widespread revolts. By 206 the Han dynasty under Gao Zu had taken power. The Han, too, presided over a highly centralized bureaucracy, their state monopoly on iron and salt, combined with the opening up of the Silk Road to Central Asia, ensuring their prosperity.

Shi Huangdi, the Qin First Emperor, imposed his autocratic rule through military force. A symbolic army of thousands of life-sized, terra-cotta soldiers was assembled to guard his tomb.

East Asia

210: Death of Shi Huangdi leads to revolts throughout Qin Empire

206: Han dynasty, under Gao Zu, assumes control

119: State monopoly on iron-working established

108: Chinese take military control of Korea

55: Xiongnu confederacy breaks up; southern group becomes tributary of Han China

221: Great Wall built as protection against northern nomadic incursions

136: Confucianism becomes state religion of China

c.112: Opening up of Silk Road across Central Asia

250 BCE — 200 — 150 — 100 — 50 — 1 CE

SEE ALSO:

North America: pp.120–121

South America: pp.144–145

Africa: pp.160–161

Europe: pp.178–179

West Asia: pp.224–225

South and Southeast Asia: pp.240–243

North and East Asia: pp.258–261

Australasia and Oceania: pp.280–281

ROMAN BUILDINGS

Architecturally, the Romans borrowed freely from the Greeks and other earlier civilizations. The most distinctive feature of their buildings, the arch, was inherited from the Etruscans. One of the Romans' major innovations was the use of *pozzolana*, concrete made of sand mixed with slaked lime and volcanic ash. This enabled them to build temples, bath houses, aqueducts, and amphitheatres on a prodigious scale.

The coffered dome of the Pantheon in Rome is made of *pozzolana*. It was still the largest in the world even when the dome of St Peter's was completed in the 16th century.

The great complex of rock-carved temples and monasteries at Ajanta in Central India became an important Buddhist center in the 1st century BCE. It is famous for its many fine ceiling paintings of the Buddha.

The World in 1 CE

- Han Empire
- Roman Empire and client states
- Empire of Pontus under Mithridates Eupator, c.100 BCE
- Numidia under Masinissa from 201 BCE
- Burebista's Dacian Kingdom, 45 BCE

South and Southeast Asia

On the death of Ashoka in 232 BCE, the Mauryan Empire disintegrated and, in 185 BCE, was supplanted by the Shunga dynasty. The Greek colony of Bactria became independent and, in the Indus Valley region, Bactrians established kingdoms where Hellenic and Indian influences mingled. Much of Southeast Asia fell under Indian cultural influence as Hinduism and Buddhism spread eastward. Chinese contact was political and military; Annam fell under Han control in the 1st century BCE.

Africa

146: Destruction of Carthage; Rome creates province of Africa from former Carthaginian possessions

105: Jugurtha, king of Numidia defeated by Roman general Gaius Marius

46: Foundation of Roman colony of Carthage

c.100: Camel introduced into Sahara by the Romans

31: Cleopatra's death marks end of Ptolemaic dynasty in Egypt

250 BCE — 200 — 150 — 100 — 50 — 1 CE

South and Southeast Asia

c.200: Bactrian Greeks establish small kingdoms

111: Annam falls to Han Empire

90: Bactrian kingdom of Gandhara falls to Scythians (Shakas)

232: Start of disintegration of Mauryan Empire

185: Pusyamitra founds Shunga dynasty

c.100: Indian influences spread to Southeast Asia via maritime trade routes

c.30: Shakas overrun Indo-Greek kingdoms of Indus Valley

250 BCE — 200 — 150 — 100 — 50 — 1 CE

TRADE IN THE CLASSICAL WORLD

Fine Chinese silks from this period, lightweight and of high value, have been found throughout Eurasia, as far west as Egypt and Greece.

BY THE BEGINNING of the 1st millennium CE, a series of commercial and political networks had evolved which combined to form a nexus of trade which linked the eastern shores of the Atlantic Ocean, the Indian Ocean, and the western shores of the Pacific. At its extremes this network linked the Roman Empire, centered on the Mediterranean, and the land-based Han Empire of China. As the commercial and territorial influences of these two power bases spread beyond their political domains, so outlying regions were drawn into the web, from sub-Saharan Africa to the East Indies. However, the most important link to emerge was the Silk Road which spanned Asia, threading through the mountain ranges and deserts of the Central Asian landmass, and along which a chain of powerful trading cities and states came into being.

Han China and the wider world

The Han Dynasty, which emerged to take over the territorial extent of the Qin Empire from 206 BCE, was largely self-sufficient. Trade was not regarded as an imperial concern, although desirable goods were drawn into Han markets by successive middlemen on the empire's fringes – spices from South and Southeast Asia, trepang (dried sea cucumber) and mother-of-pearl from the East Indies and, with the extension of the empire into Central Asia, the swift cavalry horses of Ferghana became highly prized. Conversely, Chinese products such as silk and lacquerware commanded high prices across Asia.

Decorated Han votive mirrors were used as diplomatic gifts by the Chinese, and have been found as far away as Siberia, the Caucasus, and southern Russia.

The nimble "Horses of Heaven" from Ferghana provided the Chinese with the style of cavalry needed to keep the Xiongnu at bay.

Han trade
(in approximate order of value)

Exports	Imports
silk	horses
lacquerware	spices
	precious stones

The Classical world

141: Wudi expands Han power into Central Asia
60: Establishment of Kushan Empire
c.150: Ptolemy publishes first World Atlas
200: Han dynasty collapses
396: Roman Empire divided into eastern and western halves

200 BCE — 100 BCE — 1 CE — 100 — 200 — 300 — 400

31: Roman victory at Actium consolidates control of eastern Mediterranean
117: Roman Empire at greatest extent
224: Beginning of Sassanian control in Persia
238: First Germanic incursions into Roman Empire
370: Huns enter Europe

Roman trade

Rome, in contrast to Han China, was an empire largely dependent on trade. Rome's imports were prodigious. A single currency, common citizenship, low customs barriers, and the development of a broadly secure network of roads, inland waterways, harbors, and sea-routes provided a hub of commerce which drew in produce from far beyond the imperial boundaries.

The popular Roman taste for combat with exotic wild animals in the arena saw bears, bulls, and boars being imported from northern Europe, lions and tigers from Asia, crocodiles from Egypt, and rhinoceros, hippopotami, and a variety of large cats from sub-Saharan Africa.

Roman trade
(in approximate order of value)

Exports	Imports
gold	food
silver	slaves
wine	animals
olive oil	spices
glassware	silk
	incense
	ivory
	cotton

Knowledge of Classical Eurasia

There is some evidence of direct contact between Rome and the Han Empire and Europeans clearly had extensive knowledge of the general shape of Classical Eurasia. The Greek geographer Strabo gave a detailed description of the known world in his 17-volume *Geography* (c.20 CE) and by 150 CE the Alexandrian Ptolemy's *Geography* formally laid out the topography of Eurasia. His world view (*below*) names Sinae (China), Taprobane (Sri Lanka), and Sera Metropolis (Chang'an).

The Romans built many ports and harbors around the Mediterranean, elaborate complexes with lighthouses and docks, which serviced the Roman maritime trading network.

Reconstruction of Ptolemy's map of Classical Eurasia

Central Asian trade

The development of the Silk Road saw the growth of a string of powerful cities and states which thrived, controlling the trade which passed through them. The greatest of these was the Parthian Empire of Persia (247 BCE–244 CE), while to the north Transoxiana, Bactria, and the Kushan Empire of modern Uzbekistan straddled the region in which the Silk Road converged and intersected with routes traveling north from India through the Hindu Kush, and on to the Caspian Sea and the river routes of Scythia.

The Silk Road

The campaigns by the Qin First Emperor, Shi Huangdi, and his Han successor Wudi against the nomadic Xiongnu opened a series of routes which traversed Central Asia, remaining the principal east–west trade route for centuries. The Silk Road linked Samarkand in the west with Anxi in the east; a summer route went north of the Tien Shan range, while the main route split to skirt the Takla Makan.

SEE ALSO:

Africa: pp.160–161

Europe: pp.180–181

West Asia: pp.224–225

South and Southeast Asia: pp.240–241

North and East Asia: pp.260–261

Fortified cities such as Jiaohei were established as *caravanserais* around the hostile wastes of the Takla Makan Desert.

This Greco-Roman bronze statuette of Serapis-Hercules, dating from 1st–4th century CE, was part of a hoard discovered at Bagram in the Hindu Kush, which also included Roman glassware, Chinese lacquerware, and Indian ivories.

▼ ❶ Eurasian and African trade c.1 CE

■ Roman Empire and client states	
■ Han Empire	
▨ Sinkiang (Han protectorate 73–94 CE)	

Trade routes
- Roman
- Trans-Saharan (rudimentary route)
- Indian Ocean
- Silk Road
- Scythian (rudimentary route)
- China
- East Africa
- amber
- incense
- other (rudimentary route)

Goods traded
- ⬤ amber
- 🐾 animals
- 👕 clothing
- 🟨 gold
- 🔲 silver
- 🌾 grain
- 🐎 horses
- 🔥 incense
- 🦷 ivory
- ⬭ olive oil
- ⬡ precious stones
- 🧵 silk
- 👤 slaves
- 🌿 spices
- 🪵 timber
- ▮ tin
- ◉ tortoiseshell
- 🍇 wine

Trade in the Indian Ocean

Maritime trade routes in the Indian Ocean provided important links between the Roman Mediterranean, East Africa, the Persian Gulf, India, Taprobane (Sri Lanka) and beyond into the East Indies. Greek ships hugged the coasts, but lateen-rigged dhows, propelled by the regular seasonal pattern of the monsoon winds, were the first craft to move beyond coastal trade to establish direct routes across the ocean between major trading markets. The rich variety of goods they transported was described in a Greek manual from the 1st century CE, the *Periplus of the Erythraean Sea*; hoards of Roman coins have been found in southern India, Southeast Asia, and East Africa, while silks and spices from South and East Asia were transported westward.

Cana, on the southern coast of the Arabian Peninsula, one of the strategic fortified *entrepôts* which ringed the Indian Ocean, flourished on the local trade in incense.

Scale varies with perspective

7720 km (4490 miles)

17,810 km (11,070 miles)

THE WORLD 1–250 CE

AS THE EMPIRES OF THE OLD WORLD expanded, the protection of their borders and far-flung imperial outposts became an urgent priority. Increasing threats from the mounted nomadic pastoralists of Asia, the Germanic tribes of Eastern Europe, and the Berbers of North Africa stretched resources to the limit, weakening Roman control, and leading to economic and social chaos. The empire of Han China collapsed in 220 CE, a victim of famine, floods, insurgency, and the growing power of regional warlords. By the early 3rd century CE, pressures on Rome's eastern borders precipitated a stormy century of civil wars, dynastic disputes, and army revolts. Against this troubled backdrop a new religion, Christianity, was beginning to spread throughout the Roman world. Originating with the teachings of Jesus of Nazareth in Palestine, the new religion proved remarkably resistant to Roman persecution.

Marcus Aurelius was one of the most conscientious Roman emperors: a Stoic philosopher and tireless campaigner on the German frontier.

Europe

In the 2nd century CE the Roman Empire stretched from West Asia to the Atlantic, united by one language, one coinage, a system of well-paved roads, and protected by fortified frontiers. The empire prospered under strong emperors, but stresses began to appear. Conflict over the imperial succession undermined central authority, leading to civil wars between rivals, economic breakdown, and revolts by the army. Pressure on imperial frontiers, especially from the Germanic tribes to the east of the Rhine, stretched the empire's resources, leading to inflation, famine, disease, and lawlessness.

Europe

69: The Year of the Four Emperors; order is restored by Vespasian

125: Hadrian's Wall built as defensive frontier in northern Britain

161: Accession of Marcus Aurelius

212: Roman citizenship granted to all free inhabitants of the empire

| 1 CE | 50 | 100 | 150 | 200 | 250 CE |

14: Emperor Augustus dies. Disputes over succession beset Julio-Claudian dynasty

79: Eruption of Vesuvius destroys town of Pompeii

117: Roman Empire at maximum extent on death of Trajan

192: Death of Emperor Commodus followed by civil war; rapid succession of several emperors

The most striking pottery of the early Andean civilizations was made by the Moche people. This vessel is shaped into a triple portrait of a fanged deity.

The Americas

The Moche culture of coastal Peru began to thrive in the 1st century CE, expanding through military conquest, and leaving substantial remains, such as temples of solid adobe brick. In Mexico, the vast metropolis of Teotihuacán controlled the production and distribution of obsidian throughout Central America. The city, laid out in a grid pattern on a north-south axis, housed a population of some 200,000. Ambitious projects at this time included the monumental Pyramid of the Sun, the largest structure in pre-Columbian America.

The Americas

c.1: Maya complexes start to appear at sites such as El Mirador

c.100: City of Teotihuacán begins to expand. 90% of local population move to the city

| 1 CE | 50 | 100 | 150 | 200 | 250 CE |

c.10: Moche culture, famous for substantial buildings, irrigation works, and pottery and goldwork, at its height

c.200: Hopewell moundbuilding culture flourishing in North America

The World in 250 CE

▨ Roman Empire

▨ Kushan power at peak under Kanishka, c.100 CE

THE FIRST PAPER

The traditional date for the invention of paper is 105 CE, but lightweight felted material for writing had been made in China for some time before then. The pulp was made of scraps of bark, bamboo, and hemp, finely chopped and boiled with wood ash. As techniques improved, paper replaced expensive silk and cumbersome wooden tablets.

A Chinese worker lifts a mesh screen covered with a thin layer of pulp that will drain and dry to form a sheet of paper.

Africa

Under Roman rule, Egypt experienced a remarkable economic recovery. As ancient Egyptian cults and traditions declined, Christianity found converts among the Egyptians. To the west, the Romans extended their control to the Berber kingdoms of Numidia and Mauretania. The fertile coastal plains were fully exploited, but the southern borders of Roman territory were under constant threat of Berber invasion. By 100 CE the Red Sea kingdom of Axum, its wealth based on control of the incense trade, had become a major power.

The ruined city of Petra contains remarkable rock-cut tombs. It was annexed by Rome in 106 as capital of the province of Arabia.

West Asia

In the 1st century CE the Parthian Empire was torn by internal dissent and dynastic struggles. Between 114 and 198, the Romans invaded three times, sacking the cities of Seleucia and Ctesiphon. In 224 Ardashir Papakan defeated his Parthian overlords and founded the Sassanian dynasty. He introduced a centralized administration, and transformed vassal kingdoms into provinces, ruled by Sassanian princes. His son Shapur repelled the Romans and made Sassanian Persia the most stable power of late antiquity.

70: Romans suppress Jewish revolt and destroy temple in Jerusalem

c.150: Petra, a major trading post for incense, at height of prosperity

165: Avidius Cassius sacks Seleucia and Ctesiphon

224: Sassanians take over Parthian Empire

| West Asia |
1 CE — 50 — 100 — 150 — 200 — 250 CE

c.114: Trajan annexes Armenia, takes Seleucia and reaches Persian Gulf

c.132: Second Jewish revolt precipitates diaspora

197: Septimius Severus sails down Euphrates to invade Parthian Empire

East Asia

In 25 CE, **after a brief interregnum,** Han emperors regained control of China, but their rule depended on the support of powerful landowners. The capital moved to Luoyang, and eastern and southern China exerted greater political influence. In the early 3rd century the empire, beset by rebellions and feuds, collapsed. Regional warlords carved out three new kingdoms and China remained fragmented for over 300 years. With the decline of the Han, small local states, notably Koguryo and Silla, took control of Korea.

This model horse and trap was found among the goods in the grave of a high-ranking officer of the Han period.

| East Asia |

9: Wang Mang seizes throne, founding short-lived Xin dynasty

159: Han imperial family feuds hand effective power to court eunuchs

c.220: Collapse of Han dynasty; replaced by three kingdoms: Shu, Wu, and Wei

1 CE — 50 — 100 — 150 — 200 — 250 CE

25: Han reassert control over China, but their power is limited

184: Rising of the Yellow Turbans, an insurgent group, in China

c.200: Emergence of native states in Korea

SEE ALSO:

North America: pp.120–121

South America: pp.144–145

Africa: pp.160–161

Europe: pp.180–181

West Asia: pp.224–225

South and Southeast Asia: pp.240–243

North and East Asia: pp.260–261

Australasia and Oceania: pp.280–281

MOSAIC OF THE NILE IN FLOOD

The Romans drew maps, but unfortunately only a few fragments carved on stone survive. Some others have come down to us through medieval copies. One highly imaginative representation of the contemporary world that has been preserved is this mosaic of a panoramic view of *The Nile in Flood* found at Praeneste, near Rome.

The Nile River was of great importance to Rome: its fertile floodplain was a major source of grain for feeding the city.

South Asia

In the 1st century CE the nomadic Yuezhi were pushed westward from the borders of China. One of the tribes, the Kushans, united the others, moved into Bactria, and from there expanded into northern India, founding their capital at Peshawar. The Kingdom of Kushana crumbled at the end of the 2nd century, when native peoples – the Tamils of southern India and the Satavahanas of the Deccan – were beginning to assert their power.

The Kushans' wealth came from their control of east–west trade routes. This ivory plaque was part of a famous hoard found at Begram, which contained artifacts from Rome, Africa, India, and China.

Egyptian mummy cases took on a curious hybrid appearance under Roman rule. The portrait on this 2nd-century example shows the Egyptians' Hellenistic taste in art.

| Africa |

c.50: Kingdom of Axum starts to emerge

c.100: Alexandria emerges as a center of Christian scholarship, seat of one of the earliest Christian bishoprics

c.150: Christianity starts to spread westward to Roman provinces of Numidia and Mauretania

1 CE — 50 — 100 — 150 — 200 — 250 CE

44: Mauretania annexed by Rome

69: Romans defeat powerful Saharan kingdom of Garamantes, but do not absorb it into empire

| South Asia |

99: Indian embassy to court of Trajan in Rome, probably to announce Kushan conquests

c.102: Death of Kushans' greatest ruler, Kanishka

c.200: Cities appear for first time on Deccan plateau

1 CE — 50 — 100 — 150 — 200 — 250 CE

c.60: Kushans, under Kadphises I, unite Yuezhi tribes and advance into northern India

c.150: Kushans become Persian vassals

THE EMERGENCE OF GLOBAL RELIGIONS

This 7th-century silver plaque from Hexham, England is thought to depict a Christian saint.

BY 250 CE SOME OLD WORLD religions (*see pp.36–37*) had spread far beyond their areas of origin to become substantial bodies of faith. In the west, the Roman taste for monotheistic Mithraism, derived from Persian Zoroastrianism, spread throughout the empire, although it was always a minority cult. But in its wake the cult of Christianity was becoming firmly established. Further, the Roman suppression of the Jewish revolt in 132 CE had caused a diaspora through much of the empire. In South Asia, Hinduism became deeply rooted throughout the subcontinent as Dravidians and tribal peoples adopted the practices of their Aryan conquerors; meanwhile Buddhism was spread overland to Central Asia and China and beyond by missionaries of various sectarian schools.

Mithraism, Judaism, and Christianity

The worship of Mithras was arduous and limited to males; it was popular among the Roman legions, spreading to the corners of the empire. Its monotheism paved the way for Christianity which, in parallel to the Jewish diaspora, spread to centers throughout the empire. This was inaugurated by the missionary journeys of St. Paul, in the 1st century CE. By the time of Diocletian's persecutions (304 CE) centers had been established in Asia Minor, Mesopotamia, and around the Mediterranean. The fusion of Christian theology with the ethical concerns of Greek philosophy gave it intellectual respectability; and when Constantine (306–337) adopted the faith, Christianity became the official religion of the empire.

This 5th-century pottery amphora is decorated with two versions of the Christian cross, which became the most widely used symbol of the religion.

1 The spread of Mithraism, Judaism, and Christianity by 600 CE

- border of Roman Empire 250 CE
- Mithraic center
- Jewish community by 300 CE
- Christian Patriarchate by 600 CE
- Christian Archbishopric by 600 CE
- The Seven Churches of Asia
- other Christian churches by 600 CE
- Church Council

St. Paul's journeys
- first
- second
- third
- fourth

Mithras, the creator and god of light, was frequently portrayed with signs of the zodiac, or slaying a bull, whose blood was life-giving.

The growth of early Christianity

46–57: Journeys of St. Paul	**132:** Suppression of Jewish revolt in Palestine; beginning of diaspora	**304:** Persecution of Christians by Diocletian (284–305)	**325:** Council of Nicaea assembled by Constantine	**404:** Vulgate (Latin version of Bible) completed

0	100	200	300	400	500

c.32CE: Crucifixion of Christ	**64:** Probable martyrdom of St. Paul by Nero (37–68)	**274:** Mithras admitted into pantheon of Roman Empire	**313:** Edict of Milan under Constantine (306–337) confirms Christianity as official imperial creed

The flowering of South Asian religions

By the beginning of the 1st millennium CE, Hinduism, Buddhism, and Jainism had diffused throughout the Indian subcontinent. Hinduization was a gradual process and there was no sharp dividing line between popular Hindu and pre-existing practices. Buddhism and Jainism appealed largely to a relatively elite and urbanized following. All three faiths enjoyed royal patronage; under the Guptas (320–c.540 CE) and in the 4th century, India witnessed its golden or classical age. Many texts, hitherto committed to memory by Brahmans, were put into writing, and there was a flowering of architecture, painting, music, and dance in which followers of all three religions participated.

The Hindu cosmology – some 3000 mythological beings, presided over by Vishnu, Shiva, Brahma, and Kali – became firmly established under the Guptas.

The growth of early Hinduism

1st century BCE: Initial composition of the *Ramayana*	**5th century:** *Mahabharata*, the world's longest poem, attains near final form / **5th century:** Composition of early Puranas

100 BCE	1CE	100	200	300	400	500 CE

c.100 BCE–100 CE: Composition of *Bhagavid Gita*	**2nd–3rd centuries CE:** Rules of religion (*Dharmashastras*) of Manu given final form	**5th–6th centuries:** Development of architecture in stone

2 The spread of Hinduism

- *PRACYA* Hindu cultural regions
- Holy city of the Puranas
- area of Gupta control by c.415 CE

SEE ALSO:

Africa: pp.160–161

Europe: pp.180–183

West Asia: pp.224–225

South and Southeast Asia: pp.242–245

North and East Asia: pp.260–265

A colossal rock-cut Buddha, the oldest known example of Buddhist rock carving, from Yungang Caves, Datong, c.460 CE, is approximately 14 yds high. Colossal Buddhas are common throughout China, Southeast Asia, and Ceylon.

◁ ❸ **The spread of Buddhism to 400 CE**

▨ Buddhist heartland

Holy places

○ major Buddhist center/ monastery

▥ Buddhist rock-carved temple

▲ sacred Buddhist mountain

Movement of ideas

➡ spread of Buddhism

➡ spread of Mahayana Buddhism

— trade routes

— Silk Road

The spread of Buddhism to 400 CE

Early in the development of Buddhism, various schools arose. The orthodox Theravada, also known as Hinayana (Lesser Vehicle), stresses attaining *nirvana* through monasticism, while Mahayana (Greater Vehicle) attaches great importance to Bodhisattvas, mortals who have attained *nirvana*, but who chose to remain on earth to assist others. Both schools were brought to Southeast Asia by itinerant monks, where they were adopted by local rulers – along with Hinduism – as parts of eclectic state religions. With the initial support from the Kushan emperor Kanishka, Mahayana Buddhism also spread overland, along the Silk Road to Central Asia and China, and had diffused through China and Korea by 400 CE.

The spread of Buddhism

2nd–1st century BCE: Buddhism adopted in Indo-Greek kingdoms of Central Asia; rise of Gandharan art

Late 1st century CE: Kushan emperor Kanishka propagates Buddhism over much of Central Asia

399–415: Chinese pilgrim Fa Xian travels through South Asia

200 BCE	100 BCE	1 CE	100	200	300	400	500

c.25 BCE: Buddhist canon committed to writing in Sinhala (Ceylon)

65 CE: First evidence of Buddhism in China

384: Buddhism reaches Korea

Religions of the Old World after 400 CE

Between 400 CE and the advent of Islam in the mid-7th century, the disintegration of the Old World political order was balanced by further spread and diversification of the established world religions. In South Asia, Hinduism had grown firm roots, and reformist movements such as Jainism ensured its continued vitality. Here Buddhism was declining, but further afield the faith continued to spread through maritime Southeast Asia, blending in its Zen form with traditional Shinto in Japan, and sprouting a new Tantric form within Tibet, which spread north to China and Mongolia. In the west, Christianity spawned various sects and cults, including the Coptic church in Africa, and the Mesopotamian-based Nestorian and Jacobite churches. Other cults such as Gnosticism, Manichaeism, and Arianism, originating in the Near East, spread among the Germanic successor states of the West Roman Empire.

❹ **Religions of the Old World after 400 CE** ▷

▨ area largely embracing Christianity by 600

➡ spread of Gnosticism 200–400

➡ spread of Arianism 300–500

➡ spread of Manichaeism 300–500

➡ Coptic missions by 350

➡ Nestorian/Jacobite missions 600–1000

▨ area largely embracing Zoroastrianism by 500

▨ extent of Hinduism by 400

➡ spread of Hinduism 400–600

▨ extent of Jainism by 700

▨ extent of Buddhism by 400

➡ spread of Mahayana Buddhism 400–1000

➡ spread of Buddhism 400–1000

▨ heartland of Tibetan (Tantric) Buddhism by 800

➡ spread of Tibetan (Tantric) Buddhism 800–1100

▨ Shinto

Scale varies with perspective

6670 km (4140 miles)

17,810 km (11,070 miles)

Old World religions after 400 CE

497: Franks converted to Christianity

529: Regulation of monasticism in Europe under St. Benedict

618: Rise of Tang Dynasty in China

c.800: Hindu-Buddhist temple at Borobudur founded

400	500	600	700	800

410: Visigoths sack Rome

476: Last Roman emperor in west deposed

538: Santa Sofia consecrated in Constantinople

c.550: Buddhism introduced to Japan

c.654: Buddhism established in Tibet

Jainism developed as a reformist movement within Hinduism, rejecting the latter's proliferation of divinities in favor of aspiration toward the ascetic conquest of worldly passions. Jain art is both ornate and contemplative.

THE WORLD 250–500

By 500, MIGRATIONS IN ASIA AND EUROPE had so weakened the civilizations of the Old World that only the East Roman Empire and Sassanian Persia survived. Asian nomads broke the power of the Chinese and destroyed India's Gupta Empire. The Huns even invaded Europe, where the Romans repulsed them, but only with the aid of their Gothic allies. Rome relied increasingly on the aid of the Goths and other Germanic peoples, who settled within the empire and, as central authority waned, carved out new kingdoms for themselves. In contrast to the collapsing empires of the Old World, the great urban civilizations of Central America, Teotihuacán, the Maya, and the Zapotecs, were beginning to flourish.

Much of the best late Roman sculpture is found in the carving of Christian scenes on sarcophagi.

Europe

In 284, **Diocletian** divided the Roman Empire into eastern and western halves. With the advent of Christianity and the establishment of Constantinople as a new capital in 330, the empire's center of gravity shifted eastward. Meanwhile, Germanic and Slav peoples, living on Rome's northern borders, infiltrated imperial territory, at times peacefully, often by force. The Western Empire collapsed in 476 to be replaced by a series of Germanic kingdoms and the mantle of empire passed to Constantinople in the east.

Europe			
306: Succession of Emperor Constantine. Empire briefly reunited under his rule	**378:** Visigoths under Alaric defeat Roman force under Emperor Valens	**406:** Alans, Vandals, Sueves ravage Gaul	**451:** Battle of Catalaunian Fields. Romans and Goths defeat Attila the Hun
284: Diocletian divides Empire into eastern and western halves	**391:** Christianity becomes state religion. Empire divided again	**410:** Visigoths, under Alaric, capture and sack Rome	**476:** Emperor Romulus Augustus deposed. End of Western Empire

The World in 500

- Eastern Roman Empire
- Empire of the Ostrogoths under Ermanaric, 370
- Hun Empire under Attila, 450

Maya vases usually show events in the lives of kings, often, as here, involving sacrifice. The rim is decorated with glyphs (see p.55).

Christian Egypt linked the Mediterranean world with the various kingdoms of the Upper Nile. This 5th-century linen cloth shows a heroic African figure.

The Americas

The Maya civilization of Central America, the only fully literate society in pre-Columbian America, flourished between 300 and 900. Sophisticated stone-built cities, such as Palenque and Tikal, were constructed deep in the rainforest, which was cleared by slashing and burning for agriculture. Each city retained its own architectural style and some degree of autonomy. The separate Maya states fought and traded with each other, and there is evidence of diplomatic relations with the powerful city of Teotihuacán.

The Americas		
	c.300: Beginning of Classic Age of Maya civilization; construction of cities such as Tikal and Palenque	**c.400:** Intensive building at Teotihuacán; population reaches perhaps 200,000
c.250: Important Zapotec temple complex built at Monte Albán	**c.350:** Construction of city of Tiahuanaco, near Lake Titicaca	**c.378:** Maya city of Tikal invades the city of Uaxactún
		c.450: Flourishing of Nazca people, famous for lines and giant figures drawn in desert

Africa

The kingdom of Aksum linked the Red Sea with the Ethiopian plateau and traded products by sea as far as Rome and India. In the 4th century Christianity reached Aksum from Alexandria. In West Africa, trans-Saharan trade was revolutionized by the introduction of camels for transport. Berber nomads dominated the trade, bringing West African gold, ivory, and ostrich feathers from the southern Sahara to the ports of the Mediterranean coast.

Africa			
	c.350: Aksumites under King Ezana invade kingdom of Meroe	**c.397:** Berber chief Gildo rebels against Roman rule	**439:** Fall of Carthage. Vandals set up North African kingdom
	311: Start of Donatist schism; 400 North African bishops rebel against Roman Christian church	**c.330:** Beginnings of conversion of kingdom of Aksum to Christianity	**429:** Nomadic Vandals invade North Africa from Spain

THE STIRRUP

Most technological advances in equipment for horsemen were developed by the nomadic peoples of Central Asia, where the horse had first been domesticated. The Scythians may have used leather loops as a kind of stirrup as early as 400 BCE, although these were probably just an aid for mounting. Rigid metal stirrups, which provided a stable platform for warriors to fight effectively from horseback, were adopted some time before 400 CE in China, from where their use spread across Central Asia to Europe.

This Chinese ceramic figurine of a hunter attacked by a lion demonstrates one of the advantages of the stirrup as the rider turns to deal with his aggressor.

West Asia

By the end of the 4th century, Sassanian Persia stretched from the Euphrates to the Indus. Social stability was maintained by an elaborate and efficient bureaucracy, a healthy economy based primarily on agriculture, and widespread adherence to Zoroastrianism, the state religion. The Sassanians posed a major threat to Roman interests in Asia, and for 200 years there was conflict with the Roman Empire, especially over Armenia. In the 5th century Persia had to withstand incursions by eastern nomads, notably the Hephthalites or "White Huns", but survived intact.

A Sassanian Shahanshah (King of Kings), probably Bahram V, who ruled from 421 to 439, demonstrates his authority (and prowess as a lion-hunter) on this magnificent silver dish.

SEE ALSO:

North America: pp.120–123

South America: pp.144–147

Africa: pp.160–161

Europe: pp.180–183

West Asia: pp.224–225

South and Southeast Asia: pp.242–245

North and East Asia: pp.260–261

Australasia and Oceania: pp.280–281

West Asia

296: Sassanians occupy Armenia and defeat Roman emperor Galerius. Treaty ensures peace for next 40 years

337: Shapur II embarks on new warfare against Romans

c.450: Hephthalites attack northeastern borders of Sassanian Empire

260: At Edessa, Sassanians under Shapur I defeat and capture Roman emperor, Valerian

309: Accession of Shapur II. Persian borders are threatened by nomads

484: Hephthalites defeat and kill Sassanian ruler, but the empire survives

250 — 300 — 350 — 400 — 450 — 500

MOSAIC MAP OF JERUSALEM

The sites associated with the life of Christ all lay within the East Roman Empire. Jerusalem, as the scene of Christ's Passion, was a major center of pilgrimage and source of relics from the 4th century onwards. The city was depicted in great detail in a 6th-century mosaic found at Madaba in Jordan: a bird's-eye view of the city that indicates all the important churches and pilgrimage sites.

The Madaba map shows clearly the central colonnade which dates from Hadrian's rebuilding of Jerusalem in the 2nd century CE.

This fresco of two heavenly maidens decorated Kassapa's 5th-century fortified mountaintop palace at Sigiriya in Ceylon.

China's many Buddhist monasteries of this period have all been destroyed. Only the vast cave-temples, built with imperial patronage, such as this one at Longmen near Luoyang, have survived.

South Asia

The Gupta dynasty grew in power and influence throughout the 4th century, to dominate northern India. Sanskrit literature, poetry, sculpture, and architecture all flourished under the Hindu Guptas. It was also an age noted for its religious tolerance. In the mid-5th century, however, the Hephthalites advanced into Gupta territory, ending India's "golden age". In Ceylon, meanwhile, Buddhism became established as the dominant faith.

East Asia

After a period of fragmentation, China was briefly re-united in 280 under the Jin, but when nomads sacked Chang'an in 316, the Eastern Jin dynasty moved to Nanjing. They retained control over southern China, but the north suffered successive invasions by steppe nomads. In this climate of political uncertainty, Buddhism flourished and the monastic life grew in appeal. Japan's Yamato state emerged in the 4th century, gradually gaining hegemony over the south of the country.

South Asia

c.415: High point in career of Kalidasa, one of India's greatest poets and playwrights

c.500: Collapse of Gupta Empire under renewed Hephthalite attacks

320: Expansion of Gupta family, from Magadha, heralds start of Gupta dynasty

376: Gupta rule reaches its greatest extent under Chandra Gupta II

495: Death of Kassapa, self-appointed god-king of Sigiriya in Ceylon

250 — 300 — 350 — 400 — 450 — 500

East Asia

c.300: Emergence of Yamato state in Osaka region of Japan

420: Song rule in southern China: start of period of the Southern Dynasties

c.490: Northern Wei capital moved to Luoyang

280: Sima Yan, leader of the Jin dynasty, unites China

291: Steppe peoples from beyond Great Wall allowed to settle within empire

386: Toba Wei reunify northern China, intermarry with Chinese, and adopt Chinese culture

479: Rule of southern China passes to the Qi dynasty

250 — 300 — 350 — 400 — 450 — 500

MIGRATIONS AND INVASIONS

The half-Vandal general Stilicho was regent during the reign of the child emperor Honorius.

THE GERMANIC PEOPLES who migrated into the Roman Empire during the 5th century were seeking to share in the fruits of empire, not to destroy it. They were spurred to move west in search of land by a combination of factors: famine, population pressure, and the prospects of a better standard of living. Rome initially accepted "barbarian" recruits into its depleted army as *foederati* (federates), and allowed them to retain their own leaders and laws. But when the Romans opposed the settlement of large groups or refused to reward them for their services, the results could be disastrous: campaigns of plunder, sacked cities, and the breakdown of imperial control.

Honorius succeeded his father, Theodosius, as western emperor in 395 while still a child. He lived in comfortable seclusion while senior ministers governed.

Turmoil in Italy

From the late 4th century, the Western Roman Empire was plagued by disputes over the imperial succession, which led to factionalism and civil wars. These were very destructive of Roman manpower and led to the recruitment of large numbers of barbarians under their own leaders. Emperors were often pawns in the power struggles of generals. Many of these, such as the half-Vandal Stilicho and the Suevian Ricimer, were of Germanic origin.

Turmoil in Italy

- **324:** Constantine becomes sole ruler
- **391:** Theodosius makes Christianity religion of the Empire
- **402:** Imperial court moved to Ravenna
- **476:** Child emperor, Romulus Augustulus, deposed by Odoacer, "King of Italy"
- **395:** Theodosius dies; West Roman Empire left to child emperor Honorius
- **410:** Sack of Rome by Visigoths
- **455:** Accession of Libius Severus, puppet emperor controlled by Ricimer

The aims of the migrations

The peoples who invaded the Roman Empire in the 4th and 5th centuries were driven by a variety of motives. Some, like Alaric's Visigoths, sought official acceptance by the Roman authorities. Others, such as the peoples of the Great Migration of 406, were intent on finding land anywhere and by any means. The only invaders bent purely on destruction and plunder were the Huns. As steppe nomads, the Huns' strength lay in their mobility and their skill with bow, lance, and saber. They were able to smash the overstretched imperial defenses, but were repulsed when Goths and Romans joined forces against them. The Romans relied more and more on Gothic military support, and it was the Goths who emerged as the first inheritors of the Empire's western territories.

453: On death of Attila, Empire of the Huns collapses

EMPIRE OF THE HUNS c.420

452: Attila persuaded to leave Roman Empire

c.410: Romans abandon Britain

Visigoths from 382

Ostrogoths from 450

402: Capital of West Roman Empire moved to Ravenna

KINGDOM OF THE BURGUNDIANS c.443

410: Visigoths sack Rome
455: Vandals sack Rome

410: Death of Alaric; Visigoths abandon plan to invade Africa

KINGDOM OF THE VISIGOTHS c.418

414: Athaulf, leader of the Visigoths, marries Galla Placidia, daughter of late Emperor Theodosius. She had been captured during sack of Rome.

WESTERN ROMAN EMPIRE from 395

430: City of Hippo taken by Vandals. St. Augustine, church father and bishop of the city, dies during siege.

429: Gaiseric leads Vandals into North Africa

Vandal nobles in North Africa led the same privileged life as their Roman predecessors, as this mosaic of a Vandal landowner shows.

The Great Migration

At Christmas 406, vast hordes of Vandals, Sueves, and Alans crossed the frozen Rhine River and poured into Gaul, where they greatly disrupted settled life. They then moved in a southwesterly direction and eventually reached the Iberian Peninsula. The Vandals pressed on to North Africa, crossing the Strait of Gibraltar in 429, while the Sueves and Alans set up kingdoms in Iberia.

The Great Migration

- **406:** Vandals, Sueves, and Alans cross Rhine
- **c.411:** Sueves establish kingdom in northwestern Iberia
- **439:** Vandals reach city of Carthage
- **474:** Rome recognizes Vandal kingdom
- **409:** Vandals, Sueves, and Alans cross the Pyrenees
- **429:** Vandals cross Strait of Gibraltar
- **455:** Sack of Rome by Vandal king, Gaiseric

Scale varies with perspective

6670 km
(4160 miles)

5310 km
(3310 miles)

❶ Migrations of peoples 300–500 CE

▢ extent of Roman empire, c.390 CE   ⚔ site of important battle, with date

Movements of peoples, with dates:

- → Huns
- → Goths
- → Ostrogoths
- → Visigoths
- → Alans
- → Vandals, Alans, Sueves
- → Burgundians
- → Franks
- → Jutes, Angles, Saxons
- → Irish
- → Picts

The fine mausoleum of Theodoric in Ravenna demonstrates how the Ostrogothic chief accepted and emulated the Roman heritage.

SEE ALSO:

Africa: pp.160–161

Europe: pp.180–183

West Asia: pp.224–225

North and East Asia: pp.260–261

The Goths

The Visigoths (western Goths), under a treaty of 382, were settled in Lower Moesia and many served in the imperial army. A dispute over tribute between their leader Alaric and the Senate led to an invasion of Italy and, in 410, the sack of Rome, which shook the foundations of the Empire. In 418 they secured a settlement with Rome and set up a kingdom in Aquitaine. After the death of Attila the Hun in 453, the Ostrogoths (eastern Goths) settled in Pannonia. Under their leader Theodoric, they also began to assert their independence. After campaigning in the Balkans, they moved to Italy in 489 and, after a three-year siege, captured the city of Ravenna, which they made capital of the Ostrogothic kingdom of Italy.

The Goths

376: Goths petition Emperor Valens to settle within Roman Empire

395: Alaric, Visigothic leader, seeks homeland within Roman Empire

453: Ostrogoths embark on bloody campaigns against Eastern Roman Empire

492: Ostrogothic king Theodoric defeats Odoacer at Ravenna to become king of Italy

526: Death of Theodoric

350   400   450   500   550

378: Goths defeat and kill Valens at battle of Adrianopolis

410: Visigoths, under Alaric, sack Rome

414: New leader, Athaulf, sets up Visigothic state at Narbo (Narbonne), which expands into Iberia

507: Visigoths defeated by Franks and driven out of Aquitaine

533: Beginning of reconquest of Italy by Eastern Roman Empire

The Huns

After migrating across Asia, the Huns reached Europe in the late 4th century. They settled on the Danube plain just beyond the frontier of the Roman Empire, and built a capital on the Tisza River. Under their leader, Attila, they terrorized the Romans with bloodthirsty campaigns in the Balkans, but were defeated at the battle of the Catalaunian Fields by an army of Romans and Goths. Attila then attacked Italy, sacking Aquileia and Mediolanum (Milan), but was persuaded to spare Rome by Pope Leo I. After his death in 453, the Huns' European empire disintegrated.

The Huns

c.370: First appearance of Huns in eastern Europe

c.444: Attila becomes king of the Huns

453: Death of Attila, followed by retreat of Huns

300   350   400   450   500

350: White Huns (Hephthalites) invade Persia and India

420: Huns build capital at Tisza (Theiss) on Hungarian plains

451: Attila invades Gaul; defeated at Catalaunian Fields

For steppe nomads, such as the Huns, mobility was vital. Bronze cauldrons, which could be carried on horseback, were part of the Huns' equipment, and have been found at many sites on the steppes and in central Europe.

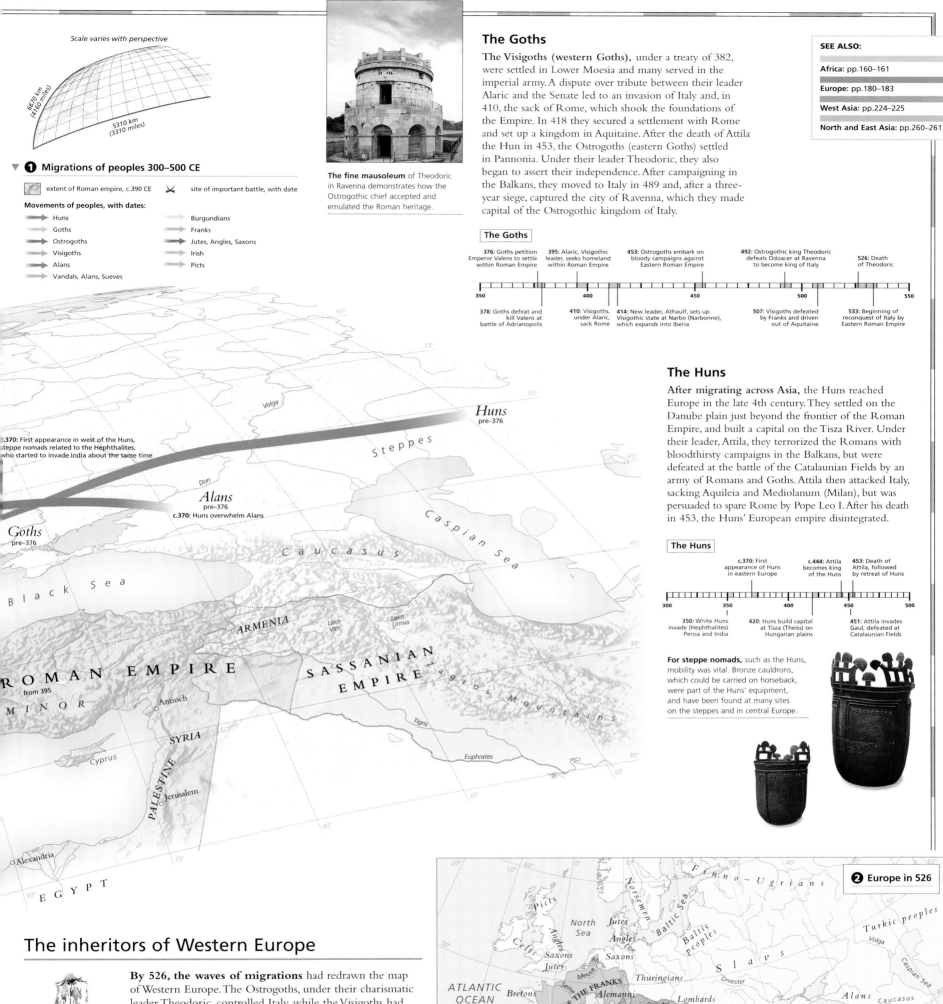

c.370: First appearance in west of the Huns, steppe nomads related to the Hephthalites, who started to invade India about the same time

Volga

Huns
pre–376

Steppes

Don

Alans
pre–376
c.370: Huns overwhelm Alans

Caspian Sea

Goths
pre–376

Caucasus

Black Sea

ARMENIA

Lake Van

Lake Urmia

ROMAN EMPIRE
from 395

MINOR

Antioch

SASSANIAN EMPIRE

Zagros Mountains

Tigris

SYRIA

Euphrates

Cyprus

PALESTINE

Jerusalem

Alexandria

EGYPT

The inheritors of Western Europe

By 526, the waves of migrations had redrawn the map of Western Europe. The Ostrogoths, under their charismatic leader Theodoric, controlled Italy, while the Visigoths had captured most of the Iberian Peninsula. The Vandals were established in North Africa, the Sueves in Galicia, and the Burgundians, who crossed the Rhine c.400, had settled in southeast France. The most enduring of the many Germanic kingdoms, however, would prove to be that of the Franks, founded in 456 by Clovis, which laid the foundations of modern France and Germany.

The magnificent votive crown of the 7th-century king Reccesuinth illustrates the importance of Christianity in Iberia under the Visigoths. Their rule lasted from the 5th century to the Arab conquest of 711.

❷ Europe in 526

Finno-Ugrians

Norsemen

Picts

North Sea

Jutes

Celts

Angles

Saxons

Jutes

Baltic Sea

Baltic peoples

Turkic peoples

Volga

Bretons

Rhine

Saxons

Elbe

Thuringians

Slavs

Dniestr

Danube

Caspian Sea

ATLANTIC OCEAN

KINGDOM OF THE FRANKS

Alemanni

Meuse

Seine

BURGUNDIAN KINGDOM

Lyon

Lombards

Milan

Gepids

Danube

Alans

Caucasus

KINGDOM OF THE SUEVES

Basques

Toulouse

KINGDOM OF THE OSTROGOTHS

Ravenna

Black Sea

Douro

Tagus

Toledo

KINGDOM OF THE VISIGOTHS

Corsica

Rome

Sardinia

Balearic Islands

KINGDOM OF THE VANDALS

Carthage

Constantinople

EASTERN ROMAN EMPIRE

SYRIA

SASSANIAN EMPIRE

Cyprus

Sicily

Crete

Mediterranean Sea

Alexandria

Arabian Peninsula

Berbers

AFRICA

EGYPT

Nile

500 km

500 miles

THE WORLD 500–750

THE RAPID RECOVERY of the ancient world from the onslaught of invading nomads is evident in the rise of two great empires in West Asia and China. The new religion of Islam was based on the teachings of Muhammad, an Arabian merchant from Mecca. Fired by a zeal for conquest and conversion, Islamic armies overran West Asia and North Africa, and by 750 had created an empire that stretched from the Indus to Spain. Under the Tang dynasty, Chinese civilization reached new heights; Tang control penetrated deep into Central Asia and Chinese cultural influence was widespread. In the Americas, the Maya remained the most advanced civilization, though their small city-states did not have the far-reaching influence of the great city of Teotihuacán.

The Byzantines were the champions of Christianity. This mosaic shows Emperor Justinian as God's representative on Earth.

Europe

The Franks became the most powerful of all Rome's Germanic successors. United under Clovis I, their overlordship was extended to the south of France and east of the Rhine. Constantinople was the Christian capital of the Byzantine Empire. The Emperor Justinian (527–65) reconquered North Africa and much of Italy, briefly creating an empire stretching from Spain to Persia. Over the next two centuries much of this territory was lost to Islam and, in the Balkans, to Slavic invaders.

Europe

- 527: Justinian becomes Byzantine emperor
- 597: Papal missionary Augustine converts the king of Kent to Christianity
- 674–78: Arabs besiege Constantinople, but fail to take it
- 732: Frankish leader Charles Martel defeats Arab armies at battle of Poitiers

| 500 | 550 | 600 | 650 | 700 | 750 |

- 511: Death of Frankish king Clovis
- 531: Frankish kingdom absorbs Burgundy
- c.590: The Avars, nomads from the steppes, establish state on Hungarian plains
- 680: Bulgars invade Balkans
- 711: Muslim invasion of Spain

The World in 750

- Tang Empire
- Byzantine Empire
- Umayyad Caliphate
- Kök Türk Empire 551–572
- East Roman Empire 554–565
- Horsha's Empire c.640
- Avar Empire c.595

Moche stirrup-spouted vessels continued to be made in the 6th and 7th centuries. The Moche culture started to die out around the time of the Huari expansion.

The Americas

Two empires emerged in South America during this period. One was centered on the city of Tiahuanaco, an Andean pilgrimage site near Lake Titicaca. The second, Huari, was a well-fortified city, the capital of a centralized power which expanded through military conquest. In Central America, the great city of Teotihuacán collapsed and was devastated by fire, though it remained a pilgrimage center until the Spanish conquest in the 16th century.

The Americas

- c.600: Maya civilization in Central America reaches its height
- c.700: Beginnings of Puebloan culture
- 750: Devastation of city of Teotihuacán

| 500 | 550 | 600 | 650 | 700 | 750 |

- c.500: Teotihuacán thriving as a major trading center
- c.600: Rise of closely-related Tiahuanaco and Huari civilizations in South America

THE CALENDAR OF THE MAYA

The Maya were the only early American people who were completely literate. They were also impressive astronomers and mathematicians and had a system of numbers based on twenty. Their calendar was made up of several cycles of different lengths, including one series of glyphs that had values denoting the days that had elapsed since the beginning of the Maya era (August 13, 3114 BCE).

The carved relief on this stone lintel from Yaxchilán commemorates an event that occurred on February 11, 526 CE.

West Asia

In the 7th century the whole of West Asia was overrun by Arabian armies, soldiers of Islam inspired to conquer and convert by the new religion founded by Muhammad. They were able to exploit the weaknesses of the two great powers in the region, the Sassanians and the Byzantines. Sassanian Persia had reached its peak under Khosrau I (531–79), who invaded Byzantine Syria and captured Antioch. But continuing conflict with the Byzantines led to a crushing defeat at Nineveh in 628.

The Dome of the Rock in Jerusalem was built in 692 over the ruins of the Jewish Temple. It is sacred to Islam as the site of Muhammad's journey to heaven.

CLASSICAL ARAB WORLD MAPS

When the Arabs took over much of the Greek-speaking eastern Mediterranean, they seized on the classical scholarship of Alexandria, including the famous *Geography* of Ptolemy (*see p.44*). Though no maps from this period survive, it seems that, while the map-making tradition died out in the west, it was kept alive by Arab scholars, albeit in the academic style of this later world map.

Al-Istakhri's world map, from the 10th century, uses a Ptolemaic projection, but with south at the top.

SEE ALSO:

North America: pp.122–123

South America: pp.142–145

Africa: pp.162–163

Europe: pp.182–185

West Asia: pp.226–227

South and Southeast Asia: pp.242–245

North and East Asia: pp.262–265

Australasia and Oceania: pp.280–281

West Asia

- 531: Beginning of reign of Sassanian ruler, Khosrau I Anohshirvanh
- 570: Prophet Muhammad born in Mecca
- 622: The Hegira: Muhammad and his followers move to Medina; start of Islamic era
- 628: Defeat of Sassanians by Byzantine emperor Heraclius
- 637: Arabian armies capture Sassanian capital, Ctesiphon
- 656: Arabians overrun Persia
- 661: Start of Umayyad dynasty. Damascus is center of Islamic empire
- 674–78: Arabian siege of Constantinople
- 698: Arabs capture Carthage
- 711: Islamic armies cross the Strait of Gibraltar and conquer Spain

500 550 600 650 700 750

Tang ceramics were of very high quality. This 7th-century figurine portrays one of the celebrated Ferghana horses, prized for their speed.

East Asia

- 538: Buddhism reaches Japan
- c.550: Kök Türk (Blue Turks) establish vast Central Asian empire
- 589: Turko-Chinese Sui reunite China
- 617: Sui dynasty collapses; succeeded in 618 by Tang
- 640: Tang armies reach Turfan in Central Asia
- 645: Buddhism reaches Tibet
- c.660: Tang forces in India and Central Asia
- 668: Korean peninsula united under Silla dynasty
- 710: Nara becomes Japanese capital

500 550 600 650 700 750

East Asia

After centuries of conflict, China was united under the Sui dynasty (581–617), which was succeeded by the Tang in 618. Chinese territory was again extended into Central Asia, protectorates were set up as far afield as eastern Persia, and they gained control of much of the Silk Road. Chinese culture exerted a strong influence over surrounding areas; Buddhism reached Japan from China in about 538. Under Chinese influence, Japan underwent a series of social and political reforms: the abolition of slavery, the creation of a civil service, and the adoption of a modified form of written Chinese.

Oceania

The island of Fiji was first settled around 1500 BCE, and it was there and in nearby islands that Polynesian culture developed. Descendants of these first settlers would eventually colonize the whole Pacific Ocean. The Polynesians sailed across the open ocean in twin-hulled outrigger canoes, using sails and paddles, with only their knowledge of the skies, winds, and ocean currents to guide them. By 400 CE they had reached Easter Island and the Hawaiian Islands, but did not colonize New Zealand until about 1200.

Oceania

- c.600: Polynesian colonists settle the Tuamotu Islands
- c.650: Easter Islanders start to build *ahus*, sacred stone platforms

500 550 600 650 700 750

Many deities with a clear common ancestry appear in slightly different forms throughout Polynesia. This wooden carving of the war-god Ku was made in Hawaii in the early 19th century.

THE IMPACT OF ISLAM

THE RAPID SPREAD OF ISLAM was one of the most decisive developments of the medieval period. The Arabian Peninsula was conquered for Islam within ten years, and following the death of Muhammad in 632, the expansion of Islam continued unabated. By the early 8th century, Arab armies fired by the concept of *jihad* (holy war) had reached the borders of India in the east and were invading Spain in the west. With the establishment of the Abbasid Caliphate, by 750 the Muslim realm was second only to that of China in extent and cultural sophistication. The Caliphate controlled Eurasian trade on land and by sea – trade which would spread the faith further afield, deep into Africa, across the Indian Ocean, and north into Central Asia, over the subsequent centuries.

This richly-decorated copy of the Koran dates from 704.

The early history of the Caliphate

Muhammad's first successors – who became known as caliphs – were early disciples (Companions of the Prophet): Abu Bakr (632–34), 'Umar (634–44), and 'Uthman, who was murdered in 656. The authority of 'Uthman's successor Ali – Muhammad's cousin and son-in-law – was challenged by 'Uthman's family, the Umayyads. Ali was murdered in 661, and the Umayyads gained power as caliphs; their supporters were known as Sunnites. A minority of Muslims, however, known as Shi'a, saw the descendants of Ali (the Imams) as the true successors of the Prophet. This fundamental division within the faith continues to this day.

Harun al-Rashid, the great Abbasid caliph, reigned from 786 to 809. This illustration shows him in an episode from the *1001 Nights* with a barber in a Turkish Bath.

The spread of Islam 623–751

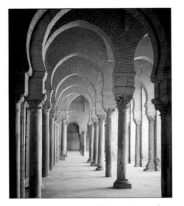

The Great Mosque at Kairouan is one of the oldest surviving Islamic buildings. It was begun in 670, shortly after Arab armies had swept through the Byzantine possessions along the North African coast.

Muhammad's vision of the Archangel Gabriel in about 610 began a process of revelation, enshrined in the Koran, the holy book which lies at the heart of Islam. His opposition to polytheism and adherence to a strict code of observance and conduct led to hostility in Mecca, and his withdrawal to Medina (the Hegira) in 622. Here the first Muslim state was established. By 630, with an army of 10,000 followers, he reentered Mecca, and began the conquest of Arabia. Conversion swelled the Muslim ranks, and Muhammad's work was continued after his death in 632 by his disciples. Within a century the heartland of Eurasia was dominated by Islam. Although Muslim warriors believed it their duty to conquer in the name of Islam, conquered peoples, especially Christians and Jews, were treated with tolerance.

❶ The growth of the Islamic world

- Muslim lands by 634
- Muslim lands by 656
- Muslim lands by 756
- Muslim raid, with date
- new city founded by Muslims
- Muslim fortress
- ✕ Muslim victory, with date
- ✕ Muslim defeat, with date
- 649 date of Muslim conquest
- Byzantine Empire c.610
- Sassanian Empire c.610
- Frankish Empire c.610

The spread of Islam

622: Beginning of Islamic calendar, marked by the Hegira of Muhammad

634: Caliphate of 'Umar (to 644)

641: Conquest of Egypt

644: Caliphate of 'Uthman (to 646)

661: Umayyad Caliphate (to 750)

670: Foundation of Kairouan

692: Dome of the Rock mosque in Jerusalem

732: Arab armies halted at Poitiers

751: Arab armies defeat Chinese on Talas River

762: Baghdad becomes Abbasid capital

632: Death of Muhammad; succession of Abu Bakr (to 634)

637: Conquest of Mesopotamia

656: Imamate of Ali (to 661)

664: Conquest of Kabul

711: Invasion of Iberian Peninsula by Tariq; rapid conquest of Visigothic kingdom

718: Christian victory at battle of Covadonga halts Muslim advance in Iberian Peninsula

750: Abbasid Caliphate established

756: Breakaway Umayyad Emirate established at Cordova (to 1031); claims status of caliphate in 928

Preaching and teaching spread the Arabic language throughout the Islamic world. This 13th-century Persian illustration shows a preacher in the mosque at Samarkand.

The impact of the Islamic advance

Water-wheels for irrigation were introduced wherever the Arabs settled. This example stands at Hamah in Syria. The Arabs also introduced Asian fruits, such as peaches and apricots.

The Islamic imprint 1000–1200

By 1000, the Islamic world had become broadly divided into two caliphates: the Abbasids, based at Baghdad, and, in the west, the Umayyads (a branch of the Abbasids' predecessors), who ruled the Iberian Peninsula. So extensive were the Abbasid domains that many subsidiary rulers wielded local power in varying degrees and were able to found autonomous dynasties. Further, the movement of peoples into the Islamic world caused further decentralization of power. In the west, the Berbers gradually established a string of local dynasties along the Maghreb coast. The Shi'ite Fatimids emerged in North Africa, conquered Egypt, and claimed caliphate status; but the most significant blow to the Abbasid Caliphate was the invasion of the Seljuk Turks from Central Asia, who moved across southwest Asia, conquered Baghdad and drove back the frontiers of the Byzantine Empire, eventually occupying Anatolia.

SEE ALSO:

Africa: pp.162–163

Europe: pp.186–187

West Asia: pp.226–227

South and Southeast Asia: pp.242–243

② The Islamic imprint c.800–1200

- Islamic world c.1000
- Abbasid Caliphate at its greatest extent c.800
- → campaigns of Seljuk Turks
- → campaigns of Berbers
- → further expansion of Islam
- ZIRIDS Muslim dynasty, with dates

935: Final text of Koran

969: Fatimids assume control of Egypt

1055: Seljuk Turks invade Baghdad

1056: Almoravids conquer North Africa and the Iberian Peninsula

1096: First Crusade; establishment of Latin kingdoms in Levant

1188: Saladin conquers Latin kingdoms in Levant

936: Buwayhids take effective control of Abbasid Caliphate

1071: Seljuks defeat Byzantine army at Manzikert

1135: Almohads control northwest Africa and the Iberian Peninsula

751: Arabs defeat Chinese army and stop Tang expansion to the west

Samarra: an Islamic city

Founded by the Abbasid caliph al-Mu'tasim, Samarra was the Abbasid capital from 836–892, and grew to sprawl some 25 miles (40 km) along the east bank of the Tigris. The new city was based around earlier settlements; it was not walled, and was organized into residential cantonments arranged around central features such as palaces and mosques, and included luxurious facilities such as racetracks and a gigantic 11.6 square miles game reserve. Later caliphs added substantial areas, notably al-Mu'tasim's successor al-Mutawakkil, who built a new center to the north, Ja'fariyya. The Abbasid court returned to its original capital at Baghdad after the death of the eighth caliph, al-Mu'tamid.

③ Samarra

- marsh
- canal
- wall
- undergound watercourse
- old towns
- cantonments
- palace
- mosque
- game reserve
- race track

The spiral minaret of the Great Mosque of al-Mutawakkil at Samarra is one of the few standing remains of the city.

THE WORLD 750–1000

THE DISINTEGRATION OF GREAT EMPIRES and conflicts between warring dynasties were widespread throughout the 9th and 10th centuries. In Europe, Charlemagne was crowned western Emperor in 800, but his Frankish Empire was broken apart by disputes over inheritance. The Abbasid Caliphate, based in Baghdad, could not maintain central control over the vast Islamic world. New Islamic dynasties, such as the Fatimids of northern Africa, broke away from Baghdad's authority. In China, the mighty Tang Empire split into small warring states while in Central America, the Maya were in decline. In contrast to this political fragmentation, powerful new states developed in many parts of the world: the Khmers in Southeast Asia, Koryo in Korea, the Toltecs in Mexico, Ghana and Kanem-Bornu in Africa, and Kievan Rus in Eastern Europe.

Ireland suffered badly from Viking raids in the 9th and 10th centuries, so monasteries built distinctive round towers, such as these at Glendalough, as lookouts and refuges.

Europe

Charlemagne, king of the Franks, incorporated most of Western Europe into a single dominion. After disputes over his inheritance, the kingdom was divided into three parts. Henry I, the Saxon successor, extended his influence over the German duchies and conquered Italy. His son, Otto I, defeated the Magyars and was crowned Holy Roman Emperor. In the west, the Carolingian Empire and the British Isles fell prey to Viking raiders.

Europe

752: Lombards capture Ravenna
800: Charlemagne crowned Holy Roman Emperor by the pope in Rome
884: Kiev becomes capital of new Russian state
896: Danish raiders besiege Paris
996: Start of war between Byzantines, led by Emperor Basil II, and Bulgaria

774: Charlemagne defeats Lombards in Italy
827: Crete and Sicily occupied by Saracen (Arab) raiders
843: Treaty of Verdun divides Carolingian empire into three
885: Saxon ruler, Alfred the Great, reconquers London from Vikings
955: Otto I defeats Magyars and halts expansion of Hungary

The World in 1000

- Song Empire
- Byzantine Empire
- Denmark and possessions
- Toltec Empire
- Kievan Rus and possessions
- Abbasid Caliphate under Harun al-Rashid, 786
- Tibet c.800
- Empire of the Franks under Charlemagne, 814
- Holy Roman Empire

In Chichén Itzá a Chac Mool, a Toltec altar in the shape of a reclining figure stands alongside the typically Maya Temple of the Jaguars.

The Americas

The nomadic Toltecs migrated into central Mexico from the northwest during the 10th century. There they became city-dwellers, expanded their territory through military conquest, and established a trading network that extended as far as South America. In the North American southwest, the Mogollon, Anasazi, and Hohokam cultures were emerging. With an economy based on efficient irrigation agriculture, these peoples built elaborate pueblos (apartment villages) in the desert canyons and established trading links which brought them into contact with the civilizations of Central America.

The Americas

c.750: First true towns appear in Mississippi valley
c.800: Hohokam, Anasazi, and Mogollon cultures emerge in American Southwest
c.900: Topiltzin, the Toltec religious leader, founds capital at Tula
990s: Exiled Toltecs take over Maya city of Chichén Itzá

c.850: Collapse of Maya civilization in Mexico's southern lowlands
c.900: Advanced Thule culture among Inuit of Alaska
987: High priest and followers expelled from Tula by rival cult that favors human sacrifice

Coptic Christianity resisted Islam in the Nubian kingdoms of Makuria and Alodia. This brightly colored altar cloth was woven during this period.

Africa

In 969, the Fatimid rulers of North Africa declared Egypt independent of Baghdad, and made Cairo their capital. Camel caravans regularly crossed the Sahara as the Arab demand for sub-Saharan gold grew. Native West African kingdoms such as Kanem-Bornu, Ghana, and Takrur all prospered as a result. In East Africa, Arab coastal trading settlements extended as far south as Zanzibar and Madagascar.

Africa

800s: Establishment of trading colonies such as Manda and Kilwa on east coast
c.950: Emergence of small kingdom of Igbo Ukwu near Niger delta
970s: Al-Azhar university established in Cairo

800: Start of Aghlabid dynasty in Tunis
868: Ahmad ibn-Tulun founds the Tulunid dynasty in Egypt
909: Shi'ite Fatimids expel Aghlabids from Tunis
969: Fatimids seize control of Egypt

PRINTING IN CHINA

The Chinese had been experimenting with ways of reproducing writing and illustrations for centuries, before they made their greatest breakthrough under the Tang in the 8th century. Carving characters and pictures in reverse onto wooden blocks was a time-consuming process, but it allowed hundreds of copies to made before the wood's surface became too worn. All kinds of documents – from religious texts to tax receipts – were printed by this method.

The earliest printed document that can be dated with certainty is *The Diamond Sutra*, a work of Buddhist doctrine printed on a scroll, produced in 868.

After the fervor of the 7th-century *jihads*, many Arab tribes subsequently turned against one another as they competed to rule the various parts of the Islamic world.

West Asia

The Abbasid dynasty came to power in 750. Though the arts, culture, and trade flourished under their rule, disagreements over the succession meant that their authority was not universally recognized. Even in Baghdad the caliphs became figureheads, real power being in the hands of Turkish mercenary or slave troops and Persian administrators. Under a new dynasty of Macedonian rulers (867–1081) the Byzantine Empire reached its apogee, and came into conflict with the Arabs to the east. Byzantine troops regained control of most of Anatolia and, in 969, reconquered Antioch.

SEE ALSO:

North America: pp.122–123

South America: pp.144–145

Africa: pp.162–163

Europe: pp.184–185

West Asia: pp.226–227

South and Southeast Asia: pp.244–245

North and East Asia: pp.262–265

Australasia and Oceania: pp.280–281

West Asia

750: Umayyad Caliphate is overthrown and succeeded by the Abbasid dynasty	**786:** Under Caliph Harun al-Rashid Baghdad becomes center of arts and learning	**863:** Byzantines annihilate Arab forces to stem Muslim advance in Anatolia	**945:** Persian Buwayhids conquer Baghdad but allow caliph to reign as figurehead	**976:** Byzantine forces threaten to take Jerusalem	
750	800	850	900	950	1000
762: Abbasid capital founded at Baghdad	**836:** Baghdad terrorized by Turkish slave troops; Abbasid Caliph al-Mutasim builds new capital at Samarra		**936:** Caliphs of Baghdad lose effective power; caliphate under control of Turkish troops		

ARAB STAR MAPS

Arab scientists and mathematicians were the finest in the world, and their astronomers added greatly to our knowledge of the heavens during this period. As well as using the night sky to set a course at sea and help them cross the desert, the Arabs continued to name stars and map constellations in the tradition of Ptolemy and other Greek astronomers. Many stars, such as Aldebaran, Rigel, and Rasalgethi, are still known by their Arab names.

The constellation of Andromeda is one of many attractive illustrations in *The Book of the Fixed Stars* compiled by Abd al-Rahman ibn Umar al-Sufi in the 10th century. The individual stars forming the constellation are shown in red.

This bronze of the god Shiva was made under the Chola dynasty. In this period cults of individual Hindu deities grew in popularity.

Buddhism affected all aspects of life in Tang China, the Buddha assuming Chinese features, as in this wall painting from Dunhuang.

South and Southeast Asia

In the north, the Islamic kingdom of the Afghan ruler Mahmud of Ghazni stretched from the Oxus to the Indus, while states such as Gurjara-Pratiharas and the Buddhist Palas vied for the Ganges plain. To the south, the Tamil Cholas and the Chalukyas fought over the Godavari and Krishna rivers. Chola conquests expanded to include Ceylon and parts of the Malay Peninsula.

East Asia

Threats of internal rebellion in the middle of the 8th century weakened the Tang dynasty's control of China. As a result the empire became more inward looking and the political and economic center of gravity began to shift south to the Yangtze valley. The Tang dynasty eventually collapsed after massive peasant uprisings in the 9th century, and China split into ten separate states until 960–79, when it was reunified under the Song. Both Korea and Japan were governed by strong, centralized Buddhist dynasties.

South and Southeast Asia

802: Angkorian dynasty founded by King Jayavarman II	**889:** Khmer King Indravarman I begins construction of Angkor	**997:** Mahmud of Ghazni extends rule into northwest India		
750	800	850	900	950	1000
c.800: Construction of Buddhist temple at Borobudur, Java	**886:** Chola dynasty rules much of southern India	**c.900:** Gurjara-Pratiharas dominates northern India	**962:** Foundation of Afghan Ghaznavid dynasty	

East Asia

751: Defeat of Chinese by Muslim forces at battle of Talas River	**794:** Kyoto becomes capital of Japan	**868:** *The Diamond Sutra*, world's oldest surviving printed work	**935:** Foundation of kingdom of Koryo in Korea	**979:** Song establish power in China
750	800	850	900	950	1000
756: Rebel general An Lushan captures Chang'an	**763:** Tang China is invaded by Tibetans	**870s:** Peasant uprisings throughout Tang China	**907:** End of the Tang dynasty	**970:** Paper money introduced by Chinese government

Map labels: Paleosiberians, Lena, Yenisey, Ob, Samoyeds, Siberia, Tungus, Mongols, Amur, KHITAN EMPIRE, Gobi, Linhuang, Kaesong, KORYO, JAPAN, Kyoto, Kaifeng, Chang'an, SONG EMPIRE, Uighurs, Dunhuang, Tanguts, TIBET, Kashmir, QARAKHANIDS, Samarkand, Oxus, GHAZNAVIDS, Ghazni, HINDU SHAHIS, QARMATIS, GURJARA-PRATIHARAS, Ganges, CHAHAMANAS, PARAMARAS, CHANDELLAS, KALACURIS, BHAUMAS, PALAS, NANZHAO, ANNAM, ARAKAN, PAGAN, SMALL STATES, CHAULUKYAS, ABHIRAS, Godavari, Krishna, Kalyani, EASTERN GANGAS, EASTERN CHALUKYAS, HARIPUNJAYA, PEGU, THATON, DVARAVATI, CHAMPA, KHMER, Angkor, Mekong, Yangtze, Yellow River, CHOLAS, Ceylon, LAMBAKANNAS, Philippine Islands, PACIFIC OCEAN, INDIAN OCEAN, SRIVIJAYA, Borneo, Malay Peninsula, Palembang, EAST JAVA KINGDOM, Borobudur, Java, Papuans, New Guinea, Australian Aborigines, Darling, New Zealand, Arabian Peninsula

EXPLORERS OF THE OCEANS

The stylized image of a ship decorates this early Viking coin, which was minted at Hedeby in the 9th century.

IN THE 1ST MILLENNIUM CE, three peoples surpassed all others as navigators of the world's oceans: the Vikings, the Arabs, and the Polynesians. The traders and raiders of Scandinavia created the fast, efficient Viking longship, which took them along the rivers of Russia to the Black Sea, and across the Atlantic Ocean to Iceland and North America. The Arabs were already accomplished seafarers; the discovery, in the 8th century, of the sea route to China via the Strait of Malacca heralded a new era of long-distance trade, and Arab ships sailed to the East Indies, East Africa, and China. Perhaps the most extraordinary seafarers of all were the Polynesians, who by 1200 CE had completed the colonization of all the islands of the Pacific.

These 12th-century walrus ivory chesspieces are from Lewis in the Outer Hebrides. The islands were settled by Norwegians in the 9th and 10th centurie

NORTH AMERICA

Region visited for timber by Greenland settlers

St Lawrence

VINLAND

L'Anse aux Meadow c.1000: Site of small Norse settlemen occupied for about 20 year

Newfoundlar

Most southerly region visited by Vikings

The Viking world

Ocean-going ships allowed the Vikings to sail in search of new lands and trading opportunities. At first they dominated their Baltic neighbors, taking tribute in the form of amber, wax, fish, ivory, and furs. Norwegians and Danes exploited weaknesses in France, England, and Ireland, using their fast, maneuverable longships to conduct lightning raids, exacting tribute, conquering, and colonizing. Eventually, in a quest for land, they crossed the Atlantic, reaching Iceland in 860 and Newfoundland c.1000. Swedish traders penetrated the navigable rivers of Russia to dominate the lucrative trade with Constantinople and the Arab world. Varangians (as these eastern Vikings were called) founded Kievan Rus, the first Russian state, and their fighting qualities were recognized by the Byzantine emperors, who employed them as their elite mercenary guard.

800 km
800 miles

Viking longships were oar-powered, ranging from 17–33 yds in length. Their light, flexible hulls "rode" the waves and made them ideal for raiding in shallow, coastal waters.

Viking voyages

793: Vikings plunder island monastery of Lindisfarne off northeast coast of England	845: Vikings sack Paris; exact tribute from Franks	866: Vikings take York	c.900: Norwegians settle in Scotland and northwest England	c.1000: Voyages from Greenland to Newfoundland and coast of North America

700 — 800 — 900 — 1000 — 1100

c.789: First recorded Viking raid on England; first raids on Ireland and Scotland recorded in 795 — 839: Swedes travel through Russia to Constantinople — 862: Novgorod founded by Rurik the Viking — c.930: Viking settlement of Iceland complete — 986: Erik the Red begins settlement of Greenland — 1042: End of Danish rule in England

The Polynesians

The first wave of colonization of the Pacific, between 2000 and 1500 BCE, took settlers from New Guinea and neighboring islands as far as the Fiji Islands. From there, they sailed on to the Tonga and Samoa groups. In about 200 BCE, the Polynesians embarked on a series of far longer voyages, crossing vast tracts of empty ocean to settle the Marquesas, the Society Islands, Hawaii, Rapa Nui (Easter Island), and New Zealand. By about 1200 CE they had discovered almost every island in the Pacific. They sailed in double-hulled canoes, laden with seed plants, chickens, and pigs. The canoes could tack into the wind, and they probably navigated by observing the sun and the stars, the direction of prevailing winds, and the flight patterns of homing birds.

Polynesian voyages 1500 BCE–1000 CE

c.1500 BCE: Earliest evidence of colonization of Fiji – by makers of incised Lapita pottery	c.500 BCE: On Samoa, Lapita style of pottery is replaced by plain, undecorated bowls	c.200 BCE: Polynesians reach Marquesas Islands from Samoa	c.400 CE: Polynesians reach Hawaiian Islands	c.700 CE: Earliest temple platforms (ahu) built on Rapa Nui (Easter Island)

1500 BCE — 1000 BCE — 500 BCE — 1 CE — 500 CE — 1000 CE

c.1300 BCE: Colonization of Tonga — c.1000 BCE: Distinct Polynesian culture starts to emerge in Fiji, Tonga, and Samoa — c.300 CE: Settlement of Rapa Nui (Easter Island) — c.400 CE: Colonization of Society Islands

On their epic ocean voyages, the Polynesians used twin-hulled canoes, similar to the one in this 19th-century engraving, up to 33 yds long. Canoes with an outrigger, attached to the hull and kept to windward for balance, were probably for inshore sailing and shorter voyages. Both types of vessel could be powered by oars or sails.

Japan

NORTH AMERICA

Tropic of Cancer

Hawaiian Islands

Tropic of Cancer

② Polynesian migrations

- before 1500 BCE
- 1500–1000 BCE
- 1000–1 BCE
- 1–500 CE
- after 500 CE

Mariana Islands

Yap

M i c r o n e s i a

Caroline Islands

Marshall Islands

Ponape

Equator

Line Islands

PACIFIC OCEAN

Equator

Admiralty Islands

New Ireland New Britain Solomon Islands

Phoenix Islands

c.400 CE

SOUTH AMERICA

New Guinea

M e l a n e s i a

Tuvalu

Santa Cruz Islands

Anuta

Futuna Uvea

Samoa Islands

c.200 BCE

Marquesas Islands

c.300 CE

Normanby Island

Coral Sea

Vanuatu

Fiji Islands

Niuatoputapu

Cook Islands

Society Islands

c.600 CE

Tahiti

c.400 CE

Tuamotu Islands

New Caledonia

Viti Levu

Lau Group

Île des Pins

Tonga Islands

c.600 CE

P o l y n e s i a

c.800 CE

Îles Gambier

Tropic of Capricorn

AUSTRALIA

Kermadec Islands

c.1000 CE

Austral Islands

c.300 CE

Rapa Nui (Easter Island)

Tropic of Capricorn

c.1200 CE

Tasman Sea

Tasmania

Aotearoa (New Zealand)

Chatham Islands

after 1200 CE

2000 km
2000 miles

SEE ALSO:

North America: pp.122–123

Europe: pp.184–185

West Asia: pp.226–227

South and Southeast Asia: pp.244–245

Australasia and Oceania: pp.280–281

Northern hunting ground of Norse Greenlanders in search of walrus ivory and polar bear skins

986: Settlements established in western Greenland, where climate mild enough for stock-rearing

Godthåb 986

Julianehåb 986

Reykjavik 873 — ICELAND

c.860

c.860

Faroe Islands c.800

793: Initial raids by Vikings

866: Danish Vikings seize city of York

911: Viking settlement becomes duchy, under Rollo

843: Noirmoutier, first Viking base in France

HELLULAND

Davis Strait

Greenland

Spitsbergen

ATLANTIC OCEAN

Shetland Islands

Orkney Islands

Lewis

SCOTLAND

IRISH KINGDOMS

Dublin

Limerick 836

841

York 866

ENGLAND

London

WELSH PRINCIPALITIES

NORMANDY

Rouen 841

Paris 845

BRITTANY

Nantes 843

Noirmoutier 842

844

FRANCE

LEÓN

NAVARRE

CASTILE

Lisbon 844

CALIPHATE OF CORDOVA

Seville 844

Balearic Islands 859

Sardinia

859–862

North Sea

Trondheim

Kaupang (Skiringssal)

NORWAY

SWEDEN

Sigtuna

Birka

DENMARK

Ringsted

Ribe 793

Lindisfarne

Hedeby

Lund

Truso

Hamburg 845

Dorestad 834

HOLY ROMAN EMPIRE

BOHEMIA-MORAVIA

POLAND

Pisa

VENETIAN REPUBLIC

Rome

PAPAL STATES

Sicily

Tunis

Baltic Sea

Staraya Ladoga (Aldeigjuborg) 750

Novgorod (Holmgard)

Gnezdovo

Paviken

Jomsborg (Wolin)

Volga

Bulgar

VOLGA BULGARIA

KIEVAN RUS

Kiev (Könugard) 882

Sarkel

Don

Dnieper

Black Sea

Constantinople (Miklagard) 839

CROATIA

BULGARIA

HUNGARY

BURGUNDY

BYZANTINE EMPIRE

Mediterranean Sea

Damascus

Cairo

FATIMIDS

ZIRIDS

Itil

Caspian Sea

Gorgan

KIEVAN RUS

GEORGIAN STATES

ARMENIA

BUWAYHIDS

Baghdad

Canary Islands c.1000

AFRICA

❶ The Viking world c.1000 CE

- area settled by Norwegian Vikings
- Danelaw 878–954
- area of Varangian influence in Russia
- area settled by Danish vikings

Viking voyages, trade routes, and raids
- → Norwegian
- ⇢ probable Norwegian voyage
- → Danish
- → Swedish

Viking settlement
- ○ Norwegian
- ○ Danish
- ● Swedish
- 981 date of Viking voyage, raid, or settlement
- ···· frontiers c.1000
- Holy Roman Empire

Arab traders in the Indian Ocean

The Arabs used the wind systems of the monsoon to propel their ships eastward from the Persian Gulf in November and to return them westward in the summer. In the 8th century, Arab traders discovered the sea route to Guangzhou (Canton) by way of the Malabar Coast, the Strait of Malacca, and Hanoi, a journey of 120 days, which nevertheless could take between 18 months and three years. The Arabs exported iron, wool, incense, and bullion in return for silk and spices. When the fall of the Tang Empire disrupted trade with China c.1000 CE, the Arabs turned to the East Indies, and Islam consequently became well established in the the islands of Southeast Asia. They also navigated the East African coast to Zanzibar and Madagascar, where they met the Malays who had colonized the island some 300 years earlier.

An Indian ship is depicted in an Arab manuscript of 1238. It has a square-rigged sail, suitable for running with the strong monsoonal winds, well known from the 1st century CE. The capacious hold could carry both passengers and cargo, essential for thriving Indian Ocean trade routes from the 8th century CE.

Baghdad c.766 CE

Aila

FATIMIDS

BUWAYHIDS

Basra

Shiraz

Kirman

GHAZNAVIDS

HINDU SHAHIS

QARMATIS

TIBET

Himalayas

SONG EMPIRE

China

Medina

Mecca

Jedda

MAKURIA

QARMATIANS

Hasa

Siraf

Thara

Daibul

Mansura

Sihar

Muscat

Persian Gulf

Red Sea

ALODIA

Athr

Zabid

YEMEN

Sana

Aden

Gulf of Aden

ETHIOPIA

DAMOT

SHOA

Ethiopian Highlands

Mogadishu

Equator

Manda

AFRICA

Zanzibar

Kilwa

SWAHILI CITY-STATES

Madagascar

to Sofala

CHAHAMANAS

GURJARA-PRATIHARAS

PARAMARAS

CHANDELLAS

CHAULUKYAS

ABHIRAS

Supara

EASTERN CHALUKYAS

EASTERN CHALUKYAS

Mandjarur

Malabar Coast

CHOLAS

Kulam Mali

Raysut

Socotra

Arabian Sea

Bay of Bengal

Ceylon

LAMBAKANNAS

Maldive Islands

Seychelles

INDIAN OCEAN

BHAUMAS

PALAS

KALCURIS

Ahina

ARAKAN

PAGAN

Hanoi

NANZHAO

GANGAS

DVARAVATI

Kusumi

PEGU

THATON

KHMER

Andaman Islands

Andaman Sea

Barus

Sumatra

Strait of Malacca

Kataha

SRIVIJAYA

East Indies

Borneo

Equator

Java

EAST JAVA KINGDOM

Guangzhou

ANNAM

HARIPUNJAYA

CHAMPA

Kadranj

Panduranga

South China Sea

c.700: Settlers from Borneo navigate to Madagascar via Sumatra (their route across Indian Ocean is unknown)

1000 km

1000 miles

❸ The Indian Ocean c.1000 CE

- → trade routes around Arabia
- → trade routes from Arabia to Africa
- → trade routes from Arabia to India and East Indies
- → trade routes from East Indies to China
- → route of first colonists of Madagascar
- ● important trade centre
- ⇒ warm monsoon (Apr to Sep)
- ⇒ cold monsoon (Oct to Mar)
- ⇒ warm ocean current

Arab and other traders in the Indian Ocean

c.632: Death of Muhammad begins the era of Arab expansion	c.700: Madagascar settled by Malays from Southeast Asia	c.900: Arab dhows (sailing ships) begin to ply the coastal routes of East Africa, as far south as Sofala	c.1000: Arab merchants begin to set up trading states in Ethiopian Highlands
600	700	800	900	1000

756: Abbasid Caliphate; new interest in seafaring, focused on Persian Gulf routes

c.800: Arab ships probably sailing as far as China

907: End of Tang Empire; disruption of Arab trade with China

THE WORLD 1000–1200

IN MANY PARTS OF THE WORLD conflict over territory and religion was intense. This was a time when the Christian West was recovering from the tumult that followed the fall of Rome. As marginal land was cleared for agriculture, the population expanded. Trade routes crossed Europe and a mercantile economy developed and prospered. Yet the resurgence of Christian Europe brought it into direct confrontation with Islam when it launched the Crusades to conquer the Holy Land. This ultimately proved a failure, but in Spain and Portugal the Christian reconquest made intermittent progress. To the east, the states of northern India fell to Muslim invaders, and Buddhism was finally driven from the subcontinent. In China the Song Empire shrank under pressure from powerful nomadic peoples to the north, such as the Xixia and the Jin.

The power of the Church was expressed in new cathedrals built first in the Romanesque and then in the Gothic style, typified by the soaring facade of Chartres.

Europe

The assimilation in the 11th century of Poland, Hungary, and the Scandinavian kingdoms into the realm of Western Christianity brought it to a new peak of power and influence. As Western Europeans began to wrest control of the Mediterranean from the Arabs and Byzantines, a new era of prosperity based on trade began. Italian merchants became middlemen in Byzantine trade, and north Italian towns, such as Venice, Genoa, and Pisa, prospered. Elsewhere, forests and marginal land were cleared for agriculture, populations grew, and new towns were founded.

1000: Hungary officially becomes a Christian state
1016: Accession of Canute unites England, Denmark, and Norway
1031: Beginning of Christian reconquest of Spain
1054: Final schism between Roman and Orthodox churches
1066: Battle of Hastings; Norman conquest of England
1077: German king, Henry IV, forced to seek absolution from Pope Gregory VII
1091: Completion of Norman conquest of Sicily
1119: Bologna University founded in Italy
1136: Independence of Russian state of Novgorod
1147: Second Crusade; Lisbon taken from Moors
1154: Building of Chartres cathedral

Europe

AL-IDRISI'S WORLD MAP

Islamic geographers led the world in medieval times. Al-Idrisi (1100–65) was a Moroccan in the service of Roger II of Sicily. The island had been under Arab rule in the 10th century and became a meeting point of two cultures where much of the knowledge of the Islamic world was transmitted to the Christian West.

Al-Idrisi's map shows the lasting influence of Ptolemy (see p.44). However, he oriented his maps, as did most contemporary Islamic geographers, with the south at the top.

The Americas

The Chimú rose to prominence in the 11th century with the construction of their capital at Chan Chan. This powerful empire, ruled by semi-divine kings, expanded by military conquest. Subject territories, linked by an advanced road system, were kept under tight economic control. In Central America, the Toltec city of Tula was sacked by Chichimec tribesmen from northwest Mexico. In turn the Chichimec established a number of small city-states, which engaged in constant, internecine warfare. North America's first true towns arose in the fertile Mississippi valley, while in the harsher climate of the arid southwest magnificent cliff dwellings were built.

The Anasazi was the most widespread of the Pueblo farming cultures of the American Southwest. Roads linked their impressive canyon villages, where they produced fine black and white pottery.

The Americas

c.1000: Leif Ericson, son of Eric the Red, sets sail from Greenland and reaches North America
c.1050: Settlements of mound-builders of Mississippi valley expand to become true towns
c.1100: Anasazi people of Southwest build fortified cliff dwellings at Mesa Verde and Chaco Canyon
1121: Bishop Eirik visits North America from Greenland
c.1175: Toltec capital, Tula, is sacked by Chichimec
c.1200: Incas, led by Manco Capac, enter and settle in Andean valley near Cuzco

The Zagwe dynasty of Ethiopia revived Christianity in the region and built astonishing churches, such as St. George's at Lalibela, which is cut directly into the local sandstone.

Africa

From the mid-11th century, the Berber Muslim Almoravids took over northwest Africa and part of Muslim Spain and, in 1076, invaded Ghana. Ghana's subsequent decline was accelerated by the desertification of the region. In 1147, the Almoravids were, in turn, overthrown by another Berber religious sect, the Almohads, who unified the Maghreb. In Ethiopia, a revival of Red Sea trade and the emergence of the Zagwe dynasty in 1150, led to a more expansionist, prosperous era. In Egypt, the military leader Saladin became ruler in 1174, ending the Fatimid dynasty and founding that of the Ayyubids.

WINDMILLS

Wind power had been harnessed in various different ways, notably in Persia and China, for grinding corn and raising water. But it was not until the 12th century that the windmill started to take on its familiar European form. The mills of northern Europe differed from earlier versions in that the shaft turned horizontally rather than vertically and the sails were turned so that they kept facing the wind. The first northern European mills were simple post-mills. These evolved gradually into bulkier tower mills with rotating caps.

In Europe windmills were used only for grinding corn up until the 15th century, as illustrated in this English woodcut from c.1340. Their power was then adapted for tasks such as land drainage, particularly in Holland.

West Asia

Byzantium's resurgence under Basil II did not last, and in the 11th century most of the empire's Asian lands fell to the Seljuk Turks. The Islamic Turks, originally from Central Asia, established themselves in Baghdad in 1055. As "men of the sword," they formed a partnership with the Persians and Arabs, the "men of the law." Tens of thousands of Europeans answered Pope Urban II's call in 1095 to recapture Jerusalem for Christendom. In 1099 the holy city was taken and the Crusaders set up states in Antioch, Edessa, Tripoli, and Jerusalem. In the following century, Muslim leaders, notably Saladin, founder of the Ayyubid dynasty in Egypt, embarked on a campaign of reconquest.

The capture of Antioch in 1098 was one of the first Christian successes on the First Crusade. The strongly fortified city held out for seven months.

SEE ALSO:

North America: pp.122–123

South America: pp.146–147

Africa: pp.162–163

Europe: pp.186–187

West Asia: pp.228–229

South and Southeast Asia: pp.244–245

North and East Asia: pp.262–265

West Asia

1055: Seljuk Turks capture Baghdad	**1099:** Jerusalem captured by Crusaders	**1174:** Founding of Ayyubid Sultanate in Egypt	**1187:** Saladin recaptures Jerusalem
1000 — 1050 — 1100 — 1150 — 1200			
1025: Death of great Byzantine emperor, Basil II	**1071:** Seljuk Turks defeat Byzantines at Manzikert	**1144:** Fall of Edessa to Muslims	**1188:** Crusader states reduced to coastal enclaves by Saladin

East Asia

By 1110, Song China was the most advanced, prosperous, and populous state in the world. However the Song alliance with the Manchurian Jin to dislodge the hostile Liao from their northern border, fatally weakened the Song Empire. The Jin overran northern China and the Song were forced to regroup in the southeast, defensive and hostile to outside influences. In Japan, the emperors lost power to the Fujiwara family in the mid-12th century. A period of violent interclan warfare followed, ending with the victory of the Minamoto clan.

This Song scroll gives a vivid depiction of the bustling street life and prosperity of Kaifeng in the 12th century. In 1105 the city's population had risen to 260,000.

East Asia

1005: Song China becomes subject state of northern Liao kingdom, with capital at Beijing	**1125:** Liao defeated by Jin from Manchuria	**1191:** Zen Buddhist order founded in Japan	
1000 — 1050 — 1100 — 1150 — 1200			
c.1045: Movable type printing invented in China	**1130:** Song capital moves to Hangzhou	**1192:** Minamoto Yoritomo becomes Shogun and forms military government in Japan	

The Khmer Empire was at its height in the 11th and 12th centuries. The artistic brilliance of the court, evident in these carvings decorating a temple at Angkor Wat, was in marked contrast to the conditions of the mass of the population.

South and Southeast Asia

Northern India was repeatedly invaded by the Ghazni Muslims of Afghanistan. In 1186 the last Ghazni ruler was deposed by the Turkish leader, Muhammad al Ghur, who continued to wage holy war in the region. Southeastern India was dominated by the Chola dynasty, who controlled the sea route between West Asia and China. The two most powerful states of Southeast Asia, the Khmer Empire and the kingdom of Pagan, both enjoyed an artistic golden age.

The World in 1200

- Byzantine Empire
- England and possessions
- Venetian Republic
- Holy Roman Empire
- Almoravid Empire 1120
- Great Seljuk Empire 1071
- possessions of Canute 1028–1035

Africa

1048: Fatimids lose control of Ifriqiya (Libya)	**c.1110:** Onset of serious desiccation of Sahel region	**1147:** Almohads established in Morocco and southern Spain	**1171:** Shi'ite Fatimid dynasty in Egypt suppressed by Saladin	
1000 — 1050 — 1100 — 1150 — 1200				
1076: Ghana falls to Almoravids	**1128:** Almohads start takeover of Almoravid dominions	**1150:** Zagwe dynasty established in Ethiopia		

South and Southeast Asia

1014: Rajendra I becomes ruler of the Cholas of southeastern India	**1018:** Rajendra conquers Ceylon	**1113:** Accession of Suryavarman II, powerful warrior king of the Khmer	**1152:** Temple of Angkor Wat completed	**1191:** Muhammad al Ghur defeats Rajput clans
1000 — 1050 — 1100 — 1150 — 1200				
c.1000: First Muslim raids into northern India, led by Sultan Muhammad of Ghazni	**1044:** Establishment of first Burmese state at Pagan	**1077:** Chola merchants send embassy to China	**1186:** Raids by Muhammad al Ghur herald end of Buddhism in northern India	

THE AGE OF THE CRUSADES

THE IDEA OF A HOLY WAR was never part of the doctrine of the early Christian church. This changed in 1095, when Pope Urban II made an impassioned speech at Clermont, urging French barons and knights to go to the aid of the beleaguered Christians of the Byzantine Empire. In return, they were promised indulgences. When they got to the Holy Land and captured Jerusalem in 1099, the aims of the Crusaders became rather less spiritual. Those rewarded with land tried to recreate the society of feudal Europe, but there was always a shortage of manpower to maintain the Crusader states in their precarious two centuries of existence. Nevertheless, the crusading ideal became firmly established in European consciousness, and there were many subsequent expeditions to defend or recapture Jerusalem, but none was as successful as the first.

The idealism of a devout Crusader is captured in this 13th-century drawing.

The most devout and determined of all the crusading kings of Europe was Louis IX of France (St. Louis). He sailed on two Crusades, once to invade Egypt, the second time to convert the King of Tunis. Both ended in disaster. In 1270, Louis and his men were struck down by disease as they camped before Tunis. Louis himself died. Here his coffin is being loaded on a ship to be carried back to France.

Scale varies with perspective
4450 km (2760 miles)
4820 km (3000 miles)

1147: Crusaders help Portuguese under Afonso Henriques to capture Lisbon

1270: Crusaders struck down by disease; death of Louis

② The Crusades 1096–1270

Muslim territory 1096	**First Crusade routes 1096–99**	**Third Crusade routes 1189–92**
Byzantine Empire 1096	Godfrey of Bouillon	Richard I
major areas of recruiting for First Crusade	Raymond of Toulouse	Richard I's fleet
Muslim/Christian frontier c.1150	Robert of Normandy	Frederick Barbarossa
Christian victory	Baldwin of Boulogne	Philip Augustus of France
Muslim victory	**Second Crusade routes 1147–49**	**Crusades of Louis IX**
Holy Roman Empire	English and Flemish Crusaders	Louis IX's Crusade 1248
frontiers c.1096	Conrad III	Louis IX's Crusade 1270
	Louis VII of France	

The major Crusades

The leaders of the First Crusade were mainly minor nobles from France and the Rhineland. Later crusades were led by emperors and kings. Rivalry between them and the rulers of the Crusader states often led to strategic blunders and ill-feeling between West and East. The Second Crusade ended in disaster under the walls of Damascus, though it had enjoyed success in the Iberian Peninsula. The Third saw valiant deeds in the face of a powerful, well-organized enemy, Saladin, but failed to retake Jerusalem. In the 13th century two crusades were organized by Louis IX of France (St. Louis), but both were ultimately unsuccessful.

Richard I of England jousts with Saladin, in a fanciful illustration of the Third Crusade. Images such as this inspired chivalric ideals in the knights of western Europe. The reality was very different: desert campaigns with terrible shortages of food and water. On the First Crusade, most of the knights had lost their horses long before reaching the Holy Land.

The Crusades 1050–1350

1095: Byzantine Empire appeals for aid to pope, who preaches in France to raise support

1099: Capture of Jerusalem

c.1130: Hospital of St. John of Jerusalem (the Hospitallers) becomes military order

1148: Crusader army abandons siege of Damascus

1187: Saladin defeats Christians at Hattin

1192: Third Crusade; Richard I of England wins back some of territory taken by Saladin

1250–54: First of Louis IX's crusades; invasion of Egypt ends in defeat at Mansurah; Louis captured and ransomed

c.1302: Last Christian territory in Levant falls to Mamluks

1071: Turks defeat Byzantines at battle of Manzikert

1085: Alfonso VI of León takes Toledo

1096: First wave of Crusaders departs

c.1118: Crusading order of Knights Templar founded

1147: Second Crusade; Emperor Conrad defeated by Turks at Dorylaeum

1204: Fourth Crusade never reaches Holy Land; Crusaders take Constantinople

1229: Emperor Frederick II regains control of Jerusalem through diplomacy

1270: Death of Louis IX outside walls of Tunis

1291: Loss of Acre

1310: Hospitallers, having taken Rhodes, make it their headquarters

The boundaries of Christianity and Islam

In the 9th and 10th centuries, the boundaries between the Islamic and Christian worlds shifted very little. A new threat to Christianity came in the mid-11th century with the advance of the Seljuk Turks, newly converted to Islam and effective rulers of the Abbasid Caliphate after reaching Baghdad in 1055. Following their victory over the Byzantines in 1071 at Manzikert, they won control of almost all Asia Minor, home to former Christian subjects of the Byzantine Empire. In the Iberian Peninsula, however, the Christian kingdoms won back land from the Muslims in the course of the 11th century.

Godfrey of Bouillon leads the attack on Jerusalem in 1099. After all the hardship and the long journey there, the capture of the Holy City was hailed as a miracle. It was followed by the murder or brutal eviction of many of the city's Muslims and Jews.

SEE ALSO:
Africa: pp.162–163
Europe: pp.186–187
West Asia: pp.228–229

❶ Islam and Christianity c.1090

- Muslim lands
- Greek Christians (Orthodox)
- Roman Church (under papal authority)
- Greek Christians in Muslim lands
- other Christians
- direction of Muslim expansion
- direction of Greek Christian expansion
- direction of Roman Church expansion
- city with important Jewish community

1000 km
1000 miles

Krak des Chevaliers was one of many heavily fortified Crusader castles. Manned by the Hospitallers, it held out against Saladin's forces, but fell to the Mamluks in 1271 after a month's siege.

Crusader states in the Holy Land

How the Crusaders' conquests should be ruled was not considered until after Jerusalem had fallen. The solution – a feudal kingdom of Jerusalem buttressed by the counties of Edessa, Tripoli, and Antioch – alienated the Byzantines, who had hoped to regain their former territories. Jerusalem was always a weak state with a small population, heavily dependent on supplies and recruits from western Christendom. When a strong Islamic ruler such as Saladin emerged, the colonists had little hope against a determined Muslim onslaught. They held on to the coast through the 13th century, but in 1291, Acre, the last major city in Christian hands, fell to the Mamluks of Egypt.

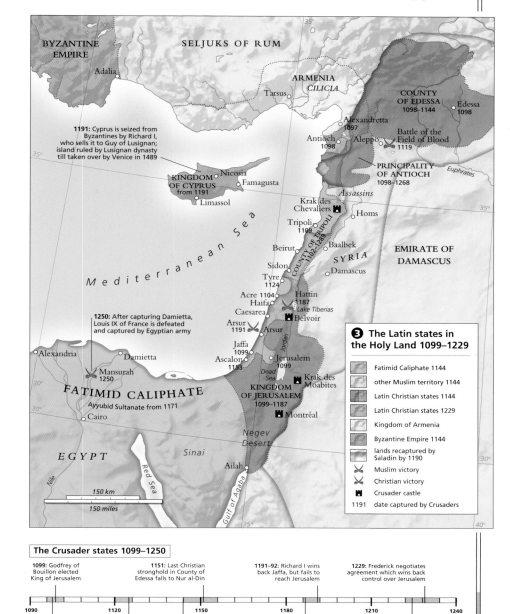

❸ The Latin states in the Holy Land 1099–1229

- Fatimid Caliphate 1144
- other Muslim territory 1144
- Latin Christian states 1144
- Latin Christian states 1229
- Kingdom of Armenia
- Byzantine Empire 1144
- lands recaptured by Saladin by 1190
- Muslim victory
- Christian victory
- Crusader castle
- 1191 date captured by Crusaders

150 km
150 miles

The Crusader states 1099–1250

1099: Godfrey of Bouillon elected King of Jerusalem
1151: Last Christian stronghold in County of Edessa falls to Nur al-Din
1191–92: Richard I wins back Jaffa, but fails to reach Jerusalem
1229: Frederick negotiates agreement which wins back control over Jerusalem

1090 1120 1150 1180 1210 1240

1098: Crusaders take Antioch
1124: Capture of important port of Tyre
1144: Edessa lost to Zangi, governor of Mosul
1187–88: Crusaders states ravaged by Saladin's armies
1225: Emperor Frederick II inherits Kingdom of Jerusalem

THE WORLD 1200–1300

IN THE 13TH CENTURY Mongol horsemen burst out of their Central Asian homeland and conquered a vast swathe of the Eurasian landmass. By 1300, they had divided their conquests into four large empires that stretched from China to eastern Europe. Mongol campaigns brought devastation, particularly to China and the Islamic states of southwest Asia but, once all resistance had been crushed, merchants, ambassadors, and other travelers were able to move safely through the Mongol realms. Though the old political order of the Islamic world, centered on the Abbasid Caliphate and Baghdad, was swept away, the influence of Islam continued to spread as many Mongols adopted the religion. Powerful new Muslim states also emerged in Mamluk Egypt and the Sultanate of Delhi. Europe remained on the defensive in the face of the Mongols and Islam, but city-states such as Venice and Genoa prospered through increased trading links with the East.

The port of Venice was the richest city in western Europe. This illustration shows Marco Polo with his father and uncle setting off in 1271 on the first stage of their incredible journey to the court of the Great Khan.

Europe

The feudal monarchies of England and France consolidated large regional states, but conflict between popes and emperors prevented any similar process in Italy and Germany. In Spain, Christian forces took Córdoba and Seville, leaving only the small kingdom of Granada in Moorish control. In eastern Europe, the Mongols of the Golden Horde collected tribute from the Russian principalities. Western Europe, in contrast, prospered economically as Italian merchants linked northern lands to the commerce of the Mediterranean basin.

Europe

- **1204:** Constantinople captured by Latin crusaders diverted from 4th Crusade
- **1236:** Christian reconquest of Córdoba
- **1261:** Byzantine Empire regains Constantinople
- **1282:** French driven from Sicily, which passes to Aragon
- **1204:** King John loses English fiefs in northern France
- **1237:** Start of Mongol conquest of Russia
- **1270:** Death of Louis IX (St. Louis) on crusade
- **1271:** Departure of Marco Polo for China

(timeline 1200–1300)

The Chimú were a coastal-dwelling fishing people. They made striking gold funerary masks to place on the mummified remains of the nobility.

The Americas

Many small city-states competed for power in central Mexico, where migrant peoples sought new lands to cultivate, among them the Mexica, who would later build the Aztec Empire. In the Andes, local rulers organized autonomous states. Chucuito dominated the highlands around Lake Titicaca, while Chimú rule extended over a long stretch of the Pacific coast. Woodland peoples east of the Mississippi River constructed increasingly elaborate ceremonial centers around massive earth mounds.

The Americas

- **c.1200:** Expansion of Chimú state
- **c.1250:** Start of decline of important Mississippian site at Cahokia
- **c.1250:** Settlement of Mexica people in Central America
- **1283:** Foundation of late Maya capital at Mayapán

(timeline 1200–1300)

The World in 1300

- Byzantine Empire
- England and possessions
- Aragon and possessions
- Venetian Republic and possessions
- Mongol Empire on death of Genghis Khan 1227
- controlled by Khwarizm Shah 1219
- Holy Roman Empire

THE MEDIEVAL MAPPAMUNDI

The world maps produced in medieval Europe were not intended as representations of the physical world. Their purpose was primarily religious and Jerusalem often appeared at the center. This circular map, oriented with Asia at the top, is full of Christian symbolism, and is decorated with grotesque faces and mythical beasts.

A 13th-century English psalter contains this tiny world map or *mappamundi*, which measures just 4 inches across.

Africa

In the 13th century, the Mali Empire displaced the Kingdom of Ghana and won control of the West African trade in gold and slaves, with caravans of as many as 25,000 camels crossing the Sahara to North Africa. Meanwhile, the Swahili city-states on the East African coast exported goods through the trading networks of the Indian Ocean. Rulers of Mali and the Swahili city-states adopted Islam and built mosques and religious schools. Islam did not reach central and southern Africa, but the trade it generated led to the establishment of wealthy inland states such as the Kingdom of Great Zimbabwe.

West Asia

This luster tile from 13th-century Persia is decorated with a verse from the Koran. The Mongols were too few to impose their beliefs on the peoples they conquered. Instead, many of them became Muslims.

In 1258 the Mongols sacked Baghdad and overthrew the Abbasid Caliphate. Their leaders established themselves as Il-Khans, nominally subordinate to the Great Khan in China. Their empire extended almost to the Mediterranean, where their westward expansion was halted by the Mamluks of Egypt. By 1300 most Mongols of the Il-Khanate had embraced Islam, as had many of their fellow Mongols of the Golden Horde. Meanwhile, the Seljuks and other Turkic peoples consolidated their position in formerly Byzantine territory by establishing regional states.

West Asia

1219: Mongol invasion of Khwarizm Empire

1260: Battle of Ain Jalut; Mamluks defeat Mongol army north of Jerusalem

1299: Osman founds Ottoman state among the small Seljuk states in western Turkey

| 1200 | 1220 | 1240 | 1260 | 1280 | 1300 |

1231: Mongols reconquer resurgent Empire of the Khwarizm Shah

1258: Sack of Baghdad and fall of Abbasid Caliphate; Hülegü founds Il-Khanate

1265: Death of Hülegü

1295: Conversion of the Il-Khan Ghazan to Islam

THE MAGNETIC COMPASS

The Chinese had long known that a floating magnetized needle always points in the same direction. Their sailors started to make regular use of this fact in about 1100. By the 13th century, the magnetic compass was probably in widespread use among the Arab navigators of the Indian Ocean. In Europe, a written account of its principles appeared as early as 1190.

In the 13th century the Chinese simply floated a magnetized needle on water. This boxed compass is an early example.

SEE ALSO:

North America: pp.122–123

South America: pp.146–147

Africa: pp.162–163

Europe: pp.186–191

West Asia: pp.228–229

South and Southeast Asia: pp.244–245

North and East Asia: pp.262–265

North and East Asia

Genghis Khan invaded northern China in 1211, but the Southern Song Empire fell only after a long campaign (1260-79) directed by Kublai Khan. China was the richest of all the Mongol conquests. Kublai became emperor and founded the Yuan dynasty. He appointed many foreigners to govern the empire and fostered both maritime and overland trade with other lands throughout East Asia. From Korea (Koryo) the Mongols made two failed attempts to invade Japan.

Ghenghis Khan receives homage from the leaders of other Mongol tribes. White horsetails flying from his tent indicated that the Mongols were temporarily at peace. Black ones meant they were at war.

North and East Asia

1206: Temujin named Genghis Khan

1233: Mongols take Jin capital, Kaifeng

1264: Kublai elected Great Khan

1279: Foundation of Yuan dynasty

1294: Death of Kublai

| 1200 | 1220 | 1240 | 1260 | 1280 | 1300 |

1211: Mongols begin conquest of northern China

1274: First Mongol attempt to invade Japan

1292: Departure of Marco Polo from China

South and Southeast Asia

In 1206 Qutb al-din, leader of the Islamic raiders who had terrorized northern India for the past 30 years, fixed the capital of a new sultanate at Delhi. The Sultanate suffered occasional Mongol raids, while the Mongols made repeated forays from China into Annam and Pagan, without ever gaining secure control of the region. They also launched a massive seaborne attack on Java, but their tactics were ineffective in the island's tropical jungles.

The spectacular royal enclosure of Great Zimbabwe was rebuilt many times between the 11th and the 15th century. The kings owed their wealth to trade in cattle, gold, and copper.

The Qutb Minar minaret rises beside the Quwwat-al-Islam mosque in Delhi. Begun in 1199, it became a powerful symbol of Islamic rule in northern India.

Africa

1228: Start of collapse of Almohad Empire in North Africa

c.1250: Building of stone mosques in Swahili city-states

1270: Expansion of Christian Kingdom of Ethiopia

| 1200 | 1220 | 1240 | 1260 | 1280 | 1300 |

1230: Establishment of the Mali Empire by Sundiata

1250: Mamluk military caste takes over Egypt

1255: Death of Sundiata

1269: Marinids inflict final defeat on Almohads in Morocco

South and Southeast Asia

1206: Foundation of Sultanate of Delhi

1258: First Mongol expedition to Annam

1288: Kublai Khan gives up attempt to subdue Annam and Champa

| 1200 | 1220 | 1240 | 1260 | 1280 | 1300 |

1293: Failed Mongol invasion of Java

THE AGE OF THE MONGOLS

Genghis Khan – the title means "universal ruler" – was born Temujin, son of a minor Mongol chief.

THE NOMADIC HERDSMEN of the Mongolian steppe traded livestock, horses, and hides with the settled agricultural civilization of China to the south, but relations between the two were usually marked by hostility and suspicion. By the 13th century, the Chinese empire had become weak and fragmented. Into this power vacuum burst the Mongols, a fierce race of skilled horsemen, their normally warring tribes united under the inspired leadership of Genghis Khan. Genghis did not seek war at all costs; he first gave his enemies a chance to submit – on his terms. If they refused, he unleashed a campaign of terror, sacking cities and massacring entire populations. Although at first the Mongols numbered no more than a million, their ranks were swelled by Turks, Arabs, and other subject peoples. Genghis's successors extended his conquests across Asia and deep into Europe, but his empire then split into four khanates. By 1400, the Mongols were a divided and weakened force and most of their conquests had been lost.

Genghis Khan, preceded by Jebe, one of his most trusted commanders, leads a cavalry charge. Jebe and another great general, Sübedei, made the astonishing raid into Russia in 1222 that first made Europe aware of the Mongols' existence.

Caravan routes across Central Asia thrived in the climate of law and order imposed by Mongol rule. This illustration from the Catalan Atlas of 1375 shows a group of European merchants riding along the Silk Road.

The Mongol peace

The Mongols' chief aim was always to exact tribute from conquered peoples, but they also brought long periods of peace; travelers were able to cross Eurasia in safety along the old Silk Road. In the reign of Genghis Khan's grandson Möngke (1251–59) it was said that a virgin with a pot of gold on her head could walk unmolested across his empire. The two most famous travelers to benefit from the Mongol peace were the Venetian merchant Marco Polo, who claimed to have spent 17 years in the employment of Kublai Khan, and Ibn Battuta, a Muslim legal scholar from Tangier in Morocco, who also traveled as far as China.

1241: Defeat of Polish-German army at Liegnitz

1241: 30,000 Mongols cross frozen Vistula to invade Poland

1241: Battle of Mohi; Batu's forces attack Béla IV's army of 65,000 Hungarians confined in their camp

1242: News reaches Mongols that Ögödei has died, so they begin journey home

1222: Battle of Kalka River; Russians' first experience of Mongol warfare

1243: Defeated Seljuks become vassals of the Mongols

1260: Hülegü invades Syria, but turns back with some of forces on news of Möngke's death. Remaining troops defeated at Ain Jalut by Mamluks

1258: Baghdad, greatest city in Islamic world, falls to Hülegü. Legends tell of 800,000 killed

1221: While evading pursuers, Muhammad II and Sübedei continue reconnaissance westward in "great raid"

1220: Genghis takes Samarkand; captives from Bukhara used as human shields

1220: Khwarizm Shah, Muhammad II, flees to west; Genghis dispatches generals Jebe and Sübedei in pursuit. They lose trail at Nishapur

1256:

1220: Genghis takes Samarkand; captives from Bukhara used as human shields

1221: Battle of the Indus against Jalal-ad-Din, son of Muhammad II

2 Eurasia and Africa c.1300

route of Marco Polo	route of Ibn Battuta
1271 ——— 1295	1325 ——— 1345

··· disputed journeys of Ibn Battuta

—— Silk Road

The Mongol peace

1235: Walled city built at Karakorum as fixed Mongol capital

1275: Marco Polo reaches Kublai's summer palace at Shangdu (Xanadu)

1325: Ibn Battuta's first pilgrimage to Mecca

1345–46: Ibn Battuta visits Southeast Asia and China

1225	1250	1275	1300	1325	1350

1264: Kublai defeats rival for title of Great Khan, ending civil war

1266: Kublai founds new capital at Khanbaliq (Beijing)

1292: Marco Polo given task of escorting Mongol princess to Hormuz

1334–41: Ibn Battuta serves as *qadi* (judge) in Delhi

The Mongol conquests

In less than 20 years, in a series of conquests without parallel in history, Genghis Khan shattered the Muslim states of Central Asia, overran northern China, and sent troops on a lightning raid into Russia. Genghis's immediate successor was his third son Ögödei, whose reign as Great Khan saw the destruction of the Jin and Khwarizm empires, continued fighting with Song China, and an invasion of Europe that reached Hungary and Poland. The conquest of the Song was completed by Kublai Khan, a grandson of Genghis, who became emperor of China, while Kublai's brother, Hülegü, founder of the Il-Khanate, destroyed the Abbasid Caliphate, sacking the great Islamic city of Baghdad. The first setback to Mongol expansion came at the hands of the Mamluks, who, in 1260, prevented their advance into Egypt at Ain Jalut.

Mongol conquests of the 13th century

1206: Mongols united by Genghis Khan
1219: Genghis attacks Khwarizm
1229: Ögödei elected Great Khan
1260: Hülegü invades Syria; Mongols suffer first major defeat at Ain Jalut
1279: Last Song resistance crushed
1281: Second failed invasion of Japan

1200 | 1220 | 1240 | 1260 | 1280 | 1300

1211: First invasion of Jin Empire
1227: Death of Genghis
1242: Batu founds Golden Horde
1258: Sack of Baghdad
1294: Death of Kublai

SEE ALSO:

Europe: pp.188–189

West Asia: pp.228–229

South and Southeast Asia: pp.244–245

North and East Asia: pp.262–265

At the siege of Hezhou in 1258–59, Mongol horsemen tried unsuccessfully to cross the Yangtze on a pontoon bridge of boats. The conquest of Song China was accomplished only after many protracted sieges.

❶ Mongol campaigns 1206–94

.... approximate state borders 1206

▨ Mongol homelands at outset of campaigns c.1206

▨ Jin Empire c.1206

▨ Southern Song Empire c.1206

▨ Kara Khitai Empire c.1206

▨ Empire of the Khwarizm Shah c.1206

▨ controlled by the Khwarizm Shah in 1219

▨ extent of Mongol Empire in 1227 on death of Genghis Khan

Routes of conquest

→ campaigns in the reign of Genghis Khan (1206–27)

→ campaigns in the reign of Ögödei (1229–41)

→ campaigns in the reigns of Güyük and Möngke (1246–59)

→ campaigns in the reign of Kublai Khan (1260–94)

✕ Mongol victory

✕ Mongol defeat

⊙ city sacked by Mongols

⊙ city captured by Mongols

This 15th-century Italian map shows Kublai Khan's capital, Cambaluc (Khanbaliq). He had the city built in 1266 near the ruined Jin capital, Zhongdu, on the site of modern Beijing.

MONGOL WARFARE

The Mongols owed their initial successes to their fast, versatile mounted archers, but also became experts in siege warfare, learned from the Chinese. City-dwellers were their natural enemies, and to defeat them they used any method to hand: cunning propaganda, bombardment with rocks and firebombs, starvation, and even flooding. Among the Mongols' many ingenious tactics were feigned retreats to lure enemies into the open, smokescreens to conceal their position, and arrows that made a whistling noise to terrify opposing armies. They achieved the only successful winter invasion of Russia in history, riding along frozen rivers, using them as roads. When crossing Asia, their massive war columns included women and children, as well as captives and slaves, with herds of cattle and spare horses – as many as four replacement mounts for each cavalryman.

Mongol horsemen, mounted on their stocky ponies, were the finest cavalrymen of the age. Disc-shaped stirrups gave the rider a steady platform, allowing him to fire his bow in any direction, even when riding at top speed.

THE WORLD 1300–1400

DURING THE 14TH CENTURY epidemics of bubonic plague swept across the Old World from China and Korea to the west coast of Europe. Dramatic demographic decline led to economic and social disruption that weakened states throughout Eurasia and North Africa. In addition, the onset of the so-called "Little Ice Age," which would last till the 19th century, brought bad weather and poor harvests to many of the regions affected by plague. The Mongol empires, which had dominated Eurasia since the conquests of Genghis Khan in the 13th century, began to disintegrate, though the Khanate of the Golden Horde maintained its hegemony in southern Russia into the 15th century. In both China and Persia the Mongols were assimilated into the local population, but in China, a new dynasty, the Ming, introduced a Han Chinese aristocratic regime.

The Black Death reached Europe from Asia in 1347. In three years it probably killed one third of the population. The fear it generated is captured in this image of Death strangling a plague victim.

Europe

Europe struggled to recover from the social and economic disruption caused by the Black Death. Scarcity of labor led peasants and workers to seek improved conditions and higher wages, but landlords and employers resisted their demands, provoking many revolts in western Europe. France suffered too from the military campaigns of the Hundred Years' War, fueled by the dynastic ambitions of English kings. Religious differences also brought disorder. Rival popes residing in Rome and Avignon both claimed authority over the Catholic Church, while in England the Lollards challenged the authority and doctrine of the Church itself.

Europe					
	1312: Order of Knights Templar suppressed by pope	**1337:** Beginning of the Hundred Years' War	**1346:** English defeat French at Battle of Crécy	**1378:** Beginning of Great Schism in Catholic church	**1381:** Peasants' Revolt in England
1300	**1320**	**1340**	**1360**	**1380**	**1400**
1309: Pope takes up residence at Avignon		**1347:** Arrival of bubonic plague in Italy	**1358:** The Jacquerie, uprising against nobility in France	**1397:** Union of Kalmar; Norway, Denmark, and Sweden united under a single monarch	

The World in 1400

- Ming Empire
- Byzantine Empire
- Ottoman Empire
- England and possessions
- Union of Kalmar
- Aragon and possessions
- Muscovy
- Genoa and possessions
- Burgundy and possessions
- Venetian Republic and possessions
- Habsburg possessions
- Luxembourg possessions
- Holy Roman Empire
- Tughluq's Empire 1335

THE CATALAN ATLAS

The Catalans were fine sailors who sailed regularly as far as the Black Sea and the Baltic. The Catalan Atlas of 1375 is a large world map on wooden panels, probably the work of the king of Aragon's mapmaker, Abraham Cresques, a Majorcan Jew. Most of the information for Europe is derived from the mariners' charts known as portolans that were used by Italian and Catalan ships' captains. The main source for China and the Far East, which are far less accurately mapped, is Marco Polo's account of his journeys (see p.68).

The Catalan map gives a comprehensive and accurate picture of the coastline and ports of Europe and North Africa.

Africa

The Islamic Mali Empire controlled the trans-Saharan caravan trade, using the profits to maintain a powerful army and dominate West Africa. Gold and slaves went north in exchange for salt, textiles, horses, and manufactured goods. Tales of the wealth of Mali spread to Europe and West Asia, especially after the ostentatious pilgrimage to Mecca made by one of the country's most powerful rulers, Mansa Musa. Many smaller states emerged in the region as rulers sought to ensure a regular supply of trade goods. The Swahili cities of East Africa were not hit by plague, but commercial traffic declined as their trading partners in Asia experienced social and economic disruption.

THE CANNON

The Chinese had a long tradition of using gunpowder weapons, including bamboo tubes that fired arrows and bullets. The English word "cannon" comes from the Italian *cannone*, meaning a large bamboo cane. Metal cannon were probably first used in China, but by the early 14th century were in action across Asia and in most of Europe. The earliest metal cannons in Europe were forged, but these were superseded by much larger ones cast using the technology initially developed for making church bells.

The cannon was primarily used as a siege weapon. Its effectiveness had a major influence on castle design.

West Asia

During the late 14th century the Turkish warrior chieftain Timur (Tamerlane), who claimed descent from Genghis Khan, carved out a vast Central Asian empire, and built himself a magnificent capital at Samarkand. Timur invaded India and sacked the city of Delhi, and he was planning an invasion of China when he died in 1405. One other empire expanded during this period – that of the Ottoman Turks, who seized Anatolia and encroached on Byzantine holdings in southeastern Europe. By 1400 the once-mighty Byzantine Empire consisted of Constantinople and a few coastal regions in Greece and western Anatolia that maintained maritime links with the capital.

Timur's ambition and cruelty revived memories of Genghis Khan. He instilled fear into conquered peoples and opponents of his rule by building towers studded with the severed heads of his victims.

SEE ALSO:

North America: pp.122–123

South America: pp.146–147

Africa: pp.162–163

Europe: pp.188–191

West Asia: pp.228–231

South and Southeast Asia: pp.242–243

North and East Asia: pp.262–267

West Asia timeline:

1326: Ottomans capture Byzantine city of Bursa and make it their capital
1347: Black Death reaches Baghdad and Constantinople
1370: Beginning of Timur's conquests
c.1380: Foundation of Janissary corps by Ottomans
1336: Birth of Timur
1354: First Ottoman conquests in southeastern Europe
1393: Sack of Baghdad by Timur

East Asia

Plague, floods, and famine all contributed to the buildup of Chinese resentment at Mongol rule. Local uprisings became increasingly frequent, culminating in 1356 in a rebellion in southeastern China, which carried Zhu Yuanzhang, founder of the Ming dynasty, to power. War with the Mongols continued for some years, but the Chinese drove them back to their original homelands in the north. Japan had successfully resisted Mongol attempts at invasion, but their own Kamakura shogunate collapsed in 1333. The new shoguns of the Ashikaga family never succeeded in exercising the same degree of control over the country.

The Ming emperors restored Chinese values after a century of Mongol rule. This statue portrays a guardian of the spirit world.

East Asia timeline:

1335: Rebellions against Mongol rule in China
1351: Massive flooding of Yellow River
1392: Foundation of Yi dynasty in Korea
1336: Foundation of Ashikaga shogunate in Japan
1368: Establishment of the Ming dynasty

South and Southeast Asia

In India, the Sultanate of Delhi reached its greatest extent in the reign of Tughluq, but by the end of the century had lost control of most of the peninsula. The small kingdoms of mainland Southeast Asia all maintained diplomatic and commercial links with Ming China. The new Thai kingdom of Siam proved especially skillful in its dealings with its powerful neighbor to the north. During the 14th century island Southeast Asia fell increasingly under the influence of the Majapahit empire based in Java. A Javanese navy, financed by taxes levied on the lucrative trade in spices, patrolled the waters of the archipelago and controlled maritime trade.

Mansa Musa, ruler of Mali, is depicted on the Catalan Atlas of 1375. Europeans were in awe of his reported wealth and the splendor of his court.

The marble dome of Tughluq's mausoleum rises above the ramparts of the fortified city he built at Delhi in 1321.

Africa timeline:

1331: Ibn Battuta's voyage to the Swahili cities of East Africa
1344: Ethiopia at its height at death of ruler Amde Sion
c.1390: Formation of the kingdom of Kongo
1324: Pilgrimage to Mecca by Mansa Musa of Mali
1347: Marinids take Tunis
1352: Ibn Battuta's travels to the Mali Empire

South and Southeast Asia timeline:

1320: Muhammad ibn Tughluq succeeds to Sultanate of Delhi
1343: Majapahit Empire completes conquest of Bali
1378: Sukhothai becomes vassal of Siam and is gradually absorbed
c.1350: Founding of Ayutthaya, capital of new kingdom of Siam
1398: Delhi sacked by Timur

TRADE AND BIOLOGICAL DIFFUSION

The peripatetic black rat, at home in a wide range of human environments, was the host for plague-carrying fleas.

CAMPAIGNS OF IMPERIAL EXPANSION, mass migration, cross-cultural trade, and long-distance travel all facilitated the spread of agricultural crops, domesticated animals, and diseases throughout much of the Old World. From 500 to 1500 CE, an array of historical processes helped introduce biological species to new regions and peoples. Chinese rulers extended their authority south of the Yangtze River; Muslim armies pushed into India, Persia, and North Africa; Bantu-speaking peoples migrated throughout most of sub-Saharan Africa; Muslim merchants pursued commercial opportunities throughout the Indian Ocean basin and across the Sahara; and missionaries, pilgrims, diplomats, administrators, and other travelers ventured throughout Eurasia and North Africa. Biological exchanges resulting from these changes profoundly influenced the development of societies throughout the eastern hemisphere.

Skulls, crossbones, and other images of death were frequently represented in both religious and secular art during the period of the so-called "Black Death."

The flea is the agent of transmission of bubonic plague between rats and humans.

1 The spread of the Black Death

- Arab trade route
- Chinese trade route
- Genoese trade route
- main Hanseatic trade routes
- Silk Road } routes opened during the
- other route } "Mongol Peace" c.1250–1350
- Venetian trade route
- other trade route
- principal route of Hajj pilgrimage to Mecca
- → progress of bubonic plague
- area of earliest outbreak of bubonic plague
- area of outbreak of bubonic plague
- recorded outbreak of bubonic plague

Scale varies with perspective

7720 km (4800 miles)

17,810 km (11,070 miles)

At the height of the Black Death in Europe, so many people died daily that it was impossible to bury them all separately. The bodies were buried together in mass graves, usually outside the settlement walls. This manuscript illustration shows plague victims carried off by agents of Death.

The plague made no concessions to status, infecting rich and poor alike. This 14th-century painting shows the deathbed of Queen Anne of Bohemia, wife of King Richard II of England.

The spread of bubonic plague

Bubonic plague has long maintained an endemic presence in rodent communities in both Yunnan in southwest China and the Great Lakes region of East Africa. In the early 14th century, Mongol armies helped infected fleas spread from Yunnan to the rest of China. In 1331 an outbreak of plague reportedly carried away 90% of the population in parts of northeast China, and by the 1350s there were widely scattered epidemics throughout China. From China, bubonic plague spread rapidly west along the Silk Roads of Central Asia. By 1346 it had reached the Black Sea. Muslim merchants carried it south and west to southwest Asia, Egypt, and North Africa, while Italian merchants carried it west to Italy and then to northern and western Europe, where it became known as the Black Death. Up to one-third of Europe's population is thought to have died in this one episode.

The spread of plague during the 14th century

1320: Outbreak of plague in Yunnan province	**1330:** Plague reaches northeastern China	**1348:** Black Death hits Greece, Italy, France, Spain, Britain, and North Africa	**1351:** Black Death reaches much of northern Europe

1310   1320   1330   1340   1350   1360

1320–30: Mongol armies help spread plague throughout China

1346: Plague reaches coast of Black Sea

1349: Black Death arrives in central Europe

The changing balance of world population

The spread of diseases and agricultural crops decisively influenced population levels throughout the Old World. In sub-Saharan Africa, for example, bananas grew well in forested regions that did not favor yams and millet, the earliest staples of Bantu cultivators. In 500 CE the population of sub-Saharan Africa was about 12 million, but following the spread of bananas it rose to 20 million by 1000 and 35.5 million by 1500. The spread of fast-ripening rice in China fueled an even more dramatic demographic surge: from 60 million in 1000, when fast-ripening rice went north from Vietnam to the Yangtze river valley, the Chinese population climbed to 100 million in 1100 and 115 million in 1200. However, beginning in the 14th century, bubonic plague raced through densely-populated lands from China to Morocco, thinning human numbers with drastic effect. By 1400, China's population had fallen to about 70 million.

SEE ALSO:

Africa: pp.162–163

Europe: pp.188–193

West Asia: pp.228–229

North and East Asia: pp.262–263

Many people were displaced by the depopulation of the Black Death and the societal changes that it wrought. Those reduced to begging often sought alms at the doors of churches or other religious foundations.

Some towns and villages suffered such depradations in population during the Black Death that they were abandoned by those who were left. The ruined church (*left*) is one of few remnants of the former village of Calceby, in the fenlands of eastern England.

❷ Distribution of world population c.1400 ▼

NORTH AMERICA
6.2 million people
2%

EUROPE
44 million people
14%

CENTRAL ASIA
312,000 people
0.1%

EAST ASIA
75 million people
24%

WEST ASIA
19 million people
6%

SOUTH ASIA
78 million people
25%

CENTRAL AMERICA AND THE CARIBBEAN
19 million people
6%

AFRICA
31 million people
10%

SOUTHEAST ASIA
22 million people
7%

SOUTH AMERICA
19 million people
6%

AUSTRALASIA AND OCEANIA
31,200 people
0.001%

ARCTIC OCEAN

ATLANTIC OCEAN

PACIFIC OCEAN

PACIFIC OCEAN

INDIAN OCEAN

Total population: 312.5 million

❸ The diffusion of staple crops to c.1500 ▶

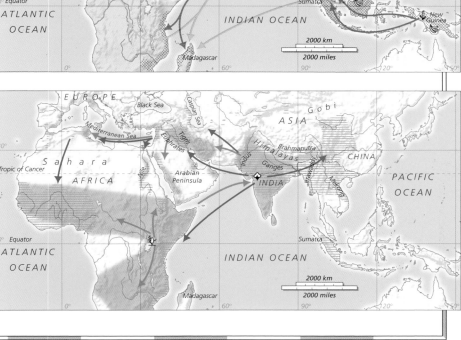

Original source areas (pre-700)
- bananas
- sugarcane
- cotton
- sorghum

Spread of crops c.700–1500
- spread of bananas
- spread of sugarcane
- spread of cotton
- spread of sorghum

Areas to which crops had spread by 1500
- bananas
- sugarcane
- cotton
- sorghum

Sugar cane was taken westward to Europe from India from c.600 CE. This 16th-century engraving of a Sicilian sugar mill shows raw sugar being transformed into sugar loaves.

The diffusion of staple crops

A massive diffusion of agricultural crops took place between about 700 and 1400 CE. Most crops spread from tropical or subtropical lands in South and Southeast Asia to the more temperate regions of the eastern hemisphere. Many crops moved with the aid of Muslim merchants, administrators, diplomats, soldiers, missionaries, pilgrims, and other travelers who visited lands from Morocco and Spain to Java and southern China. Sugar cane, native to New Guinea, arrived in the Mediterranean basin as a result of this biological diffusion, along with hard wheat, eggplants, spinach, artichokes, lemons, and limes. Other crops that dispersed widely during this era included rice, sorghum, bananas, coconuts, watermelons, oranges, mangoes, cotton, indigo, and henna.

THE WORLD 1400–1500

BY 1500 MOST OF THE EASTERN HEMISPHERE had recovered from the depopulation caused by the Black Death in the 14th century. China began the 15th century by sponsoring naval expeditions in the Indian Ocean, but in the 1430s the Ming rulers ended these voyages and concentrated on their land empire. In Southwest Asia, two Turkish peoples established strong empires – the Ottomans in Anatolia and the Safavids in Persia. European states, meanwhile, were starting to build central governments with standing armies and gunpowder weapons. In the course of the 15th century Portuguese mariners settled the Atlantic islands, explored the west coast of Africa, and completed a sea voyage to India. It was, however, a Spanish expedition under the Genoese Columbus that crossed the Atlantic to make contact with the Americas, where the Aztec and Inca empires ruled over complex organized agricultural societies.

North America

The Aztec Empire reached its height in the late 1400s, exacting heavy tribute from the small city-states it had conquered. Through trade, Aztec influence reached far beyond the borders of the empire, extending across most of Central America as far as the Pueblo farmers north of the Rio Grande. In the woodlands around the Mississippi River, mound-building peoples maintained sizeable communities based on the cultivation of corn.

Human sacrifice to the sun god Huitzilopochtli was the core of the Aztec religion. Thousands of prisoners might be killed in a single ceremony.

1428: Itzcoatl becomes ruler of Aztec Empire
1440: Motecuhzoma I becomes ruler of Aztec Empire
1487: Inauguration of great pyramid temple honoring Huitzilopochtli at Tenochtitlán
1434: Creation of the Aztec triple alliance
1473: Annexation of Tlatelolco by the Aztecs
1492: Columbus lands on Cuba and Hispaniola
North America
1400 · 1420 · 1440 · 1460 · 1480 · 1500

The World in 1500

- Ottoman Empire
- Union of Kalmar
- England and possessions
- France and possessions
- Spain and possessions
- Portugal and possessions
- Venetian Republic and possessions
- Austrian Habsburg territories
- Bahmani Kingdom to 1484
- Holy Roman Empire

The town of Machu Picchu sits on a rocky crag high in the Andes. This sacred shrine of the Incas was never discovered by Spanish *conquistadores*, but was abandoned by its inhabitants.

South America

After 1438 the rulers of the Inca state, a small regional kingdom in the Andean highlands around Lake Titicaca, embarked on a remarkable campaign of imperial expansion. Within 30 years their huge realm stretched some 2,500 miles along the Andes and the west coast, linked by an impressive network of roads. Labor to build the roads was provided by subjects of the empire as a form of tax. Elsewhere in South America, indigenous peoples lived in hunting and gathering, fishing, or small-scale agricultural societies.

South America
1471: Accession of Topa Inca; during his reign further expansion is halted by Amazon jungle
1498: Columbus, on third voyage, anchors off coast near Trinidad
1400 · 1420 · 1440 · 1460 · 1480 · 1500
1438: Beginning of period of Inca conquests under Pachacuti
c.1470: Conquest of Chimú empire by the Incas
1493: Accession of Inca ruler, Huayna Capac

MOVABLE TYPE

The use of movable metal type by printers in the German town of Mainz galvanized intellectual life in Europe, stimulating the rapid spread of ideas and a huge growth in literacy. At first type was carved on wooden blocks, as it had been in China since the 11th century, but printers soon began casting it in metal. By the end of the century, this new technology was firmly established throughout Europe.

The beautiful bible by Johann Gutenberg of Mainz (1454–55) is prized as the first European book printed using movable type.

Europe

The 15th century saw the start of the Renaissance, a flowering of architecture, art, and humanist idealism inspired by Classical models. The city-states of Italy were the cultural leaders of Europe, but political power was shifting toward the "new monarchs," who created strong, centralized kingdoms in England, France, and Spain. Poland dominated eastern Europe, but here the future lay with Muscovy, where Ivan III launched Russian expansion to the east and south and in 1472 assumed the title of "tsar."

Sixtus IV, elected in 1471, was typical of the popes of the Renaissance. A worldly, nepotistic prince, he commissioned great works of art and architecture, including the Sistine Chapel.

SEE ALSO:

North America: pp.122–123

South America: pp.146–147

Africa: pp.162–163

Europe: pp.192–193

West Asia: pp.228–231

South and Southeast Asia: pp.244–245

North and East Asia: pp.264–267

MARTIN BEHAIM'S GLOBE

Martin Behaim was a geographer of Nuremberg who visited Portugal and sailed down the west coast of Africa with Portuguese mariners in the 1480s. His globe, produced in 1490–92, is the oldest surviving globe in the world. Since he knew nothing of the existence of America, he depicted the island of "Cipangu" (Japan) and the east Asian mainland directly across the Atlantic from western Europe.

Martin Behaim's globe gives a very good picture of how Columbus must have imagined the world before he set sail across the Atlantic Ocean.

Europe timeline
1415: English defeat French at Agincourt
1429: English siege of Orléans relieved by Joan of Arc
1454: Peace of Lodi ends wars in Italy
1480: Muscovy throws off Mongol yoke
1492: Muslim Granada falls to Spain
1417: End of Schism in Catholic church
1453: Fall of Bordeaux to France ends Hundred Years' War
1469: Marriage of Ferdinand of Aragon and Isabella of Castile
1494: Invasion of Italy by Charles VIII of France

The fall of Constantinople removed the major Christian stronghold barring Islam's spread to the west. The small defending force of Byzantines and Italians was no match for the besieging army of 100,000.

West Asia

When Timur died in 1405, his empire was divided among his four sons. After a series of quarrels, Shah Rukh, who inherited the eastern part, presided over an era of peace, in which the arts and architecture flourished. The Shaybanids, who expanded south across the Syr Darya, were descendants of Genghis Khan. However, a new power was rising that would eclipse the Mongol dynasties that vied to control Persia – the Shi'ite Safavids. In the west, the Ottoman Turks, led by Sultan Mehmed II ("the Conqueror") and aided by powerful cannons, took Constantinople in 1453 and put an end to the Byzantine Empire.

West Asia timeline
1402: Ottomans defeated by Timur at Ankara
1461: Ottomans take Christian city of Trebizond
1499: Rise to power of Safavids in Persia
1405: Death of Timur
1447: Death of Shah Rukh
1453: Constantinople falls to Ottoman sultan Mehmed II

This painting on silk shows the courtyards of the Forbidden City, the compound of the imperial palace at the center of Beijing. The Ming capital was moved north from Nanjing to Beijing in 1421 during Yung Luo's campaign against the Mongols.

East and Southeast Asia

The Ming dynasty consolidated its hold on China, rebuilding the Great Wall to prevent raids by Mongol Oirats to the north. After Zheng He's epic but costly voyages in the Indian Ocean, the Ming rulers adopted a policy of self-sufficiency, discouraging travel and trade. In contrast to this defensive, inward-looking attitude, Southeast Asia thrived on trade. The most important entrepôt was Malacca. By 1500 its population was about 50,000, and it was reported that 84 languages could be heard in the city's streets.

East and Southeast Asia timeline
c.1400: Foundation of Malacca
1424: End of long Ming campaign against Mongols
1445: Conversion of Malacca to Islam
1472: Birth of Neoconfucian philosopher Wang Yangming
1405: Beginning of Zheng He's voyages in Indian Ocean
1449: Mongols defeat Chinese and capture emperor
1471: Annamites expand to south by invading Champa

Africa

Between the 1460s and 1490s the Songhay ruler Sunni Ali conquered Mali and took over the Saharan caravan trade. Meanwhile, the Portuguese explored the west coast, where African rulers, seeing opportunities for trade, laid the foundations for the small kingdoms of Akan and Benin. Sailors from the Swahili city-states in East Africa helped Vasco da Gama understand the local monsoon winds and complete his voyage to India.

This bronze statue of a Portuguese soldier was made in Benin, one of Portugal's West African trading partners.

Africa timeline
1441: First shipment of African slaves to Portugal
1464: Beginning of Songhay expansion under Sunni Ali
1415: Portuguese capture Ceuta in Morocco
c.1450: Eclipse of Great Zimbabwe by Mutapa empire
1482: Fort of Elmina founded by Portuguese

GLOBAL KNOWLEDGE

Knowledge of the world and its peoples was colored by hearsay and travelers' tales.

THE GLOBAL WORLD VIEW is a relatively modern concept. The Americas were unknown to Old World Eurasia until 500 years ago, and each of the major cultural regions had discrete world views of varying extents. Each region had developed its own means of subsistence, and technologies which were direct responses to their immediate environment. In Eurasia, ideas, faiths, and technical achievements were spread by trade, migration, and cultural or political expansion; thus the imprint of Buddhism, Christianity, and Islam was widespread, and technical ideas as diverse as printing and gunpowder, originating in East Asia, had reached Europe. Mapping in one form or another was used by all cultures as a means of recording geographical information and knowledge, although pathfinding and navigation was usually a matter of handed-down knowledge, experience, and word of mouth.

▼ ❶ Global economies and technologies c.1500

Principal economies

- hunting and gathering
- herding/pastoralism
- hand cultivation
- plow cultivation
- hand cultivation and hunting and gathering
- slash and burn farming
- terraced farming
- uninhabited

❶ Global economies and technologies c.1500

Significant technologies

- **draft animals**
  - buffalo
  - oxen
  - horse/mule
  - camel
  - elephant
  - llama/alpaca
- **transport**
  - wheeled vehicles
  - dragged vehicles
- **hydraulics**
  - canals
  - aqueducts
  - irrigation
- **architecture**
  - temporary shelters
  - post and lintel
  - barrel vaulting
  - groin vaulting
- **navigation**
  - riverine
  - coastal
  - oceanic
  - lodestone/compass
- **warfare**
  - thrown missiles
  - archery
  - gunpowder
- **power**
  - windmills
  - watermills
- X technology not developed
- **recording of knowledge**
  - knowledge recorded in writing
  - knowledge preserved orally
  - empirical cartographic tradition

The Americas

Both the Aztecs of Central America and the Incas of the Andes were still in the process of consolidating their young empires when the first Europeans arrived. Although there is evidence in both regions of extensive trading contacts, geographical obstacles (deserts, jungle) and relative immaturity meant their worlds were closely defined.

❷ The Americas ▲

- Aztec Empire
- known world 1500
- Inca Empire
- known world 1500

The size of the globe

The rediscovery of Classical texts was an important stimulus to the development of technology, science, and the arts, which flowered in the European Renaissance. European cartographers began to build a more detailed world map, using the works of Classical geographers such as Strabo and Ptolemy. The voyage of Bartolomeu Dias (1487–88) around the Cape of Good Hope established the limits of Africa; but in 1492, when Columbus made landfall in the Caribbean four weeks after leaving the Canary Islands, he assumed he had reached China (Cathay) rather than the West Indies. Although the circumnavigation by Magellan and del Cano some 30 years later (1519–22) dispelled many uncertainties, the accurate charting of the world's oceans and coasts would not be completed until the 20th century.

◀ ❽ The Ptolemaic map of the world

ASIA · OCEANUS OCCIDENTALIS · EUROPE · Sinae (China) · AFRICA · Equator
16,000 km (9940 miles)

◀ ❾ The Behaim map of the world 1492

ASIA · Cathay (China) · Beijing · Cipangu (Japan) · Venice · EUROPE · AFRICA · Equator
5300 km (3290 miles)

→ Marco Polo 1271-75
Marco Polo assumed he had travelled 16,000 miles instead of 7000 miles

◀ ❿ The modern map of the world

ASIA · NORTH AMERICA · EUROPE · AFRICA · Equator · PACIFIC OCEAN · SOUTH AMERICA · ATLANTIC OCEAN · INDIAN OCEAN
18,410 km (11,440 miles)

Coasts charted by
- 1500
- 1600
- 1700
- 1800
- 1900

The Muslim World

The most extensive and cosmopolitan of the Old World cultures, by 1500 Islam straddled large extents of three continents, stretching from the islands of the southwest Pacific to the shores of the Atlantic. Knowledge acquired from trade and travel underpinned much Muslim cultural hegemony and scholarship.

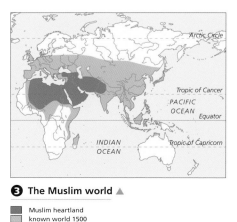

❸ The Muslim world ▲

- Muslim heartland
- known world 1500

South Asia

❻ South Asia ▼

- South Asian states
- known world 1500

In 1500, **India was about** to become subject to Muslim (Mughal) rule. Nevertheless its position on the crossroads of trade across the Indian Ocean, and overland routes from East and Southeast Asia, dated back many centuries, and its exports were known in Europe. Although essentially inward-looking, South Asian rulers and scholars had an extensive knowledge of the Old World.

Europe

By the end of the 15th century, Europe was poised on the brink of rapid territorial expansion. Technically sophisticated and resourceful, the Europeans had built up, through trade and travel, a fairly detailed knowledge of much of the Old World, from coastal Africa, through Arabia and southern Asia, to China and the many islands of the East Indies.

▲ **❺ Europe**

■ Western Christendom
□ known world 1492

East Asia

China, Korea, and Japan, although frequently isolationist – the Chinese "Middle Kingdom" regarded itself, with some justification, as the most powerful in the world – had nevertheless acquired considerable knowledge of the Old World, illustrated by the ambassadorial voyages of the Ming admiral Zheng He throughout the Indian Ocean (1405–33).

◀ **❹ East Asia**

■ charted by Chinese c.1500
□ known world c.1500

SEE ALSO:

North America: pp.118–119

South America: pp.142–143

Africa: pp.156–157

Europe: pp.172–173

West Asia: pp.218–219

South and Southeast Asia: pp.238–239

North and East Asia: 256–257

Australasia and Oceania: pp.278–279

Oceania

Some of the great early oceanic voyages were made between the scattered islands of the southwest Pacific by Polynesian sailors. By 1500, they had knowledge of most of the islands in the region, including New Zealand – settled some 800 years earlier.

❼ Oceania ▶

■ known worlds c.1500

European navigators used an astrolabe, which gave an approximate position in relation to the position of the stars. For lunar and solar measures, an almanac was also necessary.

Chinese cartographers produced detailed and very accurate maps as a navigational aid. This example showing the Philippines, Taiwan, and the East Indies is from Zhu Siben's 14th-century world atlas.

Mariners and technology

In 1500 the principal seafaring cultures were those of the Atlantic nations of western Europe – Spain, Portugal, England, and the Netherlands – the Islamic traders of the Indian Ocean, and the Chinese. Although Norsemen had crossed the North Atlantic to reach Greenland and the Americas 400 years previously, it was the navigators from Atlantic Europe who, in the 15th century, began the systematic exploration of Atlantic island groups and the African coastline. When they sailed east into the Indian Ocean, they benefited from the superior local knowledge of Arab, and later, Chinese navigators.

THE WORLD 1500–1600

IN THE 16TH CENTURY Spain seized a vast land empire that encompassed much of South and Central America, the West Indies, and the Philippine Islands. Meanwhile, the Portuguese acquired a largely maritime empire stretching from Brazil to Malacca and Macao. Ferdinand Magellan, a Portuguese in the service of Spain, demonstrated that all the world's oceans were linked and sea lanes were established through the Indian, Atlantic, and Pacific oceans, creating for the first time a genuinely global trading network. Although the Portuguese traded with the Ming Empire and Japan, cultural contact between Europeans and East Asia was limited. In Africa, too, European impact barely extended beyond the coast. Missionaries took the Catholic faith to distant parts of the Spanish and Portuguese empires, but in Europe the Church of Rome faced the threat of the Reformation, while Catholic kingdoms fought to stem Ottoman expansion in the Mediterranean and into the Habsburg lands of Central Europe.

Europe

The Protestant Reformation dominated 16th-century Europe. Rulers in Scandinavia, England, Scotland, and many German states abandoned the Roman church and took over monasteries and the running of church affairs. In France Protestants fought Catholics in a debilitating round of civil wars (1562–98) and religion was a major factor in the Dutch revolt against Spanish rule in 1565. The kings of Spain championed Catholicism and promoted missions worldwide. In the east, Russia's tsars extended their empire to the Caspian Sea and western Siberia.

Spanish troops raid a convoy in a scene typical of the atrocities of the Dutch Wars of Independence.

Europe						
	1519: Charles V elected Holy Roman Emperor	1545: Council of Trent called to counter threat of Protestantism	1580: Philip II of Spain seizes Portuguese crown	1598: Edict of Nantes ends over 30 years of religious wars in France		
1500	1520	1540	1560	1580	1600
1517: Martin Luther's 95 Theses attack abuses of Catholic church	1534: Act of Supremacy; Henry VIII of England breaks with Rome	1565: Dutch Revolt starts long series of wars to gain independence from Spain	1588: English defeat Spanish Armada			

A Spanish *conquistador* rides a llama. The prime concern for most of the Spanish colonists granted large estates in the Americas was to exploit the labor of the native peoples.

The Americas

The arrival of the Spanish transformed the Americas. Their horses, iron weapons, and guns gave the *conquistadores* a military advantage over the indigenous peoples, but these alone might not have been sufficient without the devastating effect of the lethal diseases they introduced. The Spanish won control of all the major Caribbean islands by 1511, then in 1519–22 Hernán Cortés conquered the Aztecs, and in 1531–32 Francisco Pizarro overcame the Inca Empire. The more gradual colonization of Brazil by the Portuguese began in the 1530s, when nobles and entrepreneurs established plantations along its coast.

The Americas					
1502: Start of reign of last Aztec emperor, Montezuma II	1519: Cortés reaches Tenochtitlán (now Mexico), capital of the Aztec Empire	1545: Opening of vast silver mine at Potosí	1580: Philip II of Spain becomes king of Portugal and its Brazilian empire		
1500	1520	1540	1560	1580	1600
1510: First African slaves brought to Americas	1527: Death of Inca emperor Huayna Capac ignites civil war	1533: Pizarro captures Inca capital Cuzco	1549: Portuguese royal government established in Brazil	c.1575: Brazil becomes world's largest sugar producer	

SHIPS OF THE AGE OF EXPLORATION

The ships used by Columbus and other European explorers at the end of the 16th century were usually small caravels between 60 and 200 tons. Square-rigged on the main- and foremasts, they had a lateen sail on the mizzen mast for tacking against the wind. However, once the Spanish and Portuguese had learned to use the trade winds of the Atlantic and Indian oceans, they built huge square-rigged carracks with high castles in the stern. With a laden weight of up to 1,600 tons, they were designed to maximize the cargoes of spices and precious metals shipped back from the East Indies and the Americas.

Columbus made his first crossing of the Atlantic in a square-rigged caravel similar to the model below.

This cast bronze horse and rider is an impressive example of the stylized sculpture of Benin.

Africa

While most of North Africa fell to the Ottoman Empire, Morocco remained an independent champion of Islam, dealing a mortal blow to Portuguese expansion in the region and conquering Songhay to gain control of the valuable trans-Saharan caravan trade. Many of the small West African states had trade links both with Morocco and the Portuguese, who established a fortified trading post at Elmina.

West Asia

Suleiman the Magnificent extended Ottoman rule far into southeastern Europe. In this miniature, he is seen receiving homage from his many Christian vassals.

In the 16th century the Ottoman Empire expanded into Southwest Asia, North Africa, and southeastern Europe. The Ottoman navy was the preeminent power in the Mediterranean until its defeat by a Christian fleet at Lepanto in 1571, and Muslim vessels dominated the region's shipping. Ottoman rulers clashed constantly with the Safavids in Persia, and in the late 16th and early 17th centuries the two empires fought for control of Mesopotamia and the Caucasus. Many earlier Ottoman gains were reversed during the reign of Shah Abbas the Great, the Safavid ruler from 1588 to 1629.

West Asia

1507: Portuguese victory over Ottoman and Arab fleet at Diu
1520: Suleiman the Magnificent becomes Ottoman sultan
1566: Suleiman succeeded by Selim II
1588: Abbas I the Great becomes Safavid shah

1500 — 1520 — 1540 — 1560 — 1580 — 1600

1514: Ottoman victory over Safavids at Çaldiran
1526: Battle of Mohács; Ottomans crush Hungarian army
1571: Battle of Lepanto; Ottoman navy defeated by united Christian fleet off Greek coast
1587: Isfahan becomes capital of Safavid Empire

THE NEW WORLD BY ABRAHAM ORTELIUS

Abraham Ortelius was a mapseller from Antwerp whose *Theatrum Orbis Terrarum* of 1570 is considered the first modern atlas. He was not an original cartographer, but he traveled widely in search of reliable sources and his atlas sold well throughout Europe for over 40 years. His map of the New World was a fairly accurate summary of European explorers' knowledge of the Americas and the Pacific. The vast southern continent, *Terra Australis*, a relic of the Classical geography of Claudius Ptolemy, was a feature of most maps of the period. It includes Tierra del Fuego and part of the coast of New Guinea, but the rest is pure conjecture. Ortelius was a contemporary of Gerardus Mercator. Between them, the two great mapmakers did much to shift the center of European cartography from Italy to the Low Countries.

The map gives a fairly accurate picture of Central America and the Caribbean; however, many parts of America had still not been explored by Europeans at all.

SEE ALSO:

North America: pp.124–125

South America: pp.146–149

Africa: pp.162–163

Europe: pp.194–195

West Asia: pp.230–231

South and Southeast Asia: pp.244–247

North and East Asia: pp.264–267

South and Southeast Asia

South and Southeast Asia

1510: Portuguese conquest of Goa
1526: Babur conquers Sultanate of Delhi
1563: Burmese King Bayinnaung invades Siam
1600: English East India Company founded

1500 — 1520 — 1540 — 1560 — 1580 — 1600

1511: Portuguese take Malacca
1556: Akbar becomes Mughal emperor
1565: Spanish fleet claims Philippines in name of King Philip II

In 1523 the Chagatai Turk Babur invaded northern India, founding the Mughal dynasty of Islamic rulers. The empire was consolidated by Babur's grandson, Akbar. Mughal rulers concentrated on their land empire and agriculture, allowing the Portuguese to maintain coastal trading posts and a flourishing colony at Goa. Portugal also conquered Malacca and the "Spice Islands" of the Moluccas. The dominant power in mainland Southeast Asia was Burma, which reached its largest extent under King Bayinnaung, who conquered Siam and Laos and installed puppet rulers.

The richest prize for European merchants in South and Southeast Asia was control of the valuable spice trade. This French illustration shows the pepper harvest in southern India.

The World in 1600

- Ming Empire
- Ottoman Empire
- Spain and possessions
- Portugal and possessions (ruled by Kings of Spain 1580–1640)
- England and possessions
- Austrian Habsburg territories
- France
- Denmark and possessions
- Venetian Republic and possessions
- United Provinces (fighting for independence from Spain)
- Dutch (United Provinces) possessions
- Mughal Empire at Akbar's accession, 1556
- under Burmese control, 1575
- Songhay to 1590
- Holy Roman Empire

Africa

c.1500: Establishment of forest states of Oyo and Benin
1517: Ottomans conquer Mamluks in Egypt
1578: Moroccans crush invading Portuguese

1500 — 1520 — 1540 — 1560 — 1580 — 1600

1505: First Portuguese trading posts in East Africa
1546: Songhay destroys Mali Empire
1570: Establishment of Portuguese colony in Angola
1591: Songhay Empire falls to Morocco

THE AGE OF EUROPEAN EXPANSION

The Portuguese
Vasco da Gama was the first European navigator to reach India by sea.

THE 16TH CENTURY saw the expansion of several of the great European nations far beyond their continental limits. Explorers searching for new sources of luxury goods and precious metals began to open up new territories which monarchs such as Philip II of Spain quickly built up into great empires in the "New World." The Spanish and Portuguese, inspired by the voyages of Columbus and da Gama, led the way, closely followed by the Dutch and the English. The explorers were aided by technological advances in shipbuilding, navigational equipment, and cartography. At the start of the 16th century, the Americas were virtually unknown to Europeans; by 1700, outposts of a greater European empire had been established almost everywhere the explorers landed.

European voyages of expansion and discovery

Spain and Portugal were the leaders of world exploration in the 16th century. In search of maritime trade routes to Asia, the Portuguese found sea lanes through the Atlantic and Indian oceans to India. By 1512, fortified trading posts were in place at Goa and Malacca, and they had reached the "Spice Islands" of the Moluccas in eastern Indonesia. The Spanish, taking a westward route, found the Caribbean islands and the Americas instead. Magellan's three-year global circumnavigation revealed a western route through the Strait of Magellan and across the Pacific Ocean. English and French mariners sought northern passages to Asian markets and their voyages paved the way for the establishment of European settlements in North America.

Voyages of expansion 1492–1590

1492: Columbus, in search of Asia, reaches Cuba and the Bahamas
1509–16: Portuguese voyages to Moluccas, Malacca, and Macao
1532: Cartier explores Strait of Belle Isle and St Lawrence
1576: Frobisher reaches Baffin Island

1498: Vasco da Gama rounds Cape of Good Hope and reaches India
1500: Cabral sights Brazilian coast on voyage to India
1519–22: Magellan and del Cano complete first global circumnavigation reaching Moluccas via the Philippine Islands
1553: Willoughby reaches Archangel on Northeast Passage
1577–80: Drake circumnavigates globe

① Voyages of European expansion 1492–1597

→ Spanish expeditions
→ Portuguese expeditions
→ English expeditions
→ French expeditions
→ Dutch expeditions

EAST MEETS WEST

Europeans and the peoples they encountered in the East had much to learn from one another. Jesuit missionaries were particularly successful at establishing links between China and Japan and the West. During the 1580s, the Jesuit Matteo Ricci informed the Chinese emperor and his court about many European inventions. He presented them with elaborate clocks and taught them about astronomical equipment and weapons such as cannon. His primary purpose was to convert the Chinese to Christianity, using European scientific advances to demonstrate the superiority of European religion. Despite his efforts to accommodate Chinese culture – including the celebration of the mass in Chinese – large-scale conversion eluded him. But much future scientific endeavor was due to these cultural contacts: the revival of Chinese mathematics, the development of the suspension bridge, and early Western experiments in electrostatics and magnetism.

Magellan's global circumnavigation was so extraordinary that contemporary artists portrayed him abetted on his voyage by both the latest navigational technology and weaponry, and by mythical creatures such as monsters and mermaids. He was killed by hostile local people in the Philippine Islands in 1521.

The arrival of Portuguese merchants in Japan is shown below by a Japanese artist. From the mid-16th century, Portuguese traders provided a link between a hostile China and Japan and St. Francis Xavier began a mission to gain new Christian converts. They were soon perceived as a threat to Japanese security and ships which landed were ordered to be confiscated and their crews executed.

❷ Biological exchanges ▶

Origin and movement of plants and animals

→ from Europe
→ from America
→ from Asia

Plants and animals

- bananas
- chili peppers
- horses
- corn
- manioc
- peanuts
- potatoes
- rice
- sugarcane
- sweet potatoes
- tomatoes
- wheat
- yams

Diseases

➡ bubonic plague
➡ diphtheria, influenza, measles, smallpox, and whooping cough
➡ syphilis

SEE ALSO:

North America:
pp.118–119, 122–123

South America:
pp.142–143, 148–149

Africa: pp.156–157, 162–163

South and Southeast Asia:
pp.238–239, 246–247

North and East Asia:
pp.256–257

Australasia and Oceania:
pp.278–279

Biological exchanges

The plantain, a herb with medicinal properties, was known as "Englishman's foot" by native North Americans who believed it would grow only where the English had trodden.

European expansion had a profound biological impact. Travelers transported numerous species of fruits, vegetables, and animals from the Americas to Europe. At the same time, settlers introduced European species to the Americas and Oceania. Horses, pigs, and cattle were transported to the western hemisphere where, without natural predators, their numbers increased spectacularly. The settlers consciously introduced food crops, such as wheat, grapes, apples, peaches, and citrus fruits. Some plants, such as nettles, dandelions, and other weeds were inadvertently dispersed by the winds or on the coats of animals. European expansion also led to a spread of European diseases. Vast numbers of indigenous American peoples died from measles and smallpox, which broke out in massive epidemics among populations with no natural or acquired immunity. During the 16th century, syphilis – thought now to be the result of the fusion of two similar diseases from Europe and the New World – killed a million Europeans.

Many more indigenous Americans were killed by smallpox and measles than were slaughtered by the colonizers. Up to 90% of the total population may have perished from European diseases.

❸ The Spanish Empire in 1600 ▶

- ▢ Spanish Empire
- ▢ Portugal and possessions annexed by Philip II of Spain in 1580

Trade

→ gold
→ silver
→ silk
→ spices

New Spain: conquered by Cortés in 1521, Mexico, the former Aztec city of Tenochtitlán, became the center of the Spanish Empire in North America.

South America: based around the city of Lima, the Viceroyalty of Peru was the center of the Spanish Empire in South America.

The Manila galleon: brought silver once a year from Acapulco in New Spain to Manila. The silver was used to buy silk, porcelain, and lacquerware which were transported back to New Spain and then to Spain.

The Philippine Islands: first discovered in 1521 by Magellan and claimed for Spain. A governorship and Spanish settlement of the Philippines began in 1565.

Europe: by 1600, the Spanish Empire in Europe included Portugal, Flanders, Naples, and Sicily.

The Treaty of Tordesillas (1494)

Under this treaty between Spain and Portugal, the yet-to-be-discovered world was divided, with Spain taking the western portion and Portugal the east. In 1529 a further treaty divided the eastern hemisphere.

The Spanish Empire

By the end of the 16th century the Spanish Empire included Central America, the West Indies, western South America, and most of the Philippine Islands. The need to safeguard the new lands, their precious natural resources and the new trading networks which evolved, led to the development of a colonial administration of unparalleled scope. Royal authority was vested in the twin institutions of *audiencias*, with political, administrative, and judicial functions, and a series of viceroys, who acted primarily as powerful governors, though they possessed no judicial powers. All information relating to government in the Spanish territories was controlled by specially created councils, the Council of Castile and the Council of the Indies, which met regularly to ensure communication between Spain and the distant possessions of the Spanish Empire.

The New World empire Philip II inherited from his father, Charles V, was greatly expanded after 1580 following the annexation of Portugal, which added Brazil and the East Indies.

The Expansion of the Spanish Empire

1494: Treaty of Tordesillas divides western hemisphere between Spain and Portugal

1509: Spanish settlement of mainland Central America begins

1519–21: Cortés conquers Aztec Empire

1540s: Potosí becomes greatest single source of silver in the world

1564: System of Atlantic convoys established

1580: Union of Spanish and Portuguese crowns

1480 — 1500 — 1520 — 1540 — 1560 — 1580 — 1600

1493: Columbus establishes first Spanish settlement in western hemisphere

1532–40: Pizarro conquers Inca Empire

1565–75: Spanish conquest of Philippine Islands

1571: Foundation of Manila

1590: Silver shipped to Manila almost equal in value to Atlantic trade

THE WORLD 1600–1700

DURING THE 17TH CENTURY Dutch, British, and French mariners followed Iberians into the world's seas. All three lands established colonies in North America, and all entered the trade networks of the Indian Ocean. British and French mariners searched for a northeast and a northwest passage from Europe to Asia and, although unsuccessful, their efforts expanded their understanding of the world's geography. Dutch incursions into the East Indies began to erode the dominance of the Portuguese empire in this region. Trade between Europe, Africa, North America, and South America pushed the Atlantic Ocean basin toward economic integration, while European trade in the Indian Ocean linked European and Asian markets.

Many European rulers believed that they governed by divine right. Louis XIV of France is here portrayed in a classical fashion which reflects both his supreme power and his belief in his godlike status.

Europe

The ramifications of the Protestant Reformation complicated political affairs in western and Central Europe. The Thirty Years' War (1618–48) ravaged much of Germany, but the Peace of Westphalia that ended the war established a system of states based on a balance of power. This system did not eliminate conflict but maintained relative stability until the French Revolution. The Russian Empire expanded to reach the Pacific Ocean by the mid-17th century as Cossacks and other adventurers established forts throughout Siberia while searching for furs.

Europe

| 1600 | 1620 | 1640 | 1660 | 1680 | 1700 |

1618: Start of Thirty Years' War
1643: Louis XIV becomes King of France
1648: Thirty Years' War ended by Peace of Westphalia
1682: Peter the Great becomes tsar of Russia
1611: Accession of Gustavus Adolphus signals Swedish expansion
1649: Execution of Charles I of England
1683: Siege of Vienna ends in Ottoman defeat

The World in 1700

- Ottoman Empire
- England and possessions
- France and possessions
- Denmark and possessions
- Spain and possessions
- Portugal and possessions
- Netherlands and possessions
- Hohenzollern possessions
- Sweden and possessions
- Venetian Republic and possessions
- Austrian Habsburg territories
- held temporarily by Netherlands during 17th century
- Holy Roman Empire

The French explorer Samuel de Champlain forged alliances with other Indian peoples as he fought the Iroquois in a series of violent struggles. He is seen here attacking an Iroquois fortress.

The Americas

The Spanish land empire expanded from bases in Central America and the Andes, and the Portuguese built a powerful and profitable plantation society along the coast of northeastern South America. English colonists established settlements along the Atlantic seaboard of North America, and sugar plantations on Jamaica and other Caribbean islands. French and Dutch colonists founded forts and trading posts in North America, with sugar plantations in the Caribbean and Guiana. French hunters traveled through the Great Lakes and the upper Mississippi valley in search of furs. However, indigenous peoples in the continental interior remained largely independent of European rule.

The Americas

| 1600 | 1620 | 1640 | 1660 | 1680 | 1700 |

1604–08: Foundation of French colony of Acadia
1630: Beginning of Dutch conquest of Brazil
1654: English seize Jamaica from Spain
1695: Discovery of gold in Brazil
1607: Foundation of English colony at Jamestown
1630: Foundation of English Massachusetts Bay colony
1664: English seizure of Dutch colony of New Amsterdam; renamed New York

Africa

By 1700 the Atlantic slave trade had started to affect African politics and society. In 1663 the Portuguese seized Ndongo territory to extend their colony in Angola, and made frequent attempts to conquer Kongo. The African population was boosted by the introduction of food crops from the Americas, including manioc, corn, and peanuts, but this increase was offset by the export of two million slaves from Africa – mainly to the Americas – during the 17th century. States such as Asante, Dahomey, and Oyo raided their neighbors in search of slaves to exchange for European guns.

OPTICAL INSTRUMENTS

The development of telescopes and microscopes geatly advanced human knowledge of both distant objects and those too small to see with the naked eye during the 17th century. The refracting telescope, using a combination of lenses, was first used for observation of the Moon and distant universe by Galileo in 1609. Newton's reflecting telescope, using lenses and mirrors, gave a still clearer picture of the stars and planets. In 1683, Anton van Leeuwenhoek made the first high-powered precision microscope.

A model of Newton's reflecting telescope, made in 1668.

East Asia

In 1644 a Manchu army toppled the Ming dynasty, entered Beijing, and established the Qing dynasty (1644–1911). By the 1680s they had consolidated their hold on southern China, conquered the island of Formosa, and extended Chinese influence far into North and Central Asia. The Qing adapted to Chinese ways and largely preserved the Ming administrative structure. In Japan, the Tokugawa dynasty imposed a central government for the first time. Foreign trade was strictly controlled by both the Chinese and Japanese, confined mainly to Macao in China and Nagasaki in Japan.

The Qing dynasty began their rule with great energy, encouraging many projects for the improvement of their new lands. These workers are building a new dike constructed from timber and brushwood.

SEE ALSO:

North America: pp.126–127

South America: pp.148–149

Africa: pp.164–165

Europe: pp.196–197

West Asia: pp.230–231

South and Southeast Asia: pp.244–245

North and East Asia: pp.268–269

Australasia and Oceania: pp.278–279

East Asia

- 1603: Establishment of Tokugawa dynasty in Japan
- 1633: Closure of Japan by Tokugawa shoguns
- 1644: Manchu forces topple the Ming and establish the Qing dynasty
- 1661: Kangxi becomes Qing emperor
- 1683: Conquest of Formosa by Kangxi
- 1689: Treaty of Nerchinsk between Russia and China; Russians withdraw from Amur basin

JOAN BLAEU'S EASTERN HEMISPHERE

During the 17th century, Dutch mariners and merchants pushed forward the boundaries of the world known to Europeans. Willem Blaeu and his son Joan were official cartographers to the Dutch East India Company (VOC), publishing maps and charts based on the most up-to-date and accurate information provided by explorers, as well as a series of world atlases.

The eastern hemisphere of Joan Blaeu's *Nova et accuratissima totius terrarum orbis tabula*, was first published in his *Atlas Major* in 1662. The map presents a familiar view of Africa, Europe, and most of Asia, although Australia is shown only sketchily.

The Taj Mahal was built by the Mughal emperor Shah Jahan as a mausoleum for his beloved wife, Mumtaz. Exquisitely conceived on a massive scale, it also reflects the great power and wealth of the Mughals.

South and Southeast Asia

Mughal territory was extended by Shah Jahan during the mid-17th century but the empire was increasingly riven by religious intolerance, leading to instability. English and Dutch trading companies consolidated their possessions in the Indian Ocean. The English East India Company built forts and trading posts along the coasts of India, while the Dutch East India Company established headquarters on Java to control the production and distribution of spices from the Moluccas, increasingly taking over territory held by the expansionist sultanate of Mataram.

Fort Jesus near Mombasa was built by the Portuguese in 1593. It was lost in 1698 following persistent raids by Omani Arabs on Portuguese possessions in East Africa.

Africa

- 1619: African slaves taken to the English colony at Jamestown
- 1641: Dutch capture Portuguese possessions in Angola
- 1652: Establishment of Dutch colony at the Cape of Good Hope
- 1665: Portuguese defeat Kongo at Battle of Mbwila.
- 1670: Angola gives up attempt to conquer Kongo after defeat of Portuguese army
- 1698: Omani Arabs capture Mombasa

South and Southeast Asia

- 1619: Dutch found Batavia as center of trading empire in Southeast Asia
- 1627: Shah Jahan becomes Mughal emperor
- 1641: Dutch conquest of Malacca
- 1658: Aurangzeb becomes Mughal emperor
- 1663: Dutch complete expulsion of Portuguese from Ceylon
- 1679: Fleeing Manchus settle in Mekong Delta
- 1691: South Cambodia organized into two provinces of Annam

TRADING IN HUMAN LIVES

Hugh Crow was a Liverpool trader who made a fortune from slaves in the early 19th century.

THE USE OF SLAVES seems to have been endemic in most human societies. Normally taken as prisoners of war, slaves were also acquired as a form of tribute. The establishment of European colonies and overseas empires between the 16th and 19th centuries saw the creation of a slave trade on an industrial scale, a commerce which laid the foundations for pan-global trading networks. Trading concerns such as the English and Dutch East India companies developed trade on a larger scale than ever before; but it was the need to supply labor for the plantations of the Americas which led to the greatest movement of peoples across the face of the earth.

The Atlantic slave trade

From the late 15th to the early 19th century, European merchants – especially the British and Portuguese – carried on a massive trade in African slaves across the Atlantic. As well as utilizing the established sources of slaves from the Central and West African kingdoms, they also raided coastal areas of West Africa for additional supplies of slaves. European manufactured goods, especially guns, were exchanged for slaves destined to work as agricultural laborers on plantations in the Caribbean and the tropical Americas. Slaves transported to the western hemisphere may have numbered 12 million or more.

Conditions on the terrible "Middle Passage" from the slave ports of West Africa to the New World improved little over the centuries, although the death rate declined because journey times decreased significantly. Between four and five million people are thought to have perished before reaching the Americas.

Slaves in the New World

The great plantation systems and mining concerns that arose in the New World from the 16th century onward demanded large reservoirs of labor. Though the Spanish and Portuguese initially used enslaved indigenous people, they soon required a more reliable source of labor. The Portuguese began bringing African slaves to the Caribbean and Brazil in the early 16th century. The cotton plantations of the southern US, which boomed in the early 19th century, were a key factor in sustaining the Atlantic trade.

Slaves planting sugarcane cuttings in specially-prepared plots on an Antiguan plantation in 1823 illustrate the labor-intensiveness of plantation agriculture. As European colonies, the Caribbean islands concentrated on cash crops such as sugar, coffee, and spices.

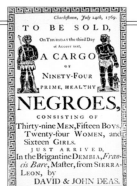

Slaves were sold at auction at ports such as Charleston, South Carolina. They swelled the population of southern North America: in the early 18th century, they comprised more than half of South Carolina's population

Other slave trades

By the 9th and 10th centuries, a number of complex slave-trading routes were in existence in Europe and the Near East. Viking and Russian merchants traded in slaves from the Balkans who were often sold to harems in southern Spain and North Africa. The Baghdad Caliphate drew slaves from western Europe via the ports of Venice, Prague, and Marseille, and Slavic and Turkic slaves from eastern Europe and Central Asia. In the 13th century, the Mongols sold slaves at Karakorum and in the Volga region. There was long-standing commerce in African slaves — primarily from East Africa before European mariners entered the slave trade. Between the 9th and 19th centuries Muslim merchants may have transported as many as 14 million across the Sahara by camel caravan and through East African ports, principally to destinations in the Indian Ocean basin.

This illustration from a 13th-century Arabic manuscript shows Africans and Europeans for sale at a slave market. Arab slave traders drew slaves from much of mainland Europe, Central Asia, and Africa.

SEE ALSO:

North America: pp.126–127, 130–131

South America: pp.148–149

Africa: pp.162–165

Slave trades

| 1502: Introduction of African slaves to the Caribbean | 1739: Stono rebellion in South Carolina | 1791: Slave revolt in Haiti | 1804: Foundation of independent Haitian state | 1867: Last known arrival of a slave ship in Cuba |

1450 — 1500 — 1550 — 1600 — 1650 — 1700 — 1750 — 1800 — 1850 — 1900

| 1479: Treaty of Alcaçovas permits Portuguese importation of slaves into Spain | 1522: First American slave revolt in Hispaniola | 1685: French *Code Noir* restricts slavery in French Caribbean colonies | 1807: Slave trade outlawed in Britain | 1850: Effective end of slave trade in Brazil | 1863: Emancipation proclamation frees slaves in Confederate states* |

* 13th Amendment to the Constitution (passed 1865) ended slavery in full in the US

① The world slave trade 1400–1860

- major slave trading nation
- export center for African slaves
- export center for Muslim slaves
- distribution of African slaves
- distribution of Muslim slaves
- African nations with active slave trade
- ⚓ number of slaves imported
- routes of European slave traders
- routes of Ottoman slave traders
- routes of Saharan slave traders
- routes of Arab slave traders
- exports of Muslim slaves from Southeast Asia
- goods exported in exchange for slaves
- goods exported for slaves
- European exports to Africa
- • slave factory

Goods produced using slaves
- cocoa beans
- coffee
- cotton
- diamonds
- gold
- silver
- sugar
- tobacco

Other goods traded
- dyestuffs
- furs and hides
- pepper
- silk and textiles
- spices
- tin

Goods imported for slaves
- salt cod

Several African rulers made immense fortunes supplying slaves to both Arab and European traders. King Alvare of Kongo traded with the Portuguese — several of whom are shown here kneeling in tribute to him.

Piracy and smuggling

High volumes of trade in lucrative commodities created abundant opportunities for piracy, privateering, and smuggling. Predators were most active in relatively unpoliced Caribbean and American waters. The numerous tiny islands, hidden harbors, and dense, tropical vegetation — and the access provided to valuable cargoes of sugar, rum, silver, and slaves — made the Caribbean a notorious hotspot for piracy and smuggling. Some predators were privateers who worked with the blessing of their home governments, such as Sir Francis Drake, but most maritime predators were freelance pirates, who selected their victims without discrimination.

Henry Morgan was a Welsh buccaneer who made a number of successful raids on Spanish ships and territory in the late 17th century – the most devastating being the destruction of Panamá in 1671.

② Piracy in the Caribbean in the 16th and 17th centuries ▶

Routes of privateers

- John Hawkins 1562
- John Hawkins 1565
- John Hawkins 1567
- Sir Francis Drake 1571
- Sir Francis Drake 1572–73
- Sir Francis Drake 1577–80
- Sir Francis Drake 1585–86
- Piet Heyn 1623–28
- Edward Mansvelt 1665
- Francois l'Olonnois 1667
- Henry Morgan 1668
- Henry Morgan 1669
- Henry Morgan 1670
- ⚓ treasure ship seized
- sack or capture of island or city (colour shows privateer)
- conflict with Spain

This iron headcollar was one of number of cruel devices designed for the restraint of slaves.

Russia: The practice of serfdom, established in 1497, by which peasant farmers were owned, and could be sold, was finally abolished in 1861

China: With the abolition of the trans-Atlantic slave trade, the labor markets of the East Indies and the Americas were supplemented by Chinese indentured laborers

THE WORLD 1700–1800

FROM THE BEGINNING of the 18th century, new ideas in science, philosophy, and political organization fueled change throughout the world. Popular reaction against the *ancien régime* in both France and North America led to the overthrow of the ruling governments. Improvements in agricultural techniques and land reform increased food production, and the population – especially in Europe – began to expand rapidly. Technological innovations in Europe led to the beginning of the Industrial Revolution and consequent urban growth. The expansion of European influence and territorial possessions throughout the world continued apace, with explorers charting the scattered islands of the Pacific and Britain establishing its power in India and Australia.

On January 21, 1793, the French king, Louis XVI, was guillotined in front of a huge Parisian crowd. His wife, Marie Antoinette, was executed later in the year.

Europe

Throughout Europe, government became more powerful, especially in the Russia of Peter the Great and the Prussia of Frederick the Great. In France, Bourbon monarchy had reached its peak during the reign of Louis XIV (1643–1715). Revolutionary ideas unleashed by the "enlightenment," combined with political relaxation, created an incendiary situation, leading in 1789 to the French Revolution whose effects reverberated throughout Europe.

Europe

- 1703: Foundation of St. Petersburg by Peter the Great
- 1715: Death of Louis XIV
- 1740: Prussia launches War of Austrian Succession and becomes major European power
- 1756–63: Seven Years' War in Europe
- 1768: War between Russia and the Ottomans
- 1774: Ottoman decline follows Treaty of Kuchuk Kainarji
- 1783: Russia conquers and annexes Crimea
- 1789: French Revolution begins
- 1799: Coup brings Napoleon to power in France

The US Constitution, ratified in 1789, enshrined the principles of liberty and democracy for all US citizens. However, for purposes of representation, slaves were only considered to be three-fifths of a person and had no voting rights.

The Americas

During the 18th century, rivalry between French, British, and Spanish colonizers and conflicts with the native American population led to a series of wars, with the British gaining more of North America. In 1775 the American Revolution against British rule led to a division between Canada, loyal to the British crown, and a republican United States of America, finally established in 1783. In South America, Portuguese and Spanish rivalry continued, with both countries seeking control of newly discovered gold deposits in Brazil. Several Native American revolts against the Spanish in Peru were unsuccessful.

The Americas

- 1713: Asiento agreement gives British control of slave trade to Spanish colonies for 30 years
- 1728: First reconnaissance of Alaska by Bering
- 1763: Treaty of Paris: France loses Canada to Britain and lands west of Mississippi to Spain
- 1775: Start of American Revolution
- 1776: American colonies declare independence from Britain
- 1783: Britain accepts American independence via the Treaty of Paris
- 1789: George Washington becomes first President of US

MEASURING LONGITUDE

Navigators had long used the Sun and stars to calculate their latitude, but the accurate calculation of longitude depended on the precise measurement of local time in relation to the time at the Greenwich meridian. The invention by John Harrison of an accurate ship's chronometer in 1762 enabled navigators to calculate their position far more precisely, greatly reducing the risk of shipwrecks, and shortening journey times.

Harrison's chronometer was used by Captain James Cook on his second round-the-world voyage. His calculation of his ship's position at the end of the journey showed an error of only 8 miles.

Africa

Islamic influence continued to expand in much of North Africa. The Asante and Yoruba were dominant in West Africa, but the slave trade which had flourished for centuries throughout much of Africa was internationalized and greatly magnified by European influence in this period. Over 13.5 million people left Africa as slaves during the 1700s. West Africans and Angolans were shipped to the New World – especially Brazil – and northern Africa traded with the Ottoman Empire. In southern Africa, Dutch and British colonists struggled for supremacy against organized Xhosa resistance.

CAPTAIN COOK'S MAP OF NEW ZEALAND

Until the 18th century Oceania and the South Seas remained a mystery to most navigators. The English sailor Captain James Cook made three exploratory voyages to the South Pacific between 1768 and 1779. This map of New Zealand was made on Cook's first voyage. His ship, the *Endeavour*, traced the coast to make this remarkably accurate map.

Cook's map was the first accurate representation of New Zealand and copies were issued to map publishers all over Europe.

South and West Asia

The Persians under Nadir Shah began to challenge the Ottomans and pushed eastward into Mughal India, even sacking the city of Delhi in 1739. By the middle of the 18th century, the Marathas were emerging as successors to the Mughals, but they were comprehensively defeated by an Afghan army at Panipat in 1761. By the end of the century, the British East India Company had established firm control over much of India via a series of effective military campaigns.

By the late 18th century, many Indian rulers, such as the Nawab of Bengal, had assigned administrative powers to the British.

SEE ALSO:

North America: pp.126–129

South America: pp.148–149

Africa: pp.164–165

Europe: pp.198–201

West Asia: pp.230–231

South and Southeast Asia: pp.246–249

North and East Asia: pp.268–269

Australasia and Oceania: pp.282–283

South and West Asia

1707: Death of Aurangzeb heralds decline of Mughal power in India
1736: Nadir Shah becomes Shah of Persia
1747: Foundation of Afghanistan by Ahmad Khan Abdali
1761: British destroy French power in India following seizure of Pondicherry
1799: Conquest of Mysore ends challenge to British power in southern India

1700 1720 1740 1760 1780 1800

1722–36: Subjugation of Afghans by Persia
1757: Robert Clive defeats Bengalis at battle of Plassey
1765: Bengal comes under British control
1775: First Anglo-Maratha war
1786: Start of Qadjar dynasty in Persia
1796: British conquest of coastal Ceylon

East Asia, Southeast Asia, and Oceania

The Qing dynasty extended its empire to include a protectorate over Tibet and the conquest of Xiankiang (Dzungaria) by 1760. By 1790, the Chinese population had virtually tripled to 300 million. Trade in tea, porcelain, and silk with Russia and the West boosted the economy, and Manchu China was able to resist European incursion. The kingdoms of Southeast Asia were frequently at war, and subject to invasion by the Chinese, as with Burma in 1765–69. Though the Portuguese and Dutch had set up trading ports, much of the East Indies had yet to be formally colonized.

East Asia, Southeast Asia, and Oceania

1716: Start of Kyoho era in Japan
1752: Start of Konbaung dynasty in Burma
1765–69: Manchus invade Burma
1768: Captain James Cook starts exploration of Pacific
1788: First British settlement at Botany Bay in Australia

1700 1720 1740 1760 1780 1800

1751: Tibet, Dzungaria, and the Tarim Basin overrun by the Chinese
1755: Alaungpaya founds Rangoon and reunites Burma
1774: Nguyen Anh becomes emperor of Vietnam

Skilled Qing artists rendered images such as this vivid portrayal of an archery contest on silk. Silk and porcelain produced to a quality unknown in the West were prized by European traders.

Finely chased gold ornaments like this were worn as insignia by officials of the Asante court.

The World in 1800

- Qing Empire
- Persia and possessions
- Ottoman Empire
- Britain and possessions
- France and possessions
- Denmark and possessions
- Spain and possessions
- Portugal and possessions
- Netherlands and possessions
- Prussia and possessions
- Russian Empire
- Austrian Habsburg territories
- Holy Roman Empire
- Persia on death of Nadir Shah 1747
- French possessions lost during 18th century

Africa

1705: Foundation of Husaynid dynasty in Tunis, which rules until 1957
1720: Dutch settlers reach Orange River from Cape
1730: Revival of ancient empire of Bornu in central Africa
1747: Oyo become main power in Niger Delta after defeat of Dahomey
1757: Muhammad III becomes Sultan of Morocco
1770s: Peak years of European slave trade with Africa
1779–80: Boers and Bantu at war in southern Africa
1787: Settlement of first freed slaves from Britain at Freetown
1795: British capture Cape of Good Hope from the Dutch
1798: Occupation of Egypt by Napoleon Bonaparte

1700 1720 1740 1760 1780 1800

EMPIRE AND REVOLUTION

João V, king of Portugal from 1706–50, used most of the gold imported from his colonies in Brazil to finance his own grandiose building schemes.

RAPID POPULATION GROWTH, the creation of the first industrial societies, the maturing of Europe's American colonies, and new ideas about statehood and freedom of the individual, combined to create an overwhelming demand for political change in the late 18th century. Royal tax demands to finance expensive wars, and their often harsh attempts to control imperial subjects, became major focuses of discontent. The success of the Americans in their rebellion against British rule, and the total rejection of royal authority in favor of representative government during the French Revolution, had profound repercussions throughout Europe, with the revolutionary flame lit on numerous occasions from the 1790s onward.

② An era of revolution 1768–1868 ▶

- area gaining independence from imperial control c.1750–1850
- area resisting imperial control or expansion c.1750–1850
- Britain and possessions
- Netherlands and possessions
- Spain and possessions
- France and possessions
- Portugal and possessions
- Denmark and possessions
- Russia and possessions
- △ independence achieved following war or revolution with date of independence
- European revolution or uprising 1750–1830 with date
- European revolution or uprising after 1830 with date
- area affected by 1848 revolutions
- important non-European uprising with date

War on a global scale

With the acquisition of new territories overseas during the 18th century, the major European powers often transferred their local conflicts to a far wider arena. The Seven Years' War (1756–63) was fought in the colonies as well as in Europe, with Britain able to take control of the Atlantic and defeat the French in North America. A few years later, however, French support for the American rebels and the resurgence of French naval power thwarted Britain's attempts to hold on to its American colonies. The position was reversed in India, where British victory at Plassey in 1757 gave her vital control of the state of Bengal, and enabled the rapid expansion of British India.

The signing of the Treaty of Paris in 1763 ended seven years of bitter fighting between Britain and France in North America. Great celebrations were held in London's Green Park to mark the agreement.

The export of European conflict

1743: King George's War between Britain and France in North America lasts until 1748	**1754:** French-Indian War between France and Indian allies and Britain	**1757:** British victory at battle of Plassey in northern India	**1760:** End of French resistance in North America; Britain gains control of much of French America

1740 — 1750 — 1760 — 1770

1744: Britain and France join Carnatic War in India | **1756:** Start of Seven Years' War in Europe parallels conflict in North America | **1758:** British take Senegal in West Africa from French / **1758–61:** British victorious over French at Fort St. David and Pondicherry in India | **1763:** Treaty of Paris ends Seven Years' War

① The European empires and the first world wars ▼

- Britain and possessions c.1750
- Dutch possessions c.1750
- Spain and possessions c.1750
- France and possessions c.1750
- Portugal and possessions c.1750
- Denmark and possessions c.1750
- Russia and possessions c.1750
- maximum area of French control in India c.1751
- ceded to Spain 1763
- ceded to Britain by 1766
- maximum area of British control in India by 1815
- ◇ Dutch acquisition
- ◇ British acquisition
- ◇ French acquisition
- ◇ Spanish acquisition
- ◇ Portuguese acquisition
- ◇ Russian acquisition
- ◇ Danish acquisition
- ⚒ colonial conflict
- ✕ battle, with date

This American cartoon from 1774, shows Bostonians protesting the Stamp Act by forcing tea into the mouth of a tax collector who has been tarred and feathered.

NORTH AMERICA

Plains Indians

RUPERT'S LAND
Hudson Bay Company

UNITED STATES
OF AMERICA
△ 1783

Hudson
Bay

1837–38: Canadians

Alaska

Arctic Circle

ARCTIC OCEAN

Greenland

Iceland

ATLANTIC
OCEAN

In 1810, Father Miguel Hidalgo, a Catholic priest, led a rebellion against Spanish rule in Mexico.

SEE ALSO:

North America: pp.126–129

South America: pp.150–151

Europe: pp.198–203

West Asia: pp.230–231

South and Southeast Asia: pp.248–249

North and East Asia: pp.268–269

Siberia

RUSSIAN EMPIRE

JAPAN

KOREA

*Yellow
Sea*

QING EMPIRE

1853–68:
Nian rebellion

1853–63:
Taiping
rebellion

1863–73: Northwest
Muslim revolts

1850–53:
Taiping advance

1855–73: Yunnan
Muslim rising

*Philippine
Islands*

local
tribes

HONG KONG
1842: to Britain
Macao

Jiantian
1850: Beginning of
Taiping rebellion

*South
China
Sea*

Celebes

PORTUGUESE
TIMOR

DUTCH
NETHERLANDS

IRELAND
1798

BELGIUM
1787
1831

DENMARK

BRITAIN

1784

POLAND
1791,
1830–31

1825: Decembrist
uprising

1831: Ostrolenka

PORTUGAL
1821

FRANCE
1789,
1830

SPAIN
1808,
1820–23

Corsica
1793

1832–47:
Abd el Kader

HOLY
ROMAN
EMPIRE

1821

HUNGARY
1790

1848–49

SERBIA
1804

SARDINIA

SICILY
1820–21

GREECE
1830 △

Berbers

1773–74: Pugachev's
and Cossack revolt

1793, 1821

1840–60:
Circassians

Kazakhs and
Turkmen

1834–59: Shamil

1844–50:
Babism

PERSIA

Pashtun

Nepal

Shan Tribes

Dayaks

Borneo

Chandernagore

*Bay
of
Bengal*

*Gulf
of
Siam*

Timor

Flores

Sumba

OTTOMAN EMPIRE

AFRICA

ALGERIA

Nile

Wahhabis

*Arabian
Peninsula*

*Arabian
Sea*

Diu
Damão

Goa

Mahé

Pondicherry
Karikal

Ceylon

Yanaon

INDIA

1857–59:
The Mutiny

Nicobar Islands
to Denmark

Achin

Sumatra

Dayaks

DUTCH POSSESSIONS AND DEPENDENCIES

1825–30:
Dipo Negoro

Java

INDIAN OCEAN

Azores
to Portugal

Canary Islands
to Spain

Equator

The era of revolution

The first serious challenges to absolutist monarchy and exploitative imperial rule came in the late 18th century, with Pugachev's revolt in Russia, the American Revolution against British colonial rule, and most influentially, the French Revolution of 1789. Uprisings continued in central and eastern Europe into the early 19th century, and the 1808 revolution in Spain spilled over into Spanish America, where a series of successful independence campaigns began in 1810. Periodic attempts to reestablish the old regime were continually met by risings, culminating in the "year of revolutions" in 1848, when the fall of Louis Philippe in France inspired uprisings across most of Europe.

Revolutions and rebellions, 1768–1868

1773: Risings in southeast Russia led by Pugachev

1784: Risings in Dutch Netherlands

1791: Revolt in Poland

1791: Revolution in Haiti

1793: Revolt in Sardinia

1793: Rebellion in Corsica

1804: Revolt in Serbia

1810: Start of revolutions in Spanish America: by 1826 all Spanish colonies in South America have gained independence

1848: Year of revolution in Europe

1850s: Taiping rebellions and control in China

1768: Revolt in Geneva

1775: Start of American War of Independence

1789: Start of French Revolution

1790: Revolt in Hungary

1798: Revolt in Ireland

1808: Revolution in Spain

1850s: Muslim rebellions in China

1853–68: Nian rebellion in China

1760 · 1780 · 1800 · 1820 · 1840 · 1860

❸ The revolution in Haiti ▽

Tortuga

Port-de-Paix
Le Cap

Fort Liberté
(Fort Dauphin)

Santiago

San Francisco de Macoris

1802: French attack

ATLANTIC OCEAN

1791:
Slave revolt

1794: British attack

SAINT
DOMINGUE

Gonâve

Jérémie

Port-au-Prince

1801–02:
Revolutionary
invasion

SANTO
DOMINGO

Hispaniola

Santo Domingo

Cayes

1790: border

1820: border between
Haiti and Santo Domingo

100 km

100 miles

Caribbean Sea

Delacroix's famous painting
Liberty on the Barricades,
became a banner of inspiration to French (and other European) revolutionary movements during the 19th century.

Haiti: a post-revolutionary state

In 1791, fired by the French Revolution, slaves in the prosperous French colony of Saint-Domingue rebelled, and by 1794, slavery was abolished. In 1801, rebel forces entered Spanish Santo Domingo, briefly uniting the whole island. Intervention by British and French forces failed to stop Haiti declaring its independence in 1804.

Toussaint l'Ouverture, a former slave, led the revolt of 1791, but did not declare Haiti fully independent. As a concession, he was appointed governor-general by the French in 1801. When French troops were sent to the island in 1802, Toussaint was forced to make terms with the commander of the invasion force. Subsequently betrayed, he died in prison in France in 1803.

THE WORLD 1800–1850

THE AFTERMATH OF THE FRENCH and American revolutions and the Napoleonic wars led to a new nationalism and demands for democracy and freedom. The colonial regimes of South America were overthrown, and in Europe, Belgium and Greece gained independence. The US and northern Europe were transformed by the Industrial Revolution, as mass production and transportation led to an economic boom. There were mass movements of peoples to the expanding cities or to new lives abroad. Hunger for raw materials to feed industry and the desire to dominate world markets was soon to lead to unprecedented colonial expansion. In the US, Australia, and New Zealand, indigenous peoples were fighting a futile battle for their homelands.

A series of major innovations put Britain at the forefront of industrial development. The Nielsen hot blast process, invented in 1824, made iron smelting more efficient.

Europe

The Napoleonic Empire convulsed the established European order, abolishing states and national institutions. While liberals preached democracy, the ruling class responded with repressive measures to restrict freedom of speech and political expression. By the late 1840s civil unrest in the growing cities, bad harvests, and economic crisis led to open rebellion. In 1848, Louis Philippe of France was forced to abdicate, and revolution broke out throughout Europe.

Europe

1805: Defeat of Russia and Austria by France at Austerlitz
1815: New map of Europe drawn up at Congress of Vienna
1830: First wave of rebellions and social unrest in Europe
1845: Irish famine; 1,170,000 people driven to emigrate

1800 — 1810 — 1820 — 1830 — 1840

1804: Napoleon becomes Emperor
1812: Napoleon's troops retreat from Moscow
1819: Carlsbad Decrees prohibit political meetings and censor press in German states
1831: Belgium becomes independent
1848: Rebellions throughout Europe are quickly suppressed

North America

The acquisition of new territories opened up the vast interior of North America to new settlement. Settlers pushing across the plains in search of fertile land and into new wealth came into bloody conflict with Native Americans who, equipped with both horses and guns, proved to be formidable foes. The mechanization of agriculture increased exports of wheat, tobacco, and cotton and as the economy prospered, cities expanded and immigrants arrived in great numbers.

The intensive plantation economy of the southern US was dependent on slave labor to pick cotton and harvest tobacco.

North America

1819: Parts of Spanish Florida conquered by US
1836: Texans rebel against Mexican rule and declare Republic of Texas
1849: California Gold Rush

1800 — 1810 — 1820 — 1830 — 1840 — 1850

1803: France sells territory between Mississippi and Rockies in Louisiana Purchase
1821: Mexico gains independence from Spanish colonists
1846–48: US victory in war with Mexico which cedes New Mexico and California to US

South America

When Spain was cut off from her colonies by the Napoleonic wars, nationalist forces took advantage of the resulting disorder and weakness of the colonial regimes. Argentina's struggle for independence was led by José de San Martín, who marched an army across the Andes to liberate Chile and Peru from royalist control. Simón Bolívar led Venezuela and New Granada to independence, and helped found the new republic of Bolivia in 1825.

The Venezuelan Simón Bolivar (1783–1830) was known as the "liberator of South America."

1810: Argentina declares independence from Spain
1821: Bolivar secures Venezuelan independence

South America

1800 — 1810 — 1820 — 1830 — 1840 — 1850

1817: San Martin wins a decisive victory over the Spanish and liberates Chile
1822: Empire of Brazil becomes independent from Portugal

Major areas of disputed/undecided status

Major areas of disputed/undecided status

RAILROADS

The steam locomotive was first developed in Britain in the early 19th century to haul heavy industrial loads. By 1830, engines were being used to pull cars on iron rails and the first steam railroad – from Stockton to Darlington – had opened. By 1850, railroads had been built throughout Britain and were being introduced throughout its empire.

The steam engine
Locomotion, built by Robert Stephenson and Co., hauled the first train at the opening of the Stockton-to-Darlington railroad in 1825.

Africa

In sub-Saharan West Africa several Islamic leaders waged *jihad* against neighboring states. Under the Ottoman leader, Muhammad Ali, the viceroyalty of Egypt extended south to incorporate Sudan. The French invasion of Algeria in 1830 led to a war of resistance, led by Abd al-Qadir. In southeastern Africa, conflict broke out between different tribal groups (the *mfecane*) as natural resources became scarce. Shaka, the Zulu leader, established a united kingdom in southern Africa. In the late 1830s the "Great Trek" of the Boers from Cape Colony extended European influence into the African interior.

East and Southeast Asia

In the early 19th century, British merchants began to exploit the Chinese desire for Indian opium. As the trade flourished and the problem of opium addiction grew, the Chinese authorities attempted to stamp out the trade. The British objected and the first Opium War ensued. Japan, ruled by the inward-looking, Tokugawa shogunate for the last two centuries, remained closed to all foreigners, except a small Dutch trading community.

Superior firepower such as that displayed by the merchant steamer *Nemesis* enabled the British to overwhelm the wooden junks used by the Chinese in the first Opium War.

GEOLOGICAL MAPS

In the 19th century newly-discovered fossil remains were used to classify rocks and determine the sequence of geological strata. Geographical names were often used in the naming of rock types; for example, the Jura Mountains gave their name to the dinosaur-bearing Jurassic rocks.

Geologists used cross sections to map the age of rocks. This one is taken from the Reverend William Buckland's *Bridgewater Treatise on Mineralogy and Geology.*

SEE ALSO:

North America: pp.128–131

South America: pp.150–151

Africa: pp.166–167

Europe: pp.200–205

West Asia: pp.232–233

South and Southeast Asia: pp.248–249

North and East Asia: pp.268–271

Australasia and Oceania: pp.282–285

East and Southeast Asia

1804: Russian envoy fails to agree commercial treaty with Japan

1819: Stamford Raffles, of the British East India company, founds Singapore

1837: Tokugawa Ieyoshi succeeds Ienari as Japanese shogun

1839–42: First Opium War in China

1800 — 1810 — 1820 — 1830 — 1840 — 1850

1802: Gia-Long proclaimed emperor of united Annam (Vietnam)

1834: Monopoly of China trade by East India Company abolished

1842: Treaty of Nanjing. Hong Kong ceded to British and five ports opened to foreign trade

Australasia and Oceania

New Zealand and Australia became British colonies in the first half of the 19th century. In Australia, settlement spread from the penal colony at Port Jackson, now part of Sydney. As settlers founded towns at Adelaide, Melbourne, and Perth, they expropriated Aboriginal lands, and infected the people with fatal diseases, destroying local Aboriginal communities.

The Treaty of Waitangi allowed the Maori to maintain control over their lands while ceding the sovereignty of New Zealand to Britain, an unequal exchange which soon led to resentment and further wars.

Australasia and Oceania

1810: Kamehameha I unites Hawaiian islands

1825: Dutch annex western New Guinea

1840: British takeover of New Zealand under Treaty of Waitangi

1800 — 1810 — 1820 — 1830 — 1840 — 1850

1829: Britain annexes the whole continent of Australia

1835–36: British found Melbourne and Adelaide

The Zulu kings Shaka and Panda were able to harness the strength and skill of their warriors to establish a Zulu kingdom in southern Africa.

Africa

1804: Muhammad Ali becomes Viceroy of Egypt

1819: Shaka, leader of the Zulus, drives his enemies northward

1820: Egyptians invade Sudan

1830: French invasion of Algeria

1838: Newly arrived Boer settlers resist attack by Zulus

1843: British annex Natal; Boers forced to make second trek

1800 — 1810 — 1820 — 1830 — 1840 — 1850

1804: Fulani leader, Uthman dan Fodio conquers Hausa city-states

1822: Freed black slaves found colony of Liberia

1847: Abd al-Qadir captured by French and exiled

The World in 1850

- Qing Empire
- Ottoman Empire
- Britain and possessions
- France and possessions
- Denmark and possessions
- Spain and possessions
- Portugal and possessions
- Netherlands and possessions
- Prussia
- Russian Empire
- Japan
- Austrian Empire
- Napoleon's French Empire 1812
- Muhammad Ali's possessions 1840
- United Provinces of Central America 1823–38
- Great Colombia 1819–30

THE WORLD'S ECONOMIC REVOLUTION

Innovative new constructions of the late-19th century included the Eiffel Tower, built in 1889.

IN THE FIRST HALF of the 19th century, world trade and industry was dominated by Britain; by the 1870s, the industrial balance was shifting in favor other nations, especially Germany, France, Russia, and the US, with rapid industrialization occurring throughout most of Europe by the end of the century. A stable currency, a standard (i.e., the price of gold) against which the currency's value could be measured, and an effective private banking system were seen as essential to the growth and success of every industrializing nation. The major industrial nations also began to invest heavily overseas. Their aims were the discovery and exploitation of cheaper raw materials, balanced by the development of overseas markets for their products.

The impact of the Industrial Revolution

The introduction of steam to oceangoing ships decreased journey times, and increased reliability because ships were no longer reliant on the wind.

World industrial output from 1870–1914 increased at an extraordinary rate: coal production by as much as 650%; steel by 2500%; steam engine capacity by over 350%. Technology revolutionized the world economy: the invention of refrigerated ships meant that meat, fruit, and other perishables could be shipped to Europe from as far away as New Zealand; sewing machines and power looms allowed the mass production of textiles and clothing; telephones, telegraphs, and railroads made communications faster.

The opening of the Suez Canal in 1869, linking the Red Sea to the Mediterranean, reduced the journey time from Europe to India by 50%.

By the 1880s almost all of the US was connected by long-distance rail networks including the Illinois Central Railroad (below).

① The impact of technology on the world trading system 1870–1910 ▶

- most highly industrialized nations
- industrializing nations
- major industrial regions c.1914

Improvements in communications
- major rail networks c.1914
- North Atlantic shipping route
- other shipping route
- underwater telegraph cable route

Location of manufacturing industry
- heavy machinery
- iron and steel
- textile production

Export markets opened up by technology
- beef cattle
- lamb and mutton
- fruit

Major cash crops
- coffee
- cotton
- rubber
- sugarcane
- tea

1859: Refrigerated container ships transport lamb and mutton to world markets

Railroads transport beef cattle from western grasslands to the populated east coast

Refrigerated container ships transport bananas to world markets

Panama Canal Opened in 1914. Journey times reduced by up to 40%.

Refrigerated container ships transport South American beef to world markets

Suez Canal Opened in 1869. Journey times reduced by up to 60%.

Inventions and the economic revolution

1856: First commercial refrigeration in US; refined technique developed in Australia by 1859

1869: Completion of Transcontinental Railroad in US

1874: Alexander Graham Bell patents telephone

1885: Development of first automobile by Daimler and Benz

1835 — 1845 — 1855 — 1865 — 1875 — 1885 — 1895

1838: Invention of first electric telegraph in Britain

1856: Bessemer invents process for mass production of steel

1863: Construction of London Underground begins

1880s: Refrigerated ships transport cheese, butter, and meat from New Zealand

1895: Invention of wireless telegraphy (radio) by Marconi

Invention of canning opens up world fruit markets

The great mineral rush

The search for new sources of minerals, both precious and functional, reached new heights of intensity in the industrial 19th century. New finds of gold and diamonds in the US, Canada, Australia, and South Africa fueled the so-called gold and diamond rushes of the later 19th century. Though individuals could pan for gold in the Australian and North American rushes, the depth of gold and diamond deposits in South Africa meant that they could only be fully exploited with mechanical diggers owned by mining companies.

SEE ALSO:

North America: pp.130–133

South America: pp.150–151

Africa: 166–167

Europe: p.204–205

West Asia: pp.232–233

South and Southeast Asia: pp.250–251

North and East Asia: pp.270–271

Australasia and Oceania: pp.282–283

▲ ❷ **Major mineral finds of the late 19th century**

cobalt	gold
copper	manganese
diamonds	silver
iron ore	tin

The Klondike and Yukon gold rushes

Gold was first discovered near the Pacific coast of Alaska in 1880 by the explorers Juneau and Harris. The mid-1890s saw frenzied activity along the Yukon river and its tributaries, with an influx of many thousands of prospectors into one of the world's most desolate regions. Though Dawson City and other settlements grew up to supply the miners, the boom had receded by 1899.

Boom towns sprang up rapidly during the Yukon gold rush. Such was the passion for gold that even the city streets were dug up by eager prospectors.

In the rush for instant riches miners such as this man, panning for gold in British Columbia in 1900, were prepared to undergo extreme hardship.

◀ ❸ **The Yukon and Klondike gold rushes**

- major gold strike
- settlement or fort

1896: Dawson City founded by Joseph Ladue. By 1898 30,000 prospecting for gold

1902: Placer gold found by Felix Pedro

1896: G.W. Carmack, Skokum Jim, and Tagish Charlie find rich source of gold

1885: Traces of gold found by Robert Henderson

1880: Gold strike by Juneau and Harris

Gold and diamond rushes

1840	1850	1860	1870	1880	1890	1900

1849–50: Comstock Lode found near Virginia City, Nevada

1851: Rich gold deposits found in southern Australia

1869: Discovery of "Star of South Africa" diamond sets off diamond rush

1896–98: Yukon and Klondike gold rushes

1848: California Gold Rush starts neaer Sutter's Mill on the Sacramento River

1858: Gold discovered on Fraser River, northwest Canada

1867: Diamonds found at Kimberley, north of Cape Colony, South Africa

1876–78: Gold found near Black Hills of Dakota Territory

1886: Deep seams of gold discovered on the Witwatersrand, South Africa

---

The politics of cotton

In the 1870s woven cotton in India was still produced on a local scale, by individuals, rather than factories, and traded at local markets (above).

❺ **The politics of cotton** ▼

- raw cotton from US to Britain
- cotton textiles to India
- raw cotton from India to Britain
- cotton producing region
- textile town
- major cotton-producing states

Cotton production was an early beneficiary of the Industrial Revolution. Eli Whitney's invention of the cotton gin led to a huge increase in the volume of cotton that could be processed; the invention of the power loom industrialized the weaving of cotton textiles. Britain's colonies in India and America supplied raw cotton for the cotton towns of Lancashire and Yorkshire; even with American independence, the southern states continued to provide much of Britain's cotton. The economic and political importance of cotton to the US was reflected in the Confederate states' decision to use it as a bargaining tool during their struggle for international recognition following secession in 1861. The ploy failed as a strategy; during the Civil War, Britain turned to India for its raw cotton supplies. British cloth woven with Indian cotton was then exported back to India, a policy which benefited British producers, while keeping the Indian textile industry at a local level until the end of the 19th century.

◀ ❹ **The cotton towns of Lancashire and Yorkshire**

- cotton town
- Peel   textile firm
- major railroad c.1850
- major canal

Cotton production in Lancashire

With plentiful water to power new machinery, Lancashire had developed as a major cotton-weaving center by the late 18th century. Textile towns such as Stockport, Blackburn, and Cromford, often containing several firms, grew up in the area around Manchester, which acted as a major market for finished cloth.

1815–60: British cotton textile production expands at a rate of 6–7% per annum and by the mid-century British cotton constitutes c.50% of world production of commercially produced cloth

1879: Abolition of all tariff duties on British textiles
1895: Britain imposes excise of 5% on Indian cotton goods
1924: Cotton excise suspended

Late 18th century: Cotton production in Lancashire is great growth industry of Industrial Revolution

1793: Invention of cotton gin leads to a massive increase in the production of short-staple cotton

1800–60: US annual raw cotton production increases from 100,000 bales to 4 million bales

1861: During Civil War, Confederate states restrict cotton exports to try and force European intervention in war

1861–65: "Cotton famine" caused by Civil War restrictions in US leads British textile manufacturers to look to India for raw materials

1820–50: As woven cloth from Britain floods into India, it loses its world market for textiles and is obliged to import machine-made cotton cloth from Lancashire

1861 onward: Boom in raw cotton production in India

THE WORLD 1850–1900

BY 1900 THE EUROPEAN POPULATION had more than doubled to 420 million, while the population of the US had reached 90 million. Industry and commerce were booming, and both Europe and the US were traversed by rail networks. The major European powers were extending their economic and political influence to the very ends of the globe, while fierce rivalries and competition were being enacted on the international as well as the domestic scene. Within two decades the European powers had colonized virtually the whole of the African continent, the British had claimed India for the Crown, and the western powers had exploited the fatal weaknesses of China's crumbling Qing dynasty to penetrate deep into the heart of Asia.

Kaiser Wilhelm II was determined to establish Germany as Europe's leading military power.

Europe

The emergence of new states, the rise of nationalism, and growing economic and political power led to rivalry and conflict. Expansionist Russia's activities in the Balkans led in 1854 to the Crimean War, between a Franco–British–Turkish alliance and Russia. In 1870 Bismarck, prime minister of Prussia, goaded the French into war; the French defeat led to the collapse of the Second Empire, providing the final impetus to the creation of the new German and Italian nations.

Europe

1854–56: Franco-British-Turkish alliance victorious against Russians in Crimea

1862: Otto von Bismarck prime minister of Prussia

1870: Franco-Prussian war; Prussian victory leads to collapse of Second Empire

1887: Bulgaria, independent of Ottoman empire, becomes leading Balkan state

1850 — 1860 — 1870 — 1880 — 1890 — 1900

1861: Abolition of serfdom in Russia

1867: Dual monarchy of Austria-Hungary established

1871: Rome becomes capital of united Italy; King Wilhelm I of Prussia declared German emperor

1896: Revival of Olympic Games at Athens, Greece

CAMPAIGN MAPS

During the American Civil War, new printing technology combined with up-to-date information from correspondents on the battlefields allowed US newspapers to produce simplified campaign maps to explain the stages of the war to a fascinated public.

This map shows the battle of Campbell's Station, Tennessee, as witnessed from the Union position by the *New York Tribune's* correspondent, Elias Smith.

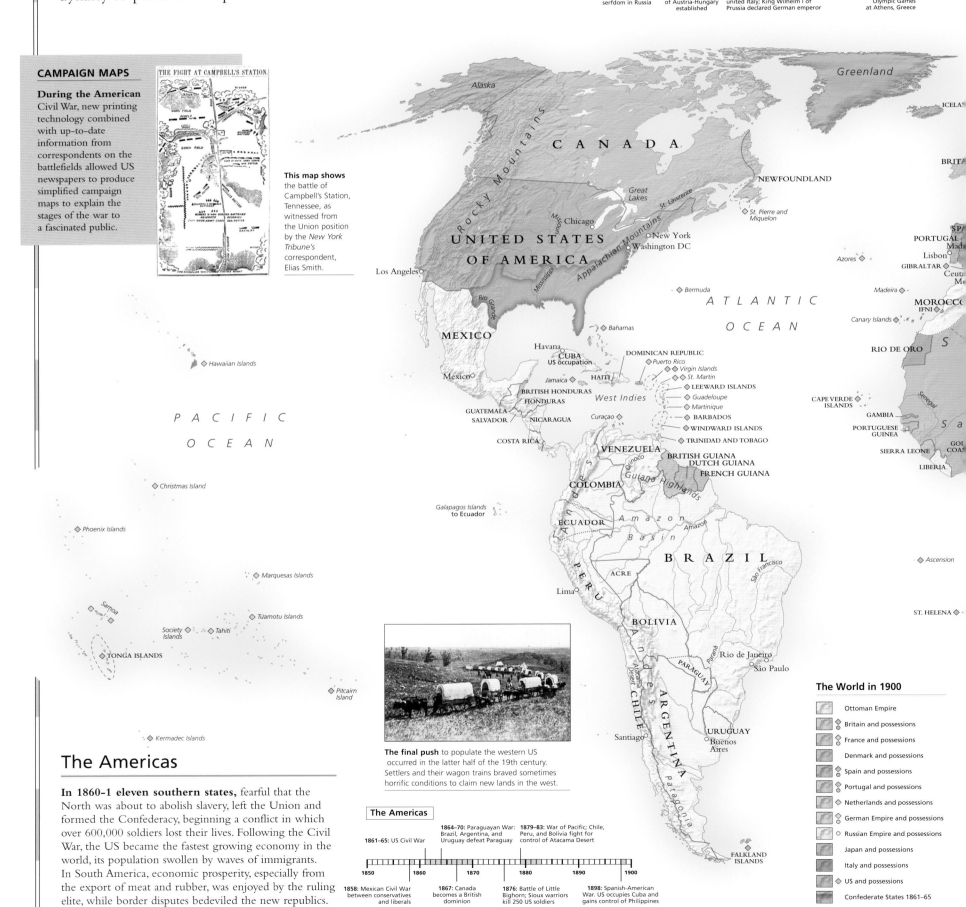

The final push to populate the western US occurred in the latter half of the 19th century. Settlers and their wagon trains braved sometimes horrific conditions to claim new lands in the west.

The Americas

In 1860-1 eleven southern states, fearful that the North was about to abolish slavery, left the Union and formed the Confederacy, beginning a conflict in which over 600,000 soldiers lost their lives. Following the Civil War, the US became the fastest growing economy in the world, its population swollen by waves of immigrants. In South America, economic prosperity, especially from the export of meat and rubber, was enjoyed by the ruling elite, while border disputes bedeviled the new republics.

The Americas

1864–70: Paraguayan War; Brazil, Argentina, and Uruguay defeat Paraguay

1879–83: War of Pacific; Chile, Peru, and Bolivia fight for control of Atacama Desert

1861–65: US Civil War

1850 — 1860 — 1870 — 1880 — 1890 — 1900

1858: Mexican Civil War between conservatives and liberals

1867: Canada becomes a British dominion

1876: Battle of Little Bighorn; Sioux warriors kill 250 US soldiers

1898: Spanish-American War. US occupies Cuba and gains control of Philippines

The World in 1900

- Ottoman Empire
- Britain and possessions
- France and possessions
- Denmark and possessions
- Spain and possessions
- Portugal and possessions
- Netherlands and possessions
- German Empire and possessions
- Russian Empire and possessions
- Japan and possessions
- Italy and possessions
- US and possessions
- Confederate States 1861–65

East Asia

From the late 19th century, the newly-modernized Japan reopened its doors to foreign trade.

Agrarian unrest in China in the 1850s led to rebellion and famine. Western powers were quick to exploit internal dissent, carving out spheres of influence and annexing territory. A wave of xenophobia led to the Boxer Rebellion of 1900. Western troops were sent to China and concessions were extracted from the weak government. In Japan, the overthrow of the Tokugawa shogunate in 1868 was followed by industrial and economic modernization.

East Asia

1850: Taiping Rebellion begins in Guangxi province
1860: British and French occupy Beijing
1871: Abolition of feudalism in Japan
1900: Boxer Rebellion: Christian missions and western legations attacked

1853: Rebels capture Nanjing – recaptured a year later
1868: Overthrow of Tokugawa shogunate
1877–79: Famine in northern China leaves at least 10 million dead
1894–95: Japanese overwhelm Chinese forces and annex Taiwan

South Asia

The railroad station in Bombay was opened in 1887. The style and scale of the building reflected the great self-confidence of India's British rulers.

By 1850 the British East India Company emerged as the major power on the subcontinent. Hostility to the British, combined with suspicions about their attitude to India's traditional faiths, led to the Mutiny of 1857–59. Following the Mutiny, the British took administrative control of India, developed an extensive rail network, and began to industrialize the Indian economy.

South Asia

1878–79: Second Afghan War; British invade Afghanistan, which is coming under Russian influence
1885: Foundation of Indian National Congress

1857: Outbreak of Indian Mutiny
1876: Queen Victoria declared Empress of India, and a Viceroy appointed as her representative
1885–86: Third Burmese War leads to British annexation of Burma

SEE ALSO:

North America: pp.128–133

South America: pp.150–151

Africa: pp.166–167

Europe: pp.202–207

West Asia: pp.232–233

South and Southeast Asia: pp.248–251

North and East Asia: pp.268–270

Australasia and Oceania: pp.282–285

THE TELEPHONE

The telephone was invented in 1876 by the Scottish-born inventor and speech therapist Alexander Graham Bell. His device used a thin diaphragm to convert vibrations from the human voice into electrical signals. These were then reconverted into sound waves. Within a few years of its invention, the telephone had been installed in many city homes in Europe and the US.

This view of Broadway in 1880 shows its skyline crisscrossed by telegraph and telephone wires.

By 1872, rich seams of gold- and diamond-bearing rock in Cape Colony were being heavily mined by European prospectors.

Africa

In 1850 Africa was a patchwork of kingdoms and states, mostly unknown to Europeans. But, by 1900, the major European powers had seized virtually the entire continent. Rivalries between European nations were played out in Africa as colonizing countries raced for territory, raw materials, and new markets. In 1898, open war between France and the British in the White Nile region was only just averted. In 1899, the Boer War, a bitter struggle between the British and Afrikaaners, began.

Africa

1869: Opening of Suez Canal
1880: White Boers have appropriated most habitable land in Cape Colony
1896: Abyssinia defeats Italians at Adowa
1899: Boer War begins

1863: Al-Hajj 'Umar clashes with French in Senegal Valley and creates a Muslim empire
1879: Zulu War with British; Zulus defeated
1882: British invade and occupy Egypt
1893: French conquer Dahomey
1898: British and French clash at Fashoda

THE ERA OF WESTERN IMPERIALISM

THE ERA OF WESTERN IMPERIALISM

This *Punch* cartoon from 1890 depicts Germany as an eagle, with Africa as her prey. The caption reads, "On the Swoop."

THE LAST TWENTY YEARS of the 19th century saw unprecedented competition by the major European nations for control of territory overseas. The balance of imperial power was changing: having lost their American empires, Spain and Portugal were no longer preeminent. From the 1830s, France began to build a new empire, and Britain continued to acquire new lands throughout the century. Newly unified Italy and Germany sought to bolster their nation status from the 1880s with their own empires. Africa was the most fiercely contested prize in this race to absorb the nonindustrialized world, but much of Southeast Asia and Oceania was also appropriated in this period. Even the US, historically the champion of anticolonial movements, began to expand across the Pacific.

Other nations were frequently critical of the behavior of European imperialists in Africa. This German cartoon (*left*) has the caption: "Even the lions weep at the way the native Africans are treated by the French."

Many British officials in India maintained rituals of extreme formality (*below*), rather than adapting to native patterns of behavior.

The scramble for Africa

The race for European political control in Africa began in the early 1880s. The Berlin Conference of 1884–85, convened to discuss rival European claims to Africa, was the starting point for the "scramble." Some governments worked through commercial companies; elsewhere, land was independently annexed by these companies; sometimes Africans actually invited Europeans in. In most cases, however, European political control was directly imposed by conquest. By 1914, Africa was fully partitioned along lines that bore little relation to cultural or linguistic traditions.

Colonial administrators often required extreme obeisance from the people they controlled. A local Moroccan sultan is shown here kneeling before a French colonel.

The scramble for Africa 1881–1900

1881: French occupation of Tunisia
1883: Start of French conquest of Madagascar
1885: King Leopold of Belgium acquires Congo
1890: Britain exchanges Heligoland with Germany for Pemba and Zanzibar
1896: Defeat of invading Italian army preserves Abyssinian independence
1900: Start of copper mining in Katanga

1880 — 1885 — 1890 — 1895 — 1900

1882: Revolt in Egypt prompts occupation by British
1884: Germany acquires South West Africa, Togo, and Cameroon
1886: Germany and Britain divide up East Africa
1889: Establishment of first Italian colony in Eritrea
1889: Cecil Rhodes' British South Africa Company begins colonization of Rhodesia
1894: Uganda occupied by Britain

▲ ❶ **Imperialism in Africa, 1880–1920**

Territory controlled by European nations by 1914

- Belgium
- Britain
- France
- Germany
- Italy
- Portugal
- Spain
- nominally Ottoman, under British control
- 1882 date of taking control
- — borders in 1914

Important mineral deposits
- coal
- copper
- diamonds
- gold

The struggle for South Africa

The British, with political control, the Afrikaners (Boers) – the first European settlers – and the Zulus all fought for control of South Africa in the 19th century. Seeking political autonomy, the Boers moved to found their own republics. The success of Transvaal, which grew rich from gold, led to annexation by Britain in 1877. British invasion of Zulu territory led to the First Zulu War, and British defeat, although this was swiftly reversed. In 1881, Boers in Transvaal rebelled against British rule, to set up the South African Republic. In 1899, the second Anglo-Boer war, broke out, lasting until 1902. The former Boer Republics became part of the British Empire as part of the Peace of Vereeniging.

It took more than 300,000 British soldiers five years to subdue 75,000 heavily-armed Boers, who were skilled in guerrilla and siege tactic, and had intimate knowledge of the terrain.

❷ **The struggle for South Africa, 1854–1914**

- Cape Colony and Natal 1854
- territory under British control 1895
- South African Republic 1895
- Orange Free State 1895
- battle in Zulu wars

Boer War 1899–1902
- Afrikaner (Boer) victory
- British victory
- Afrikaner sieges
- Union of South Africa boundary 1910
- railroad

The struggle for South Africa 1871–1910

1871: Discovery of gold in Transvaal
1879: First Zulu War: British crushed at Isandhlwana but win at Ulundi
1902: Boers forced to surrender

1875 — 1885 — 1895 — 1905 — 1915

1878: Transvaal annexed by Britain
1881: First Anglo-Boer War; British defeated at Majuba Hill; Transvaal reconstituted as South African Republic
1899: Start of Second Anglo-Boer War
1910: Formation of Union of South Africa with Afrikaners as majority white population

Imperialism in Southeast Asia

Though the Dutch East Indian Empire had existed since the early 17th century, much of Southeast Asia was not colonized until the mid-19th century. Moving east from India, British ambitions concentrated on Burma, the Malay Peninsula, and north Borneo. Renewed French interest in empire-building began in earnest with the capture of Saigon in 1858 following a concerted naval effort. By 1893, France controlled Tongking, Laos, Annam, and Cambodia, collectively known as Indochina.

Imperialism in Southeast Asia 1858–1895

1855: Start of British trade with Siam
1859: Saigon captured by France
1859: Timor divided between Netherlands and Portugal
1863: French establish protectorate over Cambodia
1867: French protectorate established in Cochin China
1873: Dutch attack on Achin sultanate
1884: Annexation of northern New Guinea and Bismarck Archipelago by Germany
1885: French protectorate established in Annam and Tongking
1886: Britain annexes Upper Burma after Third Burmese War

1850 | 1860 | 1870 | 1880 | 1890 | 1900

SEE ALSO:

North America: pp.132–133

Africa: pp.166–167

Europe: pp.202–203, p.206

West Asia: pp.232–233

South and Southeast Asia: pp.250–251

North and East Asia: pp.268–271

Australasia and Oceania: pp.282–283

3 Imperialism in Southeast Asia

Territory controlled by colonial powers by 1914
- Britain
- France
- Germany
- Netherlands
- Portugal
- USA
- frontier of Siam to 1907

Traded commodities
- aluminum
- copra
- ivory
- nickel
- oil
- rice
- rubber
- silk
- spices
- tobacco
- tin

Vietnamese dignitaries greet the arrival of the governor of French Indochina in Saigon in 1902.

The Malay Peninsula became a British possession in 1888. Vast rubber plantations provided a firm economic basis for imperial control.

BRITISH INDIA
Tropic of Cancer
Calcutta
QING EMPIRE
UPPER BURMA 1886: to Britain
ARAKAN 1826: to Britain
PEGU 1852: to Britain
Rangoon
TENASSERIM 1826: to Britain
Andaman Islands 1859: to Britain
Andaman Sea
Isthmus of Kra
19th century: Frequent proposals for building of canal to reduce shipping times.
Nicobar Islands 1859: to Britain, from Denmark
1873: Sultanate of Achin
Penang 1786: to Britain
BRITISH MALAYA 1888: to Britain
Singapore 1819: founded by Sir Thomas Stamford Raffles
Equator
Sumatra
Palembang
INDIAN OCEAN
Batavia
Java
Lombok
Sumbawa
Sumba
Timor
PORTUGUESE TIMOR
Flores Sea
Java Sea
DUTCH EAST INDIES
Banda Sea
Buru
Celebes Sea
Celebes
Borneo
SARAWAK 1888: to Britain
Sarawak
BRITISH NORTH BORNEO 1881: to Britain
BRUNEI 1888: under British protectorate
Guangzhou
Taiwan 1895: to Japan *Tropic of Cancer*
Macao 1557: to Portugal
Hong Kong 1841: to Britain 1860: Kowloon added to colony 1898: New Territories acquired
TONGKING 1885: to France
LAOS 1893
FRENCH INDO-CHINA 1887: created
Hué
KINGDOM OF SIAM
Bangkok
CAMBODIA 1867: to France
Phnomo Penh
ANNAM 1885
COCHIN CHINA 1867: to France
Saigon
Hainan
South China Sea
Luzon
Manila
Mindoro
Philippine Islands 1898: to US following Spanish-American war
Palawan
Mindanao
Halmahera
PACIFIC OCEAN
Hollandia
Bismarck Archipelago
KAISER WILHELM'S LAND 1884: to Germany
New Guinea
TERRITORY OF PAPUA 1884: to Britain 1906: to Australia
Port Moresby
1899: Bougainville and Buka to Germany
Buka
Bougainville
Solomon Islands
1893: Solomon Islands to Britain
Equator
Arafura Sea

500 km
500 miles

Reactions to imperialism

The aggressive scramble for empire provoked determined armed resistance across Africa and Asia. Local peoples rose up to repel the European intruders – for example against the British in Sudan, the Italians in Libya, and the Dutch in Sumatra – but in most cases they had to submit when faced by superior firepower. One exception was the defeat of the Italians at Adowa in Abyssinia in 1896. Imperialist meddling in countries such as China and Persia led to rebellions against the governments of the day, and the tottering Russian Empire faced a major revolt in Central Asia in 1916.

The Boxers were one of the antigovernment societies which emerged in China at the end of the 19th century. Resolutely anti-Western, they attacked communities and property, especially railroads and installations being built by Europeans. The siege of the European legations in Beijing was ended by an international expedition.

4 Movements against colonial rule, 1880–1920

Anti-colonial uprisings and incidents
- anti-British
- anti-Dutch
- anti-French
- anti-German
- anti-Italian
- anti-Portugal
- anti-Russian
- anti-Spanish
- anti-US

Other partly anti-western rebellions
- Persia
- area of Chinese revolution 1911–12
- boundary at 1914

1916: Easter Rising
BRITAIN
GERMANY
NETHERLANDS
FRANCE
PORTUGAL
SPAIN
ITALY
RUSSIAN EMPIRE
1916: Large-scale revolt in Central Asia
QING EMPIRE
1899–1900: Boxer rebellion
1891: Anti-western riots in Wuchang
1911–12: Chinese revolution
PACIFIC OCEAN
1919–26: Rif war between Spain and Rif and Jibala tribes
MOROCCO
1911: Jeliaz incident
TUNISIA
1915–16: Rebellion against French
SPANISH SAHARA
ALGERIA
1912–13: Sanusi war
LIBYA
OTTOMAN EMPIRE
1905–09: Persian revolution
PERSIA
1881–82: Arabi Pasha leads nationalist uprising
1906: Dinshaway incident
EGYPT
KUWAIT
NEJD
Tropic of Cancer
INDIA
1905–09: Terrorist campaigns in Maharashtra and Bengal
1886–91: War against British rule
BURMA
1883–88, 1893–1913: Guerrilla warfare against French
FRENCH INDO-CHINA
SIAM
1898–1902: Aguinaldo leads nationalist revolt
ANNAM 1885–87, 1916: Rebellions against French rule
PHILIPPINE ISLANDS 1885–86: Revolts against French rule
1898–1913: Moro resistance
1881–1908: Jihad against Dutch
DUTCH EAST INDIES
Sumatra
Java
1890, 1914–17: Uprising by Saminist peasant movements
1881–94: Rebellions against Dutch
FRENCH WEST AFRICA
1897–1900: Rabih leads resistance against French
1884–98: Manda resistance
NIGERIA
1904: Anyang rebellion
1900: Ashanti rebellion
GOLD COAST
FRENCH EQUATORIAL AFRICA
CAMEROON
1881–98: Mahdiyya jihad against British and Egyptian rule
ANGLO-EGYPTIAN SUDAN
BRITISH SOMALILAND
1896: Italian defeat at Adowa
ABYSSINIA
1891–1920: Sayyid Muhammad resists British and Italian rule
INDIAN OCEAN
1890–98: Bunyoro resistance
UGANDA
1895–1905: Nandi resistance
BRITISH EAST AFRICA
1911–17: Tutsi and Hutu resistance
BELGIAN CONGO
FRENCH CONGO
1888–89: Abushiri resistance
1891–98: Hehe resistance
GERMAN EAST AFRICA
1905–07: Maji-Maji resistance
BRITISH CENTRAL AFRICA (NYASALAND)
ANGOLA
NORTHERN RHODESIA
1913: Risings against Portuguese rule
1896: Revolts by Matabele and Mashona
GERMAN SOUTHWEST AFRICA
PORTUGUESE EAST AFRICA
1898–1904: Anti-French risings
MADAGASCAR
SOUTHERN RHODESIA
BECHUANALAND
1904–06: Risings by Herero and Hottentots
1906: Zulu revolt
UNION OF SOUTH AFRICA
1899–1902: Boer war between Britain and two Boer republics
ATLANTIC OCEAN
Equator
Tropic of Capricorn

1000 km
1000 miles

THE WORLD 1900–1925

THE IMPERIAL AND MILITARY RIVALRY between Britain and France, and Germany and Austria-Hungary led, in 1914, to World War I, which left millions dead and redrew the map of Europe. The Habsburg and Ottoman empires broke up, leading to the emergence of a number of smaller nation states, while the end of the Ottoman Empire also created a territorial crisis in the Middle East. In 1917, the Russian Empire collapsed in revolution and civil war, to be transformed by the victorious Bolsheviks into the world's first Communist empire. The US's participation in the war confirmed its status as a world power, cemented by the central role played by President Wilson at the Versailles Conference, and by the nation's increasing economic dominance.

German soldiers wearing gas masks emerge from a dugout. Troops on both sides endured terrible conditions in the trench warfare which dominated the war in France.

Europe

Most countries in Europe and their colonies took part in World War I, which was fought on a scale unimagined in the 19th century. Years of rivalry between the major European powers, France, Britain and Germany had created an incendiary situation, finally touched off by a crisis in the Balkans. The Versailles Settlement of 1919 altered the balance of power in Europe irrevocably, setting up the conditions for a second European war 20 years later.

Europe

1905: Revolution in Russia; Norway becomes independent of Sweden
1910: Portuguese monarchy overthrown; republic proclaimed
1915–16: Thousands killed at Somme and Verdun, northern France
1917: Bolshevik Revolution in Russia
1920: Inauguration of League of Nations

1900 — 1905 — 1910 — 1915 — 1920 — 1925

1914: Assassination of Archduke Franz Ferdinand in Sarajevo precipitates start of World War I
1918: End of World War I
1919: Versailles Settlement creates a new European order

RADIO

Radio technology was first invented by Guglielmo Marconi in 1894. In 1901 he was able to send Morse Code messages across the Atlantic, and by 1920 the first commercial radio station was set up in Pittsburgh. By the mid-1920s, radio was established as an immensely effective means of mass communication.

Bi-Acoustic Radio
It's "HIS MASTER'S VOICE" of the air!

This radio, advertised using the famous fox terrier listening to "His Master's Voice," dates from the 1920s.

Revelers mourn the passing of the Volstead Act in 1919, prohibiting the sale of alcohol in the US. Alcohol sales merely went underground, creating a profitable black market presided over by an organized criminal network.

The Americas

By 1925, the US was the world's most powerful industrial nation. Its international standing was greatly enhanced by involvement in World War I and the Treaty of Versailles of 1918, although after 1920 there was a marked return to isolation from Europe. In Mexico, Central and South America, revolt against the old rural elites ushered in a new social order and an increasingly urban society.

The Americas

1910: Start of Mexican revolution
1919: US Senate rejects entry into League of Nations
1920: US refuses to ratify Paris treaties and withdraws into isolation

1900 — 1905 — 1910 — 1915 — 1920 — 1925

1903: Panama Canal Zone ceded to US
1914: Opening of Panama Canal joins Atlantic and Pacific oceans
1917: US declares war on Germany and its allies
1921: US restricts immigration

The World in 1925

- Turkey
- Britain and possessions
- France and possessions
- Denmark and possessions
- Spain and possessions
- Portugal and possessions
- Netherlands and possessions
- Germany
- USSR
- Japanese Empire
- Norway and possessions
- Belgium and possessions
- Italy and possessions
- New Zealand and possessions
- Australia and possessions
- US and possessions

West Asia

In 1918, the Ottoman Empire collapsed after more than 400 years. A new Turkish republic was inaugurated in 1923. In the post-war period much of the former Ottoman Empire, including Transjordan, Syria, and Iraq was controlled by Britain and France. A new Arab nationalism was becoming more strident, resulting in numerous political disturbances.

Kemal Atatürk was the first leader of the new Turkish republic. From 1923–38 he radically overhauled Ottoman institutions to bring Turkey into the modern age.

West Asia	

1912–13: Ottomans lose most of their European lands in Balkan Wars
1915: Allied attack on Gallipoli
1917: Balfour Declaration commits Britain to creation of Jewish state in Palestine

1900 1905 1910 1915 1920 1925

1908: Ottoman sultan deposed in Young Turk Revolution
1914: Ottomans ally with Germany and Austria after Britan, France and Russia declare war
1918: Collapse of Ottoman Empire
1923: Foundation of modern Turkey by Kemal Atatürk

Northeast Asia

Much of North and East Asia was destabilized by the collapse of the Chinese Empire into civil war in 1911, and the Russian Revolution of 1917. The victorious Bolsheviks hoped for the spread of revolution in other countries. Meanwhile, Japanese expansionism was rewarded by territorial gains in Siberia, China, and the Pacific islands.

A Soviet propaganda poster encourages peasants to invest their savings in state projects. Much policy at this time was aimed at exerting control over the peasants.

Northeast Asia	

1910: Japanese annexation of Korea
1914: Japan takes over many German colonies in the Pacific
1918–20: Japan occupies part of Manchuria and Siberia

1900 1905 1910 1915 1920 1925

1904–05: Russo-Japanese War; series of Russian defeats
1911: Qing dynasty overthrown by Sun Yat Sen's nationalists and Republic of China declared
1922: Washington Naval Agreement limits Japanese naval power in the Pacific

SEE ALSO:

North America: pp.132–133

South America: pp.152–153

Africa: pp.166–167

Europe: pp.206–207

West Asia: pp.232–233

South and Southeast Asia: pp.250–251

North and East Asia: pp.270–271

Australasia and Oceania: pp.284–285

ROAD MAPS

The growth in automobile use, a burgeoning road network and an increasingly mobile population, necessitated the creation of a new type of road map, more detailed than any made previously.

The cover of this 1920s road map emphasizes the link between car usage and leisure pursuits.

SECTION B

MOTORING and HIKING Map

Including—
Barnard Castle, Darlington, Durham Hartlepool, Hexham, Kirkby Stephen Middlesbrough, Newcastle, Northallerton Redcar, Ripon, Stockton-on-Tees Sunderland, Tynemouth

The colonial world

By the end of the World War I, the vast overseas empires of Britain and France – which now included Germany's African lands – were becoming increasingly expensive and difficult to maintain. Colonialism was criticized by the US and the USSR, and independence movements developed in India and a number of African territories, alongside a growing nationalism in Southeast Asia.

The European colonial powers maintained substantial armies within their empires, composed of both European and colonial troops.

The colonial world	

1901: Commonwealth of Australia proclaimed
1904: Partition of Bengal: nationalist agitation in India
1910: Union of South Africa set up
1920: Mahatma Gandhi gains control of Indian National Congress

1900 1905 1910 1915 1920 1925

1902: End of Boer War in South Africa
1906: Foundation of All-India Muslim League
1911: Italian conquest of Libya
1919: Amritsar massacre leads to surge in Indian nationalism

GLOBAL MIGRATION

The Japanese shipping line *Osaka Shoshen Kaisha* carried thousands of immigrants to the US.

THE TECHNICAL INNOVATIONS of the Industrial Revolution made the 19th-century world seem a much smaller place. Railroads could quickly transport large human cargoes across continents, the Suez and Panama canals reduced travel times – sometimes by as much as 50%, and ships became larger, faster, and more seaworthy. The mechanization and centralization of industry required the concentration of labor on a scale never seen before. At the same time, the European imperial powers were exploiting their tropical possessions for economic benefit. Cash crops, grown on large plantations, needed a plentiful supply of labour as well. Political upheaval, wars, and economic hardship provided the most dramatic impetus to emigration – especially in the Russian Empire and Central Europe, and in southeastern China.

Migration in the 19th century

More than 80 million people emigrated from their country of origin during the 19th and early 20th centuries. Over half of them moved across the Atlantic to North and South America. The end of the American Civil War in 1865, and the opening up of Native American land to settlers saw the greatest period of immigration to the US and Canada. In the Russian Empire, movement was eastward from European Russia into Siberia and the Caspian region. Europeans moved south and east to take up employment in the colonies, while indentured laborers traveled to the Americas, Africa, and Southeast Asia.

Pogroms, or riots against Jews were frequent in late 19th-century Russia. Many fled following the riots; others were formally expelled from designated areas such as St. Petersburg (*above*).

❶ World migration c.1860–1920 ▶

Transatlantic migration
- ➡ to North America
- ➡ to South America and the Caribbean
- ➡ to Europe from the Americas

Other European migration
- ➡ to Australia and New Zealand
- ➡ to North Africa

Asian migration
- ➡ to the Americas and Australia
- ➡ Russian migration into Siberia
- ➡ Indian intercolonial migration

- - - - transcontinental railroad
- ▨ major exporters of people
- ▨ major importers of people

Migrants who crossed from Europe to the US and Canada were prepared to undergo extreme hardship and overcrowding (*above*).

In order to gain entry and acceptance, many immigrants made strenuous efforts to emulate the manners and dress of their new country (*left*).

Migration to the New World

1818: 20,000 Irish emigrate to US as a result of famine

1845–54: Irish Potato Famine leads 1.6 million to emigrate

1849: California Gold Rush draws large numbers of migrants from Europe, Australia, Chile, and China

1882: Beginning of major Jewish emigration from Russian Empire
1882: 80,000 Scandinavians emigrate to US

1900: Start of major Italian emigration to US and Argentina; by 1910, more than two million have arrived

1816–17: Emigration from southwest Germany following Napoleonic wars

1831–41: 200,000 people leave Ireland for Canada, many traveling on to the US

1848–49: Revolutions lead to political crackdown and exodus of democrats from Central Europe

1850s: Height of emigration from England and Scotland: more than 50,000 per year

1881–90: Peak years of German emigration to US (1,300,000)

1888: Abolition of slavery in Brazil; next decade sees over a million immigrants

`1800   1820   1840   1860   1880   1900`

② The great Jewish migration, 1880–1914

- major concentration of Jews in the Russian Empire (the "Pale")
- region with emigrating Jewish population
- region with substantial Jewish immigration
- ✹ region where pogroms occurring
- ● gateway city
- → Sephardic Jews
- → Ashkenazi Jews
- **70,000** number of Jewish immigrants 1880–1914

New York's Lower East Side became one of the most prominent areas of Jewish settlement. People were able to join up with family members who had traveled earlier.

Central and South America (excluding Argentina): 14,000

UNITED STATES 2 million

CANADA 105,000

ARGENTINA 113,000

New York

SOUTH AFRICA 43,000 Cape Town

PALESTINE 70,000

SEE ALSO:

North America: pp.132–133

South America: pp.150–151

Africa: pp.166–167

Europe: pp.202–205

West Asia: pp.232–233

South and Southeast Asia: pp.250–251

North and East Asia: pp.270–271

Australasia and Oceania: pp.282–283

Jewish migration

The French Revolution, the Napoleonic Wars, and the unification of Italy and Germany heralded an unprecedented era of liberalization for many of Europe's Jews. However, in 1795 the annexation of Poland gave the Russian Empire control over the world's largest Jewish community. Legal persecution, including military conscription, gave way to a more liberal attitude under Alexander II. His assassination in 1881 provoked more than 20 years of government-sanctioned pogroms against the Jews. Mass migration followed: to the New World - especially the US - and to western Europe.

The great Jewish migration

1791: French Revolution grants Jews political equality and full citizenship

1796: Napoleon frees Italian Jews from the ghettos

1808: Several German principalities grant citizenship to Jews, which is reversed after fall of Napoleon

1848: Partial or complete emancipation of Jews in Sweden, Denmark, Austria, and Greece

1870–71: Full emancipation of Jews throughout Italy and German Empire

1880: c.4,900,000 Jews living in "Pale of Settlement" in Russian Empire

1881: Assassination of Tsar Alexander II provokes first pogroms against Russia's Jews

1882: Jews expelled from Moscow, St. Petersburg and Karkhov

1903: Pogrom at Kishinev

1905: Jewish National Fund established to buy land in Palestine

(1775 · 1800 · 1825 · 1850 · 1875 · 1900 · 1925)

Indentured labor

The 19th-century migration of people from the Indian subcontinent dates from the abolition of slavery in the British Empire and French colonies which created a severe labor shortage on the plantations. Migrants – or indentured laborers – were hired for a period of three to five years, in exchange for the price of the passage and a given wage. During this period too, large numbers of Indians settled in eastern and southern Africa. Between about 1852 and 1900 at least 2,300,000 Chinese emigrated – on a similar basis – to North America, Australia, New Zealand, and Southeast Asia. Often fleeing famine and war, they were employed to do arduous labor, building railroads, and mining gold and tin.

The first wave of Chinese immigrants to the US came during the Gold Rush of 1849. Later, thousands of Chinese worked on the construction of the transcontinental railroads.

③ The movement of indentured labor

Migration mid-18th century to early 20th century
- core area of Indian migration
- core area of Chinese migration
- → Indian migrants
- → Chinese migrants

THE WORLD 1925–1950

THOUGH THE PARTIES to the Versailles Treaty of 1919, which followed World War I, hoped for stability, the League of Nations, set up in 1920, proved ineffective. By 1939 expansionist nationalism in Germany, Italy, and Japan led once more to war on a massive scale. World War II devastated Europe, Asia, and the USSR, killing more than 50 million people – among them perhaps 21 million Soviet citizens and more than six million Jewish civilians. The real victors of the war were the US and the USSR, who emerged as the world's most powerful nations. The great empires of Britain and France began to fragment under the financial strain of war and the rise of independence movements in their territories, beginning with India in 1947.

Adolf Hitler used vast rallies such as this one at Nuremberg to muster his followers and show the world the strength of his popular support.

Europe

Germany's humiliation at Versailles, alongside economic depression, created the conditions for a revival of aggressive German nationalism. In its efforts to create a greater Germany, Hitler's Nazi party seized much of continental Europe and launched a policy of genocide against European Jews. Only with US intervention and a resurgent Soviet Union was their advance finally halted.

Europe

1925: Josef Stalin comes to power in USSR	**1933:** Hitler becomes Chancellor in Germany	**1936:** Great Terror in the USSR	**1939:** Britain and France declare war on Germany after invasion of Poland	**1945:** German surrender ends war in Europe	**1948:** Communists take over in Czechoslovakia and Hungary
1925	1930	1935	1940	1945	1950
1931: Collapse of central European banks leads to major recession		**1936:** Spanish Civil War begins	**1938:** German invasion of Czechoslovakia	**1942:** Hitler starts mass extermination of Jews	**1948–49:** Berlin airlift to counter Soviet blockade of the city

SCHEMATIC MAPS

The subway and metro maps produced in the 1930s are some of the simplest, yet most sophisticated maps ever produced. Using bold, clearly differentiated colored lines for routes, and clear symbols to represent stations, they made no attempt to reproduce distances accurately, and showed direction only roughly. This schematic approach helped travelers to identify their destination and the quickest way to reach it.

The London Underground map devised by Harry Beck in 1931 and printed in 1933 is one of the most famous topological maps. Its design is based on electrical circuit diagrams.

The Americas

The Wall Street Crash of 1929 plunged the US into a severe depression. Only with the war effort was the economy rejuvenated: the mobilization of industry established the US as the world's leading military and industrial power. In South and Central America, a number of states sought to diversify their economies and gain control over valuable mineral reserves in neighbouring countries. The Chaco War between Bolivia and Paraguay was the most serious of these conflicts prior to World War I.

Eva Perón was the charismatic wife of the Argentinian president Juan Perón. Her immense popularity helped to mask the ruthlessness of his regime.

The Americas

	1930: Military revolution in Brazil	**1933:** Franklin Roosevelt's New Deal begins		**1945:** United Nations established in New York	**1946:** Juan Perón comes to power in Argentina
1925	1930	1935	1940	1945	1950
1929: Wall Street Crash starts Great Depression	**1932–35:** Paraguay defeats Bolivia in Chaco War		**1941:** US enters war following Japanese air attack on Pearl Harbor	**1947:** Marshall Plan drawn up to aid recovery in western Europe	

Among the first to benefit from antibiotics were US troops wounded in the Pacific theater of World War II.

ANTIBIOTICS

The discovery of penicillin in 1928 led to the creation of antibiotics, powerful drugs which were able to combat epidemic diseases such as tuberculosis. Over-prescription has led to many bacteria developing antibiotic immunity, prompting a search for new agents to combat disease.

South and East Asia

Japanese expansionism during the 1930s led to war with China in 1937, and in 1941 Japan's bombing of Pearl Harbor forced US entry into World War II. Chinese Communist and Nationalist forces held the Japanese at bay; after the war the Communists overwhelmed their former allies. In India the move to independence became irresistible following the war. In 1947 the British withdrew and the separate nations of India and Pakistan were created.

Gandhi's strategy against British rule in India was based on non-violent civil disobedience.

Southeast Asia and Oceania

In 1941–42 Japanese forces rapidly overran European troops throughout Southeast Asia, in a campaign of "liberation." Their eventual defeat by Allied forces nevertheless precipitated a widespread reluctance to return to colonial rule among the peoples of the region.

The mighty Japanese fleet was eventually destroyed by US planes launched from aircraft carriers.

SEE ALSO:

North America: pp.134–137

South America: pp.152–153

Africa: pp.168–169

Europe: pp.208–209

West Asia: pp.232–235

South and Southeast Asia: pp.250–251

North and East Asia: pp.272–273

Australasia and Oceania: pp.282–285

South and East Asia

1925: Civil war in China
1936: Japan signs anti-Comintern pact with Germany
1941: Russo-Japanese neutrality pact
1945: Atomic bombs at Hiroshima and Nagasaki force Japanese surrender
1949: Mao Zedong and Chinese Communists win Chinese Civil War

| 1925 | 1930 | 1935 | 1940 | 1945 | 1950 |

1926: Chiang Kai-shek begins Chinese reunification
1934: Start of the Chinese Communists' "Long March" to Yan'an
1937: War between China and Japan
1942: Japanese control much of South and East Asia; arrest of Congress leaders in India
1947: India and Pakistan gain independence

Southeast Asia and Oceania

1926–27: Rebellion against Dutch rule in Java and Sumatra
1942: Indonesia, Indochina, Malaya, the Philippines, New Guinea and Singapore seized by Japan
1945: Ho Chi Minh proclaims independent Vietnam
1949: Indonesia gains independence from the Dutch

| 1925 | 1930 | 1935 | 1940 | 1945 | 1950 |

1932: End of absolute monarchy in Siam (renamed Thailand in 1939)
1942: US navy halts Japanese expansion at battle of Midway in the Pacific
1946: Philippines become independent

The World in 1950

- United Kingdom and possessions
- France and possessions
- Denmark and possessions
- Spain and possessions
- Portugal and possessions
- Netherlands and possessions
- West Germany
- Japan and possessions
- Norway and possessions
- Belgium and possessions
- Italy and possessions
- New Zealand and possessions
- Australia and possessions
- US and possessions
- controlled by European Axis powers Nov 15 1942
- controlled by Japan Nov 15 1942

In 1948 the UK blockaded the seas around Israel to prevent ships carrying Jewish refugees from landing. The 700 Jews aboard this ship swam safely to shore at Haifa using a lifeline.

Africa and West Asia

At the end of World War I Britain and France gained control over much of North Africa and West Asia – especially the oil-producing nations. In World War II the Horn of Africa and North Africa became battlegrounds; Italian and German forces were eventually defeated. A new state of Israel was proclaimed for the survivors of Nazi Germany's genocide of European Jews in 1948. Conflict over Israel's disputed territorial boundaries remained unresolved for over 50 years.

Africa and West Asia

1935: Italian invasion of Ethiopia in attempt to found empire
1941: Germans advance into Egypt
1945: Foundation of Arab League
1948: Foundation of state of Israel leads to war in Middle East

| 1925 | 1930 | 1935 | 1940 | 1945 | 1950 |

1932: Foundation of kingdom of Saudi Arabia
1936: Arab revolt in Palestine against Jewish immigration
1942: British halt German advance at battle of El Alamein
1948–49: National Party wins power in South Africa with a commitment to apartheid

WORLD WAR II

Adolf Hitler's National Socialist (NAZI) party was underpinned by extreme nationalism and racism, enforced though a police state.

WORLD WAR II was a protracted struggle by a host of Allied nations to contain, and eventually destroy, the political, economic, social, and territorial ambitions of the Axis, a small group of extreme nationalist (fascist) states led by Germany and Japan. The struggle led to the mobilization of manpower and economic might on an unprecedented scale, a deployment of forces on land, sea, and air globally, and the prosecution of war far beyond the front line, deep into the civilian hinterland in all theaters. For these reasons it has been called a "Total War." Its human costs were enormous, variously estimated at between 50 and 60 million dead, and its conclusion – with the detonation of two atomic bombs over Japan – heralded the Nuclear Age.

World War II, 1939–41

Until May 1941 Japan and Germany fought and won localized conflicts: in a series of campaigns they conquered and denied isolated enemies the opportunity to gather support and mobilize potentially far superior resources. In summer 1941, with Britain isolated but for its empire, the German invasion of the Soviet Union and the Japanese move into Southeast Asia marked the point at which their separate conflicts changed and came together. Japan's provocation of the US and Germany's failure in Russia marked the end of Axis successes and the advent of global warfare.

The war to December 1941

Sep 1939: Invasion of Poland by Germany and Soviet Union	**Jun 1940:** Italy declares war on Britain and France	**Jun 1941:** Germany invades the Soviet Union (Operation Barbarossa)	**Dec 1941:** Japan attacks Pearl Harbor; US enters the war
Jan 1940	Jan 1941		Jan 1942
Sep 1939: Britain and France declare war on Germany	**Jun 1940:** German troops enter Paris; fall of France	**Jul–Oct 1940:** Battle of Britain waged in air over southern England	**Jul 1941:** Soviet Union and Britain sign pact of mutual assistance	**Dec 1941:** Germany declares war on US

① World War II, Sep 1939–Dec 1941 ▶

- political boundaries in 1939
- Axis and its allies in Mar 1940
- Allies in May 1940
- Allies by Dec 1941
- Axis territorial expansion by Jun 1940
- Axis territorial expansion by Dec 1941
- ◇ Axis satellites following the German invasion of France, May 1940
- neutral state

Japan's campaigns in Asia aimed to destroy British, US, and Dutch influence and create a "Greater East Asian Co-Prosperity Sphere" in the region.

Major battles: Dec 1941–Jul 1943

1	**Moscow**	Dec 1941	8	**Milne Bay**	Aug 1942
2	**Singapore**	Feb 1942	9	**Guadalcanal**	Aug 1942–Feb 1943
3	**Lashio**	Apr 1942	10	**El Alamein**	Oct–Nov 1942
4	**Kalewa**	May 1942	11	**Stalingrad**	Oct 1942–Feb 1943
5	**Corregidor**	May 1942	12	**Tunis**	Apr–May 1943
6	**Coral Sea**	May 1942	13	**Kursk**	Jun–Aug 1943
7	**Midway**	Jun 1942	14	**Minsk**	Jun–Aug 1943

World War II, 1941–43

By late 1942 Germany and Japan were isolated and besieged; they had to win the wars they had initiated or suffer defeat by the the massive forces ranged against them. Despite initial successes, their undoing was ensured by November 1942 with Anglo-American success in North Africa, the Soviet counter-offensive at Stalingrad, and US victories off Guadalcanal. By summer 1943 Allied consolidation in the Mediterranean, Soviet victory at Kursk and Japanese reverses at Guadalcanal and Milne Bay fatally compromised the Axis positions.

② World War II, Dec 1941–Jul 1943 ▶

- extent of Axis powers Dec 1942
- Allies Jul 1943
- Axis powers Jul 1943
- neutral state
- ● Allied base
- ● Axis base
- major battle

The war to July 1943

Feb 1942: Surrender of British forces to Japan in Singapore	**Aug 1942:** US bombing raids over Europe begin	**Oct–Nov 1942:** British defeat Germans at El Alamein
Feb 1942	Jan 1943	Apr 1943
Mar 1942: Dutch surrender East Indies to Japan	**Sep 1942:** Start of German siege of Stalingrad (ends Jan 1943)	**Jan 1943:** Roosevelt and Churchill meet at Casablanca

World War II, 1943–45

In 1943 Allied success was piecemeal and attritional; after June 1944 they achieved increasing depth of penetration and permanency of conquest. The Axis suffered escalating losses on the front line and in their heartlands. By August 1944 Germany's "Fortress Europe" was breached by the Soviets in Central Europe, and by Anglo-American forces in Italy and Normandy, while US victory in the Philippine Sea fatally split Japan's "Greater East Asian Co-Prosperity Sphere." However, Axis tenacity and the Allied insistence upon unconditional surrender, meant that peace would only be achieved with the devastation of Europe and Japan.

July 1943 to the end of the war

Jul 1943: Allied forces land in Sicily

Sep 1943: Italy surrenders to Allies; German forces occupy Milan and Rome

Aug 1944: Allied forces liberate Paris

Oct 1944: Battle of Leyte Gulf against Japan

May 1945: Germany surrenders

Aug 1945: Atomic bombs exploded over Hiroshima and Nagasaki

Oct 1943: Italy declares war on Germany

Nov 1943: Roosevelt, Stalin, and Churchill meet at Tehran

Jun 1944: D-Day: Allied landings in Normandy

Nov 1944: US begins direct aerial bombing of Japan

May 1945: Berlin surrenders to the Red Army

Sep 1945: Formal Japanese surrender

Jul 1943 — Jan 1944 — Jan 1945 — Oct 1945

SEE ALSO:

Europe: pp.210–211

West Asia: pp.234–235

South and Southeast Asia: pp.250–251

North and East Asia: pp.272–273

Heavily armored B17 or "Flying Fortress" bombers were used by US forces for high-level daylight bombing over Europe – leading to the devastation of many parts of Germany.

❸ World War II, Jul 1943–Aug 1945

- under Tripartite Pact powers control Jul 1943
- countries liberated by Allied forces by Feb 1945
- extent of Axis powers Jan 1945
- Allies in May 1945
- Axis powers in May 1945
- neutral state
- major battle

Global warfare

The spherical shape of the operational theater meant that the Allies could isolate the Axis on all fronts. Global warfare involved troops fighting far from their home nations. South Asians and Australasians fought in Africa and Europe, Europeans and Americans in Southeast Asia, and Siberians in Europe. Major shifts of population occurred in the US and USSR, producing enormous changes in patterns of trade and drawing in the economic involvement of neutrals. The powerhouse of the Allied cause was the US, which alone raised a hundred military divisions, as well as supplying aid to its allies with a cash value equivalent to 2000 infantry divisions. At peak production, US industry built an aircraft every 294 seconds and 130 merchantships in a single month.

The "Big Three" Allied leaders - Stalin, Churchill, and Roosevelt - met at Yalta in February 1945 to discuss the postwar division of the fatally weakened Nazi Empire.

Major battles: Jul 1943–Aug 1945

1	Kiev	Sep–Oct 1943
2	Anzio	Jan–Mar 1944
3	Monte Cassino	Jan–May 1944
4	Mariana Islands	Jun–Aug 1944
5	Normandy	Jun–Jul 1944
6	Arnhem	Sep 1944
7	Leyte Gulf	Oct 1944
8	Ardennes	Dec 1944–Feb 1945
9	Iwo Jima	Feb–Mar 1945
10	Königsberg	Feb–Apr 1945
11	Okinawa	Mar–Jun 1945
12	Vienna	Apr 1945
13	Prague	May 1945
14	Berlin	May 1945

The human cost of global war

More than 80 million troops were mobilized by the Allied and Axis powers during the war. Nearly one-third of them were killed or injured. The civilian cost was equally high, particularly in the Soviet Union and among Europe's Jews and other minorities, who were systematically exterminated by both the Nazis and the Soviets. The scale of Japanese atrocities in China remains unknown.

❹ Global warfare

- maximum extent of Axis powers in Europe/Russia
- maximum extent of Japanese expansion in Asia/Pacific

Movement of troops

Axis
- German
- Japanese

Allies
- British
- British Commonwealth
- American
- Soviet

The Second World War: mobilization and casualty figures

Country	Troops mobilized	Military casualties	Civilian casualties
US	11,490,000	292,100	–
Canada	780,000	39,319	–
New Zealand	150,000	12,162	–
Australia	680,000	29,395	–
South Africa	140,000	8681	–
Norway	25,000	4780	–
Finland	250,000	79,047	–
Soviet Union	20,000,000	14,500,000	c.7,000,000
Poland	1,000,000	850,000	5,778,000
Czechoslovakia	180,000	6683	310,000
Hungary	350,000	750,000 military and civilian	
Romania	600,000	519,822	465,000
Bulgaria	450,000	18,500	1500
Greece	150,000	16,357	155,300
Yugoslavia	3,740,000	1,700,000 military and civilian	
Italy	4,500,000	279,820	93,000
France	5,600,000	210,671	173,260
Belgium	800,000	9561	75,000
Netherlands	500,000	13,700	236,300
Great Britain	4,600,000	271,311	60,595
Germany	10,800,000	2,850,000	2,300,000
Japan	7,400,000	1,506,000	300,000
India	2,400,000	36,092	–
China (Nationalist)	3,800,000	1,324,000	c.10,000,000
China (Communist)	1,200,000	Not known	Not known
Denmark	Not known	4339	–
Spain	Not known	23,000 military and civilian	

Women such as these aviation engineers were enormously important to the booming US defence industry.

THE WORLD 1950–1975

WORLD POLITICS IN THE ERA following the close of World War II were defined by the tense relationship between the US and the USSR. The "Cold War" between democratic capitalism and Communism saw each side constantly attempting to contain and subvert the other. The Korean War (1950–55), the Cuban Missile Crisis of 1962, and the Vietnam War (1954–75), as well as many smaller conflicts – particularly in Central America and Africa – were all manifestations of the Cold War. Though no nuclear weapons were ever used in anger, both sides built up huge nuclear arsenals whose potential for mass destruction acted as a deterrent to conflict on a global scale.

Europe

During the Soviet era the May Day parade in Moscow's Red Square became the focus for the USSR's display of its military might. Weapons such as these ballistic rockets were wheeled through the streets.

The 1950s and 1960s were a period of widespread prosperity and political stability in Western Europe, faltering only in the early 1970s. West Germany, banned from keeping a large army, rebuilt its shattered economy and infrastructure with stunning success. Eastern Europe was overshadowed by Soviet Communism, which restricted both economic development and the personal freedom of its citizens.

Europe

1955: Warsaw Pact created as Soviet-bloc opponent of NATO
1957: Creation of European Economic Community (EEC)
1961: Berlin Wall separates East and West Berlin
1968: "Prague Spring" reforms in Czechoslovakia crushed by USSR
1973: Oil crisis causes inflation and economic slowdown

1950 — 1955 — 1960 — 1965 — 1970 — 1975

1956: Hungarian revolt crushed by Warsaw Pact
1957: First artificial satellite, Sputnik II, launched by USSR
1968: Student uprisings throughout Europe
1969: De Gaulle resigns after defeat in referendum on regional reform

SATELLITE IMAGERY

With space technology came the ability to keep artificial satellites in permanent orbit around the Earth. They are used to carry transmitters for telecommunications, as aids to navigation and as bases for space exploration. The data picked up by sensors can be digitally combined to create images of the Earth.

This satellite image of North and South America shows both vegetation cover and weather conditions at the time at which it was taken.

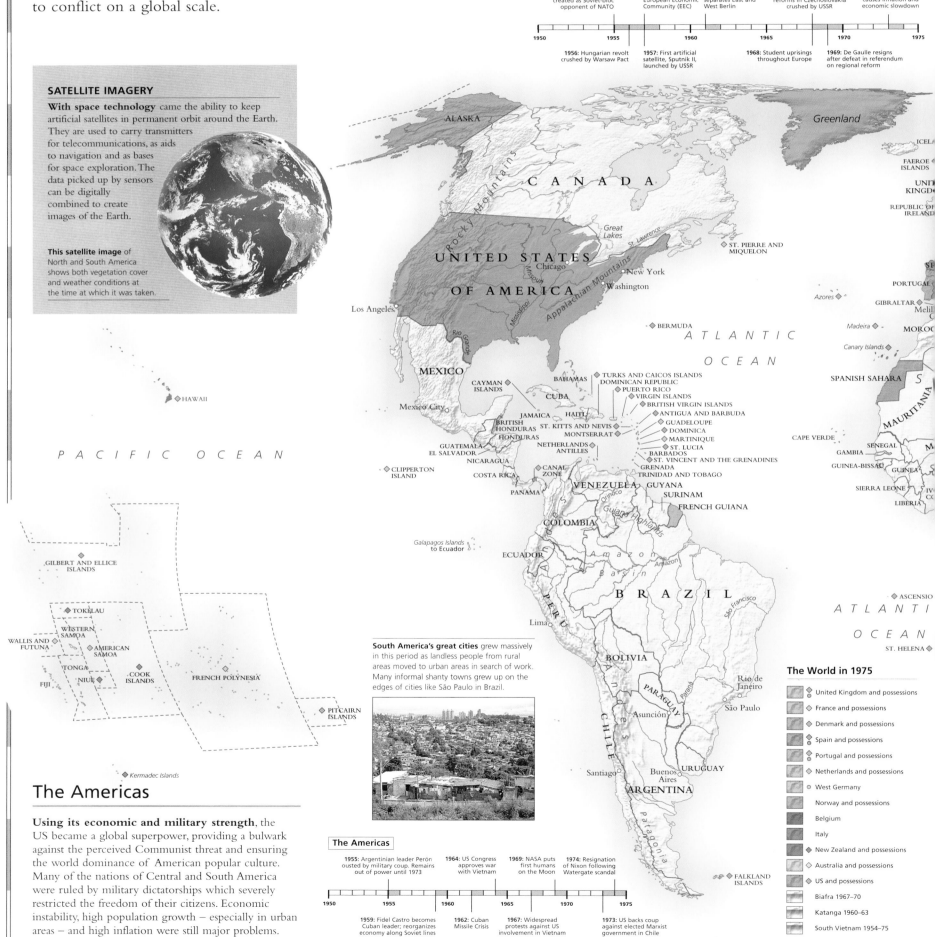

South America's great cities grew massively in this period as landless people from rural areas moved to urban areas in search of work. Many informal shanty towns grew up on the edges of cities like São Paulo in Brazil.

The Americas

Using its economic and military strength, the US became a global superpower, providing a bulwark against the perceived Communist threat and ensuring the world dominance of American popular culture. Many of the nations of Central and South America were ruled by military dictatorships which severely restricted the freedom of their citizens. Economic instability, high population growth – especially in urban areas – and high inflation were still major problems.

The Americas

1955: Argentinian leader Perón ousted by military coup. Remains out of power until 1973
1964: US Congress approves war with Vietnam
1969: NASA puts first humans on the Moon
1974: Resignation of Nixon following Watergate scandal

1950 — 1955 — 1960 — 1965 — 1970 — 1975

1959: Fidel Castro becomes Cuban leader; reorganizes economy along Soviet lines
1962: Cuban Missile Crisis
1967: Widespread protests against US involvement in Vietnam
1973: US backs coup against elected Marxist government in Chile

The World in 1975

- United Kingdom and possessions
- France and possessions
- Denmark and possessions
- Spain and possessions
- Portugal and possessions
- Netherlands and possessions
- West Germany
- Norway and possessions
- Belgium
- Italy
- New Zealand and possessions
- Australia and possessions
- US and possessions
- Biafra 1967–70
- Katanga 1960–63
- South Vietnam 1954–75

Intense rivalry between Israel and Egypt led in June 1967 to the Six Day War. Superior Israeli air power routed the Egyptian air force and the ground forces of Egypt, Jordan, Iraq, and Syria.

West and South Asia

Israel, supported by Western powers, fought a series of wars with its Arab neighbors to define its boundaries. The exploitation of extensive oil reserves brought immense wealth to the undeveloped Arabian Peninsula. Relations between India and Pakistan were strained by territorial disputes, and in 1971, the geographical separation of Pakistan proved unsustainable, with East Pakistan becoming Bangladesh.

West and South Asia

1952: First Indian general election won by Congress Party

1961: Foundation of Organization of the Petroleum Exporting Countries (OPEC)

1965: India–Pakistan War over sovreignty of Kashmir

1971: Pakistan divides; East Pakistan becomes Bangladesh

1973: OPEC restricts flow of oil to world markets

| 1950 | 1955 | 1960 | 1965 | 1970 | 1975 |

1956: Pakistan constituted as Islamic Republic

1967: Israel defeats Egypt and other Arab nations in Six Day War

1973: Arab states fail to defeat Israel in Yom Kippur War

East and Southeast Asia

In China and mainland Southeast Asia, power passed to native Communist movements. Mao Zedong's Communist China became a superpower to rival the USSR, while the US intervened in Korea and Vietnam in response to the perceived threat of Communism. Japan began rebuilding its economy with American aid to become, by the mid-1970s, one of the world's richest nations. From 1950 onward, mainland Southeast Asia was destabilized by Cold War–inspired conflict: in Laos, Vietnam, and Cambodia.

The political thoughts of Mao Zedong were published as the "Little Red Book" and distributed to all Communist Party members.

East and Southeast Asia

1950: Outbreak of Korean War

1958: Start of Mao's "Great Leap Forward" in China

1965: US troops sent to Vietnam – bombing of North begins

1975: US-backed South Vietnam regime falls

| 1950 | 1955 | 1960 | 1965 | 1970 | 1975 |

1954: Independence of Laos, Cambodia, and North and South Vietnam

1962: US military advisors sent to assist South Vietnamese regime

1966–70: Mao Zedong imposes Cultural Revolution in China

SEE ALSO:

North America: pp.136–137

South America: pp.152–153

Africa: pp.168–169

Europe: pp.212–213

West Asia: pp.234–235

South and Southeast Asia: pp.250–253

North and East Asia: pp.274–275

Australasia and Oceania: pp.284–285

THE MICROCHIP

The miniaturization of transistors and other electronic components, allowed complete electronic circuits to be created on a single slice of silicon about the size of a human fingernail. The first microprocessor chip, the Intel 4004, was produced in the USA in 1971.

Most modern electronic devices use a number of integrated circuits like this.

Africa's post-colonial era provided rich pickings for a series of corrupt military dictators such as President Mobutu, who ruled Zaire from 1965–97.

Africa

A succession of former colonies became independent from 1957 onward; by 1975, 41 African counties had become independent. Few were fully prepared for the demands of independence, and many countries remained pawns in the Cold War, armed by the opposing powers, and fighting wars on behalf of their conflicting ideologies.

Africa

1956: UK fails to block Egypt's nationalization of Suez Canal

1960: Fifteen African countries gain independence; South Africa leaves Commonwealth

1962: Nelson Mandela, leader of ANC, given life sentence in South Africa

1975: Angola and Mozambique gain independence from Portugal

| 1950 | 1955 | 1960 | 1965 | 1970 | 1975 |

1954: Algerian uprising against French rule

1957: Ghana becomes first British colony to achieve independence

1960: Katanga province secedes from Republic of Congo (Zaire); UN intervention follows

1967–70: Civil war in Nigeria over secession of oil-rich east (Biafra). Over one million die

THE COLD WAR

Spies, such as the Rosenbergs, executed in 1953 for passing US nuclear secrets to the USSR, were endemic during the Cold War.

FROM THE MEETING OF US AND SOVIET FORCES on the Elbe River in April 1945 came a division of Europe and a confrontation between the former allies which would last for almost five decades. Defensive needs – for the US the security of Western Europe, for the USSR a buffer zone in Eastern Europe – which appeared to each other to be of offensive intents, overlaid by ideological, political, and economic rivalries. Thus the Cold War took shape, with the US committed to a policy of containment and attrition by all means just short of open conflict, and the USSR intent on supporting anti-Western revolutionary movements throughout the world. Strategic and armed stalemate gave rise to détente in the 1970s, but only the collapse of Soviet system in 1989–91 ended the Cold War.

The Cuban missile crisis 1961–62

The Cold War's most dangerous single episode arose from the Castro Revolution (1956–59) and subsequent US–Cuban estrangement. Castro's alignment with the Eastern bloc provided the USSR with an opportunity to offset its strategic inferiority by the creation of Cuban bases from which missiles could strike at the heart of the continental US. This was forestalled by a US blockade, and a stand-off following which the Soviets were forced to withdraw their missiles.

Cold warriors J. F. Kennedy and Nikita Khrushchev underestimated each other's strength and determination when they met in Vienna in 1961. By 1962 they had taken the world to the verge of nuclear conflict during the Cuban missile crisis.

Cold War crises 1956–64

1956–59: Cuban Revolution under Fidel Castro

Apr 1961: USSR launches first manned space flight

1962: Cuban missile crisis

1956 1958 1960 1962 1964

1957: USSR launches first space satellite

1961: Increasing US involvement in Vietnam

1964: Kubrick's film *Dr. Strangelove* alerts public to dangers of Mutually Assured Destruction (MAD)

Scale varies with perspective

4990 km (3100 miles)

N

4440 km (2760 miles)

◀ ❷ **The Cuban missile crisis 1961-62**

potential range of Soviet missiles (1100 miles)

US blockade zone

⊕ Soviet missile and jet base

⊕ US air base

⊙ US naval base

★ Apr 1961: CIA-backed invasion force of Cuban exiles aborted at Bay of Pigs

On June 23, 1948, the Soviet army blockaded the Western-controlled sectors of Berlin, forcing the Allied powers to mount a massive airlift to supply the beleaguered enclave.

NATO and the Warsaw Pact

Deepening US–Soviet hostility, plus Western Europe's patent inability to defend itself, led to the creation of the North Atlantic Treaty Organization (NATO) in April 1949; in effect, the US provided guarantee of Western Europe's security. The latter's continuing war-weariness saw a buildup of US forces in Europe, and contributed to the decision to permit West Germany to have armed forces, admitting the nation to NATO in 1955. This in turn prompted the USSR and its satellite countries in Eastern Europe to form the Warsaw Pact. The building of the Berlin Wall in 1961 consolidated the "Iron Curtain" which divided Europe into two zones – East and West – until 1989.

The Cold War in Europe 1947–68

1948: Berlin airlift following Soviet blockade of Berlin

1948: Soviet-sponsored regimes established in Czechoslovakia and Hungary

1955: Formation of Warsaw Pact

1957: Treaty of Rome; basis of European Economic Community

1968: Reforms in Czechoslovakia suppressed by Soviets

1950 1955 1960 1965

1947: Marshall Plan for US economic aid to Europe

1955: West Germany admitted to NATO

1956: Uprisings in Poland and Hungary crushed by Soviets

1961: Berlin Wall built

❸ **The Cold War in Europe**

original NATO members in 1949

later NATO members (with dates)

Warsaw Pact members in 1955

neutral states

❶ The alliances of the Cold War

US, allies, and satellite states

- US and original NATO 1949
- later NATO
- NATO dependencies 1960
- other nations allied to the Western bloc by treaty
- ☾ CENTO Pact 1959
- major US and NATO overseas bases

USSR and allies

- USSR
- Warsaw Pact 1955
- Communist satellite states
- China
- major Soviet overseas base
- ☆ Cold War flashpoint
- major US fleet

From the early 1960s the Western allies depended increasingly on long-range nuclear-powered submarines to deliver missiles in the event of war. With the development of Trident submarines in the 1980s the range extended to 4,500 miles, a key factor in the Strategic Arms Reduction (START) negotiations of 1982–91.

SEE ALSO:

North America: pp.138–139

South America: pp.152–153

Africa: pp.168–169

Europe: pp.212–215

West Asia: pp.234–235

South and Southeast Asia: pp.252–253

North and East Asia: pp.274–275

Australasia and Oceania: pp.284–285

Strategic manoeuvres in the Cold War

1947: Truman Doctrine seeks "containment" of USSR

1949: Formation of NATO

1972: SALT I strategic arms limitation talks

1979: SALT II limitation agreement signed

1990: NATO and Warsaw Pact agree on conventional arms limitation in Europe

1945   1955   1965   1975   1985   1995

1945: Yalta Conference; division between Allies; origins of Cold War

1955: Formation of Warsaw Pact

1989–90: Collapse of Communism in Europe

1991: US and USSR sign START arms reduction treaty

The strategic balance

In the Cold War's first decade the US sought to contain the threat of global Communism by a series of regional treaties and alliances backed by economic and military strength. But by 1960, with a rift in Sino-Soviet relations splitting the Communist bloc, and as the simultaneous process of decolonization (endorsed by the US) deprived its European NATO allies of their global outreach, so the theater of the Cold War shifted from Europe to the developing world. Here a series of conflicts from Cuba to Vietnam saw both the US and the Communist world frequently fighting a war by proxy.

THE ARMS RACE

As the Cold War arms race began, the US held technological, numerical, and positional advantages over the Soviet Union. In the 1960s, as US vulnerability increased, deterrence shifted from bombers to a triad built around submarine- and land-based intercontinental missiles (ICBMs). With the USSR acquiring ICBM capability by the late 1960s, both superpowers faced the future with secure second-strikes: MAD (Mutually Assured Destruction). This situation, and the development of multiple-warhead (MRV, MIRV) technology threatened a new round in the arms race. The 1970s saw ceilings on missile and warhead numbers, and antimissile defences (ABM) were limited (SALT I in 1972, and SALT II in 1979). The brief period of détente gave way to perhaps the most dangerous phase of the Cold War, one that witnessed ABM revival with the Strategic Defence Initiative (SDI, Star Wars) which only ended with the collapse of the USSR in 1991.

The Korean War 1950–53

Reluctantly sanctioned by the USSR, North Korea's invasion of the south in June 1950 was immediately seen as a test of US global credibility. The challenge was initially countered by a US-led UN force, which was met in turn by Chinese intervention. Thereafter the front stabilized around the prewar border. The US, confronted by the need to garrison Europe, and by a reluctance to carry the war beyond Korea's borders, accepted a policy of defensive self-restraint, which formed the basis of the Western Allies' Limited War doctrine.

▲ ❹ The Korean War 1950–53

- area controlled by North Korean forces Sep 15 1950
- front line Sep 15 1950
- US forces Sep 16–Oct 24 1950
- Chinese forces Oct 1950
- front line Nov 24 1950
- front line Jan 25 1951
- cease-fire line Jul 27 1953

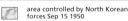

The Korean War effectively ended in stalemate in July 1953, with the partition of Korea into a Communist North and a nominally democratic South along an armistice line straddling the 38th parallel. This border has remained a heavily armed military frontier ever since. These South Korean troops were photographed in 1996.

The Angolan Civil War 1975–88

Ideological indoctrination by both East and West during the Cold War conflicts in the developing world was enforced irrespective of sex or age. The image of the child soldier is an enduring legacy of these conflicts in Africa.

By the 1970s Soviet naval and airlift capacity enabled it to give active support to anti-Western revolution globally. However, its major efforts in Africa, in Angola (1976–88) and Ethiopia (1977–89), were conducted by proxy via Cuba. In Angola, the three main organizations which had fought to end Portuguese rule were bitterly hostile to each other, and by 1975 there was a three-way civil war, the Marxist MPLA initially clearing the FNLA and UNITA from the north. The Soviets sustained the MPLA with Cuban troops, while the Western powers, through South Africa, secured southern borders in support of UNITA. The conflict lasted until 1988, the Cubans, MPLA and South Africa concluding an uneasy ceasefire. Throughout the struggle, UNITA dominated most of Angola through guerrilla warfare, but 50,000 Cuban troops ensured the survival of the MPLA.

❺ The Angolan Civil War from 1975

- under FNLA control 1975
- under MPLA control 1975
- under UNITA control 1975
- area of MPLA control by mid-1976
- area under UNITA control by mid-1976
- Cuban troops and Soviet aid to MPLA from 1975
- area of effective South African occupation
- South African attacks in support of UNITA 1976–88
- limit of UNITA guerrilla activity 1976–92

THE MODERN AGE

THE WORLD

WITH THE CLOSE OF THE COLD WAR IN 1989, rivalry between the US and the USSR ended. The USSR collapsed in 1991, and the former Eastern bloc was opened up to Western political influence and free-market forces. But hopes for a 'new world order' were premature. Russia suffered crises of confidence over democracy and capitalism. In the Middle East, disputes between Israel and her neighbours continued, while Islamic fundamentalism took hold in several countries. Saddam Hussein's regime in Iraq kept much of the region on constant standby for war. In Southeast Asia, massive investment during the 1980s fed an unsustainable economic boom, leading to depression in the late 1990s. South Africa's elections of 1994 were a triumph for democracy in Africa, but the following decade saw ethnic and resource-based conflict in many parts of the continent. After the atrocities of September 11, 2001, the US embarked on a so-called "war on terror" with military operations in Afghanistan and Iraq.

The Berlin Wall, hated symbol of division between East and West, was torn down in 1989, and Germany's two halves were reunited the following year.

Europe

While Western Europe progressed toward economic and political unity under the European Union (EU), eastern Europe was still economically constrained by Soviet Communism. But in 1989 popular movements rejected Communism, fracturing first the Eastern bloc and in 1991, the USSR itself. The fragmentation boiled over into civil war, notably in Yugoslavia and Georgia, where conflicts were fueled by ethnic nationalism.

Europe

1985: Mikhail Gorbachev becomes Soviet leader; moves to end Cold War	**1990:** East and West Germany reunited		**1995:** Ceasefire agreed in Bosnia and Herzegovina; UN troops remain		**2004:** Islamic extremist outrages in Madrid and North Ossetia, Russia

1975 — 1980 — 1985 — 1990 — 1995 — 2000 — 2005

1975: General Franco dies in Spain. He is replaced by King Juan Carlos
1989: End of Communism in Poland, Hungary, Czechoslovakia, Romania, East Germany, and Bulgaria
1991: Breakup of USSR; Start of civil war in Yugoslavia
1999: Kosovo crisis; Yugoslavia bombed

REMOTE-SENSED MAPPING

The detailed data collected by sensor-bearing satellites can be used to map changing geographic patterns. Examples include climatic conditions, soils, vegetation, pollution, and levels of urbanization.

An infrared satellite image of Buenos Aires taken from a French *SPOT* satellite shows densely populated urban areas in blue, vegetation in red, and water – including the River Plate – in black.

The Modern World

- Turkey
- United Kingdom and possessions
- France and possessions
- Denmark and possessions
- Spain and possessions
- Portugal and possessions
- Netherlands and possessions
- Russian Federation
- Japan and possessions
- Norway and possessions
- India and possessions
- Italy
- New Zealand and possessions
- Australia and possessions
- US and possessions

B-H Bosnia and Herzegovina

The traditional lifestyles of peoples such as the Yanomami of Brazil were under ever greater threat from the destruction of the rain forest and encroaching urbanization.

The Americas

From the end of the 1970s Central and South America began to move towards democracy, but economic instability and chronic inflation remained major problems. After the collapse of the USSR, the US maintained its economic dominance, but was less self-confident politically. All that changed after September 11, 2001, as the US embarked on a "war on terror" and a campaign against the "axis of evil" (Iran, Iraq and North Korea).

The Americas

1979: Start of civil war in Nicaragua between Sandinistas and US-backed Contras	**1987:** US and USSR agree to limit intermediate nuclear weapons	**1991–92:** USSR ends preferential trade agreement with Cuba	**1996:** Guatemalan civil war ends after 36 years

1975 — 1980 — 1985 — 1990 — 1995 — 2000 — 2005

1982: Falklands War between UK and Argentina
1989: Democracy restored in Chile as Pinochet steps down
1991: UN-brokered peace ends 10-year civil war in El Salvador
2001: Terrorist attacks kill almost 3000 in US

West and South Asia

Violence continued throughout the Middle East, often accompanied by the rise of fundamentalist Islam. Instability and open conflict affected much of the western region, particularly Lebanon, Iraq, Syria, Kuwait, and Saudi Arabia. The issue of Palestinian self-government proved as difficult as ever to resolve. In 2003 the EU, Russia, the UN and the US launched the "Road Map" to peace and a Palestinian state by 2005.

In 1979, an Islamic revolution led by the Ayatollah Khomeini overthrew the corrupt regime of the Shah of Iran. Iran became an Islamic state, vilifying the West, governed by religious laws, and ruthlessly suppressing political opposition.

East and Southeast Asia

From the late 1970s, China sought closer links with the West and began a program of industrial expansion and econonomic liberalization. As a result, China's economy grew rapidly, but calls for greater democracy were halted in 1989 following the massacre of students in Tiananmen Square. Elsewhere, the "tiger economies" of South Korea, Taiwan, and Singapore enjoyed a spectacular boom until the depression of the late 1990s.

Cheaper labor costs led many Western firms to relocate their production to Asia during the 1980s. In the 1990s service industries also began to outsource work to the East. British companies set up large numbers of call centers in India.

SEE ALSO:

North America: pp.136–137

South America: pp.152–153

Africa: pp.168–169

Europe: pp.214–215

West Asia: pp.234–235

South and Southeast Asia: pp.252–253

North and East Asia: pp.274–275

Australasia and Oceania: pp.284–285

West and South Asia

1979: Islamic revolution in Iran	**1980:** Start of Iran–Iraq War	**1989:** USSR withdraws from Afghanistan	**1990:** Iraqi invasion of Kuwait sparks Gulf War	**1998:** Indian and Pakistani nuclear tests	**2001:** US and allies oust Taliban from Afghanistan

1975   1980   1985   1990   1995   2000   2005

1977: Start of Middle East peace process	**1979:** Soviet invasion of Afghanistan	**1984:** Assassination of Indira Gandhi by Sikh bodyguards	**1988:** End of Iran–Iraq War	**1995:** Israeli-PLO agreement extends Palestinian self-rule within the West Bank	**2000:** Palestinian *intifada* relaunched	**2003:** US and allies invade Iraq, ousting Saddam Hussein

East and Southeast Asia

1989: Pro-democracy demonstrations in Beijing crushed	**1997:** Hong Kong returned to Chinese rule	**2000:** East Timor gains independence

1975   1980   1985   1990   1995   2000   2005

1975: Indonesia annexes East Timor	**1979:** Vietnamese invasion of Cambodia ousts Pol Pot	**1998:** Economic crisis in Indonesia leads to overthrow of government	**2001:** President Estrada ousted in Philippines

THE COMPUTER AGE

Computer technology has revolutionized the way in which business is conducted internationally. Information can be transmitted in seconds and decisions made with equal speed across continents and time zones.

Brokers in a trading office have access to information from across the world via their computers.

Africa

In South Africa, the breakdown of apartheid led to the first completely democratic elections, held in 1994. In East, Central, and West Africa, however, ongoing conflicts affected the lives of millions of people. In 2001 the Organization of African Unity launched NEPAD, the New Partnership for Africa's Development, intended to eradicate poverty and foster sustainable development and good governance.

Imprisoned from 1962–90 for his fight against apartheid, Nelson Mandela was finally able to vote for a democratic South Africa in 1994, becoming its first black premier.

Africa

1975: Independence in Angola and Mozambique followed by civil wars	**1987:** Famine in Ethiopia	**1994:** Nelson Mandela wins presidency of South Africa	**1997:** President Mobutu overthrown in Zaire	**2004:** Ethnic conflict and humanitarian crisis in W Sudan

1975   1980   1985   1990   1995   2000   2005

1986: US bombs Libya	**1994:** Massacre of 500,000 Tutsis by Hutu in Rwanda	**2001:** End of civil war in Sierra Leone	**2003:** EU intervention in Democratic Republic of Congo; peace accord signed

HIDDEN WORLDS OF TODAY

THE WORLD ECONOMY at the end of the 20th century was shaped increasingly by the investment practices and preferences of huge global businesses. The World Trade Organization (WTO), formed in 1995 and enshrining liberal free trade principles, found itself managing disputes between trade blocs as much as between individual countries. The phenomenon of globalization grew out of the rapid growth of digital processing technology and the expansion of telecommunications. But local communities continued to matter: ethnic origin, cultural affinity, shared history and religious identity connected communities across national boundaries. International terrorism, often driven by deep animosity toward the US and the Western world, together with the activities of international criminal networks, dominated the news media and public debate in the first years of the 21st century.

The production of illegal drugs occurs globally. These examples of "kef" (cannabis) and opium were made in Morocco.

The Greater African Nation

The African diaspora in the Americas, originating with the slave trade in the 16th–18th centuries, is today over 80 million strong. Only the Caribbean states have majority black populations, but African Americans in the US are the world's fourth largest black community and Brazil's population is also in the world top ten. The UK's black minority is a more recent result of post-war immigration, as is Portugal's. The black community has few political ties internationally, but a shared sense of identity and awareness of their African roots.

The developed world's inability, or unwillingness, to resource nutrition, education, and health in sub-Saharan Africa had its most dramatic effect in the establishment of HIV and AIDS in the region. By 2004, Kenya alone estimated that 14% of its population had HIV, and 1.1 million orphans had been created by AIDS.

In September 1997 the people of Scotland voted in favor of a separate Scottish parliament. These people are celebrating the 74% majority vote on the streets of Edinburgh.

❶ The greater African nation

Percentage of blacks in total population

- ◇ more than 65% (Africa)
- ◇ more than 65% (outside Africa)
- ◇ 35%–65%
- ◇ 10%–35%
- ◇ 1%–10%
- ◇ less than 1%

Devolution in Europe

Europe's new nation states of the 1990s emerged from the demise of the Soviet Union, the "velvet divorce" of Czechs from Slovaks, and the break-up of the former Yugoslavia. Eight of these countries – the Czech Republic, Estonia, Hungary, Latvia, Lithuania, Poland, Slovakia, and Slovenia – joined the EU in 2004, together with Malta and Cyprus. The Central and Eastern European countries formed a counterbalance to the supranational, federalizing inclinations of some "old Europe" members of the EU. Elsewhere, unresolved separatist aspirations and ethnic divisions resulted in armed conflict and, eventually, in uneasy peace agreements. Bosnia and Herzegovina now barely exists beyond its separate Serb and Muslim-Croat "entities", while even after the conflict of 1999 the future remained uncertain for ethnic Albanians nominally under Serbian rule in Kosovo.

❷ Devolution and statehood in Europe

- new state since 1990
- ◇ a degree of devolution acknowledged
- substantial ethnic groups without their own state
- ◉ pressure for greater self-determination

Serbian persecution of ethnic Albanians in the Kosovo region of the rump state of Yugoslavia led, in early 1999 to air strikes against Serbia by NATO and the murder or exodus of hundreds of thousands of refugees, "ethnically cleansed" from their former homes.

The pan-Islamic world

Sunni Islam is the dominant tradition in the Islamic world, encompassing some 90% of the world's one billion Muslims. The revivalist Salafi interpretation of the Sunni tradition – often known as "Wahhabism" – developed in Saudi Arabia and has taken hold in several parts of the Islamic world. In some cases, notably the activities of Osama bin Laden and the al-Qaeda movement, it has been associated with anti-Western terrorism. Shi'a Islam, with its reputation for religious zeal and martyrdom, is the majority religion in Iran.

The unity of the Muslim world is maintained by the annual pilgrimage to Mecca – the Haj. As many as two million pilgrims from all over the world congregate at the birthplace of Muhammad to perform a series of rituals at Islam's holiest shrines.

SEE ALSO:

North America: pp.138–139

South America: p152–153

Africa: pp.168–169

Europe: pp.214–215

West Asia: pp.234–235

South and Southeast Asia: pp.252–253

North and East Asia: pp.274–275

◀ ❸ The pan–Islamic World

Percentage of Muslims in population
- 91–100%
- 51–90%
- 21–50%
- 6–20%
- 1–5%
- less than 1%

Official status of Islam
- ☾ formally designated Islamic republic
- ⬤ secular state where population is more then 50% Muslim
- ☐ established religion is Islam
- ❋ membership of Organization of the Islamic Conference (OIC)
- ⚔ active conflict over militant Islam
- 💥 anti-western Islamic terrorist attack

The subterranean world of organized crime

Ease of travel and speed of communication encouraged the spread of organized crime syndicates far beyond national borders. As business became globalized, so too was corruption in business and finance; traditional criminal industries such as narcotics, prostitution, gambling, extortion, and money-laundering were transformed into global industries. Law enforcement had some successes in curtailing the Italian and US mafia, but the collapse of Communism in the Soviet Union created conditions in which a Russian mafia grew rapidly, becoming established across Eurasia and America. The big drug cartels, dealing in cocaine or heroin, fought for control of the production and distribution channels to the rich markets of North America and Europe. Profits, "laundered" through other businesses and exploiting the confidentiality of banking systems, were used to acquire increasing political influence and protection.

This "Internet Cafe" in Taiwan, offers diners access to the Internet while they eat.

THE WORLD WIDE WEB

Wide-area computer networking, developed originally for sharing information between academic institutions, expanded to become a worldwide Internet whose user numbers exploded in the 1990s. The big stimulus to its popular success was the creation of a graphical interface for "surfing" hyperlinked sites on what became known as the World Wide Web. The opportunities for anonymity, the use of encrypted communications, and the problems of authentication and copyright protection posed great difficulties for policing and control.

❹ The world of organized crime ▶

Narcotics production and trafficking
- ⬛ cannabis production
- ⬛ cocaine production
- ⬛ heroin production
- ⬛ heroin and cannabis production
- ➤ heroin trafficking
- ➤ cocaine trafficking
- ➤ cannabis trafficking

Major centers for criminal organizations
- ◆⬤ Mafia
- ◇⬤ Triads
- ⚲ major center for drug-related crime
- ☐ drug transit centers
- — "Golden Triangle"
- Ⓢ major center for money laundering
- ⬤ murder rate greater than 20 per 100,000, with figure

Extent of international organized crime
- Italian Mafia
- Chinese Triads
- Jamaican Posses
- Russian Mafia
- Colombian cartels
- Japanese Yakuzas
- United States Cosa Nostra
- Turkish Mafia

Human trafficking was, by the end of the 20th century, the single most lucrative and globalized activity for organized criminals. Slavery, the sex industry, debt bondage, economic migration, and the developed world's increasing reliance on cheap labor, fed a multi-billion dollar trade based on the recruitment, transportation, and exploitation of humans as mere commodities.

QUIBUS ADDIT.

PRO MUTATIONE HORIZONTIS

DIFFERENTES SPHÆRÆ POSI

TIONES

EARUMQUE

MUTUA CUM CIRC. CŒLESTIBUS

CONVENIENTIA ET RELATIO.

AUGUSTÆ VINDELICOR.

CURA ET STUDIO

MATTH. SEUTTERI, S.C.M.GEOGR.

PART TWO

REGIONAL HISTORY

INHABITANTS OF EACH PART of the globe view the history of the world through the lens of their regional heritage. The second section of this atlas presents the chronological story of eight principal geographic regions: North America, South America, Africa, Europe, West Asia, South and Southeast Asia, North and East Asia and, finally, Australasia and Oceania. Each regional narrative is prefaced by a map which examines its historical geography. This is followed by pages covering the exploration and mapping of the area, showing how it came to be known in its present form. Thereafter, the maps are organized to present the continuous historical development of each region through time.

By the 18th century, the modern world map was clearly emerging. This map, produced by the Dutch cartographer, Matthias Seutter in 1730, combines a series of detailed projections of the various hemispheres, with compass points depicted as a variety of different windheads.

ARCTIC OCEAN

North Pole

EURASIAN PLATE
NORTH AMERICAN PLATE

Sea of
Okhotsk

Siberia

East Siberian
Sea

BERINGIA

Kamchatka

Komandorskaya
Basin

Kuril Trench

Bering
Sea

Bering Strait

Aleutian
Basin

Bowers Ridge

Aleutian Islands

Aleutian Trench

NORTH AMERICAN PLATE
PACIFIC PLATE

Alaska Peninsula

Kodiak
Island

Gulf of
Alaska

Yukon

Greenland Sea

Norwegian Sea

Greenland

Iceland

REYKJANES
NORTH AMERICAN PLATE

Ellesmere
Island

Queen
Elizabeth Islands

Beaufort Sea

Banks Island

Parry Islands

Victoria Island

Baffin
Island

Baffin Bay

Davis Strait

Denmark Strait

Reykjanes Basin

Ice sheets stretched eastward from North America across Greenland and the northern reaches of the Atlantic Ocean as far as Europe.

North America was joined to Asia by the Beringia land bridge. The land bridge is thought to have been breached by rising sea levels 13,000 years ago.

About 12,000 years before the present, the huge ice cap began to melt, and a corridor through the ice sheet opened up.

During the last Ice Age, the global temperature was an average of 6°C cooler. Ice masses built up where the climate was both cold and moist, such as northern Europe and North America. The ice sheets in North America reached depths of 10,000 ft.

Mackenzie

Great Bear
Lake

Great Slave
Lake

LAURENTIDE
ICE SHEET

Hudson Bay

Hudson Strait

Foxe Basin

Labrador
Sea

Hudson Bay was covered with ice as recently as 8000 years ago. The land below the ice sank due to the weight of the ice cap. Water flooded the depression as the ice caps melted.

Labrador

Gulf of
St Lawrence

Mendocino Fracture Zone

Pioneer Fracture Zone

Gilbert Seamounts

Queen Charlotte
Islands

PACIFIC PLATE

JUAN DE FUCA PLATE

NORTH AMERICAN PLATE

Vancouver
Island

Cascadia
Basin

CORDILLERAN
ICE SHEET

ROCKY Mountains

Lake
Athabasca

Lake
Winnipeg

Lake
Manitoba

Canadian Shield

NORTH

Laurentian
Highlands

PACIFIC
OCEAN

Murray Fracture Zone

The 40,000 sq kms of the channel scrublands were formed when Lake Missoula's ice dam collapsed, flooding the outwash plain with water at a rate of more than 36 million cubic ft/sec, creating a deeply incised landscape. LAKE MISSOULA

LAKE
LAHONTAN

LAKE
BONNEVILLE

San Francisco Bay

Great Basin

Great Salt Lake

Columbia

Missouri

Great Plains

Lake Superior

Lake Michigan

Lake Huron

Great Lakes

Lake Ontario

Lake Erie

Mississippi

Ohio

Missouri

The Great Lakes formed in hollows created by the scouring action of massive glaciers during the Ice Age. As the glaciers and ice sheets melted, water filled the depressions.

The Great Salt Lake is all that remains of a vast glacial lake, Lake Bonneville, that occupied this part of North America during the last Ice Age.

The San Joaquin Valley in present-day California, was drowned by a vast lake towards the end of the last Ice Age.

AMERICA

Colorado
Plateau

Arkansas

Appalachian Mountains

Tennessee

New England

Berm

Tropic of Cancer

Molokai Fracture Zone

Clarion Fracture Zone

Lower California

Gulf of California

Colorado

Rio Grande

Sierra Madre Occidental

Sierra Madre Oriental

Rio Grande

Sigsbee Escarpment

The Florida peninsula was covered by a desert zone, with sandy dunes and low, scrubby vegetation.

Blake
Plateau

Blake-Bahama Ridge

Hatteras Plain

Sargas

Cedros Trench

Revillagigedo
Islands

East Pacific Rise

Campeche Bank

Gulf of Mexico

Mexico
Basin

Cuba

West

Greater Antil

Mathematicians
Seamounts

Orozco Fracture Zone

NORTH AMERICAN PLATE
COCOS PLATE

Yucatan
Peninsula

Yucatan Basin

Hispaniola

Jamaica

Tehuantepec Ridge

Middle America Trench

NORTH AMERICAN PLATE
CARIBBEAN PLATE

Nicaraguan
Rise

Caribbean
Sea

Clipperton Fracture Zone

COCOS PLATE
PACIFIC PLATE

Pacific Rise

Guatemala
Basin

Cocos Ridge

CARIBBEAN PLATE
COCOS PLATE

Isthmus of Panama

Panama
Basin

NAZCA
PLATE

Colombian
Basin

Equator

Siqueiros Fracture Zone

Colón Ridge

North America: 18,000 years ago

North America was greatly affected by the last Ice Age. Two massive ice sheets – the Cordilleran and Laurentide – merged to form an immense ice cap that covered most of the northern parts of North America. The southeast was mostly forest, and Florida was partially covered with an active desert dune system. The tropical rain forests in Central America were much smaller in area than at present.

Vegetation type

🔲	ice cap and glacier
🔲	tundra
🔲	polar and alpine desert
🔲	semidesert or sparsely vegetated
🔲	grassland
🔲	forest or open woodland
🔲	tropical rain forest
🔲	temperate desert
🔲	tropical desert
⟋	coastline (present-day)
⟋	coastline (18,000 years ago)

NORTH AMERICA
REGIONAL HISTORY

THE HISTORICAL LANDSCAPE

HUMANS FIRST ENTERED NORTH AMERICA FROM SIBERIA some 15,000 years ago. They migrated over the land bridge across the Bering Strait and, as the ice receded, moved south, into the rich gamelands of the Great Plains and onward to eventually populate Central and South America. As the ice melted and sea levels rose, these early settlers and their new homeland became isolated from Eurasia, and would remain so until the second millennium CE. The low population level and abundance of foods meant that sedentary agricultural life evolved only sporadically, some groups sustaining a hunting and gathering way of life to the present day. During this period of isolation, unique ecological, genetic, and social patterns emerged which proved disastrously fragile when challenged by the first European colonists in the 15th century CE. Within 500 years the indigenous cultures of North America had been destroyed or marginalized by waves of migrants from the Old World who, with astonishing energy and ferocity, transformed the continent into the World's foremost economic, industrial, and political power.

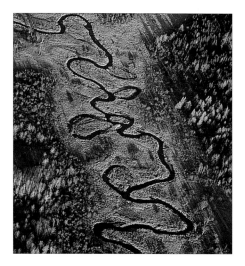

The gigantic basin drained by the Mississippi, spanning the entire tract between the Appalachians and the Rockies, provided a suitable environment for some of the first agricultural communities.

At the heart of the continent, it was the plains which provided homelands for Native North Americans, displaced and driven west by European immigrants.

The Central American mountain plateaus and uplands were where some of the earliest complex civilizations in the Americas developed. A combination of favorable climate and fertile land allowed plants to be cultivated and early agriculture to develop.

NORTH AMERICA
EXPLORATION AND MAPPING

Lewis (above) and Clark led an epic expedition to explore the west in 1805–06.

FOR MANY CENTURIES North America was untouched by contact with other continents. Viking seafarers en route from Iceland and Greenland made landfall at Newfoundland over 1,000 years ago, but their settlements were short-lived and their area of operation quite limited. Not until the early 16th century was the presence of a vast continent across the Atlantic fully accepted, and knowledge about it remained fragmentary. Once Europeans began to investigate North America, they were able to draw heavily on information from indigenous peoples, and use their preexisting trails to explore the continent.

This map of three villages showing their positions relative to the Sun and Moon was painted on a cured buffalo skin by members of the Qapaw tribe.

Native American maps

The indigenous peoples of North and Central America had detailed knowledge of the continent long before the first European expeditions. Much knowledge was undoubtedly passed on orally. But the location of early petroglyph maps carved on rocks suggests that they may have been produced as guides for traveling hunters, and to define territorial boundaries. Later maps – sometimes produced at the request of Europeans – reveal an intimate knowledge of the landscape and principles of space and distance. Several tribes used maps to show the long history of their tenure of the land when they were fighting for territory during the Indian removals of the 19th century.

Early European explorers

Though the first Europeans to visit North America were 10th-century Vikings, European exploration began in earnest in the late 15th century when improvements in shipping made the longer exploratory voyages of Columbus and Cabot viable. By the mid-16th century Spanish-sponsored expeditions in search of gold and territory founded settlements in Florida, Central America, and the Caribbean, and explored the lands of the southeast and southwest. Meanwhile, English and French expeditions traced the Atlantic coast in detail, moving north in search of new routes to Asia.

❶ The first European explorers of North America

Norse expeditions
→ Bjarni Herjolfsson 985–86
→ Leif Eriksson 1003
→ Thorvald Eriksson 1005–12

Spanish and Portuguese expeditions
→ Christopher Columbus 1492–93
→ Miguel Corte-Real 1501, 1502
→ Christopher Columbus 1502–04
→ Hernán Cortés 1519–21
→ Juan Ponce de León 1513
→ Panfilo de Narváez and Álvar Núñez Cabeza de Vaca 1528–36
→ Francisco de Ulloa 1539–40
→ Hernando de Soto 1539–43
→ Francisco Vázquez de Coronado and Garcia Lopez de Cardeñas 1540–42
→ Sebastián Vizcaíno 1602–03

English expeditions
→ John Cabot 1497
→ Martin Frobisher 1576–77
→ Francis Drake 1579
→ John Davis 1585–87
→ Henry Hudson 1610–11

French expeditions
→ Giovanni da Verrazano 1524
→ Jacques Cartier 1535–36
→ Samuel de Champlain 1604–07

○ European settlement
1608 and date of foundation

985: Bjarni Herjolfsson sights land west and south of Greenland

1610: Hudson reaches a "spacious sea"

1535: Cartier starts expedition into St. Lawrence River

1497: Cabot raises English flag on northern tip of Newfoundland

L'Anse aux Meadows c.1000

Quebec 1608

1524: Verrazano anchors close to present-day New York and is met by friendly native peoples

1579: Drake sails north after raiding ports in Pacific South America. On landing near San Francisco Bay, he names the land New Albion

1542: Coronado's expedition sees vast herd of buffalo on Great Plains

Chesapeake Bay

Jamestown 1607

Santa Fe 1609

1541: Mississippi crossed for the first time by Europeans

1513: de León's ships land at Florida, believing it to be an island

San Agustín 1565

1492: Christopher Columbus sights land now thought to be one of the Bahamian Islands

La Paz 1535

Guadalajara 1531

Tampico 1528

Tenochtitlán (Mexico City)

1521: Cortés destroys Aztec capital Tenochtitlán

Vera Cruz 1519

Acapulco 1565

1529–34: Cabeza de Vaca and three men including African Estebán are only survivors of Narváez expedition after being enslaved by coastal Indians

San Juan 1509

Santiago de Cuba 1513

Santo Domingo 1496

1513: Vasco Núñez de Balboa is first explorer to sight Pacific Ocean

1000 km
1000 miles

15th- and 16th-century European expeditions

1497: Cabot lands on Newfoundland

1501: Miguel Corte-Real enslaves 50 Indians from Beothuk

1524: Verrazano sails up Atlantic coast as far as Nova Scotia

1539–43: De Soto explores southeastern North America

1492: Columbus lands in the Bahamas thinking he has reached Asia

1513: Ponce de León traces coast of Florida

1528: Cabeza de Vaca explores Gulf of Mexico and southwest

1534: Cartier begins exploration of St. Lawrence

This map of Florida and Chesapeake Bay (above) was painted in the late 16th century. The spatial relationships are very inaccurate, with the Caribbean islands depicted much too far to the north.

European explorers were astonished by the quantity of wildlife they encountered in North America (left). Fur-bearing animals such as beavers were quickly exploited for their pelts.

Exploring the eastern interior

The rich Atlantic fisheries and the bounteous wildlife of the northeast were magnets for European hunters and fishermen, and many of the earliest settlements were fur-trading posts. Samuel de Champlain, aided by Iroquois and Montagnais, explored the St. Lawrence River and the Great Lakes, while Hudson and Davis ventured further west into Canada's great bays. Other expeditions were undertaken for missionary purposes, including Jolliet's Mississippian journey, where he was accompanied by Father Marquette. During the late 17th and early 18th centuries, several expeditions sought routes through the Appalachians, which would open up the Midwest to settlers.

One of America's great frontiersmen, Daniel Boone, is shown here leading a group of settlers through the Cumberland Gap, a pass through the Appalachian system which provided a route to the West.

❷ Journeys into the North American interior 1600–1775 ▶

British expeditions
→ John Smith 1608
-→ Thomas Batts and Robert Fallam 1671
--→ James Needham and Gabriel Arthur 1673
····→ Dr. Henry Woodward 1674, 1685

French expeditions
→ Samuel de Champlain 1609–16
-→ Medart Chouart des Groseillers and Pierre-Esprit Radisson 1659–1660
····→ Father Claude Allouez 1665–67
-→ Father Charles Albanel 1671–72
-→ Louis Jolliet and Jacques Marquette 1672–73
→ René-Robert Cavelier Sieur de La Salle 1684–87
→ Louis Hennepin 1680
····→ Chaussegros de Léry 1729

Dutch expeditions
→ Arnout Viele 1682–84
→ Johannes Rosebloom 1685–87

American expeditions
→ Christopher Gist 1750–51
-→ Thomas Walker 1750
····→ Daniel Boone 1769–71

By the late 17th century knowledge of the east coast of North America had improved significantly. This plate from Visscher's *Atlas Contractus* of 1671 shows the Atlantic coast from New England south as far as Chesapeake Bay. Detail of the lands further west and the Great Lakes remained limited.

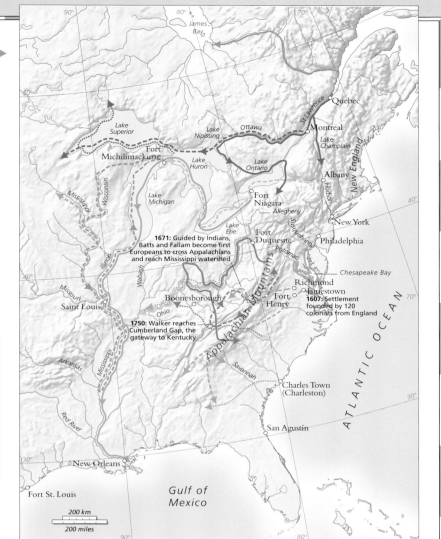

1671: Guided by Indians, Batts and Fallam become first Europeans to cross Appalachians and reach Mississippi watershed

1607: Settlement founded by 120 colonists from England

1750: Walker reaches Cumberland Gap, the gateway to Kentucky

200 km
200 miles

17th- and 18th-century expeditions in eastern North America

1609–13: Champlain explores St. Lawrence and eastern Great Lakes
1665–67: Father Allouez explores Great Lakes
1673: Jolliet and Marquette explore Mississippi and Illinois Rivers
1752: John Finley realizes that Cumberland Gap is gateway to Kentucky lowlands

1600 — 1650 — 1700 — 1750

1607–08: John Smith leads colonizing expeditions in Virginia
1673: Needham and Arthur follow Occaneechee Path across Appalachians
1682: La Salle follows Mississippi to its mouth
1729: de Léry makes first proper survey of Allegheny and upper Ohio Rivers

Charting the West

The rapid expansion of the US created the need to survey and quantify the vast territories of the new nation. Lewis and Clark's famous cross-continental expedition was funded by Congress at the express request of President Jefferson. Fremont conducted his reconnaissance of the west under the auspices of the US Army's Corps of Topographical Engineers. The highly competitive railroad surveys of the 1850s were inspired by economic and political considerations, while Clarence King's survey of the western deserts was motivated primarily by scientific curiosity.

An illustration from Lieutenant Fremont's *Memoirs* shows members of his Great Basin survey team camped on the shores of the Pyramid Lake. The lake was later surveyed in detail by Clarence King.

Lewis and Clark kept a series of illustrated notebooks on their westward journey. This map shows the mouth of the Columbia River.

❸ 19th-century exploration and surveys of the US and Canada ▶

Individual expeditions
→ Meriwether Lewis and William Clark 1804–06
→ Lt. Zebulon M. Pike 1806–07
→ Major Stephen Long 1819–20
→ Lt. John Franklin 1820–21
-→ Lt. John Franklin 1825–27
→ Lt. John C. Fremont 1842–44
→ Lt. William Emory 1846
→ Lt. James Simpson and Capt. Lorenzo Sitgreaves 1849–51
→ Lt. John Palliser 1857–59

Other expeditions and surveys
→ Russian expeditions to Alaska 1816–65
→ Western Railroad surveys 1853–55
→ Western Union Telegraph survey 1865–67
→ Canadian Yukon Exploring expedition 1887–89

Survey areas
▪ Henry Hind 1857–58
▪ George Wheeler 1867–72
▪ Clarence King 1867–73

Scale varies with perspective

This watercolor of the Kanab Desert was painted by a member of the US Geological Survey team in 1880.

Surveys in the north and west

1819: Artists on Long's expedition across Great Plains record landscape and wildlife
1821: Ill-fated expedition by Franklin along Yellowknife and Coppermine Rivers
1849–51: Simpson and Sitgreaves reveal ancient societies in southwest
1853–55: Series of surveys to find best route for railroad to the Pacific

1800 — 1810 — 1820 — 1830 — 1840 — 1850 — 1860 — 1870

1804–06: Lewis and Clark explore new land acquired in the Louisiana Purchase and reach Pacific coast
1816: Start of Russian exploration of Alaska
1842: Fremont begins series of expeditions to map American west and encourage settlement
1846: Emory surveys Spanish territory during Mexican War
1857–72: Wheeler produces first contour maps of southwest

EARLY PEOPLES OF NORTH AMERICA

The Hopewell
produced beautifully made grave offerings for burial with their dead, such as this hand, carved from a flat sheet of mica.

THE FIRST PEOPLE to settle North America are thought to have crossed over from Asia during the last Ice Age – possibly 15,000 years ago. They moved south through the corridor between the ice sheets to settle the prairies. By 11,000 BCE they had reached the southern tip of South America. By this time significant hunting activities were taking place in North America and many large mammals, such as the woolly mammoth, may have become extinct as a result of hunting and climate change. Once humans were established in Central America, they quickly became more sedentary, simple village structures evolving within a small time frame into far more complex societies. The archaeological evidence left by the Olmec and Zapotec in Central America, and the burial mounds of the Adena and Hopewell of the American Southeast reveal sophisticated societies.

The hunter-gatherers

Hunter-gatherers recorded events in their lives on the walls of caves. This series of images from Cueva Flecha in Lower California, shows humans and animals pierced by spears – perhaps as a result of conflict with other groups in the area.

The first peoples of North and Central America banded together in egalitarian, extended-family groups, living by hunting and gathering. They eventually become specialized and adapted to the continent's various ecological niches: plains, mountains, deserts, woodlands, river valleys, and coastal areas. Specially adapted spear points and other weaponry reveal the major prey species in different culture areas. The fine "Clovis" spearheads were used by plains hunters to kill bison, barbed harpoon heads were developed by coastal peoples for spearing marine creatures; and stone-tipped darts were thrown by the basin and mountain dwellers at the wildfowl which provided them with the bulk of their diet.

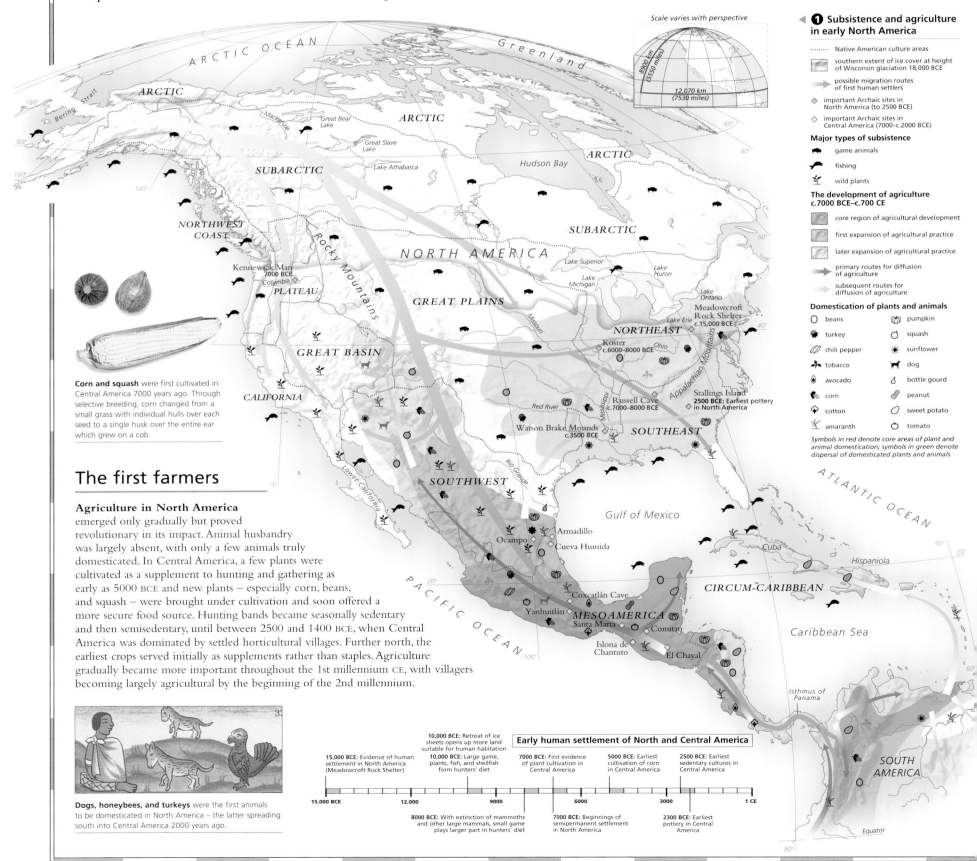

Corn and squash were first cultivated in Central America 7000 years ago. Through selective breeding, corn changed from a small grass with individual hulls over each seed to a single husk over the entire ear which grew on a cob.

The first farmers

Agriculture in North America emerged only gradually but proved revolutionary in its impact. Animal husbandry was largely absent, with only a few animals truly domesticated. In Central America, a few plants were cultivated as a supplement to hunting and gathering as early as 5000 BCE and new plants – especially corn, beans, and squash – were brought under cultivation and soon offered a more secure food source. Hunting bands became seasonally sedentary and then semisedentary, until between 2500 and 1400 BCE, when Central America was dominated by settled horticultural villages. Further north, the earliest crops served initially as supplements rather than staples. Agriculture gradually became more important throughout the 1st millennium CE, with villagers becoming largely agricultural by the beginning of the 2nd millennium.

Dogs, honeybees, and turkeys were the first animals to be domesticated in North America – the latter spreading south into Central America 2000 years ago.

◀ ❶ Subsistence and agriculture in early North America

Native American culture areas	
southern extent of ice cover at height of Wisconsin glaciation 18,000 BCE	
possible migration routes of first human settlers	
◇ important Archaic sites in North America (to 2500 BCE)	
◇ important Archaic sites in Central America (7000–c.2000 BCE)	

Major types of subsistence

game animals	
fishing	
wild plants	

The development of agriculture c.7000 BCE–c.700 CE

core region of agricultural development	
first expansion of agricultural practice	
later expansion of agricultural practice	
primary routes for diffusion of agriculture	
subsequent routes for diffusion of agriculture	

Domestication of plants and animals

○ beans	○ pumpkin
turkey	○ squash
chili pepper	sunflower
tobacco	dog
avocado	bottle gourd
corn	peanut
cotton	sweet potato
amaranth	tomato

Symbols in red denote core areas of plant and animal domestication; symbols in green denote dispersal of domesticated plants and animals

Scale varies with perspective

8900 km (5550 miles)

12,070 km (7530 miles)

Early human settlement of North and Central America

15,000 BCE: Evidence of human settlement in North America (Meadowcroft Rock Shelter)

10,000 BCE: Retreat of ice sheets opens up more land suitable for human habitation

10,000 BCE: Large game, plants, fish, and shellfish form hunters' diet

10,000 BCE: First evidence of plant cultivation in Central America

5000 BCE: Earliest cultivation of corn in Central America

2500 BCE: Earliest sedentary cultures in Central America

8000 BCE: With extinction of mammoths and other large mammals, small game plays larger part in hunters' diet

7000 BCE: Beginnings of semipermanent settlement in North America

2300 BCE: Earliest pottery in Central America

15,000 BCE	12,000	9000	6000	3000	1 CE

Early civilizations of Central America

With the establishment of village life, the earliest complex settlements occurred in the tropical lowlands from the Gulf of Mexico across the Isthmus of Tehuantepec to the Pacific coast of present-day Guatemala. Increasingly sophisticated societies were made possible by new crops and productive soils. The Olmec civilization – widely regarded as the mother culture of Central America – emerged on the Gulf Coast c.1500 BCE and persisted as an important culture until 400 BCE. Slightly later than the Olmecs, the Valley of Oaxaca witnessed the development of a sophisticated society, and by 500 BCE, complex chiefdoms or early states dominated the three interconnected valleys of central Oaxaca. At their juncture, the Zapotecs built the hilltop city of Monte Albán which would dominate the region for over 1000 years. Further south, Kaminaljuyú emerged by c.500 BCE, but a nearby volcanic eruption c.250–200 BCE, and consequent mass migration, deprived the site of much of the population in the southern part of its trading area. In the highlands south of Yucatan, the Maya civilization was starting to emerge as early as 1000 BCE.

This Olmec ceremonial adze from La Venta is carved from the pale green jade typical of the site.

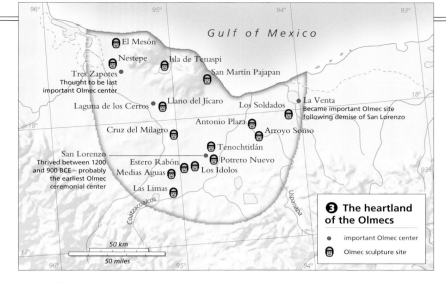

3 The heartland of the Olmecs

● important Olmec center
▣ Olmec sculpture site

50 km
50 miles

The Olmecs

The earliest civilization in Central America, the Olmecs initiated the Mesoamerican pantheon of gods, gave rise to kings and classes, and fought wars, as well as trading over vast distances and heavily influencing other cultures. They built elaborate platforms and mounds, made fine ceramics, worked precious stone, engaged in complex and sophisticated stone sculpture, established the Mesoamerican calendar, and invented the syllabary writing system. By 500–400 BCE, the Olmecs, although remaining an intellectually vibrant culture throughout the 1st millennium BCE, ceased to influence groups elsewhere directly.

2 Early civilizations of Central America

area of Olmec influence
area of Maya influence c.1000 BCE
additional area of Maya influence c.800 BCE
area of Zapotec influence

◇ site settled by, or influenced by the Olmecs
◆ other sites from formative period
→ main Olmec trade routes

Mineral resources
▣ basalt
▣ obsidian
▣ iron ore (magnetite)
▣ serpentine
▣ green jade

Early civilizations of North and Central America

c.1150: Start of Olmec civilization
800: Evidence that Maya beginning to spread northward into Yucatan peninsula
500: Settlement of Monte Albán
400: Beginning of Olmec decline

1200 BCE — 1000 — 800 — 600 — 400 — 200 BCE

1100: Establishment of Poverty Point in present-day Louisiana, an early nonagrarian settlement
700: Start of Adena culture
c.250: El Mirador, the largest early Maya city flourishing. Sites, such as Becan, fortified

The moundbuilders of the eastern river valleys

The Adena culture was found in the upper Ohio valley as early as 1000 BCE. Settlements were centered on burial mounds and extensive earthworks. Their grave goods included jewelry made from imported copper, carved tablets, and tubular pipes – which provide evidence of the early cultivation of tobacco *(see Map 1)*. The Hopewell culture had emerged by c.100 CE, and spread throughout the Mississippi Valley, sustained by small-scale agriculture. They created a complex and far-reaching trade network to source the many raw materials – including obsidian, mica sheets, quartz, shells, teeth, and copper – used in their characteristic animal and bird sculptures. Elements of Hopewell culture appear to have been adopted by many other Indian groups.

4 Moundbuilders of eastern North America c.700 BCE–c.400 CE

Adena heartland
▲ Adena site
Hopewell area of influence
OHIO Hopewell cultural area
⌂ Hopewell burial mound site
⌂ effigy mound site

Resources traded by the Hopewell
▣ chert
▣ chlorite
▣ obsidian
▣ silver
▣ copper
▣ galena
◉ mica crystals
◔ olive shell
◔ tulip shell
◔ whelks
◉ turtle
→ alligator
→ barracuda
→ shark

The Hopewell produced many objects in the shape of animals including birds, beavers, and bears. The frog adorns a platform effigy pipe; tobacco was placed in a bowl in its back and inhaled through the hole in the front of the pipe.

CITIES AND EMPIRES

Hollow pottery dogs, typical of the highly realistic ceramics of western Mexico, are common grave offerings.

CENTRAL AMERICA was split into the Highland Mexican and the Lowland Maya areas, between which there were some major differences, including languages, writing systems, and art and architectural styles. City-states dominated both areas: in the Maya area these tended to be small, multicity regional polities or autonomous cities, while Highland Mexico was dominated by a series of empires. The peoples of southern North America were turning to agriculture and establishing settled communities. Several overlapping cultures settled the desert southwest, including the Hohokam, Anasazi, and Mogollon. In the southeast, larger settlements in the Mississippi Valley replaced the Hopewell by 800 CE.

Central American civilizations 400–1400

Teotihuacan emerged as the capital of the first major empire in the 1st century CE and influenced cities throughout Mexico and Guatemala, spreading ideas and innovations. The multiethnic city reached a population of 125,000–200,000 by 500, exporting goods to the rest of Central America. By 550, Teotihuacán was in decline, and by 750, the city was largely abandoned. The resulting political vacuum encouraged the rise of several independent, fortified hilltop cities from about 650, including Cacaxtla and Xochicalco. All had extensive trade links and varying degrees of contact with other cultures. Centred at Tula, the Toltec Empire emerged in the 10th century. The Toltecs were traders, trading as far south as Costa Rica and north into the desert. Drought undermined Tula's agriculture and by 1200, it was abandoned.

Teotihuacán was centrally planned, laid out in a grid, and dominated by huge pyramids which would have held temples on their summits. It traded over much of Central America, dealing in obsidian products, ceramics, stone carvings, and featherwork.

These massive basalt figures stand on top of the central pyramid at Tula, the Toltec capital. The city reached a peak population of 60,000 inhabitants, with an equal number in the immediate hinterland.

❶ Major civilizations of Mexico ▶

The Classic period 100–900 CE
◇ important Classic site
◇ minor Classic site
◇ later cultural center

Cultural centers and direction of influence
▸ Teotihuacán
▸ Xochicalco
▸ Veracruz
▸ Remojadas
▸ Cerro de las Mesas
▸ Monte Albán

The Toltec Empire c.900–1200 CE
■ core Toltec area
■ Toltec capital
◆ other Toltec site
◆ other post-Classic site
▸ influx of Toltecs c.900 CE
▸ emigration of Toltecs 900–1200 CE

The fortified city of Xochicalco (650–900) had extensive trade connections and bears Maya influences, but was sacked and abandoned in 900. The outline of its pyramids (left), temples, and ball courts are still clearly visible.

Monte Albán was a major ceremonial center, with plazas, terraces, temple platforms, and a large pyramid. It dominated the Valley of Oaxaca until 600 CE, with a peak population of perhaps 24,000.

❷ The civilization of the Maya ▼

The late formative period c.200–400 CE
◇ Maya site
⊖ giant stucco mask site
▴ monumental architecture

The Classic period c.290–790 CE
◆ important Classic center
→ trade route
▨ area of intensive agriculture
▨ wetland

Civilizations of Central America

1 CE: Teotihuacán rises to importance	**3rd century:** Tikal rises to importance	**600:** Monte Albán begins to decline	**650:** Settlement of Xochicalco and Cacaxtla	**900:** Abandonment of Xochicalco	**1200:** Entry of Aztecs into Valley of Mexico (see p.124)

1 CE — 200 — 400 — 600 — 800 — 1000 — 1200 — 1400

290: Start of Classic Maya civilization in Yucatan — **500:** Teotihuacán at peak population — **850:** Abandonment of Cacaxtla — **900:** Rise to power of Toltecs as Classic Maya sites collapse

The city-states of the Maya

The jungle of Guatemala and Yucatan became the center for the florescence of Maya civilization. Many city-states emerged, sometimes linked by elite marriages and sometimes by descent, but political ties were few and fleeting. The Classic Maya civilization is thought to be the first fully literate culture of the Americas, developing a hieroglyphic writing system. Classic Maya cities were characterized by their massive size and structural complexity. From 800, the major cities were progressively abandoned and the focus of Maya civilization shifted to the northern lowlands.

The corbelled Arch of Labna in northern Yucatan dates from the late Classic period. Its intricate reliefs and massive size typify Maya architecture during this period.

This **Inuit knife** carved from walrus ivory was probably used for cutting blocks of snow. It is engraved with scenes showing hunters, animals, and settlements.

Cultures of the far North

The harsh landscapes of the Arctic and sub-Arctic remained sparsely populated by resourceful nomadic hunters: the Aleut and Inuit (Eskimo) of the Arctic and the Athabascan (western), Algonquian, and Beothuk (eastern) groups of the sub-Arctic. From c.1000, the Thule Inuit migrated eastward, coming to dominate the far North by c.1500. The furs, copper, and animal oils produced by northern peoples had, by c.1000, become valuable currency throughout much of the continent. They were traded along maritime and riverine routes, and with the Norse traders who settled Greenland and visited the northeast coast.

❸ Peoples of the far North to 1500 CE ▶

Aleut indigenous people
◆ Aleut site
◇ Inuit site
○ Norse settlement
▨ core region of the Inuit people
▨ sub-Arctic culture area

Inuit migration routes
⇨ from 1000
⇨ 1000–1200
⇨ 1200–1500

The far North to 1500 CE

c.700: Inuit using bows and arrows for hunting
986: Norse traders found three settlements on Greenland
c.1500: Inuit peoples are found throughout Arctic region

700 — 900 — 1100 — 1300 — 1500

c.1000 onward: Cree and other groups trading furs with southern peoples for grain

500 km / 500 miles

The American Southwest

In the Southwest, sedentary ways of life spread throughout the 1st millennium CE, producing villages and cliff dwellings, such those of the Hohokam in Arizona, after 1000, and regional polities such as Chaco Canyon and Casas Grandes. The Hohokam developed irrigation systems to allow them to grow maize in the arid semidesert and built multistoried pueblos: storehouses and dwellings of stone or adobe sometimes with ball courts and low platform mounds. The Anasazi and Mogollon peoples left evidence of pueblos constructed for defensive purposes – probably to counter other hostile groups who entered the area from c.1300. Increasing aridity caused a decline in the southwest after 1250 leaving only dispersed puebloan groups.

The Mimbres branch of the Mogollon culture produced spectacular pottery, usually for burial purposes. The pots, adorned with geometric designs, were often ritually "killed" by having a hole drilled through their base.

Settlement in the Southwest to 1500

100: Emergence of Hohokam and Mogollon cultures
800: Mimbres pottery starts to be made by Mogollon
1050: Pueblos built for defensive purposes by Anasazi
1200: Peak of importance of Chaco Canyon

1 CE — 200 — 400 — 600 — 800 — 1050 — 1200 — 1400

c.950: Flourishing pueblo culture in Southwest
1100: Construction of the Cliff Palace at Mesa Verde
1350: Most Anasazi pueblos abandoned – probably due to drought

❹ Cultures of the Southwest: 600–1500 CE

Maximum areas of influence
▨ Fremont c.400–1300
▨ Anasazi c.700–1500
▨ Patayan (Hakataya) c.500
▨ Hohokam c.300–1450
▨ Mogollon c.250–1350
▨ desert area
◆ archaeological site

1 Tonto
2 Beshbagowa
3 Points of Pines
4 Kinishba
5 Hay Hollow Valley

200 km / 200 miles

The American South and Mississippi Valley

In eastern North America there were improvements in agricultural technology, and crops such as beans and new varieties of corn were imported from Mexico. There was a developmental hiatus for about 400 years following the decline of the Hopewell interaction sphere but from c.800, settlements grew larger until, in around 1000, the Mississippian chiefdoms emerged, leading to more regional integration and significantly greater social differentiation. Many centers, including sites such as Etowah and Moundville, became regional foci, with the largest being Cahokia, with a peak population of 15,000.

▼ **❺ Mississippian cultures of eastern North America**

Areas of influence and temple mound sites
▲ Middle Mississippian
▲ South Appalachian
▲ Fort Ancient
▢ extent of secondary Mississippian influence
◆ other site
▲ Plaquemine Mississippian
▲ Caddoan Mississippian
▲ Oneota

This sculpted soapstone pipe from the Spiro mound site is thought to depict a warrior beheading his victim.

Settlement in the Southeast to 1500

c.800: Hunters in Mississippi Valley use bows and arrows
1000: Start of Mississippian culture
1200: Construction of Moundville which flourishes until 1300

400 — 600 — 800 — 1000 — 1200 — 1400 — 1600

c.400: Hopewell influence and trade network in decline
1050: Cahokia is center of Mississippian culture with population of c.10,000
c.1450: Population crash in Middle Mississippi area

COMPETING EMPIRES

Quetzalcoatl, the god of wind, was one of a pantheon of gods worshiped by the Aztecs.

UNTIL THE EUROPEAN INCURSIONS of the late 15th century, North and Central America remained largely untouched by contacts with other continents. Spanish explorers and traders, seeking new routes and markets, first reconnoitred the Caribbean islands and Central America, returning later to claim Mexico, the Caribbean and much of the southern half of America as new territory for the Spanish crown. One of their most significant conquests was the Aztec Empire that dominated central Mexico. Elsewhere European impact was slight during the 16th century; they passed through, leaving little of their own cultures behind, save for animals, such as horses, that transformed native lives, and diseases that decimated populations.

The Great Temple dominated the central plaza of Tenochtitlan. The northern temple *(left)* was dedicated to Tlaloc, god of rain and the southern temple *(right)* to the Aztec patron god of war, Huitzilopochtli.

The Aztec Empire

The Aztecs entered the already highly urbanized Valley of Mexico around 1200, establishing their island capital of Tenochtitlan on Lake Texcoco in 1325, and overthrowing their imperial masters, the Tepanecs, in 1428 to begin their own empire. By 1519, the Aztec Empire controlled most of central Mexico as well as the Maya areas of further east. The Aztecs presided over a collection of city-states which remained autonomous except for their tributary obligations to the Aztecs. The Aztec Empire maintained a state of constant military activity which served to provide a flow of tributes from neighboring states.

This turquoise mosaic pendant in the form of a double-headed serpent, was a symbol of the rain god, Tlaloc. It was probably sent by the Aztec king, Motecuzoma Xocoyotl to Cortés.

❶ The expansion of the Aztec Empire in post-Classic Central America

Growth of Aztec Empire under:
- Itzcoatl (1427–40)
- Motecuzoma Ilhuicamina (1440–68)
- Axayacatl (1469–81)
- Ahuitzotl (1486–1502)
- Motecuzoma Xocoyotl (1502–20)
- → Aztec transit route to Soconusco
- ◆ provincial center for tribute collection

The Maya in the post-Classic period
- independent northern states
- ◇ major post-Classic Maya center

The Valley of Mexico

Most Aztec settlements were located on the shores of Lake Texcoco, provisioned with food via a system of artificial islands called *chinampas* which were built up from the base of the lake. This system was not only extremely productive but allowed for a varied seasonal range of foodstuffs.

❷ Aztec rule in the Valley of Mexico

- ○ Aztec town or city
- aqueduct
- causeway
- dike
- saltwater area
- freshwater area
- marshland
- chinampas

This symbolic depiction of the Aztec cosmology is thought to show the earth monster, Tlalteuctli, at its center, although the entity is sometimes thought to be Tonatiuh, the sun god.

The rise and fall of the Aztec Empire

- c.1200: Aztecs enter Valley of Mexico
- 1325: Foundation of Tenochtitlán on island in Lake Texcoco
- 1428: Expansion of Aztec Empire begins
- 1519: Cortés captures Tenochtitlán for falls to Spanish and the first time their Indian allies
- 1520: Death of Aztec emperor, Motecuzoma Xocoyotl
- 1521: Tenochtitlán

1200 — 1300 — 1400 — 1500 — 1600

Tenochtitlán

Founded in 1325, the city of Tenochtitlán became the capital of the Aztec Empire in 1428. Water was the city's primary form of transport: Tenochtitlán was connected internally via an elaborate systems of canals and to the mainland via a series of causeways. At its height, Tenochtitlán may have had a population of more than 300,000 and was the heart of an empire of up to ten million people.

❸ Tenochtitlán and satellite towns
- street
- aqueduct
- causeway
- dyke

European exploration and conquest

The Spanish first visited the Gulf of Mexico and the Caribbean in the late 1400s and early 1500s, quickly conquering the West Indies, whose people were enslaved or impressed into forced labor and devastated by European diseases such as smallpox. The first formal expedition to Mexico, led by Córdoba, reached the Yucatán Peninsula in 1517. In 1518, Grijalva landed on the Vera Cruz coast, trading with the natives and giving Aztec emissaries their first glimpse of Europeans. The rest of the 16th century saw the replacement of Indian leaders with Spanish, the substitution of Christianity for Indian religions, and the imposition of Spanish rule in Central America. Major entries were made into North America – in the southeast by expeditions, such as de Soto's in 1539–42, and in the southwest by Coronado in 1540, leading to the initial conquest of New Mexico and the founding of Santa Fe in 1609.

Some of the earliest evidence of Spanish incursions into Mexico and North America is in the form of religious buildings. The church of St. Francis at Tlaxcala dates from 1521.

Spanish colonizing expeditions in the New World

1	Sebastian de Ocampo	1508
2	Juan Ponce de León	1508 and 1512
3	Juan de Esquival	1509
4	Diego Velasquez	1511
5	Vasco Núñez de Balboa	1513–14
6	Pedrarias Dávila	1514–19
7	Hernández de Córdoba, Juan de Grijalva, Alonso Álvarez de Peneda, and Francisco de Garay	1517–23
8	Pedrarias Dávila	1519
9	Hernán Cortés	1519
10	Gonzalo de Sandoval	1521
11	Luis Marín	1521–24
12	Francisco Orozco	1521
13	Francisco Gordillo and Pedro de Quexos	1521
14	Pedro de Alvarado	1522
15	Hernán Cortés	1522
16	Cristóbal de Olid	1522
17	Gil González Dávila and Andrés Niño	1522–23
18	Pedro de Alvarado	1523–24
19	Cristóbal de Olid	1524
20	Francisco Hernández de Córdoba	1524
21	Esteban Gomez	1524–25
22	Lucas Vázquez de Ayllón	1526
23	The Montejos	1527
24	Pánfilo de Narváez and Álvar Núñez Cabeza de Vaca	1528
25	Nuño de Guzmán and Cristóbal de Oñate	1529
26	Hurtado de Mendoza, Becerra, Grijalva, Cortés, Tapia, Ulloa, Alarcón	1532–42
27	Hernando de Soto	1539–42
28	Francisco Vásquez de Coronado	1540
29	The Montejos	1545
30	Francisco de Ibarra	1554
31	Pedro Menéndez de Avilés	1565
32	Juan de Oñate	1595
33	Sebastián Vizcaino	1596

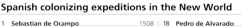

San Agustin, Florida, was founded by Pedro Menéndez de Avilés in 1565. Its massive coastal fort, the Castillo de San Marcos was a classic example of 16th-century military technology.

❹ Spanish exploration and colonization in the New World 1492–c.1600

Spanish expansion

→ 1492–1514
→ 1514–20
→ 1520–25
→ 1525–30
→ 1530–1600

Spanish settlement

○ Spanish town
⚔ fort
✝ Jesuit mission
⛏ silver mine
Yuma Native American people
1632 date of foundation

600 km
600 miles

The Spanish colonization of Mexico and North America

1492: Columbus' first expedition lands in the Bahamas

1509: Founding of San Juan on Puerto Rico

1517: Córdoba leads expedition to Mexico

1518: Grijalva lands on Vera Cruz coast

1539: De Soto leads expedition into south-eastern North America

1565–67: Spanish found San Agustin and build other fortified towns on east and Gulf coasts of Mexico

1496: Foundation of Santo Domingo on Hispaniola

1519–21: Cortés' expedition into Mexico leads to collapse of Aztec Empire

1540: Coronado leads expedition into south-western North America

1560s: Jesuit missions established in the Southeast (Florida) and in the Southwest

1490   1510   1530   1550   1570

The conquest of the Aztecs

In 1519, Hernán Cortés, sponsored by the Governor of Cuba, landed on the Vera Cruz coast with about 450 soldiers. Forging alliances with the Totonacs and the Tlaxcaltecs, he was able to seize the Aztec capital, Tenochtitlán, in November 1519. Governor Velasquez then attempted to punish Cortés for disobeying his orders, sending a force to retrieve him which ultimately led to his being forced out of Tenochtitlán, but he was able to maintain his alliances with groups such as the Chalcas and the Acolhua. In 1520 Cortés again led expeditions around the Valley of Mexico and beseiged Tenochtitlán, defeating the Aztecs in August 1521.

❺ Cortés' invasion and conquest of Mexico, 1519–21

→ Cortés' march to Tenochtitlán, Apr–Nov 1519
→ retreat to Tlaxcala, 1520
→ final conquest of Tenochtitlán, 1520–21

50 km
50 miles

While Cortés claimed victory for Spain, the battles against the Aztecs were actually won by his tens of thousands of Indian allies. With several major allied groups, no one group was able to take power and Cortés reaped the benefits.

FROM COLONIZATION TO INDEPENDENCE

George Washington, the first US president, came to prominence in the Anglo-French conflicts of the 1750s.

FROM THE EARLY 17TH CENTURY, British, French, and Dutch migrants settled along the Atlantic seaboard and in the Gulf of St. Lawrence. As they grew in numbers, they displaced Native American peoples from their lands. Though the French were able to form mutually beneficial alliances with local peoples, relationships elsewhere were characterized by conflict, and by 1759, most of the surviving Native Americans had been driven westward. By the second half of the 18th century, the British emerged as the major political power in North America. By 1775, and with the elimination of French power in Canada, the American desire for self-determination led to revolution and the creation of an independent United States of America by 1783.

European colonial settlement 1600–1750

The site of Montreal was first visited by Jacques Cartier in 1535. In 1642, when this map was drawn, the first French settlement was set up.

During the 17th century, the British established a string of Atlantic colonies with a population that grew to about a million settlers, including African slaves. They produced and exported tobacco, timber, fish, and food, and ran a thriving colonial merchant fleet that dominated Atlantic trade, along with sugar colonies in the West Indies. To the north and west, a small number of French settlers forged strong alliances with native peoples, traded in fur, and established an arc of territories designed to stop further British expansion.

Settlement and conflict in 17th-century North America

1608: Champlain colonizes Quebec for France
1609: Champlain allies with Algonquins and initiates war with Iroquois
1637: Local tribes defeated in Pequot War
1661: French-Iroquois war resumes
1675: Native American forces under "King Philip" wiped out by British

1607: Foundation of Jamestown
1609–14: War between English and Powhatan
1620: Settlement of New England begins
1648–51: Iroquois destroy French allies, the Huron
1653–60: Temporary French-Iroquois peace
1690: Iroquois neutrality is followed by alliance to British

| 1600 | 1620 | 1640 | 1660 | 1680 | 1700 |

European traders made use of the fur trade routes established by native peoples. In 1670, the Hudson's Bay Company established fur "factories" to tap the fur trade of the far interior.

Changing populations

The population composition of North America changed radically with the European incursion. Indigenous peoples succumbed to European diseases such as plague and measles, and to the settlers' superior firepower and ability to organize themselves quickly. Only small numbers of Africans were brought to North America as slaves in the 17th century, but the growth of labor-intensive plantation agriculture in the south and the West Indies led to the burgeoning of the Atlantic slave trade.

❶ The colonization of North America to 1750

- British control and settlement
- Spanish control and settlement
- French control and settlement
- French influence
- approximate western limit of French claim
- Dutch control and settlement
- migration from Britain
- migration from France
- migration from Spain
- movement of slaves
- fur trade routes
- **1682** date of foundation
- conflict with Native Americans
- fur trading post
- *Houma* indigenous people

1713: to Britain via Treaty of Utrecht

1600–1700: 100 migrants per year

1713: to Britain via Treaty of Utrecht

1600–1700: 2000 migrants per year

1600–1700: 1500 slaves imported per year to British territories

1600–1700: 300 slaves imported per year to French territories

1600–1700: 2500 migrants per year

1600–1700: 100,000 slaves imported per year to Spanish territories

	European and native conflicts	
1	Jamestown	1622, 1644
2	Pequot War	1636–37
3	New Haven	1637
4	Kieft's War	1643–46
5	King Philip's War	1675–76
6	Bacon's Rebellion	1676
7	Boston	1676
8	Montreal	1689
9	Deerfield	1704
10	Tuscarora War	1711–13
11	Yamasee War	1715–28

500 km
500 miles

Competition for North America 1690–1761

Conflict between France and Britain in North America at first mirrored the wars of Louis XIV in Europe in the 1690s. In the late 1730s Britain and Spain clashed in the Spanish colonies. Serious fighting between the British and French resumed in 1744–48, but the decisive struggle for the continent occurred between 1754–61. In July 1755, General Braddock, aided by provincial troops including George Washington, marched on Fort Duquesne but was repelled by the French. It took the full weight of the British army until 1759 to gain ascendancy over the French and their native allies. General Wolfe's capture of Quebec in September 1759 was followed by the surrender of Montreal. With peace agreed at the Treaty of Paris in 1763, Britain became the dominant colonial power in the New World.

Anglo-French conflict in North America 1754–1760

1754: French capture British Fort Necessity

1755: British capture French Fort Beauséjour

1756–57: French capture British forts Oswego and William Henry

1758: French successfully repel British attack on Ticonderoga; British capture Fort Duquesne

1759: British amphibious forces advance up St. Lawrence to capture Quebec

1755: Braddock beaten back by French at Fort Duquesne

1757: French abandon forts along Lake Champlain

1758: Louisbourg captured by British

1760: Montreal surrenders to massed British forces

The brief but fierce battle for Quebec in September 1759, claimed the lives of the commanders of both sides: the British General Wolfe (left), and the French Marquis de Montcalm the following day. Final victory belonged to the British who had been advancing up the Gulf of St. Lawrence for over a year.

② Anglo-French conflict 1754–60

- British town
- French town
- British fort
- French fort
- French ring of defense
- British line of attack
- French line of attack
- British victory
- French victory

400 km
400 miles

The Revolutionary War 1775–1783

By the 1760s, the inhabitants of the British colonies had grown rapidly in population, wealth, and self-confidence and were increasingly resistant to conventional methods of colonial control, such as taxation. In addition, the British government was perceived to be keeping all the fruits of victory against the French for itself, including the Canadian fur trade and the western lands. In 1775, the first shots of the Revolutionary War were fired near Boston. Almost all of the early campaigns ended in stalemate: British forces were superior in numbers and weaponry, but the Patriots gained support with every campaign as the struggle moved south. The American victory at Saratoga in 1777 convinced the French government to support the Americans with troops and ships. Later the Dutch and Spanish also joined against Britain. In 1781 George Washington forced General Cornwallis to surrender at Yorktown, Virginia, and the new nation was secure.

❸ The American Revolutionary War

- The Thirteen Colonies, 1775
- The United States, 1783
- British movements
- French movements
- US movements
- British victory
- French victory
- US victory
- indecisive outcome
- fort

Scale varies with perspective

1371 km (1230 miles)

1667 km (1040 miles)

Battles of the Revolutionary War

1	Concord	Apr 19 1775
2	Lexington	Apr 19 1775
3	Bunker Hill (Boston)	Jun 17 1775
4	Fort Ticonderoga	Autumn 1775
5	Quebec	Dec 30–31 1775
6	Charleston	Jun 28 1776
7	Long Island	Aug 27 1776
8	White Plains	Oct 28 1776
9	Trenton	Dec 25 1776
10	Princeton	Jan 3 1777
11	Oriskany	Aug 6 1777
12	Brandywine	Sep 11 1777
13	Freeman's Farm	Sep 19 1777
14	Bemis Heights	Sep 19, Oct 7 1777
15	Paoli	Sep 20 1777
16	Germantown	Oct 4 1777
17	Bennington	Oct 14 1777
18	Saratoga	Oct 17 1777
19	Wyoming Massacre	Autumn 1778
20	Savannah	Dec 29 1778
21	Monmouth Court House	Jun 28 1778
22	Augusta	Jan 29 1779
23	Briar Creek	Mar 3 1779
24	King's Mountain	Oct 7 1780
25	Blackstock	Nov 20 1780
26	Camden	Jan 16 1781
27	Cowpens	Jan 17 1781
28	Guilford Court House	Mar 5 1781
29	Hobkirk's Hill	Apr 25 1781
30	Jamestown	Jul 6 1781
31	Virginia Capes	Sep 5 1781
32	Eutaw Springs	Sep 8 1781
33	Yorktown	Oct 19 1781

At the Battle of Bunker Hill on June 17, 1775, British forces attempted to loosen the American encirclement of Boston. The British eventually gained the position, but their heavy losses and the ability of the colonists to stand firm under fire was an important boost to American morale.

The road to independence

1764: Sugar Act imposes tax on molasses brought from non-British colonies

1770: Soldiers shoot five colonists in "Boston Massacre"

1772: Committees of Correspondence promote American identity

1775: Start of Revolutionary War

1778: France enters war as American ally

1781: Washington defeats British at Yorktown

1765: Stamp Act inspires the slogan "taxation without representation is tyranny"

1767: Townshend Acts tax tea, paper, and other imports

1773: Militants destroy shipments of tea in "Boston Tea Party"

Jul 4 1776: Adoption of Declaration of Independence

1783: End of Revolutionary War. Treaty of Paris recognizes new United States

---

This cartoon, published in 1776, shows the British government killing their "golden goose" – the American colonies. Unpopular taxes combined with the harsh suppression of opposition alienated many colonists and hardened American resistance to the British government.

BUILDING NEW NATIONS

Thomas Jefferson was the principal author of the Declaration of Independence and the third US president.

BY 1783, THE NEWLY-FORMED United States of America operated under the Articles of Confederation and had a border which soon extended as far as the Mississippi, causing considerable alarm among its Native American, Spanish, and Canadian neighbors. In the War of 1812, Canada successfully fended off invasion by the United States, but remained fearful of the growing power to its south. In Mexico and Central America, Creole dissenters launched a disastrous war for independence from Spain starting in 1810. Mexico plunged into a bloody race war that killed hundreds of thousands and wrecked the colonial infrastructure. The nations of Central America and Mexico became independent during the 1820s, though greatly weakened from their former colonial status.

The growth of the US

The Louisiana Purchase of 1803 added to the US a huge swathe of western lands formerly controlled by France. After the War of 1812, all hope of annexing Canada was abandoned, and the US began the great push westward.

The consolidation of western lands encouraged millions of pioneers to forge new lives in the West. The spirit of aggressive progress which drove settlers westward soon became known as "manifest destiny".

Settlers poured into the Great Plains, the Pacific Northwest, and the northern periphery of the Republic of Mexico, including Texas and California. The Santa Fe trail, open for trade by 1823, brought New Mexico under US influence. By mid-century, the US boasted an extensive communications network. Steamboat traffic dominated the riverine highway system, augmented by canals and railroads running cross-country.

② **North America 1783–1905: struggles for nationhood and the seizing of the West**

The plains of Texas and the west were swiftly populated with beef cattle. They were driven to railheads such as Abilene and Dodge City, Kansas, for shipment by rail to eastern cities. Chicago, for example, had a thriving meat-packing industry.

The expansion of the US

1803: Louisiana Purchase — 1820: Missouri Compromise — 1821: Austin leads settlers to Texas — 1853: Gadsden Purchase — 1867: US purchases Alaska from Russia for $7.2 million — 1877–87: Peak of the buffalo slaughter — 1890: US western frontier declared to exist no longer

1811: Annexation of West Florida — 1821: Mexico becomes independent — 1824: First Mexican constitution produced — 1846: Oregon settlement — 1867: First cattle drives to Kansas — 1869: Transcontinental railroad completed — 1885: Completion of Canadian trans-continental railroad

Territorial conflict and US expansion

Although involved in conflicts with Britain over the boundary with Canada, the US managed to solve these issues peacefully. A weak, divided Mexico, however, feared US territorial demands, especially after President Andrew Jackson offered to purchase Texas. By 1835 the Texans had seceded. Suspicion between the US and Mexico turned quickly to crisis, and in 1846, to war. In 1848 Mexico yielded about a third of its territory to the US as terms of peace, and descended into civil war. The cession of the northern Oregon Country by Britain in 1846 and James Gadsden's 1853 purchase of 30,000 square miles south of the Gila river from Mexico, completed the westward expansion of the US. The last piece of continental land added to the US was the northwestern territory of Alaska in 1867.

Destruction of Native Americans

From the 1790s, Native Americans were removed from their Eastern homelands and forced to migrate west of the Mississippi River. Some, like the Seminole in Florida, resisted stoutly. The settlement of the West from the 1860s was met with serious armed resistance from Native Americans. With the final loss of their lands, traditional societies were reorganized so as to pave the way for their integration into the national population.

◄ ❶ The growth of the US, 1783–1896

Thirteen Colonies 1776
Addition of 1783
Louisiana Purchase 1803
Red River Cession 1818
Purchase of Florida 1819
Texas Annexation 1845
Oregon Country Cession 1846
Mexican Cession 1848
Gadsden Purchase 1853
1812 date of admission to statehood
— modern state boundary

Sitting Bull (*above*), chief of the Teton tribe of the Lakota (Sioux) nation, attempts to retain a homeland in the western lands and predicted the deaths of Custer and his men at the Battle of Little Bighorn.

White Cloud (*left*) was chief of the Iowa tribe, who pursued a semisedentary agricultural existence alongside their hunting and battle activities. In 1836, the Iowa ceded their lands to the US and moved to a reservation on what is now the Kansas-Nebraska border.

Territorial conflicts 1783–1890, including Native American wars

1794: Battle of Fallen Timbers paves way for white settlement
1828: Start of Federalist/Centralists wars in Mexico. These last until 1859
1846–48: US–Mexican War
1861–65: US Civil War (see pp.130/131)
1873–75: Red River War
1890: Massacre at Wounded Knee

1810: Grito de Dolores (Father Hidalgo's Revolution) in Mexico
1812: War of 1812: US foils British attempt to restrain US navy
1835–36: Texas Revolution
1857–59: War of the Reform in Mexico
1866–76: First Sioux War
1871: Start of Apache wars
1877: Nez Percé War

Texas Revolution 1835–36:
US settlers in Mexican province of Texas rebel, declaring independence from Mexico and driving out troops – led by General Santa Ana – sent in to quell the uprising

The US–Mexican War 1846–48:
Admission of Texas to the US in 1845 leads to war with Mexico. US quickly wins California and by 1848, Mexico has ceded 33% of its US territory for a fee of $15M

In the latter half of the 19th century, western Canada and the US prioritized the building of transcontinental railroads. These opened up the West to hunters who killed millions of buffalo for their hides, almost destroying the North American herd by the end of the century.

THE AMERICAN CIVIL WAR

Abraham Lincoln's 1863 Emancipation Proclamation freed the slaves of the south.

BETWEEN INDEPENDENCE in 1776 and 1860 there developed within the United States two very different regional societies. In the North there emerged an industrialized society, committed to liberal banking and credit systems, and protective tariffs. The south was a less populous agrarian society opposed to the sale of public land in the Midwest, high duties, and restrictions upon the institution of slavery. Moreover, the libertarian North increasingly resented Southern political and judicial overrepresentation. The Democratic Party held the two parts together until 1859; its split, and the election of a Republican president committed to opposing the spread of slavery, provoked the Union's collapse – even before Lincoln's inauguration, seven southern states had seceded, and war became inevitable.

The cotton gin invented by Eli Whitney in 1793 enabled the swift processing of short-staple cotton. Cotton production increased massively in the southern states, with a resultant rise in the number of slaves required to work the burgeoning plantations.

6 The Civil War to the fall of Vicksburg Apr 1861–Jul 1863

- Union states 1861
- Confederate states 1861
- Union front line to Dec 1861
- Union front line to Dec 1862
- Union movement
- Confederate movement
- Union fort
- Confederate fort
- Union naval blockade
- Union victory
- Confederate victory
- Apr 12 1865 date of battle or attack

An unequal nation

By 1860 the US was composed of 18 "free" states – mainly in the North, and 15 "slave" states – mainly in the South. On the issue of slavery, as well as economics, the expanding nation was divided. Industry and finance dominated the North which also had 71% of the population, 81% of bank deposits, 72% of railroad mileage, and 85% of the country's factories. The South concentrated on farming, in particular on the production of cotton, tobacco, and sugar for export to Europe. In 1850, 347,000 Southern families out of a total population of 6,000,000 were slaveowners. The West was developing an agricultural economy, but produced a greater variety of crops, and sold most of its produce to the North.

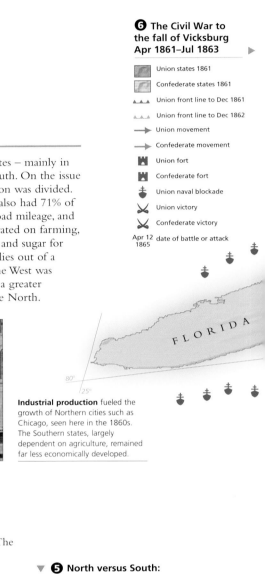

Industrial production fueled the growth of Northern cities such as Chicago, seen here in the 1860s. The Southern states, largely dependent on agriculture, remained far less economically developed.

Compromises on the road to civil war

The addition of Missouri in 1820 was the first extension of Union territory west of the Mississippi. The question of whether slavery should be allowed in the new state was settled by the so-called Missouri Compromise, with an artificial limit of 36° 30' marking the boundary between slave and free territory. In 1854 the Kansas-Nebraska Act established two new territories and proposed to allow territorial legislatures to decide the issue of slavery. The Dred Scott decision of 1857 – in which a slave who had been taken west by his master claimed that he was free because slavery was not legal in the new territory – led to the ruling that slavery could not be excluded from new territories.

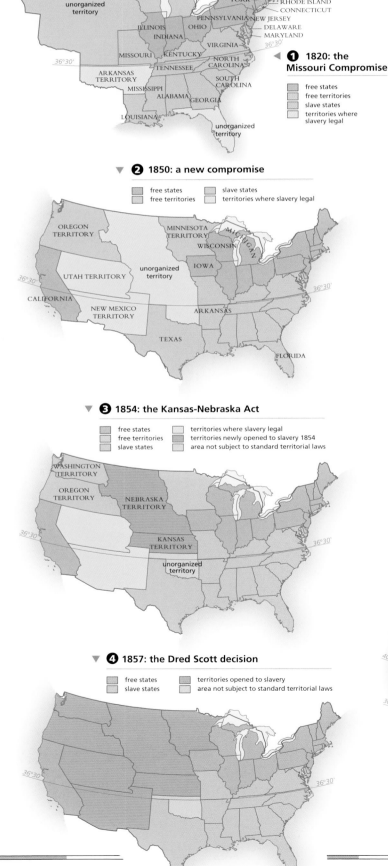

1 1820: the Missouri Compromise
- free states
- free territories
- slave states
- territories where slavery legal

2 1850: a new compromise
- free states
- free territories
- slave states
- territories where slavery legal

3 1854: the Kansas-Nebraska Act
- free states
- free territories
- slave states
- territories where slavery legal
- territories newly opened to slavery 1854
- area not subject to standard territorial laws

4 1857: the Dred Scott decision
- free states
- slave states
- territories opened to slavery
- area not subject to standard territorial laws

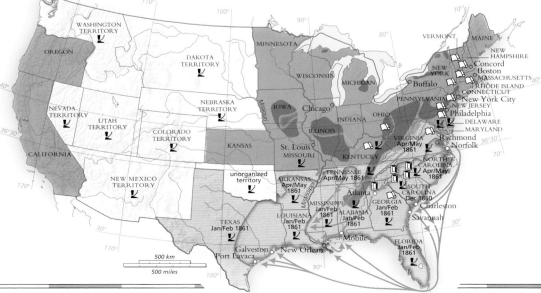

5 North versus South: the state of the Union in 1861
- Union states
- Confederate states
- slavery legal
- major slave trade routes
- Jan 1861 date of secession from the Union

Resources and industry
- southern cotton belt
- northern corn belt
- coal
- iron ore
- precious metal
- textile production
- manufacturing city

The Civil War 1861–65

In 1860, seven Southern states, fearing restrictions on slavery, seceded from the US. By 1861, they had been joined by four more and became known as the Confederacy. The remaining 23 so-called Union states remained loyal to the US. In April 1861, an attack on Fort Sumter in Charleston Harbor started a war for which neither side was prepared. The Civil War became a war of exhaustion. The superior demographic, industrial, and positional resources of the North, combined with sea power that ensured the Confederacy's isolation, slowly destroyed the capacity and will of the Confederacy to wage war. The Confederacy rarely tried to carry the war to the North, meeting crushing defeat at Gettysburg in July 1863. For the most part it waged a defensive war in order to sap the will of the Union. Certainly by 1864 war-weariness had set in in the North, but the successes of the 1864 campaign ensured Lincoln's reelection and sealed the South's defeat.

The Civil War was among the first wars to be recorded using photography. Field photographers such as Matthew Brady were able to record the true horrors of battles such as Gettysburg, the dead from which are seen above.

The Civil War to the fall of Vicksburg

During 1861–62 Union forces lost a series of battles to an enemy with superior military skills. However, the Northern naval blockade began to cut off both Southern exports and essential supplies. With no Confederate offensive on the upper Ohio which might have split the Union, the North was able to undertake offensives against the Confederate capital, Richmond, Virginia, and along the Tennessee and Mississippi. Repulsed before Richmond and obliged thereafter to move directly against the city, Union forces secured Memphis and New Orleans, capturing Vicksburg on July 4, 1863, to divide the Confederacy.

Black fighting troops were not used by the Union army until 1863. The passage of the Militia Act in 1862 allowed them to enlist as soldiers. By the end of the war, more than 180,000 blacks had fought for the Union, although only about 100 had been able to achieve officer rank.

From Gettysburg to Petersburg

After Confederate victories at Fredericksburg and The Wilderness, the Confederate offensive into Pennsylvania was defeated at Gettysburg, on the same day as Vicksburg fell. Thereafter on the defensive, Confederate armies were increasingly outnumbered: with Grant's appointment as commander, they were also increasingly outfought. Grant undertook an offensive against Richmond that broke the Confederate freedom of action in a series of battles and the siege of Petersburg: at the same time, Sherman's army broke into Georgia and South Carolina. With defeat in front of Petersburg, Confederate resistance collapsed in April 1865.

Ulysses S. Grant was appointed supreme commander of the Union forces in 1864.

Scale varies with perspective

2070 km (1290 miles)

1890 km (1170 miles)

❼ Grant's War: the Civil War Jul 1863–Apr 1865

- Union states 1861
- Confederate states 1861
- ▲▲▲ Union front line to Dec 1863
- ▲▲▲ Union front line to Dec 1864
- → Union movement
- → Confederate movement
- 🏰 Union fort
- 🏰 Confederate fort
- ⚓ Union naval blockade
- ✕ Union victory
- ✕ Confederate victory
- ✕ inconclusive battle
- Apr 12 1865 date of battle or attack
- ✕ city destroyed
- ✕ destruction by Sherman's forces

The progress of the American Civil War 1861–65

Date	Event
12 Apr 1861	Fort Sumter shelled by Confederate troops
15 Apr 1861	President Lincoln issues call for troops
19 Apr 1861	Lincoln proclaims blockade of South
6–7 Apr 1862	Battle of Shiloh: heavy casualties on both sides
16 Apr 1862	Start of draft in Confederate states
1 May 1862	Union fleet captures New Orleans
22 Sep 1862	Preliminary Emancipation Proclamation issued
13 Dec 1862	Severe Union defeat at Fredericksburg
1 Jan 1863	Emancipation Proclamation frees slaves in Confederate states
3 Mar 1863	Draft law passed in North
May 1863	Grant's army defeats Confederates in Mississippi and starts to besiege Vicksburg
1–3 Jul 1863	Confederate defeat at battle of Gettysburg
4 Jul 1863	Vicksburg captured by Union troops
19 Nov 1863	Gettysburg Address
2 Sep 1864	Sherman's troops enter Atlanta
15 Nov 1864	Sherman begins 'March to the Sea'
15–16 Dec 1864	Battle of Nashville destroys western Confederate army
9 Apr 1865	Lee surrenders to Grant at Appomattox
14 Apr 1865	Assassination of Lincoln

NORTH AMERICA 1865–1920

THE NATIONS OF NORTH AMERICA focused on the development of their own resources after 1865. The US worked to reconstruct itself after the Civil War and, like Canada, concentrated on the completion of transcontinental railroads to further exploit the continent's immense resources. Abroad, the US extended its influence in Central America and west across the Pacific, gaining new territory and economic advantage. In Mexico, Benito Juárez and his Republican forces felled the regime of Maximilian, ushering in a period of relative calm. Under Porfirio Díaz, Mexico attracted foreign investment and immigration, but its population remained brutally suppressed.

The Statue of Liberty came to symbolize the hope and freedom offered by the US.

Industrialization and urbanization

US manufacturing techniques and machinery were refined throughout the second half of the 19th century.

The growth of the railroads and industrialization transformed the North American landscape. The economic boom turned the continent into a magnet for immigration: thousands came to its shores seeking a better life. Inventions and innovations abounded; cities arose across the continent, supporting factories that had expanded rapidly because of the demands of the American Civil War. The new industrial cities became pressure cookers of societal and political discontent, with often bloody confrontations between organized labor, police, and even the military.

Theodore Roosevelt, president 1901–09, presided over the economic boom of the early 20th century.

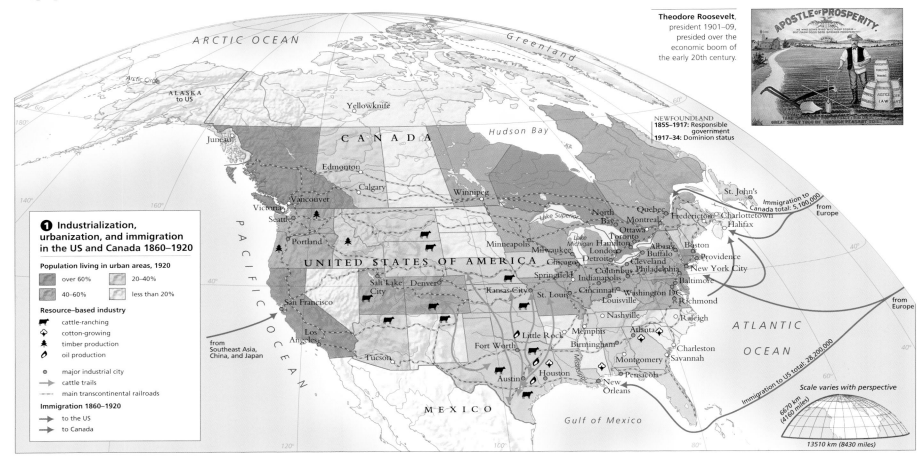

NEWFOUNDLAND
1855–1917: Responsible government
1917–34: Dominion status

① Industrialization, urbanization, and immigration in the US and Canada 1860–1920

Population living in urban areas, 1920
- over 60%
- 40–60%
- 20–40%
- less than 20%

Resource–based industry
- cattle-ranching
- cotton-growing
- timber production
- oil production
- major industrial city
- cattle trails
- main transcontinental railroads

Immigration 1860–1920
- to the US
- to Canada

from Southeast Asia, China, and Japan

Immigration to Canada total: 5,100,000 from Europe

from Europe

Immigration to US total: 28,200,000

Scale varies with perspective
6670 km (4160 miles)
13510 km (8430 miles)

② Ethnic neighborhoods in Manhattan c.1920

- African-American
- Chinese
- Czech, Hungarian
- French
- German
- Irish
- Italian
- Jewish
- Scandinavian, Finnish
- Syrian, Turkish, Armenian, Greek

2 km
2 miles

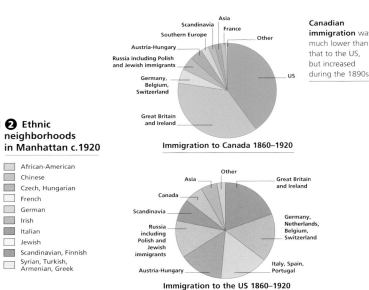

Canadian immigration was much lower than that to the US, but increased during the 1890s.

Immigration to Canada 1860–1920

Immigration to the US 1860–1920

The era of mass migration

During the 19th century nearly 50 million immigrants swelled the populations of Canada and the US. Immigration was initially from northern Europe: Germany, Scandinavia, Britain, and Ireland. From the 1880s, the bulk of migrants came from eastern and southern Europe. Most settlers were lured by the economic opportunities offered by the Americas, but others sought freedom from religious persecution and political uncertainty. After World War I, immigration was severely curtailed.

The majority of new arrivals to the Americas were able to gain entry. Only about 2% were refused entryy.

New York

New York City's Ellis Island was the point of entry for millions of immigrants between 1892 and 1920. Many people remained within the city, finding comfort and support in the ethnic neighborhoods which had grown up there. By the 1920s, the diversity of nationalities on Manhattan was a reflection of the diverse strains that made up the population of the US.

The US: 1865–1914

1869: 15th Amendment gives vote to freed slaves in US

1866: Railroad Act permits appropriation of Native American lands by railroad companies

1881–85: Start of migration to the US by nearly 400,000 Canadians

1882: Chinese immigration into US is banned

1896: Klondike gold rush: more than 100,000 people come to Yukon territory

1889: Two million acres of Native American land in Oklahoma given to settlers

1903: Flight of the Wright brothers at Kitty Hawk

1917: Asian laborers excluded from entering US by Immigration Act

1860 1870 1880 1890 1900 1910 1920

The Mexican Revolution 1910–20

Long-term government mismanagement of Mexico's natural resources combined with political repression under Porfirio Díaz produced an explosive situation by 1910. Francisco Madero's *Plan de San Luis Potosí* called for a revolt against the government; revolutionary armies led by Pascual Orozco and Pancho Villa raided government garrisons in the north, while Emiliano Zapata waged a campaign against local political bosses in the south. From 1911–1915, Madero, Victoriano Huerta, Venustiano Carranza, and Eulalio Gutierrez all held the post of president but all failed to control the bloody anarchy which had been unleashed. The US, alarmed by the potential damage to its business interests, intervened militarily from 1915–17. In 1917, a new constitution was drawn up, which, while allowing the president dictatorial powers, gave the government the right to confiscate land from wealthy landowners, guaranteed workers' rights, and limited the rights of the Catholic church.

The Mexican revolution was conducted largely at a local level with bands of guerrilla fighters loyal to a factional leader waging war against government troops.

❸ The Mexican Revolution 1910–17

Areas of control
- Venustiano Carranza
- Pancho Villa
- Emiliano Zapata
- Francisco Madero
- → route of US expedition
- US/Mexican clash
- major incident in revolution
- state boundary
- railroad

Map labels (Mexican Revolution):
- 1915: Villa's raids claim lives of 18 Americans
- Columbus, NEW MEXICO, ARIZONA
- Cullerson's Ranch
- Nogales, Ascension
- Spring 1911: City seized by revolutionary forces; Madero declared President in place of Diaz
- El Paso, Ciudad Juárez
- Colonia Dublán, Carrizal
- 1916: Mexican government troops defeat US force
- Namiquipa, SONORA, TEXAS
- San Antonio
- 1910: Francisco Madero calls for revolt from prison
- Guaymas, Bachiniva
- Dec 1913: Pancho Villa becomes governor of Chihuahua
- Tomochic, CHIHUAHUA, Chihuahua
- Eagle Pass
- Ciudad Porfirio Díaz
- Mar 1916: US forces on punitive mission fired on by Mexicans
- Parral, Jiménez, COAHUILA, Laredo
- Rosario, Escalón, NUEVO LEÓN
- Torreón, Parras, Monterrey, Saltillo
- DURANGO, Culiacán, Durango
- Tropic of Cancer
- ZACATECAS, TAMAULIPAS
- Mazatlán, Tropic of Cancer
- SAN LUIS POTOSÍ
- Ciudad Madero, Tampico
- Apr 1914: Arrest of crew of USS Dolphin
- Gulf of Mexico
- Progreso, Mérida, YUCATÁN
- Aguascalientes, GUANAJUATO
- Apr 1914: Landing of US marines sent by President Wilson; Nov 1914: Withdrawal of marines
- Tepic, NAYARIT, QUERÉTARO, HIDALGO
- Campeche, QUINTANA ROO
- JALISCO, Guadalajara, Celaya
- Apr 1915: Villa routed by Obregon in bloody battle
- Gulf of Campeche
- CAMPECHE
- COLIMA, MICHOACÁN, MEXICO, Puebla, Veracruz
- Mexico City, PUEBLA, TLAXCALA
- Feb 1913: Military coup: Huerta assumes presidency with US approval; Madero assassinated
- Aug 1914: Carranza declares himself president despite Villa's objections
- TABASCO, BRITISH HONDURAS
- GUERRERO, Tehuacán
- San Cristóbal, CHIAPAS
- Oaxaca, OAXACA, Tehuantepec
- Salina Cruz, GUATEMALA
- Gulf of Tehuantepec
- PACIFIC OCEAN
- 300 km / 300 miles

US imperial ambitions

US expansion in the Pacific was fueled partly by missionary zeal – especially in the case of the Philippines – and by a desire for access to the immense possibilities of the Chinese market. The US continued to dominate Latin American affairs, with frequent political and economic intervention becoming a feature of the relationship. The Spanish–American war resulted in Cuban independence and US control of Puerto Rico and the Philippines.

In 1898, the destruction of the USS Maine in Havana Harbor with the loss of 266 of her crew led to war between the US and Spain.

The US, Central America, and the Caribbean

- 1867: Archduke Maximilian shot in Mexico; Benito Juárez becomes president
- 1876: Start of dictatorship of Porfirio Díaz in Mexico. He has US support
- 1895: Uprising in Cuba against Spanish rule
- 1897: Cuba becomes autonomous but not fully independent from Spain
- 1898: Spanish–American War
- 1899: Cession of Cuba and Puerto Rico to US by Spain
- 1903: US leases Panama Canal Zone
- 1911: Overthrow of dictator Díaz in Mexico
- 1915–16: US intervention in Mexico and invasion of Haiti and Dominican Republic
- (Timeline: 1860, 1870, 1880, 1890, 1900, 1910, 1920)

❺ US intervention in Cuba
- major battle
- US naval base after war
- → Spanish forces
- → US forces
- outbreak of war

Map labels (Cuba):
- US forces from Tampa and Norfolk
- Tropic of Cancer
- Havana, Feb 15 1898: USS Maine sunk
- Bahía Honda
- US forces from Puerto Rico
- Santa Clara
- CUBA
- Jul 3 1898
- US naval blockade
- San Juan Heights, Jul 1 1898
- Guantánamo, Jun 1898: US established supply base
- Santiago de Cuba, Jul 16 1898: Santiago surrenders
- Caribbean Sea
- May 19 1898: Spanish forces, Jul 3 1898
- 200 km / 200 miles

---

❹ US territorial expansion and imperialism, 1860–1920
- US protectorate/temporary occupation by US
- acquired as a result of Spanish-American War 1898
- ◆ New territory acquired by US
- → US forces
- major battle

**Map labels (world/Pacific):**
- RUSSIA, ARCTIC OCEAN, EUROPE
- 1917: US enters World War I 2 million US troops serve in Europe
- ATLANTIC OCEAN
- 1867: Alaska Purchase (from Russia)
- CANADA
- 1900: US sends troops as part of foreign force to crush Boxer Rebellion
- Beijing, Bering Sea, Aleutian Islands
- 1897–1903: Alaska border dispute between US and Canada
- CHINA, Andong, INDIA
- AFRICA
- CUBA 1868–78, 1895–98: Revolution in Cuba; 1898: Spanish-American War; 1901–34: US protectorate under Platt Amendment established
- JAPAN, USA
- Hong Kong, Taiwan
- HAITI 1915–1934: occupied and under US protectorate
- 1915: US troops under General Pershing intervene in Mexican Revolution
- DOMINICAN REPUBLIC 1868: US attempts purchase; 1916–24: US occupation
- New Orleans, Miami, MEXICO
- VIRGIN ISLANDS 1916: purchased by US from Denmark
- PHILIPPINE ISLANDS
- April–May 1898: Spanish-American War
- Dec 1898: US annexes the Philippines
- 1898–1901: US-Filipino War
- Manila Bay May 1 1898, Manila
- PUERTO RICO 1898: annexed by US
- Midway Islands 1867: annexed by US
- HONDURAS 1907: US intervention; 1924–25: US occupation
- INDIAN OCEAN
- Wake Island 1899: annexed by US
- Hawaiian Islands 1898: annexed by US
- GUATEMALA 1898: United Fruit Co. founded for banana trade; 1906: US intervention
- Caracas
- Guam 1898: ceded to US
- Johnston Island 1898: annexed by US
- Bogotá, COLOMBIA, VENEZUELA 1895–98: Venezuelan crisis
- NICARAGUA 1906, 1909–10: US intervention; 1912–1925: US occupation and financial supervision
- ECUADOR, BRAZIL
- PANAMA 1903: US acquires Canal Zone; 1903–39: US protectorate; 1914: Completion of Panama Canal
- DUTCH EAST INDIES
- PACIFIC OCEAN
- PERU, BOLIVIA
- AUSTRALIA
- American Samoa 1899: US control
- CHILE, ARGENTINA, Equator

AN ERA OF BOOM AND BUST

The NRA, set up in 1933, was the first New Deal recovery program.

INVOLVEMENT IN WORLD WAR I confirmed the US's position as a world power in the first quarter of the century. Immigration greatly magnified the population, but during the 1920s, laws were enacted to control the tide of European settlers. The economy grew quickly, but the boom proved vulnerable and in 1929 the stock market collapsed. Between 1930 and 1932, the number of unemployed rose from 4 million to between 12 and 15 million – 25% of the total workforce. The Republican government, which had promoted the boom and was blamed for the crash, was rejected by the electorate, leading to the political dominance of a Democrat, Franklin Delano Roosevelt, for 13 years.

The industrial boom

This Model-A Ford was the successor to the Model-T Ford, the first car to be built using production line techniques and initially produced only in black. By the 1930s, Henry Ford achieved his dream of "a car so low in price that no man making a good salary will be unable to afford one."

The early 1920s saw a massive growth in US production. Traditional industries such as iron and steel were in relative decline, but automobiles, petrochemicals, construction, and the service industries grew rapidly, as did speculation on the stock market. But the boom was built on shaky foundations. High rates of small business failure in the 1920s gave the first signs of fragility and it was clear that production was outstripping consumption. Paper fortunes that had accrued in stocks and shares were wiped out by the Wall Street Crash of 1929.

The depression and the New Deal

The stock market crash of 1929 shattered millions of dreams and left many Americans destitute. Farmers were particularly hard hit, as banks withdrew funding. So were black people in both cities and rural areas. The Roosevelt administration devised a series of relief programs known as the "New Deal" to restart the economy and provide new jobs. Though millions of dollars of federal funding were spent on relief, 20% of Americans were still unemployed in 1939. Not until World War II did the economy recover.

The Works Progress Administration (WPA) provided work relief for 8.5 million unemployed. Projects included the building and repair of roads, bridges, schools, and hospitals.

❶ Major US industries c.1925

- iron and steel
- meat processing
- oil and gas
- textile production
- timber
- vehicle manufacture
- coalfield
- major industrial city

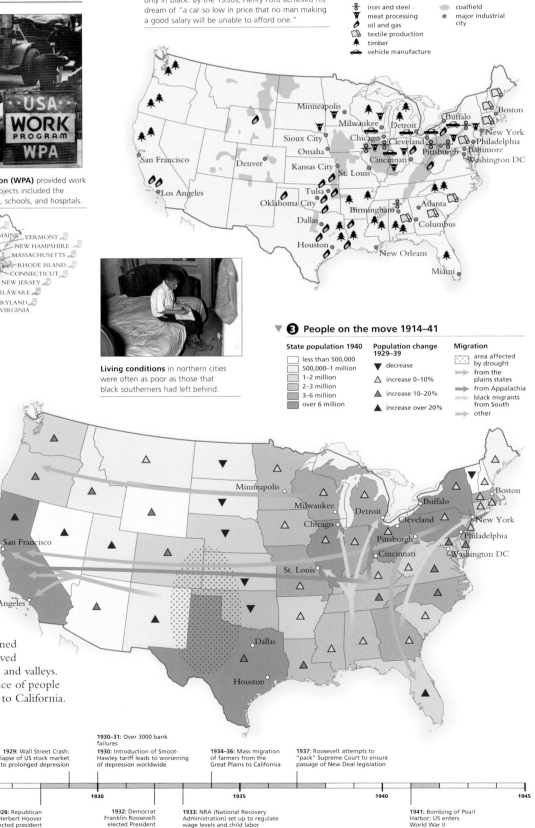

❷ The impact of the Great Depression 1933–34

Unemployed	Families receiving relief
less than 10%	less than 10%
11–15%	10–15%
16–25%	over 15%
over 25%	

Living conditions in northern cities were often as poor as those that black southerners had left behind.

❸ People on the move 1914–41

State population 1940	Population change 1929–39	Migration
less than 500,000	decrease	area affected by drought
500,000–1 million	increase 0–10%	from the plains states
1–2 million	increase 10–20%	from Appalachia
2–3 million	increase over 20%	black migrants from South
3–6 million		other
over 6 million		

Migration in the US, 1914–41

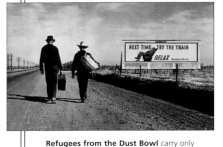

Refugees from the Dust Bowl carry only the bare essentials as they walk towards Los Angeles in search of work (1939).

By the 1920s, more than 50% of Americans lived in urban areas. From 1917–20, more than 400,000 rural black southerners moved to northern cities, and 600,000 more went in the 1920s. In the mid-1930s, farmers from the drought-affected plains states abandoned their farms by the thousands and moved west – primarily to California's cities and valleys. Appalachia also saw a mass transference of people north to Indiana and Ohio and west to California.

The US 1914–1941

1917–20: Start of migration of southern blacks to northern cities	
1918: Armistice ends World War I	1920: American women granted the vote
1923: More than 13 million cars on US roads	1929: Wall Street Crash: collapse of US stock market leads to prolonged depression
1930–31: Over 3000 bank failures	1930: Introduction of Smoot-Hawley tariff leads to worsening of depression worldwide
1934–36: Mass migration of farmers from the Great Plains to California	1937: Roosevelt attempts to "pack" Supreme Court to ensure passage of New Deal legislation

1915	1920	1925	1930	1935	1940	1945

1917: US enters World War I	1919: Influenza kills 500,000 Americans
1923: Republican Calvin Coolidge becomes president after death of Warren Harding	1928: Republican Herbert Hoover elected president
1932: Democrat Franklin Roosevelt elected President	1933: NRA (National Recovery Administration) set up to regulate wage levels and child labor
1941: Bombing of Pearl Harbor; US enters World War II	

Popular culture in the US

Developments in technology during World War I improved communications throughout the US. By the 1920s virtually all of the nation was connected to the Bell Telephone network. Radio sets enabled news and information to reach even isolated areas. The movies became the first mass entertainment industry. From small beginnings in the early 1900s, by the 1930s, the film industry in Hollywood was exporting its glamorous products worldwide. During the Depression, cheap movie tickets kept audience numbers buoyant despite an initial downturn. Professional sports such as football, baseball, and boxing became of national interest for the first time, with huge attendances and highly paid celebrities.

❹ The major Hollywood studios in 1919

- Nestor
- Famous Players – Lasky Clater Paramount
- National Film Corporation of America
- Metro
- Chaplin
- Brunton
- Fox
- D.W. Griffith
- Vitagraph
- Mack Sennett
- Universal
- Ince
- Goldwyn

By 1919, most of the major movie studios had established themselves to the north of Los Angeles. Hollywood became the heart of the world motion picture industry and a magnet for all aspiring filmmakers.

Annual consumer expenditure on moviegoing ($ millions)

The growth in spending on movie tickets reflected wartime prosperity.

Number of radio sets in the US (millions)

By 1924, more than 2.5 million radios had been sold to American consumers.

Sales of records in the US ($ millions)

The growth in popularity of the radio led to a dramatic decline in record buying: within five years sales had virtually halved.

Though musicals and comedies took audiences away from the realities of the Depression, other films such as John Ford's *The Grapes of Wrath* dealt with themes inspired by the harshness of people's lives.

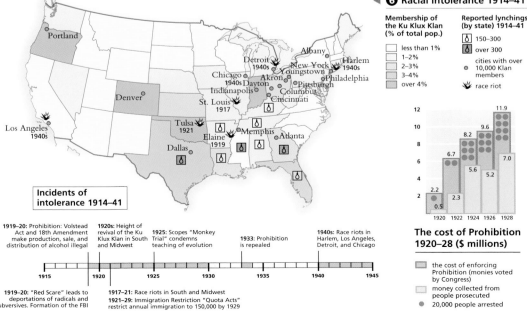

The growth of US popular culture spawned a new wave of national heroes including movie stars and athletes like the baseball star Babe Ruth, who scored 60 home runs in a season for the New York Yankees.

Walt Disney's Mickey Mouse first appeared as an animated cartoon in 1928. He became the symbol of the world's first international entertainment empire.

© Disney

Entertaining the masses 1914–41

- 1915: D.W. Griffith directs *The Birth of a Nation*
- 1917: First jazz recording made
- 1921: Charlie Chaplin produces *The Kid*, his first full-length film
- 1927: Al Jolson launches the talking picture with *The Jazz Singer*
- 1928: Mickey Mouse makes his first appearance on film
- 1929: First Academy Awards ceremony introduces the "Oscar"
- 1930: Weekly movie ticket sales reach more than 100 million
- 1934: More than 583 radio stations established nationwide
- 1935: Gate receipts exceed $1 million at World Heavyweight Boxing Championship
- 1939: *Gone With the Wind* becomes the highest-grossing film yet
- 1940: 86% of US population own radio sets

1915 — 1920 — 1925 — 1930 — 1935 — 1940 — 1945

THE FDR EFFECT

The political complexion of the US altered radically during the 1930s. Hoover's Republican party, so dominant at the height of the 20s boom, was routed by the Democrats in 1932. The patrician Franklin Delano Roosevelt attracted a "New Deal coalition" of Blacks, women, labor groups, and southern whites which dominated American politics for over 30 years.

Roosevelt spoke regularly to the American people via his "fireside chats" which were broadcast on national radio.

❺ Presidential elections

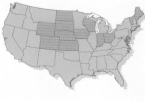

- Republican
- Democrat

1928

1932   1936

1940   1944

Intolerance

This period, particularly the 1920s, was marked by diverse displays of intolerance against perceived threats to the "American Way of Life." "New" immigrants, black migration, the increased freedom of women, and economic instability all fueled anxieties. The prohibition of alcohol, immigration "Quota Acts," and the formation of the FBI in response to the "Red Scare" of 1919–20 and the fear of Communism, were official responses to this new intolerance. Other – unofficial – reactions included race riots in the southern states and Midwest, and the revival of the white supremacist Ku Klux Klan, whose membership increased to more than two million in the 1920s.

The growth of the Ku Klux Klan in this period was largely an expression of insecurity among small-town White Anglo-Saxon Protestants toward a multitude of apparent threats to their power and influence.

Incidents of intolerance 1914–41

- 1919–20: Prohibition: Volstead Act and 18th Amendment make production, sale, and distribution of alcohol illegal
- 1919–20: "Red Scare" leads to deportations of radicals and subversives. Formation of the FBI
- 1920s: Height of revival of the Ku Klux Klan in South and Midwest
- 1917–21: Race riots in South and Midwest
- 1925: Scopes "Monkey Trial" condemns teaching of evolution
- 1921–29: Immigration Restriction "Quota Acts" restrict annual immigration to 150,000 by 1929
- 1933: Prohibition is repealed
- 1940s: Race riots in Harlem, Los Angeles, Detroit, and Chicago

1915 — 1920 — 1925 — 1930 — 1935 — 1940 — 1945

❻ Racial intolerance 1914–41

Membership of the Ku Klux Klan (% of total pop.)
- less than 1%
- 1–2%
- 2–3%
- 3–4%
- over 4%

Reported lynchings (by state) 1914–41
- 150–300
- over 300
- cities with over 10,000 Klan members
- race riot

The cost of Prohibition 1920–28 ($ millions)
- the cost of enforcing Prohibition (monies voted by Congress)
- money collected from people prosecuted
- 20,000 people arrested

SOCIETIES IN TRANSITION

Martin Luther King, Jnr. harnessed the spontaneous protests of the 1950s to create a massive civil rights movement.

IN THE 1950S, THE UNITED STATES was labeled "the affluent society." This phrase reflected the experience of unprecedented economic prosperity and social progress in the years since World War II ended the Great Depression. Most Americans enjoyed rising incomes on the back of the postwar boom. The quality of life was further enhanced by the availability of new consumer goods, new leisure opportunities, and suburban housing. The people of Mexico, Central America, and the Caribbean continued to have a much lower standard of living than the US and Canada. And within the US, itself, not all regions and social groups experienced equal advances in affluence and status.

Postwar prosperity in the US

The idealized family unit, headed by a male breadwinner, became a favorite image for advertisers and politicians during the 1950s.

The economic stimulus provided by the war and, later, the arms race with the Soviet Union were key factors in creating the affluence of the immediate postwar decades. As manufacturing switched to a peacetime mode, consumer durables flowed into the domestic marketplace. Consumerism generated a flourishing service sector. America's position at the hub of the international trading system gave her access to foreign markets and raw materials crucial to economic success. The boom ended in the early 1970s, with the Vietnam War and the energy crisis producing prolonged inflation and recession. Europe and Japan were also challenging American economic dominance.

❶ Average family income by region, 1949

Rocky Mountains $13,857
New England $13,328
Far West $15,416
Great Plains $12,635
Great Lakes $14,997
Mid-Atlantic $15,722
Southwest $11,656
Southeast $8856

By no means all of the US benefited from the prosperity of the postwar period. While California and the industrial north boomed, the South in particular remained depressed, with an average income only half that of other parts of the US.

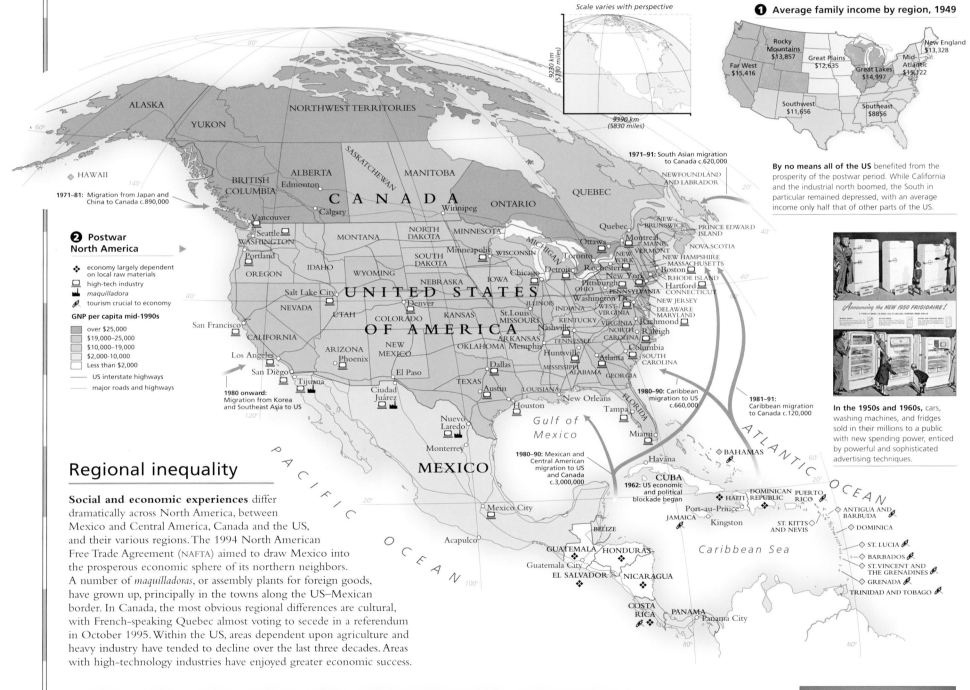

Scale varies with perspective

9230 km (5730 miles)

9390 km (5830 miles)

❷ Postwar North America

- economy largely dependent on local raw materials
- high-tech industry
- *maquilladora*
- tourism crucial to economy

GNP per capita mid-1990s
- over $25,000
- $19,000–25,000
- $10,000–19,000
- $2,000-10,000
- Less than $2,000

— US interstate highways
— major roads and highways

1971–81: Migration from Japan and China to Canada c.890,000

1971–91: South Asian migration to Canada c.620,000

1980 onward: Migration from Korea and Southeast Asia to US

1980–90: Mexican and Central American migration to US and Canada c.3,000,000

1962: US economic and political blockade began

1980–90: Caribbean migration to US c.660,000

1981–91: Caribbean migration to Canada c.120,000

In the 1950s and 1960s, cars, washing machines, and fridges sold in their millions to a public with new spending power, enticed by powerful and sophisticated advertising techniques.

Regional inequality

Social and economic experiences differ dramatically across North America, between Mexico and Central America, Canada and the US, and their various regions. The 1994 North American Free Trade Agreement (NAFTA) aimed to draw Mexico into the prosperous economic sphere of its northern neighbors. A number of *maquilladoras*, or assembly plants for foreign goods, have grown up, principally in the towns along the US–Mexican border. In Canada, the most obvious regional differences are cultural, with French-speaking Quebec almost voting to secede in a referendum in October 1995. Within the US, areas dependent upon agriculture and heavy industry have tended to decline over the last three decades. Areas with high-technology industries have enjoyed greater economic success.

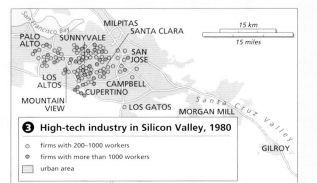

❸ High-tech industry in Silicon Valley, 1980
- firms with 200–1000 workers
- firms with more than 1000 workers
- urban area

SILICON VALLEY

Without specific locational needs, many high-tech firms were able to site their businesses in nonurban areas in the South and West, helping to revitalize the economy of these regions. Silicon Valley near San Francisco, California, contains one of the world's highest concentrations of computing and electronics industries. Initially, many high-tech manufacturers relied upon contracts from the US military, but the age of the personal computer has allowed these manufacturers to play a key role in sustaining American exports and growth.

New high-tech industries including aerospace and electronics, as at Silicon Valley *(right)*, grew up in the late 1970s to fill the gaps left by the decline of traditional US heavy industries.

Changes in urban life

As black Americans migrated from the rural South to urban centers in the 1940s and 1950s, many whites abandoned city life for the suburbs. These areas became increasingly detached from the cities; instead of petitioning for access to the cities' municipal facilities, postwar suburban residents fought fiercely against annexation proposals. The tax dollars of prosperous whites were no longer available to maintain the city infrastructure. The financial crisis was made worse by the decline of traditional US industries, and many of America's cities sank into crisis during the 1960s and 1970s. Housing stock deteriorated, roads were not repaired, and poverty, crime, and racial tension were common features of many urban areas in the US. Poverty was not confined to the inner cities: people in rural areas in the deep South and the Appalachians were some of the most deprived in the US.

The centers of many of America's great cities declined physically as people move to the suburbs. Old housing stock was torn down but not replaced, and the infrastructure declined through lack of funding.

The growth of the suburbs

The 1950s saw the growth of suburban America. New construction techniques lowered the cost of new homes, and expressways improved access to and from urban centers. In the postwar era, cities like Chicago absorbed ever more of their surrounding areas.

The new suburbs provided a safe haven away from the cities. Mortgage assistance was readily available to those wishing to move to suburban areas. Until the 1960s, money was siphoned into the suburbs by federal housing officials, who simultaneously denied loans to people still living in urban areas.

❹ Chicago: 1850–1969

Urban growth
- 1850
- 1875
- 1900
- 1925
- 1950
- 1969

LAKE COUNTY
McHENRY COUNTY
ILLINOIS
KANE COUNTY
DU PAGE COUNTY
Chicago
COOK COUNTY
KENDALL COUNTY
WILL COUNTY
INDIANA
LAKE COUNTY
PORTER COUNTY
Lake Michigan

20 km
20 miles

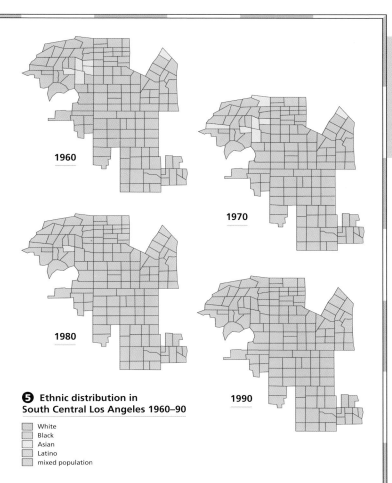

1960
1970
1980
1990

❺ Ethnic distribution in South Central Los Angeles 1960–90
- White
- Black
- Asian
- Latino
- mixed population

Poverty and ethnic balance in inner city Los Angeles

Los Angeles demonstrates how wealth and poverty live separate lives in postwar urban America. The central neighborhoods in an otherwise prosperous city have a massively disproportionate number of poor residents, with an ethnic mix in constant flux. In 1960, a substantial white population remained in South Central Los Angeles. By 1970, whites had largely left the area, which had a now predominantly black population. Twenty years later, Latinos formed a majority in many South Central neighborhoods.

Civil Rights and other protest movements

1955: Bus boycott against segregation in Montgomery, Alabama
1961: Student freedom riders go into South to protest against segregation
1963: March on Washington led by Martin Luther King, Jr.
1965: Voting Rights Act increases number of black voters; Watts Riots in Los Angeles
1968: Assassination of Martin Luther King, Jr. sparks riots in 124 US cities
1970: Four students killed at Kent State University, Ohio in protest over US involvement in Cambodia

1955 — 1960 — 1965 — 1970 — 1975

1957: Martin Luther King, Jr. heads coordinated resistance movement
1964: Civil Rights Act forbids segregation in public places
1966: Race riots in Atlanta
1968: Riots and protests follow Democrat rally in Chicago
1969: 250,000 people march on Washington in protest against war in Vietnam
1974: High Court gives go-ahead to busing for integration of US schools

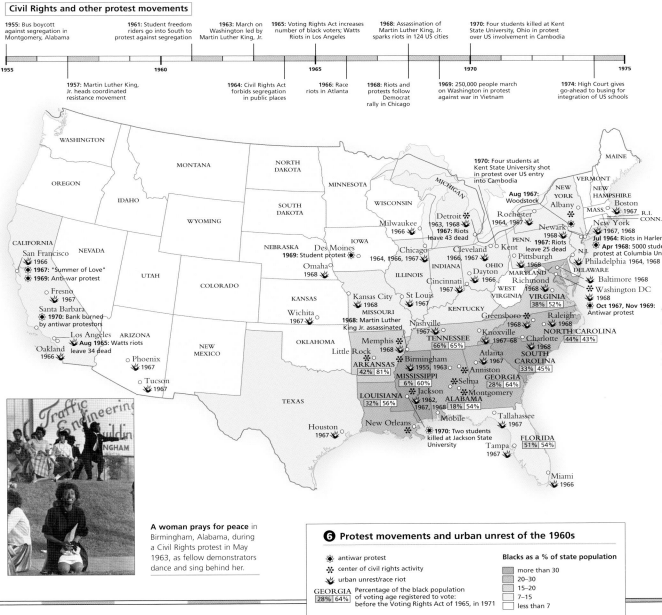

A woman prays for peace in Birmingham, Alabama, during a Civil Rights protest in May 1963, as fellow demonstrators dance and sing behind her.

❻ Protest movements and urban unrest of the 1960s

☀ antiwar protest
✳ center of civil rights activity
☙ urban unrest/race riot

GEORGIA 28% | 64% Percentage of the black population of voting age registered to vote: before the Voting Rights Act of 1965, in 1971

Blacks as a % of state population
- more than 30
- 20–30
- 15–20
- 7–15
- less than 7

In August 1969, 400,000 people gathered at a farm near Bethel in upstate New York to form the "Woodstock Nation," at a music festival which was also a celebration of peaceful, antiestablishment coexistence.

Moves for freedom

The opportunities presented by postwar America were denied to many black Americans, particularly in the still-segregated South, where they were prevented by whites from voting. Inspired by decolonization movements abroad, and aided by a 1954 Supreme Court judgement that segregation was unconstitutional, black Americans began to challenge discrimination. In 1955, a bus boycott in Montgomery, Alabama forced the bus company to end segregation. The success inspired similar protests throughout the South. In 1964 and 1965, the US Congress passed legislation banning racial discrimination and protecting the democratic rights of all Americans. The 1960s also saw a rise in political consciousness among other groups; protests against the Vietnam War grew in number throughout the late 1960s, as did the movement for women's rights.

THE USA: GROWTH OF A SUPERPOWER

John F. Kennedy, a charismatic and popular US president, was assassinated in 1963.

THE JAPANESE ATTACK on Pearl Harbor in December 1941 and the subsequent US entry into the Second World War caused a shift in the US view of the world. Thereafter, through alliances, military interventions, and trade, the United States dominated world affairs. Although challenged by the Cuban Revolution in 1959, the US maintained its position in the Americas, a secure base from which to fight the Cold War. The collapse of the Soviet Union in 1991 left the US as the world's only superpower. After the atrocities of 11 September 2001, the US embarked on a new phase of unilateralist interventionism, determined to stamp out terrorist and other threats to US security.

America and the world

During World War II, the US established military bases around the world, which remained important throughout the Cold War with the Soviet Union. The Cold War also encouraged the US to form alliances, such as the North Atlantic Treaty Organization (NATO) of 1949. After the Vietnam War, the US retreated from international politics, but the Soviet invasion of Afghanistan in 1979 revived the Cold War for another decade. With the collapse of the Soviet Union in 1991, the US was left as the sole superpower. After 11 September 2001, the United States took on a more assertive and unilateralist role in international affairs.

US soldiers with a Viet Cong suspect during the Vietnam War (1950–73), the longest and most costly of US attempts to contain the perceived Communist threat during the Cold War.

On September 11, 2001, two aircraft hijacked by Muslim terrorists were flown into the World Trade Center, New York, killing over 2,700. The response of US President George W. Bush was to declare a 'War on Terror', stepping up security at home and invading Afghanistan (2001) and Iraq (2003).

▲ ① Strategic alliances 1948–89

US collective defense treaties
- NATO from 1983
- Rio Treaty by 1975
- ANZUS Pact 1951
- Southeast Asia Collective Defense Treaty 1954
- Bilateral defense treaties (Japan 1960; South Korea 1953; Philippines 1951, Taiwan 1954)
- US troops on active service
- COMECON members
- other Communist states 1977
- Military Air Transit Rights, Eastern Hemisphere

US involvement in world affairs since 1950

1950: Korean War	1955: US intervention in Iran
1962: Cuban missile crisis	1973: US withdraws troops from Vietnam
1979: Iran hostage crisis	1990: US sends troops to the Gulf in response to Saddam Hussein's invasion of Kuwait
1994: US intervenes in Haiti	1999: Ethnic cleansing in Kosovo prompts US to bomb Yugoslavia

1950: Start of US involvement in Vietnam — 1958: Eisenhower Doctrine commits US to prevent spread of Communism in Middle East — 1973: US assists in right-wing coup in Chile — 1978: US-brokered peace deal between Egypt and Israel — 1983: US intervention in Grenada — 1995: US troops withdraw from Somalia after failing to restore democracy — 2001: Taliban ousted in Afghanistan by US-led forces — 2003: US leads invasion of Iraq

US investment overseas

During the Cold War, investment overseas was seen as a way to bind other nations to the capitalist sphere. The Marshall Plan of 1948 aimed both to aid the postwar recovery of Western Europe and reduce the chances of Communist subversion. American firms also tried to secure access to valuable raw materials, most importantly oil in the Middle East. Since the end of the Cold War, US investment in Western Europe has grown significantly, as American companies have sought industrial partnerships and a share of the growing European economy.

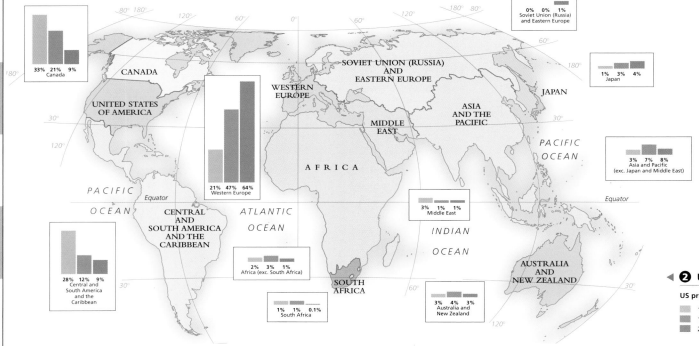

◀ ② US investment overseas

US private direct investment abroad
- 1960
- 1984
- 2003

The decline of the Democratic South

The migration of Southern blacks to northern cities in the 1940s and 1950s (in part due to the mechanization of cotton farming) killed off most of the remaining cotton plantations in the South, which had depended on their cheap labor, leading to a decline in the Southern economy. In the North, black Americans became an important political constituency. The Democratic Party tried to reconcile its desire for their votes with its desire for the continued support of white Southerners who traditionally voted Democrat. By the late 1960s, after the Civil Rights legislation of President Lyndon Johnson, many Southerners abandoned their traditional commitment to the Democratic Party.

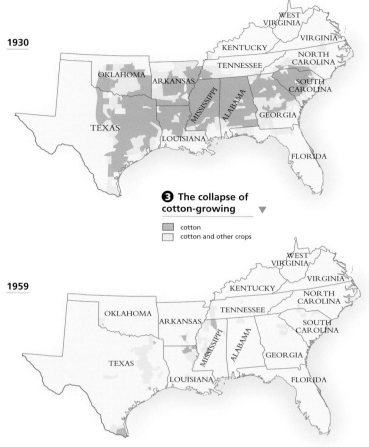

1930

1959

❸ **The collapse of cotton-growing** ▼

- cotton
- cotton and other crops

US intervention in Central America

Historically the US has acted under the "Monroe Doctrine" to ensure stability and protect its business interests in Central America. During the Cold War, the US feared Communist subversion in its own backyard. In 1954, US agents organized the downfall of a left-wing government in Guatemala. In 1962, a crisis over Soviet nuclear arms in Cuba (*see p.108*) almost caused nuclear war. During the 1980s, President Reagan acted against leftists in Grenada and Nicaragua. After the Cold War, the US became more constructively engaged in combating the drugs trade in the region.

❺ **US intervention in Central America and the Caribbean** ▼

- ☙ Cuban-sponsored guerrilla activities 1959–68
- ▰ US intervention

KEY ELECTIONS 1948–2000

In 1948 Democrat President Harry Truman won a shock victory over the Republican Thomas Dewey. However, the success of the pro-segregationist States Rights Party indicated that the Democrats might have problems maintaining the support of both blacks and Southerners, and in 1968 the Democrats lost every Southern state except Texas. Though Republicans held the Presidency throughout the 1980s, the elections of 1992 and 1996 proved that the Democrats could still win despite a largely Republican South. The 2000 election was the most controversial for over a century. Republican George W. Bush secured a smaller share of the popular vote (49.8 million) than his Democrat rival, Al Gore (50.2 million). Only when the bitterly disputed result for Florida finally went his way, did Bush win the Presidency on the votes of the states in the electoral college (271 votes to 267).

1948

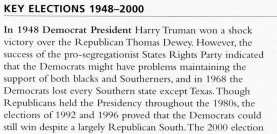
1968

Alaska ◆
Hawaii ◆

2000

Alaska ◆
Hawaii ◆

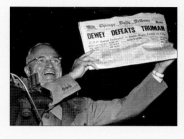

The Chicago Daily Tribune was so confident of the outcome of the 1948 US Presidential elections that the paper was printed without confirmation of the results, leaving the victorious Democratic candidate Harry Truman to revel in the premature headline.

George W. Bush had to wait five weeks after the election in 2000 before his opponent, Al Gore, conceded. All depended on the extremely close result in Florida, where, amid a flurry of legal actions, votes were counted and recounted manually until the US Supreme Court stepped in to call a halt.

❹ **Presidential elections**

States won by each party
- Republicans
- Democrats
- States Rights
- American Independent

US election results 1944–2000

1944: Roosevelt (Democrat) elected for a fourth term but dies in April 1945
1952: Eisenhower (Republican) wins election
1960: John F Kennedy (Democrat) elected
1968: Nixon (Republican) elected. Reelected 1972
1976: Jimmy Carter (Democrat) elected
1992: Bill Clinton (Democrat) elected
2000: George W. Bush (Republican) wins closely-fought election after recount in Florida

1944   1952   1960   1968   1976   1984   1992   2000

1948: Roosevelt's successor, Truman (Democrat), is surprise winner
1956: Eisenhower wins second term
1963: Assassination of Kennedy. Johnson becomes President. Reelected in 1964
1974: Nixon resigns over Watergate scandal. Replaced by Gerald Ford
1980: Ronald Reagan (Republican) wins. Wins second term in 1984
1988: George Bush (Republican) wins
1996: Bill Clinton wins second term
2004: George W Bush reelected after another close campaign, endorsing his "War on Terror"

The Sandinista revolution of 1978 put an end to more than 40 years of military dictatorship in Nicaragua. The left-wing Sandinistas were distrusted by the US which sponsored Contra guerrillas based in Honduras (*left*) against the government.

US military advisors have been active, often working with the Drug Enforcement Administration (DEA), in training local troups in many Central and South American countries since its invasion of Panama in 1989.

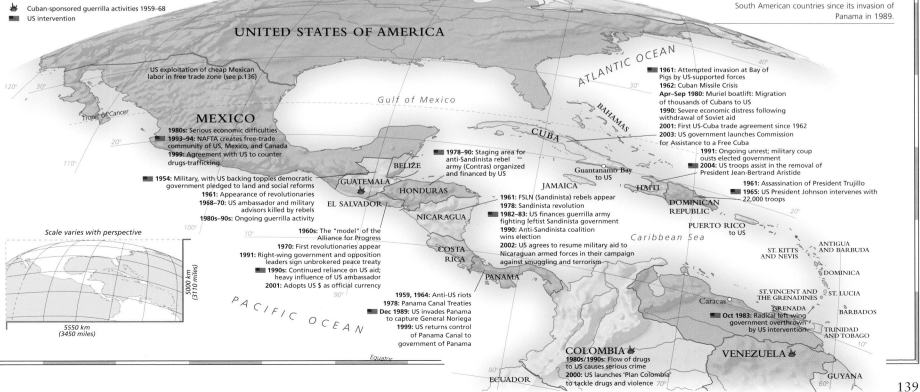

Scale varies with perspective

5550 km (3450 miles)
5000 km (3110 miles)

UNITED STATES OF AMERICA

ATLANTIC OCEAN

US exploitation of cheap Mexican labor in free trade zone (see p.136)

Tropic of Cancer

Gulf of Mexico

MEXICO
1980s: Serious economic difficulties
▰ **1993–94:** NAFTA creates free-trade community of US, Mexico, and Canada
1999: Agreement with US to counter drugs-trafficking

BAHAMAS

CUBA

1961: Attempted invasion at Bay of Pigs by US-supported forces
1962: Cuban Missile Crisis
Apr–Sep 1980: Muriel boatlift: Migration of thousands of Cubans to US
1990: Severe economic distress following withdrawal of Soviet aid
2001: First US-Cuba trade agreement since 1962
2003: US government launches Commission for Assistance to a Free Cuba

Guantanamo Bay to US

BELIZE

1978–90: Staging area for anti-Sandinista rebel army (Contras) organized and financed by US

▰ **1954:** Military, with US backing topples democratic government pledged to land and social reforms
1961: Appearance of revolutionaries
1968–70: US ambassador and military advisors killed by rebels
1980s–90s: Ongoing guerrilla activity

GUATEMALA
HONDURAS
EL SALVADOR
NICARAGUA

JAMAICA
1961: FSLN (Sandinista) rebels appear
1978: Sandinista revolution
▰ **1982–83:** US finances guerrilla army fighting leftist Sandinista government
1990: Anti-Sandinista coalition wins election
2002: US agrees to resume military aid to Nicaraguan armed forces in their campaign against smuggling and terrorism

HAITI
1991: Ongoing unrest; military coup ousts elected government
▰ **2004:** US troops assist in the removal of President Jean-Bertrand Aristide

DOMINICAN REPUBLIC
1961: Assassination of President Trujillo
▰ **1965:** US President Johnson intervenes with 22,000 troops

PUERTO RICO to US

Caribbean Sea

1960s: The "model" of the Alliance for Progress
1970: First revolutionaries appear
1991: Right-wing government and opposition leaders sign unbrokered peace treaty
▰ **1990s:** Continued reliance on US aid; heavy influence of US ambassador
2001: Adopts US $ as official currency

COSTA RICA

PACIFIC OCEAN

1959, 1964: Anti-US riots
1978: Panama Canal Treaties
▰ **Dec 1989:** US invades Panama to capture General Noriega
1999: US returns control of Panama Canal to government of Panama

PANAMA

ANTIGUA AND BARBUDA
ST. KITTS AND NEVIS
DOMINICA
ST. VINCENT AND THE GRENADINES
ST. LUCIA
GRENADA
▰ **Oct 1983:** Radical left-wing government overthrown by US intervention
BARBADOS
TRINIDAD AND TOBAGO

Caracas

COLOMBIA ☙
1980s/1990s: Flow of drugs to US causes serious crime
2000: US launches 'Plan Colombia' to tackle drugs and violence

VENEZUELA ☙

ECUADOR

GUYANA

Equator

SOUTH AMERICA
REGIONAL HISTORY

THE HISTORICAL LANDSCAPE

THE LAST CONTINENT – APART FROM ANTARCTICA – to be colonized by humans (the first settlers arrived from North America no more than 13,000 years ago), South America remains a realm of harsh extremes of climate, environment, and human society. The cordillera spine of the Andes was the heartland of the first complex societies and civilizations. Early settlers spread through the fertile tracts of the Amazon Basin, but few ventured to the sterile salt pans of the Atacama Desert – one of the driest places on Earth – or Patagonia – one of the least hospitable. European contact in the 16th century brought, as elsewhere in the Americas, the decline of indigenous cultures. Although here widespread intermarriage and the enforced importation of African slaves to work on plantations created an extraordinarily varied genetic, linguistic, and cultural pool. The continent struggled free of European colonialism in the 19th century only to be confronted by the challenge of economic, social, and political modernization, which was met with varying success. This process brought wealth for some, marginalization for many – especially in the continent's burgeoning but scattered centers of population – and a threat to the global ecosystem, as the resources of the Amazonian wilderness were increasingly placed under pressure.

The Andes were one of the sites of the earliest agricultural civilizations in South America, perhaps as many as 10,000 years ago. The mountains and temperate climate provided a wide range of habitats for wild plants. Tubers – such as potatoes and sweet potatoes – grew naturally and were simple to cultivate.

The Amazon rain forests now cover about 116,000 sq miles of South America. At the height of the last Ice Age, around 18,000 years ago, the cool arid climate, unsuitable for rain forest plants, had reduced the forest to only about 10% of its present area. Over the past 10,000 years, wetter climates have enabled the forest to grow in size.

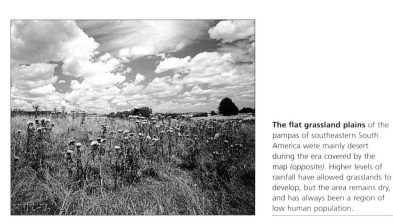

The flat grassland plains of the pampas of southeastern South America were mainly desert during the era covered by the map *(opposite)*. Higher levels of rainfall have allowed grasslands to develop, but the area remains dry, and has always been a region of low human population.

Vegetation type

- ice cap and glacier
- tundra
- polar and alpine desert
- semi-desert or sparsely vegetated
- grassland
- forest or open woodland
- tropical rain forest
- temperate desert
- tropical desert
- coastline (present day)
- coastline (18,000 years ago)

AMERICA

Sargasso
Sea

Hatteras Plain

Nares Plain

West Indies

Bahamas

Great Bahama Bank

Cuba

Yucatan
Basin

Hispaniola

Puerto Rico Trench

Cayman Trough

Jamaica

Puerto Rico

Mid-Atlantic Ridge

Tropic of Cancer

NORTH AMERICAN PLATE
SOUTH AMERICAN PLATE

Cape Verde
Basin

ATLANTIC

AFRICAN PLATE

Doldrums Fracture Zone

Gambia
Plain

Caribbean Sea

Grenada Basin

Demerara
Plain

Guiana
Basin

Four North Fracture Zone

Saint Paul Fracture Zone

Equator

NORTH AMERICAN
PLATE

CARIBBEAN
PLATE

Middle America Trench

Guatemala
Basin

Colombian
Basin

Nicaraguan Rise

Colón Ridge

Panama
Basin

Panama
Basin

CARIBBEAN PLATE
SOUTH AMERICAN
PLATE

Llanos

Orinoco

The Llanos region was a
sandy desert during the
last Ice Age, with this
scrubby vegetation.
Today it is covered
by rough grasslands.

Guiana
Highlands

Ceará Plain

Pernambuco
Plain

Putumayo

Japurá

Rio Negro

Amazon

Amazon

Marañón

Juruá

Ucayali

A
n
d
e
s

SOUTH AMERICAN PLATE

NAZCA PLATE

Peru-Chile Trench

Atacama Desert

Amazon
Basin

Madeira

Tapajós

Xingu

Roosevelt

SOUTH AMERICA

Rain forest only covered a small
portion of the Amazon Basin – the
rest was vegetated by temperate
forests, woodlands and scrub.

Planalto de
Matto Grosso

Madeira

Mamoré

São Francisco

Brazilian Highlands

Brazil
Basin

Abrolhos
Bank

Tropic of Capricorn

Santos
Plateau

OCEAN

Mendaña Fracture Zone

Peru
Basin

Nazca Ridge

Chile
Basin

Gran Chaco

Xingu

Paranaíba

Sala y Gómez Fracture Zone

Roggeveen
Basin

The Pampas was a vast
sandy region covered with
dunes 18,000 years ago.
Today this flat area is
widely cultivated, and
covered with cereals
and natural grasslands.

Paraná

Uruguay

Paraná

Río de la Plata

Pampas

Lower sea levels resulted
in much of the continental
shelf off the southeastern
coast of the continent
turning to dry land.

Rio Grande
Rise

Argentine
Basin

East Pacific Rise

NAZCA PLATE
ANTARCTIC PLATE

Colorado

Ice sheets in the far south
of the continent covered
the southernmost peaks
of the Andes, reaching
from the mountain tops
all the way down to
the Pacific Ocean.

A
n
d
e
s

Argentine
Plain

Patagonia

Falkland Escarpment

Falkland
Plateau

Falkland
Islands

SOUTH AMERICAN PLATE

South Sandwich Trench

ANTARCTIC PLATE
PACIFIC PLATE

Scotia Ridge SOUTH AMERICAN PLATE
SCOTIA PLATE

Scotia
Sea

SCOTIA PLATE
ANTARCTIC PLATE

Antarctic Circle

South Shetland Trough

Weddell
Sea

South America: 18,000 years ago

At the height of the last Ice Age (18,000 years ago),
South America was both colder and more arid. In addition,
lower sea levels exposed most of the continental shelf
in the southeast. The Amazon rain forest retreated into
a smaller area in central and southwestern Amazonia,
leaving much of the remaining land covered with grasslands.
Sandy deserts appeared in the Llanos region in the
north and in the Pampas region in the southeast.

141

SOUTH AMERICA

EXPLORATION AND MAPPING

THOUGH THE INCAS left no maps, their Andean empire's extensive road system was testimony to their topographical skills. It was a long time before any Europeans had a similar understanding of the continent. When Columbus first sighted the South American coast in 1498, he realized he had found a continental landmass, but thought it was part of Asia. This was disproved by the voyages of Vespucci and others along the Atlantic coast, culminating in Ferdinand Magellan's reaching the Pacific in 1520.

The name America was coined to honor Amerigo Vespucci, an Italian explorer in the service of Portugal.

In the wake of Pizarro's conquest of Peru and theft of the Incas' gold, many explorers were fired by dreams of instant riches. The net products of most expeditions, however, were the alienation of native tribes and the spread of European killer diseases. From the mid-17th century to the late 18th century, when serious scientific surveys began, exploration was largely the preserve of intrepid missionaries, notably the Jesuits, and slave-raiders from Brazil.

European conquerors and explorers

Throughout the first two decades of the 16th century Portuguese and Spanish explorers of the Atlantic coast sailed into every wide estuary in the hope that it would prove to be a passage to the Indies. Magellan eventually demonstrated that

such a route existed, but it proved impracticable for the purpose of trade with the East. As a result, the Atlantic coastal regions of the continent were soon well understood and mapped, further information coming from Portuguese traders who sailed there in search of brazil wood, a tree that produced a valuable red dye and gave its name to the region. In the Andes, Pizarro, Benalcázar, and their fellow *conquistadores* were able to follow the well-maintained roads of the Inca Empire; but in most other parts of the continent, expeditions were forced back by hostile indigenous peoples, trackless swamps and forests, or impassable rapids.

This detail from a map of South America produced by John Rotz in 1542 shows Native Americans carrying logs of brazil wood for trade with Europeans.

1500: Cabral claims Brazil for Portugal; Pinzón discovers mouth of the Amazon

1520: Magellan discovers strait that now bears his name and enters Pacific

1540: Valdivia crosses Atacama Desert to extend Spanish conquests to south

1550: Spanish crown forbids new expeditions against indigenous peoples; ban lasts 10 years

1498: Columbus is first European to sight South American mainland

1507: Waldseemüller's world map gives name America to continent in honor of Amerigo Vespucci

1528: Charles V grants lands around Coro to German bankers, the Welsers

1531–33: Francisco Pizarro conquers the Inca Empire

1542: Orellana sails length of the Amazon

European exploration

The Cantino planisphere, the earliest known map showing South America, was produced in Lisbon in 1502. It shows part of Brazil and the line agreed by the Treaty of Tordesillas in 1494, dividing the world between Portugal and Spain.

① **First European explorers of South America** ▶

Principal journeys

→ Spanish expedition
→ Portuguese expedition
→ German expedition
→ English expedition
→ Dutch expedition

Recife 1535 European settlement and date of foundation

Jesuit missions in the interior

Spanish Jesuits created frontier settlements – often of three or four thousand people – known as *reducciones*. These had their own churches, workshops, foundries, even armories, and lands where the Native Americans grew crops and raised herds of cattle. Money was not used, but the Jesuits traded with local Spanish settlers, who envied their success, especially among the Guaraní tribes. For the authorities, however, the *reducciones* formed a defense against Portuguese encroachment on Spanish lands; Native Americans fought many battles with the slave-raiders from São Paulo known as Paulistas or *mamelucos*.

From the 17th century, most serious exploration and mapping of the interior of South America was the work of missionaries. This detail is from a map of the Amazon compiled by Samuel Fritz, a Bohemian-born Jesuit, and published in 1707. Note the Jesuits' IHS monogram above the Equator.

② South America 1750 ▶

Areas colonized

- Spanish by 1650
- Spanish by 1750
- Portuguese by 1650
- Portuguese by 1750
- Dutch
- French

Missionary activity

- principal areas of Jesuit *reducciones*
- ✝ other major Jesuit missions
- ✝ major Franciscan missions
- *CHACO* *reduccion* with date of foundation
  1732
- 1630–32 active between these dates

Exploration of the interior

- → Jesuits
- → Franciscans
- → Paulista raids

The area covered by the detail from Father Fritz's map (*shown left*).

The Jesuits in South America

1550: First Jesuits reach Brazil	**1607:** Jesuits found province of Paraguay around Asunción	**1641:** Indians and Jesuits defeat slave-raiders from São Paulo on Uruguay River	**1649:** Viceroy grants *reducciones* virtual independence

1573: Rules drawn up for planning Jesuit towns — **1631:** Father Ruiz de Montoya descends Paraná River with 12,000 Indians to escape slave-raiders — **1640s:** Long-running quarrel between Jesuits and governor of Asunción — **1690:** Foundation of first Chiquito *reduccion* — **1711:** Jesuits banned from entering Minas Gerais region — **1750:** Treaty of Madrid: territory of seven Guarani *reducciones* ceded to Portugal — **1754–55:** Guarani War in protest at terms of treaty — **1759:** Expulsion of Jesuits from Brazil — **1767:** Expulsion of Jesuits from all Spanish colonies

Timeline: 1550 1575 1600 1625 1650 1675 1700 1725 1750 1775

Later scientific exploration

Humboldt endured far greater hardship than this studio portrait suggests, as he traveled with French botanist, Aimé Bonpland, by canoe and on foot through the rainforests of the Orinoco.

For three centuries, the colonial authorities in South America did little to encourage scientific exploration. In the 19th century, however, scientists of all kinds began to explore the peaks of the Andes, the Amazon Basin, and even the wilds of Patagonia. The Prussian Alexander von Humboldt amassed unparalleled data on the geography, geology, meteorology, and natural history of South America. He mapped the course of the Casiquiare, a most unusual river in that it links the Amazon and Orinoco drainage basins. Of later travelers, the most famous was Charles Darwin, whose observations as a young naturalist aboard *HMS Beagle* in 1831–36 would inspire his theory of evolution expounded in *On the Origin of Species*. The French paleontologist Alcide d'Orbigny, who spent eight years studying the continent's microfossils, published the first detailed physical map of South America in 1842.

③ Scientific explorers

Humboldt's journey
Aug 1799 ——— Mar 1803

Darwin's journey
Feb 1832 ——— Sep 1835

The Galapagos Islands are a volcanic group that lies on the equator. This chart was drawn by the officers of the *Beagle*, who were surveying the coast of South America for the British Navy. Darwin's interest was aroused by the peculiarities of the islands' fauna, such as the giant tortoises, which had evolved slightly different forms on each of the main islands, and the curious marine iguanas.

Large-billed seed-eating finch

Insectivorous warbler finch

The finches Darwin collected on the Galapagos Islands later provided powerful evidence for his theory of natural selection. Several closely related species had diverged from a common ancestor to occupy the various ecological niches on the islands.

Scientific exploration

1802: Humboldt climbs to record height on the mountain of Chimborazo; correctly attributes altitude sickness to lack of oxygen	**1826–34:** D'Orbigny studies continent's fossil-bearing strata	**1835:** Darwin encounters unique island fauna of the Galapagos Islands	**1859:** Naturalist Henry Bates returns to England with 8,000 insects new to science after 11 years in Amazon region	

Timeline: 1725 1750 1775 1800 1825 1850 1875 1900

1735: Expedition to Quito led by French scientist La Condamine to test sphericity of the Earth — **1783:** Spanish crown sponsors botanical expedition to South American colonies — **1832:** Darwin discovers fossils of giant mammals near Bahía Blanca, including *Megatherium* — **1835–44:** Guiana region explored by Sir Robert Schomburgk, who fixes boundary of British colony — **1872:** German Wilhelm Reiss scales Cotopaxi, which Humboldt had pronounced unclimbable

EARLY CULTURES OF SOUTH AMERICA

SOUTH AMERICA WAS COLONIZED by settlers from the north, possibly more than 13,000 years ago. By 10,000 BCE, hunter-gatherers had reached its southern tip and, by 5000 BCE, communities were beginning to exploit local resources, such as corn, manioc, and potatoes. Successful agriculture led to growing populations and increasingly stratified societies. The distinctive temple mounds of Peru appeared by c.2500 BCE, and characteristic elements of South American religious iconography were disseminated all over Peru from the site of Chavín de Huantar, from c.1200 BCE. By 300 CE, Peru was dominated by two major civilizations: the Nazca and the more expansionist Moche.

The Bahía people of coastal Ecuador made clay sculptures such as this figure holding a swaddled child.

The earliest settlements

The first South American settlers were hunter-gatherers, exploiting the big game which flourished following the last Ice Age. Spearheads and arrowheads found at Fell's Cave indicate that this way of life had reached the far south of the continent by 10,000 BCE. In Chile, the site of Monte Verde (c.11,000 BCE) is a village of timber huts draped with animal hides. Finds of medicinal plants, potato peelings, digging sticks, wooden bowls, and mortars, reveal an intimate knowledge of plant resources which supplemented a diet of small game and mastodon.

Monte Verde, the earliest known settlement in the southern half of the continent, is thought to have existed by at least 11,000 BCE. Stone tools found there include devices for chopping, scraping, and pounding *(left)*.

Earliest settlements in South America

c.11,000 BCE: Evidence of settlement at Monte Verde in present-day Chile

6000 BCE: Maize is cultivated in Ecuador

3000 BCE: Cotton cultivated in Central Andes. Large village settlements begin to appear

c.1750 BCE: Massive ceremonial architecture at Sechín Alto

11,000 BCE	10,000	9000	8000	7000	6000	5000	4000	3000	2000 BCE

10,000 BCE: Evidence of hunter-gatherers at site of Fell's Cave, Patagonia

c.2500 BCE: Masonry building and temple architecture at sites such as Caral, Aspero, and Kotosh

① Settlement and agriculture in early South America

- ········· Native American culture areas
- ◇ archaeological site before 10,000 BCE
- ◇ archaeological site 10,000– 2500 BCE
- ⚒ early ceremonial center 2500 BCE–1000 BCE
- ⚱ finds of early pottery, with date

The development of agriculture c.6000 BCE–c.1000 BCE

- earliest agricultural development
- early expansion of agriculture
- later expansion of agriculture
- ➡ initial diffusion of agriculture
- → subsequent dispersal of agriculture
- distribution of shell middens

Domestication of plants and animals

🌿 tobacco	🥑 avocado
squash	manioc
uxalis	maize
ullucu	pumpkin
cacao	quinoa
sweet potato	groundnut
cotton	chili pepper
potato	amaranth
guinea pig	dog
llama/alpaca	sunflower
beans	

Symbols in red denote core areas of plant and animal domestication; symbols in green denote dispersal of domesticated plants and animals

Monumental centers

Spectacular improvements in plant yields sustained growing populations; villages grew into small towns, and the large temple mounds which appeared on the coast of central Peru from c.2500 BCE are evidence of organized, stratified societies. Major sites of this kind include Huaricoto, La Galgada, Caral, and Aspero, and the later El Paraíso.

This painted ceremonial vase shows a man hunting wild llamas. These versatile creatures were among the first animals to be fully domesticated by the early farmers of the Andes.

Scale varies with perspective

3560 km (1816 miles)

6224 km (3864 miles)

This water vessel, dating from 900–200 BCE, was found near Cupisnique in the north of the Chavin region.

Agriculture

The first farmers of South America were located on the northern Pacific coast. Corn, the staple crop of the Americas, was cultivated in Ecuador c.6000 BCE; and the major high-altitude crop in the Andes, the potato, may have been grown by 4000 BCE. Llamas and alpaca, domesticated for their wool, were used as Andean pack animals. Manioc, which became a staple of tropical forest farmers, was cultivated in the Amazon Basin by 3000 BCE.

The peoples of the Amazon Basin and the Atlantic coast

Rock shelters and flaked stone tools dating to c.10,000 BCE provide the earliest evidence of settlement east of the Andes. The transition from hunting and gathering to agriculture – principally the cultivation of manioc – probably began c.3000 BCE. Large shell middens at the mouths of the Amazon and Orinoco rivers contain remains of pottery dating to c.5000 BCE – far earlier than the first pottery of Peru. When corn was introduced into the river flood plains in the 1st millennium BCE, populations expanded and hierarchical societies (chiefdoms) developed. Drainage earthworks on the Llanos de Mojos suggest that large populations were cooperating to farm the landscape.

◀ **2 Early settlement of Amazonia and eastern South America**

◇ early archaeological site 12,000–6000 BCE
⬱ early ceramic site 5000–1000 BCE
⚒ early lithic site
⬳ earthworks and hydrological systems
🐚 shell midden

The cultures of Peru 1300 BCE–600 CE

The most influential culture of the middle Andes was that of the Chavín, which flourished at and around the major religious center of Chavín de Huantar between 850 BCE and 200 BCE. The Chavín were distinguished by the sophistication of their architecture and sculptural style and by technological developments including the building of canals. As Chavín influence waned, from c.200 BCE, many distinctive regional cultures developed in the Andean highlands. Coastal Peru, however, was dominated by two major civilizations, Nazca in the south, and Moche in the north. As these cultures developed a strong identity, military rivalries intensified, paving the way for the appearance of other major states from 500 CE including Tiahuanaco and Huari.

Large cemeteries in the Paracas region contained thousands of mummified bodies wrapped in colorful wool. The motif of a large-eyed deity, the Oculate Being, on these textiles shows a strong affinity with the Chavín deity, known as the Smiling God.

4 Coastal Peru c.600 BCE–600 CE

◻ Paracas cultural region c. 600–350 BCE
◆ major Paracas sites
◻ Ecuadorian cultural region c.500 BCE–500 CE
◻ Lima cultural region c.400 BCE–500 CE
◻ Nazca cultural region c.350 BCE–450 CE
◻ earliest Moche sites c.1 CE
◻ Moche cultural region c.1–600 CE
◻ Recuay cultural region c.500 CE
▽ irrigated river valley

Moche

Moche culture was centered on the capital of Moche, dominated by the famous Temple of the Sun, a massive structure of solid adobe 40 m high. The Moche state was powerful, well-organized, and expanded by military conquest. Mass labor was organized to participate in major public works and civil engineering projects and the construction of "royal" tombs.

The stirrup-spout on this drinking vessel is a typical feature of Moche pottery, as is the marvelously realistic and sensitive modeling of the facial features.

Nazca

Based on the south coast of Peru, Nazca culture is famous for its superb and graphic pottery, textiles, and above all, the enigmatic "Nazca lines," straight, geometric, or figurative designs etched onto the surface of the desert, possibly as offerings to the gods.

This aerial view shows Nazca lines etched into the shape of a hummingbird. Some of these images can be over 100 m across.

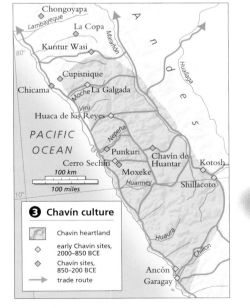

3 Chavín culture

◻ Chavín heartland
◇ early Chavín sites, 2000–850 BCE
◇ Chavín sites, 850–200 BCE
→ trade route

The Chavín

Chavín de Huantar (c.1200–200 BCE), with its large stone sculptures and grand temples, became a cult center. Chavín motifs, in architecture, textiles, pottery, and goldwork, are found throughout Peru.

Cultures of Peru 1300 BCE–1 CE

850 BCE: Florescence of Chavín de Huantar; Chavín style widely disseminated

500 BCE: Paracas culture in southern Peru produces textiles woven with Chavín-style images

c.1 CE: Emergence of Moche culture of coastal Peru

1400 BCE · 1200 · 1000 · 800 · 600 · 400 · 200 · 1 CE

1300 BCE: Cerro Sechin is earliest central Andean site with Chavín-style iconography

200 BCE: Regional cultures begin to appear in central Andes

THE EMPIRES OF SOUTH AMERICA

This gold knife in the form of a Chimú (or Sicán) sun god dates from c.1100 CE. The body is decorated with turquoises.

THE EMPIRES WHICH DOMINATED the Andes between 500 and 1450, Tiahuanaco, Huari, and Chimú, were important precursors of the Inca, laying down the religious and social foundations, and the authoritarian government which were to serve the Inca so well. The Inca Empire (1438–1532) was the greatest state in South America exercising stringent control over its subjects through taxation, forced labor, compulsory migration, and military service. With its unyielding hierarchy and ill-defined line of succession, the empire was fatally weakened by a leadership crisis at the very point when Pizarro arrived in 1532, and was unable to prevent its own destruction at the hands of the Spanish *conquistadores*.

Empires of the Andean coast 250–1375

The empires of Tiahuanaco and Huari, which together dominated the Andes from 500 CE, shared a similar art style, and probably the same religion. The city of Tiahuanaco, on the windswept Altiplano of modern Bolivia, was a major pilgrimage center, and its cultural influence diffused throughout the south-central Andes from 500–1000. The contemporary Huari Empire, which controlled the coast around present-day Lima, was, by contrast, centralized and militaristic, expanding its influence through conquest. The Inca owed most to their direct predecessor, the Chimú Empire of the northern Andes, with its efficient administration, colonial expansionism, irrigation projects, and stress on an effective communication system.

1 The empires of the Andean coast

- Nazca culture 350 BCE–500 CE
- Moche culture 1–600 CE
- Tiahuanaco c.700
- area of Tiahuanaco influence c.700
- Huari Empire at its height c.650
- Huari gains after c.650
- Chimú Empire c.1200
- Chimú gains by 1475
- ▽ irrigated river valley
- — Huari roads

c.450: Tiahuanaco influence evident in pottery and architecture at secondary centers

c.500: Huari becomes a major center; perhaps following a war

c.700: Emergence of Chimú on northern Peruvian coast

c.1000: Sicán culture flourishes around El Purgatório in northern Peru

1375: Beginnings of Chimú conquests

250: Tiahuanaco becomes a large town, both an economic and cult center

600: Huari leaders conquer territory stretching 560 miles along Andean coast

800: City of Huari abandoned

Empires of the Andes 250–1375 CE

Tiahuanaco

By **500 CE** the city of Tiahuanaco on Lake Titicaca's southeastern shore had become a major population center, housing up to 40,000 people, and a focus of pilgrimage for the entire Andean region. It was dominated by palaces and a cult center, consisting of temples, monumental gateways, and large monolithic sculptures. The city's iconography, with its symbolism of water, sun, and weather, spread throughout the south-central Andes.

Carved from a single slab of andesite, the Gateway of the Sun at Tiahuanaco is a representation of the cosmos, with the creator god at the center of the frieze.

Huari

Thriving from 500–800 CE, the empire based on the city of Huari shared many of Tiahuanaco's cultural characteristics, but was a much more militaristic state which grew through conquest, reflected in finds of major trunk roads and regional centers with military barracks. Public works, such as road-building, were carried out as a labor tax by the empire's subjects.

The back of this Huari hand mirror contains a central face, with small heads at each side. The reflecting surface is of pyrite and the mosaic back of a variety of stones of contrasting texture and color.

Chimú

The **Chimú Empire** which ruled over the coast of northern Peru (c.700–1476) was centered on the capital of Chan Chan. A series of great royal compounds within the city served as both the palaces and tombs of ten successive monarchs. The empire stretched for 1,600 miles along the Peruvian coast, administered by a series of regional centers.

The Chimú people were skilled metalworkers, producing a wide variety of ceremonial objects such as this gold dove with turquoise eyes.

This small figure reflects the intricate casting and polishing typical of the goldsmiths of the Quimbaya chiefdoms. They also produced masks, spear tips, pendants, and helmets

Chiefdoms of the northern Andes

By the **15th century**, many peoples of the northern Andes were organized into chiefdoms, based on large villages, supported by wetland farming, and capable of mobilizing sizable armies. Their gold-working skills gave rise to myths of "El Dorado" *(see p.149)*. Gold and copper resources were exploited by efficient mining operations – an indication of their impressive organizational ability.

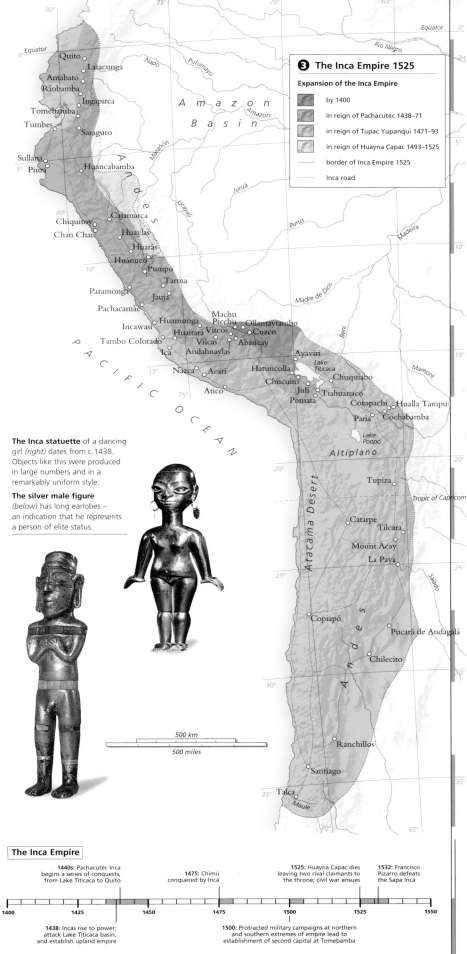

The Inca Empire

The Inca emerged, in less than a century, as the preeminent state in South America; from 1470 they ruled vast territories from their capital, Cuzco. Their hierarchical society, ruled by the Sapa Inca (believed to be descended from the sun), depended on the mass organization of labor. Adult men were liable for forced labor, and worked in the fields, on public works (terracing, building, mining), and served in the army. An extensive road network, interspersed with way stations and regional centers, bound the empire together. Yet this complex bureaucracy had no form of writing, although arithmetic records were used for administration, tribute, and taxation.

The Inca *quipumayoc*, or grand treasurer, is shown holding a *quipu*, a device made of knotted strings, used to record administrative matters and sacred histories. Information was encoded in the colors of the strings and the style of the knots.

◄ ❷ South America c.1500

- .... border of Inca Empire
- high civilization
- chiefdoms
- tropical forest farming villages
- other farming villages
- nomadic hunter-gatherers
- *Ona* indigenous people

The peoples of South America c.1500

The golden raft, bearing a godlike figure surrounded by attendants, is a detailed example of a *tunjo* or offering piece, produced by the Muisca (Chibcha) people of the northeastern Andes.

A great diversity of indigenous cultures existed in South America by the start of the 16th century, ranging from the high civilization of the Incas to the hunter-gatherers of Patagonia. Large populations lived along the Amazon, the upper river dominated by the Omagua people, its lower reaches controlled by the warlike Tapajosó. Many chiefdoms held sway over huge areas, some extracting forced labor from subject peoples, who were often engaged on extensive building projects. Ancestor cults, based on the mummified bodies of chiefs, were widespread.

❸ The Inca Empire 1525

Expansion of the Inca Empire
- by 1400
- in reign of Pachacutec 1438–71
- in reign of Tupac Yupanqui 1471–93
- in reign of Huayna Capac 1493–1525
- .... border of Inca Empire 1525
- Inca road

The Inca statuette of a dancing girl *(right)* dates from c.1438. Objects like this were produced in large numbers and in a remarkably uniform style.

The silver male figure *(below)* has long earlobes – an indication that he represents a person of elite status.

THE VERTICAL ECONOMY OF THE ANDES

This stylized carving in the shape of a tree is etched on a hillside in the coastal desert above present-day Paracas.

The rugged terrain of the Andes provided a series of contiguous, but contrasting environments, fully exploited by the Incas and their predecessors. High, treeless, grassy plains (the *puna*) were used for grazing llamas. Below this, at heights up to 4,400 yds above sea level, lay the *suni*, where potatoes and tubers could be cultivated. Corn, squash, fruits, and cocoa grew in lower, frost-free valleys (the *quechua*), while the lower slopes of the mountains (the *yunga*) were planted with peppers, coca plants, and other fruits. Sources of shellfish and fish from the ocean were periodically disrupted by El Niño, an irregular climatic disturbance which warmed the ocean, leading to torrential rains and disastrous flooding.

- *puna*: over 4,400 yds above sea level
- *suni*: 3,500–4,400 yds above sea level
- *quechua*: 2,520–3,500 yds above sea level
- forested eastern slopes
- dry coastal region
- *yunga*: 820–2,520 yds above sea level
- dry coastal region: 0–820 yds above sea level

The Inca Empire

- 1440s: Pachacutec Inca begins a series of conquests, from Lake Titicaca to Quito
- 1475: Chimú conquered by Inca
- 1525: Huayna Capac dies leaving two rival claimants to the throne; civil war ensues
- 1532: Francisco Pizarro defeats the Sapa Inca
- 1438: Incas rise to power; attack Lake Titicaca basin, and establish upland empire
- 1500: Protracted military campaigns at northern and southern extremes of empire lead to establishment of second capital at Tomebamba

1400 | 1425 | 1450 | 1475 | 1500 | 1525 | 1550

COLONIAL SOUTH AMERICA

Christianity in South America blended with local traditions to produce colorful spectacles such as this 18th-century Corpus Christi procession in Cuzco.

IN THEIR CONQUEST of South America, the Spanish were so driven by the quest for gold and silver that it took the *conquistadores* less than ten years to take over the rich, organized states of the Andes. The Portuguese were slower to settle Brazil, first trading with the Indians, then turning to sugar production. Wherever Europeans settled, the native population declined rapidly, mainly through lack of resistance to alien diseases. There were also periodic wars against the colonists. Large cattle stations that destroyed native arable smallholdings were a further factor in their decline. Emigration to South America from both Spain and Portugal was light; settlers mixed with the natives, creating a mixed-race *mestizo* population. To make up for shortages in labor, they imported African slaves. Catholic missionaries, notably the Jesuits, were active throughout the colonial era, often defending the rights of the Indians against the settlers. Both colonial empires collapsed in the 19th century, but the religion and languages of the conquerors survived.

The silver mine at Potosí was the prime source of revenue to the Spanish crown between 1550 and 1650. At first the native population supplied all the labor and technology. The silver was extracted using mercury, mined at Huancavelica.

The conquest of Peru

In 1531 Francisco Pizarro sailed from Panama to conquer Peru. By the time the expedition had penetrated inland to Cajamarca, where the reigning Inca, Atahualpa, and 40,000 men were camped, Pizarro had only 180 men. Yet he succeeded in capturing Atahualpa, whom he held for ransom. When this was paid, Atahualpa was executed, and the *conquistadores* moved on to capture the Inca capital, Cuzco. The Incas were in awe of the Spanish horses and guns, but this astonishing feat of conquest would have been impossible had the Inca Empire not been weakened by a smallpox epidemic and civil war.

Atahualpa was given a summary trial by Pizarro and then garrotted, or – as this contemporary Inca illustration shows – beheaded.

◀ ❶ Pizarro's conquest of the Inca Empire

→	1524 expedition
→	1526 expedition
→	1531–33 expedition
⋯⋯	extent of Inca Empire
1526	date of foundation

The founder of Spain's South American empire, Pizarro was an aging soldier of fortune. Some of his own lieutenants rebelled against him and he was killed in a riot in Lima in 1541.

Spanish South America

Spain ruled her American colonies through two great viceroyalties, New Spain (centered on Mexico) and Peru. The viceroys' principal duty was to guarantee a steady flow of bullion for the Spanish Crown. When booty from the native empires was exhausted, the colonists turned to the region's mineral resources, using forced native labor (*mita*) to extract precious metals, in particular silver. Smaller administrative units called *audiencias* were presided over by a judge who enacted the complex laws devised in Spain for the running of the colonies. Attempts to expand the empire were thwarted in the south by the fierce Araucanian people, elsewhere by the inhospitable nature of the terrain.

Inca ornaments, such as this gold llama, are very rare because most were melted down and shipped to Spain.

◀ ❷ Spanish South America

▨	Spanish territory before 1650
▨	Spanish territory after 1650
▨	region disputed by Spain and Portugal up to 1777
▨	Jesuit mission states, with dates
○	border with Brazil by Treaty of Madrid 1750
⋯⋯	border with Brazil where modified by Treaty of San Ildefonso 1777
●	Portuguese settlement
▣ gold	◡ drugs
▣ silver	✕ hides
▣ copper	▨ cocoa
▣ mercury	

Spanish South America 1500–1800

1533: Pizarro takes Inca capital, Cuzco	1535: City of Lima founded	1607: Jesuits found first mission villages on Paraguay River	c.1680: Start of serious slump in economy of Spanish South America	1750: Treaty of Madrid defines boundary between Spanish colonies and Brazil	1776: New viceroyalty of Río de la Plata centered on Buenos Aires	
1500	1550	1600	1650	1700	1750	1800
1541: Pedro de Valdivia founds Santiago	1545: Discovery of silver at Potosí	1630s: Intense Jesuit missionary activity in Paraguay region		1739: Viceroyalty of New Granada established to defend Caribbean coast	1777: Treaty of San Ildefonso	

Portuguese South America

Brazil was formally claimed by Portugal in 1500. There were no conspicuous mineral resources, so colonization depended on agriculture. In the 1530s, in an attempt to encourage settlement, João III made grants of land to 12 hereditary "captains," each captaincy consisting of 50 leagues of coastline. Some failed completely and little of the coastal plain was settled before 1549 when a royal governor-general was sent to Bahia. The captaincy system continued, but the colonists' fortunes changed with the success of sugar. The native population living near the coast had been almost wiped out by disease and wars. The few that remained had no wish to labor on sugar plantations, so slaves were imported from Africa. In the 18th century, a gold boom opened up the Minas Gerais region, but apart from slave-raiders hunting for natives and prospectors searching for gold and diamonds, penetration of the interior was limited.

Between 1550 and 1800, some 2.5 million African slaves were taken to Brazil, more than 70% of them to work for the sugar plantations and mills which were the backbone of the economy.

Slaves were also employed at the gold and diamond mines of the interior. This early 19th-century print shows slaves washing diamond-bearing rock.

❸ Portuguese South America

- Portuguese territory by 1600
- Portuguese territory by 1750
- Portuguese frontier territory
- region disputed by Spain and Portugal up to 1777
- PARÁ 1616 captaincy and date of foundation
- □ capital city
- 🏛 gold
- ◯ diamonds
- ◆ dyes
- ✕ hides
- ↓ sugar

Brazil 1500–1800

- 1502: First expedition sent from Lisbon to exploit newfound coastline
- 1532: First captaincies granted for purposes of settlement
- 1549: Direct royal rule imposed from new capital at Bahia
- 1562–63: War and disease kill much of Indian population
- 1580: Portugal and her empire come under rule of Spanish kings
- 1621: Formation of separate Estado do Maranhão with its own governor-general
- 1663: Brazil becomes viceroyalty
- 1674: Foundation of Manaus, 995 miles from mouth of Amazon
- 1680s: Portuguese found Colônia do Sacramento
- 1695: Gold discovered in Minas Gerais region
- 1750: Portugal renounces claim to Colônia do Sacramento
- 1763: Rio de Janeiro becomes Brazilian capital

From the 1530s until well into the 17th century, fantastic tales of the kingdom of El Dorado (the gilded man) inspired many foolhardy expeditions through the Andes, the Orinoco basin, and the Guiana Highlands. The English sea captain Walter Raleigh twice sailed to the Orinoco, but both his voyages ended in failure, and on the second in 1617 his teenaged son was killed by the Spanish.

The legend of El Dorado took many forms. The most persistent was of a chieftain so rich that he was regularly painted in gold by his subjects.

Other colonial powers

For 150 years Portugal's hold on Brazil was far from secure. The French, who traded along the coast with the natives, made several attempts to found colonies. In the first half of the 17th century, the defense of Portuguese colonies was neglected by the ruling Spanish kings. This allowed the Dutch to capture a long stretch of the northeast coast. They were finally expelled in 1654 and had to be content, like the English and French, with a small colony in the Guianas.

Dutch Brazil thrived under the governorship of Prince Maurits of Nassau (1636–44), when many new towns were built. The artist Franz Post painted idealized views of the colony during this period. This detail shows the slave quarters on a plantation.

❹ Brazil and the Guianas c.1640

- ○ Portuguese possession and settlement
- ○ Dutch possession and settlement
- ○ French possession and settlement
- temporary French colonies in Brazil

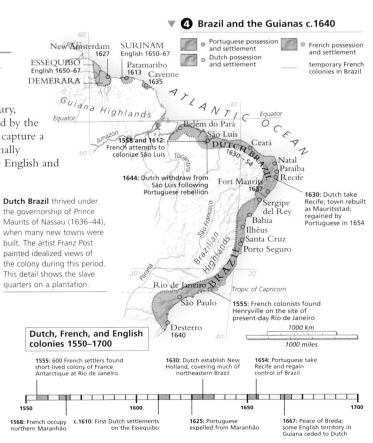

1558 and 1612: French attempts to colonize São Luís

1644: Dutch withdraw from São Luís following Portuguese rebellion

1630: Dutch take Recife; town rebuilt as Mauritsstad; regained by Portuguese in 1654

1555: French colonists found Henryville on the site of present-day Rio de Janeiro

Dutch, French, and English colonies 1550–1700

- 1555: 600 French settlers found short-lived colony of France Antarctique at Rio de Janeiro
- 1568: French occupy northern Maranhão
- c.1610: First Dutch settlements on the Essequibo
- 1625: Portuguese expelled from Maranhão
- 1630: Dutch establish New Holland, covering much of northeastern Brazil
- 1654: Portuguese take Recife and regain control of Brazil
- 1667: Peace of Breda; some English territory in Guiana ceded to Dutch

THE AGE OF INDEPENDENCE

Pedro I became the emperor of an independent Brazil in 1822, when his father and the royal family returned from exile to Portugal.

AFTER THREE CENTURIES of rule by Spain, the colonial families of South America began to demand more autonomy. When Spain was invaded by Napoleon in 1808, it was cut off from its empire, and in 1810 several colonies established independent ruling juntas. The struggle for independence lasted until 1826, when the last Spanish troops departed. The heroic deeds of the Liberators, Simón Bolívar, José de San Martín, and others passed into legend, but the task of forming new republics proved harder. Liberals and Conservatives fought numerous civil wars and military dictators ran countries as their personal fiefs. The economies of the new states were dominated by foreign trading powers, especially Britain. Brazil gained its independence from Portugal more peacefully, a result of the royal family's flight to Brazil in 1807. The two states separated when they returned to Portugal in 1822.

The liberation of Spanish South America

The wars of liberation were fought between patriots and those who remained loyal to the Spanish crown. The longest struggle was that of Simón Bolívar in his native Venezuela and neighboring Colombia. The first states to achieve independence were Paraguay and Argentina, from where in 1817 José de San Martín led an army over the Andes to help liberate Chile. Bolívar's campaigns regained momentum in 1818–22 in a triumphal progress from Venezuela to Ecuador. The armies of liberation from north and south then joined forces for the liberation of Peru and, in honor of Bolívar, Upper Peru was renamed Bolivia.

The llanero lancers from the plains of Venezuela were praised by Bolívar as his "cossacks." They continually harrassed the army sent from Spain in 1815 to oppose the liberation movement.

Bolívar enters Caracas in triumph in 1829 after putting down the uprising of his former lieutenant Antonio Páez. But it was Páez who became dictator of the new republic of Venezuela on Bolívar's death in 1830.

The break-up of Great Colombia

The personality of Simón Bolívar and the need for military unity in confronting the Spanish created the republic of Great Colombia. It proved an unwieldy state with a very remote capital at Bogotá. Commercial links and communications between the three former Spanish colonies of New Granada, Venezuela, and Quito (Ecuador) were very limited, and in 1830, the year of Bolívar's death, they became separate states under the leadership of generals Santander, Páez, and Flores respectively.

② The dissolution of Great Colombia

- Republic of Great Colombia 1819–30
- New Granada 1830
- Ecuador 1830
- Venezuela 1830
- present-day international borders

① The independence of South America 1810–30

- Spanish territory in South America 1810
- VICEROYALTY OF NEW GRANADA — Spanish administrative region
- 1821 — date of independence of new state

Principal campaigns of liberators

- Bolívar 1812–14
- O'Higgins 1817–18
- San Martín 1817–18
- Bolívar 1819
- San Martín 1820–22
- Sucre 1821–22
- Bolívar 1822
- Bolívar 1823–26
- Sucre 1824
- ✗ victory for armies of liberation
- ✗ defeat for armies of liberation

The Wars of Liberation 1808–30

1805	1810	1815	1820	1825	1830
1808–09: Napoleon invades Iberian Peninsula	**1810:** Independent juntas established	**1815:** General Morillo sent from Spain to reconquer Venezuela	**1822:** Brazilian independence	**1824:** Spanish defeated in Peru	**1830:** Venezuela and Ecuador withdraw from Great Colombia; death of Bolívar
1807: Portuguese royal family flees to Brazil	**1811:** Bolívar starts fight to liberate Venezuela	**1816:** United Provinces of La Plata set up as independent state	**1823:** US recognizes new South American states	**1825:** Founding of Bolivia	**1828:** Uruguay becomes independent
		1817: O'Higgins becomes 'supreme director' of Chile			

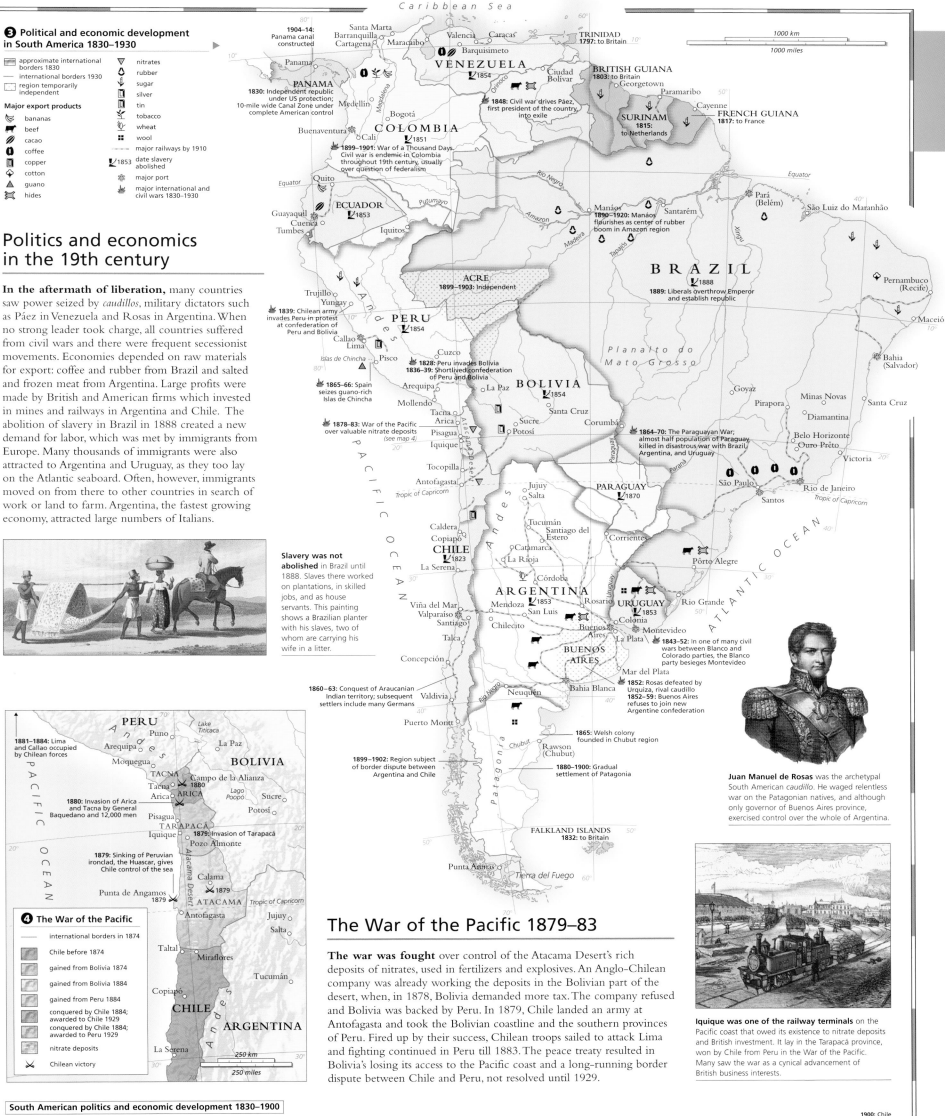

❸ Political and economic development in South America 1830–1930

- ▱ approximate international borders 1830
- — international borders 1930
- ▢ region temporarily independent

Major export products

🌿 bananas	▽ nitrates
🐄 beef	⬇ rubber
◿ cacao	🧂 sugar
◉ coffee	🔲 silver
▦ copper	⬇ tin
✿ cotton	🌿 tobacco
△ guano	🌾 wheat
✖ hides	🐑 wool

- ⋯ major railways by 1910
- ⚰1853 date slavery abolished
- ⚓ major port
- ⚔ major international and civil wars 1830–1930

Politics and economics in the 19th century

In the aftermath of liberation, many countries saw power seized by *caudillos*, military dictators such as Páez in Venezuela and Rosas in Argentina. When no strong leader took charge, all countries suffered from civil wars and there were frequent secessionist movements. Economies depended on raw materials for export: coffee and rubber from Brazil and salted and frozen meat from Argentina. Large profits were made by British and American firms which invested in mines and railways in Argentina and Chile. The abolition of slavery in Brazil in 1888 created a new demand for labor, which was met by immigrants from Europe. Many thousands of immigrants were also attracted to Argentina and Uruguay, as they too lay on the Atlantic seaboard. Often, however, immigrants moved on from there to other countries in search of work or land to farm. Argentina, the fastest growing economy, attracted large numbers of Italians.

Slavery was not abolished in Brazil until 1888. Slaves there worked on plantations, in skilled jobs, and as house servants. This painting shows a Brazilian planter with his slaves, two of whom are carrying his wife in a litter.

The War of the Pacific 1879–83

The war was fought over control of the Atacama Desert's rich deposits of nitrates, used in fertilizers and explosives. An Anglo-Chilean company was already working the deposits in the Bolivian part of the desert, when, in 1878, Bolivia demanded more tax. The company refused and Bolivia was backed by Peru. In 1879, Chile landed an army at Antofagasta and took the Bolivian coastline and the southern provinces of Peru. Fired up by their success, Chilean troops sailed to attack Lima and fighting continued in Peru till 1883. The peace treaty resulted in Bolivia's losing its access to the Pacific coast and a long-running border dispute between Chile and Peru, not resolved until 1929.

Juan Manuel de Rosas was the archetypal South American *caudillo*. He waged relentless war on the Patagonian natives, and although only governor of Buenos Aires province, exercised control over the whole of Argentina.

Iquique was one of the railway terminals on the Pacific coast that owed its existence to nitrate deposits and British investment. It lay in the Tarapacá province, won by Chile from Peru in the War of the Pacific. Many saw the war as a cynical advancement of British business interests.

❹ The War of the Pacific

- — international borders in 1874
- Chile before 1874
- gained from Bolivia 1874
- gained from Bolivia 1884
- gained from Peru 1884
- conquered by Chile 1884; awarded to Chile 1929
- conquered by Chile 1884; awarded to Peru 1929
- nitrate deposits
- ✖ Chilean victory

**Map annotations:**
- 1904–14: Panama canal constructed
- 1830: Independent republic under US protection; 10-mile wide Canal Zone under complete American control
- TRINIDAD 1797: to Britain
- BRITISH GUIANA 1803: to Britain
- 1848: Civil war drives Páez, first president of the country, into exile
- SURINAM 1815: to Netherlands
- FRENCH GUIANA 1817: to France
- 1899–1901: War of a Thousand Days. Civil war is endemic in Colombia throughout 19th century, usually over question of federalism
- ACRE 1899–1903: Independent
- 1890–1920: Manáos flourishes as center of rubber boom in Amazon region
- 1889: Liberals overthrow Emperor and establish republic
- 1839: Chilean army invades Peru in protest at confederation of Peru and Bolivia
- 1828: Peru invades Bolivia
- 1836–39: Shortlived confederation of Peru and Bolivia
- 1865–66: Spain seizes guano-rich Islas de Chincha
- 1878–83: War of the Pacific over valuable nitrate deposits (see map 4)
- 1864–70: The Paraguayan War; almost half population of Paraguay killed in disastrous war with Brazil, Argentina, and Uruguay
- 1843–52: In one of many civil wars between Blanco and Colorado parties, the Blanco party besieges Montevideo
- 1852: Rosas defeated by Urquiza, rival caudillo
- 1852–59: Buenos Aires refuses to join new Argentine confederation
- 1860–63: Conquest of Araucanian Indian territory; subsequent settlers include many Germans
- 1865: Welsh colony founded in Chubut region
- 1880–1900: Gradual settlement of Patagonia
- 1899–1902: Region subject to border dispute between Argentina and Chile
- FALKLAND ISLANDS 1832: to Britain

War of the Pacific map annotations:
- 1881–1884: Lima and Callao occupied by Chilean forces
- 1880: Invasion of Arica and Tacna by General Baquedano and 12,000 men
- 1880: Campo de la Alianza
- 1879: Invasion of Tarapacá
- 1879: Sinking of Peruvian ironclad, the Huascar, gives Chile control of the sea
- 1879: Punta de Angamos

South American politics and economic development 1830–1900

- 1829: Juan Manuel de Rosas becomes *caudillo* or dictator of Buenos Aires for next 23 years
- 1840: Guano boom helps stabilize Peru
- 1860: Ecuador's president, theocrat García Moreno, launches ambitious program of public works
- c.1865: Chile producing 44% of world's copper
- c.1870: European investment and immigration into Argentina starts to accelerate
- 1881: Patagonia becomes part of Argentina
- 1888: Slavery in Brazil at last completely abolished
- 1896: Height of Brazilian rubber boom; Manáos builds opera house
- 1900: Chile and Argentina agree border protocol
- 1839: Confederation of Bolivia and Peru shattered at battle of Yungay by Chileans and Peruvian nationalists
- 1851: Railway track completed from Copiapó to port of Caldera in Chile
- 1853: Slave traffic to Brazil ceases
- 1864–70: Paraguayan War; catastrophic defeat of Paraguay by Brazil, Argentina, and Uruguay
- 1879–83: War of the Pacific
- 1889: Brazil gains republican status as emperor is forced to leave
- 1900: Brazil produces 66% of the world's coffee; tin supersedes silver as Bolivia's chief export.

MODERN SOUTH AMERICA

POLITICAL AND ECONOMIC instability arose in South America as a result of the great depression of the 1930s. Border disputes persisted, although few flared up like the Chaco War of 1932–35. In most states, a sharp rise in population, together with rapid urbanization and industrialization, exerted great pressures on weak democratic institutions. Opposition to the conservative status quo was pronounced among intellectuals and trade unionists. In the late 1960s, social conflicts and ideological battles shook governments and set many countries on a new course of repressive, conservative authoritarianism. In the 1980s, South America began to turn towards democracy, free markets and international trade. By the start of the 21st century, most countries were benefiting from improved levels of social, political and economic stability.

Augusto Pinochet headed Chile's military government from 1974 to 1990.

South America: from instability to democracy

After killing some 35,000 people in the 1980s and 1990s, the Maoist Sendero Luminoso (Shining Path) terrorist movement was largely defeated by the Peruvian government. However, drug-trafficking and kidnapping enabled a resurgence of terrorism in the early 2000s.

In response to the global recession of the 1930s, populist governments promoted economic nationalism and industrial development. By the late 1950s, economic and social progress had led to greater democracy, but the Communist-inspired Cuban Revolution threatened the status quo. Fearing the spread of Communism, the US pledged $10 billion in aid, but massive population growth soon absorbed this. As conflict mounted between ruling elites and leftist guerrillas, military regimes, backed by the US, took control. The tide of military rule began to recede in the 1980s. By the end of the 20th century, most states were functioning multi-party democracies, although in some cases authoritarian tendencies remained.

Political development from 1935

1937: "New State" in Brazil launched by Vargas		**1968:** Tupamaros urban guerrilla group founded in Uruguay. Military junta takes over in Peru		**1974:** Brutal dictatorship of Pinochet in Chile	**1989:** Free elections in Brazil; democracy restored in Chile	**1998:** Left-wing Hugo Chávez wins election in Venezuela	**2001:** Economic crisis in Argentina
1935	**1940**	**1950**	**1960**	**1970**	**1980**	**1990**	**2000**
	1946: Peron comes to power in Argentina			**1976:** 15,000 political subversives killed during "Dirty War," by military and right-wing death squads in Argentina	**1982:** Argentina occupies Falkland Islands; troops surrender to UK forces	**1995:** Fujimori re-elected in Peru after "self-coup"	**2003:** Peru elects first female prime minister

### Map labels

Scale varies with perspective
4450 km (2770 miles)

1987: Fighting almost erupts over maritime border dispute in the Gulf of Venezuela

1966: Independence from UK

1975: Independence from Netherlands

Caribbean Sea

TRINIDAD AND TOBAGO Iron, oil, and gold rich area claimed by Venezuela

Maracaibo

Caracas

VENEZUELA
- 1908–35 Gómez ● 1958
- 1945, 1948 ● 1959
- 1952–58 Pérez/Jiménez ● 1962–66
- **1992:** Failed military coup led by Col. Higo Chávez
- **1998:** Chávez begins his "Bolivarian Revolution" reorganizing constitution
- **2002:** Unsuccessful coup

San Cristóbal

PANAMA

Paramaribo
Georgetown
Cayenne

GUYANA 1966

SURINAM 1980
- 1980–87
- 1990
- 1992

FRENCH GUIANA

French overseas department

Hostilities mainly over illegal gold prospecting

claimed by Surinam

claimed by Surinam

Macapá

COLOMBIA
- 1930
- 1953
- 1953–57 Rojas Pinilla
- 1957
- from 1964
- **2002:** Conflict with guerrillas intensifies

Bogotá
Cali

Belém
São Luís
Natal

Equator 0°

ECUADOR
- 1930 Guayaquil
- 1944, 1942, 1963
- 1963–66, 1972–79
- 1979
- **1995–98:** Border war with Peru

Quito

Previously claimed by Ecuador

Río Negro
Manaus

Amazon Basin

Recife

1998: Delineation of 77 km stretch of border between Peru and Ecuador; intended to give Ecuador navigation and trade rights in the Amazon region

Trujillo

Porto Velho

BRAZIL
- 1930
- 1937–45 Vargas' Estado Novo
- 1945, 1964
- 1960s, early 1970s
- 1964–85
- 1985

Aracaju

PERU
- 1930
- 1936–39 Benavides
- 1948–56 Odría
- 1962
- 1968
- 1968–75 General Velasco
- 1968–80
- 1980
- from 1980 Shining Path

Callao
Lima
Ayacucho
Río Branco
Río Branco

Salvador

BOLIVIA
- 1930 ● 1952
- 1936 ● 1964
- 1940 ● 1964–82
- 1943 ● 1967 Che Guevara
- 1946 ● 1969, 1971, 1978, 1979, 1981
- 1951 ● 1982

Brasília
Cuiabá
Belo Horizonte

1981–98: Border dispute with Ecuador
1992: Presedent Fujimori satges "self coup"
2000: Fujimori flees amid corruption scandal

Lake Titicaca
La Paz
Sucre

Clashes over coca eradication and gas export policy

Campo Grande
Rio de Janeiro

Bolivia had negotiated with Chile and Peru for corridor to Pacific Ocean since Atacama area was lost to Chile in 1884

Atacama Desert

São Paulo

Tropic of Capricorn

Chaco War 1932–35 (see Map 2)

PARAGUAY
- 1930 ● Asunción
- 1936, 1937, 1940
- 1940–48 Morínigo
- 1948, 1954
- 1954–89 Stroessner
- 1989
- 1989

Short section of boundary has not been precisely delimited

Short section of boundary disputed

Short section of boundary disputed

1982: allow UK to use ports during Falklands War

CHILE
- 1936
- 1973
- 1974–89 under General Pinochet
- 1989

Córdoba

URUGUAY
- 1930
- 1933–38 President Terra (soft dictatorship)
- 1963–72 Tupamaros
- 1976
- 1976–84
- 1985

Montevideo
Buenos Aires

ARGENTINA
- 1930, 1943
- 1943–45
- 1946–55 Perón
- 1955
- 1955–58
- 1962, 1966
- 1966–73
- 1969–79 Montoneros and 1970–77 People's Revolutionary Army
- 1976–83
- 1983
- **2001:** government brought down by financial crisis

Valparaíso
Santiago

1982: Chile gives clandestine communications information and support to British forces during Falklands War

1978: Territorial dispute with Chile over islands in Beagle Channel almost leads to war; settled 1984 with Vatican mediation

FALKLAND ISLANDS to UK claimed by Argentina

Falklands War
1982: Argentina attempt to take Falklands from UK by military action

❶ Political change in South America from 1930

- 🌿 civilian-led revolution
- 🌿 social revolution
- ⚖ democratic government
- 🤝 border/territorial dispute
- 🌿 full-scale war
- 🗡 successful military coup
- ⊖ personal dictatorship
- 🗡 military regime
- 🗡 guerrilla activity
- frontiers 1999
- ☐ capital city

Urban population as a percentage of total population, 2002
- 0–49%
- 50–69%
- 70–80%
- over 80%

The urban explosion

After 1930, the large cities of Latin America which had been predominantly commercial and administrative centers became increasingly industrialized. Rapid population growth, coupled with worker migration, led to the growth of slum areas in most cities.

Population (in 1000's)

	1930	1970	2004
Lima	250	3318	8250
Rio de Janeiro	1500	6870	11,900
São Paulo	1000	7838	19,850
Buenos Aires	2000	8353	12,600

The Chaco War

Bolivian claims to the Chaco territory, north of the Pilcomayo river, led to a three-year war with Paraguay from 1932. The conflict grew out of Bolivia's desire to gain access to the Atlantic coast via the river system which ran across the region to the Plate River, and Paraguay's interest in potential oil deposits. At the end of the war, Paraguay, the supposedly weaker militarily of the two countries, had gained more territory than its pre-war claims.

Bolivian machine-gunners are shown wearing gas masks in action against Paraguay in 1934 during the offensive on the Gran Chaco front.

❷ The disputed territory of the Chaco 1887–1938

- Bolivia's claim
- Paraguay's claim
- Tamayo-Aceval Treaty 1887
- Quijarro-Decoud Treaty 1879
- Ichazo-Benites Treaty 1894
- Pinilla-Soler Treaty 1907
- frontiers 1932
- ++++ ceasefire front line
- peace conference boundary award 1938 and final frontier
- 🌿 major battle
- ○ fort
- ⛏ oilfield
- ⌁ railway

BOLIVIA
Santa Cruz
Altiplano
Camiri
Villa Montes
Sanandita
Mar–Nov 1934
Fortín Ballivián
Jun–Sep 1932
Fortín Boquerón
Fortín Nanawa
Bahía Negra
Puerto Casado

BRAZIL

Gran Chaco

PARAGUAY
Asunción

Tropic of Capricorn

ARGENTINA

250 km
250 miles

Pilcomayo
Paraná
Uruguay
Iguaçu

The Chaco War

Aug 1932: Paraguayans mobilized in major offensive against Boquerón	**May 1933:** Paraguay formally declares war	**Mar–Jul 1934:** Heaviest fighting of the war occurs near Fortín Ballivián	**Nov 1934:** Fortín Ballivián falls to Paraguayans
1932	**1933**	**1934**	**1935**	**1936**
Jun 1932: Chaco War begins; Bolivians seize Paraguayan positions; they successfuly attack Fortín Boquerón	**Sep 1932:** Fortín Boquerón falls to Paraguay	**Oct 1933:** Paraguay makes spectacular gains along the war front	**Jun 1935:** Truce arranged; peace treaty signed in 1938

Economic development

After 1930, many South American nations adopted industrial development policies in an attempt to restructure their economies. Trade tariffs were imposed from the 1940s to accelerate industrialization while high inflation was tolerated in the hope of maintaining a strong demand for goods and services. Manufacturing industries became concentrated in a number of locations, yet income distribution remained unequal. From the 1980s, more open economies attracted investment. Economic reforms in the 1990s, aimed at defeating spiralling inflation, saw the privatization of many state–run enterprises. However, a number of states still suffer from underdevelopment, as well as debt and inflation. The Argentine economy collapsed in 2001, though recovery is underway.

Semi-skilled assembly line work, as in this car manufacturing plant in Argentina, was the main type of employment offered by foreign multinational corporations to South American workers in the 1990s.

❸ Industry and resources in modern South America ▶

Industry
- ✈ aerospace
- 🚗 car/vehicle manufacture
- chemicals
- electronics
- engineering
- $ finance
- food processing (includes brewing, fish processing, meat processing, and sugar processing)
- gas
- hi-tech industry
- iron and steel
- metal refining
- narcotics
- oil
- pharmaceuticals
- printing and publishing
- shipbuilding
- textiles
- timber processing
- tobacco processing
- main industrial areas

Agricultural resources
- cattle
- cocoa
- corn (maize)
- cotton
- coffee
- fishing
- fruit
- oil palms
- peanuts
- rubber
- sheep
- shellfish
- soya beans
- sugar cane
- vineyards
- wheat

Mineral resources
- bauxite (aluminium)
- copper
- diamonds
- gold
- iron ore
- lead
- manganese
- nickel
- silver
- tin
- coal field
- gasfield
- oilfield

Gross national product per capita, 2002
- no data available
- less than $1000
- $1000–$2500
- $2501–$4500

Development and deforestation in Amazonia

In the 1950s, the Brazilian government attempted to alleviate poverty among landless rural populations by granting resettlement plots along new roads in the Amazonian rain forest. From the 1960s, the government pursued vigorous economic policies which encouraged the development of the region. Subsidies and tax incentives made the clearing of Amazonia especially profitable for large land-holders involved in cattle ranching, and these farms were responsible for 80% of the destruction of the forest. By 2004, 16% of Brazil's rainforest had been cleared.

1964: Plans for highway network throughout Amazon Basin

1967: Daniel Ludwig sets up Jari Project in north Brazil; includes a wood-pulp plant and rice growing

1978: Trans-Amazon Highway completed. It extends 5000 km from Recife to Peruvian border

1981: United States provides $1.5 billion for conversion of forest land into pastures in Brazil

1992: United Nations Conference on the Environment in Rio de Janeiro; Indians granted title to one million hectares in Amazonia

2002: Sharp increase in rate of deforestation due to clearance of land to plant soya beans

| 1960 | 1970 | 1980 | 1990 | 2000 |

Economic development of the Brazilian rainforest from 1960

▼ ❹ Development and deforestation in Amazonia

Environmental issues
- tropical forests
- forest under medium / high threat
- deforested areas

Transportation network
- major Amazonian railway
- major Amazonian road

Mineral resources
- bauxite (aluminium)
- gold
- copper
- iron ore
- manganese
- nickel
- tin

Development programs
- development area with type of development

Scientists believed that gas released during the burning of the Brazilian rain forest contributed to global warming. Burning resulted in the release of carbon dioxide which the destroyed forest could not absorb to produce free oxygen.

A child harvests the coca crop in Colombia, where the shrub thrives in the tropical climate. Coca has been traditionally chewed by the people of Andean South America to cope with altitude sickness.

❺ The drugs trade ▶
- coca-growing areas
- poppy-growing areas
- provinces of Colombia
- border 2004

The narcotics trade

From the 1970s, Latin America began to ship massive quantities of cocaine to its main overseas market, the United States. The Andean countries, Bolivia, Colombia, and Peru, produced the coca leaf from which cocaine was derived, and the trade was organized and directed by the Medellín and Cali drugs cartels in Colombia. International intervention did little to depress the profits of drug barons, who later diversified into poppy growing in Colombia, for the production of heroin. By 1995, some 90% of the world's cocaine was being produced in Bolivia and Peru. South America also became the main source for the US heroin market.

AFRICA
REGIONAL HISTORY

THE HISTORICAL LANDSCAPE

THE GEOGRAPHY AND CLIMATE OF AFRICA has, to possibly a greater extent than in any other continent, determined its role in world history. The earliest human remains have been found here in the arid geological block faults of the Great Rift Valley and southern Africa. Although unaffected by the glaciation of the last Ice Age, attendant climatic changes witnessed a transformation of the Sahara from a desert during the Ice Age, into a belt of temperate grassland, inhabited by herds of game and groups of hunter-gatherers by 8000 years ago. By around 4000 BCE, the process of desiccation began which continues today, effectively isolating sub-Saharan Africa from the Mediterranean. Only the Nile Valley provided a link, and here one of the world's oldest civilizations emerged. South of the Sahara, a wide range of isolated cultures developed, their nature determined largely by their environment, linked by rich nonliterate oral traditions. The plateau nature of much of Africa, and the desert and jungle which dominate much of the landscape, meant that Africa was one of the last continents to be colonized by Europeans, and their brief and callous century of tenancy left a legacy of underdevelopment and political strife.

The Great Rift Valley was home to one of the earliest known human ancestors, *Australopithecus afarensis*, 3.8 million years ago. Modern humans *(Homo sapiens)* evolved here about 100,000 years ago before migrating to Asia and Australasia, Europe, and finally the Americas.

The Sahara covers much of northern Africa, although sand dunes account for only a quarter of the desert's area. The rest is made up of barren, rock-strewn surfaces. Desert has existed in this part of Africa for almost five million years, and the harsh climate and inhospitable landscape have prevented the establishment of permanent settlements.

The Nile River winds its way across the hostile Sahara to the Mediterranean Sea, flanked by fertile floodplains. Humans have inhabited the Nile region since the early Stone Age, making use of the fertile soils that have built up as a result of the annual flooding of the river.

Vegetation type

	semidesert or sparsely vegetated
	grassland
	forest or open woodland
	tropical rain forest
	tropical desert (18,000 years ago)
	desert (8000 years ago)
	coastline (present-day)
	coastline (18,000 years ago)

EUROPE

ASIA

Mediterranean Sea

Ionian
Basin

EURASIAN PLATE
AFRICAN PLATE

Anatolia

ANATOLIAN PLATE
AFRICAN PLATE

Atlas Mountains

Tigris

Euphrates

Dead
Sea

ARABIAN PLATE
IRANIAN PLATE

Tropic of Cancer

Sea levels at the Strait of Gibraltar, between Africa and Europe, were lower, but the two continents were not joined. It is thought that seawater breached this narrow gap about 5.5 million years ago, flooding the deep basins of the Mediterranean.

Ahaggar

DESERT MARGIN 9000 YEARS AGO

S a h a r a

Arabian
Peninsula

Nile

Red Sea

Lower sea levels meant that the Red Sea was narrower and shallower than it is today.

ARABIAN PLATE
AFRICAN PLATE

DESERT MARGIN 9000 YEARS AGO

Tibesti

East Sheba Ridge

Owen Fracture Zone

The swampy inland delta of the Niger River is all that remains of this lake today.

Niger

MEGA
CHAD
(8000 YEARS AGO)

Lake Chad

Much of the Chad Basin was filled by the huge lake Mega Chad, as the climate warmed at the end of the last Ice Age. The deserts receded about 8000 years ago, allowing nomads and pastoralists to inhabit the Sahara.

Nile

Blue Nile

White Nile

Ethiopian
Highlands

Horn of
Africa

Ogaden

Alula-Fartak Trench

Socotra

Chain Ridge

**ARAOUANE
LAKE**
(8000 YEARS AGO)

Lake Volta

Niger

A F R I C A

Uele

Congo

Somali Basin

Somali
Plain

Equator

During the last Ice Age, the Congo Basin was not covered by dense rain forests as it is today. The colder, drier climate meant that most of the basin was covered by grassland and scrub.

Guinea
Basin

Bioko

São Tomé

Ogooué

Congo Basin

Lualaba

White Nile

Lake
Rudolf

Lake
Albert

Lake
Victoria

INDIAN

OCEAN

Amirante Trench

Chain Fracture Zone

Congo
Canyon

Congo

Great Rift Valley

Lake
Tanganyika

Lake Rukwa

Great Rift Valley

Zanzibar

Comoro
Islands

ATLANTIC OCEAN

SOUTH AMERICAN PLATE
AFRICAN PLATE

Mid-Atlantic Ridge

Angola
Basin

Lake
Mweru

Comoro
Basin

18,000 years ago Madagascar was covered with great temperate forests in place of the lush tropical forests that exist today.

Mascarene Plain

Mascarene Ridge

Deserts extended from southern Africa as far north as the Congo River.

Cuango

Lake
Nyasa

Lake Cabora
Bassa

Zambezi

Madagascar

Wilshaw Ridge

Cubango

Walvis Ridge

Kalahari
Desert

LAKE
MAKGADIKGADI

Sabi

Limpopo

Runde

Tropic of Capricorn

Madagascar
Basin

The area once covered by this vast lake is now occupied by the Okavango Delta.

Orange River

Vaal

Orange River

Olifants

Natal
Basin

Madagascar
Plateau

Mozambique Plateau

Natal Valley

Southwest Indian Ridge

Discovery II Fracture Zone

Indomed Fracture Zone

Drakensberg

Du Toit Fracture Zone

AFRICAN PLATE
ANTARCTICA PLATE

Prince Edward Fracture

Atlantic-Indian Ridge

Crozet Plateau

Cape
Basin

Agulhas
Plateau

Cape Rise

Agulhas
Basin

Africa: 18,000 years ago

Africa was both colder and drier during the Ice Age. These two factors produced a marked change in the vegetation of the continent. The Sahara expanded southward, and rain forests shrank to a fraction of their present size, surviving in small strips next to rivers in the Congo Basin, and replaced for the most part by open grasslands and scrub. Deserts also spread in southwestern Africa, advancing northward and inland from the dry coastal zone.

AFRICA
EXPLORATION AND MAPPING

IN THE ABSENCE OF A WRITTEN historical record, little is known of early local knowledge of Africa south of the Sahara. Writing in the 5th century BCE, the Greek historian Herodotus reported an attempt by a Phoenician crew to circumnavigate the continent in 600 BCE. By 150 CE, the Greek geographer Ptolemy had mapped the area north of the line between Mombasa and the Canary Islands (*see p.44*). From 600 CE Arab merchants crisscrossed the Sahara establishing Muslim settlements. Several trading nations of Europe had secured coastal toeholds by 1600; however, by 1800, the African land mass remained relatively uncharted. The great 19th-century explorers of the interior meticulously recorded those features they encountered.

To stake a territorial claim, Portuguese sailors would place a stone cross (*padrão*) on the African shore.

MEDIEVAL ACCOUNTS OF THE INTERIOR OF WEST AFRICA

Though the West Africans did not have maps, travelers in the region built up a considerable store of topographic information. It was this knowledge that Arabs and later the Portuguese tapped as their source for maps of the interior. Al-Idrisi, in 1154 reported a single river in West Africa. The Egyptian geographer al-'Umari had an account of a Nile of the Blacks which divided into two rivers, one flowing to the ocean, the other to the East African Nile via Lake Chad. Writing in 1456, a Portuguese squire called Diogo Gomes recounted the testimony of Buquer, an African merchant, who talked of a great river called Emin. The reports of Mandinka merchants in 1585 agreed with Buquer's account and gave additional detail.

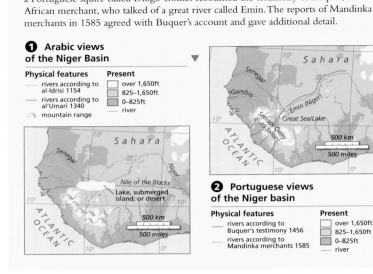

❶ Arabic views of the Niger Basin

Physical features	Present
—— rivers according to al-Idrisi 1154	▢ over 1,650ft
—— rivers according to al'Umari 1340	▢ 825–1,650ft
⋀ mountain range	▢ 0–825ft
	—— river

❷ Portuguese views of the Niger basin

Physical features	Present
—— rivers according to Buquer's testimony 1456	▢ over 1,650ft
—— rivers according to Mandinka merchants 1585	▢ 825–1,650ft
	▢ 0–825ft
	—— river

The caravel was a light sailing ship developed by the Portuguese for the exploration of coastal Africa. Its lateen sails allowed it to sail close to the wind.

❸ 14th- and 15th-century exploration

Moroccan
→ Ibn Battuta 1325–53

Chinese
--→ Zheng He 1417–31

Portuguese
→ Gonçalo Cabral 1432
→ Gil Eanes 1433–35
→ Alfonso Baldaya 1436
→ Alvise Cadamosto 1455–56
→ Diogo Gomes 1458–60
→ Diogo Cão 1482
--→ Diogo Cão 1485
→ Bartolomeu Dias 1487
→ Pero de Covilhã 1487–1520
→ Vasco da Gama 1497–99
→ Pedro Cabral 1500 (with Diogo Dias)
→ Pedro Cabral 1500
····→ Diogo Dias 1500–01

▨ area known to Greeks and Romans c.150
▨ area known to Muslim traders c.1500
—— trade routes
✝ mariners' milestone (padrão)

1352: Ibn Battuta takes last journey crossing Sahara to West Africa

1434: Eanes is first European to successfully navigate the cape; area is subsequently explored by Portuguese for slaves

1325: Ibn Battuta begins travels by undertaking pilgrimage to Mecca

1327–30: Ibn Battuta visits Muslim settlements on east coast of Africa

1417–31: Zheng He undertakes three voyages which include journeys along the east coast of Africa

Jan 6–Feb 3 1488: Dias rounds the stormy cape by sailing away from land and then returning to a coastal route

By the mid-16th century, European navigators had considerable knowledge of the coasts of Madagascar and East Africa, as depicted in this Portuguese map of 1558.

Portuguese exploration

Systematic voyages of discovery were undertaken by the Portuguese along the western coast of Africa. These and later expeditions were made in the hope both of making contact with the gold-producing centers known to exist in West Africa and of establishing a trade route to India around the tip of the continent. In consequence, the lower reaches of the rivers Gambia and Senegal were explored, contact was made with the Empire of Mali, and the Cape Verde Islands were discovered.

Portuguese voyages of discovery

1416: Prince Henry of Portugal founds school of navigation to seek sea route to Asia

1434: Eanes rounds the dreaded Cape Bojador

1445: Mouth of the Senegal River discovered

1446: Portuguese reach Senegal River and Cape Verde islands

1482: Portuguese build fort São Jorge da Mina (Elmina) on Gold Coast; Diogo Cão discovers mouth of Congo River

1488: Dias navigates the Cape of Good Hope

1497: Vasco da Gama despatched to inaugurate trade with India

1500: Cabral reaches Brazil and sails on to India

1420 1440 1460 1480 1500

Exploration of the African interior

The European exploration of the African interior is largely the story of the search for the sources of some of the world's greatest rivers. The Scottish explorer, James Bruce, toured Ethiopia between 1768 and 1773, discovering the source of the Blue Nile in 1772. Systematic exploration may be said to have begun in 1788, under the auspices of the African Association, a group of English scientists and scholars. In 1795 the association sponsored Mungo Park's first journey to West Africa; he investigated the Gambia River and reached the Niger, showing that it flowed eastward. British exploration intensified in the first half of the 19th century culminating in John Hanning Speke's triumphant discovery of the source of the Nile at Ripon Falls, Lake Victoria, in 1862. In anticipation of the scramble for territorial control, a number of continental Europeans also embarked on investigative expeditions.

French explorer René Caillié made this sketch of Timbuktu in 1828, when he fulfilled his great ambition to visit the Saharan city and secured a 10,000-franc prize for his efforts. The sum had been offered by the Société Géographique to the first European to return from the city.

The 19th century saw the systematic and scientific exploration of the African interior. As a result, cartographers were reluctant to represent uncertain data. Published in 1808, this map of Africa shows less information than its more speculative predecessors.

④ 19th-century exploration ▶

British
- → James Bruce 1768–73
- → Mungo Park 1795–96
- --→ Mungo Park 1805–06
- → Hugh Clapperton, Dixon Denham, and Walter Oudney 1821–25
- --→ Hugh Clapperton and Richard Lander 1825–27
- → David Livingstone 1841–53
- --→ David Livingstone 1849
- --→ David Livingstone 1853–56
- → David Livingstone 1866–73
- → Samuel and Florence Baker 1861–65
- → Henry Stanley 1871–89
- → Mary Kingsley 1895

French
- → René Caillié 1827–28
- --→ Pierre Savorgnan de Brazza 1875–78
- → Jean-Baptiste Marchand 1897–98

German
- → Heinrich Barth 1850–55

Italian
- → Vittorio Bottego 1892–97

Portuguese
- → Alexandre Serpa Pinto 1877–79

Swedish
- → Charles Andersson 1853–59

1000 km
1000 miles

⑤ Tracking the Nile
- → Richard Burton and John Speke 1856–59
- --→ John Speke 1858
- → John Speke and James Grant 1860–63
- → Samuel and Florence Baker 1863–65

300 km
300 miles

John Hanning Speke journeyed with Richard Burton in 1856–59. In 1862, James Grant and Speke came across the source of the Nile at Lake Victoria.

Livingstone carefully noted the dimensions of those physical features he encountered. He annotated this map of Victoria Falls with precise measurements and descriptive detail.

The source of the Nile

The quest for the source of the Nile captured the imagination of 19th-century Europe. The adventure stimulated intellectual debate and provoked fierce personal jealousies. After Speke had identified the source as Ripon Falls, Lake Victoria, persistent attempts were made to discredit his discovery. The political and economic importance of the region made it the objective of rival imperialists.

Sir Henry Morton Stanley, the British-American journalist, was sent to Africa by the *New York Herald* in 1871 to find David Livingstone, of whom nothing had been heard for several months. In the 1880s he helped create Léopold's Congo Free State.

European exploration of Africa from 1772

1788: African Association founded in London by Sir Joseph Banks	**1806:** Scottish explorer Mungo Park dies negotiating rapids on Niger	**1828:** Caillié reaches Timbuktu	**1853:** Barth arrives at Timbuktu / Livingstone crosses Africa; he encounters and names Victoria Falls	**1858:** Burton and Speke reach Lake Tanganyika	**1876–77:** Stanley travels down Congo to Atlantic

1760 — 1780 — 1800 — 1820 — 1840 — 1860 — 1880

1772: Bruce encounters the source of the Blue Nile
1823: Denham and Clapperton reach Lake Chad
1849: Livingstone reaches Lake Ngami
1859: Livingstone reaches Lake Nyasa
1862: Speke reaches Nile source
1875: Stanley confirms Nile source as Ripon Falls

THE EARLY HISTORY OF AFRICA

Hatshepsut seized the throne in Egypt from her stepson and reigned from 1472 to 1458 BCE.

THREE EVENTS contributed to the growth and spread of farming in Africa: the spread of cattle pastoralism in the Sahara, the domestication of indigenous crops further south, and the introduction of cereals to Egypt. Asian wheat and barley spread along the Mediterranean coast, up the Nile Valley to the Sudan, and the Ethiopian Highlands. Drier conditions from 3000 BCE forced Saharan pastoralists to migrate to the Nile Valley, where from 5000 BCE crops had thrived in fertile soil deposited by annual floods. Egypt thereafter emerged as a powerful state, organized conventionally into 30 "Dynasties," broken down into three "Kingdoms" separated by two "Intermediate Periods" of disunity and instability.

The development of agriculture

From 4000 BCE bulrush millet was cultivated alongside sorghum in southern Sudan.

Both the herding of wild cattle in the Sahara and the cultivation of indigenous plants farther south began c.6000 BCE. From 5000 BCE, Asian wheat and barley were grown in Egypt. By 2000 BCE pastoralism was widespread north of the Equator. Farming and herding south of the Equator however, were impeded by dense forests and the presence of the parasitic tsetse fly. As a result, pastoralism progressed only slowly down the east coast, reaching southern Africa by 1000 CE.

Saharan rock art provide vivid pictures of what life was like in the region. This example from the Tassili n'Ajjer plateau dates from c.6000 BCE. It depicts the hunting of giraffes, now only found south of the Sahara.

❶ The development of agriculture and technology 10,000–500 BCE ▶

Vegetation c.6000 BCE

- semidesert
- Mediterranean scrub
- savanna
- tropical grassland and scrub
- tropical rain forest
- tropical woodland
- ---- ancient lake c.7000–6000 BCE
- .... ancient coastline c.10,000 BCE

Archaeological evidence of early societies

- site with bone harpoons
- site with wavy-line pottery
- distribution of bone harpoons and wavy-line pottery
- areas wih Saharan rock art 6000–1000 BCE
- distribution of early copper and bronze metallurgy
- early iron working site
- early copper working site

Subsistence lifestyles 10,000–1000 BCE

- hunting and gathering site throughout 10,000–5000 BCE
- hunting and gathering site throughout 10,000–1000 BCE
- early food production site
- early food production site with cattle

The spread of plants and animals

- West Asian cereals c.6000–4500 BCE
- sheep and goats c.6000–4500 BCE
- limit of cattle domestication, with date

Domesticated indigenous crops

- bulrush millet
- ensete
- finger millet
- fonio
- guinea corn
- sorghum
- teff
- yam

Africa from the Neolithic period to the Iron Age

18,000: At the end of last Ice Age tropical forest limited to small areas of Congo Basin	9000: Wavy-line pottery making and village settlement in central Saharan region	6000: Agriculture and pastoralism expecially along the Nile River	4000: Agriculture in West Africa at Taruga	800: First Iron working in Sub-Saharan Africa

18,000 BCE	15,000	12,000	9000	6000	3000	1 CE

8000: Herding of wild animals in the Sahara	1500: Copper worked in the Saharan region	500: Iron working in the Great Lakes region

c.700 BCE: island uninhabited until colonized by Malays from Borneo

❷ Predynastic Egypt
c.5000–3000 BCE

- Confederacy of Thinis c.3500–3000 BCE
- Confederacy of Nubt c.3500–3000 BCE
- Confederacy of Nekhen c.3500–3000 BCE
- predynastic kingdom of Hieraconpolis
- military expansion of Hieraconpolis
- ○ early predynastic site
- ○ middle predynastic site
- △ middle predynastic Nubian site
- ◇ late predynastic site
- ◇ late predynastic Nubian site
- 🌴 oasis

Egypt 3200–1285 BCE

c.3000: Egyptian state ruled by 1st–3rd Dynasties
c.2795 Old Kingdom (to c.2180): 4th–6th Dynasties
c.2150: Series of low floods brings famine and discontent
c.1965: Nubia conquered by Egypt; frontier at 2nd Cataract
c.1530: New Kingdom (to 1070): 18th–20th Dynasties

c.3200: Earliest hieroglyphic script in Egypt
c.2650: Pyramid of Zoser; start of great period of pyramid building
c.2180: First Intermediate Period
c.2134: Middle Kingdom (to 1640): 11th–13th Dynasties
c.1640: Second Intermediate Period
1285: Advance into Levant halted by Hittites

❸ Old Kingdom
Egypt c.2795–2180 BCE

- regions of Egyptian control
- regions of contact
- Nubian chiefdoms
- ■ kingdom capital
- △ pyramid
- ○ oasis
- — trade route

Traded materials
- gold
- copper
- limestone
- turquoise
- red granite
- alabaster

The growth of Egypt 3500–2180 BCE

From 5000 BCE settled communites of farmers in the Nile valley gradually coalesced into urban centers under local rulers who developed efficient administrations. Narmer of the 1st Dynasty established the Egyptian state c.3000 BCE. From this time the use of hieroglyphic writing spread and Memphis was founded. With greater centralization of power the Old Kingdom emerged and the building of the great pyramids, which served as royal burial places, began. From 2400 BCE royal power began to decline and by 2180 BCE the Old Kingdom was divided between two rival dynasties in Upper and Lower Egypt. The years of political instability that followed became known as the First Intermediate Period.

The step pyramid of Zoser dating from c.2650 BCE was the earliest pyramid built in Egypt. Its construction required the large-scale mobilization of thousands of workers

❹ Middle Kingdom
Egypt c.2134–1640 BCE ▶

- regions of Egyptian control
- regions of contact
- ✳ trading center
- ⌂ Nubian fort
- ♒ Middle Kingdom temple
- 🌴 oasis
- — trade route

Traded materials
- gold
- copper
- turquoise

Hatshepsut's temple at Deir el-Bahri was built c.1473 BCE. A fine example of architecture from the 18th Dynasty, the building has a series of colonnades and courts on three levels.

Expansion and division in Egypt

The governors of Thebes emerged from the First Intermediate Period as rulers of Upper Egypt. They later successfully challenged Lower Egypt for control of the entire region, and the Middle Kingdom was established by c.2134 BCE. Its army and administration systematically enriched Egypt's economy by dominating, and eventually annexing, Wawat and northern Kush. The Second Intermediate saw Nubia lost from Egyptian control, and the division of the Nile Delta region into several kingdoms. From 1640 BCE much of Egypt was ruled by the Hyksos from the Mediterranean coast. They were later expelled by Ahmose, king of Thebes, who became the first ruler of the New Kingdom. During the New Kingdom Egypt embarked on a policy of expansion both north and south which made it the major commercial power in the ancient world. By 1000 BCE, however, the New Kingdom was in decline.

❺ New Kingdom
Egypt c.1530–1070 BCE

- regions of control under Thutmosis III
- regions of contact
- Hittite area of influence
- Mitannian influence
- — trade route
- ✕ battle, with date
- 🌴 oasis
- ♒ New Kingdom temple

THE SPREAD OF COMPLEX SOCIETIES

The Nok culture of West Africa was noted for its terra-cotta sculptures.

ALTHOUGH TRADE ROUTES connected sub-Saharan Africa to the Mediterranean civilizations of the north, the two regions developed very much in isolation. The southward migrations of Bantu-speakers from 2000 BCE may have contributed to the diffusion of settled agriculture in sub-Saharan Africa. Sheep-herding and ironworking spread south at a later date. The Nok of West Africa were smelting iron by 600 BCE. In North Africa, the rich lands of the Mediterranean coast and Egypt attracted foreign invaders, including the Greeks and Romans. However, from 300 BCE, powerful native states also emerged, notably Aksum, which dominated the Red Sea, and the Berber states which competed with Rome for the lands of northwest Africa.

The Bantu influence

From their homeland in modern-day Nigeria on Africa's west coast, the Bantu-speaking peoples dispersed along eastern and western routes into the equatorial rain forests and then on to southern Africa during the 1st millennium BCE. The migrating Bantu cleared forests and engaged in mixed farming. From the late 1st century BCE, their knowledge of ironworking gave them a distinct advantage over hunter-gatherers such as the Khoisan people. They established an economic basis for new societies which could sustain greater populations than those based on hunting and gathering. Thus, the period from 500 BCE to 1000 CE saw the transfer of Bantu traditions to much of sub-Saharan Africa.

During the first millennium BCE the Bantu settled in villages on the edge of the rain forest in Central Africa, engaging in mixed farming.

The spread of ironworking

The earliest evidence for ironworking south of the Sahara is found at the settlements of the Nok culture in West Africa, including Taruga and Samun Dukiya and dates from c.600 BCE. By 300 BCE, ironworking had spread as far south as the Congo river. From 1 CE, dates from sites on the subequatorial west coast correspond with those in East Africa. It is possible, therefore, that iron smelting diffused southward along two separate routes: one along the eastern part of the continent and the other along the west. In addition to its use for tools such as hoes, axes, knives, and spears, iron was also a luxury trade item, and helped to sustain intercommunity relations in the sub-Saharan region.

Paintings of chariots are found along ancient trans-Saharan routes. They may provide evidence for the transport of iron-working to sub-Saharan Africa.

The development of iron technology and social organization

c.600 BCE: First known ironworking in Nok region	c.400 BCE: Beginnings of ironworking in Ethiopian Highlands	c. 200 BCE: Earliest settlement in Jenne	c.1 CE: Sheep herded by Khoisans in southern Africa	c.400 CE: Jenne a substantial city with population of 12,000	c.600 CE: Cattle and iron-working widespread in southern Africa

600 BCE — 400 — 200 — 1 CE — 200 — 400 — 600 CE

c.300 BCE: Berber states begin to emerge in North Africa

c.300 CE: Bantu cereal cultivators in southeast Africa begin to herd cattle

❶ The development of complex societies in Africa

- Bantu homeland 2000 BCE
- Northwestern Bantu by 500 CE
- Eastern Bantu by 500 CE
- Western Bantu by 500 CE
- → spread of Bantu, with date
- Nok early Iron Age culture, 6th century BCE–5th century BCE
- → possible route of spread of ironworking c.600 BCE–400 CE
- area of sub-Saharan rock art from 1000 BCE
- East African pastoral Neolithic site
- early Iron Age settlement 600 BCE–600 CE
- early ironworking site with date
- Late Stone Age settlement, c.3000–600 BCE
- evidence of sheep domestication of the late Stone Age
- chariot rock art 1200 BCE
- frontiers at 500 CE
- equatorial rain forest

Scale varies with perspective

Berber states in North Africa

From 300 BCE, the Berber inhabitants of North Africa, including the Mauri, Masaesyli, and Massyli, began to form states, building cities and developing administrative structures. In alliance with Rome, the kingdoms were largely united to form Numidia by Masinissa of the Massyli in 201 BCE. Masinissa's grandson Jugurtha later incited war with Rome and was defeated in 104 BCE. His territory was subsequently absorbed into the Roman Empire as a client state. In 33 BCE King Boccus II of Mauretania willed his kingdom to the empire thus completing the annexation of the region. The entire North African coast supplied Rome with agricultural products, primarily wheat and olives; cities on the coast, such as Carthage, were centers of exchange.

The Berber states issued their own coinage. This coin dating from the 2nd century BCE depicts Jugurtha, ruler of Numidia from 118 BCE until his defeat at the hands of the Romans in 104 BCE.

An enduring consequence of the Roman Empire was the spread of the Latin language and Roman architecture. As towns sprang up in North Africa, they acquired characteristic features of Roman cities and architecture, such as this Roman amphitheater at Thysdrus (El Djem) in present-day Tunisia. Built in 225 CE, the building could seat 50,000 people.

2 States of North Africa

- area controlled by Carthage 500 BCE
- area controlled by Carthage 202 BCE
- area controlled by Carthage 201 BCE
- Ptolemaic Empire 202 BCE
- Roman province of Africa Nova 146 BCE
- Roman Empire at the death of Trajan 117 CE

Berber kingdoms of Mediterranean North Africa

- Massyli kingdom under Masinissa to 201 BCE
- Masaesyli kingdom under Syphax 201 BCE
- Massyli kingdom to 104 BCE
- Mauretanian kingdom under Boccus I to 104 BCE
- reduced territory of Massyli after Jugurtha's defeat 104 BCE
- Mauri Kingom of Mauretania 104–33 BCE

✕ battle, with date
→ trade route

Trade
gold		carpets	
silver		pottery	
copper		cloth	
timber		wine	
salt		olives	
marble		incense	
glass		wheat	
slaves		fish	
ivory		papyrus	

The Berber states and the Roman Empire

500: Foundation date for Carthage based on archaeological evidence
300: Development of the pre-Roman Berber states
201: Masinissa unites the kingdoms of Massyli and Masaesyli by Romans, called Numidia
104: King Jugurtha of Numidia is defeated by Marius

332: Alexander of Macedonia conquers Egypt, beginning Greek domination
255: Roman invasion of Carthaginian territory in North Africa ends in defeat
146: Rome conquers Carthage
112: The Roman-Jugurthian war begins
33: King Boccus II of Mauretania wills kingdom to Roman Empire

(Map labels include: Narbo, Massilia, Ancona, Salonae, Dioscurias, Black Sea, Iberian Peninsula, Tarraco, Corsica, Ostia, Rome, ITALY, Sardinia, Thessalonica, Sinope, Amisus, Trapezus, Gades, Rusaddir, Caesarea, Cirta, Bagradas, 255 BCE, Carthage, Lilybaeum, Syracuse, Sicily, Croton, Crete, CAPPADOCIA, Anatolia, Ephesus, Antioch, Cyprus, Euphrates, Tigris, MAURETANIA, Atlas Mountains, NUMIDIA, Zama 202 BCE, AFRICA NOVA, Leptis, Mediterranean Sea, Cyrene, Damascus, Caesarea Maritima, Alexandria, Memphis, Aelana, EGYPT, CYRENAICA, Sahara, Nile, to Nubia, Red Sea, Tropic of Capricorn.
Dated events: 112 BCE: Jugurtha provokes war with Rome when he kills Italians helping a rival defend Cirta; 255 BCE: Unsuccessful Roman attempt to invade Africa; 146–48 BCE: Roman province grows in stages beginning with Africa Nova; 48–47 BCE: Julius Caesar puts Cleopatra on throne of Egypt; 44 CE: Romans divide Mauretania into Mauretania Tingitana and Mauretania Caesariensis provinces; 104 BCE: Jugurtha defeated by Gaius Marius; Numidian territory reduced following Jugurthan war; 96 BCE: bequeathed to Rome; 74 BCE: Province of Rome; 30 BCE: Province of Rome; to Arabian Peninsula, East Africa, and India.)

The rise of Aksum 100 BCE–600 CE

Aksum, the center of the Ethiopian state, began its rise around 100 BCE, becoming a major trading power by the end of the first century CE. The kingdom grew wealthy through its control of the incense-trading port of Adulis on the Red Sea (see p.225). Aksum provided Egypt, India, Persia, and Arabia with tortoiseshell, ivory, and rhinoceros horn. The kingdom reached its peak during the reign of King Ezana, who converted to Christianity c.350 CE. By 500 CE most of the country had adopted the new religion. In 525 CE Kaleb, one of Ezana's successors, conquered the southern part of the Arabian Peninsula, and Aksum occupied this territory until 574 CE. With the spread of Islam in the 7th century, Aksum lost its monopoly of the Red Sea to Muslim traders, and began to decline.

Aksum's rulers commemorated their victories with stone stelae, sometimes up to 100 ft high, which were built above subterranean royal tombs.

The rise and fall of kingdoms in northeast Africa

500 BCE: Foundation of Kingdom of Daamat, the first state of the Ethiopian Highlands
100 BCE: Rise of Aksum
330 CE: Fall of Meroe to Aksumites
c.540 CE: Nubians convert to Christianity

300 BCE: Capital of Napata moved to Meroe; the kingdom expands
350 CE: Conversion of Ezana of Aksum to Christianity
525–574 CE: Aksumite armies occupy southern Arabian Peninsula

3 Northeast Africa 100 CE

frankincense and myrrh	rhinoceros horn
gold	slaves
ivory	tortoiseshell
obsidian	→ trade route
precious stones	

(Map 3 labels: SYRIA, Palmyra, Tyre, Euphrates, Tigris, PARTHIAN EMPIRE, Babylon, Charax, Mediterranean Sea, Alexandria, Gaza, Aelana, Petra, NABATAEA, Gerrha, ROMAN EMPIRE, EGYPT, Myos Hormus, Thebes, Leucecome, Medina, Persian Gulf, Ommana, to India, Tropic of Cancer, Berenice, Mecca, Arabian Peninsula, Dongola, KUSH, Meroe, Sahara, Sennar, Timna, Najran, Samhar, Adulis, Zafar, Cana, AKSUM, Muza, Avalites, Mundus, Socotra, Emporion, Lake Tana, Malab, to Zanzibar, Opone, Ethiopian Highlands, Gulf of Aden.)

4 Northeast Africa 350 CE

(Map 4 labels: SYRIA, Palmyra, Tyre, Euphrates, Tigris, SASSANIAN EMPIRE, Babylon, Charax, Mediterranean Sea, Alexandria, Gaza, Petra, Aelana, ROMAN EMPIRE, EGYPT, Myos Hormus, Thebes, Leucecome, Medina, Persian Gulf, Tropic of Cancer, Berenice, Mecca, Arabs, Arabian Peninsula, Kerma, Dongola, KUSH, Meroe, first Christian church, Soba, Sahara, Kassala, Adulis, HIMYARITES, Himyar, Zafar, Saba, AKSUM, Muza, Avalites, Lake Tana, Socotra, Ethiopian Highlands, Gulf of Aden.)

5 Northeast Africa 500 CE

✝ early Christian church 350 CE–600 CE

(Map 5 labels: SYRIA, Palmyra, Tyre, Euphrates, Tigris, SASSANIAN EMPIRE, Babylon, Charax, Mediterranean Sea, Alexandria, EASTERN ROMAN EMPIRE, Gaza, Aelana, Petra, NABATAEA, Gerrha, EGYPT, Myos Hormus, Thebes, Leucecome, Medina, Persian Gulf, Ominana, Tropic of Cancer, Gebel Adda, Berenice, Mecca, Arabs, Arabian Peninsula, NUBIA, Kerma, Dongola, MAKURIA, Meroe, Soba, ALWA, Sennar, Sahara, Kassala, Himyar, Najran, Samhar, HIMYARITES, Aksum, Zafar, Cana, AKSUM, Muza, Avalites, Fur, Lake Tana, Socotra, Emporion, Kushites, Malab, Opone, Mundus, Ethiopian Highlands, Gulf of Aden.)

ISLAM AND NEW STATES IN AFRICA

FROM THE 10TH CENTURY, A SERIES of empires arose in the sub-Saharan savannah. They attracted Muslim Arab traders who traveled south in search of salt, gold, and slaves. Through frequent contact, Islam gradually infiltrated the region by means of peaceful conversion. When the Muslim Berber Almoravids captured the capital of Ghana in 1076, causing the collapse of the empire, their conquest did little to advance the spread of Islam. Christian Ethiopia also withstood Muslim advances. However, Ghana's successors, Mali and Songhay, owed much of their wealth and civilization to the advent and adoption of Islam, as did the Kanem-Bornu Empire around Lake Chad, and, after the 15th century, the Hausa city-states. From the late 10th century, Arab merchant colonies were established in the coastal towns of East Africa, stimulating African trade with Arabia and India, and accelerating the southward spread of Islam.

Unearthed on the island of Pemba, these North African gold coins testify to Swahili trade with the Arab world.

African trade and the spread of Islam

Built in the 14th century, the great mosque at Jenne in Mali was constructed with sun-dried mud bricks.

Islamic expansion out of Arabia began in earnest following the death of the Prophet Muhammad in 632. By 640 Egypt had fallen into the hands of Muslim soldiers and settlers. From the 8th century, traders and clerics were the agents of Islam, spreading the religion along the commercial arteries of the Sahara which extended into West Africa, and up the Nile. By the 13th century the Saifawa kings of Kanem had adopted the faith. Islam had also traveled down the east coast of Africa, taken by seafaring Arabs who set up coastal trading centers. Trade between Arabs and Bantu necessitated a new language, so Swahili became the *lingua franca* of the east coast.

Carved by West African craftsmen, this 16th-century ivory horn *(above)* was produced for the European market. This is confirmed by its Portuguese-style inscriptions.

Dating from the 16th century, this blue and white Ming dynasty bowl *(left)* was found on the east coast of Africa, providing evidence of trade with China.

Islamic expansion in Africa from 600

632: Death of Muhammad
635–40: Conquest of Egypt by Arabs
c.800: Emergence of trading towns on East African coast.
909: Fatimid dynasty founded by Ubaydullah
1050: King of Takrur converts to Islam
1270: Beginning of Solomid dynasty in Ethiopia

| 600 | 700 | 800 | 900 | 1000 | 1100 | 1200 | 1300 |

625: First Islamic Arab invasion of Makuria
680: Arab armies reach Atlantic at Morocco
1076: King of Ghana converts to Islam

① African trade and the spread of Islam 500–1500 ▶

- ----- frontiers 1500
- → Muslim trade routes
- limit of Muslim influence by 900
- limit of Muslim influence by 1100
- limit of Muslim influence by 1300
- limit of Muslim influence by 1500
- limit of Muslim influence in Spain 1492
- Christians c.1100
- Christians c.1500
- ○ Portuguese possession in 1500

- copper
- gold
- dates
- fish
- flour
- ivory
- kola nuts
- leather
- porcelain
- perfume
- saffron
- salt
- silk
- slaves
- spice
- wax
- wool

Scale varies with perspective

N

4730 km (2940 miles)

8890 km (5520 miles)

to India

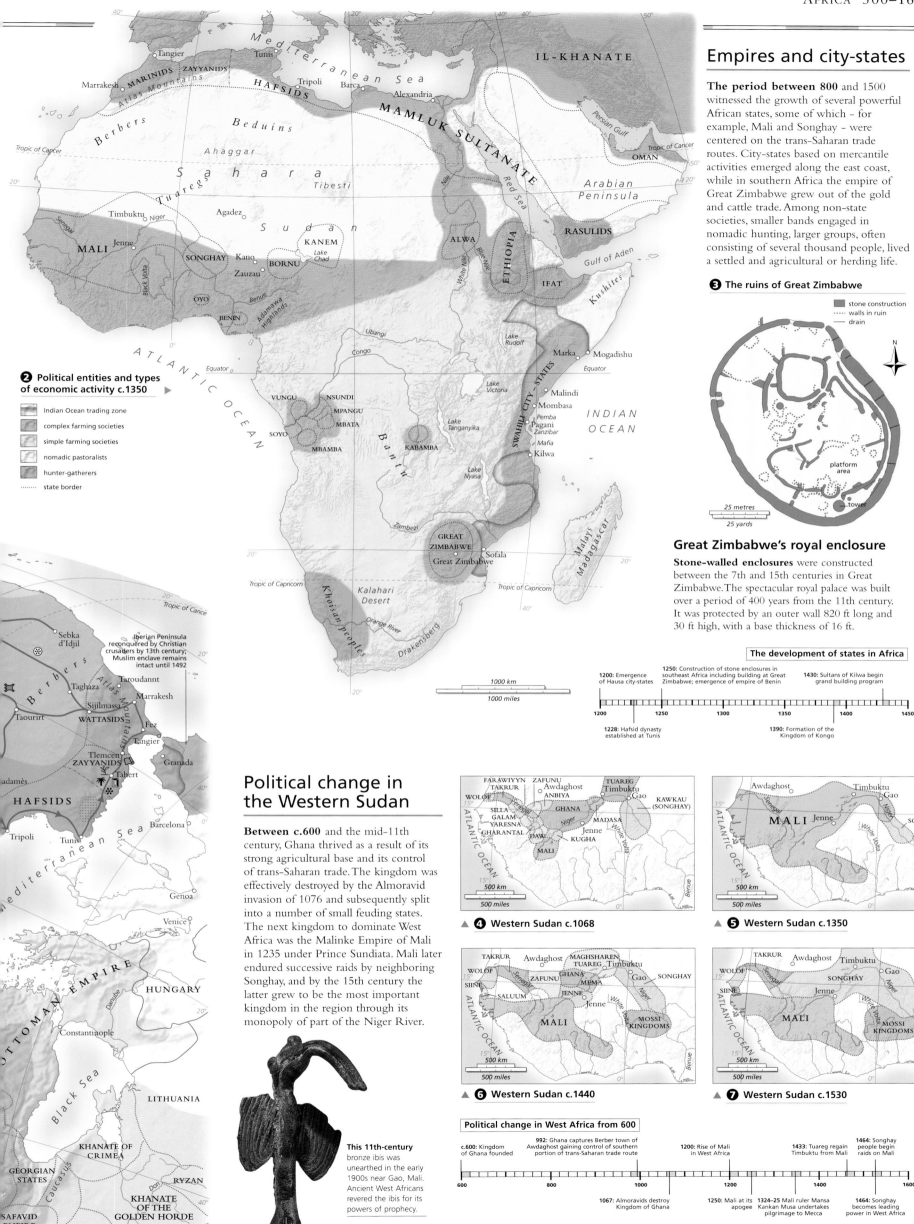

Empires and city-states

The period between 800 and 1500 witnessed the growth of several powerful African states, some of which – for example, Mali and Songhay – were centered on the trans-Saharan trade routes. City-states based on mercantile activities emerged along the east coast, while in southern Africa the empire of Great Zimbabwe grew out of the gold and cattle trade. Among non-state societies, smaller bands engaged in nomadic hunting, larger groups, often consisting of several thousand people, lived a settled and agricultural or herding life.

❸ The ruins of Great Zimbabwe

- ▮ stone construction
- ⋯ walls in ruin
- ▬ drain

Great Zimbabwe's royal enclosure

Stone-walled enclosures were constructed between the 7th and 15th centuries in Great Zimbabwe. The spectacular royal palace was built over a period of 400 years from the 11th century. It was protected by an outer wall 820 ft long and 30 ft high, with a base thickness of 16 ft.

The development of states in Africa

1200: Emergence of Hausa city-states	1250: Construction of stone enclosures in southeast Africa including building at Great Zimbabwe; emergence of empire of Benin		1430: Sultans of Kilwa begin grand building program
1200	**1250** 1228: Hafsid dynasty established at Tunis	**1300** **1350** 1390: Formation of the Kingdom of Kongo	**1400** **1450**

❷ Political entities and types of economic activity c.1350 ▶

- Indian Ocean trading zone
- complex farming societies
- simple farming societies
- nomadic pastoralists
- hunter-gatherers
- ⋯ state border

Political change in the Western Sudan

Between c.600 and the mid-11th century, Ghana thrived as a result of its strong agricultural base and its control of trans-Saharan trade. The kingdom was effectively destroyed by the Almoravid invasion of 1076 and subsequently split into a number of small feuding states. The next kingdom to dominate West Africa was the Malinke Empire of Mali in 1235 under Prince Sundiata. Mali later endured successive raids by neighboring Songhay, and by the 15th century the latter grew to be the most important kingdom in the region through its monopoly of part of the Niger River.

This 11th-century bronze ibis was unearthed in the early 1900s near Gao, Mali. Ancient West Africans revered the ibis for its powers of prophecy.

❹ Western Sudan c.1068

❺ Western Sudan c.1350

❻ Western Sudan c.1440

❼ Western Sudan c.1530

Political change in West Africa from 600

c.600: Kingdom of Ghana founded	992: Ghana captures Berber town of Awdaghost gaining control of southern portion of trans-Saharan trade route	1200: Rise of Mali in West Africa	1433: Tuareg regain Timbuktu from Mali	1464: Songhay people begin raids on Mali
600	**800** **1000** 1067: Almoravids destroy Kingdom of Ghana	**1200** 1250: Mali at its apogee 1324–25 Mali ruler Mansa Kankan Musa undertakes pilgrimage to Mecca	**1400** 1464: Songhay becomes leading power in West Africa	**1600**

163

EARLY MODERN AFRICA

Asante's well-armed warriors made it the most powerful state on the Gold Coast.

AFTER THE PORTUGUESE had led European expansion into Africa in the 15th century, a few colonies were established – in Angola, along the Zambezi Valley, and in the region of the Cape of Good Hope – but for the most part, African rulers contained and controlled the activities of the newcomers. In parts of West Africa they allowed Europeans to establish coastal forts and trading posts. With this new presence came increased opportunities for external trade, principally in gold, ivory, and slaves. After 1700, however, the importance of all other goods was totally eclipsed by the value of the Atlantic slave trade.

The 16th century saw the Ottoman Empire advance across North Africa as far as the Atlas Mountains. To the south, the great empire of Songhay yielded to Moroccan invaders in 1591, though the cycle of empires continued in West Africa with Great Fulo. In the early 18th century powerful coastal kingdoms arose in Asante and Dahomey, while Rozwi replaced Mwenemutapa in southeast Africa.

Southern and East Africa

The Portuguese presence in the region was challenged in the 17th century by the Rozwi empire, which drove them from the highlands of Zimbabwe, while Omani fleets captured many of their coastal forts in East Africa. Portugal was left with the semi-independent *prazos* (estates) of the Zambezi valley and the coastal towns of Sofala, Mozambique, and Inhambane. In 1652 the Dutch East India Company founded its colony at Cape Town. Rapid expansion in the 18th century brought Dutch settlers into conflict with the many small states of the Nguni region.

Fort Jesus, built in 1593 to protect Portuguese trading interests in Mombasa, fell to the Omanis in 1698.

1652: Dutch establish colony at Cape of Good Hope

1696: Dombo Changamire expands Rozwi over Zimbabwe region

1729: Portuguese leave East Africa in wake of attacks from Oman

1779: Start of series of wars between Dutch settlers and Nguni

| 1650 | 1675 | 1700 | 1725 | 1750 | 1775 | 1800 |

1720–30: Dutch occupy Portuguese settlement at Delagoa Bay

1795: British capture Cape Town from the Dutch

Southern and East Africa

① Southern and East Africa c.1700

- Portuguese possessions
- Dutch possessions
- ⌕ ruined city

500 km
500 miles

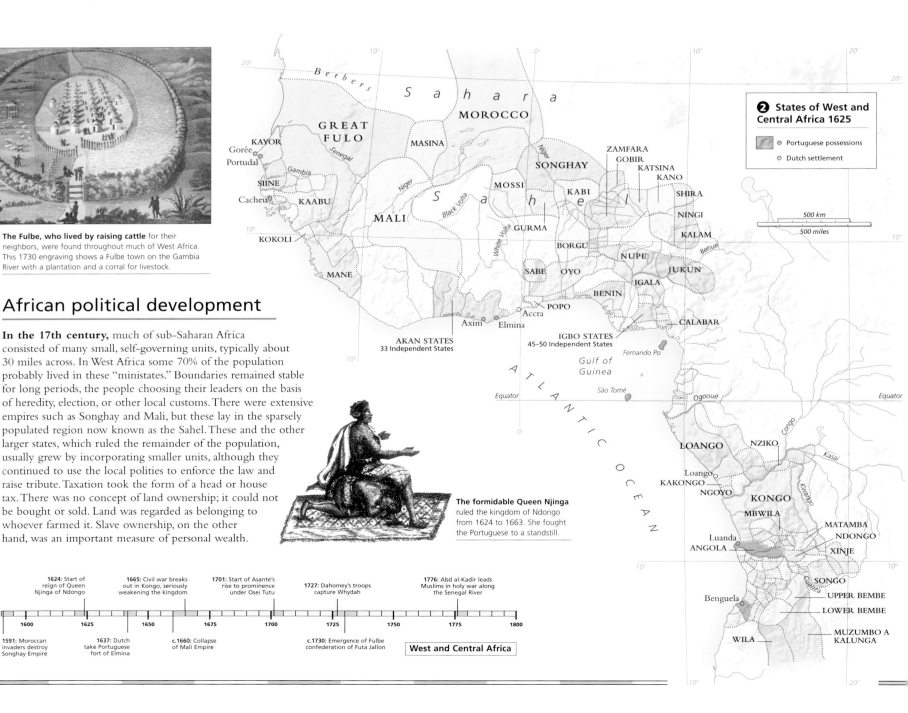

The Fulbe, who lived by raising cattle for their neighbors, were found throughout much of West Africa. This 1730 engraving shows a Fulbe town on the Gambia River with a plantation and a corral for livestock.

African political development

In the 17th century, much of sub-Saharan Africa consisted of many small, self-governing units, typically about 30 miles across. In West Africa some 70% of the population probably lived in these "ministates." Boundaries remained stable for long periods, the people choosing their leaders on the basis of heredity, election, or other local customs. There were extensive empires such as Songhay and Mali, but these lay in the sparsely populated region now known as the Sahel. These and the other larger states, which ruled the remainder of the population, usually grew by incorporating smaller units, although they continued to use the local polities to enforce the law and raise tribute. Taxation took the form of a head or house tax. There was no concept of land ownership; it could not be bought or sold. Land was regarded as belonging to whoever farmed it. Slave ownership, on the other hand, was an important measure of personal wealth.

② States of West and Central Africa 1625

- Portuguese possessions
- Dutch settlement

500 km
500 miles

The formidable Queen Njinga ruled the kingdom of Ndongo from 1624 to 1663. She fought the Portuguese to a standstill.

1624: Start of reign of Queen Njinga of Ndongo

1665: Civil war breaks out in Kongo, seriously weakening the kingdom

1701: Start of Asante's rise to prominence under Osei Tutu

1727: Dahomey's troops capture Whydah

1776: Abd al-Kadir leads Muslims in holy war along the Senegal River

| 1600 | 1625 | 1650 | 1675 | 1700 | 1725 | 1750 | 1775 | 1800 |

1591: Moroccan invaders destroy Songhay Empire

1637: Dutch take Portuguese fort of Elmina

c.1660: Collapse of Mali Empire

c.1730: Emergence of Fulbe confederation of Futa Jallon

West and Central Africa

The struggle for the Horn of Africa

Ethiopia's domination of the region came to an end in the 16th century. The Christian empire's expansion into Muslim lands to the south had often involved forced conversion and the destruction of Islamic literature and places of worship. In 1529 a dynamic imam from Adal, Ahmad Grañ, proclaimed a holy war against Ethiopia, winning many striking victories. In 1540 the Ethiopians sought aid from Portugal and Grañ was killed in battle in 1543. This ultimately inconclusive war laid waste the region, which allowed the Oromo to invade from the south. Organized in many independent mobile bands, they took over both Christian and Muslim lands and founded new kingdoms of their own. Many Oromo embraced Islam and some fought as mercenaries in civil wars in Ethiopia. The fortunes of the Ethiopian empire revived somewhat in the Gondar period in the 17th century, but its lands were much reduced.

1529: Ahmad Grañ leads *jihad* against Ethiopia	1540: Portuguese come to the aid of Ethiopia	1597: Start of period of civil war	1636: King Fasiladas founds permanent capital at Gondar	1682: Accession of Iyasu I, last great king of Gondar period

The decline of Ethiopia

1543: Death of Ahmad Grañ, shot by a Portuguese musketeer	1590: Oromo bands begin occupation of southern Ethiopia	1632: End of civil wars. Jesuit missionaries expelled from Ethiopia

❸ Horn of Africa 1500–1700

→ Jihad of Ahmad Grañ 1529–43 ⇒ Oromo expansion 1550–1700
······ approximate state border 1500

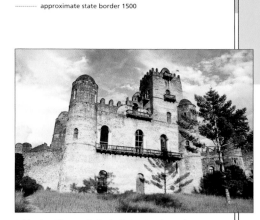

Ethiopian King Fasiladas built the city of Gondar and this magnificent castle in 1636. Before his reign, the rulers of Ethiopia had never had a fixed residence, instead setting up a tented court for periods of six months to a year, then moving on to another part of the kingdom.

❹ The African slave trade c.1750

- Ottoman Empire
- ◉ Portuguese possessions
- ◉ Dutch possessions
- ◉ French settlement
- ◉ British settlement

Principal slave routes
- Arab routes
- British routes
- Danish routes
- Dutch routes
- French routes
- Moroccan routes
- Portuguese routes

A group of slaves is led to the West African coast by traders using a coffle, a device that secured the slaves by the neck while leaving their legs free.

The slave trade

Between 1500 and 1800 some 15 million people were sold as slaves from Africa. The majority were carried across the Atlantic on European and American ships, though significant numbers were also taken across the Sahara and the Horn of Africa for sale in North Africa, the Middle East, and southern Europe. African traditions recognized the right of states and private individuals to establish control over others, and this provided the legal basis for the trade. Most Africans who were sold were taken prisoner in warfare, typically between African states, though some were captured illegally or seized through judicial punishments.

1441: Portuguese export slaves from Atlantic coast to Europe	1502: First slaves taken to the New World	c.1550: Importance of slave trade starts to outweigh trade in gold	c.1700: Rapid increase in numbers of slaves sold annually to the Americas	1787: Establishment of Sierra Leone for freed slaves in Africa

The African slave trade

1592: English ships join in slave trade	1619: Slaves shipped to English North America	1788: British Privy Council begins investigation of slave trade

THE COLONIZATION OF AFRICA

THE 19TH CENTURY was a period of revolutionary change in Africa. The states of West Africa were convulsed by a series of reformist Islamic *jihads*, while in the south the rise of Zulu militarism had catastrophic consequences for neighboring peoples. By the mid-19th century Africa was also undergoing a commercial revolution. Europeans could now offer high-quality machined goods in large quantities. As a result, Africa was condemned to the role of producer of primary goods. By the end of the century, many African kingdoms and clan-based communities were being replaced by states organized along indigenous lines. However, this process was forestalled by the decision of the major European powers to carve up the continent between them.

Cecil Rhodes, the embodiment of colonialism, planned to extend British rule in Africa from Cairo to Cape Town.

Commerce in the 19th century

The development of new export goods in Europe had social implications for Africa. Reduced shipping costs brought about by the introduction of the steamship meant that European textile and metal goods arrived in force. The resultant decline in local industries was accompanied by a growth in the internal slave trade. The substantial carrying trade, especially the porterage trade of East and Central Africa, was run by small-scale entrepreneurs. While such ventures did not bring large profit, those involved enjoyed new and elevated social positions. Often the carrying trade was organized from a particular region, giving it an ethnic character. Enterprising African traders took advantage of the expanding economy to gain political power – for example, the copper trader Msiri won himself a kingdom.

The Arab slave trader Tibbu Tib organized his own state and security system in 1875 with the help of armed followers.

❶ Commercial and political Africa c.1830

- cloves
- cocoa
- coffee
- copper
- cotton
- diamonds
- gold
- gum arabic
- honey and wax
- ivory
- olives
- palm products
- peanuts
- rubber
- slaves/ migrant workers
- wheat
- wine
- → trade route

- British possession
- French possession
- Ottoman territory
- Portuguese possession
- Spanish possession
- commercial group

Commercial Africa from 1815

1816: Wool mills, flax mills, sugar refineries, indigo factories, and glassworks established in Egypt

c.1850: Atlantic slave trade, including clandestine operations, begins to die out

1875: Tibbu Tib establishes trading principality

1815 1825 1835 1845 1855 1865 1875

1830: 20,000 slaves exported from central African ports to Brazil

1866: Copper trader Msiri establishes trading principality

Zulu and Afrikaner expansion

Under the leadership of Shaka, the Zulu were organized into a highly militarized kingdom. They conquered neighboring Nguni tribes and set off a series of wars which depopulated large parts of the southern interior, leaving it vulnerable to Afrikaner expansion. Afrikaners left Cape Colony between 1835 and the 1840s in search of pastureland and to escape from unwelcome British rule. They successfully defeated powerful military kingdoms as they progressed northward.

British reforms, such as the abolition of slavery, caused the exodus of many Boers from Cape Colony. They undertook the "Great Trek" in ox-drawn wagons.

❷ The Afrikaner treks and the Mfecane wars

- the nuclear Zulu chiefdom
- Shaka's Zulu kingdom 1817
- Sobhuza's Swazi kingdom 1820
- Moshoeshoe's Lesotho kingdom 1824
- Mzilikazi's Ndebele kingdom 1826
- ⚔ Nguni victory
- ⚔ British victory
- ⚔ Boer victory
- → main Boer trek route 1836–54
- → Nguni migrations
- — borders 1895

Shaka armed the Zulu with long-bladed stabbing *assegais*, which forced them to fight at close quarters. Shield markings and headdress distinguished different regiments.

Zulu and Afrikaner expansion

1820: Nguni clans disperse to avoid Mfecane wars brought about by rise of Zulu Empire

1835: Zwangendaba crosses the Limpopo taking the Mfecane northward

1843: Short-lived Boer republic of Natal annexed by Britain

1852: Independence granted by British to Voortrekkers in Transvaal

1820 1830 1840 1850 1860

1816: Shaka becomes leader of the Zulu, a clan of the Nguni

1836: Start of the Great Trek

1854: Boers found the Orange Free State

Islamic wars in western Africa

1807: Hausa kings replaced by Fulani emirs
1820: Usuman dan Fodio establishes Sokoto Fulani Kingdom
1852: 'Umar Tal conquers the Senegal valley
1861: 'Umar Tal's forces conquer Segu

1800 · 1810 · 1820 · 1830 · 1840 · 1850 · 1860 · 1870

1804: *Jihad* of Usuman dan Fodio
1816: Inspired by Usuman dan Fodio, Amadu Lobbo launches *jihad* in Masina
1863: Timbuktu falls to 'Umar Tal; he founds Tukulor Empire
1864: 'Umar Tal is killed attempting to suppress Fulani rebellion

The text of this richly decorated 19th-century Koran is written in West African Sudani script. The large rectangular design marks the end of a chapter.

Islamic reform in West Africa

The *jihads* of West Africa were a source of major turmoil in the 19th century. The idea that reformers could overthrow governments they thought were unjust was deeply rooted in the region, and dated back to the 11th century Almoravid movement. Holy men challenged rulers, often because of their tyranny and corruption, and demanded change. Social problems also promoted reform, for example, Fula herdsmen often backed reformers against those who taxed and mistreated them. In other cases, it was humble peasants or slaves who converted to Islam. Tukulor cleric Usuman dan Fodio's *jihad* in Hausaland in 1804 led to the establishment of the Islamic Sokoto Fulani Kingdom in 1820. Fulani cleric al-Hajj 'Umar Tal set about reforming the Segu region in 1851 and by 1863 had founded the Tukulor Empire.

❸ 19th-century West African *jihads* ▶

- Sokoto Fulani Kingdom c.1820
- Tukulor Empire c.1864
- ◉ British possession
- ◉ French possession
- ◉ Portuguese possesssion
- → *jihad* route of al-Hajj 'Umar Tal
- ···· borders c.1850
- ✕ conflict

The conquest of the interior

The years after 1885 saw a race to complete the conquest of the African interior *(see p.96)*. International rivalries between European powers, coupled with local merchant competition and the popularity of African conquest in the home arena, ensured European governmental interest in the continent. In many cases, initial conquests were funded by commercial interests, such as Cecil Rhodes' De Beers Consolidated Mines company. Most of the fighting personnel were Africans, hired mercenaries, or militarily trained slaves. The use of commercial contacts with African traders and the exploitation of local rivalries were as effective as brute force and the machine gun.

The conquest of Africa from 1880

1883: France begins its conquest of Madagascar
1884: Berlin Conference on Africa; Samore Touré proclaims his Islamic theocracy
1894: Britain occupies Buganda
1896: France takes Madagascar
1900–01: Britain annexes Asante
1908: Belgium takes over Congo Free State

1880 · 1890 · 1900 · 1910

1882: Britain occupies Egypt; Congo Free State formed by King Leopold of Belgium
1889: Italy establishes its first colony in Eritrea
1892: France destroys the Tukulor Empire
1904: French create federation of French West Africa

❹ European penetration of Africa ▼

Colonial territory c.1880
- Ottoman suzerainty
- British
- Portuguese
- French
- Spanish
- Boer Republics
- frontier of Christian missionary activities c.1880

European routes of expansion
- → Belgian
- → British
- → French
- → German
- → Italian
- → Portuguese
- → Spanish
- → main lines of missionary advance
- **1888** foundation date of colonial settlement

Colonial settlements
- ◉ Belgian
- ◉ Boer
- ◉ British
- ◉ French
- ◉ German
- ◉ Italian
- ◉ Portuguese
- ○ other settlement

Armed and trained by France, these African soldiers, known as the Senegalese Rifles, helped France win territory in Africa.

POST-COLONIAL AFRICA

Julius Nyerere led the fight for independence in Tanganyika.

MOST AFRICAN COUNTRIES gained independence between 1956 and 1968. The new states, with few exceptions, were territorially identical to the European colonies they replaced. Following independence, leaders often became dictators, or the army seized power; many governments were corrupt and a number of countries were devastated by war. Moves were made towards multiparty democracy, most notably in South Africa where apartheid was dismantled in 1990. During the 1990s and 2000s, many western and central African states were gripped by bitter conflicts, stemming from ethnic rivalries and disputes over natural resources, such as timber and diamonds.

African independence

After World War II the colonial powers in Africa faced demands for self-determination, and most countries gained independence around 1960. In the face of widespread opposition, Portugal clung on to its territories through the 1960s. This resulted in long and bloody wars in Angola, Guinea-Bissau, and Mozambique. There were also protracted struggles for majority rule in the former British colonies of Zimbabwe and South Africa. The presidential election victory of Nelson Mandela in 1994 marked the end of white minority rule in South Africa.

The national flag is raised in Ghana during an independence ceremony. The country was declared a republic on July 1, 1960, with Dr. Kwame Nkrumah as the first president.

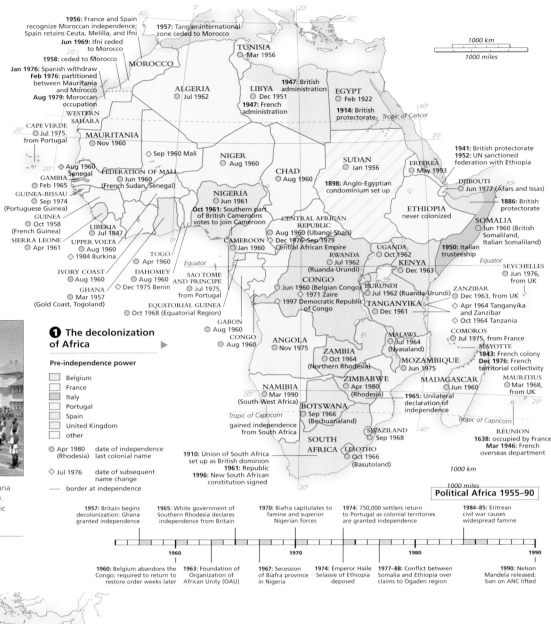

❶ The decolonization of Africa ▶

Pre-independence power
- Belgium
- France
- Italy
- Portugal
- Spain
- United Kingdom
- other

⊙ Apr 1980 (Rhodesia) — date of independence / last colonial name
◇ Jul 1976 — date of subsequent name change
— border at independence

Political Africa 1955–90

1957: Britain begins decolonization: Ghana granted independence
1965: White government of Southern Rhodesia declares independence from Britain
1970: Biafra capitulates to famine and superior Nigerian forces
1974: 750,000 settlers return to Portugal as colonial territories are granted independence
1984–85: Eritrean civil war causes widespread famine

1960 | 1970 | 1980 | 1990

1960: Belgium abandons the Congo; required to return to restore order weeks later
1963: Foundation of Organization of African Unity (OAU)
1967: Secession of Biafra province in Nigeria
1974: Emperor Haile Selassie of Ethiopia deposed
1977–88: Conflict between Somalia and Ethiopia over claims to Ogaden region
1990: Nelson Mandela released; ban on ANC lifted

The African economy

Industrial growth is government policy in a number of countries in Africa, and is seen as the way to progress economically. Countries with large manufacturing sectors include South Africa and oil-rich states such as Nigeria, Algeria, and Libya. Many other states rely on a single resource or cash crop for export income, leaving them vulnerable to market fluctuations.

❷ Industry in Africa, 2004

Primary resources
- bauxite
- coal
- copper
- diamonds
- gas
- gold
- iron
- oil
- phosphates
- tin
- uranium

Secondary industry
- car/vehicle manufacture
- chemicals
- electronics
- engineering
- finance
- food processing
- palm oil processing
- pharmaceuticals
- textiles
- major industrial areas

Major cash crops
- cocoa
- coffee
- cotton
- dates
- fruit
- olives
- rice
- rubber
- shellfish
- spices
- timber
- tobacco
- vineyards

Ecological tourism
- national parks

Percentages of total export earnings
40–59 | 60–80 | more than 80
- agriculture and fishing
- crude oil and petroleum products
- metals and minerals

○ Main export product

The burden of debt

The HIPC (Highly Indebted Poor Countries) initiative was proposed by the World Bank and IMF in 1996. It aims to lessen the debt burden of the poorest countries, with the promise to erase $100 billion of debt. Forty-two countries were deemed eligible, 27 of which (23 of them African) have joined the scheme so far. There was significant early progress, but the fairness and effectiveness of the initiative are vigorously debated.

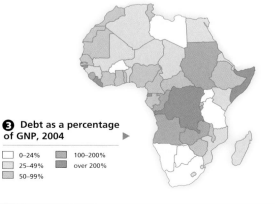

❸ Debt as a percentage of GNP, 2004 ▶
- 0–24%
- 25–49%
- 50–99%
- 100–200%
- over 200%

4 Post-independence conflict and crisis

- famine
- anti-colonial war
- civil war
- interstate war
- successful coup d'état
- South African tribal homelands
- independent South African homelands

Map labels (Post-independence conflict and crisis):

MOROCCO 1960
WESTERN SAHARA 1957
ALGERIA 1962 / 1954–62 / 1965, 1992
TUNISIA 1958 / 1957, 1988
LIBYA 1969
1969: King Idris I overwhelmed by Colonel Moammar Gadhafi
1986: US bomb five sites in retaliation for terrorist activities in Germany
2003: Renounces nuclear weapons
EGYPT 1967, 1973 / 1974 / 1952, 1954
1992: Violence between Muslims and Christians
de facto border
political border
MAURITANIA 1960, 1971–74, 1983, 2002 / 1978, 1979, 1984
MALI 1960, 1971–74, 1983, 2002 / 1968, 1991 / **2003:** Failed Coup
NIGER 1971–74 / 1974, 1996
1990–95: Tuareg Rebellion
1999: Gen. Mainassara assassinated
CHAD 1971–74, 1983 / from 1968 / 1975, 1979,1982, 1990
1985: Intensive fighting between Libyan-backed and French-backed forces
1999: Rebellion in the north
1973–90
from 1984: Guerrilla activities undertaken by National Democratic Alliance in northern Sudan
2004: Ethnic conflict in Darfur
ERITREA **1972:** Armed struggle for independence / 2002–04 / 1970–93
1984–85: Civil war leads to famine in Ethiopia
2000: Failed Coup
DJIBOUTI 1998–2000 / 1977
SUDAN 1971–74, 1983, 2004 / 1955–72, 1983–2004 / 1958, 1964, 1969,1984, 1989
SENEGAL 1971–74, 2002
1982: Rebellion in southern Casamance region
2000: Failed Coup
GAMBIA 1973 / 1994
CAPE VERDE
GUINEA-BISSAU 1998 / 1959–74 / 1980, 1999 / **2000:** Failed Coup
GUINEA 2000 / 1984
BURKINA 1971–75, 1977 / 1966, 1980, 1982, 1983, 1987
2000–03 / 1999 / **2000:** Gen. Guei ousted in popular revolution
SIERRA LEONE 1991–2001 / 1967, 1968, 1992, 1997
LIBERIA **2003:** President Taylor flees into exile / 2000–03 / 1980, 1990
IVORY COAST 1966, 1972, 1978, 1979,1981
GHANA 1971–74, 1977, 1983 / 1981 / 1963,1965,1967,1969,1972
TOGO 1967, 1963
BENIN 1971–74
1972: Marxist-Leninist state proclaimed
1990: Country steers towards pluralist democracy
NIGERIA 1967–70, 1971–74, 1967–69 / 1966, 1966, 1975, 1983, 1985 / 1967–69
1967–70: Secession of Biafra
1999: Nigeria returns to democracy
2000: Ethnic conflict escalates
2002: Religious conflicts
Biafra
CAMEROON
CENTRAL AFRICAN REPUBLIC 1974 / 1996–97, 2001–02 / 1965, 1979, 1981,2003
from 1989: Guerrilla activities undertaken by rebel Sudanese People's Liberation Army in southern Sudan
EQUATORIAL GUINEA 1979
CONGO 1960–61 / 1997–99,2002 / 1963, 1968, 1977, 1997
DEM. REP. CONGO 1960–65, 1977–78, 1992–93, 1996–97, 1998–2003 / 1960, 1965
1960–63: Katanga secession
1996–97: Government overthrown
Katanga
GABON
SAO TOME AND PRINCIPE 2003
UGANDA 1980 / 1966, 1971,1979, 1985,1986
1972: President Amin gives 8000 Asians 48 hours to leave the country
1979: Tanzanian forces expel President Amin
1987: Civil war with LRA
KENYA 1952–60 / **1982:** Failed Coup
1990's: Ethnic conflict
2002: Daniel arap Moi and KANU voted out after over 30 years in power
ETHIOPIA 1973–79, from 1980–2004 / from 1962 / 1974,1991 / 1964, 1977–78
SOMALIA 1969, 1991 / from 1982
1991: Somali National Movement declares secession of an independant Somaliland Republic; Somalian government rejects secession
Ogaden
RWANDA 1995–96 / 1962–65,1995–96 / 1973
1994: 300,000 Tutsi massacred; 2 million Hutus flee to nearby states
BURUNDI 1972,1995 / 1962–65, 1994 / 1966, 1966, 1976, 1987, 1996
1972: 150,000 Hutus massacred by rival Tutsi ethnic group
TANZANIA 1983
COMOROS 1997,1999 / 1977,1989
1995: President Djohar held prisoner by insurrectionists
2002: New Constitution
MAYOTTE to France
ANGOLA 1971–74,1983, 2002–04 / 1975–92, 1992–94, 1998–2002 / 1961–75
1974–92: Civil war between Soviet and Cuban-backed MPLA and US and South African -backed UNITA
MALAWI 2002–04
ZAMBIA 2002–04
ZIMBABWE 2002–04
2000: President Mugabe begins appropriation of white farms; widespread fod shortages
MOZAMBIQUE 1971–74, 1983, 2001, 2002–04 / 1964–75 / 1980–92
MADAGASCAR **2002:** Over disputed election, President Ratsiraka forced from office after 27 years / 1972
NAMIBIA 1966–90
1985–86: South African raids
BOTSWANA
SWAZILAND 1983
LESOTHO 1974, 1983, 2002–04 / 1970, 1986, 1991
SOUTH AFRICA 1983 / 1964–94
1948: System of racial segregation (Apartheid) begins
1985: State of emergency
1990: Nelson Mandela released after 26 years
1994: First multiracial elections

1000 km
1000 miles

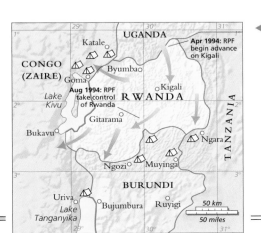

Rebel troops from Guinea-Bissau take cover behind a sand barrier amidst fierce fighting with government forces during an army mutiny in 1998.

The colonial legacy

In attempting to emulate European–style political systems, newly emerging African states experienced much upheaval. Fragile government institutions accounted for many of the civil wars that occurred in the years following independence. Changes of government were more often than not the result of military coups. The colonially-induced switch from subsistence crops to cash crops for export led to the dependence of many countries on unaffordable imports. Parts of Africa suffered severely from drought, particularly the lands of the Sahel region. The effects were exacerbated by a rapid increase in population which led to the widepread erosion of over crowded lands. Urban growth brought poverty and political tension, even though cities were often favored economically at the expense of rural areas.

Political Africa 1990–2005

1991: Somalia descends into civil war and chaos
1994: South Africa holds first multi-racial election
1997: Mobutu relinquishes power in Zaire. New president Laurent Kabila faces continuing civil war
2000: International AIDS conference in Durban. Number of people in Africa infected with HIV continues to rise
2001: President Kabila of Congo assassinated; replaced by his son
2004: Refugee crisis in Darfur, W Sudan, amid accusations of ethnic cleansing

1990 — 1995 — 2000 — 2005

1991: Start of civil war in Sierra Leone
1994: Massacre of Tutsis in Rwanda
1999: Ivory Coast begins period of civil unrest
2000–03: Civil war in Liberia
2003: Libya renounces nuclear weapons

The Rwandan crisis

Following a violent revolt in 1959 the Hutu ethnic group in Rwanda grasped political power from the Tutsi minority. In 1990, the Tutsi Rwandan Patriotic Front (RPF) mounted an invasion from Uganda. Genocidal violence broke out in 1994 and an estimated 500,000 Tutsi were massacred. Two million Hutus subsequently fled the country. An international criminal tribunal, set up to investigate the genocide, has indicted only a handful of those responsible.

Rwanda crisis map:
UGANDA
CONGO (ZAIRE)
Katale / Goma / Byumba / Kigali
Apr 1994: RPF begin advance on Kigali
Aug 1994: RPF take control of Rwanda
RWANDA
Bukavu / Gitarama / Ngara
TANZANIA
Ngozi / Muyinga
Uvira
Lake Kivu
Lake Tanganyika
Bujumbura / Ruyigi
BURUNDI
50 km
50 miles

5 Crisis in Central Africa
- advancing RPF (Tutsi) forces
- migrating Hutu refugees
- refugee camp

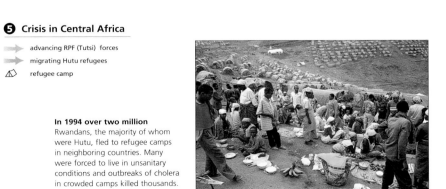

In 1994 over two million Rwandans, the majority of whom were Hutu, fled to refugee camps in neighboring countries. Many were forced to live in unsanitary conditions and outbreaks of cholera in crowded camps killed thousands.

Europe: 18,000 years ago

At the height of the last Ice Age, northern Europe was covered by immense sheets of ice which blanketed most of the continent as far south as Berlin and the British Isles. Forest cover was virtually wiped out by the harsh climate, to be replaced by hardy tundra grasses and scrub. Ice caps also developed on the mountains of the Pyrenees and on the tops of the Alps. As the ice caps began to melt about 8000 years ago, a huge lake – Lake Ancylus – filled the space where the Baltic Sea now lies.

ARCTIC OCEAN

North Pole

Laptev Sea

Severnaya Zemlya

Franz Josef Land

Kara Sea

Spitzbergen

EURASIAN PLATE

NORTH AMERICAN PLATE

Greenland

Greenland Sea

Barents Sea

Bjørnøya

Novaya Zemlya

West Siberian Plain

Jan Mayen

Denmark Strait

Kolbeinsey Ridge

Barents Trough

North Cape

Murmansk Rise

Ob'

Irtysh

Iceland Plateau

Arctic Circle

Faeroe-Iceland Ridge

Vøring Plateau

Kola Peninsula

Ural Mountains

Iceland

Norwegian Sea

White Sea

ASIA

Iceland Basin

Faeroe Islands

Karelia

Scandinavia

Hatton Ridge

Faeroe-Shetland Trough

Shetland Islands

Viking Bank

Gulf of Bothnia

An immense lake built up in front of the ice sheet 9000 years ago, as the climate warmed and the ice sheet began to melt.

The weight of the ice depressed the surface of the land by as much as 2,150m in some places. Today, without the ice, the land is rising back up to its original height at rates of a few fractions of an inch a year.

Volga Upland

The Caspian Sea flooded much of what is now the low-lying region around the Volga delta.

Rockall Rise

Feni Ridge

Orkney Islands

Norwegian Trench

Gulf of Finland

Iceland

North Sea

Jylland

LAKE ANCYLUS

Baltic Sea

North European Plain

Volga

Caspian Depression

Porcupine Plain

British Isles

Ireland

Irish Sea

Pennines

Britain

Europe's ice cap was about 6,600 ft thick and stretched from the pack ice of the frozen Arctic Ocean, south to the British Isles and the Netherlands. Today, Northern Europe is littered with moraines, which mark the farthest advance of the huge ice sheet.

Dnieper

Don

Central Russian Upland

Celtic Shelf

English Channel

EUROPE

Carpathian Mountains

Dniester

Caspian Sea

After the ice receded, the British Isles were for a time still connected to mainland Europe. Evidence of settlements now beneath the North Sea has recently been detected.

Rhine

Global climatic changes affected Europe radically, forming the immense ice sheet in the north, but also altering the vegetation. South of the ice sheet, a great swathe of the continent was covered with sparse tundra vegetation, and soils were permanently frozen – making it less suitable for habitation.

Great Hungarian Plain

Sea of Azov

Crimea

Caucasus

Loire

ATLANTIC OCEAN

Charcot Seamounts

Biscay Plain

Bay of Biscay

Massif Central

Alps

Drava

Transylvanian Alps

Danube

Balkan Mountains

Black Sea

The Black Sea was an isolated lake, not yet joined to the Mediterranean Sea via the Bosporus. It was permanently linked to the Mediterranean c.4500 years ago.

Galicia Bank

Garonne

Adriatic Sea

Dinaric Alps

Rhodope Mountains

EURASIAN PLATE

ANATOLIAN PLATE

Iberian Plain

Iberian Peninsula

Pyrenees

Sistema Central

Sistema Ibérico

Apennines

Adriatic Basin

Carpathian Mountains

Aegean Sea

Anatolia

LAKE KONYA

ARABIAN PLATE

Tagus Plain

Corsica

Tyrrhenian Sea

Balearic Islands

Balearic Plain

Sardinia

Tyrrhenian Basin

Taurus Mountains

AFRICAN PLATE

Horseshoe Seamounts

Sistemas Béticos

Desertlike steppe conditions prevailed throughout southern Europe.

Sicily

Ionian Sea

Crete

Cyprus

Cyprus Basin

Seine Plain

EURASIAN PLATE

AFRICAN PLATE

Malta

Ionian Basin

Lower sea levels meant far more of the Mediterranean coast was exposed 18,000 years ago. In Greece, this created land bridges between many of the islands

Mediterranean Sea

Mediterranean Ridge

Agadir Canyon

Atlas Mountains

Gulf of Sirte

Grand Erg Occidental

Grand Erg Oriental

Libyan Desert

Western Desert

Nile

Sinai

AFRICA

Sahara

Vegetation type

- ice cap and glacier
- polar or alpine desert
- tundra
- semidesert or sparsely vegetated
- forest or open woodland
- temperate desert
- tropical desert
- desert
- coastline (present-day)
- coastline (18,000 years ago)

EUROPE
REGIONAL HISTORY

THE HISTORICAL LANDSCAPE

EUROPE, THE SECOND SMALLEST OF THE WORLD'S CONTINENTS, has a great diversity of topography, climate, and ecology, a rich pattern which contributed greatly to its inordinate influence on global history. Extensive oceanic and inland shorelines, abundantly fertile soils, and broadly temperate conditions provided innumerable heartlands for a wide array of cultures. Internecine rivalries created shifting patterns, themselves frequently overlaid by successive waves of migration and incursion. The shores of the Mediterranean provided a cradle for many powerful cultural groups, which formed myriad states and several empires until the 15th century, when the power base shifted to the emergent nations of the Atlantic coast. It was these aggressive, mercantile and pioneering maritime powers who vaulted Europe to a globally dominant position, through trade and colonialism, during the closing centuries of the 2nd millennium. As they collapsed, a seemingly ineradicable linguistic, economic, technological, and cultural imprint remained, which in the 20th century was widely adopted and adapted, creating an almost universal global culture.

During the Ice Ages, the Alps were covered with extensive glacier systems, vestiges of which remain today. As the ice receded, the mountains provided a barrier between the cultures of the Mediterranean and those of Northern Europe.

The fertile plains of rivers such as the Danube provided the setting for early agricultural settlements, which spread north from the shores of the Aegean Sea from around 7000 BCE.

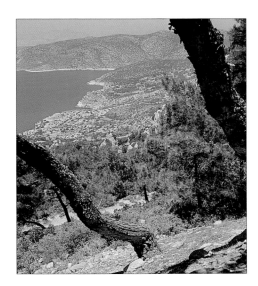

Europe's first cultures spread westward from Anatolia, reaching the fertile, often isolated coastal valleys around the Aegean between 7000 and 6000 BCE.

EUROPE

EXPLORATION AND MAPPING

EUROPEANS LEARNED TO KNOW their lands by practical experience and scientific study. Trade and the acquisition of new land provided an impetus for travel and exploration. Phoenician traders moving west in the 9th century BCE, and the Greeks from the 8th century BCE explored the Mediterranean. They were followed by the Romans, whose road system eventually covered much of southern and western Europe. Long-range travel was next developed by the wide-ranging Scandinavians of the 9th and 10th centuries. The emphasis was on sea and river, not road transport. The Greeks were the earliest people to begin to codify their knowledge of Europe, and the sailors of the Mediterranean produced the most sophisticated charts and maps of Europe until the flowering of Dutch cartography in the 16th century, which laid the foundations for modern mapmaking.

The theodolite was first used in the 17th century. This model, dating from 1765 could measure both altitude and azimuth.

The Vikings in the North Atlantic

The extraordinary Viking voyages of the 9th and 10th centuries were primarily for plunder – trade and the acquisition of new land came later. Sailing west from Norway into treacherous northern waters, the Vikings settled the Shetland islands and the Faeroes. Iceland was discovered in the mid-9th century, and despite the ice-logged winters, further travelers returned to colonize the island, founding settlements c.873, and establishing bases for voyages to Greenland and Labrador.

Viking ships were built with great care and attention to detail. The tiller *(left)* is carved in the shape of a snake, while the weather vane *(below)*, made from polished bronze, is topped with a figure of a dog.

Mapping in the Classical era

This map reconstructs the Europe known to Pytheas. His journey was the first scientific exploration of northern Europe by Greeks. The map is based on Eratosthenes' three-continent (Europe, Africa, and Asia) world view. The Mediterranean familiar to the Greeks is accurately plotted; the northern topography is far more speculative.

The peoples of the Mediterranean made the earliest attempts at a survey of Europe. In 340 BCE, the Greek Pytheas traveled from Massalia to Britain, visiting the Orkneys and Shetlands; he later visited Norway and north Germany. The first attempts at scientific mapping were made in the Mediterranean: Eratosthenes successfully measured the diameter of the earth; Hipparchus suggested lines of latitude and longitude as reference points, and Ptolemy tried to show the surface of the earth using two conical projections, and provided points of reference for more than 8000 places.

❶ Defining the boundaries of ancient Europe

→ supposed route of Himilco 6th century BCE
→ route of Pytheas 340 BCE
→ Roman routes in northern Europe and West Asia c.48 BCE–68 CE
→ Viking expansionist exploration 8–10th centuries CE
— major Roman roads by c.120 CE

320 BCE: Pytheas sails towards Arctic Circle while searching for new sources of tin

597 CE: Augustine travels from Rome to Britain on early Christian mission

9th century BCE: Phoenicians found colonies at Gades and Massalia

c. 858: Viking expedition reaches Balearics and southern France

Early 9th century: Swedes (also known as the Rus) travel south using Volga and Lovat'–Dnieper river system to make contact with Persia and the Byzantine Empire

838: First Swedes arrive in Constantinople

500 km
500 miles

❷ The Viking discovery of Iceland

→ Gardar Svavarsson c. 860
→ Naddod c. 870
→ Floki Vilgerdarsson
→ other Viking explorers

Floki lands in the far northwest, inspired by Naddod's earlier sighting. Sea ice forces him to winter there. He names the new land 'Iceland'

Gardar travels round the whole of Iceland

Naddod, blown off course, lands on the east coast but finding no human settlement, soon leaves

c. 900: First sighting of Greenland by Viking sailors

Early 9th century: Faeroes settled by Norse peoples

1,000 mile journey to Iceland from Faeroes through stormy seas

Late 9th century: Shetland Islands under direct rule from Norway

The Peutinger Table, a strip map 23 ft long and 1 ft wide, showed roads in the Roman Empire – such as the Via Appia – with little reference to the surrounding countryside. It was probably first drawn in the 3rd century CE and was a useful tool for actually planning journeys. Some 5000 places are recorded, mostly in Europe.

The Vikings in the North Atlantic

c.825: First settlement in the Faeroes
c.860: First trip round Iceland by Gardar Svavarsson
c.900: First sighting of Greenland by Viking seamen

750   800   850   900

795: First recorded Viking raid on isle of Iona
c.825: Irish monks probably first to discover Iceland
Late 860s: Brothers Ingolf and Hjerleif reconnoitre East Fjords
873: First permanent settlement started by Ingolf
Late 9th century: Shetlands come under direct Viking rule

Medieval mapping of Europe

Most of Europe was well known to travelers by the 11th century, but the accuracy with which it was mapped was extremely variable. The literate sailors of the Mediterranean were able to draw on the relatively sophisticated Portolan charts, which were made chiefly by Italian and Catalan navigators, but nothing comparable existed for the sailors of the north. Inland, largely imaginary wall maps represented Christian beliefs and the known world, with Jerusalem at the center of the earth, Europe at left, and Africa on the right. A second type of map was based on accumulated knowledge, and gave a recognizable, if distorted, picture of Europe. Examples include Gough's map, and the maps of Matthew Paris (1200–1259 CE). From the 15th century, Ptolemy's map of Europe *(see p.44)* was once again available and it was added to, and corrected in the light of new knowledge and re-published in the *Tabulae Modernae*. In 1425, Clavus, a Dane who had visited Iceland and Southern Greenland, added these, plus Norway, to the Ptolemaic base map.

The Hereford wall map *(left)* is perhaps the best known of the 600 or so "T-in-O maps" which are known to have survived. The T-shape of the Mediterranean Sea which divides the world into Europe, Africa and Asia is contained within a circle – the O.

Medieval mapping

1276: Hereford wall map designed by Richard of Haldingham and Lafford

1321: Pietro Vesconte's *Mappamundi* incorporates some features of portolan charts

1475: Publication of Ptolemy's *Geography*

1485: Bartolommeo dalli Sonetti's *Isolario*, based on observation by navigators, is published

1276: Publication of *Il Compasso da Navigare*, a collection of verbal descriptions of key routes

1472: First publication of the *Etymologiae* by Archbishop Isidore of Seville, devisor of the concept of the T-in-O map in 7th century

16th century: Latitude scales added to portolan charts

1539: First printed portolan chart made in Venice by Giovanni Andrea di Vavasore

| 1200 | 1300 | 1400 | 1500 | 1600 |

Portolan charts *(above)* were available to Mediterranean sailors from early Medieval times. They recorded the ports of the Mediterranean and Black Sea, giving landmarks, bearings, and distances, based on the Roman mile of 1000 paces.

The beginnings of modern cartography

In early modern Europe, increasing trade and a growing gentry class interested in their surroundings encouraged a new phase of mapmaking. Overseas territories and the possessions of the rich were mapped using surveying instruments such as the theodolite. Dutch cartographers made some of the most important innovations. Gerardus Mercator was the first to break from the Ptolemaic model. Mercator's projection rejected Ptolemy's conical model to show bearings with a scale identical in all directions. This made it particularly useful for navigators, and it is still widely used today. Another Dutchman, Willebrord Snell (Snellius), was the first to use triangulation to survey a large area. After carefully measuring a base line, he then employed trigonometry to calculate the distances to far off landmarks.

This map of Europe was produced by Mercator in 1554. It gives a detailed picture of settlement patterns, river networks, forest cover, and country boundaries, but some of the surrounding details - for example the proportions of Scandinavia - are far from accurate.

This detailed aerial view of Paris dates from 1576. It shows the original city wall, as well as building on the outskirts, agricultural areas – including windmills – and rough pasture on the edge of the city.

The Netherlands and the origins of modern cartography

1530: Jacob van Deventer commissioned to survey and map five provinces and regions of the Netherlands

1569: Mercator's new projection used for the first time in a world map

1606: Mercator's *Atlas sive cosmographicae meditations* is first use of term "atlas" applied to book of maps

| 1530 | 1540 | 1550 | 1560 | 1570 | 1580 | 1590 | 1600 | 1610 |

1533: Gemma Frisius publishes description of concise method of triangulation

1554: Mercator publishes large wall map of Europe; establishes new standard of latitudinal accuracy

1570: *Theatrum orbis terrarum* of Abraham Ortelius brings together elements of modern atlas for the first time

1606: Later edition of Ortelius' *Atlas* contains superbly detailed mapping of northern Europe

Saxton's county map of England and Wales, published in 1579, shows the detail and accuracy which was being achieved by the 16th century. Other similar examples include Norden's county maps of 1593, and Ogilvie's road map published in *Britannia*.

In England, fear of Napoleonic invasion and a need for detailed information about the land, led to a survey on a scale of two inches to the mile and publication on a scale of one inch to the mile. The first map of this series was sold as four sheets in 1801.

J.D. and C.F. Cassini continued Snellius' triangulation surveys in France. By 1744 all of France was covered by some 2000 triangles. The first sheets of a map of France on a scale of 1:86,400 were produced in 1756, but it was not until the Revolution that the last of the 182 sheets was published.

Surveyors from the Royal Engineers were responsible for making accurate maps of Britain and its Empire during the 19th century. Here they are shown undertaking a triangulation.

PREHISTORIC EUROPE

Mycenaean pottery, such as this goblet from Rhodes (c.1300 BCE), was traded throughout the eastern Mediterranean.

IN 7000 BCE, postglacial Europe, with its deciduous forests and increasingly temperate climate, was rich in natural resources and thinly populated by hunter-gatherers. By 1000 BCE, villages stretched from the Balkans to Scandinavia, and agriculture had reached even the marginal regions of the continent; there was a flourishing transcontinental traffic in salt, metals, and amber; and the first palace-based states had emerged on Crete and the Greek mainland. Although remains of settlements are rarely well preserved, a wide range of burials reveal, through grave goods as varied as woven textiles, ceramic vessels, and bronze axheads, an increasingly stratified society, in which individual possessions were a reflection of status.

The introduction of farming 7000–5000 BCE

The first potters of Central Europe used fired clay to make stylized human figures.

As agriculture spread from Anatolia into the Balkans and beyond, farming practices were adapted to more northerly latitudes, with an increased reliance on cattle and pigs and new, hardy strains of cereal. The mud-brick hill villages (tells) of the Middle East were replaced, in the thickly forested river valleys of Central Europe, by clusters of timber longhouses. The location of early farming communities can be charted by different pottery styles; incised Bandkeramik pottery is found from Hungary to the North Sea, while Cardial pottery, decorated with shell impressions, is found along the Mediterranean.

The spread of farming 7000–5000 BCE

c.7000: Farming spreads from Anatolia to southeastern Europe	**c.6000:** Farming starts to spread along the western coast of Mediterranean	**c.5000:** Agriculture well established in southern France and in the Netherlands

7000 BCE — 6500 — 6000 — 5500 — 5000 BCE

c.6500: Rising postglacial sea levels separate British Isles from the rest of the European continent — **c.6000:** First farming villages appear in southern Italy and Sicily — **c.5600:** Farming communities using Bandkeramik pottery in Central Europe

Timber longhouses, such as this example from Bylany in the Czech Republic, were built by the earliest farmers of Central Europe. The basic framework, made from plentiful timber supplies, was covered with wattle and daub. The buildings could be up to 150 ft long, and housed one or more families, as well as livestock and stores of food.

❶ The introduction of farming 7000–5000 BCE ▶

→ spread of farming
▧ cultivated land by c.7000 BCE
▨ cultivated land by c.6000 BCE
▩ cultivated land by c.5000 BCE
▨ concentrations of Mesolithic settlements c.5000 BCE
○ early farming settlement
⚱ Balkan painted ware site
⚱ Bandkeramik pottery site
⚱ Cardial and incised pottery site

Europe in the Copper Age 4500–2500 BCE

This was an era of technological innovation and contact between communities. Both horses and wheeled vehicles spread westward from the steppes, reaching western Europe by c.2500 BCE, while the introduction of the scratch plow increased productivity. Copper technology, which was developed in eastern Europe c.5000 BCE, spread throughout Europe over the next millennium. Finds of high prestige metalwork in some individual burials indicate that society was becoming more hierarchical, while distinctive pottery styles, known as Beaker Ware and Corded Ware, became widespread in central and western European burials, indicating the existence of a network of contact and exchange.

Marble figurines, made in the Cycladic Islands of Greece from c.2600 BCE, were placed in burials.

Western Europe: Distinctive Beaker pottery found in male graves with copper knives and flint arrowheads

Northern Europe: Distinctive Corded Ware pottery found in male graves alongside battleaxes denoting status

Balkans: Spectacular finds of copper and gold in cemetery burials indicate stratified society

Cucuteni-Tripolye: Farming villages of as many as 150 houses appear on the steppes of southern Ukraine

Central Italy: Copper-working based on exploitation of local resources

Southern Iberia: 3rd-millennium fortified settlements and elaborate tombs with rich grave goods indicate a stratified society

Greece: Settlement in islands; beginnings of palace-based societies, bronze industry, and wide-ranging trade

❷ Europe in the Copper Age 4500–2500 BCE

▢ early copper-working areas c.5000–4000 BCE
■ copper resources
→ spread of copper-working, with date
▨ area of Corded Ware burials c.2900–2000 BCE
▨ area of Beaker burials c.2500–2000 BCE
◆ important archaeological site

Europe in the Copper Age 4500–2500 BCE

c.4000: Farming villages of the Cucuteni-Tripolye group appear in southern Ukraine	**c.3500:** Stone circles and alignments, henges, and menhirs appear throughout northwestern Europe	**c.3000:** Copper-working begins in southern France	**c.2500:** Copper-working reaches British Isles. Bell beaker pottery found in individual burials in western Europe

4000 BCE — 3500 — 3000 — 2500 BCE

c.4000: Copper mines being exploited in Bulgaria and Yugoslavia — **c.3500:** First wheeled vehicles in Central Europe — **c.2900:** Appearance of Corded Ware pottery and stone battleaxes in burials in northern Europe

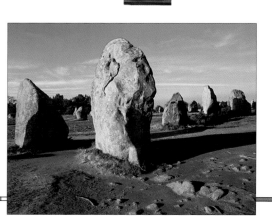

The stone alignments at Kermario in northwestern France date to c.3000 BCE. They were probably associated with processions and seasonal rituals.

Europe in the Bronze Age 2300–1500 BCE

The Bronze Age in Europe was a period of remarkable cultural and technological uniformity. Limited tin resources in western Europe, vital for bronze manufacture, were transported along long distance trade routes in exchange for other valued commodities – Baltic amber and salt. Access to these resources was a major factor in creating a distinct social elite, interred under large burial mounds, replete with a rich array of grave goods. By 1500 BCE, marginal land was being brought into cultivation to feed growing populations. These social and economic pressures led to increasing conflict, evident in the appearance of fortified settlements and the emergence of a warrior elite.

Many of the bronze artifacts made in Europe during the 2nd millennium BCE, such as this ritual bronze ax from Teteven in the Balkan Mountains, were status objects for the emerging warrior elite.

Scale varies with perspective

3880 km (2420 miles)
4570 km (2840 miles)

❸ **Europe in the Bronze Age 2300–1500 BCE** ▶

- ⬭ burial mounds
- ● lakeside village
- ▣ fortification
- ▣ palace
- ▣ farming settlement
- ▣ area of burial mounds in Central Europe
- ▣ area of burial mounds in Scandinavia
- ▣ area of Alpine lakeside villages
- ✿ salt mine
- ✿ sea-salt processing
- ▣ tin
- ▣ copper
- ▣ amber deposit
- ▽ mining complex
- → trade route

Scandinavia: Sophisticated bronze-using society, dependent on imports of copper and tin exchanged for Baltic amber

Baltic: Amber is widely sought after and traded throughout Europe

trade with steppe cultures

Bavaria: Marginal upland areas increasingly brought into cultivation as pressure of population on land increases

Southern Poland: Natural deposits of rock salt are mined and extensively traded

Northwestern Europe: Small hamlets and farmsteads

Eastern Europe: Fortified settlements increasingly common from c.2000 BCE onward

Western Europe: Tin is transported to bronzesmiths throughout Europe

Central Europe: Individuals buried under large mounds with rich grave goods of gold and bronze

Greece and Aegean islands: Palace-based societies with trading contacts extending to the Middle East and North Africa

Alpine lakes: Lakeside villages of wooden houses, with evidence of use of plow

trade with Levant

trade with Egypt

Places on map: Hallunda, Kvärnby, Egtved, Voldtofte, Perleberg, Salzkammergut, Spišský Štvrtok, Barca, Ockov, Tószeg, Blučina, Vattina, Gomolava, Donja Slatina, Ezero, Troy, Cyprus, Helmsdorf, Leubingen, Hallstatt, Wasserburg, Mitterberg, Custrasta, Ledro, Polada, Scoglio del Tonno, Mycenae, Pylos, Phaistos, Knossos, Borg in-Nadur, Barumini, Filitosa, Lumi, Narce, Kernonen, Cortes de Navarra, Cortaillod-Est, Etaules, Haguenau, Downpatrick, Great Orme, Black Patch, Bush Barrow, Flag Fen, Elp, Toterfout, Cerro de Real, El Argar

Shetland Islands, North Sea, Baltic Sea, Vistula, Elbe, Danube, Dniester, Don, Carpathian Mountains, Balkan Mountains, Black Sea, Caucasus, Anatolia, Mesopotamia, Euphrates, Adriatic Sea, Aegean Sea, Peloponnese, Crete, Mediterranean Sea, Nile Delta, EGYPT, Sahara, Atlas Mountains, AFRICA, Iberian Peninsula, Tagus, Douro, Rhône, Seine, Meuse, Rhine, Po, Corsica, Sardinia, Sicily, Malta, ATLANTIC OCEAN, British Isles, Britain, Ireland, Pyrenees

Bronze Age Europe 2300–1500 BCE

c.2300: Beginning of European Bronze Age – bronze objects begin to appear in tombs	**c.2000:** Fortified settlements begin to appear in eastern and central Europe, a sign of increased social and economic pressure	**c.1900:** Potter's wheel introduced to Crete	**c.1800:** Finds of wooden plows in Scandinavian bogs. Bronze artifacts suggest sun worship

2300 BCE — 2200 — 2100 — 2000 — 1900 — 1800 BCE

c.2200: Defensive enclosures built in southern Britain as communities compete for land and resources

c.2000: First palace built at Knossos on Crete. Palace-based societies develop throughout island

These bronze slashing swords made in Europe toward the end of the 2nd millennium BCE, along with the widespread appearance of fortified settlements, were indications that society was becoming more militaristic.

Minoan Crete and Mycenaean Greece

The palaces of Minoan Crete were flourishing economic, royal and ritual centers. When catastrophe, possibly a volcanic eruption, struck c.1450 BCE, the Mycenaean kingdoms of mainland Greece gained supremacy. The Mycenaeans were able sailors and long-distance traders. Their well-fortified palaces, and the evidence of painted pottery, armor, and weapons, all attest to their military technology. But internal disorder and, possibly, foreign invasion precipitated their downfall, c.1100 BCE.

The snake goddess was revered as a household guardian in Minoan Crete. This figure is from Knossos, c.1500 BCE.

❹ **Mycenaean Greece c.1550–1150 BCE** ▶

- ▣ Mycenaean major palace
- ◇ Minoan and Mycenaean sites
- → major routes within the Mycenaean heartland
- → import routes
- → export routes

to Balkans, THRACE, Black Sea, Sea of Marmara, MACEDONIA, Olympus, Lemnos, Dardanelles, Troy, THESSALY, Iolcus, to Southern Italy, Lesbos, Anatolia, Sporades, Orchomenus, Gla, Eubœa, Thebes, Aegean Sea, Chios, Athens, Dendra, Mycenae, Aegina, Argos, Tiryns, Cyclades, Naxos, Miletus, Ionian Islands, Ionian Sea, Paros, Pylos, Peloponnese, Menelaion, Vapheio, Melos, Phylakopi, Dodecanese, Thera, Akrotiri, Rhodes, Sea of Crete, pottery to Anatolia, pottery to Italy, Sicily, and Sardinia, copper from Sardinia, pottery to Levant and Egypt, Knossos, Phaistos, Zakros, Crete, gold and alabaster from Egypt, ivory, tin from Syria, copper from Cyprus, Mediterranean Sea, Gulf of Corinth

Mycenaean Greece

c.2000: Palace-based societies emerge on Crete	**c.1450–1250:** Mycenae at height of power and prosperity linked by trading networks from the Levant to Sicily	**c.1250:** Defenses strengthened at several Mycenaean palaces, suggesting troubled conditions	

2000 BCE — 1800 — 1600 — 1400 — 1200 — 1000 BCE

c.1550: Kingdom of Mycenae rises to prominence

c.1450: Destruction of Minoan palaces of Crete. Mycenaeans take control of island

c.1100: Mycenaean palaces and towns sacked or abandoned

200 km / 200 miles

THE MEDITERRANEAN WORLD

This Phoenician carved ivory plaque was found at the Assyrian city of Nimrud.

BETWEEN 700 AND 300 BCE, the Mediterranean world shaped western civilization. The impact of Classical Greek ideas on art, architecture, literature, philosophy, science, and, through the revolutionary innovation of democratic government, on political institutions was profound and wide ranging. The conquests of Philip of Macedon and his son Alexander the Great *(see pp.40–41)* took the fundamental features of Greek culture as far as the borders of India. Of other major civilizations, the Etruscans were undoubtedly influenced by the Greeks, both in the layout of their grid-plan cities and in their lifesize terracotta statues. The Phoenicians, an energetic, maritime people based in city-states in the Levant, took their culture, through trade and colonization, to the western shores of the Mediterranean.

The colonization of the Mediterranean

This magnificent Attic red-figure vase, which illustrates the Homeric myth of Odysseus and the Sirens, dates from c.490 BCE.

Both the Phoenicians and the Greeks founded colonies during the 1st millennium BCE. The limited fertile terrain of the Greek homelands could not support the growing population, and many Greek cities sent colonists to western Anatolia, the Black Sea shores, Sicily and southern Italy, and even southern France, where Massalia (Marseille) was founded. The city of Miletus alone was responsible for establishing over 80 colonies. The Phoenicians set out in search of metals, initially setting up a colony in Cyprus to mine copper, and eventually founding Gades (Cadiz) because of nearby silver deposits. Their greatest colony was Carthage, which became a major power in its own right.

▲ **1 The Mediterranean world 700–300 BCE**

Greek homeland	○ city of the Greek homeland	♠ timber
area of Greek colonization	○ city founded by Greeks	🌿 grain
Phoenician homeland	○ city founded by Phoenicians	iron
area of Phoenician colonization	○ Etruscan city	copper
area of Etruscan city-states	✕ Phoenician trade route	silver
under Etruscan control by 530 BCE	✕ Greek trade route	gold
	✕ Greek victory over Persians	
	✕ Macedonian victory over Greeks	

This Etruscan tomb painting from Tarquinia shows dancing and feasting.

The Etruscans

The Etruscan civilization flourished in the hilltop cities of Tuscany between 800 and 300 BCE, its wealth was based on agriculture and rich deposits of copper and iron. Most of our knowledge of their civilization comes from tomb paintings, which depict evocative scenes of feasting, hunting, dancing, and wrestling, while their grave goods are a testament to their skill in bronzeworking and sculpture. Ultimately, however, they succumbed to the growing power of Rome.

The Etruscans 1000 BCE–1 CE

c.616: Etruscan king Tarquin I rules Rome
509: Romans expel Etruscan king Tarquin II
396: Etruscan city of Veii taken by Rome
250: Whole Italian peninsula under control of Rome

| 1000 BCE | 800 | 600 | 400 | 200 | 1 CE |

c.800: Emergence of Etruscan city states
c.690: Etruscan script developed from Greek
c.530: Etruscan expansion into Po valley
c.100: Language and culture of Etruscans in terminal decline

The Greeks 1000–300 BCE

c.1000: Colonists begin to migrate from Greece to Asia Minor and eastern Aegean
733: Corinth founds the colony of Syracuse; start of Greek colonization of Mediterranean
c.700: Beginning of Archaic period; rise of city-states
480: Vast Persian army under Xerxes sent to Greece; defeated at Salamis, Plataea, and Mycale
431–404: Peloponnesian War between Sparta and Athens
338: Macedonia gains control of Greece at battle of Chaeronea

| 1000 BCE | 900 | 800 | 700 | 600 | 500 | 400 | 300 BCE |

776: First pan-Hellenic athletics festival held at Olympia
c.650: Rise of 'tyrants' in many Greek cities
490: Greeks defeat Persians at Marathon
448: Construction of Parthenon in Athens begins
356: Philip II becomes King of Macedonia; starts to extend territory

The Greek colonies in Sicily were large, populous cities. When Selinus was captured in 409 BCE during the Peloponnesian War, 30,000 prisoners taken. Its impressive ruins include six temples like this one, all dating from the 6th and 5th centuries BCE.

The Greeks

The cornerstone of Greek civilization was the *polis*, or city-state. These independent, self-governing communities, frequently isolated by Greece's rugged terrain, were based on walled cities, with outlying villages and farmland. Yet, despite the multiplicity of city-states, Greece was united by language, religion, and culture, reflected in harmonious architecture, sculpture, philosophy, and drama. Politically, the city-states swung between the extremes of oligarchy and democracy. While Athens was the birthplace of democracy, in Sparta a militaristic society was ruled by kings, supported by an underclass of serfs *(helots)*.

The Phoenicians

A Semitic people, whose home cities lay along a narrow strip of the eastern Mediterranean coast, the Phoenicians were the foremost traders and craftsmen of the Mediterranean, renowned for their skill in ivory carving, metalworking and glass manufacture. Perhaps their greatest legacy was their alphabetic writing system, which formed the basis of both the Greek and Roman scripts. The city of Carthage, founded as a colony, became a great power in its own right, leading a confederation of Phoenician cities which controlled southern Iberia, the western Mediterranean islands, and North Africa.

The limestone bust of 'the Lady of Elche', from southern Iberia, shows the artistic influence of the Phoenician city of Carthage, which had close links with cities throughout the western Mediterranean.

The Phoenicians and the Carthaginians 1000–200 BCE

c. 1600: The Phoenicians begin to use the Canaanite script, the first alphabetic script

c. 1000: Phoenicians become main maritime power in Levant region

814: Traditional date for foundation of Carthage

264–241: First Punic War; Rome gains control of Carthaginian Sicily

c. 900: Phoenician ships sail westwards in search of metals, and found colonies near rich metal deposits

218–201: Second Punic War; Carthaginians invade Italy, but Rome eventually wins war to become regional superpower

1600 BCE — 1400 — 1200 — 1000 — 800 — 600 — 400 — 200 BCE

The fiercely patriotic, militaristic culture of Sparta is embodied in this small bronze of a soldier.

The Athenian Empire

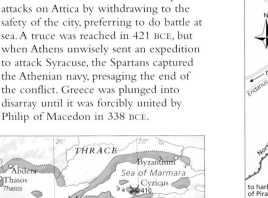

The city of Athens claimed a special affinity with its patroness Athene, goddess of wisdom, war, and arts and crafts.

The city-states of Greece were united in their bid to repulse the Persians, which culminated in famous victories at Marathon (490) and Salamis (480). In 478, Athens emerged as the leader of a loose maritime confederation of eastern Aegean states, based on the tiny island of Delos. Membership of the Delian League involved participating in a common military policy, and contributing to a common treasury. Athens came increasingly to dominate the League, transferring the treasury to the city in 454, and ruthlessly crushing any attempts at revolt. Greatly enriched by League funds, Athens now entered its greatest period of power and prosperity. The League had, in effect, become an Athenian empire, much resented in many Greek cities.

❷ The Athenian Empire 454–428 BCE

Areas paying tribute to Athens: (number of tribute-paying states in brackets)

- Islands (29)
- Thrace (62)
- Hellespont (45)
- Ionia (35)
- Caria (81)
- Athenian homeland
- non-tribute paying areas belonging to Delian League
- states with tribute assessment of over 5 silver talents per annum (454–428 BCE)
- states with tribute assessment of 1–5 silver talents per annum (454–428 BCE)
- overseas dependencies of Athens
- states in revolt against Athens

The Peloponnesian War

Athens' high-handed imperialism made war with Sparta inevitable, and a system of alliances embroiled much of Greece in the conflict. The Athenians withstood Sparta's attacks on Attica by withdrawing to the safety of the city, preferring to do battle at sea. A truce was reached in 421 BCE, but when Athens unwisely sent an expedition to attack Syracuse, the Spartans captured the Athenian navy, presaging the end of the conflict. Greece was plunged into disarray until it was forcibly united by Philip of Macedon in 338 BCE.

❸ The Peloponnesian War 431–404 BCE

- Athenian Empire
- Athenian ally
- Sparta and allied states
- neutral territory
- ✗ Athenian victory
- ✗ Spartan victory

❹ The city of Athens

- remains from 6th–5th century BCE
- remains from 4th century BCE–2nd century CE
- road
- aqueduct
- city wall

Athens

The mid-5th century was Athens' golden age. Governed by the eminent statesman, Pericles, and the home of such great intellectuals such as Plato, Sophocles, and Euripides, the city was dominated by the Parthenon temple, built of local marble by the sculptor Phidias, and approached by the monumental Propylea Gate. The Acropolis was the military and religious centre of the city, while commercial and municipal life dominated the agora, or town square.

THE RISE OF ROME

ROME BEGAN THE 5TH CENTURY BCE as the most powerful city of the regional alliance known as the Latin League. By conquering the Etruscan city-state of Veii in 396 BCE, the Romans doubled their territory, and after the breakup of the Latin League in 338, they incorporated the whole Latin region. This gave them the manpower to defeat a coalition of Samnites, Etruscans, and Gauls in 295. When they faced the army of the Greek general Pyrrhus, they were able to sustain two crushing defeats before achieving victory in 275 BCE. With Italy now under its control, Rome turned its attention to foreign rivals. Following victory over Carthage in 202, it took less than a century to add North Africa, most of Iberia, southern Gaul, Macedon, Greece, and Asia Minor to its empire.

The legionaries of Rome's citizen army were unmatched in discipline and skill.

Rome and the Italian confederacy

From the 5th to the 3rd century BCE, the city of Rome extended its area of domination to create a confederacy that united all Italy. Some cities were simply annexed and their inhabitants enjoyed the status of full Roman citizens, while others were granted a halfway form of citizenship that did not include the right to vote or hold office in Rome. Other peoples were considered "allies" and united to Rome by individual treaties. New towns known as "Latin colonies" extended the Roman presence throughout Italy, while "Roman colonies," where the inhabitants were full citizens, were established for defensive purposes, primarily along the Tyrrhenian coast. Beginning with the Via Appia in the 4th century BCE, the Romans built a road network that linked the whole peninsula.

Traditionally, this bronze bust of a stern Roman aristocrat has been identified as Lucius Junius Brutus, one of the founders of the Roman Republic in 509.

Rome and its Latin allies c.495 BCE

Rome was the most powerful of the Latin city-states when the Republic was established in 509, though it controlled just 320 sq miles of territory.

The peoples of Italy in 500 BCE

Latin, the language Rome would spread throughout western Europe, was just one of many closely related Italic languages spoken by the tribes of central Italy. The most powerful peoples in the peninsula were the Greek colonists and the Etruscans, a sophisticated city-state people whose language suggests eastern Mediterranean origins. It had been the Etruscans' arrival in Rome in the 7th century BCE that transformed a cluster of small villages into a city.

1 Italy in 240 BCE

Territory under Roman control 240 BCE

- full Roman citizens
- Roman citizens without right to vote
- ◇ Latin colonies
- Allies (Socii) of Rome
- ● Roman colony
- ○ other settlement
- 295 date of foundation
- — administrative boundary
- — Roman territory (Ager Romanus) 495 BCE
- — Rome and allies c.300 BCE
- — Roman road
- ···· modern coastline

2 The peoples of Italy in 500 BCE

- Greeks
- Etruscans
- Carthaginians
- Italic-speaking peoples
- ● city of the Etruscan League

This sarcophagus of a husband and wife shows the artistic skill and the playful spirit typical of Etruscan monuments to the dead.

The Greek colonies around the coast of southern Italy left impressive monuments such as Paestum's Temple of Neptune.

The emerging power of Rome 800–200 BCE

- **753:** Traditional date for founding of Rome by Romulus
- **c.700:** Start of Etruscan expansion to the south
- **616:** Traditional date for accession of Tarquin I, Etruscan king of Rome
- **509:** Roman Republic founded
- **496:** Rome defeats Latins at battle of Lake Regillus
- **396:** Romans capture Veii
- **390:** Gauls take Rome
- **340–338:** War against Latins ends in dissolution of Latin League
- **312:** Building of Via Appia
- **290:** Roman victory in Third (and final) Samnite War
- **280–275:** Romans twice defeated by invading army of Pyrrhus, but emerge victorious

800 BCE — 700 — 600 — 500 — 400 — 300 — 200 BCE

Rome and Carthage: the Punic Wars

Founded by Phoenicians *(Punici)* in 814 BCE, Carthage grew to be the preeminent naval power in the western Mediterranean. Rome came into conflict with the Carthaginians in 264, the start of a series of three wars. In the first, the Romans pushed their enemies out of Sicily. Then, in 218, Rome forced a second war by opposing Carthaginian actions in Iberia. Despite many defeats at the hands of Hannibal, the Romans won this war and stripped Carthage of its navy. The final war (149–146) ended in the destruction of Carthage and the enslavement of its people.

3 The First and Second Punic Wars 264–201 BCE

- Carthaginian Empire 264 BCE
- Carthaginian gains in Iberia to 218 BCE
- Carthaginian territory 200 BCE
- Roman territory 264 BCE
- Roman gains by 238 BCE
- Roman gains by 200 BCE
- Massalian territory 218 BCE

✕ Roman victory
✕ Carthaginian victory

Campaigns of the Second Punic War
→ Hannibal (219–202)
→ Hasdrubal (208–207)
→ Scipio Africanus (210–206 and 204–202)

The First and Second Punic Wars

280 BCE · 260 · 240 · 220 · 200 BCE

- **264:** Outbreak of First Punic War over control of Strait of Messina
- **262:** Romans capture Agrigentum
- **256:** Romans win huge naval battle off Ecnomus
- **255:** Failure of Roman invasion of North Africa
- **241:** Romans force peace and gain control of Sicily
- **238:** Romans occupy Corsica and Sardinia
- **226:** Iberus River (Ebro) is agreed as limit of Carthage's expansion in Iberian Peninsula
- **218:** Siege of Saguntum sparks Second Punic War
- **218:** Hannibal crosses Alps
- **206:** Scipio Africanus concludes successful campaign in Iberia
- **207:** Hasdrubal's attempt to reinforce Hannibal in Italy ends in defeat
- **202:** Decisive Roman victory at Zama

The Carthaginian general Hannibal *(left)* fought the Romans for 15 years in Italy. The smaller coin *(right)* shows an African elephant, used by the Carthaginians to strike terror into opposing armies.

The subjugation of Greece by Rome

In 200 BCE the major powers of the Greek world were Macedon and the Seleucid Empire. Two Greek federations had also emerged: the Aetolian League and the Achaean League, which included Corinth, largest of the mainland Greek cities. Other city-states, such as Athens and Sparta, maneuvered to maintain their independence, as did the Asian kingdom of Pergamum. Political tensions and appeals to Rome for help gave the Romans excuses for five major military interventions in the 2nd century. Macedon became a Roman province in 148; Greece succumbed in 146 after the Achaean War.

4 Greece in 200 BCE
- Macedon
- ally of Macedon
- Aetolian League
- ally of Aetolian League
- Achaean League
- Seleucid Empire
- Ptolemaic Empire
- independent Greek states and cities
- Roman Empire
- ally of Rome
- ✕ Roman victory

Corinth was first an ally of Rome, then an enemy. It was razed to the ground in 146 by the Roman general Mummius. The ruined temple *(left)* dates from the 6th century BCE.

This fine mosaic of a lion hunt decorated the royal palace in the Macedonian capital of Pella. Even before annexing Macedon and Greece, Rome eagerly embraced Hellenistic culture and customs.

Rome's overseas provinces in 120 BCE

Following the defeat of Carthage in 202 BCE, Rome's empire expanded rapidly. Greece and the Greek states of Asia Minor were won through a combination of diplomacy and war, but long, costly campaigns were needed to subdue the tribes of the Iberian Peninsula. Carthage itself was added to the empire in 146. As the Romans extended their rule beyond Italy, they largely abandoned the principles of incorporation that they had applied in Italy and instead set up provinces. These were ruled by governors, who served short one- or two-year terms, maintained order, and oversaw the collection of taxes. Corruption and plundering by governors were common enough for a special permanent court to be set up to try such cases in 149.

Roman expansion 200–120 BCE

200 BCE · 180 · 160 · 140 · 120 BCE

- **200–196:** Second Macedonian War
- **172–167:** Third Macedonian War
- **148:** Roman victory in Fourth Macedonian War
- **139:** Defeat of Lusitani
- **133:** Romans take Iberian city of Numantia
- **192–189:** War with Seleucid king Antiochus; Roman victories at Thermopylae and Magnesia
- **168:** Romans crush Macedonians at Pydna
- **146:** Roman armies destroy conquered cities of Corinth and Carthage
- **133:** Rome bequeathed province of Asia by king of Pergamum

5 Roman conquests to 120 BCE
- Roman Empire c.200 BCE
- Roman gains by c.120 BCE
- Massalia and possessions
- independent Greek states and cities
- Ptolemaic Empire and possessions
- Seleucid Empire
- ASIA 133 Roman province and date of foundation
- *Volcae* 121 people and date of conquest by Rome

THE ROMAN EMPIRE

Constantine sealed the Empire's fate by moving the center of power to the east.

REPUBLICAN ROME asserted military control over most of the Mediterranean, but a century of internal political conflict and civil war prevented the development of an orderly imperial system. The first emperor, Augustus (27 BCE–14 CE), ended this period of disorder with his defeat of Mark Antony in 31 BCE and established the Principate – the military and political system that defended and governed the empire until the reforms of Diocletian and Constantine at the end of the 3rd century. At the height of its power in the 2nd century, Rome ruled over some 50 million people scattered in over 5000 administrative units. For the most part, subjects of the Empire accepted Roman rule, and, at least in the west, many adopted Roman culture and the Latin language. After 212 CE all free inhabitants of the Empire had the status of Roman citizens.

The Empire under Hadrian

The Empire reached its greatest extent early in the 2nd century under Trajan, who conquered Dacia, Arabia, Armenia, Assyria, and Mesopotamia. However, when Hadrian succeeded in 117 CE, he abandoned the last three provinces and adopted a defensive frontier strategy that would be followed by most of his successors. A professional army – under Hadrian it numbered just 300,000 – defended the frontiers and suppressed rebellions in trouble spots such as Britain and Judaea, while the navy kept the Mediterranean free of pirates. Fleets were also based on the Rhine and the Danube on the northeastern frontier.

The Pont du Gard, part of the aqueduct that supplied Nemausus (Nîmes) in the south of France, is a fine example of the Romans' skill in civil engineering.

❶ The Roman Empire under Hadrian c.120 CE

- ····· boundary of Roman Empire c.120 CE
- DACIA province in reign of Hadrian
- 45 CE date of conquest or annexation by Rome
- ⦿ provincial capital
- legion headquarters
- major naval base
- fortified frontier (limes)
- major road
- region temporarily held by Rome, with dates

The wealth of Thugga (Dougga) in North Africa is evident in the ruins of its magnificent theater. The region grew rich by shipping grain to Rome.

The Roman Empire

51 BCE: Julius Caesar completes conquest of Gallia (Gaul)	30 BCE: Egypt annexed following Octavian's defeat of Mark Antony	9 CE: New province of Pannonia secures Danube frontier	43 CE: Roman invasion of Britain	66–73 CE: First Jewish revolt against Roman rule	106 CE: Trajan conquers Dacia	132–35 CE: Second Jewish Revolt; Jerusalem refounded as Roman city, Aelia Capitolina

50 BCE — 1 CE — 50 CE — 100 CE — 150 CE

27 BCE: Assuming the title Augustus, Octavian becomes first Roman emperor

9 CE: After defeat by Germans, Romans retreat to Rhine frontier

14 CE: Death of Augustus

44 CE: Client kingdom of Mauretania absorbed into empire

70 CE: Destruction of Jerusalem by Titus

115–17 CE: In war against Parthia, Trajan extends Roman rule to Persian Gulf

138 CE: Death of Hadrian

The city of Rome

As the empire grew, so did Rome, reaching a population of about one million in the 2nd century CE. The city was sustained by food shipped up the Tiber from Ostia and aqueducts that delivered 100 gallons of water per head per day. Many Romans did not work, but were eligible for the *annona*, a free handout of grain. Following the example of Augustus, every emperor aimed to leave his mark on the city by building magnificent forums, theaters, arenas, and temples.

The Colosseum, completed in 80 CE, vied with the Circus Maximus racetrack as Rome's most popular stadium. It regularly attracted a full house of 50,000 to its gladiatorial and wild animal combats.

Earthenware amphorae were used to transport and store wine, olive oil, and fish sauce.

❸ Supply routes to Rome

Supplying the city of Rome

Feeding the citizens of Rome required regular shipments of grain from Egypt and North Africa. These were landed at Ostia and Portus, a new port built by Trajan at the mouth of the Tiber, from where they were shipped on smaller galleys up river to the capital. Goods were carried by ship wherever possible, as this was much cheaper and faster than road transport. Rome imported food and raw materials from all over its empire. Marble for the pillars and statues that graced the city's temples and palaces often came from as far afield as Greece and Africa. Unusual imports included *garum*, a fermented fish sauce which the Romans used, much like ketchup, to add flavor to a wide variety of dishes, and murex, a shellfish that produced the purple dye used for imperial togas. To give an idea of the volume of goods imported to the city, Mons Testaceus, a large hill, 165 ft in height, was created in imperial times from the shards of broken amphorae from the rows of warehouses that lined the banks of the Tiber in the southwest of the city.

❷ Imperial Rome c.300 CE

The Tetrarchy of Diocletian and the final division of the Empire

In the 3rd century CE the Empire was threatened by invasions by the Persians and Germanic peoples and by breakaway states such as the Kingdom of Palmyra. To counter this, Diocletian (284–305) and Constantine (307–337) reorganized the imperial administration. The existing provinces were divided into 100 smaller units, grouped in twelve larger regions called dioceses, each governed by a vicar. To share responsibility for defending the empire and to provide for an orderly succession, Diocletian established the Tetrarchy: two emperors with the title Augustus, one in the east, one in the west, each assisted by a junior emperor with the title of Caesar.

The later Roman Empire 250–400 CE

❹ The Roman Empire 240–395 CE

The four tetrarchs ruled the Empire from 293 to 305. Similar forms of joint rule were tried during the 4th century until the Empire finally split in 395.

This gold coin shows the heads of Diocletian and Maximian, first co-rulers of the Roman Empire.

This floor mosaic of Orpheus decorated a villa in Daphne, a wealthy suburb of Antioch, capital of the province of Syria.

EUROPE AFTER THE FALL OF ROME

THE END OF THE WESTERN ROMAN EMPIRE in 476 did not signal an immediate descent into barbarism. The rulers of the new kingdoms maintained relations with the eastern emperor in Constantinople, and most pretended to govern on his behalf. In much of western Europe, Roman laws and institutions were retained and, sooner or later, the so-called "barbarians" all converted to Christianity. The Eastern Roman (Byzantine) Empire continued to exert influence in the west. In the 6th century, Justinian, the most powerful emperor of the period, won back some of the Western Roman Empire. But, after failing to halt the Lombard invasion of Italy in 568, the Byzantines were unable to reassert their authority. The eventual successors to the Romans in the west were the Franks and the papacy.

This glass drinking horn would have been used at feasts of the Lombard rulers of Italy.

The kingdoms of the new order

On the death of the emperor Theodosius in 395, the Roman Empire was divided definitively in two. The 5th century saw the transfer of power in western Europe from the emperors to Germanic immigrants, for the most part groups recruited by the Romans to help them defend their lands (see pp.52–53). Chief beneficiaries were the Goths. By 480 the Visigoths had established a large kingdom in Aquitaine and Iberia, with its capital at Toulouse. In 492 the Ostrogoths took Italy and the Dalmatian coast.

Christianity maintained a sense of continuity between the Western Roman Empire and the kingdoms that replaced it. This late Roman sarcophagus is from Ravenna, capital of the Ostrogoths, successors to the Romans in Italy.

Classis was the port of Ravenna, capital of Ostrogothic and Byzantine Italy. This detail from a 6th-century mosaic shows the castle and ships riding at anchor in the harbor.

Europe in 500

One of the most powerful of the new kingdoms established in western Europe in 500 was that of Theodoric the Great, leader of the Ostrogoths. Though he ruled from Ravenna, the Senate still sat in Rome and relations between Romans and Goths were largely amicable. Royal marriages helped forge alliances with the Vandal and Visigothic kings in North Africa and Iberia. Theodoric hoped to create a power bloc to counter the might of the Eastern Roman Empire, but after his death in 526 he was succeeded by his infant grandson, who died young, and the dynasty collapsed.

❶ The inheritors of the Roman Empire at 500

- Frankish expansion
- Ostrogothic expansion
- Byzantine reconquests
- Sassanian expansion

❷ The new kingdoms at 600

- Lombard Kingdom and duchies
- Kingdom of the Franks
- Frankish overlordship
- Visigothic conquests
- Lombard conquest of Liguria
- expansion of the Slavs (from 580s)

This Visigothic cross dates from the 6th century. Although Christian, the Visigoths were Arians (they denied the Trinity). This changed in 589, when King Reccared converted to the orthodox Catholicism of his Hispano-Roman subjects.

Europe in 600

The political map of Europe changed dramatically in the 6th century. In 600 the Visigoths still controlled the Iberian peninsula, but the Franks now ruled most of modern France. The Eastern Roman Empire had reconquered North Africa, Italy, Illyria, and even part of southern Iberia. The destruction of the Roman heritage was far greater during the long war waged by the Byzantines against the Goths than during the previous century. Italy then fell prey to the Lombards (Langobardi), Germanic invaders from the northeast.

Kingdoms of the new order 400–650

410: Sack of Rome by Visigoths
418: Visigoths settled in Aquitaine
476: Deposition of last western emperor in Rome; Odoacer becomes ruler of Italy
492: Conquest of Italy by Theodoric
508: Ostrogoths occupy Provence
526: Death of Theodoric; succeeded by grandson with daughter as regent
540: Byzantines take Ravenna
568: Lombards invade Italy
597: Mission of St. Augustine to England
624: Visigoths expel last Byzantine garrisons from southern Iberia

407: 'Great Invasion' of the Roman Empire by Alans, Vandals, and Sueves
439: Vandals capture Carthage
455: Vandals plunder Rome
493: Theodoric takes Ravenna
507: Franks expel Visigoths from Aquitaine
533: Eastern Roman Empire conquers Vandal kingdom
535: Byzantine general Belisarius invades southern Italy
555: Byzantines complete reconquest of Italy; also conquer south coast of Visigothic Iberia
585: Visigoths conquer Sueves
617: Slavs migrating south appear at walls of Constantinople

400 | 425 | 450 | 475 | 500 | 525 | 550 | 575 | 600 | 625 | 650

❸ Britain c.750 ▶

- Anglo-Saxon kingdoms
- Mercia and dependencies
- Celtic kingdoms
- Pictish kingdoms
- ⚔ battle
- † important monastery

This gem-studded gold buckle is typical of the jewelry worn by the Lombard nobles who ruled Italy for two centuries.

PICTISH KINGDOMS

Iona †
DALRIADA
Nechtansmere 685 ⚔

Melrose
Degsastan 603 ⚔
Hexham †
NORTHUMBRIA
BERNICIA
† Lindisfarne
† Bamburgh
† Jarrrow
† Monkwearmouth
† Whitby

REGED
DEIRA
York
Winwaed 655 ⚔
Humber
Irish Sea
North Sea

Chester 616 ⚔
LINDSEY
Lincoln
Nottingham
MERCIA
Lichfield
Tamworth
Elmham
POWYS
WELSH PRINCIPALITIES
Middle Angles
Oundle
EAST ANGLIA
Worcester
Offa's Dyke
Magonsaetas
Hwicce
Sutton Hoo
DYFED
Cirencester
Colchester
ESSEX
London
Thames
Glastonbury
Winchester
KENT
Canterbury
WESSEX
Dorchester
SUSSEX
WEST WALES (DUMNONIA)
Exeter

English Channel

100 km
100 miles

Excavation of a burial site at Sutton Hoo unearthed the treasure of a 7th-century Anglo-Saxon king or chieftain, including this striking gilt bronze helmet.

Early Anglo-Saxon kingdoms

597: St. Augustine begins conversion of Anglo-Saxon kings to Roman Christianity
655: Northumbrians defeat Mercians at Winwaed
663: Synod of Whitby. "Roman" Christianity adopted instead of "Celtic"
716: Ethelbald fights way to crown of Mercia; kingdom dominates all England south of Humber

600	650	700	750	800

603: Northumbrians defeat Scots at Degsastan
616: Northumbrians defeat Britons at Chester
679: Mercians conquer Lindsey from Northumbrians
685: Last great king of Northumbria killed by Picts at Nechtansmere
757: Accession of Offa, most powerful of Mercian Kings; treated as equal by Charlemagne

Anglo-Saxon Britain 600–800

For the two centuries that followed the Roman withdrawal in 410, there are no reliable accounts of events in Britain. The Celtic Britons fought each other, as well as Scottish invaders (from Ireland) and Angles, Saxons, and Jutes, who invaded across the North Sea from Denmark and north Germany. Around 600, following St Augustine's mission from Rome to convert the Anglo-Saxons, records appear of a number of kingdoms ruled by Anglo-Saxon kings (though some of these have British names). The west, notably Wales and West Wales (Dumnonia), remained in the hands of Celts. For most of the 7th century, the most powerful kingdom was Northumbria, whose kings briefly controlled much of Scotland. By 700, however, supremacy had passed to the midland kingdom of Mercia.

Byzantine and Lombard Italy

After the expulsion of the Goths, control of Italy was contested by the Byzantines and the Lombards, the latter gradually winning more and more territory after their invasion of 568. Only rarely did the Lombard kings, based at Pavia, exercise authority over the southern dukedoms of Benevento and Spoleto. Similarly, representatives of Byzantium, including the pope, often acted independently according to their own interests. The Byzantines were ousted from Ravenna in 751, but Lombard rule there lasted only until 756. At the pope's request, Pepin, king of the Franks, invaded northern Italy and crushed the Lombards.

KINGDOM OF THE FRANKS
Alps
Following Lombard invasion of Italy in 568, their former territories are occupied by Avars and Slavs
DUCHY OF FRIULI
Forum Julii (Cividale)
NEUSTRIA
AUSTRIA
Monza
Milan
Turin
Pavia
KINGDOM OF THE LOMBARDS
Verona
Padua
Cremona
Parma
Genoa
Bologna
EMILIA
Ravenna
Rimini
EXARCHATE OF RAVENNA
Siena
PENTAPOLIS
TUSCIA
Perugia
Spoleto
DUCHY OF SPOLETO
c.700: conquered by Lombards
Corsica
Rome
DUCHY OF ROME
DUCHY OF BENEVENTO
Monte Cassino
Benevento
Sardinia
Naples
Salerno
APULIA
Brindisi
Amalfi
Adriatic Sea
Tyrrhenian Sea
Sicily
Syracuse
Mediterranean Sea
100 km
100 miles

❹ The struggle for Italy 565–750

- East Roman Empire 565
- Lombard territories 565
- under Lombard rule 590
- Lombard gains by 650
- Lombard gains by 744
- East Roman territory 744

External threats to Italy in the 7th century
→ Franks
→ Avars and Slavs

The struggle for Italy 550–750

568: Lombard invasion of Italy
590–604: Papacy of Gregory the Great, who negotiates with Lombards to save Rome
653: Conversion of Lombards to Christianity
712: Liutprand becomes Lombard king; tries to unite Italy
751: Lombards under Aistulf take Ravenna; end of Byzantine rule
753–56: Italy invaded by Pepin

550	600	650	700	750

554: Frankish invasion defeated; Italy under Byzantine control
643: Edict of Rothari: first book of Lombard law
663: Byzantine Emperor Constans II invades Italy and sacks Rome
773–74: Conquest of Lombards by Charlemagne; northern Italy comes under Frankish rule

The early Frankish kingdoms 481–650

The only Germanic kingdom of any permanence established in this period was the Kingdom of the Franks, foundation of modern France. The first Frankish dynasty, the Merovingians, expanded from lands around Tournai under Clovis, who pushed southwest to the Loire, then defeated the Visigoths in Aquitaine. Clovis's sons destroyed the Burgundians and exercised control over several Germanic tribes to the east. When a powerful king such as Clovis died, his territories were divided between his heirs, provoking dynastic civil wars. The three major kingdoms were Neustria and Austrasia (together referred to as Francia), and Burgundy.

Dagobert I's throne is a powerful emblem of the continuity of the French kingdom, which lasted till the Revolution in 1790.

The early Frankish kingdoms 481–650

c.481: Accession of Clovis I
c.497: Clovis converts to Christianity
558: Chlothar I sole king of the Franks
573: Beginning of major civil wars between the Franks
629: Chlothar II dies; succeeded by son, Dagobert I,
639: Death of Dagobert; kingdom divided between two sons

450	500	550	600	650

507: Clovis defeats Visigoths at Vouillé
511: Death of Clovis; his kingdom divided between four sons
561: Death of Chlothar I; kingdom divided between his four sons
613: Chlothar II king of all Gaul; civil wars end

200 km
200 miles

Frisians
Saxons
Thuringians
Ripuarian Franks
Cologne
Tournai
Salian Franks
c.486 ⚔ Soissons
Meuse
Rhine
Bretons
Rheims
Metz
Alemanni
Paris
Strasbourg
Orléans
Loire
KINGDOM OF BURGUNDY
Tours
Chalon
Vouillé 507 ⚔
Bourges
Lyon
Poitiers
AQUITAINE
Clermont
Vézeronce 526 ⚔
KINGDOM OF THE OSTROGOTHS
Bordeaux
Garonne
Avignon
Rhône
Arles
Basques
Toulouse
Marseille
SEPTIMANIA
KINGDOM OF THE VISIGOTHS

❺ The Kingdom of the Franks 486–537 ◀

- Frankish lands 486
- conquered by Clovis by 507
- conquered by 511
- Kingdom of Franks at the death of Clovis 511
- conquered by Clovis's sons 534
- conquered by Clovis's sons 537
- ⚔ battle

Frisians
Saxons
Cologne
Tournai
AUSTRASIA
Thuringians
Rhine
Meuse
Soissons
Metz
Bretons
Rheims
Strasbourg
Paris
Alemanni
Seine
NEUSTRIA
Orléans
Bourges
Chalon
Bavarians
Poitiers
Loire
BURGUNDY
RAETIA
Clermont
Lyon
Bordeaux
AUVERGNE
Garonne
EASTERN ROMAN EMPIRE
AQUITAINE
Rhône
Basques
Toulouse
Arles
PROVENCE
SEPTIMANIA
Marseille
KINGDOM OF THE VISIGOTHS
200 km
200 miles

❻ Division of the Frankish kingdoms 561 ▶

- Charibert
- Sigebert
- Guntram
- Chilperic
- territory of Frankish overlordship
- ○ royal residence

THE HOLY ROMAN EMPIRE

This bronze statue of Charlemagne is an idealized 9th-century portrait, created after the Emperor's death.

THE FRANKISH KINGS Pepin and Charlemagne crushed the Lombards in Italy, granted lands to the pope, and extended the frontiers of Christian Europe. The coronation of Charlemagne as Holy Roman Emperor in 800 was an ambitious attempt by the papacy to recreate the central authority of imperial Rome. Yet by 843, the empire was divided. In the 10th century, a smaller Holy Roman Empire was established under the Saxon Ottonian dynasty. Otto I, who, like Charlemagne, was crowned in Rome, helped convert the Bohemians, Danes, and Poles to Christianity and stopped the advancing Magyars. Meanwhile, Viking raiders terrorized much of western Europe and in Russia, Swedish Vikings helped establish the new state of Kievan Rus.

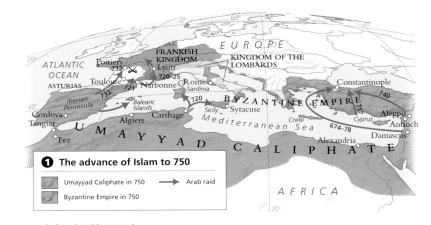

❶ The advance of Islam to 750

- Umayyad Caliphate in 750
- Byzantine Empire in 750
- → Arab raid

Scale varies with perspective

4670 km (2900 miles)

4100 km (2550 miles)

The empire of Charlemagne

Charlemagne was both a warrior and a reformer. By 800, he had established Christian hegemony over much of western Europe, his conquest and conversion of Saxony and defeat of the Avars taking the eastern borders of his empire to the Slav world. "Marches," or buffer zones, protected the empire from the Slavs and from the Moorish Emirate of Cordova. The unity of western Christendom did not last: after the death of Louis the Pious in 840, the empire was divided between his three sons, and by 900 it had fragmented into smaller kingdoms. Local dukedoms and counties, the precursors of feudal domains, started to gain power at the expense of central authority.

Charlemagne's throne still stands in a vaulted chapel at Aachen (Aix-la-Chapelle), the most important of the emperor's many royal residences.

Pope Leo III crowned Charlemagne emperor in 800. This confirmed the Carolingians' right to their lands. When Charlemagne was born c.744, his father Pepin was not even king of the Franks, but mayor of the palace. He was elected king in 751.

The advance of Islam

In the 7th century, Arab armies carried Islam across the Middle East and North Africa, then, in 711, to the Iberian Peninsula. The Byzantine Empire suffered severe losses and Constantinople had to withstand determined sieges in 674 and 717. In the west, an Islamic invasion of France was turned back in 732 at Poitiers by Charles Martel, the grandfather of Charlemagne. This stemmed the Muslim advance, but Arab raids on all the Christian states of the Mediterranean continued.

❷ The empire of Charlemagne

- Frankish kingdom in 751
- conquest of Pepin
- conquest of Charlemagne
- regions recognizing Charlemagne as overlord, at least nominally
- states of the Church, part of Charlemagne's empire
- marches
- Byzantine possessions

Major campaigns

- → in reign of Pepin 751–68
- → in reign of Charlemagne 768–814
- ◼ royal palace

SAXONY 804 division of Charlemagne's empire, with date of final conquest

The empire of Charlemagne

772: Charlemagne embarks on conquest of Saxony (complete 802)

800: Imperial coronation of Charlemagne by Pope Leo III in Rome

840: Death of Louis the Pious; war between his sons

751: Pepin the Short crowned king, the founder of Carolingian dynasty

771: Charlemagne becomes sole king of Franks

774: Charlemagne conquers Lombardy

814: Accession of Charlemagne's son, Louis the Pious

843: Treaty of Verdun divides Empire into three. Eastern and western parts roughly correspond to Germany and France

200 km

200 miles

Europe 800–1000

The fragmentation of the Carolingian Empire led, by 900, to its division into eastern and western parts. In 919, the East Frankish crown passed to Henry I of Saxony, who established the Ottonian dynasty, which was to dominate Europe for the next two centuries. The decisive Ottonian defeat of the Magyars earned the respect of rival noblemen, and Otto I's conquest of Italy, and coronation as Holy Roman Emperor (962), legitimized his rule. Otto's successors reinforced their power in Germany by constant movement around their empire. They controlled bishoprics and churches, encouraged learning and literature, and presided over the formation of Christian states in Poland, Hungary, and Bohemia.

Carvings of Viking ships appear on a picture stone in Gotland, dating from the 8th century, just before the raids began. This scene shows the spirits of dead heroes.

The Vikings of Scandinavia

The Vikings earned a fearsome reputation when they began their raids on Europe in the late 8th century. Their leaders were probably warlords who had been displaced by more powerful kings. They targeted the wealth of towns, monasteries, and churches in England, Ireland, and France. By the late 9th century, they ruled kingdoms in England and Ireland, and the Duchy of Normandy in France. Once settled, they adopted Christianity and established commercial towns. The Swedish Vikings raided and traded along the rivers of Russia, making contact with the Byzantine Empire and the Islamic world, a rich source of silver. They founded a merchant town at Novgorod and won control of Kiev, which became capital of the extensive state of Kievan Rus.

Otto II, who reigned from 973 to 983, receives homage from the subject nations of his empire. Portraits of Holy Roman Emperors emulated those of the Byzantine emperors, who were portrayed as God's representatives on earth.

3 Europe c.800–1000

- ····· frontiers c.1000
- Muslim lands
- Hungary
- Denmark
- Sweden
- Norway (under Danish rule)
- Byzantine Empire (under direct Byzantine rule)
- Byzantine dependencies (effectively independent)
- Holy Roman Empire

Viking settlement
- Danish
- Swedish
- Norwegian
- Danelaw 878–954

Expeditions and raids
- Danish
- Swedish
- Norwegian
- Magyar migration
- Magyar raid
- Muslim raid

Eastern Europe

The Magyars and the Bulgars were migrants from western Asia. They established powerful kingdoms in mainly Slav lands, and harried and threatened Christian Europe, Magyar raids penetrating as far west as France. Throughout the 9th and 10th centuries, Christian rulers embarked on the conquest and assimilation of these pagan peoples: the Magyars, the Danes, the Poles, and the Czechs (Bohemians) were all part of the Catholic church by 1000, while the Byzantine Empire had crushed the Bulgars by 1018.

Stephen I of Hungary favored the Roman church over the Orthodox and in 1001 was recognized as king by the pope, who sent him a crown (above).

Europe 800–1000

- **790s:** Beginnings of Viking raids on western Europe
- **816:** Byzantines make peace with Bulgars after prolonged military campaigns
- **841:** Vikings establish settlement at Dublin
- **844:** Vikings raid as far as Toulouse
- **863:** Saints Cyril and Methodius sent as missionaries to Moravia
- **874:** Viking "Great Army" creates kingdom of York
- **896:** Magyars start to settle in Danube basin
- **911:** Vikings found Duchy of Normandy
- **919:** Henry of Saxony elected king of eastern kingdom of the Franks (Germany)
- **933:** Henry defeats Magyars at Riade
- **936:** Henry is succeeded by his son, Otto I; Bohemians rebel (made tributary 950)
- **955:** Otto defeats Magyars decisively at Lechfeld
- **962:** Otto I crowned Emperor by John XII; spends later years in Italy
- **980:** Effective end of Viking dynasty at Dublin
- **980–83:** Otto II campaigns against Arabs in Italy
- **990:** Ottonian campaign against Bohemians
- **1000:** Poland joins Catholic church
- **1001:** Coronation of Stephen I of Hungary
- **1018:** Defeated Bulgars submit to Byzantine Empire

EUROPE IN THE AGE OF THE CRUSADES

Emperor Frederick
Barbarossa is shown in Crusader dress. He drowned in 1190 on his way to the Third Crusade.

FOLLOWING THE SUCCESS of the First Crusade *(see pp.64–65)*, the spirit of the venture captured the imagination of Christian Europe. Expeditions to subdue the pagans of the Baltic and campaigns against the Muslims in Iberia were undertaken with papal blessing. Ideals of chivalry inspired the new religious orders of warrior clerics established to protect pilgrims to the Holy Land, such as the Templars and Hospitallers. These organizations became immensely wealthy with hundreds of priories and estates in Europe. At the same time, it was a period of great intellectual excitement. The rediscovery of Classical texts inspired an interest in philosophy; universities were founded and new religious orders gave renewed energy to the Catholic Church.

The crusading ideal in Europe

The Knights Templar were so well rewarded for their services in the Holy Land that they became a powerful political force throughout Europe.

The ideal of Holy War which inspired the Crusaders to fight in the Iberian Peninsula and the Holy Land was used to justify other wars, conflicts, and even racist atrocities. In 1096, German mobs attacked and massacred as "unbelievers" the Jews in their own communities. Missionary efforts to convert the pagan peoples of Livonia, Lithuania, and Prussia became a crusade, preached by Pope Innocent III. One crusade was mounted against "heretics" within Christian Europe – the Cathars (Albigensians) of southern France. In 1212 a French shepherd boy even set out to lead a children's crusade to Jerusalem. Most of his followers got no further than Genoa and Marseille.

The crusading ideal

1118: Founder of Knights Templar granted site close to Solomon's temple in Jerusalem
1126: Hospitallers of St. John adopt a military role
1208: Crusade against Cathars, or Albigensians, in southern France
1283: Conquest of Prussia completed by Teutonic Knights
1312: Templar Order accused of heresy and suppressed by Pope

1050 — 1100 — 1150 — 1200 — 1250 — 1300 — 1350

1096: Attacks on Jewish communities by Crusaders and their supporters
1197: Order of Teutonic Knights established in the Holy Land
1233: Inquisition established in Toulouse
1306–10: Hospitallers conquer Rhodes, which becomes their base

❶ The crusading ideal in Europe 1100–1300

- predominantly pagan lands c.1100
- Muslim lands c.1180
- main Cathar region
- Waldensian strongholds
- direction of Reconquest in Spain

Crusades in the Baltic
- Danish expeditions
- Swedish expeditions
- direction of advance of Sword Brothers
- direction of advance of Teutonic Knights

Other crusades
- Albigensian Crusade 1209–13
- Children's Crusade 1212
- massacre of Jews 1096
- major Templar house 1300
- headquarters of crusading orders in Spain
- frontiers 1180
- Holy Roman Empire
- first state of Teutonic Knights 1211–15

The Norman conquest of England

The Duchy of Normandy was established in northern France by 911. In 1066, William, Duke of Normandy led an expedition to win the English throne from Harold, the last Anglo-Saxon king. Harold had seen off the threat of another claimant, Harald Hardrada of Norway, but, after a long march south, he was defeated by William at Hastings. Once England had been conquered, it was parceled out in fiefs amongst William's Norman knights.

❷ The Norman conquest of England 1066–1095

- Harald Hardrada's route 1066
- Harold's route 1066
- William's route 1066
- William's possessions 1066
- conquered by 1070
- additional conquest by 1095
- area of uprising against Norman rule c.1070
- × battle

The Norman conquest of England 1066

5 Jan: Death of Edward the Confessor, king of England; Harold assumes throne
Apr: Harold's fleet drives off Tostig; guards English Channel until September
25 Sep: Harold defeats his brother Tostig and Harald Hardrada at Stamford Bridge
14 Oct: Battle of Hastings; Harold defeated and killed
25 Dec: William crowned in London

Jan 1066 — Apr 1066 — Jul 1066 — Oct 1066 — Jan 1067

Apr: Raids along south coast of England by Harold's exiled brother Tostig
Aug–Sep: William assembles fleet and army at Dives-sur-Mer
28 Sep: William lands at Pevensey

William's success depended on a large fleet to ship men and horses across the English Channel, but the Normans had long abandoned the seagoing life of their Viking forebears. Yet they managed to build a fleet, depicted here in a scene from the Bayeux Tapestry, large enough to transport an army of perhaps 7000 men to England.

3650 km (2270 miles)
3890 km (2420 miles)

❸ The 12th-century renaissance in Europe ▶

- 🔲 university with date of foundation
- 🔲 other important theological school
- ▨ Muslim lands reconquered by Christians 1030–1200
- ▨ Muslim lands reconquered by Christians 1200–1300
- ⦿ center of contact with Arab scholarship
- ✝ major Cistercian house with date of foundation
- ------ frontiers 1200
- Holy Roman Empire

NORWAY; SWEDEN; ✝Alvastra 1143; North Sea; Baltic Sea; DENMARK; SCOTLAND; IRELAND; ✝Newbattle 1140; ✝Melrose 1142; Mellifont 1142; ✝Rievaulx 1150; ✝Fountains 1132; ✝Rievaulx 1132; ✝Kirkstall 1147; WALES; ENGLAND; Oxford early 12th century; Cambridge c.1209; ✝Waverley 1128; London; Canterbury; ✝Camp 1132; Cologne; KINGDOM OF GERMANY; POLAND; ✝Wagrowiec 1143; RUSSIAN PRINCIPALITIES; Bec; Paris; Rheims; Prague 1348; ✝Jedrzejów 1149; Chartres; Worms; Angers; Orléans c.1236; Clairvaux 1115; Ebrach 1127; Tours; Meung; Morimond 1115; Lützel 1124; Eberbach 1135; Pontigny 1114; La Ferté 1113; Citeaux 1098; Heiligenkreuz 1137; FRANCE; ✝Czikador 1142; HUNGARY; Grenoble 1339; Milan; Vicenza 1204; Padua (law) 1222; Cahors 1332; Toulouse 1229; Avignon 1303; Piacenza 1248; Venice; Pamplona; Narbonne; Montpellier (medicine) 12th century; Genoa; Bologna (law) 1088; Arezzo 1215; VENETIAN REPUBLIC; Marseille; Pisa; LEÓN; León; NAVARRE; ✝Moreruela 1132; Salamanca 1218; Lérida 1300; Siena 1246; Perugia 1308; Assisi; SERBIA; BULGARIA; Coimbra Alcobaça 1148; Lisbon 1290; PORTUGAL; Segovia; CASTILE; Toledo; Tarazona; ARAGON; Barcelona; Corsica; Rome c.1140 1245; PAPAL STATES; Danube; Seville 1254; Cordova; Balearic Islands; Sardinia; Naples 1224; Salerno (medicine) since 9th century; BYZANTINE EMPIRE; ALMOHAD EMPIRE; Mediterranean Sea; Palermo; Sicily; KINGDOM OF SICILY; ATLANTIC OCEAN

c.1200: University of Paris has colleges for students from all over western Europe

1308: University of Lisbon transferred to Coimbra

500 km / 500 miles

The 12th-century renaissance

Christian idealism in this period was reflected in the growth of new monastic and teaching orders. The Cistercians, founded at Cîteaux in 1098, spread throughout Europe under the charismatic leadership of St. Bernard of Clairvaux. The early 13th century saw the even more rapid expansion of the orders founded by St. Francis of Assisi and St. Dominic. At the same time a renewed interest in scholarship led to the founding of new universities. The increased availability of the seminal texts of the ancient world, obtained through the medium of Arabic translations, was critically important for medieval scholars. By reconciling the science of Aristotle with Christian faith, St. Thomas Aquinas (d. 1274) gave Catholic theology an intellectual basis that lasted for centuries.

The Cistercians were founded in reaction to the idle life of monasteries financed by tithes. They worked their own land and were self-supporting, though they accepted gifts of marginal or recently conquered land. Their graceful architecture was plain and unadorned, as seen here in the refectory of Fountains Abbey in northern England.

The 12th-century renaissance

1126: Birth of Muslim philosopher Averroes in Cordova	1158: Frederick Barbarossa grants imperial protection to University of Bologna		1249: Foundation of Merton College, Oxford
1100	1150	1200	1250	1300
1098: Foundation of new monastery at Cîteaux	1115: Bernard founds Cistercian daughter house at Clairvaux	1210: St. Francis of Assisi gains papal recognition of his order of friars dedicated to poverty	1220: First chapter of the Dominican order of friars

The Angevin Empire

The laws of inheritance of feudal Europe enabled Henry II, Count of Anjou and King of England, to acquire lands that included England, Ireland, and most of western France. His marriage to Eleanor of Aquitaine meant that he ruled more of France than the French king, even though he was nominally the latter's vassal. He spent much of his reign defending his empire against Louis VII of France and the ambitions of his children. After his death in 1189, the Angevin empire soon disintegrated. In 1214, Philip II of France defeated Henry's son, John, ending English rule in Normandy. England, however, did keep western Aquitaine, and, in the 14th century, would renew its claims to France in the Hundred Years' War.

English possessions 1154–89

1152: Henry marries Eleanor of Aquitaine	1154: Succession of Henry II to English crown	1173–74: Henry quells French-backed rebellion by his sons	1199: Accession of John	
1140	1160	1180	1200	1220
1151: Henry succeeds Geoffrey as Count of Anjou		1189: Succession of Richard the Lionheart	1214: Defeat of English and German allies at Bouvines

Henry II and Eleanor of Aquitaine had an intense, stormy relationship. She was imprisoned for intriguing against him on behalf of their eldest son Henry in 1173–74.

Map labels: KINGDOM OF MAN to Norway; SCOTLAND notional fief of English crown; Scone; Stirling; Edinburgh; Berwick; IRELAND granted to Henry II by papal bull 1155; Carrickfergus; Dublin; Cork; Waterford; Wexford; York; WELSH STATES notional fiefs of English crown; Warwick; Bristol; Oxford; London; Winchester; Canterbury; ENGLAND; North Sea; Irish Sea; English Channel; Cherbourg; Rouen; Bouvines 1214; Brest; BRITTANY; NORMANDY; MAINE; Rennes; Nantes; ANJOU; Paris; CHAMPAGNE; La Roche-aux-Moines; 1214; Tours; BURGUNDY; Bay of Biscay; FRANCE; Limoges; Dijon; Bordeaux; GASCONY; Périgueux; AQUITAINE; HOLY ROMAN EMPIRE; LEÓN; Bayonne; NAVARRE; Toulouse; TOULOUSE; Avignon; Carcassonne; CASTILE; ARAGON

◀ ❹ The possessions of Henry II, 1180

- ▢ lands acquired through marriage to Eleanor of Aquitaine 1152
- ▨ territory controlled by Henry 1180
- ▨ other lands notionally fiefs of Henry 1180
- ▨ French Royal domain 1180
- ▨ Norwegian possessions
- ---- border of the Holy Roman Empire

Venice and the Latin Empire

As well as being the principal emporium for east-west trade, Venice also made money shipping Crusaders to the Holy Land. When the Fourth Crusade gathered in Venice in 1203, the leaders did not have enough money to pay. The Venetians diverted the fleet first to capture the Adriatic port of Zara, long coveted by Venice, then to Constantinople, where in 1204, the Crusaders sacked the city and installed their own emperor. The Empire was divided into Venetian colonies and Latin fiefs. There were now two empires in the east; the "Latin" empire, ruled from Constantinople, and a rump Byzantine Empire, ruled from Nicaea.

The Crusaders' motive for attacking Constantinople in 1203 was financial reward for restoring Alexius IV (son of deposed emperor Isaac Angelus) to the imperial throne. When the population rebelled and killed Alexius in 1204, the Crusaders took over the city for themselves.

Map labels: HOLY ROMAN EMPIRE; HUNGARY; Buda; Black Sea; TREBIZOND; GEORGIA; SELJUK SULTANATE OF RUM; BULGARIA; Adrianople; Constantinople; Nicomedia; Nicaea; PRINCIPALITY OF ANTIOCH; Antioch; Venice; Milan; Zara; Spalato; SERBIA; Salonica; ROMANIA; SALONICA; EMPIRE OF NICAEA; LITTLE ARMENIA; COUNTY OF TRIPOLI; Tripoli; SYRIA; Genoa; Pisa; PAPAL STATES; Durazzo; NEGROPONTE; Aegean Sea; Rhodes; RHODES; KINGDOM OF CYPRUS; Acre; KINGDOM OF JERUSALEM; Jerusalem; ITALY; Adriatic Sea; Bari; DESPOTATE OF EPIRUS; DUCHY OF ATHENS; Athens; DUCHY OF NAXOS; Naxos; Corsica; Rome; Naples; Amalfi; Taranto; ACHAIA; Mistra; Coron; Monemvasia; Modon; Maina; Candia (Crete); Scarpanto (Karpathos); AYYUBID SULTANATE; EGYPT; Cairo; Sardinia; KINGDOM OF SICILY; Palermo; Catania; Mediterranean Sea

Venice and the Latin Empire 1204–1300

1204: Constantinople taken by Fourth Crusade		1261: Michael Palaeologus recaptures Constantinople and restores Byzantine Empire	
1200	1220	1240	1260	1280	1300
1212: Venetians occupy Crete	1224: Latin kingdom of Salonica conquered by Despotate of Epirus	1275: Principality of Achaia inherited by Philip of Anjou; ruled from Naples	

▲ ❺ The eastern Mediterranean c.1214

- ▨ Byzantine Empire on eve of Fourth Crusade 1202
- ▨ Venetian Republic and possessions
- ▢ Latin Empire
- ▢ Crusader states
- ▢ Byzantine states
- ▢ Muslim states
- → route of Fourth Crusade
- ---- border of Holy Roman Empire

EUROPE IN CRISIS

THE CONSOLIDATION of nation states on the eastern and western edges of Europe was matched, in the 13th century, by the decline of the Holy Roman Empire, its power depleted by long struggles with the papacy and the Italian city-states. In the east, raids by Mongols destroyed Kiev in 1240, and Russia, subject to Mongol overlords, developed in isolation until the 15th century. In the northeast, German colonization brought political and economic change, with a new trading axis around the Baltic Sea. During the 14th century, however, social unrest swept through Europe, compounded by famines, economic decline, dynastic wars, and the Black Death of 1347 *(see pp. 72–73)*, which wiped out a third of Europe's population in just two years.

This silver pfennig shows the Emperor Frederick II, whose claim to rule Italy alienated the popes.

The Empire and the papacy

Under the Hohenstaufen dynasty, the aspirations of the Holy Roman Emperors to universal authority were blocked by the papacy in central Italy, and the city-based communes of northern Italy. Emperor Frederick II (1211–50) clashed with Rome at a time when popes exercised great political power. After his death, the papacy gave the Kingdom of Sicily to Charles of Anjou, and Frederick's heirs were eliminated. Confronted with the growing power of France and England, the Empire lost any pretence to political supremacy in Europe; in Germany, a mosaic of clerical states, principalities, and free cities continued to undermine imperial authority.

Under Innocent III (1198–1216) the medieval papacy was at the height of its spiritual authority and temporal power.

England, Scotland, and Wales

The Scottish king, Robert Bruce, pictured here with his second wife, was a noble of Norman descent like his English enemies.

After a century of peace along the Anglo-Scottish border, Edward I (1272–1307) set out to assert his overlordship over all the British Isles. In 1284 he annexed Wales, bestowing the title of Prince of Wales on his son, but Scotland proved more intractable; Edward's attempts to subdue the Scots were met with resistance led by Robert Bruce, the victor at Bannockburn (1314). Hoping to extend his domains, Bruce sent an expedition to Ireland in 1315. His brother Edward continued fighting there until his death in 1318. In 1328, after a devastating period of guerrilla warfare and border raiding, England acknowledged Scottish independence.

England, Scotland, and Wales 1284–1337

1284: Edward I invades Wales

1305: Execution of William Wallace, Scottish nationalist leader

1322: Scottish barons assert independence in Declaration of Arbroath

1329: Death of Robert Bruce

1337: Start of Hundred Years' War; Scots ally with French against England

1296: Edward I invades Scotland

1314: English defeated at Bannockburn

1318: Edward Bruce killed in Ireland

1328: Scottish independence confirmed by Treaty of Northampton

(timeline: 1280 1290 1300 1310 1320 1330 1340 1350)

▼ ❷ The British Isles 1200–1400

- frontiers 1070
- to England 1092; to Scotland 1136
- southern limit of Scotland 1139–57
- to Scotland from Norway 1266
- northern limit of English control 1400
- Welsh Principalities, brought under English control gradually by 1247
- campaigns of Edward I, with dates
- Robert Bruce's campaign 1307–08
- region affected by Edward Bruce's invasions of Ireland 1315–18
- Irish overkingdom c.1100
- Irish states brought under English control by Papal grant 1155; subdued gradually by 1169
- autonomous Irish chiefdoms 1300
- core area of Peasants' Revolt 1381

❶ The Empire of Frederick II ▲

- frontier of Holy Roman Empire 1250
- Kingdom of Germany
- Kingdom of Italy
- under effective Hohenstaufen control 1250
- German lands largely under imperial or Hohenstaufen ownership
- Papal States 1178
- added by 1219
- added by 1278
- Venetian Republic and possessions
- ● member of Lombard League 1167
- frontiers 1250

The Hohenstaufens and the papacy

1167: Lombard League formed to oppose Emperor Frederick I Barbarossa in northern Italy

1198: Accession of Pope Innocent III

1211: Frederick II becomes Emperor

1245: Innocent IV excommunicates Frederick

1268: Charles of Anjou defeats Conradin, Frederick's grandson, at Tagliacozzo

1282: Sicilian Vespers; Charles of Anjou defeated by Aragonese

1194: Emperor Henry VI crowned King of Sicily

1237: Frederick II defeats Italian communes at Cortenuova

1250: Death of Frederick

1305: Pope Clement V takes up residency at Avignon, under French supervision

(timeline: 1150 1170 1190 1210 1230 1250 1270 1290 1310)

Eastward expansion in the Baltic

A German-led wave of migration, from 1100–1350, transformed eastern and Baltic Europe. As peasants moved east in search of land and resources, German language and law became predominant; New towns were bound together in the Hanseatic League, a trading association with links from Muscovy to London. Crusades in the east were spearheaded by the Knights of the Teutonic Order, who began to wage war on the pagans of Prussia and Lithuania in 1226. They also took over the Sword Brothers' lands in Livonia. The Livonians and Prussians were subdued, but Lithuania expanded to the southeast to become a powerful state. It was united with Poland in 1386.

Marienburg was the headquarters of the Teutonic Knights from 1309. Part abbey, part fortress, it was built of brick like many of the castles erected by the crusading order in Prussia and Livonia.

The Baltic 1200–1400

c.**1200**: Bishopric of Riga established

1242: Russians defeat Teutonic Knights at Lake Peipus

1309: Teutonic Order's subjugation of Prussia complete

1386: Poland and Lithuania joined through marriage alliance

1226: Teutonic Knights invited to crusade in Prussia

1237: Start of Mongol invasion of Russia

1342: Death of Gedymin, founder of Lithuania

▲ ❸ **The Baltic states 1100–1400**

frontier of Kievan Rus c.1100
Holy Roman Empire, 1100
added to Holy Roman Empire by 1380
Sweden
added to Sweden by 1323
main thrusts of Danish expansion
under Danish control c.1225
eastern frontier of ethnic German settlement 1100
frontier of ethnic German settlement 1400
possessions of the Hungarian Angevins
member of Hanseatic League (not all shown)
frontiers 1380

Central and southeastern Europe

After the setbacks of the early 13th century, when eastern Europe was devastated by Mongol invasions, the consolidation of powerful new states began. In Bohemia, the imperial ambitions of Ottakar II (1253–78) briefly expanded his domain from Silesia to the Adriatic, but he came into conflict with Bohemian and German princes, and the Habsburgs were able to seize power in Austria on his death. Powerful monarchies were established in Lithuania under Gedymin (c.1315–42), in Poland under Casimir the Great (1333–70), and in Hungary under Louis the Great (1342–82). Bohemia under the Luxembourg dynasty remained an influential state, especially when the king was elected as the Emperor Charles IV. In the Balkans, Stefan Dušan (1331–55) forged for himself a substantial Serbian Empire, but it fell to the Ottomans in 1389.

The Emperor Charles IV is shown with his Electors. His Golden Bull of 1356 set out clear rules for electing the emperor.

Central and southeastern Europe 1200–1400

1212: Golden Bull establishes Kingdom of Bohemia

1260: Ottakar II of Bohemia defeats Bela IV of Hungary

1306: Luxembourg dynasty acquires Bohemia

1389: Battle of Kosovo; Ottomans gain control of Balkans

1241: Mongols invade Poland and Hungary

1278: Emperor Rudolf I of Habsburg defeats and kills Ottakar II

1333: Accession of Casimir the Great of Poland

1342: Accession of Louis the Great of Hungary

◀ ❹ **Central and Southeast Europe 1200–1400**

Byzantine Empire
Habsburg possessions
Latin states
Polish states
Russian principalities, vassals of the Golden Horde
Venetian Republic and possessions
Bulgaria 1230
Mongol-Tartar campaigns 1240–42
possessions of Ottakar II of Bohemia at his death, 1278
frontiers 1320
Serbian Empire of Stefan Dušan at his death, 1355
possessions of Casimir the Great of Poland at his death, 1370
possessions of Louis the Great of Hungary at his death, 1382
frontier of Ottoman Empire and dependencies
frontier of Lithuania 1400
frontier of Holy Roman Empire

TRADE IN MEDIEVAL EUROPE

The seal of Lübeck shows a cog, the ship used for large cargoes in northern Europe.

THE EXPLOSION IN EUROPE'S POPULATION, which nearly doubled between the 10th and 14th centuries, was caused by greatly increased agricultural productivity, enhanced by technological innovations, in particular the use of the iron plow, and large land clearance projects, which brought marginal land, such as marshes and forests, under cultivation. This demographic surge inevitably led to increased trading activity; merchants traversed the continent, using the trans-Alpine passes which provided arterial routes between Italy and the North and, from c.1300, new maritime routes which opened up the North and Baltic seas. Trade and commerce went hand in hand with urban development. Commercial wealth had a cultural impact; cities were enhanced with magnificent buildings and churches and, from c.1200, universities. As cities prospered, a new class, the bourgeoisie, emerged.

Medieval trade

From the 11th century the Alpine passes had linked the textile towns of Lombardy and manufacturing centers of the Po valley with northern Europe, rich in natural resources, such as timber, grain, wool, and metals. Merchants converged from all over Europe to trade at vast seasonal fairs. International bankers, such as the Florentine Peruzzi, facilitated payments and promoted business. Around 1300, the Genoese opened a new sea route to the North Sea through the Strait of Gibraltar; Bruges, at the end of the route, became a major city. In the Mediterranean, Genoa competed with Venice for the carrying trade. Venice controlled the valuable eastern routes, profiting from trade in silks, sugar, spices, and gemstones from India and East Asia. In northern Germany, an association of trading cities centered on Lübeck, the Hanseatic League, promoted monopolies and sought exclusive trading rights with towns in England, Scandinavia, and Flanders.

Italian towns

Northern Italy was well-endowed with populous, wealthy cities, such as Milan and Florence. The Italian cities did not develop under the direct rule of kings, emperors, or the nobility, and took advantage of this to assert their municipal rights, evolving their own constitutions, codes of law, and military forces, the "communal movement."

The textile industry flourished in Flanders and northern Italy. The horizontal loom (above) was introduced to Europe in the 11th century.

Medieval trade 1100–1400

	1245: Italian merchants granted own courts to settle trading disputes at Champagne fairs	**1291:** Genoese open sea route through Strait of Gibraltar to Bruges	**c.1300:** Venetians improve Brenner Pass, so suitable for vehicles	**1340s:** Bankruptcy of Peruzzis; economic chaos compounded by arrival of Black Death in 1347		
1143: Foundation of Lübeck						

1100	1200	1300	1400

1167: Lombard League opposes Frederick Barbarossa's attempt to abolish liberties of Italian communes

c.1200: Silver coins, notably the grosso, introduced in northern Italy

1237: Opening of St. Gotthard pass through Alps

1275: Establishment of Peruzzi trading company in Florence

1320: Flanders loses wool monopoly to Brabant; start of decline of Champagne fairs

MONEY AND BANKING

Many gold and silver currencies circulated freely in Medieval Europe, irrespective of where they were minted, so money changing was inevitably an important profession. Traveling merchants left currency on deposit with money changers in exchange for a receipt, the first stage in the evolution of banking. By the 14th century the use of the bill of exchange, where one person instructs another to pay a sum of money to a third party, was widespread. The organization of bills of exchange was lucrative, and banking families, such as the Peruzzi and Bardi of Florence, became rich and powerful.

Venetian coinage included the silver grosso and the widely circulated gold ducat.

Medieval Italy gave the world the word "bank" from the *banco* (counter) where bankers transacted their business, as shown in this 14th-century illustration.

Medieval cities

Many of the cities of Medieval Europe owed their development to trade and commerce. The cities of northern Italy emerged from the 10th century onward, as entrepôts in the trade between Europe, Byzantium, and the Islamic world. In the 13th century, the demand for manufactured goods, such as glassware, textiles, and metalwork, led to the emergence of industrial centers, notably the Lombard textile towns and the wool centers of Flanders, such as Ghent, Bruges, and Ypres. By the mid-13th century, German expansion eastward had led to the growth of a thriving network of Baltic trading cities, including Lübeck, Hamburg, Danzig, and Riga.

The Seine was vital to the economy of Paris. Boats of all sizes delivered goods along the river and the fortified bridges carried a constant flow of traders.

② Paris c.1400

- ☐ university and colleges
- ■ other important building
- ☐ built-up area
- ✝ church
- ⌓ city gate
- wall of Philip Augustus c.1200
- wall of Charles V 1357

Medieval Paris

From the 11th century, Paris benefited from the return of order and stability under the Capetian kings. Streets were paved, city walls enlarged and three "divisions" of the city emerged; the merchants were based on the right bank of the Seine, the university (recognized in 1200) on the left bank, with civic and religious institutions on the Île de la Cité. In the 14th century, however, the city stagnated under the dual blows of the Black Death *(see pp.72–73)* and the Hundred Years' War; repeatedly fought over by the contending forces, it was beset by riots and civil disorder.

1312: Knights Templar suppressed and property confiscated

Medieval Paris

1100 | 1200 | 1300 | 1400

c.1200: Paris undergoes improvements; streets are paved

1257: Foundation of Sorbonne; it soon becomes most famous college of Paris University

1382: Tax riot is brutally suppressed; municipal government suspended

1171: King Louis VII grants river-merchants' guild a monopoly of river trade

1220: Citizens of Paris granted right to collect import duty

1356: Provost of merchants, Étienne Marcel, takes over running of Paris and orders building of new city wall

Medieval Venice

Venice was perceived as the symbolic center of a liberal government and divinely ordered religious, civic, and commercial life. Its political focus was the Doge's Palace, residence of the elected Doge and center of government. Since the city's wealth depended on maritime trade, the government maintained a vast shipyard – the Darsena – to build galleys for war and for merchant ventures.

A 13th-century mosaic in St. Mark's Basilica shows the Doge in a procession led by a bishop.

❸ Venice in the 14th century

- ■ houses (palazzi) of the nobility
- ☐ built-up area
- ✝ church
- navigable channels
- main sea routes

976: Fire destroys Doge's Palace; rebuilt over next five centuries

1204: Sack of Constantinople; Venetian gains in Adriatic and Greece

1295: Foundation of oligarchic Grand Council (Maggior Consiglio)

900 | 1000 | 1100 | 1200 | 1300 | 1400

Medieval Venice

1071: Completion of St. Mark's Basilica; focus of public religious life

1284: First gold ducats minted in Venice

1354: Peace concluded with Genoa, after over 50 years of warfare over trade supremacy

❶ Trade in Europe c.1300

Principal trade routes

— Venetian
— Genoese
— Catalan
— Hanseatic
— main overland route

- 🌾 region of commercially produced cereals
- 🍇 region of commercially produced wine
- ⊙ town with population over 50,000
- ○ other trading center
- ☐ major textile town
- ✳ important fair
- Ⓟ branch or agency of Florentine Peruzzi company
- ⛏ silver mine
- wax
- timber
- salt
- fish
- furs
- frontier of Islamic world 1300

250 km
250 miles

Reval
Dorpat
Riga
Pskov
Novgorod
Kovno
TEUTONIC ORDER
Vitebsk
Smolensk
Western Dvina
RUSSIAN PRINCIPALITIES
Moscow
LITHUANIA
Mogilev
Lublin
L'vov
Kiev
Dnieper
KHANATE OF THE GOLDEN HORDE
Dniester
Carpathians Mountains
Tana
to New Sarai
Moncastro
Danube
Kaffa
Black Sea
BULGARIA
Varna
Trebizond
TREBIZOND
to Tabriz
Pera
Constantinople
BYZANTINE EMPIRE
Aegean Sea
Anatolia
RUM
Phocaea
SELJUK STATES
Ephesus
Egroponte
IL-KHANATE
to Baghdad
Taurus Mountains
LITTLE ARMENIA
Aleppo
Antioch
Modon
Rhodes
Famagusta
CYPRUS
Beirut
Crete
Acre
Jerusalem
Damietta
Alexandria
Nile
MAMLUKS
Cairo

THE EMERGENCE OF MODERN STATES

Joan of Arc (1412–31) led the French to a famous victory against the English at Orléans in 1429 during the Hundred Years' War.

THE MAP OF EUROPE was redrawn throughout the 15th century as new nation-states appeared. France emerged, bruised but victorious, from the Hundred Years' War, soon to become the model of a modern nation state. Newly unified Spain vanquished the last Iberian outpost of Islam in 1492, emerging as a formidable power. The vast realm of Poland-Lithuania dominated Eastern Europe, while the Bohemians threw off imperial control. Feudal models of government were disappearing everywhere, and monarchies increasingly relied on the endorsement of the "estates," representative bodies of nobility, clergy, and the newly emerging bourgeoisie. Commercial centers such as the Netherlands and Italy saw a flowering of humanist philosophy, science, literature, and art, known as the Renaissance.

The Hundred Years' War

Over a century of intermittent conflict between France and England (1337–1453) was precipitated by the English kings' possessions in France and their claims to the French throne. Six major royal expeditions to France, starting with Edward III's landing in Antwerp in 1338 and ending with the death of Henry V in 1422, were interspersed with skirmishes and provincial campaigns led by independent war parties. After many setbacks, the triumphs of Joan of Arc (1429–30) led to a resurgence of French confidence and ultimately to English defeat.

The skill of 10,000 English longbowmen proved the deciding factor against the French cavalry at the battle of Crécy in 1346.

▼ ❷ The Hundred Years' War after 1400

→ campaign of Henry V, 1415
→ campaign of Henry V, 1421–22
held by England or Burgundy, 1429
→ campaign of Earl of Salisbury autumn 1428
possessions of House of Burgundy 1429
→ campaign of Joan of Arc 1429
under Burgundian control by 1453
added to France 1477
added to France 1481
acquired or occupied by France temporarily, with dates
— frontiers 1493

◀ ❶ The Hundred Years' War to 1400

limit of lands held by England 1300
held by England at outbreak of war 1337
added at Treaty of Brétigny 1360
under English influence at outbreak of war
····· remained under English control 1380
→ campaign of Edward III, 1339–40
→ campaign of Edward III, 1342
→ campaign of Edward III, 1346
→ campaign of Black Prince, 1355
→ campaign of Black Prince, 1356
→ campaign of Edward III, 1359–60
added to France gradually, 1301–16
added to France 1349
area of the Jacquerie 1358
area affected by plundering of Great Companies 1360–66
— frontiers 1380

The Hundred Years' War 1337–1453

1337: Philip VI of France confiscates Guyenne; Edward III claims kingdom of France
1356: English victory at Poitiers
1360: Treaty of Brétigny; peace lasts nine years, but bands of mercenaries, the Great Companies, ravage southeastern France
1420: Treaty of Troyes; Henry V marries Catherine of France
1435: Congress of Arras; Burgundy, an English ally, makes terms with France
1450: English lose Normandy

1346: English victory at Crécy
1358: Jacquerie: popular uprising against exploitation of countryside by soldiers
1396: 28-year truce agreed. Richard II marries Isabelle of France
1415: Henry V invades France; English victory at Agincourt
1429: Joan of Arc relieves Orléans
1453: English lose Guyenne

1300 — 1350 — 1400 — 1450

The *Reconquista*

The Christian reconquest of Moorish Spain began in earnest in the 11th century, led by the kingdoms of Navarre, Aragon, León-Castile, and Portugal. Despite strong Muslim counterattacks, the Christians had reconquered all but the small kingdom of Granada by 1260. León-Castile now dominated Iberia, and Aragon acquired extensive possessions in the western Mediterranean. These kingdoms, united by the marriage of Ferdinand II of Aragon and Isabella of Castile, embarked on a final crusade, and Granada fell in 1492.

The Alhambra at Granada was built as a palace and fortress by the Moorish kings who ruled there until 1492. Following the expulsion of the Moors, much of the magnificent decoration was effaced or destroyed.

◀ ❸ The reconquest of Spain

— limit of Umayyad Caliphate 732
under Christian control by 1030
Almoravid campaigns 1080–1100
lands controlled by El Cid 1092
under Christian control by 1100
— frontier of Almoravid Empire 1115
under Christian control by 1180
— frontier of Almohad Empire 1180
under Christian control by 1280
under Christian control by 1492
— frontiers 1493
✗ Muslim victory with date
✗ Christian victory with date
→ major campaigns of reconquest with date

The *Reconquista*

1085: Christian forces capture Toledo
1094: "El Cid" takes Valencia
1147: Lisbon taken by Christians
1248: Seville falls to Christians
1410: Ferdinand, regent of Castile, takes Antequera; becomes king of Aragon
1469: Marriage of Ferdinand II and Isabella
1492: Capture of Granada

1000 — 1100 — 1200 — 1300 — 1400 — 1500

1137: Union of Aragon and Catalonia
1212: Battle of Las Navas de Tolosa; defeat of Almohads
1282: Peter III of Aragon captures Sicily
1479: Union of Castile and Aragon

Central Europe in the 15th century

In Bohemia, the preachings of Jan Hus, which railed against the abuses of the clergy, were taken up by the Hussites, who called for a free Bohemia, and established a national Czech church. A new state in Bohemia was forged by Czech resistance to a series of bitter crusades launched by the Holy Roman Empire. The union of Poland and Lithuania in 1386 had created the largest realm in Christendom, its future secured by the defeat of the Teutonic Order in 1410. In the Holy Roman Empire, the Habsburgs sowed the seeds of future domination, acquiring by treaty, marriage, and conquest domains stretching from Austria and Styria to the Netherlands, and encompassing, from 1477, the lands of the Valois dukes of Burgundy.

The civil war initiated by the Hussites led to the deposing of Sigismund, king of Bohemia, who was forced to wage war on the Hussites on an almost annual basis until 1436. The picture (left) shows Hussite battle wagons drawn up in a defensive circle.

This coin was minted to honor Jan Hus, who was burned at the stake for heresy in 1415.

4 Central Europe 1400–1500

- lost by Habsburgs during 14th and 15th centuries
- approximate extent of core Hussite area
- limit of area affected by Hussite campaigns 1425–34
- → campaign of János Hunyadi, 1443
- limit of direct Ottoman control, 1451
- Burgundian control 1477
- possessions of Matthias Corvinus of Hungary at his death 1490
- Jagiello possessions 1500
- Habsburg possessions 1500
- Papal States and notional dependencies 1500
- Venetian Republic 1500
- --- frontiers 1500
- — notional frontier of Holy Roman Empire 1500

Central and Eastern Europe 1400–1500

1410: Battle of Tannenberg Grunwald; Polish defeat of Teutonic Order

1415: Jan Hus burned for heresy at Constance

1419: Defenestration of Prague; German bürgermeister thrown from window by Czech crowds

1434: Battle of Lipany; victory of moderate Hussites over extremists

1454: Beginning of Thirteen Years' War between Poland and Teutonic Order

1456: Death of János Hunyadi, leader of Hungarians

1466: Second Treaty of Toruń; Prussia becomes a fief of Poland

1477: Death of Charles the Bold. Habsburgs acquire former Burgundian lands including the Netherlands and Franche Comté

1490: Polish Jagiello dynasty controls Poland, Bohemia, and Hungary

The formation of Switzerland

The forest cantons of Switzerland were strategically placed to control vital Alpine passes, the route for pilgrims and merchants traveling between Italy and northern Europe. Increasingly, they resented attempts by their powerful neighbors to exert political control. In 1291, a union was formed by Uri, Schwyz, and Unterwalden, later joined by other cantons and cities, to defend a growing autonomy. The Swiss, in their conflicts with the Habsburgs and Burgundy, gained a formidable military reputation.

Victory in the Swabian War by 1499 brought *de facto* independence from the Empire. Membership of the Union continued to expand until the 16th century.

At the battle of Morgarten in 1315, a Swiss peasant army was able to defeat a Habsburg attack led by Leopold I of Austria and an army of knights.

The formation of Switzerland

1291: Union of Uri, Schwyz, and Unterwalden

1315: Battle of Morgarten; defeat of Habsburgs

1332: Luzern joins Union

1352: Berne joins Union

1386: Habsburg emperor, Leopold III defeated and killed at Sempach

1476: Battles of Grandson and Morat against Charles the Bold of Burgundy

1477: Battle of Nancy; Charles the Bold killed

1499: Swiss victory in Swabian War

5 The growth of the Swiss Confederation

- first three cantons 1291
- added to Swiss Confederation by 1501
- added further by 1579
- frontier of Switzerland 1579
- — frontiers 1815

The growth of Hungary

Following the ravages of the Mongol campaigns of 1241, which reduced the population in some areas by up to 60 percent, a succession of Angevin and German princes were elected to the Hungarian throne. The growing threat from the Ottomans, who had taken Constantinople in 1453, precipitated a revolt led by János Hunyadi. In 1458 he secured the throne for his son, Matthias Corvinus (1458–90), who subsequently achieved many notable military successes against the Ottoman Turks.

Matthias Corvinus brought many of the ideas of the Renaissance to the business of government, simplifying the administration and laws. However, his subjects bore a heavy tax burden, partly to finance his huge standing army, which was kept in readiness for campaigns against the Ottomans and other foreign adversaries.

THE AGE OF THE REFORMATION

A SERIES OF PROFOUND CHANGES in theological doctrine and practice were to have violent political consequences in 16th-century Europe. The religious reformation, spearheaded by Martin Luther in 1517, divided much of the continent along religious lines, precipitating a series of wars which permanently sapped the strength of the Catholic Habsburg Empire. In northern Europe, new nations came to prominence; Sweden, Russia, and Denmark struggled for control of the Baltic, while in the Netherlands, a rising against the Catholic rule of Spain led to the independence of the Calvinist north. In the east, the expansion of the Ottoman Empire brought Christian Europe into conflict with Islam; the Turks exploited European disunity, penetrating as far as Vienna.

Martin Luther's questioning of the doctrine and practice of Christianity led to the creation of the Protestant faith.

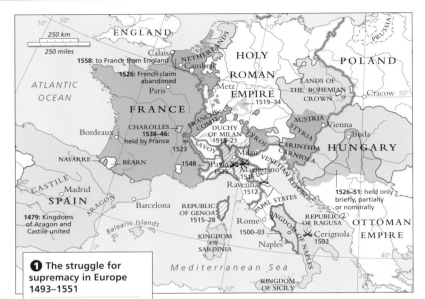

① The struggle for supremacy in Europe 1493–1551

- ▨ Habsburg possessions 1493
- ☐ added by 1551
- ☐ held temporarily, with details
- ▨ France 1493
- ☐ added by 1551, with date
- ▨ Bishoprics of Metz, Nancy, and Toul, to France 1552
- ▨ held temporarily 1499–1512
- — held temporarily with date
- — occupied by France 1536–39
- --- frontiers 1551
- — frontier of Holy Roman Empire 1551

The Reformation

The spiritual complacency, material wealth, and abuses of power of the Roman Catholic church provoked a revolution in Christianity, inspired by the teachings of Martin Luther (1483–1546). His reformed theology, with its emphasis on study of the Bible, spread rapidly through northern Europe. Some opportunistic rulers, such as Henry VIII of England, embraced "Protestant" forms of religion in order to seize church lands. By 1570, Protestantism prevailed over much of central and northern Europe. In 1545, the Catholic Church summoned the Council of Trent, which reaffirmed fundamental doctrine, but condemned the worst clerical abuses.

St. Ignatius Loyola founded the Society of Jesus in 1534 to champion the Catholic Counter-Reformation. Highly-educated and assertively evangelical, the Jesuits took Catholic teachings to territory throughout the rapidly expanding Spanish Empire.

The Habsburg defeat of France at the battle of Pavia in 1525 is here commemorated in a contemporary tapestry. Even though Francis I of France was captured by the Spanish, the French finally abandoned their claim to Italy at the Treaty of Cateau-Cambrésis in 1559.

The Habsburgs and France

Charles V, Emperor from 1519–56, ruled Spain, Flanders, and much of Italy as well as the Habsburg lands of Central Europe. He was opposed by the German princes, especially the Protestant ones, and Francis I and Henry II of France, who pursued the claims of their predecessors to Italy. Constant wars wasted many lives and much money, but gained nothing. In 1556, Charles V abdicated, dividing his empire between his brother and his son.

French-Habsburg rivalry 1515-59

- **1519:** Charles V elected German Emperor
- **1525:** Francis I captured at Pavia
- **1529:** Francis I signs Treaty of Cambrai, abandoning his ambitions in Italy
- **1559:** Henry II accepts Treaty of Cateau-Cambrésis; Habsburgs victorious
- **1515:** Francis I invades nothern Italy; defeats Swiss at Marignano
- **1521:** War between Francis I of France and Charles V
- **1543:** Francis attacks Charles V in Netherlands and northern Spain
- **1552:** Francis' successor, Henry II, forces Charles to abandon Siege of Metz (truce in 1556)

The Reformation in Europe 1517–55

- **1529:** At Diet of Speyer, Charles V attempts to reach compromise with Lutheran princes
- **1535:** John Calvin formulates doctrine of predestination in Geneva
- **1545:** Start of Council of Trent, which defines modern Catholicism
- **1517:** Martin Luther posts 95 Theses condemning abuses of Catholic church at Wittenberg
- **1532:** Henry VIII of England declares himself head of Church of England
- **1555:** At Peace of Augsburg; Lutheran princes win right to choose their religion

② The religious map of Europe 1590 ▶

- ▨ almost exclusively Catholic, with just minimal Protestant presence in northern areas
- ☐ overwhelmingly Catholic, with appreciable Protestant minority
- ▨ Catholic majority, but with very strong Protestant presence
- ☐ exclusively or overwhelmingly Protestant, with only slight Catholic presence in places
- ☐ Protestant majority, with some Catholic presence
- ▨ mainly Catholic, with strong Greek Orthodox presence
- ▨ Greek Orthodox, with significant Muslim presence in some areas of the Balkans
- ▨ Muslim majority
- --- frontiers 1590
- — frontier of Holy Roman Empire 1590
- *Calvinist* locally dominant Protestant denomination

Conflict in the Baltic 1500–1595

The collapse of the Union of Kalmar, which bound Sweden, Denmark, and Norway together, in 1523, precipitated a century of warfare around the Baltic Sea, bringing the growing power of Sweden into conflict with Russia and Denmark, which controlled the narrow outlet to the North Sea, vital for Swedish trade interests. The Reformation had led to the collapse of crusading orders such as the Teutonic Knights, opening up Livonia to the ambitions of Russia, Sweden, and Poland-Lithuania.

Ivan Vasilievich, Tsar of Russia from 1547 to 1584, was known as "the Terrible" for his drastic reforming of the hereditary aristocracy. Although his wars with Sweden and Poland were largely unsuccessful, he was able to expand the Russian Empire to include non-Slav states.

❸ The Baltic in the 16th century ▶

- area controlled by Teutonic Order 1450
- Poland-Lithuania and dependent territory 1558
- added to Poland by 1585, with date
- added to Sweden by 1583, with date
- to Sweden 1583–95
- Danish control 1558
- added to Denmark 1573
- possessions of Prince Magnus of Holstein 1564
- ▲▲ deepest advance of Russian forces into Livonia at various times during 1558–73
- to Russia 1563–70
- → campaigns of Polish King István Báthory 1579, 1580, 1581
- frontier of Holy Roman Empire
- ---- frontiers 1595

Conflict in the Baltic 1500–1582

1561: Collapse of Teutonic Order in Livonia; region partitioned into Russian, Swedish, and Polish-Lithuanian spheres of interest

1567: Swedes take Oslo from Danes

1581: Swedes recapture Estonia

1582: Ivan IV forced to conclude peace with King István Báthory of Poland, after the latter's successful campaigns against Russia

1563: Denmark and Sweden go to war. Gothenburg (Sweden's sole outlet to North Sea) falls to Danes

1576: Ivan IV of Russia conquers most of Livonia, but his army is crushed by Polish-Swedish alliance at Wenden (1578)

1595: Treaty of Teusina: Russia renounces all claim to Estonia

---

The expansion of Ottoman power

By 1500, the Ottomans controlled the lands to the south and west of the Black Sea. With the accession of Suleyman I – "the Magnificent" – (1520–66), they turned their attention to Europe, increasing naval pressure on the eastern Mediterranean, and pushing northward into Moldavia, the Danube valley, and Hungary. In 1529, they were turned back after their unsuccessful siege of Vienna, but continued to maintain their pressure on the frontier of the Habsburg Empire, exploiting conflict in Europe by forming alliances with France against the Habsburgs, and gaining control of Transylvania in 1562.

This detail from an Italian manuscript records the victory of Habsburg forces over the Ottomans at the siege of Vienna in 1529. The illumination is one of a series entitled "Triumphs of Charles V."

❹ The Ottoman frontier in 16th century ◀

- Ottoman Empire 1500
- added to Ottoman Empire by 1606, with dates
- Ottoman vassals 1606
- Habsburg possessions 1606
- temporary conquest by Ottoman Empire, with dates
- → Ottoman and Tartar attacks with dates
- ---- frontiers 1606
- Holy Roman Empire

The expansion of Ottoman power 1453–1571

1484: Turks capture Akkerman at mouth of Dniester

1529: Unsuccessful Turkish siege of Vienna

1562: After inconclusive skirmishes, Ottomans gain Transylvania

1453: Constantinople falls to Ottomans

1526: Ottoman invasion of Hungary; Battle of Mohács

1547: Negotiated peace acknowledges Ottoman control of most of Hungary

1571: Naval battle of Lepanto; a decisive Christian victory

The Dutch Revolt

Philip II of Spain, a fierce champion of the Roman Catholic cause, was determined to suppress Calvinism in the Netherlands. He reacted harshly to demands by Dutch nobles for autonomy and religious freedom, and his reprisals, combined with onerous taxes, led to a general revolt under the leadership of William of Nassau, which the Spanish could not quell. In 1579, ten southern Catholic provinces were promised liberty; in reply, seven Calvinist northern provinces formed the Union of Utrecht. In a 1609 truce, their independence was conceded by Spain.

The Sea Beggars were Dutch rebels who took to the sea to combat the Spanish from foreign ports. In 1572, they mounted a successful attack on the fortress of Brill in southern Holland *(above)*, encouraging Holland and Zeeland to join the revolt.

The Dutch Revolt 1565–1609

1568–72: Raids by Dutch "Sea Beggars" on Spanish naval transports and bases

1574: Dutch capture Middelburg and force Spanish to retreat from siege of Leiden

1585: The Duke of Parma captures rebel town of Antwerp. English intervene on side of rebels

1600: Victory of United Provinces at Nieuwpoort

1609: 12-year truce negotiated with Spanish

1566: Riots in Netherlands against Philip II's unpopular religious and fiscal policies

1576: Unpaid Spanish army mutinies in Antwerp and sacks city

1579: Catholic nobility in the south sign Treaty of Arras with Philip II

1590: Dutch rebels make major gains in northeast

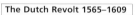

❺ The Dutch Revolt 1568–1609

- frontier of Holy Roman Empire 1568
- Spanish Netherlands at outbreak of revolt 1568
- joined Union of Utrecht 1579 and 1581
- Union of Arras 1579
- limit of Spanish advance by 1589
- Netherlands in terms of 1609 truce
- ✕ Dutch victory
- ✕ Spanish victory

EARLY MODERN EUROPE

Cardinal Richelieu, was Louis XIII's chief minister and the architect of royal absolutism in France.

IN THE 17TH CENTURY, following years of destructive warfare, the modern European state system began to evolve. States were ruled centrally by autocratic (or absolutist) monarchs and bounded by clear, militarily secure frontiers. The Thirty Years' War laid waste large parts of central Europe, causing a decline in population from some 21 million in 1618 to 13 million in 1648. Under Louis XIV, France was involved in four costly wars, but emerged as the leading nation in Europe, eclipsing Spain, which entered a long period of decline. After a period of expansion under the Vasa kings, Sweden lost much of its Baltic empire by 1721. The Ottoman Turks struck once again at the heart of Europe, but were met by an increasingly powerful Austria, whose main rival in the region was Russia.

The Thirty Years' War

The Thirty Years' War provoked great advances in methods of mass destruction, and involved an unprecedented number of soldiers, over a million of whom died before it ceased. Much of Germany was devastated, towns were sacked, and their inhabitants raped and murdered.

The Thirty Years' War saw Protestant-Catholic rivalry and German constitutional issues subsumed in a wider European struggle. Habsburg attempts to control Bohemia and crush Protestantism coincided with the breakdown of constitutional mechanisms for resolving conflict in the Holy Roman Empire. Spain intervened to secure supply lines to the Netherlands; Danish and Swedish involvement followed as they competed for control of the Baltic. Fear of imperial absolutism, prompted by Austrian Habsburg victories in 1621 and 1634–35, led France to intervene in 1635 in support of Sweden. Prolonged negotiations from 1643 culminated in the Treaty of Westphalia, which fused attempts to secure peace in Europe with curbs on the emperor's authority in Germany.

The Thirty Years' War 1618–48

1620: Battle of the White Mountain; Habsburgs defeat Bohemians	1629: Habsburgs triumphant in much of northern Germany	1630: Swedish king, Gustavus Adolphus, intervenes in war	1635: Peace of Prague strengthens position of Habsburg emperor, Ferdinand II	1648: Peace of Westphalia

1620 — 1630 — 1640 — 1650

| 1618: Bohemian revolt against Habsburg authority sparks off Thirty Years' War | 1629: Danes forced out of war by imperial armies | 1631: Habsburg army crushed by Gustavus Adolphus at Breitenfeld | 1636: Open war between France and Holy Roman Empire | 1644–48: Imperial armies defeated by French, Swedish, and Dutch |

❶ The Treaty of Westphalia, 1648

- Austrian Habsburg possessions
- Spanish Habsburg possessions
- Brandenburg possessions
- Danish possessions
- Swedish possessions
- Church lands
- ◆ electorate
- boundary of Holy Roman Empire, 1648
- — frontiers 1648
- ⚔ major battle of Thirty Years' War

Political consolidation and resistance

European states were transformed in a process of internal political centralization and external consolidation. The legitimacy of these developments was often questioned, leading to civil wars and popular resistance. Foreign intervention turned local disputes into international conflicts, as in the Thirty Years' War. In western Europe, Spain's dominant position was broken by Portuguese and Dutch independence. The two rising powers in the region, France and England, developed in very different ways. In France, Louis XIV assumed absolute power, while in England, Charles I was arrested and executed for disregarding parliament, and although the English monarchy was restored, its powers were drastically curbed.

❷ Political consolidation and resistance in 17th-century Europe

- Austrian Habsburg possessions 1683
- Spanish Habsburg possessions 1683
- ⚜ civil war or widespread disturbance
- ⚜ local revolt or unrest
- ⚙ civic autonomy suppressed by territorial rulers
- — frontiers 1683
- — Holy Roman empire 1683

Expansionist tendencies
- → Sweden
- → Russia
- → England
- → Ottoman Empire
- → Austrian Habsburgs
- → France
- → United Provinces

The union of Spain and Portugal was ended in 1640 when the native House of Braganza led a nationalist revolt. The relief of the siege of Elvas during the War of Independence is depicted in a Portuguese tile painting *(above)*.

As one of the leading generals of the Parliamentary army, Oliver Cromwell *(left)* played a decisive role in the English Civil War. After the execution of Charles I, he quelled the Royalists in Scotland and Ireland. Dissolving the "Rump" Parliament, he became Lord Protector of the Commonwealth.

Civil wars and revolts 1625–65

1628–29: Siege of Protestant stronghold of La Rochelle	1640: Portugal declares independence from Spain — 1640: Catalan Revolt	1649: Execution of Charles I of England	1660: Restoration of English monarchy

1625 — 1635 — 1645 — 1655 — 1665

| 1640: Civil War breaks out in England | 1648–53: The Fronde: resistance to royal authority throughout France |

❸ The Swedish Empire 1560–1721

- Sweden at the death of Gustavus Vasa 1560
- conquests by 1645
- conquests by 1658
- temporary Swedish acquisitions, with dates
- Russian gains from Sweden by treaty of Nystad, 1721
- → Swedish campaigns
- → Russians campaigns under Peter the Great
- trade routes
- frontiers, 1658

Habsburg–Ottoman conflict 1663–1718

In the mid-17th century, the Ottoman Empire resumed its expansion into southeastern Europe. Austrian attempts to challenge the Ottomans' control of Transylvania led to full-scale war in 1663. The Turkish advance on Vienna in 1664 was halted, but in 1683 the Turks besieged the city. The siege failed, and by 1687 the war had become a Habsburg war of conquest. The acquisition of Transylvania and Turkish Hungary transformed Austria into a great European power and loosened its traditional ties to the Holy Roman Empire.

In 1683 the Ottomans began their greatest onslaught on the Habsburg Empire by besieging Vienna with a huge army. Poland and the Papacy joined the German princes in an international relief effort which ended in Ottoman defeat.

Habsburg-Ottoman wars 1663–1718

1660	1680	1700	1720	1740

- 1672: Greatest extent of Ottoman Empire
- 1699: Peace of Karlowitz confirms Austrian conquests
- 1716–18: Further Austrian victories, including capture of Belgrade
- 1664: Turkish advance on Vienna turned back at battle of St. Gotthard
- 1683: Siege of Vienna starts Great Turkish War

❹ The Ottoman frontier 1683–1739

- Ottoman Empire 1683
- Habsburg possessions 1683
- Venetian Republic 1683
- Russia 1683
- Habsburg gains, with date
- temporary Habsburg gains, 1718–39
- acquired by Russia 1739
- Venetian gains 1699
- Habsburg-Ottoman frontier 1718
- ✕ Habsburg victory
- frontiers 1683
- Holy Roman Empire border

Sweden, Russia, and the Baltic

The 17th century witnessed the phenomenal growth of Sweden as an imperial power: by defeating regional rivals Denmark, Poland and Russia, it had by 1648 established a Baltic empire, the high point of which was reached during the reign of Charles X (1654–60). Lacking indigenous resources, however, Sweden's strength rested on its control of strategic harbors and customs points along the Baltic shore. Defense of these positions forced Sweden into a series of costly wars from 1655. After the Great Northern War, much of the empire was lost to the rising powers of Russia, Prussia, and Hanover.

Founded in 1703 by Peter the Great, St. Petersburg was modelled on European cities, its classical architecture and orderly street grid symbolizing the Tsar's westernizing policies.

The rise and fall of the Swedish Empire

1625	1645	1665	1685	1705	1725

- 1629: Sweden gains Livonia
- 1643: Sweden invades Denmark
- 1654: Start of reign of Charles X
- 1658: Peace of Roskilde; Denmark loses southern Sweden
- 1700: Great Northern War
- 1721: Peace of Nystad; Sweden cedes Ingria, Livonia, and Karelia to Russia
- 1632: Gustavus Adolphus dies at victorious battle of Lützen
- 1648: Substantial Swedish gains confirmed by Treaty of Westphalia
- 1675: Brandenburg defeats Sweden at Fehrbellin
- 1709: Charles XII's attempt to invade Russia halted at Poltava

The French state under Louis XIV, 1660–1715

Under Louis XIV, France pursued an expansionist, anti-Spanish policy. The expense of maintaining a large army and building a ring of frontier fortresses was met by administrative reforms, and tax collection in the provinces was overseen by royal officials (intendants). In 1667–68 Louis' armies secured parts of the Spanish Netherlands. Although this provoked international opposition to French aggression, further gains were made in the Dutch War (1672–79). The occupation of various territories in 1679–84 (known as the Réunions) rationalized France's eastern frontier, but after defeat in the Nine Years' War (1688–97), most of these had to be given up. The War of the Spanish Succession (1701–14) brought France no further gains.

A ring of defensive fortresses was built by Vauban, a great military engineer, to secure French territory.

During his long reign, Louis XIV (left) established France as cultural and political leader of Europe.

❺ France 1648–1715

- France 1648
- frontier of Holy Roman Empire 1648
- French frontier 1713/14
- administrative regions under Louis XIV (intendances or généralités)
- French gains confirmed 1659
- French gains confirmed 1661
- French gains confirmed 1668
- French gains confirmed 1678–79
- areas temporarily annexed under the Réunions, 1684–97
- further French gains by 1697
- Vauban fortress
- fortified town
- barrier fortress
- administrative center

The growth of France under Louis XIV

1660	1680	1700	1720

- 1667–68: France acquires parts of Flanders from Spain
- 1679–84: Réunions: annexation of territory west of the Rhine
- 1701–14: War of the Spanish Succession
- 1661: Louis XIV assumes personal rule
- 1672–79: Dutch War brings significant territorial gains
- 1688–97: Nine Years' War: Peace of Ryswick (Rijswijk) partially reverses the Réunions
- 1715: Death of Louis XIV

THE AGE OF ENLIGHTENMENT

Catherine the Great ruled the Russian Empire as an enlightened despot from 1762 to 1796.

THE 18TH CENTURY was a period of relative stability, when well-established monarchies ruled most of Europe and almost all the land was controlled by the nobility or the state. The Russian Empire and Prussia became leading powers. The rest of Germany remained a jigsaw of small states, as did Italy, while Poland was swallowed up by its powerful neighbors. Improved methods of cultivation fed Europe's escalating populations; towns and cities increased in size and number; trade and industry expanded to reach global markets; philosophy, science, and the arts flourished. Intellectual curiosity encouraged the radical political theories of the "Enlightenment," but alarmed reaction set in when the flag of liberty was raised in France in the last decade of the century. Though ultimately unsuccessful, the French Revolution would inspire many social and political reforms in the 19th century.

Cities and economic life 1700–1800

Despite the beginnings of industrialization in the 18th century, principally in textile production, in 1800 four out of five Europeans still depended on agriculture for their livelihood. The growing population – largely due to a fall in the death rate as a result of better health and hygiene – led to a rapid increase in the size of cities; in 1700 Europe had ten cities with over 100,000 inhabitants; by 1800 there were 17. At the same time, farmers adopted a more scientific approach to agriculture, introducing new, more productive crops and livestock. A general improvement in transportation by sea, road, river, and canal greatly stimulated trade throughout Europe and, as colonialism developed, with the rest of the world.

Thomas Coke of Norfolk, England, was known as "the father of experimental farms." He pioneered new agricultural techniques and developed breeds of sheep, pigs, and cows that gave higher wool, meat, and milk yields.

Population growth in major European states 1650–1800

- France *
- Sweden *
- Russian Empire
- Spain*
- Britain *
- Italian states
- Dutch Republic *
- Holy Roman Empire

* Excluding overseas territories

❶ Cities and economic life c.1750

Population per sq mile
- over 100
- 50 to 100
- less than 50

- city with population over 500,000
- city with population over 100,000
- other settlement
- major textile area
- major metallurgical area
- major grain producing area
- cotton
- linen
- silk
- wool
- furs
- shipbuilding
- major overseas trade routes

The partitions of Poland

17th-century Poland was one of Europe's largest states, but suffered frequent territorial losses to its neighbors, especially Russia. The elective monarchy allowed foreign powers to interfere in Polish affairs, and in the late 18th century the Russians, the Habsburgs, and Prussia settled their differences at Poland's expense in three partitions which removed the country from the map.

◀ ❷ The partitions of Poland 1772–95

- frontier of Poland in 1699

Partition of Poland in 1772
- to Prussia
- to Russian Empire
- to Habsburg Empire

Partition of Poland in 1793
- to Prussia
- to Russian Empire

Partition of Poland in 1795
- to Prussia
- to Russian Empire
- to Habsburg Empire
- frontiers in 1795

The decline of Poland 1550–1795

- **1569:** Poland united with Lithuania
- **1660:** East Prussia gains independence from Poland
- **1697:** Start of rule by Electors of Saxony
- **1772:** First partition of Poland
- **1795:** Third partition

- **1629:** Sweden acquires Livonia
- **1667:** Russia acquires East Ukraine
- **1764:** Russia secures Polish crown for Stanislas Poniatowski
- **1793:** Second partition

THE ENLIGHTENMENT

The 18th-century "enlightened" writers, or *philosophes*, such as Voltaire and Diderot, appealed to human reason to challenge traditional assumptions about the Church, state, monarchy, education, and social institutions. "Man is born free, but everywhere he is in chains," wrote Jean-Jacques Rousseau in his *Social Contract* (1762), in which he sought to show how a democratic society could work.

Voltaire (1694–1778) used poetry, drama, and satire to express his political views, including his opposition to the Catholic Church. His radicalism often led to periods of exile from his native France.

Published in 28 volumes from 1751–72, the *Encyclopédie* spread the philosophic and scientific ideas of the Enlightenment. It gave a comprehensive account of contemporary institutions and technologies, while fine engravings illustrated the work of all kinds of craftsmen, such as the instrument makers above.

The rise of Brandenburg Prussia

After the Peace of Westphalia in 1648, Germany consisted of some 300 small principalities, some Catholic, some Protestant. By the end of the 17th century Brandenburg was the dominant Protestant state. Frederick William (the "Great Elector") gained full sovereignty in Prussia and created a powerful state with a huge standing army. With the accession of Frederick II (the "Great") in 1740, expansion continued, including the acquisition of Silesia from the Habsburg Empire. With additional territory from the partitions of Poland, by the end of the century Prussia had become one of Europe's Great Powers.

❸ The rise of Brandenburg Prussia 1648–1795

- Brandenburg in 1648
- acquisitions 1648–1707
- area held 1713–42
- acquisitions 1715–20
- acquisitions by Frederick the Great 1740–86
- temporary acquisitions by Frederick the Great 1740–86
- acquisitions from Poland 1793
- acquisitions from Poland 1795
- Habsburg possessions in 1795
- frontier of Holy Roman Empire, 1789

The growth of Prussia in the 18th century

1713: Accession of Frederick William I, King of Prussia	1720: Treaty of Stockholm gives part of Western Pomerania to Prussia	1740: Accession of Frederick II (the "Great")
1742: Frederick completes rapid conquest of Silesia	1760: Austrian and Russian troops occupy Berlin, but Prussia survives	1772: First partition of Poland; Prussian lands in the east now linked to Brandenburg
1795: Third partition of Poland		

1713: Treaty of Utrecht: Prussia gains Upper Gelderland and Neuchâtel	1715: Prussia takes Stralsund in Great Northern War against Sweden	1740–48: War of the Austrian Succession
1756–63: Seven Years' War: Prussia faces coalition of Austria, Russia, and France	1763: Treaty of Hubertusburg allows Prussia to keep Silesia	1786: Death of Frederick the Great
1793: Second partition of Poland		

1700 — 1720 — 1740 — 1760 — 1780 — 1800

These splendidly uniformed cavalry officers are representative of the highly disciplined and efficient army which, by 1763, enabled Prussia to emerge as the dominant military force in 18th-century Europe.

The French Revolution 1789–95

In May 1789, a political crisis forced Louis XVI to summon the Estates–General, a parliament of nobles, clergy, and commoners. The third estate (the commoners) demanded reform and declared itself a National Assembly. Noble and clerical privileges were abolished; provincial uprisings were directed against landowners, many of whom fled into exile. In 1792 the Revolution gathered momentum: Louis was imprisoned, the monarchy abolished, and France declared a republic. Mass conscription was introduced to meet the threat of invasion by Austria and Prussia and the king was executed. Power shifted to the radical Jacobins, who ruled by means of "the Terror," executing all "enemies of the people." Many regions opposed these excesses, notably the Vendée in the west, but resistance was crushed. In 1794 the Jacobins shared the fate of their victims. France, however, had been saved from invasion, and there followed a period of moderate rule – the Directory.

Although France's political crisis had begun a year earlier, the storming of the Bastille by a Paris mob on 14 July 1789 signaled the true start of the French Revolution. Chosen by the mob as a symbol of repression, the fall of the ancient prison demonstrated the power of the people to force change.

❹ The French Revolution 1789–95

- French territory 1789
- Vendée uprising 1793
- other areas of counterrevolutionary resistance 1792–99
- centre of revolution 1789
- centre of Federalist revolt 1793–94
- centre of execution
- 300 numbers executed by revolutionaries
- émigré centre

War of the First Coalition
- ✕ French victory
- ✕ French defeat
- → offensives by French forces against Allies 1792–94
- → offensives by Allies 1792–94
- territories annexed by France 1789–97

French Revolution

May 5 1789: Opening of the Estates-General	Jul 12 1790: Civil Constitution of the Clergy	Apr 20 1792: War of First Coalition
Jan 21 1793: Louis XVI executed	Mar 10 1793: Vendée uprising	

Jul 14 1789: Fall of the Bastille	Aug 26 1789: Declaration of the Rights of Man	Oct 1 1791: Meeting of newly-elected Legislative Assembly
Aug 10 1792: Louis XVI overthrown	Sep 22 1792: Republic proclaimed	May 31 1793: Left-wing Jacobins take power; start of Terror
Jul 27 1794: Fall of Robespierre and end of the Terror		

1789 — 1790 — 1791 — 1792 — 1793 — 1794 — 1795

NAPOLEONIC EUROPE

THE BRILLIANT REVOLUTIONARY GENERAL Napoleon Bonaparte returned from his Egyptian campaign in 1799 to stage a *coup d'état* which made him ruler of France as First Consul. During the Consulate he began reforms of the administration, the legal system, the Church, and education. In 1804, just over ten years after revolutionaries had executed Louis XVI, Napoleon took the title of emperor and began to create a dynasty, members of his family being given the crowns of conquered states.

His imperial ambitions were ultimately thwarted by Britain: its navy was used to blockade France and overrun French colonies, while a series of alliances completed an encirclement that contained and gradually reduced Napoleon's empire.

The Code Napoléon of 1804, the first modern law code, embraced many of the principles of the French Revolution.

The battle of Eylau in 1807 was fought in a blizzard, with the French heavily outnumbered and outgunned by the Russians. Though both sides claimed victory, the French lost more men. For the first time in his career, Napoleon had failed to win a major battle.

In this cartoon of 1812, Napoleon tries desperately to bridge the 2000 miles between Madrid and Moscow. The impossibility of personally masterminding both the Peninsular campaign in Spain and Portugal and the Russian campaign led to his downfall.

The rise and fall of Napoleon

Napoleon established his military reputation with his bold, unexpected maneuvers leading the French Revolutionary army against Austria in Italy (1796–97). His expedition to Egypt in 1798 was doomed by the loss of the French fleet, but his subsequent European campaigns were a series of triumphs, culminating in his victory at Austerlitz in 1805. By 1809, he controlled Central Europe, but the Peninsular War (1808–14) and the winter retreat from Moscow (1812) were blows from which he could never recover. Defeated in 1814, he was exiled to Elba, but escaped to fight one last campaign. This ended with defeat at Waterloo in 1815. This time he was exiled to the island of St. Helena in the South Atlantic, where he died in 1821.

The campaigns of the Napoleonic Wars 1794–1815

The War at Sea, 1794–1805
In a series of engagements, both in European seas and the West Indies, the British navy proved its supremacy over the French, culminating in Nelson's historic victory at Trafalgar.

The Italian Campaign, Apr 1796–Jan 1797
In late 1795 Napoleon took command of the French Army of Italy. Though badly equipped and heavily outnumbered by the Austrians, Napoleon won battle after battle, finally driving them out of northern Italy.

The War of the Second Coalition, 1798–1801
The Allies planned to drive the French from northern Italy, but Napoleon marched his army through the Great St. Bernard Pass in midwinter and defeated Austrians at Marengo. Further victories at Zurich and Hohenlinden forced Austrians to sue for peace.

The Egyptian Campaign, 1798–1801
Napoleon's expedition to Egypt was intended to open a route to India. Despite early successes on land, his plan was wrecked by British seapower, and France's brief rule in Egypt ended in 1801.

The War of the Third Coalition, 1805–1807
The Allies planned an invasion of France. Napoleon marched his army from Boulogne to Ulm and defeated Austria, then won a brilliant victory against Austria and Russia at Austerlitz. Austria surrendered and Prussia entered the war. After a series of victories, Napoleon became virtual ruler of western and central Europe.

The Peninsular War, 1808–1814
In order to impose the Continental System on the Iberian Peninsula, Napoleon invaded Portugal, then Spain. The Spanish people revolted; Britain entered the war and a six-year guerrilla struggle ensued.

The War with Austria, 1809
Emboldened by Napoleon's concentration on Spain, Austria tried to liberate Germany from French rule. Within three months, the Austrians were forced to seek an armistice.

The War with Russia, 1812
Napoleon's relations with Russia, now France's only major Continental rival, deteriorated. Tsar Alexander was persuaded by Britain to renounce the Continental System, a serious economic blow to France. Napoleon invaded Russia with some 450,000 men.

The Leipzig Campaign, 1813
Allies united to end Napoleon's grip on Europe. Despite crushing defeat at Leipzig, Napoleon refused peace terms offered by the Allies.

The Defense of France, 1814
Napoleon rejected Allies' peace offer. His armies scattered across Europe, Napoleon mustered some 118,000 men while three Allied armies converged on Paris. Despite early victories, Napoleon was forced to abdicate in April.

"The Hundred Days", Mar–Jun 1815
Escaping from Elba, Napoleon returned to Paris, mustered an army and marched north to Ligny. On June 18, he was defeated by the Allied armies at Waterloo.

### Map labels

NORWAY

BRITAIN

Edinburgh
Dublin
Bristol
London

Killala Bay 1798
1796–98: attempted French invasions of Ireland

Bantry Bay

ATLANTIC OCEAN

Jun 1 1794: French convoy sails from US. French send fleet to protect it; intercepted by Howe and defeated

Jul 1805: Outmaneuvered in West Indies by Nelson, Villeneuve returns; defeated at Cape Finisterre

Brest

Corunna
Jan 16 1809: Moore repulses French, but British army evacuated

Cape Finisterre
Vigo

Sep 1805: Nelson sails from Portsmouth to Trafalgar

Vimeiro
Aug 21 1808: Wellington defeats Junot

Feb 14 1797: Spanish fleet, sailing to join French for invasion of Britain, intercepted and defeated

May 1805: Villeneuve to West Indies

Oporto May 1809
Sahagún
Santander
Burgos 1807
Ciudad Rodrigo Jan 1812
Salamanca Jul 1812
Badajoz Apr 1812
Lisbon
Lines of Torres Vedras
PORTUGAL
Talavera Jul 1809
Madrid **1808:** captured by Napoleon **1812:** retaken by Wellington
Saragossa **1809:** captured
Vitoria **Jun 1813:** French defeated in decisive battle of the war
Wellington 1814
Bordeaux
FRANCE

Iberian Peninsula
SPAIN
Seville
Guadalquivir
Bailén **1808**
Valencia 1812
Barcelona

Cádiz
Cartagena
Gibraltar to Britain
Tangier
Trafalgar
Oct 21 1805: In a 5-hour battle British destroy Franco-Spanish fleet. Nelson mortally wounded

MOROCCO

May 1798: Napoleon, with 40,000 men and escorted by 13 ships under Admiral Brueys, sails for Egypt

May 1805: Nelson pursues Villeneuve to West Indies

Algiers
ALGIERS
Tunis

North Sea
DENMARK
Apr 2 1801: Nelson smashes Danish fleet
Copenhagen
Lübeck
SWEDISH POMERANIA
Hamburg
Bremen
HANOVER
Hanover
Leipzig
BATAVIAN REPUBLIC
PRUSSIA
Oct 16–19 1813: Allies win great victory, but Napoleon escapes with remnant of army
Oct 1806: Napoleon captures Berlin
Berlin
Boulogne
Waterloo Jun 18 1815
Brussels
Ligny/ Quatre-Bras Jun 16 1815
Château-Thierry Feb 12 1814
Amiens
Rouen
Jena-Auerstädt **Oct 14 1806:** Prussians defeated
Bautzen **May 20–21 1813**
SAXONY
Lützen May 2 1813
Dresden **May 7–8 1813:** captured by Nap **Aug 26–27 1813:** Napoleon repuls Allied attack
SMALL GERMAN STATES
Paris
Rheims Mar 13 1814
Champaubert Feb 10 1814
Montereau Feb 18 1814
Orléans
Montmirail Feb 11 1814
Vauchamps Feb 14 1814
La Fère-Champenoise Mar 25 1814
Sep 1805: Napoleon crosses Rhine
Oct 1805: Austrians encircled and capitulate
Lunéville
Strasbourg
Ulm
Ratisbon Apr 23 1809
BOHEMIA
Prague
Eckmühl Apr 22 1809
MORAVIA
Auste Dec 2
NEUCHÂTEL
Zurich 1799
SWISS CONFEDERATION
Geneva
Hohenlinden 1800
Munich
BAVARIA
Vienn **May 18** capture French
AUSTRIA
Leoben
HABSBUR
Lyon
Marengo **Jun 14 1800:** Napoleon defeats Austrians
Great St. Bernard Pass
Turin
Rivoli 1797
Lonato 1796
Milan
Dego 1796
Lodi 1796
Castiglione 1796
Arcole 1796
Campo Formio
Mondovi 1796
Mar 1796
Cannes
Genoa
Venice
Bassano 1796
Toulon
Nice
Montenotto 1796
Mantua **Jun 1796–Feb 1797:** besieged by French
Bologna
Florence
Mar 1797: Napoleon invades Austria
TUSCANY
Marseille
Montebello
Corsica
Elba
PAPAL STATES
Rome
Adriatic Sea
RAGUS
MONTENE
Toulouse Apr 1814
Toulon 1808
ANDORRA
Pyrenees
Naples
KINGDOM OF SARDINIA
KINGDOM OF NAPLES AND SICILY
Mediterranean
Palermo
Sicily
Mos
Wellington 1814
Wagram Jul 5–6 1809
Campo Formio

1801 (arrow)
1794
1805

Jun 12 1798: occupied by Napoleon
Malta

Tripoli

TRIPOLITANIA

250 km
250 miles

The campaigns of Napoleon 1796–1815

1796–97: Italian campaign	May 1798: Start of Egyptian campaign	Jun 14 1800: French defeat Austrians at Marengo	Mar 27 1802: Peace of Amiens between Britain and France	Oct 19 1805: Napoleon defeats Austrians at Ulm; Oct 21 1805: Nelson destroys Franco-Spanish fleet off Trafalgar	7–8 Feb 1807: Battle of Eylau	1808: France invades Spain; start of Peninsular War	1810: Russia withdraws from Continental System	Sep–Oct 1812: French occupy Moscow, then retreat; Sep 7 1812: Battle of Borodino	Jun 18 1815: Napoleon defeated by British and Prussians at Waterloo
	Jul 1798: Defeat of Egyptians at Battle of the Pyramids								

1796	1798	1800	1802	1804	1806	1808	1810	1812	1814

Oct 1797: Peace of Campo Formio between France and Austria	Aug 1798: Battle of the Nile	1799: Directory overthrown and First Republic dissolved; Napoleon elected First Consul	1801: Peace of Lunéville between Austria and France; May 18 1803: Britain declares war on France	Dec 2 1804: Napoleon becomes "Emperor of the French"	2 Dec 1805: Battle of Austerlitz; Oct 14 1806: Defeat of Prussians at Jena and Auerstadt	Jul 1807: Peace treaty between Napoleon and Russia at Tilsit; Jan 16 1809: British defeated at Corunna	May 1812: Napoleon invades Russia	Oct 16–18 1813: Napoleon defeated by Allies at Leipzig; Mar 30 1814: Allies enter Paris; Napoleon abdicates

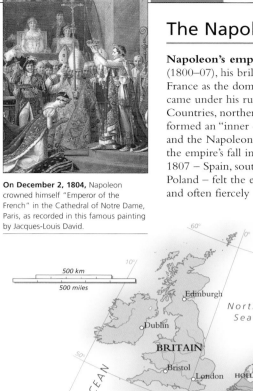

On December 2, 1804, Napoleon crowned himself "Emperor of the French" in the Cathedral of Notre Dame, Paris, as recorded in this famous painting by Jacques-Louis David.

The Napoleonic Empire

Napoleon's empire grew in two stages. In the first (1800–07), his brilliant military victories established France as the dominant power in Europe. Lands that came under his rule before 1807 – France, the Low Countries, northern Italy, and western Germany – formed an "inner empire." Here, French institutions and the Napoleonic legal code took root, surviving the empire's fall in 1814–15. Those areas taken after 1807 – Spain, southern Italy, northern Germany, and Poland – felt the effects of Napoleonic rule less, and often fiercely rejected French influence.

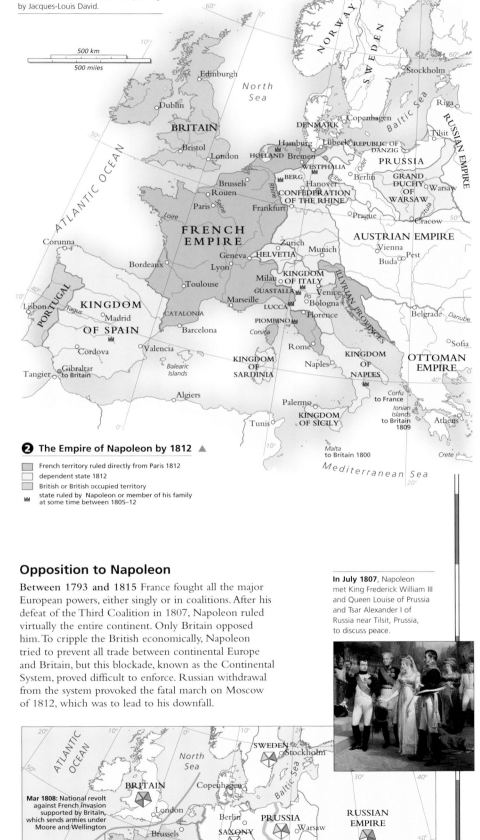

② The Empire of Napoleon by 1812 ▲
- French territory ruled directly from Paris 1812
- dependent state 1812
- British or British occupied territory
- ⚜ state ruled by Napoleon or member of his family at some time between 1805–12

Opposition to Napoleon

Between 1793 and 1815 France fought all the major European powers, either singly or in coalitions. After his defeat of the Third Coalition in 1807, Napoleon ruled virtually the entire continent. Only Britain opposed him. To cripple the British economically, Napoleon tried to prevent all trade between continental Europe and Britain, but this blockade, known as the Continental System, proved difficult to enforce. Russian withdrawal from the system provoked the fatal march on Moscow of 1812, which was to lead to his downfall.

In July 1807, Napoleon met King Frederick William III and Queen Louise of Prussia and Tsar Alexander I of Russia near Tilsit, Prussia, to discuss peace.

① The campaigns of Napoleon 1794–1815
- → British forces
- ✗ French victory (colored by campaign)
- ✗ French defeat (colored by campaign)
- ⚓ British blockade
- ▲ defensive lines
- ⊙ French siege
- -- frontiers 1797
- Holy Roman Empire 1797

③ Alliances in opposition to France 1792–1815 ▶

Alliances against France in the Napoleonic Wars:
- ✗ wars of Second Coalition 1798–1800
- ✗ wars of Third Coalition 1805–07
- ✗ war with Austria 1809
- ✗ war with Russia 1812
- ✗ Wars of Liberation of France 1813–15
- France 1792
- annexed by France 1802
- satellites of France 1802
- Napoleon's Continental System
- Holy Roman Empire
- frontiers c.1802

Napoleon's invasion of Egypt in July 1798 was intended to secure an overland route to India, but the destruction of his fleet by the British under Nelson at the battle of the Nile left the French forces stranded.

THE GROWTH OF NATIONALISM

Otto von Bismarck, prime minister of Prussia 1862–1890, was chief architect of the unification of Germany.

TO RESTORE PEACE and stability after the turmoil of the Napoleonic Wars, the Congress of Vienna was convened in 1814. Attended by all the major European powers, but dominated by Austria, Britain, Russia, and Prussia, the Congress redrew the political map of Europe and restored many former ruling houses. The result was three decades of reactionary rule, during which nationalist and republican movements, inspired by the American and French models, challenged the status quo. In eastern Europe, Greece and the Balkan states took advantage of the weakness of the Ottoman Empire to gain independence. In the west, Italy and Germany finally achieved their dreams of unification. But traditional rivalry between royal houses was now replaced by rivalry between industrialized nation states – a rivalry which led, ultimately, to World War I.

Europe under the Vienna system

The Congress of Vienna met to share out the spoils of victory over Napoleon, though painful compromise was required to achieve a workable balance of power in Europe. Political stability was reestablished by restoring the hereditary monarchs overthrown by Napoleon. France, though deprived of all its conquests, once more had a Bourbon on the throne. But the restored monarchs ruled with too heavy a hand: liberal, republican, and nationalist revolts began to break out, reaching a crescendo in 1848 when the governments of France, Italy, and Austria were all shaken by insurrection.

The Congress of Vienna was attended by five monarchs and the heads of 216 princely families. It was dominated by the Austrian chancellor, Prince Metternich, seen here standing on the left at the signing of the final settlement.

Threats to the Vienna system 1814–50

1806: Abolition of Holy Roman Empire
1814: Napoleon abdicates; opening of Congress of Vienna
1820–23: Revolts in Spain, Portugal, Naples, Sicily, Piedmont, and the Balkans
1830–31: Belgian War of Independence
1848: Second Republic in France with Louis-Napoleon as president

1815: Napoleon escapes from exile, but is defeated at Waterloo; restoration of French monarchy
1821: Start of Greek War of Independence which lasts until 1833
1830: Revolution in Paris
1833–39: First Carlist War in Spain
1848: Revolutions throughout Europe

1800 — 1810 — 1820 — 1830 — 1840 — 1850

❶ Europe after the Congress of Vienna 1815–52

MAIN MAP

- small German states
- areas in revolt against Louis-Napoleon in 1851
- German Confederation
- ⚔ threat to Vienna System 1817–39
- ✹ revolution in 1848–49
- ---- frontiers 1815

▼ **INSET: Belgian independence 1831–39**

- United Netherlands 1815–31
- boundary of German Confederation 1815
- boundary of German Confederation 1839
- ······ boundary between French and Flemish speakers

400 km
400 miles

ATLANTIC OCEAN

North Sea

SCOTLAND
Edinburgh
IRELAND
Dublin
1822–29: Catholic Emancipation campaign
BRITAIN
ENGLAND
WALES
London
1830–32: First Reform Act crisis
1840s: Chartist agitation
Amsterdam
1831: Belgium gains independence from United Netherlands
Brussels
UNITED NETHERLANDS
Hamburg
HANOVER in personal union with Britain Hanover
1817–31: German student protests
Berlin
PRUSSIA
Cologne
SAXONY
Prague

NORWAY
1814: Denmark forced to cede Norway to Sweden
SWEDEN
Stockholm
DENMARK
Copenhagen
Bornholm
SCHLESWIG-HOLSTEIN

FINLAND
1808–09: Russia invades, then annexes Finland
Helsingfors
St. Petersburg
Riga
Moscow
Baltic Sea
Danzig
EAST PRUSSIA
Posen
Vistula
Warsaw
Brest-Litovsk
POLAND
1830–31: national revolt
Cracow
REP. OF CRACOW **1847:** to Austria
1847: Peasant uprising
GALICIA
Kiev
Dnieper
RUSSIAN EMPIRE

Bay of Biscay

1830: Revolution
Paris
Rhine
Jan–Mar 1848: Fighting at the barricades
Loire
1831: Vendean uprising
FRANCE
Bordeaux
BAVARIA
Stuttgart
WÜRTTEMBERG
BADEN
BAVARIA
Munich
PR. OF NEUCHÂTEL
Geneva SWITZERLAND
1847–48: Swiss Civil War
Lyon
Marseille
AUSTRIAN EMPIRE
Vienna
Buda Pest
HUNGARY
MILITARY FRONTIER
TRANSYLVANIA
Odessa
Dniester
WALLACHIA
MOLDAVIA
1829: to Russia
Sebastopol
Black Sea

Oporto
1820: Revolution in Portugal against British control of country
PORTUGAL
Lisbon
1820: Revolution Madrid
1833–39: First Carlist War
ANDORRA
SPAIN
1846–48: Second Carlist War
Barcelona
GIBRALTAR to Britain
Corsica
SARDINIA
MASSA AND CARRARA
LUCCA
MODENA
SARDINIA
Milan
LOMBARDY-VENETIA
1821: Piedmontese revolution
PARMA
Venice
ILLYRIAN KINGDOM
DALMATIA
BOSNIA
SAN MARINO
TUSCANY PAPAL STATES
Rome
1807–33: Serbian revolts
Belgrade
SERBIA
Bucharest
1821: Revolts in Wallachia and Moldavia
Danube
MONTENEGRO
BULGARIA
RUMELIA
ALBANIA
THRACE
Constantinople
Salonica
ANATOLIA
Smyrna
OTTOMAN EMPIRE

Balearic Islands
Mediterranean Sea
Palermo
1821: Revolution
KINGDOM OF THE TWO SICILIES
1820: Revolution Naples
1815: to Britain
Corfu
Ionian Islands
1815: to Britain
GREECE
1821–33: War of Independence
Athens
Crete
Malta **1800:** to Britain
Cyprus

Belgian independence

With the aim of preventing further French expansion, the Congress of Vienna created a buffer state by uniting the former Austrian Netherlands (Belgium) with Holland as the United Netherlands. Belgian opposition to this move led in 1830 to revolution, and 1831 saw the creation of the new kingdom of Belgium.

50 km
50 miles

Amsterdam
The Hague
Utrecht
NETHERLANDS
Bruges
Antwerp
HANOVER
Rhine
BELGIUM
1831: achieves independence
Brussels
LIMBURG
Maastricht
Namur Meuse Liege
PRUSSIA
FRANCE
1839: Eastern Luxembourg ruled by Dutch kings
1890: independent
LUXEMBOURG
Luxembourg

The unification of Germany

In 1815 Germany's states were reduced to a Confederation of 39 under Austrian leadership. These states were further united in 1834 by the formation of a customs union (Zollverein). In 1866 Bismarck, prime minister of Prussia, proposed a German Confederation which would exclude Austria. When Austria refused, Bismarck – bent on German unification – declared war on Austria. Following Austria's defeat, Bismarck established the North German Confederation. The German Empire, including Bavaria and other south German states, was created after Prussia's victory in the Franco-Prussian War in 1870.

Spiked helmets such as this one worn by a dragoon officer became emblems of German militarism.

In 1870, alarmed at the intentions of Prussia, Napoleon III declared war, but the French were defeated. Here, Napoleon surrenders to the Prussian king Wilhelm I.

The unification of Germany

1864: German-Danish War
1867: Prussia forms North German Confederation
1870: French defeated at Sedan
1871: Wilhelm I of Prussia proclaimed Emperor of Germany

1860 — 1865 — 1870 — 1875

1862: Bismarck prime minister of Prussia
1866: Austro-Prussian War
1870: Siege of Paris begins
1871: Germany adds Alsace-Lorraine to newly-created empire

❷ The unification of Germany

- boundary of German Confederation of 1815
- Prussia in 1815
- Prussian gains by 1866
- other states in North German Confederation 1867
- other German states 1866
- Austro-Hungarian Empire 1867
- frontiers in 1866
- → attack on Denmark by Austro-Prussian forces 1864
- --→ Prussian armies in war with Austria 1866
- --→ Prussian invasion of France in Franco-Prussian War 1870–71
- boundary of German Empire 1871

The unification of Italy

The restoration of the old order in 1815 provoked a movement to liberate and unite Italy. In 1859 Cavour, prime minister of Sardinia-Piedmont, enlisted the help of French emperor Napoleon III to drive the Austrians out of Lombardy. In 1860 Sicily and Naples were conquered by Garibaldi and his 1000 "Redshirts," then handed over to Victor Emmanuel II of Sardinia, who became king of a united Italy in 1861. Rome was finally added to the new kingdom in 1870.

◄ ❸ Italy 1815–70

- Kingdom of Sardinia 1815
- territory annexed 1859
- territory annexed 1860
- territory lost to France 1860
- territory annexed 1866–70
- frontier of newly-created kingdom of Italy 1861
- → Garibaldi and the Thousand 1860
- → Sardinian army 1860

The unification of Italy 1848–71

1848: Short-lived Roman Republic established by Garibaldi and Mazzini
1860: France takes Nice and Savoy in exchange for Lombardy
1861: Victor Emmanuel becomes king of Italy
1870: Italian army takes Rome and remaining Papal States

1845 — 1850 — 1855 — 1860 — 1865 — 1870 — 1875

1859: French and Piedmontese defeat Austrians at battles of Magenta and Solferino
1860: Garibaldi conquers Sicily and Naples
1866: Austria forced to cede Venetia
1871: Rome made capital of unified Italy

At the meeting in 1860 between Victor Emmanuel II and Garibaldi at Teano, Garibaldi – a lifelong Republican – effectively presented the king with half of Italy.

In this cartoon of 1908, Ottoman sultan Abdul Hamid II sulks as more Balkan territory is whipped from under his feet by Austria and Bulgaria.

Nationalism in the Balkans

Nationalism proved most volatile in the Balkans, where many subject peoples aspired to independence from the Ottomans. Initially only the Greeks were successful. Meanwhile, Austria and Russia vied to replace the Turks as the dominant power in the region. Russian expansionism provoked the Crimean War in 1854, when Russia was defeated by Britain, France, Austria, and Turkey, and the Russo-Turkish War of 1877–78. At the Congress of Berlin in 1878, Turkey was forced to abandon all claims to Montenegro, Romania, and Serbia. In 1912, intent on seizing the Ottomans' last remaining European territories, Serbia, Bulgaria, and Greece were victorious in the First Balkan War. Resentment over the division of the spoils sparked a new war, from which Serbia emerged triumphant, but the precarious situation would be a major cause of World War I.

❹ The Balkans and the Black Sea to 1913

- international boundaries 1913
- Ottoman Empire 1913
- Russian Empire 1913
- Austro-Hungarian Empire 1913
- Italy and possessions 1913
- Serbia 1833
- Serbian gain 1878
- Serbian gain 1913
- Greece 1830
- Greek gain 1864
- Greek gain 1881
- Greek gain 1913
- Romania 1861
- Romanian gain 1878
- Romanian gain 1913
- Bulgaria 1878
- Bulgarian gain 1885
- Bulgarian gain 1913
- Montenegro 1878
- Montenegrin gain 1913
- Albania 1913
- → Russian forces in Crimean War
- → Allied forces in Crimean War
- → Russian forces in 1877–78
- ✕ significant Ottoman defeat

The Balkans and the Black Sea 1850–1913

1854–56: Crimean War
1877–78: Russia, Serbia, and Montenegro at war with Turkey
1878: Congress of Berlin alters terms of San Stefano treaty; Bulgaria becomes autonomous principality within Ottoman Empire
1908: Bulgaria declares full independence
1913: Treaty of London confirms independent Albania

1850 — 1860 — 1870 — 1880 — 1890 — 1900 — 1910 — 1920

1878: Treaty of San Stefano negotiated by Russia and Turkey
1885: Bulgaria granted Eastern Rumelia
1912: Serbia, Bulgaria, Greece, and Montenegro form Balkan League; First Balkan War
1913: Second Balkan War

THE INDUSTRIAL REVOLUTION

Matthew Boulton's metal works in Birmingham developed the steam engine for industrial use.

IN THE LATTER HALF of the 18th century, rapid technological, social, and economic changes began to transform Britain from an agrarian into a largely urban, industrial society. This process, which became known as the Industrial Revolution, spread to Europe in the course of the 19th century. The population of the continent doubled in this period and was fed by a similar growth in agricultural production. Changes included the use of new power sources such as coal and steam; new building materials, chiefly iron and steel; and technical innovations and improved systems of transportation. These developments led to large-scale production and the growth of the factory system.

Industrial chimneys dominate the Manchester skyline in this 19th-century engraving. Industry in Britain concentrated in cities where rich coal and iron deposits were in close proximity.

The move to the towns

Urban development was inextricably linked to the process of industrialization. The most marked 19th-century urban growth occurred in areas where labor-intensive, mechanized, and often factory-based industries were emerging. Rapid urbanization first occurred in Britain, where the urban population grew from 20% of the total population in 1800, to 41% in 1850. By the 1850s, many other European countries experienced urban growth at a rate comparable with that of Britain in the first half of the century.

The Industrial Revolution in Britain

The replacement of water power with steam power greatly increased efficiency. Huge fly-wheels could drive machinery, such as that used here to make cable, at greater speeds.

A combination of geographical, political, and social factors ensured that Britain became the first industrial nation. The country possessed a number of natural ports facing the Atlantic, an established shipping trade, and a network of internal navigable waterways. It was richly endowed with coal and iron ore and could draw on a large market both at home and overseas. British colonies supplied raw materials and custom and an expanding population ensured buoyant demand at home. The textile industry in Britain was the first to benefit from new technical innovations which brought about greater production efficiency and output.

Built 1887–94 to provide economic transport link to coastal docks

▲ ❷ **The growth of Manchester 1840–1900**

- railroad
- railroad station
- Manchester South junction viaduct
- park
- built-up area 1840
- growth of city 1840–1900

The advance of British technology from 1733

1733: John Kay invents the flying shuttle

1765: James Hargreaves invents "spinning Jenny" which increases the output of spun cotton

1765: James Watt builds improved steam engine with separate condenser

1785: Power loom for cloth making revolutionizes weaving

1811–12: Luddite rioters wreck new textile machinery in Derbyshire

1825: First passenger steam railroad from Stockton to Darlington

1837: First practical electric telegraph system produced by Cooke and Wheatstone

1838: Launch of I.K. Brunel's Great Western steamship

1832: Outbreak of cholera kills 31,000 people in Britain

1842: Lord Shaftesbury's Mines Act; underground employment of women and children prohibited

1840: Cheap postal system introduced; one penny per letter to anywhere in Britain

◀ ❶ **The industrial revolution in Britain 1770–1870**

- coalfields 1870
- canals 1870
- railways 1870

Population 1850
- over 500,000
- 200,000–500,000
- 100,000–200,000
- less than 100,000

Economic activities 1870
Extractive industries
- iron mining and smelting
- tin mining and smelting
- copper mining and smelting
- lead mining and smelting
- quarrying

Manufacturing
- wool
- cotton textiles
- hosiery
- silkworking
- jute
- food processing
- shipbuilding

URBANIZATION AND PUBLIC HEALTH

From the 1850s, industrial cities in Britain began to grow faster than the infrastructure needed to support the growing populations. Poorly built workers' tenement housing became severely overcrowded, and people drank water contaminated by sewage and industrial effluent. These poor standards of living resulted in the proliferation of diseases such as cholera, smallpox, dysentery, tuberculosis, and rickets. In 1854 and 1855, cholera broke out in Newcastle, where steep banks produced a concentration of settlement in the commercial areas along the river. Families lived five to a room, without sanitation or ready access to clean water, and of the 9453 houses in the city in 1854, 8032 were without toilets. During the cholera epidemic of 1854, 1500 of the 90,000 population died of the disease in a period of five weeks.

◀ ❸ **The Newcastle cholera epidemic of 1854**

Mean number of people per house
- over 12
- 10–11.99
- 8–9.99
- less than 8
- one death from cholera

The Public Health Act of 1848 was a turning point for public health in Britain. It allowed for the formation of local Boards of Health and the appointment of medical officers. This public health poster entitled *Cholera Tramples the Victor and the Vanquish'd Both*, warned people that no class was immune from the disease.

The **Industrial Revolution** could not have occurred without developments in large-scale, efficient transportation. From the 1830s railroad lines spread rapidly and by 1870 most of Europe had basic rail networks, linking ports, inland sources of raw materials and manufacturing centers. This print depicts the Manchester and Liverpool Railway in 1831.

Scale varies with perspective
6220 km (3870 miles)
5980 km (3710 miles)

◀ **4 The industrialization of Europe by 1914**

Land use 1914
- ☐ mountain/wasteland
- ☐ agriculture and stock rearing
- ☐ forest
- ☐ industrial area

Resources
- ▨ coalfield
- ◧ lignite (brown coal)
- ◪ iron ore
- ⬤ oil
- △ potash

Manufacturing industry
- cotton
- linen
- silk
- wool
- iron smelting
- machinery
- shipbuilding

Population growth
- • city with population over 500,000 in 1850
- ◦ city with population over 500,000 in 1890
- ○ city with population over 500,000 in 1914
- ○ city with population under 500,000 in 1914
- ⊕ major port
- --- principal rail lines 1914
- ⋯ frontiers 1914

The development of industry in Europe 1850–1914

In the 1830s, most European countries still relied on handicraft production in towns and villages. By the 1840s railroad construction was beginning to create a strong demand for iron and coal. By 1850, much of northern Europe, especially Belgium, Germany, Russia, and France, had developed factory textiles, and were exploiting mineral resources such as coal and iron. As transportation improved, technologies spread to southern Europe. By 1900, Germany had outstripped Britain in many areas of manufacturing, including high-grade engineering, machine tools, and chemicals.

The area around the Ruhr river became the center of German heavy industry. Essen (left) was the headquarters of the Krupp steel and armaments factories.

Industrial relations

Industrial development introduced a new relationship between capital and labor. Changes in labor organization often brought unrest and protest. Many craftworkers found their trades rendered obsolete by mechanization and machine-wrecking became a form of resistance. Trade unionism, which was initially confined to skilled craftworkers, began in Britain with the rise of the factory system. By the 1870s, less skilled workers had also joined the labor movement.

In the 19th century industry became inspiration for art. This copper foundry at Toulon was painted by Realist artist Ignace François Bonhomme.

Industrial developments in Europe from 1840

1847: Siemens lays first telegraph line between Berlin and Frankfurt

1851: Great Exhibition of Industry at Crystal Palace, London

1870: Industrial expansion begins in Germany

1878: Gilchrist-Thomas method for steel production; internal-combustion engine constructed by Nikolaus Otto

1891: Construction of Trans-Siberian railroad begun

1840 · 1850 · 1860 · 1870 · 1880 · 1890 · 1900 · 1910

1844: Engels' *The Condition of the Working Class in England* is published

1867: Publication of Marx's *Das Kapital*, an analysis of the economic injustices of the Capitalist system

1868: First British Congress of Trade Unions meet in Manchester

1889: Eiffel Tower completed for centennial exhibition

1908: First radio transmitter built by Marconi

WORLD WAR I

Dynamic recruiting posters appealed directly to the patriotism of Europe's young men.

WORLD WAR I is one of history's watersheds. Austria-Hungary's attempt to assert its power developed into a protracted struggle that swept up most of Europe and the rest of the world in its train. The conflict mobilized 65 million troops, of whom nine million died and over one-third were wounded. Civilians also died – as a result of military action, starvation, and disease. The war was won by the Allied Powers, but at great cost. The German, Austro-Hungarian, Ottoman, and Russian empires were destroyed; European political and financial supremacy ended; and by 1918 the US had emerged as the greatest power in the world. The debt and disillusionment that followed paved the way for the revolutionary forces of the left and right that emerged in the 1930s in the wake of the Great Depression.

The start of World War I

World War I began in Europe in August 1914. A decade of increasingly severe political crises, combined with military and naval arms races among Europe's major powers, created an incendiary situation. The murder of Austrian Archduke Franz Ferdinand in Sarajevo in June 1914 proved the catalyst. Serbia, Montenegro, Russia, France, Belgium, and Britain (the Allied Powers) found themselves opposed to Austria-Hungary, Germany, and Turkey (the Central Powers). The Central powers were joined by Bulgaria in 1915, while the Allied powers gathered Italy by 1915 and Romania in 1916. In 1917, the US joined the war as an "associated power" on the Allied side.

❶ The balance of power in Europe, 1879–1918

- ◆ Austro–German alliance 1879–1918
- ◆ Three Emperors' alliance 1881–87
- ◆ Austro–Serbian alliance 1881–95
- ◆ Triple alliance 1882–1915
- ◆ Austro–German–Romanian alliance 1883–1916
- ◆ Reinsurance treaty 1887–90
- ◆ Franco–Russian alliance 1894–1917
- ◆ Russo–Bulgarian military convention 1902–13

Alliances on the eve of the war
- ☐ Allied Powers 1914
- ☐ Central Powers 1914
- ☐ neutral states 1914

War on the Western Front

By November 1914 the war on the Western Front had become largely static. A German offensive against Paris via Belgium was rapidly met by French and British forces, who forced them back to Flanders. For three years, the British and French armies, and the Germans at Verdun, undertook a series of futile and exceptionally costly offensives in which gains were generally no more than a few miles. The front was marked by long lines of trenches, from which the two sides sought to defend their positions. It was impossible for them to achieve any measure of surprise, or, with no room for maneuver, to shift their position at all.

For several years, the war in western Europe was fought along a barely shifting frontline, marked by a series of trenches. These British troops, from the Border Regiment are squatting in "funk holes" near Thiepval Wood during the battle of the Somme in 1916.

Tanks were first used at the end of the 1916 battle of the Somme and later during the Allied advance in the summer and autumn of 1918. Though they could cope with difficult terrain, the trench system provided considerable obstacles (left).

Aircraft were used initially for reconnaissance and artillery spotting; later, in 1917–18 Germany and Britain used heavy bombers to destroy industrial and civilian targets.

The Western Front

Aug 1914: Battle of the Frontiers | Oct 1914: The "race to the sea" | May 1916: Battle of Jutland in North Sea | Feb–Mar 1917: Germans withdraw to Hindenburg Line | Apr–May 1917: Allied offensives | Mar–Jul 1918: German offensives on Somme, Aisne, Noyon-Mondidier, and Champagne-Marne lines

1915 | 1916 | 1917 | 1917 | 1919

Sep 1914: Battle of the Marne; first battle of the Aisne | Feb–Dec 1916: Battle of Verdun | Jul–Nov 1916: Battle of the Somme | Apr 1917: US declares war on Central powers | Aug–Nov 1917: Third battle of Ypres | Jul–Oct 1918: Counteroffensives by Allies | Nov 1918: Armistice ends war on Western Front

The German offensive leads to stalemate

Facing a war on two fronts against enemies with larger armies, Germany sought to defeat France before Russia could fully mobilize. They planned to outflank the main French defenses by moving through Belgium and then through northern France to encircle France within six weeks. However, supply lines proved inadequate, and communications to, and between, the two main armies no better. The plan ignored British intervention, relying on the likelihood of French immobilization as the offensive progressed. French success at the battle of the Marne ended German hopes of a quick victory, and paved the way for the trench warfare that lasted until spring 1918.

❷ The Western Front 1914–17

Offensives and counteroffensives in 1918

When Russia withdrew in 1917, Germany needed to defeat Britain and France before US forces could be mustered in sufficient strength on the Western Front. The 1918 offensives were a strategic failure, sapping German resources and morale. The Allied Powers took advantage of their superior manpower and resources to counterattack successfully. With Germany's allies collapsing, its commanders were forced to seek the armistice that ended the war.

❸ The Western Front 1916–18

The Western Front 1914–1918

- → German invasion of France and Belgium, 1914
- ▲▲ farthest extent of German advance, 1914
- → German retreat
- ▬ line from end of 1914–Jul 1916
- – – – Hindenburg line
- ☐ gains by Allied powers 1916–17
- ☐ Kaiserschlacht ("the Kaiser's battles") 1918
- ▲▲ German offensive Mar–Jul 1918
- → Allied counterattacks, 1918
- ▬ line at the Armistice Nov 11 1918

Major battles
- ⚜ 1914
- ⚜ 1915
- ⚜ 1916
- ⚜ 1917
- ⚜ 1918

The Eastern Front

The Eastern Front

Sep–Oct 1914: German operations in southwestern Poland

Feb 1915: Second Battle of Masurian Lakes

Jul–Sep 1915: Russian withdrawal

Aug–Sep 1916: Romanian offensive

Mar 1917: Russian Revolution

Jul 1917: Second Brusilov Offensive

Dec 1917: Russian armistice

1914 | 1915 | 1916 | 1917 | 1918

Aug 1914: Battle of Tannenberg
Sep 1914: First Battle of Masurian Lakes

Nov 1914: Battle of Lodz

May 1915: German breakthrough at Gorlice-Tarnow

Jun–Aug 1916: Brusilov Offensive by Russia

Sep–Dec 1916: Elimination of Romania

Mar 1918: Treaty of Brest-Litovsk allows Germany to occupy Ukraine and gain access to food supplies

The Eastern Front map

4 The Eastern Front

- Russian advances, 1914
- front line in 1914–15 (limit of Russian advance)
- limit of Austro–German advances, 1915–16
- Brusilov offensives, 1916
- Armistice line Dec 1917
- German landings, 1917–18
- German offensives into Russia 1918
- German penetration into Russia by Jun 1918
- Area occupied by Central Powers under Treaty of Brest-Litovsk

Major battles:
- 1914
- 1915
- 1916
- 1917

250 km / 250 miles

War on the Eastern Front

There was far more movement on the Eastern Front than in the West, partly because of the much greater distances involved. Though the Russian army was generally superior to Austria–Hungary militarily, they were invariably defeated by the force of German arms. By the end of 1915, Russia had lost most of Poland, with more than two million troops taken prisoner. Inadequate military supplies and poor leadership produced a consequently high casualty rate: war-weariness and mutiny were key factors in bringing the Bolsheviks to power in 1917.

During the first German onslaught on the Eastern Front, casualty numbers were such that even churches were converted into makeshift field hospitals. The priest is giving a blessing to sick and wounded troops.

CASUALTIES OF WAR

The toll of military dead and wounded was appalling; of the millions mobilized on the Allied side, fewer than half escaped death or injury. The Central Powers' losses were even higher, particularly in Austria–Hungary. In total, nearly nine million men died in four years, with 23 million left physically or psychologically scarred. Civilians died too, from bombing raids, malnutrition, and disease.

Military casualties (millions)

- troops mobilized
- troops killed
- troops wounded

Allied powers: Russia, British Empire, France, Italy, US, Others

Central powers: Germany, Austria-Hungary, Turkey, Bulgaria

War in the Balkans

Serbia survived three invasion attempts in 1914, but succumbed in 1915 to an Austro–German offensive supported by Bulgaria, which checked an Anglo-French attempt to support the Serbian army from Salonica. In 1916, having successfully contained Allied forces at Salonica and invaded Romania, Bulgarian armies were joined by Austro–German forces that captured Bucharest in December. The Bulgarians were able to defeat several Allied offensives in front of Salonica until September 1918 when a major offensive broke the Bulgarian front and morale. Forced to sue for an armistice, the Bulgarians saw their capital occupied by British forces, while French and Serbian forces liberated Belgrade on November 1.

Lying in a key position at the head of the Gulf of Salonica, the port city of Salonica was a major focus for Allied operations in the Balkans during the First World War.

The war in the Balkans

Aug 1914: First invasion of Serbia

Nov–Dec 1914: Third invasion of Serbia

Oct–Dec 1915: Establishment of Salonican front

Aug 1916: Bulgarian surprise attack starts Allied counteroffensive

Dec 1917–Sep 1918: Advance to Greek frontier and limited offensive operations

Sep 1918: Allied offensive against weakened Bulgarian army

1915 | 1916 | 1917 | 1918 | 1919

Sep 1914: Second invasion of Serbia

Oct–Nov 1915: Final invasion and elimination of Serbia

Aug 1916: Entry of Romania into war

Nov 1917: Fall of Monastir to Allied forces

Sep 1918: Bulgarian armistice

6 The war in Southeast Europe and the Balkans

- route of Austrian, German, Bulgarian forces into Serbia Oct–Nov 1915
- Anglo–French forces Oct 1915
- retreating Serb forces Nov 1915
- Salonican front Sep 1918
- Allied offensive Sep 1918

Major battles
- 1914
- 1915
- 1916
- 1917
- 1918

100 km / 100 miles

The Italian Front

Italy entered the war in 1915 in an opportunistic arrangement engineered by its leaders with the Allies to secure territory at the expense of Austria–Hungary. Fighting on the Italian Front was some of the most bitter of the war, with much of the fighting occurring in a series of battles close to the Isonzo River. The great battle of Caporetto in 1917 almost led to Italian defeat. Italy was more successful in subsequent fighting, but the terrible disillusionment after the war over the price paid for Italy's gains contributed heavily to the rise to power of Benito Mussolini and the Fascists.

5 The Italian Front 1915–1918

- Italian offensives on the Isonzo River, 1915–17
- Austro–German campaigns, 1917
- front line in Sep 1917
- front line Dec 1917–Oct 1918
- Allied offensive, Oct 1918
- Armistice line Nov 4 1918

Major battles
- 1915
- 1917
- 1918

Italian civilians suffered great privations during the years of warfare in the north of the country. Here, women – wheeling handcarts – and children flee following the 6th battle of the Isonzo.

The war in Italy

Jun–Sep 1915: 1st and 2nd Battle of the Isonzo

Mar 1916: 5th Battle of the Isonzo

Aug–Sep 1916: 6th and 7th Battles of the Isonzo

May–Jun 1917: 10th Battle of the Isonzo

Oct–Nov 1917: Battle of Caporetto

Jun 1918: Battle of the Piave

1915 | 1916 | 1917 | 1918 | 1919

Oct–Nov 1915: 3rd and 4th Battles of the Isonzo

May–Jun 1916: Asiago Offensive by Austria

Oct–Nov 1916: 8th and 9th Battles of the Isonzo

Aug–Sep 1917: 11th Battle of the Isonzo

Nov 1918: Battle of Vittorio Veneto

EUROPE BETWEEN THE WARS

Vladimir Illich Lenin
was the architect of
the Bolshevik
Revolution.

AS WORLD WAR I drew to its close, the three
great conservative empires of Europe – Russia,
Austria-Hungary, and Germany – suffered
cataclysmic change. Revolution in 1917 in
Russia led to the seizure of power by Lenin
and the Bolsheviks. After the end of the war,
the victorious allies imposed peace treaties
which dismembered Austria-Hungary and sliced
territory from Germany – as well as imposing
punitive financial penalties. New states sprang
up right across Europe as nationalist aspirations coincided
with the collapse of multinational empires.

Europe after World War I

Following the end of World War I, Finland, Estonia, Latvia,
and Lithuania gained independence from Russia;
Czechoslovakia and Yugoslavia emerged from the wreckage
of Austria-Hungary, while Poland reappeared as an
independent state for the first time since its partition in
1794. In western Europe too, long-frustrated national
discontent finally brought about the establishment of an
independent Irish Free State in 1921. The birth of new states
and changes in regime did not happen easily, and Finland
and the new Irish state were both engulfed by civil war.

The immense reparations imposed
on Germany by the Treaty of Versailles
proved an impossible burden to a
nation already crippled by the costs
of the war. Hyperinflation during
the 1920s so devalued the national
currency that it became totally
worthless. These children are using
Deutschmarks as building blocks.

The aftermath of World War I

1919: Treaty of Versailles forces Germany to admit guilt for starting war and pay reparations to Allies	1923: Hyperinflation begins in Germany	1924: German reparations reduced by Dawes Plan

1919	1921	1923	1925
1920: League of Nations founded	1921: Birth of Irish Free State	1923: France occupies Ruhr region of Germany	1925: European boundaries stabilized by Treaty of Locarno

❶ Europe after World War I

European empires in 1914

German Empire	frontiers 1923
Austro-Hungarian Empire	new states
Russian Empire	

Revolution and civil war in Russia

In 1917, Russia's Tsarist regime, ravaged by war and a failing economy, collapsed. The
provisional government which replaced it failed to improve the economy, and in
October 1917, the socialist Bolsheviks seized key installations in Petrograd and took
control of a number of important towns. Civil war broke out as anti-Bolsheviks and
pro-monarchists (the "Whites"), aided by troops from other European nations (the Entente
powers), tried to overthrow them. However the well-organized Bolsheviks (the
"Reds") held the heartland of Russia and by 1921 had defeated their weak, disunited
opponents. Meanwhile, national groups on the periphery of Russia strove for
independence. Finland, Estonia, Latvia, Lithuania, and Poland broke free and were able to
remain so, but the independence of Armenia, Azerbaijan, and Georgia was short-lived. By
1924 the Bolsheviks were firmly in control and the Soviet Union came into being.

Scale varies with perspective

The Russian Civil War

	Russian boundary after Treaty of Brest-Litovsk Mar 1918
→	Bolshevik forces
→	White Russian forces
→	Entente forces

❷ The Russian Revolution, the Russian Civil War, and the formation of the Soviet Union 1917–24

	the Russian Empire in 1914
	countries/republics which declared independence from Russia in 1917–18

The Bolshevik revolution

●	towns where Bolsheviks gained control 1917
●	towns where Bolsheviks gained control 1918

The formation of the Soviet Union

★	republics temporarily independent from Russia 1917/18–21
	occupied by Japan 1918–22
	extent of Bolshevik territory in mid-1919
	Soviet Union by 1924
	frontiers 1924
-----	Trans-Siberian railroad

Revolution and civil war in Russia 1917–24

Mar 1917: Abdication of Tsar Nicholas II	1918: Start of civil war between Bolsheviks and White Russians; 1918: Treaty of Brest-Litovsk ends World War I in the east	1920: White Russia, Ukraine, and Caucasus Republics return to Russian control	1922: USSR (Union of Soviet Socialist Republics) is formed	

1917	1919	1921	1923	1925
Nov 1917: Bolsheviks begin to take control of European Russia	1920: Start of peasant revolts throughout Russia	1921: Russian civil war ends with Bolshevik victory. New economic policy encourages peasants to produce more food while modernization is taking place		1924: Lenin dies and is later succeeded by Josef Stalin

Economic crisis and political extremism

The US economic crisis of 1929 hit a Europe suffering from the aftermath of wartime dislocation. Industrial output and agricultural production fell sharply across the world, but the industrial nations were hardest hit. Farmers survived by retreating to subsistence production, but the collapse in industrial output brought unemployment on a massive scale. Without proper systems of social security to support the unemployed, poverty became widespread. The economic and social problems of the 1930s encouraged the growth of extreme political movements on both Left and Right, especially in Germany and Italy, where Fascism under Hitler and Mussolini became the defining political force.

In 1936 more than 200 men marched from Jarrow in northern England to London to draw attention to the plight of their town – formerly a center for shipbuilding – where male unemployment had reached more than 70%.

③ The Great Depression in Europe and the growth of political extremism

- Fascist regime
- Communist regime
- other dictatorship
- △ more than 20% unemployment by 1932
- ⚑ right-wing activity
- ⚒ strikes and riots during the 1930s
- 60% decrease in industrial output since 1929 (1932 figures as a percentage of 1929)

*Map labels:*
- **1931:** Formation of the fascist "Blueshirts" (Ireland)
- **1932:** Oswald Mosley founds fascist "Blackshirts" (Britain) — 89%
- **1933:** Nazi leader Adolf Hitler becomes German chancellor — 60%
- 63% (Poland)
- **1934:** Fascist activity (Belgium)
- 73% (France)
- **1934:** Failed coup by Austrian Nazis
- **1934:** Murder of Dollfuss (Austria)
- **1930:** King Carol finances fascist Iron Guard (Romania)
- **1930, 1932:** Lapua attempt coups (Finland)
- **1933:** Right wing constitution adopted under Salazar (Portugal)
- **1939:** Nationalists under General Franco win civil war (Spain)
- **1922:** "March on Rome" Fascists under Mussolini seize power (Italy) — 61%

The Great Depression in Europe

- **1929:** Wall Street Crash precipitates worldwide depression
- **1930:** Almost 40% of German workforce unemployed
- **1931:** European central banks collapse leading to further economic downturn
- **1933:** Almost 25% of British workforce unemployed

Timeline: 1925 · 1927 · 1929 · 1931 · 1933 · 1935

Revolution and nationalism in Europe

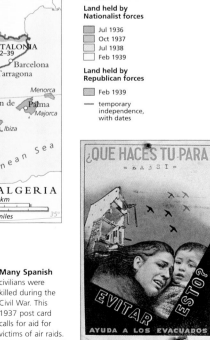

In March 1939 Nazi troops took control of the Czech lands and a puppet state was established in Slovakia. This photograph shows the entry of German troops into Prague, watched by wary Czech civilians.

On achieving power in 1933, Hitler began a campaign to restore Germany to its position as a great international power. In 1936, German troops marched back into the Rhineland. The response from the western powers was weak, and in March 1938, Nazi Germany annexed Austria in the *Anschluss*. At Munich six months later, Britain and France allowed Germany to annex the Czech Sudetenland, signaling the breakup of the Czechoslovak state. Fascist Italy aped Hitler, conquering Ethiopia in 1935–36 and occupying Albania in 1939. Finally, bolstered by the Nazi–Soviet Pact Hitler ignored British and French protests to invade Poland in September 1939.

⑤ Territorial expansion in Central Europe 1936–39

Territory taken over by Germany
- 1936
- 1938
- 1939

Territory taken over by Italy
- 1939

Territory taken over by Hungary
- 1938
- 1939

— frontiers 1936

*Map labels:*
- **1939:** Memel annexed by Germany
- **1936:** Rhineland reoccupied by Germany
- **1935:** Saar region granted by plebiscite to Germany
- **1938:** Czech territory (Sudetenland) granted to Germany by Munich Agreement
- **1939:** Poland invaded by Germany
- **1939:** Whole of western Czechoslovakia occupied by Germany
- **1938:** Czechoslovakian territory granted to Poland
- **1939:** Ruthenia occupied by Hungary
- **1938:** Slovak territory granted to Hungary
- **1924:** Fiume annexed
- **1938:** Austria annexed by Germany (the *Anschluss*)
- **1939:** Albania annexed by Italy

④ The Spanish Civil War 1936–39

Land held by Nationalist forces
- Jul 1936
- Oct 1937
- Jul 1938
- Feb 1939

Land held by Republican forces
- Feb 1939

— temporary independence, with dates

Map labels: BASQUE REPUBLIC 1936–37; CATALONIA 1932–39

The Spanish Civil War

The Spanish elections of 1936 brought in the left-wing Popular Front government, precipitating a military revolt by conservative groups. A brutal civil war followed, with the right-wing Nationalists, led by General Franco and supported by Germany and Italy, triumphant against Republican groups.

Many Spanish civilians were killed during the Civil War. This 1937 post card calls for aid for victims of air raids.

¿QUE HACES TU PARA EVITAR ESTO? AYUDA A LOS EVACUADOS

The growth of nationalism in Europe

- **1931:** Republican success in Spanish elections leads to flight of king
- **1933:** Hitler becomes Chancellor of Germany
- **1934:** Murder of Austrian Chancellor Dollfuss by Nazi supporters
- **1936:** Start of Spanish Civil War
- **1936:** Germany reoccupies Rhineland
- **1938:** Breakup of Czechoslovakia
- **1938:** Germany occupies Austria (*Anschluss*)
- **1938:** Munich Agreement allows Germany to occupy Czech Sudetenland
- **1939:** Signing of Nazi-Soviet Pact
- **1939:** German invasion of Poland

Timeline: 1931 · 1933 · 1935 · 1937 · 1939

WORLD WAR II IN EUROPE

Women were encouraged to join the war effort both as civilians and in the armed forces.

THE GREATEST WAR in Europe's history was initiated by a series of aggressive annexations and conquests by Hitler's Nazi Germany between 1939 and 1941. When the conflict ceased to be a series of campaigns and became a war, however, Germany was checked and then stripped of the initiative by an Allied force headed by two nations on the lateral extremes of Europe – Britain and the USSR – and from December 1941, a non-European nation, the US. Each of the latter proved more than Germany's equal in military and economic resources. The eventual Allied victory, following concerted assaults from the west, south, east, and the air, saved Europe from the scourge of Nazism but also completed Europe's devastation, bringing to an end 400 years of European global domination.

Blitzkrieg in Europe 1939–42

Between 1939 and 1941, lightning campaigns on land and in the air enabled Nazi Germany to conquer many of its weaker neighbors. In temporary alliance with the USSR, Germany annihilated Poland in the autumn of 1939. Denmark, Norway, Belgium, France, and the Netherlands were overrun in April–June 1940. Yugoslavia and Greece were occupied in April–May 1941, Britain was isolated, and Bulgaria, Romania, and Hungary brought under Nazi domination. Although a large contingent of German forces was committed to support Italy in North Africa, in June 1941 Hitler ordered a surprise attack on the USSR, hoping to destroy it in a single campaign. The attempt ended in failure because of the distances involved and unexpected Soviet resistance. In mid-winter 1941, the Nazi invasion forces were halted outside Moscow.

Following the Blitz
(September 1940–May 1941) London became the first city in history to undergo ballistic missile attack from V1 flying bombs and V2 rockets (1944–45).

① Blitzkrieg in Europe 1939–42

- Axis territory Sep 1939
- German offensive, 1939–41
- Italian offensive, 1939–41
- airborne attacks
- cities severely bombed
- Axis conquests 1939
- Axis conquests 1940
- Axis conquests 1941
- Soviet conquests 1939–40
- Axis satellites
- Allied territories Dec 1941
- British retreats
- Allied offensive 1941
- neutral states

The Second World War 1939–42

Aug 1939: Germany and USSR sign non-aggression pact

Apr 1940: German invasion of Denmark and Norway

Jul–Oct 1940: Battle of Britain in skies over southern England

Apr 1941: German invasion of Yugoslavia and Greece

Dec 1941: Germany declares war on US

Sep 1942: Start of German siege of Stalingrad

Nov 1942: Germans occupy Vichy France

Sep 1939: Germany and USSR invade Poland; France and Britain declare war on Germany

May–Jun 1940: Germany invades France, Netherlands, and Belgium

Oct 1940: Italy invades Albania and Greece

Jun 1941: Operation Barbarossa: German invasion of USSR

Nov 1941: USSR counterattacks against Germany

Oct–Nov 1942: UK defeats Germany at El Alamein

The Battle of the Atlantic

The battle over the supply of Europe was fought in the Atlantic. British destruction or containment of German surface warship raiders, following the sinking of the *Bismarck* in May 1941 and the blockade of supplies to "Fortress Europe," was followed by a German submarine (U-Boat) campaign against British shipping in western waters. Once the US entered the war in December 1941, U-boat attacks spread across the Atlantic. By summer 1943, US mass production of "Liberty" merchant ships, the use of the convoy system, increasing air cover, and the Allied interception of German radio traffic critically inhibited the effectiveness of the U-Boat "wolfpacks."

This Enigma encoding machine is being used by German naval personnel. By summer 1940, British counterintelligence experts had managed to crack the Enigma code, enabling them to interpret German radio traffic and disperse the intercepted messages (codenamed Ultra) throughout Allied High Command.

The battle of the Atlantic

Total U-Boat fleet

Sep 1939–Jun 1941: Anti-surface raider escort only; wolf packs operating in western Atlantic

Independently sailed ships sunk

May 1944: Convoy system reaches its peak

Jul 1942–May 1943: Wolf packs operating in mid-Atlantic air escort gap

May 1943: Mid-Atlantic air escort gap closed

Jun 1941: Shore-to-shore antisubmarine escort introduced

Allied ships sailing

Operational U-Boats

Dec 1941–Jul 1942: Wolf packs operating in US waters

U-Boats sunk

The Greater German Reich 1939–1943

The creation by the Nazis of a Greater German Reich encompassing their conquered and allied territories was based on five basic principles: pure "Aryan" regions were annexed or occupied and integrated into Germany under the aegis of the Gestapo secret police; nonincorporated areas were placed under military control; puppet and satellite states were strictly controlled and exploited by coercion; the conquered areas of the East were ravaged and cleared for German settlement; and underlying all these policies a principle of ethnic cleansing, targeting Jews, Gypsies, political dissidents, and "social deviants," began with imprisonment, concentration camps or enslaved labour, but escalated by 1943 into a policy of systematic extermination.

② The Greater German Reich 1942

- Greater German Reich
- areas occupied by Germany and Finland
- Italy and areas occupied by Italy
- Axis satellites
- Allied territories
- neutral states

③ The organization of persecution

- ▽ concentration camp
- ⊗ extermination camp
- ■ site of mass killing
- ⊗ ghetto
- 8000 number of Jews killed

The Nazi impact on Europe

Nov 1938: *Kristallnacht*: coordinated Nazi attacks on Jews in Germany

Sep–Oct 1939: Invasion of Poland; mass murder of Jews; establishment of ghettoes

Jun 1941: Invasion of Russia; *Einsatzgruppen* murder squads active in Eastern Europe

Jul 1941: Hitler orders Final Solution (extermination of Europe's Jews)

Dec 1941: First death camp opened at Chelmno

Jan 1942: Plans for Final Solution agreed

mid-1942: Auschwitz death camp opened

Apr 1943: Jewish uprising in Warsaw

Jul 1944: Majdanek camp liberated by Soviet Army

Jan 1945: Auschwitz liberated by Soviet Army

The Allied invasion of Europe 1943–45

A final German attempt to conquer the USSR brought their forces to Stalingrad by August 1942. The following winter saw their defeat there which, with Anglo-US victories in North Africa, brought the strategic initiative to the Allies. July 1943 witnessed Soviet victory at Kursk and Anglo-US landings in Sicily, initiating a Soviet onslaught in the East and the collapse of Italy. A sustained Anglo-US bombing offensive (from January 1943) and landings in southern France and Normandy meant, by summer 1944, that Germany was in retreat on all fronts. With its infrastructure, industry, capital, and leadership effectively destroyed, by May 1945 Germany was powerless to stop Soviet and Anglo-US forces finally meeting on the Elbe River and enforcing an unconditional surrender.

World War II 1942–45

Jan 1943: Germans surrender at Stalingrad

Jul 1943: Allied forces land in Sicily

Jun–Aug 1943: USSR defeats Germans in tank battle at Kursk

Sep–Oct 1943: Italian surrender to Allies; Germany occupies Rome and Milan. Italy declares war on Germany

Jan 1944: End of 900-day siege of Leningrad

Jul 1944: USSR enters Poland

Jun 6 1944: D-Day: Allied forces land in Normandy

Oct–Nov 1944: Allies liberate Greece

Jan 1945: Soviet troops enter Budapest, Warsaw, and Auschwitz

Mar 1945: Allied forces cross Rhine

May 1945: Germany surrenders

May 1945: Berlin surrenders to Soviet troops

The Allied invasion of northern Europe began with Operation Overlord, the largest combined operation and successful shore-to-shore invasion in history; eight seaborne and airborne divisions established a beachhead in Normandy, on D-Day (June 6, 1944) supported by 6500 ships and 12,000 aircraft.

④ The Allied invasion of Europe 1942–45

- under Axis control by 1942
- Allied territory 1942
- areas occupied by Germany by Nov 1942
- Axis satellites
- → German offensive from 1942
- → Allied offensive 1942–43
- → Allied offensive 1944
- → Allied offensive 1945
- Ⓥ Allied victory
- city severely bombed by Allies
- city severely bombed by Germans
- partisan resistance
- neutral states

Concentration camps were established by the Nazis as detention centers from 1933 and used as resources of slave labor from 1940. Actual extermination of local populations, directed by *Einsatzgruppen* murder squads began in Poland and occupied Russia from 1941. The *Endlösung*, or Final Solution, involving the mass deportation of Jews to extermination camps such as Auschwitz-Birkenau began at the same time. By 1945 six million Jews, Poles, and other "undesirables" had been systematically murdered.

THE DIVISION OF POSTWAR EUROPE

Josef Stalin, leader of the Soviet Union 1929–53, headed a regime of terror and totalitarian rule.

AFTER WORLD WAR II, Europe was divided into the democratic West and Soviet-dominated Communist East. Germany, which by 1947 was partitioned along the same lines, played a pivotal role in the tensions between the two blocs. From 1945–52, millions of people were forcibly resettled, while many others fled persecution. The US, fearing that Communism would be an attractive alternative to postwar poverty and dislocation, financed the "Marshall Plan," an economic recovery programme for Europe. By 1948 a pro-Soviet bloc, bound by economic and military agreements, had been established in Eastern Europe. Attempts to challenge Soviet dominance in the Soviet bloc in the 1950s and 1960s were brutally suppressed.

The Allied occupation of postwar Germany

Following Germany's surrender in May 1945, the occupying powers – America, Britain, France and the USSR – divided Germany into four zones. Berlin, which lay within the Soviet zone, was similarly divided. In March 1948 the Western powers decided to unite their zones into a single economic unit. The USSR responded by launching a land blockade of Berlin in protest against the unification. The Western nations frustrated the blockade by airlifting essential supplies to their sectors of Berlin. The blockade was abandoned in 1949.

❶ The partition of Germany and Austria ▶

Occupation zones
- American
- British
- French
- Soviet
- Soviet allies
- ☐ checkpoint between East and West
- --- air corridor
- ● four-sector city

The occupation of Berlin

In accordance with agreements made at the Potsdam Conference in 1945, Berlin was partitioned in a similar way to Germany. Between 1949 and 1961, around 2.5 million East Germans fled from East to West Germany, including skilled workers and professionals. Their loss threatened to destroy the economic viability of the East German state. In response, East Germany built the Berlin Wall in 1961 to prevent migrations and possible economic catastrophe.

With Soviet consent, the East German authorities constructed the Berlin Wall in 1961. For 28 years the wall served to segregate East Germans from West Germany, becoming a potent symbol of the Cold War.

❷ The division of Berlin

Occupation zones
- American
- British
- French
- Soviet
- ● checkpoint
- Berlin Wall 1961–89

Inter-zonal transport
- --- railroad
- — road

- ☐ American command headquarters
- ☐ British command headquarters
- ☐ French command headquarters

1948: Soviets begin Berlin blockade

1952: Total number of Germans fleeing to West reaches 985,000

1955: Allies sign treaty in Vienna reestablishing Austrian republic in its pre-1938 borders

1961: Berlin Wall erected on the night of Aug 12–13

1945 — 1950 — 1955 — 1960

1945: Potsdam Conference confirms partitioning of Berlin

1949: Soviets abandon Berlin blockade; Soviet occupation zone becomes German Democratic Republic

Germany in Cold War Europe

Refugees and resettlement 1945–52

World War II left millions of Europeans displaced. In an attempt to reestablish ethnic and linguistic uniformity within political boundaries, more than 31 million people were resettled between 1945 and 1952. Under the Potsdam agreement, Cossacks and Russian prisoners of war were forcibly repatriated, often to death or imprisonment. Millions of Germans fled Eastern Europe ahead of the Red Army. Mutual transfers of peoples were organized to coincide with shifts in boundaries - for example between Poland and the Baltic republics, and between Hungary and Yugoslavia. Finns were displaced by the Soviet occupation of Karelia, and many Jewish Holocaust survivors fled to Palestine and the US.

These children were among millions forced to live in refugee camps while they waited to learn whether they could return to their former homes.

❸ Displaced peoples in East and Central Europe ▶

- ☐ USSR 1945
- ☐ Communist states by 1948
- --- pre-war boundary
- — post-war boundary
- ▬ "Iron Curtain" 1948

Movement of peoples 1945–52
- (300) number of refugees in thousands (with color of peoples)
- → Baltic peoples
- → Czechs
- → Finns
- → Germans
- → Greeks
- → Hungarians
- → Italians
- → Poles
- → Romanians
- → Russians
- → Russians forcibly repatriated
- → Turks
- ✴ Jewish emigration to Israel 1945–50 in thousands

Soviet expansionism under Stalin

To establish firm buffers against possible threat to the USSR, Stalin annexed territories in Eastern Europe after World War II. Between 1952 and 1976 military spending was one-fifth of the budget as a nuclear arsenal to rival that of the US was developed. A return to the modernization program, begun in 1928, saw industrial output increase remarkably. Prison camps were used as a labor resource and by 1956 Soviet influence had extended into Africa and Asia.

Opponents of Stalin's regime were sent to labor camps to work for the benefit of the state. Among those populating the camps were Germans, peasants, and repatriated Russians whom Stalin believed to have been treacherous during World War II.

Movements against Communism 1950–1970

In the 1950s and 1960s a number of East European countries challenged Soviet domination. Riots erupted in Poland and East Germany in 1953. A more serious insurrection in Hungary in 1956 was quashed by Soviet troops. In January 1968, Communist Party leader Alexander Dubček began a process of liberalization in Czechoslovakia, but in August an invasion by the Warsaw Pact returned Communist hardliners to positions of power.

On the evening of August 20, 1968, Soviet, East German, Polish, Hungarian, and Bulgarian armed forces invaded Czechoslovakia and occupied it with little opposition. An important tactic used by Czech protestors was that of passive resistance (*above*).

④ Soviet expansionism 1949–59

- prewar Soviet territory
- prewar Soviet Satellite states
- territory annexed to USSR 1939–40
- territory annexed to USSR 1944–45
- postwar Soviet satellite states
- under temporary Soviet occupation
- influenced by Soviet Union from 1954
- Soviet nuclear base
- important Soviet military airfield
- US nuclear base
- Communist takeover with date
- Cold War conflict with date
- prewar boundary
- postwar boundary

Soviet repression
- labor camp by 1947
- labor camp administrative region (gulag)
- isolation camp administrative region (gulag)
- labor region
- deportations 1942–45
- areas affected by deportations

Scale varies with perspective

5560 km (3450 miles)
11,580 km (7200 miles)

The USSR 1945–65

1945: Stalin begins transfer of ethnic-minority peoples to labor camps

1946: Stalin confiscates land and savings of peasants in USSR

1948: Yugoslavia breaks ties with Soviet Union; Communist takeovers in Hungary and Czechoslovakia

1949: USSR tests its first atomic bomb

1953: Stalin dies while head of Soviet Union

1956: Hungarian uprising suppressed by Soviet Union

1956: Kruschchev denounces Stalin at Party Congress

1962: Cuban missile crisis (*see pp.108–109*)

1964: Kruschchev ousted; succeeded by Brezhnev

1945 | 1955 | 1960 | 1965

Military blocs in Europe

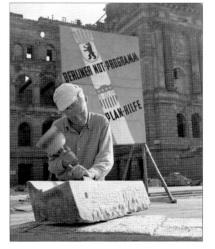

The US Marshall Plan granted over $12.5 billion to friendly European countries between 1948 and 1951 to assist postwar economic recovery. The North Atlantic Treaty Organization (NATO) grew out of this partnership, committing the US, Canada, and several Western European countries to joint defense against any Soviet aggression. The Soviet equivalent, the Warsaw Pact was established in 1955, and was a response to the decision of western powers to allow West Germany to rearm.

A poster advertising Marshall aid forms a backdrop as a stonemason works on a major reconstruction project in postwar Berlin.

❺ Marshall aid and military alliances in Europe 1948–55

- Marshall aid recipient, with amount in US $
- applied for aid but withdrew application
- unsuccessful applicant
- did not apply
- ◆ Warsaw Pact 1955–1991
- ◈ members of North Atlantic Treaty Organisation (NATO) 1949 (date of entry given for countries that joined after 1949)

The polarization of Eastern and Western Europe

Jan 19 1948: Soviet-sponsored Communist "Lublin Committee" monopolizes power in Poland

Jun 5 1948: US Secretary of State announces Marshall Plan

1949: Foundation of the Council for Mutual Economic Assistance (COMECON), an economic association for Communist countries

Apr 4 1949: North Atlantic Treaty signed in Washington

Oct 6 1949: US President Truman signs Mutual Defense Assistance Act

1948 | 1949 | 1950

UK receives nearly 25% of the programme's allocation of $12.5 billion

NORWAY $236 million
SWEDEN $107 million
FINLAND
IRELAND $148 million
UNITED KINGDOM $3190 million
DENMARK $273 million
North Sea
Baltic Sea
NETHERLANDS $1084 million
BELGIUM
WEST GERMANY $1391 million 1955
EAST GERMANY
POLAND
U S S R
Luxembourg and Belgium together receive $546 million
LUXEMBOURG
Foreign minister Georges Bidault canvasses European support of the Marshall Plan despite opposition from the nation's Communist Party
FRANCE $2714 million
SWITZERLAND
AUSTRIA $678 million
CZECHOSLOVAKIA
HUNGARY
ROMANIA
PORTUGAL $51 million
SPAIN 1982
ITALY $1509 million
YUGOSLAVIA
Black Sea
Corsica
Sardinia
Balearic Islands
US already supplying aid towards reconstruction of Italy before implementation of Marshall Plan
ALBANIA until 1968
BULGARIA
GREECE $707 million 1952
TURKEY $225 million 1952
Sicily
Crete
Mediterranean Sea

500 km
500 miles

MODERN EUROPE

BETWEEN 1948 AND 1989, the ideological divide between Communist Eastern Europe and the West stood firm. Divisions within Europe were compounded by economic growth in the West and stagnation in the East. In November 1989, the fall of the Berlin Wall signalled the end of the Cold War, and a rise of nationalism in Eastern Europe brought about the collapse of Communism and the Soviet bloc. A range of newly-independent states moved toward free elections, but political freedom had other consequences. In 1991, historical ethnic tension fractured Yugoslavia. Conflict escalated into war in Bosnia in 1992, and atrocities in the Serbian province of Kosovo prompted NATO intervention in 1999. In 2004 both NATO and the EU accepted new members from Central and Eastern Europe.

In January 1999, the Euro was formally adopted as currency of the European Union.

The European Union

The European Economic Community (EEC) was established in 1957 to guarantee the economic success of its members, and to develop a union of states in an attempt to lessen the risk of another war. The success of the EEC's liberalized trade policies encouraged further integration. In December 1991, the Maastricht Treaty created the European Union (EU) and expanded the focus of the community to issues such as justice, citizens' rights, security, and the environment. From an initial six members in 1957, the EU now has 25, twelve of which have adopted the European single currency, the Euro. The EU aims to produce a constitution to help define and reaffirm its role.

The flags of the ten new members the European Union are unfurled, ready to be hoisted to join those of the 15 existing members at a ceremony in Brussels on May 1, 2004.

▲ ❶ The growth of the European Union

- members of European Coal and Steel Community (ECSC), European Atomic Energy Community (EAEC) and European Economic Community (EEC) 1957
- EU original members 1957
- EU members by 1973
- EU members by 1986
- EU members by 1995
- EU members by 2004
- applicants to EU (with date of application)
- members of Council for Mutual Economic Assistance (COMECON) 1949
- € countries using the EURO
- ⊕ members of NATO

The disintegration of the Communist bloc

By the 1970s it became clear that Communist economic policies were failing the nations of Eastern Europe. Economic instability throughout the 1970s and 1980s brought much of the Eastern bloc to the point of bankruptcy. The Soviet leader, Gorbachev, abandoned the satellite states in an effort to save the economy of the USSR. Beginning with protests in East Germany in 1989 which brought down the Communist government, nation after nation asserted their independence in a series of massive popular demonstrations which swiftly ended more than 50 years of Soviet control in Eastern Europe.

The decline of the Russian economy from 1990 forced many people to work within the "informal economy" for income. This street vendor is selling toys from a makeshift stall.

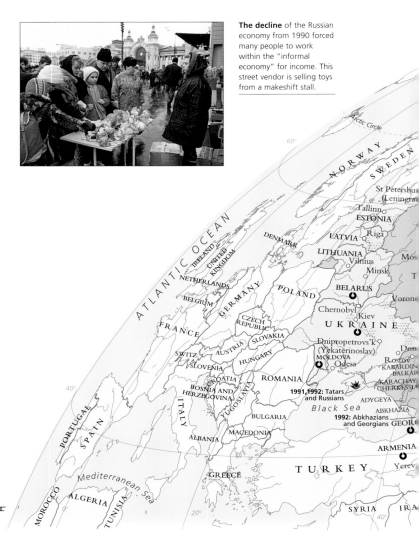

▲ ❷ The collapse of Communism in Eastern Europe

- Soviet Union to 1991
- Soviet-dominated Eastern Europe to 1989
- German Democratic Republic (GDR), united with Federal Republic of Germany 1990
- Czechoslovakia to Dec 1992
- Yugoslavia to 1991
- other Communist state before 1991
- 1990 date of first free election

In November 1989, these peaceful demonstrators in Prague united with other cities across Czechoslovakia in their protest against Communist rule to bring about the so-called "Velvet Revolution."

The rise of nationalism

The wave of nationalism which began in the German Democratic Republic was repeated throughout Eastern Europe. The reunification of Germany in 1990 was followed by the collapse of the USSR and its division into 15 independent states. In 1993, Czechoslovakia split into two new republics: Slovakia and the Czech Republic. New governments were forced to implement strict economic measures to stem decline, and moderate socialism replaced Communism as the main political force in Eastern Europe. Nationalism continued to create tension in the Balkans, where internal ethnic conflict eventually led to the break-up of the state of Yugoslavia.

Conflict in Yugoslavia from 1991

Following the death of Communist premier Josip Broz (Tito) in 1980, the fragility of the multinational Federal People's Republic of Yugoslavia quickly became apparent. The election of Serbian leader Slobodan Milošević in 1987 brought an upsurge of Serb nationalism which struck fear in the multi-ethnic republics. In 1991, the provinces of Slovenia, Croatia and Bosnia declared their independence. Serbian forces attacked both republics in an effort to compel their return to the federation. In January 1992, Serbs in Bosnia and Herzegovina began the persecution, or "ethnic cleansing," of Bosnia's Muslims. Bitter fighting between Serbs, Muslims, and Croats ensued, until foreign intervention brought the war to an end in 1995. In 1999, the persecution of ethnic Albanians in Kosovo provoked military intervention by NATO. The state of "Yugoslavia" officially ceased to exist in 2003.

Bosnian Muslim refugees take up temporary residence on a basketball court as they flee Serbian forces at the height of the "ethnic cleansing" campaign in 1993.

❸ Conflict in former Yugoslavia 1990–99

The ethnic composition of Yugoslavia, 1991
- Albanian
- Bulgarian
- Croat
- Hungarian
- Macedonian
- Muslim
- Romanian
- Serb and Montenegrin
- Slovene
- Yugoslav regions

(Nov 1992) date of secession from Federal Republic of Yugoslavia

The Croatian conflict
- Serb advances by Dec 1991
- Serb-controlled regions 1991–95/96
- Croat advances, autumn 1995

The Bosnian War
- secured by Yugoslav army and Bosnian Serb forces by Dec 1992
- area controlled by Bosnian Croat forces, Dec 1992
- attacking Serbs 1993
- attacking Bosnian Muslims 1993
- Autonomous Province of Western Bosnia Sep 1993–Aug 1994
- area remaining under control of breakaway Serbian forces, Oct 1995
- areas of combat between Croats and Bosnian Muslims
- Muslim secure zone

The Kosovan crisis
- Kosovo Liberation Army (KLA) stronghold
- Serb forces attacking KLA, 1999

The collapse of the Soviet Union

From 1985, Mikhail Gorbachev, leader of the Soviet Union, launched a series of political and economic reforms under the banner of *perestroika* (restructuring). The Supreme Soviet Council was replaced with a Congress of People's deputies and a parliament was elected in 1989. Russian president Boris Yeltsin quashed an attempted coup by hard-line Communists in 1991, which accelerated the end of the USSR. Russia and 14 other Soviet republics became independent in 1991, although 12 of them maintained a loose federation as the CIS (Commonwealth of Independent States). Russia and other states, such as Georgia, are beset by problems with separatist movements. There has been a bitter conflict between Russia and Chechnya since 1991.

War and ethnic tension in Yugoslavia from 1980

- **1980:** Death of Tito
- **1987:** Slobodan Milošević rises to power in Yugoslavia
- **1989:** Milošević strips Kosovo of autonomy it has enjoyed since 1974; tension between Serbs and ethnic Albanians escalates
- **1991:** Croatia, Slovenia, and Bosnia declare independence from Yugoslavia
- **1992:** All out war in Bosnia
- **1995:** Peace agreement ends the Bosnian war
- **1998:** Milošević sends troops into areas controlled by Kosovo Liberation Army (KLA)
- **1999:** Peace talks collapse; NATO begins bombing campaign
- **2000:** Milošević surrenders power
- **2001:** Milošević extradited to The Hague to stand trial for war crimes
- **2003:** Rump state of Yugoslavia renamed Serbia and Montenegro

Scale varies with perspective

5560 km (3450 miles)

12,320 km (7660 miles)

❹ The legacy of the Soviet Union
- territory controlled by USSR in 1945
- Russian federation from 1991
- autonomous regions
- major concentration of minority Russians
- Commonwealth of Independent States 1991
- interstate conflict
- civil war
- ethnic conflict (with date)
- Islamic separatist attack
- autonomous district

1994: Chechen declaration of independence provokes war with Russia

1989: Kazakhs and Lezgians

1989–90: Uzbeks and Meskhetians

1990: Kirghiz and Uzbeks

1989: Kirghiz and Tajiks

1988: Armenians and Azerbaijanis

The decline of Soviet influence

- **1985:** Gorbachev initiates *perestroika* and *glasnost*
- **1987:** Washington arms control treaty decommissions one-fifth of Soviet arms
- **1989:** Anti-Communist protests across Eastern Europe
- **1990:** Germany reunified
- **1990–91:** Baltic republics declare independence
- **1991:** Unsuccessful coup attempt in USSR; disintegration of Soviet Union
- **1992:** Civil war in Georgia
- **1993:** Czech Republic and Slovakia become separate states
- **1994:** Russian troops march on Chechnya
- **1996:** Peace accord in Chechnya
- **1999:** New Russian offensive in Chechnya. Separatist violence in Dagestan
- **2000:** Russia starts to withdraw troops from Georgia
- **2002:** Chechen fighters occupy Moscow theatre
- **2004:** Chechen rebels occupy school in Beslan, N Ossetia; over 350 killed
- **2004:** Chechen president assassinated

WEST ASIA
REGIONAL HISTORY

THE HISTORICAL LANDSCAPE

A SEEMINGLY INHOSPITABLE REALM, arid, largely desert or mountainous plateau, West Asia lays claim to a panoply of grand names – the Garden of Eden, the Fertile Crescent, the Promised Land, the Cradle of Civilization, the Crossroads of History. Lying at the meeting point of the three Old World continents - Africa, Europe, and Asia - the region was blessed with the fertile soils, beneficent climate, and diverse demography to earn these titles. As such it remained a pivotal point of Old World, or Afro-Eurasian, urbanization, culture, communications, trade, and – inevitably – warfare, until relatively recent times. In addition, possibly as a consequence of these factors, the region was also the birthplace of Judaism, Christianity, and Islam, which became three of the most widely observed world religions. Despite the attentions of European colonial powers, West Asia has upheld its inherent qualities and traditions; rivalries and divisions persist alongside ways of life and artistic traditions now centuries old, a cultural longevity sustained by religion on the one hand and, in the 20th century, by the region's control of the world's most valuable commodity – oil.

West Asia, apart from its fertile riverine lowlands, is a combination of dry sandy deserts and mountainous plateaus that remain sparsely populated, or totally uninhabited even today.

The mountainous Iranian Plateau is cut off from the moist ocean air, and temperatures fluctuate greatly between winter and summer and night and day. Humans lived in the mountain fringes, but did not settle in the plateau's interior because of the cold, dry climate.

The banks of the Euphrates and Tigris rivers were where the world's first towns and cities were established.

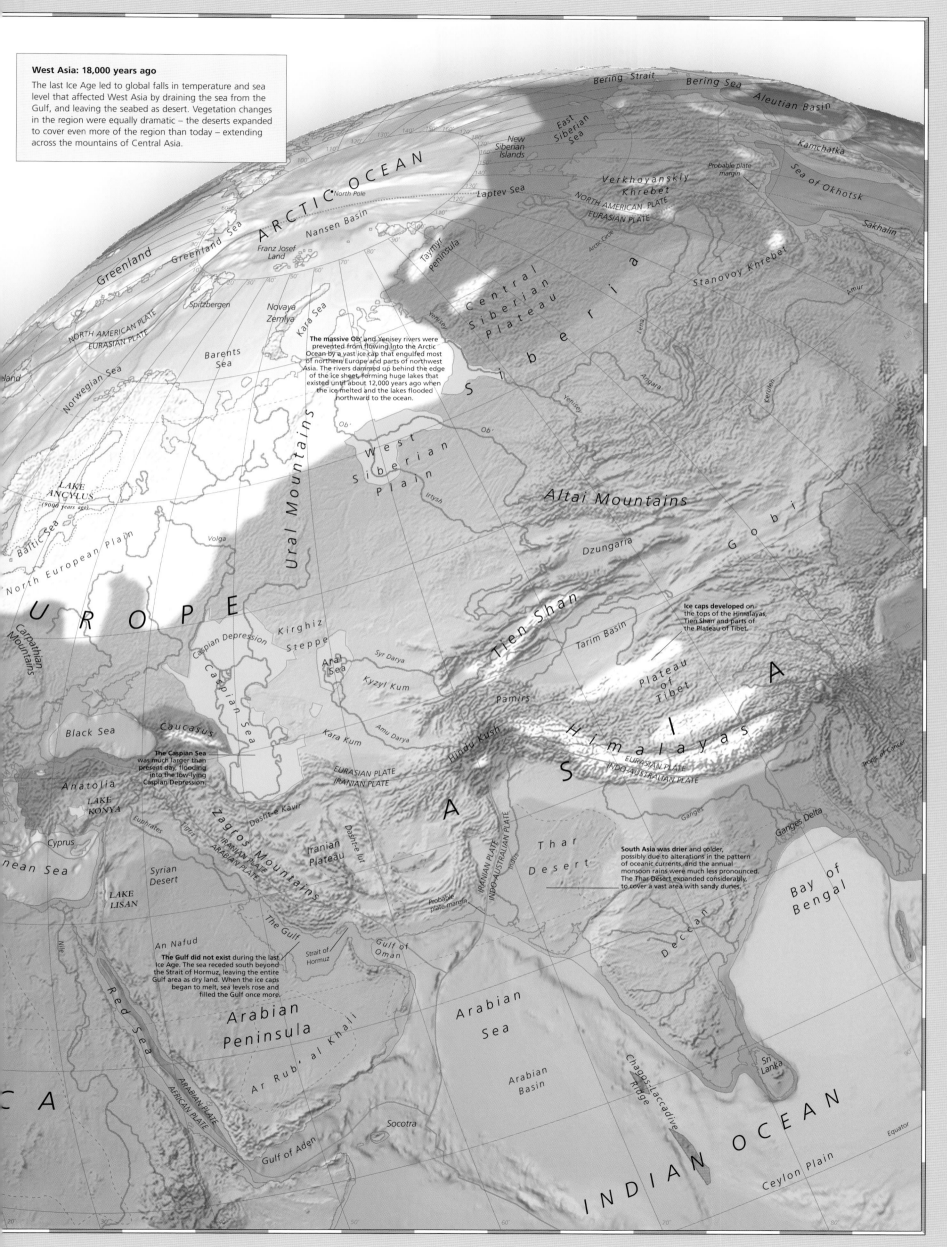

West Asia: 18,000 years ago

The last Ice Age led to global falls in temperature and sea level that affected West Asia by draining the sea from the Gulf, and leaving the seabed as desert. Vegetation changes in the region were equally dramatic – the deserts expanded to cover even more of the region than today – extending across the mountains of Central Asia.

The massive Ob' and Yenisey rivers were prevented from flowing into the Arctic Ocean by a vast ice cap that engulfed most of northern Europe and parts of northwest Asia. The rivers dammed up behind the edge of the ice sheet, forming huge lakes that existed until about 12,000 years ago when the ice melted and the lakes flooded northward to the ocean.

Ice caps developed on the tops of the Himalayas, Tien Shan and parts of the Plateau of Tibet.

The Caspian Sea was much larger than present day, flooding into the low-lying Caspian Depression.

South Asia was drier and colder, possibly due to alterations in the pattern of oceanic currents, and the annual monsoon rains were much less pronounced. The Thar Desert expanded considerably, to cover a vast area with sandy dunes.

The Gulf did not exist during the last Ice Age. The sea receded south beyond the Strait of Hormuz, leaving the entire Gulf area as dry land. When the ice caps began to melt, sea levels rose and filled the Gulf once more.

ARCTIC OCEAN

Bering Strait
Bering Sea
Aleutian Basin
Kamchatka
Sea of Okhotsk
Sakhalin
East Siberian Sea
Laptev Sea
New Siberian Islands
Verkhoyanskiy Khrebet
NORTH AMERICAN PLATE
EURASIAN PLATE
Stanovoy Khrebet
Amur
Probable plate margin
North Pole
Nansen Basin
Taymyr Peninsula
Central Siberian Plateau
Siberia
Franz Josef Land
Greenland
Greenland Sea
Spitzbergen
Novaya Zemlya
Kara Sea
Ob'
Yenisey
Angara
Lena
Kerulkh
Arctic Circle
Barents Sea
Norwegian Sea
West Siberian Plain
Altai Mountains
Gobi
Ural Mountains
Irtysh
Dzungaria
LAKE ANCYLUS (9000 years ago)
Baltic Sea
Volga
North European Plain
Kirghiz Steppe
Aral Sea
Syr Darya
Tien Shan
Tarim Basin
Plateau of Tibet
ASIA
EUROPE
Carpathian Mountains
Caspian Depression
Caspian Sea
Kyzyl Kum
Pamirs
Black Sea
Caucasus
Kara Kum
Amu Darya
Hindu Kush
Himalayas
EURASIAN PLATE
INDO-AUSTRALIAN PLATE
Ganges
Ganges Delta
Anatolia
LAKE KONYA
Cyprus
Euphrates
Tigris
Zagros Mountains
IRANIAN PLATE
ARABIAN PLATE
Dasht-e Kavir
Iranian Plateau
Dasht-e Lut
EURASIAN PLATE
IRANIAN PLATE
IRANIAN PLATE
INDO-AUSTRALIAN PLATE
Indus
Thar Desert
Bay of Bengal
nean Sea
Syrian Desert
LAKE LISAN
Nile
An Nafud
The Gulf
Strait of Hormuz
Gulf of Oman
Probable plate margin
Deccan
Red Sea
Arabian Peninsula
Ar Rub' al Khali
Arabian Sea
Arabian Basin
Chagos-Laccadive Ridge
Sri Lanka
CA
ARABIAN PLATE
AFRICAN PLATE
Socotra
Gulf of Aden
Ceylon Plain
INDIAN OCEAN
Equator

WEST ASIA

EXPLORATION AND MAPPING

Invented by the Greeks, the astrolabe was developed by the Arabs into an indispensable tool of navigation.

SINCE THE EMERGENCE of city–states and trade, West Asia has formed the crossroads between Europe, Africa, and Asia. The Sumerians and Babylonians accumulated local geographical knowledge, but it was the Greeks, following the conquests of Alexander the Great, who began a systematic recording of the region's geography. The Romans built on the knowledge of the Greeks, as did the Arabs when, in the 7th century, Islam spread throughout West Asia. In the 13th century, when the Mongols controlled Central Asia, traffic between China and the West flourished, leaving the way open for the great journeys of Marco Polo and William of Rubruck. The region least well-known to outsiders, though its geography was well understood by its desert tribes, was Arabia, finally mapped in the 19th and 20th centuries.

Islamic travelers

Within a century of the death of Muhammad in 632, the Muslim world stretched from the Iberian Peninsula to the borders of Tang China. Building on knowledge acquired by earlier civilizations, in particular the Greeks, and incorporating information gathered by merchants, sailors, and other travelers, Arab geographers were able to create maps of the vast Islamic realms. By the 12th century they had an excellent understanding of West Asia, Europe, and North Africa. In 1325 Ibn Battuta *(see p.68)* began the first of the great journeys which were to take him to all corners of the Islamic world.

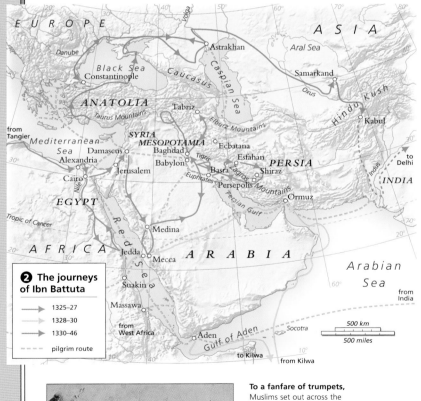

②The journeys of Ibn Battuta

- 1325–27
- 1328–30
- 1330–46
- pilgrim route

To a fanfare of trumpets, Muslims set out across the Arabian desert to make their pilgrimage to Mecca.

The Moroccan al-Idrisi was one of the most famous geographers of his day. The map shown here is a facsimile of the West Asian section of the beautiful world map he produced for Roger of Sicily c.1154. South is at the top, so the Mediterranean is on the right.

The Greco-Roman view

Many merchants from Greek colonies in Asia Minor traded eastward to the Caspian Sea. Then, in the 4th century BCE, Alexander the Great led his army into West Asia, accompanied by a team of surveyors who recorded the route. Though none survive today, these records were a major source for subsequent geographers. Extending his quest for knowledge to the ocean, Alexander sent his admiral, Nearchus, to explore a route from the Indus to the Persian Gulf. The Greek merchant Hippalus was the first European sailor to recognize the regularity of the monsoon winds, harnessing them for his voyage to India. Arabia remained largely unknown, despite an exploratory expedition led by the Roman general Aelius Gallus.

This reconstructed map shows the world known to the Greeks in 5th century BCE. It is based on descriptions in the *History* of Herodotus, who traveled in Europe, Egypt, and West Asia, and gathered additional information from people he met en route.

Greek and Roman journeys to West Asia

c.410: Xenophon leads army of 10,000 Greek mercenaries from Babylon to Black Sea	334–323: Alexander the Great extends his empire from Mediterranean to Himalayas	120: Eudoxus first Greek to reach India from Egypt	63: Birth of Strabo, author of a famous *Geography*	14–37 CE: Hippalus sails through Red Sea to the Indus	

500 BCE — 400 BCE — 300 BCE — 200 BCE — 100 BCE — 1 CE — 100 CE — 200 CE

6th century: Scylax reaches Indus, returning via Red Sea	325: Nearchus sails from the Indus to the Persian Gulf	c.146: Eudoxus sails from Black Sea to West Africa	25–24: Aelius Gallus explores western Arabia
			c.150: Ptolemy of Alexandria writes his *Geography*

①Greek and Roman expeditions

- Alexander the Great 334–323 BCE
- Nearchus 326–325 BCE
- Aelius Gallus 25–24 BCE
- Hippalus 14–37 CE
- main trade route
- Persian Royal Road
- ✕ battle

25–24 BCE: Aelius Gallus, Prefect of Egypt, leads an expedition into the Arabian desert

325–324 BCE: Alexander commissions his admiral, Nearchus, to explore the coast from the Indus to the Head of the Persian Gulf

14–37 CE: During his voyage to India, Greek merchant Hippalus is the first westerner to recognize the regularity of the monsoon winds; this knowledge transformed trade routes from Egypt to the East

Medieval and Renaissance travelers from Europe

In the late 13th century, in the lull following the first Mongol invasions, Europeans began to venture east across Asia. Both William of Rubruck's mission to the Mongol Khan for Louis IX of France and Marco Polo's epic journeys yielded a wealth of geographical information. But with the rise to power of the Ottoman Turks, Central Asia's trade routes were once more closed to Europeans. Later explorers such as Sir Robert Sherley focused their attention on Persia, sworn enemy of the Turks.

European pilgrims visit the Holy Sepulchre in Jerusalem in this illustration from an illuminated manuscript of the travels of Marco Polo.

Juan de la Cosa's early 16th-century world map demonstrates how little Europeans of the period knew of West Asia to the east of the Holy Land. Inland from the Mediterranean coast, the cartographer compensated for lack of detail with an attractive illustration of the Three Kings on their journey to Bethlehem.

3 Medieval and Renaissance travelers

William of Rubruck 1253–55
possible route of Marco Polo 1271–95
Anthony Jenkinson 1557–64
John Newbery 1581–82
Robert Sherley 1598–1600
Thomas Herbert 1627–29

500 km
500 miles

MAPS FOR PILGRIMS

The Holy Land has possibly been the subject of more maps than any other part of the world. To medieval Christians, the holy city of Jerusalem was the center of their world, a concept depicted by many medieval maps which show a circular walled city, instead of a rectangular one, to symbolize the perfection of the Heavenly Jerusalem. Pilgrims and crusaders traveling to the Holy Land carried with them maps which were little more than illustrated itineraries of the towns they would pass through on their journey through Europe.

A 13th-century French map depicts the walled city of Jerusalem schematically, showing just the city's most important features, including the Holy Sepulchre and the Tower of David. Below, a crusader puts mounted Saracens to flight.

European travelers in West Asia 1200–1700

1502: Italian Lodovico di Varthema visits Arabia disguised as an Arab
1581–82: Newbery visits Mesopotamia and Persia
1598: Anthony and Robert Sherley travel to Persia, where they meet Shah Abbas

1200 | 1300 | 1400 | 1500 | 1600 | 1700

1253–55: William of Rubruck crosses Asia to Karakorum
1271–95: Marco Polo travels throughout Asia, returning by ship through Persian Gulf
1487–89: Portuguese Pero de Covilhã sails through Red Sea to India
1557–64: Jenkinson travels through Russia to Caspian Sea
1627: Herbert's travels in Persia

European travelers in Arabia

Although crisscrossed by Muslim pilgrim routes, maps of the interior of Arabia were rare until the 19th century. The region's hostile terrain and reputation for religious fanaticism remained considerable barriers to exploration by Europeans, despite the peninsula's wealth of valuable raw materials. Those that successfully penetrated Arabia did so armed with fluent Arabic and disguised as Muslims, particularly those who entered Islam's holy cities. The 19th century brought a rush of European explorers, especially the British, to Arabia. The last area to be explored was the Rub' al Khali (Empty Quarter), crossed first by Bertram Thomas in 1930–31 and explored more thoroughly by Wilfred Thesiger. The most detailed maps of the peninsula were made from the late 1920s following surveys by oil companies.

Europeans in the Arabian Peninsula 1800–1950

1812: Burckhardt discovers Petra, ancient capital of Nabataea
1853: Richard Burton visits Mecca and Medina in Arab disguise
1864: Guarmani travels through northern Nejd
1879: Wilfrid Scawen Blunt and his wife, Anne, travel to Nejd to buy horses
1930: Thomas first European to cross Empty Quarter
1946–48: Thesiger's double crossing of Empty Quarter

1800 | 1850 | 1900 | 1950

1814: Burckhardt visits Mecca
1818: Sadleir makes first east-west crossing
1862–63: Palgrave makes first west-east crossing through the Nafud
1876–78: Doughty's Arabian journeys
1888: Publication of Doughty's classic *Travels in Arabia Deserta*
1932: Philby crosses Empty Quarter

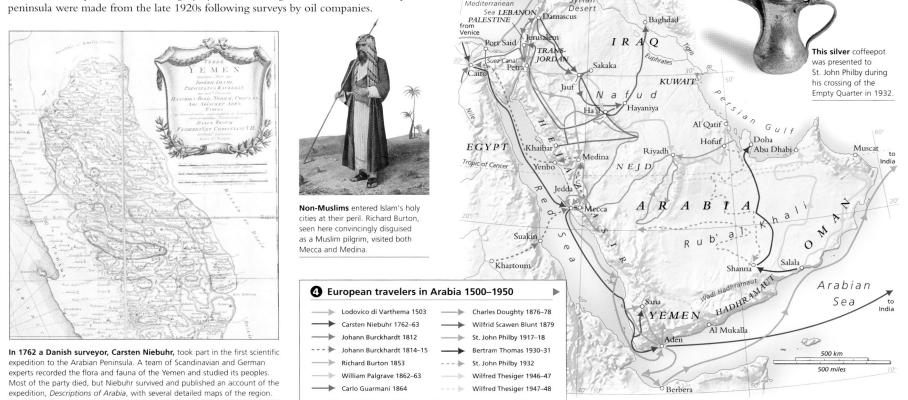

This silver coffeepot was presented to St. John Philby during his crossing of the Empty Quarter in 1932.

In 1762 a Danish surveyor, Carsten Niebuhr, took part in the first scientific expedition to the Arabian Peninsula. A team of Scandinavian and German experts recorded the flora and fauna of the Yemen and studied its peoples. Most of the party died, but Niebuhr survived and published an account of the expedition, *Descriptions of Arabia*, with several detailed maps of the region.

Non-Muslims entered Islam's holy cities at their peril. Richard Burton, seen here convincingly disguised as a Muslim pilgrim, visited both Mecca and Medina.

4 European travelers in Arabia 1500–1950

Lodovico di Varthema 1503
Carsten Niebuhr 1762–63
Johann Burckhardt 1812
Johann Burckhardt 1814–15
Richard Burton 1853
William Palgrave 1862–63
Carlo Guarmani 1864
Charles Doughty 1876–78
Wilfrid Scawen Blunt 1879
St. John Philby 1917–18
Bertram Thomas 1930–31
St. John Philby 1932
Wilfred Thesiger 1946–47
Wilfred Thesiger 1947–48

500 km
500 miles

FROM VILLAGE TO EMPIRE

This inlaid chlorite vessel is decorated with a cat fighting a serpent Made in southern Persia, it was found at Nippur in Mesopotamia.

THE "FERTILE CRESCENT" extends from the Persian Gulf along the flanks of the Zagros Mountains, then swings west across northern Mesopotamia and down the Mediterranean coast to Egypt. It was in this region that the first farming settlements were established, expanding into fortified walled towns. By 3500 BCE the first city-states, centres of production and trade *(see pp. 24–25)*, had grown up in Mesopotamia. In 2300 BCE, a number of these were united by Sargon of Akkad to form the first empire. Other empires followed: the empire of Ur, the first Assyrian Empire, the first Babylonian Empire. In the 2nd millennium BCE, a new center of power developed in Anatolia: the Hittite Empire, which battled with Egypt for control of the region.

The development of agriculture in the Fertile Crescent

Bounded by mountains to the north and east and desert to the south, the Fertile Crescent is relatively well-watered. Wild grains, such as einkorn wheat and barley, grew on the moist mountain uplands, also home to the ancestors of domestic sheep and goats. By 10,000 BCE, this combination of resources enabled local groups to establish the first settled agricultural communities; cereals were cultivated and stored, and animals domesticated.

Larger settlements, such as Jericho (8000 BCE) in the Jordan valley and Çatal Hüyük (7000 BCE) in Anatolia, became regional centers, surrounded by cultivable land and showing evidence of crafts and long-distance trade.

A number of skulls, with features modeled in gypsum and cowrie shells for eyes, were found beneath the floors of houses at Jericho.

The wall of a shrine at Çatal Hüyük was decorated with this painting of a stag's head, seen here in an artist's reconstruction. One of the oldest towns in the world, Çatal Hüyük had tightly-packed houses built of mud bricks with flat roofs.

❶ Early farming in southwest Asia 8000–5000 BCE ▷

Vegetation
- floodplain
- Mediterranean forest
- forest
- steppe
- semi-desert
- desert
- more than 250 mm mean annual rainfall

Areas of domestication of principal staple crops
- barley
- einkorn wheat
- emmer wheat
- present-day coastline/river
- ○ site of major farming settlement

The first cities of West Asia

Farmers from northern and central Mesopotamia began to settle the alluvial plain of the Tigris and Euphrates around 6000 BCE. Irrigation enabled enough food to be produced to support large settled communities. In time, some settlements developed into cities. Each had at its heart a mud-brick temple raised on a high platform. These structures later became ziggurats like the one at Ur *(see pp. 24–25)*, one of the great Sumerian cities of the 3rd millennium BCE. While sharing a common culture, each city remained an independent city-state.

After 3500: Development of first urban civilization at Sumer; rise of Uruk — 3100: Cuneiform script emerges in Mesopotamia — 2700: Gilgamesh rules Sumerian city of Uruk — 2500: "Royal Graves" of Ur

| 3500 BCE | 3300 | 3100 | 2900 | 2700 | 2500 BCE |

3250: Pictographic clay tablets used for temple accounts — 3200: Evidence of use of wheeled transport in Sumer

The first cities

This Sumerian gaming-board (c.2500 BCE), made of wood and inlaid with shell, bone, and lapis lazuli, was found in the "Royal Graves" at Ur. Players cast dice or threw sticks before moving their counters, which were kept in a drawer set into the board.

The growth of Uruk

From 4000 BCE, Uruk expanded into one of the leading Sumerian cities. Its closely-packed mud-brick houses were enclosed by a 6 mile wall. Beyond the wall, crops such as barley, sesame, and onions grew in fields irrigated by a network of canals from the Euphrates. Two ceremonial complexes dominated the city; the Anu ziggurat and the Sanctuary of Eanna. The latter contained a columned hall 100 ft wide, the columns decorated with mosaics of colored stone cones set in mud plaster. Many of the works of art found at Uruk, Ur, and other Sumerian cities used materials such as alabaster, gemstones, and lapis lazuli, from as far afield as Central Asia and the Indus Valley.

❷ The first cities c.4300–2300 BCE
- fertile zone
- ziggurat or temple
- ○ city or important site
- irrigation and ancient water course
- present-day coastline/river
- trade route

❸ Uruk
- built before 2500 BCE
- built between 2500–500 BCE
- built after 500 BCE
- remaining ruins of city wall
- original city wall
- road

The first empires of West Asia

Around 2300 BCE, an Akkadian official seized power at Kish, and, as Sargon I, founded a new capital, Agade, and a new Akkadian dynasty. From Agade, Sargon embarked on a series of remarkable military campaigns; he conquered Elam, parts of Syria and Anatolia, and united the independent city-states of southern Mesopotamia to form the world's first empire. Sargon's empire collapsed under the impact of internal conflict and invasion by the Gutians. After a period of revival of the Sumerian city-state system, Ur emerged as the dominant power in the region. It too was overthrown c.2004 BCE, to be replaced early in the 2nd millennium by the Babylonian Empire founded by Hammurabi.

This bronze head probably represents King Sargon of Akkad. Known as "ruler of the four quarters of the world." In 2300 BCE Sargon founded the first empire.

❹ The first empires c.2300–1750 BCE

- Sumer during Early Dynastic period c.3000–2360
- Empire of Sargon I of Akkad c.2360–2230
- Ur III Empire c.2112–2004
- Kingdom of Shamshi-Adad c.1813–1781
- Babylonian Empire of Hammurabi c.1782–50
- → migration of Semites
- → campaigns of Sargon
- → campaigns of Naram Sin c.2330–2270
- → invasion by Gutians
- --- present-day coastline/river

Migration of Semites to Sumer

c.1775–1760: Palace completed during reign of Zimri-Lim

2150: Gutians conquer Sumer, ruling it until 2050

Unconfirmed site of Sargon's capital Agade (2371–2230); sacked by Gutians

Ur-Nammu's capital, where he built the largest ziggurat in Sumer

ELAM conquered by Sargon
Susa Elamite capital

The first empires of West Asia

c.2340: Sargon I founds and rules city of Agade	**2150:** Gutians conquer Sumer, ruling it until 2050	**1950:** Foundation of Assyrian trading colonies in Anatolia, e.g. Kanesh	**c.1763:** Hammurabi of Babylon conquers all of Sumer

2350 BCE — 2250 — 2150 — 2050 — 1950 — 1850 — 1750 BCE

2300: Sargon of Akkad unites city-states of southern Mesopotamia	**2111:** Ur-Nammu founds Third Dynasty of Ur	**c.2000:** Ur destroyed by Elam	**c.1750:** Hammurabi writes his Code of Laws, the first in world history

The Hittite Empire c.1650–1200 BCE

The Hittites were the major Anatolian power of the 2nd millennium BCE. Establishing their capital at Hattushash, they extended their empire through much of Anatolia and into Syria. In 1595 BCE they captured Babylon, but then retreated, leaving the city to the Kassites. The high point of Hittite rule was achieved under Suppiluliumas who led a successful campaign against the Mitanni, their main rivals in northern Syria, then extended their rule south along the Levantine coast. But Egypt, determined to regain lost territory in Syria, met the Hittites in battle at Kadesh. The battle was inconclusive and a peace treaty was signed by the two nations c.1284 BCE. In c.1200 BCE the Hittite Empire collapsed under invasions from their Anatolian neighbors, the Phrygians.

This small silver bull with gold inlays was found in a grave at Alaca Hüyük, north of Hattushash, the Hittite capital. It was probably the decorative finial of a canopy pole or a ceremonial staff.

The religion of the Hittites was remarkably eclectic; in their texts they refer to the "thousand gods" in their realm. Here, on a relief at the rock sanctuary of Yazilikaya in Anatolia, the Hittite king Tudhaliyas IV is held in the protective embrace of the god Sharruma.

❺ Southwest Asia 1650–1200 BCE

- Hittite heartland
- Hittite sphere of influence
- Mitannian heartland
- Mitannian sphere of influence
- Egyptian state
- Egyptian sphere of influence
- Babylonia
- Babylonian sphere of influence
- region disputed between Egyptians and Hittites
- → Hittite campaign
- → Egyptian campaign
- → invasion of "Sea Peoples"

1350: destroyed by Hittites

c.1275: Border agreed between Egyptians and Hittites

1595: Babylon conquered by Hittites

Power struggles in West Asia, 1650–1200 BCE

1600: Kassites conquer most of Mesopotamia	**1500:** Egyptians, Hittites, and Mitannians compete for control of Levantine city-states	**1200:** Widespread disruption owing to raids by the "Sea Peoples," Hittite Empire collapses
	1595: Hittites sack Babylon	

1700 BCE — 1600 — 1500 — 1400 — 1300 — 1200 BCE

1650: City-states of Central Anatolia united to form Hittite kingdom	**c.1375:** Accession of Suppiluliumas	**c.1285:** Hittites meet the Egyptians in battle at Kadesh

221

EARLY EMPIRES OF WEST ASIA

The Ishtar Gate, the entrance to the great city of Babylon, was built by King Nebuchadnezzar II.

THE FIRST MILLENNIUM BCE saw a succession of powerful empires in West Asia. The first, established in the 10th century, was the Assyrian Empire. The Assyrians built their empire on the prowess of their armies and their administrative efficiency. After their overthrow by a Babylonian-Mede coalition in 612 BCE, Babylon became the dominant regional power, until it was overthrown in turn by the Persians. Founded by Cyrus the Great, the Persian Empire expanded to become the largest the world had yet seen, stretching from the Aegean to the Indus. While its empires rose and fell, West Asia was responsible for an invention of lasting value to the wider world. From its early beginnings in Mesopotamia, writing was developed into an alphabet by the Phoenicians, who carried it into the Mediterranean world, where it was adopted by the Greeks.

THE HISTORY AND LEGENDS OF MESOPOTAMIA

Much modern knowledge of the early history of West Asia is based on the libraries of clay tablets found at the palaces of the great rulers of Mesopotamia. The Royal Library of the Assyrian king Ashurbanipal at Nineveh yielded a spectacular find of some 20,000 clay tablets dealing with almost every aspect of life. One of the great literary compositions is the story of Gilgamesh, a legendary Sumerian king, based on an epic that dates back to the early 2nd millennium BCE. There is also an account of the creation, and another of a great deluge that covers the face of the earth with water. There are clear similarities between the account of the flood and the Biblical account of Noah's Flood in Genesis.

Gilgamesh was the legendary king of the Sumerian city-state of Uruk, and the hero of an epic in which he recounts his exploits during his search for immortality.

Israel c.1000–500 BCE

c.1020: Saul becomes first king of the Israelites	c.965: Start of reign of Solomon
c.882: Foundation of kingdom of Israel by Omri	842: Jehu seizes power in Israel, but becomes tributary of Assyria
701: Assyrians invade Judah	597: Nebuchadnezzar captures Jerusalem
538: Jews return from exile	

Timeline: 1000 BCE — 900 — 800 — 700 — 600 — 500 BCE

- c.1006: David succeeds as king of the Israelites
- c.926: Death of Solomon; nation divides into Israel and Judah
- 871–852: Reign of Ahab, who marries Jezebel, princess of Sidon
- 722–21: Israel conquered by Assyrians; becomes an Assyrian province
- 587: Jerusalem and Temple destroyed by Nebuchadnezzar; Jews exiled to Babylon

Israel in the time of David

According to the Bible, when David became king of Israel, he moved the capital from Hebron to Jerusalem, making it the political and religious center of the Israelites. By defeating the Philistines, David extended Israelite rule in the region. Under his successor, Solomon – traditional builder of the Temple at Jerusalem – the nation prospered, but subsequently divided into two kingdoms, Judah and the larger kingdom of Israel under Omri and his son Ahab. In 721 BCE Israel was absorbed into the Assyrian Empire; Judah, having resisted repeated invasions, fell to Nebuchadnezzar of Babylon in 597 BCE. Jerusalem was destroyed and the Jews forced into exile in Babylon for almost 50 years.

This ivory plaque was found at Megiddo, a small but important palace/fortress in northern Israel. It shows that Egyptian influence was still strong in the Levant.

❶ Biblical Palestine at the time of David

- Judah and Israel
- conquered kingdom
- vassal
- boundary of David's empire
- boundary between kingdoms of Judah and Israel from 926

The Assyrian and Babylonian empires

950: Assyrian Empire founded	880: Nimrud becomes capital of Assyria
722: Accession of Sargon II; Israel absorbed into Assyria	689: Babylon destroyed by Assyrian king Sennacherib
612: Assyrian Empire falls; destruction of Nineveh	539: Conquest of Babylonia by Persian king, Cyrus II

Timeline: 1000 BCE — 900 — 800 — 700 — 600 — 500 BCE

- 900: Establishment of Kingdom of Urartu, which lasts till its defeat by Assyrians in 714
- 744: Accession of Tiglath-Pileser III
- 705: Capital of Assyria moves to Nineveh
- 669: Assyrian king Esarhaddon conquers north Egypt
- 605: Nebuchadnezzar II succeeds to throne of Babylon

The Assyrian and Babylonian empires c.950–600 BCE

The first Assyrian Empire was established early in the 2nd millennium BCE, but collapsed under attacks from Babylon and the Mitanni. Under a series of powerful and ruthless kings it was revived, reaching its apogee during the reigns of Tiglath-Pileser III, Sargon II, and Ashurbanipal. Babylon was reconquered, the Kingdom of Urartu defeated, and the empire extended to the Mediterranean, and, briefly, into northern Egypt. These conquests were achieved by a well-equipped, well-disciplined army which made skilful use of cavalry. But in the mid-7th century BCE, attacks by Medes and Scythians, combined with a revolt in Babylonia, sent the empire into a terminal decline. In 625 BCE the Chaldaeans took control of Babylon, and under Nebuchadnezzar II, the Babylonian Empire took over most of the former provinces of Assyria, including Syria and Palestine.

A relief from the Assyrian capital at Nineveh shows Assyrian soldiers using scaling ladders during King Ashurbanipal's siege of an Elamite city.

❷ The Assyrian and Babylonian Empires 950–539 BCE

- under Ashur-dan II (934–912)
- added by death of Shalmaneser III (858–824)
- added by death of Sargon II (745–705)
- added by death of Ashurbanipal (668–626)
- New Babylonian Empire (625–539)
- present-day coastline/river

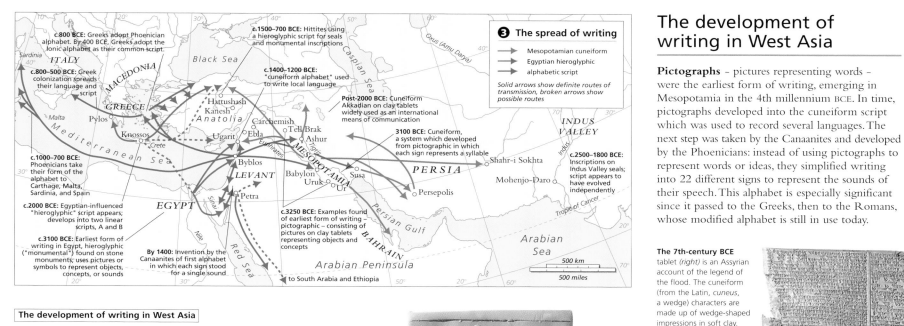

The development of writing in West Asia

c.800 BCE: Greeks adopt Phoenician alphabet. By 400 BCE, Greeks adopt the Ionic alphabet as their common script.

c.800 BCE: Greek colonization spreads their language and script

c.1000–700 BCE: Phoenicians take their form of the alphabet to Carthage, Malta, Sardinia, and Spain

c.2000 BCE: Egyptian-influenced "hieroglyphic" script appears; develops into two linear scripts, A and B

c.3100 BCE: Earliest form of writing in Egypt, hieroglyphic ("monumental") found on stone monuments; uses pictures or symbols to represent objects, concepts, or sounds

c.1500–700 BCE: Hittites using a hieroglyphic script for seals and monumental inscriptions

c.1400–1200 BCE: "cuneiform alphabet" used to write local language

Post-2000 BCE: Cuneiform Akkadian on clay tablets widely used as an international means of communication

3100 BCE: Cuneiform, a system which developed from pictographic in which each sign represents a syllable

c.2500–1800 BCE: Inscriptions on Indus Valley seals; script appears to have evolved independently

c.3250 BCE: Examples found of earliest form of writing – pictographic – consisting of pictures on clay tablets representing objects and concepts

By 1400: Invention by the Canaanites of first alphabet in which each sign stood for a single sound

to South Africa and Ethiopia

❸ The spread of writing
→ Mesopotamian cuneiform
→ Egyptian hieroglyphic
→ alphabetic script
Solid arrows show definite routes of transmission, broken arrows show possible routes

500 km
500 miles

The development of writing in West Asia

Pictographs – pictures representing words – were the earliest form of writing, emerging in Mesopotamia in the 4th millennium BCE. In time, pictographs developed into the cuneiform script which was used to record several languages. The next step was taken by the Canaanites and developed by the Phoenicians: instead of using pictographs to represent words or ideas, they simplified writing into 22 different signs to represent the sounds of their speech. This alphabet is especially significant since it passed to the Greeks, then to the Romans, whose modified alphabet is still in use today.

The 7th-century BCE tablet (right) is an Assyrian account of the legend of the flood. The cuneiform (from the Latin, *cuneus*, a wedge) characters are made up of wedge-shaped impressions in soft clay.

The language on the 5th-century BCE cylinder seal (left) is Aramaic, which used the Phoenician-Hebrew alphabet. Aramaic became the administrative language of the Persian Empire and was thus in use from Anatolia to the Indus.

The development of writing in West Asia

c.3250: First pictographic writing from Tell Brak, Mesopotamia

c.2500: Earliest syllabic script used in Sumerian literature

c.2000: Egyptian-influenced "hieroglyphic" script in Crete; develops into two linear scripts, A and B

c.1000–700: Phoenicians take alphabet to Carthage, Malta, Sardinia, and Spain

c.3100: Cuneiform writing emerges in Mesopotamia; hieroglyphic writing appears on Egyptian stone monuments

c.2500: Indus Valley civilization marks seals with inscriptions

c.1400: Development of first alphabets in Sinai and Levant

c.800: Greeks adopt Phoenician alphabet

3500 BCE — 3000 — 2500 — 2000 — 1500 — 1000 — 500 BCE

The first Persian Empire

Babylonian rule in Mesopotamia was ended by Cyrus the Great. Uniting the Medes and Persians, he founded the Persian Empire, naming it the Achaemenid Empire after an ancestor. Once in power, Cyrus defeated the Lydians, then unseated Nabonidas, King of Babylon. A tolerant ruler and magnanimous victor, Cyrus released the Jews from captivity in Babylon and authorized the rebuilding of the Temple in Jerusalem. Under Darius I ("the Great") and Xerxes I, the empire was extended, organized into 20 provinces ruled by satraps (governors), and a major road network constructed. But both rulers failed in their attempts to conquer Greece. Weakened from without by raiding nomads, and from within by ambitious satraps, the empire was defeated at Issus in 333 by Alexander the Great.

The simple but imposing tomb of Cyrus the Great at Pasargadae, where Cyrus built himself a permanent residence, commemorates an outstanding leader and founder of the Achaemenid Persian Empire.

The first Persian Empire

547–46: Cyrus defeats Croesus, King of the Lydians

530: Cyrus killed in battle against the nomads of Central Asia

521: Darius the Great ruler of Persian Empire

500: Building of the Persian Royal Road

486: Xerxes I becomes ruler of Persian Empire

c.550: Persian Empire established by Cyrus the Great

539: Conquest of Babylon by Cyrus

525: Cambyses II conquers Egypt and advances to Nubia and Libya

513: Darius invades Scythia

490: Persian invasion force defeated by Athenians at Marathon

480: Xerxes brings huge army to Greece, but is defeated at Salamis

545 BCE — 535 — 525 — 515 — 505 — 495 — 485 — 475 BCE

The great palace in Persepolis was begun in 518 BCE by Darius, but built mainly under Xerxes I. The wide staircase leading to the audience hall, or *apadana*, was decorated with carved reliefs of subject peoples bearing tribute.

❹ The Achaemenid Empire c.550–331 BCE
- Persian homeland under Cyrus before 550 BCE
- Kingdom of Medes, annexed 550 BCE
- Kingdom of Lydians, annexed c.547 BCE
- Kingdom of Babylonians, annexed 539 BCE
- Kingdom of Egyptians, annexed 525 BCE
- annexed by Darius I and Xerxes I
- ⋯⋯ Persian Empire at greatest extent
- —— Persian Royal Road
- Persian administrative district (satrapy) ruled by governor
- → major campaigns of Cyrus and Darius I
- ✕ battle with date

Wars with Greece 490–479 BCE
- → Persian campaigns against Greece
- ✕ Greek victory
- ✕ Persian victory
- ✕ indecisive battle
- ⋯⋯ present-day river/coastline

500 km
500 miles

GREEK AND ROMAN EXPANSION

ALEXANDER THE GREAT'S CONQUESTS (see pp.40–41) briefly united a vast tract of West Asia. Subsequently, empires competed and dynasties fell, but a widespread Hellenistic culture survived. In Persia and Mesopotamia, the Seleucids were ousted by the Parthians, who then clashed with an expansionist Rome. By 1 CE, Rome's empire formed a single vast trading area; its West Asian Greek-speaking provinces were the richest of all. A particularly valuable trade was in incense from southern Arabia. Unrest in the Roman Empire was often religious. Rome suppressed two Jewish revolts, provoking a diaspora, but it was a new offshoot of Judaism, Christianity, that spread most effectively through the region (see pp.48–49). In the east, c.226 CE, the Sassanians succeeded the Parthians, establishing a new capital at Ctesiphon.

This opalescent vase of molded glass was produced in Roman Syria in the 1st century CE.

Seleucus I took the largest portion of Alexander's empire. His dynasty lasted until 129 BCE, most of his lands falling to Rome and the Parthians.

Alexander's successors

The death of Alexander was followed by a long struggle for his empire between his generals. With the elimination of three principal contenders – Antigonus at the battle of Ipsus, Lysimachus at Corupedium, Cassander through disease – three great monarchies were established: Macedonia under the Antigonids; Egypt under the Ptolemies; Mesopotamia and Persia under Seleucus I. During the reign of Antiochus III, the greatest of the Seleucids, the Seleucid Empire was extended, but his invasion of Greece in 192 BCE led to conflict with Rome and he was forced to make peace. Thereafter the Seleucid Empire declined.

Parthia and Rome

In about 240 BCE a Scythian people from the steppes of Turkmenistan broke away from Seleucid rule and established the Parthian state. A century later, under Mithridates I, they took Mesopotamia and founded a new capital at Ctesiphon. Roman expansion in the 1st century BCE brought conflict with Parthia; in 53 CE the Parthians defeated them at Carrhae. In the 2nd century CE, a weakened Parthia was invaded by Rome. Finally, 400 years of Parthian rule was ended by Ardashir, the first Sassanian ruler.

The Parthians were renowned for their heavily armored cavalry and the skill of their mounted bowmen.

3 Red Sea trade in the 1st century CE

▭ limit of Roman Empire 117 CE	● major port
⬮ myrrh	→ trade route
⬮ frankincense	

Arabia's Red Sea trade

The aromatic gums frankincense and myrrh were prized commodities in the early civilizations of Egypt and West Asia. Both were widely used to make incense, perfumes, and cosmetics, while myrrh was also used for embalming. Mainly cultivated in southern Arabia, Ethiopia, and the island of Socotra, frankincense and myrrh were carried north by camel caravan to the cities of the eastern Mediterranean. Occupying a key point on this overland route, Petra, capital of the Nabataeans, became a wealthy city. As navigational skills improved and sailors learnt to harness the monsoon winds, frankincense and myrrh were increasingly transported by sea, thus benefiting those Arab states with major ports around the Gulf of Aden, such as Cana, Muza, and Eudaemon Arabia.

Incense consists of a mixture of gums and spices. The fragrant odor of burning incense was associated with religious rites and prayer throughout West Asia and the eastern Mediterranean, hence its great value. It was burned on small stone altars, such as this example from southern Arabia.

Roman Palestine

In 63 BCE Judaea was conquered by Rome, and it was in an atmosphere of anti-Roman protest by Jewish Zealots that Christianity developed in the 1st century CE. In 66 CE, discontent flared into open revolt, suppressed by a force of 60,000 men under Vespasian, and then by his son, Titus, who destroyed and looted the Jewish Temple in Jerusalem. Diehard Zealots took refuge on the rock fortress at Masada and, rather than submit to Rome, committed mass suicide. In 132 CE Bar Cochba led another revolt, which ended with the Roman destruction of Jerusalem.

After Christianity won acceptance under Constantine, many Roman artists turned from secular to sacred themes, such as the biblical scene depicted on this early Christian sarcophagus.

4 Jewish revolts 66–74 CE

—	frontier of Roman Empire and client states 66 CE
	Kingdom of Herod 20 BCE
	Roman province of Judaea
	Kingdom of Agrippa II, 61 CE
	area of major revolt 66 CE
	area of revolt in 69 CE
→	army of Vespasian 67–68 CE
→	army of Titus 70 CE
→	army of Bassus and Silva 71–74 CE
⊚	siege
✗	Jewish victory

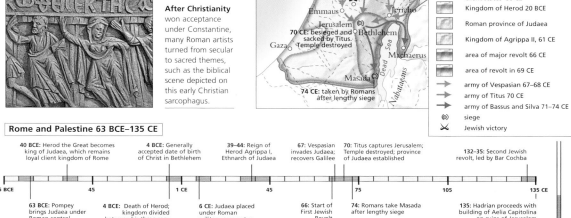

Rome and Palestine 63 BCE–135 CE

40 BCE: Herod the Great becomes king of Judaea, which remains loyal client kingdom of Rome
4 BCE: Generally accepted date of birth of Christ in Bethlehem
39–44: Reign of Herod Agrippa I, Ethnarch of Judaea
67: Vespasian invades Judaea; recovers Galilee
70: Titus captures Jerusalem; Temple destroyed; province of Judaea established
132–35: Second Jewish revolt, led by Bar Cochba

75 BCE — 45 — 1 CE — 45 — 75 — 105 — 135 CE

63 BCE: Pompey brings Judaea under Roman control
4 BCE: Death of Herod; kingdom divided between his three sons
6 CE: Judaea placed under Roman military procurator
66: Start of First Jewish Revolt
74: Romans take Masada after lengthy siege
135: Hadrian proceeds with building of Aelia Capitolina on ruins of Jerusalem

The Jewish diaspora 66–135 CE

The failed revolts of 66 and 132 CE precipitated a diaspora (Greek for "dispersion") of Jews from Palestine. Vast numbers were sold into slavery, became refugees in Galilee, or fled abroad, many to long-established centers in Babylonia and Mesopotamia. Jews were banished from Jerusalem, which was refounded as a Roman city (Aelia Capitolina). By the 2nd century CE Jews may have made up some 5–10% of the population of the Roman Empire; in some eastern cities, perhaps 25%. Remaining loyal to their faith, the exiled Jews continued to regard Judaea as their homeland.

A detail from the triumphal arch of Titus shows the great candlestick (menorah) and other treasures being looted from the Temple at Jerusalem by Roman soldiers.

5 The Jewish world c.150 CE

Areas of Jewish settlement

	dense
	less dense
●	major center of Jewish settlement
→	major trade route

Sassanian Persia

Ardashir I rebelled against the Parthian king, Artabanus V, c.226 CE, and founded the Sassanian Empire. He kept Ctesiphon as his capital and reintroduced Zoroastrianism as the state religion. The empire reached its peak of prosperity under Khosrau I. In the 7th century, his son, Khosrau II, invaded the Byzantine Empire, but was met by a successful counteroffensive. The weakened empire then fell to the Muslim Arabs.

A cameo depicts the capture of the Emperor Valerian by Shapur I, following the great Persian victory against the Romans near Edessa in 259 CE.

Sassanian Persia c.226–642 CE

c.226: Sassanian dynasty founded by Ardashir I
259: Sassanians defeat and capture Roman emperor Valerian
400: Invasion by Hephthalites (White Huns)
531: Accession of Khosrau I
611: Arabs invade Mesopotamia
637: Arabs capture Ctesiphon

200 — 300 — 400 — 500 — 600 — 700

230: Ardashir invades Syria
253: Sassanians defeat Romans and take Antioch
350: Invasion by Kidarites (Huns)
611–626: Persian armies capture Jerusalem and overrun Asia Minor
642: Arabs crush Sassanians at Nehavend

6 Sassanian Persia c.224–642

	Sassanian Empire at greatest extent
	East Roman Empire in 3rd century
	area disputed by Sassanians and East Roman Empire during 6th century
→	Sassanian expedition
→	Arab invasion
→	Hunnish attack
⚔	Sassanian victory over Romans
✗	Arab victory over Sassanians

THE ADVENT OF ISLAM

This gold dinar shows Abd al-Malik, caliph from 685 to 705. He reorganized the army and the Islamic state.

IN 610, IN A CAVE south of Mecca, the Prophet Muhammad received the first of the messages from God which led him to found the Islamic faith. The clear, monotheistic message of Islam appealed to the Arabs, and within 30 years they had carried it to Persia and Palestine. The early Islamic empire was a single political entity, ruled by the caliph, or "successor" of Muhammad *(see pp. 56–57).* By 750 CE, Arab armies had carried Islam west to the Iberian Peninsula and east to Central Asia. The Abbasid Caliphate, with its capital usually at Baghdad, was founded in 750. It was an era of great prosperity, especially in the reign of Harun al-Rashid, but later caliphs lost all political power, ruling in name only over a steadily diminishing Caliphate.

Religions in West Asia c.600

Fine textiles decorated with the Cross and other Christian imagery were woven by Egypt's Copts under Byzantine and Islamic rule.

By 600 CE three major religions were firmly rooted in West Asia: Christianity, Judaism, and Zoroastrianism. Orthodox Christianity was the state religion of the Byzantine Empire; other Christian sects, such as the Nestorians, had strong followings in Mesopotamia and Persia. Jewish communities were scattered throughout the region. The most populous was probably in Babylonia, which was also the leading cultural center of the Jewish world. The Sassanian rulers of Persia tolerated Christians and Jews, although Zoroastrianism was the state religion. The Islamic invasion led to the emigration of many Zoroastrians, mainly to India.

The religions of West Asia c.600

381: Theodosius establishes official religion of Roman Empire	**489:** Nestorian Christians expelled from Egypt and settle in Persia
	c.570: Birth of Muhammad
	636: Byzantine army routed by Muslims on Yarmuk River
	642: Muslims invade Persia; Sassanian Empire falls

313: Constantine ends persecution of Christians — **451:** Council of Chalcedon; Orthodox Church denounces Monophysite sects, such as Copts and Nestorians — **476:** Fall of West Roman Empire; Constantinople center of Christian orthodoxy — **622:** Muhammad's flight to Medina, the Hegira; start of the Islamic era — **633–37:** Muslims conquer Syria and Mesopotamia

THE KORAN

A fragment from a copy of the Koran (c.900) shows the beauty of Arabic calligraphy, regarded as the supreme art in the Islamic world. It is written in Kufic script, with the vowels indicated in red.

The Koran (Qur'an) is the name given to the collected revelations transmitted to the Prophet Muhammad by the Archangel Gabriel, believed by Muslims to be the infallible word of Allah (God). Together, the revelations form the basis of Islam, the authority Muslims consult not only on questions of theological doctrine and ethics, but also on practical legal, political, and social matters. The Koranic revelations were committed to memory by the first disciples of the Prophet, and in 651 CE the first authorized Arabic text was prepared. The Koran is about the length of the New Testament of the Bible, and is divided into 114 *suras* or chapters as revealed to the Prophet at Mecca or Medina.

The spread of Islam

In 622 Muhammad and his followers, faced with hostility in Mecca, fled to Medina. In 630 he returned to Mecca with an army and took the city, thenceforth the religious center of Islam. At his death, he ruled almost half the Arabian Peninsula. His successors, who took the title "caliph" (successor or deputy), continued to spread his message through conquest: Syria, Mesopotamia, Persia, and Egypt were overrun by armies fired by the spirit of *jihad* (holy war). In 661 control of the Caliphate was gained by the Umayyad dynasty, who set up a new political capital at Damascus and extended the empire west to the Atlantic and east to the Indus.

Pilgrims in the ritual costume of two pieces of white cloth gather around the Ka'ba in the Great Mosque at Mecca.

① The religions of West Asia c.600

- area converted to Christianity by 600
- area of Jewish settlement
- area predominantly Zoroastrian
- principal trade routes
- dispersal of Jews to 500 CE

The spread of Islam

632: Death of Muhammad	**637:** Arabs defeat Persians at Al Qadisiya; Jerusalem seized
	642: Conquest of Egypt completed
	656: Murder of 'Uthman; first civil war
	661: Umayyads seize control
	669: Conquest of North Africa extended beyond Tripoli to the west

634: 'Umar appointed caliph — **636:** Rout of Byzantines on Yarmuk river — **644:** Death of 'Umar; 'Uthman appointed caliph — **656:** Ali, son-in-law of Muhammad, attempts to gain control of caliphate

The Hegira *(hijra)*

Muhammad's flight from Mecca to Medina in 622 marks the start of the Islamic calendar. It was from Medina that Muhammad started to preach with success and spread the message of Islam. In recognition of this, the city's name was changed from Yathrib to Medina (the City), and it became the first political capital of the Islamic world. Mecca, however, had long been a holy city among the pagan tribes of the Arabian Peninsula and an important place of pilgrimage. Since it was also the birthplace of Muhammad and the site of his first revelations, it became the holiest city of Islam.

627: Army of 10,000 from Mecca; defeated by Muhammad and his followers

632: Death of Muhammad

624: Muhammad and 300 followers defeat 1000 Quraysh warriors

622: Muhammad journeys to Yathrib; journey known as the Hegira (or *hijra* – the flight)

570: Birth of Muhammad

② The Hegira 622

- road
- route of Hegira

③ The diffusion of Islam to 661

- residence of the Caliph
- diffusion of Islam with date

④ The Abbasid Caliphate c.850

- Abbasid Caliphate at greatest extent 786–809
- other Muslim dynasties
- Islamic expansion 750–850
- Byzantine Empire
- → Saffarid incursions
- → Abbasid campaigns
- → Qarmatian expansion
- → Islamic naval attacks

⑤ The inner city of Baghdad c.800

outer wall
Basra Gate
Syrian Gate
government offices
guard house
inner wall
houses and shops
houses and shops
palace
mosque
guard house
government offices
Kufa Gate
Khurasan Gate

500 meters
500 yards

Baghdad at the time of Harun al-Rashid

Founded in 762 by al-Mansur, Baghdad had an inner citadel, based reputedly on the circular armed camps of the ancient Assyrians. In the outer ring were houses and shops. At the city's heart lay the caliph's palace, crowned by a shimmering green dome, and a mosque. Under Harun al-Rashid, Baghdad achieved its greatest brilliance, becoming a center of learning, culture, and prosperity.

In the early 9th century, the Abbasid court was moved from Baghdad to Samarra, a luxurious new city on the banks of the Tigris (see p.57). This reconstructed fragment of a wall painting comes from the Jawsak palace.

The Abbasid Caliphate

Claiming descent from Abbas, uncle of the Prophet, the Abbasids overthrew the Umayyads in 750. The caliphs claimed no spiritual authority, but ruled a prosperous empire, in which a great diversity of peoples and nations were united by Islam. Their capital at Baghdad became the center of a trading network that linked India, Africa, and China. In the reign of the fifth caliph, Harun al-Rashid (786–809), the empire reached the height of its power, but, on his death, the division of empire among his heirs led to rivalry and conflict.

The Abbasid Caliphate 750–809

750: Abbasids seize power from Umayyads	756: Umayyad dynasty established at Cordova by Abd al-Rahman	786: Harun al-Rashid becomes Caliph	800: Aghlabids gain independence in North Africa

740 — 760 — 780 — 800 — 820

754: al-Mansur becomes Caliph	762: Abbasid capital moved to Mesopotamia; founding of Baghdad	789: Idrisids establish power in northwest Africa	809: Death of Harun al-Rashid; start of Abbasid civil war

The fragmentation of the Caliphate

Civil war on the death of Harun al-Rashid accelerated the Abbasids' loss of power, though they ruled in name until 1258. The lands of Islam, once ruled by a single caliph, fragmented into semiautonomous dynasties. Among these were the Fatimids of Egypt, the Samanids of Transoxiana, and the Ghaznavids of Afghanistan, who played a major role in the introduction of Islam to India. In 946, a Persian dynasty, the Buwayhids, invaded and occupied Baghdad. They became protectors of the Caliphate, an event that inspired a revival of Persian national identity.

All mosques share certain features, modeled on Muhammad's house at Medina. These include the *kibla*, the wall facing Mecca, the *minbar*, or pulpit, and the minaret – the tower from which the faithful are called to prayer. The minaret shown here is from the 9th-century mosque of Ibn Tulun at Cairo.

⑥ The fragmentation of the Caliphate c.900–1030 ▶

- Abbasid Caliphate c.900
- ⊙ residence of the Caliph c.900
- Byzantine Empire c.900
- → Samanid expansion in early 10th century
- → Ghaznavid expansion

Areas controlled in 1028 by
- Ghaznavids
- Fatimids
- Buwayhids

500 km
500 miles

The fragmentation of the Caliphate 800–1055

819: Founding of Samanid dynasty	867: Founding of Saffarid dynasty	899–905: Abbasid campaign against Egypt	928: Ruler of Cordova, Abd-al Rahman III, claims the Caliphate	977: Founding of Ghaznavid dynasty	1055: Seljuk Turks take Baghdad

800 — 850 — 900 — 950 — 1000 — 1050

868: Tulunids govern Egypt and Syria	909: Founding of Fatimid dynasty	946: Buwayhids occupy Baghdad	969: Fatimids conquer Egypt	1041: Zirids of Ifriqiyah gain independence

The 10th-century mausoleum of the Samanids at Bukhara is one of the earliest monumental tombs in Islamic architecture. The decorative effect is achieved entirely by means of patterns in the brickwork.

TURKISH AND MONGOL INVADERS

The Islamic warrior was armed with a long curved sword, often of highly-tempered steel and finely engraved.

IN THE 11TH CENTURY West Asia was invaded by the Seljuk Turks, nomads from Central Asia. Reuniting the central Abbasid lands, they emerged as the dominant power in Mesopotamia, Persia, and Anatolia. Their crushing victory at Manzikert in 1071 drove the Byzantines out of Asia Minor and provoked the Crusades. The Crusaders set out to regain the lands lost to Islam, but their capture of Jerusalem in 1099 was countered a century later by Saladin, who had become ruler of Egypt. In the mid-13th century, a new threat was presented by the Mongols, who conquered much of the region, but were halted by the Mamluks, who now ruled Egypt. In the late 14th century, Timur, the last Mongol conqueror, launched a series of campaigns which took him from Ankara to Delhi.

The Seljuk Turks and the Byzantines

The Seljuks were great builders. Their architectural forms and intricate abstract designs had a lasting influence on Islamic art. This glazed tilework in Isfahan's Friday Mosque dates from the late 11th century.

In about 1040, a group of Turkish tribes swept out of the lands north of the Oxus. The Seljuks were the dominant clan. By 1055 they reached Baghdad, where they ruled in the name of the Abbasid caliph. Recent converts to Sunni Islam, the Seljuks planned to subdue all Shi'ites and infidels. Conquering Armenia, they then struck at the Byzantines in Asia Minor, defeating them at Manzikert in 1071. The seizure of Syria and much of Palestine from the Fatimids followed. After a period of civil war, the Seljuk Empire was split in two by the establishment in Anatolia of the independent Sultanate of Rum, with its capital at Konya. The Seljuks' control over their empire waned and they were crushed by the Mongols at Köse Dagh in 1243.

Saladin and the Ayyubid Sultanate

Saladin was a Kurdish general in the army of Nur al-Din, Zangid ruler of Mosul, who fought successfully against the Crusaders (see pp.64–65) and his Muslim neighbors. Ousting the Fatimids from Egypt, he united Egypt and Syria under his rule. Hostilities with the Crusader states led in 1187 to Saladin's annihilation of Christian forces at Hattin and the capture of Jerusalem and Acre. This provoked the Third Crusade, in which the Crusaders recaptured most of the coastal plain of Palestine. The dynasty founded by Saladin, the Ayyubids, dominated the region until it fell to the Mamluks in 1250.

Saladin and the reconquest of Jerusalem

1171: Fatimids overthrown	**1174:** Saladin becomes sultan of Egypt	**1183:** Saladin takes Aleppo		**1191:** Crusaders recover Acre	**1193:** Death of Saladin
1170	1175	1180	1185	1190	1195
	1174: Saladin takes Damascus		**1187:** Saladin defeats Christians at Hattin; takes Jerusalem and Acre	**1189:** Start of Third Crusade	**1192:** Richard I of England makes treaty with Saladin

The growth of the Great Seljuk Empire

c.1040: Seljuks conquer Afghanistan and eastern Persia	1069: Seljuks take Konya (Iconium)	1071: Alp Arslan, Seljuk leader defeats Byzantines at Manzikert	1084: Fall of Antioch to Seljuks	1092: Vizier Nizam al-Mulk murdered by Ismaili Assassin	1099: Crusaders recover Jerusalem
1040	1050	1060	1070	1080	1090	1100
	1055: Seljuks established in Baghdad, ruling in the name of the Abbasid Caliph	1077: Province established in Anatolia with capital first at Nicaea and then Konya; dynasty comes to be known as the Seljuks of Rum (Rome)		1094: Seljuk dynasty of Syria founded with capital at Aleppo	1098: Crusaders recover Antioch

▲ **❶ The Seljuk Turks and the Byzantine Empire from c.1025**

Byzantine frontier in Asia c.1025	route of Seljuk invasion from Asia c.1038
Byzantine Empire 1095	route of Byzantine army
Seljuk Empire c.1095	stronghold of the sect of the Assassins
Seljuk tributary states	
Byzantine territory overrun by Seljuks by 1095	
eastern frontier of area recovered by the Byzantine Empire by 1180	
other Muslim dynasty	

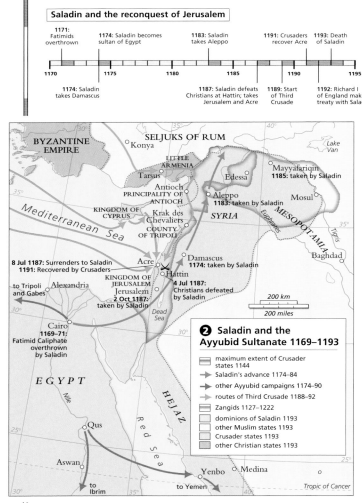

❷ Saladin and the Ayyubid Sultanate 1169–1193

	maximum extent of Crusader states 1144
	Saladin's advance 1174–84
	other Ayyubid campaigns 1174–90
	routes of Third Crusade 1188–92
	Zangids 1127–1222
	dominions of Saladin 1193
	other Muslim states 1193
	Crusader states 1193
	other Christian states 1193

At the head of an army from Egypt, the Muslim leader Saladin (1138–1193) drove the Crusaders out of most of Palestine and Syria and recaptured Jerusalem, restoring the Dome of the Rock, one of Islam's oldest surviving shrines, to Muslim worship. Though a formidable leader, Saladin was recognized by the Crusaders as a chivalrous opponent.

In this Persian illustration, Timur leads his army through the Hindu Kush in 1398 before falling upon the cities of the Punjab and sacking Delhi. This, like most of his conquests, was carried out in the name of Islam.

Mamluks and Mongols

The Mamluks, who seized power in Egypt in 1250, were chiefly Circassians from the Caucasus, captured in childhood and trained as slave bodyguards. Once in power, they extended their rule into Syria and built up a trading network in Africa and the Indian Ocean. Within five years of the Mamluks' rise to power, the Mongol Hülegü (see pp.68–69) led a powerful army into West Asia. After destroying Alamut, the stronghold of the Assassins (an Ismaili Shi'ite sect), Hülegü sacked Baghdad. The Mongol threat was averted by the death of the Mongol khan, Möngke which required Hülegü to withdraw his main army. Seizing their advantage, in 1260 the Mamluks marched north in the defence of Islam, and crushed the Mongol army at Ain Jalut.

The Mamluk warrior was superbly trained, studying both the theory and practice of combat in military manuals, such as this one showing four cavalrymen exercising around a pool.

❸ The rise of the Mamluks and the Il-Khanate 1250–1300

- boundary of Ayyubid Sultanate c.1247
- Mamluk territory in 1250
- annexed by Mamluks 1253
- annexed by Mamluks 1260
- Christian territory in the Levant conquered by Mamluks 1263–1291
- Christian territory after 1291
- Il-Khanate and vassals c.1259
- → route of Mongol invasion under Hülegü
- ⚔ sacked by Mongols

The Mongols and Mamluks in West Asia

1250: Mamluks seize power from Ayyubids	1256: Hülegü crosses Oxus (Amu Darya)	1258: Hülegü sacks Baghdad; last Abbasid caliph executed	1260: Mamluks defeat Mongols at Ain Jalut; take Aleppo and Damascus		1265: Death of Hülegü	
1250	**1255**		**1260**		**1265**	**1270**
1251: Mamluks defeat Syrians at al-'Abbasa	1256–57: Assassins' stronghold at Alamut falls to Hülegü	1259: Great Khan Möngke dies			1268: Mamluks capture Antioch from Crusaders	

The Il-Khanate c.1260–1353

The first Il-Khan, Hülegü, entered a period of conflict with Berke, Khan of the Golden Horde. Berke, who had converted to Islam and allied himself with the Mamluks, resented Hülegü's new empire. By 1262 the situation had stabilized, and Hülegü settled on the well-watered plains of Azerbaijan and built a capital at Maragheh, from where he ruled the lands he had gained in Persia, Mesopotamia, Asia Minor, and the Caucasus. The Mongol dynasty established by Hülegü – the Il-Khanate – ruled Persia until 1353.

In 1258 the Mongols under Hülegü sacked the great city of Baghdad, the very heart of Arab civilization, and reputedly murdered 800,000 of its inhabitants. The last Abbasid caliph was captured, rolled in a carpet, and then trampled to death by galloping horses.

The dominions of Timur

Claiming descent from Genghis Khan, Timur the Lame became master of Transoxiana in 1369. Making Samarkand his capital, he embarked on a series of campaigns against Persia, the Golden Horde, the Sultanate of Delhi, the Mamluks, and the Ottomans. At Ankara in 1402, he defeated and captured the Ottoman Sultan Bayezid. In 35 years Timur created a vast empire; plans for invading China ceased with his death. Though his conquests struck fear into Muslim Asia, Timur's empire proved short-lived.

The campaigns of Timur 1379–1405

	1380: Timur launches series of attacks on Persia	1384: Herat rebels; Timur suppresses ruling dynasty	1392–94: Further campaigns in Persia	1395: Sack of New Sarai, capital of Golden Horde	1400: Sack of Aleppo and Damascus		1405: Death of Timur
1375	**1380**	**1385**	**1390**	**1395**	**1400**	**1405**
1379: Timur marches on Urgench	1387: Isfahan rebels; in reprisal, Timur kills 70,000, building towers with their skulls	1388–91: War against Mongol Khanate of the Golden Horde	1393: Capture of Baghdad	1398: Invasion of India; sack of Delhi	1401: Sack of Baghdad	1402: Defeat of Ottomans at Ankara

Timur is buried beneath a slab of jade in the Gur-i Mir, Samarkand.

❹ The dominions of Timur

- Empire of Timur
- Ottoman Empire
- Mamluk Sultanate

Campaigns of Timur: 1379–1405
- → against Khwarizm and Persia 1379–88
- → against Golden Horde 1388–91 and 1395
- → against Sultanate of Delhi 1398–99
- → against Mamluk Sultanate and Baghdad 1399–1401
- → against Ottomans 1402
- → planned invasion of China 1404–05
- ⚔ city sacked by Timur

Scale varies with perspective

THE OTTOMAN EMPIRE

THE OTTOMAN EMPIRE was one of the great world powers of the early modern age. At its height, the empire stretched from the Indian Ocean to Algiers, Hungary, and the Crimea. Constantinople, captured from the Byzantines in 1453 was a key center of power that had resisted non–Christian attack for 1000 years. Turkish expansion in the Balkans led to shifts in religious, ethnic, linguistic, and economic frontiers, which still have serious consequences in the modern world. The conquest of Egypt and Syria established a powerful presence in Africa and West Asia, although, in the east, the Ottomans faced powerful opposition from Safavid Persia, which flourished in the 16th and 17th centuries.

The rise of the Ottomans

The Ottoman state started as a small frontier principality dedicated to raids on Christian Byzantium. In the 14th century, led by a succession of warrior sultans, Osman I, Orkhan, and Murad I, the Ottomans began a series of rapid conquests. Sultans often waged war to obtain more land and money to reward their loyal troops. In an attempt to halt their progress, the threatened Christian states of the Balkans amassed an army, but were defeated at Kosovo in 1389. Sultan Bayezid I exploited this victory by annexing Bulgaria and invading Hungary, but expansion eastward was temporarily halted by Timur in 1402. Constantinople was finally taken by Mehmed II (the "Conqueror") in 1453.

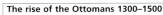

The rise of the Ottomans 1300–1500

- c.1300: Ottoman state founded by Osman
- 1326: Ottomans conquer Bursa
- 1356: Capture of Gallipoli; Ottomans advance into Europe
- 1361: Capture of Edirne (Adrianople)
- 1396: Bayezid defeats Crusader army at Nicopolis
- 1389: Serbs and Bosnians defeated at Kosovo
- 1389: Accession of Bayezid I
- 1402: Bayezid defeated by Timur at Ankara
- 1453: Turks take Constantinople
- 1459: Annexation of Serbia

The Ottomans' rise to become a world power was based on their highly-trained army, seen here besieging Belgrade in 1456. The most feared troops were the janissaries, drawn from young slaves given in tribute and trained from childhood.

① Rise of the Ottoman Empire c.1300–1500

- nucleus of Ottoman Empire c.1300
- conquests of Osman I, c.1300–26
- conquests of Orkhan, 1326–62
- conquests of Murad I, 1362–89
- conquests of Bayezid I, 1389–1402
- Ottoman eastern frontier following Timur's invasion 1402
- Ottoman territory by 1451
- further Ottoman conquest by 1481
- vassal of Ottoman Empire by 1481
- under Venetian control c.1450
- Holy Roman Empire c.1480
- ...... frontiers in 1481
- ✕ battle, with date
- ⊙ siege, with date

- 1517: Selim I orders construction of Ottoman fleet at Suez; Portuguese attack on Jedda repulsed
- 1516–17: Ottomans conquer Syria, Egypt, the Hejaz, and Yemen
- 1525: Ottomans again defeat Portuguese fleet in Red Sea
- 1538: Ottomans subjugate Yemen and Aden and take occupy port of Basra on Persian Gulf
- 1538: Failure of Ottoman blockade of Portuguese at Diu
- 1546: Ottomans retake Basra after revolt
- 1551–52: Ottomans fail to oust Portuguese from Hormuz

Ottoman attempts to control trade in the Indian Ocean

Trade in the Indian Ocean

With their conquest in the early 16th century of Egypt, Mesopotamia, the Hejaz, and Yemen, the Ottomans gained control of trade through the Persian Gulf and the Red Sea. Ships carrying goods such as spices from India and the Moluccas and slaves from East Africa, docked at Aden and Jedda; from there they were transported overland to the markets of Cairo, Aleppo, Damascus, and north into Anatolia. Responding to persistent threats to their trade from the Portuguese, the Ottomans assembled fleets at Suez and Basra and made several attempts to oust the Portuguese from the region, but without lasting success.

② Trade in the Indian Ocean in the 15th and 16th centuries

- → main trade route
- ⇢ Ottoman naval campaigns in the Indian Ocean in 16th century

Commodities and raw materials exported

- ambergris
- aromatic woods
- carpets
- porcelain
- coconuts
- copper
- cotton
- gems
- gold
- grain
- horses
- incense
- indigo
- iron/steel
- ivory
- manufactured goods
- metalware
- pearls
- perfumes
- rice
- silk
- silver
- slaves
- spices
- sugar
- tea
- textiles
- timber
- tin
- wine

Scale varies with perspective

Iznik pottery, developed in the late 15th century, was among the finest made by the Ottomans. Designs were largely figurative, such as this Portuguese ship.

3 The height of Ottoman power 1512–1639
- Ottoman Empire and vassals 1512
- conquests of Selim I, 1512–20
- conquests of Suleyman I, 1520–66
- Ottoman conquest, 1566–1639
- Austrian Habsburg possessions
- Spanish Habsburg possessions
- Venetian Republic and possessions
- major campaigns of Selim I, 1512–20
- major Ottoman campaigns, 1520–1639
- Christian counter-offensive against Ottomans
- Ottoman victory
- 1538 battle, with date
- Knights of St. John
- siege, with date
- vassal border
- frontiers 1600
- Holy Roman Empire

The Selimiye mosque at Edirne was designed by Suleyman's imperial architect, Sinan.

The height of Ottoman power

Selim I came to power in 1512, pledged to defend Sunni Islam against Shi'ite encroachment from the east. After crushing the Persians at Çaldiran, Selim turned his armies south and swept into Syria, Egypt, and the Hejaz. Selim's son, Suleyman I, prosecuted the Holy War against the Christians by conquering Hungary and reaching the gates of Vienna. His capture of Baghdad confirmed his preeminence in the Islamic world, while his navy established supremacy in the eastern Mediterranean.

Built by Mehmed II in the 1460s, Constantinople's Topkapi Palace was the sultan's residence and the seat of government.

The height of Ottoman power

1514: Selim defeats Safavids at Çaldiran	1520: Accession of Suleyman I (the "Magnificent")	1529: First Ottoman siege of Vienna	1538: Ottoman navy defeats combined Venetian, Spanish, and papal armada at Preveza		1571: Ottomans take Cyprus from Venetians, but are defeated by Holy League at Lepanto
1510	1520	1530	1540	1550	1560	1570
1512: Accession of Selim I	1517: Capture of Cairo	1521: Suleyman takes Belgrade	1526: Defeat of Hungarians at Mohács	1534: Suleyman retakes Baghdad from Safavids	1565: Ottoman siege of Malta fails

This mural from Isfahan shows a man and a girl taking refreshment in a garden. Figurative art flourished at the cultured Safavid court in the reign of Shah Abbas I.

Safavid Persia

Ottoman expansion to the east was halted by the sudden rise to power around 1500 of a new Persian dynasty, the Safavids. The first Safavid ruler, Shah Ismail I, rapidly united Persia, converting it from Sunni to Shi'ite Islam. Expansion west into Kurdistan was checked by the Ottomans, but in the east the Uzbeks were driven from Khurasan. During the enlightened reign of Shah Abbas I (the "Great"), Safavid domains were extended as far as Balkh, and the Ottomans expelled from Mesopotamia.

4 Safavid Persia 1501–1736
- Safavid possessions c.1500
- Safavid Empire 1512
- territory contested by Uzbek Shaybanids and Safavids in 16th century
- Safavid Empire 1722
- territory under Ottoman control 1722
- territory under Uzbek control 1722
- easternmost limit of area contested by Ottomans to 1736
- major Ottoman campaign
- Uzbek invasion 1587
- Safavid victory
- Ottoman victory

Safavid Persia 1500–1620

1501: Accession of Shah Ismail I	1528: Safavids take Baghdad from Kurdish usurper	1553–55: War with Ottomans	1578–90: War with Ottomans	1598: Isfahan becomes imperial capital	1604: Abbas conquers Erivan, Shirvan, and Kars
1500	1520	1540	1560	1580	1600	1620
1514: Ottomans defeat Ismail at Çaldiran	1534–35: War with Ottomans, who capture Tabriz and Baghdad	1588: Accession of Abbas I (the "Great")	1603–19: War with Ottomans; in first year Abbas retakes Tabriz

THE DECLINE OF THE OTTOMANS

Abdul Hamid II failed to modernize his empire and was deposed by the Young Turks in 1908.

AT THE HEIGHT OF ITS POWER in the 16th century, the Ottoman Empire stretched from the gates of Vienna to the Indian Ocean and from the Crimea to Algiers. By the end of the 18th century the empire was shrinking, its power eroded by a loss of internal authority and by the ambitions of the major European powers. Attempts to westernize and strengthen the empire foundered, and when the Turks entered World War I *(see pp. 206–207),* on the side of the Central Powers, they had lost all their territories in Africa, and most of them in Europe. Defeat in the war brought the empire to an end: British and French mandates were imposed in Mesopotamia and the Levant, and Saudi Arabia became independent. The Turks, however, established a new national identity for themselves by driving the Greeks from Anatolia and creating the modern republic of Turkey in 1923.

The empire in decline 1800–1913

By 1900 Turkey was attracting European tourists, seen here against the backdrop of Constantinople's domes and minarets. Many Turks now wore Western dress and had adopted Western habits.

Under pressure from the West, attempts were made to modernize the empire, notably in the period 1839–76. In 1908 a movement for more liberal government, led by the Young Turks, succeeded in deposing the sultan, Abdul Hamid II. The Ottomans' hold over the Balkans was broken by Greece gaining independence in 1830, followed by Serbia, Montenegro, and Romania in 1878, while Russia challenged Turkish control of the Black Sea. In Africa, the French seized Algeria and Tunisia, Britain occupied Egypt, and the Italians conquered Libya.

❶ The Ottoman Empire 1800–1913

- area lost by 1832
- area autonomous or under only nominal control by 1833
- area lost by 1882
- autonomous 1878; lost 1908
- area lost by 1913
- Ottoman Empire 1913

Scale varies with perspective

4850 km (3014 miles)

7250 km (4505 miles)

The Ottoman Empire 1815–1913							
	1840: Empire under threat from Egypt; saved by British and Austrian intervention	**1854–56:** Crimean War; French and British come to aid of Turks against Russia	**1878:** Cyprus occupied by British	**1881:** Tunisia occupied by French	**1908:** Bosnia-Herzegovina annexed by Austro-Hungarian Empire	**1912–13:** Balkan Wars	
1830: Algiers occupied by France							
1815 — 1825 — 1835 — 1845 — 1855 — 1865 — 1875 — 1885 — 1895 — 1905 — 1915							
1821–30: Greek War of Independence	**1839–61:** Sultan Abdul Majid I makes series of liberal *Tanzimat* decrees	**1853:** Russians defeat Turkish navy at Sinop	**1878:** Independence of Serbia, Montenegro, and Romania recognized at Berlin Congress	**1882:** Egypt occupied by British	**1908:** Bulgaria declares independence	**1911:** Libya occupied by Italy	

Emir Faisal, seen here with his bodyguard, united the Arabs and in 1916, together with Colonel T. E. Lawrence, led a successful revolt against the Turks. After the war Faisal became king of Iraq under the British mandate.

EGYPT AND THE SUEZ CANAL

An early sign of Ottoman decline was Muhammad Ali's establishment of a virtually independent Egypt after 1805. He and his successors encouraged European investment and in 1859 Egypt became the site of one of the century's greatest feats of engineering. The brainchild of a French diplomat, Ferdinand de Lesseps, who supervised its construction, the 105-mile Suez Canal linked the Mediterranean to the Red Sea. Cutting the sea journey from Britain to India by 6,000 miles, the canal opened in 1869 and became one of the world's most heavily used waterways. In 1875 Britain paid the bankrupt Khedive of Egypt four million pounds for a controlling interest in the canal, thus securing a lifeline to its empire in the east.

On the day after the opening ceremony in Port Said, 68 ships, headed by the *Aigle* with Empress Eugénie of France on board, sailed the length of the Suez Canal. This painting is from Eugénie's souvenir album of the event.

World War I					
Feb 1915: First Turkish attempt to capture Suez	**Feb 1916:** Russians take Erzurum	**Apr 1916:** British surrender at Kut al Amara	**Mar 1917:** British take Baghdad		**Oct 1918:** Turks surrender
1914 — 1915 — 1916 — 1917 — 1918 — 1919					
Oct 1914: Turkey closes Dardanelles	**Feb 1915:** Gallipoli landings	**1915:** About one million Armenians massacred or deported by Turks	**Jun 1916:** Arab Revolt	**Dec 1917:** British take Jerusalem	**Sep 1918:** Battle of Megiddo

The partition of the Ottoman Empire 1918–23

Following the Turkish surrender in 1918, Syria became a French mandate while Palestine, Iraq, and Transjordan became British mandates. By the Treaty of Sèvres (1920), Turkey was forced to give up all her non-Turkish lands; eastern Thrace and Smyrna were given to Greece. The Turkish sultan accepted the Treaty's conditions, but the Allies had underestimated the fervor of the Turkish Nationalists; led by Kemal Pasha, they launched an attack on the Greek invaders, driving them out of Anatolia. The present frontiers of Turkey were recognized by the Treaty of Lausanne in 1923. In the same year the last Ottoman sultan, Mehmed VI, was overthrown and Turkey became a republic.

❸ Southwest Asia after the First World War

- British mandate
- French mandate
- Turkey after Treaty of Sèvres (1920)
- area annexed by Turkey 1921
- area restored to Turkey by Treaty of Lausanne (1923)
- international border 1926

In an attempt to cover the retreat of their own troops, a Greek cavalry detachment charges a Turkish force near Smyrna in 1922. Under the inspired leadership of Mustafa Kemal Pasha, Turkish Nationalists fought a fierce three-year campaign, eventually regaining eastern Thrace and Smyrna.

Postwar Turkey

- **May 1919:** Greek forces land at Smyrna
- **Aug 1919:** Kemal Pasha breaks away from authority of Istanbul government
- **Aug 1920:** Treaty of Sèvres
- **Dec 1920:** Armenia cedes half its territory to Turkey
- **1921:** Turkish Nationalist government established in Ankara
- **Sep 1922:** Turks recapture Smyrna
- **Jul 1923:** Treaty of Lausanne recognizes Turkish sovereignty over Smyrna and eastern Thrace
- **Oct 1923:** Turkish Republic proclaimed with Kemal Pasha as first president

The First World War in Southwest Asia

❷ The First World War in Southwest Asia

- Ottoman Empire 1914
- British Empire 1914
- Russian Empire 1914
- area of Arab revolt (1916–18)
- Russian/Turkish front 1917
- Turkish lines at surrender, 1918
- Turkish forces
- Allied forces
- Allied forces under Col T.E. Lawrence
- French forces
- Russian forces
- rail line

British and Australian troops (left) land on the Gallipoli peninsula. They abandoned the offensive in January 1916, having lost over 250,000 men.

French General d'Esperey lands in Istanbul in 1919 to be greeted by British General Wilson (below). Behind Wilson stands Kemal Pasha (later known as Atatürk), who was to lead Turkey in its struggle to become a modern state.

World War I 1914–18

The Turks began the war well, pinning down an Allied force on the Gallipoli peninsula for nine months and halting the British in Mesopotamia. But they twice failed to take Suez, and in 1916 their Third Army was virtually destroyed by the Russians at Erzurum. The end came in 1918 when British forces, supported by Arab irregulars, drove north in a two-pronged attack, capturing Baghdad and Jerusalem, and eventually reaching Damascus.

The emergence of Saudi Arabia 1800–1932

The modern Saudi state has its origins in the 18th century when the Wahhabis – an orthodox sect attempting to preserve the "purity of Islam"– united the previously divided Arab tribes. Led by the Saud family, the Wahhabis raided into Mesopotamia, the Hejaz, and Syria, capturing Mecca in 1806. But in a series of campaigns (1812–18), the Wahhabis were crushed by armies from Egypt and Ottoman forces from the north. In 1902, Abd al-Aziz Ibn Saud led a Saudi resurgence. The Saud family gradually consolidated its power within the peninsula and, in 1932, the kingdom of Saudi Arabia was proclaimed.

Abd al-Aziz Ibn Saud regained his family's homelands around Riyadh, then founded a kingdom that he ruled until his death in 1953.

The Arabian Peninsula 1750–1950

- **c.1750:** Emergence of Wahhabi movement
- **1806:** Wahhabis take Mecca
- **1812:** Egyptian forces retake Mecca and Medina
- **1818:** Wahhabi resistance crushed by Egyptian forces
- **1843:** Fortunes of Saud family restored by Faisal
- **c.1880:** Birth of Abd al-Aziz Ibn Saud in Kuwait
- **1887:** Riyadh taken by Rashidis, who dominate Nejd
- **1902:** Ibn Saud reclaims his patrimony by capturing Riyadh
- **1926:** Ibn Saud crowns himself King of the Hejaz and Sultan of Nejd
- **1932:** Kingdom of Saudi Arabia proclaimed
- **1938** First oil exported from Saudi

❹ The formation of Saudi Arabia

MAIN MAP: 1912–1932

- Ottoman Empire c.1912
- Saudi territory c.1912
- Saudi gains 1913
- Saudi gains 1920
- Saudi gains 1921–22
- Saudi gains 1924–25

INSET: 1800–1812

- Ottoman Empire c.1800
- Wahhabi territory c.1800
- Wahhabi expansion in early 19th century
- 1805 date captured by Wahhabis

MODERN WEST ASIA

Yasser Arafat, the chairman of the PLO from 1969, led the fight for recognition of Palestinian rights.

THE HISTORY OF WEST ASIA after the Second World War was dominated by two things: oil, and the creation of the state of Israel. The discovery of huge oil reserves in the Gulf region influenced the economics and politics of all the states concerned. The UN decision of 1947 to partition Palestine and form the Jewish homeland of Israel sparked off Arab-Israeli wars in 1948, 1967, and 1973. Israel remains technically at war with all its Arab neighbors except Egypt and Jordan. The emergence of Islamic fundamentalism in the region, with the Iranian revolution (1979), the Palestinian *intifada* (from 1987) in Israel, and the international anti-Western campaign by al-Qaeda (from the 1990s), led to a seemingly intractable confrontation between Islamic and Western values. This provoked the invasion, without UN approval, of Saddam Hussein's Iraq by the US and its allies in 2003.

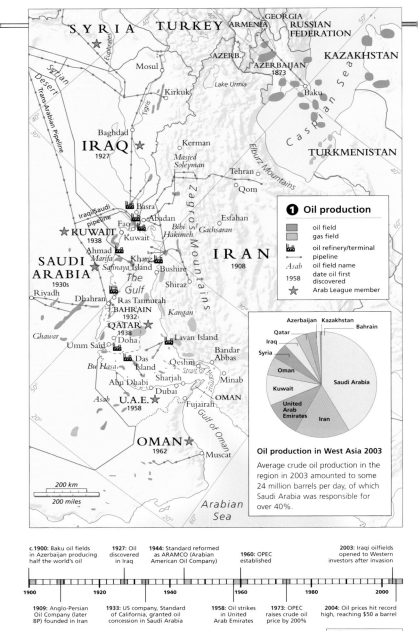

① Oil production

- oil field
- gas field
- oil refinery/terminal
- pipeline
- *Asab* oil field name
- 1958 date oil field first discovered
- ★ Arab League member

Oil production in West Asia 2003

Average crude oil production in the region in 2003 amounted to some 24 million barrels per day, of which Saudi Arabia was responsible for over 40%.

Oil production in the Gulf

The Gulf is the world's most valuable region of oil and natural gas, producing some 35% of the world's requirements. The Gulf states exert a powerful influence: increases in the price of crude oil, such as that imposed by OPEC in 1973–74, had worldwide repercussions. Regional conflicts that disrupt oil supplies, such as Iraq's invasion of Kuwait (1990) and the US-led intervention in 1991, and the toppling of Saddam Hussein's regime in 2003, seriously affected global confidence in the security of oil supplies. This was further undermined in the early 2000s by uncertainty over the durability of Saudi Arabia's ruling family.

The vulnerability of supplies in the Middle East in the current political climate can lead to huge rises in oil prices on the world market. Here Iraqi firemen put out the blaze after a bomb attack on an oil pipeline, just one of many such attacks in 2004.

c.1900: Baku oil fields in Azerbaijan producing half the world's oil	1927: Oil discovered in Iraq	1944: Standard reformed as ARAMCO (Arabian American Oil Company)	1960: OPEC established		2003: Iraqi oilfields opened to Western investors after invasion

1900	1920	1940	1960	1980	2000

1909: Anglo-Persian Oil Company (later BP) founded in Iran	1933: US company, Standard of California, granted oil concession in Saudi Arabia	1958: Oil strikes in United Arab Emirates	1973: OPEC raises crude oil price by 200%	2004: Oil prices hit record high, reaching $50 a barrel

Oil in West Asia

Arab-Israeli wars

The state of Israel was established in May 1948. The next day, five Arab armies invaded; Israel survived, but its refusal to acknowledge Palestinian claims, and the refusal of Arab states to recognize Israel, led to a succession of wars in which the Arabs were defeated and Israel occupied more territories. A succession of initiatives, such as the Oslo Accords of 1993 and the "Road Map" of 2003, tried to find a viable arrangement between Israel and the Palestinians. However, the Israeli settlements in the West Bank and Palestinian suicide bombing campaigns remain obstacles to any peace agreement.

Jewish and Palestinian Migrations

③ Migration 1947–96

▲ SMALL MAP:
Palestinian emigration
→ 1947–48

▼ LARGE MAP:
Jewish migration to Israel
→ 1948–71
→ 1972–96

Jewish immigration to Palestine from Europe increased sharply in the 1930s and 1940s as a result of persecution and the Holocaust. While the Jews accepted the UN partition plan, the Arabs declined it; in the subsequent civil war and Israel's 1948–49 war against the invading Arab states, tens of thousands of Palestinians fled their homes and became refugees (*left*). Since 1948 Israel has absorbed even greater numbers of Jewish immigrants (*below*).

② Arab-Israeli Wars 1947–82

▲ MAIN MAP: Arab-Israeli Wars

- Israel in 1949
- occupied by Israel after 1967 war
- occupied by Israel after 1973 war
- occupied by Israel after 1967 war reoccupied by Egypt after 1973 war
- demilitarized zone held by UN after Israel-Syria agreement, 1974, and 2nd Sinai agreement, 1975
- → route of Israel's invasion of Lebanon 1982
- Palestinian refugee camps 1982
- +++++ disputed border

INSET: UN Partition plan 1947 ▲
- border of British mandate 1923
- proposed Arab State
- proposed Jewish State
- proposed international zone

Arab-Israeli wars

1947: UN partition of Palestine	1956: Suez crisis; Israel, France, and Britain invade Egypt	1973: Yom Kippur War	1979: Egypt and Israel sign peace treaty based on Camp David accords	1991: Israel subjected to Iraqi missile attack	2000: Israeli withdrawal from Lebanon

1950	1960	1970	1980	1990	2000

1948: Invading Arab armies repulsed; some 725,000 Arabs flee Palestine	1967: Six Day War; Israel takes Sinai, Gaza, Golan Heights, West Bank, and Jerusalem	1982: Israel invades Lebanon	1993: Oslo peace accords	2002: Work starts on West Bank barrier

In 2001, Israel's prime minister, Ariel Sharon, proposed a plan to withdraw troops from Palestinian-administered areas and authorized the construction of a 300-mile security wall in the West Bank. This provoked an intensification of the *intifada*, characterized by a renewed suicide bombing campaign, and harsh Israeli reprisals.

USSR:
51,282 (1948–71)
821,396 (1972–96)

Eastern Europe:
494,440 (1948–71)
59,687 (1972–96)

Western Europe:
59,754 (1948–71)
50,514 (1972–96)

USA and Canada:
24,616 (1948–71)
56,545 (1972–96)

Turkey:
58,491 (1948–71)
6028 (1972–96)

Iran:
57,111 (1948–71)
18,037 (1972–96)

North Africa:
(Morocco, Algeria, Tunisia, Libya, Egypt)
395,268 (1948–71)
24,079 (1972–96)

Lebanon:
3289 (1948–71)
743 (1972–96)

Iraq:
128,489 (1948–71)
1050 (1972–96)

Syria:
6686 (1948–71)
1837 (1972–96)

Central and South America:
25,840 (1948–71)
46,663 (1972–96)

Yemen:
50,551 (1948–71)
68 (1972–96)

Ethiopia:
167 (1948–71)
49,862 (1972–1996)

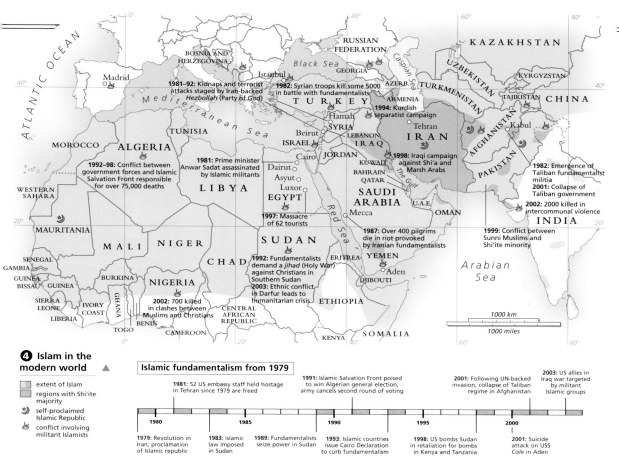

Map labels (Islam in the modern world):

1981–92: Kidnaps and terrorist attacks staged by Iran-backed Hezbollah (Party of God)

1982: Syrian troops kill some 5000 in battle with fundamentalists

1994: Kurdish separatist campaign

1998: Iraqi campaign against Shi'a and Marsh Arabs

1982: Emergence of Taliban fundamentalist militia

2001: Collapse of Taliban government

2002: 2000 killed in intercommunal violence

1981: Prime minister Anwar Sadat assassinated by Islamic militants

1992–98: Conflict between government forces and Islamic Salvation Front responsible for over 75,000 deaths

1997: Massacre of 62 tourists

1987: Over 400 pilgrims die in riot provoked by Iranian fundamentalists

1999: Conflict between Sunni Muslims and Shi'ite minority

1992: Fundamentalists demand a *jihad* (Holy War) against Christians in Southern Sudan

2003: Ethnic conflict in Darfur leads to humanitarian crisis

2002: 700 killed in clashes between Muslims and Christians

1000 km / 1000 miles

④ Islam in the modern world

- extent of Islam
- regions with Shi'ite majority
- self-proclaimed Islamic Republic
- conflict involving militant Islamists

Islamic fundamentalism from 1979

1981: 52 US embassy staff held hostage in Tehran since 1979 are freed

1991: Islamic Salvation Front poised to win Algerian general election; army cancels second round of voting

2001: Following UN-backed invasion, collapse of Taliban regime in Afghanistan

2003: US allies in Iraq war targeted by militant Islamic groups

1980 — 1985 — 1990 — 1995 — 2000

1979: Revolution in Iran; proclamation of Islamic republic

1983: Islamic law imposed in Sudan

1989: Fundamentalists seize power in Sudan

1993: Islamic countries issue Cairo Declaration to curb fundamentalism

1998: US bombs Sudan in retaliation for bombs in Kenya and Tanzania

2001: Suicide attack on USS *Cole* in Aden

Islamic revivalism

Shi'a Islam was the driving force behind the Iranian Revolution of 1978–79. Under the leadership of Ayatollah Khomeini, political, social, educational, and cultural life in the Islamic Republic of Iran, were to be governed by the basic elements ("fundamentals") of the Sharia or Islamic law. The revivalist Salafi interpretation of the Sunni tradition – often known as "Wahhabism" – developed in Saudi Arabia. In one form or the other, revivalist Islam has been associated with terrorism and conflict. "Wahhabism," for example, has been linked to anti-Western terrorism, especially the activities of Osama bin Laden and the al-Qaeda movement.

Amid scenes of uncontrollable grief, Ayatollah Khomeini, Iran's leader and symbol of the Iranian revolution, is escorted to his grave by mourners in June 1989.

Al-Qaeda

Founded in the late 1980s by Osama bin Laden and his associates, al-Qaeda soon became the most notorious international terrorist network. Al-Qaeda organized a number of high-profile attacks, including the bombing of US embassies in Kenya and Tanzania in 1998, the suicide attack on the USS *Cole* in Aden in 2000, and the destruction of the World Trade Center in New York on September 11, 2001. Meaning "the base" in Arabic, al-Qaeda latterly became more like a movement or ideology, inspiring terrorist groups and individuals around the world.

Osama bin Laden came from a wealthy Saudi Arabian family. His campaign against Western values and the process of globalization nevertheless relied, with considerable ingenuity, upon the products of his enemies – the internet, digital credit transactions, cellphones, videotapes, and television broadcasts.

Conflict in the Gulf

In September 1980, Iraq launched a massive attack against Iran. The war lasted until 1988, left over one million dead or injured, and wrecked the economies of both countries. The reasons for Iraq's aggression were complex: border disputes with Iran, long-standing rivalry in the region, and the opposition of Saddam Hussein's Arab nationalist regime to the revolutionary Islamic theocracy in Iran. In 1990, Saddam invaded Kuwait, aiming to gain control of its oil reserves to rebuild his war machine. With UN approval, a US-led coalition of 29 states liberated Kuwait in 2001. In 2003, US-Iraqi hostility culminated in the invasion of Iraq by US-led forces, ostensibly to destroy Iraqi weapons of mass destruction. The collapse of Saddam's regime left a power vacuum.

Saddam Hussein's Ba'athist regime controlled Iraq through a ministry of fear and the cult of the leader. His continued defiance of the West after the first Gulf War (1990–91) led to the US invasion of 2003.

The plight of the Kurds

Numbering over 20 million, the Kurds inhabit large areas of Turkey, Iran, and Iraq, and some of Syria. But "Kurdistan" is not officially recognized and Kurds have long experienced persecution over their aspirations for independence. From 1987 Saddam Hussein unleashed the "al-Anfal" pacification/extermination campaign against the Iraqi Kurds, in which chemical weapons were used. After the 1990–91 Gulf War, they had some protection under a "no fly zone" imposed by the US and its allies. The destruction of Saddam Hussein's regime in 2003 prompted debate on the place of the Kurds in the new Iraq.

Kurdish refugees flee across the mountains to Turkey in 1991 in the wake of Saddam Hussein's chemical attacks on their communities in northern Iraq. Over one million Kurds fled into Turkey and Iran. In May 1992 the Iraqi Kurds elected their own government and became a semi-independent political entity.

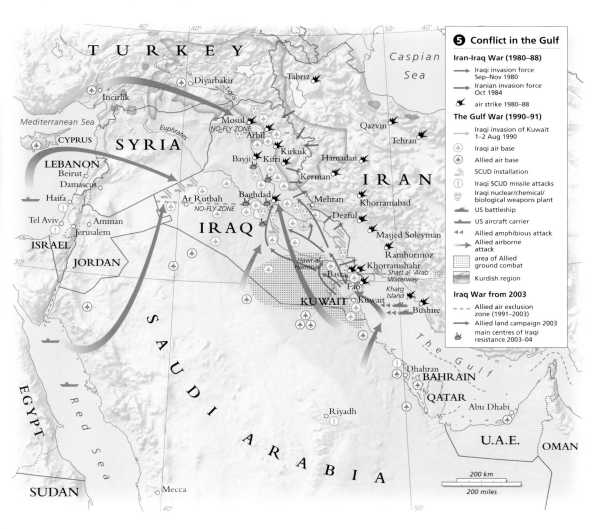

⑤ Conflict in the Gulf

Iran-Iraq War (1980–88)
- Iraqi invasion force Sep–Nov 1980
- Iranian invasion force Oct 1984
- air strike 1980–88

The Gulf War (1990–91)
- Iraqi invasion of Kuwait 1–2 Aug 1990
- Iraqi air base
- Allied air base
- SCUD installation
- Iraqi SCUD missile attacks
- Iraqi nuclear/chemical/biological weapons plant
- US battleship
- US aircraft carrier
- Allied amphibious attack
- Allied airborne attack
- area of Allied ground combat
- Kurdish region

Iraq War from 2003
- Allied air exclusion zone (1991–2003)
- Allied land campaign 2003
- main centres of Iraqi resistance 2003–04

200 km / 200 miles

The invasion of Iraq 2003–04

20 Mar: War begins with series of massive bombing raids

13 Dec: Saddam Hussein found hiding near home town, Tikrit

28 Jun: Interim government sworn in

Jan 2005: Scheduled democratic election

Mar 2003 — Jan 2004 — Jan 2005

9 Apr: US troops control most of Baghdad

31 Jul: Shi'a cleric Moqtada al-Sadr claims 10,000 men have joined "Islamic army" in Najaf

29 Apr: Photographs of torture of Iraqis in Abu Ghraib prison shown on US television

SOUTH AND SOUTHEAST ASIA

REGIONAL HISTORY

THE HISTORICAL LANDSCAPE

LYING LARGELY BETWEEN THE TROPICS, this region enjoys a complex geography incorporating the world's greatest mountains, some of the world's largest river systems and tropical rain forests, and the globe's most extensive archipelago. During the last Ice Age, lower sea levels rendered the shallow seas surrounding Southeast Asia into dry land, allowing humans to migrate from the Asian mainland through the islands of Southeast Asia. From 3000 BCE, the Indian subcontinent was home to some of the world's earliest civilizations, founded on the banks of the Indus and Ganges rivers. Historically, the sheer size of the Indian subcontinent and variety of its peoples have attracted and resisted political unity in equal parts, and Hinduism, Buddhism, and Islam have provided the inspiration for remarkable eras of cultural, economic, and political efflorescence. The region is well-endowed with valuable natural resources and has attracted and fostered trade since the earliest times. Only in the recent centuries of colonial rivalry have concerns about self-determination been overtaken by the need to meet the demands of soaring population growth.

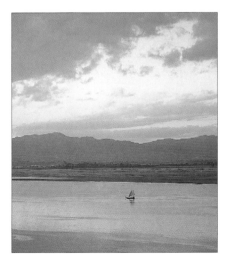

The Mekong is one of many great rivers which radiate south and east from the Plateau of Tibet. The alluvial soils that accumulate around the lower reaches of these rivers are exceptionally fertile, and have long been utilized by humans for agriculture – especially the cultivation of rice.

The Himalayas have always been a barrier to human migration between South and East Asia. The first settlers entered southern Asia by passes that still provide the only means of traversing the mountains.

The Indus River flows from the Himalayas, through mountain meadows and down across fertile plains to the sea. The Indus Valley civilizations were the most sophisticated early societies in southern Asia.

The **Thar Desert** in western India is a small remnant of the larger Great Indian Sand Desert, that covered much of western India at the end of the last Ice Age.

South and Southeast Asia: 18,000 years ago

Climatic changes and a global fall in sea level affected South and Southeastern Asia. The drop in sea levels turned much of the continental shelf surrounding the islands of Southeast Asia into dry land, forming a wide land bridge that encompassed Java, Sumatra, and Borneo. Rain forests covered a much smaller area, and many forested zones became grasslands and scrub. In India, sand dunes in the Thar Desert expanded to occupy a much larger area than today.

Arctic Circle

Central
Siberian
Plateau

Kamchatka

Sea of Okhotsk

NORTH AMERICAN PLATE

EURASIAN PLATE

Ural Mountains

West
Siberian
Plain

S i b e r i a

Sakhalin

Kurile Islands

Great Khingan Range

Manchurian
Plain

Amur

Hokkaido

Kurile Trench

Aral
Sea

Altai Mountains

Dzungaria

G o b i

Sea of Japan
(East Sea)

Honshu

Japan Trench

Tien Shan

A S I A

Yellow River

Ordos
Desert

Bo Hai

Korea

Tarim
Basin

Qilian Shan

Yellow River

Yellow
Sea

Kunlun Mountains

Great Plain
of China

East China
Sea

Plateau
of Tibet

Qin Ling

Yangtze

Ryukyu Islands

EURASIAN PLATE

PHILIPPINE PLATE

Tropic of Cancer

PACIFIC PLATE

Himalayas

Red
Basin

Nan Ling

Taiwan

PHILIPPINE PLATE

Ganges

Brahmaputra

Patkai Range

Xi Jiang

Irrawaddy

Arakan Yoma

Ailao Shan

P A C I F I C

O C E A N

Salween

Gulf of
Tongking

Hainan

Philippine
Basin

Western Ghats

Bay of
Bengal

Mekong

Colder, drier climates affected the vegetation of Southeast Asia. The rain forests that grew to blanket much of the area, covered much smaller portions of the continent.

South
China
Sea

Luzon

Philippine Trench

Yap Trench

Andaman
Islands

Isthmus of Kra

Gulf of
Thailand

South China Basin

Palawan

Sulu
Sea

Mindanao

Sri Lanka

Sri Lanka and India were linked by dry land at the end of the last Ice Age. Rising sea levels flooded the link between them, and made Sri Lanka an island, although even today the two are only separated by a narrow expanse of shallow sea.

Andaman
Sea

Nicobar
Islands

EURASIAN PLATE

INDO-AUSTRALIAN PLATE

Malay Peninsula

Strait of Malacca

18,000 years ago, many of the shallow seas surrounding maritime Southeast Asia were dry land. The Sunda Shelf was a low-lying, thickly forested plain, and many of the East Indian islands were joined together as a long peninsula which stretched eastward to Australia.

Celebes
Sea

Halmahera

Moluccas

PACIFIC PLATE

INDO-AUSTRALIAN PLATE

Equator

Ceylon Plain

Ninetyeast Ridge

Cocos
Basin

Sumatra

Sunda
Shelf

Borneo

S U N D A

The Sunda Shelf was dissected by a complex river system; all of these ancient rivers were drowned when sea levels rose.

Makassar Strait

Celebes

Seram

New
Guinea

O C E A N

Java Trench

Java

E a s t   I n d i e s

Bali

Flores

Timor

Banda
Sea

Arafura Sea

SOUTH AND SOUTHEAST ASIA

EXPLORATION AND MAPPING

THE RELIGIONS OF SOUTH ASIA all have a long tradition of cosmography, though surviving maps are of relatively recent date. While some early maps may have related to secular themes, most would have been associated with religion and the place of humankind in a greater universe, reflecting the sacred geography of the Hindu, Jain, and Buddhist traditions. Despite the sophistication of Indian science and the great distances traveled by Indian – especially Buddhist – missionaries and merchants, there is little evidence of conventional geographical mapping until well after the establishment of Islam in the region. Following the establishment of the Portuguese in western India after 1498, European colonists, with competing territorial claims, spurred on the Western mapping of South and Southeast Asia. Commercial, economic, and military motives, combined with a zeal for knowledge, led to the British Survey of India from 1767, an epic project to map and define their eastern empire.

This 18th-century Hindu globe shows the heavens *(in the top half)* and the earthly realm *(below)*.

The cosmographic tradition

A Jain diagram of the universe shows Mount Meru surrounded by concentric circles representing different continents and oceans.

The cosmographic conceptions of Hinduism, Buddhism, and Jainism, which attempted to locate the sacred places of this world in an imagined universe, were remarkably complex. Within each of them, Jambudvipa – the world inhabited by humans – formed only a very small part. In all cultures of Asia there is a strong belief that the fortunes of humans are affected by extraterrestrial forces whose influence can be foretold, in part, through astrology, with which astronomy was closely associated. Thus, mapping the heavens (on an astrolabe or other astronomical instruments) was a much more important concern than the geographic mapping of topography.

The lotus flower, redrawn here by Francis Wilford in 1805, was for Buddhists a symbol of the universe.

The astronomical observatory at Jaipur was one of five built by the Rajput king Sawai Jai Singh between 1722 and 1739. It contained remarkably accurate masonry instruments.

Indigenous mapping of South and Southeast Asia

Scarcely any surviving indigenous maps of the region are earlier than the 16th century. Maps were drawn for a variety of reasons: to provide information for the military; to illustrate itineraries or journeys; to legitimize territorial possessions. Maritime navigation charts from Gujarat date to the 17th century. Yet few surviving maps are strictly geographical, and virtually none are drawn to a fixed scale. Cosmographic views were sometimes combined with geographical knowledge of the known world.

Indigenous South and Southeast Asian mapping

c.1660: Gujaratis make earliest known Indian nautical charts

c.1700: Probable commencement of Mughal military mapping

c.1800: Extensive military and administrative mapping by Marathas and Burmese

1600 — 1650 — 1700 — 1750 — 1800

c.1647: Completion of Atlas of India by Sadiq Isfahani

1776: Trai Phum (*Story of Three Worlds*), Thai manuscript containing world's longest map (172 m)

The sacred map of the Sundanese chiefdom of Timbanganten in western Java *(left)* was drawn in the late 16th century. It is still venerated by local villagers for its protective powers against the volcano clearly depicted on the left of the map.

The Mughal Emperor Jahangir is shown embracing Shah Abbas of Persia on a geographic globe, based on an Elizabethan model brought to the court by the first English ambassador in 1615 *(right)*.

An encyclopedic work in Persian by Sadiq Isfahani of Jaunpur in northern India was finished in 1647. The section on travel contains a map *(left)* of the "inhabited quarter" (Africa and Eurasia), drawn in the traditional style of Islamic cosmography.

The detail *(right)* is from a Mughal map showing the route from Delhi to Kandahar by means of a system of straight lines and nodal points.

Niccolò dei Conti: Venetian merchant explored sea routes between India and Saigon. His journey was the subject of a famous book by Poggio Bracciolini, published in 1439

Ibn Battuta: Islamic scholar set out from Mecca on 75,000-mile, 30-year journey, which may even have taken him to Beijing as the ambassador of a Delhi sultan

Magellan: First European to cross Pacific. Killed after fighting in Philippines, his around-the-world voyage was completed by del Cano. 18 men, out of an original 270, survived voyage

Serrão: Left behind by Abreu/Rodrigues mission; subsequently made his way by native ship to Spice Islands

Abreu/Rodrigues: Expedition to find fabled Spice Islands, turned back at Banda Sea

Da Gama: Via Cape of Good Hope, then from Mombasa. First discoverer of continuous sea route from Europe to India.

① Travelers and explorers in South and Southeast Asia

Major routes

→ Ibn Battuta, 1325–54
→ Niccolò dei Conti, 1414–37
→ Pêro da Covilhã 1487–90
→ Vasco da Gama, 1497–99
→ Antonio de Abreu/ Francisco Rodrigues, 1512
→ Francisco Serrão, 1512
→ Ferdinand Magellan/Juan Sebastian del Cano, 1519–22
→ Ralph Fitch 1583–91
→ Jean Baptiste Tavernier 1639–67 (five visits)

1000 km
1000 miles

Travelers in South and Southeast Asia

1498: Vasco da Gama's voyage to Calicut; secret Portuguese mapping follows
1535: Waldseemüller's map improves on shape of India
1596: J.H. Van Linschoten's *Itinerario* includes numerous large– and small-scale maps

1400 — 1450 — 1500 — 1550 — 1600

1439: Poggio Bracciolini records Asian journeys of Niccolò dei Conti
1502: First published map to show correct general shape of India, by Alberto Cantino
1512: Francisco Serrão (Portuguese) makes his way to Moluccas
1619: William Baffin's map of Mughal Empire, the first by an English cartographer

Travelers in South and Southeast Asia

The most celebrated medieval traveler in the region was Ibn Battuta of Tangier in the 14th century, even if his claim to have journeyed as far China may not be true. A century later Vasco da Gama was piloted across the Indian Ocean by a Gujarati Muslim. An even more southerly route opened up the richest prize of Southeast Asia – the fabled Spice Islands, subject of a Portuguese monopoly from 1512. In the 1590s the Dutch began to probe the southern Indian Ocean, using Mauritius as a staging-point.

This map of India and Ceylon dating from 1596 appears in Jan Huygen van Linschoten's *Itinerario*, a work instrumental in encouraging Dutch and English trade with India.

A Portuguese map of the Moluccas (1646) shows major settlements, volcanoes, and types of vegetation on the islands (*left*).

This 17th-century French map shows the Kingdom of Siam, the Malay Peninsula, Sumatra, and Java, including political boundaries and areas of influence (*right*).

The Survey of India

Although European mapping of India began in the wake of Vasco da Gama's 1498 landfall, it was not until after James Rennell's 1767 appointment as the first Surveyor General of the newly acquired province of Bengal that the British began to survey and map the country systematically. Initially, maps were based on observation, reports, and intelligence. From the late 18th century, British Army officers, such as Colin Mackenzie and William Lambton, began formal trigonometrical surveys. Sir George Everest, Lambton's successor, planned a vast network of triangulations, operated by a huge staff. He was careful to placate local princes, who feared that land surveys would infringe on their already eroded sovereignty.

James Rennell, surveyor of Bengal and Bihar, published this map in 1782, four years after his return to England. The cartouche depicts Britannia receiving the sacred scriptures of India from a Brahmin.

George Everest planned his trigonometrical triangulations on a grid overlying the entire subcontinent. His predecessor, William Lambton laid down the central north-south axis.

The Indian Atlas of J. & C. Walker was commissioned by the East India Company in 1823. It was produced at a scale of four miles to one inch.

The Survey of India

1792: Colin Mackenzie completes first maps of the territories of Tipu Sultan (Hyderabad)
1800: William Lambton commences triangulation of India
1823: George Everest becomes Superintendent of the Great Trigonometrical Survey

1750 — 1775 — 1800 — 1825 — 1850 — 1875

1767: Appointment of James Rennell as first Surveyor General of Bengal
1852: Mount Everest, named after Sir George Everest, recognized as world's highest peak

The scientific exploration of Southeast Asia

In 1854, the British naturalist Alfred Wallace set out for Singapore, and spent the next eight years traveling around the islands of the East Indies and New Guinea. He observed and collected a vast number of animal species, many previously unknown to western science. Most importantly, he observed a dramatic change in fauna at the center of the region; the eastern species are distinctly Australian, the western, Asian. He argued that the eastern part of the archipelago was therefore once part of a Pacific continent. The boundary between the two faunal regions came to be called the Wallace Line.

Alfred Wallace's account of his Southeast Asian travels, published in 1869, contains many fine illustrations of the species encountered on his journey, such as this black cockatoo from the Aru Islands.

The series of maps published in Alfred Wallace's account of his journey to Southeast Asia show, in great detail, the terrain which he explored. This map, of Ceram in the Moluccas, shows the region where he encountered and carefully observed many different types of birds of paradise, and first began to devise his theories about species evolution.

② The scientific journeys of Alfred Wallace in Southeast Asia

→ journeys of Alfred Wallace, 1854–62
— Wallace "line"
--- inferred ancient coastline
▨ eastern limit of transitional faunal zone

EARLY CIVILIZATIONS OF SOUTH ASIA

THE DEVELOPMENT of copper and bronze technology in South and Southeast Asia during the 5th to 3rd millennia BCE preceded the emergence of urban civilizations in these regions. The cities of the Indus established trade networks which extended to Mesopotamia. Some time after the collapse of the Indus civilization c.1800 BCE, Sanskrit-speaking Aryans settled in the region and their influence spread across northern India over the next thousand years. In the 6th century BCE the region of Magadha gained ascendancy over the small states of the Ganges plain. Chandragupta Maurya established a vigorous new dynasty with its capital at Pataliputra in 321 BCE, which reached its apogee in the following century in the reign of Ashoka. In Southeast Asia, Sanskrit inscriptions from c.400 BCE are evidence of early Indian influence in the region.

This perforated pot from Mohenjo-Daro was used for carrying perfume.

The development of Harappan culture

Harappan (Indus) culture arose from agricultural and pastoral cultures in the hills of nearby Baluchistan during the late 4th millennium BCE and expanded from its core area on the Indus valley as far east as the Ganges River and south to present-day Maharashtra. Indus civilization is marked by regularly laid-out cities, built of baked brick, and dominated by imposing citadels, which contained religious, ceremonial and administrative buildings. Many of the streets of the residential areas had brick-roofed drains with regular inspection holes. Weights, measures, and bricks were all standardized, indicating a high level of cultural uniformity. The demise of the Indus civilization may have been caused by environmental change which disrupted the delicate balance between the cities and their agricultural base.

This bust of a bearded man from Mohenjo-Daro c.2100 BCE, may represent a priest-king.

Pre-Mauryan cultures in South Asia

c.2600: Harappan Bronze Age civilization centered on Indus plain until c.1800 BCE

c.1500: Vedic Aryans begin to spread over much of northwest and north of Indian subcontinent

c.1000: Iron technology starts to diffuse over much of India

Mid-6th century: Magadha emerges as preeminent state in India

c.1800: Collapse of Harappan civilization, probably due to drying up of Saraswati river

c.1000: Aryans begin shift from pastoral to agricultural lifestyle and establish a number of small states

Late 6th–early 5th century: Emergence of Buddhism and Hinduism

❶ The citadel at Mohenjo-Daro

"college"

Great Bath

"granary"

200 meters
200 yards

❷ The development of Harappan culture, late 4th– early 2nd millennium BCE ▶

Baluchistan hill cultures
- hill cultures of Baluchistan, late 4th–late 3rd millennium BCE
- ◆ major site
- ◇ other site (selected)

Harappan cultures
- area of early Harappan culture, c.3000-2600 BCE
- limit of mature Harappan culture, c.1800 BCE
- ◆ principal cities
- ◇ other settlements
- major clusters of urban sites
- ◇ other important contemporary site

Bronze tools and weapons from Mohenjo-Daro reveal the city's high level of technological sophistication.

Mohenjo-Daro

This ancient city, along with Harappa, was one of the two greatest urban centers of Harappan civilization. With an area of more than 500 acres, the city's population may have been as high as 50,000. The houses of the lower town were divided into blocks by regular streets. The city was a major center of both trade and manufacture.

Stylish Harappan bronzes include this elegant dancer.

The Bronze Age in Southeast Asia to 1000 BCE

Archaeologists have unearthed numerous and diverse bronzes from Southeast Asia, some possibly dating as far back as 2000 BCE. The presence of bronze artefacts in some burials of the period, notably at Non Nok Tha and Ban Chiang in Thailand, indicates that society was becoming increasingly stratified. The background to this development, however, coming before the region was influenced by the civilized societies of India and China, is poorly understood. Sophisticated techniques, such as lost-wax casting and closed moulds, were used, and earthenware crucibles found near the burials indicate local mastery of complex bronze technology.

❸ Bronze Age Southeast Asia from c.1500 BCE
- ◇ major Bronze Age site
- ◇ find of Dong Son-type drum

This pottery urn mounted on four supporting legs was made in Thailand c.3000–2000 BCE.

Bronze Dong Son drums, such as this one from Vietnam, c.500 BCE have been found throughout the region.

④ The Nanda and Mauryan empires 365–181 BCE

- maximum extent of Nanda Empire
- maximum extent of Mauryan Empire

GAUDA name of province/region

⬦ Ashokan pillar edicts

▦ Ashokan rock edicts

Invasions from Central Asia

➜ Northern Shakas/Sai Wang (mid- to late 2nd century BCE)

➜ Yuezhi (Tocharians), c. 165–100 BCE

➜ Scythians (under pressure from Yuezhi) (late 2nd century BCE)

➜ Scythians (after defeat by Parthians) (late 2nd century BCE)

➜ Shakas (under pressure from Scythians) 110–100 BCE

Shakas peoples

The central narrative of the *Mahabharata* tells the story of the struggle for supremacy between two groups of cousins – the Kauravas and the Pandavas. This manuscript illustration shows a chariot battle between the two forces.

The Nanda and Mauryan empires c.365–181 BCE

By c.600 BCE, the Ganges plain was dominated by 16 distinct political units which, over the next century, all came under the control of the state of Magadha. By the time of the Nanda dynasty (c.365–321 BCE) the extent of the Magadhan Empire was already substantial. The succeeding Mauryan Empire (321–181 BCE), however, was the first to achieve pan-Indian status and its political and cultural influence extended well beyond the subcontinent. When the Mauryan leader Ashoka converted to Buddhism (c.260 BCE), he foreswore war. Following the decline of the empire, northwest India suffered a series of invasions by peoples from northeast Asia, propelled into migration by the expansion of Han China.

A Buddhist stupa still stands at Sarnath, a Mauryan city on the northern Ganges plain.

The Mauryan Empire and successor states in South Asia

321: Chandragupta Maurya founds Mauryan Empire

c.190: Establishment of several Greek kingdoms in northwestern South Asia

Early 1st century CE: Kushans invade northwestern India

c.90 CE: Shakas invade northwestern South Asia

c.269: Mauryan Emperor Ashoka ascends throne

c.181: End of Mauryan and start of Shunga dynasty

c.50: Powerful Satavahana dynasty arises in Deccan, lasts until 250 CE

c.200 CE: India's trading links with Classical Western world and China at their height

The Mahabharata War

India's two Sanskrit epics, the *Mahabharata* and the *Ramayana*, may have been composed as early as 400 BCE. The works recount events which seem to relate to a great war fought in northwestern India several centuries earlier. The later magnification of this conflict into a pan-Indian struggle is probably the result of post-Mauryan mythology. The peoples identified in this map are among those who came within the ambit of expanding Mauryan power.

⑤ Realms mentioned as participants in the Mahabharata War

- ▦ Kaurava capital
- ▦ Pandava capital
- ▦ Janapadas (realms) in the Kaurava alliance
- ▦ Janapadas (realms) in the Pandava alliance
- ▦ Janapadas (realms) divided in allegiance, or changing allegiance during the course of the war

⑥ Areas influenced by India in Southeast Asia to 650 CE

- areas influenced by India
- ● major city of Indianized state

TUN-SUN ancient Indianized state

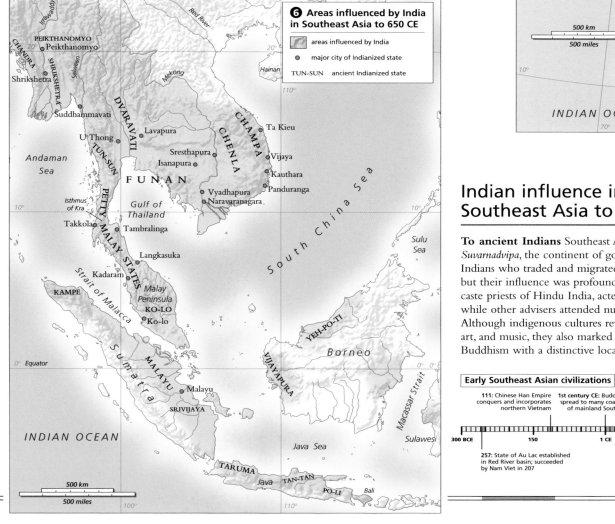

Indian influence in Southeast Asia to 650 CE

To ancient Indians Southeast Asia was known as *Suvarnadvipa*, the continent of gold. The number of Indians who traded and migrated there was not great, but their influence was profound. Brahmins, the high-caste priests of Hindu India, acted as ritual specialists, while other advisers attended numerous royal courts. Although indigenous cultures revered Indian traditions, art, and music, they also marked Hinduism and Buddhism with a distinctive local character.

A bronze statue of the Hindu deity Vishnu from Thailand (7th century CE) reflects the impact of Indian civilization on Southeast Asia.

Early Southeast Asian civilizations

111: Chinese Han Empire conquers and incorporates northern Vietnam

1st century CE: Buddhism starts to spread to many coastal localities of mainland Southeast Asia

c.192: Establishment of Lin-yi/ Champa, longest-lived Hinduized state of Southeast Asia

6th century: Rise of Indianized Mon state of Dvaravati in what is now Thailand

257: State of Au Lac established in Red River basin; succeeded by Nam Viet in 207

1st century CE: Funan, precursor of Cambodia, arises as first Hinduized state of Southeast Asia

c.550: Khmer state of Chenla overthrows its former suzerain, Funan

THE RELIGIONS OF SOUTHERN ASIA

THE HISTORY OF SOUTH AND SOUTHEAST ASIA is inextricably linked to the diffusion and development of religions, and the interaction between different systems of belief. Indeed, the identity of most of the region's populations has long been defined by religion. India was the cultural birthplace of both Hinduism and Buddhism, as well as other less widespread faiths, such as Jainism and Sikhism. Buddhism once enjoyed substantial political patronage from Indian rulers, but ultimately failed to become established among the population at large. The resurgence of Hinduism in the course of the 1st millennium CE and the spread of Islam in the 8th–13th centuries also contributed to the demise of Buddhism in the land of its birth. Many imported faiths, including Buddhism, Hinduism, Islam, and, most recently, Christianity, have planted roots in the receptive soil of various parts of Southeast Asia.

This relief of the Buddha is in the Gandhara style, inspired by Greco-Roman sculpture.

◀❶ India of the early Vedas

☐ Vedic Aryan settlement by c.900 BCE
PRACHYA broad cultural region
Kashi Mahajanapada (one of 16 domains noted in later Buddhist texts)

India of the early Vedas, 1500–1000 BCE

The *Rig Veda* (completed c.900 BCE) is the great literary monument left by the early Aryan settlers of northern India. This collection of sacred hymns traces the development of religious ideas as they were passed down orally from generation to generation. They depict the Aryans as chariot-driving warriors, formerly nomadic pastoralists, gradually adapting to a settled way of life. Later Buddhist texts abound in geographic references and mention the 16 great domains of north and central India – the *Mahajanapadas*.

c.900 BCE: Composition of later *Vedas*, *Brahmanas*, and *Upanishads* begins	c.400 BCE: Start of Hindu diffusion to southern India and Sri Lanka	c.50 BCE: Start of composition of *Bhagavad Gita*	c.450: Composition of early *Puranas* and near-final form of *Mahabharata*
1500 BCE	**1000 BCE**	**500 BCE**	**1 CE**	**500 CE**
c.1500 BCE: Composition of hymns of *Rig Veda* begins	c.500–300 BCE: Codes of religious laws (*Dharmashastra*) composed	c.400 BCE: Composition and compilation of *Mahabharata* and *Ramayana* epics begins	**Vedic India**

India of the Puranas

During the 1st millennium BCE, as the Aryan tribes coalesced into small kingdoms and republics, their religion became more comparable to the current form of Hinduism. As non-Aryan peoples were conquered and absorbed, a caste-based social order dominated by a Brahman priesthood, who oversaw increasingly elaborate rituals, and by a warrior caste (*Kshatriyas*) emerged. At first conquered peoples formed the lower strata of society. The expansion of Hindu culture can be traced through sacred texts; the collection of encyclopedic works – known as the *Puranas* – are rich in geographic content. They divide India up into a series of states or realms known as *janapadas*.

This bronze figure of Shiva, dating from the 11th century CE, depicts him as Lord of the Dance. He is surrounded by a circle of fire, which symbolizes both death and rebirth.

The hearth of Buddhism and Jainism

Buddhism and Jainism arose in the Gangetic Plain during the 6th century BCE, partly in reaction to the ritual excesses and social inequalities within Brahmanism. Both faiths stress *ahimsa* (nonviolence), detachment from worldly possessions, and religious meditation. Both diffused widely and enjoyed the patronage of numerous political rulers before the advent of Islam in northern India, although the number of followers, especially of Jainism, may not have been great.

India's largest collection of Buddhist monuments is found at Sanchi in Central India. They were built from the 3rd century BCE to the 11th century CE.

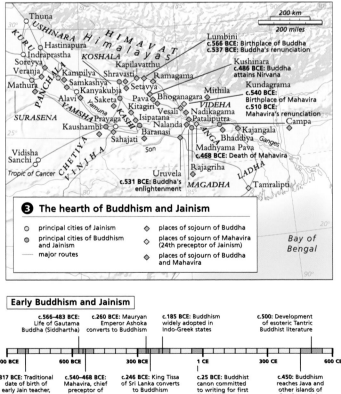

❸ The hearth of Buddhism and Jainism

○ principal cities of Jainism
◑ principal cities of Buddhism and Jainism
— major routes
◆ places of sojourn of Buddha
◇ places of sojourn of Mahavira (24th preceptor of Jainism)
◆ places of sojourn of Buddha and Mahavira

Early Buddhism and Jainism

c.566–483 BCE: Life of Gautama Buddha (Siddhartha)	c.260 BCE: Mauryan Emperor Ashoka converts to Buddhism	c.185 BCE: Buddhism widely adopted in Indo-Greek states	c.500: Development of esoteric Tantric Buddhist literature
900 BCE	**600 BCE**	**300 BCE**	**1 CE**	**300 CE**	**600 CE**
817 BCE: Traditional date of birth of early Jain teacher, Parshvanatha	c.540–468 BCE: Mahavira, chief preceptor of Jain religion	c.246 BCE: King Tissa of Sri Lanka converts to Buddhism	c.25 BCE: Buddhist canon committed to writing for first time in Sri Lanka	c.450: Buddhism reaches Java and other islands of Southeast Asia

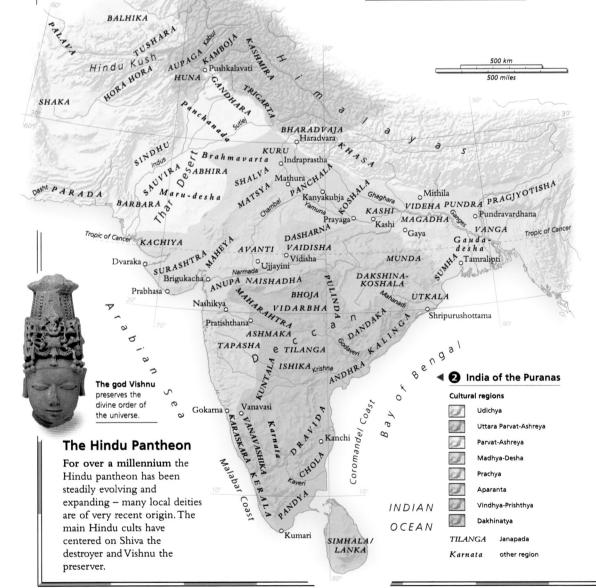

◀❷ India of the Puranas

Cultural regions
☐ Udichya
☐ Uttara Parvat-Ashreya
☐ Parvat-Ashreya
☐ Madhya-Desha
☐ Prachya
☐ Aparanta
☐ Vindhya-Prishthya
☐ Dakhinatya

TILANGA Janapada
Karnata other region

The god Vishnu preserves the divine order of the universe.

The Hindu Pantheon

For over a millennium the Hindu pantheon has been steadily evolving and expanding – many local deities are of very recent origin. The main Hindu cults have centered on Shiva the destroyer and Vishnu the preserver.

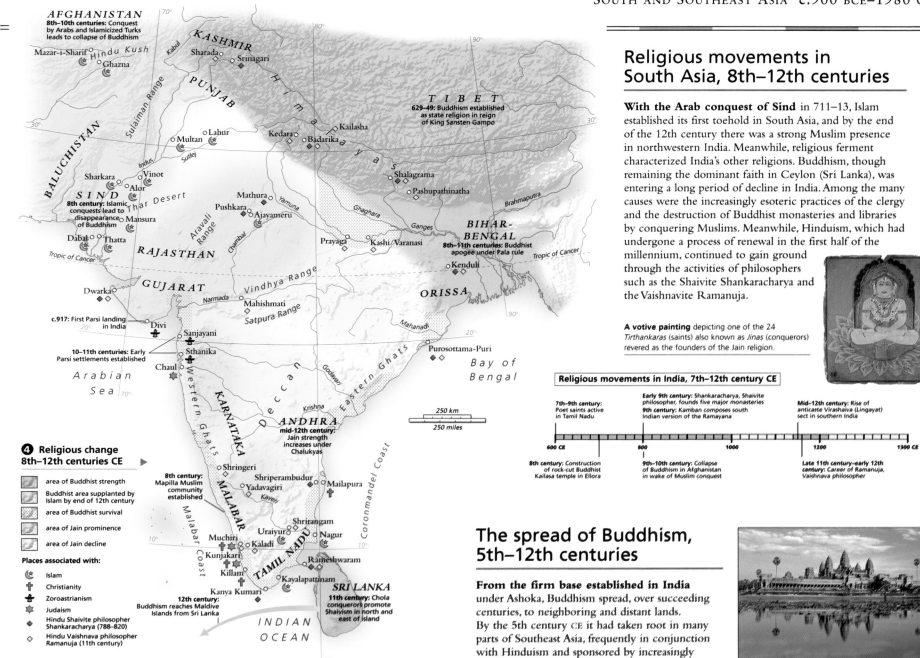

AFGHANISTAN
8th–10th centuries: Conquest by Arabs and Islamicized Turks leads to collapse of Buddhism

629–49: Buddhism established as state religion in reign of King Sansten Gampo

8th century: Islamic conquests lead to disappearance of Buddhism

c.917: First Parsi landing in India

10–11th centuries: Early Parsi settlements established

8th–11th centuries: Buddhist apogee under Pala rule

mid-12th century: Jain strength increases under Chalukyas

8th century: Mapilla Muslim community established

12th century: Buddhism reaches Maldive Islands from Sri Lanka

11th century: Chola conquerors promote Shaivism in north and east of island

④ Religious change 8th–12th centuries CE

- area of Buddhist strength
- Buddhist area supplanted by Islam by end of 12th century
- area of Buddhist survival
- area of Jain prominence
- area of Jain decline

Places associated with:
- ☾ Islam
- ✝ Christianity
- ☩ Zoroastrianism
- ✡ Judaism
- ◆ Hindu Shaivite philosopher Shankaracharya (788–820)
- ◇ Hindu Vaishnava philosopher Ramanuja (11th century)

Religious movements in South Asia, 8th–12th centuries

With the Arab conquest of Sind in 711–13, Islam established its first toehold in South Asia, and by the end of the 12th century there was a strong Muslim presence in northwestern India. Meanwhile, religious ferment characterized India's other religions. Buddhism, though remaining the dominant faith in Ceylon (Sri Lanka), was entering a long period of decline in India. Among the many causes were the increasingly esoteric practices of the clergy and the destruction of Buddhist monasteries and libraries by conquering Muslims. Meanwhile, Hinduism, which had undergone a process of renewal in the first half of the millennium, continued to gain ground through the activities of philosophers such as the Shaivite Shankaracharya and the Vaishnavite Ramanuja.

A votive painting depicting one of the 24 *Tirthankaras* (saints) also known as *Jinas* (conquerors) revered as the founders of the Jain religion.

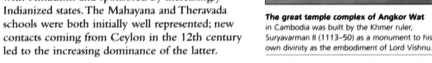

Religious movements in India, 7th–12th century CE

7th–9th century: Poet saints active in Tamil Nadu

Early 9th century: Shankaracharya, Shaivite philosopher, founds five major monasteries

9th century: Kamban composes south Indian version of the Ramayana

Mid-12th century: Rise of anticaste Virashaiva (Lingayat) sect in southern India

8th century: Construction of rock-cut Buddhist Kailasa temple in Ellora

9th–10th century: Collapse of Buddhism in Afghanistan in wake of Muslim conquest

Late 11th century–early 12th century: Career of Ramanuja, Vaishnava philosopher

| 600 CE | 800 | 1000 | 1200 | 1300 CE |

The spread of Buddhism, 5th–12th centuries

From the firm base established in India under Ashoka, Buddhism spread, over succeeding centuries, to neighboring and distant lands. By the 5th century CE it had taken root in many parts of Southeast Asia, frequently in conjunction with Hinduism and sponsored by increasingly Indianized states. The Mahayana and Theravada schools were both initially well represented; new contacts coming from Ceylon in the 12th century led to the increasing dominance of the latter.

The great temple complex of Angkor Wat in Cambodia was built by the Khmer ruler, Suryavarman II (1113–50) as a monument to his own divinity as the embodiment of Lord Vishnu.

⑤ The spread of Buddhism, 5th–12th centuries

Areas penetrated by Buddhism:
- by 1 CE
- 1st–5th centuries CE
- 6th–12th centuries CE
- → spread of Buddhism by 5th century CE
- → diffusion of Singhalese form of Theravada Buddhism, 12th century
- ○ major Buddhist centre
- 🛕 major stupa
- 🛕 major pagoda

The spread of Islam in Southeast Asia

Indian Muslim traders settled in the mercantile centers of Southeast Asia as early as the 10th century, but it was only after the conversion to Islam of the ruler of the powerful Sumatran state of Achin that the mainly peaceful process of Islamization began in earnest. In rapid succession, the princes of other small trading states also embraced the new faith. From their coastal capitals, Islam gradually penetrated inland, a process still underway in parts of present-day Indonesia.

A Dutch engraving of 1596 shows an envoy from Mecca meeting the governor of Bantam in west Java, an example of the East Indies' strong links with the Muslim world.

The diffusion of Islam in South and Southeast Asia

711–12: Arab conquest of Sind introduces Islam to South Asia

c.1000: Mahmud of Ghazni conquers northwest India

1295: Conversion of Sultan of Achin to Islam, which spreads over much of the East Indies

| 700 CE | 800 | 900 | 1000 | 1100 | 1200 | 1300 CE |

c.750: Muslim merchants establish Islam in Kerala, southwest India

c.1200: Muslim Sufi saint, Mu'in al-Din Chishti, founds first Sufi order in subcontinent

⑥ The spread of Islam in Southeast Asia

Areas penetrated by Islam:
- 13th–14th centuries
- 15th century
- 16th century
- 17th–18th centuries
- 19th–20th centuries
- → spread of Islam

The Buddhist stupa at Borobudur, Java, symbolizes via its structure, the Buddhist transition from reality at its base – for example in this panel showing sailing vessels – to the achievement of spiritual enlightenment at the summit.

STATES AND EMPIRES 300–1525

SOUTH ASIA WAS ruled by a great diversity of regional powers for much of this period. However, in the 4th century CE, the Gupta dynasty succeeded in uniting much of the Indian subcontinent. The next 200 years are often described as a "golden age" of Indian civilization. It was not until the 13th century that so much of India again came under the control of a single state, the Delhi Sultanate. The Turkish dynasties that ruled the Sultanate were unable to maintain effective control over so vast an area, and its power declined in the 14th century. Southeast Asia also witnessed the rise and fall of numerous states. Kambujadesha, with its magnificent capital at Angkor, dominated the mainland, while the two greatest states of the Indonesian archipelago were Srivijaya and, later, Majapahit.

Bajang Ratu was the capital of the Majapahit kingdom in Central Java.

The imperial Guptas c.300–550

The authority of the Guptas extended over many conquered states whose rulers remained on their thrones in a tributary relationship to the Gupta sovereign. They held sway over other regional powers by virtue of diplomacy and marital alliances. Peace, prosperity, scholarly debate, and religious tolerance all encouraged a florescence of Indian art – in particular, in sculpture, painting, poetry, and drama. But Gupta rule was shattered by the invasion of Hunas Huns Hephthalites), nomads from Central Asia, in the 6th century.

This wall painting depicting a scene from the life of the Buddha is from the spectacular cave sanctuaries at Ajanta, central India.

❶ Imperial Guptas and contemporary powers, 300–550

- core area of Gupta Empire
- maximum extent of Gupta Empire
- core area of Vakataka state
- core area of Pallava state
- → major Huna penetration of India, with initial date
- ○ important city or town
- *Hephthalites* Central Asian people

Medieval states 550–1206

This rock carving depicts a scene from the epic poem *Mahabharata*.

The multiplicity of regional powers that dominated India during this period all developed distinctive cultural styles, whose legacy survives in architecture, literature, and tradition. Some of them achieved, for brief periods, quasi-imperial status. The struggle for control of the Ganges plain was dominated by three major states: the Gurjara-Pratiharas, the Palas, and the Rashtrakutas. In the south, two major powers emerged; the Chalukyas in the west, and the Tamil Cholas in the east. Under Rajaraja (985–1014), the Cholas conquered much of southern India and Ceylon (Sri Lanka), their rule extending to the Malay Peninsula.

The Brihadeshwana temple at Thanjavur (Tanjore) is one of several fine Dravidian temples in the city, dating from the 11th century when it was the capital of the Chola kingdom.

Medieval states

- **320:** Chandra Gupta I founds Gupta Empire; India's "golden age"
- **c.495:** Huna invasions weaken Guptas in northern India
- **c.880:** Gurjara-Pratiharas rule over virtually the whole of northern India
- **c.1025:** Apogee of Tamil Chola dynasty

(timeline 300–1100)

- **c.540:** King Harsha restores mighty Hindu state in Kanyakubja, northern India
- **c.750:** Apogee of Pala dynasty, the last major Buddhist state in South Asia
- **c.825:** Rashtrakuta dynasty rules over south India and Sri Lanka

❷ The medieval states of South Asia

- core areas of principal states (dates indicate period of independent power)
- (630–856) dates of states' greatest territorial extent

The Delhi Sultanate 1206–1526

The invasion of Mahmud of Ghazni in the 11th century, highlighted India's political and military vulnerability, and subsequent invasions by Turkish peoples from Central Asia led to the establishment of the Mamluk dynasty of the Delhi Sultanate in 1206. The territory controlled by the five successive dynasties that ruled the Sultanate fluctuated greatly, reaching its greatest extent under the Tughluqs. Administrative inefficiency and an ill-advised attempt to move the capital south to Daulatabad hastened the Sultanate's decline, and much of India fragmented once again into warring kingdoms.

The Delhi Sultanate

- **c.1025:** Conquest of Punjab by Ghaznavids
- **1192–93:** Afghan Ghurids defeat Rajputs and seize Delhi and much of northern India
- **1206:** Breakaway Mamluk (Slave) dynasty, under Aibak, establishes Delhi Sultanate
- **1398:** Sack of Delhi by Timur (Tamerlane) leads to fall of Tughluq dynasty

(timeline 1000–1400)

- **1336:** Rebellion against Tughluqs marks beginning of Vijayanagara Empire
- **1345:** Hasan Gangu, governor of Tughluq Deccani domains, revolts and founds Bahmani kingdom

Delhi's first congregational mosque, known today as the Quwwat al-Islam mosque was built by Qutb ud-Din Aibak, after the capture of Delhi in 1192.

The ornate sandstone pillar of Delhi's Qutb Minar, built c.1200, is adorned with Arabic calligraphy.

❸ The Delhi Sultanate

- area of Sultanate at accession of Jalal ud-Din Khalji, 1290
- additional territory at some time under direct Khalji administration
- limit of nominal Khalji vassals
- → possible route of Khalji raids against Mongols
- extent of Sultanate at accession of Ghiyas ud-din Tughluq, 1320
- maximum extent of Sultanate under direct Tughluq administration
- limit of nominal Tughluq vassals
- *Ahoms* peoples and dynasties
- *SIND* cultural region

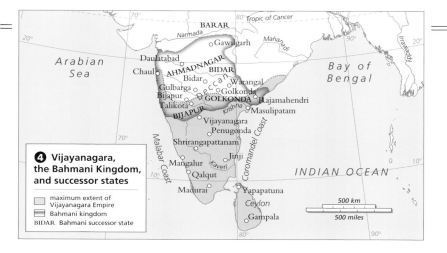

④ Vijayanagara, the Bahmani Kingdom, and successor states

maximum extent of Vijayanagara Empire
Bahmani kingdom
BIDAR Bahmani successor state

The Vijayanagara Empire 1335–1570

The decline of the Delhi Sultanate led to the breakaway of the Muslim-controlled areas of the Deccan and the creation, in 1347, of the Bahmani Kingdom. To the south, in the Krishna valley, the powerful new Hindu kingdom of Vijayanagara was firmly established by 1345. Its splendid capital, Vijayanagara (modern Hampi), was a magnificent temple city, with massive fortifications and a royal palace. Vijayanagara successfully withstood repeated attempts by the Bahmani Kingdom to expand southward. The Bahmani Kingdom divided into five sultanates in 1518, and Vijayanagara finally succumbed in 1570, after a disastrous defeat at Talikota in 1565.

The royal capital of Vijayanagara ("city of victory"), founded in the mid-14th century, was destroyed by invaders from the Deccan sultanates in 1565.

Principal states of Southeast Asia 650–1250

The major states of mainland Southeast Asia, although extensive, were loosely controlled and included substantial tribal populations. Their civilizations frequently displayed a strong Indian influence, most obviously in Hindu-Buddhist centers such as Borobudur. The Khmer state of Kambujadesha, with its impressive capital at Angkor, dominated the mainland. In the East Indies, the leading states were bound together largely by commercial ties. The maritime empire of Srivijaya, with its capital at Palembang in Sumatra, controlled international trade through the straits of Malacca and Sunda.

This carved relief from the 13th-century temple complex at Angkor Thom, part of the Khmer capital of Angkor, shows mounted soldiers accompanying a war elephant being transported in a cart pulled by donkeys.

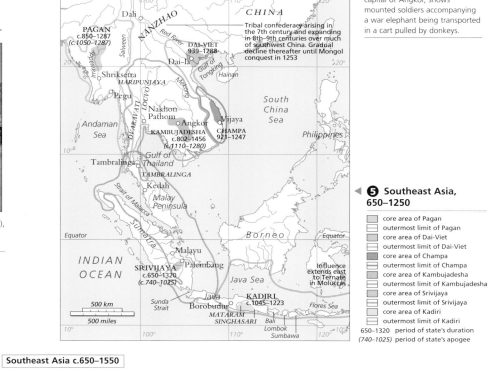

⑤ Southeast Asia, 650–1250

core area of Pagan
outermost limit of Pagan
core area of Dai-Viet
outermost limit of Dai-Viet
core area of Champa
outermost limit of Champa
core area of Kambujadesha
outermost limit of Kambujadesha
core area of Srivijaya
outermost limit of Srivijaya
core area of Kadiri
outermost limit of Kadiri
650–1320 period of state's duration
(740–1025) period of state's apogee

Southeast Asia c.650–1550

802: Founding of Khmer state of Kambujadesha by Devaraya II, with capital at Angkor

c.1200: Zenith of Kambujadesha under reign of Jayavarman VII

c.1280: Mongol invasions destroy Pagan and eclipse Dai Viet

c.1450: Islam spreads over much of East Indies

c.700: Srivijaya power extends over most of Sumatra, Malay Peninsula and western Java

939: Nam Viet throws off Chinese rule

c.1250: Thai state established in Sukhothai

c.1350: Majapahit exercises sway over most of East Indies

1471: Final collapse of Hindu state of Champa in southern Vietnam

Principal states of Southeast Asia 1250–1550

During this period there was a marked increase in the number of medium-sized contenders for power throughout the region. The decline of Kambujadesha was matched by the rise of several ethnically Thai states and the destruction of the long-lived state of Champa by the sinicized kingdom of Dai-Viet. In the East Indies, dominance passed from Srivijaya to Majapahit which, in the 14th century, established the most extensive commercial empire that the area was to see in precolonial times.

⑥ Southeast Asia, 1250–1550

Outer limits of areas at some time subject to the following major states:

Toungoo | Champa
Ava | Dai-Viet
Pegu | Singhasari
Sukhothai | Melaka
Ayuthia | Majapahit
Kambuja | BALI other states

A bronze water vessel in the shape of a duck, from Thailand, demonstrates the technological sophistication of the metal-workers of Southeast Asia.

The Garai Cham tower from the city of Phan Rang, in the Hindu-Buddhist kingdom of Champa, which flourished in southern Vietnam (7th–12th centuries), but was absorbed by Dai-Viet in 1471.

MUGHALS, MARATHAS, EUROPEANS

Shah Jahan (1627–58) was one of the greatest of the Mughal emperors.

THE CONQUEST OF NORTHERN INDIA in 1526 by the Muslim Mughal chief, Babur, was to usher in a new era, marked by orderly government, economic prosperity, and great achievements in the arts, notably architecture, miniature painting, and literature. When, after the stern rule of Aurangzeb, the empire fell into disarray, the Hindu Marathas expanded rapidly from their Deccan base and dominated Indian affairs until their defeat by the British early in the 19th century. Vasco da Gama's voyage to India in 1498 opened up new trade routes, enabling European powers to establish commercial toeholds; spices, textiles, and jewels were soon being exported to western markets.

The Mughals, 1526–1857

This miniature shows Shah Jahan with his four sons. His third son, Aurangzeb, deposed him in 1658.

In 1526 the Mughals, led by Babur, a descendant of Timur (see p.229), swept across much of northern India. His successor, Humayun, expelled by the governor of Bihar in 1539, returned in 1555 to establish a long-lived dynasty and an expansionist empire. The reign of Akbar (1556–1605) was a time of cultural florescence and religious tolerance. Later in the 17th century, Aurangzeb's long and harsh rule led to revolt. Many provinces seceded, and the rise of the Maratha confederacy from 1646 eventually reduced the Mughals to puppet rulers.

The tomb of Sheikh Salim lies in the Great Mosque at Fatehpur Sikri. Construction of the spectacular red limestone city began in the 1570s in the reign of Akbar.

Emperor Shah Jahan built the Taj Mahal c.1654 as a mausoleum for his beloved wife, Mumtaz. This exquisite structure of white marble is one of the masterpieces of Mughal architecture.

The Mughal Empire

1526: Babur conquers Delhi and founds Mughal Empire

1556–1605: Reign of Akbar marked by territorial expansion and cordial Hindu-Muslim relations

1658–1707: Empire reaches maximum extent during reign of Aurangzeb

1724: Independent rule over Deccan by Nizam of Hyderabad hastens disintegration of empire

1739: Sack of Delhi by Persians and Afghans under Nadir Shah

1788: Mughal emperors become puppets of Marathas

1803: British occupy Delhi

1857: Last Mughal Emperor, the puppet Bahadur Shah II, dethroned and exiled by British

① The Mughal Empire, 1526–1707

- Babur's domains, 1525
- Babur's acquisitions prior to Mughal expulsions, 1539
- Akbar's domains, 1556
- areas held by Mughals at Akbar's death 1605
- areas partially integrated into Mughal domains, 1605
- additional areas acquired up to the death of Aurangzeb, 1707
- ○ British possessions
- ○ Dutch possessions
- ○ Portuguese possessions
- SIND 1574–81 regions acquired by Mughals 1556–1696, with dates of acquisition

Nadir Shah of Persia is shown sacking Delhi in 1739. His invasion, and the growing power of the Marathas, led to the downfall of the Mughals.

◀ ② Maratha expansion 1708–1800

- territories at some time in the possession of Shivaji or Venkaji, 1646–80
- areas at some time under the direct rule of the Marathas, 1708–1800
- areas nominally under Maratha rule, but not administered by them
- — outermost limit of territory under Maratha rule
- other areas in which Marathas levied taxes
- 1739 date of acquisition by Marathas
- (–75) date of subsequent loss by Marathas to c.1800
- *BHONSLE* principal member of Confederacy
- ○ capital city of principal member of Confederacy
- → Maratha campaigns into neighboring territory, with date

The Marathas, 1646–1818

The origins of the Hindu Maratha state lie with a heroic chieftain, Shivaji, who, from his heavily fortified base in the Western Ghats, led a large force of highly mobile, lightly armored horsemen who engaged in relentless battle with the Mughal Empire and the sultans of Bijapur. After the death of the Mughal emperor Aurangzeb, in 1707, Maratha campaigns resumed, and a loose confederacy gained control over most of India. Until their final defeat in 1818, the Marathas presented the last obstacle to growing British supremacy.

The Marathas

1674: Shivaji crowned king; career marked by widespread conquests

1728: Marathas defeat Nizam of Hyderabad and gain supremacy over Deccan; with subsequent territorial expansion

1761: Defeat by Afghans temporarily ends Maratha hegemony over northern India

1782: Treaty ending first Anglo-Maratha war results in territorial losses for Marathas

1788: Occupation of Delhi; Maratha territorial apogee

1803: Second Anglo-Maratha war results in loss of Delhi

1818: Third Anglo-Maratha war ends in Maratha defeat

❸ European commerce with South Asia 16th–18th centuries ▶

1505 date of first European trading contact
● important manufacturing center

Colonial holdings
◇ Portuguese
◇ Dutch*
◇ British
◇ French*
◇ Austrian
◇ Danish*

on the map, diamonds reflect the chronological order in which European powers asserted control

*All French, Dutch, and Danish holdings in India were seized by the British during various wars between 1765–1815 and subsequently restored. Dutch and Danish possessions were ceded to Britain in 1825 and 1846 respectively.

Main commodities manufactured and traded

▦	embroidery	✸	indigo
⚒	arms	⚶	jute
⟿	carpets	⚕	rice
▤	woodwork	△	ships
⚱	perfume	✾	opium
◗	ghee	△	saltpeter
◑	oils	⚓	sugar
▭	paper	⚘	wheat
▥	cotton	⚘	pepper
▦	silk	⚘	cinnamon
▦	other textiles	⚘	cardamom
⚘	yarn	⚘	coir
▨	glass	⚘	ginger
✕	leather goods	⚙	iron
⚬	coconuts	▣	precious stones
⚱	tobacco	▤	quilts and blankets
♨	brassware, gold, and silver inlay wares		
♙	pottery		

European commerce with South Asia 1500–1800

In 1510, the Portuguese chose Goa to be capital of all their Indian possessions, and throughout the 16th century they were the sole European power to conduct significant trade with India. During the 17th century, Dutch, English, French, and Danish companies also established coastal trading centers, and Indian exports soon found their way onto world markets. During the multisided and sometimes lucrative commercial rivalry that ensued, control over large territorial holdings was long seen as neither necessary nor economically feasible. This view, however, was to change by the mid-18th century.

The Portuguese seized Goa in 1510; making it the capital of their Asian trading empire. This map of the city was engraved c.1600.

The Dutch were the main commercial power in Asia in the mid-17th century. They built trading posts in India – such as Cranganur near Cochin (right) – and in the East Indies.

Fort St. George, founded in 1639 by Francis Day of the British East India Company, became the city of Madras (now Chennai).

Early European commercial contacts with South and Southeast Asia

1511–12: Portuguese establish base in Malacca and reach Moluccas

1600: Founding of British East India Company

1650–90: Dutch seize many Portuguese posts and become dominant mercantile power

1811–15: During Napoleonic Wars, British take over French and Dutch possessions

1500 — 1600 — 1700 — 1800 — 1900

1510: Goa made capital of all Portuguese possessions in Asia

1585: Spain establishes first permanent European settlement at Cebu, in Philippines

1744–63: Anglo-French wars eclipse French power in Asia

1819: Sir Stamford Raffles obtains cession of Singapore for British East India Company

❹ South East Asian contacts with Europe c.1550–1800

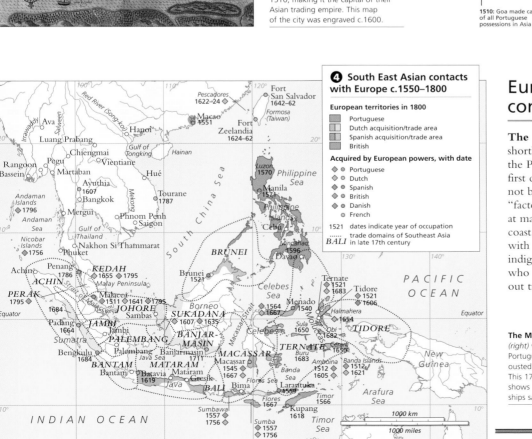

European territories in 1800
▨ Portuguese
▦ Dutch acquisition/trade area
▧ Spanish acquisition/trade area
▩ British

Acquired by European powers, with date
◇ Portuguese
◇ Dutch
◇ Spanish
◇ British
◇ Danish
◇ French

1521 dates indicate year of occupation
..... trade domains of Southeast Asia
BALI trade domains of Southeast Asia in late 17th century

European and Southeast Asian contacts 1500–1800

The commercial penetration of Southeast Asia by Europeans began shortly after the Portuguese arrival in India. The Spanish established links with the Philippines after Magellan's discovery of the islands in 1521 during the first circumnavigation of the globe. Dutch and British trade in the region did not begin until the 17th century. As in India, the European powers established "factories," often fortified, at many points along the coast. They cooperated with local magnates, both indigenous and Chinese, who had already carved out trading domains.

The Moluccan island of Ambon (right) was reached by the Portuguese in 1512. They were ousted by the Dutch in 1605. This 17th-century engraving shows Dutch East India Company ships sailing near the island.

THE AGE OF COLONIAL EXPANSION

Sir Stamford Raffles refounded the port city of Singapore in 1819.

BETWEEN 1765 AND 1914 the European powers completed their conquest and annexation of most of South and Southeast Asia. Nepal and Afghanistan were greatly reduced in size and made protectorates of Britain, while Siam, though shorn of most of its outer territories, maintained its independence, acting as a buffer between the British and the French. There were many reasons for European conquest, including commercial disputes, the desire to control resources, diplomatic entanglements, and strategic considerations. All were the inevitable result of interaction between nations with vastly differing military and naval resources in an age of imperial expansion.

Major indigenous powers confronting British and French colonizers

1749: Mysore starts to become major power in southern India

1754: Powerful Burmese dynasty established on capture of Ava by Alaungpaya

1802: With French aid, Nguyen Anh unites and becomes emperor of Vietnam

1857–59: Revolt ("Mutiny") attempts to oust British from India

1700 · 1750 · 1800 · 1850 · 1900

c.1720: Marathas start to expand over most of India

1757: Expansion of Gurkha (Nepali) domains over much of Himalayas

1782: Siam reaches territorial apogee under Rama I

1785: Burmese invasion of Siam and counterinvasion by Siam of Burma

1839–42: Afghans under Dost Mohammed defeat British in First Afghan War

Warren Hastings, the first British governor-general of India (1774–85), is shown here dining with Indian princes. He was forced to confront both the Marathas and Mysore during the first phase of British expansion in India.

Indigenous powers and colonization

Even after the collapse of the Mughal Empire in 1761, significant states stood in the path of Western colonial expansion in both India and Southeast Asia. In India, the foremost power was the Maratha Confederacy, while in Southeast Asia, Burma, Siam, and Vietnam expanded in size and strength. At the dawn of the 19th century no large states remained over most of the East Indies, but Dutch commercial dominance was not yet reflected in territorial holdings.

British control in South Asia 1757–1914

Britain's imperial ventures in India began with the commercial activities of the East India Company. In 1757, the victory of Robert Clive at Plassey over a French and Mughal force and the acquisition of the right to collect taxes in Bengal began an era of territorial expansion which ended with British claims to the Northeast Frontier Agency in 1914. With a pivotal role in the British Empire, India became enmeshed in European rivalries; from 1848, colonial acquisitions along the periphery of the subcontinent had greater strategic than economic impact.

① South and Southeast Asia 1765

- area under British control and possessions 1765
- Danish possessions
- area under Dutch control and possessions 1765
- French possessions
- area under Portuguese control and possessions 1765
- petty tribal polities
- other states
- ----- frontiers c.1765

This miniature of 1830 shows an Englishman hunting tigers, an activity greatly enjoyed by the British ruling class.

② British territorial expansion 1757–1914

- areas under British rule, pre-1800
- areas under British rule, 1800–50
- areas under British rule, post-1850
- Muslim princely state
- non-Muslim princely state
- British protectorate, with dates
- Portuguese colony
- French colony

Native bearers are shown carrying a British officer in a palanquin, c.1828.

Territorial expansion of British in South Asia and Burma

1757: Battle of Plassey; British victory over combined French and Mughal force

1803: Second Anglo-Maratha war leads to British acquisition of Delhi

1815: Victory in Anglo-Gurkha war extends British possessions into the Himalayas

1849: British annex Punjab after two Sikh wars

1885: Third Anglo-Burmese War; British annex Upper Burma

1750 · 1770 · 1790 · 1810 · 1830 · 1850 · 1870 · 1890

1799: British-led coalition defeats and partitions Mysore; British obtain the Carnatic coast

1815: British annex Ceylonese kingdom of Kandy

1826: First Anglo-Burmese War; British acquire coastal areas

1852: Second Anglo-Burmese War; British occupy Lower Burma

The Revolt of 1857–59

Much more than a mutiny, the revolt of 1857–59 involved not merely the defection of large sections of the British Indian army, but also a series of peasant insurrections, led either by local rulers or *zamindars* (great landlords), aimed at throwing off the imperial yoke. The revolt failed because of its lack of a coordinated command structure and British superiority in military intelligence, organization, and logistics.

British troops are shown rushing to quell the revolt at Umballa in 1859. The reforms made after the Revolt helped secure the British presence in India for another 90 years.

❸ **The Revolt of 1857–59** ▶

- princely states in rebellion
- states in which princes were loyal to British, but troops were in rebellion
- neutral princely states
- states actively aiding British
- British India
- areas in which British administration was disputed
- post at which Indian Sepoy troops mutinied
- site of major revolt, Mar 29 1857–Aug 31 1858
- site of significant British victory, Aug 16 1857–May 21 1859

The Revolt of 1857–59

May 10: Initial mutiny of troops at Meerut
May 11: Delhi seized by rebels. Retaken by British, Sep 30

Jun 4: Mutinies in both Benares and Cawnpore (retaken by British Jul 17)
Jun 7: Fyzabad mutiny. Maulavi Ahmad Shah becomes major rebel leader

Nov 23: British take stronghold of Firoz Shah, rebel leader from Delhi

Apr 3: British capture rebel leader the Rani of Jhansi
Apr 22: Kalpi, a rebel gathering place, taken by British

Jun 21: British take city of Gwalior, ending Central India rebellion

1857

Mar 29 1857: Mutiny of Mangal Pande, a sepoy from Oudh, initiates revolt

May 30: First battle of Revolt at Hindan River
May 30: Lucknow mutiny

Jun 18: Fatehgarh mutiny. Reoccupied by British, Jan 1858
Jun 27: Massacre of British evacuees at Cawnpore

Aug 16: British capture place of exile of Maratha rebel leader Nana Sahib
Aug 17: 8th Madras Native Regiment disbanded after refusing to go north

1858

Mar 22 1858: British retake Lucknow after 20-day siege

May 6: British take Bareilly, capital of Rohilkhand leader

Aug 31: Disarmed troops revolt at Multan

1859

❹ **The economy of India and Ceylon, 1857** ▶

Agriculture
- mainly peasant agriculture
- scattered cultivation, hunting and gathering, and limited pastoralism
- predominantly pastoralism, with scattered pockets of agriculture
- forested areas

Industry
- coal-mining areas
- sites of extraction of other minerals

Manufacturing centers
- metalworking
- arms
- ship building
- textiles
- glazed pottery, tiles, and ceramics
- woodworking and furniture making
- jewelry
- ivory carving

Transportation
- important road
- railroad
- railroad under construction

Population
- city with population of over 500,000
- city with population of 100,000–500,000
- city with population of 50,000–100,000
- important city with population of less than 50,000

Principial types of agricultural produce
- areca
- cacao
- cinnamon
- coconuts
- coffee
- cotton
- dates
- fruits
- indigo
- jute
- mustard
- opium
- palm sugar
- pepper
- potato
- rape
- salt
- sandalwood
- sesame
- spices
- sugar
- sunflower
- tea
- teak
- tobacco

Cotton was grown over much of the Indian subcontinent. In the 19th century, large quantities were exported to British mills, and the cloth then reimported, to the detriment of the local weavers. These men are ginning raw cotton to remove the seeds.

The economy of India and Ceylon by 1857

India became an essential part of a global economic network created by Britain during the 18th and 19th centuries. In some cases, British imports wiped out Indian industry – India was obliged to import woven cotton from Lancashire by 1853. India was an overwhelmingly peasant society in 1857, but railroads, canals, plantations, mines, small-scale factories, and the growth of busy port cities and administrative centres were transforming its economic landscape.

The first locomotive in India, not yet mounted on rails, is delivered by a string of elephants. Following the Revolt of 1857–59, an extensive program of railroad-building helped secure Britain's military and economic hold on India.

THE COLONIAL APOGEE AND DEMISE

M.K. Gandhi (1869–1948) was the hero of India's independence movement.

TWO NEW COLONIAL POWERS, the US and Japan, entered Southeast Asia at the beginning of the 20th century. The Philippines were annexed by the US following the Spanish-American War of 1898; the Japanese took over the German Pacific island colonies north of the equator in 1919 and acquired virtually the whole of Southeast Asia by force in World War II. Though the early 20th century can be seen as the apogee of colonialism in the region, especially in British India, there was already strong opposition to foreign rule. The Indian National Congress, founded in 1885, initially sought reforms, but by the 1930s demanded complete independence. In the Philippines, a revolutionary independence movement was well established when the Americans took over. But while India's freedom struggle was, on the whole, peaceful, the struggle in most of Southeast Asia was bloody, nowhere more so than in Vietnam.

The partition and reunification of Bengal 1905–12

Lord Curzon's 1905 partition of India's most populous province, Bengal, was fiercely opposed on many grounds by both Hindus and Muslims. Some upper-class Hindus, for example, feared that the creation of East Bengal and Assam, a Muslim-majority province, would restrict their access to government employment. The Muslim League, formed in 1906, urged that legislation should provide for separate electorates for Muslim minorities, to guarantee their representation in Hindu-majority areas. In 1912, the Bengali-speaking areas of the old province were reunited.

The independence struggle 1879–1947

Indian nationalist movements took many forms in the course of the long struggle for independence. The Indian National Congress, originally an organization of the Western-educated elite, became a mass popular movement after the return to India in 1915 of the charismatic Mohandas K. Gandhi. By the 1930s, cautious calls for self-rule had become unequivocal demands for independence.

British officers serving in India led lives of conspicuous ease, their lifestyles supported by domestic staff, as this photograph of a servant giving a pedicure shows.

▼ **②** The partition and reunification of Bengal, 1905–12

— national border
— provincial boundary
······ provincial boundary prior to 1905
▬ line of 1905 partition

▨ Muslim majority area
▧ British districts
☐ native states and protectorates
☐ frontier area

The freedom movement in India

1885: Founding of the Indian National Congress
1906: Foundation of Muslim League
1920: Start of civil disobedience campaigns by M. K. Gandhi in support of independence struggle
1918: Indian contribution to World War I earns it membership in League of Nations
1939: Congress ministries resign because India given no voice in respect to participation in World War II
1937: Burma is separated from India and made crown colony
1945: India becomes UN charter member
1947: New independent dominions of India and Pakistan are born
1948: Burma and Ceylon become independent; former withdraws from Commonwealth

◀ **①** The independence struggle, 1879–1947

Areas of widespread disturbance:

☐ 1919 hartal (general strike) and Punjab disturbances
☐ 1920–22 Noncooperation Program
☐ 1942 Quit India Campaign
☐ areas of widespread communal riots, 1946–47
✷ major riot with political consequences, with date
◉ political activities associated with Mohandas K. Gandhi
△ secret revolutionary group, with date of foundation
⚓ chief sites of Royal Indian Navy mutiny

☐ British India
☐ princely states
☐ French India
☐ Portuguese India

World War II in South and Southeast Asia

The Japanese swiftly overran Southeast Asia, occupying the whole region by March 1942. The Allied counteroffensive consisted of US advances across the western Pacific from 1943, and the advance of British and Indian troops through Burma from 1944. But Japanese occupation had unleashed a tide of nationalism which was to have a grave impact on the postwar maintenance of the status quo, leading to the creation of new nations and the end of the European empires.

These Japanese prisoners of war were taken after the capture of Guadalcanal in 1942 – a key campaign in the US amphibious offensive.

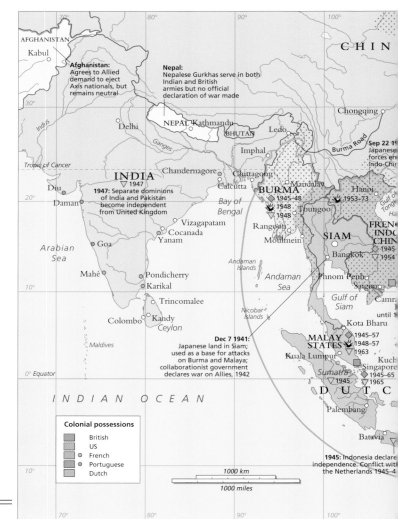

Colonial possessions

☐ British
☐ US
☐ French
☐ Portuguese
☐ Dutch

Political changes in Southeast Asia

1945: Sukarno and Ho Chi Minh declare independence for Indonesia and Vietnam respectively

1954: Geneva accords allow separate governments in North and South Vietnam

1957: Malaya granted independence, despite ongoing Communist insurrection

1963: Federation of Malaysia incorporates Singapore, Sarawak, and Sabah, along with Malaya

1975: Communist regimes come to power in South Vietnam, Laos, and Cambodia

1945 — 1955 — 1965 — 1975

1946: Philippines obtain their independence

1954: Sukarno abrogates union with Dutch and declares unitary state of Indonesia

1964: Gulf of Tonkin resolution authorizes US air strikes against North Vietnam and Viet Cong; war soon spreads to Laos and Cambodia

US troops are landed from a helicopter in Vietnam in 1967. Media coverage hardened public opposition to the war.

The decolonization of South and Southeast Asia

The global wave of decolonization swept over the region with remarkable speed. In 1946, the Philippines became the first country to be granted independence; India and Pakistan followed in 1947; and by 1948 all of South Asia was free. The last colonial territory in Southeast Asia, East Timor, was evacuated by Portugal in 1975. Grants of independence, however, did not always mean freedom from a foreign military presence, as Britain, France, and the US all sought to retain involvement in the region both commercially and through the maintenance of military bases.

❹ The decolonization of South and Southeast Asia

Former colonial powers
- ◆ United Kingdom
- ○ France
- Netherlands
- US
- Portugal
- Australia
- 1948 end of colonial/ dependent status
- ⊗ member of British Commonwealth 1971

British troops bring Communist insurgents out of the jungle during the Malaysian rebellion of 1947–48.

Jubilant citizens swarm through the streets of Calcutta, climbing over trucks and trams to celebrate Independence Day.

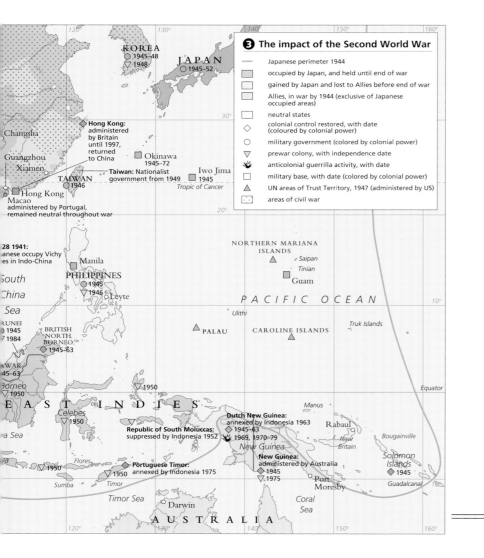

The impact of the Cold War 1946–89

The Vietnam War, the most violent and protracted conflict in Southeast Asia in the 20th century, was, in many ways, a proxy struggle for the US, China, and the USSR within the global context of the Cold War. Although Vietnam's independence was proclaimed at the end of World War II, it took three decades of bloody struggle – affecting both Vietnam and the neighboring states of Laos and Cambodia – before the French, and then the Americans who replaced them, were evicted from French Indochina.

❸ The impact of the Second World War

- Japanese perimeter 1944
- occupied by Japan, and held until end of war
- gained by Japan and lost to Allies before end of war
- Allies, in war by 1944 (exclusive of Japanese occupied areas)
- neutral states
- colonial control restored, with date (coloured by colonial power)
- ○ military government (colored by colonial power)
- ▽ prewar colony, with independence date
- ☐ anticolonial guerrilla activity, with date
- ☐ military base, with date (colored by colonial power)
- △ UN areas of Trust Territory, 1947 (administered by US)
- areas of civil war

❺ The Vietnam War ▶

The First Vietnam War, 1946–54
- ⚔ major battle
- French border posts, captured by Viet Minh 1951

The Second Vietnam War, 1964–75

Major battles with US involvement:
- ⚔ 1965–66
- ⚔ 1967–69
- western limit of Pathet Lao areas, 1967
- Tet offensive 1968
- Viet Cong Easter offensive, 1972
- Final offensive, 1974–75

Communist supply lines
- → Ho Chi Minh trail
- → Sihanouk trail

Nov 1946: French naval bombardment drives Viet Minh from city, precipitating first attack on French

1965–69: Communist-controlled areas bombed by US

1954: North-South Demarcation Line agreed at Geneva Conference

Aug 1964: North Vietnamese attacks reported on US destroyers; Gulf of Tongking Resolution, commits US forces to war

Mar 1965: First US ground forces in Vietnam, ostensibly to protect air base

Mar 1968: Notorious massacre of 300-400 South Vietnamese civilians by US soldiers in My Lai

Apr 1975: North Vietnamese Army encircles city. US civilians are evacuated by helicopter from embassy rooftop. Final surrender

MODERN SOUTH AND SOUTHEAST ASIA

Jawaharlal Nehru, his daughter Indira Gandhi, and grandson Rajiv Gandhi *(above)* all served as Indian prime ministers.

IN MOST OF THE COUNTRIES of the region, securing independence failed to usher in an era of political peace and stability. The ethnic, religious, and linguistic heterogeneity of their populations quickly led to demands for readjustment of the political map and, in many instances, to secessionist movements and wars for independence. Notwithstanding all these internal and external stresses, most of the countries in South and Southeast Asia took great strides on the path of economic, social, and cultural development under a variety of political systems and economic philosophies. Life expectancy, levels of literacy, and per capita material consumption, especially for the growing middle and upper classes, were far higher than during the colonial era and the economic infrastructure greatly expanded, with the development of a varied commercial base. In 1998 both India and Pakistan successfully tested nuclear weapons, bringing a new level of risk to the subcontinent.

South Asia from 1948

In creating Pakistan, the 1947 partition of India established a political entity which could not withstand the many subsequent stresses between its two distant wings. In 1971 Pakistan was split between its eastern and western halves, and the new state of Bangladesh was formed. There were also a series of international disputes over areas whose borders were not adequately defined during the colonial era or, in the still-unresolved case of Kashmir, over an area whose future was left undecided when the British left India.

❷ Jammu and Kashmir

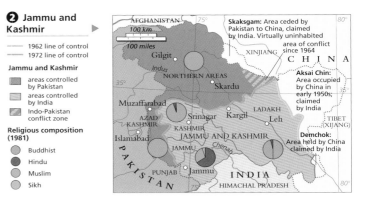

- 1962 line of control
- 1972 line of control

Jammu and Kashmir
- areas controlled by Pakistan
- areas controlled by India
- Indo-Pakistan conflict zone

Religious composition (1981)
- Buddhist
- Hindu
- Muslim
- Sikh

Skaksgam: Area ceded by Pakistan to China, claimed by India. Virtually uninhabited area of conflict

Aksai Chin: Area occupied by China in early 1950s; claimed by India since 1964

Demchok: Area held by China claimed by India

Conflict over Jammu and Kashmir

India and Pakistan have contested possession of the Muslim-majority state of Kashmir since 1947 and fought wars over the territory in 1947–48 and 1965. Since 1989, there has been an independence movement in the Indian-held portion of the state, although India insists this is the handiwork of terrorists aided by Pakistan. The Kashmir conflict continues, with tension heightened by the fact that both India and Pakistan now have nuclear capabilities.

Territorial changes since 1947

The urgent task of integrating more than 600 largely autonomous princely states into the new Indian union was accomplished by 1950. But demands for more linguistically homogeneous states soon surfaced. The partition of the multilingual state of Madras in 1954 was the first in a long series of changes, including the creation of a number of tribal states, that have altered India's political map.

In 1984 the Indian army attacked Sikh militants who were occupying the Golden Temple of Amritsar, the Sikhs' holiest shrine.

Territorial conflicts in South Asia

1947: Start of Indo-Pakistani War fought over Jammu and Kashmir; UN ceasefire line agreed in 1949	1962: India set back in brief Sino-Indian border war after years of intermittent clashes	1971: Successful rebellion leads to creation of Bangladesh. Third Indo-Pakistani war as India intervenes in Bangladesh freedom struggle
1955: Afghan government supports movement for separation of Pakhtunistan from Pakistan	1965: Second inconclusive Indo-Pakistani war over Jammu and Kashmir	1989: Start of violent insurrection against Indian rule in Jammu and Kashmir

1950   1960   1970   1980   1990

The birth of Bangladesh

The two sectors of Pakistan had little in common apart from their Muslim faith, and the stresses on federalism and parliamentary democracy in the union caused its rupture. The Bangladeshi independence struggle was led by the Awami League, with active military support from India.

❸ The birth of Bangladesh

- ▽ site of violent clash between Bengalis and Pakistan army, Mar 1–2 1971
- △ site of Pakistan army "crackdown" Mar 25–26 1971
- ◇ site of major act of sabotage by Mukti Bahini guerrillas (Bengal Liberation Army)
- area of marked guerrilla activity
- □ site of Indo-Pakistani border incident
- → refugees fleeing Bangladesh (with number of refugees)

❶ The formation of contemporary South Asia, 1947–2000

Boundaries in 1975
- agreed or de facto international boundaries, demarcated
- extent of international territorial claim
- line of control in Kashmir
- state or province after 1975

Territories
- Union territories created after 1956, now fully-fledged states
- East and West Pakistan 1967
- Area disputed between India and Pakistan
- former protectorate
- former French colonial possessions
- former Portuguese colonial possessions
- contemporary Indian state, with date of formation
- □ national capital
- ○ state capital
- (1947) achievement of statehood

NORTHWEST FRONTIER PROVINCE
1947: became part of Pakistan

AZAD KASHMIR
1971: Ceasefire line agreed after third Indo-Pakistani War

Centrally administered tribal areas

AFGHANISTAN
1979–89: occupied by Soviet Union from 1992: Civil war

Pakhtunistan:
1948–63: Area of ethnic Pathans; claims to independence supported by Afghanistan

PAKISTAN

WEST PAKISTAN
1956: Declared single province
1971: dissolved

(EAST) PUNJAB (1947)
Former province divided between India and Pakistan
1966: Indian portion partitioned

(WEST) PUNJAB
1947: formed from former Punjab province of India

BALUCHISTAN
1952: Baluchistan States Union formed;
1970: reconstituted as separate province

Gwadar:
1958: ceded by Oman to Pakistan

SIND
1947: Became part of Pakistan

Rann of Kutch:
1968: Minor border adjustments based on tribunal award of 1968

Junagadh:
Aug 1947: Decision to accede to Pakistan; taken over by India in Nov

1969: Tribal areas absorbed into Pakistan

NORTHERN AREAS

Nominally independent, but recognized only by Pakistan
1963: Area ceded to China by Pakistan but claimed by India

Aksai Chin:
early 1950s: occupied by China
1962: Ceasefire line following Sino-Indian conflict

JAMMU AND KASHMIR (1949)
Princely state partitioned into two parts. Northwest area controlled by Pakistan; remainder constituted as Indian state

HIMACHAL PRADESH (1971)
Former princely states reconstituted as fully-fledged state

TIBET
1949: Chinese proclaim 'liberation' of Tibet
1950: Chinese invasion of eastern Tibet

1961: Minor adjustments of Sino-Nepali border based on treaty

CHINA

ARUNACHAL PRADESH (1987)
formerly Northeast Frontier Agency. Most of this state claimed by China, but all is integrated within India; 1962: fought over by China and India

BHUTAN
1949: Indian protectorate
1971: Sovereignty broadened on admission to UN

1950: made Indian protectorate
1974: associate state
1975: annexed as a state

HARYANA (1966)
created on partition of Punjab

UTTARANCHAL (2000)

DELHI
1956: Union territory
1995: National capital territory

NEPAL

SIKKIM (1975)

ASSAM (1950)

NAGALAND (1961)

MEGHALAYA (1972)

UTTAR PRADESH (1947)
before 1950: called United Provinces

BIHAR (1948)

MANIPUR (1972)

TRIPURA (1972)

MIZORAM (1986)

JHARKHAND (2000)

WEST BENGAL (1947)

1951: ceded to India

BANGLADESH
Former East Pakistan.
Mar 1971: Declared independence from Pakistan
Dec 1971: Independence secured following civil war and Indian military intervention

RAJASTHAN (1949)

INDIA

MADHYA PRADESH (1948)
1948: formed incorporating Madhya Bharat, a union of 20 princely states
1956: incorporated former state of Bhopal

GUJARAT (1960)
created on division of Bombay

Diu
1961: became Union territory with Goa

Daman
1961: became Union territory with Goa

CHHATTISGARH (2000)

ORISSA (1948)

BURMA

DADRA AND NAGAR HAVELI
1961: Union territory

BOMBAY
1956: incorporated part of former state of Hyderabad
1960: divided into Gujarat and Maharashtra

MAHARASHTRA (1960)
created on division of Bombay

GOA (1987)
1961: annexed by India

ANDHRA PRADESH (1953)
1953: separation from Madras
1956: incorporated part of former state of Hyderabad

Yanam
1955: ceded to India

KARNATAKA (1947)
1947–73 called Mysore
1953: boundaries altered
1956: part of former state of Hyderabad was incorporated

Mahe
1955: ceded to India

KERALA (1956)
1949: Travancore and Cochin state formed
1956: incorporated former state of Travancore and Cochin

TAMIL NADU (1947)
1947–69: called Madras

Pondicherry
1955: ceded to India

Karikal
1955: ceded to India

Palk Strait:
Indo-Sri Lankan accord on division of water and islands

SRI LANKA (CEYLON)
1947: dominion status
1948: full independence

Arabian Sea

INDIAN OCEAN

Bay of Bengal

In 1949 refugees were driven from their homes by Indo-Pakistani border clashes in Kashmir.

NEPAL

ASSAM 375,000

NAGALAND

MEGHALAYA

BANGLADESH 1.8 million

BIHAR 25,000

WEST BENGAL 6.4 million

TRIPURA

MIZORAM

MANIPUR

675,000

Madhya Pradesh (off map) 125,000

Nov 1970: Area seriously devastated by cyclone. Inadequate government response provokes eastern opposition to martial law regime imposed from West Pakistan

Secessionist movements and regional cooperation

The post-independence era in South and Southeast Asia has been characterized by a multitude of internal movements among subnational groups who have called for greater recognition, autonomy, and even independence. These have been treated with varying degrees of tolerance by the national governments. At the same time, the nations of South and Southeast Asia have embarked upon endeavours to bring about greater supranational and extra-regional cooperation. The latter efforts have been, in varying degrees, military, political, and economic in nature.

The Communist Khmer Rouge operated from a rural power base.

Cambodia

From 1975, Pol Pot's Communist Khmer Rouge conducted a social program in Cambodia which led to the deaths of two million people, and the 're-education' of millions more. Parliamentary elections are now held in Cambodia. The UN is to set up a tribunal for the "killing fields" genocide of the Pol Pot years.

Indonesian army troops are seen looting rice from paddy fields in East Timor, where repression of prosecessionists was particularly brutal.

East Timor

Originally a Portuguese colony, East Timor was invaded by Indonesia in 1975. Resistance by the East Timor Revolutionary Liberation Front (FRETILIN) eventually led to independence in 2002, but a quarter of the population is thought to have died during the Indonesian occupation.

The Tamil Tigers fought for Tamil independence from the rest of Sri Lanka through the 1980s and 1990s. They remain the most feared militant group, notorious for suicide bombings.

Sri Lanka

Since Sri Lanka gained independence in 1948, relations have deteriorated between the Sinhalese majority and the Tamil minority. A bloody civil war was fought from 1984 until a fragile cease-fire agreement was reached in 2002.

④ Secessionist movements and regional cooperation

- secessionist movements
- violent protests against existing borders on linguistic grounds
- tribal/ethnic minority conflict with ruling power
- conflict between indigenous groups
- other violent uprisings

Membership of Asian Regional Movements:

ADB	Asian Development Bank, est. 1966
APEC	Asia-Pacific Economic Cooperation, est. 1989
ASEAN	Association for Southeast Asian Nations, est. 1967
CP	Colombo Plan, est. 1951
ESCAP	Economic and Social Commission for Asia and Pacific, est. 1947
SAARC	South Asian Association for Regional Cooperation, est. 1985

Afghanistan: Complete civil war since 1992; ethnic divisons between majority Pathans and minority tribes lie behind much of the conflict

Afghanistan: 2001 Taliban government falls after US-led strikes

Pakistan: Non-Punjabi minority secessionist movements

Bhutan: Ethnic tension between indigenous Drupka people and Nepali immigrants in the south

Burma: Numerous dissident minorities in rebellion. Ethnic rebel groups (Karens) have joined forces with political groups to end military rule and bring in the democratic government which was legally elected in 1990.

Vietnam: Mountain minorities (Montagnards) and Chinese ethnic groups regarded with suspicion by Communist government

Laos: Small pockets of resistance by Hmong (mountain tribes) to Communist government since 1975

Cambodia: Following withdrawal of Vietnamese troops in 1989, Khmer Rouge resumed armed struggle in central and western Cambodia, provoking government counter-offensives

India: Internal riots and uprisings since the 1950s have been directed at reorganizing state boundaries mainly on linguistic grounds. Most civil disorder is confined to the larger cities. Tribal conflict in the northeast and secessionist movements in Kashmir are ongoing

Bangladesh: Tribes are demanding autonomy in the Chittagong Hills

Thailand: Secessionist movement amongst Muslim Malays

Sri Lanka: Ongoing conflict between majority Sinhalese government and Tamil minority who are fighting for an independent state, Tamil Eelam

Aceh: Aceh people of northern Sumatra in conflict with Indonesian government

Malaysia: Malay/Chinese immigrant tension stimulated by positive discrimination laws introduced in 1970

Singapore: Multiparty democracy in name only; opposition faces severe restrictions

Indonesia: Java-dominated government suppresses local culture and politics, leading to secessionist movements. Conflict with ethnic Chinese

Philippines: Communist and Muslim separatists have been fighting government for over 25 years

Brunei: Ruled by Sultan's decree following a failed rebellion in 1962

Irian Jaya: Free Papua movement seeking autonomy from Indonesia. Outbreaks of violence in 1977, 1978 and 1981

East Timor: Repression and persecution by Indonesian government from declaration of independence in 1985. Independent 2002

Secessionist movements and political coups

1955: Naga uprising in northeastern India, the first of numerous tribal insurrections

1958: Abortive secessionist uprisings in Baluchistan, Pakistan

1962: Military take over rule of Burma

1965: Failed Marxist coup and military countercoup in Indonesia ends Sukarno regime

1972: Ferdinand Marcos declares martial law in Philippines

1975: Khmer Rouge take over Cambodia; impose regime of extreme terror

1979: Deposition of monarchy in Afghanistan; Soviet invasion and civil war

1981: Start of struggle for independent Sikh state of Khalistan in Indian Punjab

1982: Start of struggle in Sri Lanka for independent state of Tamil Eelam

1986: "People power" uprising ousts President Marcos of Philippines

1988: Military seizes power in Burma; renames country Myanmar

1991: Indian prime minister Rajiv Ghandi assassinated

1996: Islamist Taliban take control of most of Afghanistan

1999: General Musharraf overthrows the government of Pakistan

2001: Crown Prince Dipendra murders most of royal family in Nepal

2002: East Timor gains independence. Cease-fire agreed in Sri Lanka

2003: Major offensive against Aceh separatists in Indonesia

The urbanization of South and Southeast Asia

The development of South and Southeast Asia is reflected dramatically in its burgeoning cities, some of which, notably Bombay (Mumbai), are among the largest in the world. Of the roughly 1.8 billion people now inhabiting the region about 500 million live in urban areas. However, growing populations, the majority still dependent on agriculture and living in densely settled areas such as the great river valleys of the Ganges, Indus, and Mekong, place an increasing burden on fragile ecosystems, with potentially disastrous consequences for the environment.

Poverty drives many of India's rural poor to the increasingly overcrowded cities.

The modern financial centre of Singapore towers over the harbor, a reminder of the island state's origins as a strategic trading settlement.

◀ ⑤ The urbanization of South and Southeast Asia

Urban centers (populations in 2004)
- over 16 million
- 8–16 million
- 4–8 million
- 2–4 million
- under 2 million
- capital city

Population density per square kilometre (2002)
- 300–1000
- 100–299
- 50–99
- 10–49

The urban/rural divide (2002)
- urban population
- rural population

NORTH AND EAST ASIA
REGIONAL HISTORY

THE HISTORICAL LANDSCAPE

THE FRAGMENTED GEOGRAPHY of this, the world's largest uninterrupted land mass, has produced a wide variety of historical scenarios. The mountainous massifs at its heart – the Plateau of Tibet, the Altai, Tien Shan, and Pamir ranges – enclose the arid Takla Makan, Gobi, and Ordos deserts, which together comprise a hostile and sparsely inhabited realm. Stretching in a wide arc around this region are the massive steppes, long home to pastoral nomads whose turbulent history was punctuated by sorties against their sedentary neighbors and, occasionally, violent irruptions which impelled their skilled and fast-moving horsemen across Eurasia. Broad rivers flow north across Siberia to the Arctic, and west to inland deltas and landlocked seas such as the Aral and Caspian. To the east, the fertile floodplains of the Yellow River and the Yangtze were the focus of one the world's oldest civilizations, that of China, an enormous demographic and cultural fulcrum which dominates East Asia, and whose influence has been cast far across the peninsulas and archipelagos of the Pacific Rim.

Japan was settled by hunter-gatherers about 30,000 years ago. At the the time of the last Ice Age, most of the Japanese islands were densely forested, with settlement only in the coastal regions.

The Yellow River flows down to the plains of eastern China across a plateau of fertile *loess* – fine silty soils laid down along the edges of glaciers. The river cuts down through the soft sediments, washing them downstream and depositing them on the Great Plain of China, resulting in exceptionally fertile soils, suitable for a wide range of crops.

Siberia was a cold, frozen region at the time of the last Ice Age, sparsely inhabited by hunter-gatherers. Unlike northern Europe and North America, Siberia was not covered by an ice cap because of the lack of moisture across the region. The extreme cold preserved the remains of creatures such as mammoths, along with evidence of the shelters built by the people who hunted them.

North and East Asia: 18,000 years ago

North Asia was relatively ice-free during the last Ice Age, except for the extension of the European ice sheet to the east of the Ural Mountains, covering only a small part of the West Siberian Plain. The climate, however, was still bitterly cold, far colder than it is today. Extreme temperatures in southern Siberia limited vegetation to scrubby tundra plants across most of North Asia. Along the Ob' and Yenisey rivers, two large lakes were formed where the rivers dammed up behind the edge of the European ice sheet.

The Ob' and Yenisey rivers were dammed by an ice cap, forming huge lakes.

The extent of the ice cap over northern Asia is still unclear. Many scientists believe that the ice sheet terminated near the Yenisey River, but other hypotheses suggest the ice sheet was much more extensive, stretching much further eastward across the Central Siberian Plateau.

Siberia was a vast, windswept polar desert – temperatures and conditions were similar to those found in the dry valleys of Antarctica today. Tree cover was virtually nonexistent; afforestation of this barren region only began around 9000 years ago, when global climate became warmer.

Central Asia was much drier, with a belt of desert lying just to the north of the main mountain ranges, stretching well into southern Siberia. Here, deposits of sand and loess were piled into dunes by high winds, and rocks and stones were eroded and sculpted by wind-borne sediments, to form extraordinary structures.

A scattering of ice caps existed on the Himalayas and the Plateau of Tibet, but there was insufficient moisture for full-scale glaciation. Some scientists however, have suggested that the glaciation may have been far more extensive, and ice caps may have covered most of the plateau.

Northern China and the Manchurian Plain were mainly dry, covered by sparse, scrubby vegetation and tundra.

The Sea of Japan (East Sea) was almost totally enclosed, forming a huge lake that drained into the sea via a narrow channel between Japan and Korea.

China was much drier than at present, suggesting that monsoon conditions then did not reach as far north as they do today.

As sea levels fell at the height of the Ice Age, broad plains were exposed on the Chinese continental shelf.

The Japanese islands were joined together, and linked to mainland Asia by a peninsula of land that today forms the island of Sakhalin.

NORTH AND EAST ASIA
EXPLORATION AND MAPPING

This 3rd-century Chinese view of the world placed the imperial capital at the center of a grid, with outlying areas organized in a regular, diminishing hierarchy.

THE GROWTH OF KNOWLEDGE of Central Asia was very gradual. Mountain barriers, extensive deserts, and climatic extremes hemmed in and defined the cultures of the region. The rulers of both China and India rarely looked beyond their frontiers, while remote states such as Tibet and Japan actively shunned external contact. In the Classical and Medieval eras perilous trade routes provided limited passage for missionaries and entrepreneurs, supplanted in the 16th century by the growth of maritime trade and European colonialists. In the 19th-century imperial European powers vied for control of Asia's land and wealth, a struggle echoed today as rich mineral resources attract increasing attention.

The early mapping of Japan

Following the introduction of Chinese administrative ideas during the 7th century CE, the southern Japanese islands were divided into 68 provinces. The limited size of Japan made it possible to conduct surveys of land and population in order to raise taxes; the first maps were of individual estates, but with the creation of centralized government in 710, the Buddhist priest Gyogi began to draw up national diagrams featuring the provinces. Gyogi-style maps typically show south at the top, and often include fantastical lands.

A Gyogi-style map of Honshu from 1305, orientated with south at the top, naming and listing the 68 Japanese provinces.

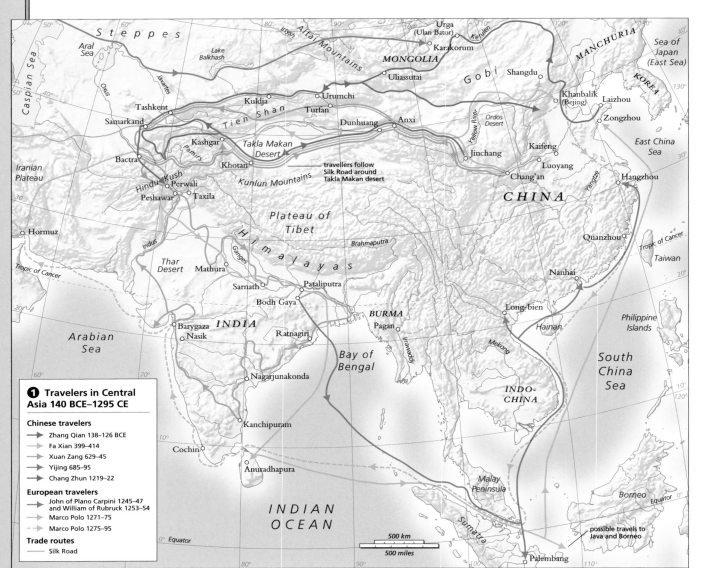

❶ Travelers in Central Asia 140 BCE–1295 CE

Chinese travelers
→ Zhang Qian 138–126 BCE
→ Fa Xian 399–414
→ Xuan Zang 629–45
→ Yijing 685–95
→ Chang Zhun 1219–22

European travelers
→ John of Plano Carpini 1245–47 and William of Rubruck 1253–54
→ Marco Polo 1271–75
--→ Marco Polo 1275–95

Trade routes
— Silk Road

Mapping was an essential tool in administering the vast Chinese empire. Here a cartographer presents a Tang emperor with a map of his domains.

The conquest of Central Asia by the Mongols in the 13th century re-opened the Silk Road for trans-Asian trade. This Persian painting shows some Chinese merchant traders.

Travelers in Central Asia

The first recorded travelers in Central Asia were diplomatic missions, such as Zhang Qian, or Chinese Buddhist priests on pilgrimage to India, such as Fa Xian and Xuan Zang. Over 1000 years later the "Mongol Peace" encouraged further missions (Chang Zhun), while the secure trading routes drew Christian missionaries and traders such as Marco Polo to the east. Their extensive accounts contributed greatly to knowledge of the region.

A 17th-century European copy of a Chinese map by Zhu Siben, a leading 14th-century Chinese cartographer. It is notable for the details of coastline and drainage – knowledge of river systems was regarded as a vital means of controlling China; the use of a grid to establish a projection was a Chinese invention.

c.1000 BCE: Western Zhou sponsor exploration and recording of China's geography
2 CE: First census of Chinese population
105 CE: Invention of paper in Han China
607: First record of Japanese diplomatic mission to China
751: Arabs reach Central Asia, and defeat Tang
c.1220: Zhao Rugua publishes account of travels in Southeast Asia

1000 BCE — 500 BCE — 1 CE — 500 CE — 1000 CE

Early knowledge of Asia

1st century BCE: Silk Road develops, linking southwest Asia and China
c.250: Lodestone compass used in China
c.900: First maps of Japan, showing provinces
1206: Mongols begin conquest of Central Asia

❷ European exploration of North and East Asia ▶

- routes used by fur trappers in 16th and 17th centuries
- Sir Hugh Willoughby and Richard Chancellor 1553
- Willem Barents 1596–97
- Vitus Bering 1728–30
- Great Northern Expedition 1733–42
- Baron Ferdinand von Wrangel 1820–24
- Alexander von Middendorff 1842
- Alexander von Middendorff 1844
- Adolf Nordenskjöld 1878–79
- voyages of the *Taymyr* and *Vaygach* 1914–15
- voyage of the *Sibiryakov* 1932
- 1860 date of foundation

Russian traders and colonists in Siberia frequently traveled by sled, following the frozen courses of the vast river systems, which in summer they traversed by boat portage.

The Northeast Passage and Siberia

The repeated failure to find a Northeast passage to Asia, and the abundance of furs and minerals beyond the Urals, led to a sudden and rapid expansion of the Russian Empire across Siberia. Military forays such as the great Northern Expedition followed fur traders' routes, subdued local tribes, and paved the way for colonists. Between the 1580s and 1650 Russians gained the largest land empire yet seen, crossed the Bering Strait, and claimed Alaska. Only in the 20th century did icebreakers open the maritime route across the Arctic Ocean.

The conquest of Siberia 1580–1932

1581–82: Yermak begins Russian conquest of Siberia	**1649:** Russians reach Pacific coast	**1733–42:** Great Northern Expedition under Bering surveys northern coasts of Siberia	**1914–15:** First icebreakers complete navigation of Northeast Passage from east

1550 — 1650 — 1750 — 1850 — 1950

| **1689:** Treaty of Nerchinsk agrees Russian and Chinese spheres of influence in east Asia | **1728:** Vitus Bering navigates Bering Strait | **1878–79:** Nordenskjöld completes first navigation of Northeast Passage from west | **1932:** First single-season traverse of Northeast Passage by icebreaker *Sibiryakov* |

On the roof of the world

Nominally under Chinese control during the 19th century, in effect Tibet remained independent, closed to the outside world. This 18th-century Tibetan painting maps the splendor of the Dalai Lama's Potala palace in Lhasa.

Both Russia and Britain regarded accurate mapping (below) as essential to imperial control. The maps of Nepal and Tibet produced covertly by local "pundits," provided essential intelligence for Anglo-Indian imperialists.

As the imperial world map was filled in during the 19th century, so the most remote regions of Central Asia began to be explored and claimed. Jesuit missionaries and diplomatic missions (frequently backed by force) had limited success in penetrating the fastnesses of Tibet. In India, the British recruited local guides as secret agents (pundits) to conduct clandestine surveys. Only during the last century did scientists (often Russian) such as Przhevalsky and Roerich explore the plateaux and mountains in any detail.

❸ Exploring Asia's great mountains 1873–1929

- international borders, 1914

Russian explorers
- Nikolai Przhevalsky 1879–80
- Nikolai Przhevalsky 1883–85
- Gombozhab Tsybikov 1889–1902
- Nicolas Roerich 1925–28

British explorers
- Francis Younghusband 1886–87

Other explorers
- Sven Anders von Hedin 1890–97
- Area surveyed by pundits

The penetration of Tibet

1661: First Jesuit mission to Lhasa	**1750s:** Qing China conquers Tibet and Turkestan	**1792:** Qing China closes Tibet to visitors	**1846:** French monks visit Lhasa	**1904:** Younghusband defeats Tibetan army; Anglo-Tibetan treaty

1650 — 1700 — 1750 — 1800 — 1850 — 1900 — 1950

| **1774:** First British mission to Tibet | **1865:** Nain Singh begins survey of Tibet |

THE FIRST EAST ASIAN CIVILIZATIONS

THE EMERGENCE OF ORGANIZED CULTURES in East Asia took a variety of forms. The fertile soils of the Yellow River basin and Yangtze valley provided the potential for the region's first agricultural communities 8000 years ago. Pottery working with kilns and bronze technology developed, accompanied by the first Chinese states and empires; the region remains to this day the heartland of China's culture and population. In Japan, the abundance of natural resources, especially fish and seafood, meant that hunter-gathering persisted, alongside features normally associated with sedentary agriculture – the world's earliest pottery is found here. Across the steppe grasslands of Central Asia, dominated by seasonal migration in search of pasture, communities developed a mobile culture now revealed through elaborate burials and decorated grave goods.

Some of the earliest Chinese script is preserved on Shang period oracle bones (c.1400 BCE).

The agricultural revolution in Central and East Asia from c.10,000 BCE

The hardy yak provided abundant meat, furs for clothing and tents, and dairy products for the nomadic pastoralists of Central Asia.

A wide range of crops and plants was domesticated across East Asia from c.10,000 BCE. The pig was the most widely domesticated animal, and varieties of cattle such as oxen, yak, and banteng supported migratory herders. It was the domestication of staple crops such as millet and rice that provided the basis for population growth and, later the first Chinese cities and states. Rice was cultivated in the Yangtze Valley around 6000 BCE, reaching Korea some 4000 years later and Japan in the 1st millennium BCE. In the Yellow River Valley of northern China, millet was domesticated.

❶ The agricultural revolution 6000–2000 BCE

- distribution of Yellow River loess soils
- northern limit of wild rice distribution
- → spread of rice cultivation
- area of early wet rice cultivation
- area of early millet cultivation
- ● early farming site
- ⊙ Japanese hunter-gatherer site
- ◇ pottery site before 10,000 BCE
- ◇ pottery site before 8000 BCE
- ◇ pottery site before 6000 BCE
- ● steppe site c.4500–2000 BCE
- ○ steppe site c.2000–1000 BCE

Domesticated plants and animals

○	rapeseed		coconut
○	soybean		breadfruit
○	adzuki bean		tea
⊛	cucumber		sago palm
☸	ginger		sugar cane
◗	taro		jute
◖	arrowroot		nutmeg
○	turnip		buffalo
○	lemon		banteng
○	peach		yak
○	grapefruit		pig
◖	banana		

Early technology and agriculture in East Asia

c.6000: First Chinese agricultural communities in Yellow River Basin
c.5000: Millet, dogs, and pigs widely domesticated in Yellow River Basin
c.3500: First jadeworking, Hongshan culture
c.3000: Sheep and cattle domesticated in northern China; water buffalo in southern China; use of plowshare
c.5000–3000: Yangshao culture in Yellow River Basin
c.4500: Horse domesticated in Central Asia
c.3500: First Chinese cities, with walls and rammed-earth platforms
c.3000–2000: Longshan culture in northeast China

6000 BCE	5000	4000	3000	2000

Scale varies with perspective

Neolithic China c.4000–2000 BCE

The early agricultural communities in the Yellow River Basin developed common cultural characteristics known to us through settlement patterns, burial practices, and pottery. The Yangshao regional grouping was one of the earliest to be identified. By about 3000 BCE this was replaced by the more prosperous and sophisticated Longshan culture, which spread throughout the basin and the coastal plain. Technological advances occurred in pottery, copperworking was introduced, the plowshare was in use, and by 2000 BCE silk weaving had begun.

The geometric decoration of Yangshao pottery probably had a ritualistic significance.

❷ Neolithic China

- area of Yangshao culture
- area of Longshan culture by c.2500 BCE
- ● major neolithic site
- ◇ site with pottery kilns from c.4000 BCE

200 km
200 miles

Shang China 1800–1027 BCE

In about 1800 BCE, the nucleus of the first Chinese state emerged in the Yellow River Valley of northern China. The Shang state was feudal, with its core territory under the direct control of the kings, but outlying areas less securely attached. The Shang kings used ancestor worship and divination to confirm their dynastic status. Their successive capitals were mainly ritual centers with palace complexes and elaborate royal burial places. The Shang were skilled in writing, and were exponents of martial conquest, divination, and human sacrifice. Bronzeworking (often for military purposes), stonecarving, and potterymaking were harnessed to religion and the state.

Although the Shang used bronze widely for everyday objects and armaments, they produced sophisticated vessels – often in the shape of animals – for specific ritualistic and sacrificial functions.

c.2000: Xia dynasty, probable forerunners of the Shang, established
c.1800: Beginnings of Shang state
1400: Anyang becomes Shang capital
1027: Western Zhou dynasty supplants Shang

2000 BCE — 1800 — 1600 — 1400 — 1200 — 1000 BCE

c.1700: First bronze vessels cast
c.1400: Earliest evidence of Chinese writing on oracle bones
c.1200: Wheeled chariots spread to China from Central Asia

Shang China

Zhou China 1027–403 BCE

The 11th century BCE saw political control wrested from the Shang by the Zhou (Chou), based west of the Shang capital. Under the Western Zhou greater political unity developed, the royal family assigning territories to their vassals to create a proto-feudal state. Human sacrifice declined, defensive walls began to be built, and the first literary records of Chinese history emerged. Constant rivalry and dissent gradually eroded centralized power, and from 770 BCE a new capital was established at Luoyang under the Eastern Zhou. A looser political federation came about, bound together by the need for defense against hostile neighbors, and by common cultural values reflected in the use of coinage, in richly decorated tombs, and in the writings of Confucius.

The first Chinese coins came into use around 500 BCE, and were normally cast in bronze in the form of tools.

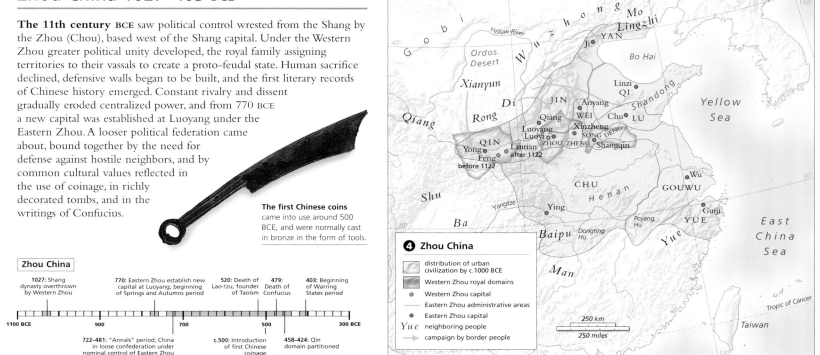

4 Zhou China

	distribution of urban civilization by c.1000 BCE
	Western Zhou royal domains
●	Western Zhou capital
—	Eastern Zhou administrative areas
●	Eastern Zhou capital
Yue	neighboring people
→	campaign by border people

Zhou China

1027: Shang dynasty overthrown by Western Zhou
770: Eastern Zhou establish new capital at Luoyang; beginning of Springs and Autumns period
520: Death of Lao-tzu, founder of Taoism
479: Death of Confucius
403: Beginning of Warring States period

1100 BCE — 900 — 700 — 500 — 300 BCE

722–481: "Annals" period; China in loose confederation under nominal control of Eastern Zhou
c.500: Introduction of first Chinese coinage
458–424: Qin domain partitioned

Qin China 221–206 BCE

The Zhou confederation eventually collapsed into bitter civil war. The Warring States period (403–221 BCE) was gradually brought to an end by the Qin dynasty, who created by alliance, diplomacy, and conquest, the first unified Chinese empire. A series of ruthless campaigns by Shi Huangdi (the First Emperor) extended Qin domains far to the north and to the south beyond the Yangtze valley to the borders of modern Vietnam; in their wake, a process of centralization and standardization was introduced to minimize regional differences and tribal dissent. The area of the Qin state was effectively tripled in 16 years, while the constant threat to the northern borders by nomadic steppe peoples such as the Xiongnu led to the construction of the first Great Wall.

247: King Zheng (later Shi Huangdi) becomes ruler of Qin domain
230: Campaigns of Shi Huangdi begin
221: Qin Empire established, organized into 36 commanderies
214: Slave labor used to link ramparts to form Great Wall
210: Death of Shi Huangdi, entombed with vast terra-cotta army

250 BCE — 240 — 230 — 220 — 210 — 200 BCE

221–207: General disarmament, standardization of weights, measures, and axle widths to facilitate commerce
213: Proscription of nonscientific books; standardization and simplification of Chinese script
206: Beginning of Han dynasty

Qin China

Thousands of life-size terra-cotta soldiers and horses were buried near Shi Huangdi's tomb outside Xianyang, a testament to his military might and concern for his destiny in the afterlife.

5 Qin China

	original Qin territory c.350 BCE
	Qin expansion by 288 BCE
	Qin expansion by 220 BCE
HAN 230	Qin acquisition with date
	areas under Qin control after unification
●	Qin state capitals and administrative center
	defensive wall
Yue	people

Scale varies with perspective

THE HAN AND THE GREAT MIGRATIONS

A ceremonial bronze bridle from the Han period reflects the importance of Chinese cavalry skills.

THE UNIFICATION OF CHINA under an authoritarian centralized regime by the Qin in 221 BCE paved the way for the Han, who assumed control in 206 BCE. The Han consolidated Chinese control of the south, pushing indigenous populations into more marginal areas, as well as expanding far into Central Asia along the Silk Road. In doing so, the Han established a domain by far the greatest the world had ever seen, and provided a template for Chinese territorial aspirations for the next two millennia. The Han benefited from trans-Asian trade *(see pp. 44–45)*, but were constantly troubled by the steppe peoples, especially the Xiongnu, mounted pastoralists who harassed their northern borders.

Han China 206 BCE–220 CE

Tomb pottery from the Han period often celebrates daily life, as in this model of a farm building, complete with sheep and donkey.

The Han, who ruled China for over 400 years (apart from a brief interregnum under Wang Mang from 9–25 CE), established China as the most dominant cultural, political, and economic force in Asia. They constructed a new Great Wall to protect their northern borders, and established military garrisons from Korea in the east to Champa (Vietnam) in the south and Ferghana in the west to protect their expanding empire. Trade – along the great trans-Eurasian land routes and by sea – flourished; Buddhism entered China during this period (although the Han bureaucracy was structured on Confucian principles); and by 2 CE the first imperial census revealed a Chinese population of over 57 million, living mainly in the river valleys of the north.

The Han dynasty

141 BCE: Han emperor Wudi expands into Central Asia	138–126 BCE: Embassy of Zhang Qian to Xiongnu and Central Asia	11 CE: Yellow River changes course to south of Shandong Peninsula	91 CE: Han defeat Xiongnu	184 CE: Yellow Turbans revolt

250 BCE — 150 BCE — 50 BCE — 50 CE — 150 CE — 250 CE

221 BCE: The First Emperor (Shi Huangdi) unites China under Qin dynasty (to 207) · 206 BCE: Foundation of Han dynasty; capital at Chang'an · 9 CE: Xin Dynasty under Wang Mang (to 25 CE) · 25 CE: Restoration of the Han dynasty; capital at Luoyang · 105 CE: First recorded use of paper in China · 220 CE: Collapse of Han Dynasty

Han Commanderies (administrative districts)

1 JINGZHAOYIN	6 HENEI	11 HEJIAN	16 YUNZHONG	21 GUANGYANG	26 JINAN	31 GAOMI	36 DONG	41 CHENLIU
2 YOUFUFENG	7 WEI	12 JULU	17 DINGXIANG	22 YUYANG	27 QIANCHENG	32 JIAODONG	37 DONGPING	42 HUAIYANG
3 ZUO PINGYI	8 GUANPING ZHAO	13 ZHONGSHAN	18 YANMEN	23 YOUBEIPING	28 QI	33 LANGYA	38 JIYIN	43 YINGCHUAN
4 HEDONG	9 QINGHE	14 CHANGSHAN	19 DAIZHUO	24 BOHAI	29 ZICHUAN	34 CHENGYANG	39 SHANYANG	44 HENAN
5 SHANGDANG	10 XINDU	15 WUYAN	20 SHANGGU	25 PINGYUAN	30 PEIHAN	35 TAISHAN	40 LIANG	45 HONGNONG

① The Han Empire 140 BCE–220 CE

- Qin China 206 BCE
- Kingdom of Nanyue 206–113 BC
- early Han Empire by 2 CE
- Han principalities
- Tanyang Han commanderies
- Great Wall under the Han
- imperial canals
- imperial highways
- territories added by the Later Han, c.25–200 CE (with date)
- Han expeditions against their neighbors

500 km
500 miles

During the Han period Chinese architecture acquired its characteristic qualities of finely jointed wooden structures supporting many broad-eaved stories, here represented in a clay tomb model.

❷ The Three Kingdoms c.250 CE ▲

❺ China c.560 CE ▲

❸ The later Sixteen Kingdoms period c.400 CE ▲

❹ The Toba Wei c.440–500 CE ▲

Imperial Toba Wei pastures   Toba Wei conquests c.500 CE

The fragmentation of China 220–589 CE

The threat posed by the steppe warriors' extraordinary horsemanship is illustrated in this relief tile from Sichuan. The mounted archer is performing a "Parthian" shot at full gallop, in full control of both his weapon and his speeding horse.

A series of revolts, the inability to collect taxes from northern vassals, and an increasing reliance on mercenaries recruited from steppe tribes led to the collapse of the Han dynasty and a prolonged period of turmoil in China. The north fell prey to a succession of non-Chinese peoples, the most notable being the Turkic Toba (or Northern) Wei, while the Chinese aristocracy withdrew to the south. During this period the collapse of Chinese institutions saw a decline in respect for Confucian values and the growth of Taoist cults and Buddhism.

The fragmentation of China

220: Emergence of Three Kingdoms
265: Western Jin take over Wei state
280: Western Jin conquer southern China
304: Sixteen Kingdoms period (to 439)
439: Northern (Toba) Wei dominate northern China (to 534)
490: Northern Wei rebuild Luoyang
524: Invasion of Wei by Ruanruan and Turks
552: Northern Qi dynasty (to 577)
557: Beginning of Northern Zhou dynasty (to 581)
589: China reunited under Sui dynasty (to 617)

The steppe kingdoms of Central Asia

The collapse of Han China was only one product of the emergence of organized, militaristic confederations among the steppe peoples of northern and Central Asia. Between the 3rd and 6th centuries, jostling for territory and opportunistic campaigns against the more sedentary states to their south – the most serious being those of the Xiongnu – caused a domino pattern of migratory movements south and west, the effects of this irruption being felt across all Eurasia.

The Xiongnu owed much of their military success to their understanding of cavalry tactics. In addition to the fast, lightly armored skirmishers associated with steppe peoples, they maintained a heavy cavalry capable of breaking through massed infantry. This figurine of an armored horseman dates from the 5th century CE when the Toba Wei competed with other steppe peoples for control of northern China.

❻ The steppe kingdoms of Central Asia ▼

area occupied by nomadic agriculturalists
Xiongnu homeland
Han Empire at greatest extent c.200 CE
Gupta Empire at greatest extent c.400 CE
Sassanian Persia c.250 CE
Kushan Empire c.275 CE
Toba Wei c.500 CE
Eastern Turks c.600 CE
Western Turks c.600 CE
— Silk Road

Major movements of steppe peoples:
1st–3rd century CE
300–350
350–500
after 500

This iron Bactrian plaque plated in sheet gold with turquoise gems, and depicting a horseman, is typical of the intricate but very portable art of the steppe peoples.

Steppe kingdoms of Central Asia

91: Han defeat Xiongnu, forcing them westward
c.50: Foundation of Kushan Empire
c.300: Invention of stirrup in Central Asia increases efficiency of steppe cavalry
304: Xiongnu invade China, inaugurating a century of civil war in north (Sixteen Kingdoms period)
c.350: Black Huns invade Persia and India
370: Huns begin to invade Europe

EARLY MEDIEVAL EAST ASIA

THE TANG BROUGHT CHINA under a unified administration in 618, and rapidly extended its domains far into Central Asia, briefly achieving by 742 a territorial extent and era of stable growth comparable to that of their Han forebears. The influence of Chinese culture also spread during this period, which in turn saw the establishment of similarly organized states around their frontiers on all sides. Chinese forces were defeated in 751 by Arab armies on the Talas River, which inaugurated a process of Islamicization in Central Asia and loosened Tang control in the region. But China's greatest threats continued to lie to the north, where coalitions of steppe peoples began to establish expansionist regimes, eager to control the Chinese heartland.

This porcelain incense burner in the shape of a duck dates from the Song period. Song pottery was widely traded.

Tang China

Tang China was unified under a centralized government, political and commercial integration established by a network of highways and canals centered on the capital Chang'an. The Yangtze Valley became an increasingly important economic region, while commerce focused on the coastal plain. The stability and prosperity of Tang China attracted both emulation and envy among its neighbors. But the Tang dynasty was fatally weakened by peasant revolts from the 870s and the empire eventually fragmented into local regimes which vied for power for over a century.

Scale varies with perspective

❶ Tang China and its neighbors c.750

- Tang Empire
- areas of temporary Tang control
- area of Chinese cultural influence
- Tibetan Empire c.800
- Western Turks 552–745
- Eastern Turks 552–745, Uighur Empire 745–840
- ⊚ metropolitan prefecture
- ⊙ city of over 300,000 population
- ○ other major city
- Great Wall
- imperial highway
- imperial canal
- ⊛ under Chinese influence
- ⊛ under Indian influence
- ☾ under Islamic influence

KHWARIZM
TRANSOXIANA from 750
SOGDIANA from 750
FERGHANA 659–65: Tang protectorate (Islamic influence from 750)
Bactra
751: Talas River: Tang forces defeated by Arabs
WESTERN TURKESTAN
DZUNGARIA 645–769: occupied by Tang China
Western Turks
Yarkand, Kashgar, Aksu, Beshbalik
Taxila, Khotan, Turfan
Uighurs
Karakorum
EASTERN TURKESTAN
Shazhou, Guazhou, Anxi
Dunhuang
711: Arabs invade northwest India
Plateau of Tibet
Ganzhou
GANSU 763–843: occupied by Tibet
⊛ NINGXIA
TIBET c.600: unified from 650: begins rapid expansion c.840: Empire collapses
Liangzhou
Lhasa ⊛ to 750 / from 750
Qiang
GUANNEI
Kirghiz
Khitan
BOHAI (Parhae) 710: State established by exiled Koguryo 934: destroyed by Khitan
Malgal
Shiwei
Taiyuan
HEBEI Cangzhou
INDIA ★
Pataliputra
Ganges
Brahmaputra
JINGJI
Chang'an
Luoyang Jizhou
Weizhou
Xiangzhou
DUJI Bianzhou
HENAN
Bo Hai
Korea
SILLA 668: Unified state emerges after Tang invasion destroys Koguryo and Paekche states in northern Korea
Sea of Japan (East Sea)
Hokkaido
Kuril Islands
PACIFIC OCEAN
Sea of Okhotsk
Sakhalin
Kyoto, Nara, Nagoya
JAPAN 7th century: unified, except for Hokkaido
Arabian Sea
SHANNAN XIDAO
Hanzhou
JIANNAN Chengdu
SHANNAN DONGDAO
TANG CHINA
JIANZHONG
HUAINAN Xuanzhou
NANZHAO ⊛ c.700: unified; begins expansion
Tanzhou
Hongzhou
Runzhou
Changzhou
Yellow Sea
East China Sea
PYU 8th–9th century: invaded by Nanzhao
Pagan, Pegu
LINGNAN
Yangzhou
JIANGNAN XIDAO
JIANGNAN DONGDAO
Shaozhou, Fuzhou, Wuzhou
Bay of Bengal
Hanoi (Lang-pien)
Annanduhufu
Guangzhou (Canton)
Hainan
Thaton
Hué
KHMER EMPIRE Angkor
ANNAM
South China Sea
Taiwan
CHAMPA

Chang'an

The great city of Chang'an had been a Chinese capital since the Han period. By the 8th century there were around a million people within the city walls, with the same number close by outside, making it the largest city in the world at the time. The rigorous grid structure accommodated a variety of districts, each with its own function.

The stability of the Tang period saw a revival of trans-Asian trade. Bactrian camels with exotic traders, who entered China via the Silk Road, provided a common motif in Tang art *(above)*.

Tang domination of their neighbors is recorded here as caricatured Uighurs pay homage to an unarmed Tang general *(left)*.

❷ Chang'an

Daming Palace and Park
Xingqing Palace
East Market
Taiji (Imperial) Palace
Imperial City
Imperial Granary
Imperial Observatory
West Market
Great South Gate
N

- imperial building
- government building
- upper class district
- middle class district
- working class district

2 km
2 miles

Tang China and its neighbours

618: Tang begin to unite China
751: Battle of Talas River; Arabs defeat Tang
870: Series of peasant revolts in China

607: Tibet unified (to 842)
645: Introduction of Chinese institutions to Japan
745: Foundation of Uighur Empire (to 840)
868: The *Diamond Sutra*, world's oldest surviving printed work

600 — 650 — 700 — 750 — 800 — 850 — 900

Song China

The anarchy which followed the fragmentation of the Tang Empire was followed by the period known as the Five Dynasties and Ten Kingdoms, when China was broken up into as many as ten states. The Song arose in northern China in 960, expanding to form a Chinese empire by 979, although they lost control of the north to the Khitans, who established the Liao Empire in Manchuria, balanced to the west by another steppe empire, the Tangut Xixia Empire. The Jurchen, vassals of the Liao, established the Jin state, which seized the Song capital of Kaifeng, restricting Song rule to the south. The Song period was nevertheless one of great prosperity.

The growth in trade under the Tang and Song brought a need for currency. The mercantile practice of issuing paper receipts in place of weighty bullion transactions was adopted by the government in the 1120s, resulting in the world's first paper money; this printed banknote dates from 1287.

❸ The Five Dynasties 881–979 ▲

- Chinese states
- states occupied by non-Chinese peoples

❹ Song China 960–1127 ▲

— imperial canal
— imperial highway
□ national capital
● provincial capital

916: Foundation of Khitan Empire

947: Khitans invade northern China, establishing Liao Dynasty at Beijing

1038: Foundation of Xixia Empire

1126: Jin take control of northern China

900 · 950 · 1000 · 1050 · 1100 · 1150 · 1200

907: Beginning of Five Dynasties and Ten Kingdoms period (to 960)

939: Annam independent

979: Song dynasty unites China

Song China

Fine porcelain and stoneware was produced in a range of regional centers in Song China, where mass-production techniques developed to meet international demands.

❺ The Southern Song 1127–1234
- □ capital city
- Song empire
- other states/empires

POPULATION CHANGE IN CHINA

A shift in population distribution had occurred by the Song period: the Yellow River remained heavily populated, while the area south of the Yangtze became more intensively agricultural.

742

❻ Chinese population
- high density
- low density

1102

The Yuan (Mongol) invasion

The Mongol conquest of Jin in 1234 occasioned enormous violence and destruction. But the Mongols rapidly adopted Chinese customs and institutions *(see pp. 68–69)*, and the eventual conquest of the Song south in 1278 was less brutal. Subsequent campaigns brought outlying areas under temporary Mongol control, and expanded Chinese administration far to the southwest, but the Mongols exercised only temporary control over Tibet and Southeast Asia and never conquered Japan.

This illustration from an early military manual shows a portable scaling ladder used in siege warfare. Other innovations of this period included the catapult.

The Japanese defeat of Kublai's armies in 1274 (30,000 troops) and 1281 (140,000 troops), the largest amphibious invasion forces of premodern times, were recorded in an illustrated scroll in the 1290s *(left)*.

❼ The Mongol (Yuan) period c.1300
- southern extent of Mongol conquest to 1279
- Mongol conquest 1280–1368
- □ imperial capital
- ● provincial capital
- GANSU Yuan province
- area of loose or temporary Mongol control

The Yuan Dynasty

1264: Foundation of Yuan dynasty by Kublai Khan

1281: Second attempted invasion of Japan

1287: Expedition to Pagan

1292: Expedition to Java

1230 · 1250 · 1270 · 1290 · 1310

1234: Mongols invade Jin Empire

1274: First attempted invasion of Japan

1279: Yuan take over Southern Song

1283: Expeditions against Annam and Champa

THE FIRST STATES IN JAPAN AND KOREA

DURING THE FIRST CENTURIES CE a group of powerful states developed to the east of China. Yamato, centered on what was to became the traditional heartland of Japan, grew to dominate the southern Japanese islands, while Korea saw the development of three states – Paekche, Silla, and Koguryo. Both areas came under the influence of Buddhism and of Chinese culture and politics during the 5th and 6th centuries. The various states of Korea would continue to be regarded by the Chinese as vassals, but Japan affirmed its independent status, maintaining an imperial court, albeit dominated by a succession of warrior lords.

Dotaku ceremonial bells, c.100 BCE, are typical of early Japanese bronze casting.

State formation in Japan and Korea

The basis for state formation in East Asia was the agricultural surplus provided by the spread of rice cultivation, associated with Yayoi culture in Japan. In southeast Japan, the Yamato state began to expand from about 500 CE, and in doing so provoked neighboring cultures such as Kibi and Izumo, to become more politically organized in defense of their territory. In Korea, partly occupied by Han China in the 1st century BCE, the states of Koguryo, Paekche, and Silla emerged, Silla growing to dominate the peninsula by the end of the 7th century. Yamato came under increasing Chinese influence and the introduction of Buddhism in the mid-6th century began a transformation of Japanese society.

Japanese *haniwa* warrior figures, placed on tombs, reflect the martial qualities of Japan in the 5th and 6th centuries CE.

The first states

500 BCE: Rice cultivation spreads to Japan from China

108 BCE: Han China occupies northern Korea

c.300 CE: Rice cultivation reaches northern Honshu

c.550 CE: Buddhism introduced to Japan

c.200 CE: End of Chinese occupation of Korea; growth of Koguryo, Paekche, Silla

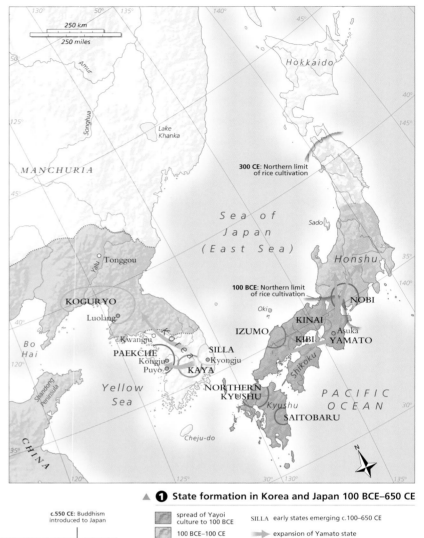

▲ ❶ **State formation in Korea and Japan 100 BCE–650 CE**

- spread of Yayoi culture to 100 BCE
- 100 BCE–100 CE
- after 100 CE
- Han Empire c.108 BCE
- SILLA early states emerging c.100–650 CE
- → expansion of Yamato state
- → expansion of Silla state
- ○ state capital

◄ ❷ **The first empires c.300–900 CE**

YANGJU administrative divisions of Silla

- extent of Paekche to 660
- furthest southern extent of Chinese (Han and Wei) control in Korea
- extent of Silla power 670–935
- extent of Nara state by 600
- — trade route

Phases of Japanese settlement and expansion

- by mid-8th century
- by late 8th century
- by early 9th century
- by mid-9th century

This Shinto shrine at Hakata in Kyushu is typical of traditional Japanese religion. Shinto observes the *kami*, the combined forces of nature and ancestral spirits. Shrines are often located on rocks, islands, and waterfalls, and include a *torii* or sacred gateway, significant features being linked by a straw rope replaced each year.

The first empires c.600–900 CE

Early imperial ambitions from about 500 CE focused on the Korean Peninsula. The Japanese Yamato state had exercised some influence in the south, and formed an alliance with Paekche against Silla. Tang China, which regarded all these states as effectively vassals, provided Silla with forces to overwhelm Paekche and the northern mountain state of Koguryo in the 660s. Thereafter, Japan withdrew and began to establish formal diplomatic relations with China, while the defeated Koguryo retreated north to establish an empire in Manchuria — Pohai which was similarly based on the Chinese model.

The struggle for Korea

554: Yamato supports Paekche against Silla

c.600: Yamato controls Japan south of Central Honshu

660: Tang forces support Silla in destruction of Paekche

668: Silla takes control of Korean peninsula

698: Pohai Empire formed in Manchuria by Koguryo refugees

668: Tang forces destroy Koguryo; refugees flee to Manchuria

The Taika Reform and the Ritsuryo state

From the 6th century, the increasing influence of Chinese institutions and of Buddhism began to transform Japan from a clan-based society into an imperial state. Under Prince Shotoku a new imperial structure was introduced (based on Chinese criminal (*ritsu*) and civil (*ryu*) law). Provinces were linked by highways and there was a centralized tax system. New capitals were built at Fujiwara then Heijo-kyo, and Buddhism formalized as a state religion alongside traditional Shinto. By the 10th century the provincial governors, tasked with quelling regional rebellion, were also involved in internecine warfare, conflict which also drew in other groups such as the substantial armies of warrior priests maintained by Buddhist temples.

❸ Japan under the Nara Ritsuryo state ▶

- ┄┄ district boundaries after Taika Reform (646)
- ○ provincial center
- ── highway
- ── seaway
- ▲ sacred Buddhist mountain

This gilded bronze Buddha dates from the 8th century. Buddhism, introduced to Japan during the 6th century, had a profound impact on all aspects of Japanese life.

❹ The rise of Taira and the Bushi ▼

Bushido warrior clans
- Taira
- Minamoto
- Fujiwara
- Buddhist temple army
- → Minamoto campaigns to suppress the north 1051–62, 1083–87
- Taira fiefdoms c.1150
- daimyo boundary

The rise of the warrior lords

645: Taika Reform under Prince Shotoku	**794–1185:** Heian Period; transition from Chinese influence to warrior lords	**c.1160:** Taira clan gain political control

600 CE — 700 — 800 — 900 — 1000 — 1100 — 1200 CE

710–784: Nara Period. Establishment of new capital, imperial court, and Japanese Buddhism
858–1160: Ascendency of the Fujiwara clan
1051–1087: Minamoto clan gain control of north and east Honshu

❺ The age of the Shoguns ▶

- ┄┄┄ daimyo boundaries

Areas of control in early 1180s
- Taira
- Northern Fujiwara
- Minamoto Yoritomo
- Minamoto Yoshinaka
- area of Yoritomo control 1190
- Later Paekche 892–930
- → Mongol invasion 1274
- → Mongol invasion 1281
- → Minamoto campaigns
- Noriyori Minamoto generals
- ⚔ battle, with date

LIAO
early 10th century: Khitan peoples establish state in Manchuria

fortified barrier wall to keep Liao at bay

KORYO
from 935: under Gaoli Dynasty
1196–1392: accepting Jin, Yuan (Mongol), and Ming overlordships

1281: Mongols fight sea battles in Hakata Bay. Invasion again fails as fleets devastated overnight by typhoon. Japanese attribute good fortune to "divine winds" (*kamikaze*)

1274: Mongols land at Hakata Bay. They return to ships after battle but fleet is dispersed by gales

1185: Taira leaders killed

Scale varies with perspective

Minamoto Yoritomo, founder of the Kamakura Shogunate, an outstanding general who wrested power from the Taira, is here represented in stylized form as an enlightened administrator and politician.

The Kamakura Shoguns 1160–1333

The ascendency of the Taira clan in Japan proved short-lived. They had gained effective power in the imperial court by destroying the Hogen (1156) and Heiji (1159) uprisings, and went on to defeat a revolt led by Minamoto Yoritomo in 1180. But he regrouped and marched on the capital. In a series of campaigns led by generals from his family, Yoritomo crushed the Taira clan, and the child emperor. Yoritomo founded the Kamakura Shogunate (1192–1333), which was charged by the imperial government to oversee the military affairs of the state. Noted for administrative wisdom and justice, the state was able, under the Minamoto successors, the Hojo, to repel Mongol invasion attempts in 1274 and 1281.

The samurai military elite observed the cult of the warrior (*bushido*), and were noted for their military, administrative, and literary skills. Eventually, they were allowed to wear two finely wrought steel swords (*daisho*), while commoners were forbidden to wear any.

The Kamakura Shogunate

1185: Taira clan eliminated	**1192:** Start of Kamakura Shogunate	**1274:** First Mongol invasion defeated	

1150 CE — 1200 — 1250 — 1300 — 1350 CE

1180–1185: Campaigns of Minamoto Yoritomo
1189: Yoritomo destroys Fujiwara rising in northern Honshu
1219: Minamoto line ends; Hojo clan act as regents for Fujiwara shogun
1281: Second Mongol invasion defeated
1333: End of Kamakura Shogunate

EAST ASIA AND THE MING

Zhu Yuanzhang, founder of the Ming Dynasty, ousted the Mongols to become emperor.

WITH THE ESTABLISHMENT of the Ming by Zhu Yuanzhang in 1368, China came under the unified control of a native dynasty for the first time in over 400 years. After an initial phase of expansionism and international diplomacy, most notably the missions of the great admiral Zheng He, the haughty and aristocratic Ming rulers became passive, inward-looking, and dominated by eunuch bureaucrats. Nevertheless, Ming China prospered greatly from the creation (largely by Europeans) of a global trading network, and the population boomed to some 150 million by 1600. Ming consolidation was emulated by their neighbors, with the growth of wealthy trading states across Central Asia, and the reunification of Japan under the Ashikaga Shogunate and their successors.

China under the Ming dynasty

The Great Wall had its origins in the Qin dynasty (221 BCE) but it was the Ming who, after ejecting the Mongol (Yuan) dynasty, rebuilt it and extended it in its current form.

The Ming arose from the increasing chaos which attended the decline of the Mongol Yuan dynasty. One rebel leader, Zhu Yuanzhang (or Taizu), eventually overcame his rivals and established a capital at Nanjing in 1356, and within 12 years had ousted the remaining Mongols. An initially aggressive foreign policy led to the reincorporation of the southwest and campaigns in Annam and Mongolia, but by the mid-15th century the empire became increasingly defensive and factionalized. However, the Chinese infrastructure grew under imperial patronage, and the impact of trade led to the growth of great industrial centers – including Yangzhou and Nanjing – at the mouth of the Yangtze, linked to Beijing by the Grand Canal. The unwieldy Ming bureaucracy was to prove incapable of responding swiftly to change.

① China under the Ming c.1600

- — Ming provinces c.1600
- ● provincial capital
- ■ regional military center
- ○ other important city
- △ frontier defense area
- ⛩ Great Wall
- ⟋⟋ Willow Palisade
- — imperial highway
- — canal

1557: Portuguese colony

200 km
200 miles

Under Taizu's son, Chengzu, Ming expansionism reached its apogee with the voyages of Zheng He to Southeast Asia and the Indian Ocean. Conceived on a grand scale (the fourth voyage, 1413–15, involved over 60 large vessels and 28,000 men), these missions were designed to exact tribute to the Ming court. This silk painting records a giraffe brought back from Africa on the seventh voyage (1431–33).

Revolts under the Ming

The ineffective government of the Ming was beset by internal dissent, often arising from crop failures and floods, exacerbated by resistance to taxation and the pressures of rapid urban growth and inflation. Rebellions in the 1440s led to over a million deaths, but two major revolts in the 1640s directly challenged Ming authority. When Li Zicheng's rebel forces took Beijing in 1644, the last Ming emperor committed suicide.

② Revolts under the Ming

- Ming China
- widespread agrarian unrest 1626–41
- area controlled by Zhang Xianzhong 1641–44
- area controlled by Zhang Xianzhong 1644–47
- area controlled by Li Zicheng 1641–45
- ⚔ urban riots

1625: White Lotus Rebellion

China under the Ming dynasty 1368–1644

1368: Foundation of Ming Dynasty	
1440s: Widespread agrarian rebellions	
1449: Mongols capture Ming emperor	
1641–45: Revolt of Li Zicheng ousts Ming rulers	
1641–47: Revolt of Zhang Xianzhong disrupts Ming control in Central China	
1644: Manchus gain control of Beijing	

1350   1450   1550   1650

1406–27: Occupation of Annam

1626–44: Widespread agrarian unrest

1636: Qing dynasty established at Mukden

The states of Central Asia

By the mid-16th century, a range of largely Islamic states had evolved across Central Asia, thriving on control of the revitalized east-west trade that had emerged under the so-called "Mongol Peace." Some of these were devolved successor states to the brief era of Mongol dominance but others, such as the Uzbek Empire, were of Turkic origin. Although rulers constantly vied for territorial control, the region enjoyed an era of cultural wealth and continuity, thriving on the periphery of, and exhange between, older and more stable civilizations.

Pastoral sheep herders of the plateaus and steppes of Central Asia are illustrated here in an Indian manuscript showing Mughal troops raiding their herds.

Though trading junks continued to ply the East and South China seas, the construction of larger oceangoing vessels was prohibited after Zheng He's seventh voyage.

❸ The Ming and the outside world

- Ming Empire
- Ming tributary peoples
- Spanish area of control in the Philippines
- transcontinental trade route
- coastline known to Chinese sailors
- Portuguese trade routes
- Dutch trade routes
- Spanish trade routes
- Chinese Manila trade routes
- voyages of Zheng He
- Japanese raids
- campaigns against the Mongols
- ◇ Dutch territory/trading station with date
- ◇ Portuguese territory/trading station with date
- ○ English territory/trading station with date
- ○ Spanish trading station with date
- ○ major Chinese port

The Ming and the outside world

Despite its isolationism, Ming China was continually affected by external forces. In the early 16th century its sheer wealth and productivity made it a magnet for global trade. By the beginning of the 17th century, its territorial size had been outstripped by that of Spain, the most powerful of several European maritime states who were drawn to East Asia by trading opportunities; but this allure also brought the unwelcome attentions of Japanese pirates and warlords, who raided China's eastern coasts throughout the Ming period.

Trade and the first European contacts

1349: First Chinese settlement at Singapore; beginning of oceangoing trade	**1405–33:** Zheng He's seven voyages	**1523:** Japanese pirates repulsed from Chinese mainland	**1557:** Foundation of Portuguese colony at Macao
c.1433: Construction of oceangoing junks banned	**1517:** First Portuguese trading mission to China	**1555:** Japanese pirates besiege Nanjing	

1300 · 1400 · 1500 · 1600

❹ The reunification of Japan

- daimyo boundaries
- *Oda* major clans following Onin War (1467–77)
- area unified by Oda Nobunaga by 1582
- Toyotomi Hideyoshi's campaigns of unification
- campaigns in Korea 1592
- campaigns in Korea 1597
- centers of Korean resistance
- Ming campaigns in defence of Korea
- area of Korea occupied by Japan 1593–98
- □ capital city

Pre-Edo Japan

The militaristic hegemony imposed by the Kamakura Shogunate and then by the Ashikaga was undermined by almost constant internecine warfare between *bushido* warlords, which culminated in the Onin War of 1467–77. This struggle for supremacy led to the emergence in the next century of two shoguns: Oda Nobunaga, who enforced national unification under a virtual dictatorship, and his successor Toyotomi Hideyoshi, whose imperial ambitions led to repeated campaigns in Korea. This period was accompanied by the first contacts with European trade and Christian missions.

Ieyasu (r.1603–05) founder of the Tokugawa Shogunate, (1603–1868), benefited from the centralizing policies of his predecessors, Oda Nobunaga and Toyotomi Hideyoshi.

Himeji castle, Hyogo, was one of over 200 heavily fortified castles built between 1570 and 1630 to enforce imperial authority, and designed in response to the challenge of gunpowder.

Japan in transition

1333: Decline of Minamoto (Kamakura) rule	**1467–77:** Onin War begins "Era of Warring States"	**1543:** First Portuguese trading mission	**1597–98:** Second Japanese invasion of Korea	**c.1600:** Edo (Tokyo) becomes capital
c.1350: Ashikaga shoguns dominant		**1570:** Nagasaki opened to foreign trade	**1592–93:** Japanese campaigns in Korea	**1603:** Foundation of Tokugawa Shogunate

1300 · 1400 · 1500 · 1600

The Edo period

The death of Hideyoshi in 1598 ignited a brief power struggle which was settled at the battle of Sekigahara (1600) by the victory of Tokugawa Ieyasu. Under the Tokugawa the imperial capital was established at Edo (Tokyo), European missions were violently suppressed, and Japan entered a 250-year period of isolationism.

❺ The rise of Edo Japan

- daimyo boundaries
- Tokugawa domain from 1560

Shimabara 1638: Uprising of Christian converts suppressed

Hirado 1609: Dutch trading post

Nagasaki 1570: Opened to European trade
1641: Dutch traders confined to Deshima island

Sekigahara 1600

Osaka 1615

Edo (Tokyo) 1600: Capital
1651, 1652: abortive coups
1675: destroyed by fire

Tanegashima 1543: First Portuguese trade mission

THE ERA OF THE QING EMPIRE

Qing China produced porcelain, jade, intaglio, carpets, and silk goods specifically for Western markets.

THE MANCHUS had already built a state along Chinese lines in southern Manchuria, based at Mukden, and were poised to take advantage of the Ming collapse in 1644. They swiftly suppressed the rebels and by the end of the 17th century had reduced Ming resistance in the south. The 18th century was a stable period of expansion and prosperity, as the Manchu, or Qing dynasty, adopted Chinese ways. Successive campaigns established an enormous empire and an array of tributary states, while regional uprisings were ruthlessly crushed. But by the 19th century the pressures of European imperial expansion and internal dissent on an unprecedented scale brought regression, isolationism, resistance to reform, and political decay.

China under the Qing

The military expansion of the Qing Empire continued throughout the 17th and 18th centuries, provoked in part by the threat of Russian, British, and French moves into Asia. Only part of the vast Qing realms were directly governed by the Manchus or settled by the Chinese, but were secured through military garrisons. The cost of this expansion was huge, and was funded by trade, largely paid for in bullion. In the 19th century, as the Qing economy faltered under pressure from European manipulation, so did the Manchu ability to administer their domains.

The Manchu rulers of the Qing Dynasty rapidly adopted the courtly manners, customs, and aristocratic aloofness of their Ming forebears. Here Kangxi (r.1662–1722) is portrayed in formal imperial splendor.

The expansion of Qing China

1636: Manchus establish Qing imperial rule at Mukden	1683: Conquest of Taiwan	1689: Treaty of Nerchinsk; acquisition of Amur and Ussuri regions from Russia	1758–59: Campaigns against Kalmyks	1792: Invasion of Nepal

1600 — 1700 — 1800

1644: Qing forces enter Beijing	1696–97: Suppression of Mongolia	1720: Formal control of Xinjiang established	1751: Invasion of Tibet	1765–69: Attempted invasion of Burma; establishment of suzerainty	1788: Attempted invasion of Annam

Scale varies with perspective

6830 km (4500 miles)
6670 km (4140 miles)

① Qing China 1644–1911

- under Manchu control by 1644
- under Manchu control by 1660
- Qing acquisitions by 1770
- 1788 date of Qing control
- → main Qing campaigns
- border of Qing Empire at its greatest extent
- tributary states c.1800
- Kalmyk realm in 17th century
- Great wall

(map labels) Kalmyks · TURKESTAN c.1750–1864: loose Qing control · KALMYKIA · Lake Balkhash · Hindu Kush · Kashgar · Indus · Yarkand · Khotan · Takla Makan Desert · Aksu · Kuldja · Dzungars · Irtysh · Ob · ILI PROTECTORATE 1755–67 · XINJIANG 1720 · Turfan · Urumchi · Tien Shan Mountains · Altai Mountains · URIANKHAI · Yenisey · NEPAL 1792–1908 · TIBET 1720: suzerainty 1751: protectorate · Hami · 1788–92 · Himalayas · Kathmandu · Plateau of Tibet · Lhasa · 1758–59 · INDIA · BHUTAN · QINGHAI 1724 · 1720–24, 1751 · OUTER MONGOLIA (KHALKHA) 1697 · Urga · RUSSIAN EMPIRE · Lake Baikal · Kheta · Ganges · Brahmaputra · GANSU 1649–59 · Lanzhou · Gobi · 1696 · Ordos Desert · Vitim · Lena · 120 · Bay of Bengal · SICHUAN 1646 · Chengdu · SHAANXI 1645–46 · SHANXI 1644–45 · Yellow River · Ordos · INNER MONGOLIA 1635 · Aldan · BURMA 1769–1886 · 1766–69: Attempted invasions · Irrawaddy · Chongqing · Xi'an · Beijing ZHILI 1644 · 1644 · Amur · INDIAN OCEAN · Pegu · YUNNAN 1659 · GUIZHOU 1658 · HUBEI 1645 · HENAN 1644–45 · Jinan SHANDONG 1645 · Mukden (Shenyang) 1689 · MANCHURIA · AMUR 1689 · 1788: Attempted invasion · HUNAN 1647–50 · ANHUI 1645 · Nanjing · 160 · SIAM 1767–c.1800: invaded by Burma · Hanoi · GUANGXI 1650–52 · Changsha · Nanchang · Yangtze · JIANGXI 1649–52 · KOREA 1627: vassal state · USSURI · LAOS · Guangzhou · Macao 1557: to Portugal · JIANGSU 1645 · Hangzhou · Suzhou · Yellow Sea · Sakhalin · Mekong · Hainan · GUANGDONG 1650–55 · FUJIAN 1646 · ZHEJIANG 1646 · Fuzhou · 1683 · Sea of Japan (East Sea) · Sea of Okhotsk · ANNAM 1666–1884 · TAIWAN 1683 · 120 · East China Sea · Kamchatka · Anadyr · Arctic Circle · South China Sea · Tropic of Cancer · PACIFIC OCEAN · Kyoto · JAPAN · Edo · 140 · 160 · 180 · 60

The decline of the Qing

The Manchus successfully suppressed a major rebellion by Ming supporters in southern China, largely by reduction and coercion, early in their reign. Subsequent revolts took a variety of forms: tribal uprisings, Muslim *jihads,* and millenarian sects. In most instances these were provoked by population pressures and economic distress. The great Taiping and Nian peasant rebellions in the mid-19th century left some 25 million dead, and although they vitally threatened Qing stability they were ultimately unsuccessful. The former, led by a Christian visionary, invoked tacit support among the hawkish European powers. In contrast, the populist Boxer rebellion was explicitly anti-European and enjoyed covert support from the Qing rulers.

The Taiping rebellion began in southern China in 1850; by 1853 the rebel armies had moved north to establish a base at Nanjing (above). From here they courted foreign powers based at Shanghai, to threaten the Qing in Beijing.

Revolts against the Qing

	1850: Start of Taiping rebellion; widespread uprising in southern China; ends 1863	1855: Jihad of Yunnan Muslims; ends 1873	1900–01: Boxer rebellion; popular anti-Western rebellion

1700 — 1800 — 1900

1674: Start of pro-Ming revolts in southern China; finally suppressed 1683	1853: Nian peasant rebellion around Kaifeng; ends 1868	1863: Start of Northwest uprising; largest Muslim jihad; ends 1873

② Revolts under the Qing Empire

- area of Three Feudatories and other pro-Ming rebellions, 1674–83
- Qing Empire
- tribal risings
- Muslim revolts
- area of Northwestern Muslim rising 1863–73
- sectarian uprising
- area controlled by Taiping rebels 1853–63
- → Taiping rebellion
- area of Nian rebellion 1853–68
- → Nian rebellion
- area of Boxer uprising 1900–01
- Guizhou Muslim uprising 1854–72
- frontier of Qing Empire 1850

(map ② labels) 500 km · 500 miles · Irtysh · Yenisey · Lake Baikal · Amur · MANCHURIA · Lake Balkhash · Dzungars 1765 · Olot 1750–57 · OUTER MONGOLIA · Gobi · INNER MONGOLIA · Sea of Japan (East Sea) · Tien Shan · XINJIANG · Aksu 1758–59 · Kashgar 1758–59 · Takla Makan Desert · Hui 1781–84 · Beijing · ZHILI · Tianjin · Eight Trigrams Sect 1786–88 · KOREA · QINGHAI · Hui 1781–84 · Lanzhou · SHANXI · SHANDONG · Yellow River · Yellow Sea · Kaifeng · Heavenly Principle Sect 1811–14 · TIBET · Tibetans 1707–49, 1755–79, 1807 · GANSU · SHAANXI · HENAN · Nanjing · mid-1850s: Taiping base · Shanghai · ANHUI · JIANGSU · Indus · Jinchuan 1746–76 · White Lotus 1795–1804 · SICHUAN · HUBEI · Hankou · ZHEJIANG · East China Sea · Brahmaputra · Ganges · Tropic of Cancer · Miao 1726–29 · GUIZHOU · HUNAN · JIANGXI · FUJIAN · TAIWAN Taiwanese 1787–88 · Yao 1790 · YUNNAN Yunnan 1855–73 · GUANGXI · GUANGDONG · Miao 1795–1806, 1833, 1850–72 · Jintian 1850: Outbreak of Taiping uprising · Bay of Bengal · South China Sea · PACIFIC OCEAN · 20 · 40 · 80 · 100 · 120 · 140

Russian expansion in North Asia 1600–1914

The Russian march across Siberia, in the wake of fur trappers, involved physical hardship but provoked little resistance from native peoples. The expansion to the south and east was more hard-fought, against the Kazakhs and Turkic peoples of Central Asia, but western military techniques prevailed. Further east, the conquest of the Amur and Ussuri regions from Qing China gave Russia access to the Pacific. With the abolition of serfdom in 1861, a wave of Russian migrants swept east. Russian progress resulted in an Anglo-Japanese alliance (1902), and was only finally halted by the Russo-Japanese War of 1904–05 *(see page 270)*.

The Trans-Siberian Railway, covering 4,500 miles between Moscow and Vladivostok, was designed to bind Russia's Asian provinces together and to reinforce its presence in the Pacific.

The growth of Russia in Asia

1697: Start of conquest of Kamchatka; completed in 1732 it gives Russian control of Siberia

1858–60: Russia regains control of Amur-Ussuri region
1860: Foundation of Vladivostok

1868–70: Suppression of Muslim states of Bukhara and Samarkand

1900–05: Occupation of Manchuria

1689: Treaty of Nerchinsk settles territorial dispute with Qing China

1730–34: Suppression of Khazaks

1864: Establishment of control in Kalmykia (Semipalatinsk)

1891: Construction of Trans-Siberian Railway started; completed 1917

1904–05: Russo-Japanese war halts Russian expansion

③ Russian expansion in Asia 1600–1914

Russian Empire c.1600	acquisitions 1877–1914
acquisitions 1600–1725	temporary acquisition, with dates
acquisitions 1726–1855	Russian sphere of influence, 1914
acquisitions 1856–76	

1788 date of foundation or acquisition
Trans-Siberian Railway, built 1891–1917
borders 1914

Foreign imperialism in East Asia

The rapidly expanded Qing economy of the 18th century made it prey to foreign ambitions. The dynasty's failure to halt the highly profitable illegal British trade in opium in 1839–42 revealed its weaknesses. Hong Kong was the first of many territorial and trading concessions which gave not only the Europeans but the Russians and Japanese valuable toeholds in the Middle Kingdom. Qing complacency, resistance to modernization, and their inability to counter growing internal dissent played into their adversaries' hands. By the end of the 19th century, despite belated attempts to reform, the Qing were a power in name only.

Foreign incursions into China

1841: Foundation of British colony at Hong Kong

1860: Anglo-French forces occupy Beijing forcing further cessions

1904–05: Russo-Japanese war; Russian occupied territories taken over by Japan

1840–42: Opium War; British attacks force trading concessions

1858–60: Loss of Amur-Ussuri region to Russia

1898–1905: Port Arthur leased to Russia

1900–05: Russian occupation of Manchuria

④ Foreign imperialism in East Asia, 1840–1910

Area of control

Russian
Japanese
French
British
Dutch
American
Portuguese

1893 date of acquisition by foreign power

Area of influence

Russian
Japanese
French
British
German

Leased territory

Japanese
French
British
Portuguese
German

Treaty ports

Japanese
French
British
American
open port

Qing Empire at its greatest extent c.1850

Foreign attacks on China

British (Opium War 1840–42)
Anglo-French campaigns 1858–60
French 1883–85

Western warehouses and shipping dominated the Guangzhou waterfront from the 1830s onward.

THE MODERNIZATION OF EAST ASIA

BOTH JAPAN AND CHINA entered the 19th century under feudal, courtly, isolationist, and reactionary regimes which had held power since the 17th century. By 1900 their development stood in stark contrast. Japan under the Tokugawa Shogunate was a prosperous, sophisticated society, socially developed, universally literate, and ready for modernization. When this came – through international trade pressure – Japan adopted the role of a progressive industrialized state, keen to dominate East Asian affairs. It was aided by the Qing dynasty's rejection of external pressures and internal demands for reform in China. The end of the Qing dynasty coincided with Japanese territorial aspirations, widespread factionalism among reforming groups in China itself, and the rise of Communism in its largest neighbor, Russia.

Jiang Jieshi (Chiang Kai-shek) assumed control of the Chinese Nationalist Party in 1925.

Japanese modernization 1868–1919

When US Commodore Perry's fleet entered Tokyo Bay in 1853 to demand international trading rights with Japan, the 200-year policy of isolationism under the Tokugawa Shogunate (Bakufu) effectively ended. Reformist forces based in the south conducted a campaign (the Boshin War 1868–69) which restored the Meiji ("enlightened rule") emperor, and inaugurated political, social, and economic reform. The nation was divided into prefectures, and a centralized bureaucracy introduced a new constitution, the construction of a railroad system, and the creation of modern industries, such as shipbuilding.

The modernization of Japan

- 1854: First foreign trade treaties
- 1868–69: Boshin War; Tokugawa Bakufu defeated by modernizing imperialists
- 1877: Satsuma rebellion, led by reformer Saigo Takamori, in defense of traditional values
- 1889: New constitution balances imperial authority with parliamentary government
- 1894–95: Sino–Japanese War; increases sphere of influence on mainland
- 1904–05: Russo–Japanese War consolidates influence in Korea and Manchuria
- 1918: Japan occupies areas of Russia during civil war
- 1919: League of Nations accords German Pacific territories under mandate to Japan

1840 · 1860 · 1880 · 1900 · 1920

Visitors to Japan were confined to Nagasaki for almost 400 years. In 1853, when Commodore Perry took warships into Tokyo Bay to enforce US trading treaties with Japan, the confrontation between Japan and the West reached crisis point.

① Japanese modernization 1868–1918

Boshin War 1868–69
- imperial (anti–Bakufu) alliance
- route of imperial army
- battle, with date

Modernization under the Meiji
- KOCHI prefectures established 1871
- main industrial areas by 1918
- railroads built 1868–1918

Traditional industries
- ceramics
- textiles
- silk

Industries developed after 1868
- manufacturing
- machine-building
- shipbuilding
- chemicals
- city of over 500,000 in 1918
- city of over 100,000 in 1918
- other major city

Japanese expansion 1868–1936

The entry of Japan onto the world's stage in 1868 was accompanied by an active policy of territorial expansion to support its rapidly expanding economy. Supported by the US (its principal trading partner by 1918), Japan claimed neighboring islands and gained territory as a result of wars against China (1894–95) and Russia (1904–05) – leading to the annexation of Formosa and Korea. Japan's firm commitment to the Allies during World War I (1914–18) gave her lands in the Pacific, and she rapidly gained other substantial footholds on mainland Asia.

After the Meiji revolution Japanese transportation modernized rapidly; steamships, railroads, and automobiles were introduced.

③ The Sino-Japanese War 1894–95

- area of Tonghak rebellion
- Japanese advance
- Japanese victory
- area leased to Japan 1895

The Sino-Japanese War 1894–95

Upon the outbreak of a populist, quasi-religious nationalist rebellion, the Tonghak Revolt (1894), the Korean court appealed to both Qing China and Japan for support. The Japanese forces compromised the Korean royal family, and open conflict with China erupted; the modern equipment and tactics employed by the Japanese forced Qing forces back to the Liaodong Peninsula, which with Taiwan was ceded to the victors, and Korea entered the Japanese sphere of influence.

The Russo-Japanese War 1904–05

Territorial rivalry and mutual animosity between Russia and Japan, already overheated by Russia's adventurist occupation of Manchuria in 1897, came to a head when Japanese vessels bombarded Russian ships at Port Arthur in 1904. The Japanese moved rapidly to secure a series of successes in southern Manchuria, exploiting their effective control of Korea, and victory was sealed when the Russian Baltic Fleet was savaged by Japanese ships in the Tsushima Strait (1905).

④ The Russo-Japanese War 1904–05

- Qing China
- to Russia 1897, to Japan 1905
- area leased to Japan 1895
- Japanese advances 1904–05
- route of Russian Baltic fleet
- Japanese victory, with date

② Japanese expansion 1868–1936

- Japan in 1868
- gains by 1894
- gains by 1910
- spheres of influence by 1918
- Japanese treaty ports
- granted by Treaty of Versailles 1919
- occupied by 1936

Scale varies with perspective

National victories against China and Russia in the 1890s were celebrated in a dynamic manner by Japanese artists whose style influenced the development of 20th-century graphic art.

The Chinese Revolution of 1911

After a century of almost continual internal dissent, and some ten attempted revolutions since 1890, the Qing dynasty finally recognized the need for reform in 1911. An almost spontaneous eruption of revolt across China (orchestrated by telegraph) led within five months to the abdication of the boy emperor in favour of a reformist Qing general, Yuan Shikai. Meanwhile, the leader of the Nationalist uprising, Sun Zhongshan, proclaimed a republican constitution in Nanjing. The fragile situation, with Yuan rapidly adopting dictatorial measures, began to collapse into bitter regional strife.

The Dowager Empress Cixi was photographed in regal splendor as the Qing dynasty drew to its close. Her regency between 1861 and 1908 represented the last bastion of Qing conservatism in the face of reform and modernization.

◀ **⑤ The Chinese Revolution 1911**

- joined revolt Oct 1911
- joined revolt Nov 1911
- joined revolt after Nov 1911
- rest of Qing Empire
- occupied by Japan

Oct 16 1911: Mutiny by reformist army officers sparks nationwide revolt

1913: Parliamentary elections; Nationalists win over 50% of seats. Yuan refuses to endorse constitution

May 4 1919: Movement revives Nationalist cause, provoked by international support for Japan's claims in mainland China

1926–28: Nationalist Northern Expedition unites Chinese heartland

1927–28: Nationalist purge of Communist allies

1910 — 1915 — 1920 — 1925 — 1930

Jan 1912: Sun Zhongshan declares republican constitution in Nanjing
Feb 1912: Abdication of last Qing emperor; Yuan Shikai assumes power as president

1915: Yuan announces plans to become emperor

1925: Sun Zhongshan dies, succeeded by Jiang Jieshi

Revolution in China 1911–28

The Red Flag over Asia

Bolshevik "Agitation-Instruction" trains decorated with revolutionary themes traveled to every corner of the USSR to spread the gospel of Communism.

In the wake of the Civil War (1918–21), the Russian Bolsheviks moved swiftly to consolidate their control of Asian areas of Russia. They harnessed technology and modernism with propaganda techniques to achieve the socialist revolution. Communist republics had been set up in the Far East, at Tannu–Tuva, and in Central Asia. These were gradually coerced into merging with the Soviet Union, while military support was provided to oust Chinese troops from Mongolia. The active export of Bolshevik Communism (Comintern) continued in various forms, notably in China and India.

The spread of Communism in Asia

1917: Bolshevik revolution in Russia

May 4 1919: Movement in China, resurgence of Nationalism

1921: Chinese Communist Party founded

1925: Asiatic borders of USSR consolidated

1927–28: Chinese Nationalists purge Communists

1915 — 1920 — 1925 — 1930

1918–22: Civil war and foreign intervention in Russia

1919: Third International (Comintern); Bolsheviks commit to international revolution

1924: Death of Lenin

1926: Jiang Jieshi leads Nationalist campaign to unify China

Scale varies with perspective

⑧ The Red Flag over Asia 1917–30 ▶

- independent Communist states
- active Bolshevik influence (Comintern)
- 1921 date of formation of Communist party

Maps panel (top right)

1920

1924

1926

⑥ The Chinese Civil War 1920–26

Factions during the civil war

- Fengtian Clique
- Anhui Clique
- Zhili Clique
- Zhili faction
- Nationalist (Kuomintang)
- pro-Nationalist (Kuominchung)
- Guangxi Clique
- independent warlords
- nonaffiliated regions

The Chinese Civil War 1920–26

Following the death of **Yuan Shikai** in 1916, the Chinese republic faltered. The nation fragmented further into regional power groups, often dominated by local warlords. Over the next 12 years a constantly shifting pattern of factionalism and alliance dominated the map of China. The 4 May Movement of 1919 in Shanghai provoked an upsurge of nationalist fervor, in the wake of which the Chinese Communist Party was formed (1921); Sun Zhongshan's Nationalists (Kuomintang) formed an alliance with the Communists, and began a campaign of unification which culminated in the Northern Expedition of 1926–28. This was led by Sun's successor, Moscow-trained Jiang Jieshi (Chiang Kai-shek), who then inaugurated a bloody purge of the Communists.

▲ **⑦ Nationalist China**

- under direct control of Nationalist government at Nanjing 1928
- Nanjing control 1929–34
- Nanjing control 1935–37
- Japanese sphere of influence by 1935
- → route of Northern Expedition
- → pro-Nationalist forces

THE WAR IN THE PACIFIC

Japanese expansionism in Manchuria and Jehol accelerated in 1937 with a full-scale invasion of China.

FOLLOWING WORLD WAR I, Japan was accorded an extended sphere of territorial control in the Pacific. The Chinese Civil War enabled Japan to extend its territorial ambitions on the East Asian mainland, culminating in outright warfare in China by 1937. But international sanctions, designed to limit Japan's aspirations resulted, by 1940, in a political standoff. Next year, Japan went to war, calculating its chances on the basis of its rapid industrial development, the colonial powers' involvement in Hitler's war in Europe, and the bounty which would accrue from the establishment of an anti-Western "Greater East Asia Co-Prosperity Sphere." By June 1942 Japan was trying to maintain a front line over 22,000 miles in extent – inevitably, it proved indefensible.

The Japanese offensive 1941–42

Almost simultaneous preemptive strikes in December 1941 against the US naval base at Pearl Harbor, Hawaii, the US-controlled Philippines, the Dutch East Indies, and the British Malayan states created at a stroke and for a brief

historical moment, the largest contiguous empire the world has ever seen. Campaigns in New Guinea, the Solomons, and Burma extended it even further. The combination of surprise (Japan attacked before declaring war), detailed strategic planning, the use of innovative aggressive methods (amphibious landings, aircraft carriers, tactical bombing, jungle tactics), and a disregard for the "acceptable" rules of warfare proved initially irresistible.

The Japanese army's comprehensive training in military techniques such as jungle warfare and amphibious assaults proved an essential element in their initial successes in China and tropical Southeast Asia.

The surprise Japanese bombing raid on the US naval base at Pearl Harbor on December 7, 1941, was designed, at least temporarily, to destroy US sea power in the Pacific. Only 18 of the 94 warships at anchor were actually put out of action, but as a result, the US was drawn into war against Japan and its Axis allies.

① **The Japanese offensive 1941–42**

— international borders 1940–42

- - - areas of territorial control (colored as country of origin)

☐ military bases (colored as country of origin)

China
British possessions
French possessions
Portuguese possessions
Dutch possessions
USSR
Japan and possessions
Australia
US and possessions

⟹ Japanese campaigns Dec 1941
⟹ Japanese campaigns Jan–Jun 1942
Ⓥ Japanese victory
⚓ Japanese air raid 1942
Ⓥ Allied naval victory
⚓ Allied carrier/air raid
▬ Japanese front line Jun 1942

The Japanese offensive 1937–41

Dec 12 1937: Japanese take Nanjing, massacring population

Oct 21 1938: Japanese take Guangzhou

Aug 23 1939: Nazi-Soviet Non-Aggression Pact

Sep 23 1940: Japanese forces occupy French Indo-China

Sep 27 1940: Japan, Germany and Italy form Tri-Partite Pact

Dec 7 1941: Japanese raid Pearl Harbor

Dec 10–24 1941: Japanese forces land on Philippines

Jul 7 1937: Sino-Japanese War breaks out

Mar 28 1938: Japanese establish puppet government at Nanjing

Aug 25 1939: Japanese leave Anti-Comintern Pact

26 July 1940: Proclamation of New Order in Far East

Apr 13 1941: Japan and USSR sign neutrality pact

Dec 25 1941: Hong Kong surrenders

1937 1938 1939 1940 1941 1942

The Allied counteroffensive 1942–45

In mid–1942 the Allied defeat of naval forces in the Coral Sea and at Midway halted the Japanese advance. Over the next year, bitter campaigns on and around Guadalcanal in the Solomons proved a turning point. American industrial mobilization on a massive scale fed a selective island-hopping campaign designed to disrupt the internal communications of the Japanese empire and to bring air power within striking distance of the Japanese home islands. Japanese resistance was so fierce that it took the US explosion of two newly developed atomic bombs over Japan, which was followed by a Soviet land campaign in Manchuria, to force a surrender.

The war in the Pacific 1942–45

May 6 1942: US forces on Philippines surrender
Jun 4 1942: Japanese defeated at Midway
Aug 1943: Allied victory in New Guinea
Oct 1944: Battle of Leyte Gulf, US begin reconquest of Philippines
Jun 1945: Allied forces secure Okinawa
Aug 8 1945: USSR declares war on Japan

1942   1943   1944   1945   1946

Mar 9 1942: Dutch East Indies capitulate
May 4–8 1942: Japanese repulsed at Coral Sea
Feb 1943: Japanese evacuate Guadalcanal after six months of US offensive
Jun 19–20 1944: Japanese defeat at Philippine Sea
Aug 6 1945: Atom bomb dropped on Hiroshima
Sep 2 1945: Japanese surrender

The US refinement of amphibious operations, landing large forces supported by naval bombardment and carrier-borne air power, was a key element in their reconquest of the Pacific.

② The Allied counter-offensive 1942–45

→ Japanese offensives
→ Allied offensives 1943
→ Allied offensives 1944
→ Allied offensives 1945
▨ Japanese front line Jun 1942
▨ Japanese front line Sep 1944
▨ Japanese front line Aug 1945
▪ Chinese military base
▫ British military base
▫ US military base
Ⓥ Allied naval victory
◩ Allied amphibious assault
◼ Japanese base isolated by Allies
◼ Japanese air/naval base taken by Allies

The "Big Six" bomb targets
Mar 10–Jun 15, 1945

City	Number of raids	Approx % of city destroyed
Tokyo	5	50
Nagoya	4	31
Kobe	2	56
Osaka	4	26
Yokohama	2	44
Kawasaki	1	33

③ The bombardment of Japan 1945

🔥 "Big Six" firebomb targets
🔥 other firebomb targets
✺ main minelaying operations
⚓ naval bombardment targets
☁ atomic bomb targets

The bombardment of Japan

The Allied air assault began in June 1944 with raids from Chengdu in China. With the capture of the Marianas, Iwo Jima, and Okinawa, greater air power could be brought to bear, bombing cities and sowing mines in Japan's home waters. Complemented by carrier-supported raids from March 1945, which inaugurated the "Big Six" firebomb raids against key cities, over 50 other cities were attacked; merchant shipping was reduced by over 80%, over half of Japan's urban area was devastated, one-third of all buildings destroyed, and 13 million people made homeless. It culminated in the atomic bomb attacks against Hiroshima and Nagasaki, killing over 150,000 people.

As the Allied forces closed in on the home islands, Japanese resistance became more tenacious. Volunteer squadrons of suicide (*kamikaze*) fighter-bomber pilots were recruited to attack the Allied fleet.

COMMUNISM AND CAPITALISM

FROM 1945, EAST ASIA was dominated by the conflicting ideologies of Communism and capitalism, which brought international war in Korea (1950–53) and Vietnam (1946–75). In China, Mao Zedong and his successors sought social revolution through centralization, collectivization, and the ruthless elimination of dissent, while attempting to manage phenomenal population growth. Meanwhile, spurred by the example of post-war Japan, and supported by the US in an attempt to contain Communism, capitalist economic growth spread around the Pacific Rim. By 2000, only North Korea remained isolated as China embraced market economics with dramatic results. In Central Asia, the collapse of the USSR in 1991 saw a resurgence of ethnic rivalries and Islamic revitalization, sparking another international conflict in Afghanistan.

A high-speed train passing Mount Fuji exemplifies Japan's rapid development as one of the world's leading economies

Mao Zedong's vision of a Communist revolution in China was underpinned by the mobilization of the masses down to a family level, spread by his writings, mass education, and by propaganda (above).

China under the Communists

The victorious Chinese Communists moved from moderation to a radical agenda of socialist reform, creating a centralized, Party-led, political and economic infrastructure, and modernizing industry, after almost 40 years of turmoil. Mao Zedong used propaganda and coercion to mobilize the peasants through collectivization of agriculture and mass labor projects. The Great Leap Forward (1958–60) resulted in famine and 30 million deaths. Ideological purges continued, notably during the Cultural Revolution (1966). After Mao's death in 1976, China steadily reversed many economic and social policies, although the Communists brutally guarded their monopoly on power, massacring pro-democracy protestors in 1989. By 2000, China's "open door" trading policy had led to a second industrial revolution, making it the fastest-growing economy in the world.

The Great Leap Forward (1958–60) redirected peasant labor to massive public works projects to transform China from an agricultural to an industrial economy. Yet the nation's agricultural capacity was drastically reduced, causing widespread famine in the 1960s.

The Communist revolution in China 1927–49

Following the schism with the Guomindang Nationalists in 1927, the Communists fled to remote mountain bases. Harried by the Nationalists under Chiang Kai-shek (Jiang Jieshi), Mao Zedong and fellow Communists retreated north in 1934 to Yenan (the Long March). The war against Japan saved them, allowing Mao to rebuild the Party, hone its ideology and extend its influence, while the Nationalists withdrew to Chongqing in the southwest. Upon the Japanese surrender, Soviet forces occupied Manchuria. This gave the Communists an advantage, allowing them to gain control of China's northeast heartland. By 1948, open warfare had erupted, but, with the collapse of their forces north of the Yangtze, the Nationalists withdrew to Taiwan. The People's Republic of China was established in 1949.

① The Communist Revolution in China ▶

- Communist centers 1934
- Long March Oct 1934–Oct 1935
- area under Japanese control 1944
- area under Communist (PLA) control 1946
- area under Communist (PLA) control by mid-1949
- area of Communist guerrilla operations 1944–49
- battle
- principal Communist campaigns
- city with date of Communist control

② Chinese economic development from 1950 ◀

- boundary of Autonomous Regions

Percentage population growth 1950–90
- over 100%
- 75–100%
- 55–75%
- less than 55%

Economic development under Mao Zedong
- oilfield
- coalfield
- nuclear plant
- industrial centre

Economic development since 1980
- Special Economic Zone
- open port
- average income more than 80% of national average, 1990s
- average income less than 80% of national average, 1990s

The Communist Revolution

1921: Chinese Communist Party founded	**Oct 1934–Oct 1935:** Long March unites Communists	**1937:** Sino-Japanese war breaks out	**1945:** Japanese surrender in Second World War	**1949:** Republic of China set up in Taiwan

1920 — 1925 — 1930 — 1935 — 1940 — 1945 — 1950

| **1923:** First United Front: Guomindang and Communists unite against warlords | **1927:** Split between Nationalists and Communists | **1937–45:** Second United Front: Guomindang and Communists unite against Japanese | **1946–49:** Civil war between Nationalists and Communists | **1949:** People's Republic of China established |

The Long March of 1934–35 was a scramble for survival that succeeded in strategically relocating and uniting the Communist forces. The 8000 or so survivors of 100,000 who set out) later became the core of the Party. Mao Zedong, seen here addressing his troops, only became supreme leader after a power struggle en route.

China under Communist rule

1950–56: Land reform and collectivization of agriculture; millions of landowners executed

1960–65: Pragmatists such as Deng Xiaoping work to revive economy

1968: Red Guard disbanded

1978: Beginnings of economic liberalization under Deng Xiaoping

1979: One child per family policy introduced to limit population growth

1989: Suppression of pro-democracy movement; Tiananmen Square massacre

1990: Shanghai stock exchange reopens

1997: Death of Deng Xiaoping. UK hands over Hong Kong

1999: Portugal returns Macao to China

2004: Greatest mass migration in history speeds urbanization and industrialization

1950 — 1960 — 1970 — 1980 — 1990 — 2000

1958–60: Great Leap Forward; attempt to increase productivity and boost industry

1959: Start of Three Hard Years; widespread famine

1966: Cultural Revolution; massive purges, formation of revolutionary Red Guard

1976: Death of Mao Zedong

1982: Census reveals 1 billion Chinese, justifying "one child policy"

1984: Record harvest

1992: Deng Xiaoping's reforms start to rejuvenate economy

1993: Jiang Zemin president

2001: China admitted to WTO. 'Strike Hard' anti-corruption policy

2002: Hu Jintao Party leader

RUSSIAN FEDERATION
prior to 1991: called USSR

Chinese expansionism from 1949

The cooling of relations between the West and the Communist bloc was further chilled by China's involvement in the Korean War, its covert support for Communist guerrillas elsewhere, and by its ideological split with the Soviet Union in 1960, sparked off by the Amur–Ussuri border dispute. Chinese isolationism was balanced by an aggressive foreign policy. Tibet was invaded and occupied, and the divine ruler, the Dalai Lama, exiled in 1959. It was formally absorbed as an Autonomous Region of China in 1965. Border disputes brought a brief war with India in 1962, the highest in the history of warfare, and a temporary invasion of North Vietnam in 1979. Taiwan has remained a thorn in China's side, while the need to control potential oil and gas deposits has seen China defending remote claims in the South China Sea.

The invasion of Tibet in 1950 was the most significant incident of Chinese expansionism since the Communist Revolution. Traditional ways of life and beliefs were suppressed and, following a revolt in 1959, Tibet's spiritual and political leader, the Dalai Lama, was forced into exile.

❸ Chinese expansion from 1949

- ☐ Chinese provinces
- ☐ Autonomous Regions (Zizhiqu)
- territorial/border dispute
- → Chinese invasion
- ★ Chinese support for Communist insurgents
- Soviet support for Communists after 1960
- suppression of anti-Communist movements

The expansion of China, 1950–1980

- 1950: Chinese invasion of Tibet
- 1950: Chinese troops invade Korea
- 1959: Tibetan rebellion crushed, religious institutions banned
- 1960: Amur-Ussuri border dispute; ideological split with USSR
- 1962: Sino-Indian War over border claim at Arunachal Pradesh; rectification of border claims with Pakistan, Nepal, and Burma
- 1971: China admitted to United Nations; Taiwan expelled
- 1979: US severs relations with Taiwan in return for detente with China
- 1979: Invasion of North Vietnam

The "Tiger" economies from 1960

During the US occupation of Japan (1945–52) a new conservative pro-capitalist constitution was created, along with the conditions for rapid economic growth. As a standing army was banned, greater investment could be made in industry. Japan's phenomenal growth focused on shipbuilding, electronic goods, cameras, and cars. By the 1970s Japan, the world's third- largest industrial nation, had launched a global outward investment program. The Japanese example encouraged the development of a string of economic successes around the Pacific Rim over the next 20 years, but China's spectacular growth in the early 21st century threatened to overshadow them all.

❹ The "Tiger" economies from 1960

- ☐ Communist states 1976
- ⟳ ASEAN membership
- ⊛ over 50% of workforce employed in primary industries by mid-1980s
- △ average GDP growth rate of over 8% in 1970s
- ◉ major industrial city

4390 km (2730 miles)
5560 km (3450 miles)

Growth of "Tiger" economies of the Pacific Rim 1980–2002

GDP in $US billion
☐ 1980 ☐ 1996 ☐ 2002

China, Hong Kong, Indonesia, Japan, Malaysia, Philippines, Singapore, South Korea, Thailand

Japan emerged in the 1960s as a beacon of modernization, dominating many of the world's industries. The economy faltered in the 1990s, but remains the second strongest in the world.

Economic growth in East Asia

- 1951: Treaty of San Francisco; Japan regains independence
- 1965: Singapore independent; rapid growth in service and electronics sector
- 1967: ASEAN created to promote economic cooperation
- 1973: Global oil crisis leads Japan to focus on high-tech industries
- 1975: End of Vietnam War
- 1980s: Rapid growth of South Korean economy
- 1986: Collapse of pro-US Marcos regime in Philippines
- 1989: Tokyo stock market crash ends period of exponential economic growth
- 1997: Domino effect of Japanese crash throughout Pacific Rim
- 1997: Hong Kong returned to China; end of boom

Islam and nationalism in Central Asia

The Islamic states of Central Asia inherited widespread environmental damage, especially in Kazakhstan, where the Soviet nuclear testing and space center at Baykonur (above) was based.

Islam in Central Asia survived suppression and political change, to re-emerge as a vital force in the region's politics. Signalled by the *mujahedin* rebellion in Afghanistan (from 1973), and the establishment of an Islamic Republic in Iran in 1979, the revival progressed with the *mujahedin* defeat of a Soviet invasion (1979–89). Following the collapse of the USSR in 1991, ethnic and religious rivalry flared up across the new republics. The fundamentalist Taliban conquered Afghanistan in 1995–98, but were ousted by the US in 2001 for harboring Islamic terrorists.

❺ Islam and nationalism in Asia

- ▨ predominantly Muslim populations
- ☾ Muslim minorities
- ▨ Shia majority
- ethnic conflict
- Islamic revolution/civil war

North and Central Asia since 1979

- 1979: Soviet invasion of Afghanistan
- 1979: Islamic revolution in Iran
- 1989: Soviet troops withdraw from Afghanistan
- 1990–91: Collapse of USSR; creation of Central Asian republics
- 1995: Taliban militia reignites Afghan civil war
- 1998: Taliban control 90% of Afghanistan. Tajik civil war ends after seven years
- 1999: Increase in Islamist militancy in Uzbekistan
- 2001: US-led force removes Taliban from power after 9/11 attacks
- 2004: Free elections for Afghan president

AUSTRALASIA AND OCEANIA

REGIONAL HISTORY

THE HISTORICAL LANDSCAPE

THE INSULAR CONTINENT OF AUSTRALIA and the myriad island groups of Melanesia, Micronesia, and Polynesia, strewn across the Pacific Ocean, share the most unlikely chapter in world history. Australia and New Guinea were first colonized some 60,000 years ago by migrants crossing the Southeast Asian landbridge, who completed their journey by boat – the world's first navigators. As sea levels rose after the last Ice Age, they became divided and isolated, maintaining simple, sustainable lifestyles in remote communities until European contact in the 18th century when their vulnerability was fatally exposed. The settlement of the Pacific islands, beginning some 30,000 years ago, again depended on navigational skills, and developed from about 1500 BCE into a process of active colonization. By 1200 CE, Polynesians were the most widely distributed ethnic group on the face of the earth, with settlements from New Zealand to Hawaii. The region was the penultimate target of European imperialists, leaving only the barren tracts of the Arctic ice cap and continental Antarctica as the final, ephemeral prizes in Europe's race for global domination – a race of heroic futility played out across the opening years of the 20th century.

Initially settlements were concentrated around the coasts; then, as the population grew, people moved inland to colonize the flat glacial plains of the interior.

Australia's deserts were more extensive during the last Ice Age. As the land bridge between Australia and New Guinea was flooded, settlers retreated south into the desert margins of Australia.

Most Pacific islands are volcanic, formed by eruptions on the sea floor which accumulate a cone of volcanic material, eventually rising above the ocean surface. As the volcano becomes extinct, coral reefs grow around the island's fringes. Humans first sailed to the Pacific islands from New Guinea and the Solomon Islands, reaching Fiji by 1500 BCE.

Vegetation type

	ice cap and glacier
	tundra
	semidesert or sparsely vegetated
	grassland
	forest or open woodland
	tropical rain forest
	tropical desert
	desert
	coastline (present-day)
	coastline (18,000 years ago)

PACIFIC OCEAN

SOUTHERN OCEAN

ANTARCTICA

PACIFIC PLATE

Midway Islands
Wake Island

Hawaiian Islands
Necker Ridge
Johnston Atoll
Schjetman Reef
Hawaii

Tropic of Cancer

Central Pacific Basin

Christmas Ridge

Kiritimati

Line Islands

Equator

Phoenix Islands

Polynesia

Tuamotu Islands

Northern Cook Islands
Manihiki Plateau
Samoa
Samoa Basin
Penrhyn Basin

Society Ridge
Society Islands
Tahiti

Southern Cook Islands

Iles Australes
Iles Gambier
Tropic of Capricorn

Southwest Pacific Basin

Agassiz Fracture Zone

Eltanin Fracture Zone
Udintsev Fracture Zone

PACIFIC PLATE
ANTARCTIC PLATE

Pacific-Antarctic Ridge

Antarctic Circle

Philippine Sea
West Mariana Basin
South Honshu Ridge
Mariana Islands
Mariana Trench
East Mariana Basin

Kyushu-Palau Ridge
CAROLINE PLATE
Yap Trench
PHILIPPINE PLATE
Caroline Islands

East Caroline Basin
Eauripik Rise
PACIFIC PLATE

Micronesia

Mid-Pacific Seamounts

Marshall Islands
Marshall Seamounts

Melanesian Basin
Nauru
Banaba
Tungaru
Gilbert Islands

Admiralty Islands
Bismarck Sea
New Britain
BISMARCK PLATE
Solomon Sea
SOLOMON PLATE
Solomon Islands
South Solomon Trench

Melanesia

Vityaz Trench

Tuvalu

Coral Sea Basin

Coral Sea

North New Hebrides Trench
Vanuatu
Tanna
Iles Loyauté
New Caledonia
New Hebrides Trench
FIJI PLATE
Cook Fracture Zone

North Fiji Basin

Fiji
Vitu Levu
Vanua Levu

PACIFIC PLATE
FIJI PLATE

Robbie Ridge

Samoa

Lau Basin
Tonga

South Fiji Basin

New Caledonia Basin
Norfolk Ridge
West Norfolk Ridge
Norfolk Island
Three Kings Rise

Lord Howe Seamounts
Lord Howe Rise

Kermadec Ridge
Kermadec Trench
Tonga Trench

Louisville Ridge

New Guinea
Torres Strait
LAKE CARPENTARIA
Cape York Peninsula

Great Barrier Reef

Great Dividing Range

Australia

Eyre
Darling
Murray

Bass Strait

Tasmania
Tasman Plain
Tasman Sea
Tasman Basin
Tasman Plateau

INDO-AUSTRALIAN PLATE
ANTARCTIC PLATE
Southeast Indian Ridge

Tasman Fracture Zone

Macquarie Ridge
Auckland Islands
Macquarie Island

New Zealand
North Island
Southern Alps
South Island

Chatham Rise
Chatham Islands

Bounty Trough
Campbell Plateau

Glaciers covered the tops of New Zealand's Southern Alps, carving deep valleys into the mountains that today have filled with water to form lakes.

New Zealand's North Island and South Island were joined together by a narrow land bridge.

...mania was attached to ...land Australia across ...ass Strait, forming the ...ernmost peaks of the Great Dividing Range.

Australasia and Oceania: 18,000 years ago

During the last Ice Age, Australia and New Guinea were joined by a land bridge. New Zealand's North Island was covered by grassland and scrub while tundra covered the South Island – in marked contrast to the forests that cover much of the islands today. The Australian climate was cooler and drier – and the deserts expanded to cover more than three-quarters of the continent.

AUSTRALASIA AND OCEANIA
EXPLORATION AND MAPPING

Abel Tasman reached Tasmania and New Zealand in 1642 in his search for a great southern continent.

ALMOST ALL THE PACIFIC ISLANDS had been discovered and, when habitable, settled by Polynesian voyagers some 500 years before European explorers ventured into the ocean. After Magellan's pioneering crossing of 1521, it took three centuries to chart the whole Pacific. The continent of Australia presented even greater problems. Ever since Classical times, European world maps had included a vast southern continent, *Terra Australis Incognita*. It was not until James Cook's voyages in the 18th century that the true extent of Australia was established. New Guinea's mountainous interior was not explored by Europeans until the 20th century.

STICK CHARTS OF THE MARSHALL ISLANDS

The **Melanesian** and Polynesian peoples who have been sailing the Pacific for four millennia have built up a vast store of knowledge of its islands, winds, and currents. The inhabitants of the Marshall Islands make charts of sticks and shells. Some are actual maps of surrounding islands and are carried aboard their canoes. Others are teaching aids. The *mattang*, for example, is not a map as such; it demonstrates the way islands affect patterns in the ocean's swell, an invaluable means of detecting the presence of low-lying atolls.

This typical *mattang* chart is made of the midribs of coconut fronds. Shells mark the location of islands and the sticks show variations in ocean swell.

❶ **Oceania: the major European voyages**

Spanish expeditions
— Ferdinand Magellan 1520–21
--- Pedro Fernández de Quirós 1605–07
...... Luis Váez de Torres 1606–16

Dutch expeditions
— Isaac Le Maire and Willem Schouten 1615–16
--- Abel Tasman 1642–44

British expeditions
— James Cook's first voyage 1768–71
--- James Cook's second voyage 1772–75
...... James Cook's third voyage 1776–79

French expeditions
— Louis Antoine de Bougainville 1767–68
--- J.F. Galaup de La Pérouse 1785–88

1778 date of first European sighting or landing

European voyages of discovery

In the 16th century the Spanish sailed into the Pacific out of curiosity and greed, seeking routes to the riches of China and the "Spice Islands." At first they did not intrude too greatly on the life of the islands, using them as stopovers to pick up food and water. In Australasia the Dutch led the way, but, seeing no potential profit in Australia or New Zealand, left them alone. Things changed in the 18th century when the French and the British were competing for domination of the globe. The three voyages of Captain James Cook transformed Europe's understanding of Oceania, and it was in part the popularity of accounts of Cook's voyages that spurred European and American exploitation and colonization of the region in the 19th century.

Dutch mariners provided the data for this 1593 map. It gives a reasonably accurate picture of the Solomon Islands and part of the north coast of New Guinea, but the shape and extent of Australia are still a mystery. Here, it is at least divided from New Guinea by a strait – many later maps show the two islands attached.

The *Resolution*, James Cook's ship on his epic second voyage of 1772–75, was originally built to carry coal.

European exploration of the Pacific

1520: Magellan enters the Pacific

1606: Torres sails through strait that now bears his name and proves New Guinea is an island

1642: Tasman, searching for a southern continent, finds Tasmania and New Zealand

1699: Dampier surveys west coast of Australia, but is unimpressed

1768: Cook's first voyage

1788: La Pérouse sunk off Vanikoro

1500 — 1550 — 1600 — 1650 — 1700 — 1750 — 1800

1526: Jorge de Meneses first European to sight New Guinea

1567–69: Alvaro de Mendaña explores Solomon Islands

1688: William Dampier first Englishman to visit Australia

1721–22: Jacob Roggeveen visits many Polynesian islands

1779: Cook killed in Hawaii on third voyage

Burke and Wills set off in 1860 to cross Australia from south to north in a fanfare of publicity. Their confidence was misplaced; Aboriginals they encountered helped them find food and water, but eventually they died of hunger.

❷ Exploration in Australia and New Guinea 1798–1928

→ George Bass and Matthew Flinders 1798–99
→ Matthew Flinders 1802–03
→ Charles Sturt 1828–46
→ Thomas Mitchell 1836–46
→ Edward Eyre 1839–41
→ Ludwig Leichhardt 1844–45
→ Edmund Kennedy 1848
→ Robert Burke and William Wills 1860–61
→ John Stuart 1861–62
→ Peter Warburton 1872–73
→ John Forrest 1874
→ Ernest Giles 1875–76
→ Luigi Maria d'Albertis 1876
→ Alexander Forrest 1879
→ Charles Karius 1927–28

Exploring Australia and New Guinea

1802–03: Flinders circumnavigates Australia	**1829–30:** Sturt's journeys pave way for founding of colony of South Australia in 1836	**1875:** D'Albertis makes first of three trips up Fly River	**1927–28:** Karius expedition crosses New Guinea from south to north

1800 — 1825 — 1850 — 1875 — 1900 — 1925 — 1950

1813: Route found across Blue Mountains
1841: Eyre is first European to cross Nullarbor Plain
1879: Forrest explores from Port Hedland across Kimberley Plateau

Australia and New Guinea: explorers of the interior

Australia never aroused the curiosity of the Dutch who knew only the hostile west coast. The British, who settled in the more temperate southeast, were gradually drawn to the interior, first by the lure of gold and the search for grazing land, later by curiosity about the vast deserts of the interior. Expeditions such as those of Burke and Leichhardt used imported camels. New Guinea was even more unwelcoming to intruders with its mountains and dense rain forest. Most 19th-century explorers of the island followed the courses of rivers, while parts of the highlands remained inaccessible until the age of the airplane.

James Cook took a copy of this French map of 1756 with him on his voyage of 1768–71. The west coast of Australia is well charted because Dutch ships bound for the East Indies were often blown ashore there. The east was unexplored until Cook himself charted it and the fact that Tasmania was an island was established by Flinders and Bass in 1798–99.

Sealers, whalers, and traders

The first outsiders to have a significant impact in the Pacific were American sealers in the late 18th century. Traders soon followed to supply their sailing ships, establishing stations throughout the Pacific. By the 1820s, with Atlantic whale stocks depleted, whalers were also starting to arrive in large numbers, with calamitous results: introduced diseases caused the destruction of entire island societies. In the 1860s came a further threat – "blackbirders," slave raiders operating initially out of Peru, later carrying off the young males of many islands to work in the canefields of Queensland, Australia.

Sperm whales were the chief quarry of Pacific whalers, due to the growing market for their oil, used in industrialized Europe and the US for lubricating machinery.

❸ Europeans and Americans in the Pacific 1800–50

⌁ major whaling ground
● whaling station
⚓ sealing station
✿ trading station

Knowledge of the Pacific expanded rapidly with the arrival of American and European whaling ships in the 19th century. By 1837, when this map was published, the picture was almost complete.

Exploitation of the Pacific 1800–1850

1800: Tahiti starts supplying Port Jackson (Sydney) with pigs	**1820:** American whalers based on Îles Wallis	**c.1825:** Whaling and sealing stations on east coast of New Zealand	**1840s:** Copra becomes mainstay of trade on Society Islands	**1849:** US alone has 760 whaling ships operating in Pacific

1800 — 1810 — 1820 — 1830 — 1840 — 1850

1804: Sandalwood traders arrive in Fiji
1825: Solomon Islands attract traders in turtleshell and mother-of-pearl
1841: At least 35 whaling stations in Tasmania

PREHISTORIC OCEANIA

This fine carving from Rurutu in the Austral Islands shows the local god A'a.

DURING THE ICE AGES, Australia, New Guinea, and Tasmania were linked by land bridges to form the continent of Sahul. The first people to inhabit the region were Australoids, ancestors of today's Papuans and Australia's Aborigines, who may have reached Sahul as early as 60,000 years ago. The next significant wave of immigrants did not come until 6000 BCE, when Austronesian people fanned out through the Philippines and the East Indies. They mixed with the resident Australoids to produce the heterogeneous population of Melanesia. Around 1500 BCE the Austronesians, the greatest seafarers of prehistory, reached Fiji, and soon after that Samoa, starting point for later Polynesian expansion to the eastern Pacific and the eventual settlement of islands as far apart as Hawaii and New Zealand.

THE DREAMTIME

Australian Aboriginal cultures vary greatly; however, nearly all share the concept of "dreamtime" – the time of creation. Aboriginal lore maintains that, before creation, basic matter existed, but then the spirits of dreaming imbued the world with physical features and spiritual substance. The landscape can be read as a complex system of signs revealing the truth of these ancestral spirits.

The spirit figure in this rock painting in Kakadu National Park is Barrginj, wife of Lightning Man.

The settlement of Australia, Tasmania, and New Guinea

No one knows exactly when or by what route the first settlers reached Australia and New Guinea. What is certain is that they would have had to cross a stretch of open sea. In the case of Australia, this was probably from the island of Timor, 45 miles from the mainland, when sea level was at its lowest. Although Australia enjoyed a better climate with higher rainfall than today, settlement would have been largely near the coast. Valuable archaeological evidence was lost when sea levels rose again at the end of the last Ice Age. At this point the Tasmanians, who may have been an early wave of immigrants, were cut off from the mainland.

❶ The settlement of Australia, Tasmania, and New Guinea

Archaeological sites with approximate date of earliest human presence
◇ pre 20,000 BCE
◈ post 20,000 BCE

→ probable migration routes
→ possible migration routes
- - - maximum extent of Sahul landmass c.16,000 BCE
- - - maximum extent of Sunda landmass c.16,000 BCE

The settlement of Australia and New Guinea

60,000: Possible date of partial male skeleton found at Kow Swamp on Murray River

40,000: Australoids start voyaging out toward Solomon Islands

30,000: Careful burial of male body near Lake Mungo, one of the Willandra Lakes sites

10,000: First human-like figures in Australian rock art

c.8000–6000: Rising sea level covers New Guinea land bridge

38,000: Campfire site on New Guinea's Huon Peninsula

18,000: Fraser Cave on southern tip of Tasmania occupied

c.10,000: Land bridge connecting Australia and Tasmania starts to disappear

| 60,000 BCE | 50,000 | 40,000 | 30,000 | 20,000 | 10,000 | 1 CE |

Within their home range, most Aborigines led a largely nomadic life, following the food supply according to the seasons. The men were armed with spears for hunting, as in this rock painting; the women carried digging sticks and baskets.

Prehistoric agricultural development on New Guinea

The Australoids of Sahul were hunter-gatherers. However, as early as 6000 BCE, New Guineans began clearing dense forests, placing them among the world's first crop gardeners. Remains of pigs and dogs dating from 4000–3000 BCE suggest these were brought to New Guinea by Austronesian immigrants, who also introduced techniques of taro cultivation and swamp drainage and management. These soon spread from coastal regions to the Western Highlands. The inhabitants of the Eastern Highlands, however, grew a different staple rootcrop, *Pueraria lobata*, while continuing to hunt and gather.

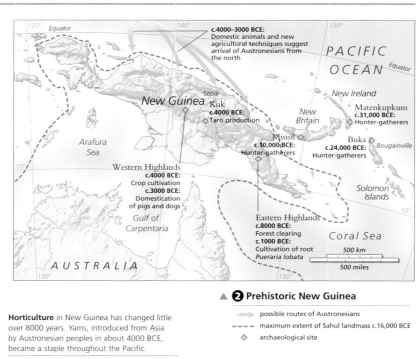

▲ ❷ Prehistoric New Guinea
→ possible routes of Austronesians
- - - maximum extent of Sahul landmass c.16,000 BCE
◇ archaeological site

Horticulture in New Guinea has changed little over 8000 years. Yams, introduced from Asia by Austronesian peoples in about 4000 BCE, became a staple throughout the Pacific.

The peopling of the Pacific

Settlement of the Pacific was accomplished in two epic series of migrations. From about 2000 BCE Austronesian peoples settled Melanesia, sailing from the Philippines, the Bismarck Archipelago, the Solomons, and ultimately Fiji. Their spread can be charted by their distinctive Lapita pottery. The Fiji-Tonga-Samoa crescent was the cradle of a new, equally dynamic culture: the Polynesians. A major migration, probably from Samoa, to the Marquesas, was the springboard that launched the Polynesians to the remaining far-flung islands of the Pacific, from New Zealand in the south to Hawaii in the north and Rapa Nui (Easter Island) in the east.

Prehistoric migrations in the Pacific

c.6000: Migrations from Southeast Asia give rise to Austronesian culture
c.4000: Austronesians reach southwestern Pacific islands
2000: Austronesians settle New Caledonia
c.1000: Emergence of archaic Polynesian society in Fiji, Tonga, and Samoa
c.1200 CE: Settlement of New Zealand; almost all Pacific islands inhabited

6000 BCE   5000 BCE   4000 BCE   3000 BCE   2000 BCE   1000 BCE   1 CE   1000 CE

1600: Earliest datable Lapita pottery from Bismarck Archipelago
c.200: Migration of Samoans to the Marquesas
c.300 CE: Rapa Nui (Easter Island) settled

This greenstone *heitiki* is a traditional ornament of the Maori, one of the most recent cultures of Polynesia.

The boats used by the Polynesians for their great migrations were double-hulled canoes like this modern reconstruction. As well as staple crops, they took with them pigs, chickens, and dogs.

This ornate carved head of a Maori war canoe was recorded by a 19th-century illustrator. In cool, temperate New Zealand, the Maori way of life was very different from that of societies on smaller, warmer islands to the north, but in their arts and beliefs the Maori still display many aspects of their Polynesian roots.

Scale varies with perspective

11,580 km (7200 miles)
N
8890 km (5520 miles)

Rapa Nui (Easter Island)

Rapa Nui's history reflects its geographical isolation. Settled around 300 CE, it once supported a population of perhaps 7000. The society that erected the famous giant statues started to collapse around 1680. The once palm-covered island was by then denuded of trees. With no wood for boats and therefore no fish, islanders fought for control of the scarce food resources: chickens, bananas, sweet potatoes, and yams. Another catastrophe came in 1862 when some 1300 islanders, one-third of the population, were carried off by Peruvian slavers.

Rapa Nui's statues were made to stand on stone platforms, altars sacred to the island's various clans. Many had topknots of red tufa. These examples were left near the quarry, when the society collapsed in the 17th century.

❹ Rapa Nui (Easter Island) ▼

▪ main area of statues
◇ restored statue site
● ceremonial centre
○ settlement
⬭ quarry for red topknots
⬮ quarry for statues
△ mountain

❸ Austronesian and Polynesian migrations

→ migration between 2000 BCE and 1000 BCE
→ migration between 1000 BCE and 1 CE
→ migration between 1 CE and 500 CE
→ migration between 500 CE and 1200 CE
→ back migration c.500 CE

▢ Melanesia
▢ Micronesia
▢ Polynesia

◇ Lapita pottery site
◼ source of obsidian

Crops cultivated
- - - area of cultivated breadfruit
· · · area of cultivated taro
⬭ atoll taro
⬭ taro
⬭ cassava
⬭ yams
⟋ sweet potato
⟋ rice
↓ sugar cane
⯭ bananas
⯭ coconuts
⯭ roots of native fern and cabbage tree

### Map labels

Marquesas Islands
Tuamotu Archipelago
Îles Gambier
Rapa Nui (Easter Island)
Line Islands
Society Islands
Tahiti
Austral Islands
Cook Islands

PACIFIC OCEAN

Phoenix Islands
Samoa Islands
Niuatoputapu
Tonga Islands
Vava'u Group
Uvea
Ha'apai Group
Futuna
Tongatapu Group
Tuvalu
Lau Group
Fiji Islands
Viti Levu
Kermadec Islands
Chatham Islands
Kiribati
Aotearoa (New Zealand)
Anuta
Efaté
Vanuatu
Eretoke
Santa Cruz Islands
Malo
Île des Pins
Lapita
New Caledonia
Solomon Islands
Rennell
Bellona
Guadalcanal
Coral Sea
Sohano Island
Green Islands
Feni Islands
New Ireland
Duke of York Islands
Watom
New Britain
Elouae Island
Normanby Island
Talasea
Kandrian
Arawe Islands
Bismarck Archipelago
Admiralty Islands
Yule
New Guinea
AUSTRALIA

Equator
Tropic of Capricorn
Tropic of Capricorn

Rapa Nui inset map

Hamea
Miru
'Anakena
Ma'unga Terevaka
Miru
Ahu Ra'ai
Tu'u
Rapa Nui (Easter Island)
VAITEA
'Otu'Iti
Pu'a Katiki
POIKE
Ahu 'Akivi
Rano Raraku
Ahu Tongariki
Motu Marotiri
Puna Pau
Ahu Tahai
Hanga Roa
Marama
Ngaure
Ahu Akahanga
Haumoana
Ngatimo
Ahu Vinapu
Rano Kao
'Orongo
Motu Nui

5 km
5 miles

109°20'
27°10'

THE COLONIZATION OF AUSTRALASIA

Australian convicts working in road gangs wore distinctive dress and were chained.

THE BRITISH COLONIES in Australia and New Zealand rank with the US as the most successful transplantations of European culture to another continent. Neither colony had auspicious beginnings: Australia was where Britain transported its unwanted criminals; New Zealand was a convenient base for sealers and whalers in search of quick profits. In time, both started to attract emigrants from Europe in their tens of thousands. As in the US, the colonists simply drove out the native peoples by any means available. The Aborigines of Australia and the Maori of New Zealand were treated as obstacles to the progress of settlers who wanted to raise familiar European crops and livestock on their lands. In Tasmania, settlers wiped out the entire population in the space of 70 years.

THE FIRST FLEET AND BOTANY BAY

In January 1788, to the astonishment of the local Aborigines, a fleet of 11 British ships sailed into Botany Bay. On board were 778 convicts and their jailers. After his visit in 1770, Captain Cook had described Botany Bay as well-watered and fertile, but this proved untrue and the convicts were moved to Port Jackson, a natural harbor to the north. The penal settlement at Port Jackson grew to become Australia's largest city – Sydney. However, it was the name Botany Bay that stuck in the British imagination as the time-honored destination for transported convicts.

A detachment of ships from the First Fleet sails to join the others anchored in Botany Bay.

▲ ❶ Early European impact in Australia

Colony boundaries
— 1788 (western boundary of New South Wales only)
— 1825
--- 1836
--- amended in 1859
1859 date colony established
□ colony capital

Convict settlements
▨ main areas where ex-convicts settled
■ ● penal settlement

Areas of Aboriginal resistance
▦ before 1855
▦ after 1855

Spread of agricultural settlement
▨ by 1845
▨ by 1860
▨ by 1880
▨ by 1900
▨ since 1900
▨ area unsuitable for agriculture

Map labels: Arafura Sea; Timor Sea; Melville Island; Darwin; Katherine; Wyndham; Halls Creek; Broome; Tennant Creek; Port Hedland; INDIAN OCEAN; Gulf of Carpentaria; Coral Sea; Cairns; Normanton; Burketown; Cloncurry; Mount Isa; Townsville; Hughenden; Mackay; Longreach; Rockhampton; Gladstone; Charleville; Maryborough; Moreton Bay; Brisbane; Toowoomba; Bourke; Inverell; Grafton; WESTERN AUSTRALIA; QUEENSLAND 1859; SOUTH AUSTRALIA 1836; Oodnadatta; Marree; Copper Creek; Wiluna; Carnarvon; Mount Magnet; Menzies; Kalgoorlie; Geraldton; Perth; Fremantle; Bunbury; Busselton; Albany; Esperance; Ceduna; Port Augusta; Port Pirie; Broken Hill; Port Lincoln; Adelaide; Great Australian Bight; NEW SOUTH WALES 1788; Wellington; Bathurst; Goulburn; Albury; Port Macquarie; Port Stephens; Newcastle; Sydney; Bendigo; VICTORIA 1851; Melbourne; Warrnambool; Port Phillip; Western Port; Tasman Sea; Bass Strait; Port Dalrymple; Launceston; Macquarie Harbour; Maria Island; Hobart; Port Arthur; VAN DIEMEN'S LAND 1825

1825–63: Region administered by New South Wales
1863–1911: Part of South Australia

1825–61: Region administered by New South Wales
1861: Part of South Australia

1831: Colony receives its own governor
1890: Western Australia granted constitution as separate colony

1829: First settlement in Western Australia
1850–69: Nearly 10,000 male convicts transported to Western Australia

1788–1852: Over 75,000 convicts landed

1803–53: Over 65,000 convicts landed

1825: New colony established, separate from New South Wales
1853: renamed Tasmania

European impact in Australia

Britain's decision to colonize New South Wales was in part a result of the loss of its North American colonies, where convicted criminals had been transported in the past. The impact of the first convict settlement at Port Jackson (Sydney) indicated the course Australia's history would take. Aborigines living nearby were nearly wiped out by introduced disease, then driven off by force of arms. Further penal colonies were established, the most notorious being on Tasmania (Van Diemen's Land), where convicts were first landed in 1803. In 1821 over half the island's population consisted of convicts. Free immigrants came to New South Wales as early as 1793 and free colonies were established in Western Australia in 1829 and South Australia in 1836. The former suffered from a labor shortage, so convicts were shipped there in the 1850s. As the immigrant population grew, both with freed convicts and new settlers, pressure for new land for grazing resulted in frequent clashes between drovers and Aborigines.

The impact of Australia's penal settlements

1788: First penal settlement established at Port Jackson (Sydney)

1832: Inquiry concludes penal system still "too lenient"; infamous Port Arthur penal colony opened

1869: Last convict ship to arrive in Australia delivers cargo in Fremantle

1789: Smallpox ravages Aborigines of coastal New South Wales

1803: "Incorrigible" convicts first transported to Van Diemen's Land (Tasmania)

1829: Britain annexes western third of Australian continent

1876: Truganini, said to be the last full-blooded Tasmanian Aborigine, dies

(timeline: 1780 1800 1820 1840 1860 1880)

The lure of gold

The event that accelerated the growth of the Australian colonies was the discovery of gold in New South Wales and Victoria in 1851. The richest finds were at Bendigo and Ballarat, and in the 1850s more than 1000 tons of gold were dug up in Victoria. In a gold rush to rival that of California in 1849, the population of Australia trebled in less than a decade. A later gold rush occurred in the 1890s when gold was discovered at Kalgoorlie in the remote deserts of Western Australia.

Gold rushes in Australia 1851–1900

1851: First gold strike at Bathurst, New South Wales

1861: At Lambing Flat, white miners burn camps of 3000 Chinese miners

c.1890: Gold discovered at Kalgoorlie, Western Australia

1854–55: Eureka uprising by Ballarat miners; police kill 45. In following year New South Wales and Victoria granted parliaments

1890: Western Australia last state to be granted self-government

(timeline: 1850 1860 1870 1880 1890 1900)

Population growth in Victoria and New South Wales 1851–91

□ Victoria
□ New South Wales

(bar chart, y-axis: 0 to 1,100,000; x-axis: 1851 1861 1871 1881 1891)

Miners pump water for gold-panning on a claim near Bathurst. Many who arrived in Australia in the 1850s were experienced prospectors from the California gold rush.

❷ Australian goldfields 1850–90

Discovery of goldfields
▨ 1850–60   ▨ 1860–70   ▨ 1870–90

Map labels: QUEENSLAND; Great Dividing Range; Tropic of Capricorn; Gympie; Brisbane; SOUTH AUSTRALIA; NEW SOUTH WALES; Cobar; Hillgrove; Forbes; Gulgong; Hargraves; Newcastle; Grenfell; Bathurst; Adelaide; Echunga; Lambing Flat; Sydney; Adelong; Araluen; Murray; Darling; INDIAN OCEAN; VICTORIA; Bendigo; Ovens; Ararat; Omeo; Clunes; Walhalla; Ballarat; Hill End; Castlemaine; Melbourne; Bass Strait; Beaconsfield; Launceston; Mount Lyell; Lefroy; Hobart; TASMANIA; Tasman Sea

Federation Australia

The Commonwealth of Australia was established in 1901 after referendums in the six states had voted for a federation. Throughout the 20th century, traditional agriculture and stock-rearing met problems through lack of water, and disasters such as a plague of introduced rabbits. After World War II, however, the country enjoyed a period of prosperity with the discovery of valuable mineral reserves and immigration was encouraged. In the late 1980s the Aboriginal population found a new political consciousness and began to lodge claims to traditional tribal lands.

Aboriginal protesters at the Australian bicentennial celebrations of 1988 display the Aboriginal flag to draw attention to two centuries of neglect and marginalization.

Federation Australia from 1901

1901: Australia becomes self-governing federation within British Empire	**1930s:** Australia hit hard by global depression	**1948:** White immigration, especially from UK, becomes post-war policy	**1975:** Restrictions imposed on immigration	**2001:** "Pacific Solution" of farming out asylum seekers to other countries adopted	
1900	**1920**	**1940**	**1960**	**1980**	**2000**
1914–18: Over 60,000 Australian troops lose lives in First World War	**1942:** Australia under threat of invasion as Japanese bomb Darwin	**1972:** Labour government of Gough Whitlam challenges paternalistic attitude of UK to Australia	**1988:** Aboriginal protests at Bicentennial celebrations	**1993:** Native Title Act recognizes Aborigine rights to land	

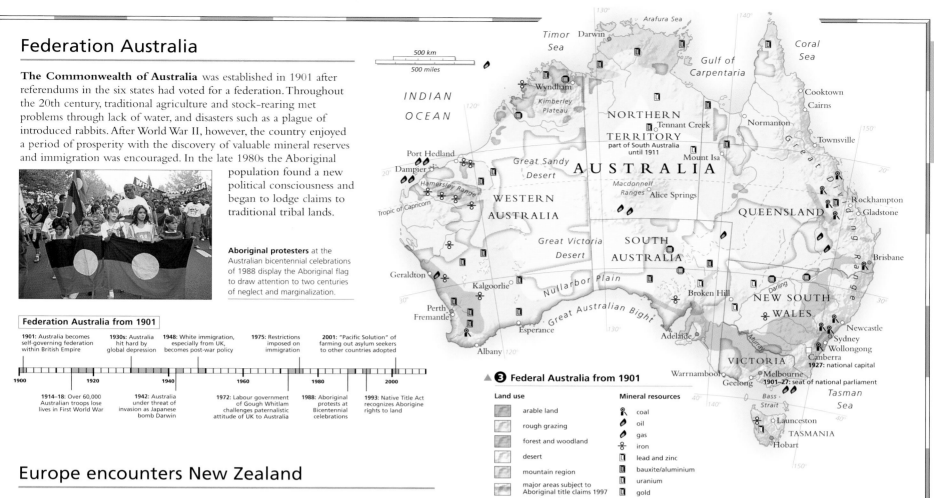

❸ Federal Australia from 1901

Land use
- arable land
- rough grazing
- forest and woodland
- desert
- mountain region
- major areas subject to Aboriginal title claims 1997
- ——— state boundary
- ◦ state capital

Mineral resources
- coal
- oil
- gas
- iron
- lead and zinc
- bauxite/aluminium
- uranium
- gold
- precious stones

1927: national capital
1901–27: seat of national parliament

Europe encounters New Zealand

The first European settlements in New Zealand were sealing and whaling stations, set up around 1800. At first they enjoyed good relations with the local Maori, who were eager to trade so they could get hold of metal axes and muskets. The results were disastrous: intertribal warfare took on a totally new character, tribes with muskets being able to massacre those without, and migrations spread the conflict throughout both islands. It was against this background that the New Zealand Company was set up to encourage British immigrants with assisted passages.

In this portrait drawn on Captain Cook's first voyage in 1769, the artist captures the pride and composure of a tattooed Maori warrior.

c.1820: Maori living near stations acquire muskets; resulting intertribal wars kill nearly a quarter of all Maori males and prompt major migrations

1820s: Raids by Ngapuhi and Waikato

1820–35: Migration of Ngati Raukawa, Ngati Toa, and Ngati Awa southward due to raids in the north

1835: Ngati Awa invade Chatham Islands, nearly annihilating indigenous Moriori

1820–40: Major movements of Maori to South Island, hitherto sparsely inhabited

1820s–30s: Raids by Ngati Toa

1820s–30s: Raids by Ngai Tahu

◀ ❹ New Zealand 1800–40
- main areas of Maori settlement 1800
- ◦ European settlement established by 1850
- Maori intertribal battle 1820–36
- whaling station before 1840
- sealing station before 1840
- Maori migration
- Maori raid on other Maoris in area

New Zealand 1800–40

1802: First British and American sealing stations operating on east coast	**1818:** Start of Maori 'Musket Wars'	**1830:** A mere 200 foreigners, mostly British, permanently resident in New Zealand	**1837:** New Zealand Company founded	
1800	**1810**	**1820**	**1830**	**1840**
1814: Samuel Marsden establishes mission in the Bay of Islands	**1825:** Musket Wars at their peak; Christian missionaries attempt to mediate	**1833:** British Resident appointed in Kororareka to challenge attempted French colonization		

New Zealand becomes British

The Treaty of Waitangi, signed in 1840 by over 500 Maori chiefs, gave sovereignty over New Zealand to Britain, while guaranteeing Maori ownership of the land. In practice, the Crown – and later private individuals – purchased the land for trifling sums. In response to this, the Maori fought long, bloody wars against the intruders. Unlike Australia's Aborigines, who used hit-and-run tactics, the Maori waged sustained battles from fortified stockades and earthworks. After their defeat, they were reduced to marginal existence. Only in the 1990s did the Maori, some 15% of the population, start to receive substantial compensation for the wrongs of Waitangi.

New Zealand 1840–70

1840: Treaty of Waitangi	**1845–46:** Northern War, started by Ngapuhi chiefs deprived of trade when capital moved from Russell to Auckland	**1860:** Settler population over 100,000; Europeans outnumber Maori	**1861:** Gold discovered in Otago province	**1870:** Maori resistance effectively crushed
1840	**1850**	**1860**		**1870**
1841: New Zealand becomes a separate Crown Colony	**1852:** Constitution Act divides New Zealand into six provinces	**1858:** King Movement demands Maori state and opposes further land sales	**1862:** Second Maori War	**c.1865:** Some 14,000 British troops deployed in New Zealand

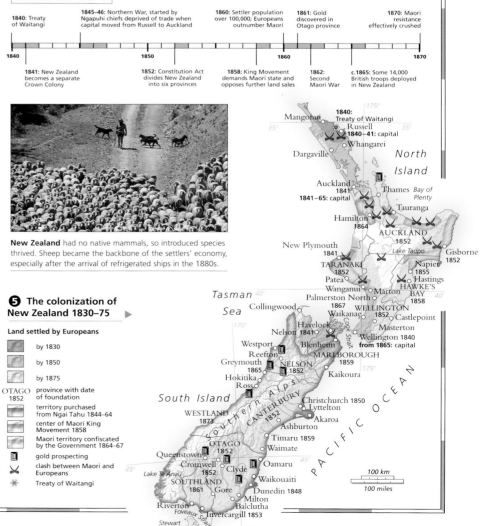

New Zealand had no native mammals, so introduced species thrived. Sheep became the backbone of the settlers' economy, especially after the arrival of refrigerated ships in the 1880s.

1840: Treaty of Waitangi
1840–41: capital
1841: capital
1841–65: capital
1852
from 1865: capital

❺ The colonization of New Zealand 1830–75 ▶

Land settled by Europeans
- by 1830
- by 1850
- by 1875
- OTAGO 1852 province with date of foundation
- territory purchased from Ngai Tahu 1844–64
- center of Maori King Movement 1858
- Maori territory confiscated by the Government 1864–67
- gold prospecting
- clash between Maori and Europeans
- Treaty of Waitangi

THE COLONIZATION OF THE PACIFIC

THE 19TH CENTURY WITNESSED the near annihilation of many Pacific island societies. Firearms made intertribal warfare more lethal, but many more deaths were caused by alien diseases, especially measles and influenza. Killings by colonial powers as they asserted their authority, and "blackbirding" (slave-raiding for laborers in the sugarcane fields of Queensland and elsewhere) also contributed to the rapid depopulation of the islands. Many demoralized communities experienced an alarming fall in birth rate. However, subsequent repopulation by immigrant Europeans, Indians, Chinese, Japanese, North and South Americans rebuilt many island societies with new forms of trade, culture, and administration. European and American governments put in place political structures that, over time, enabled remnant Pacific peoples to survive as a host of new nations, territories and federations. Many of these now seek a wider forum. In the 1990s governments started to make calls for a "United States of the Pacific."

A Hawaiian surfer typifies the modern image of the Pacific as a vast playground for leisure pursuits.

MISSIONARIES IN THE SOUTH SEAS

Throughout most of the Pacific, a region that had hitherto known only nature and ancestor worship, ancient values and practices were swept away by the arrival of Christianity. In the 17th century the Spanish founded missions in Micronesia, but by the mid-19th century Roman Catholic, Anglican, and Methodist missions were operating across Polynesia. Often the islanders' first contact with European customs, the missions paved the way for the wholesale Europeanization of Pacific cultures. Today a conservative, communal Christianity is the dominant feature of many Pacific island communities.

The high priest of Tahitian ruler Pomare II kneels before representatives of the London Missionary Society. The conversion of Pomare, who took control of Tahiti in 1815, was seen as a triumph for the society.

Imperialism in the Pacific

The expense of administering far-flung islands in the Pacific did not always appeal to the great 19th-century colonial powers. As a rule, they preferred to promise friendly rulers the status of protectorate. Toward the end of the century, however, colonial rivalry, especially between the French, Germans, and British led to the formal annexation of many territories. In larger territories, such as Fiji and Hawaii, where there was the possibility of establishing plantations, annexation was followed by the importation of large numbers of migrant workers.

① Imperialism in the Pacific ▶

Period of first European contact
- 16th century
- 17th century
- 18th century

European and US trading posts
- ✳ by 1700
- ✳ by 1850

Protectorates and colonies
- ○ protectorate with date established
- ◇ colony with date established
- ◇ Australian
- ◉ British
- ◇ Chilean
- ◇ Dutch
- ○◇ French
- ○◇ German
- ◇ Japanese
- ◆ NZ
- ◇ Spanish
- ○◇ US
- — Australian mandate 1920
- — frontiers 1900

This pictorial proclamation, issued in Australia in 1829, aimed to show the fairness of British justice. If an Aborigine killed a European, he would be hanged; if a European killed an Aborigine, he would suffer the same fate. In practice, this ideal was very rarely implemented in any of the European colonies in the Pacific.

The colonization of the Pacific

- **1840:** Start of influx of British settlers into New Zealand
- **1865–66:** 1000 Chinese brought to Tahiti to work cotton plantation
- **1874:** Indian sugarcane workers arrive in Fiji
- **1888:** Chile starts colonization of Easter Island
- **1788:** The "First Fleet" of convict settlers lands in New South Wales
- **c.1850:** Migrant workers begin arriving in Hawaii from China, Japan, the Philippines
- **1864:** First French convict settlers in New Caledonia
- **c.1870:** Germans start to buy up large tracts of Western Samoa
- **1898:** US annexes Hawaii and seizes Guam from Spain

1780 · 1800 · 1820 · 1840 · 1860 · 1880 · 1900

The abuse of Pacific resources

From the late 18th century, with Britain's decision to use Australia as a penal colony, European and American contacts with the Pacific produced a continuous catalog of violation and abuse. In the 19th century, the islands' isolation suggested their use as penal and leper colonies. In more recent times, their remoteness was exploited for experiments with weapons that could not be tested elsewhere. US nuclear tests in the Marshall Islands robbed islanders of a homeland for at least 50 years, while the French destroyed the islands of Mururoa and Fangataufa in the Tuamotus. Phosphate mining on Nauru created a moonscape that will take centuries to heal.

A nuclear bomb of 13 kilotons was detonated at ground level on Enewetak atoll in the Marshall Islands in 1956 as part of the US weapon-testing program.

② The use and abuse of Pacific resources

19th century
- ■ penal center
- ▫ leper colony

20th century
- ☢ nuclear test site 1946–63
- ☢ nuclear test site 1966–90

The exploitation of the Pacific from 1800

1814: In ten years Australian cutters have denuded Fiji of sandalwood reserves

1862–63: Thousands of islanders "blackbirded" to Peru

1895: More than 50,000 Melanesians indentured to Australia's canefields

1912: Start of phosphate mining on Nauru

1985: South Pacific Forum declares nuclear-free Pacific; US and France reject this

1996: France halts Pacific nuclear tests

1815: First kauri gum exported from New Zealand to Sydney

: Copra becomes mainstay of Society Islands' economy

1870: First shipload of lepers transported to Kalaupapa Peninsula, Molokai, Hawaii

c.1890: Kauri gum, for varnish, becomes New Zealand's chief export

1946: US begins nuclear tests at Enewetak and Bikini atolls in Micronesia

1966: France begins nuclear tests in Tuamotu Islands

1992: Australia agrees to compensate Nauru for phosphate extraction

Decolonization and nationhood

Australia achieved nationhood on January 1, 1901, New Zealand six years later. However, in both countries the native peoples had been dispossessed by colonists. It was many years before colonized Pacific peoples were deemed to have reached political majority. World War II loosened colonial ties and encouraged a sense of national identity. In 1962 Western Samoa became the first indigenous Pacific state to achieve full nationhood. Within 18 years, eight others had followed. Today, a wide variety of political systems and free associations with former colonial powers coexist – from Tonga's independent monarchy to Hawaii's US statehood.

Western Samoa became fully independent from New Zealand in 1962. The capital Apia, with its post office and town clock, still has the look of a colonial town. Ties with New Zealand remain strong: the rising population and a shortage of jobs compel many islanders to migrate there in search of work.

The Pacific from 1945

1945: War in Pacific ends

1971: First South Pacific Forum, annual meeting of heads of government

1987: Two military-led coups disrupt Fijian democracy

1998: End of bloody civil war in Bougainville

1951: ANZUS security pact between Australia, New Zealand, and US

1962: Western Samoa gains independence

1983: Federated States of Micronesia and Marshall Islands enter free association with US

1997: First settlements in New Zealand's review of 1840 Treaty of Waitangi

2000: Nationalist coup in Fiji

③ Decolonization and nationhood

- ○ independent from (with date)
- ◇ dependency of
- ○◇ Australia
- ○◇ France
- ○ Netherlands
- ◉◆ New Zealand
- ○◇ UK
- ○◇ US
- ☀ conflict since 1980

THE ARCTIC AND ANTARCTICA
EXPLORATION AND MAPPING

The Norwegian
Roald Amundsen led expeditions to the Arctic and Antarctica.

THE FROZEN LIMITS OF THE GLOBE – the Arctic an icy ocean, the Antarctic an ice-capped mountainous continent – were not fully explored until the 20th century. Their hostile environment still provides a challenge for explorers. Viking sailors traveled to Iceland and Greenland in the 9th and 10th centuries, establishing settlements on both islands. Not until the 16th century were serious attempts made to forge a passage around the Arctic Ocean. Despite the efforts of those who braved the turbulent southern waters in search of a new continent, the Antarctic remained mysterious until the 20th century, when it was confirmed that it was indeed a continent rather than an ice mass linking a series of islands. Further knowledge of both the Arctic and the Antarctic was gained by air exploration and of the Arctic by the use of submarines.

The search for northern routes to Asia

Aiming to circumvent Iberian control of the central Atlantic, Dutch and British sailors sought northern routes to Asia and the Pacific during the 16th century. Early attempts to find a northeast route were sponsored by the Muscovy Company, and Richard Chancellor was able to set up a trading partnership with Russia. Willem Barents, experienced in Arctic conditions, reached Novaya Zemlya in 1596. Martin Frobisher's 1576 journey was the first to attempt a western passage. In 1585–87, John Davis traveled between Greenland and Baffin Island, reaching 72°N. Henry Hudson bore west to enter the vast bay that bears his name in 1610, and William Baffin, piloting Hudson's ship, *Discovery*, traced the northern reaches of Baffin Bay, although all attempts to find a viable northern passage to the Pacific were unsuccessful until the 19th century.

② Charting the Arctic coast and the race to the North Pole ▶

The western Arctic
→ James Clark Ross (British) 1829–33
→ John Franklin (British) 1845–47
→ Roald Amundsen (Norwegian) 1903–06
→ Vilhjalmur Stefansson (Canadian) 1913–18

The eastern Arctic
→ Edward Parry (British) 1827
→ Nils Nordenskjöld (Swedish) 1878–79
→ Fridtjof Nansen (Norwegian) 1893–96

Exploring the North Pole
→ Robert Peary (American) 1909
→ Richard Evelyn Byrd (American) 1926
→ Umberto Nobile (Italian) 1926

Russian icebreakers
-→ voyages of the *Taymyr* and *Vaygach* 1914–15
⋯→ voyage of the *Sibiryakov* 1932

① The search for new routes to Asia: explorers of the far north 1550–1820

Northeast passage
→ Sir Hugh Willoughby and Richard Chancellor (English) 1553–54
→ Willem Barents (Dutch) 1556

Northwest passage
→ Martin Frobisher (English) 1576
→ John Davis (English) 1585–87
→ Henry Hudson (English) 1610–11
→ William Baffin (English) 1616
→ Alexander Mackenzie (British) 1789
→ John Franklin (British) 1819
→ Vitus Bering (Danish-Russian) 1728–30

1867: to US (Alaska)

1909: Peary sets off from Cape Columbia, reaching North Pole on April 6

500 km
500 miles

In 1576, Martin Frobisher took three ships from England to Labrador and then to Baffin Bay in search of the Northwest Passage. Several of his crew were killed in an encounter with hostile Inuit (*left*).

The Dutchman Willem Barents traveled via Spitzbergen to Novaya Zemlya in 1596, where he and his crew were forced to spend the winter. They built a wooden shelter and hunted walrus (*below*) and polar bears.

Exploring the top of the world

During the 19th century a series of British expeditions again tried to find a northwest sea passage to the Pacific, a feat only achieved in 1906 by the Norwegian Roald Amundsen. A northeastern route was found by Nils Nordenskjöld in 1878–79. From Edward Parry in 1827, attempts had been made to reach the North Pole on foot over the ice. Fridtjof Nansen with three dog sledges tried unsuccessfully in 1895–96, and in 1908–09 Robert Peary and Frederick Cook both claimed to have been first to the Pole, with Peary eventually declared the victor.

Somerset House was headquarters to Captain Ross and his men during their 1820 Arctic expedition.

The conflicting polar claims of Peary and Cook in 1909 was a popular subject for cartoonists.

The exploration of the Arctic

1553: Willoughby and Chancellor seek Northeast Passage
1576: Frobisher reaches Baffin Island
1610: Hudson discovers Hudson Bay
1728: Bering finds strait between North America and Asia
1819–22: Franklin traces northern coastline of North America
1833: James Clark Ross reaches magnetic North Pole
1850–53: Possible route for Northwest Passage discovered by McClure
1878: Nordenskjöld navigates Northeast Passage
1909: Peary reaches North Pole on April 6
1926: First dirigible balloon flight over North Pole
1926: First flight over North Pole by Byrd

1550 | 1650 | 1750 | 1850 | 1950

Exploring the Antarctic

Though James Cook sailed close to the Antarctic in 1775, he did not actually sight land. Forty-four years later, the Russian, Bellingshausen, sighted Antarctica but did not land. In the 1830s a series of expeditions charted stretches of the coast of Antarctica. These culminated in James Clark Ross's discovery of a spectacular ice shelf; his sturdy ships were the first to make their way through pack ice. The early 20th century saw the start of a series of expeditions to explore the interior of the Antarctic and reach the South Pole, with the veteran Norwegian, Amundsen, winning the race over Robert Scott's ill-fated expedition in 1911.

In 1915, Ernest Shackleton's ship *Endurance* became entombed in ice in the Weddell Sea. The crew had to camp on the ice until they could launch their boats.

Robert Scott's British National Antarctic Expedition (1901–04) used lightweight sledges, designed by the Norwegian explorer Fridtjof Nansen, which could be pulled by both dogs and men. Scott met his death near the Pole in 1912.

❸ Exploring the Antarctic ▶

Thaddeus Bellingshausen (Russian) 1819–21
James Weddell (British) 1822–24
John Biscoe (British) 1830–33
Jules Dumont d'Urville (French) 1837–40
Charles Wilkes (American) 1838–42
James Clark Ross (British) 1839–43
Ernest Shackleton (British) 1907–9
Roald Amundsen (Norwegian) 1910–12
Robert Scott (British) 1910–13
Douglas Mawson (Australian) 1911–14
Ernest Shackleton (British) 1914–16

The exploration of the Antarctic

1773–75: Cook crosses Antarctic Circle and circumnavigates continent
1819–21: Bellingshausen's expedition sights Antarctica
1823: Weddell sails into Weddell Sea
1839–45: Ross leads three Antarctic voyages
1840: Terrre Adélie named by Dumont d'Urville
1898: First winter camp on Antarctica at Cape Adare
1909: Mawson reaches magnetic South Pole
1912: Amundsen's expedition reaches South Pole ahead of Scott
1929: Byrd flies over South Pole for first time

1775 | 1825 | 1875 | 1925

KEY TO MAP FEATURES

PHYSICAL FEATURES

- coastline
- ancient coastline
- major river
- minor river
- major seasonal river

- ancient river course
- canal
- aqueduct
- dam
- spring / well / waterhole / oasis

- perennial lake
- seasonal lake
- perennial salt lake
- ancient lake
- marsh / salt marsh

- ice cap / sheet
- ice shelf
- glacier
- summer pack ice limit
- winter pack ice limit

- elevation above sea level (mountain height)
- volcano
- pass

GRATICULE FEATURES

- Equator
- lines of latitude / longitude
- tropics / polar circles
- *45°* degrees of longitude / latitude

BORDERS

- international border
- undefined border
- vassal state border
- disputed border

- maritime border
- internal border

COMMUNICATIONS

- major road
- minor road
- major railroad
- railroad under construction

SETTLEMENT / POSSESSION

- o settlement symbol
- ◇ colonial possession

TYPOGRAPHIC KEY

REGIONS

state / political region...**LAOS**

administrative region within a state.... HENAN

cultural / undefined region / group...............*FERGHANA*

SETTLEMENTS

settlement / symbol location / definition............Farnham

PHYSICAL FEATURES

continent / ocean..............*AFRICA*

INDIAN OCEAN

landscape features........*Mekong*

Lake Rudolf

Tien Shan

Sahara

MISCELLANEOUS

tropics / polar circles.................... *Antarctic Circle*

people / cultural group.. *Samoyeds*

annotation......................**1914:** British protectorate

POLITICAL COLOR GUIDE

- ◇ o China
- ◇ o Persia / Iran
- ◆ o Rome
- ◆ o Japan
- ◆ o Norway
- ◆ o USA

- ◆ ● Italy
- ◆ ● Ottoman / Turkey
- ◆ ● England / Britain / UK
- ◆ ● France
- ◆ ● Denmark
- ◆ ● Spain (Castile)

- ◇ ● Spain (Aragon)
- ◆ ● Portugal
- ◆ ● Netherlands
- ◆ ● Germany
- ◇ o Russia
- ◇ o India

- ◆ ● New Zealand
- ◇ o Australia
- ◆ ● Belgium
- ◇ other state / cultural region

RELIGION COLOUR GUIDE

- Buddhism
- Islam
- Hinduism
- Confucianism / Taoism
- Christianity
- Roman Catholic
- Judaism
- other religion

(NB. the colors which identify political regions have, as far as possible, been used consistently throughout the atlas. Any variations are clearly identified in the individual map keys)

GUIDE TO MAP INTERPRETATION

Contemporary historical names are used throughout; modern equivalents or variants can be found in the index.

Major land borders are shown using a solid line, while sea borders use a dashed style.

Colors are used to indicate major political areas and states.

Broad arrows indicate general movement or spread.

Vignetted colors are used to show a general, undefined region.

Annotations provide additional explanatory information.

Political control of a settlement is identified by color.

Arrows indicate journeys or campaigns.

Borders are shown in a variety of styles and individually keyed.

SUBJECT INDEX AND GLOSSARY

In addition to acting as a page reference guide to the people, events, and themes referred to in the Atlas, the Subject Index and Glossary is intended to provide supplementary information and explanation of those features which appear in the Atlas.

Page references are indicated using the following symbols:

❖ text reference ● timeline reference

◆ map reference, indicating page number and map number;

❏ picture/caption reference.

Dates in the Atlas are expressed in the following way:

BP Before Present. Generally used for dates more than 10,000 years ago.

BCE Before Common Era (indicating number of years before the supposed year of Christ's birth).

CE Common Era (indicating number of years since the supposed year of Christ's birth).

A

Abbas I (*aka* Abbas the Great) (c.1571–1629) Safavid shah of Persia (r.1588–1629). Crushed the Uzbek rebellions, and recovered Persian territories from the Ottomans, expelling them from Mesopotamia. In 1598 he established the Persian capital at Isfahan. ❖79, ❖219●, ❖231, ❖231●, ❏238

Abbasid Caliphate (c.750–1258). The second great Islamic dynasty, replacing the Umayyads in 750 CE. The Abbasid capital from 762 was Baghdad, from where they exercised control over the Islamic world until the 10th century. The last Abbasid Caliph was killed by the Mongols in 1258. ❖56, ❖57 (2), ❖58–9, ◆227 (4)
dynasty founded (750) ❖59, ❖61
fragmentation (800–1055) ◆227, ◆227 (6)
overthrown by Mongols (1258) ❖67●
rulers of Baghdad ❖228

Abd al-Qadir (1830s). Algerian resistance leader ❖90, ❖91●

Abd al-Rahman ibn Umar al-Sufi 10th-century astronomer ❖59

Abdul Hamid II (1842–1918) Ottoman sultan (r.1876–1909).
An autocratic ruler, noted for suppression of revolts in the Balkans, which led to wars with Russia (1877–78), and for the Armenian massacres (1894–96). His failure to modernize his realm led to his deposition in 1909, following a revolt by the Young Turks. ❏232

Abdul Majid I (1823–61) Ottoman sultan (r.1839–61). Urged by Western Powers, Abdul Majid I issued a series of liberal decrees, known as the Tanzimat (1839–61), to reform the judiciary and administration of the Ottoman Empire. ❖232●

ABM see Anti-Ballistic Missile

Aborigines Native people of Australia, who probably first settled the continent c.60,000 years ago. From c.8000 BCE, when the land bridge to New Guinea was severed by rising sea levels, they lived in more or less complete isolation until the 18th century CE. In the north, there was occasional contact with sailors from the islands of the Torres Strait and Indonesia. ❖280 (1), ❖282
armed for hunting ❏280
bicentennial celebrations ❏283
British justice ❏284
civilization destroyed ❖91
dreamtime ❖280
resistance to colonization ❖282 (1)

rock carving ❏15
spirit figure rock painting ❏280

Abreu, António de 16th-century Portuguese explorer. Embarked on a voyage to India in 1508. He set out for the Spice Islands in 1511, exploring Amboina, Sumatra, Java, and parts of New Guinea. He was appointed governor of Malacca in 1526.◆239 (1)

Abydos Royal tombs ❖25

Abyssinia (*var.* Ethiopia). Italian defeat at ✕ of Adowa (1896) ❖95●

Academy Award first Oscar ceremony (1929) ❏135●

Acadia Founded (1604–08) ❖82●

Achaean League Confederation of Greek city-states of the northern Peloponnese, dating back to the 4th-century BCE. The league's traditional enemy was Sparta. It was after the league attacked Sparta in 150 BCE that the Romans destroyed Corinth, the leading city of the league, and made Achaea a Roman province. ❖179

Achaemenids see Achaemenid Empire

Achaemenid Empire (c.550–330 BCE). Greek name for the Persian royal dynasty named after Achaemenes (Hakhamani), an ancestor of Cyrus II "the Great." From c.550 BCE, Cyrus presided over the expansion of the Persian empire, conquering Lydia, Phrygia, Ionia, and Babylonia. The empire lasted until 330 BCE, when Darius III was killed after his defeat by ✕ at Gaugamela. ❖35, ❖34–5, ❖39●, ❖223, ❖223●, ◆223 (4)

Achin (*var.* Atjeh). The Indonesian island of Sumatra became, from the 7th century CE, the center of a powerful Hindu kingdom, established by Indian emigrants. In the 13th century CE, Arabs invaded the Sumatran kingdom of Achin, which converted to Islam. At the end of 16th century, the Dutch attempted to gain supremacy in Achin, a struggle which was to last for the next three centuries. ◆245 (1) (2) ◆248 (1)

Acolhua, Aztec civilization ❖125

Acre Crusader loss (1291) ❖64●, ❖65, ❖64–5 (1) (2)

Acropolis Ancient Greek fortified hilltop citadel, the best-known being that of Athens, rebuilt by Pericles after the Persian invasion in the second half of the 5th century BCE. It comprised a complex of buildings including the national treasury and many shrines, mostly devoted to Athena, the city's patron goddess. ❖177

Act of Supremacy (1534). Parliamentary act which recognized King Henry VIII, and every British sovereigns thereafter, as supreme head of the Church of England. ❖78●

Adelaide Founded 1835–36 ❖91, ◆279 (2)

Adena culture (c.1000–100 BCE). A series of North American communities, based around what is now southern Ohio, formed the Adena culture. Principally hunter-gatherers, they built circular houses with conical roofs constructed of willow and bark, used stone tools, and produced simple pottery. Finds of copper and shell ornaments indicate long-distance trade.
BCE culture ◆30●, ❖34, ◆36 (1), ◆38●, ❖42●
moundbuilders ◆121 (4)

Adowa ✕ of Italian invasion of Abyssinia (1896). Serious Italian defeat put an end to Italian colonial ambitions in Ethiopia. A settlement after the battle acknowledged the full sovereignty and independence of Ethiopia, but preserved Italian rights to Eritrea. 95●, ❖97, ❖97 (4)

Adrianopolis ✕ (378). Visigothic victory over Romans. ◆52–3 (1)

Aegospotami ✕ of Peloponnesian Wars (405 BCE). Spartan victory over Athens. ◆177 (3)

Aelfred see Alfred the Great

Aelius Gallus Roman general of the 1st century BCE, who led his troops on an exploratory expedition into Arabia. ◆218 (1)

Aetolian League Federal state of Aetolia, in ancient Greece, which by c.340 BCE became a leading military power. Having successfully resisted invasions by Macedonia in 322 BCE and 314–31 BCE, the league rapidly grew in strength expanding into Delphi and allying with Boeotia c.300 BCE. ❖179

Afghanistan
British protectorate ◆248 (2)
founded (1747) ❖87●
emergence of Taliban ❖235 (4)
Mahmud of Ghazni's kingdom ❖59, ❖63, ◆227 (6)
Marathas defeated at Panipat (1761) ❖87
Persian subjugation (1722–36) ❖87●
Second Afghan War (1878–79) ❖95●
Soviet invasion (1979–89) ❖111●, ❖138

Africa 154–169
BCE ❖14, 15●, ❖16, ❖19, ❖30, ❖34
(c.1300) ◆68 (2)
diaspora ❖112
exploration and mapping
14th–15th century ◆156 (3)
Niger Basin ◆156 (1) (2)
African interior (19th century) ◆157 (4)
Boer (Afrikaner) treks ❖90, ◆166 (2)
history
colonization ◆39●, ❖42, ◆62, ❖66–7, ❖95, ◆169, ◆166–67 (1) (2) (4)
complex societies ◆160–1, ◆160 (1)
early history ◆158–9
early modern ◆154–5
historical landscape ◆154–5, ❏154, ◆154–5
Islam and new states ◆162–3, ◆163●
Muslim empire (1863) ❖95●
post-colonial ◆168–9
Roman province ◆43●, ❖46
home affairs
agriculture ❖82
conflict and crisis ◆169, ◆169 (4)
independence ◆107, ❖168, ◆168 (1)
tribal conflict ❖90
Zulu War (1879) ❖95
innovations
Nok sculpture (BCE) ❏38
Northeast Africa
rise and fall of kingdoms ◆161 (4) (5)
trade ◆161 (3)
political development ◆164, ◆166, ◆166 (1), ◆168●, ◆169●,
religion
Donatist schism (311) ◆50●
struggle for the Horn (1500–1700) ◆165 (3)
trade and industry
economy in 1999 ❖168, ◆168 (2) (3)
Arab coastal settlements ❖58
commerce (19th century) ◆166, ◆166 (1)
Eurasian and African ◆44–5
gold ❖66, ❖70
Indian Ocean network (13th century) ❖66
ironworking ❖38
links with Morocco ❖78
links with Portugal ❖78, ❖79●
and the spread of Islam ◆162 (1)
see also Boers; individual countries; slavery; trans-Saharan trade

Africa Nova Roman province (146 BCE) ◆161 (2)

African Association Club formed in London in 1788 "for promoting the discovery of the interior parts of Africa." ❖157●

African National Congress (ANC). Organization founded in S. Africa in 1912 to promote equality for Africans. It was banned by the South African government in 1961, and although its leaders were jailed or forced into exile, became the focus for resistance to the apartheid regime. The ANC signed an agreement with the ruling Nationalists in 1990 and came to power under Nelson Mandela at the election of 1994. ❖111, 169●

Afrikaner South African of European descent whose first language is Afrikaans, a development of Dutch. See Boers

Aghlabids (*var.* Banu Al-aghlab). Arab Muslim dynasty that ruled Ifriqiyah in present-day Tunisia and eastern Algeria from 800 to 909 CE. The Aghlabids were nominally subject to the Abbasid caliphs of Baghdad but were in fact independent. ◆227 (4)
dynasty founded (800) ❖58●
expelled by Fatimids (909) ❖58●

Agincourt ✕ of Hundred Years' War (1415). French defeat by English. ❖75●

agriculture
advent and spread of ❖20–1, ◆18–19, ❖21 (2), ❖22–3, ❖34
African ❖158 (1), ◆166 (1)
Andean ❖147, ❏147
Australian (1845–1900) ◆22 (1)
development of technology ❖158 (1)
diffusion of staple crops ❖73, ❖73 (3)
domestication ❖21, ❖21●
early settlements ◆120, ◆121 (1), ❏171
E. Asian revolution (6000–2000 BCE) ◆258 (1)
Europe ❖62, ❖198, ❖198 (1)
grindstones ❖16
Maya civilization ❖50
mechanized ❖90
Pacific ◆281 (3)
prehistoric New Guinea ❖280, ❏280, ◆280 (2)
source of Egypt's wealth (BCE) ❏27
S. America ◆144 (1), ◆153 (3)
See also farming; irrigation

Ahmad ibn Fadi Allan Al-'umari see al 'Umari

Ahmad Khan Abdali (*var.* Ahmad Shah) (1724–73)
founds Afghanistan (1747) ❖87●

Ahmad Shah see Ahmad Khan Abdali

Ahuitzotl Aztec ruler (1486–1502) ◆124 (1)

Ahura Mazda Zoroastrian god ❏36
Silver disc ❏21

Ai Khanoum Hellenistic city. ❖21

Ain Jalut ✕ of Mongol invasions (1260). Mongol defeat ❖67●, ❖69, ❖229

Aistulf (d.756) Lombard king, who captured Ravenna and threatened to take Rome. The pope summoned the Frankish King Pepin to defeat him. 183●

Ajanta Buddhist center ❏43

Akbar (*aka* Akbar the Great) (1542–1605) Mughal emperor (r.1556–1605). Became emperor at the age of 14. For the first seven years of his reign Akbar was engaged in permanent conflict, which left him the undisputed ruler of an empire which stretched from Bengal to Sind, and Kashmir to the Godavari river. He evolved a standardized tax system, incorporated the rulers of conquered territory into his own army, and introduced a policy of marriage alliances between the Mughal nobles and the Rajput princely families. He was tolerant toward the Hindu religion, and encouraged a great florescence in the arts, particularly in miniature painting and architecture, which was remarkable for its synthesis of western and Islamic styles. ❖79●, ❖246, ❏246, ❖78–9, ◆246 (1)

Akhenaten (*var.* Akhenaton, Ikhnaton, Amenhotep, Amenophis IV) 18th Dynasty pharaoh of Egypt (r.1352–1333 BCE). A religious and cultural revolutionary who replaced the existing Egyptian pantheon with a monotheistic cult of the solar disc – Aten. He changed his name to reflect his beliefs, replaced the capital at Thebes with his own, El-Amarna (*var.* Akhetaten), and persecuted the older gods, expunging Amon's name from monuments across the country. A significant change in artistic style is representative of his rule, with both royals and commoners portrayed in a naturalistic rather than a formalized way. His unpopular religious reforms, and this artistic tradition, were reversed by Tutankhamun.
Egyptian pharaoh ❖26, ❖27●, ❏28
founds the city of El-Amarna ❖29, ◆29 (5)
Great Palace fragment ❏29

Akkad see Sargon I of Akkad

Aksum (*var.* Axum). ◆161 (3) (4) (5)
converts to Christianity (c.330) ❖50●
incense trade ❖46
kingdom emerges (c.50) ❖47●
major trading power ❖161
Meroë kingdom invasion (c.350) ❖50●
Roman-Indian trading link ❖50
stone stelae ❏161

Al-Azhar University established (970s) ❖58●

Al-Hajj Umar Ibn Said Tal see 'Umar Tal, Al-Hajj

Al-Idrisi see Idrisi

Al-Istakhri 10th-century Islamic geographer. ◆218 (1)

Al-Mu'tasim (794–842) Abbasid caliph (r.833–842). A son of Harun al-Rashid, al-Mu'tasim moved the Abbasid capital from Baghdad to Samarra. He waged war successfully against the Byzantines in Asia Minor and employed large numbers of Turkish slave soldiers, who subsequently became a powerful force in the Caliphate. (c.836) ❖59●

al-Rashid, Harun (*var.* Harun Ar-rashid, Ibn Muhammad al-Mahdi, Ibn al-mansur al-'Abbasi) (766/763–809). The fifth caliph of the Abbasid dynasty (786–809), who ruled Islam at the zenith of its empire. ❖58●, ❖227, ❖227●, ❏56, ❏227, ❖58–9

al 'Umari (*var.* Shihab Ad-din, Ahmad Ibn Fadl Allah Al-'umari) (1301–1349). Scholar and writer descended from 'Umar, the second Islamic caliph. His works on the administration of the Mamluk dominions of Egypt and Syria became standard sources for Mamluk history. ❖156

Alamo, The ✕ of Texas Revolution (1836). Mexican victory. ◆129 (2)

Alans People who migrated to Europe from the steppes near the Caspian Sea. They joined the Vandals and Sueves in the Great Migration of 406 from Germany to the Iberian Peninsula. They briefly established a kingdom there, but were ousted by the Visigoths.
migrations and invasions (300–500 CE)
❖50●, ❖182●, ◆52–3 (1)

Alaric (c.370–410). Chief of the Visigoths from 395 and leader of the army that sacked Rome in 410, an event that came to symbolize the fall of the Western Roman Empire. ❖50●, ❖53

Alaska
Bering's first reconnaissance (1728) ❖86●
discovery of gold (1880) ❖93
Eskimos' Thule culture (c.900) ❖58●
Russian expeditions ◆257, ◆119 (3) ◆128, ◆128–9(2)

Alaska Purchase (aka Seward's Folly). In 1867, US Secretary of State William H. Seward organized the purchase of Alaska from Russia for $7,200,000. ◆128–9

Alaung Phra see Alaungpaya

Alaungpaya (*var.* Alaung Phra, Alompra, Aungzeya) (1714–1760). King (r.1752–60) who unified Burma, and founded the Alaungpaya dynasty which held power in Burma until the British annexed the northern part of the region in 1886.
founds Rangoon (1755) ❖87●

Albanel, Father Charles (1616–96). French Jesuit who traveled in E. Canada, reaching Hudson Bay and traveling along the Saguenay River, in search of fur-trading routes. ◆119 (2)

Albert, Prince of Saxe-Coburg-Gotha see Victoria

Albertis, Luigi Maria d' (1841–1901) Italian explorer of New Guinea. ◆279 (2)

Albigensians (*aka* Cathars). Heretical sect which flourished in southern France in the 12th century. It had little to do with Christianity; its most extreme followers believed in the evil of matter and aspired to reach the state of the "perfect," those who had forsaken the material world. The Albigensian Crusade (1210–26) not only stamped out the heretics but also placed Toulouse and much of southern France under the control of the French crown.
Albigensian Crusade ◆186●, ◆186 (1)

Aleut
Arctic nomadic hunters ◆123
sites ◆123 (3)

Alexander I (1777–1825) Tsar of Russia (r.1801–25). The early years of his reign were marked by attempts to reform Russia, but he failed to abolish serfdom. Initially a member of the coalition against Napoleon, but defeats at Austerlitz and Friedland led to Alexander concluding the Treaty of Tilsit (1807) with France. When Napoleon's invasion of Russia (1812) broke the treaty, Russia joined the Allied pursuit of the French to Paris. ❏201

Alexander the Great (*aka* Alexander III) (356–323 BCE) Greek emperor (r.336–323 BCE). Son of Philip II of Macedon, Alexander led one of the most rapid and dramatic military expansions in history, extended Hellenistic culture and conquest as far as India, founding cities and vassal-states throughout West Asia.
bust ❏40
conquests ❖38, ❖40, ❖223
empire ◆38–9, ◆40–1 (1)
expeditions ◆218 (1)
legacy ❖41, ❖41l
oracle worship ❖37
Pompeii mosaic ❏39 ❏40
sarcophagus ❏40
successors ❖224, ❖224●, ◆224 (1)
death ❖38l, ❖39

Alexandria City founded by and named after Alexander the Great, on the delta of the Nile River. From the 3rd century BCE, for over a thousand years, the city of Alexandria became the commercial, cultural, and scientific hub of all Eurasia, boasting the world's greatest library and generating important schools of literature, poetry, drama, medicine, philosophy, and cosmology.
founded (332 BCE) ❖39●, ◆40●
Christian center (100 CE) ◆47●
Classical scholarship ❖55
Muslims at prayer ❏113

Alexius IV (d.1204) Byzantine emperor (r.1203–1204). He ascended the throne with the help of the Fourth Crusade but was deposed a year later by a national revolt. ❖187

Alfonso VI (*aka* Alfonso the Brave, *Sp.* Alfonso El Bravo) (1040–1109). King of León (r.1065–1109) and king of reunited Castile and León (1072–1109), who by 1077 had proclaimed himself "emperor of all Spain." His oppression of his Muslim vassals led to the invasion of Spain by an Almoravid army from North Africa in 1086.
takes Toledo (1085) ◆64●

Alfred the Great (*var.* Aelfred) King of Wessex (r.871–899). Ruler of a Saxon kingdom in S.W. England. He prevented England from falling to the Danes and promoted learning and literacy. Compilation of the Anglo-Saxon Chronicle began during his reign, c. 890. reconquers London (885) ❖58●

Algeria
French invasion (1830) ❖90, ❖232
industrial growth ◆168, ◆168 (2)
Islamic fundamentalism ❖235●
uprising against France (1954) ❖107●

Algonquin N. American subarctic nomadic hunters ◆123
war with Iroquois (1609) ◆126●

Alhambra Moorish palace in Granada, S. Spain ❏192

Allegheny River Survey (1729) ❖119●

Allies (*aka* Allied Powers). General term applied to the victorious Great Powers at the end of WW I (after the US joined the Entente Powers – Britain, France, Russia – in 1917). More generally used to describe the alliance ranged against the Axis powers during WW II headed by Britain, France, Poland, and the USSR and US (from 1941). ❖104–5●, ❖❖206–211●

Allied Powers see Allies

Allouez, Father Claude (1622–89). French Jesuit missionary who explored the Great Lakes region of N. America as well as the St. Lawrence River, setting up missions in present-day Wisconsin.
expedition (1665–67) ◆119 (2)

Almagro, Diego de (1475–1538) Spanish *conquistador*. Companion of Pizarro in the conquest of Peru in 1532. In 1535 he set off southward in an attempt to conquer Chile. He later quarreled with Pizarro and civil war broke out between their followers. ◆142 (1)

Almohad dynasty (1130–1269). Muslim dynasty. Founded by a revival Muslim revival movement, the Almohads eventually commanded North Africa as far east as Tripoli, as well as controlling most of the Iberian peninsula. ◆186 (1), 192●, ◆192 (3)
defeated by Marinids (1269) ❖67●
empire collapses (1228) ❖67●
in Morocco and Spain (1147) ❖63●
takeover of Almoravids (1128) ❖63●

Almoravid Empire Confederation of Berbers whose religious zeal and military enterprise built an empire in N.W. Africa and Muslim Iberia in the 11th and 12th centuries. ◆192 (3)
12th century ❖62–3
invasion of Ghana ❖163
in N. Africa and Iberia (c.1050) ❖63

Key to index: ❖ text ❏ picture *var.* variant name *f/n* full name *r.* ruled WW I World War I
● timeline ◆ map *aka* also known as *prev.* previously known as ✕ battle WW II World War II

289

reconquest of Spain ✛192, ✛192●, ◆192 (3)
takeover by Almohads (1128) ✛63●
Alodia Coptic Christianity ✛58
Alompra see Alaungpaya
alphabet see writing
Altai Mountains
  burial sites (BCE) ✛39
  wooden carving (BCE) ❑39
Alvarado, Pedro de (c.1485–1541) Spanish *conquistador*. Took part in the expeditions of Juan de Grijalva and Hernán Cortés in Mexico and Central America, later gaining control over highland Guatemala and El Salvador, and becoming governor of Honduras and Guatemala. ✛125
Alvare (d.1614) King of Kongo who was restored to his throne with the help of Portuguese troops after his country had been invaded in 1568.
  as slave trader ❑85
Alvarez de Peneda, Alonso 16th-century Spanish explorer of the Yucatan Peninsula (1517–23). ✛125
Amadu Lobbo (1775–1844). Fulani leader who established a Muslim state in Masina, western Africa, in the 19th century. ✛167●
Amazon River
  mouth discovered (1500) ✛142●
  sailed by Orellana (1542) ✛142●
Amazonia
  development and deforestation ✛153●, ◆153 (4)
  early settlements ◆145 (2)
amber Eurasian and African trade (c.1 CE) ◆44–5
Amde Sion Ruler of Ethiopia (d.1344) ✛71●
Amenhotep see Akhenaten
Amenophis III see Amenophis III
Amenophis III (*var.* Amenhotep) (c.1390–1353 BCE) Egyptian pharaoh. His reign saw peaceful progress at home and effective diplomacy abroad. ✛27●
Amenophis IV see Akhenaten
America 116–153
  historical landscape ✛117–18, ❑117, ◆116
  BCE ✛18, ✛30, ✛34, ✛38
  Committees of Correspondence (1772) ✛127●
  Declaration of Independence adopted (1776) ✛82, ✛90
  killer epidemics ❑81
  Revolutionary War ✛86, ◆126–7, ◆127 (3)
  road to independence ✛127●
  Southwest, cultures, ✛58, ◆123 (4)
  Stamp Act (1765) ✛127●, ❑88
  Sugar Act (1764) ✛127●
  Townshend Acts (1767) ✛127●
  See also Central America; N. America; S. America; slavery; USA; other individual countries
American Civil War (1861–65). Civil war between the northern states (the Union) and the southern Confederate states over the extension of slavery and the rights of individual states to make their own laws. Broke out in Apr 1861 following the secession of seven Confederate states from the Union. The war was won by the Union and slavery was made illegal throughout the US. ✛130–31●
Amphipolis ✕ of Peloponnesian War (422 BCE). Spartan victory over Athens. ◆177 (3)
amphitheaters Arenas of Etruscan origin, developed for a variety of open air entertainment. They consisted of tiered seats around a central round or oval performance space. The best known and largest is Rome's Colosseum, built 72–80 CE. ✛181, ❑181
amphora Two-handled ceramic jar with pointed base, commonly used to transport olive oil and wine. They are often stamped with a maker's mark, indicating their origin and compliance with size regulations. ❑48, ❑181, ◆181
Amritsar massacre (Apr 13, 1919) India. Followed riots on the streets of Amritsar in the Punjab, protesting against the Rowlatt legislation (anti-sedition laws). British troops fired at the demonstrators, killing nearly 400 people, and wounding over 1,000. The massacre caused widespread outrage. ❑99●
Amundsen, Roald (1872–1928) Norwegian explorer. Explored both the N. and S. Poles, tracing the Northwest Passage in 1903–06 and discovering the magnetic North Pole. He later attempted to reach the S. Pole in 1911. Explored the Arctic by air in the 1920s.
  Antarctic exploration (1910–12) ◆287 (3)
  Arctic explorer ◆286–7 (2)
Amur basin Russia withdraws (1689) ✛83●
An Lushan (703–757). Chinese general who assembled an army of 160,000 and rebelled against the Tang. He captured Chang'an in 756, but was murdered the following year. ✛59●
Anasazi culture (200–1500 CE). Ancient culture of the

southwestern US. The later period saw the development of complex adobe-built settlements known as pueblos.
  ✛58, ◆123 (4)
  defensive pueblos (1050) ✛123●
  fortified cliff dwellings (c.1100) ✛62●
  pottery ❑62
Anatolia The Asian part of Turkey. A plateau, largely mountainous, which occupies the peninsula between the Black Sea, the Mediterranean, and the Aegean.
  Arab forces annihilated (863) ✛59●
  BCE villages ✛19
  Europe's first cultures ❑171
  seized by Ottomans ✛71
  See also Asia Minor
ancestor worship ✛31, ✛36
Andersson, Charles (1827–67). Swedish explorer of southwest Africa (1853–59). ◆157 (4)
Andes
  autonomous states ✛66
  ceremonial vase ❑144
  coastal empires (250–1375) ✛146, ◆146 (1)
  early agricultural development ❑140
  northern chiefdoms ✛146, ❑146
  plant domestication (BCE) ◆180●, ✛144
  temple complexes (2600 BCE) ✛220●
  vertical economy ✛147, ❑147
  see also Chavín; Inca; Moche; Nazca
Andronovo steppe cultures (1250 BCE) ✛26–7
Angevins Kings of Hungary between 1308 and 1387.
  Baltic States (1100–1400) ◆144●, ◆187 (4), ◆189 (3)
Angevin dynasty (*aka* Plantagenets). English ruling dynasty established by Henry II, Count of Anjou in 1154. ◆186
Angkor Capital of the Khmer Empire (Kambujadesha), located in central Cambodia. Angkor was an extensive city, covering over 25 sq km, of stone temples dedicated to the Khmer god kings. The most impressive temples are Angkor Wat (12th century) and Angkor Thom (13th century).
  Angkor Thom, temple complex ❑245
  Angkor Wat, temple complex ✛59●, ✛63●, ❑63, ❑243
Angkorian dynasty Founded (802) ✛59●
  See also Kambujadesha
Angles Germanic people who invaded England in the 5th century along with the Jutes and Saxons.
  migrations and invasions ✛183, ✛52–3 (1)
Anglo-Burmese Wars (1824–26, 1852, 1885). In 1824, after Burmese encroachments on their territory, the British declared war on Burma. After two years of intermittent conflict the king of Ava signed the treaty of Yandabo, abandoning all claim to Assam and ceding the provinces of Arakan and Tenasserim. Further conflict in 1852 led to the annexation of the Irrawaddy valley. A third clash in 1885 led to the annexation of Upper Burma and (in 1890) the Shan states. ✛248●
Anglo-Gurkha War (1814–15). Conflict between the Gurkhas of Nepal and Britain in Sikkim and the Ganges plain. By the terms in the Treaty of Segauli, the Nepalis were obliged to withdraw from Sikkim and the lower ranges of the western Himalayas. ✛248●
Anglo-Japanese alliance (1902–23) ✛269
Anglo-Maratha Wars (1775–82, 1803–05, 1817–18). The first Maratha war began when Britain became involved in struggles between Maratha leaders. Though the British were crushed at Wadgaon in 1778, they conquered Gujarat and stormed Gwalior to end the war, which concluded with the Treaty of Salabai (1782). During the Second Maratha war, Maratha artillery was particularly effective at the battles of Assaye and Argaon (1803). British conquest of the three great Maratha powers in the third war in 1818 allowed Britain to incorporate Maratha territory into their growing domains. ✛248●
Anglo-Persian Oil Company founded ✛234●
Anglo-Tibetan Convention see Anglo-Tibetan Treaty
Anglo-Tibetan Treaty (*var.* Anglo-Tibetan Convention) (Sep 6, 1904). Agreement of mutual support between Britain and Tibet, following the opening of commercial relations and establishment of boundaries under the Sikkim Convention (1890, 1893). ✛257●

independence (1975) ✛107●, ✛111●, ✛168
animals
  biological exchanges ◆81 (2)
  biological origin and movement ◆81 (2)
  domestication (BCE) ◆18, ✛21, ✛23 (2), ✛39, ❑120, ◆120 (1), ◆144 (1), ✛258●
  exotic animal combat ❑44
  used for draft ◆76–7 (1)
An Nafud Arabian Peninsula crossed by Palgrave (1862–63) ◆219●
Annam Historic state of mainland Southeast Asia, in area of modern North Vietnam; under Chinese suzerainty at various times from the 2nd century CE to independence (1428), part of French Indochina from 1880s.
  ✛43, ✛43●, ✛59, ◆61 (3), ◆63, ◆67, ✛67●, ◆69 (1), ✛71, ✛75, ✛75●, ✛79, ◆83, ✛83●, ◆243 (5), ◆263 (7)
  See also Dai-Viet, Vietnam
Anne of Bohemia (1366–94). First wife of Richard II of England. She died of plague without producing an heir. ❑72
Anpu see Anubis
Anschluss (1938). Nazi Germany's annexation of Austria, despite an express prohibition of such a union under the terms of the 1919 Versailles Treaty. ✛209●
Antarctic exploration ✛287●, ◆287 (3)
anthropomorphism The attribution of human characteristics to gods, animals, or objects.
Anti-Ballistic Missile (ABM). Defense systems, developed by the US in the late 1960s. ✛109●
antibiotics Discovered and used in WW II. ✛102
Anti-Comintern Pact (Nov 25, 1936). Joint declaration by Germany and Japan of opposition to Soviet Communism and Communist International; acceded to by Italy (Oct 1937). ✛103●
Antietam ✕ of American Civil War (Sep 17, 1862). Union victory. ✛131 (6)
Antigonid dynasty (c.306–168 BCE). Dynasty of Macedonian monarchs established by one of Alexander's generals, Antigonus Cyclops – so called because he had lost an eye – after the death of Alexander. It established dominance over the Greek portion of Alexander's Empire. ✛41, ◆224, ✛224●, ◆224 (1)
Antigua, slave plantation (1823) ❑84
Antioch
  captured by Khosrau I (628) ✛55
  Crusader state ◆63, ◆65, ❑63
  floor mosaic of Orpheus ❑181
  reconquered by Byzantium (969) ✛59
Antiochus III (d.187 BCE) Seleucid emperor (r.223–187 BCE). Ruled over Syria and much of Asia Minor. His interference in Greek affairs brought him into conflict with Rome and he was defeated at Thermopylae in 191. ◆224, ✛224●
Anubis (*var.* Anpu). Ancient Egyptian god of the dead, represented by a jackal or the figure of a man with the head of a jackal. ❑37
Anxi Silk Road ✛45
Anyang Shang capital (1400 BCE) ✛27●
Anzio (*var.* Anzio Beach) ✕ of WW II (Jan–May 1944). Allied (US) landings in central Italy established a bridgehead north of German defensive lines. ◆211 (4)
Anzio Beach see Anzio
Anzus Pact (*var.* Anzus Treaty) (1951). Formerly known as the Pacific Security Treaty, and signed by the US, Australia, and New Zealand, it aimed to protect the countries of the Pacific from armed attack. ◆138 (1)
Anzus Treaty see Anzus Pact
Aornos ✕ of Alexander the Great's expansionist campaigns (327 BCE). ◆40–1 (3)
Aotearoa see New Zealand
Apache Native American people of the US southwest. Their remote location meant that they suffered less initial disruption from European expansion. Led by Geronimo, they fought a series of wars (the Apache Wars) against the US army during the mid-19th century before they were eventually forced into reservations in 1887. ◆125 (4), ◆126 (1), ✛129●, ◆129 (2)
apartheid (apartness). Policy in South Africa from the 1960s to 1990 that sanctioned racial segregation and social, political, and economic discrimination against the black majority.
  See South Africa
Appalachia Migration (1917–20) ✛134, ◆134 (3)
Appalachians Occaneechee Path explored (1673) ◆119●
Appomattox (1865) Confederate surrender in American Civil War. ✛131●

aqueducts Artificial water channels, built by classical Roman engineers to supply their towns. Many were carried on vast arched bridges, some of which still survive. ❑180
Aquileia Sacked by the Huns ✛53
Aquinas, St. Thomas (*var.* Aquinas, Doctor Angelicus, *It.* San Tommaso D'Aquino) (c.1224–74). Italian scholar and Dominican theologian whose doctrinal system became known as Thomism. ◆187
Aquitaine
  captured by Franks (507) ✛53●, ✛182●
  Visigoth kingdom (418) ✛53, ✛182, ✛183
Ara Pacis (*var.* Altar of Peace) ❑42
Arab-Israeli Wars (1948–9, 1956, 1967, 1973, 1982). Series of five wars between Israel and the Arab states over the territorial and strategic consequences of the creation of a Jewish state. *See also* Six-Day War, Suez Crisis, Yom Kippur War, Lebanon, Invasion of ✛234●
Arab League Association of Arab states founded in 1945 with the aim of encouraging Arab unity. The original members were Egypt, Syria, Lebanon, Transjordan, Iraq, Saudi Arabia, and Yemen. By 1994 the League had 22 member states, including Palestine, represented by the Palestine Liberation Organization (PLO).
  founded (1945) ✛103
Arab Revolt, the (1915–18). Uprising against Turkish rule during WW I by several Arab tribes. Centered on the Hejaz, the revolt subsequently helped the British to capture Palestine. ✛232–3●, ◆233 (2)
  See also Lawrence, T.E. and Faisal, Emir.
Arabia
  aromatic gum trade (1st century CE) ✛225, ❑225, ◆225 (3)
  desert explored by Aelius Gallus (BCE) ◆218 (1)
  European travelers ◆219 (4)
  See also Saudi Arabia
Arabian American Oil Company (ARAMCO). Founded in 1936 by Standard Oil of California and Texaco to exploit petroleum concessions in Saudi Arabia, it is now among the most powerful oil groups in the world. In 1979 the Saudi Arabian government took complete control of the company. ✛234●
Arabs Semitic people originally of the Arabian Peninsula, but now widespread throughout the S.W. Asia and N. Africa.
  Classical world maps ❑55
  coastal trading settlements ✛58
  era of expansion from c.632 CE ✛61●
  Indian Ocean trade (to c.1000 CE) ◆61, ◆61 (3)
  lose control of Mediterranean (11th century) ✛62
  mapping Niger Basin ◆156 (1)
  skilled astronomers ❑59
  tribal conflicts ❑59
Arafat, Yasser (1929–2004). Palestinian resistance leader, cofounder in 1959 of the Palestine Liberation Organization (PLO), and its chairman from 1969. In 1988 he persuaded the majority of his colleagues in the PLO to acknowledge the right of Israel to coexist with an independent state of Palestine. In 1993, together with the prime minister of Israel, Yitzhak Rabin, he negotiated a peace agreement by which Israel agreed to withdraw from Jericho and the Gaza Strip. ❑234
Aragon
  control of Sicily ✛66●
  and possessions ◆66–7, ◆70–1
Araucanians People of central Chile. The Araucanians resisted European conquest for over 300 years. They quickly learned to ride the horses introduced by the Spanish and proved formidable opponents in war. They were finally subdued by the Chilean army in the 1870s. ◆151 (4)
Arbela ✕ of Wars between Parthia and Rome (216 BCE). ◆224 (2)
Archangel Reached by Willoughby (1553) ✛80●
Archimedes (c.287–212 BCE). Greek scientist and mathematician who made many valuable contributions to theories of mechanics and hydrostatics; among them Archimedes' Principle, which states that the volume of a body can be found by measuring the volume of the fluid it displaces. ✛38
  Archimedean screw ❑38
Arcole ✕ of (1796) Napoleonic Wars, Italian campaign. French victory. ✛200–1
Arctic Ocean
  charting the coast ✛286, ✛286–7 (2)
  exploration ✛287●
  new routes to Asia ✛286, ◆286 (1)
  Northeast Passage navigated ◆257 (2)

Ardashir I (d.241 CE) Persian king (r.208–241 CE). In c.224 Ardashir overcame the Parthian, Artabanus V, and invaded Syria, establishing the Sassanian dynasty and empire. He made Ctesiphon on the Tigris River his capital (near modern Baghdad) and revived Zoroastrianism.
  ✛47, ✛225, ✛225●, ◆225 (6)
Ardennes ✕ of WW II (Dec 1944–Feb 1945). Final and unsuccessful German counteroffensive in western Europe. ◆211 (4)
Ardipithecus ramidus Early hominid, dating from 4.4 million years ago. ◆12 (1), 12●
Ares (*var.* Mars) Greek god of war. ◆37 (3)
Argentina 148–153
  Falklands war (1982) ◆110●
  governed by Perón (1946–55) ◆102●, ◆106●
  independence ◆90, ◆150, ◆150 (1)
  Paraguayan War (1864–70) ◆94●
Arianism Christian doctrine developed by Arius (c.318) which regarded Jesus Christ as a demigod, less divine than God; widely observed by successor states to W. Roman Empire (Visigoths, Vandals), but declared heretical at Council of Nicaea (325). ◆49 (4)
Arica ✕ of War of the Pacific (1880). Chilean victory. ✛151 (4)
Armenia
  annexed by Rome ✛47●, ✛51
  kingdom ◆65 (3)
  occupied by Sassanians ✛51●
  solar system bronze (BCE), ❑31
  Urartu kingdom ✛31
Arms Race General term for the technical development and stockpiling of weapons of mass destruction by the Western and Eastern blocs during the Cold War. ✛109●
Arnhem ✕ of WW II (*var.* Operation Market Garden, Sep 1944). Unsuccessful Allied airborne operation intended to secure bridges across the Rhine in advance of land forces. ◆211 (3)
Arras, Congress of (1435) ✛192●
Arsaces I (d.211 BCE). Founder of the Parthian Empire, which he ruled (c.250–211 BCE) by leading a rebellion against the Seleucids. ✛43●, ◆224 (1)
Arsur ✕ of crusades in the Holy Land (1191). Crusader victory. ◆65 (3)
Arthur, Gabriel 17th-century explorer of North America. In 1673, Arthur accompanied James Needham southwest across the Blue Ridge Mountains of North America, and into territory occupied by the Cherokee. During his travels he was captured by natives. ◆119 (2)
Aryans Nomadic Indo-European-speaking people who migrated into northwest India some time after c.1500 BCE. Originally cattle pastoralists, they became sedentary farmers and gradually spread eastward. They were divided into various tribes, often warring among themselves. The early Aryan settlers of northern India coalesced, by c.600 BCE, into sixteen distinct political units (*see* Magadha), which dominated the Ganges plain.
  religious practices ✛36
  settle N. India ✛35, ✛36●
Asante (*var.* Ashanti).
  annexed by Britain (1900–01) ✛167●
  court insignia ❑87
  rise to prominence begins (1701) ✛164●
  slave trade ✛82
  well-armed warrior ❑164
  W. African dominance ✛86
ASEAN see Association of South-East Asian Nations
Ascalon ✕ of crusades in the Holy Land (1099), city captured by crusaders (1153). ◆65 (2) (3)
Ashanti see Asante
Ashikaga Shogunate (1336–1573) Line of military governors of Japan.
  founded (1336) ✛71●
Ashoka (*var.* Asoka) (d.227 BCE) Mauryan emperor (r.264–227 BCE). The grandson of Chandragupta Maurya, Ashoka established his rule over most of the Indian subcontinent. After his victory in Kalinga by the Bay of Bengal, he became an enthusiastic convert to Buddhism, and published the fundamental principles of the faith on pillars or rock-carved edicts, found throughout India.
  ✛38–9, ✛241, ✛242●, ✛243
  promulgator of Buddhism ✛36●, ✛36 (2)
Ashur City-state ✛27
Ashurbanipal Last of the great kings of Assyria (r.668–627 BCE), who assembled the first systematically organized library in the ancient Middle East in Nineveh. ✛222, ✛34–5, ✛222 (2)
Asia
  See East Asia, South and Southeast Asia, West Asia.

Asiento Slave Agreement Contract in use from the 16th to the mid-18th century with the Spanish crown, which for an agreed sum of money granted a contractor (*asentista*) a monopoly in supplying African slaves for the Spanish colonies in the Americas. 86●
Asoka see Ashoka
Assassins Ismaili Shi'ite sect ✛229
Association of South-East Asian Nations (ASEAN), established in 1967 to promote economic, social, and cultural cooperation. ◆253 (5)
Assyrian Empire (*var.* Neo-Assyrian Empire) (c.950–612 BCE). State based on Assur on the Tigris in upper Mesopotamia, which conquered its neighbors to establish a vast empire. At its height between the 9th and 8th centuries BCE, Assyria reached the Mediterranean in the west to Persia in the east, and from the Persian Gulf northward to the eastern Anatolian mountains. Overthrown by the Medes and Babylonians in 612 BCE.
  (BCE) ✛31, ✛222, ✛222●, ✛34–5, ◆222 (2)
  invade Egypt (667 BCE) ✛35●
  ivory sphinx ❑31
  legend of flood ✛222, ❑223
astronomy
  astrolabe ✛238, ❑218
  Babylonian ❑31
  Babylonian Venus tablet ❑33
  Islamic knowledge ❑77
  Jaipur observatory ❑238
  mapping fixed stars ✛39
  Maya civilization ✛54
  Rigel (star) ✛59
  stone alignment at Newgrange ❑33
Asunción Conflict with Jesuits (1640s) ✛143●
Atacama Desert ✕ of War of Pacific (1879–83). ✛94●
Atahualpa (1502–1533). Last emperor of the Inca, who was victorious in a civil war with his half brother. He was later captured, held for ransom, and then executed by Francisco Pizarro. ❑148
Atatürk, Mustafa Kemal (*prev.* Mustafa Kemal Pasha) (1881–1938). Founder and first president of the republic of Turkey. Participated in the revolt of the Young Turks (1908). Served with distinction in WW I. In 1919 he broke away from the authority of the Istanbul government and established a provisional government in Ankara. As leader of the Turkish Nationalists he drove the Greeks from western Anatolia (1919–22). In 1922 the Ottoman Sultanate was formally abolished and Turkey became a secular republic, with Kemal as president. He launched a program of social and political reform intended to transform Turkey into a westernized modern republic. In 1934 he took the name Atatürk, "Father of the Turks." ❑99, ◆233●
Aten (*var.* Aton). Originally the Egyptian sun disc, subsequently the sun god with which Pharaoh Akhenaten replaced the existing Middle Kingdom pantheon. ✛26, ✛28
Athabascan (*var.* Athapaskan, Athapascan). N. American peoples, subarctic nomadic hunters, mainly of western Canada, and the name given to the language group linking a number of peoples from this area. ◆123, ◆123 (3)
Aten race riots (1966) ✛137●
Athaulf Visigothic leader (*fl.*414) ✛53●
Athenian Empire (454–428 BCE) ✛177, ◆177 (2)
Athens The most celebrated of the city-states of Ancient Greece, both for its unrivaled cultural achievements and for its position under Pericles in the 5th century BCE as the most powerful Greek city-state. In 431 BCE Athens' role as leader of the Delian League provoked the hostility of Sparta, leading to the Peloponnesian War, in which Athens was completely defeated. Under the Romans (from 146 BCE), Athens was more important culturally than politically. In modern times it was chosen as capital of the new kingdom of Greece in 1834.
  Athene patroness ❑177
  city-state ✛179
  conflict with Sparta ✛38
  democracy established (505 BCE) ✛34●
  Olympic Games revived (1896) ✛94●
  plan showing BCE remains ◆177 (4)
Atjeh see Achin
athletics Pan-Hellenic festival (776 BCE) ✛31●
Atlanta ✕ of American Civil War (Jul 20–Sep 2, 1864). Union victory. ✛131●
Atlanta race riots (1966) ✛137●
Atlantic, Battle of the Naval and air ✕ of WW II. Protracted German campaign (1939–45) to disrupt

Key to index: ✛ text ❑ picture *var.* variant name *f/n* full name *r.* ruled WW I World War I
● timeline ◆ map *aka* also known as *prev.* previously known as ✕ battle WW II World War II

290

Key to index: ✦ text ❑ picture *var.* variant name *f/n* full name *r.* ruled WW I World War I
● timeline ◆ map *aka* also known as *prev.* previously known as ⚔ battle WW II World War II

demise in the 1st century BCE when the Romans and Germanic tribes marginalized them. Celtic dialects survive in several parts of Europe; including Wales, Brittany, and Ireland.
Anglo-Saxon Britain (600–800) ✛183, ✛183●
invade British Isles ✛38●
Iron Age (800 BCE) ✛31●
lunisolar calendar ❑33
sack Rome ✛38●
tribal societies ✛34
censorship Carlsbad Decrees (Aug 6–31, 1819) ✛90●
CENTO Pact see Central Treaty Organization
Central Africa
interethnic warfare ✛111
Rwandan crisis ✛169, ✛169 (5)
Central America
Communist subversion ✛139
cotton growing (BCE) ✛22●
cultures
Kaminalijuyú, (c.500 BCE) ✛121
Maya ✛46●, ✛50, ✛54, ❑58, ✛36 (1), ✛121 (2)
Olmec ✛30●, ✛34, 30, ✛36 (1), ◆121 (2) (3)
Toltec Empire ✛58, ✛62, ✛58–9
Zapotec ✛34, ✛121 (2)
early civilizations ✛120●, ✛121●, ✛122
moves toward democracy (1970s) ✛110
plant domestication (BCE) ✛18
revolt against rural elites ✛98
Spanish colonization (16th century) ✛78, ✛82, ✛118, ✛81 (3)
United Provinces 1823–38 ✛90–1
US intervention ✛139
See also individual countries
Central Asia
classical world trade ◆44–5●
Islam and nationalism ✛275, ◆275 (5)
Islamic states (16th century) ✛267
steppe kingdoms ✛261, ✛261●, ◆261 (6)
Central Intelligence Agency (CIA). Established in 1947 in the US to gather intelligence information abroad and report to the president and National Security Council. ✛113
Central Powers Term used for the members of the Triple Alliance in WW I: Germany and Austria-Hungary, together with their allies Turkey and Bulgaria. ✛206–7, ◆206–7
Central Treaty Organization (CENTO Pact) (1955). Defense alliance originally known as the Baghdad Pact, between Iran, Iraq, Pakistan, Turkey and the United Kingdom. ◆108–9 (1)
ceramics
Chinese (650 BCE) ✛35●
hunter attacked by lion ❑51
molds used for casting bronze (BCE) ✛27●
Tang Ferghana horse ❑55
Ceuta Captured by Portuguese (1415) ✛75●
Ceylon
British conquest (1796) ✛87●
Buddhism dominant faith ✛51
Chola conquests ✛59
economy (1857) ✛249, ◆249 (4)
Portuguese expelled by Dutch (1663) ✛83●
Chacabuco ⚔ of wars of S. American independence (Feb 1817). Spanish forces defeated by San Martin. ✛150 (1)
Chaco Canyon
cliff dwellings (c.1100) ✛62●
peak importance (1200) ❑123●
Chaco War (1932–35). Conflict between Bolivia and Paraguay over the Chaco Boreal, a wilderness region that forms part of the Gran Chaco. A peace treaty was arranged by the Chaco Peace Conference and was signed in Buenos Aires on Jul 21, 1938. Paraguay gained clear title to most of the disputed region, but Bolivia was given a corridor to the Paraguay River. ✛152●, ✛152 (2), ❑152
Chaco Ju-kua see Zhao Rugua
Chad, Lake Reached by Denham and Clapperton (1823) ✛157●
Chaeronea ⚔ of Alexander's campaigns in Europe (338 BCE). Decisive confrontation which left the Macedonians in effective control of all Greece. ◆40●
Chagatai (var. Jagatai) Mongol ruler, the second son of Genghis Khan. On the death of Genghis in 1227, Chagatai was granted a large vassal khanate in Central Asia, centered on Transoxiana. Despite this eclipse by Timur at the end of the 14th century, the Chagatai Khanate survived into the 16th century. ✛261
Chaka Zulu see Shaka Zulu
Chalcas Aztec civilization ✛125
Chaldean tribe ✛31
Chaldean dynasty (626–539 BCE). Originating in the area at the head of the Persian Gulf, the Chaldeans established a Babylonian dynasty in 626 BCE. After their overthrow in 539 BCE the Babylonian and Chaldean dynasties became synonymous. ✛222, ◆222 (2)

Chaldiran see Çaldiran
Chaldiron see Çaldiran
Chalukya Dynasty (550–750 BCE). Deccan-based dynasty, founded in about 550 CE. The Chalukyas were eventually superseded by the Rashtrakutas in 750. The Rashtrakutas were overthrown in 973 CE by Taila II, a scion of the Chalukyas dynasty who founded a second dynasty known as the Chalukyas of Kalyani, which went into decline during the 11th century. ✛59, ✛244
chamber tombs (var. dolmens). Megalithic monuments constructed of upright stones (orthostats) and capstones, beneath an earth mound. Often used for collective burials they comprise a series of chambers which can contain collections of different skeletal parts. Evidence suggests they were used over successive generations, during the Neolithic period in Europe, from c.5000 BCE. ✛23●
Champa South Vietnamese Hindu-Buddhist kingdom with its capital at Vijaya (modern Binh Dinh). The capital was annexed by the expanding north Vietnamese kingdom of Dai-Viet in 1471.
✛67●, ✛75●, ✛245, ◆245 (5) (6)
Champagne fairs ✛190●
Champlain, Lake French abandon forts (1757) ✛127●, ✛127 (2)
Champlain, Samuel de (1567–1635). French explorer of N. America. Founded the colony of New France, later to become Canada. Explored the St. Lawrence River, establishing a colony at Port Royal in 1604, founding Quebec in 1608, and discovering Lake Champlain in 1609. ❑82, ✛118, ✛126●, ✛118–19 (1) (2)
Chan Chan Chimú capital (11th century) ✛62, ✛146 (1)
Chancellor, Richard (d.1556). British navigator and pioneer of Anglo-Russian trade. Appointed pilot-general in 1553 to Sir Hugh Willoughby's expedition seeking a Northeast passage to China. Separated from them by bad weather, he continued into the White Sea and went overland to Moscow. The Muscovy Company was founded in 1555 to carry out the trade. ◆257 (2), ◆286 (1)
Chancellorsville ⚔ of American Civil War (May 1–4, 1863). Confederate victory. ◆131 (6)
Chandragupta II (380–415) Gupta dynasty king (r.c.375–415). Famous for the long campaign he waged against the invading Shakas (Scythians), from 388 to 409. He extended the Gupta domains, both by military conquest and marriage alliance. ✛244
Chandragupta Maurya (var. Candra Gupta) Founder of the Mauryan dynasty (r.c.321–297 BCE) and the first emperor to unify most of India under one administration. Having seized the Magadhan throne in 327 BCE, Chandragupta Maurya annexed all the lands east of the Indus, occupied much of north-central India and captured much of Afghanistan from Seleucus Nicator, the successor of Alexander the Great. ✛36●, ✛39, ✛240
Chang'an
captured by An Lushan (756) ✛59●
nomad sacking (316) ❑51
plan of city ❑262
Chang Ch'ien see Zhang Qian
Chang Zhun (Ch'iu Ch'ang-ch'un) (1148–1227). Chinese Taoist sage summoned to attend the court of Genghis Khan and sent on a mission from Beijing, via the Altai Mountains, Samarkand, and the Tien Shan, to just south of Kabul. ◆256, ◆256 (1)
Chao Ju-kua see Zhao Rugua
Chaplin, Charlie (Sir Charles Spencer Chaplin) (1889–1977). English film actor and director, who won international fame in American-made silent comedy films.
first full-length film (1921) ✛135●
Charlemagne (var. Lat. Carolus Magnus) (c.742–814). King of the Franks and Holy Roman Emperor. Charlemagne's kingdom comprised France, much of Germany, and northern Italy, and became the first medieval Holy Roman Empire. The pope crowned him emperor in 800.
empire ✛184●, ✛184 (2)
bronze statue ❑184
Frankish king ✛58●
throne ❑184
Charles I (1600–49) King of England, Scotland, and Ireland (r.1625–49). His marriage to the Catholic Henrietta Maria aroused public hostility. He dissolved three parliaments in the first four years of his reign, and then ruled without one for 11 years until rebellion in Scotland forced him to recall it. Conflict with the Long Parliaments led to the Civil War (1642–46). He was defeated

at ⚔ Naseby in 1645 by Parliamentarian forces. He escaped briefly, but was recaptured, tried for treason, and beheaded.
✛82●, ✛196
Charles IV (1316–78) Holy Roman Emperor (r.1347–78) and King of Bohemia (as Charles I). The greatest of the Luxembourg rulers of Bohemia. He briefly made Prague center of the Empire. ✛189, ❑189
Charles Martel (c.688–741). Frankish leader, Mayor of the Palace to the late Merovingian kings (r.719–741). He was the effective ruler of the Frankish kingdom and defeated Muslim invaders at Poitiers in 732. ✛54●, ✛184
Charles the Bold (1433–77) Last reigning duke of Burgundy (r.1467–77). Continually at war with Louis XI, he almost succeeded in creating a kingdom independent of France. His death while fighting the Swiss ended Burgundy's resistance to France. ✛193●, ◆193 (4)
Charles V (1500–58) Holy Roman Emperor. Charles inherited the Netherlands from his father, Spain (which he ruled as Charles I) from his mother, and the German Habsburg territories from his grandfather, all before he was 20. Elected emperor in 1520, to protect his lands he had to fight France and the Ottoman Turks, while his reign also saw Germany torn apart by the wars of the Reformation. He abdicated in 1555, leaving his Spanish possessions and the Netherlands to his son Philip II and his Austrian and German lands to his brother Ferdinand. ✛78●, ✛142●, ✛192, ✛192●, ✛194
Charles VII (1403–61) King of France (r.1422–61). Not actually crowned until 1429 when Joan of Arc raised the siege of Orléans. By 1453 he had expelled the English from all France except Calais, thus ending the Hundred Years' War. ◆192 (2), ✛194 (1)
Charles VIII (1470–1498). King of France (r.1483–1498), remembered for beginning the French expeditions into Italy that lasted until the middle of the 16th century. ✛75●
Charles X (1622–60) King of Sweden (r.1654–60). Invaded Poland in 1655. In a successful war with Denmark (1657–58), Sweden reached the limit of its territorial expansion. ✛177●
Charleston ⚔ of American Revolutionary War (Jun 28, 1776). British victory. ◆127 (3)
Chartres Construction of cathedral begins (1154) ❑62
Chateau-Thierry ⚔ of Napoleon's defense of France (Feb 12, 1814). ◆200 (1)
Chattanooga ⚔ of American Civil War (Nov 23–25, 1863). Union victory. ◆131 (7)
Chavin culture (1000–200 BCE). From its birth around 1000 BCE this culture united around 800 sq km of Peruvian coast from its base at Chavín de Huántar in the eastern Andes. This unity was religious rather than political, and was at its height around 400–200 BCE. Noted for their stone carvings of deities with jaguar fangs, the Chavin also made improvement in corn cultivation, metallurgy, and weaving.
decorative motif (900 BCE) ❑30
influential Peruvian culture ✛145, ✛145 (3)
state religion (BCE) ✛38, ◆36 (1)
water vessel ❑144
Chavin de Huántar (c.850–200 BCE). The earliest urban civilization in the Andes, which flourished in the central highlands. The site of Chavín de Huántar was dominated by a central temple complex adorned by a 4.5-m-high carving of a deity, the Oculate Being, with projecting fangs and a snarling mouth. Elements of this iconography spread throughout the Andean region and permeated the art and religion of later Andean cultures. ✛30, ✛145, ◆145 (3)
chemical warfare
used against Kurds ✛235
WW I gas masks ❑98
Cheng Ho see Zheng He.
Ch'eng Tsu see Chengzu
Chengzu (var. Yonglo) (1360–1424) (r.1402–24). Son of Zhu Yuanzhang, the founder of the Ming dynasty in China. Ruled China in the early 15th century.
✛266, ❑266
Cherokee Native people of N. America. Formerly ranged across much of the southern US. Removed to reservations in Oklahoma and N Carolina in the late 19th century. ✛125 (4), ✛126 (1)
Chesapeake Bay
painted map (16th century) ❑118
plate from Atlas Contractus ❑119

Chester ⚔ (616). Britons defeated by Northumbrians. ◆183 (3)
Chiang Kai-shek see Jiang Jieshi.
Chibcha see Muisca
Chicago
in the 1860s ❑130
Democratic rally riots (1968) ✛137●
growth of the suburbs (1850–1950) ✛137, ◆137 (4)
race riots (1940s) ✛135●
Chichén Itzá Toltec altar ❑58
Chichimec People of N.W. Mexico (c.12th century CE). They created small city-states and were in constant conflict with each other. In the 1170s, as their homeland became increasingly desiccated and famine-struck, they sacked the Toltec city of Tula. ✛62●
Chickamauga ⚔ of American Civil War (Sep 19–20, 1863). Confederate victory. ◆131 (7)
Children's Crusade ✛186, ✛186 (1)
Chile 148–153
colonization, Rapa Nui (Easter Island) ✛284●
environmental survival strategies (BCE) 16
foreign affairs, War of Pacific (1879–83) ✛94●, ✛151, ✛151 (4)
home affairs
coup against Marxists (1973) ✛106●, ◆138●
democracy restored (1989) ✛110●
liberated (1817) ✛90●, ✛150, ✛150 (1)
trade and industry
economic development (1950) ✛274, ◆274 (2)
with Arab world (c.800–907 CE) ✛61
exports to Russia and the West (18th century) ✛87
Chimú culture (c.700–1476). Civilization of N. Peru. Flourished for over 700 years until its defeat by the Incas in 1476. The Chimú empire was built around military conquest, efficient communications, and social control. Chimú craftsmen were noted for their metalwork, pottery, and textiles.
11th century ✛62
conquered by Incas (1470) ✛74●
empire ✛146, ✛146 (1)
expansion (1200) ✛66●
funerary mask ❑66
gold dove ❑146
gold knife ❑146
Ch'i Dynasty see Qi Dynasty
Ch'in Dynasty see Qin Dynasty
Chin Dynasty see Jin Dynasty
China
conflicts, revolution (1911) ✛271, ✛271●, ◆271 (5)
conflicts
Boxer Rebellion (1900) ✛95, ❑96
Civil War (1920–26) ✛103●, ✛271, ◆271 (6)
Communist revolution (1927–49) ✛274, ✛274●, ◆274 (1)
Cultural Revolution (1966–70) ✛107●
famine (1877–79) ✛95●
fragmentation (220–589) ✛261, ◆261 (2) (3) (4) (5)
"Great Leap Forward" ✛107●, ❑274
"Long March" ✛103●, ❑274
peasant uprisings (870s) ✛59●
rebellions against Mongols (1335) ✛71●
cultures
Banshan ✛23●
Longshan ✛23●
dynasties, see Han; Hongshan; Jin; Ming; Qi; Qin; Qing; Shang; Song; Sui; Tang
exploration and mapping
cartographers' map grids ❑256●
geography recorded (c.1000 BCE) ❑256●
travelers in Central Asia ◆256 (1)
Zhou sponsored (c.1000 BCE) ✛256●
foreign affairs
closer links with West ✛111
control of Korea (108 BCE) ✛43●
expansionism from 1949 ✛275, ✛275●, ◆275 (3)
influence on Japan ✛55, ✛256, ✛265
Japanese diplomatic mission (607) ✛256●
Taiwan annexed (1894–95) ✛95
Treaty of Nerchinsk with Russia (1689) ✛83●, ✛257●
war with Japan (1937) ✛103
home affairs
agriculture (BCE) ✛19, ✛21
empire collapses ✛99
empire expanded and unified ✛259 (5)
Hong Kong returned (1997) ✛111●
Mongol conquest begins (1211) ✛67●
Nationalists (Kuomintang/Guomindang) ✛271, ✛271 (7)
Republic declared (1911) ✛99●
reunification by Chiang Kai-Shek (Jiang Jieshi) ✛103●
Sixteen Kingdoms (c.400) ✛261 (3)
Three Kingdoms (c.250) ✛261 (2)
Tiananmen Square massacre (1989) ✛111●
Toba Wei (c.440–500) ◆261 (4)

innovations
boxed compass (13th century) ❑67
bronze casting ✛22, ✛31●, ❑27
bronze coins ❑34, ❑259
crossbow ✛39
gunpowder weapons ✛71
introduced by 16th-century Jesuit missionary ✛80
lodestone compass (c.250) ✛256●
metal stirrups ❑51
movable type printing invented (c.1045) ✛63●
neolithic ◆258 (2)
paper money ✛59●, ❑263
planned villages (c.4000 BCE) ✛23●
pottery wheel (c.3000) ✛22
printing ✛63●
silk (BCE) ✛23, ✛34
timber and brushwood dike ❑83
wind power ✛63
writing paper ❑46
population
(1790) ✛59
first census (2 CE) ✛256●
Song period ✛263 (6)
religion
Buddhist cave temple ❑51
state (BCE) ✛36 (1)
trade and industry
economic development (1950) ✛274, ◆274 (2)
with Arab world (c.800–907 CE) ✛61
exports to Russia and the West (18th century) ✛87
Han dynasty and the wider world ◆44–5
industrial expansion (late 1970s) ✛111
iron technology ✛35●, ◆43●
silk trade (BCE) ✛34
toy factory near Guangzhou ❑111
trade with Europe (BCE) ✛39
See also Silk Road
World War II
human cost of global war ✛105
mobilization and casualty figures ✛105
chinampas Artificial islands, used by peoples of Central America (e.g. the Aztecs) for raising crops. ✛124, ◆124 (2)
Chinese script see calligraphy
Ch'in dynasty see Qin dynasty
Ching dynasty see Qing dynasty
Ching Empire see Qing dynasty
Ching-Ghis Khan see Genghis Khan
Chingis Khan see Genghis Khan
Chiquito Reducción founded (1690) ✛143●
Choga Mami Irrigation system (5500 BCE) ✛20●
Chola dynasty (var. Cola dynasty) (c.860–1279). The Chola kingdom, mentioned in the inscriptions of Ashoka, came into prominence in southern India in c.860 CE. Under Rajaraja the Great, who came to the throne in 985, Chola control extended to Ceylon and parts of the Malay Peninsula. Chola power gradually declined after the 11th century.
conquers Ceylon (1018) ✛63●
dominates southeastern India ✛63
in India ✛59●, ✛63, ✛244, ✛224●, ❑244 (2)
sends embassy to China ✛63●
Shiva bronze ❑59
Chou dynasty see Zhou dynasty
Chou En-lai see Zhou Enlai
Christ, Jesus see Jesus of Nazareth
Christianity One of the world's great religions, an offshoot of Judaism that emerged in Palestine in the 1st century CE, based on the life and teachings of Jesus of Nazareth. The early Christian faith diverged into many sects, but by the 8th century there were two main branches: the Eastern Orthodox and the Roman Catholic Churches. In 16th-century Europe, a reaction to the Roman Church known as the Reformation, led to the foundation of many breakaway Protestant churches which refused to recognize the authority of the pope in Rome.
origins ✛37, ✛46, ✛225
spread (600 CE) ✛226, ✛226●, ◆48 (1), ◆226 (1)
early growth (to 500 CE) ✛48●
in Africa
✛47●, ✛50, ✛67●, ◆161 (5)
Augustine converts Britain (597) ✛54●
Byzantine Empire ◆54–5
11th–12th-century Europe ✛62●
Roman Empire state religion ✛50●, ✛182
12th-century renaissance in Europe ◆187 (3)
the Crusades (1096–1270) ◆64–5, ◆64–5 (1) (2) (3), ✛186 (1)
in Anglo-Saxon England ✛183●
crucifixion of Christ (c.32 CE) ✛48●
depictions
amphora with two versions of the cross ✛48
carved sarcophagus ❑50, ✛225
Coptic weaving ❑58

Corpus Christi procession ❑148
and Islam (c.1090) ◆65 (1)
missionaries
in Africa (c.1880) ◆167 (4)
Chinese missions attacked (1850) ✛95●
journeys of St. Paul ◆48 (1)
in the South Seas ✛284, ◆284 (1)
to pagans of Europe ✛186
persecutions, Diocletian (304 CE) ✛48●
Protestant Reformation ✛78, ✛82, ✛194, ✛194●
religious map of Europe (1590) ◆194 (2)
Roman-Orthodox schism (1054) ✛62●
See also Catholicism
Chu-ssu-pen see Zhu Siben
Chu Yuan-chang see Zhu Yuanzhang
Chucuito culture South American people of the Andes. 13th century ✛64
Churchill, Sir Winston Leonard Spencer (1874–1965) British statesman. Service in Omdurman campaign (1897–98) and as a journalist during the Boer War (1899–1900) preceded his entry to Parliament (1900). Became Home Secretary (1910) and First Lord of the Admiralty (1911–15), bearing responsibility for the Dardanelles campaign, thereafter serving in the trenches and entering political "wilderness." Formed coalition government (1940) and oversaw Britain's policy and strategy during WW II. Lost election upon Allied victory (1945), but returned as Prime Minister (1951–55).
Casablanca conference (1943) ✛104●
Tehran conference ✛105●
Yalta "Big Three" conference (1945) ❑105
CIA see Central Intelligence Agency
cinema Major Hollwood studios (1919) ✛135, ◆135 (4)
Cipangu see Japan
CIS see Commonwealth of Independent States
Cistercians Roman Catholic monastic order that was founded in 1098 and named after the original establishment at Cîteaux, France. The order's founding fathers, led by St. Robert of Molesmes, were a group of Benedictine monks who wished to a live a solitary life under the strictest interpretation of the Rule of St. Benedict. ✛187, ✛187●, ◆187 (3)
cities
BCE growth ✛28–9, ◆28–9 (2) (3) (4) (5)
Central American civilization ✛122, ❑122
development ✛24, ✛28●
first Chinese ✛28, ✛258●
first on Deccan plateau (c.200) ✛47●
growth in Europe (18th century) ✛198, ◆198 (1)
medieval ✛190–1
Mongol warfare ✛69
Toltec ✛58, ✛122
and trade (BCE) ✛24●
urbanism ✛28, ✛28–9 (1)
city-state A single urban center and its hinterland. Although politically autonomous, they frequently shared cultural traits – such as language and religion – with neighboring city-states.
African (800–1500) ✛163, ✛163●
Greek ✛31, ✛34, ✛176, ✛179
Italian ✛75
Maya ✛50, ✛58●, ✛122, ✛122 (2)
Mesopotamia ✛23–4, ✛27
Mexican ✛66, ✛122●, ✛122 (1)
Swahili ✛66, ✛67●, ✛75
Civil Rights Movement US mass movement to combat segregation and discriminatory practices against Black people. Arose in the US in the 1950s and 1960s. The movement began with the Montgomery bus boycott of 1956, following the arrest of Rosa Parks, for refusing to move to the "Negro" section of the bus. The movement gained momentum with the involvement of Martin Luther King Jr., who advocated the principle of nonviolent protest, culminating in the 1963 March on Washington by more than a million people. The Civil Rights Act of 1964 and the Voting Rights Act of 1965 were legal responses to the pressure generated by the movement. ✛137, ✛137●, ◆137 (6)
Cixi, Dowager Empress (var. Tz'u-Hsi) (1835–1908) Manchu empress (r.1861–1908). Became regent in China and opposed all modernization. Helped foment the Boxer Rebellion in 1900 and organized the murder of her successor, the emperor Guangxu, in 1908. ❑271
Clapperton, Hugh (1788–1827). The first European explorer in W. Africa to return with a first-hand account of the region around present-day N. Nigeria. He journeyed with explorers Dixon Denham and Walter Oudney (1821–25). ✛157 (4)

Key to index: ✛ text ❑ picture var. variant name f/n full name r. ruled WW I World War I
● timeline ◆ map aka also known as prev. previously known as ⚔ battle WW II World War II

Clark, William (1770–1838). US explorer. With Meriwether Lewis he was sent by President Thomas Jefferson to explore the lands acquired in the Louisiana Purchase of 1803, and to find a land route to the Pacific Ocean. ◆119 (3)

Classical Age Greece (5th–3rd centuries BCE). An era of city-states characterized by stone or marble monumental architecture – the zenith of architecture, art, and sculpture, which set the standards of beauty and proportion for figurative art for the next 2,500 years. This era also saw the flowering of literature, philosophy, and science. ✤34, ✤37, ✤38, ✤44–5

Claudius Ptolemaeus see Ptolemy

Clavus 15th-century Danish mapmaker. Added detail of northern Europe to the Ptolemaic map of the world (1425). ✤173

Cleopatra VII (var. Thea Philopator) (69–30 BCE) Queen of Egypt (r.51–30 BCE). The last of the Ptolemaic dynasty which ruled Egypt after Alexander the Great's death. Cleopatra was a Macedonian, and ruled alongside her brothers, Ptolemy XIII, Ptolemy XIV, and subsequently, her son Ptolemy XV Caesar. She alone among her dynasty learned to speak Egyptian. She used her famed charm and beauty to delay Egypt's annexation by Rome, bearing children by two of its statesmen, Julius Caesar and Mark Antony. The latter restored much of the old Ptolemaic empire to her, and awarded areas of Rome's eastern provinces to their children, a policy which led to their defeat by Octavian at Actium in 31 BCE. Soon after, both she and Antony committed suicide. ✤42–43●

Clermont Urban II initiates First Crusade (1095) ✤63, ✤64

Clinton, William Jefferson (Bill) (1946–) 42nd president of the US (Democrat, 1992– 2000). The youngest-ever governor of Arkansas, in 1992 he defeated George Bush to become the first Democrat president since Jimmy Carter. Despite a number of scandals, remained enormously popular at home due to the buoyant US economy, and was reelected in 1996. Became first 20th-century president to undergo an impeachment trial in 1999. ◆139●

Clive, Sir Robert (1725–74). Originally a clerk in the British East India Company, Clive commanded British troops at the defense of Arcot (1751), and defeated a combined French and Mughal force at the battle of Plassey (1757), which laid the foundations of the British empire in India. He became the governor of the company's settlements in Bengal (1757–60, 1765–67), and instituted major reforms of the company's administration. ✤87●, ✤248

Clovis I (c.465–511). King of the Franks, responsible for creating the kingdom of France from the old Roman province of Gaul. He defeated the Visigoths in Aquitaine. ✤53, ✤54, ✤183●, ◆183 (5)

Clovis point Heavy clovis point, usually in the shape of a leaf, dating from the 10th millennium BCE, specifically in eastern New Mexico. They are often found close to finds of mammoth bones. □114●

cobalt see metallurgy

cocaine White crystalline alkaloid obtained from the leaves of the coca plant, cultivated in Africa, northern S. America, S.E. Asia, and Taiwan. A widespread recreational drug. ◆153 (4), ◆153, ◆153 (5),□153

Codomannus see Darius III

coins
Athenian tetradrachma □33
Bactrian King Demetrios □41
BCE Chinese □34, □259
Berber (c.118 BCE) □161
Carthage African elephant □179
dinar showing Abd al-Malik □226
Diocletian and Maximian □181
evolution ✤33
first issued by Lydia (BCE) ✤33, ✤35
gold ducats ✤191●
grosso introduced (c.1200) ✤190●
honoring Jan Hus □193
N. African □162
Seleucus I □224
silver pfennig □188
Theban □33
Venetian □191
Viking (9th century) □60

Coke, Thomas William (1752–1842) English agriculturalist who developed new and more robust strains of cattle, pigs, and sheep on his experimental farm. He also helped to initiate the switch from rye to wheat-growing in N.W. Norfolk. □198

Cola dynasty see Chola dynasty

Cold Harbor ✕ of American Civil War (Jun 3, 1864). Inconclusive result. ◆131 (7)

Cold War (c.1947–1991). Period of ideological, political, economic, and military confrontation between Communist bloc, dominated by Soviet Union and China, and Western free market economy nations bound to the US by NATO. Effectively ended by the dissolution of the Soviet Union in 1991.
politics of ✤106–7, ✤108–9
alliances ◆108–9 (1)
Angolan Civil War ◆109 (5)
arms race ✤109
Cuban Missile Crisis (1961–62) ✤106, ◆109 (2)
in Europe ◆108 (2)
ideological indoctrination □109
Korean War (1950–53) ✤106, ✤107●, ◆109 (4)
NATO and the Warsaw Pact ✤108
strategic balance ✤109
Vietnam War (1954–75) ✤106, ✤107●

Colònia do Sacramento
founded (1680s) ✤149●
Portuguese renounce claim (1750) ✤149●

Columbus, Christopher (var. It. Cristoforo Colombo) (c.1451–1506) Genoese explorer. In 1492, having been financed by Ferdinand and Isabella of Spain, Columbus crossed the Atlantic in search of China and Japan, but made a landfall (probably) in the Bahamas, sailed on to Cuba, and then founded a colony on Hispaniola. He made three more voyages which greatly increased European knowledge of the Caribbean, but his governorship of the expanding colonies was never successful and once, in 1500, he was arrested and sent back to Spain in chains.
anchors near Trinidad (1498) ✤74●
expands Spanish empire (1493) ✤81●
N. American expeditions (1492–93) □102–04
✤125●, ✤80 (1), ✤118 (1)
reaches Cuba and Hispaniola (1492) ✤74●, ✤76, ✤80●
ships used in exploration ✤78
sights S. America ✤142●

Combined Bombing Offensive Joint strategic bombing campaign by US and RAF against Nazi-occupied Europe during WW II; inaugurated in 1942, reached a climax with the destruction of Dresden Feb 13–15, 1945. ✤211, ◆211 (4)

COMECON see Council for Economic Assistance

Comintern (aka Communist International). International socialist organization established in 1919, promulgated by the leadership of Bolshevik Russia, envisioning export of Soviet Communism worldwide. Split the world socialist movement and led to uprisings in Europe and elsewhere. Dissolved in 1943. ✤271●

Committee of Correspondence Set up by legislatures in Britain's 13 American colonies to provide leadership to the colonial cause and aid cooperation. The first group was organized by Samuel Adams in Boston in Nov, 1772. ✤127●

Commodus, Caesar Marcus Aurelius (161–192 CE) Commodus' tenure as Roman emperor between 180–192 CE ended 84 years of stability and prosperity in Rome. As he lapsed into insanity, he renamed Rome "Colonia Commodiana," and believed himself to be the god Hercules. When he took to appearing in gladiatorial garb his advisors in desperation had him strangled by a champion wrestler. ✤46●

Common Market see European Union.

Commonwealth of Independent States (CIS) (var. Rus. Sodruzhestvo Nezavisimykh Gosudarstv). Free association of sovereign states formed in 1991, and comprising Russia and 11 other republics that were formerly part of the Soviet Union. ✤215
See also Russian Federation

communications
improvements (1870–1910) ◆92 (1)
and organized crime ✤113, ◆113 (4)

Communism Political and social ideology developed by Karl Marx (1818–83) and Friedrich Engels (1820–95) whereby all property and goods are owned communally and distributed according to need. Implemented under socialist revolutionary conditions with escalating degrees of failure by Lenin and Stalin in Russia, and by Mao Zedong in China.
Bolshevik ✤98, ✤271●, □271

China under Communist rule ✤274●
Chinese ✤103, ✤107, ✤271, ✤271●, ◆271 (7)
Czechoslovakian ✤102●
Eisenhower Doctrine (1958) ✤138●
European collapse (1989–90) ✤109●, ✤110●
Hungarian ✤102●, ✤213
Khmer Rouge □253
in Middle East ✤138●
movements against (1950–70) ✤213, ✤213 (4)
Red Flag over Asia ✤251●, ✤271, ✤271●, ◆271 (8)
revolution in China (1927–49) ✤274●, ◆274 (1)
Soviet ✤106, ✤213, ✤215●, ✤213 (4)
US fear the "Red Scare" ✤135, ✤138–9

Communist Bloc (var. Eastern Bloc, the East). General geopolitical term for the group of socialist (Communist) states in military and economic alliance following WW II, led by the USSR and China. Soviet hegemony was formalized by COMECON (1949) and the Warsaw Pact (1955) binding the Soviet-dominated nations of central and eastern Europe into a military grouping, although the Communist bloc was weakened by the Sino-Soviet dispute (1960). The Soviet alliance collapsed in 1989–90, and was partly replaced by the Commonwealth of Independent States (CIS, 1991). ✤213, ✤214

compass see navigation

computer technology
□111
microprocessor chip □107
World Wide Web □113

Comstoke Lode Nevada, gold find (1849–50) ◆93●

Concepción ✕ of wars of S. American independence in Chile (May 1817). ◆150 (1)

Concord ✕ of American Revolutionary War (Apr 19, 1775). American victory. ◆127 (3)

Confederacy (Confederate states) The 11 Southern states which seceded from the United States in 1860–61 to form a separate government, so leading to civil war. The states were Alabama, Arkansas, Florida, Georgia, Louisiana, Mississippi, N. Carolina, South Carolina, Tennessee, Texas, and Virginia. These were reincorporated into the Union in 1865 following the Confederate surrender.
✤130–131, ◆130–131
✤130–131, ◆130–131

Confucius (var. K'ung-fu-tzu, Kongzi) 551–479 BCE). Chinese accountant, administrator, and philosopher whose teachings and writings (Analects) espoused the inherent common good in correct conduct, morality, ethics, education, and respect, which codified the Chinese social and political system and acquired the status of a religion. BCE Chinese philosopher ✤35, ✤38, ✤39●, ✤259, ✤37 (4)
principles used in Han China ✤260–1
teachings □37

Congo
abandoned by Belgium (1960) ✤168●
Free State, formed (1882) ✤167●
river mouth discovered (1482) ✤156●
See also Zaire

conquistador (conqueror). Leaders in the Spanish conquest of America, especially of Mexico and Peru, in the 16th century. □78
See also individual entries on explorers of N. and S. America.

Conrad III (1093–1152). German king (r.1138–1152) who was the first sovereign of the Hohenstaufen family. ✤64–5 (2)

Constantine I (Constantine the Great) (c.280–337) Roman emperor (r.307–337). Constantine eliminated various rivals and co-emperors to emerge as sole ruler in 324. His reign was remarkable for his conversion to Christianity and the Edict of Milan (313), which granted toleration of Christianity throughout the empire. His creation of a new capital at Constantinople in 330 also had momentous consequences for the Roman Empire.
Christian Roman Emperor (c.280–337) ✤50●, ✤180, □180
assembles Council of Nicaea (325) ✤48●
division of Roman Empire ✤181 (4)
Edict of Milan (313 CE) ✤48●

Constantinople (var. Byzantion, Byzantium, mod. Istanbul).
besieged by Arabs (674–78) ✤54●, ✤55●, ✤184
Black Death (1347) ✤71●
Byzantine capital ✤54
captured by Latin crusaders (1204) ✤64●, ✤66●, ✤187, □187, ◆187 (5)
European tourists (1900) □232

regained by Byzantium ✤66●
Roman capital (324) ✤50
Swedish trading monopoly ✤60
taken by Ottomans (1453)
✤195●, ✤230, □75
Topkapi palace □231

Conti, Niccolò dei (c.1395–1469). Venetian merchant who embarked on journeys through Arabia, Persia, India, Burma, and the East Indies. He was forced to convert to Islam on his travels, but on his return to Europe embraced Christianity. ✤239●, ✤239 (1)

Contras Nicaraguan counter-revolutionaries, supported by the US in the 1980s. From bases in Honduras, they mounted guerrilla actions against the ruling left-wing Sandinistas. ✤110●

Cook, Captain James (1728–79). English explorer of the Pacific. Cook's three epic voyages to the Pacific added immeasurably to European knowledge of the region. The ostensible purpose of the first (1768–71) was to observe the transit of Venus across the face of the sun from Tahiti, but Cook also mapped the whole of New Zealand and the uncharted east coast of Australia. The second (1772–75) included the circumnavigation of Antarctica, and the third (1776–79) took him north to the Bering Strait. On the way, he discovered the Hawaiian Islands. Returning there, he was killed in an argument between islanders and his crew.
18th-century navigator and explorer ✤86
explores Pacific (1768) ✤87●, ✤278●
map of New Zealand □87
Oceania voyages ◆278 (1)
second voyage ship □278

Cook, Frederick Arctic explorer (20th century) □287

Coolidge, (John) Calvin (1872–1933) 30th president of the US (Republican,1923–28). Became president on death of Warren Harding. His laissez faire policies, including tax cuts and business deregulation, were later thought to have been responsible for the stock market crash of 1929. His administration presided over the Dawes Plan, reducing German reparations, and the Kellogg-Briand Pact. □287

Copper Age Name given to the period in European history – the 5th and 4th millennia BCE – before the Bronze Age, when many societies started to work metal first by hammering, then by smelting. The metals used were chiefly copper and gold, the objects made were generally ornamental rather than practical. ✤174, ✤174●, ◆174 (2)

copper
African trade (1868) ✤166●, ◆166 (1)
in the Balkans (5000 BCE) ✤20●
finds in 19th century ◆96 (2)
first use ✤18–19, ✤20●, ✤24●, ✤258
smelting at Çatal Hüyük (6500 BCE) ✤20●
trade ✤25

Copts Members of the Coptic Church, an ancient Monophysite branch of Christianity founded in Egypt in the 5th century which has survived to the present day.
altar cloth □58
missions (by 350 CE) ✤49●, ◆49 (4)

Coral Sea Naval ✕ of WW II (May 1942). US forces halted Japanese advance in southwest Pacific. ◆272 (1)

Córdoba, Hernández de 16th-century Spanish explorer of N. America (1517–24).
✤125, ◆125 (4)

Cordova, Caliphate of (756–1031). After the Umayyad Caliphate fell to the Abbasids in 749, one branch of the Umayyad dynasty won control of the Iberian Peninsula. In 929 Abd al-Rahman proclaimed himself Caliph. The rule of the Umayyads ended in the 10th century, as the Caliphate splintered into many small kingdoms. ✤57 (2), ✤227 (4)
Christian reconquest ✤66●

cord scoring Method of decoration created by imprinting unfired ceramic objects with a length of cord. □19

Corinth
Roman rule (146 BCE) ✤42●
ruins of the later Roman city □179

Cornwallis, General, Charles Cornwallis, 1st Marquis (1738–1805). English soldier. Despite opposing the taxation of American colonists, he led British forces against the Americans in the American Revolution, winning at Camden (1780). He was forced to surrender after the siege of Yorktown (1781) paving the way for British defeat in the war. He

later held senior government and military posts in France, Ireland, and India where he twice held the post of Governor-General. ✤127, ◆127 (3)

Coronado, Francisco Vázquez de (1510–54) Spanish explorer of N. America. Appointed governor of New Galicia province in Mexico. In 1540 he set out to find the "seven treasure cities of the north" on the orders of the viceroy. In 1541 he traveled north of the Arkansas River. ✤118 (1), ✤125, ◆125 (4)

Corregidor ✕ of WW II (May 1942). Took place on island in Manila Bay, marking last defeat of US forces in Philippines by Japan. ◆104 (2)

Corsica Devolution ✤112

Cortenuova ✕ (1237). Italian communes defeated by Frederick II. ◆189 (1)

Corte-Real, Gaspar and Miguel (d.1501 and 1502) Portuguese explorers. Gaspar traveled down the N. American coast from Greenland c.1500 but his ship was lost on a subsequent expedition. On a later expedition in 1502, Miguel's ship was also lost. Spanish recognition of the lands they discovered allowed Portuguese exploitation of the rich fisheries in the Newfoundland banks. ◆118 (1)

Cortés, Hernán (var. Cortéz) (1485–1547). Spanish conquistador who overthrew the Aztec empire (1519–21) and won Mexico for the Spanish crown.
colonizing expeditions (1519, 1522, 1532–42) ✤125, ◆125 (4) (5)
conquers Aztec Empire (1519–22) ✤78, ✤81, ✤124, ✤81 (3)
Indian allies □125
invasion and conquest of Mexico (1519–21) ◆125 (3)
mosaic serpent pendant □124
N. American expedition (1519–21) ✤118 (1)

Cortéz, Hernán see Cortés, Hernán

Corupedium ✕ of (281 BCE). Lysimachus defeated by Seleucus. ◆224 (1)

Cosa, Juan de la (d.1509) Spanish cartographer and navigator who accompanied Columbus on his second expedition in 1493. In 1500 he compiled a world map which records Columbus's discoveries. □219

Cosa Nostra see Mafia

cosmology ✤22, □22, □124, ✤238

Cossacks Inhabitants of the northern hinterlands of the Black and Caspian seas. They had a tradition of independence and finally received privileges from the Russian government in return for military services. ✤82

Cotopaxi Scaled by Wilhelm Reiss (1872) ✤143●

cotton
beneficiary of Industrial Revolution ✤93
British, Indian, and American politics ✤93, ✤93 (5)
in central Andes (3000 BCE) ✤144●
collapse of cotton-growing ✤139, ✤139 (3)
commercial Africa (19th century) ◆166 (1)
market trading in India □93
plantation economy □90
production in Lancashire ◆93 (4)

Council for Economic Assistance (COMECON). Communist organization, established (1949), under auspices of Soviet Union, to create sphere of economic and trade links within Eastern Bloc countries. See also Communist bloc. ✤213●, ✤138 (1)

Counter-Reformation (var. Catholic Reformation, Catholic Revival). Efforts directed, in the 16th and early 17th centuries, both against the Protestant Reformation and toward internal renewal of the Catholic Church. ✤78●, ✤194, ✤194 (2)

Courland (var. Courland Pocket) ✕ of WW II (Feb–May 1945). Led to reduction of German troops and military resistance by Soviet forces in Baltic region. ◆211 (4)

Courland Pocket see Courland

Covilhã, Pêro da (var. Pedro de Covilham, Covilhão). Portuguese explorer. In 1487 he went in search of the mythical "Prester John," sailing down the Red Sea and exploring the west coast of India and E. Africa. Established relations between Portugal and Ethiopia. ✤156 (3), ✤239 (1)

Covilham, Pedro de see Covilhã, Pêro da

Cowpens ✕ of American Revolutionary War (Jan 17, 1781). American victory. ◆127 (3)

Crécy ✕ of Hundred Years' War (1346). English defeat French. ✤70●, □192

Cree Native peoples of northwest N. America. ✤123●, ✤123 (3), ✤126 (1)

cremation First known (26,000 BP) ✤16●

Creole Name given to descendants of European settlers in Central and S. America and the Caribbean. Also language which is a mixture of a European and another, especially African, language.

Cresques, Abraham 14th-century Majorcan cartographer to King Peter IV of Aragon, creator of the so-called "Catalan Atlas." ✤70

Crete
Linear A script (1650 BCE) ✤27●
Minoan civilization established (2000 BCE) ✤27●, ✤175, ◆175 (4)
Minos bull cult ✤37
occupied by Saracens (827) ✤58●
palace-based societies (c.2000) ✤175
potter's wheel introduced (c.1900) ✤175

crime Global organization of ✤113, ✤113 (4)

Crimea Conquered and annexed by Russia (1783) ✤86●

Crimean War (1853–56). War fought by France, Britain, and Turkey against Russia. The origins of the war lay in Russia's claim to be the protector of all Greek Christians in the Turkish Empire and from British and French distrust of Russia's ambitions in the Black Sea area, which posed a threat to their overland routes to India. Following a series of battles fought in the Crimean peninsula and a prolonged siege of the Russian fortress at Sebastapol, the Russians withdrew their forces from the peninsula. Peace negotiations at Paris checked Russian influence in southeast Europe. ✤203●, ◆203 (5)

Cristoforo Colombo see Christopher Columbus

Cromford Textile town ✤93, ✤93 (5)

cromlechs see megaliths

Cromwell, Oliver (1599–1658) English soldier and statesman. A sincere Puritan, he was an effective leader of the anti-royalist forces in the English Civil War. After the battle of Naseby (1645) he led the demand for the execution of Charles I. After the king's execution, he quelled the royalists in Scotland and Ireland. In 1653 he dissolved the "Rump" Parliament and established the Protectorate, which he ruled as Lord Protector (1653–58). □196

Crusades Series of campaigns by western European armies to recapture the Holy Land from the Muslims. The success of the First Crusade in 1099 led to the foundation of the Kingdom of Jerusalem and other "Latin" (i.e. western European, not Greek) states. Subsequent expeditions to defend these territories or reconquer land lost to the Muslims were less successful. The name crusade was given to campaigns in other parts of Europe, notably Spain and the Baltic.
the age of the Crusades ✤64–5, ◆64–5 (1)
major Crusades ✤64
capture of Antioch (1098) □63
Constantinople captured (1204) ✤66●
crusading ideal in Europe (1100–1300)
✤186, ✤186●, ◆186 (1)
Islam and Christianity (c.1090) ✤65 (1)
Latin states in the Holy Land ✤65 (3)
Lisbon taken from Moors ✤62●
medieval mapping ◆219 (3)
Saladin recaptures Jerusalem (1187) ✤63●, ✤64●, ✤228●
states in the Mediterranean ✤63, ◆187 (5)
Venice and the Latin Empire ✤187, ✤187●

Ctesiphon
Parthian capital (90 BCE) ✤43●, ✤224
sacked by Romans (c.114) ✤47
Sassanian capital (637) ✤55●, ✤225, ✤225●

Cuba
Columbus lands (1492) ✤74●, ✤80●
Fidel Castro leader (1959) ✤106●
last slave ship (1867) ✤85●
preferential trade ends (1991–92) ✤110●
Revolution ◆89 (3), ✤152
role in Angolan civil war ✤109, ◆109 (5)
Spanish-American War (1898) ✤94●, ✤133, ✤133 (5)
US tightens blockade (1991–92) ✤110●

Cuban Missile Crisis (1961–62). Major Cold War confrontation between the US and the Soviet Union over the siting of Soviet ballistic missile launching sites in Cuba. ✤106●, ✤108, ✤138●, ✤139, ◆108 (2), ◆139 (5)

Cúcuta ✕ of wars of S. American independence in Colombia (Feb 1813). ◆150 (1)

Cucuteni-Tripolye Villages (c.4000 BCE) ✤174

Key to index: ✦ text   ❏ picture   var. variant name   f/n full name   r. ruled   WW I World War I
● timeline   ◆ map   aka also known as   prev. previously known as   ⚔ battle   WW II World War II

Habuba Kabira Trading post (c.3100 BCE) ✛24●

Habyarimana Juvénal (1937–94) President of Rwanda (r.1973–94) ✛169

Hadrian (*var.* Publius Aelius Hadrianus) (76–138). Roman Emperor (r.117–138), under whom the Roman Empire consolidated its defenses and enjoyed a period of peace and prosperity. Hadrian traveled extensively around the empire, not as a soldier, but as an administrator and connoisseur of the arts. He commissioned many new buildings, notably in Athens and Rome, and new cities, such as Aelia Capitolina, built on the ruins of Jerusalem. ✛180●, ◆180 (1)

Hadrian's Wall 117-km-long wall built by emperor Hadrian (r.117–38 CE) to consolidate the northern frontier of the Roman Empire. Constructed between 122–28 CE, it straddles northern England from the Solway Firth to the Tyne River, and was defended by 16 forts, 80 milecastles, and numerous signal turrets and stretches of ditch. Despite attacks by northern tribes it survived until c.400 CE. 46●, ✛180●, ◆180 (1)

Hafsid dynasty Berber dynasty of the 13th–16th century in Ifriqiyah (Tunisia and eastern Algeria), founded by the Almohad governor Abu Zakriyya' Yahya about 1229. ✛163●, ◆162–3 (1)

Hagia Sofia *see* Santa Sofia.

Haile Selassie I (1892–1975) (r.1930–74) Emperor of Ethiopia, formerly Prince Ras Tafari. Driven out of Ethiopia by the Italian occupation of 1936–41, but led the reconquest, helped by Britain, and began to modernize Ethiopia. A revolution provoked by famine in 1974 deposed him and he died under house arrest. He is still revered by certain groups, notably the Rastafarians. ✛169●

Haiti
   independent state (1804) ✛85●
   slave revolt (1791) ✛85●, ◆89, ✛89 (3)
   US invasion ✛133●

Haj (*var.* Hajj). Pilgrimage to Mecca. Every adult Muslim is required to make the journey to the Islamic holy city of Mecca in Saudi Arabia at least once in his or her lifetime. The object of the pilgrimage is the Kaaba, the sacred shrine of Islam containing the "black stone" in the middle of the great mosque.
   pilgrim routes to Mecca ◆218 (2)

Hajj *see* Haj

Hakataya culture *see* Patayan culture

Haldingham and Lafford 13th-century English mapmakers. ✛173●

Hallstatt Iron Age (800 BCE) ✛31

Hamah Syria, water wheel ❑57

Hammurabi Babylonian king (1790–1750 BCE) ❑32

Han dynasty Ruling dynasty of China, successors to the Qin. The Former or Western Han (206 BCE–9 CE), with their capital at Chang'an, greatly expanded Chinese realms under emperor Wudi (140–87 BCE) The Later, or Eastern Han (25–220 CE), made their capital at Luoyang, during which Buddhism was introduced, and extended their domains into Central Asia; but their empire eventually collapsed under pressure from northern peoples. ✛46, ✛260, ◆42–3, ◆260 (1)
   architecture ❑260
   bronze bridle ❑260
   collapses ✛47, ❑261
   commanderies ❑260
   dynasty ✛260●
   tomb pottery ❑260
   trade links ◆44–5

Han Empire *see* Han dynasty.

Hangzhou Song capital (1130) ✛63●

Hannibal (247–183 BCE). Carthaginian general who, in 218, invaded Roman Italy by marching his army (including elephants and cavalry) over the Alps. His initial campaigns were all successful, but he became pinned down in the south of Italy. He was eventually summoned to return to Africa, where he was defeated at Zama in 202. Hannibal fled to the court of Antiochus III, the Seleucid king of Syria. ✛179, ✛179●

Hanseatic League Trading association of north German and Baltic towns, which flourished between the13th and 15th centuries. Important members of the league included Lübeck, Cologne, Danzig, and Brunswick.
   trade routes (c.1300) ◆190, ◆190–1 (1), ✛189, ◆189 (3)

Hapsburg dynasty *see* Habsburg dynasty

Harald Hardrada (*var.* Haardraade) (1015–66) King of Norway. After fleeing Norway as a young man, he commanded the Varangian Guard in Constantinople, where he won a reputation as a fearsome warrior (Hardrada meant ruthless). On his return home, he first shared the

kingdom with his nephew, then became sole ruler in 1048. In 1066, he claimed the throne of England but was defeated by Harold Godwinson, and killed at the battle of Stamford Bridge. ✛186, ◆186 (2)

Harappan culture The first urban communities of the Indian subcontinent developed c.2500 BCE in the Indus plain, with two major cities at Harappa and Mohenjo-Daro. Over 100 urban settlements are known, most of them major towns of baked brick buildings, dominated by citadels containing religious and ceremonial buildings. The Harappan cities had extensive trade links, reaching as far as southern Mesopotamia. The urban civilization ended c.2000 BCE; the reasons for its demise could be connected to Aryan invasion, or to changed environmental conditions disrupting Indus agriculture.
   BCE burials ✛19
   culture ✛23, ❑240, ◆240●, ❑240, ◆240 (1) (2)
   irrigation techniques (BCE) ✛23●
   pictograph writing ❑23
   trade (c.2500 BCE) ✛24●
   trading links (BCE) ◆24●, ✛25
   two-wheeled bullock cart ❑22
   urban civilization ✛23

Harding, Warren Gamaliel (1865–1923) 29th president of the US (Republican, 1921–23). On his election, Harding promised a return to normal life after WW I. His administration oversaw the completion of peace treaties with Germany, Austria, and Hungary. However, the exposure of serious corruption by his cabinet colleagues in 1923 (which became the so-called "Teapot Dome" scandal) is thought to have contributed to his death. ✛134●

Hargreaves, James (c.1720–78). English inventor of the spinning jenny (c. 1764), the first practical application of multiple spinning by a machine, one of the major innovations of the Industrial Revolution. ◆204●

Harlem race riots (1940s) ✛135●

Harold II (*var.* Harold Godwinson) (c.1022–66). *See* William I

Harris, Richard T. 19th-century explorer of Alaska.
   first gold strike in Alaska (1880) ✛93

Harrison, John (1693–1776). British clockmaker who made a clock accurate and reliable enough to be used to calculate longitude. ✛86

Harrison, William Henry See main entries.

Hastings ✕ of Norman invasion of England (1066). Victory of William, Duke of Normandy, over Harold, King of England. ✛62●, ✛186 (2)

Hastings, Warren (1732–1818). First governor-general of India (1774–85). He instituted reforms in the system of revenue collection and civil courts. He was impeached on corruption charges, but finally acquitted in 1795. ❑248

Hatshepsut (*aka* Hatshopitu) (r.1472–1458 BCE). Pharaoh of Egypt.
   Deir el-Bahari temple ❑159
   Egyptian ruler ❑158

Hattin ✕ of the Crusades (1187). Saladin defeats Christians of the Crusader States. ✛64●

Hattushash
   Hittite fortified citadel ✛27
   plan of city ✛28, ◆28 (3)

Hausa city-states ✛163●

Hausaland Usman dan Fodio's *jihad* (1804) ✛167

Havana destruction of the USS Maine ❑133

Hawaii
   annexed by US ✛284●
   settled by Polynesians ✛55, ✛60
   surfing ❑284
   united by Kamehameha I (1810) ✛91

Hawkins, Sir John (1532–95). English admiral who made three voyages to the New World (1562, 1564, and 1567), during which he made piratical attacks on Portuguese slavers, and forced the Spanish colonies to trade with him. From 1573 he became the principal administrative officer of the English navy. In 1588 he served as rearadmiral against the Spanish Armada and was knighted. He died, on an expedition with Sir Francis Drake, off the coast of Puerto Rico in 1595. ◆85 (2)

Hebrews ✛31
   See also Jews

Hedeby Viking coin (9th century) ❑60

Hedin, Sven Anders von (1865–1952). Swedish explorer and geographer of uncharted regions of Central Asia, Tibet, and China. ◆257 (3)

hegemony Leadership, or more specifically dominance, of one social group over another.

Hegira (*var.* Hijra). Muhammad's flight from Mecca to Medina (622) ✛55●

Heian Period (794–1185) Period of Japanese history that began with

the transfer of the capital to Heian-kyo. ✛265●

Heijn, Piet *see* Heyn, Piet

Hejaz Mountainous plateau in western Saudi Arabia covering an area of some 388,500 sq km. It contains the holy cities of Islam, Mecca and Medina. ◆227 (4)

Hellenic age
   cities of W. Asia ◆40
   culture ✛37
   empires and kingdoms ✛41●, ◆41 (2)
   outpost in the East ✛41, ❑41

henge Ritual monument, normally a circular space defined by an earthen bank with one or more entrances, with an internal ditch providing a symbolic separation between activities inside and outside the henge. Henges are sometimes further defined by arrangements of standing stones or menhirs, often precisely located along astronomical alignments. ✛22, ❑22, ✛174●

Hennepin, Father Louis (1640–c.1701) Belgian explorer. Sailed to Canada in 1675 as a Franciscan missionary. Explored the upper course of the Mississippi River with the Frenchman La Salle, but did not, as he claimed in a memoir of his travels, discover the river's mouth. ◆119 (2)

Henry II (1133–89) King of England (r.1154–89). French-born, he inherited the Duchy of Normandy from his mother and became Duke of Anjou on the death of his father, gaining Poitou and Guyenne on his marriage to Eleanor of Aquitaine. When he succeeded Stephen in 1154, he added England to his possessions. He extended the judicial and administrative power of the crown, but clashed with Thomas á Becket over his attempts to restrict church authority, and later with members of his own family. ✛187, ❑187, ◆187 (4)
   See also Angevin Empire

Henry V (1387–1422) King of England (r.1413–22). A skillful military leader, in 1415 he invaded France and defeated the French at Agincourt. By 1419 he had conquered Normandy, and was recognized as heir to the French throne. ◆192 (2)

Henry VIII (1491–1547) King of England (r.1509–1547). The Pope's refusal to allow his marriage to his first wife, Catherine of Aragon, because of her failure to produce male heirs, led to England's break with the Roman Catholic Church, and to Henry becoming supreme head of the Church in England. The dissolution of the monasteries followed. In 1536 he executed his second wife, Anne Boleyn, for infidelity. Successive marriages were to Jane Seymour (died), Anne of Cleves (divorced), Catherine Howard (beheaded), and Catherine Parr (survived after Henry's death).
   Act of Supremacy (1534) ✛78●
   breaks with Rome (1534) ✛78●
   embraced Protestant religion ✛194

Henry II (1519–59) King of France (r.1547–59). His marriage to Catherine de Médicis produced three future kings of France. Dominated by his mistresses, Diane de Poitiers and Anne de Montmorency. Through the influence of the de Guise family he formed an alliance with Scotland, and declared war on England, which ended with the seizure of Calais in 1558. Continued wars against Emperor Charles V and Spain. ✛194, ✛194●

Henry IV (1050–1106). German Emperor (son of Henry III), who inherited the kingdoms of Germany, Italy, and Burgundy in 1056 under his mother's regency. His conflict with Pope Gregory VII over the investiture question led to his excommunication in 1075; in 1077, his public abasement at Canossa restored him to the Church. He appointed Clement III as anti-Pope in 1084 and was crowned emperor. Repeated conflict with the German nobles, eventually led by his younger son (Henry V), led to his forced abdication in 1105. ✛62●

Henry I (*aka* Henry the Fowler) King of Saxony (r.919–936). Henry was elected King of Germany, which he transformed into a viable state. His imperial ambitions were realized by his son Otto. ✛58, ✛185●

Henry the Navigator (*aka* Henry of Portugal) Founded school of navigation (1416). ✛156●

Hepthalites *see* Huns

Heracles (*var. Lat.* Hercules). Most popular demigod of Greek pantheon, noted for his immense strength. ✛37, ❑37

Hijra *see* Hegira

hillforts Earthwork monuments located on hilltops or high ground and comprising a central occupation area accessed through often complex "gates" through the

610, he defeated the Persian armies that were threatening his empire, and victory in the Tigris plain in 627 forced the Persians to make peace. In 629 Arab armies made their first incursion into Syria and, by 637, they had occupied Syria, Palestine, and Egypt. Heraclius was ill and did little to confront the new threat. ✛55●

Herbert, Sir Thomas (1602–82) English traveler and author. In 1627 he embarked on a voyage to the Cape, Madagascar, Goa, and Surat, and made extensive journeys throughout Persia. He returned via Sri Lanka, the Coromandel coast, and St. Helena. His service to the king in the Civil War was rewarded with a baronetcy at the Restoration (1660). He described his journeys, which included an account of the ruins of Persepolis, in his *Description of the Persian Monarchy* (1634). ◆219 (3)

Hercules *see* Heracles

Hereford "T-in-O map" ❑173

Herjólfsson, Bjarni 10th-century Viking explorer, the first European to sight the New World. Icelandic sagas relate how, in c.985, Herjolfsson was blown off course from Greenland and sighted land to the west, the coast of Labrador. Some 15 years later, Leif Eriksson set sail from Greenland to investigate Herjolfsson's sightings. ◆118 (1)

Herod the Great (c.73–4 BCE). Herod's father served under Caesar in Egypt and appointed him ruler of Galilee. In 40 BCE Herod led the Roman army's expulsion of the Parthians from Jerusalem, became King of a Judea loyal to Rome. ◆43●

Herodotus (c.484–420 BCE) Greek historian, writer, and geographer, known as the "Father of History." He claimed to have made extensive journeys throughout the ancient world, but is best known for his history of the Persian Wars.
   African report (600 BCE) ✛156

heroin (*var.* Diacetylmorphine). Morphine derivative that makes up a large portion of the illicit traffic in narcotics. Morphine is an alkaloid found in opium, which is the dried milky exudate obtained from the unripe seedpods of the poppy plant. ◆113 (4)

Heyn, Piet (*var.* Heijn) (1577–1629) Dutch naval commander. As viceadmiral of the Dutch East India Company in 1624, he defeated the Spanish near San Salvador, Brazil, and in 1626 off Bahia. His 1626 capture of the Spanish silver fleet let to his appointment as Admiral of Holland in 1629. ◆85 (2)

Hezbollah (*var.* Hizbullah, Hizbollah, "Party of God"). The largest of the Shi'ite Islamic political groups in Lebanon. Under Iranian sponsorship, they have been associated with the kidnapping of Westerners and terrorist attacks to further their political aims, and have been in conflict with Israeli forces since Israel's invasion of Lebanon in 1982. ◆235 (4)

Hezhou siege (1258–59) ❑69

Hidalgo, Father Miguel y Costilla (1753–1811). Mexican priest, celebrated as beginning the revolution against Spain which resulted in Mexican independence. He led a force of 80,000 against the Spanish before turning back at Mexico City in 1811. He was later executed. ❑89

Hieraconpolis founded (c.3300) ✛24●, ✛69 (2)

hieratic writing ❑32
   See also writing

hieroglyphic Ancient system of writing using symbols or hieroglyphs, named from the Greek "sacred carving." They were originally pictographs, usually written right to left and giving three kinds of information: an object or concept in the real world; a consonant or sequence of consonants; or an explanation of an otherwise ambiguous associated symbol. The first evidence for hieroglyphs comes from c.3250 BCE and they continue in use into the late 3rd century CE. They mainly appear in religious and monumental contexts.
   Central American glyph ❑32
   Cretan ✛32●
   Egyptian ✛23●, ✛32, ✛32●, ✛32 (1), ◆223 (3)
   Harappa pictographs ❑23
   inscriptions ✛34
   Maya calendar ❑54
   Maya system ✛122
   pictographs (BCE) ✛23, ✛24●, ✛25, ✛32, ◆223, ❑25
   Rosetta stone ✛42
   tomb paintings ❑37

Hijra (*var.* Hijra) *see* Hegira

Ho Chi Minh (1890–1969). Vietnamese statesman. In 1930 Ho Chi Minh founded the Indochina Communist Party. He became the leader of the Viet Minh guerrillas and at the end of WW II

surrounding series of one or more banks and ditches. Built by Iron Age populations across western Europe, they acted as defensive centers when communities were under threat, and the scale of the earthworks was a declaration of the power and prestige of their builders. ✛174●

Himeji Japanese fortified castle ❑267

Hind, Henry, 19th-century surveyor of the western US.
   US surveys (1857–58) ◆119 (3)

Hindenburg Line (*var.* the Siegfried Line). German fortified line of defense (named for Field Marshal Hindenburg) on the Western Front during WW I, to which German forces retreated following their initial thrust into France. The line remained unbroken until 1918. ◆206 (2) (3)

Hinduism The dominant religion in India, it involves belief in destiny (Karma) and cycles of reincarnation (Samsara) and adherence to a particular moral law (Sharma). It is associated with a class system of social organization (caste) and includes ritual ceremonies, mystical contemplation, and self-denying practices. All-embracing in its forms, capable of including extreme polytheism and high monotheism, animal sacrifice and refusal to take any form of life. Unique among world religions in having no single founder, but has grown over a period of 4,000 years. The Vedas are accepted as the most sacred scriptures. ✛36, ◆43
   bronze deities ❑59, ❑241, ❑242
   establishment of cosmology ✛238, ❑48
   Puranic India ❑242, ◆242 (2)
   resurgence ✛243, ✛243●, ◆243 (4)
   spread (to 600 CE) ✛48●, ✛49 (4)
   statue of Surya ❑35
   trimurti ❑36

Hippalus 1st century CE Greek merchant who was the first westerner to recognize the regularity of the monsoon winds, harnessing them for his voyage through the Red Sea to the Indus from 14–37 CE. ◆218 (2)

Hipparchus (*var.* Hipparchos) (c.180–125 BCE). Greek astronomer and mathematician. He was the first to use latitude and longitude to define the position of places on the earth. ✛172

Hiroshima atom bombs dropped (1945) ✛103●, ◆105●

Hispaniola
   Columbus lands (1492) ✛74●
   slave revolt (1522) ✛85●

History, The (Herodotus) ✛218
   See Herodotus

Hitler, Adolf (1889–1945). German dictator. Following service in the trenches in WW I, he became a political agitator during the Weimar period, building support for his National Socialist (Nazi) party, based on extreme nationalism, anti-Communism, and racism. He became chancellor in 1933, rapidly disposing of parliamentary constraints, and establishing dictatorship (as *Führer*, through the Enabling Law of 1933). Hitler transformed the German economy by placing it on a war footing, and recovered pre-WW I territories, annexing Austria, and invading Poland (1939), to precipitate WW II. He adopted personal responsibility for the conduct of the war, and inaugurated the Final Solution against the Jews. He committed suicide as Soviet forces entered Berlin.
   annexation of Austria and Czechoslovakia ◆209 (5)
   becomes chancellor (1933) ✛102●, ◆209
   begins mass extermination of Jews (1942) ✛102●
   Nuremberg rally ❑102
   portrait ❑104
   World War II ◆210–11 (1)–(4)

Hittite Empire (*fl.*1450–1200 BCE). Indo-Europeans, who probably came from north of the Black Sea to settle in Anatolia and northern Syria, establishing their capital Hattushash near modern Boğazköy. After the indecisive battle of Kadesh against the Egyptians (c.1285 BCE) they established peace, but were overthrown c.1200.
   (1200 BCE) ✛31●
   (1250 BCE) ◆26–7
   conflict with Egypt ✛27
   gold figurine of a king (c.1400 BCE) ✛27●

Hizbollah *see* Hezbollah

Hizbullah *see* Hezbollah

Ho Chi Minh (1890–1969).

established a government in Hanoi. When the French tried to regain control of their former colony, he led the resistance that forced them to withdraw from the north. President of North Vietnam from 1954, he successfully countered American intervention in Vietnam in the 1960s. When the Vietnam War ended with the fall of Saigon in 1975, it was renamed Ho Chi Minh city in his honor.
   proclaims independent Vietnam (1945) ✛103●

Hobkirk's Hill ✕ of American Revolutionary War (Apr 25, 1781). American victory. ◆127 (3)

Hohenlinden ✕ of Napoleonic Wars – the War of the 2nd Coalition (1800). French victory forced Austrians to sue for peace.◆200 (1)

Hohenstaufen dynasty (*var.* Staufer dynasty). German dynasty that ruled the Holy Roman Empire from 1138 to 1208 and from 1212 to 1254.
   dynasty ✛188, ◆188 (1)
   and the papacy ◆188●

Hohokam Native American people of the US southwest.
   ✛58, ◆123, ✛123 (4)

Hojo Japanese family of warrior regents which dominated Japan in the 13th century, especially during the Mongol invasions of Japan in 1274 and 1281. ◆265 (5)

Hollywood
   annual consumer expenditure (1919–45) ❑135
   film industry (1919) ✛135, ❑135, ◆135 (4)

Holocaust Name given to persecution of the Europe's Jews by Nazi Germany from 1933–45, which led ultimately to the deaths of about six million Jews.
   cause of Jewish migration ✛234

Holy Land Latin states (1099–1229) ✛65, ◆65 (3)

Holy Roman Empire Complex of European territories under the rule of the Frankish or German king who bore the title of Roman emperor, founded by Charlemagne in 800. After Charlemagne, imperial power was at its greatest under the Hohenstaufens in the 12th–13th centuries. It was dissolved by Napoleon in 1806.
   800–1000 ◆185 (3)
   1100–1400 ◆189 (3), ✛189 (4)
   1200 ◆62–3, ◆187 (3)
   1300 ◆66–7
   1400 ◆70–1
   1500 ◆74–5
   1600 ◆78–9
   1700 ◆82–3
   1800 ◆86–7
   184–5, ✛185 (3)
   abolished (1806) ✛202●
   Baltic conflict (16th century) ✛195, ✛195●, ◆195 (3)
   conflict in Bohemia ✛192, ◆193 (4)
   Crusades (1096–1270) ◆64–5 (2), ✛186 (1)
   Dutch revolt (1568–1609) ✛195, ✛195●, ◆195 (5)
   population growth (1650–1800) ❑198
   Treaty of Westphalia ◆196 (1)

Homer (*var. Gk.* Homeros). 9th-century BCE Greek poet, credited with writing the greatest early Greek poems, including *The Iliad* and *The Odyssey*. His work formalized the long oral traditions of recounting the stories and legends of ancient Greece. ✛37

Homo Term used for creatures belonging to the same group as modern humans. The earliest known homo is *Homo habilis*, which evolved about 2.5 million years ago.
   ✛12–13, ❑13, ◆13 (2)

Homo erectus ("upright man," c.1.6 million to 300,000 years ago and in some regions perhaps to 50,000 years ago). Species found in many regions of Asia, thought to have evolved there from *Homo ergaster*. By 500,000 years ago they had mastered the use of fire. ✛12–13, ◆13 (2)

Homo ergaster (c.1.8 million ago to perhaps 200,000 years ago). Species that appeared in Africa, distinguished by large brain size, tall, long-legged physique, and tool-making skills, including the invention of the hand-ax. ✛12–13, ❑13, ◆13 (2)

Homo habilis ("handy man," c.2.5 to 1.6 million years ago), so called because of its stone toolmaking abilities. *H. habilis* was the earliest member of the genus *Homo*, with a brain capacity about half the size of modern humans', but about 50% larger than any known Australopithecine. ✛12–13, ❑13, ◆13 (2)

Homo heidelbergensis (c.800,000 to c.200,000 years ago). Species probably descended from *Homo ergaster*, the first human inhabitants of Europe, formerly confusingly known as archaic *Homo sapiens*. The earliest fossils,

J

exodus from Egypt (c.1200 BCE) ✣31●

formal expulsion from St. Petersburg ❏100

human cost of global war ✣105

mass extermination under the Nazis ✣102●, ✣211 (3)

migration (1880–1914) ✣101, ✣101●, ◆101 (2)

migration to Israel ◆234 (3)

settlement in New York ❏100

Jiang Jieshi (var. Chiang Kai-shek) (1887–1975). Chinese general and political leader. Leader of the Kuomintang from 1926, president of the republic 1928–31. Opposed the Chinese Communist Party until defeated in 1949 when he withdrew to Taiwan. ✣103●, ❏270–1

Jiang Qing see Cultural Revolution

jihad Holy war ✣56, ◆167, ◆235 (4)

Jin dynasty Chinese dynasty of the Sixteen Kingdoms period. ◆261 (3)

dynasty unifies China (280) ✣51●

Eastern dynasty moves to Nanjing ✣51

Jin dynasty (var. Chin dynasty) (r.1115–1234). Dynasty of northern China.

founded by the Jurchen ✣263

alliance with Song China ✣63 (c.1206) ◆68–9 (1)

capital city ✣69

conquered by Mongols ✣263, ◆263 (7)

first Mongol invasion (1211) ✣69●

Jin Empire see Jin dynasty

Jinghis Khan see Genghis Khan

Joan of Arc (var. Fr. Jeanne d'Arc, aka the Maid of Orleans, Fr. La Pucelle) (c.1412–31). French national heroine. Claiming to hear voices urging her to rid France of English domination, she led an army which raised the siege of Orleans (1429), enabling the dauphin to be crowned Charles VII at Rheims. Captured and sold to the English, she was convicted of heresy and burned at the stake. She was canonized in 1920. ❏192

campaigns ◆192 (2)

saves Orléans (1429) ✣75●, ◆192, ✣192●

João III (1502–57) King of Portugal (r.1521–57). His kingdom suffered, both socially and economically, because of his subservience to the clerical party. He tried to stimulate the colonization of the new Portuguese territory in Brazil by granting captaincies. ✣148

João V (1689–1750) King of Portugal (1707–50). A supporter of the Triple Alliance (between Britain, Austria, and the Netherlands), he embarked on a series of unsuccessful campaigns in Castile during the War of the Spanish Succession. Though his treasury benefited from the recent discovery of gold in Brazil, João V was entirely under the influence of the clergy and the administration suffered from his neglect. ❏88

John (1167–1216) King of England (r.1199–1216). His reign saw the renewal of war with Philip II Augustus of France, to whom he had lost several continental possessions. Tensions between John and Pope Innocent III led to the imposition of an interdict over England in 1208 and the king's excommunication in 1212. He was also forced to grant the Magna Carta at Runnymede. ◆66●

Johnson, Lyndon Baines (1908–73) 36th president of the US (Democrat, 1963–68). Became president following the assassination of John F. Kennedy in 1963. His administration passed the Civil Rights Act (1964), the Voting Rights Act (1965), aimed at improving the position of African Americans, and introduced a series of economic and social reforms under the slogan "Great Society," but his personal standing was severely weakened by public protests against the escalation of the Vietnam War.

Democrat President ✣139

Civil Rights legislation ✣139

Jolliet, Father Louis (1645–1700). Explorer of N. America. Born in Canada, Jolliet discovered the source of the Mississippi River with Jacques Marquette. In 1672–73 they traveled along the river to within 640 km of the Gulf of Mexico. ◆119 (2)

Jolson, Al (prev. Asa Yoelson) (1886–1950) Russian-born American actor and singer. He toured with various stage and minstrel shows, making his Broadway debut in 1911. In 1927, he made screen history when he starred in the first full-length "talkie," *The Jazz Singer*. In 1928, his first big record hit "Sonny boy/there's a rainbow round my shoulder" sold over three million copies. ✣135●

Jomon culture Hunters, fishers, and gatherers who lived in Japan from c.7500 to 250 BCE. They fully exploited an abundance of fish,

---

animal, and plant resources and, in the densely populated east, lived in permanent villages, but there is no evidence of plant cultivation. Jomon pottery dates back to c.10,000 BCE, the earliest known anywhere in the world. The culture is named from the cord-decorated pottery found at the Omori shell mounds near Tokyo. ✣19

Jordan Six Day War (1967) ◆107●

Juan Carlos I (1938–) King of Spain (r.1978–). The grandson of Alfonso XIII (who abdicated in 1931), he was named successor to the dictator, General Franco in 1969, and proclaimed king in 1975. Juan Carlos presided over a rapid, and peaceful, transition to democracy; by 1978 Spain was declared a parliamentary monarchy. In 1981 King Juan Carlos foiled a Francoist military coup by taking preventative action and winning pledges of loyalty from military commanders. ◆110●

Juan-juan see Ruanruan

Juárez, Benito (Pablo) (1806–72) Mexican statesman (r.1861–72). As part of the Liberal government which replaced the Conservative Santa Anna, Juárez helped pass the anticlerical and liberal constitution of 1857. In 1861 he assumed the role of president of Mexico, a post he held until his death. A French invasion under Maximilian forced him to retreat to the north, but after the French were defeated in 1867 he was able to restore Republican rule.

◆128–129 (2), ◆129

Judaism Religion of the Jewish people, developed among the ancient Hebrews and characterized by a belief in one God, its ethical system and its ritual practices are based on the Pentateuch as interpreted by the rabbis of the Talmudic period in the first five centuries CE and their successors up to the present day.

candelabra ❏37

origins ◆36–7

spread of (600 BCE) ◆48 (1)

Jugurtha (160–104 BCE) King of Numidia (r.118–105 BCE). Struggled to free his N. African kingdom from Roman rule. ◆43●

Julio-Claudian dynasty The four successors of the Roman Emperor Augustus (r.31 BCE–14 CE), all indirectly descended from Julius Caesar. The Emperor Augustus, who had extended the frontiers of the empire and introduced stable and efficient government, was succeeded by Tiberius (14–37 CE), the most able of the dynasty. Caligula (37–41 CE) was famous for his excesses and capricious behavior. He was succeeded by Claudius (41–54 CE), who devoted himself to public works and administrative reforms, although he never gained the respect of his subjects. The tyrannical Nero (54–68) was notorious for his ruthless murders, and the revenge he took on the Christians for the great fire of Rome (64 CE) which, it was rumored, he had started himself. ◆46●

Julius Caesar see Caesar, Gaius Julius

Juneau, Joe 19th-century French explorer of Alaska. Founded town of Juneau.

finds gold in Alaska (1880) ✣93, ◆93 (3)

Jupiter (var. Gr. Zeus). Most powerful god in the Greco-Roman pantheon. ✣37

Jurchen People originating in the mountains of eastern Manchuria, Central Asia. Established the Jin state and seized northern China in 1126, restricting Song rule to the south of China. ✣263, ◆263 (5)

See also Jin dynasty

Justinian I (483–565) Byzantine Emperor. Born in what is now Yugoslavia, he was adopted by his uncle Justin I, who ascended the throne in 518, and succeeded him in 527. He is famous for his reforms of the Roman law codes and imperial constitutions, and the publication of the Codex Justinianus (534). His program of costly public works included the building of the church of Hagia Sophia in Constantinople. He engaged in major campaigns against the Vandals in Spain and North Africa and the Goths in Italy, but his victories proved fragile. ❏54

reconquests ◆182, ◆182 (1)

Jutes Germanic people who, with the Angles and Saxons, invaded Britain in the 5th century CE. ◆183, ◆52–3 (1)

Jutland Naval ⚔ of WW I (May 31, 1916) between the British and German fleets in the North Sea. Though the result was inconclusive, the Allies thereafter retained control of the North Sea. ◆206●

K

K'ang-hsi see Kangxi

Kabul Captured by Taliban (1996) ✣111●

Kadesh ⚔ between the Egyptians and Hittites (c.1285 BCE). First recorded battle in world history. ✣27●, ◆221, ◆221 (5)

Kadphises I (var. Kujula Kadphises, Chiu-Chiu-Chueh) Kushan ruler who achieved political unity of the Yuezhi tribes in the 1st century CE, and ruled over northern India, Afghanistan, and parts of central Asia. ✣47

Kaifeng

captured by Mongols (1233) ✣67●, ◆68–9 (1)

scroll depicting 12th-century street life ❏63

Song capital ◆263, ◆263 (7)

Kairouan Great Mosque ❏56

Kalahari Desert Environmental survival strategies (BCE) 16

Kalewa ⚔ of WW II (May 1942). Marked furthest point of Japanese advance in Burma. ◆104 (2)

Kalhotia Mesolithic painting ❏14

Kali Important goddess in Hinduism, associated with death, disease, and destruction. ❏48

Kalidasa 4th-century Indian poet and playwright. ✣51●

Kalmar, Union of (Jun 1397). Scandinavian union that brought the kingdoms of Norway, Sweden, and Denmark together under a single monarch until 1523. ◆70●, ◆195, ✣70–1, ✣74–5, ◆195 (3)

Kalmyks Buddhist Mongolian people of Central Asia who came under pressure from Qing China 1758–59. ✣268●, ◆268 (2)

Kamakura Shogunate (1185–1333) Military rulers of Japan. ✣71, ✣265, ✣265●

Kambujadesha The Khmer state of Kambujadesha, founded by Devaraya II in 802, controlled most of S.E. Asia for the next four centuries from the magnificent city of Angkor in southern Cambodia. Although Hinduism was the state religion, it combined many elements of Buddhism, as can be seen in the magnificent monumental architecture of Angkor, which reached its zenith under the rule of Jayavarman VII (c.1200). ◆245●, ◆245 (5)

Kamehameha I (1782–1819). The king of one of the four kingdoms of Hawaii who, with superior vessels and firearms, as well as foreign aid, succeeded in conquering all the islands, with the exception of Kauai and Niihau, by 1795. He reorganized government, encouraged industry, while withstanding foreign cultural influence and adhering to traditional Hawaiian religious practices (abolished after his death by his favorite queen, Kaahumanu). ✣91●

kami The combined forces of nature and ancestral spirits, central to Shinto religious observance. ❏264

kamikaze Japanese term for "divine wind," a typhoon which halted second Mongol invasion attempt (1281); adopted as name by Japanese suicide fighter-bomber squadrons during final campaigns of WW II. ✣273, ❏273

Kaminaljuyú (fl. 500 BCE) Central American civilization ❏121

Kanab Desert US Geological Survey sketch (1880) ❏119

Kandahar see Gandhara

Kanem-Bornu W. African kingdom ✣58

See also Bornu

Kangxi (var. K'ang-hsi) (1654–1722) Emperor of the Manchu (Qing) dynasty of China (r.1661–1722). ✣83●, ❏268

Kanishka (var. Kaniska) (r.c.78–96 CE). Ruler of the Kushan, or Kushana, Empire of south central Asia whose adoption of (Mahayana) Buddhism was instrumental in the spread of the faith to Central Asia and along the Silk Road to China. ✣47●, ◆48

Kansas-Nebraska Act (1854). The third of the critical decisions regarding the extension of slavery in the US, the Kansas-Nebraska Act applied the principle of popular sovereignty to the territorial organization of Kansas and Nebraska. The passage of the act led to the formation of the Republican Party to oppose the expansion of slavery into new territories. ❏130, ❏130 (3)

Kao Tsu see Gao Zhu

Kara Khitai Muslim empire in central Asia which rose to prominence in the 12th century. In 1141 the Kara Khitai defeated the Seljuk Turks at Samarkand. ◆68–9 (1) (2)

Karakorum ◆68–9 (1)

Mongol capital built (1235) ✣68●

slave trade center (13th century) ✣85

Karius, Charles 20th-century British explorer of New Guinea (1927–28). ◆279 (2)

Karlowitz, Peace of (var. Carlowitz) (1699). Peace settlement that ended hostilities (1683–99) between the Ottoman Empire and the Holy League (Austria, Poland, Venice, and Russia) which significantly diminished Turkish influence in east-central Europe, making Austria the dominant power there. ◆197●, ◆197 (4)

Kashmir

Indian-Pakistan war (1965) 107● and Jammu ◆252, ◆252 (2)

refugees ❏252

Kassapa (447–495). Ruler of Sigiriya in Sri Lanka, who usurped power and believed he was a god-king.

god-king of Sigiriya ✣51●

palace, two heavenly maidens (5th century) ❏51

Katanga Secedes from Congo (1960) ✣107●

Kay, John Inventor of flying shuttle (1733) ◆204●

Kazakhs People of Central Asia. Traditionally pastoral nomads; incorporated into the Russian Empire in the mid-19th century, now mainly settled in Kazakhstan. ◆89 (3), ◆267 (3)

Kebara Neanderthal burial site ❏12

Kemal Pasha, Mustafa see Atatürk

Kennedy, Edmund (1818–48). Born in the Channel Islands, he migrated to New South Wales in 1840. Trained as a surveyor, he joined Sir Thomas Mitchell's expedition into central Queensland in 1847. In 1848 he led an expedition up the eastern coast of Queensland to Cape York. During the course of the arduous journey all his party perished – Kennedy was speared by Aborigines while within sight of his supply ship. ◆279 (2)

Kennedy, John Fitzgerald (1917–1963) 35th president of the US (Democrat, 1960–63). Following service in US navy during WW II, became the youngest elected US president at the age of 43. He aimed to introduce legislation for the improvement of civil rights and for the extension of funding for healthcare and education. Foreign policy issues included the unsuccessful invasion of the Bay of Pigs in Cuba, the Cuban Missile Crisis which brought the world to the brink of nuclear war, and the continuing involvement of the US in Vietnam. He was assassinated in Dallas, Texas, on Nov 22, 1963. ✣139●, ❏108

Kennesaw Mountain ⚔ of American Civil War (Jun 27, 1864). Confederate victory. ✣131 (7)

Kent King converted to Christianity (597) ✣54●

Kenya 167–169

British penetration in 19th century ◆167 (3)

independence ◆168 (1)

terrorist bombing (1998) ✣235●

Kermario Stone alignments (c.3000 BCE). ❏174

Khanbaliq (var. Beijing, Cambaluc). founded by Kublai Khan (1266) ✣68●

Italian map (15th century) ❏69

Khedive of Egypt The title, granted by the Sultan of Turkey in 1867, to his viceroy in Egypt, Ismail. "Khedive" is a Persian word meaning prince, or sovereign. The title was abandoned in 1914 when the title "Sultan" was adopted. ✣232

Khitans (var. Liao) (907–1125). People of Mongolia who established the Liao Empire in Manchuria in the 10th century. ✣263, ◆263 (3) (4)

Khmer Rouge A Marxist party in Cambodia, led by Pol Pot, organized to oppose the right-wing government of Lon Nol, 1970–75. They overthrew the government in 1975 and instituted a reign of terror which led to the death of over two million Cambodians. They were overthrown in 1979 following a Vietnamese invasion. ✣253●, ◆253 (4), ❏253

Khmer state ✣245, ✣245●, ◆245 (5)

temple carvings ❏63

See also Kambujadesha

Khomeini, Ayatollah Ruhollah (1900–1989). Iranian religious and political leader. A Shi'ite Muslim whose bitter opposition to the pro-Western regime of Muhammad Reza Shah Pahlavi led to his exile from Iran in 1964. Following a popular revolution and the overthrow of the Shah's government in 1979, he returned to Iran and was proclaimed religious leader of the Islamic Revolution. Islamic law was once more imposed, and a return to strict fundamentalist Islamic tradition enforced. ❏235

Khosrau I (var. Khosrow I, aka Khosrau the Just) (r.531–579). Sassanian Persian Shah who quelled the Mazdakite rebellion and successfully resisted the Byzantines. ✣55, ◆225

Khosrau II (var. Khosrow II, aka Khosrau the Victorious) (r.591–628). Persian Shah at the apogee of the Sassanian era. In 601 he attacked Byzantium, capturing Antioch, Jerusalem, and Alexandria. ◆225

Khrushchev, Nikita Sergeyevich (1894–1971) Soviet statesman and successor to Stalin. First Secretary of the Communist Party (1953–64). Deposed in a coup and replaced by Leonid Brezhnev. ❏108

Khufu (c.2575–2465 BCE) Egyptian pharaoh of the 4th dynasty who initiated the building of the largest pyramid at Giza: 147 m high, consisting of c.2.3 million blocks, each weighing c.2.5 tons. ❏51

Khwarizm Empire (aka Empire of the Khwarizm Shah, Uzbek Empire) State of Turkic origin, broadly corresponding with ancient Chorasmia, N. Persia, based around Samarkand from the 12th century. Overrun by Mongols, then forming part of Khanate of the Golden Horde, and subsequently conquered by Timur (1378), the state fragmented into a number of Muslim khanates based around Bukhara and Samarkand which were finally absorbed into the Russian Empire during the 19th century.

(1219) ◆66–7

(c.1206–19) ◆68–9 (1)

invaded by Mongols (1219) ✣67●, ✣69●

Kibi Ancient people of southern Honshu, Japan. ◆264

Kiev ⚔ of WW II (Sep–Nov 1943) Soviet forces defeat German counteroffensive in Ukraine. ◆105 (3), ◆211 (4)

Kiev

captured by Vikings ✣185

Russian capital ◆58●

Kievan Rus State established in 840 by Vikings from Sweden who were trading along the rivers between the Baltic and the Black seas. Kiev became a flourishing capital; through trading links with Byzantium the Christian faith became established there at the end of the 10th century. Repeated sackings by nomads from the east reduced Kiev to a number of independent and warring principalities from the middle of the 11th century. ✣185, ✣185 (3), ◆189 (3)

possessions ◆58–9

founded by Varangians ◆60

Kilwa

building program ✣163●

coastal trading colony (c.800) ✣58

Kimberley South Africa, gold finds (1867) ◆93●

King, Clarence (1842–1901). American explorer and geologist. In 1867, as director in charge of the United States Geological Exploration of the Fortieth Parallel he began an extensive ten-year survey of a 100-mile-wide strip of land running from Cheyenne, Wyoming, to the eastern Sierra Nevada. ◆119 (3)

King, Martin Luther (1929–1968) US civil rights leader. A baptist minister in Alabama, Martin Luther King Jr. founded the Southern Christian Leadership Conference in 1957 to coordinate activities for the promotion of black civil rights throughout the US. He advocated a policy of nonviolence and passive resistance which undoubtedly helped the passage of the Civil Rights Act of 1964 and the Voting Rights Act of 1965. He was awarded the Kennedy Peace Prize and the Nobel Prize. In 1968 he was assassinated in Memphis, Tennessee. The third Monday in January is now celebrated as Martin Luther King Day in the US.

assassination (1968) ✣137●

heads protest movement (1957) ✣137●

portrait ❏136

Washington march (1963) ✣137●

King Movement A Maori king movement of the late 1850s that opposed land sales to European settlers and demanded a Maori state. It was led by chief "King" Te Wherowhero. ◆283●

King Philip's War (1675–76) Conflict between English colonists and Native Americans in New England following the rapid expansion of European settlement into Native American territory from 1640 onward. The conflict involved most of the tribes of New England, including the Wapanoag and the Narragansett, and may have led to the loss of perhaps 600 settlers and 3,000 Indians. The Indians thereafter fled north and west. ✣126, ◆126 (1)

King's Mountain ⚔ of American Revolutionary War, Oct 7, 1780. American victory. ◆127 (3)

Kingsley, Mary (1862–1900). English traveler who journeyed through western and equatorial Africa and became the first European to enter parts of present-day Gabon. ◆157 (4)

Kisesse Decorated caves (29,000 BP) ◆17●

Klerk, F.W. de (fln Frederik Willem de Klerk) (1936–). Politician who, as president of South Africa (1989–94), brought the apartheid system of racial segregation to an end. Both he and Nelson Mandela jointly received the Nobel Peace Prize in 1993, in recognition of their efforts to establish nonracial democracy in South Africa.

begins dismantling of apartheid (1990) ◆169●

Klondike Gold rush ✣93, ✣93 (3)

Knights Hospitaller (var. Knights of St. John). Military/religious order established in Jerusalem during the early 12th century following the success of the First Crusade. Its purpose was to care for pilgrims to the Holy Land, but the Knights also played an important role in the defense of the Crusader states. In 1310, the Hospitallers took Rhodes, which remained their base until 1522, when it was taken by the Ottomans. They were then granted the island of Malta by Charles V. ✣186, ◆189 (3)

conquer Rhodes (1306–10) ✣186●

fall of Rhodes to Ottomans ◆231 (3)

military order (c.1130) ✣64●, ❏186●

Knights of St. John see Knights Hospitallers

Knights Templar Military/religious order founded c.1118 to protect pilgrim routes to Jerusalem. In the 12th and 13th centuries, knights of the order fought in all the major campaigns against Islam. They acquired estates all over Christian Europe, but their wealth and influence made them enemies. In 1307, Philip IV of France had the order accused of heresy and other crimes, and it was suppressed in 1312.

Order founded (c.1118) ✣64●, ❏186●

European political force ❏186

Order suppressed (1312) ◆70●

Templar houses ✣186 (1)

Knossos Bronze Age city on Crete, a focus of the Minoan civilization, and known for the artistic and architectural brilliance of its palace, built c.2000 BCE, which dominated the city's mansions, houses, and paved roads. Knossos flourished for some 1,500 years, despite its palace being destroyed several times (once by the eruption of Thera), and invasion by the Mycenaeans c.1450. It was finally destroyed by the Romans 66–67 BCE. See Minoan civilization.

Knut see Canute

Koguryo North Korean ruling clan destroyed by the Tang in 668. See also Korea.

controls Korea (c.220) ✣47●

establishes Pohai empire ✣264

Kök Türk (Blue Turk) Empire (551–72) ✣54–5●

Konbaung dynasty Founded (1752) in Burma. ◆87●

Kongo

Kingdom formed (c.1390) ✣71●, ✣163●

outbreak of civil war (1665) ✣164●

Portuguese attempt colonization ✣82

Kongzi see Confucius

Königsberg ⚔ of WW II (Feb–Apr 1945). Prolonged siege of German forces by Soviet troops. ◆105, ◆211 (4)

Koran (var. Qu'ran). The holy book of Islam. ✣226, ❏56, ❏67, ❏167 See also Islam.

Korea Peninsula of E. Asia, frequently under Chinese and Japanese influence and control; early states included Koguryo (c.150–668 CE), Paekche (c.250–663 CE), and Silla (from 313 CE). Silla Period (676–935). Koryo Period (936–1392). I (or Li) dynasty, capital at Kyongsang, ruled often as Ming or Qing vassals (1392–1910). Annexed to Japan 1910–1945. Partitioned into independent states of N. and S. Korea (1948).

agriculture (BCE) ✣23●, ✣31, ✣258

dynasties

Buddhist ✣59

Yi (1392) ✣71●

home affairs

annexed by Japan (1910) ◆99●

BCE subsistence ✣19●

controlled by native states (c.200) ✣47●

first empires ◆264 (2)

Ludwig, Daniel Keith (1897–1992). American entrepreneur who began a billion-dollar development of the Jari River valley in Brazil, but in 1982 he abandoned the costly project, which had led to the destruction of large tracts of tropical rain forest. ✤153●

Luoyang
conquered by Qin (256 BCE) ✤39
northern Wei capital (c.490) ✤51●

Luther, Martin (1483–1546). German scholar and priest whose questioning of certain church practices led to the Protestant Reformation. He first clashed with the Catholic authorities in 1517 after his *95 Theses*, attacking the sale of indulgences, denied that the pope and clergy could forgive sins. He inspired a movement that revolutionized religious thought, incidentally provoking much social and political upheaval in northern Europe.
✤78●, ✤194, ✤194●

Luxembourg dynasty The counts of Luxembourg were a powerful dynasty in the late Middle Ages. They were also kings of Bohemia and four of their number were elected emperor, the most famous being Charles IV.
possessions ◆70–1, ✤189, ◆189 (4), ◆194 (2)
creation of modern duchy ◆202, ◆202 (1 inset)

Luxor see Thebes ❑29

Lydia
(BCE) ✤35, ✤223, ◆34–5, ◆223 (4)
issues first coins (BCE) ✤35

Lysimachus (var. Gre. Lysimachos) (360–281 BCE) General of Alexander the Great. Following Alexander's death in 323, Lysimachus became ruler of Thrace. He extended his territories in the wars between Alexander's successors, but was killed in battle against Seleucus, with whom he had formerly been allied. ✤224●, ◆224 (1)

M

Maastricht Treaty (var. European Union Treaty) (Dec 1991). International agreement between the states of the European Community (EC) in Maastricht, Netherlands, which established the European Union (EU), with Union citizenship for every person holding the nationality of a member state. It provided for the establishment of a central banking system and the implementation of a common foreign and security policy. ✤214

Macao Portuguese colony in China.
16th-century voyages by Portuguese ✤80
returned to China (1999) ◆111

Macedonia
Antigonid dynasty
◆41, ✤224, ✤224●, ◆224 (1)
(BCE) ✤34–5, ◆38–9
Byzantine rulers (867–1081) ✤59
growth of power ◆40●

Machu Picchu Inca sacred shrine ❑74

MacKenzie, Colin (c.1753–1821) Officer in the British East India Company's army, whose accurate mapping led to his appointment as surveyor-general of India in 1819. ✤239, ◆239●, ❑239

Mackenzie, Sir Alexander (c.1755–1820) Explorer and fur-trader. In 1789, on behalf of the Northwestern Company, he ventured to Great Slave Lake and down what was to become the Mackenzie River to the Arctic Ocean. His next expedition, starting from Lake Athabasca in 1792, eventually reached the Pacific Ocean, making him the first white man to cross N. America north of Mexico. ◆286 (1)

MAD see Mutually Assured Destruction

Madaba 6th-century mosaic ❑51

Madagascar
Arab trading settlements
✤58, ✤61, ✤61 (3)
colonized by Malays ✤61
French conquest (1883–96) ✤167●, ◆167
Portuguese map (1558) ❑156

Madero, Francisco Indalecio (1873–1913) Mexican revolutionary and statesman. In 1908, Madero launched a presidential campaign against the dictator, Porfirio Díaz. Imprisoned by Díaz, he then fled to the US and launched a military campaign, capturing Ciudad Juárez, which he made his capital in May 1911. He made moderate reforms as president, but was increasingly faced by revolts demanding land reform. He was murdered in Feb 1913 following a military coup by Victoriano Huerta, assisted by the US ambassador. ✤133, ✤133 (3)

Mafia (aka Cosa Nostra). International criminal organization, originally based in Sicily and dating from the 13th century. In the US, the Mafia became one of the major forces in the development of organized crime, especially during the Prohibition era.
✤113, ✤113 (4)

Magadha One of the 16 mahajanapadas (great realms) which dominated the Ganges plain from c.600 BCE. Gradually all the other kingdoms were absorbed into Magadha, with its capital at Pataliputra (Patna), which dominated the lucrative Ganges trade routes. Magadha became the nucleus of the first Indian empire, the Mauryan Empire, when its throne was seized by Chandragupta Maurya in 327 BCE. Magadha was the scene of many of the incidents in the life of Gautama Buddha. Later the center of the Gupta dynasty. ✤36, ✤39, ✤241, ◆241 (4)

Magellan, Ferdinand (c.1480–1521). Portuguese navigator, who undertook his most famous voyage in the service of the Spanish crown. In 1519 he sailed with five ships to discover a westward route to the Indies. He achieved this, sailing through the Strait of Magellan, then crossing the Pacific to the Philippines. There, Magellan was killed after intervening in a local war. One of his ships, captained by Sebastián del Cano, made the journey back to Spain, thus completing the first circumnavigation of the globe.
16th-century Portuguese navigator ✤78, ◆239 (1)
global circumnavigation ✤76, ❑80
Oceania voyages ◆278 (1)
reaches the Pacific (1520) ✤142

Magnesia ✕ (190 BCE). Roman victory over Seleucid king Antiochus III. ◆179 (4)

Magyars People of the steppes, the ancestors of today's Hungarians, who migrated into present-day Hungary in the late 9th century. Their raids at first struck fear into western European states, but following their defeat by Otto I at Lechfeld in 955, the Magyars started to lead a more settled existence and in the 11th century Hungary became a Christian kingdom.
defeated by Otto I ✤58, ✤58●
raids (c.800–1000) ◆185 (3)
settle in Danube basin ✤185●

Mahabharata Sanskrit epic which, along with the *Ramayana*, was composed c.450 BCE. It tells the story of an epic struggle for supremacy between two groups of cousins, the Kauravas and the Pandavas. The battle was fought in northwestern India, and is probably an account of Mauryan expansion.
✤241, ❑241, ❑244, ◆241 (5)

Mahavira (c.540–468 BCE) Brought up as a pious Jain near Patna, Mahavira became a monk, who instructed 11 disciples, and became the foremost preceptor of the Jain religion.
✤242●, ◆242 (3)

Mahayana Buddhism (aka Greater Vehicle). Interpretation of Buddhism developed from 1st century CE, which spread from N.W. India into China, Korea, Japan, and Tibet; focusing on the concept of the Bodhisattva, who would postpone entry into *nirvana* until all others are similarly enlightened, Mahayana regards the historical Buddha as a temporary manifestation of the eternal and innate nature of the Buddha. *See also* Buddhism.
✤49 (4)

Mahmud of Ghazni (var. Muhammad of Ghazni) (r.971–1030). Ruler of an empire, consisting of Afghanistan, northeastern Persia, and northwest India (r.998–1030). Mahmud was the son of a Turkish ruler of Khurasan, a vassal of the Samanids. His reign was notable for the frequent raids he made on northern India. The Ghaznavid dynasty continued to rule until the late 12th century when they were overthrown by the Ghurids. ✤59●, ✤63, ◆227 (6)

Mainz First use of movable metal type ✤74

Majapahit Empire Javanese empire from the late 13th to the 16th centuries. Although Majapahit probably exercised direct rule only over Java and nearby small islands, in its heyday in the 14th century, its powerful fleets controlled trade over a far wider area, including the Moluccan Spice Islands.
✤71●, ✤245●, ❑244, ◆245 (6)

Makura
Arab invasion ✤162●
Coptic Christianity ✤58

Malacca
founded (c.1400) ✤75●
captured by Dutch (1641) ✤83●

captured by Portuguese (1510) ✤79●, ◆247 (4)
converts to Islam (1445) ✤75●
trading center ✤75

Malay Peninsula
Chola conquests ✤59
rubber plantations ❑97

Malaya (now Malaysia)
Independence (1957) ✤251, ◆251 (4)
rebellion (1947–48) ❑251
seized by Japan (1942) ✤103●

Mali Empire West African state at its most powerful in the 13th and 14th centuries. The empire was founded by Sundiata c.1235, though a small state had existed there for some two centuries before. ✤162 (1)–(7)
founded ✤67●, ✤163●
collapses (c.1660) ✤163●
conquered by Songhay (1546) ✤79●
conquered by Sunni Ali ✤75
control of caravan trade ✤70, ✤163
Ibn Battuta's visit (1352) ✤71●
Jenne mosque ❑162
Mansa Musa 14th-century ruler ❑71
usurps Kingdom of Ghana (13th century) ✤66

Malinke West African people, the most influential of the Mali Empire, famous as traveling merchants. ✤163

Mamluks (var. Mamelukes). Slave soldiers in many medieval Islamic states, frequently of Turkish origin, noted for their skill and bravery. Mamluks often rose to occupy positions of great power. In Egypt they ruled the country from 1250 until 1517, when it was conquered by the Ottomans.
and Mongols in W. Asia ✤67●, ✤69, ✤229, ✤229●, ◆229 (3)
conquered by Ottomans (1517) ✤79●
superbly trained warriors ❑229
Manassas see Bull Run
takeover of Egypt (1250) ✤67●

Manaus Founded (1674) ✤149●

Manchester
expansion in 19th century ◆204 (2)
market for finished cloth ✤93

Manchuria
army topples Ming dynasty (1644) ✤83
invasion of Burma (1765–69) ✤87●
Mekong Delta settlement (1679) ✤83●
rulers of the Qing dynasty ✤268
occupied by Japan (1918–20) ✤99●
Song–Jin alliance ✤63
trade
BCE jade imports ✤19●
bronze technology ✤19●

Manchu dynasty see Qing dynasty

Manda Coastal trading colony (c.800) ✤58

Mandela, Nelson (f/n Nelson Rolihlahla Mandela) (1918–). South African Black nationalist and statesman, who was imprisoned for 28 years (1962–90) but was subsequently elected to the presidency in 1994.
imprisoned (1964–90) ✤107●, ✤111, ✤169●
portrait ❑111
wins presidency (1994) ✤111●, ✤168

Mandinka Merchants' topographic reports ✤156

Manichaeism Dualist religion founded in Persia in the 3rd century CE by Mani, who tried to integrate the messages of Zoroaster, Jesus, and Buddha into one universal creed. Often regarded as a Christian heresy. ✤49 (4)

Manila galleon Every year, from the late 16th century, the Spanish sent a galleon laden with silver from Acapulco to Manila in the Philippines to pay for silk and other luxury goods from China. The galleon returned to Mexico, laden with silks and oriental luxury goods that were then shipped on to Spain. ✤81, ✤81 (3)

Mansa Musa Ruler of Mali Empire (r.c.1312–1337). Under Mansa Musa, the Mali Empire reached the height of its power, largely through its control of the West African gold trade. He demonstrated his country's great wealth on his pilgrimage to Mecca in 1324.
pilgrimage to Mecca (1324) ✤70
ruler of Mali (14th century) ❑71

Mansurah ✕ of the Crusades (1250). Defeat of the crusader army of Louis IX as it advanced into Egypt.
✤64●, ✤65 (3)

Mansvelt, Edward 17th-century Dutch sailor, who raided Spanish colonies in the Caribbean. ✤85 (2)

Manzikert ✕ of 1071. Decisive victory of the Seljuk Turks over the Byzantines which resulted in the collapse of Byzantine power in Asia Minor. ✤228●, ◆228 (1)

Mao Tse-tung see Mao Zedong

Mao Zedong (var. Mao Tse-tung) (1893–1976). Chinese Communist leader and first chairman of the People's Republic of China (1949). Ruthlessly ambitious, he held an unprecedented seven consulships, and reformed the army by recruiting men of no property to create a professional fighting force, with the legions divided for the first time into cohorts and centuries. ✤43●
Chinese Communists win civil war (1949) ✤103●, ✤274, ◆274 (1)
"Great Leap Forward" begins (1958) ✤107●, ✤274, ❑274
imposes Cultural Revolution (1966–70) ✤107●
"Little Red Book" ✤107
portrait ❑107

Maori Indigenous people of New Zealand of Polynesian origin. They reached New Zealand (Aotearoa) c.700 BCE, making it one of the last Pacific island groups to be colonized. ✤283
carved canoe head ❑281
resistance to colonization ✤283●
Maori "Musket Wars" ✤283 (4) (5)
migration ◆283 (4)

mappamundi ✤173●, ❑66

maquilladora Name given to foreign-owned (often US) assembly plants in Mexico which are used for the import and assembly of duty-free items. ✤136 (1)

Maranhão
established as separate colony from Brazil (1621) ✤149●, ◆149 (3)
occupied by France (1568) ✤149●
Portuguese expelled by Dutch (1625) ✤149●

Maratha Confederacy Hindu state, based in the rock forts of the Western Ghats, the Maratha Confederacy was founded by Sivaji. Although the Mughal emperor Aurangzeb checked the advance of the Marathas during his lifetime, after his death in 1707 the confederacy gained control over much of India. In 1761 the Marathas confronted invading Afghans and were routed at ✕ Panipat. Yet the Marathas continued to present a formidable military obstacle to the growing power of the British. The three Anglo-Maratha wars, which took place from 1775–1818, ultimately led to Maratha defeat.
✤87●, ✤246, ✤246●, ◆246 (2)

Marathon ✕ (490 BCE). Athenian defeat of Persians. ◆223 (4)

Marchand, Jean-Baptiste (1863–1934). French soldier and explorer who in 1898 occupied Fashoda in the Sudan. ◆157 (4)

Marconi, Guglielmo Marchese (1874–1937) Italian physicist and inventor of wireless telegraphy (1895). ✤92●

Marcos, Ferdinand (1917–89). US-sponsored president of the Philippines (r.1965–86), accused of repression, fraud, and corruption. Died in exile in Hawaii following electoral defeat. ✤252●

Marcus Antonius see Mark Antony

Marcus Aurelius (121–180 CE) Roman emperor, adopted son of Antoninus Pius. As emperor, he worked conscientiously for what he considered the public good, but his reign (161–180) was marked by warfare and plague. War with the Parthians was followed by a highly infectious "plague". The emperor then fought a long campaign to secure the Danube frontier against incursions by Germanic tribes. While on campaign, he wrote his reflections on Stoic philosophy, the *Meditations*. ❑46

Marcus Ulpius Traianus see Trajan

Mari Ancient Mari was the most important city on the middle Euphrates in the 3rd and 2nd millennia BCE, until its destruction by the Babylonians in 1759 BCE. Its importance as the center of a vast trading network covering northwest Mesopotamia is evidenced by around 20,000 cuneiform tablets which were found there. ✤27

Mariana Islands ✕ of WW II (Jun–Aug 1944). Scene of a series of major US amphibious assaults during the "island-hopping" campaign in the central Pacific.
◆105 (3), ◆272 (1), ◆273, ◆273 (2)

Marie Antoinette (1755–93) Queen of France. The daughter of Maria Theresa of Austria, she married the future Louis XVI of France in 1770. As an Austrian, she was never popular with the French. Her reputation sank even lower with the Revolution and she was tried and executed in 1793. ✤86

Marienburg Teutonic Knights headquarters ❑189

Marignano ✕ (1515). Swiss defeated by Francis I of France. ◆194 (1)

Marin, Luis 16th-century Spanish colonizer of Mexico. ✤125

Marinids Berber dynasty that ruled Morocco from the 13th to the 15th centuries.
defeat Almohads (1269) ✤67●
take Tunis (1347) ✤71●

Marius, Gaius (157–86 BCE). Roman general and politician who married into the aristocracy and achieved high position due to his military talents, including his role in

suppressing the rebellious Numidian king, Jugurtha. Ruthlessly ambitious, he held an unprecedented seven consulships, and reformed the army by recruiting men of no property to create a professional fighting force, with the legions divided for the first time into cohorts and centuries. ✤43●

Mark Antony (var. Marcus Antonius) (83 BCE–30 BCE). A relative and staunch supporter of Julius Caesar. After Caesar's death in 44 BCE, he almost assumed absolute power in Rome, laying the foundations of future power struggles with Caesar's heir, Octavian. While reorganizing the government of the eastern provinces he met Cleopatra, by whom he had several children. When he started giving large areas of Rome's eastern territories to his children, declaring Cleopatra's son by Julius Caesar heir in Octavian's place, Octavian rallied Rome against him. Antony was defeated at Actium in 31 BCE, and committed suicide soon after. ✤180

Market Garden, Operation see Arnhem

Marne ✕ of WW I (Sep 1914). Saw the Allied halting of the German advance on Paris. ◆206 (2)

Marne ✕ of WW I (Jul 1918). Ended the German offensive on the Western Front. ◆206 (3)

Marquesas Islands Settled by Polynesians ✤60

Marquette, Father Jacques (1637–75) French Jesuit missionary who accompanied Louis Jolliet down the Mississippi River in 1673, coming to within 400 miles of its mouth. ◆119 (2)

Marshall Plan (aka European Recovery Program) (Apr 1948–Dec 1951). US-sponsored program designed to rehabilitate the economies of 17 European nations in order to create stable conditions in which democratic institutions could survive.
✤102●, ✤108●, ✤138, ✤213, ❑213, ◆213 (5)

Martínez de Irala, Domingo (c.1512–56) Commander of the precarious Spanish colony at Asunción in the 1540s and 1550s. He explored the Gran Chaco region and discovered a route across the continent to Peru. ◆142 (1)

Masada Mass suicide of Zealots ✤225

Masina Amadu Lobbo's *jihad* (1816) ✤167●

Masinissa (c.240–148 BCE). Masaeyli ruler of the N. African kingdom of Numidia who assisted Rome conquer Carthaginian territory. ✤161●, ◆161 (2)

Massachusetts Bay English colony founded (1630) ✤82●

Massalia (var. Lat. Massilia, mod. Marseille). Greek colony in the south of France that was a significant political and economic power in the 3rd and 2nd centuries BCE. Gradually absorbed by Rome.
✤34●, ◆38–9
possessions in 3rd century BCE ◆179 (3)
possessions in 120 BCE ◆179 (4)

mastodon relative of the elephant, hunted to extinction c.10,000 years ago. ✤18

Mataram Sultanate of Java expansion in 17th century ✤83●, ◆245 (5), ◆247 (4)

mathematics
Babylonian text ❑33
16th-century revival of Chinese ✤80
calculating device ❑147
Egyptian counting stick ❑33
evolution of numerical systems ✤33, ✤33 (2)
Maya civilization ✤54
Rhind mathematical papyrus ❑33

Matthias Corvinus see Matthias I Hunyadi

Matthias I Hunyadi (aka Matthias Corvinus) (1443–90) King of Hungary (r.1458–90). During his reign, Hungary was almost continually at war against Bohemia and the Turks. In 1477 his armies invaded Austria, besieging and capturing Vienna. Patron of learning and science and founder of the Corvina Library at Buda. ❑193, ◆193 (4)

Mauretania
Christian converts (c.150 CE) ✤47●
Roman control ✤46

Mauri Berber inhabitants of the Roman province of Mauretania. ◆161 (2)

Maurits of Nassau (1604–79). Sent by his cousin, the stadholder, Frederick Henry, to govern the colony in Brazil which the Dutch had taken from the Portuguese. After his successful governorship (1636–44) he returned to Europe and fought in wars against Britain and France. ✤149

Mauryan dynasty (321–180 BCE). Ancient Indian dynasty and the first to establish control over all

India. Founded by Chandragupta Maurya in 321 BCE and extended by his son Bindusara and his grandson Ashoka. The dynasty's power declined under Ashoka's successors and finally ended in c.180 BCE. ✤43, ✤241, ✤241●, ◆38–9, ◆241 (4)

Mauryan Empire see Mauryan dynasty.

Mawson, Sir Douglas (1882–1958) Australian explorer and geologist. Accompanied Shackleton to the Antarctic in 1907–09 and reached the magnetic S. Pole. Led the Australasian Antarctic Expedition 1911–14, and a joint British, Australasian, and New Zealand Antarctic expedition in 1929–31. ◆287 (3)

Maya People of Central America, and the dominant culture of Central America, between 250 and 900 CE, in present-day southern Mexico, Guatemala, northern Belize, and western Honduras. The Maya are famed for their skills in astronomy, including developing solar and sacred calendars, hieroglyphic writing, and ceremonial architecture. An elite of priests and nobles ruled the agricultural population from political centers, characterized by plazas, vast palaces, and pyramid temples.
(200–790 CE) ◆122 (2)
Arch of Labna ❑122
calendar ✤54
Classic Age (c.300–600) ✤50, ✤54●
collapse in southern lowlands (850) ✤68●
controlled by Aztecs (1519) ✤124
early Central America ◆121 (2)
El Mirador complex (1 CE) ✤46●
Mayapán founded (1283) ✤66●
in post-Classic period ◆124 (1)
state religion ✤36 (1)
Temple of the Jaguars ❑58
vase ❑50

Meadowcroft Rock Shelter (15,000 BCE) ✤14●, ✤120●, ◆120 (1)

Mecca Holy city in the Hejaz region of western Saudi Arabia. The birthplace of the prophet Muhammad, it is Islam's holiest city and the center of pilgrimage.
annual Muslim pilgrimage ❑218
captured by Wahhabis (1806) ✤233
Ibn Battuta's first pilgrimage (1325) ✤70
Islamic religious center ✤226, ✤56, ❑226, ◆226 (2) (3)
pilgrimage by Mansa Musa (1324) ✤70
See also Haj

Medes Ancient people who lived to the southwest of the Caspian Sea. They were at their peak during the 7th century BCE when, alongside the Babylonians, they conquered the Assyrians and extended their power westward to central Anatolia and eastward through most of Persia. Their empire was overwhelmed by the Persians in the mid-6th century BCE. ✤31, ◆34–35

Medina Muhammad's capital (622) ✤55●, ✤56, ✤226

Mediterranean
700–300 BCE ◆176–7, ◆177 (1)
colonization ✤176
religions (BCE) ◆37 (3)

megaliths (var. cromlechs, Gr. mega lithas: large stones). – European prehistoric structures, often tombs, were constructed of massive, roughly dressed stone slabs and were built across Europe during the Neolithic period, from c.5000 BCE. They are comparable, although unrelated, to megalithic monuments found in S. India, Tibet, and S.E. Asia. ✤22

Megiddo ✕ of WWI (Sep 18–23, 1918). Final battle of the Palestine campaign fought by British and Commonwealth troops against Turkey. A British and Commonwealth victory, it also marked the last use of massed cavalry in warfare.
✤232●, ◆233 (2)

Mehmet II "the Conqueror" (1432–1481) Ottoman Sultan (r.1451–81) who in 1453 captured Constantinople (Istanbul) and pursued the rapid expansion of the empire into Greece, the Balkans, and Hungary.
fall of Constantinople (1453) ✤75, ✤230
Topkapi palace ❑231

Mehmet VI (1861–1926) Ottoman Sultan (r.1918–22). His failure to suppress the Turkish Nationalists, led by Mustafa Kemal (Atatürk), resulted in the abolition of the sultanate and his subsequent exile. ✤233

Mehmet Ali see Muhammad Ali

Mehrgarh Early pottery discovered ✤19, ✤20●, ✤23●

Meiji Japanese term meaning "enlightened rule." The restoration of the Meiji emperor in 1868 ended Japan's two centuries of isolationism under the Tokugawa Shogunate and initiated a period

305

of political and economic reform. modernization of Japan ◆270 (1)

Melanesia One of three broad geographical divisions of the Pacific, the others being Micronesia and Polynesia. Melanesia includes New Guinea, New Caledonia, the Solomons, and Vanuatu. ✦276

Melbourne Founded (1835–36) ✦91

Memphis ⚔ of American Civil War (Jun 5, 1862). Union victory. ✦131 (6)

Memphis (Egypt) founded (3100 BCE) ✦23● BCE invasions ✦34, ◆35●

Mena see Narmer

Mencius (var. Meng-tzu) (c.371–c.289 BCE) Chinese philosopher who continued the teachings of Confucius. Developed a school to promote Confucian ideas, and from the age of 40 traveled China for 20 years searching for a ruler to implement Confucian morals and ideals. Believed that man was by nature good, but required the proper conditions for moral growth. ✦37

Mendaña, Álvaro de (c.1542–95) Spanish explorer of the Pacific. On Mendaña's first Pacific voyage in 1568, he discovered the Solomon Islands. He was attempting to return there and establish a colony in 1595, but he could not find the islands. He died on Santa Cruz Island. ✦278●

Mendoza, Hurtado de 16th-century Spanish explorer of Lower California. ✦125, ◆125 (4)

Menéndez de Avilés, Pedro 16th-century Spanish conquistador and explorer of N. America. Founded San Agustín in Florida (1565). ✦125, ◆125 (4)

Menes see Narmer

Meneses, Jorge de 16th-century Portuguese traveler in the East Indies. Sighted New Guinea (1526). ✦278●

Meng-tzu see Mencius

Meni see Narmer

Mercator, Gerardus (prev. Gerhard Kremer) (1512–94) Flemish cartographer. Originator of the Mercator projection and publisher of the first book to use the word "Atlas" to describe a set of maps. ✦79, ✦173, ◆173●, ❑173

Meroë BCE–CE capital of Egypt ✦34–5, ◆42 Cushite temple relic ❑35 invaded by Axumites (c.350) ✦50●

Merovingians (c.448–751) The first dynasty of Frankish kings of Gaul, named after Merovech, grandfather of Clovis I. ✦183, ◆183 (5) (6)

Mesa Verde cliff dwellings (c.1100) ✦62●, ✦123●

Mesolithic Literally the "middle stone age," this is a term applied to the transitional period between the Paleolithic (old stone age) and Neolithic (new stone age) in western Europe. The Mesolithic covers the period from the end of the last Ice Age, c.10,000 BCE, to the adoption of farming, c.7000–6000 years ago. It is characterized in the archaeological record by chipped stone tools, in particular microliths, very small stone tools intended for mounting on a shaft. These, as well as tools made of bone, antler, and wood, were used by hunter-gatherer communities, roughly contemporary with Neolithic farming groups further east. ✦14, ❑14, ✦18●

Mesopotamia The area between the Tigris and Euphrates, literally "land between the rivers." Lower Mesopotamia covered Baghdad to the Persian Gulf, and was home to the world's first urban civilizations in the 4th millennium BCE. Upper Mesopotamia extended from Baghdad northwest to the foothills of eastern Anatolia. ◆222 (1) BCE ✦19, ✦35, ◆43, ◆36 (1) city-states ✦27 history and legends ✦222, ❑222 Ottoman and Safavid clashes ✦79 pictograph writing (c.3250) ✦23 Seleucid Empire ✦41, ✦224, ◆38–9, ◆224 (1) trading links ✦25 urban expansion and revolution (BCE) ✦23, ✦24●, ✦28, ◆28 (1)

metallurgy The range of techniques associated with metalworking: extracting metals from their ores, converting them into useful forms such as alloys, and fabricating objects. BCE use ✦18–19, ✦23●, ◆30–1, ✦34, ✦174–5 development ✦26● Eurasian and African tin trade (c.1 CE) ✦44–5 gold rushes ✦90●, ✦93 See also bronze; copper; gold; silver

Metaurus River ⚔ of Punic Wars (207 BCE). Roman victory. ◆179 (3)

Metternich, Clemens Fürst von (1773–1859) Austrian statesman. In 1809 he became Austrian foreign minister and was instrumental in the fall of Napoleon. He was the architect of the "Vienna system" in 1814–15, and the major force in European politics from 1814 until he was forced from office by the Viennese revolution of 1848. ◆257 (2)

Mexican Civil War (1858–60). Broke out between conservatives and liberals in 1858. The liberal leader Benito Juárez became president. His defeat of the conservative forces in 1860 was dependent on loans from western powers. France, Spain, and Britain invaded Mexico to enforce loan repayments; in 1863 a French army occupied Mexico City. The French appointed Archduke Maximilian of Austria as Mexican emperor. He was ousted in 1867 by Juárez' forces, and Juárez was reelected as president (1867–72). ✦94●, ✦128–9●

Mexican Revolution (1910–20). Beginning in 1910 with a revolt against the incumbent dictator, Porfirio Díaz, and the entrenched interests of landowners and industrialists, the Mexican Revolution drew in a range of different factions in a protracted struggle which eventually led to the creation of Mexico as a constitutional republic. ✦133, ◆133 (3) See also Victoriano Huerta, Francisco Madero, Pancho Villa, Emiliano Zapata

Mexican-American War (var. Sp. Guerra de 1847, Guerra de Estados Unidos) (Apr 1846–Feb 1848). The result of the US annexation of Texas in 1845 and a subsequent dispute over the territorial extent of Texas. A series of battles on land and sea resulted in US victory, and the military phase of the war ended with the fall of Mexico City. Via the Treaty of Guadalupe Hidalgo, the US gained the territory that would become the states of New Mexico, Utah, Nevada, Arizona, California, Texas, and western Colorado for $15,000,000. ✦129●, ◆128–9 (2)

Mexico 118–129,133,136–139 cultures Aztec ✦66, ◆124●, ◆124 (2), ❑124 city-states ✦66, ✦122 major civilizations ◆122 (1) Maya ✦50●, ❑50, ✦122● Mexica ✦66 Olmec (1200 BCE) ✦30 Teotihuacán ✦50●, ◆122●, ❑122 Toltec ✦58, ◆122 (1) foreign affairs Texan rebellion (1836) ✦90● US war (1846–48) ✦90●, ✦128, ✦129●, ◆128–9 (2) home affairs center of Spanish Empire in N. America (1521) ✦81 Civil War (1858) ✦94●, ✦129● Federalist-Centralist wars ✦129● gains independence (1821) ✦90● regional inequality ✦136 revolution (1910) ✦98●, ✦128, ✦129●, ✦132–3, ◆133 (3), ❑133 Spanish colonization ✦125●, ◆125 (4), ❑125 church of St. Francis at Tlaxcala ❑125 Cortés' invasion and conquest (1519–21) ◆125 (5)

Mfecane (var. Difaqane, "the Crushing"). A series of Zulu and other Nguni wars and forced migrations in southern Africa during the first half of the 19th century which were set in motion by the rise of the Zulu military kingdom under Shaka. ✦166●, ◆166 (2)

Michael Palaeologus (r.1277–1320). Byzantine co-emperor with his father, Andronicus II, from 1295, who failed to stem the decline of the empire, despite his efforts in fighting the Turks and in resisting the invasions of Catalan mercenaries. ✦187●

Mickey Mouse First appearance (1928) ❑135

microliths Tool technology which developed in Africa c.30,000 years ago, and some time after the peak of the last Ice Age, c.16,000 years ago, in Europe. Small (microlithic) flints were mounted in a range of bone or wooden hafts, to make "composite" tools, which could be used to exploit the much wider range of food resources becoming available as the last Ice Age ended. ✦16●

Micronesia Region of the western Pacific, dotted with tiny archipelagos, including the Marianas and the Marshall Islands. The peoples of Micronesia are of more mixed ancestry than those of Polynesia to the east, having had

---

more frequent contact with mainland E. Asia. ✦276, ◆281 (3)

microscopes see optical instruments

Middendorff, Alexander von 19th-century Russian explorer of Siberia. ◆257 (2)

Middleburg ⚔ of Dutch Revolt (1574). Dutch victory over Spain. ◆195 (5)

Middle East Arab-Israeli wars ✦234●, ◆234 (2) (3) peace process begins (1977) ✦111● spread of Communism (1958) ✦138● territorial crisis ✦98 See also individual countries, West Asia

Middle Kingdom Division of ancient Egyptian history, c.2134–1640 BCE, which saw some expansion into Palestine, and fortification of the Nubian frontier. ✦27●, ✦159●, ◆159 (4)

Midway Naval ⚔ of WW II (Jun 1942). Defeat of Japanese by US forces in mid-Pacific Ocean, marking turning point in Pacific War. ✦103●, ◆104 (2), ◆272 (1)

migration aims ✦52 of peoples (300–500 CE) ✦92–3●, ◆92–3 (1) (2) (3) 19th century ✦100 depictions Chinese construction workers ❑101 hardship and overcrowding on ships ❑100 settlers populate western US ❑94 to the US ✦100 from Ireland (1845) ✦90● German-led ✦189 global ✦100–1 indentured labor ✦101, ✦151, ◆101 (3) inheritors of western Europe (526 CE) ✦53, ◆53 (2) and invasions ✦52–3 Jewish (1880–1914) ✦101, ✦101●, ◆101 (2) Jewish and Palestinian (1947–96) ◆234 (3) Magyar ✦185 (3) mass ✦90 Native Americans "Trail of Tears" ✦129, ❑129 Polynesian ✦60, ◆60 (2) steppe kingdoms of Central Asia ✦261, ◆261 (6) to the New World ✦100● in the US ✦134–5, ✦134●, ◆134 (3) world (c.1800–1920) ◆100 (1)

Milan, Edict of (313 CE). Proclamation that permanently established religious toleration for Christianity within the Roman Empire. It was the outcome of a political agreement concluded in Milan between the Roman emperors Constantine I and Licinius in Feb 313 CE. ◆48●

Milne Bay ⚔ of WW II (Aug 1942). Defeat of Japanese landing force in southeastern New Guinea. ✦104, ◆104 (2)

Milošević, Slobodan (1941–). Politician and administrator who, as leader of the League of Communists of Serbia (from 1987) and president (1989–97), pursued Serb nationalist policies that led to the breakup of Yugoslavia. ✦215

Milvian Bridge ⚔ (312). Constantine defeated his rival Maxentius just north of Rome to become master of the western half of the Roman Empire. He attributed his victory to a vision of the cross of Christ he had seen on the eve of the battle. ✦181●

Min see Narmer

Minamoto Yoritomo (1147–99). Founder of the Kamakura Shogunate in Japan, who crushed the Taira clan. ✦63●, ❑265

Minas Gerais rich gold-mining area of Brazil, which helped prop up the Portuguese economy in the 18th century. Gold was first discovered there in 1695. gold discovered (1695) ◆149● Jesuits banned from region (1711) ✦143●, ◆143 (3), ✦149 (3)

minerals deposits in Africa ◆96 (2) early Central American resources ◆121 (1) late 19th-century finds ◆93 (3) S. American resources ◆153 (3)

Mines Act (1842) Act passed by British parliament, forbidding employment of women and children underground. ✦204●

Ming dynasty (1368–1644) Ruling dynasty of China. rulers of China ✦266–7, ✦70–1, ◆78–9, ◆266–7 (1) bowl (16th century) ❑162 campaign against Mongols ✦75●, ◆266 guardian of the spirit world ❑71 and the outside world ✦267●, ◆266 (1) restores Chinese values ✦71 revolts ✦22, ◆266 (2) self-sufficiency policy ✦75●

---

toppled by Manchus (1644) ◆83 Zhu Yuanzhang founder of dynasty ✦71, ◆266

Ming Empire see Ming dynasty

Minoan civilization Named after the legendary King Minos of Crete, the Minoans were the first great European civilization, c.2000 BCE, whose main cities were Knossos and Phaestus. They had strong trade links with Egypt, and flourished due to their control of sea routes c.2200–1450 BCE. Evidence from their complex palaces attests their high standards of art, metalworking and jewelry-making. Early Minoan pictorial writing has been found, dating to around 1880 BCE, which was superseded by the still undeciphered Linear A and then early Greek writing known as Linear B. civilization (2000 BCE) ✦27●, ◆175●, ◆175 (4) frescoes of bull-leaping game ❑27 palace built (2000 BCE) ✦27● snake goddess (c.1500 BCE) ❑175

Minos The first king of Crete, according to legend, the son of Zeus and Europa, and husband of Pasiphae. Knossos was said to have been his capital from where he ruled a powerful seafaring empire. The ancient civilization of Crete, Minoan civilization, is named after him. His palace at Knossos was built c.2000 BCE. bull cult ✦37

Minsk ⚔ of WW II (Jun–Aug 1943). Encirclement of German forces by Soviets in Belorussia. ✦211 (3) (4)

MIRV see Multiple Independently Targeted Warhead Reentry Vehicle.

Mississippian culture (c.1000–1500 CE). Based in the river valleys of the present-day states of Mississippi, Alabama, Georgia, Arkansas, Missouri, Kentucky, Illinois, Indiana, and Ohio, with scattered populations in Wisconsin and Minnesota and on the Great Plains. A settled agricultural culture, they are distinctive for the oval earthworks which dominated most settlements. ✦66●, ◆123 (5) first towns (c.750) ✦58● true towns (c.1050) ✦62●

Mississippi River earth mounds ✦66, ✦74 explored by Jolliet and Marquette (1673) ✦119● explored by La Salle (1682) ✦119●

Missouri Compromise (1820). The measure which allowed for the admission of Missouri as the 24th US state in 1821. James Tallmadge's attempt to add an antislavery amendment to the admission of new states to the US led to a major debate over the right of the government to restrict slavery in new states. The issue remained unresolved in Dec 1819 when the northern state of Maine applied for statehood. The Senate passed a bill allowing Maine to enter the Union as a free state and Missouri to be admitted with no restriction on slavery. A further amendment was then added that allowed Missouri to become a slave state but banned slavery in the rest of the Louisiana Purchase north of latitude 36°30'. ✦130, ◆130 (1)

Mitanni Indo-Persian people whose empire in northern Mesopotamia flourished between c.1500–1360 BCE. Their capital, Wahshukanni, was probably in the Khabur River region, and at their height they ruled over lands from the Zagros Mountains west to the Mediterranean. conflict with Egyptians and Hittites (1250 BCE) ✦27●, ◆26–7

Mitchell, Thomas (1792–1855) Scottish-born soldier and explorer. Surveyor-General of New South Wales from 1827, he led several important expeditions into the Australian interior. ◆279 (2)

Mithradates II (d.88 BCE). After recovering the eastern provinces that had been overrun by his father's reign, Mithradates was one of the most successful Parthian kings, concluding the first treaty between Parthia and Rome in 92 BCE. ◆42–3

Mithraism Worship of Mithras, an ancient Indian and Persian god of justice and law. Spread as a mystery cult in the Roman Empire, with Mithras as a divine savior. Ousted by Christianity in the 4th century CE. BCE cult ❑37 (3) portrayal of Mithras ❑48 spread of (600 BCE) ✦48, ◆48 (1)

Mithras see Mithraism

Mobile (⚔ of Mobile Bay). ⚔ of American Civil War (Aug 5, 1864). Union victory. ✦131 (7)

Mobutu, Sese Seko Koko Ngbendu wa za Banga (Joseph-Désiré) (1930–97). President of Zaire. Mobutu staged a coup to become president in 1965 and held on to power for over 30 years despite the flagrant corruption of his regime. He finally lost control of Zaire while in Europe for medical treatment in 1997 and never returned. overthrown (1997) ✦111 portrait ❑107

Moche culture (var. Mochica). The earliest major civilization on the north coast of Peru, based in the ancient city of Moche around 200 BCE–550 CE. It is best known for the twin brick pyramids of the Sun and Moon, Huaca del Sol and Huaca de la Luna, which were richly decorated with multicolored murals. The Moche people also carried out extensive irrigation, fortified their ceremonial centers, and produced cast, alloyed, and gilded metalwork. ✦42●, ✦145, ◆145 (4), ✦146 (1) fanged deity pot ❑54 stirrup-spouted vessel ❑54, ❑145

Mochica see Moche culture

Mogollon Native American culture of the US Southwest. ✦58, ◆123 (4) defensive pueblos (1050) ✦123● Mimbres pottery ❑123

Mogul dynasty see Mughal dynasty

Mohács ⚔ (1526). Ottomans crush Hungarian army. ✦79●, ◆195 (3)

Mohammed see Muhammad

Mohenjo-Daro ✦23, ❑240, ◆240 (1)

Moluccas (Spice Islands) ✦79, ✦80, ❑239, ❑247

money see coins; economy

Möngke (d.1259) Mongol leader, a grandson of Genghis Khan, elected Great Khan in 1251. Möngke's rule saw the start of the so-called "Mongol Peace," when travel and trade across Central Asia flourished. ✦68 See also Mongols

Mongols Pastoralist, nomadic people of Central Asia. Their conquests from the 13th century onward were the last assault by nomadic armies inflicted upon the settled peoples of western Asia. ✦68–9 (1) (2) age of the Mongols ✦68–9 campaigns ✦69, ✦75●, ◆68–9 (1), ◆263 (7), ◆265 (5) capital of Karakorum founded (1235) ✦68● cavalryman ❑69 conquests 13th century ✦69● Central Asia (1206) ◆256● Chinese (1449) ✦75● Kaifeng captured (1233) ◆67● Khwarizm Empire (1219) ◆67● northern China (1211) ✦67● Russian ✦66●, ✦69, ✦75, ✦189● sacking of Baghdad (1258) ✦67, ✦69●, ✦229, ❑229 Song resistance crushed (1279) ✦69● converts to Islam ✦67 defeats Ain Jalut (1260) ✦67●, ✦69● Annam and Pagan forays ✦67 invasions of Japan (1274, 1281) ✦67●, ✦69● Java (1293) ✦67 Mamluk ✦67●, ✦69, ✦229, ✦229●, ◆229 (3) periods of peace ✦68, ✦68●, ◆267 Yuan period (c.1300) ◆263, ◆263 (7)

Monmouth Court House ⚔ of American Revolutionary War (Jun 28, 1778). Inconclusive result. ◆127 (3)

monotheism ✦37, ◆36 (1)

monsoon Wind system involving seasonal reversal of prevailing wind direction. Occurs mainly in the Indian Ocean, the western Pacific, and off the W. African coast. The term also applies to the rainy seasons of much of southern and eastern Asia, and of E. and W. Africa.

Montagnais Native American peoples of northeastern N. America. ✦119, ◆126 (1)

Montcalm, Louis Joseph, Marquis de (1712–59). Commander of the French troops in Canada in the Seven Years' War. He was mortally wounded defending Quebec. ✦127, ◆127 (2)

Monte Albán influential Mexican city ❑122, ◆122 (1) Los Danzantes ❑34 Zapotec culture ✦38●, ✦121

Monte Cassino see Cassino

Monte Verde early settlements ✦144●, ◆144 (1) environmental survival strategies (BCE) ✦14● 16 stone tools ❑144

Montejos, the 16th-century Spanish explorers of N. America (1527, 1545). ✦125, ◆125 (4)

Montenegro ✦203, ◆203 (4), ◆232 (1), ◆232 See also Balkans, nationalism

Montezuma II see Motecuzuma Xocoyotl

Montgomery, Alabama Boycott against segregation (1955) ✦137●, ◆137 (2)

Montmirail ⚔ of Napoleon's defense of France (Feb 11, 1814). French victory. ◆200 (1)

Montoya, Father Ruiz de 17th-century Jesuit missionary in South America. ◆143●

Montreal captured by British (1760) ✦127●, ◆127 (2) European and native conflict (1689) ◆126 French settlement map (1642) ❑126

Morgan, Sir Henry (c.1635–88) Welsh buccaneer who operated in the West Indies, preying primarily on Spanish ships and territories including Panama, which he captured in 1671. Though arrested and transported to London to placate the Spanish, he returned to the West Indies and became a wealthy planter. ❑85, ◆85 (2)

Morgarten ⚔ (1315). Austrian Habsburg forces defeated by Swiss peasant army. ◆193 (5)

Morocco 165–169 Almohad sect established (1147) ✦63● Almohads defeated by Marinids (1269) ✦67● Ceuta captured by Portuguese (1415) ✦75● French occupation ◆167 (4) independence ◆168 (1) Muhammad III becomes Sultan (1757) ✦87● Portuguese invasion crushed (1578) ✦79● Songhay Empire captured (1591) ✦79●

Morse Code Code consisting of dots and dashes devised by American painter and inventor Samuel Morse (1791–1872), for use with the electric telegraph he had designed. ✦98

mosaics Aztec serpent pendant ❑124 castle, ships, and harbor of Ravenna (6th century) ❑182 Darius III at ⚔ Issus ❑40 floor mosaic of Orpheus ❑181 Macedonian lion hunt ❑179 map of Jerusalem ❑51 Roman ❑47 The Nile in flood ❑47 Vandal landowner ❑52

Moscow ⚔ of WW II (Dec 1941). Soviet forces halted German advance during Operation Barbarossa. ◆210 (1)

Moscow Napoleon's retreat (1812) ✦90●

Moshoeshoe Lesotho kingdom (1824) ◆166 (2)

Moslem see Muslim

Motecuzoma I Aztec ruler (1440–68) ✦74●, ◆124 (1)

Motecuzoma Xocoyotl (aka Montezuma II) (1466–1520) 9th emperor of the Aztec Empire (1502–20). During the Spanish conquest of Mexico by Hernán Cortés and his conquistadors, he was deposed as ruler and imprisoned. Aztec ruler (1502) ✦78●, ◆124, ◆124 (1) last Aztec emperor ✦78●

moundbuilders see earthworks

Moundville Mississippian cultural site ✦123, ◆123 (5)

Mount Olympus cult center ◆37

Mozambique independence (1975) ✦107●, ✦111●, ◆168, ◆168 (1) post-independence ◆169 (2)

MPLA see People's Movement for the Liberation of Angola

MRV see Multiple Reentry Vehicle

Msiri 19th-century trade who settled with his Nyamwezi followers in southern Katanga, central Africa, in 1856. Msiri dominated the area by about 1870. ✦166

Mughal dynasty (var. Mogul dynasty) (1526–1857). The victory of Babur, an Afghan Muslim, at Panipat in 1525, was the beginning of the Mughal Empire, which was to dominate India until 1739. The empire reached its peak during the reign of Akbar, when it extended from Bengal to Sind and Gujarat, and from Kashmir to the Godavari river. From the 1670s, confrontation with the Marathas, a new Hindu power, depleted the power of the Mughals and decline soon set in. In 1739 Nadir Shah of Persia marched into India, and sacked Delhi, and from this point the Mughals were merely puppet emperors. ✦79, ✦246, ✦246●, ◆78–9, ◆246 (1) Persian incursions ✦87 powers declines (1707) ✦87

Key to index: ✦ text ❑ picture var. variant name f/n full name r. ruled WW I World War I
● timeline ◆ map aka also known as prev. previously known as ⚔ battle WW II World War II

route map ❑238
troops raiding sheep herds ❑267
Mughal Empire see Mughal dynasty.
Muhammad (var. Mohammed)
(c.570–632). Founder of Islamic
religion, born in Mecca (Saudi
Arabia). In 610 a vision of the
Angel Gabriel revealed messages
from God. These messages,
written down as the Koran
(meaning "Reading" or
"Recitation"), are revered as the
holy book of Islam. In 622
Muhammad and his followers
were forced to move to Medina, a
migration (Hegira) which marks
the beginning of the Islamic
calendar. As a religious leader, he
conquered Mecca in 630,
destroyed the pagan idols, and
unified much of Arabia. His legacy
passed to his father-in-law, Abu
Bakr, the first caliph. ✣55, ✣56,
✣66, ✣61●, ✣218, ✣226
Hegira ◆226 (2)
Muhammad III Sultan of Morocco
(r.1757–90), who introduced
administrative reforms and
reopened trade with Europe after
a long embargo. ✣87●
Muhammad al Ghur see Muhammad
of Ghur
Muhammad Ali (c.1769–1849) (var.
Mehmet Ali, Mohammed Ali).
Viceroy of Egypt (1805–48), who
made Egypt the leading power in
the eastern Mediterranean. An
Albanian military officer, he went
to Egypt (1801) in command of an
Ottoman army sent to face
Napoleon. After many successful
military campaigns, he turned
against the Ottomans, defeating
them in Asia Minor (1839), but
European intervention prevented
the overthrow of the sultan.
✣232
possessions 1840 ◆90–1
Viceroy of Egypt (1804) ✣90
Muhammad Ibn Adullah see Ibn
Battuta
Muhammad of Ghazni see Mahmud
of Ghazni
Muhammad of Ghur (var. Ghiyas al-
Din) (d.1202) (r.1173–1202). Leader
of an Afghan army, in 1191 he
defeated the Rajput clans of
northern India, and in 1206 his
general, Qutb al-Din Aybak,
established the first Turko-Afghan
dynasty in Delhi, ruling it as sultan.
defeats Rajput clans (1191)
✣63●
Ghurid dynasty ◆244 (2)
Muisca (var. Chibcha). Native people
of the highlands around Bogotá. It
was in Muisca lands that the
legend of El Dorado caught the
imagination of Spanish
conquistadores. ❑147
Mujahedin (var. Mujahideen). Islamic
nationalist forces during Afghan
civil war (from 1973) who
spearheaded resistance to Soviet
invasion (1979–89) with Pakistani
backing, forming a government
(1983), but opposed by Taliban
from 1995. ◆235 (4)
Mujahideen see Mujahedin
Multiple Reentry Vehicle (MRV) ICBM
developed by US in the early 1960s
that could deliver a "footprint" of
warheads in a selected area,
greatly increasing US nuclear
potential during the Cold War.
✣109
**Multiple Independently Targeted
Warhead Reentry Vehicle** (MIRV)
ICBM developed by US in late
1960s, that could select several
targets, greatly escalating US
nuclear potential during the Cold
War. ✣109
Mumbai see Bombay
mummification Preservation of
human and animal bodies by
embalming and wrapping in
lengths of cloth, after removal of
the internal organs.
Mummification is associated with
belief in life after death, and was
practiced by the ancient Egyptians
among others.
ancestor cults ✣147
Chimú funerary mask ❑66
Egyptian ❑31
goddess Anubis ❑37
Paracas region ❑145
Roman mummy case ❑47
Mungo, Lake Site of first known
cremation (26,000 BP) ✣16●
Murad I (c.1326–89) Third Ottoman
Sultan, who pursued the expansion
of the empire in the Balkans,
annexing Bulgaria and much of
Serbia. He was killed at the battle
of Kosovo Polje. ✣230, ◆230 (1)
Muret ⚔ of Albigensian Crusade
(1213). Peter II of Aragon killed by
crusading army. ◆186 (2)
Murfreesboro (⚔ of Stones River,
⚔ of American Civil War (Dec 31,
1862–Jan 2, 1863). Union victory.
◆131 (6)
Muscovy State created by the grand
princes of Moscow in the 13th
century. Though isolated, Muscovy
became increasingly powerful
through the annexation of
Novgorod and the proclamation of
independence from the Mongols in

1480. By 1556 Muscovy had
annexed the Khanate of Astrakhan,
controlling the Volga down to the
Caspian Sea. In 1571 Moscow was
sacked by Crimean Tatars.
14th century ✣70–1
throws off Mongol yoke (1480)
✣75●
Muscovy Company Formed in 1555
by the navigator and explorer
Sebastian Cabot and various
London merchants in order to
trade with Russia, the company
was granted a monopoly of Anglo-
Russian trade.
sponsors of Arctic exploration
✣286
Musket Wars A series of conflicts
between Maori tribes in the 1820s,
sparked by the introduction of
European firearms into New
Zealand. ✣283●, ◆283 (4)
Muslim (var. Moslem, Mussulman) Of
or pertaining to the Islamic faith.
See Islam
Muslim League Formed in 1906, as a
result of the conflicts created
within Bengal by Lord Curzon's
1905 partition of the province. The
league's original aim was to
promote separate electorates for
Muslim minorities within Hindu
majority areas, but by the 1940s it
had started to demand a separate
Muslim state. It was pressure from
the league that led to the creation
of Pakistan in 1947. ✣250●
Mussolini, Benito Amilcare Andrea
(1883–1945) Italian dictator
(1925–43). Expelled from the
socialist party for pressing for
support of the Allies during WW I;
after the war Mussolini founded
the Fasci di Combattimento (Fascist
movement). Aided by Blackshirt
supporters, he attacked
Communism, and in 1922 marched
on Rome. He was appointed prime
minister by King Victor Emmanuel
III, and by 1925 had declared
himself Il Duce (the leader) and
swiftly established a totalitarian
regime within Italy. In 1935 he
invaded Ethiopia as part of a plan
to form an Italian empire, and by
1936 had formed the Rome-Berlin
axis with Hitler, declaring war on
the Allies in 1940. Dependence on
Hitler broke support for Mussolini
and he was deposed in 1943 and
executed by partisans in 1945.
✣207, ✣209, ◆209 (3)
Mutapa Empire (var. Muwenutapa).
Kingdom of southern Africa that
flourished between the 15th and
18th centuries. ✣164
absorbs Great Zimbabwe (c.1450)
✣75●
Mwenemutapa see Mutapa Empire
Mycale (var. Gre. Mykale) ⚔
(479 BCE) Defeat of the Persian
navy by the Greeks off the coast of
Asia Minor. ✣39, ◆176 (1)
Mycenaean Greece Named after its
capital Mycenae, a Bronze Age
Greek culture which dominated
mainland Greece between
1580–1120 BCE. The Mycenaeans
appear to have conquered Knossos
in Crete around 1450 BCE, and they
traded widely in Asia Minor,
Cyprus, and Syria. Their sacking of
Troy c.1200 BCE was later
mythologized in Homer's Iliad.
Archaeological evidence points to
great wealth and skill, with palaces
at Mycenae, Tiryns, and Pylos at
the center of a system of
government by a distinct warrior
class overseeing a redistributive
economy. The final destruction or
abandonment of these palaces is
now thought to be due to internal
unrest rather than external
conquest. 175●, ◆175 (4)
bronze dagger blade ❑26
civilization (1250 BCE) ◆26–7
dominant power on Greek
mainland (1550 BCE) ✣27●
mythology ✣37
pot ❑31
ritual sprinkler ❑37
Mysore Conquered by Britain (1799)
✣87●
mythology Origins of religion ✣36–7
Mzilikazi Ndebele kingdom (1826)
◆166 (2)

N

Naddod 9th-century Viking explorer
who visited Iceland (c.870).
◆172 (2)
Nadir Shah (1688–1747). A bandit
chieftain of Turkish origin, in 1736
he seized the Safavid throne of
Persia, immediately embarking on
campaigns against neighboring
states. In 1739 he attacked Delhi,
capital of Mughul India,

slaughtered its citizens and stole
the Koh-i-noor diamond. Cruel and
ruthless, he was eventually
assassinated by his own troops.
✣87, ✣246, ✣246●, ◆246
NAFTA see North American Free
Trade Agreement
Nagasaki ⚔ of American Civil War
(Dec 15–16, 1864). Union victory.
◆131 (7)
Nagasaki Atom bombs dropped
(1945)
✣103●, ✣105●, ✣273●, ◆273 (3)
Nain Singh 19th-century Indian
surveyor, who made an epic
journey in disguise through Tibet
on behalf of the Survey of India.
✣257●, ◆257 (3)
Nanda Empire ✣241, ◆241 (4)
Nanjing
center of Jin dynasty ✣51
rebellion (1853) ✣91●
Treaty (1842) ✣91●
Nanjing, Treaty of see Opium War
Nansen, Fridtjof (1861–1930).
Norwegian scientist, explorer, and
statesman. Crossed Greenland
icecap in 1888 on foot. In his
specially-designed ship, the Fram,
he explored the Arctic from
1893–96, stopping to take part in a
bid for the North Pole. In 1918 he
became a commissioner to the
League of Nations and was
awarded the Nobel Peace Prize in
1923 for his work in assisting
famine-struck regions of the Soviet
Union. ◆286–7 (2)
Nantes, Edict of (1598). Order signed
by Henry IV of France granting
Huguenots the right to practice
their own religion. It was revoked
in 1685 by Louis XIV, and as a result
many non-Catholics fled the
country. ✣78●
Napoleon I, Bonaparte (1769–1821)
French military and political leader,
and Emperor of France
(1804–1815). Following a successful
Italian campaign (1796–7) and an
invasion of Egypt (1798), he
assumed power as First Consul in
1799. A brilliant general, he
defeated every European coalition
which fought against him. Decline
set in with failure of the Peninsular
War in Spain and a disastrous
invasion of Russia (1812). Defeated
at Leipzig (1813) by a new
European alliance, he went into
exile but escaped and ruled as
emperor during the Hundred Days.
Finally defeated at Waterloo (1815)
and exiled to St. Helena. As an
administrator, his achievements
were of lasting significance and
include the Code Napoléon, which
remains the basis for French law.
◆200–1 (1) (2)
abdicates (1814) ◆202●
aftermath of wars ✣90
campaigns ◆200–1, ✣200●,
❑200, ◆200–1 (1)
Code Napoléon ❑200
coup brings power in France
✣86●
defeated at Waterloo (1815)
✣200, ✣202●
Emperor of France ❑201
French Empire 1812
✣90–1, ◆201 (2)
occupies Egypt (1798)
✣87●, ✣200, ❑201
opposition alliances
✣201, ◆201 (3)
retreats from Moscow (1812)
✣90●, ◆200
rise and fall ◆200
Tilsit peace talks ❑201
Napoleon III var. Charles Louis
Napoléon Bonaparte) (1808–1873).
Nephew of Napoleon I, Emperor of
the French (1852–71). Involved
France in the Crimean War
(1853–6) and allowed Bismarck to
provoke him into the Franco-
Prussian War (1870–1), which
ended in France's defeat and
Napoleon's exile to Britain. See
also Crimean War, Franco-Prussian
War.
president of Second Republic
(1848) ✣202●
revolts against his rule ◆202 (1)
surrenders to Wilhelm I ✣203
Naqa Cushite temple relic ❑35
Naqada Founded (c.3300) ✣24●
Nara period (710–784). Period of
Japanese history that began with
the establishment of a capital at
Heijo-kyo (to the west of the
modern city of Nara).
✣55●, ✣265●, ✣265, ◆265 (3)
Narbo (Narbonne), Visigothic state
(414) ✣53●
Narmer, King (var. Menes, Mena,
Meni, Min). The first pharaoh of
the Old Kingdom in Egypt. Narmer
unified the formerly discrete
fortified towns of Upper and
Lower Egypt into a powerful state,
and is credited with founding the
capital at Memphis near Cairo.
According to the 3rd-century BCE
historian Manetho, Narmer ruled
for 62 years and was killed by a
hippo. ✣22
Narváez, Panfilo de (c.1478–1528)
Spanish conquistador. Involved in
conquest of Cuba and Cortés's
conquest of Mexico. Commissioned
to conquer Florida in 1526. The
journey took ten months and
decimated the crew, and Narváez

himself died on the Texas coast,
although survivors of the party did
go on to complete the map of the
northern Gulf coast.
✣125, ✣118 (1), ✣125 (4)
NASA see National Aeronautics and
Space Administration
Nashville ⚔ of American Civil War
(Dec 15–16, 1864). Union victory.
◆131 (7)
Nassau, William I, Prince of Orange
(aka William of Nassau,1533–84)
Dutch statesman who marshaled
resistance to Spanish Catholic rule
in the Netherlands.
Dutch revolt (1568–1609)
✣195, ✣195●, ◆195 (5)
Natal ✣96 (2), ◆166 (2)
annexed by Britain ✣91●
annexed by Britain (1843) ✣166●
**National Aeronautics and Space
Administration** (NASA)
space program (1969) ✣106●
**National Front for the Liberation of
Angola** (FNLA). Political party of
Angola. ◆109 (5)
National Recovery Administration
(NRA). US government agency set
up as part of Roosevelt's New Deal
program. The National Industrial
Recovery Act authorized the
introduction of industry-wide
codes to reduce unfair trade
practices and cut down
unemployment, establish minimum
wages and maximum hours, and
guarantee the right of collective
bargaining. The NRA ended when
it was invalidated by the Supreme
Court in 1935, but many of its
provisions were included in
subsequent legislation. ❑134
nationalism
European growth ✣202–3, ✣214
movements ✣90, ✣94, ✣99
Serb ✣215
NATO see North Atlantic Treaty
Organization
Natufian peoples Levantine people,
named after the site of Wadi en-
Natuf in Israel. From c.13,000 BCE,
Natufian peoples harvested wild
cereals, using grindstones to crush the grains.
They were the precursors of the
first farmers. ✣15●
navigation
Arab traders in the Indian Ocean
◆61 (3)
harnessing winds
✣61, ✣75, ✣78, ✣218
instruments
astrolabe ❑77, ❑218
Chinese magnetized needle
(13th century) ❑67
Harrison's chronometer ❑86
lodestone compass used in
China (c.250) ✣256●
measuring longitude ✣86
Magellan's global
circumnavigation ❑80
mapping
latitude scales (16th century)
✣173
medieval ✣173
Portolan charts
✣70, ✣173, ❑173
stick chart ❑173
Northeast Passage ◆257 (2)
Polynesian ✣55, ✣60
technology
global (c.1500) ◆76–7 (1)
and mariners ✣77
satellite imagery ❑106
trading network ✣78
Nazca culture Coastal culture of
southern Peru which flourished
between c.200 BCE and 500 CE. The
Nazca are noted for their ceramic
human and animal figures but are
best known for the "Nazca lines,"
large abstract designs and animal
shapes which they laid out on a
huge scale by clearing and aligning
stones, and which are best seen
from the air. ✣38●, ❑42, ✣145 (4),
◆146 (1)
desert figures (c.450)
✣51●, ❑145
empire ◆146 (1)
pottery figure ❑42
Nazi Party (var. National-
Sozialistische Deutsche
Arbeiterpartei) see Nazism
Nazi-Soviet Non-Aggression Pact
Treaty signed Aug 1939 arranging
for division of Poland. Paved way
for outbreak of WW II in Europe.
✣209●
Nazism Political creed developed by
Adolf Hitler in the 1920s and
implemented by his National
Socialist (Nazi) party after Hitler
became chancellor of Germany in
1933. Based on extreme
nationalism, anticommunism and
racism (especially anti-semitism),
Nazi policies of social and
economic mobilization led to the
dramatic recovery of Germany in
the 1930s, but also led the nation
into a program of territorial
aggression which plunged Europe
into WW II. ◆209●, ◆209 (3)
Nationalist Socialist ✣102, ✣104
concentration camps ❑138, ❑211
impact on Europe ✣211●
Yalta "Big Three" conference
(1945) ◆103●
Ndebele African Kingdom (1826)
◆166 (2)

Ndongo Portuguese seize territory
(1663) ✣82
Neanderthals (c.120,000 to 28,000
years ago). Species of human,
Homo neanderthalensis,
contemporary with Homo sapiens.
Named after the Neander Valley in
Germany, where the first skull cap
of their type was recognized, the
Neanderthals lived in Europe and
the Middle East. Distinguished by
their strong, heavy skeleton,
projecting face, broad nose, and
large teeth, their brain capacity
was at least the size of modern
humans. They were accomplished
toolmakers, and were the first type
of human known to bury their
dead. They demonstrated, in their
cultural behavior and social
organization, many of the
characteristics of modern humans.
✣12, ❑12, ✣15●, ✣13 (2)
Nearchus (d.312 BCE) Admiral of
Alexander the Great's fleet. In 325
BCE he was instructed to sail west
along the coast from the mouth of
the Indus to the mouth of the
Euphrates. His voyage opened a
coastal trading route to India for
Greek merchants. ◆218 (1)
Nebuchadnezzar II (r.c.630–562 BCE).
Babylon's most famous king and
founder of the new Babylonian
empire, (r.605–562 BCE) during
which time the Babylonian
civilization reached its peak.
Nebuchadnezzar instituted many
major building projects including
the Hanging Gardens, one of the
seven wonders of the ancient
world. He led his father's army to
victory over the Egyptians at
Carchemish, and famously exiled
the Jews after capturing Jerusalem
in 586 BCE.
✣35●, ✣222, ❑222
Needham, James (d.1673) 17th-
century explorer of N. America.
Gained experience of the frontier
with Henry Woodward and then
accompanied Gabriel Arthur on the
journey to find a route to the
"South Sea." ◆119 (2)
Nehru, Jawaharlal (1889–1964) First
prime minister of independent
India (r.1947–64). He joined the
nationalist movement in 1920, and
was president of the Indian
National Congress Party 1929–30,
1936–7, 1946, 1951–4. ❑252
Nekhen Confederacy (BCE) ◆159 (2)
Nelson, Horatio, Viscount
(1758–1805) British admiral. On the
outbreak of war with France in
1793, he achieved a series of
brilliant and decisive victories on
the Nile (1798) and at Copenhagen
(1801). His defeat of a combined
Spanish and French fleet at
Trafalgar (1805) saved Britain from
the threat of invasion by
Napoleon. He was mortally
wounded in the battle.
◆200 (1), , ✣200●
Nemausus (var. Nîmes) Pont du Gard
❑180
Neo-Assyrian Empire see Assyrian
Empire
Neolithic The last subdivision of the
Stone Age, the period when crops
and animals were domesticated,
pottery was manufactured, and
stone tools were made by grinding
and polishing.
Africa ◆160 (1)
China ◆258 (2)
Nepal Mapping and exploration
◆257 (3)
Nerchinsk, Treaty of (1689). Peace
agreement between Russia and
China, in which Russia withdrew
from the area north of the Amur
river. First treaty between China
and a European power.
✣83, ◆275●
Nero (37–68 CE) Roman Emperor. The
last of the family of Augustus
Caesar to rule Rome (r.54–68).
Palace intrigues and murders
(including that of his mother) gave
Nero's reign a notoriety unmatched
by that of any previous emperor.
He committed suicide as provincial
governors joined in revolt against
him. ✣48●
Nestorian Church Followers of
Nestorius, whose Christian
teachings, condemned by the
councils of Ephesus (431) and
Chalcedon (451), emphasized the
independence of the divine and
human natures of Christ.
Represented today by the Syrian
Orthodox Church.
✣226, ✣226●, ✣49 (4)
Netherlands
foreign affairs
voyages of expansion
(1492–1597) ◆80–1 (1)
possessions
1600 ◆78–9
1700 ◆82–3, ◆164 (1)
Africa
British seize Cape colony
(1795) ✣87●
Cape of Good Hope colony
established (1652) ✣83●
Central Africa (1625) ◆164 (2)
Orange River settled (1720)
✣87●

Portuguese possessions in
Angola captured (1641) 83●
S. and E. Africa (c.1700)
◆164 (1)
America
colonization and settlement
of N. America
✣126, ◆126 (1)
New Amsterdam colony
seized (1664) ✣82●
S. American exploration
✣142–3 (1) (2)
trading posts in north ✣82
Asia
Indonesia gains
independence (1949) ✣103●
Malacca captured (1641)
✣83●
rebellion against Dutch rule
(1926–27) ✣103●
Southeast trading
✣83●, ❑247
Brazil, colonization (1630–54)
✣82●, ✣149, ✣149 (4)
Guiana, colony (c.1640)
✣149, ✣149 (4)
Pacific imperialism ◆284 (1)
home affairs
Dutch revolt (1568–1609) ✣195,
✣195●, ◆195 (5)
population growth (1650–1800)
❑198
World War II see Wars
Netjerykhet see Zoser
New Amsterdam
colonized ◆126 (1)
Dutch colony in America ✣82●
seized by English; renamed New
York (1664) ✣82●
New Caledonia Settled by French
(1864) ✣284●, ◆284 (1), ◆285 (2)
New Deal see Roosevelt, Franklin
New England Settlement begins
(1620) ✣126●, ◆126 (1)
New Granada
Viceroyalty established (1739)
✣148●
independence secured ✣90●
New Guinea
BCE drainage and cultivation
✣19●
Dutch annex west (1825) ✣91
exploration and mapping
✣279, ◆279 (2)
prehistoric agricultural
development
✣280, ❑280, ◆280 (2)
seized by Japan (1942) ✣103●
settlement
✣280, ✣280●, ◆280 (1)
New Haven European and native
conflict (1637) ✣126, ◆126 (1)
New Holland Established by Dutch
(1630) ✣149●
New Kingdom (c.1530–1070 BCE).
Period of ancient Egyptian history
marked by strong central
government control, and one
which saw the height of Egyptian
power. Punctuated by the El-
Amarna period of Akhenaten.
✣26●, ✣26, ✣159●
New Spain (var. Sp. Virreinato de
Nueva España). Spanish Viceroyalty
established in 1535 to govern
Spain's conquered lands north of
the Isthmus of Panama and regions
in present-day Lower California.
◆126 (1), ◆148 (2)
New State (var. Port. Estado Novo).
Dictatorship (1937–45) of President
Getúlio Vargas of Brazil, initiated
by a new constitution issued in Nov
1937. Vargas himself wrote it with
the assistance of his minister of
justice, Francisco Campos.
✣82●, ◆152 (1)
New York
English colony (1664) ✣82●
See also New Amsterdam
New Zealand
Captain Cook's map ❑87
colonization
British
✣91, ✣283, ✣284●, ◆283 (5)
European (1840)
✣283, ◆283 (4)
Pacific decolonization and
nationhood ◆285, ◆285 (3)
Pacific imperialism ◆284 (1)
Polynesian colonization
✣55●, ✣60, ◆60 (2), ✣281,
◆280–1 (2)
Maori carved canoe head ❑281
possessions
1925 ✣98–9
1975 ◆106–7
trade and industry
refrigerated shipping
✣92●, ❑283
sheep farming ❑283
whaling ✣283●, ◆283 (4)
World War II, mobilization and
casualty figures ✣105
Newbery, John 16th-century English
explorer and merchant. Traveling
to Hormuz in 1581–83 to survey its
commercial prospects, he became
the first Englishman to sail down
the Euphrates and visit Hormuz,
Shiraz, and Isfahan. He returned
overland through Persia to
Constantinople. ◆219 (3)
Newfoundland Reached by Vikings
(c.1000 CE) ✣60
Newton, Sir Isaac (1642–1727).
English mathematician and
physicist. His work on calculus, the
laws of motion, gravity, and light
made him the most celebrated
scientist of his age. ❑83

Nez Percé War (1877) War which broke out between the Nez Percé people of the N.W. plains and the US army. It was the result of a long-running dispute over the drastic reduction of the Nez Percé reservation in 1863 after gold was discovered on their lands, and incursions by European settlers. Led by Chief Joseph, a band of 250 Nez Percé kept US forces at bay for more than five months. They were subsequently forced to relocate to Oklahoma. ✢128–9 (2)

Ngami, Lake Reached by Livingstone (1849) ✢157●

Nguni
dispersal of clans (1816) ✢166●
Mfecane wars ◆166 (2)
wars with Dutch begin (1779) ✢164●

Nguyen Anh Emperor of Vietnam (1774) ✢87●

Nguyen Puc Anh see Gai Long

Nian Rebellion (var. Nien) (1853–68) Chinese peasant rebellion of the mid-19th century. ◆268 (2)

Nicaea Council assembled by Constantine (325) ✢48●

Nicaragua, civil war (1978–89). After 40 years of dictatorship, a revolution in 1978 by the left-wing Sandinistas, who drew on the support of a rural peasant base, began 11 years of civil war. Despite losing the first free elections of 1990, the Sandinistas remain a potent force in the country, increasingly threatening the stability of the government.
civil war (1979) ✢110●
US intervention ✢139●, ◆139 (5)

Niebuhr, Carsten (1733–1815). German-born surveyor who took part in an international scientific expedition in 1761, financed by the King of Denmark, to explore the Arabian Peninsula. Niebuhr was the only survivor. His systematic accounts of the expedition, containing maps and illustrations, were published in 1772 and 1774. ◆219 (4)

Nielsen hot blast process (1824) ❑90

Nieuwpoort ⚔ of Dutch Revolt (1600). Dutch victory over Spain. ◆195 (5)

Niger Basin, Arabic and Portuguese views ✢156 (1) (2)

Niger Delta
Nok culture (BCE) ✢38
Oyo main tribe (1747) ✢87●

Nigeria
independence ◆169 (1)
industrial growth ✢168, ◆168 (2)
secession of Biafra and civil war (1967–70) ✢107●, ◆169 (4), ✢169●

Nimrud
(BCE) ✢31, ✢35●
Phoenician carved plaque ❑176

Ninety-five Theses (1517). Document demanding ecclesiastical reforms, especially with regard to the sale of indulgences, nailed to a church door in Wittenberg by Martin Luther. ✢95●
See also Martin Luther

Nineveh (BCE) ✢31, ✢35●

Niño, Andreas 16th-century Spanish explorer of Central America. ✢125, ◆125 (4)

Nippur Plan of city (BCE) ✢28, ❑28, ✢28 (2)

Nirvana see Buddhism

Nisa Parthian capital ✢43

Nixon, Richard Milhous (1913–94) 37th president of the US. (Republican, 1969–74). Came to political prominence as a member of HUAC (the House Committee on Un-American Activities) investigating the Alger Hiss case. He served as vice president under Dwight D. Eisenhower from 1952–59, but lost the 1960 presidential election to John F. Kennedy. He was eventually elected president in 1968 and won a second term in 1972 by a narrow margin. Nixon's term of office saw the invasion of Cambodia in 1970, the ending of the Vietnam War, the initiation of arms limitation talks with the Soviet Union and the reestablishment of US relations with China. His involvement in the Watergate scandal led to his resignation in 1974, although he was granted a full pardon by his successor, Gerald Ford. ✢139●

Njinga Queen of the Ndongo kingdom in southwest Africa (r.1624–63). She resisted Portuguese attempts to expand their control of the Angola region. ❑164

Nkrumah, Dr. Kwame (1909–72). Ghanaian nationalist leader who led the Gold Coast's drive for independence from Britain and presided over its emergence as the new nation of Ghana. He headed the country from independence in 1957 until he was overthrown by a coup in 1966. ✢168

Nobile, Umberto (1885–1978) Italian aviator. Crossed the N. Pole in his dirigible balloon in 1926, along with Amundsen and 14 others. A second expedition ended in disaster with the loss of seven lives. ✢286–7 (2)
See also USA, Canada

Noin Ula Burial site (BCE) ✢39●

Nok culture var. Nok figurine culture. Ancient Iron Age culture that existed on the Benue plateau of Nigeria between about 500 BCE and 200 CE. They produced the earliest known ironworking south of the Sahara, and distinctive terra-cotta figurines.
✢160, ❑38, ✢160 (1)

Nok figurine culture see Nok culture

Norden's county maps ✢173

Nordenskjöld, Baron Nils Adolf Erik (1832–1901) Swedish explorer and scientist. Made several expeditions to Spitzbergen. In 1870 led expedition to explore Greenland ice cap. In 1878–79, he sailed through the Northeast Passage on the ship Vega. ✢286–7 (2)

Noriega, General Manuel Antonio Morena (1940–) Panamanian politician and soldier. As commander of the National Guard and de facto ruler of Panama (1982–89), Noriega enjoyed US support until 1987. In 1988 he was indicted by a US grand jury on charges of drug trafficking, and in 1989 he was arrested during a US military operation in Panama, and deported to the US. ❑139

Normans Name given to the Vikings, chiefly of Danish origin, who, under their leader Rollo, settled in northern France from the early 10th century. Originally the word meant Northmen or Norsemen. The Viking settlers of Normandy soon became French speakers, well integrated with the local population, but their adventurous spirit showed itself in the 11th century in their conquests of England and of Southern Italy and Sicily.
conquest of England (1066) ✢62●, ◆186, ◆186●, ❑186, ◆186 (2)
of Sicily (1091) ✢62●

Normandy Landings (var. D-Day, Operation Overlord) ⚔ of WW II (Jun–Jul 1944). Allied combined operation, the largest amphibious landing in history, which initiated the Allied invasion of Nazi Europe. ✢105, ✢105●, ◆105 (3), ◆211 (4)

Normandy
Duchy founded by Vikings (911) ✢185●, ◆185 (3)

Norsemen see Vikings

North Africa 158–169
Berber states ✢161, ◆161 (2)
colonized by Vandals ✢52–3, ◆52 (1) (2)
Fatimid rulers ✢58
reconquered by Justinian ✢54
Roman amphitheater ❑161
Roman Empire ✢42
spread of Islam ✢56 (1), ✢86, ✢111

North America 116–139
1865–1920 ◆132–3
Anglo-French conflict ✢126–7, ◆127 (2)
big game hunting (BCE) ✢18
boom and bust (1914–41) ✢134–5
California Gold Rush (1849) ✢90●, ✢93
cemetery (BCE) ✢18●
cities and empires ✢122–3
colonization ✢86, ◆126 (1)
cultures
Adena (1000 BCE) ✢30
Anasazi ✢58, ✢62●
Aztec ✢66, ✢74, ✢78, ✢124 (1) (2) (3)
Hopewell (BCE) ✢38●, ✢46●, ◆120, ◆123, ✢36 (1)
Maya ✢46●, ✢50, ✢54, ✢58●, ✢66●, ✢124
Mogollon ✢58
Olmec (BCE) ✢30●, ✢34
decline of the Democratic South ✢139
early peoples ✢120–1, ◆121 (4)
early subsistence and agriculture ✢26, ✢90, ◆120 (1)
eastern interior ✢119, ◆119 (2)
expansion ✢82, ✢90, ✢128, ◆128 (2)
exploration and mapping ◆60●, ✢118, ◆118 (1) (2) (3)
historical landscape ✢116–17
indigenous people ✢90, ✢118, ✢123, ✢126, ✢128–9
population changes ✢126
seizing of the West ✢128, ✢128●, ◆128–9 (2)
settlement and conflict ✢126–7, ✢128–9, ✢136–7, ◆128 (2)
settlers populate the West ❑94, ✢128
societies in transition ✢136–7
Spanish exploration and colonization ✢125●, ◆125 (4)
struggle for nationhood ✢128, ✢128●, ◆128–9 (2)
wagon trails ◆128 (2)
wildlife ✢118

North American Free Trade Agreement (NAFTA). Agreement betwen the US, Canada, and Mexico to remove trade barriers between the three nations for a ten-year period. It came into force in Jan 1994. ✢136●
See also USA, Canada

North Atlantic Treaty Organization (NATO). Established in 1949 as security coalition among Western Allies, dominated by the US. Frequently deployed troops from member states as peacekeeping forces, but played a large role in Gulf War (1991) and Yugoslav conflict (1999).
created 1949 ✢108●, ◆109●, ✢213
Cold War alliances ✢109, ✢138, ◆138–9 (1)
conventional arms limitation (1990) ✢109●
US collective defense treaties (1983) ◆138 (1)
Warsaw Pact (1955) ✢106●, ✢108, ◆108 (3)

North Korea see Korea

North Vietnam see Vietnam

Northeast Passage Maritime route along the northern coast of Europe and Asia between the Atlantic and Pacific oceans, not fully navigated until 20th century.
✢257 (2)
search for routes to Asia (1550–1807) ✢80●, ✢257●, ✢286, ◆286 (1)

Northern Chou see Northern Zhou

Northern Expedition (1926–28) An attempt by the Kuomintang (Guomindang) to unify China, led by Jiang Jieshi (Chiang Kai-shek). ✢271●

Northern Song see Song dynasty

Northern Wei see Toba Wei

Northern Zhou (var. Northern Chou) Ruling dynasty of northern China (557–581) that overthrew the Northern Qi.
✢261●, ◆261 (5)

Norway
800–1000 ◆185 (3)
accession of Canute (1016) ✢62●
foreign affairs
possessions
1925 ◆98–9
1950 ◆102–3
1975 ◆106–7
Norwegians settle in Scotland (c.900 CE) ✢60●
WW II, mobilization and casualty figures ✢105
Union of Kalmar (1397) ◆70●

Novgorod
founded by Rurik the Viking (862 CE) ✢60●, ✢185
granted independence (1136) ✢62●

NRA see National Recovery Administration

Nubia The name given by the Egyptians to the area extending from the First Cataract of the Nile south to the Sudan. Its capital was first at Napata then at Meroë. In the 2nd millennium BCE the Nubians were under Egyptian rule, but themselves ruled Egypt in the 1st millennium, making Napata briefly the center of the ancient world. Egypt's 25th dynasty, 751–668 BCE, came from Cush and 300 of their pyramids remain.
BCE ✢30, ✢31●, ✢34
confederacy of chiefdoms ◆159 (3)
Coptic Christianity ✢58
gold deposits (BCE) ✢26

Nubt Confederacy (BCE) ◆159 (2)

Nuclear Age General term for the period since the end of WW II when nuclear fission technology, used for power generation and weapons of mass destruction, was developed by a coterie of powerful nations.
bombing of Japan ◆104, ◆273, ◆273 (3)
Pacific test sites ❑285, ✢285 (2)

numerical systems
evolution ✢33, ◆33 (2)
See also mathematics

Numidia Roman province north of the Sahara in N. Africa.
Berber state ✢161 (2)
Christian converts (c.150 CE) ✢47●
Roman control ✢46
under Masinissa (c.210 BCE) ✢46

Nur al-Din (d.1174). Turkish leader of Muslim resistance to the crusader states from his territories in Syria. He sent his pupil Saladin to Egypt, where he brought the Fatimid Caliphate to an end in 1169. ✢65●

Nyasa, Lake Reached by Livingstone (1859) ✢157●, ◆168 (1)

Nyasaland (now Malawi). Granted independence (1963) ✢169●

Nyerere, Julius (1922–1999) The first prime minister of independent Tanganyika (1961), who became the first president of the new state of Tanzania (1964). Nyerere was also the major force behind the Organization of African Unity (OAU). ❑168

O

Oaxaca Region of southern Mexico which was the site for the some of the earliest civilizations of Central America including the Olmec. ◆36 (1), ✢121

Ocampo, Sebastián de Early 16th-century Spanish conquistador, leader of expedition from Hispaniola to Cuba. ✢125, ◆125 (4)

Occaneechee Path Exploration (1673) ✢119●

Oceania General geographic term for the island groups of the Pacific Ocean, sometimes including Australia and New Zealand. 276–285
✢55, ✢91
Austronesian and Polynesian migrations ◆280–1 (3)
and Australasia, historical landscape ✢276–7, ◆276–7
exploration and mapping ✢278–9, ◆278–9 (1) (3)
peopling the Pacific ◆280–1 (3)
prehistoric ✢15, ◆280–1

Octavian see Augustus Caesar

Oda Nobunaga (1534–82) Provincial leader who initiated the unification of Japan (r.1568–82). ✢266, ◆266 (4)

Odoacer 5th-century barbarian chieftain, who in 476 deposed the last Roman emperor, Romulus Augustulus, to become ruler of Italy with his capital at Ravenna. He was killed in 493 after surrendering to Theodoric.
rules Italy (476) ✢182●
defeated by Ostrogoths (492) ✢53●

Offa (r.757–96). King of Mercia, which during Offa's reign became the most powerful of the Anglo-Saxon kingdoms of Britain. ✢183●

Offa's Dike Rampart and ditch built c.785 by Offa of Mercia to define the border between the English and the Welsh. ◆183 (3)

Ogedei see Ögödei

Ogilvie's road maps ✢173

Ögödei (var. Ogedei) (d.1241). Mongol leader, son of Genghis Khan, who led successful campaigns against the Khwarizm Shah and the Jin of northern China. He was elected Great Khan in 1229.
elected Great Khan (1229) ✢69●
Mongol campaigns (1229–41) ✢68–9 (1)

O'Higgins, Bernardo (1778–1842) Liberator of Chile. Son of an Irish-born soldier who emigrated to Chile, O'Higgins rose to be leader of the patriotic forces that fought for liberation from Spain from 1810. Defeated and driven from Chile in 1814, he received support from the newly independent Republic of Río de la Plata, crossed the Andes with José de San Martin, and won the decisive battle of Chacabuco in 1817. He became the first president of Chile, but his authoritarian rule was unpopular and he was driven from office in 1823. He died in exile in Peru. ◆150 (1)

Ohio
Kent State University protest (1970) ✢137●, ✢137 (7)
migration (1917–20) ✢134

Ohio River
Adena culture (1000 BCE) ✢30
first proper survey (1729) ✢119●

oil
crisis causes inflation (1973) ✢106●
exploitation ✢107, ✢138
OPEC founded ✢107●
pollution ❑235
production in Gulf region ✢234 (1)

Oirats Nomad raids on China ✢75

Okinawa ⚔ of WW II (Mar–Jun 1945). Major US amphibious assault which, with Iwo Jima, secured an island base for strategic bombing campaign against Japan. ◆272 (1), ✢273 (2)

Old Kingdom (2795–2180 BCE). Period of Egyptian history encompassing the 4th to the 8th Dynasties which was especially notable for the building of the pyramids. ◆36 (1), ✢159●, ✢159 (3)

Old World General geohistoric term for Africa and Eurasia, prior to European discovery of Americas and Australasia.

Olid, Cristóbal de Early 16th-century Spanish conquistador, leader of expedition from Mexico to Honduras. ✢125, ◆125 (4)

oligarchy In the ancient Greek city-states an oligarchy was in place when power was in the hands of a minority of male citizens, as contrasted with democracy when power was held by the majority. ✢176

Olmec culture Elaborate Central American native culture based on the Mexican Gulf coast, which flourished between 1200 and 600 BCE. The Olmecs influenced the rise and development of other great civilizations and are credited with having the first planned religious centers, with monumental sculptures and temples, and with devising the 260-day Mesoamerican calendar.
civilization (1200 BCE) ✢30●, ✢34, ❑30, ✢121 (2)
heartlands ◆121 (3)
jade ceremonial adze ❑121
state religion (BCE) ◆36 (1)

Olustee ⚔ of American Civil War (Feb 20, 1864). Union victory. ◆131 (7)

Olympia Athletics festival (776 BCE) ✢31●

Olympic Games Revived (1896) ✢94●

Omaha People of the Upper Amazon region of S. America. ✢147, ◆147 (5)

Omani Sultans
attack Portuguese in E. Africa (1729) ✢164●
capture Mombasa (1698) ✢83●

Oñate, Cristóbal de 16th-century Spanish explorer, leader of an expedition from Mexico to New Mexico and Arizona. ✢125, ◆125 (4)

Oñate, Juan de (c.1550–1630) Spanish conquistador. Led colonizing expedition into New Mexico in 1598 establishing settlements north of the Rio Grande. Reached mouth of Colorado River in 1605. Governor of New Mexico from 1605–08. ✢125, ◆125 (4)

Onin War (1467–77). Struggle between Japanese warlords. ✢267●, ◆267 (4)

OPEC see Organization of Petroleum Exporting Countries

Operation Market Garden see Arnhem

Operation Overlord see D-Day, Normandy Landings

Opium Wars Confrontations (1839–42) (1850–60) arising from Chinese (Qing) attempts to limit the profitable British opium trade in south and east China. British naval forces attacked or blockaded several Chinese ports (Guangzhou, Xiamen, Fuzhou, Ningbo, Tianjin, Shanghai) wresting the first of many territorial trading cessions (Treaty Ports) in the peace settlement, the Treaty of Nanjing (1842). ✢91●, ✢269●, ◆269 (4)

optical instruments Newton's reflecting telescope ❑83

oracles
bones for divination ✢27●
Shang dynasty interpretations ❑32

Orange Free State founded (1854) ✢166●

Orange River, reached by Dutch settlers (1720) ✢87●

Orbigny, Alcide Dessalines d' (1802–57). French paleontologist, who spent eight years (1826–34) traveling in South America, producing a 10-volume account of his travels and the first detailed map of the whole continent. His observations on fossils in sedimentary rocks gave rise to the science of micropaleontology. ✢143

Orellana, Francisco de (c.1490–1546) Spanish conquistador. Orellana was a member of an expedition to the eastern slopes of the Andes led by Gonzalo Pizarro, brother of Francisco. He and companions became separated from the main party and sailed the length of the Amazon. ✢142●, ◆142 (1)

Organization of African Unity (OAU). Founded (1963). ✢169●

Organization of Petroleum Exporting Countries (OPEC). International organization seeking to regulate the price of oil. Founded in 1960, it consists of thirteen oil-producing countries which include Saudi Arabia, Iran, Iraq, Kuwait, Venezuela, Libya, and Algeria.
founded ✢107●, ✢234
restricts supplies (1973) ✢107●

Orinoco Raleigh's expeditions ✢149

Oriskany ⚔ of American Revolutionary War (Aug 6, 1777). American victory. ◆127 (3)

Orléans Siege (1429). Turning point in Hundred Years' War. The city, under siege from the English, was relieved by the French, inspired by Joan of Arc. ✢75●, ✢192, ✢192●

Oromo People of East Africa who migrated north into Ethiopia in large numbers in the 16th and 17th centuries. ✢165, ◆165 (3)

Orozco, Francisco de Early 16th-century Spanish explorer of N. America. colonizing expedition (1521) ✢125, ◆125 (4)

Orozco, Pascual Mexican revolutionary leader ✢133

Ortelius, Abraham (1527–98) Dutch cartographer and publisher. Publisher of the first "modern" atlas, the Theatrum Orbis Terrarum in 1570. ✢79, ✢173●

Osaka Emergence of Yamato state (c.300) ✢58

Osei Tutu (d. 1712). Founder and first ruler of the Asante nation. ✢164●

Osman I (c.1258–1326) Founder of the Ottoman dynasty, which grew powerful in the regions of northwest Anatolia bordering Byzantium. By the time of his death the Ottomans controlled most of Bithynia. ✢67●, ❑230

Ostrogoths The "Eastern Goths" first emerged as a threat to Rome in 453, after the death of Attila and the dispersal of the Huns. Under their leader, Theodoric the Great, they conquered Italy in 493, establishing a kingdom that lasted until 553. ✢182
See also Goths

Otto I (aka Otto the Great) (912–73). He was elected king of the Germans in 936 and crowned emperor in 962. His defeat of the Magyars at Lechfeld in 955 put an end to their raids on western Europe. Made Germany the most powerful political entity in western Europe.
defeats Magyars (955) ✢58●, ✢185, ✢185●
Holy Roman Emperor ✢58, ✢185, ◆185 (3)

Otto II (955–83) Holy Roman Emperor. Joint emperor with his father Otto I from 967.
Italian campaign ✢185●

Ottokar II (1230–78). King of Bohemia, who extended Bohemian rule almost to the Adriatic. He was defeated by the Emperor Rudolf of Habsburg at the battle of Marchfeld. ✢189●, ◆189 (4)

Ottoman Empire Islamic empire established in Anatolia in the late 13th century by Turkish tribes. It rapidly spread into Europe, reaching its peak in the 16th century when it stretched from the Persian Gulf to Morocco in the south, and from the Crimea to the gates of Vienna in the north. After the unsuccessful siege of Vienna (1683), the empire began a protracted decline, collapsing altogether when Turkey was defeated in WW I. 230–233
1200–1400 ◆189 (4)
1300–1500 ◆230 (1)
1400 ✢70–1, ◆229 (4)
1500 ✢74–5, ◆193 (4)
1512–1639 ◆231 (3)
1600 ✢78–9
1700 ✢82–3
1800 ✢86–7
1800–1913 ✢232, ✢232●, ◆167 (4), ◆232–3 (1)
1850 ✢90–1
1900 ✢94–5, ◆166 (1)
founded (1299) ✢67●, ◆230
Bursa becomes capital (1326) ✢71●
decline and collapse ✢86●, ✢98, ✢232
partition (1918–23) ✢233●
defeats
by Timur (1402) ✢95●
European lands lost (1912–13) ✢99●
⚔ Lepanto (1571) ✢79, ✢231●
Safavid Persia (1501–1736) ✢231, ◆231 (4)
siege of Vienna (1683) ✢82●, ✢195
expansion
rise of the empire ✢230, ✢230●, ◆230 (1)
consolidation and resistance (17th century) ✢196, ✢196●, ◆196 (2)
frontier (16th century) ◆195 (4)
height of power (1512–1639) ✢231, ✢231●, ◆231 (3)
Mamluks conquered in Egypt (1517) ✢79●
naval campaigns (15th–16th century) ◆230 (2)
of power (1453–1571) ✢194, ✢194●
seizes Anatolia ✢71
southeastern Europe (1354) ✢71●
Trebizond (1461) ✢75●
WW I ✢99●
Habsburg conflict (1663–171) ✢197, ✢197 (4)
Indian Ocean trade ✢230, ◆230 (2)
Janissary corps (c.1380) ✢71●, ❑230
sultan deposed (1908) ✢99●
See also Balkans; Turkey

Ottonian dynasty Saxon dynasty, named after Otto I, Holy Roman Emperors in the 10th and 11th centuries. ✢185, ✢185●

Oudney, Walter (d.1824) British naval officer and explorer. He accompanied Denham and Clapperton across the Sahara to Lake Chad in 1822, but died during the journey. ✢157 (4)

Oyo West African state that dominated the region between the Volta and the Niger in the 18th century.
main power in Niger Delta (1747) ✢87●
slave trade ✢82
state established (c.1500) ✢79●

P

Rajaraja the Great (r.985–1014). Chola king who extended Chola control into the eastern Deccan, Ceylon, and the Malay Peninsula. By the time he died, he was the paramount ruler of southern India. ✛244, ◆244 (2)

Rajendra I (r.1014–44). King of the Chola dynasty of southern India. Under his rule the Chola navy took control of the eastern sea route between Arabia and China. He ruled from the city of Tanjore. Chola rule (1014) ✛63●
conquers Ceylon (1018) ✛63●

Rajput clans People of Rajputana, N. India. Defeated in 1191 by the Afghan leader Muhammad of Ghur. ✛63●, ◆244 (3)

Raleigh, Sir Walter (c.1554–1618). English adventurer. He found favor under Elizabeth I and named the colony he founded on Roanoke Island in 1584 Virginia after the "virgin queen." Fell out of favor with Elizabeth and under James I was imprisoned. Released in 1616 to undertake a voyage to Guiana in search of El Dorado. This ended in disaster and Raleigh was executed on his return to England. ✛149

Ramayana Classical Sanskrit epic of India relating the adventures of Rama, probably composed in the 3rd century BCE. Based on numerous legends, the epic was revised and set down in its best known form by the poet Tulsi Das (1532–1623). ✛241, ◆36 (3)

Rameses III (var. **Ramesses**) (r.c.1184–53 BCE) Second king of the 20th dynasty of Egypt. Went to war with the Philistines and the "Sea Peoples." ✛31●

Ramesses see Rameses III

Rangoon Founded (1755) ✛87●

Rapa Nui (var. Easter Island) colonized by Chile ◆284●
settled by Polynesians
✛55●, ✛60, ✛281, ✛281 (4)
temple platforms
✛600●, ❏281

Rashtrakutas A powerful kingdom established in 753 CE in the northern Deccan. At its peak, Rashtrakuta control extended from southern Gujarat to Tanjore. ✛244●, ◆244 (2)

Ravenna Capital of Italy under the Ostrogoths and Byzantines.
captured by Lombards (752) ✛58●
captured by Ostrogoths (492) ✛53, ✛182
detail from mosaic (6th century) ❏182
sarcophagus ❏182

Raymond of Toulouse Crusade route (1096–99) ◆64–5 (2)

Reagan, Ronald Wilson (1911–2004). 40th president of the United States (Republican, 1981–89). A former movie actor, as president of the Screen Actors' Guild Reagan cooperated with efforts to combat alleged Communist influences in the American film industry. He was governor of California from 1967–74. In 1980 he won the presidential election in a landslide victory. During his tenure he greatly increased military spending while reducing taxes and cutting back on general government expenditure. He introduced the controversial SDI (Strategic Defense Initiative) and signed the INF treaty with the Soviet Union, which limited intermediate range missiles. His administration was damaged by revelations that profits from arms deals with Iran had been used to support the Contra rebels against the Sandinista government of Nicaragua. ✛139, ✛139●

Recife Taken by Portuguese (1654) ✛149●

Reconquest of Spain (var. Sp. Reconquista). The reconquest of Muslim Spain by the Christian states, from the 11th to the 15th century. ✛192, ✛192●, ◆186 (1), ✛192 (3)

Reconquista see Reconquest of Spain

Reconstruction (1865–77). Period following the US Civil War in which the southern states were controlled by the Federal government and social legislation including the granting of new rights to Blacks was introduced. But a new Republican government returned power to white leaders who reintroduced segregation in the South. ✛132

Recuay Cultural region ◆145 (4)

Red River Indian War (1874–75). Major uprising by members of the Arapaho, Cheyenne, Comanche, Kiowa, and Kataka tribes from reservations in Oklahoma and Texas against white settlers in the area. US forces led by General William Sherman were forced to fight 14 battles against the natives in the Red River Valley, before their eventual surrender. ✛128–9●, ◆128–9

Red Scare Name given to the fear of Communist subversion in the US which arose in the late 1940s, leading to the setting up of schemes such as the Federal Employee Loyalty Program, and Senator Joseph McCarthy's list of government employees whom he claimed had Soviet sympathies. The scare led to a significant degree of persecution of those suspected of Communist sympathies, and many people – especially in the government, schools, universities, and the mass media – found themselves unable to work because of their suspected beliefs. ✛135●

Red Sea trade (1st century CE) ✛225, ◆225 (3)

reducciones Jesuit frontier settlements in Spanish S. America ✛143, ◆143 (2)

Reformation Religious revolution of the 16th century which took place in the Roman Catholic church, led by Martin Luther and John Calvin. The Reformation had long-term political, economic, and social effects, and laid the groundwork for the foundation of Protestantism. ✛194–5, ✛195●

refrigeration First commercial units (1856) ✛92●

refugees and resettlement ✛212, ✛212 (3)

Reiss, Wilhelm 19th-century German explorer of S. America, who scaled the volcano Cotopaxi in 1872. ✛143●

religion
Buddhism (to 400 CE) ◆49 (3)
characteristics ◆36 (1)
development of organized ◆36–7
global ◆48–9
Mediterranean cults ◆37 (3)
Mithraism, Judaism, and Christianity (to 600 CE) ◆48 (1)
old world ◆49, ◆49 (4)
South Asian ◆36 (2)
state ◆36 (1)
Taoism and Confucianism ◆37 (4)

Remojadas Early Mexican civilization (c.600–900 CE) ✛122 (1)

Renaissance (var. **Renascence**, c.1300–1550). Period of cultural, economic, and political efflorescence in medieval Europe, characterized by the rediscovery of classical Greek and Roman culture, which found expression, initially in Italy, in the growth of humanist studies and in writing, and a revitalization of architecture, painting, sculpture, and the arts in general.
comes into being ✛75
in Europe (12th century) ✛187, ✛187●, ✛187 (3)
travelers in W. Asia ◆219 (3)

Renascence see Renaissance

Rennell, James (1742–1830). British naval officer who became the surveyor-general of Bengal in 1764. He was responsible for the first consistent mapping of the Indian subcontinent, the Survey of India. ✛239●, ❏239

Republican Party One of the two major political parties of the US. Formed in 1854 to support anti-slavery policies prior to the Civil War, Abraham Lincoln was its first president. Today, it favors limited government and interventionist foreign policy and is generally considered to be more right-wing than the Democratic Party. ✛130–1, ✛135 (5), ✛139 (4)

Rio de Janeiro
Brazilian capital (1763) ✛149●
Carnival dancers ❏112
France Antarctique colony (1555) ✛149●

Rio de la Plata Viceroyalty established (1776) ✛148●

Réunions Lands occupied by France during the reign of Louis XIV following the decisions of a special court convened for the purpose, the Chambre des Réunions. Important annexations included Luxembourg (1679) and Strasbourg (1684). Most of the territories had to be returned by the Treaty of Ryswijk (1697). ✛197●, ✛197 (5)

revolts
against rule of Louis-Napoleon ✛202, ✛202●
Boxer rebellion (1898) ✛95, ✛97, ❏97, ✛268 (2)
Dutch (1568–1609) ✛195, ✛195●, ✛195 (5)
English Peasants' (1381) ✛70●, ✛188 (2)
European students (1968) ✛106●
following Black Death ✛70
fragmentation of China (220–589) ✛261
Hungarian Hunyadi ✛193●
Indian Mutiny ✛95●, ✛249, ✛249●, ◆249 (3)
movements against colonial rule (1880–1920) ✛97, ✛97 (4)
Taiping rebellion (1850–64) ✛95●, ❏268
Warsaw Pact crushes Hungarian (1956) ✛106●
Yellow Turbans (147 CE) ✛47●

revolutions
American (1775) ✛86, ✛126–7, ✛127 (3)
Chinese (1911) ✛271, ✛271 (5)
Cuban ✛152
economic ✛92–3
era of revolution 1768–1868 ✛89, ✛89●, ✛88–9 (2)
in Europe (1900) ✛202●, ✛209
factors leading to industrial ✛86
French ✛82, ✛86, ✛90, ✛199, ❏199, ✛199 (4)

impact of industrial ✛92, ✛92 (1)
inventions and world economy (1835–95) ✛92●
Liberty on the Barricades (painting) ❏89
political crackdowns ✛100●
Russian (1905, 1917) ✛98●, ✛99●, ✛208, ◆208 (2)
See also industrial revolution

Rhodes Greek island
Hospitallers headquarters (1310) ✛64●

Rhodes, Cecil (1853–1902). Financier, statesman, and empire builder of British South Africa. He was prime minister of Cape Colony (1890–96) and founder of the diamond mining company De Beers Consolidated Mines Limited (1888).
De Beers Consolidated Mines ✛167
portrait ❏166

Rhodesia ◆168 (1)
Northern Rhodesia granted independence (1963) ✛168●
See also Zimbabwe

Ri dynasty see Yi dynasty

Ricci, Matteo (1552–1610) Italian Jesuit missionary and cartographer. Joined Jesuit mission in Macao in 1582, and then established mission on Chinese territory, eventually settling in Beijing in 1601. His maps and other data gave the Western world unprecedented access to information about China. ✛80

Richard I of England (aka Richard the Lion-Heart, Lion-Hearted, Fr. Richard Coeur de Lion) (1157–1199). Duke of Aquitaine from 1168 and of Poitiers from 1172 and king of England, duke of Normandy, and count of Anjou (r.1189–99). His prowess in the Third Crusade (1189–92) made him a popular king in his own time.
Crusade route (1189–92) ◆64–5 (2)
jousts with Saladin ❏64
succession (1189) ✛187●

Richard II (1367–1400) King of England (r.1377–99). Son of Edward the Black Prince. Deposed in 1399 by his cousin, Henry of Lancaster, later crowned Henry IV. He died in prison, probably murdered. ✛192●

Richelieu, Cardinal Chief minister of Louis XIII with whom he collaborated to make France a leading European power. ✛196

Riel Rebellions (1869) (1885). Rebellions by the Metis (mixed race descendants of the Cree tribes and French fur traders) and their native allies against incursions of European settlers into their lands. ✛129 (2)

Rig Veda Completed c.900 BCE, this is the great literary monument of Aryan settlers of the Punjab. A collection of sacred hymns, it traces the religious development of Aryan India and depicts the Aryan settlers as chariot-driving warriors who gradually adapt to a more sedentary life. It is rich in geographical references. ◆36, ✛242, 242●, ◆242 (1)

Rio de Janeiro
Brazilian capital (1763) ✛149●

roads
maps ❏99
Ogilvie's maps ✛173
Peutinger Table ❏172
Roman (by c.120 CE) ◆172 (1)

Robert I "the Bruce" (1274–1329) King of Scotland (r.1306–29). Crowned in 1306 in defiance of King Edward I of England. Decisively defeated the English at the battle of Bannockburn (1314). English acknowledgment of Scottish independence and Robert's right to the throne came in 1328.
victor at Bannockburn ✛188●, ❏188, ✛188 (2)

Robert of Normandy (c.1054–1134) Duke of Normandy (r.1087–1106). Eldest son of King William I of England. Inherited Normandy upon the death of his father, while his brother William inherited the throne of England. Took part in the First Crusade (1096–1100). Crusade route (1096–99) ◆64–5 (2)

Robespierre, Maximilien François Marie-Isidore de (1758–94). French revolutionary and Jacobin leader who played a key role in the overthrow of the moderate Girondins. A member of the Committee of Public Safety which instituted the Reign of Terror (1793–4). Overthrown by the Convention, he was tried and guillotined. ✛199●
See also French Revolution, Jacobins, Terror, Reign of

rock art The oldest known art form, dating back to c.30,000 BCE in Western Europe, usually depicting hunting scenes and found in caves or, commonly in African examples,

rock shelters and exposed rock faces. The images are either painted or etched into the rock surface, and are not purely decorative: some occur in recesses so difficult to access that they are thought to have played a part in ritual activities. Rock art is more abundant in the Saharan region than anywhere else in the world. ✛17●, ✛17 (3) (5)

Roerich, Nicolas (1874–1947) Russian traveler and painter in Central Asia. ✛257 (3)

Roger II of Sicily (1095–1154) (r.1101–54) First Norman king of Sicily, whose court at Palermo was one of the most magnificent in Europe, a meeting place for Christian and Arab scholars. Commissioned the *Book of Roger*, a medieval book of maps. ✛62, ✛218

Roggeveen, Jacob (1659–1729). Dutch explorer. His voyage across the Pacific in 1722 established the first European contact with a number of islands, including Rapa Nui (Easter Island) and Samoa. ✛278●

Roman Catholicism see Catholicism

Roman Empire The largest empire ever established in Europe, stretching from northern Britain to Egypt. From its apogee in the 2nd century CE, the empire became increasingly difficult to govern, and in 395 it was divided into two. The Western Empire fell in 476, but the Eastern Roman (or Byzantine) Empire, with its capital at Constantinople, survived until 1453. ✛42–3, ✛46–7, ✛50–1, ✛52–3, ✛54–5
51 BCE to 138 CE ◆180●
c.117 CE at the death of Trajan ◆161 (2)
c.120 CE under Hadrian ◆180 (1)
240–395 CE ✛181, ✛181 (4)
250–400 CE ✛180●
476 CE end of the Empire ✛182
Attila the Hun defeated (451) ✛50●
and Carthage: the Punic Wars ✛42, ✛179, ◆179 (3)
conflict with Sassanian ✛50
conquests (to 120 BCE) ✛179, ◆179 (5)
depictions
exotic animal combat ❏44
maritime trade ❏44
mummy case ❏47
The Nile in Flood mosaic ✛47, ❏47
Europe after the fall ✛182, ✛182 (1)
expansion program ✛42, ✛179●, ✛224–5, ◆224 (2)
exploration and mapping ✛42, ✛47, ✛218 (1)
Africa (c.150) ◆156 (3)
boundaries of ancient Europe ◆172 (1)
Hadrian's defensive strategy ✛180
Italian confederacy (264 BCE) ✛38●
mythological pantheon ✛37
overseas provinces (120 BCE) ✛179
Palatine Hill village (BCE) ✛31●
subjugation of Greece ✛179, ✛179 (4)
territory (240 BCE) ◆178 (1)
Tetrarchy of Diocletian ✛50, ✛181, ❏181, ✛181 (4)
trade, classical world ◆44–5
Western Empire collapses (476) ✛50●
See also Rome

Romania
end of Communism (1989) ✛110●
granted independence ✛232
See also Balkans, nationalism; Wars, World War I; World War II

Rome Rome began as a small city-state which, through military might combined with skilful use of threats and alliances, conquered first the Italian Peninsula, then, by the 1st century BCE, the entire Mediterranean world. The city of Rome's importance declined from the 4th century CE. From the 7th century, it regained prestige as the seat of the papacy and headquarters of the Roman Catholic Church. It was ruled by the papacy until it became the capital of the newly united kingdom of Italy in 1871.
earthenware amphora ❏181
Imperial Rome (c.300 CE)
✛181, ✛181 (2)
legionary ❏178
politics
capital of united Italy (1871) ✛94●
and the Italian Confederacy ✛178
and Latin allies (c.495 BCE) ◆178
ruins of Colosseum ❏181
sacked by Vandals (455) ✛52●
sacked by Visigoths (410) ✛53●, ✛182●
saved from Huns ✛53
saved from Lombards ✛183●
supply routes ✛181, ◆181 (3)
See also Roman Empire.

Rome, Treaty of see European Union

Romulus Augustus Last Roman emperor in the West, deposed (476) ✛50●

Roosevelt, Franklin Delano (aka FDR) (1882–1945) 32nd president of the US (Democrat, 1932–45). Roosevelt became president in 1932, on the cusp of the worst years of the Great Depression. He immediately launched a series of reforms collectively known as the "New Deal" to combat the depression; these included the abandonment of the gold standard and agricultural price support, as well as programs such as the Works Progress Administration, aimed at providing work for the unemployed, and the creation of a Social Security Act. His "common touch" and immense personal popularity saw him elected for an unprecedented four terms. Though initially opposed to involvement in conflict in Europe, by the outbreak of WW II, he broke with neutrality to support the Allied position, bringing the US fully into the war following the bombing of Pearl Harbor in Dec 1941.
American President (1932–45) ✛134, ✛139
New Deal ✛102, ✛134, ✛134●, ✛135
FDR effect ✛135
NRA recovery program ❏134
WPA (Works Progress Administration) ❏134
portrait ❏135
World War II
Casablanca conference (1943) ✛104●
Tehran conference ✛105●
Yalta "Big Three" conference (1945) ❏105

Roosevelt, Theodore (Teddy) (1858–1919) 26th president of the US (Republican, 1901–09). After commanding the "Roughriders" in the Spanish-American War (1898), Roosevelt returned as governor of New York from 1898–1900, and was subsequently elected vice president. He became president following the assassination of William McKinley. He initiated the building of the Panama Canal, strengthened the US navy, and won the Nobel Peace Prize in 1906 for his part in ending the Russo-Japanese war. He formed a "progressive" movement within the Republican party but was defeated on the Progressive ticket in the elections of 1910.
US President 1901–09 ✛132
era of economic boom ❏132

Rosas, Juan Manuel de (1793–1877) Argentinian dictator. Although his official title was only governor of Buenos Aires province, Rosas was the effective ruler of Argentina from 1829–52. He owed his position to his loyal force of gauchos, and his wars of conquest against the Patagonian native tribes. ❏151

Rosebioom, Johannes 17th-century explorer in N. America. Employed by Governor Thomas Dongan to discover new routes for the fur trade. Reached Michilimackinac between Lakes Huron and Michigan in 1685 after traveling for three months. ◆119 (2)

Rosenberg, Ethel and Julius (1915–53), (1918–53). American Communists and part of a transatlantic spy ring. Convicted of passing on atomic secrets to the Soviet Union and executed. They were the first US citizens to be executed for espionage. ❏108

Rosetta stone Basalt slab inscribed by priests of Ptolemy V of Egypt in hieroglyphic, demotic, and Greek. Found near the city of Rosetta in Egypt in 1799 and taken by the British in 1801; now in the British Museum in London. Served as the key to understanding Egyptian hieroglyphics. ❏42

Ross, Sir James Clark (1800–62) British naval officer and explorer of the poles. Accompanied both Edward Parry and his uncle John Ross on expeditions in the Arctic. In 1839–43 he led the navy's first major Antarctic expedition. He discovered the Ross Sea, the Ross Ice Shelf, Ross Island, and Victoria Land.
Antarctic exploration (1839–43) ✛287 (3)
Arctic explorer (1829–33) ✛287, ◆286–7 (2)

Rotz, John Early map of S. America (1542) ❏142

Rousseau, Jean Jacques (1712–78) French philosopher and writer. Believed in the original goodness of human nature and that it was society that created inequality and misery. His most famous work, *Du Contrat Social* (1762), profoundly influenced French revolutionary thought. ✛198

Royal Road Road constructed under the Persian Achaemenid Empire in the 6th century BCE from Susa, the ancient capital of Persia, to Sardis,

on the Aegean Sea. construction ✛35, ✛223●, ◆223 (4)

Rozwi Empire Empire of southern Africa (c.1684–early 19th-century) challenges Portuguese (17th century) ✛164
replaces Mwenemutapa ✛164

Ruanruan (var. Juan-juan, Avars). Nomadic steppe peoples whose expulsion from Mongolia by the Blue (Celestial) Turks in the 4th century CE impelled them westward, entering Europe in the mid-6th century. See also Avars. ✛261●, ✛261 (4)

Rub' al Khali (var. the "Empty Quarter"). Area of waterless desert covering some 250,000 sq miles (650,000 sq km) of the southern Arabian Peninsula.
19th- and 20th-century explorers ✛219●

Rudolf I (1218–91) Count of Habsburg and Holy Roman Emperor. The first Habsburg to be elected Emperor, Rudolf secured Austria as the center of the Habsburg domains through his defeat of Ottokar II of Bohemia in 1278. ✛189●

Rukh (1377–1447). Mongol shah, son of Timur ✛75

Rum Seljuk Sultanate in Anatolia in the 12th and 13th centuries, with its capital at Konya (Iconium). Its name is derived from Rome, because its lands had been captured from the Byzantine (East Roman) Empire.
◆65 (1) (2), ✛225

Rurik the Viking (r.c.862–79). Semi-legendary Swedish ruler of the merchant town of Novgorod, seen as the founder of the Russian state (named after "Rus," the Finnish word for Swede). ✛60●

Russia State originating in rise of Muscovy in the 16th century under Ivan IV, who defeated the Tatars and united neighboring principalities, proclaiming himself Tsar. Consolidated power in eastern Europe and expanded beyond Urals in 17th century (notably under Peter the Great), to dominate northern and central Asia by 18th century. Tsarist rule toppled by Bolshevik (Communist) revolution in 1917. 194–215, 257–273
See also USSR
foreign affairs
Alaskan expeditions (1816–65) ✛119 (3)
Balkan nationalism ✛203, ✛203 (4)
Baltic states, conflict ✛195, ✛195●, ✛197, ✛195 (3), ✛197 (3)
Bering Strait-Alaska exploration (16th–17th century) ✛257
claim on N. America (1821) ◆128 (2)
conquers and annexes Crimea (1783) ✛86●
Crimean War (1854) ✛94, ✛203
Empire see below
France, opposition alliances (1792–1815) ✛90●, ✛201, ✛201 (3)
neutrality pact with Japan (1939) ✛103●
Treaty of Nerchinsk with China (1689) ✛83●, ✛257●
Turkey and the Black Sea ✛203, ✛232, ◆203 (4)
withdraws from Amur basin (1689) ✛83●
World War I see Wars, World War I
World War II see Wars, World War II
Golden Horde vassals (1200–1480) ◆189 (4)
home affairs
Bolshevik Revolution (1917) ✛98●
Mongol conquest begins (1237) ✛66●
Mongol raids (1222) ✛68
population growth (1650–1800) ❏198
revolutions (1905, 1917) ✛98●, ✛99●, ✛208, ◆208 (2)
serfdom abolished (1861) ✛94●, ✛269
trade and industry, Japanese commercial talks (1804) ✛91●
Russian Empire ✛195, ✛208
1800 ✛86–7
1850 ✛90–1
1900 ✛94–5
expansion ✛78, ✛82, ✛257, ✛269, ✛269●, ◆269 (3)
European, consolidation and resistance (17th century) ✛196, ✛196●, ✛196 (2)

Russian Revolution (1917). Revolution which saw the overthrow of the provisional government that had replaced the regime of Tsar Nicholas II by the Communist Bolsheviks, who took over the Winter Palace and swiftly established strongholds in towns throughout European Russia. In 1918, a new constitution was

311

Key to index: ✤ text ❑ picture var. variant name f/n full name r. ruled WW I World War I
● timeline ◆ map aka also known as prev. previously known as ⚔ battle WW II World War II
312

Key to index: ✦ text   ❑ picture   *var.* variant name   *f/n* full name   r. ruled   WW I World War I
● timeline   ◆ map   *aka* also known as   *prev.* previously known as   ⚔ battle   WW II World War II

U

V

they made Toledo their capital, controlling most of the Iberian Peninsula until the Muslim invasion of 711. *See* Goths.

Visscher's *Atlas Contractus* ❑119

Vittorio Veneto ⚔ of WW I (Oct 1918). Final battle of the Italian Front, resulted in victory for the Italians against Austrian forces, who obtained an armistice in Nov 1918. ✦207●, ◆207 (6)

Vizcaíno, Sebastián 16th–17th century Spanish navigator. Sailed regularly on the Manila treasure galleon from 1586. In the early 17th century made expeditions to trace the Pacific coast of N. America, identifying a useful harbor at Monterey and making a detailed survey of the coast. Later commissioned to search the north Pacific for the islands of Rica de Oro and Rica de Plata and to establish diplomatic relations with Japan. ✦125, ◆118 (1)

Volga Slave trade center (13th century) ✦85, ◆84 (1)

Volstead Act (Oct 28, 1919). Law to enforce the 18th Amendment, which prohibited the sale and manufacture of alcoholic drinks in the US. ✦135●, ❑98

Voltaire Pseudonym of François-Marie Arouet (1694–1778). Wit, poet, dramatist. His outspoken belief in political, social, and religious freedom made him the embodiment of the 18th-century Enlightenment. His major works include *Lettres Philosophiques* (1734) and his satire *Candide* (1759). ❑198

Voortrekker *see* Boers

Voting Rights Act (1965) ✦137●

voting rights Slave ✦86

votive mirror Han decorated ❑44

Vouillé ⚔ (517). Visigoths defeated by Clovis I. ◆183 (5)

Vulgate Latin version of Bible completed (404) ✦48●

W

Wahhabis Followers of Muhammad ibn 'Abd al-Wahhab (1703–92), who founded an ultra-orthodox sect in Nejd to preserve the "purity of Islam." An alliance between the Wahhabis and the Saud family led in the 18th century to the unification of most of the Arabian Peninsula under the Saudi banner. In 1902 Abd al-Aziz ibn Saud began to reform and expand the modern kingdom of Saudi Arabia. The Wahhabi form of Islam remains Saudi Arabia's official faith. ✦233
See also Abd al-Aziz ibn Saud.

Waitangi, Treaty of (Feb 6, 1840) Treaty drawn up to facilitate British annexation of New Zealand. The Maori acknowledged British sovereignty in return for ownership of their lands, which could only be purchased from them by crown agents. The initial ceremony at Waitangi was followed by further signings at sites all over N. Island, and the treaty was eventually signed by over 500 Maori chiefs. The Maori translation of the English text led them to believe that they would retain authority over their lands and peoples. ❑91

Waldenses *see* Waldensians

Waldensians (var. Waldenses, *aka* Poor Men of Lyons) Reformist Christian sect founded c.1170, based on teachings of Peter Waldo/Valdez (c.1140–1217), based on simplicity, poverty, and evangelical zeal. Highly critical of clerical behavior, Waldo was condemned by the Council of Verona (1184), and his followers were subject to persecution during the period of the Albigensian Crusade (1209). ◆186 (1)

Waldseemüller, Martin (1470–1521) Cartographer from Lorraine. Famous as the man who coined the word "America" after the Italian explorer Amerigo Vespucci for his world map of 1507. He also published an edition of Ptolemy's *Geography* in 1513. ✦142●, ◆239●

Wales, England, and Scotland (1284–1337) ◆188●

Walker, J & C 19th-century British cartographers.
Indian Atlas ❑239

Walker, Thomas (1715–94) American land speculator and public official. Rediscovered the Cumberland Gap in 1748. ◆119 (2)

Wall Street Crash (1929) Collapse in the price of stocks and shares on the New York Stock Exchange which created panic in financial markets across the world and was a major contributory factor in the Great Depression in the 1930s. ✦102, ❑134

Wallace, Alfred Russel (1823–1913) English naturalist who traveled to the Amazon (1848–52) and Malay archipelago (1854–62). He

developed theories of natural selection which had a profound influence on Charles Darwin. The Wallace Line, which divides the different types of fauna found to the east and west of the archipelago, was named after him. ✦239, ❑239, ◆239 (2)

Wallace, William (c.1270–1305). Scottish national hero who led Scottish resistance forces during the first years of the long struggle against English rule. ◆188 (2)

Wandiwash ⚔ of Seven Years' War in India (1760). French defeated by British. ✦88 (1)

Wang Mang *see* Xin dynasty.
founds Xin dynasty ✦47●

Wang Yangming (var. Wang Yang-ming) (1472–1529). Chinese Neo-Confucian philosopher of Ming dynasty, who taught that Confucian ethics of correct behavior and morality were innate, and could be discovered and promoted through contemplation and self-awareness rather than the study of classical texts and ancestral tradition. His teachings are frequently compared to tenets of Zen Buddhism. ✦75

Wang Yang-min *see* Wang Yangming

Warburton, Peter (1813–89) English-born explorer of Australia. After emigrating in 1853, he set out north from Adelaide, exploring the Simpson Desert and S. Queensland; in 1872 he traveled west from Alice Springs across the Great Sandy Desert to the west coast. ◆279 (2)

warfare
amphibious invasion (1281) ❑263
the cannon ❑71
Chinese weapons (BCE)
✦35●, ✦39●
crossbow ✦39
defensive fortresses ❑197
global technologies (c.1500)
✦76–7 (1)
gunpowder weapons ✦71
Mongol ✦69
portable scaling ladder
❑222, ❑263
prehistoric technology ❑12
two-wheeled chariot ❑24
USSR May Day parade ❑106

Warring States period (403–221 BCE) A time of civil war in China when the Zhou confederation collapsed into rival factions: the Qi in the northeast, Chu in the south, and Qin in the northwest. Brought to an end by the Qin dynasty. ✦37, ✦39●, ✦259●

warrior clans Rise of Japanese ✦265●, ✦259 (4), ✦265 (4)

wars
Achaean ✦179
American Civil War (1861–65)
✦130–1, ❑94, ◆130–1 (1–7
Anglo-Maratha (1775) ✦87●
Arab-Israeli ✦234●
Austrian Succession (1740) ✦86●, ✦199●
Austro-Prussian (1866) ✦203●
Balkan
✦99●, ✦203, 203●, ✦232●
Belgian War of Independence (1830–31) ✦202●
Boer (1899–1902)
✦95●, ✦96, ✦96●, ✦96 (2)
Boer-Bantu (1779–80) ✦87●
Boshin (1868–69)
✦270, ✦270 (1)
Chaco (1932–35)
✦102●, ◆152 (2)
Chinese Civil War (1920–26)
✦271, ✦271 (6)
"Cold War"
✦106–7, ✦108–9, ✦138, ✦212, ✦214, ✦212 (4), ◆251 (5)
Crimean (1854)
✦94, ✦203, ✦232●
Dutch War (1672–79) ✦197●
Dutch Wars of Independence ❑78
English Civil War ✦196●, ❑196
Falklands (1982) ✦110●
Franco-Prussian (1870)
✦94●, ✦203
German-Danish (1864) ✦203●
Great Northern (1700) ✦197●, ✦199●
Great Turkish ✦197●
Greek War of Independence (1821) ✦202●, ✦232●
Gulf War (1990–91)
✦111●, ✦138●, ✦235 (5)
Hundred Years' War
✦70●, ✦75●, ✦187, ✦191, ✦192, ◆192 (1) (2)
Indian-Pakistan (1965) ✦107●
Iran-Iraq (1980–88) ◆235 (5)
Kieft's (1643–46) ✦126
King Philip's (1675–76) ✦126
Korean (1950–53)
✦106, ✦107●, ✦138●, ◆109 (4)
Macedonian ✦179●
Mexico Civil (1858) ✦94●
Mexico-US (1846–48) ✦90●, ✦128, ✦129●, ◆128–9 (2)
Napoleonic (1794–1815)
✦90, ◆200–1, ◆200–1 (1) (3)
Nine Years' (1688–97) ✦197●
Onin (1467–77) ✦267
Opium (1839–60) ✦91●, ✦269 (4)
Pacific (1879–83)
✦94●, ✦151, ✦151 (4)
Paraguayan (1864–70) ✦94●
Parthian ✦224, ◆224 (3)
Peloponnesian (431–404)
✦38●, ✦177, ✦177 (3)

Peninsular (1808–14) ✦200
Pequot (1636–37) ✦126
Punic ✦42●, ✦177●, ✦179, ✦179 (3)
Revolutionary (1775–83)
✦127, ✦127 (3)
Riel Rebellion (1869–85)
✦128–9 (2)
Russian-Ottoman (1768) ✦86●
Russo-Japanese (1904–05)
✦269, ✦270, ✦270 (4)
Russo-Turkish (1877–78) ✦203
Second Afghan (1878–79) ✦95●
Seven Years' (1756–63)
✦86●, ✦88, ✦199●
Sino-Japanese (1894–95)
✦270, ✦270 (3)
Six Day War (1967) ✦107●, ✦234●
of South American liberation (1808–30) ✦150●
Spanish Carlist (1833–39) ✦202●
Spanish Civil War (1936–39)
✦102●, ✦2–9, ✦209 (4)
Spanish Succession (1701–14)
✦197●
Spanish-American War ✦94●
Texas Revolution (1835–36)
✦128–9 (2)
Thirty Years' (1618–48) ✦82, ✦196, ✦196●, ❑196, ◆196 (1)
Tuscarora (1711–13) ✦126
US natives' and settlers' conflicts
✦128, ✦129●, ✦128 (2)
US international conflicts
✦128, ✦129●, ✦128 (2)
Vietnam,
✦106●, ✦107●, ✦108●, ✦137●, ✦138●, ✦251, ❑138, ◆251 (5)
War of 1812,
✦128, ✦129●, ✦128–9 (2)
World War I
casualties ❑207
causes ✦98, 206, ◆206 (1)
Eastern Front ✦207, ✦207●, ❑207, ◆207 (4)
Italian Front ✦207, ✦207●, ❑207, ◆207 (5)
Southeast Europe and Balkans
✦207, ✦207●, ❑207, ◆207 (6)
in Southwest Asia
✦232●, ◆233 (2)
Western Front ✦206, ◆206●, ❑98, ❑206, ◆206 (2) (3)
World War II
Sept 1939–Dec 1941 ◆104 (1)
Dec 1941–July 1943 ◆104 (2)
July 1943–Aug 1945 ◆105 (3)
global warfare ◆105 (4)
battle of the Atlantic ✦210
Greater German Reich (1942)
✦211, ◆211 (2)
Allied invasion (1943–45) ✦211, ◆211 (4)
Allied counteroffensive
✦273, ◆273 (2)
bombardment of Japan
✦273, ◆273 (3)
causes and consequences
✦102–3
human cost of global war ❑105
impact on South and S.E. Asia
◆250–1, ◆250–1 (3)
Japanese offensive
✦272, ✦272●, ◆272 (1)
liberation of POWs ❑138
major battles ◆104–5
mobilization and casualty
figures ◆105
Pacific ✦272–3, ◆273●
Yamasee (1715–28) ✦126
Yom Kippur (1973)
✦107●, ✦234●
Zulu ✦95, ✦96●

Warsaw Pact (var. Warsaw Treaty Organization) (1955). Cold War political and military alliance, dominated by USSR, including Poland, E. Germany, Czechoslovakia, Hungary, Romania, Bulgaria, Albania (to1968).
created by Soviet bloc (1955)
✦106●, ✦109●, ✦213, ◆213 (5)
conventional arms limitation
(1990) ✦109●
crushes revolts ✦106●, ✦213
and NATO ◆108 (3)

Warsaw Treaty Organization *see* Warsaw Pact

Washington, George (1732–99) 1st president of the US (1789–97). Born in Virginia, Washington served with distinction on the British side during the Seven Years' War against France (1754–61). He later represented Virginia in the House of Burgesses, and in the Continental Congresses of 1774 and 1775. When war broke out between Britain and the American colonists, Washington was the first choice to lead the colonial army. Important successes included the battles of Trenton and Princeton, and the key battle of Yorktown in 1781 which virtually ended the American Revolution. From 1783, Washington sought to establish a constitutional government for the new nation. In 1789 the first government under the new constitution was assembled, with Washington as its president. He was elected to a second term, retiring in 1797 in the face of increasing disputes between the Democratic Republicans of Thomas Jefferson and the Federalists, led by Alexander Hamilton.
first US president (1789) ✦86●
forces Cornwallis to surrender (1781) ✦127

Washington Naval Agreement (1922) After the concession of various Pacific territories to Japan at the Treaty of Versailles, this agreement was designed to limit and balance the level of naval power in the region, assuring predominance to the Western Powers. ✦99●

WASP (White Anglo-Saxon Protestants) ✦135

Watergate (aka Watergate Affair). Scandal sparked by involvement of US Republican President Richard M. Nixon's administration in a break-in at the Democratic Party national headquarters (the Watergate building, Washington) during the presidential elections (June 1972). The televised hearings of a special Senate committee revealed escalating degrees of White House involvement and attempted cover-up. This ultimately led to a House Judiciary Committee investigation, the release and publication of sensitive tapes, and the erosion of confidence in Nixon's administration (and Washington practices in general). The imprisonment of three of Nixon's senior aides preceded the adoption of three articles of impeachment against the president, resulting in Nixon's resignation (Aug 9, 1974), although he was subsequently pardoned by his successor, Gerald R. Ford. ✦106●

Waterloo ⚔ of Napoleonic Wars (Jun 18, 1815). Final defeat of Napoleonic forces. ◆200 (1)

wattle and daub Mixture of clay plastered over a framework of interlaced wooden rods and twigs, used for the walls of huts or houses. It can last for several hundred years if adequately protected from the elements by overhanging eaves. ❑21

Watt, James Improves steam engine (1765) ◆204●

wavy-line pottery The first pottery to be made in Africa (c.7000 BCE) by the hunters and fishers of the southern Sahara, who lived in a broad swathe stretching from Mali to the Nile Valley. The pottery was decorated by parallel wavy-lines; these could be made by dragging the spine of a fish across the clay while it was still wet, or using bone or wooden points. ✦19●,

Weddell, James (1787–1834). English navigator whose claim to have sailed into the vast bay in W. Antarctica (1823), bounded by the Antarctic Peninsula, Coats Land and the Ronne Ice Shelf, led to it being named after him. ◆287 (3)

Wei Kingdom *see* Shu

weights and measures ✦33, ❑33

Wellington, Arthur Wellesley, 1st Duke of (1769–1852) British general and statesman; prime minister (1828–30). Campaigned in India, then commanded the British forces in the Peninsular War (1808–14), driving the French out of Portugal and Spain. After Napoleon's escape from Elba, he defeated the French at Waterloo. ◆200 (1)

West, the Geopolitical term relating to the free market economies and countries of US/NATO alliance during the Cold War.

West Africa 156–169
BCE development ✦34
exploration and mapping, medieval interior ✦156
Islamic reform (19th century) ✦167
Islamic wars (1806–70)
✦167●, ✦167 (3)
native kingdoms ✦58
political change
◆163 (4) (5) (6) (7)

West Asia 216–235
Arsacid (Parthian) dynasty founded (247 BCE) ✦43●
BCE ✦14, ✦14●, ✦31●, ✦35●, ✦39
collapse of Ottoman Empire (1918) ✦99●
development of writing
✦223, ❑223, ◆223 (3)
early empires ◆222–3
historical landscape
❑216, ◆216–17
modern history ◆234–5
oil production ◆234 (1)
overrun by Islam ✦55
plant domestication (BCE) ✦19
religions (c.600) ✦226, ✦226●
Sassanian Empire
✦44●, ✦51, ✦55

West Bank Taken by Israel in Six Day War (1967) ✦234●

West Germany (var. Federal Republic of Germany, FRG, Bundesrepublik Deutschland, BRD) Established 1949 following Soviet partition of postwar occupied Germany. Joined NATO (1955), and founding member of EEC enjoying huge economic growth until dissolution upon German reunification (1990).
1950 ✦102–3
1975 ◆106–7
entry into NATO (1955) ✦108
postwar recovery (1961) ✦106
✦212, ✦214

West Indies
colonization by Spain (16th century) ✦78, ✦125, ✦125 (4)
colonization by other European powers ✦126 (1)
piracy ✦85, ✦85 (3)
US intervention ✦139, ◆139 (5)

Western Allies' Limited War doctrine ✦109
See also Limited War Doctrine

Western Front The western theater of war during WW I, based primarily in northeast France and western Belgium.
✦206●, ◆206 (2) (3)

Western Goths *see* Visigoths

Western Han *see* Han dynasty.

Western Jin Ruling dynasty of China (265–304 CE) who overthrew the Wei and briefly established Chinese unity. ◆260 (3)

Western Railroad Surveys of US (1853–55) ◆119 (3)

Western Samoa Achieves independence (1962)
✦285, ✦285●
See also Samoa

Western Union Telegraph Surveys of US (1865–67) ◆119 (3)

Western Zhou *see* Zhou dynasty.

Westphalia, Peace of (1648) General name for the 11 separate treaties, negotiated 1643–48, between the Habsburgs and their adversaries, bringing to an end the Thirty Years' War, which recognized religious tolerance and secularization of Church lands in much of Germany, and the independence of the United Provinces and the Swiss Confederation. ✦82, ✦199

wheat
agricultural mechanization ✦90
commercial Africa (19th century) ◆166 (1)
domestication ✦19●

Wheeler, George Montague (1842–1905) US army officer and explorer. After completing a survey for the military of the area east of the Sierras in 1869, he set up his own organization: the United States Geographical Surveys West of the One-Hundredth Meridian, and surveyed thousands of miles of the West. ◆119 (3)

Whitby, Synod of (663). Ecclesiastical council which led to Britain's Christian communities adopting the practices and doctrines of Rome rather than those of Celtic Christianity. 183●

White Cloud Iowa chief, portrait ❑129

White Huns (var. Hephthalites) *see* Huns

White Mountain ⚔ of Thirty Years's War (1620). Bohemians defeated by Habsburg armies. ✦196 (1)

White Plains ⚔ of American Revolutionary War (Oct 28, 1776). British victory. ✦127 (3)

Whitney, Eli (1765–1825). US inventor, whose development of the cotton gin to separate cotton fiber from cotton seed (1793) transformed the efficiency of the Southern cotton industry and the conditions of its slave work force. Never properly patented, his invention was widely copied. He later manufactured firearms using a prototype production line system. ✦93, ❑130

Whydah Captured by Dahomey (1727) ✦164●

Wilderness, The ⚔ of American Civil War (May 5-7, 1864). Inconclusive result. ◆131 (7)

Wilhelm I (1797–1888) King of Prussia (r.1861–88) and first German Emperor (r.1871–88). Dominated by chancellor Bismarck, whose policies led to creation of German Empire. ✦94●

Wilhelm II (1859–1941) German emperor and king of Prussia (r.1888–1918). He dismissed Bismarck (1890) and, in a long period of personal rule, asserted Germany's claim to world leadership. Forced to abdicate at the end of WW I. ❑94

Wilkes, Charles (1798–1877) US explorer of Antarctica. After appointment as head of Depot of Charts and Instruments (1834) he commanded the US Exploring Expedition (1838–42) in the Southern Ocean, surveying the part of Antarctica now named after him, Wilkes Land. Court-martialled for cruelty, he retired during the American Civil War, retiring as rear admiral. ◆287 (3)

William I (aka William, Duke of Normandy, William the Conqueror) (c.1028–87). First Norman king of England (r.1066–87), who inherited dukedom of Normandy in 1035, annexing Maine (1063) and invading England, defeating Harold Godwinson at the battle of Hastings (1066), ending the era of Saxon rule. His victory was recorded, and claims to the English throne justified, in the Bayeux Tapestry. He introduced religious, political, and social reform, and began the process of English

unification. Although largely based in Normandy, he commissioned the first systematic survey of English property, the Domesday Book (1085), the foundation of the English feudal system.
✦186●, ◆186 (2)

William, Duke of Normandy *see* William I

William of Nassau *see* Nassau

William the Conqueror *see* Willam I

William of Rubruck (c.1215–1295). A Franciscan friar, in 1253 he was sent on a religious mission to the Mongols by Louis IX of France. His description of his travels and his meeting with the Great Khan Möngke were contained in his Itinerary, one of the best-known works of travel of the medieval period.
explorer of Central Asia (1253–54) ◆256 (1)
W Asia (1253–55) ◆219 (3)

Willoughby, Sir Hugh (d.1554) British military officer and explorer. Appointed captain-general of a fleet of three ships sent by London merchants to seek a Northeast Passage. One of the ships, commanded by Richard Chancellor, reached the White Sea. ✦80●, ◆257 (2), ◆286 (1)

Wills, William (1834–61) English explorer of Australia who accompanied Robert Burke on his journey across Australia from south to north. Died of starvation at base camp, Cooper's Creek, after reaching swamps at the Gulf of Carpentaria. ❑279, ◆279 (2)
See also Burke, Robert O'Hara.

Wilson (Thomas) Woodrow (1856–1924) 28th president of the US (Democrat, 1912–21). Under Wilson's administration, women's right to vote was added to the Constitution, along with the prohibition of the sale of alcohol. Wilson took the US into WW I in 1917 and intervened in the Mexican Revolution following Pancho Villa's attacks on US territory and citizens. He laid out the "fourteen point" plan for peace which led to the Armistice in Nov 1918, and gave vigorous support to the League of Nations. His health was broken by the Senate's refusal to ratify the Treaty of Versailles. ✦98

Wilson's Creek ⚔ of American Civil War (Aug 10, 1861). Confederate victory. ✦131 (6)

windmills ✦63, ❑63

Witwatersrand
gold finds (1886) ✦93●

Wolfe, General James (1727–59) English general. Led British forces during the Seven Years' War against France in N. America. He was instrumental in the capture of Louisburg in 1758, but was killed during the Battle of Quebec in 1759 which resulted in British victory. ❑127

Woodstock (1969) Huge rock festival in upstate New York, often seen as the culmination of the so-called "Summer of Love." ❑137

Woodward, Dr. Henry (d.c.1686) 17th-century explorer of N. America. From 1668 he explored much of the Carolinas, including the Savannah River. ◆119 (2)

Works Progress Administration (WPA) (var. from 1939–43, Work Projects Administration) Set up in 1935, as part of the Roosevelt administration's New Deal, the WPA aimed to provide work for the unemployed on a series of government projects, including the building of new roads, public buildings, bridges, parks, and airports, as well as the employment of writers, artists, and actors in community arts and theater projects. ❑134

World Trade Organization (WTO). Organization for the regulation and liberalization of world trade, set up in January 1995 as a successor to GATT (the General Agreement on Tariffs and Trade) which had been in existence since 1947. 104 countries were founding members of the WTO, which is responsible for making sure that GATT agreements are adhered to, as well as the setting up of new trade agreements.

World War I (var. First World War, the Great War) (1914–18). Major conflict in which expansionist aggression by Germany, Austria-Hungary, and the Ottoman Empire in Europe and their colonial holdings (the Central Powers), was countered by an Allied coalition led by France, Britain, Russia, Italy and (from 1917) the US. The first war to be fought on a truly industrial scale, involving mass mobilization of population and industry, and the innovative use of airplanes, gas, and tanks on the battlefield, it was also a war of attrition on a massive scale. It heralded the end of European imperialism, the Communist

(Bolshevik) Revolution in Russia, the redrafting of the map of Europe, and the dismemberment of the Ottoman Empire. +206–207●, ◆206–207 (2)–(6), +232

World War II (var. Second World War). Major conflict (1939–45) arising from territorial expansion and aggressive racist policies of Germany, Italy, and Japan (the Axis), who were countered by an Allied coalition led by Britain and the Commonwealth, forces from Axis-occupied nations, USSR, and US (from 1941). Mass mobilization of the population and industry by all belligerents, the gradual involvement of most countries in the world, the prosecution of the war on land, sea, and air, the widespread involvement of partisans, technological innovation, and the impact of the war on civilian populations led to its characterization as a "Total War." The insistence by the Allies on unconditional surrender, and their deployment of nuclear weapons over Japan proved decisive. The final stages saw the destruction and partition of Europe, the occupation of Japan, and the emergence of USSR and US as ideologically opposed superpowers during the Cold War. +104–5●, ◆104–5, +210–11●, ◆210–11, +272–3●, ◆272–3 (1) (2)

World Wide Web International computer network offering a huge interface for the storage, retrieval, and exchange of information. +113 *See also* Internet.

Wounded Knee, Massacre at (1890). More than 200 Sioux were killed by US army troops in what was to be the last major confrontation between Native Americans and the US army. +128 (2)

Wrangel, Baron Ferdinand von (1797–1870) Russian vice admiral and explorer of Arctic waters and coasts of Siberia. ◆257 (2)

writing 32, 223
  evolution +32●, +223, +223●, +32 (1), ◆223 (3)
  alphabet +31●, +44●, ◆223 (3)
  Canaanite script (1600 BCE) +27●
  Chinese +259●, ❑258, +32 (1)
  counting and calendars +32–3
  cuneiform +24●, +25, +32●, +223, ❑25, ❑34, +32 (1), ◆223 (3)
  Etruscan script (c.690) +176●
  first alphabetic script (1600 BCE) +27●
  first texts +25, ❑25
  Indus script +32 (1)
  Linear A script (1650 BCE) +27●
  Mesoamerican script +32 (1)
  Olmec syllabary writing system +121
  Phoenician +27●, +31, +32●, ❑32, +32 (1)
  recording of knowledge +76–7 (1)
  Roman lapidary inscription ❑32
  Runic script +32 (1)
  Zapotec +32
  See also hieroglyphics

Wu Kingdom *see* Shu, Wu, and Wei Kingdoms
Wu-ti *see* Wudi.
Wudi (var. Wu-ti) (156–87 BCE). Most powerful of Former Han rulers (r.140–87 BCE), whose campaigns in south and southwest China, Vietnam, and against the Xiongnu of Central Asia greatly extended Chinese realms. He established the role of emperor and Confucianism as state religion, and revived a central bureaucracy. +44●, +45

X

Xanadu *see* Shangdu
Xenophon (c.431–350 BCE). Greek historian and disciple of Socrates. A skilled soldier, he fought with 10,000 Greek mercenaries under the Persian prince, Cyrus, in the 401 BCE campaign against Cyrus' brother, the King of Persia. Cyrus' death left the Greeks stranded 900 miles from home. Elected leader, Xenophon led them safely to the Black Sea. +218●

Xerxes I (var. Xerxes the Great) (519–465 BCE). The son of Darius I, Achaemenid King of Persia, Xerxes (r.486–465 BCE) is known mainly for his massive and unsuccessful invasion of Greece from the Hellespont in 480 BCE. +39●, +223, +223●

Xhosa Bantu-speaking people of southern Africa, inhabitants of South African homeland of Transkei until late 20th century. resist European colonists +86

Xia dynasty (var. Hsia, c.2000–1800 BCE) Ruling dynasty of first Chinese proto-state, forerunners of the Shang. +259●

Xiankiang (var. Dzungaria), conquered by Qing (1760) +87
Xin dynasty (var. Hsin dynasty) Ruling dynasty of China (9–23 CE) under sole emperor Wang Mang (former Han regent 1–8 CE) who introduced major reforms, including taxation, money lending, nationalization of estates, and government monopolies on main industries (salt, coinage, iron, wine) during his brief interregnum before accession of Later Han. +47●

Xiongnu (var. Hsiung-nu). Chinese name for federation of largely nomadic steppe peoples that dominated central Asia from c.3rd century BCE to the 4th century CE, constantly threatening China's northern borders. Disrupted by campaigns of Former Han, they split into eastern and western hordes; after decline of Han dynasty, Xiongnu generals established dynastic kingdoms in N. China during the Sixteen Kingdoms period. Sometimes associated with the Huns.
  confederacy breaks up (55 BCE) +43●
  nomadic steppe people +259
  steppe cavalry tactics ❑261

Xixia Empire (var. Hsihsia) *See also* Tanguts.
  founded by the Tangut +263
Xochicalco Influential fortified city ❑122, +122 (1)
Xuan Zang (var. Hsuan-tsang, 596–664) Chinese pilgrim and traveler whose search for original Buddhist texts took him across the Gobi and Takla Makan deserts, to Bactria and the Punjab to the Gangetic Plain, returning overland. His account of his 16-year journey, and its geographical descriptions, were published by imperial command. ◆256 (1)

Y

yak Early domestication ❑258
Yalta Conference (Feb 4–11, 1945) Meeting of Allied war leaders led by Roosevelt, Churchill, and Stalin. Reaffirmed the decision to demand unconditional Axis surrender and planned a four-power occupation of Germany. Also discussed the plans for the United Nations.
  "Big Three" conference (1945) +105, +109●

Yamasee War (1715–16). Conflict between British colonists and the Yamasee tribe and its allies in S.E. South Carolina, a result of European incursions into native lands and the fur trade. ◆126 (1)

Yamato state Ancient Japanese state and clan on the island of Honshu.
  Chinese influence +264
  emergence (c.300) +51
  expansion ◆264 (1)

Yan'an (var. Yenan) End of Chinese Communists "Long March" +103●

Yangshao culture (c.5000–3000 BCE) Early agricultural culture of China centered around the Yellow River basin, later replaced by Longshan culture. The Yangshao is characterized by square and round timber and thatch houses and handmade red burnished pottery, finished on a slow wheel. Yangshao communities grew millet, had domesticated pigs and dogs, and lived across much of the Yellow River valley in the 4th and early 3rd millennium BCE.
  geometrical decorated pot ❑258
  neolithic China ◆258 (2)

Yangtze
  delta rice cultivation +19
  first agricultural communities +258
  siege of Hezhou (1258–59) ❑69

Yanomani Hunter-gatherer tribal people of Amazonian rain forest, whose traditional lifestyle was threatened by commercial concerns developing in the region in the late 20th century. ❑110

Yayoi culture (c.300 BCE–300 CE). Period in Japanese history when rice, pottery, and metals were introduced. +264, +264 (1)

Year of the Four Emperors (68–69 CE) When the Roman emperor Nero was overthrown in 68 CE the struggle for succession plunged the empire into civil war. The following twelve months saw Galba proclaimed as emperor in Spain, but murdered on his return to Rome. His successor, Otho, committed suicide when Vitellius was proclaimed emperor in Germany. Finally Vespasian was declared emperor by his troops, invaded Italy and successfully claimed the throne. +46●

Yellow River
  BCE agricultural revolution ◆258 (1)
  massive floodings (1351) +71●
Yellow Turbans (var. Zhang Yue). Religious sectarian revolt of Later Han (184 CE), whose communal lifestyle and vision of a forthcoming age of "Great Wellbeing" made them the most significant of the peasant revolts which attended Han decline. +47●, +260 (1)
Yellowknife River Expedition by Franklin (1821) +119●, ◆119 (3)
Yeltsin, Boris (1931–) First president of Russia after the break-up of the Soviet Union in 1991. He oversaw the transformation of the Russian economy to a free market. In increasingly poor health and faced with the threat of impeachment, he resigned at the end of 1999. +214
Yenan *see* Yan'an
Yermak, Timofeyevich (d.1585) Russian Cossack whose campaign against the Tartar khanate across the centrals Urals (1581) led to the first Russian settlement of Siberia. Killed in a counteroffensive, his achievement initiated the systematic Russian exploration, occupation, and settlement of Siberia. +257●, ◆257 (2)
Yi dynasty (var. I, Li, Ri, 1392–1910). Ruling dynasty of Korea, founded by Yi Songgye with Ming support. +71●
Yijing (var. I-ching). Chinese Buddhist pilgrim of late 7th century CE who visited the hearth of Buddhism by sea (685–695). ◆256 (1)
Yi Songgye *see* Yi dynasty
Yom Kippur War (Oct 6, 1973). War in which Egypt and Syria launched a joint surprise attack on Israel on the Jewish festival of Yom Kippur. The war ended three weeks later when Israel had repulsed Syria, and crossed the Suez Canal, encircling an Egyptian army. Following UN ceasefire, Israel withdrew from Egyptian side of canal and, after 1979 treaty, from Sinai. +234, ◆234 (2)
York Viking stronghold +60●, +185●
Yorkshire Cotton towns ◆93 (4)
Yorktown, Siege of ⚔ of American Revolutionary War (Sep 28–Oct 19, 1781). American victory. ◆127 (3)
Yoruba People of W. Africa, noted for urban cultures on lower reaches of Niger, whose kingdom of Oyo emerged as one of the most powerful in the region until the early 18th century. +86, ◆164 (2), ◆165 (4), ◆166 (1), ◆167 (3) (4)
Young Turks The failure of the Ottoman sultan, Abdul Hamid II, to modernize the empire led in 1908 to a revolution by the Young Turks, an association of army officers and reformers. The sultan was forced to restore the suspended constitution before his deposition in 1909. The Young Turks subsequently became the empire's dominant political party. +232
  See also Atatürk.
Younghusband, Francis (1863–1942) British explorer of Central Asia. In 1902 led the expedition which opened up Tibet to the western world, leading to Anglo-Tibetan Treaty (1904). ◆257 (3)
Yuan dynasty (1206–1367) Ruling Mongol dynasty of China. +67●, +263, +263●, +266, ◆263 (7)
Yuan Shih-k'ai *see* Yuan Shikai
Yuan Shikai (var. Yuan Shih-k'ai) (1859–1916). First president of the Republic of China in 1912 after the 1911 revolution. Precipitated civil war in 1913 by murdering the revolutionary party chairman and trying to create a new imperial dynasty. +271●
Yucatan
  Maya city-states +122, ◆122 (2)
  Maya civilization (1000 BCE) +121, +122●, ◆122 (2)
  Olmec civilization (1200 BCE) +30, ◆121 (4)
  ◆124 (1)
Yuezhi Tribal people of S.C. Asia who were unified under the Kushanas (c.60 CE) +47
Yugoslavia 208–215
  civil war (1991) +110●
  conflict +215, +215●, ◆215 (3)
  copper mines (c.4000 BCE) +174
  creation ◆208 (1)
  World War II *see* Wars, World War II
Yukon
  Bluefish Cave settlement (13,000 BCE) +14●
  gold rush +93, ❑93, ◆93 (3)
Yungang Caves Datong, north central China, site of first colossal Buddhist rock-carvings, c.460 CE ❑49

Z

Zagwe dynasty (1137–1270). Ruling dynasty of Ethiopia, whose interregnum in the Solomonian line was marked by fragmentation and a move away from the ancient capital of Axum.
  church ❑62
  established in Ethiopia (1150) +63●
Zaire
  as Congo, Katanga secedes from Republic +107●
  President Mobutu overthrown (1997) +111●
  See also Congo.
Zama ⚔ of Punic Wars (202 BCE). Decisive Roman victory. ◆179 (3)
Zangi (aka Imad al-Din Zangi, 1084–1146). Seljuk governor of Mosul (1126), who carved out an independent state around Aleppo, and whose capture of Edessa from the Franks (1144) caused the Second Crusade. Assassinated by associates while campaigning to capture Damascus. Succeeded by his son, Nur al-Din (1144) +65●
Zanzibar Arab trading settlements +58, +61, ◆162 (1)
Zapata, Emiliano (1879–1919) Mexican revolutionary. Following the outbreak of the Mexican Revolution (1910–17), Zapata organized the occupation of large estates, demanding the return of land to the people. His forces were mainly responsible for bringing down the dictatorship of Porfirio Diaz, and he later opposed the government of Venustiano Carranza. He continued agrarian reform in the south, setting up the Rural Loan Bank. +133, ◆133 (3)
Zapotec culture Pre-Columbian Middle American natives whose culture flourished in southern Mexico between 300 BCE–300 CE. They were centred on Monte Albán and produced the earliest hieroglyphic inscriptions in the Americas. +34, +38●, +121, ◆121 (2)
Zen Buddhism Sectarian form of Buddhism developed and practiced in China, Korea, and Japan, based on intense meditation, austere discipline, and monasticism, seeking to achieve enlightenment through nonrational forms of thought. Frequently associated with martial arts and intense aestheticism. +49●, +63●
Zeus Greek god ❑37
  Sanctuary of (776 BCE) +31●
  See also Jupiter.
Zhang Qian (var.Chang Ch'ien) (d.c.114 BCE). Han diplomat and ambassador whose travels in Central Asia seeking Han allies against the Xiongnu make him the earliest recorded explorer. Imprisoned by the Xiongnu for ten years (139–129 BCE), he escaped and traveled to Ferghana and Bactria, returning to China in 126 BCE. Reports of his journeys, which marked out the Silk Road, including a second trip to Parthia (115), encouraged Han expansion in Central Asia.
  explorer of Central Asia (138–126 BCE) +256, ◆256 (1), +260
Zhang Yue *see* Yellow Turbans
Zhao Rugua (var. Chao Ju-kua) 13th-century Chinese traveller, contemporary of Marco Polo, who recorded his journeys in Southeast Asia. +256●
Zheng He (var. Cheng Ho) (1371–1435) Chinese admiral and emissary of the emperor Chengzu. Undertook expeditions to S.E. Asia, India, Arabia, and Africa.
  exploration of Africa ◆156 (3)
  Indian Ocean voyages +75●, +77
  silk painting of a giraffe ❑266, ◆267 (3)
Zhengzhou
  plan of city +29, ◆29 (4)
  Shang capital +27●
Zhongdu Jin capital +69
Zhou dynasty (var. Chou). (1111–256 BCE) Chinese dynasty that overthrew the Shang dynasty in 1027 BCE. The Western Zhou developed political unity until 770 BCE, when the Eastern Zhou established a new capital at Luoyang and rivalry and dissent between the states eroded centralized power. The Zhou confederation collapsed into civil war (the Warring States period, 403–221 BCE) and was brought to an end by the Qin dynasty. +35, ◆30–1, +259 (4)
  bronze ritual vessel ❑31
  exploration of BCE China +256●
  Taoism +37 (4)
Zhou Enlai (var. Chou en-lai) (1898–1976) Chinese statesman, founding member of the Chinese Communist Party, and loyal supporter of Mao Zedong. Active during Japanese and Civil wars, became prime minister upon Communist victory (1949) until his death, also serving as foreign minister (1949–58). Generally moderate, in favor of detente, he established the Four Modernizations program (1975). +270–271●
Zhu Siben (var. Chu-ssu-pen) (1273–1337). Chinese mapmaker of Yuan (Mongol) dynasty, whose Atlas comprised a single-scale map of China and its neighbors, with details extending to the Indian Ocean, and most of the African coastline. ❑77, ❑256
Zhu Yuanzhang (var. Taizu, Hung-wu [mightily martial] emperor, Chu Yuan-chang) (1328–98). Founder and first emperor of Chinese Ming dynasty (r.1366–98). Born into poverty, he became a monk in 1344, before joining a bandit gang. Rose to become leader of a rebel army which seized Nanjing (1356) and over the next 12 years overthrew the Mongol (Yuan) rulers, proclaiming the Ming imperial dynasty in 1366. +71, +266, ❑266
ziggurat Built in Sumeria and adjacent Elam, these are temples constructed on a high pyramidal mound with a series of external stairways on all sides leading to a surmounting shrine. +220
Zimbabwe
  decolonizaton ◆168 (1)
  struggle for majority rule +168
  See also Great Zimbabwe, Rhodesia.
Zimri-Lim Palace constructed (2300 BCE) +27●
Zirids Muslim dynasty ◆57 (2)
zodiac Thracian fresco (BCE) ❑39
Zollverein The customs union of German states organized in 1834 under Prussian auspices. It marked an important step toward German unification +203, ◆203 (3)
Zoroastrianism A monotheistic religion dating back to the Achaemenid era founded by Zoroaster (Zarathustra, Zardushi), a Persian or Bactrian prophet who lived from about 628–551 BCE. The roots of Zoroastrianism lay in the ancient polytheistic folk-myths of India, from which Zoroaster abstracted a single Wise God, Ahura Mazda, opposed by the Evil Spirit Angra Mainyu. After the Greek and Roman eras, the Sassanians restored Zoroastrianism as Persia's state religion. Its modern adherents are the Parsees. +51, +226, ❑36, +49 (4), ◆226 (1)
Zoser, King (var. Djoser, Netjerykhet) (c.2650–c.2575 BCE) Egyptian ruler of the 3rd dynasty. His reign was a period of technical innovation and cultural flowering, including the construction of Egypt's first stone buildings; formerly they were made of bricks and mud. He initiated the building of the first step pyramid at Saqqara, the first structure of its size in the world. +23●, ❑159
Zulu kingdom Kingdom in southern Africa which arose under Zulu leader Shaka (r.1816–28), who with a well-disciplined and efficient fighting force, conquered most of present-day Natal.
  expansion +166●
  struggle for South Africa +92●, ◆92 (1), ◆166 (2)

318

Key to index: ✛ text ❑ picture *var.* variant name *f/n* full name *r.* ruled WW I World War I
  ● timeline ◆ map *aka* also known as *prev.* previously known as ⚔ battle WW II World War II

INDEX-GAZETTEER

Glossary of Abbreviations

This glossary provides a comprehensive guide to the abbreviations used in this Atlas, in the Subject Index and Glossary and in the Index-Gazetteer.

A
abbrev. abbreviated
Afr. Afrikaans
aka also known as
Alb. Albanian
Amh. Amharic
anc. ancient
approx. approximately
Ar. Arabic
Arm. Armenian
ASEAN Association of South East Asian Nations
ASSR Autonomous Soviet Socialist Republic
Aust. Australian
Az. Azerbaijani
Azerb. Azerbaijan

B
Basq. Basque
BCE before Common Era
Bel. Belorussian
Ben. Bengali
Ber. Berber
B-H Bosnia-Herzegovina
Bibl. Biblical
bn billion (one thousand million)
BP British Petroleum
Bret. Breton
Brit. British
Bul. Bulgarian
Bur. Burmese

C
C central
C. Cape
Cam. Cambodian
Cant. Cantonese
CAR Central African Republic
Cast. Castilian
Cat. Catalan
Chin. Chinese
CIS Commonwealth of Independent States
Cro. Croat
Cz. Czech
Czech Rep. Czech Republic

D
Dan. Danish
Div. Divehi
Dom. Rep. Dominican Republic
Dut. Dutch

E
E east
EC see EU
EEC see EU
ECU European Currency Unit
EMS European Monetary System
Eng. English
est estimated
Est. Estonian
EU European Union (previously European Community [EC], European Economic Community [EEC])

F
Faer. Faeroese
Fij. Fijian
Fin. Finnish
Flem. Flemish
fl. Floruit
Fln. full name
Fr. French
Fris. Frisian
ft foot/feet
FYROM Former Yugoslav Republic of Macedonia

G
Gael. Gaelic
Gal. Galician
GDP Gross Domestic Product (the total value of goods and services produced by a country excluding income from foreign countries)
Geor. Georgian
Ger. German
Gk Greek
GNP Gross National Product (the total value of goods and services produced by a country)

H
Heb. Hebrew
HEP hydro-electric power
Hind. Hindi
hist. historical
Hung. Hungarian

I
I. Island
Icel. Icelandic
In. Inuit (Eskimo)
Ind. Indonesian
Ir. Irish
Is Islands

It. Italian

J
Jap. Japanese

K
Kaz. Kazakh
Kir. Kirghiz
km kilometre(s)
km² square kilometre (singular)
Kor. Korean
Kurd. Kurdish

L
L. Lake
Lao. Laotian
Lapp. Lappish
Lat. Latin
Latv. Latvian
Liech. Liechtenstein
Lith. Lithuanian
Lux. Luxembourg

M
m million/metre(s)
Mac. Macedonian
Maced. Macedonia
Mal. Malay
Malg. Malagasy
Malt. Maltese
mi. mile(s)
mod. modern
Mong. Mongolian
Mt. Mountain
Mts Mountains

N
N north
NAFTA North American Free Trade Agreement
Nep. Nepali
Neth. Netherlands
Nic. Nicaraguan
Nor. Norwegian
NZ New Zealand

O
off. officially/ official name

P
Pash. Pashtu
Pers. Persian
PNG Papua New Guinea
Pol. Polish
Poly. Polynesian
Port. Portuguese
prev. previously known as

R
r. ruled
Rep. Republic
Res. Reservoir
Rmsch. Romansch
Rom. Romanian
Rus. Russian
Russ. Fed. Russian Federation

S
S south
SCr. Serbo-Croatian
Sinh. Sinhala
Slvk. Slovak
Slvn. Slovene
Som. Somali
Sp. Spanish
St., St Saint
Strs Straits
Swa. Swahili
Swe. Swedish
Switz. Switzerland

T
Taj. Tajik
Th. Thai
Thai. Thailand
Tib. Tibetan
Turk. Turkish
Turkm. Turkmenistan

U
UAE United Arab Emirates
Uigh. Uighur
UK United Kingdom
Ukr. Ukrainian
UN United Nations
Urd. Urdu
US/USA United States of America
USSR Union of Soviet Socialist Republics
Uzb. Uzbek

V
var. variant
Vtn. Vietnamese

W
W west
Wel. Welsh
WWI First World War
WWII Second World War

Y
Yugo. Yugoslavia

This index lists all the place names and features shown on the maps in this Atlas.

Place name spelling

The policy followed throughout the Atlas is to use the contemporary historical name or spelling appropriate for the period or theme of the map. English conventional names, where they exist, have been used for international features e.g. oceans and country names.

All European language spellings use full diacritics, but no diacritics have been used for transliterated spellings (e.g. from Chinese or Cyrillic).

In translating Chinese names, the Pinyin system has been used throughout the Atlas, although alternative spelling systems have been cross referred.

In spelling pre-Columbian Central and South American names, the later addition of Spanish accents has been avoided.

The index also contains commonly-found alternative names and variant spellings, which are fully cross-referenced.

Index structure

All main entry names are those of settlements unless otherwise indicated by the use of italicized definitions.

In order to avoid unnecessary repetition, the names of frequently recurring states on the World Era Overview maps have been omitted. Those places which *only* appear on the World Era Overview maps have been included.

A

Aachen *anc.* Aquae Grani, Aquisgranum; *Dut.* Aken, *Fr.* Aix-la-Chapelle Central Europe (Germany) early modern states 193 (4) economy 190 (1) Franks 184 (2) medieval states 188 (1), (2) Reformation 195 (5) WWI 206 (3)
Aarhus *var.* Århus Scandinavia (Denmark) medieval states 185 (3)
Abadan *oil terminal* Southwest Asia (Iran) economy 234 (1)
Abai *see* Blue Nile
Abaj Takalik Central America (Mexico) first civilizations 121 (2)
Abancay South America (Peru) Incas 147 (3)
Abay Wenz *see* Blue Nile
Abbasid Caliphate *state* Southwest Asia early Islam 57 (2) medieval states 185 (3) Mongols 68–69 (1)
Abbeville France medieval states 192 (2)
Abdera Greece ancient Greece 177 (1), (2), (3)
Abéché *see* Abeshr
Abenaki *people* North America colonization 126 (1)
Abensberg *battle* Central Europe (Germany) Napoleon 200–201 (1)
Aberbrothock *see* Arbroath
Aberdeen *anc.* Devana British Isles (United Kingdom) medieval states 188 (2)
Abergwaun *see* Fishguard
Abertawe *see* Swansea
Aberteifi *see* Cardigan
Aberystwyth British Isles (Wales) medieval states 188 (2)
Abeshr *mod.* Abéché Central Africa (Chad) Islam 163 (1)
Abhiras *dynasty* South Asia first empires 241 (5) medieval states 242 (2)
Abhisara *state* South Asia first empires 241 (5)
Abidjan West Africa (Ivory Coast) economy 168 (2)
Abina South Asia (India) medieval voyages 61 (3)
Abitibi *people* North America cultural groups 123 (3)
Abkhazia *region* Southwest Asia Soviet Union 214–215 (4)
Åbo Scandinavia (Finland) early modern states 195 (3) medieval states 189 (3)
Åbo *see* Surabaya
Abodrites *people* Central Europe Franks 184 (2)
Aboriginal Hunter-Gatherers of Australia *people* Australia the world in 2500 BCE 22–23 *see also* Australian Aborigines
Abu Dhabi *var.* Abū Ẓabī; *Ar.* Abū Ẓaby Southwest Asia (United Arab Emirates) 20th-century politics 233 (4) economy 234 (1) exploration 219 (4)
Abu Dulaf Southwest Asia (Iraq) early Islam 57 (3)
Abu Hurayrah *see* Abu Hureyra
Abu Hureyra *var.* Abu Hurayrah Southwest Asia (Syria) the world in 5000 BCE 18–19
Abuja South West Africa (Nigeria) first civilizations 24 (3)
Abu Rawash Egypt ancient Egypt 159 (3)
Abu Salabikh Southwest Asia (Iraq) first cities 220 (2)
Abu Simbel *early food production site* Egypt early agriculture 158 (1)
Abusir Egypt ancient Egypt 159 (2), (3)
Abū Ẓabī *see* Abu Dhabi
Abū Ẓaby *see* Abu Dhabi
Abydos *var.* Abydus Egypt ancient Egypt 159 (2), (3), (4), (5) first cities 28–29 (1) first civilizations 24 (2)
Abydos *var.* Abydus *settlement/state* Southwest Asia (Turkey) ancient Greece 177 (2) first civilizations 177 (1)
Abydus *see* Abydos
Abyssinia *mod.* Ethiopia *state* East Africa 20th-century politics 233 (4) European imperialism 96 (1), 97 (4) trade 165 (3), 167 (1) WWII 104 (2) *see also* Ethiopia
Acachinamoco Central America (Mexico) Aztecs 124 (3)
Acadia *mod.* Nova Scotia *region* North America the world in 1700 82–83 *see also* Nova Scotia
Acalbixca Central America (Mexico) Aztecs 124 (3)
Acancéh Central America (Mexico) first civilizations 123 (2)
Acanthus *settlement/state* Greece ancient

Greece 177 (2), (3)
Acapulco *var.* Acapulco de Juárez Central America (Mexico) European expansion 80–81 (1), 81 (3), 84–85 (1) exploration 143 (3) first civilizations 122 (1) US economy 136 (2)
Acapulco de Juárez *see* Acapulco
Acari South America (Peru) Incas 147 (3)
Acarnania *state* Greece ancient Greece 179 (4)
Acatitla Central America (Mexico) Aztecs 124 (3)
Acatlan Central America (Mexico) first civilizations 122 (1)
Acayocan Central America (Mexico) Aztecs 124 (3)
Accho *see* Acco, Acre
Acco *mod.* ʿAkko; *Bibl.* Accho, Ptolemais; *Eng.* Acre, *Fr.* Saint-Jean-d'Acre Southwest Asia (Israel) ancient Egypt 159 (5)
see also Acre
Accra *var.* Fort James West Africa (Ghana) colonization 167 (4) economy 168 (2) empire and revolution 88 (1) slave trade 165 (4) trade 164 (2)
Aceh *see* Achin
Acemhüyük Southwest Asia (Turkey) first cities 28–29 (1)
Achaea *see* Achaia
Achaean League *var.* Principality of Achaia *state* Greece the world in 250 BCE 38–39
see also Achaia
Achaia *var.* Achaea Greece ancient Greece 177 (3)
Achaia, Principality of *see* Achaean League
Achalapura South Asia (India) early medieval states 244 (2)
Acheh *see* Achin
Achin *var.* Aceh, Atchin, Atjeh; *mod.* Aceh Maritime Southeast Asia (Indonesia) colonialism 247 (4) early medieval states 245 European imperialism 97 (3) postwar politics 253 (4) trade 267 (3)
Acolapissa *people* North America colonization 126 (1)
Acolhuacan *state* Central America Aztecs 124 (1)
Acoma *people* North America colonization 126 (1)
Açores *see* Azores
Açores, Arquipélago dos *see* Azores
Açores, Ilhas dos *see* Azores
Acragas Italy first civilizations 177 (1)
Acre *mod.* ʿAkko; *prev.* Acco; *Bibl.* Accho, Ptolemais; *Fr.* Saint-Jean-d'Acre Southwest Asia (Israel) crusades 228 (2), 65 (3) economy 190 (1) exploration 219 (4) medieval states 187 (5) Mongols 229 (3), 68 (2) Napoleon 200–201 (1)
see also Acco
Acre *state* South America empire and revolution 152 (1)
Acropolis *temple* Greece ancient Greece 177 (4)
Acrothooi *state* Greece ancient Greece 177 (2)
Actaeon Islands *island group* Pacific Ocean exploration 278 (1)
Actium *Gk.* Aktion Greece the world in 1 CE 42–43
Acton *battle* North America (USA) the growth of the US 129 (2)
Adab Southwest Asia (Iraq) first cities 220 (1) first civilizations 24 (3)
Adal *state* East Africa Islam 163 (1) trade 165 (3)
Adalia *mod.* Antalya; *prev.* Attalia; *anc.* Attaleia Southwest Asia (Turkey) 20th-century politics 233 (3) crusades 65 (3), 64–65 (2)
see also Attalia
Adamawa *region* West Africa Islam 167 (3)
Adamawa Highlands *Mountain range* West Africa economy 163 (2)
Adamello *mountain* Italy WWI 207 (5)
ʿAdan *see* Aden, Eudaemon Arabia
Adana *var.* Seyhan Southwest Asia (Turkey) 20th-century politics 233 (3) early Islam 57 (3) Ottomans 230 (1)
Adare, Cape *headland* Antarctica Antarctic Exploration 287 (3)
Ad Dawhah *see* Doha
Addis Ababa *Amh.* Ādīs Ābeba East Africa (Ethiopia) colonization 167 (4) economy 168 (2)
Adelaide Australia colonization 282 (1), (2), 283 (3), 284–285 (1) exploration 279 (2), (3) imperial global economy 92 (1)
Adélie, Terre *physical region* Antarctica Antarctic Exploration 287 (3)

Adelong *goldfield* Australia colonization 282 (2)
Aden *var.* Eudaemon Arabia; *Ar.* ʿAdan, *Chin.* A-tan Southwest Asia (Yemen) ancient trade 44–45 (1) biological diffusion 72–73 (1) early Islam 56–57 (1), 57 (2) European expansion 84–85 (1) exploration 156 (3), 219 (4) imperial global economy 92 (1) Islam 163 (1), 226 (2), 227 (4) medieval voyages 61 (3) Mongols 68 (2) Ottomans 231 (3) trade 230 (2), 267 (3) 20th-century politics 233 (4) *see also* Eudaemon Arabia
Adena North America (USA) first religions 36 (1)
Adena *burial mound* North America (USA) first civilizations 121 (4)
Adena/Hopewell Culture *people* North America the world in 250 BCE 38–39 the world in 1 CE 42–43
Adige *Ger.* Etsch *river* Italy WWI 207 (5)
Ādīs Ābeba *see* Addis Ababa
Admiralty Islands *island group* Pacific Ocean early cultures 280–281 (3) medieval voyages 60 (2) WWII 272 (1), 273 (2)
Adobe Walls *battle* North America (USA) the growth of the US 129 (2)
Adrar Bous West Africa (Niger) early agriculture 158 (1)
Adrar Tioueine North Africa (Algeria) early agriculture 158 (1)
Adria *see* Hadria
Adrianople *mod.* Edirne; *anc.* Adrianopolis, Hadrianopolis Christian *archbishopric/settlement* Southwest Asia (Turkey) Roman empire 182 (1) crusades 64–65 (2) medieval states 187 (5), 189 (4) Ottomans 195 (4), 230 (1), 231 (3) Reformation 194 (2) world religions 48 (1) WWI 207 (6)
see also Adrianopolis, Edirne, Hadrianopolis
Adrianopolis *battle* Southwest Asia (Turkey) great migrations 52–53 (1)
Adriatic Sea *sea* Southeast Europe Roman empire 179 (3) Bronze Age 175 (3) Copper Age 174 (2) early agriculture 174 (1) early modern states 193 (4) early states 178 (1), (2) economy 190 (1) empire and revolution 202 (3) first civilizations 177 (1) civil war 209 (5) medieval states 183 (4), 187 (5), 188 (1), 189 (4) Ottomans 230 (1) postwar economy 213 (5), 214 (2), 215 (3) postwar politics 212 (3) Reformation 194 (2) WWI 207 (5), (6)
Adulis *settlement/state* East Africa (Eritrea) ancient trade 44 (2), 44–45 (1) early cultures 160 (1), 161 (3), (4), (5) early trade 225 (3)
Adventure Bay *bay* Australia exploration 278 (1)
Adwuku West Africa (Ghana) early agriculture 158 (1)
Adygeya *region* Eastern Europe Soviet Union 214–215 (4)
Aegae Greece Hellenistic world 40–41 (1)
Aegates *mod.* Isole Egadi *island group* Italy Roman empire 179 (3)
Aegina *var.* Aiyina, Egina Greece ancient Greece 177 (3) first civilizations 175 (4)
Aegospotami Southwest Asia (Turkey) ancient Greece 177 (3)
Aegyptus *province* North Africa Roman empire 180–181 (1) ancient trade 44 (2)
Ahe *island* Pacific Ocean exploration 278 (1)
Ah Kin Chel *state* Central America Aztecs 124 (1)

Aelaniticus, Sinus *see* Aqaba, Gulf of
Aelia Capitolina *see* Jerusalem
Aemona *see* Ljubljana
Aenea Greece ancient Greece 177 (2)
Aenus Greece first civilizations 177 (1), (2)
Aequi *people* Italy early states 178 (1), (2)
Aesernia *mod.* Isernia Italy early states 178 (1)
Aethiopia *region* East Africa ancient trade 44 (2)
Aetolia *region* Greece Hellenistic world 40–41 (1)
Afalou Bou Rhummel North Africa (Algeria) the world in 10,000 BCE 14–15
Afars and Issas, French Territory of the *mod.* Djibouti; *prev.* French Somaliland *state* East Africa the world in 1975 106–107 *see also* Djibouti, French Somaliland
Afghanistan *region/state* Central Asia Cold War 109 (1) colonialism 248 (1), (2), 269 (3), (4) Communism 271 (4) decolonization 250 (1), 251 (4) early cultures 161 (3), (4), (5) early trade 225 (3) economy 205 (2), (3) exploration 218 (2) Islam 163 (1) Ottomans 231 (3) slave trade 165 (4) Timur 229 (4) trade 165 (3), 230 (2) 20th-century politics 233 (4) Aden Protectorate *colonial possession/state* Southwest Asia 20th-century politics 233 (4) Cold War 109 (1) WWII 104 (1) Afifko early food production site West Africa (Nigeria) early agriculture 158 (1)
Africa *continent* 154–169
Africa, Exarchate of *state* North Africa medieval states 183 (4)
Africa, Horn of *physical region* East Africa European expansion 84–85 (1) slave trade 165 (4) trade 165 (3)
Africa Nova *province* North Africa early cultures 161 (2)
Afudofo *mod.* Nimule East Africa (Sudan) exploration 157 (4), (5)
Afyeh *early food production site* Egypt early agriculture 158 (1)
Agadès *see* Agadez
Agadez *Fr.* Agadès West Africa (Niger) colonization 167 (4) early agriculture 158 (1) economy 163 (2) exploration 157 (4) Islam 163 (1)
Agadir North Africa (Morocco) exploration 157 (4)
Agartala South Asia (India) postwar politics 252 (1), (3)
Agatha *see* Agathe
Agathe *var.* Agatha; *mod.* Agde France first civilizations 177 (1)
Agde *see* Agathe
Agendicum *see* Sens
Aggassiz, Lake *lake* North America the world in 10,000 BCE 14–15
Aghlabids *dynasty* North Africa early Islam 57 (2) Islam 227 (4)
Agincourt *battle* France medieval states 192 (2)
Aginsky Buryat AD *autonomous region* Siberia (Russian Federation) Soviet Union 214–215 (4)
Agordat *early food site* East Africa (Eritrea) early agriculture 158 (1)
Agra South Asia (India) colonialism 248 (1) early medieval states 244–245 (3) economy 249 (4) Mughal Empire 246 (1) postwar economy 253 (5) trade 267 (3)
Agra *state* South Asia Mughal Empire 246 (1)
Agra and Oudh, United Provinces of *see* Uttar Pradesh
Agram *see* Zagreb, Zágráb
Agri Decumates *region* Central Europe Roman empire 181 (4)
Agrigento *see* Agrigentum
Agrigentum *mod.* Agrigento Italy Roman empire 179 (3), 180–181 (1) first religions 37 (3)
Aguascalientes Central America (Mexico) Mexican Revolution 133 (3)
Agulhas, Cape *Afr.* Kaap Agulhas *headland* South Africa European imperialism 96 (2)
Agulhas, Kaap *see* Agulhas, Cape
Agulhas mountain range North Africa ancient trade 44–45 (1) early cultures 160 (1) economy 163 (2) first humans 13 (2) historical geography 154–155 (1)

Ahmad *oil terminal* Southwest Asia (Kuwait) economy 234 (1)
Ahmadābād *see* Ahmadabad
Ahmadnagar *var.* Ahmednagar South Asia (India) Mughal Empire 246 (1)
Ahmadnagar *state* South Asia early medieval states 245 (4) Mughal Empire 246 (1)
Ahmadabad *var.* Ahmadābād South Asia (India) colonialism 247 (3), 248 (1) decolonization 250 (1) economy 249 (4) imperial global economy 93 (5) postwar economy 253 (5)
Ahmednagar *see* Ahmadnagar
Ahoms *dynasty* South Asia early medieval states 244–245 (3) Mughal Empire 246 (1)
Ahtena *people* North America cultural groups 123 (3)
Ahteut North America (USA) cultural groups 123 (3)
Ahu Akahanga *archaeological site* Pacific Ocean (Easter Island) early cultures 281 (4)
Ahu ʿAkivi *archaeological site* Pacific Ocean (Easter Island) early cultures 281 (4)
Ahuehuetlan Central America (Mexico) Aztecs 124 (3)
Ahuilizapan Central America (Mexico) colonization 125 (5)
Ahu Raʿai *archaeological site* Pacific Ocean (Easter Island) early cultures 281 (4)
Ahu Tongariki *archaeological site* Pacific Ocean (Easter Island) early cultures 281 (4)
Ahu Vinapu *archaeological site* Pacific Ocean (Easter Island) early cultures 281 (4)
Aichi *var.* Aiti *prefecture* Japan economy 270 (1)
Aigaion Pélagos *see* Aegean Sea
Aigaío Pélagos *see* Aegean Sea
Aigues-Mortes France crusades 64–65 (2)
Aigun *see* Aihun
Aihun *var.* Aigun East Asia (China) colonialism 269 (4)
Ai Khanoum *see* Alexandria ad Oxum
Aikudi South Asia (India) early medieval states 244 (1)
Aila *var.* Elath; *mod.* Eilat, Elat Southwest Asia (Israel) medieval voyages 61 (3) *see also* Eilat, Elath
Ailah Southwest Asia (Israel) crusades 65 (3)
Ain Jalut *battle* Southwest Asia (Israel) Mongols 229 (3), 68–69 (1)
Ainu *people* Japan early modern states 265 (5) medieval states 262–263 (1), (2), 265 (3) trade 267 (3)
Air *state* West Africa slave trade 165 (4)
Airgialla *state* British Isles medieval states 188 (2)
Ais *people* North America colonization 125 (4), (5), (1)
Aisne *river* France WWI 206 (2), (3)
Aiti *see* Aichi
Aix-en-Provence France early modern states 197 (5)
Aix-la-Chapelle *see* Aachen
Aiyina *see* Aegina
Aizawl South Asia (India) postwar politics 252 (1)
Aizu Japan early modern states 267 (4)
Ajanta *Buddhist center/settlement* South Asia (India) first religions 36 (2) world religions 49 (3)
Ajayameru *var.* Ajmer, Ajmere South Asia (India) early medieval states 244 (2) world religions 243 (4) *see also* Ajmer
Ajdabiya North Africa (Libya) early Islam 56–57 (1)
Ajman Southwest Asia (United Arab Emirates) first civilizations 24 (3)
Ajmer *var.* Ajayameru, Ajmere South Asia (India) colonialism 247 (3) Mughal Empire 246 (1) *see also* Ajayameru
Ajmer *var.* Ajmere *state* South Asia colonialism 248 (2) Mughal Empire 246 (1)
Ajmere *see* Ajmer, Ajayameru
Ajnadain Southwest Asia (Israel) Islam 226 (2)
Ajnadain *battle* Southwest Asia (Israel) early Islam 56–57 (1)
Akaba *see* Akaba, Aqaba
Akamagaseki *see* Shimonoseki
Akan States *state* West Africa Islam 163 (1) trade 164 (2)
Akaroa New Zealand colonization 283 (5)
Akbarpur South Asia (India) colonialism 247 (3)
Aken *see* Aachen
Akermanceaster *see* Bath
Akhaura South Asia (Bangladesh) postwar politics 252 (3)
Akhenaten Egypt ancient Egypt 159 (5)
Akhetaten *var.* Tell el-Amarna Egypt ancient Egypt 159 (5)
Akhisar *see* Thyatira
Akhmim *var.* Ipu Egypt ancient Egypt 159 (5)
Akira *early food production site* East Africa (Kenya) early agriculture 158 (1)
Akita Japan economy 270 (1) medieval states 264 (2), 265 (3), (4)
Akita *prefecture* Japan economy 270 (1)
Akjoujt *prev.* Fort-Repoux West Africa (Mauritania) early agriculture 158 (1)
Akkad Southwest Asia (Iraq) the world in 1250 BCE 26–27
Akkad *state* Southwest Asia first civilizations 221 (4)
Akkerman Eastern Europe (Ukraine) Ottomans 195 (4)
ʿAkko *see* Acco, Acre
Ak Koyunlu *var.* Akkoyunlu, Aq Qoyunlu *state* Southwest Asia Islam 163 (1)
Akmola Central Asia (Kazakhstan) Soviet Union 214–215 (4)
Akmolinsk *region* Central Asia/Siberia colonialism 269 (3)
Akron North America (USA) US politics 135 (6)
Akrotiri Southwest Asia (Cyprus) first civilizations 175 (4)
Aksai Chin *Chin.* Aksayqin *region* South Asia postwar economy 275 (3) postwar politics 252 (1), (2)
Aksayqin *see* Aksai Chin
Aksha Egypt ancient Egypt 159 (5)
Aksu *var.* Aqsu East Asia (China) ancient trade 44–45 (1) early modern states 268 (1) empire and revolution 268 (2) medieval states 262–263 (1) world religions 49 (3)

Aksum East Africa (Ethiopia) ancient trade 44–45 (1) early cultures 160 (1), 161 (3), (4), (5) early trade 225 (3) world religions 49 (4)

Aktion see Action

Akwamu state West Africa the world in 1700 82–83

Akwe Shavante people South America early cultures 147 (2)

Akyab Mainland Southeast Asia (Burma) trade 230 (1) WWII 272 (1), 273 (2)

Ala WWI 207 (5)

Alabama state North America imperial global economy 93 (5) the growth of the US 129 (1) US Civil War 130 (2), (3), (4), (5), 131 (6), (7) US economy 134 (2), 139 (3) US society 137 (6) US superpower 139 (5)

Alabama people North America colonization 125 (4), 126 (1)

Alabama river North America US Civil War 131 (6)

Al-'Abbasa Egypt Mamluks 229 (3)

al Abyaḍ, Al Baḥr see White Nile

al Abyaḍ, An Nil see White Nile

Alaca Hüyük Southwest Asia (Turkey) first cities 28–29 (1) first civilizations 221 (5)

Alacant see Alicante

Alaka people South America early cultures 145 (2)

Alalakh Greece ancient Egypt 159 (5)

Alalia mod. Aleria France first civilizations 177 (1)
see also Aleria

Alamanni see Alemanni

Al 'Amārah see Amara

Alamgirpur archaeological site South Asia (India) first cities 240 (2)

Alamo, The battle North America (USA) the growth of the US 129 (2)

Alamut assassins site/settlement Southwest Asia (Iran) Mongols 229 (3), 68–69 (1) Seljuks 228 (1)

Alans people Eastern Europe Roman empire 181 (4) great migrations 52–53 , (1)

Al 'Arabiyah as Su'ūdiyah see Saudi Arabia

Alarcos Iberian Peninsula (Spain) Islam 192 (3)

Al 'Aşab see Asab

Alasca, Golfo de see Alaska, Gulf of

Alashiya see Cyprus

Alaska prev. Russian America colonial possession/state North America Cold War 109 (1) colonialism 269 (3) Communism 273 (3) empire and revolution 88–89 (2) exploration 257 (2) imperial global economy 93 (3) the growth of the US 129 (2), 132 (1) US economy 136 (2) WWII 104 (1), 273 (2)

Alaska, Gulf of var. Golfo de Alasca gulf North America cultural groups 123 (3) exploration 118 (1), 119 (2), (3), 286 (1) the growth of the US 129 (2)

Alaska Range mountain range North America the growth of the US 129 (2)

Alavi South Asia (India) world religions 242 (3)

Albacete Iberian Peninsula (Spain) Civil War 209 (4)

Al Baḥrayn see Bahrain

Albania Alb. Shqipëria state Southeast Europe Cold War 108 (3), 109 (1) early 20th century 206 (1) economy 205 (4) civil war 209 (3), (5) Ottomans 202 (4), 230 (1) postwar economy 213 (5), 214 (1), (2), 215 (3) postwar politics 212 (3) Soviet Union 213 (4) the modern world 112 (2), 113 (3), (4) WWI 208 (1) WWII 104 (1), 211 (2), (4)

Albanians people Southeast Europe the modern world 112 (2)

Albanus, Lacus lake Italy early states 178 (1)

Albanus, Mons mountain Italy early states 178 (1)

Albany penal colony/settlement Australia colonization 282 (1), 283 (3) environmentalism 285 (2) exploration 279 (2)

Albany North America (USA) colonization 126 (1) empire and revolution 127 (2), (3) exploration 119 (2) the growth of the US 129 (2), 132 (1) US politics 135 (6) US society 137 (6)

Alba Regia see Székesfehérvár

Al Başrah see Basra

Albert France WWI 206 (2), (3)

Alberta province North America the growth of the US 129 (2), 132 (1) US economy 136 (2)

Albert Edward Nyanza see Edward, Lake

Albert, Lake var. Albert Nyanza, Lac Mobutu Sese Seko lake East Africa early agriculture 158 (1) exploration 157 (4), (5) historical geography 154–155 (1) Islam 163 (1) slave trade 165 (4)

Albert Nyanza see Albert, Lake

Albi anc. Albiga France economy 190 (1)

Albiga see Albi

Albigensian crusade France crusades 186 (1)

Albion region British Isles ancient trade 44 (2)

Albis see Elbe

Alborz, Reshteh-ye Kühhâ-ye see Elburz Mountains

Albreda West Africa (Gambia) the world in 1700 82–83 empire and revolution 88 (1)

Albury Australia colonization 282 (1)

Alcacer Iberian Peninsula (Portugal) Islam 192 (3)

Alcántara Iberian Peninsula (Spain) crusades 186 (1) Islam 192 (3)

Alcobaça cistercian house Iberian peninsula (Spain) medieval states 187 (3)

Alcudia Iberian Peninsula (Spain) economy 190 (1)

Aldan river Eastern Europe early modern states 268 (1) Soviet Union 214–215 (4)

Aleksandrovka archaeological site Siberia (Russian Federation) early agriculture 258 (1)

Alemanni var. Alamanni people Central Europe Roman empire 181 (4), 182 (1) Franks 183 (5), (6) great migrations 53 (2) medieval states 182 (2)

Alemannia region Central Europe Franks 184 (2)

Alençon France early modern states 197 (5)

Alep see Aleppo

Aleppo var. Yamkhad; anc. Beroea; Ar. Halab, Fr. Alep Southwest Asia (Syria) ancient Persia 223 (4) trade 72–73 (1) crusades 228 (2), 65 (1), (3) economy 190 (1) exploration 219 (3) first cities 28–29 (1) first civilizations 221 (4), (5) Islam 184 (1) Mongols 229 (3), 68–69 (1) Napoleon 200–201 (3)

Aleria Roman empire 179 (3), 180–181 (1) early states 178 (2)

Alessandria Fr. Alexandrie Italy economy 190 (1), 190–191 medieval states 188 (1)

Aleut people North America cultural groups 123 (3)

Aleutian Islands island group North America cultural groups 123 (3) exploration 257 (2) the growth of the US 129 (2) US superpower 138 (1) WWII 272 (1), 273 (2)

Alexander, Empire of state Southwest Asia Hellenistic world 224 (1)

Alexandretta Turk. İskenderun Southwest Asia (Turkey) crusades 65 (3) WWI 233 (2)

Alexandria North America (USA) empire and revolution 127 (2)

Alexandria Ar. Al Iskandariyah Egypt ancient Persia 225 (6) Roman empire 179 (5), 180–181 (1), 181 (3), (4), 182 (1), 224 (2), 225 (5) ancient trade 44 (2), 44–45 (1) plague 72–73 (1) colonization 167 (4) crusades 228 (2), 65 (3) early cultures 160 (1), 161 (2), (3) early Islam 57 (2) early trade 225 (3) economy 163 (2), 190 (1) exploration 156 (3), 157 (4), 218 (1), (2) first cities 240 (2) first empires 241 (4) Hellenistic world 224 (1), 41 (2) Islam 163 (1), 226 (2), 227 (4), (5) medieval states 185 (3) Mongols 229 (3) Napoleon 200–201 (3) Ottomans 232–233 (1) slave trade 165 (4) world religions 226 (1), 49 (4) WWI 233 (2) WWII 104 (1), 211 (4) 20th-century politics 233 (3)

Alexandria battle Egypt early Islam 56–57 (1) Islam 226 (2)

Alexandria ad Oxum var. Ai Khanoum Central Asia (Afghanistan) Hellenistic world 40–41 (1)

Alexandria Arachoton Central Asia (Afghanistan) Hellenistic world 40–41 (1)

Alexandria Areion var. Aria; mod. Herat Central Asia (Afghanistan) ancient trade 44–45 (1) exploration 218 (1), 219 (3) Hellenistic world 40–41 (1), 41 (2)
see also Herat

Alexandria Eschate var. Kokand Central Asia (Uzbekistan) Hellenistic world 40–41 (1)

Alexandria Margiana mod. Merv Central Asia (Turkmenistan) Hellenistic world 40–41 (1)

Alexandrie see Alessandria

Alexandroupolis see Dedeagach

Al Fáshir see El Fasher

Al Faw var. Fao Southwest Asia (Iraq) economy 234 (1) see also Fao

Al Fujayrah see Fujairah

Al Furât see Euphrates

Al Fustat Egypt early Islam 56–57 (1)
see also Fustat

Algarve region Iberian Peninsula (Portugal) Islam 192 (3)

Alger see Algiers

Algeria prev. Algiers; anc. Icosium colonial possession/state North Africa early Islam 57 (2) economy 168 (2), (3) European imperialism 96 (1), 97 (4) Civil War 209 (4) Islam 235 (4) Ottomans 232–233 (1) the modern world 112 (1), 113 (3), (4) WWII 104 (1), 211 (4) Cold War 109 (1) colonization 167 (4) decolonization 168 (1) early 20th century 206 (1)
see also Algiers

Algiers var. Al Jazair; Fr. Alger North Africa (Algeria) trade 72–73 (1) colonization 167 (4) crusades 186 (1) economy 168 (2), 190 (1) European expansion 84–85 (1) exploration 157 (4) Islam 184 (1) medieval states 185 (3) Napoleon 200–201 (1), 201 (2) Ottomans 231 (3), 232–233 (1) slave trade 165 (4) trade 167 (1) US superpower 138 (1) WWII 211 (4)

Algiers var. Algeria; anc. Icosium state North Africa Napoleon 200–201 (1) slave trade 165 (4) trade 167 (1)
see also Algeria

Algoa Bay bay South America exploration 156 (3)

Algonquin people North America colonization 126 (1) cultural groups 123 (3)

Al Hadhar see Hatra

Al Hadr see Hatra

Al-Hajj Umar Ahmadu Sefu state West Africa colonization 167 (4)

Al Hamad see Syrian Desert

Al Hijaz see Hejaz

Al Hira Southwest Asia (Iraq) early Islam 56–57 (1)

Al Hufūf see Hasa

Alicante Lat. Lucentum; Cat. Alacant Iberian Peninsula (Spain) economy 190 (1), 205 (4) Franks 184 (2) Civil War 209 (4) Islam 192 (3)

Alice Boër archaeological site South America (Brazil) early cultures 145 (2)

Alice Springs Australia colonization 283 (3) exploration 279 (2)

Alids dynasty Southwest Asia Islam 227 (4)

Aligarh South Asia (India) economy 249 (4)

Ali Kosh Southwest Asia (Iraq) early agriculture 220 (1)

Al Iskandarìyah see Alexandria

Al Jawf see Jauf

Al Jizah see Giza

Al Kūfah see Kufa

Al-Kuwait see Kuwait

Al Kuwayt see Kuwait

Allada state West Africa the world in 1700 82–83

Allahabad South Asia (India) colonialism 247 (3), 248 (1) decolonization 250 (1) economy 249 (4) Mughal Empire 246 (1) postwar economy 253 (5)

Allahabad state South Asia Mughal Empire 246 (1)

'Allaqi, Wadi el- river Egypt ancient Egypt 159 (4)

Allen's Cave Australia exploration 280 (1)

Allia Bay archaeological site East Africa (Kenya) first humans 12 (1)

Allobroges people France Roman empire 179 (5)

Al Lubnān see Lebanon

Alma battle Eastern Europe (Ukraine) Ottomans 202 (4)

Alma-Ata Central Asia (Russian Federation) Soviet Union 213 (4)

Al Madain Southwest Asia (Iraq) early Islam 56–57 (1)

Al Madinah see Medina

Al Mahdìyah see Mahdia

Almalyk var. Almalyq East Asia (China) biological diffusion 72–73 (1) Mongols 68–69 (1)

Al Manāmah see Manama

Al-Mariyya see Almeria

Al Mawşil see Mosul

Almeria anc. Unci; Lat. Portus Magnus; Ar. Al-Mariyya Iberian Peninsula (Spain) economy 190 (1) Civil War 209 (4) Islam 192 (3)

Almohad Empire state North Africa crusades 64–65 (2), 186 (1)

Almohads dynasty North Africa crusades 186 (1) early Islam 57 (2)

Almoravid Empire state Iberian Peninsula/North Africa crusades 64–65 (2) early Islam 57 (2)

Al Mukalla Southwest Asia (Yemen) exploration 219 (4)

Al Mukallã see Al Mukalla

Alodia state East Africa the world in 750 CE 54–55 the world in 1000 58–59

Alor South Asia (Pakistan) early medieval states 244 (2) world religions 243 (4)

Alpes Cottiae province France Roman empire 180–181 (1)

Alpes Graiae et Poeninae var. Alpes Penninae province France Roman empire 180–181 (1)

Alpes Maritimae province France Roman empire 180–181 (1)

Alpes Penninae see Alpes Graiae et Poeninae

Alpi see Alps

Alpi Giulie see Julian Alps

Alps Fr. Alpes, Ger. Alpen, It. Alpi mountain range Central Europe Roman empire 179 (3), 180–181 (1), 181 (3) Bronze Age 175 (3) Copper Age 174 (2) crusades 186 (1), 64–65 (2) early agriculture 174 (1) early states 56–57 (1), 57 (2) early modern states 193 (4), (5) economy 190 (1) European expansion 84–85 (1) exploration 172 (1) first religions 37 (3) Franks 183 (5), (6), 184 (2) great migrations 52–53 (1) medieval states 185 (3), 192 (1), (2) Napoleon 200–201 (1) Ottomans 232–233 (1) prehistoric culture 17 (3), (4) world religions 48 (1), 49 (4) WWI 207 (5) WWII 210 (1), 211 (4)

Al Qadisiya Southwest Asia (Iraq) ancient Persia 225 (6)

Al Qadisiya battle Southwest Asia (Iraq) Islam 226 (2)

Al Qāhirah see Cairo, Fustat

Al Qatif Southwest Asia (Saudi Arabia) exploration 219 (4)

Al Qayrawān see Kairouan

Al Quds see Jerusalem

Al Quds ash Sharif see Jerusalem

Al Raydaniyya Egypt Ottomans 231 (3)

Alsace-Lorraine region France empire and revolution 202 (1ii), (2) WWI 208 (1)

Alsium Italy early states 178 (1)

Alt see Olt

Altai see Altai Mountains

Altai Peoples people East Asia the world in 750 BCE 34–35

Al Ṭa'if see Taif

Altai Mountains var. Altai; Chin. Altay Shan, Rus. Altay mountain range East Asia/Siberia ancient trade 44–45 (1) colonialism 269 (3), (4) early agriculture 258 (1) exploration 256 (1), 257 (3) first humans 13 (2) first states 260 (1) Hellenistic world 40 (1) medieval states 261 (6) Mongols 68–69 (1) trade 267 (3) world religions 49 (3), (4)

Altamira Central America (Mexico) first civilizations 121 (2)

Altamira archaeological site/settlement Iberian Peninsula (Spain) prehistoric culture 17 (3)

Altar de Sacrificios Central America (Mexico) first civilizations 121 (2)

Altar de Sacrificios site de Sonoran Desert
see also Altar Mountains

Altar Shan see Altai Mountains

Altay Central America (Mexico) Aztecs 124 (2)

Altiplano physical region South America early cultures 145 (2), (4) politics 152 (2)

Alto Paraná see Paraná

Alto Ramirez South America (Chile) early cultures 146 (1)

Altun Shan mountain range East Asia early agriculture 258 (1) first states 260 (1)

Altxerri archaeological site Iberian Peninsula (Spain) prehistoric culture 17 (3)

Al Urdunn see Jordan

Alvastra monastery Scandinavia (Sweden) medieval states 187 (3)

Alwa state East Africa early medieval states 160 (1), 161 (5) economy 163 (2)

Al Wajh see Wejh

Alwar South Asia (India) colonialism 247 (3)

Amabato South America (Ecuador) Incas 147 (3)

Amadzimba South Africa (South Africa) the world in 5000 BCE 18–19

Amakusa Japan early modern states 267 (4)

Amalfi Italy Franks 184 (2) medieval states 182 (2), 183 (4), 185 (3), 187 (5), 188 (1)

Amantlan Central America (Mexico) Aztecs 124 (2)

Amaquemecan Central America (Mexico) colonization 125 (5)

Amara var. Al 'Amārah Southwest Asia (Iraq) WWI 233 (2)

Amaravati Buddhist center/settlement South Asia (India) early medieval states 244 (1) world religions 49 (3)

Amasia mod. Amasya Christian archbishopric Southwest Asia (Turkey) world religions 48 (1) see also Amasya

Amasya anc. Amasia Southwest Asia (Turkey) Ottomans 231 (3) see also Amasia

Amathus Southwest Asia (Cyprus) first civilizations 177 (1)

Amazon Port/Sp. Amazonas river South America colonization 148 (2), 149 (3), (4) early agriculture 20–21 (2) early cultures 144 (1), 145 (2), 146 (1), 147 (2) economy 153 (3) empire and revolution 150 (1), (2), 151 (3), 88 (1), 88–89 (2) environment 153 (4) exploration 142 (1), 143 (2), (3) global immigration 100 (1) global knowledge 76–77 (1) imperial global economy 92 (1) Incas 147 (3), 148 (1) narcotics 153 (5) prehistoric culture 16 (1)

Amazonas see Amazon

Amazon Basin basin South America colonization 149 (3) early agriculture 20–21 (2) early cultures 145 (4), 147 (2) environment 153 (4) Incas 148 (1)

Ambala see Umballa

Ambianum see Amiens

Amboina prev. Ambon, Amboyna Maritime Southeast Asia (Indonesia) colonization 284–285 (1) empire and revolution 88 (1) WWII 272 (1), 273 (2)

Amboina var. Ambon; mod. Pulau Ambon island Maritime Southeast Asia (Indonesia) empire and revolution 247 (4) Islam 243 (6) postwar politics 253 (4)

Ambon see Amboina

Ambon, Pulau see Amboina

Amboyna see Amboina

Ambracia Greece ancient Greece 177 (3), 179 (4)

Ameca Central America (Mexico) first civilizations 122 (1)

Amekni West Africa (Algeria) early agriculture 158 (1)

America see United States of America, North America, South America

American Samoa prev. Pago Pago colonial possession Pacific Ocean colonization 284–285 (1) decolonization 285 (3) exploration 279 (3) the growth of the US 133 (4) US superpower 138 (1)

American Virgin Islands var. Virgin Islands of the United States; prev. Danish West Indies colonial possession West Indies Cold War 108 (2)

Amery Ice Shelf ice feature Antarctica Antarctic Exploration 287 (3)

Amida mod. Diyarbakir Christian archbishopric Southwest Asia (Turkey) world religions 48 (1) see also Diyarbakir

Amiens anc. Ambianum, Samarobriva France early modern states 197 (5) economy 190 (1) Franks 184 (2) medieval states 192 (2) Reformation 195 (5) WWI 206 (2), (3)

Amirante Islands var. Amirantes Group island group Indian Ocean the world in 1850 90–91 the world in 1900 94–95 the world in 1925 98–99

Amirantes Group see Amirante Islands

Amisus mod. Samsun Christian archbishopric/settlement Southwest Asia (Turkey) early cultures 161 (2) Hellenistic world 40–41 (1) world religions 48 (1)

Amjhera state South Asia empire and revolution 249 (3)

Amman var. Philadelphia, Bibl. Rabbah Ammon, Rabbath Ammon Southwest Asia (Jordan) early Islam 56–57 (1) Ottomans 232–233 (1) WWI 233 (2) 20th century 234 (2) 20th-century politics 233 (3), (4), 235 (5)

Ammon state Southwest Asia first civilizations 222 (1)

Amnok-kang see Yalu

Amol var. Amul Southwest Asia (Iran) Hellenistic world 40–41 (1) Mongols 68–69 (1)

Amoy see Xiamen

Amphipolis battle/settlement/state Greece ancient Greece 177 (2), (3)

Ampuras see Emporiae

Amri archaeological site South Asia (Pakistan) First cities 240 (2)

Amritsar South Asia (India) colonialism 247 (3), 248 (1) decolonization 250 (1) economy 249 (4) postwar politics 252 (1)

Amsa-dong archaeological site East Asia (South Korea) early agriculture 258 (1)

Amsterdam Low Countries (Netherlands) Cold War 108 (3) early modern states 193 (4) economy 198 (1), 205 (4) empire and revolution 202 (1), (1i), (2) European expansion 84–85 (1) global immigration 100 (1) Reformation 195 (5), 196 (1)

Amu Darya anc. Oxus; Rus. Amudar'ya, Taj. Dar"yoi Amu, Turkm. Amyderya, Uzb. Amudaryo river Central Asia ancient trade 44–45 (1) colonialism 248 (1), 269 (3) early Islam 56–57 (1), 57 (2) exploration 257 (2) first civilizations 24 (2), 25 (3) first humans 13 (2) medieval Persia 231 (4) Mongols 68 (2), 68–69 (1) Ottomans 232–233 (1) world religions 226 (1) see also Oxus

Amudaryo see Amu Darya

Amudar'ya see Amu Darya

Amur region/state Siberia colonialism 269 (3), (4) early modern states 268 (1)

Amur/Chin. Heilong Jiang river Siberia/East Asia ancient trade 44–45 (1) biological diffusion 72–73 (1) Chinese revolution 271 (5) colonialism 269 (3), (4) Communism 271 (8) early agriculture 20–21 (2), 258 (1) early modern states 265 (5) empire and revolution 268 (2) exploration 256 (1), 257 (2), (3) first states 260 (1) imperialism 270 (2) medieval states 261 (6), 262–263 (1), 263 (6), 264 (1), (2) Mongols 68–69 (1) postwar economy 275 (3) postwar politics 274 (2) Soviet Union 214–215 (4) trade 267 (3) world religions 49 (4)

Amyderya see Amu Darya

Ana Southwest Asia (Iraq) early Islam 56–57 (1)

Anadolu see Anatolia

Anadyr' Siberia (Russian Federation) exploration 257 (2)

Anadyr' Siberia (Russian Federation) exploration 257 (2)

Anaghia see Anadyrsk

Anadyrsk var. Novomarinsk; mod. Anadyr' Siberia (Russian Federation) exploration 257 (2)

Anahilapataka South Asia (India) medieval states 244 (1)

'Anakena Easter Island early cultures 281 (4)

Ananatuba archaeological site South America (Brazil) early cultures 144 (1), 145 (2)

Anartta state South Asia first empires 241 (5)

Anasazi Culture state North America the world in 1200 62–63

Anatolia region Southwest Asia plague 72–73 (1) Bronze Age 175 (3) crusades 64–65 (2) early agriculture 174 (1) early cultures 161 (2) early Islam 56–57 (1), 57 (2) economy 163 (2) empire and revolution 218 (2), 219 (3) first cities 28–29 (1) first civilizations 175 (4), (5), 222 (1) first humans 13 (2) first religions 37 (4) global knowledge

An tSionainn see Shannon

Antung see Andong, Dandong

Antwerp Fr. Anvers Low Countries (Belgium) early modern states 193 (4) economy 190 (1), 205 (4) empire and revolution 202 (1) global immigration 100 (1) medieval states 188 (1), 192 (2) Reformation 195 (5) WWI 206 (2), (3)

Anglo-Egyptian Sudan see Sudan

Anglo-Egyptian Sudan state East Africa 20th-century politics 233 (3), (4) WWII 104 (1)
see also Sudan

Anglo-Saxon Kingdoms state British Isles medieval states 182 (2)

Anglo-Saxons people British Isles Roman empire 182 (1) medieval states 182 (2)

Angola prev. People's Republic of Angola, Portuguese West Africa state Southern Africa Cold War 109 (1), (5) decolonization 168 (1) economy 168 (2), (3) European expansion 84–85 (1) European imperialism 96 (1), 97 (4) slave trade 165 (4) the modern world 112 (1), (2) WWII 104 (1)
see also Dondo

Angora mod. Ankara; anc. Ancyra Southwest Asia (Turkey) 20th-century politics 233 (3) Ottomans 232–233 (1)
see also Ancyra, Ankara

Ango-Saxons people British Isles Roman empire 182 (1) medieval states 182 (2)

Angostura mod. Ciudad Bolívar South America (Venezuela) empire and revolution 150 (1), (2) exploration 143 (3)
see also Ciudad Bolívar

Angoulême anc. Iculisma France Franks 184 (2)

Anguilla colonial possession West Indies Cold War 108 (2)

An-hsi see Anxi

Anhui var. Anhwei, Wan province East Asia Chinese revolution 271 (5) early modern states 268 (1) empire and revolution 271 (7), 274 (2) postwar politics 271 (6)

Anhwei see Anhui

Anhui Clique movement East Asia Chinese Civil War 271 (6)

Aniba var. Miam Egypt ancient Egypt 159 (4)

Anio river Italy early states 178 (1)

Anjengo South Asia (India) colonialism 247 (3)

Anjidiv Island South Asia (India) colonialism 247 (3)

Anjou France medieval states 187 (4)

Anjou region France medieval states 187 (4)

Anji East Asia (North Korea) Sino-Japanese War 270 (3)

Ankara prev. Angora, anc. Ancyra Southwest Asia (Turkey) early Islam 56–57 (1) first civilizations 221 (4) Napoleon 200–201 (1), 201 (2) Ottomans 230 (1) Timur 229 (4) WWI 233 (2) WWII 210 (1), 211 (4) Cold War 108 (3)
see also Angora, Ancyra

Ankole state East Africa colonization 167 (4)

An Loc battle Mainland Southeast Asia (Vietnam) postwar politics 251 (5)

Annaba prev. Bône North Africa (Algeria) economy 168 (2) see also Bône

Annam mod. Trung Phân state Mainland Southeast Asia biological diffusion 72–73 (1) colonialism 269 (4) early modern states 266 (1), (2), 268 (1) European expansion 80–81 (1) European imperialism 97 (3) exploration 239 (1) medieval voyages 61 (3) Mongols 68–69 (1) postwar economy 253 (5) postwar politics 253 (4) world religions 243 (5)

Annandūfu East Africa (Djibouti) early medieval states 262–263 (1)

Annapolis North America (USA) the growth of the US 129 (2)

Anniston North America (USA) US society 137 (6)

Annomadu West Africa (Ghana) empire and revolution 88 (1)

Anping East Asia (China) first states 260 (1)

Anshan Southwest Asia (Iran) first cities 28–29 (1) first civilizations 24 (2), 25 (3)

Antakya see Antioch

Antalya see Adalia, Attalia

Antananarivo Madagascar economy 168 (2) politics 169 (4)

Antandros see Antandrus

Antandrus var. Antandros state Greece ancient Greece 177 (2)

Antarctica continent 286–287

Antarctic Peninsula coastal feature Antarctica Antarctic exploration 287 (3)

Antequera see Oaxaca

Antietam North America (USA) US Civil War 131 (6)

Antigua island West Indies empire and revolution 88 (1) WWII 104 (2)

Antigua South America colonization 125 (5)

Antigua and Barbuda state West Indies the modern world 112 (1) US economy 136 (2) US politics 139 (4)

Antioch mod. Antakya; anc. Antiochia Southwest Asia (Turkey) ancient Persia 225 (6) Roman empire 180–181 (1), 181 (3), (4), 224 (2), 225 (5) ancient trade 44–45 (1) crusades 228 (2), 65 (3) early cultures 161 (2) early states 178 (1) Hellenistic world 40 (1) medieval states 185 (3), 187 (5) Mongols 229 (3), 68 (2) Seljuks 228 (1) world religions 226 (1)

Antioch mod. Antakya; anc. Antiochia Southwest Asia (Turkey) ancient Persia 225 (6) Roman empire 180–181 (1), 181 (3), (4), 224 (2), 225 (5) ancient trade 44–45 (1) crusades 228 (2), 65 (3) early cultures 161 (2) early states 178 (1)

Antioch, Principality of state Southwest Asia crusades 228 (2), 65 (3) medieval states 187 (5)

Antioquia South America (Colombia) empire and revolution 150 (2)

Antissa state Greece ancient Greece 177 (2)

Antium mod. Anzio Italy early states 178 (1) see Anzio

Antô see Andong, Dandong

Antofagasta South America (Chile) empire and revolution 151 (3) environment 153 (4) politics 151 (4)

Antonine Wall Lat. Vallum Antonini wall British Isles Roman empire 180–181 (1)

Antoniniana, Aqua aqueduct Italy Roman empire 181 (2)

Antoniniana, Thermae see Caracalla, Baths of

Antonini, Vallum see Antonine Wall

Antonio Plaza archaeological site Central America (Mexico) first civilizations 121 (2)

Antwerp Fr. Anvers Low Countries (Belgium) early modern states 193 (4) economy 190 (1), 205 (4) empire and revolution 202 (1) global immigration 100 (1) medieval states 188 (1), 192 (2) Reformation 195 (5) WWI 206 (2), (3)

Anyang archaeological site/settlement East Asia (China) early agriculture 258 (1) early systems 32 (1), 33 (2), (3) first cities 259 (3), (4), 28–29 (1)

Anyi East Asia (China) first cities 259 (3), (5) first religions 37 (4)

Anyi vassal state East Asia first cities 259 (3)

Anzio battle/settlement Italy WWII 105 (3), 211 (4)

Aomen see Macao

Aomori Japan Communism 273 (3) economy 270 (1)

Aomori prefecture Japan economy 270 (1)

Áoos see Vjosë

Aornos battle Central Asia (Tajikistan) Hellenistic world 40–41 (1)

Aotearoa mod. New Zealand state New Zealand early cultures 280–281 (3) medieval voyages 60 (3)

Ao Thai var. Siam, Gulf of; Thailand, Gulf of

Apache people North America colonization 126 (1)

Apalachee people North America colonization 125 (4), 126 (1)

Apamea Southwest Asia (Turkey) Hellenistic world 40–41 (1), 41 (2) world religions 48 (1)

Aparanta region South Asia first empires 241 (4)

Aparanta/Pascad-Desa region South Asia early religions 48 (2)

Apatzingán Central America (Mexico) first civilizations 122 (1)

Apennines mountain range Central Europe Roman empire 179 (3) early states 178 (1), (2) economy 190 (1) medieval states 183 (4) Napoleon 200–201 (1)

Aphrodisias Southwest Asia (Turkey) Hellenistic world 40–41 (1)

Aphytis settlement/state Greece ancient Greece 177 (2)

Apollo religious site Southwest Asia (Turkey) first religions 37 (3)

Apollo II Cave archaeological site Southern Africa (Namibia) prehistoric culture 17 (2)

Apollonia mod. Sozopol; prev. Sizebolu Southeast Europe (Bulgaria) ancient Greece 179 (4) first civilizations 177 (1) Hellenistic world 40–41 (1)

Apollonis Southwest Asia (Turkey) Hellenistic world 41 (2)

Apologos Southwest Asia (Kuwait) early trade 225 (3)

Appalachian Mountains mountain range North America colonization 126 (1) cultural groups 122 (5) early agriculture 120 (1), 20–21 (2) exploration 118 (1), 119 (2), (3) first civilizations 121 (4) the growth of the US 129 (2)

Appia, Aqua aqueduct Italy Roman empire 181 (2)

Appian Way see Via Appia

Appia, Via Eng. Appian Way road Italy Roman empire 181 (2) early states 178 (1)

Appomattox North America (USA) US Civil War 131 (7)

Apuli people Italy early states 178 (1), (2)

Apulia region Italy medieval states 183 (4)

Apulum prev. Bălgrad, Karlsburg, Károly-Fehérvár; Ger. Karlsburg, Weissenburg Hung. Gyulafehérvár, Rom. Alba Iulia Southeast Europe (Romania) Roman empire 180–181 (1) world religions 48 (1)
see also Gyulafehérvár

Apure river South America empire and revolution 150 (1) exploration 143 (3) politics 152 (1)

Aqaba, Gulf of var. Gulf of Elat; anc. Sinus Aelaniticus; Ar. Khalij al 'Aqabah gulf Southwest Asia crusades 65 (3) 20th century 234 (2)

Aqaba, Khalij al see Aqaba, Gulf of

'Aqabah, Khalij al see Ak Koyunlu

Aq Qoyunlu see Ak Koyunlu

Aqsu see Aksu

Aqua Antoniniana aqueduct Italy Roman empire 181 (2)

Aqua Appia aqueduct Italy Roman empire 181 (2)

Aqua Claudia aqueduct Italy Roman empire 181 (2)

Aquae Calidae see Bath

Aquae Granni see Aachen

Aquae Solis see Bath

Aqua Marcia aqueduct Italy Roman empire 181 (2)

Aqua Traiana aqueduct Italy Roman empire 181 (2)

Aqua Virgo aqueduct Italy Roman empire 181 (2)

Aquila Italy medieval states 189 (4)

Aquileia Italy Roman empire 179 (5), 180–181 (1), 181 (3) ancient trade 44–45 (1) great migrations 52–53 (1) medieval states 182 (2), 185 (3) world religions 48 (1)

Aquiles Serdán Central America (Mexico) first civilizations 121 (2)

Aquincum mod. Budapest legion headquarters Central Europe (Hungary) Roman empire 180–181 (1) see also Buda, Budapest

Aquisgranum see Aachen

Aquitaine anc. Guyenne; anc. Aquitania region France Franks 183 (6), 184 (2) medieval states 187 (4)
see also Aquitania, Guyenne

Aquitania province France Roman empire 180–181 (1)

Arabia region Southwest Asia ancient Persia 223 (4) Roman empire 180–181 (1) ancient trade 44–45 (1) crusades 65 (1) exploration 156 (3), 157 (4), 218 (1), (2), 219 (3), (4), 239 (1) Islam 226 (2), 227 (4), (5) medieval voyages 61 (3) Mongols 68 (2) the modern world 113 (4) world religions 226 (1)

Arabian Desert var. As Şaīrā' ash Sharqīyah; Eng. Eastern Desert desert Egypt ancient Egypt 159 (4), (5) early agriculture 20–21 (2) early trade 225 (3) first cities 220 (2) first civilizations 221 (4)
see also Eastern Desert

Arabian Peninsula physical region Southwest Asia ancient Egypt 159 (5) ancient Persia 223 (4) plague 72–73 (1) early agriculture 20–21 (2) early cultures 160 (1), 161 (3) early Islam 57 (2) early systems 223 (3) economy 163 (2) first civilizations 222 (1) Hellenistic world 41 (2) imperial global economy 92 (1) Islam 163 (1) medieval Persia 231 (6) Ottomans 231 (3), 232–233 (1) prehistoric culture 16 (1) slave trade 165 (4) trade 165 (3), 230 (2), 267 (3) world religions 49 (4) WWI 233 (2)

Arabian Sea var. Sinus Arabicus sea Indian Ocean ancient Persia 225 (6)

Colônia do Sacramento var. Colonia; Eng. Colonia del Sacramento South America (Uruguay) colonization 148 (2) exploration 143 (2) see also Colonia

Colonia Dublán Central America (Mexico) Mexican Revolution 133 (3)

Colorado state North America the growth of the US 129 (1) US economy 134 (2)

Colorado river North America colonization 125 (4), 126 (1) cultural groups 123 (4) exploration 118 (1), 119 (2), (3) the growth of the US 129 (2)

Colorado, Rio river South America environment 153 (4)

Colosseum building Italy Roman empire 181 (2)

Coltonoco Central America (Mexico) Aztecs 124 (3)

Columbia North America (USA) the growth of the US 129 (2) US society 137 (6)

Columbia river North America early agriculture 120 (1)

Columbia, Cape coastal feature North America exploration 287 (2)

Columbia, District of region North America the growth of the US 132 (1)

Columbus North America (USA) Mexican Revolution 133 (3) the growth of the US 129 (2) US Civil War 131 (6) US economy 134 (1) US politics 135 (6)

Comalcalco Central America (Mexico) first civilizations 122 (1), 123 (2)

Comana religious site Southwest Asia (Turkey) first religions 37 (3)

Comanche people North America colonization 126 (1)

Comani people South America the world in 250 CE 46–47

Comilla Ben. Kumillā South Asia (Bangladesh) decolonization 250 (1) postwar politics 252 (3)

Commagene state Southwest Asia the world in 1 CE 42–43

Como anc. Comum Italy economy 190 (1) medieval states 188 (1)

Comodoro Rivadavia South America (Argentina) environment 153 (4)

Comoro Islands var. Comoros colonial possession/island group East Africa European imperialism 96 (1) see also Comoros

Comoros prev. Comoro Islands state East Africa decolonization 168 (1) economy 168 (2) the modern world 112 (1), 113 (3) see also Comoro Islands

Compiègne France Franks 184 (2) medieval states 192 (2) WWI 206 (2), (3)

Compniacum see Cognac

Compostela Central America (Mexico) colonization 125 (4)

Compostella see Santiago de Compostela

Comum see Como

Conakry West Africa (Guinea) economy 168 (2)

Concelho de Ribeira Grande see Ribeira Grande

Concepción var. Villa Concepción South America (Paraguay) exploration 143 (2)

Concepción South America (Chile) colonization 148 (2) empire and revolution 151 (1) environment 153 (4) exploration 143 (3)

Concepción battle South America (Chile) empire and revolution 150 (1)

Concho people Central America colonization 125 (4), 126 (1)

Concord North America (USA) empire and revolution 127 (3) the growth of the US 129 (2) US Civil War 130 (5)

Concord battle North America (USA) empire and revolution 127 (3)

Condate see Rennes

Condivincum see Nantes

Conestoga see Susquehanna

Confederate States of America state North America 130–131

Congo prev. French Congo, Middle Congo; Fr. Moyen-Congo state Central Africa Cold War 109 (1) economy 168 (2), (3) the modern world 113 (3) see also French Congo

Congo var. Kongo; Fr. Zaïre river Central Africa ancient trade 44–45 (1) early agriculture 158 (1), 20–21 (2) early cultures 160 (1) early systems 33 (2) economy 163 (2) European expansion 84–85 (1) exploration 156 (3), 157 (4) first humans 12 (1), 13 (2) first religions 36 (1) global immigration 100 (1) Islam 163 (1) prehistoric culture 16 (1) slave trade 165 (4) trade 164 (2), 167 (1)

Congo (Zaïre) free state/state Central Africa decolonization 168 (1) economy 168 (2), (3) the modern world 112 (1)

Congo Basin basin Central Africa first humans 12 (1), 13 (2) slave trade 165 (4)

Congo Free State var. Belgian Congo, Zaïre; mod. Democratic Republic of Congo state Central Africa the world in 1900 94–95 see also Belgian Congo, Congo (Zaïre), Zaïre

Conimbria see Coimbra

Conimbriga see Coimbra

Conjeeveram see Kanchipuram

Connacht region British Isles medieval states 186 (2)

Connecticut state North America empire and revolution 127 (2), (3) the growth of the US 129 (1) US Civil War 130 (2), (3), (4), (5) US economy 134 (2)

Connecticut river North America empire and revolution 127 (3)

Consentia see Cosentia

Constance var. Constanz; hist. Kostnitz, anc. Constantia; Ger. Konstanz Central Europe (Germany) early modern states 193 (4) Franks 184 (2) medieval states 188 (1)

Constance, Lake Ger. Bodensee lake Central Europe early modern states 193 (5)

Constanţa Southeast Europe (Romania) WWI 207 (6)

Constantia see Constance

Constantine, Baths of Lat. Thermae Constantini building Italy Roman empire 181 (2)

Constantini, Thermae see Constantine, Baths of

Constantinople anc. Byzantium; Bul. Tsarigrad, Eng. Istanbul, Turk. Istanbul, Norse. Mikligard settlement Southwest Asia (Turkey) Roman empire 182 (1) plague 72–73 (1) crusades 186 (1), 64–65 (2), 65 (1) early Islam 56–57 (1), 57 (2) economy 190 (1), 205 (4) empire and revolution 202 (1) European expansion 84–85 (1) exploration 172 (1), 218 (2), 219 (3) global immigration 100 (1) great migrations 52–53 (1) imperial global economy 92 (1) Islam 163 (1), 226 (2), 227 (4), (5) medieval states 182 (2), 185 (3), 187 (5), 189 (4) medieval voyages 60–61 (1) Mongols 229 (3),

68 (2) Napoleon 200–201 (1), 201 (3) Ottomans 195 (4), 230 (1), 231 (3), 232–233 (1) Seljuks 228 (1) Timur 229 (4) world religions 226 (1), 49 (4) WWI 207 (6), 233 (2) 20th-century politics 233 (3) see also Byzantium, Istanbul

Constantinople battle Southwest Asia (Turkey) early Islam 56–57 (1) Islam 226 (2)

Constanz see Constance

Con Thien battle Mainland Southeast Asia (Vietnam) postwar politics 251 (5)

Conway British Isles (United Kingdom) medieval states 188 (2)

Cooch Behar region South Asia decolonization 250 (2)

Cook County region North America

Cook Islands colonial possession Pacific Ocean colonization 285 (3) decolonization 285 (3) early cultures 280–281 (3) environmentalism 285 (2) exploration 279 (3) medieval voyages 60 (2)

Cook Strait var. Raukawa sea waterway New Zealand colonization 283 (5)

Cooktown Australia colonization 283 (3)

Coomassie see Kumasi

Coondapoor var. Barcelore South Asia (India) colonialism 247 (3)

Cooper North America first civilizations 121 (4)

Cooper Creek var. Barcoo, Cooper's Creek river Australia colonization 282 (1) see also Barcoo, Cooper's Creek

Coorg state South Asia colonialism 248 (2)

Coosa people North America colonization 126 (1)

Copán Central America (Honduras) first civilizations 121 (2), 122 (2)

Copena region North America first civilizations 121 (4)

Copenhagen anc. Hafnia; Dan. København Scandinavia (Denmark) early modern states 193 (4), 195 (3) economy 190 (1), 205 (4) empire and revolution 202 (1), (2) medieval states 189 (3) Napoleon 200–201 (1), 201 (2), (3) postwar politics 212 (3) Reformation 194 (2) WWII 210 (1), 211 (2), (3), (4) Cold War 108 (3)

Copiapó prev. San Francisco de Selva South America (Chile) empire and revolution 151 (3) exploration 143 (3) Incas 147 (3) politics 151 (4)

Copper Inuit people North America cultural groups 123 (3)

Coppermine river North America exploration 286 (1), 287 (2)

Coquimbo South America (Chile) colonization 148 (2)

Coral Sea sea Australia colonization 282 (1) decolonization 251 (4), 285 (3) early cultures 280–281 (3) environmentalism 285 (2) exploration 280 (1) medieval voyages 60 (2) postwar economy 253 (5) WWII 104 (2), 251 (3), 272 (1), 273 (2)

Coral Sea Islands colonial possession Pacific Ocean the modern world 110–111

Corcaigh see Cork

Corcyra Southeast Europe (Croatia) first civilizations 177 (1)

Corcyra var. Kérkira; mod. Corfu island Greece ancient Greece 177 (3), 179 (4) see also Corfu

Corcyra Nigra see Korčula

Corded Ware Burials cultural region Northeast Europe The World in 2500 BCE 22–23

Cordillera Central mountain range South America early cultures 145 (2)

Cordilleran Ice Sheet ice feature North America historical geography 117 (1)

Cordillera Occidental mountain range South America early cultures 145 (2)

Cordillera Oriental mountain range South America early cultures 145 (2)

Córdoba anc. Corduba; Eng. Cordova Iberian Peninsula (Spain) economy 190 (1) civil war 209 (4) Napoleon 201 (2) see also Corduba, Cordova

Córdoba South America (Argentina) colonization 148 (2) empire and revolution 150 (1), 151 (3) environment 153 (4) exploration 143 (2) politics 152 (1)

Córdoba state Iberian Peninsula Franks 184 (2) medieval states 185 (3) medieval voyages 60–61 (1) the world in 1000 58–59 Islam 226 (2), 227 (4)

Cordova Iberian peninsula (Spain) Roman empire 182 (1) crusades 186 (1), 64–65 (2), 65 (1) early Islam 56–57 (1), 57 (2) Franks 184 (2) Islam 184 (1), 192 (3) medieval states 182 (2), 185 (3) medieval voyages 60–61 (1) the World in 1000 58–59 (1)

Corduba mod. Córdoba; Eng. Cordova Iberian Peninsula (Spain) Roman empire 181 (4) great migrations 52–53 (1) world religions 48 (1) see also Córdoba, Cordova

Corfinium Italy Roman empire 180–181 (1) early states 178 (1)

Corfu var. Kérkira; Eng. Corfu island Greece empire and revolution 202 (1) Napoleon 201 (3) Ottomans 230 (1), 231 (3) see also Corcyra

Corinium, Corinium Dobunorum see Cirencester

Corinth North America (USA) US Civil War 131 (7)

Corinth anc. Corinthus; Gr. Kórinthos Greece ancient Greece 177 (3), 179 (4) Roman empire 179 (5), 180–181 (1), 181 (3), 182 (1) exploration 172 (1) first civilizations 177 (1) great migrations 52–53 (1) Hellenistic world 40–41 (1) medieval states 182 (2) world religions 48 (1)

Corinth, Gulf of anc. Corinthiacus Sinus gulf Greece ancient Greece 177 (2), (3) first civilizations 175 (4)

Corinthiacus Sinus see Corinth, Gulf of

Cork Ir. Corcaigh British Isles (Ireland) economy 205 (4) medieval states 186 (2), 187 (4)

Corneto see Tarquinia

Coro prev. Santa Ana de Coro South America (Venezuela) exploration 142 (1)

Coromandel Coast physical region South Asia colonialism 247 (3), 248 (1), (2) decolonization 250 (1) early medieval states 244 (1), (2), 244–245 (3), 245 (4) economy 249 (4) first empires 241 (4), (5) Marathas 246 (1) Mughal Empire 246 (1) postwar politics 252 (1) world religions 242 (2), (3), 243 (4)

Coromandel Peninsula coastal feature New Zealand colonization 283 (4)

Coron Greece medieval states 187 (5)

Corozal people South America the world in 1 CE 42–43 the world in 250 CE 46–47

Corregidor battle Philippines WWII 104 (2)

Correntes, Cape headland Southern Africa exploration 156 (3)

Correo Mexicano battle Gulf of Mexico the growth of the US 129 (2)

Corrientes prev. San Juan de Vera South America (Argentina) empire and revolution 151 (3) environment 153 (4) exploration 143 (2)

Corse see Corsica

Corsica Fr. Corse island France Roman empire 179 (3), 180–181 (1), 181 (3), (4), 182 (1) Bronze Age 175 (3) crusades 186 (1), 64–65 (2) early cultures 161 (2) early Islam 56–57 (1) economy 190 (1) empire and revolution 199 (4), 202 (1), (3), 88–89 (2) first religions 37 (3) Franks 184 (2) civil war 209 (5) Islam 226 (2), 227 (4) medieval states 183 (4), 185 (3), (5), 188 (1) Napoleon 201 (2) Ottomans 231 (3) postwar economy 213 (5), 214 (1) postwar politics 212 (3) Reformation 196 (1), (2) the modern world 112 (2) world religions 48 (1) WWII 210 (1), 211 (2), (4)

Corsica and Sardinia province Italy Roman empire 179 (5)

Corsicans people France early states 178 (2) the modern world 112 (2)

Cortaillod-Est France Bronze Age 175 (3)

Cortellazzo Italy WWI 207 (5)

Cortenuova battle Italy early states 188 (1)

Cortes de Navarra Iberian Peninsula (Spain) Bronze Age 175 (3)

Cortez, Sea of see California, Gulf of

Cortina see Hayden

Cortona Italy early states 178 (2) first civilizations 177 (1)

Corumbá South America (Brazil) colonization 148 (2) empire and revolution 151 (3)

Coruña Sp. La Coruña Iberian Peninsula (Spain) Napoleon 200–201 (1), 201 (2) Corupedium battle Southwest Asia (Turkey) Hellenistic world 40–41 (1)

Corvo, Passo di Italy early agriculture 174 (1)

Cos settlement/state Greece ancient Greece 177 (1) first civilizations 177 (1)

Cosa Italy early states 178 (1)

Cosentia var. Consentia Italy early states 178 (1)

Cosquer archaeological site France prehistoric culture 17 (2)

Cossack Revolt war Eastern Europe Reformation 196 (2)

Cossimbazar South Asia (India) colonialism 247 (3)

Costa Rica state Central America Cold War 108 (2), 109 (1) the growth of the US 129 (2) the modern world 112 (1) US economy 136 (2), 139 (4) US superpower 138 (1)

Costermansville see Bukavu

Côte d'Ivoire see Ivory Coast

Côte Française des Somalis see Djibouti, French Somaliland

Côtière, Chaîne see Coast Mountains

Cotopachi South America (Bolivia) Incas 147 (3)

Cotrone see Croton

Courland Ger. Kurland state Eastern Europe/Scandinavia early modern states 195 (3) Reformation 194 (2)

Courtrai Low Countries (Belgium) WWI 206 (2), (3)

Cova Negra archaeological site Iberian Peninsula (Spain) first humans 13 (2)

Coventry British Isles (United Kingdom) economy 190 (1) WWII 210 (1)

Coveta de l'Or Iberian Peninsula (Spain) early agriculture 174 (1)

Cowpens battle North America (USA) empire and revolution 127 (3)

Coyoacán Central America (Mexico) Aztecs 124 (3) colonization 125 (5)

Coyolapan state Central America Aztecs 124 (1)

Coyotepec Central America (Mexico) Aztecs 124 (1)

Coyotera Apache people North America colonization 125 (4)

Cozumel, Isla island North America Aztecs 124 (1) first civilizations 123 (2)

Crab Orchard region/burial mound North America first civilizations 121 (4)

Cracovia see Cracow

Cracow Lat. Cracovia; Ger. Krakau, Pol. Kraków settlement Central Europe (Poland) biological diffusion 72–73 (1) early modern states 193 (4), 194 (1) economy 190 (1) empire and revolution 198 (2), 202 (1) civil war 209 (3) medieval states 188 (1), 189 (3), (4) Mongols 68–69 (1) Napoleon 200–201 (1), 201 (2) Ottomans 195 (4) postwar politics 212 (3) Reformation 194 (2) WWI 207 (4) WWII 211 (3), (4) 20th-century politics 233 (3)

Cradle of Humankind see Sterkfontein

Craig Harbour North America (Canada) cultural groups 123 (3)

Cranganur South Asia (India) colonialism 247 (3)

Cravant battle France medieval states 192 (2)

Crécy battle France medieval states 192 (1)

Cree people North America colonization 126 (1) cultural groups 123 (3)

Creek people North America colonization 125 (4), 126 (1)

Crema Italy economy 190 (1)

Cremera river Italy early states 178 (1)

Cremona Italy Roman empire 180–181 (1) economy 190 (1) Franks 184 (2) medieval states 183 (4)

Crépy France Reformation 194 (2)

Crestaulta Central Europe (Switzerland) Bronze Age 175 (3)

Creta anc. Candia; Eng. Crete, Gr. Kriti island Greece Roman empire 180–181 (1), 181 (4) see also Candia, Crete

Crete region/island Greece ancient Egypt 159 (5) ancient Greece 177 (2), 179 (4) ancient Persia 223 (4) Roman empire 179 (5), 181 (4), 182 (1), 24 (2), 225 (5) ancient trade 44–45 (1) Bronze Age 175 (3) crusades 186 (1), 64–65 (2) early cultures 161 (2) early Islam 56–57 (1) early systems 223 (3) Hellenistic world 224 (1) Islam 184 (1), 226 (2), 227 (4), (5) Napoleon 200–201 (1), 201 (2) Ottomans 230 (1), 231 (3), 232–233 (1) postwar economy 213 (5), 214 (1) postwar politics 212 (3) Reformation 196 (1) world religions 226 (1) WWI 233 (2) WWII 210 (1), 211 (2), (4) 20th-century politics 233 (3)

Crete, Sea of sea Greece ancient Greece 179 (4) first civilizations 175 (4)

Crewe British Isles (United Kingdom) economy 204 (1)

Criel Mound burial mound North America (USA) first civilizations 121 (4)

Crimea Rus. Krym region/coastal feature Eastern Europe exploration 219 (3) historical geography 170–171 (1) Ottomans 202 (4), 232–233 (1) the modern world 112 (2) WWI 207 (4)

Crimea, Khanate of state/vassal state Eastern Europe Islam 195 (4), 230 (1), 231 (3)

Crimean Tartars people Eastern Europe Soviet Union 213 (4)

Crna Gora see Montenegro

Croatia Ger. Kroatien, SCr. Hrvatska region/state Southeast Europe medieval states 185 (3), 189 (4) Ottomans 197 (4), 230 (1) postwar economy 214 (1), (2), 215 (3) Soviet Union 214–215 (4) the modern world 112 (2), 113 (3) WWII 210 (1), 211 (2), (4)

Croats people Southeast Europe Franks 184 (2)

Crocodile see Limpopo

Cromford British Isles (United Kingdom) imperial global economy 93 (4)

Cromwell New Zealand colonization 283 (5)

Crooked Creek battle North America (USA) the growth of the US 129 (2)

Croquants rebel faction France Reformation 196 (2)

Cross, Cape headland Southern Africa exploration 156 (3)

Croton var. Cotrone; mod. Crotone; anc. Crotona Italy Roman empire 179 (3) early cultures 161 (2) early states 178 (1), (2) first civilizations 177 (1)

Crotona see Croton

Crotone see Croton

Crow people North America (USA) colonization 126 (1)

Crown Point North America (USA) empire and revolution 127 (2), (3)

Crozet Islands island group Indian Ocean the world in 1800 86–87

Crusader States archaeological site Southwest Asia Mongols 68–69 (1)

Cruz del Milagro archaeological site Central America (Mexico) first civilizations 121 (3)

Cruzeiro do Sul South America (Brazil) environment 153 (4)

Crystal II North America (Canada) cultural groups 123 (3)

Ctesiphon var. Tayspun Southwest Asia (Iraq) ancient Persia 225 (6) Roman empire 180–181 (1), 224 (2) ancient trade 44–45 (1) Islam 227 (4), (5) Sasanian empire 225 (5) early cultures 161 (1) economy 190 (1) Hellenistic world 224 (1) trade 230 (2)

Cuahtitlan state Central America Aztecs 124 (1)

Cuando var. Kwando river Southern Africa exploration 157 (4)

Cuangar Southern Africa (Angola) Cold War 109 (5)

Cuango var. Kwango river Southern Africa trade 164 (2) see also Kwango

Cuanza var. Kwanza river Southern Africa Cold War 109 (5) exploration 157 (4) trade 164 (2)

Cuarte Iberian Peninsula (Spain) Islam 192 (3)

Cuatepec see Coatepec

Cuauhatitlan Central America (Mexico) colonization 125 (5)

Cuauhquecholan Central America (Mexico) colonization 125 (5)

Cuauhtepec Central America (Mexico) Aztecs 124 (3)

Cuauhtochco state Central America Aztecs 124 (1)

Cuautitlán Central America (Mexico) Aztecs 124 (2)

Cuautlapan Central America (Mexico) Aztecs 124 (3)

Cuba colonial possession/state/island West Indies colonization 125 (4), 126 (1) early agriculture 120 (1) empire and revolution 88 (1), 85 (2) exploration 143 (3) global immigration 100 (1), 101 (3) historical geography 117 (1) imperial global economy 92 (1) the growth of the US 129 (2), 133 (4) the modern world 112 (1) US economy 136 (2) US politics 135 (6) US superpower 138 (1) WWII 104 (1), 109 (1)

Cubango var. Kuvango; Port. Vila Artur de Paiva, Vila da Ponte river Southern Africa Cold War 109 (5) exploration 157 (4)

Cuckadoo Australia the world in 10,000 BCE 14–15

Cúcuta var. San José de Cúcuta South America (Colombia) empire and revolution 150 (2)

Cúcuta battle South America (Venezuela) empire and revolution 150 (1)

Cuello Central America (Belize) first civilizations 121 (2)

Cuenca South America (Ecuador) colonization 148 (2) empire and revolution 151 (3)

Cuera see Chur, Curia

Cuernavaca Central America (Mexico) Aztecs 124 (2) colonization 125 (5)

Cuetlachtlan Central America (Mexico) colonization 125 (5)

Cuetlaxtlan state Central America Aztecs 124 (1)

Cueva people South America early cultures 147 (2)

Cuiabá prev. Cuyabá South America (Brazil) environment 153 (4) politics 152 (1)

Cuicatlán Central America (Mexico) first civilizations 122 (1)

Cuiculco Central America (Mexico) first civilizations 121 (2)

Cuihuacan Central America (Mexico) first civilizations 122 (1)

Cuiry-les-Chaudardes France early agriculture 174 (1)

Cuitlahuac Central America (Mexico) Aztecs 124 (2) colonization 125 (5)

Culara see Grenoble

Culhuacan Central America (Mexico) Aztecs 124 (2), (3)

Culiacán var. Culiacán Rosales, Culiacán-Rosales Central America (Mexico) Mexican Revolution 133 (3)

Culiacán Rosales see Culiacán

Culfavera archaeological site Iberian Peninsula (Spain) prehistoric culture 17 (2)

Cullerson's Ranch North America (USA) Mexican Revolution 133 (3)

Culver Lake North America (USA) US economy 135 (4)

Cumae Italy early states 178 (1), (2) first civilizations 177 (1)

Cumana South America (Venezuela) colonization 148 (2) empire and revolution 150 (1), (4)

Cumans var. Kipchaks; Rus. Polovtsy people Eastern Europe crusades 186 (1) Mongols 68–69 (1)

Cumberland River river North America the growth of the US 129 (2)

Cunaxa battle Southwest Asia (Iraq) ancient Persia 223 (4)

Cunjamba Southern Africa (Angola) Cold War 109 (5)

Cupertino North America (USA) 136 (3)

Cupisnique archaeological site South America (Peru) early cultures 145 (3)

Cupul state Central America Aztecs 124 (1)

Curaçao island West Indies European expansion 85 (2)

Curia mod. Chur; anc. Curia Rhaetorum; Fr. Coire, It. Coira, Quera Central Europe (Switzerland) Roman empire 180–181 (1)

Curia Rhaetorum see Chur, Curia

Curitiba South America (Brazil) environment 153 (4)

Curium Southwest Asia (Cyprus) first civilizations 177 (1)

Curpeutaria, Lake ancient lake Australia the world in 10,000 BCE 14–15

Currarong Australia the world in 5000 BCE 18–19

Curzola see Korčula

Cusco var. Cuzco South America (Peru) environment 153 (4) narcotics 153 (5) see also Cuzco

Cush see Kush

Cushites see Kushites

Cutch, Gulf of see Kachchh, Gulf of

Cuttack South Asia (India) colonialism 247 (3), 248 (1) economy 249 (4)

Cuyabá see Cuiabá

Cuyutec people Central America colonization 125 (4)

Cuzco mod. Cusco South America (Peru) colonization 148 (2) early cultures 146 (1) empire and revolution 151 (3) exploration 142 (1) Incas 147 (3), 148 (1) see also Cusco

Cuzco state Central America the world in 250 CE 46–47 the world in 1000 58–59 the world in 1200 62–63

Cyclades var. Kiklādhes; Eng. Cyclades island group Greece ancient Greece 177 (2), (3) first civilizations 175 (4)

Cyme state Greece ancient Greece 177 (2)

Cymru see Wales

Cynoscephalae battle Greece ancient Greece 179 (4)

Cynossema battle Southwest Asia (Turkey) ancient Greece 177 (3)

Cyprus Gk. Kypros, Turk. Kıbrıs state Southwest Asia ancient Egypt 159 (4), (5) ancient Greece 177 (2) ancient Persia 223 (4), 225 (6) Roman empire 179 (5), 180–181 (1), 181 (3), (4), 182 (1), 224 (2), 225 (6) ancient trade 44–45 (1) Bronze Age 175 (3) crusades 228 (2) early agriculture 220 (1) early cultures 161 (2) early Islam 56–57 (1) early trade 225 (3) economy 190 (1) empire and revolution 202 (1) exploration 172 (1) first cities 220 (2) first civilizations 177 (1), 221 (4), (5), 222 (1), (2) first religions 37 (3) Hellenistic world 224 (1) historical geography 170–171 (1) Islam 184 (1), 226 (2), 227 (4), (5) medieval states 182 (2), 185 (3), 187 (5) kingdom 229 (3), 68–69 (1) Napoleon 200–201 (1) Ottomans 202 (4), 230 (1), 231 (3), 232–233 (1) postwar politics 212 (3) Seljuks 228 (1) the modern world 112 (2), 113 (3), (4) world religions 226 (1) WWI 233 (2), 207 (6), 211 (2), (4)20th-century politics 233 (3), (4), 235 (5)

Cyprus, Kingdom of state Southwest Asia crusades 65 (3)

Cyrenaica var. Barqah region/state North Africa Roman empire 225 (5) early cultures 161 (2) first civilizations 177 (1) Islam 227 (4) Ottomans 232–233 (1) slave trade 165 (4)

Cyrene North Africa (Libya) ancient Persia 223 (4) Roman empire 179 (5), 180–181 (1), 181 (3), (4), 225 (5) ancient trade 44–45 (1) early cultures 160 (1), 161 (2) first civilizations 177 (1) Hellenistic world 40–41 (1) world religions 48 (1)

Cyrene and Creta province North Africa Roman empire 180–181 (1)

Cyrrhus legion headquarters Southwest Asia (Syria) Roman empire 180–181 (1)

Cyrus river Southwest Asia ancient Persia 223 (4)

Cytorus Southwest Asia (Turkey) first civilizations 177 (1)

Cyzicus state Southwest Asia (Turkey) ancient Greece 177 (2), 179 (4) Roman empire 180–181 (1)

Czechoslovakia state Central Europe civil war 209 (3), (5) postwar economy 213 (5) postwar politics 212 (1), (3) Soviet Union 213 (4) WWII 208 (1) WWII 211 (3) Cold War 108 (3), 109 (1)

Czech Republic Cz. Česká Republika state Southeast Europe postwar economy 214 (1), (2) Soviet Union 214–215 (4) the modern world 112 (2), 113 (4) see also Czechoslovakia

Czernowitz Eastern Europe (Ukraine) WWI 207 (4)

Czikador major cistercian house Central Europe medieval states 187 (3)

D

Daamat state East Africa the world in 500 BCE 34–35

Dabal South Asia (Pakistan) world religions 243 (4)

Dacca mod. Dhaka South Asia (Bangladesh) colonialism 247 (3) decolonization 250 (1), (2) economy 249 (4) imperial global economy 93 (5) see also Dhaka

Dachau concentration camp Central Europe WWII 211 (3)

Dacia province/state Southeast Europe Roman empire 180–181 (1), 181 (4) ancient trade 44–45 (1) world religions 48 (1)

Dacians people Southeast Europe the world in 1 CE 42–43

Dade's Battle battle North America (USA) the growth of the US 129 (2)

Dading East Asia (China) medieval states 263 (4)

Dadiwan archaeological site East Asia early agriculture 258 (1)

Dadra and Nagar Haveli region South Asia postwar politics 252 (1)

Dadri South Asia empire and revolution 249 (3)

Dadu East Asia (China) medieval states 263 (6)

Dagden see Dagö

Dagestan state Eastern Europe Soviet Union 214–215 (4)

Daghestan mod. Dagestan state Eastern Europe/Southwest Asia Mongols 68–69 (1) see also Daghestan

Dagö Est. Hiiumaa; Ger. Dagden, island Southeast Europe early modern states 195 (3) WWI 207 (4)

Dagomba state West Africa the world in 1800 86–87 the world in 1850 90–91

Dagon see Rangoon

Dagushan var. Takushan East Asia (China) Russo-Japanese War 270 (4)

Dahecun archaeological site East Asia early agriculture 258 (1)

Dahlak island East Africa Islam 163 (1)

Dahomey mod. Benin state West Africa colonization 167 (4) European imperialism 96 (1) Islam 167 (3) slave trade 165 (4) trade 167 (1) see also Benin

Dahshur Egypt ancient Egypt 159 (3), (4)

Daibul var. Daybul South Asia (Pakistan) medieval voyages 61 (3) see also Daybul

Dai Do battle Mainland Southeast Asia (Vietnam) postwar politics 251 (5)

Daifang East Asia (Korea) medieval states 264 (2)

Daijun East Asia (China) first cities 259 (5)

Dai-la mod. Hanoi; prev. Thang Long Mainland Southeast Asia (Vietnam) early medieval states 245 (5), (6) see also Hanoi

Daima archaeological site/settlement West Africa (Nigeria) ancient trade 44–45 (1) early agriculture 158 (1) early cultures 160 (1)

Dainzú Central America (Mexico) first civilizations 121 (2)

Dairen var. Dalian, Dalian, Jay Dairen, Lüda, Ta-lien; Rus. Dalny East Asia (China) colonialism 269 (4) imperialism 270 (2) Russo-Japanese War 270 (4) Sino-Japanese War 270 (3) Soviet Union 213 (4)

Dai-sen mountain Japan medieval states 265 (3)

Dai Viet state Mainland Southeast Asia early medieval states 245 (5) world religions 243 (5)

Daju state Central Africa the world in 1200 62–63 the world in 1300 66–67 the world in 1400 70–71

Dakar West Africa (Senegal) economy 168 (2) European imperialism 96 (1) global immigration 100 (1) US superpower 138 (1) WWII 104 (2)

Dakhla Oasis var. Wāhat el Dākhla oasis Egypt ancient Egypt 159 (2), (3), (5)

Dākhla, Wāhat el see Dakhla Oasis

Dakota colonization 126 (1)

Dakovica Southeast Europe (Yugoslavia) postwar economy 215 (3)

Dakshina Koshala region South Asia world religions 242 (2)

Daksinapatha region South Asia ancient India 242 (1) first empires 241 (4)

Daksinatya/Daksinapatha region South Asia world religions 48 (2)

Dak To battle Mainland Southeast Asia (Vietnam) postwar politics 251 (5)

Dalautabad South Asia (India) early medieval states 244–245 (3)

Dali var. Xiaguan East Asia (China) early humans 13 (2) early medieval states 245 (5) medieval states 263 (4), (5) Mongols 68–69 (1)

Dalian East Asia (China) Islam 275 (4) postwar politics 274 (2)

Daliang East Asia (China) first cities 259 (5)

Dalien see Dairen, Dalian

Dallas North America (USA) Cold War 108 (2) imperial global economy 93 (5) US economy 134 (1), (3), 136 (2) US politics 135 (6)

Dalmatia region Southeast Europe Roman empire 180–181 (1), 225 (5) early cultures 161 (2) empire and revolution 202 (1) Ottomans 230 (1)

Dalny see Dairen, Dalian

Dalriada state British Isles medieval states 183 (3)

Dalstroi region Siberia Soviet Union 213 (4)

Daluo Mainland Southeast Asia (Vietnam) Mongols 68–69 (1)

Daman settlement/colonial possession South Asia (India) colonialism 247 (3) postwar politics 252 (1) trade 230 (2)

Damão mod. Daman colonial possession/settlement South Asia empire and revolution 88–89 (2) trade 267 (3) WWII 251 (3)

Damaraland region West Africa the world in 1850 90–91

Damas see Damascus

Damasco see Damascus

Damascus var. Ash Shām, Esh Sham; Ar. Dimashq, Fr. Damas, It. Damasco Southwest Asia (Syria) ancient Egypt 159 (5) ancient Persia 223 (4), 225 (6) Roman empire 180–181 (1), 224 (2), 225 (4), (5) ancient trade 44–45 (1) plague 72–73 (1) crusades 228 (2), 65 (1), (3) early cultures 161 (2) early Islam 56–57 (1), 57 (2) early trade 225 (3) exploration 156 (3), 218 (2), 219 (4) first civilizations 221 (4), (5), 222 (1), (2) Hellenistic world 224 (1) Islam 184 (1), (2), 226 (2), 227 (4), (5), 68–69 (1) Napoleon 200–201 (1) Ottomans 231 (3), 232–233 (1) Seljuks 228 (1) Timur 229 (4) trade 230 (2) world religions 226 (1) WWI 233 (2) 20th-century 233 (3), (4), 20th-century politics 233 (3)

Damascus, Emirate of state Southwest Asia crusades 65 (3)

Damb Sadaat archaeological site South Asia (Pakistan) first cities 240 (2)

Damghan Southwest Asia (Iran) early Islam 56–57 (1)

Damietta Ar. Dumyāt Egypt crusades 64–65 (2), 65 (3) Islam 163 (1)

Daming var. Ta-ming East Asia (China) first cities 259 (5)

Damot state East Africa the world in 1000 58–59 the world in 1200 62–63

Dampier Australia colonization 283 (3)

Dan settlement/state Southwest Asia (Israel) first civilizations 222 (1)

Dana Eastern Europe (Russian Federation) biological diffusion 72–73 (1)

Da Nang battle Mainland Southeast Asia (Vietnam) injustwar politics 251 (5)

Dandaka region South Asia world religions 242 (2)

Dandanqan Central Asia (Turkmenistan) Seljuks 228 (1)

Dandong var. Tan-tung; prev. Antung; Jap. Antō East Asia (China) Cold War 109 (4) see also Andong

Danelaw state British Isles medieval states 185 (3) medieval voyages 60–61 (1)

Danes people Scandinavia Roman empire 182 (1) Franks 184 (2) medieval states 185 (3) the modern world 112 (2)

Danger Cave North America (USA) the world in 5000 BCE 18–19

Dangerous Archipelago see Tuamotu Islands

Daning East Asia (China) medieval states 263 (6)

Danish March region Central Europe Franks 184 (2)

Danishmends state Southwest Asia crusades 64–65 (2)

Danish West Indies see American Virgin Islands

Danmark see Denmark

Danmarksstraedet see Denmark Strait

Dantapura South Asia (India) ancient India 242 (1)

Danube Lat. Danubius, Danuvius, Ister; Bul. Dunav, Cz. Dunaj, Ger. Donau, Hung. Duna, Rom. Dunărea; river Southeast Europe ancient Persia 225 (6) Roman empire 180–181 (1), 181 (3), (4), 224 (2), 225 (5) ancient trade 44–45 (1) Bronze Age 175 (3) Copper Age 174 (2) crusades 186 (1), 64–65 (2) early agriculture 174 (1), 20–21 (2) early Islam 56–57 (1), 57 (2) early modern states 193 (4) economy 190 (1) empire and revolution 199 (3), 202 (1), (2) exploration 172 (1) first civilizations 177 (1) first humans 13 (2) first religions 36 (1), 37 (3) Franks 184 (2) great migrations 52–53 (1), 53 (2) Hellenistic world 224 (1) Islam 163 (1), 226 (2), 227 (4) medieval states 182 (2), 185 (3), 188 (1), 189 (4) Napoleon 200–201 (1), 201 (2), (3) Ottomans 197 (4), 230 (1), 231 (3), 232–233 (1) postwar economy 215 (3) postwar politics 212 (3) Reformation 196 (1), (2) Seljuks 228 (1) world religions 226 (1), 49 (4) WWI 207 (6) WWII 210 (1), 211 (4) civil war 209 (5) postwar economy 215 (3) see also Danuvius

Danubius see Danube

Danum see Doncaster

Danuvius var. Danube river Southeast Europe ancient trade 44 (2)

Danyang East Asia (China) first cities 259 (5) first religions 37 (4)

Danyang province East Asia first cities 260 (1)

Danzig mod. Gdańsk Central Europe (Poland) trade 72–73 (1) early modern states 193 (4), 195 (3) economy 190 (1), 205 (4) empire and revolution 198 (2), 199 (3), 202 (1), (2) medieval states 189 (3), (4) Napoleon 200–201 (1) WWI 207 (4) WWII 210 (1), 211 (4)

Dapenkeng archaeological site East Asia early agriculture 258 (1)

Darada state South Asia first empires 241 (5)

Daradus river West Africa (Senegal) ancient trade 44 (2)

Dar al Baida, al see Rabat

Darbelo South Asia (Pakistan) colonialism 247 (3)

Dardanelles var. Hellespont; Turk. Çanakkale Boğazı sea waterway Southwest Asia/Europe first civilizations 175 (4) WWI 207 (6), 233 (2)

Dar-el-Beida see Casablanca

Dar es Salaam East Africa (Tanzania) colonization 167 (4) economy 168 (2) exploration 156 (3), 157 (4), (5)

Dar es-Soltan archaeological site North Africa (Morocco) first humans 13 (2), 14 (1)

Darfur state East Africa colonization 167 (4) slave trade 165 (4) trade 167 (1)

Darfar region East Africa (Sudan) colonialism 247 (3)

Darién, Golfo del see Darién, Gulf of

Darién, Gulf of Sp. Golfo del Darién gulf South America colonization 148 (2) Incas 148 (1)

Darién, Isthmus of see Panama, Isthmus of

Dariorigum France Roman empire 180–181 (1)

Dar'īyah see Deraya

Darjeeling South Asia (India) exploration 257 (3)

Darling river Australia colonization 282 (1), (2), 283 (3) early agriculture 20–21 (2) exploration 279 (2) prehistoric culture 17 (5)

Darlington British Isles (United Kingdom) economy 204 (1)

Dar Tichit West Africa (Mauritania) early agriculture 158 (1)

Darwin prev. Palmerston, Port Darwin Australia colonization 282 (1), 283 (3) exploration 279 (2) WWII 251 (3), 272 (1)

Dar'yoi Amu see Amu Darya

Dās island Southwest Asia economy 234 (1)

Dasapura South Asia (India) early religions 48 (2)

Dasharna region/state South Asia first empires 241 (5) world religions 242 (2)

Dashkhovuz see Dashkhovuz

Dashiqiao var. Tashihkiao East Asia (China) Russo-Japanese War 270 (4)

Dashkevur prev. Tashauz; Turkm. Dashhowuz Central Asia (Turkmenistan) Soviet Union 214–215 (4)

Dasht river South Asia first cities 240 (2) first civilizations 24 (2), 25 (3) first empires 241 (4), (5) Mughal Empire 246 (1) world religions 242 (2)

Dating East Asia (China) medieval states 263 (4)

Datong East Asia (China) first modern states 266 (1) medieval states 263 (5) world religions 49 (3)

Daugava see Western Dvina

Daugavpils see Dünaburg

Daulatabad South Asia (India) early medieval states 244 (4)

Dauni people Italy early states 178 (2)

Dauphiné region France medieval states 192 (1), (2)

Davao off. Davao City Philippines colonialism 247 (4)

Davao City see Davao

Davis Strait sea waterway North America exploration 286 (1), 287 (2) the growth of the US 129 (1)

Dawa var. Daua river South Asia the world in state 163 (4)

Dawaro state East Africa the world in 1200 62–63 the world in 1300 66–67

Dawenkou archaeological site East Asia early agriculture 258 (1), (2)

Dawson see Dawson City

Dawson City mod. Dawson North America (Canada) imperial global economy 93 (3)

Dawston *see* Degsastan
Daybul *var.* Daibol South Asia (India) medieval voyages 61 (3) trade 230 (2)
Daybul *see* Daibul
Dayi Shang *vassal state* East Asia first cities 259 (3)
Dayton North America (USA) US politics 135 (6)
Da Yunhe *see* Grand Canal
Dazaifu Japan early modern states 265 (5) medieval states 264 (2), 265 (3)
Dazhangheguo *state* East Asia medieval states 263 (3)
DDR *see* German Democratic Republic
Dead Sea *var.* Bahret Lut, Lacus Asphaltites; *Ar.* Al Bahr al Mayyit, Bahrat Lut, *Heb.* Yam HaMelah *salt lake* Southwest Asia 20th century 234 (2) 20th-century politics 234 (2) Roman empire 225 (4) crusades 65 (3) first civilizations 221 (4), 222 (1)
De Blicquy North America (Canada) cultural groups 123 (3)
Debrecen *prev.* Debreczen; *Ger.* Debreczin, *Rom.* Debreţin Central Europe (Hungary) Reformation 194 (2)
Debreczen, Debreczin *see* Debrecen
Debreţin *see* Debrecen
Decapolis *state* Southwest Asia Roman empire 225 (4)
Deccan *plateau/region* South Asia colonialism 247 (3), 248 (1) early medieval states 244 (1), (2), 244–245 (3) economy 249 (4) first empires 241 (4), (5) first religions 36 (1) imperial global economy 93 (5) Marathas 246 (2) Mughal Empire 246 (1) postwar politics 252 (1) world economy 92 (2), 243 (4)
Deccan States *state* South Asia colonialism 248 (2)
Dedeagach *mod.* Alexandroupolis Greece WWI 207 (6)
Dego *battle* Italy Napoleon 200–201 (1)
Degsastan *var.* Dawston *battle* British Isles (United Kingdom) medieval states 183 (3)
Dehli *see* Delhi, Indraprastha
Dehra Dun South Asia (India) decolonization 250 (1) exploration 257 (3)
Deira *region* British Isles medieval states 183 (3)
Deir el-Bahri Egypt ancient Egypt 159 (4)
Deir el-Balah Southwest Asia (Israel) ancient Egypt 159 (5)
Deir el-Bersha Egypt ancient Egypt 159 (4)
Deir el-Gabrawi Egypt ancient Egypt 159 (3)
Delagoa Bay *var.* Baía de Lourenço Marques *bay* Southern Africa slave trade 165 (4)
Delaware *state* North America empire and revolution 127 (2), (3) the growth of the US 129 (1) US Civil War 130 (2), (3), (4), (5), 131 (6), (7) US economy 134 (1)
Delaware *people* North America colonization 126 (1)
Delgado, Cape *headland* Southern Africa exploration 156 (3)
Delhi *var.* Dehli, *Hind.* Dilli; *prev.* Indraprastha; *hist.* Shahjahanabad South Asia (India) trade 72–73 (1) colonialism 247 (3), 248 (1), 269 (4) Communism 271 (8) decolonization 250 (1) early medieval states 244–245 (3) economy 249 (4) empire and revolution 249 (3) exploration 239 (1), 257 (3) global immigration 101 (3) imperial global economy 92 (1), 93 (5) Mongols 68 (2) Mughal Empire 246 (1) postwar economy 253 (5) Timur 229 (4) trade 267 (3) US superpower 138 (1) WWII 251 (3) *see also* Indraprastha
Delhi *region* South Asia postwar politics 252 (1)
Delhi, Sultanate of *state* South Asia Mongols 68–69 (1) Mughal Empire 246 (1) Timur 229 (4)
Delhi United Provinces *state* South Asia colonialism 248 (2)
Delium *battle* Greece ancient Greece 177 (3)
Delos *religious site/settlement* Greece ancient Greece 177 (3), 179 (4)
Delphi *religious site/settlement* Greece ancient Greece 177 (3), 179 (4) Roman empire 180–181 (1) first religions 36 (1), 37 (3)
Demchok *var.* Dêmqog *region* South Asia postwar politics 252 (1)
Demerara *colonial possession* South America colonization 149 (4)
Demetrias Greece Hellenistic world 41 (2)
Demnat North Africa (Morocco) exploration 157 (4)
Demotika *state* Southeast Europe WWII 211 (2)
Dêmqog *see* Demchok
Dendra Greece first civilizations 175 (4)
Deng *state* East Asia first cities 259 (4)
Dengchong East Asia (China) medieval states 263 (6)
Dengkil *archaeological site* Mainland Southeast Asia (Malaysia) Bronze Age 240 (3)
Dengyue *var.* Tengchung East Asia (China) colonialism 269 (4)
Dengzhou *var.* Teng-chou East Asia (China) early modern states 265 (5), 266 (1) medieval states 263 (6) Mongols 68–69 (1)
Denison, Cape *headland* Antarctica Antarctic Exploration 287 (3)
Denjong *see* Sikkim
Denkyera *state* West Africa the world in 1700 82–83 (1)
Denmark *anc.* Hafnia; *Dan.* Danmark; *state* Scandinavia crusades 186 (1), 64–65 (2) early modern states 193 (4), 197 (3) economy 190 (1), 205 (4) empire and revolution 199 (3), 202 (1), (2) European expansion 84–85 (1) civil war 209 (3), (5) medieval states 185 (3), 188 (1), 189 (3), (4) medieval voyages 60–61 (1) Mongols 68–69 (1) Napoleon 200–201 (1), 201 (2) postwar economy 213 (5), 214 (1), (2) postwar politics 212 (1), (3) Reformation 196 (1) Soviet Union 213 (4) the modern world 112 (2) US superpower 138 (1) WWII 210 (1), 211 (2), (4) Cold War 108 (3), 109 (1) early 20th century 206 (1)
Denmark–Norway *state* Scandinavia early modern states 195 (3) Reformation 194 (2)
Denmark Strait *var.* Danmarksstraedet *sea waterway* Atlantic Ocean exploration 172 (2)
Denver North America (USA) the growth of the US 129 (1), 132 (1) US economy 134 (1), 136 (2) US politics 135 (6)
Deptford Culture *people* North America the world in 250 BCE 38–39
Deraya *Ar.* Dar'iyah Southwest Asia (Saudi Arabia) 20th-century politics 233 (4)
Derbend *see* Derbent

Derbent Eastern Europe (Russian Federation) Islam 226 (2), 227 (4), (5) medieval Persia 231 (4) Mongols 68 (2), 68–69 (1) Ottomans 231 (3) Timur 229 (4)
Derby British Isles (United Kingdom) economy 204 (1)
Derbyshire *region* British Isles imperial global economy 93 (4)
Dereivka *archaeological site* Eastern Europe (Ukraine) Copper Age 174 (2)
Derna North Africa (Libya) colonization 167 (4)
Dertosa *mod.* Tortosa Iberian Peninsula (Spain) Roman empire 179 (3), 180–181 (1) *see also* Tortosa
Derwent *river* British Isles economy 204 (1)
Desalpur *archaeological site* South Asia (India) first cities 240 (2)
Deseado *river* South America colonization 148 (2)
Desert Gatherers *people* North America the world in 250 CE 46–47 *passim*.
Des Moines North America (USA) the growth of the US 129 (2)
Desmumu *state* British Isles medieval states 188 (2)
Desna *river* Eastern Europe WWI 207 (4)
Desterro *mod.* Florianópolis South America (Brazil) colonization 149 (3), (4)
Detroit *prev.* Fort Pontchartrain North America (USA) colonization 126 (1) the growth of the US 129 (2), 132 (1) US economy 134 (1), US politics 135 (6)
Deutschland *see* Germany
Deutsch-Südwestafrika *see* Southwest Africa, German Southwest Africa
Deva *var.* Legacaester, Devana Castra; *mod.* Chester; *Wel.* Caerleon; *legion headquarters/mithraic site* British Isles (United Kingdom) Roman empire 180–181 (1) world religions 48 (1) *see also* Chester
Devagiri South Asia (India) early religions 48 (2)
Devagiri *region* South Asia early medieval states 244–245 (3)
Devana *see* Aberdeen
Devana Castra *see* Chester, Deva
Devapattana South Asia (Nepal) early medieval states 244 (1) first empires 241 (4)
Deventer Low Countries (Netherlands) economy 190 (1)
Devils Lake *burial mound* North America (USA) First civilizations 121 (4)
Dez *river* Southwest Asia first cities 220 (2) first civilizations 221 (4)
Dezful Southwest Asia (Iran) 20th-century politics 235 (5)
Dezhnev, Cape *headland* Siberia exploration 287 (2)
Dhahran *Ar.* Az Zahran Southwest Asia (Saudi Arabia) 20th-century politics 233 (4), 235 (5) economy 234 (1) US superpower 138 (1)
Dhaka *prev.* Dacca South Asia (Bangladesh) postwar economy 253 (5) postwar politics 252 (1), (3) *see also* Dacca
Dhanbad South Asia (India) postwar economy 253 (5)
Dharangaon South Asia (India) colonialism 247 (3)
Dharwar South Asia (India) economy 249 (4)
Dhlo Dhlo Southern Africa (Zimbabwe) trade 164 (1)
Dhodhekánisos *see* Dodecanese
Dhofar Southwest Asia (Yemen) trade 267 (3)
Dholavira *archaeological site* South Asia (Pakistan) first cities 240 (2)
Dhualdadr *see* Dulkadir
Dhu Qar Southwest Asia (Iraq) ancient Persia 225 (6)
Di *people* East Asia first cities 259 (4) first states 261 (2)
Diamantina South America (Brazil) colonization 149 (3) empire and revolution 151 (3)
Dian *people/state* East Asia/Mainland Southeast Asia first cities 259 (5) first states 260 (1) medieval states 261 (6)
Dias Point *see* Volta, Cape da
Díbio *see* Dijon
Dickson North America (USA) cultural groups 122 (5)
Dicle *see* Tigris
Didyma *religious site* Southwest Asia (Turkey) first religions 37 (3)
Diedenhofen *var.* Thionville France Franks 184 (2)
Dieguño *people* North America colonization 125 (4)
Die Kelders *archaeological site* Southern Africa (South Africa) early cultures 160 (1) first humans 13 (2)
Dien Bien Phu *battle* Mainland Southeast Asia (Vietnam) postwar politics 251 (5)
Dieppe France WWI 206 (2), (4)
Dieu, Hôtel *building* France economy 191 (2)
Dihang *see* Brahmaputra
Dijlah *see* Tigris
Dijon *anc.* Díbio France early modern states 193 (4), 197 (5) empire and revolution 199 (4) Franks 184 (2) medieval states 187 (4), 192 (1)
Dikbosch *archaeological site* Southern Africa (South Africa) early cultures 160 (1)
Diksmuide *see* Dixmude
Dikson Siberia (Russian Federation) exploration 287 (2)
Dikwa West Africa (Nigeria) exploration 157 (4)
Dili *var.* Dilli, Dilly Maritime Southeast Asia (Indonesia) WWII 272 (1), 273 (2)
Dilli, Dilly *see* Dili
Dilli *see* Delhi, Indraprastha
Dilmun Arabian Peninsula first civilizations 24 (2), 25 (3)
Dimasha *see* Damascus
Dinajpur South Asia (Bangladesh) postwar politics 252 (3)
Dinant Low Countries (Belgium) WWI 206 (2), (3)
Dingcun *archaeological site* East Asia (China) first humans 13 (2)
Dinghai West Africa (Guinea) Islam 167 (3)
Dingliao *military base /rebellion* East Asia early modern states 266 (1), (2)
Dingtou East Asia (China) medieval states 263 (7)
Dioacaesarea *Christian archbishopric* Southwest Asia (Syria) world religions 48 (1)
Diocletian, Baths of *Lat.* Thermae Diocletiani *building* (Italy) Roman empire 181 (2)
Diocletiani, Thermae *see* Diocletian, Baths of
Dion *state* Greece ancient Greece 177 (2)
Dionysus, Theatre of *building* Greece ancient Greece 177 (4)
Dioscurias Southwest Asia (Georgia) early cultures 161 (2) first civilizations 177 (1)

Diospolis Magna *see* Thebes
Dipylon *see* Dipylum
Dipylum *var.* Dipylon *building* Greece ancient Greece 177 (4)
Dire Dawa *archaeological site* East Africa (Ethiopia) first humans 13 (2)
Dishasha Egypt ancient Egypt 159 (5)
Dispur South Asia (India) postwar politics 252 (1)
Diu South Asia (India) colonialism 247 (3), 248 (1), 269 (4) decolonization 251 (4) empire and revolution 88–89 (2) exploration 239 (1) postwar politics 252 (1) trade 230 (2), 67 (3) WWII 251 (3)
Divi *var.* mod. Diu South Asia (India) world religions 243 (4) *see also* Diu
Divodurum Mediomatricum *see* Metz
Divostin Southeast Europe (Yugoslavia) early agriculture 174 (1)
Dixmude Low Countries (Belgium) WWI 206 (2), (3)
Diyala *var.* Rudkhaneh-ye Sirvan, Sirwan, Diyálá, Nahr river Southwest Asia first cities 220 (2), 221 (4), (5)
Diyarbakir Southwest Asia (Turkey) 20th-century politics 235 (5)
Djailolo *see* Halmahera
Djakarta *see* Batavia, Jakarta
Djambi *see* Jambi
Djawa *see* Java
Djenné *see* Jenne
Djerba *island* North Africa Ottomans 231 (3)
Djibouti East Africa (Djibouti) colonization 167 (4) European imperialism 96 (1)
Djibouti *var.* Jibuti; *prev.* French Somaliland, French Territory of the Afars and Issas; *Fr.* Côte Française des Somlis *state* East Africa decolonization 168 (1) economy 168 (2) Islam 235 (4) the modern world 112 (1), 113 (3) *see also* French Somaliland, French Territory of the Afars and Issas
Dmanisi *archaeological site* West Asia early humans 13 (2)
Dnepr *see* Dnieper
Dnepropetrovsk *see* Dnipropetrovs'k, Yekaterinoslav
Dnestr *see* Dniester
Dnieper *Bel.* Dnyapro, *Rus.* Dnepr, *Ukr.* Dnipro *river* Eastern Europe ancient trade 44–45 (1) biological diffusion 72–73 (1) crusades 64–65 (2) early Islam 56–57 (1) empire 190 (1) empire and revolution 198 (2), 202 (1) exploration 172 (1) first humans 13 (2) Islam 227 (4) medieval states 185 (3) medieval voyages 60–61 (1) Mongols 68–69 (1) Napoleon 200–201 (1) Ottomans 202 (4), 230 (1), 231 (3), 232 (1) prehistoric culture 17 (4) Timur 229 (4) WWI 207 (4) WWII 210 (1), 211 (4)
Dniester *anc.* Tyras; *Rom.* Nistru, *Rus.* Dnestr, *Ukr.* Dnister *river* Eastern Europe Bronze Age 175 (3) Copper Age 174 (2) crusades 64–65 (2) early agriculture 174 (1) economy 190 (1), 205 (4) empire and revolution 198 (2), 202 (1) exploration 172 (1) great migrations 52–53 (1), 53 (2) medieval states 189 (4) Mon gols 68–69 (1) Napoleon 200–201 (1) Ottomans 197 (4), 230 (1), 231 (3) WWI 207 (4) WWII 210 (1), 211 (4)
Dnipro *see* Dnieper
Dnipropetrovs'k *var.* Yekaterinoslav; *Rus.* Dnepropetrovsk Eastern Europe post-Soviet Union 214–215 (4) *see also* Yekaterinoslav
Dnister *see* Dniester
Dnyapro *see* Dnieper
Doboj Southeast Europe (Bosnia and Herzegovina) postwar economy 215 (3)
Dobro Polje *battle* Southeast Europe (FYR Macedonia) WWI 207 (6)
Dobruja *region* Southeast Europe Ottomans 202 (4), 230 (1)
Dodecanese *var.* Dodecanese Islands, Nóties Sporádes; *prev.* Dhodhekánisos *state/island group* Greece ancient Greece 177 (2), (3) first civilizations 175 (4) medieval states 187 (5) Ottomans 202 (4), WWII 211 (2), (4) 20th-century politics 233 (3)
Dodecanese Islands *see* Dodecanese
Do Dimmi West Africa (Niger) early agriculture 158 (1)
Dodoma East Africa (Tanzania) economy 168 (2) exploration 157 (5)
Dodona *religious site* Greece first religions 37 (3)
Dogale *Palace* building Italy economy 191 (3)
Dogrib *people* North America cultural groups 123 (3)
Doha Southwest Asia (Qatar) economy 234 (1) exploration 219 (4)
Dojran *battle* Southeast Europe (FYR Macedonia) WWI 207 (6)
Dolni Věstonice *archaeological site/settlement* Central Europe (Poland) prehistoric culture 17 (4)
Dolomites *var.* Dolomiti; *It.* Dolomitiche, Alpi *mountain range* Italy WWI 207 (5)
Dolomiti, Dolomitiche, Alpi *see* Dolomites
Dominica *colonial possession/state/island* West Indies empire and revolution 150 (1) European expansion 85 (2) the growth of the US 129 (2) the modern world 112 (1) US economy 136 (2) US politics 139 (4)
Dominican Republic *state* West Indies Cold War 108 (2), 109 (1) the growth of the US 129 (2), 133 (4) the world in 1850 90–91 the world in 1900 94–95 the world in 1925 98–99 the world in 1950 102–103 the modern world 110–111 , 112 (1), 113 (4) US economy 136 (2) US politics 139 (4) US superpower 138 (1)
Domitian, Stadium of *building* Italy Roman empire 181 (2)
Domrémy France medieval states 192 (2)
Don *anc.* Tanais *river* Eastern Europe ancient trade 44–45 (1) biological diffusion 72–73 (1) Bronze Age 175 (3) early agriculture 174 (1) early Islam 56–57 (1) economy 205 (4) first humans 13 (2) great migrations 52–53 (1) Islam 163 (1), 227 (4) medieval states 185 (3), Mongols 68–69 (1) Napoleon 200–201 (1) Ottomans 230 (1), 231 (3), 232–233 (1) prehistoric culture 17 (4), 17 (4) WWI 207 (4) WWII 210 (1), (1) *see also* Douro
Donau *see* Danube
Donbas *region* Eastern Europe economy 205 (4)
Doncaster *anc.* Danum British Isles (United Kingdom) economy 204 (1)

Don Cossacks *people* Eastern Europe/Siberia Reformation 196 (2)
Donets *river* Eastern Europe WWI 207 (4)
Donets's Eastern Europe (Ukraine) Soviet Union 214–215 (4)
Dong Ap Bia *see* Hamburger Hill
Dong Dau Mainland Southeast Asia (Vietnam) the world in 2500 BCE 22–23
Dong Duong Mainland Southeast Asia (Vietnam) world religions 243 (5), 49 (4)
Dong Hai *see* East China Sea
Donghu *state* East Asia first cities 259 (5)
Dong Khe *fort* Mainland Southeast Asia postwar politics 251 (5)
Dongola *var.* Dongola, Dunqulah East Africa (Sudan) ancient trade 44–45 (1) colonization 167 (4) early cultures 161 (3), (4), (5), Islam 163 (1) first cities 260 (1)
Dongyi *state* East Asia first cities 259 (3), (5) first states 260 (1)
Dongzhen *state* East Asia (Manchuria) 263 (5)
Donja Slatina *fort* Southeast Europe (Yugoslavia) Bronze Age 175 (3)
Donja *see* Dongola
Doornik *see* Tournai
Dorchester *anc.* Durnovaria British Isles (United Kingdom) economy 204 (1) medieval states 183 (3)
Dordogne *river* France first civilizations 177 (1)
Dordrecht *var.* Dordt, Dort Low Countries (Netherlands) economy 190 (1)
Dordt *see* Dordrecht
Dorestad Low Countries (Netherlands) medieval states 185 (3) medieval voyages 60–61 (1)
Dori West Africa (Burkina) exploration 157 (4)
Dornach *battle* Central Europe (Switzerland) early modern states 193 (5)
Dorpat Eastern Europe (Estonia) early modern states 195 (3) economy 190 (1) medieval states 189 (3)
Dorsoduro Italy economy 191 (3)
Dort *see* Dordrecht
Dortmund Central Europe (Germany) medieval states 188 (1)
Dorylaeum Southwest Asia (Turkey) Roman empire 180–181 (1)
Dorylaeum *battle* Southwest Asia (Turkey) crusades 64–65 (2)
Douai *anc.* Duacum; *prev.* Douay France economy 190 (1)
Douala *var.* Duala Central Africa (Cameroon) colonization 167 (4) economy 168 (2)
Douanas *river* Mainland Southeast Asia ancient trade 44 (2)
Douay *see* Douai
Doullens France WWI 206 (2)
Douro *Sp.* Duero *river* Iberian Peninsula Bronze Age 175 (3) Copper Age 174 (2) crusades 64–65 (2) early agriculture 174 (1) economy 190 (1) first civilizations 177 (1) great migrations 52–53 (1), 53 (2) *see also* Duero
Dove Creek *battle* North America (USA) the growth of the US 129 (2)
Dover British Isles (United Kingdom) economy 204 (1), 205 (4) WWI 206 (2), (3)
Dover, Strait of *var.* Straits of Dover; *Fr.* Pas de Calais *sea waterway* Western Europe WWI 206 (2), (4)
Dover, Straits of *see* Dover, Strait of
Downpatrick *Ir.* Dún Pádraig British Isles (United Kingdom) Bronze Age 175 (3)
Drač *see* Durazzo
Drag *see* Durazzo
Drakensberg *physical region* Southern Africa economy 163 (2) first humans 12 (1) slave trade 165 (4) trade 164 (1)
Drancy *ghetto* France WWII 211 (3)
Drangiana *region* Central Asia Hellenistic world 40–41 (1)
Drapsaca Central Asia (Afghanistan) Hellenistic world 40–41 (1)
Drau *var.* Drava; *Eng.* Drave, *Hung.* Dráva *river* Southeast Europe WWI 207 (5), (6) *see also* Drava
Drava *var.* Drau; *Eng.* Drave, *Hung.* Dráva *river* Southeast Europe postwar economy 215 (3) *see also* Drau, Dráva
Dráva, Drave *see* Drau, Drava
Dravida *region/state* South Asia world religions 48 (2) first empires 241 (5) world religions 242 (2)
Drenthe *province* Low Countries Reformation 195 (3)
Drepanum *see* Trapani
Dresden Central Europe (Germany) early modern states 193 (4) economy 205 (4) empire and revolution 199 (3) postwar politics 212 (1) Reformation 196 (1) WWII 211 (4)
Dresden *battle* Central Europe (Germany) Napoleon 200–201 (1)
Drina *river* Southeast Europe exploration 257 (2) postwar economy 215 (3) WWI 207 (6)
Drontheim *see* Trondheim
Druk-yul *see* Bhutan
Dry Creek *archaeological site* North America the world in 10,000 BCE 14–15
Duacum *see* Douai
Duala *see* Douala
Dubai *Ar.* Dubayy Southwest Asia (United Arab Emirates) economy 234 (1)
Dubayy *see* Dubai
Dublin South Asia (Ireland) biological diffusion 72–73 (1) economy 190 (1), (3) empire and revolution 202 (1) civil war 209 (3) medieval states 185 (3), 186 (2), 187 (4), 188 (2) medieval voyages 60–61 (1) Napoleon 200–201 (1), 201 (2) postwar politics 212 (3) Reformation 194 (2) WWI 207 (3)
Dubris *see* Dover, Dubrae
Dubrovnik *It.* Ragusa Southeast Europe (Croatia) postwar economy 215 (3) *see also* Ragusa
Ducie Island *island* Pacific Ocean exploration 278 (1)
Duero *Port.* Duero *river* Iberian Peninsula crusades 186 (1) early Islam 56–57 (1) Franks 184 (2) civil war 209 (4) Islam 192 (3) Napoleon 200–201 (1) world religions 48 (1) *see also* Douro
Duff Islands *island group* Pacific Ocean exploration 278 (1)

Dufile East Africa (Uganda) exploration 157 (4)
Duinekerke *see* Dunkirk
Duji *var.* Tuchi *province* East Asia medieval states 262–263 (1)
Dukang East Asia (China) first cities 259 (5)
Duke of York Islands *island group* Pacific Ocean early cultures 280–281 (3)
Dulkadir *var.* Dhualdadr Southwest Asia the world in 1400 70–71 the world in 1500 74–75
Dumbarton British Isles (United Kingdom) medieval states 186 (2)
Dumyât *see* Damietta
Duna *see* Danube
Düna *see* Western Dvina
Dünaburg East Africa (Latvia) early modern states 195 (3) medieval states 189 (3)
Dunaj *see* Danube, Vienna
Dunärea, Dunav *see* Danube
Dundee British Isles (United Kingdom)
Dunedin *settlement/whaling station* New Zealand colonization 283 (4), (5)
Dunholme *see* Durham
Dunhuang *settlement* East Asia (China) ancient trade 44–45 (1) exploration 256 (1), 257 (3) first states 260 (1), 261 (3) medieval states 261 (6), 262–263 (1), 263 (6) world religions 49 (3), (4)
Dunhuang *province* East Asia first states 260 (1)
Dunkerque *see* Dunkirk
Dunkirk *prev.* Dunquerque; *Flem.* Duinekerke, *Fr.* Dunkerque, France Reformation 195 (3) WWI 206 (3)
Dún Pádraig *see* Downpatrick
Dunqul Egypt ancient Egypt 159 (4)
Dunqulah *see* Dongola
Dura Europos *settlement* Southwest Asia (Iraq) ancient Persia 225 (6) Roman empire 180–181 (1), 224 (2), 225 (5) early trade 225 (5) Hellenistic world 41 (2) world religions 226 (1)
Durango Central America (Mexico) colonization 125 (4) Mexican Revolution 133 (3)
Durango *state* Central America Mexican Revolution 133 (3) the growth of the US 129 (2)
Durazzo *anc.* Dyrrachium; *mod.* Durrës, Dursi; *SCr.* Drač, *Turk.* Drač Southeast Europe (Albania) crusades 64–65 (2) early modern states 193 (4) medieval states 185 (3), 187 (5), 188 (1), 189 (4) Ottomans 230 (1) WWI 207 (6) *see also* Dyrrachium
Durban *var.* Port Natal Southern Africa (South Africa) colonization 166 (2), 167 (4) economy 168 (2) European imperialism 96 (2)
Durham *prev.* Dunholme British Isles (United Kingdom) medieval states 186 (2)
Dürnkrut *battle* Central Europe (Austria) medieval states 189 (4)
Durnovaria *see* Dorchester
Durocortorum France Roman empire 180–181 (1), 181 (4)
Durostorum *var.* Silistria; *mod.* Silistra; *legion headquarters* Southeast Europe (Bulgaria) Roman empire 180–181 (1) *see also* Silistria
Duroverrum *see* Canterbury
Durrës *see* Durazzo, Dyrrachium
Dursi *see* Durazzo
Dushanbe *var.* Dyushanbe; *prev.* Stalinabad, *Taj.* Stalinobod Central Asia (Tajikistan) Soviet Union 214–215 (4)
Dusky Sound *sealing station* New Zealand colonization 283 (4)
Düsseldorf Central Europe (Germany) WWI 206 (2), (3) WWII 211 (4)
Dust Bowl *drought* North America US economy 134 (2)
Dutch Brazil *colonial possession* South America colonization 149 (4)
Dutch East Indies *mod.* Indonesia; *prev.* Netherlands East Indies *colonial possession* Maritime Southeast Asia colonialism 269 (4) colonization 284–285 (1) European imperialism 97 (3), (4) exploration 279 (3) empire and revolution 88–89 (2) global immigration 100 (1) the growth of the US 133 (4) WWII 104 (1), 251 (3), 272 (1), 273 (2)
Dutch Guiana *var.* Netherlands Guiana; *mod.* Surinam, Suriname *colonial possession/state* South America Cold War 109 (1) WWII 104 (1) *see also* Surinam
Dutch Harbor *military base* North America (USA) WWII 104 (2), 272 (1), 273 (2)
Dutch Netherlands *rebellion* Low Countries empire and revolution 88–89 (2)
Dutch New Guinea *colonial possession/state* New Guinea Cold War 109 (1) European imperialism 97 (3)
Dutch Republic *see* Batavian Republic, Netherlands, United Provinces
Dutch South Africa *colonial possession* Southern Africa slave trade 165 (4) trade 164 (1)
Dutch West Indies *see* Netherlands Antilles
Dvaraka South Asia (India) world religions 242 (2)
Dvarasamudra South Asia (India) early medieval states 244 (2), 244–245 (3)
Dvaravati South Asia (India) ancient India 242 (1) early religions 48 (2)
Dvaravati *region/state* South Asia ancient India 241 (4) early medieval states 245 (5) world religions 243 (5), 49 (4)
Dvin *Christian archbishopric* Southwest Asia (Armenia) world religions 48 (1)
Dvina *river* Eastern Europe early modern states 197 (3) WWII 207 (4)
Dvinsk *see* Dünaburg
Dvinsk Eastern Europe (Latvia) WWI 207 (4)
Dvorak *region* South Asia early medieval states 244–245 (3) world religions 243 (4)
Dyed *region* British Isles medieval states 183 (3)
Dyrrhachium *mod.* Durrës; *It.* Durazzo, *SCr.* Drač, *Turk.* Drač Southeast Europe (Albania) Roman empire 179 (5), 180–181 (1) *see also* Durazzo
Dyubis *see* Dover, Dubrae
Dyushanbe *see* Dushanbe
Dza Chu *see* Mekong
Dzhruchula *archaeological site* Eastern Europe (Russian Federation) first humans 13 (2)
Dzibilchaltún Central America (Mexico) first civilizations 122 (1), (2) prehistoric culture 17 (3)
Dzungaria *region* Central Asia ancient trade 44–45 (1) medieval states 262–263 (1)
Dzungars *people/rebellion* Central Asia early modern states 268 (1) empire and revolution 268 (2)
Dzungars, Khanate of the *state* East Asia early modern states 268 (1)
Dzvina *see* Western Dvina

E

Eagle Pass North America (USA) Mexican Revolution 133 (3)
Eagle Rock North America (USA) US economy 135 (4)
Eanna *building* Southwest Asia (Iraq) first cities 220 (3)
Early Kalachuris *dynasty* South Asia early medieval states 244 (2)
Early Man Shelter Australia exploration 280 (1)
Early Mississippian Culture *people* North America the world in 1000 58–59
East Anglia *state* British Isles medieval states 183 (3)
East Antarctica *see* Greater Antarctica
East Asia *region* East Asia biological diffusion 72–73 (1)
East Bengal and Assam *region* South Asia colonization 250 (2)
East Berlin Central Europe (Germany) postwar politics 212 (2)
East Cape *headland* Australia colonization 283 (4)
East China Sea *Chin.* Dong Hai *sea* East Asia ancient trade 44–45 (1) biological diffusion 72–73 (1) decolonization 251 (4) early agriculture 20–21 (2), 258 (1), (2) early modern states 244 (1), (2) economy 274 (1) first cities 259 (3), (4), (5) first states 260 (1) Islam 275 (4) medieval states 262–263 (1), 263 (6) world religions 49 (3), (4)
Dunhuang province East Asia first states 260 (1)
Eastern Chalukyas *dynasty* South Asia early medieval states 244 (1)
Eastern Desert *var.* As Sahrá' ash Sharqiyah, *Eng.* Arabian Desert *desert* Egypt ancient Egypt 159 (5) *see also* Arabian Desert
Eastern Europe *region* Eastern Europe US economy 138 (2)
Eastern Gangas *dynasty* South Asia early medieval states 244 (1), 244–245 (3) Mongols 68–69 (1)
Eastern Ghats *mountain range* South Asia early medieval states 244 (1), 244–245 (3) economy 249 (4) first empires 241 (4) first religions 36 (1) Mughal Empire 246 (1) colonialism 247 (3), 248 (1)
Eastern Jin *state* East Asia first states 261 (3)
Eastern March *region* Eastern Europe Franks 184 (2)
Eastern Pomerania *region* Central Europe empire and revolution 199 (3)
Eastern Rumelia *region* Southeast Europe Ottomans 202 (4), 232–233 (1)
Eastern Sierra Madre *see* Sierra Madre Oriental
Eastern Solomons *battle* Pacific Ocean (Solomon Islands) WWII 273 (2)
Eastern States *state* East Asia colonialism 248 (2)
Eastern Thrace *region* Southwest Asia 20th-century politics 233 (3)
Eastern Turkistan *state* East Asia medieval states 262–263 (1)
Eastern Woodland Culture *people* North America the world in 500 CE 50–51 the world in 750 CE 54–55
East Fjords *fjords* Atlantic Ocean (Iceland) exploration 172 (2)
East Florida *colonial possession* North America empire and revolution 127 (3)
East Friesland *see* East Frisia
East Frisia *var.* East Friesland *region* Central Europe empire and revolution 199 (3)
East Germany *state* Central Europe Cold War 109 (1) postwar economy 213 (5) postwar politics 212 (3) Soviet Union 213 (4)
East Greenland Inuit *people* North America cultural groups 123 (3)
East Indies *island group* Maritime Southeast Asia ancient trade 44–45 (1) biological diffusion 72–73 (1) decolonization 251 (4) early modern states 92 (1) Islam 163 (1), 226 (2), 227 (4), (5), 235 (4) medieval states 187 (5) medieval voyages (1) Mamluks 229 (3), 68 (2) Napoleon 200–201 (1) Ottomans 231 (3), 232–233 (1) Seljuks 228 (1) slave trade 165 (4) the modern world 112 (1), 113 (3), (4) US superpower 138 (1) world religions 226 (1), 49 (4) WWI 233 (2) WWII 104 (1), 210 (1), 211 (4) 20th century 234 (2) 20th-century politics 233 (3), (4), 235 (5) *see also* Aegyptus
Egyptians *people* East Africa trade 167 (1)
Ehime *prefecture* Japan economy 270 (1)
Eichstätt Central Europe (Germany) Franks 184 (2)
Eight Trigrams Sect *rebellion* East Asia empire and revolution 268 (2)
Eilat *var.* Aila, Elat, Elath Southwest Asia (Israel) 20th century 234 (2) *see also* Aila, Elath
Éire *see* Hibernia, Ireland
Éireann, Muir *see* Irish Sea
Eivissa *see* Ibiza
Ekain *archaeological site* Iberian Peninsula (Spain) prehistoric culture 17 (3)
Ekapa *see* Cape Town
Ekven North America (USA) cultural groups 123 (3)
El Abra Cave *archaeological site* South America (Colombia) early cultures 144 (1)
El Agheila North Africa (Libya) WWII 211 (4), 211 (4)
Elaine *incident* North America (USA) US politics 135 (6)
El Alamein *battle* Egypt WWII 104 (2), 211 (4)
Elam *var.* Susiana, Uvja; *mod.* Khuzistan, Khuzistan *state* Southwest Asia first civilizations 221 (4), (5), 222 (1)
El-Amarna Egypt first cities 28–29 (1), 29 (5)
Eland's Bay *archaeological site* Southern Africa (South Africa) early cultures 160 (1)
Elandslaagte *battle* Southern Africa (South Africa) European imperialism 96 (2)
El Argar *fort* Iberian Peninsula (Spain) Bronze Age 175 (3)
Elat *see* Aila, Eilat, Elath
Elatea Greece first civilizations 177 (1)
Elat, Gulf of *see* Aqaba, Gulf of
Elath *var.* Aila, Elat; *mod.* Elat Southwest Asia (Israel) early trade 225 (3) *see also* Aila, Eilat
Elath *see* Aelana, Aqaba
Elba *island* Italy Napoleon 200–201 (1) Elba

Ecatepec Central America (Mexico) Aztecs 124 (2)
Ecbatana *mod.* Hamadan Southwest Asia (Iran) ancient Persia 223 (4), 225 (6) Roman empire 224 (2), 225 (5) ancient trade 44–45 (1) early trade 225 (3) exploration 218 (1) Hellenistic world 224 (1) world religions 226 (1) *see also* Hamadan
Echunga *goldfield* Australia colonization 282 (2)
Eckmühl Central Europe (Germany) Napoleon 200–201 (1)
Ecuador *state* South America economy 153 (3) empire and revolution 150 (2), 151 (3) environment 153 (4) imperial global economy 92 (1) politics 152 (1) the growth of the US 133 (4) the modern world 112 (1), 113 (4) US superpower 138 (1)
Edendale North America (USA) US economy 135 (4)
Edessa *mod.* Şanliurfa, Urfa *Christian archbishopric/settlement* Southwest Asia (Turkey) Roman empire 224 (2), 225 (5) crusades 228 (2), 65 (3) Hellenistic world 41 (2) Islam 227 (4) world religions 226 (1) *see also* Urfa
Edfu *var.* Idfu Egypt ancient Egypt 159 (3) first cities 28–29 (1) first civilizations 24 (2)
Edinburgh British Isles (United Kingdom) biological diffusion 72–73 (1) economy 190 (1), 205 (4) empire and revolution 202 (1) medieval states 186 (2), 187 (4), 188 (1) Napoleon 200–201 (1), 201 (2) Reformation 194 (2)
Edirne Greece Ottomans 202 (4)
Edmonton North America (Canada) the growth of the US 129 (1), 132 (1) US economy 136 (2) US superpower 138 (1)
Edo *mod.* Tokyo, Tôkyô (Japan) early modern states 267 (4), 268 (1) economy 270 (1) trade 267 (3) *see also* Tokyo
Edom *state* Southwest Asia first civilizations 222 (1)
Edward, Lake *var.* Albert Edward Nyanza, Edward Nyanza, Lac Idi Amin, Lake Rutanzige *lake* East Africa exploration 157 (4) first humans 12 (1)
Edward Nyanza *see* Edward, Lake
Edzna Central America (Mexico) first civilizations 122 (2)
Eems *see* Ems
Eesti *see* Estonia
Éfaté *settlement/island* Pacific Ocean (Vanuatu) early cultures 280–281 (3) environmentalism 285 (2) medieval voyages 60 (2)
Efes *see* Ephesus
Eflâk *see* Wallachia
Egadi, Isole *see* Aegates
Egbaland *state* West Africa Islam 167 (3)
Ege Denizi *see* Aegean Sea
Eger *mod.* Cheb Central Europe (Czech Republic) medieval states 188 (1)
Egina *see* Aegina
Egmont, Cape *headland* New Zealand colonization 283 (4)
Egoli *see* Johannesburg
Egtved *burial mound/settlement* Scandinavia (Denmark) Bronze Age 175 (3)
Egypt *prev.* United Arab Republic; *anc.* Aegyptus *region/state* Egypt ancient Egypt 159 (4) ancient Persia 223 (4) Roman empire 181 (4), 224 (2), 225 (5) ancient trade 44–45 (1) plague 72–73 (1) colonization 167 (4) crusades 65 (1), 228 (2), 65 (3) decolonization 168 (1) early 20th century 206 (1) early agriculture 220 (1) early cultures 161 (2), (3), (4), (5) early Islam 57 (2) early systems 223 (3), 32 (1), 33 (2), (3) early trade 225 (3) European expansion 84–85 (1) European imperialism 96 (1), 97 (4) exploration 157 (5), 218 (1), (2), 219 (3), (4) first cities 220 (2) first civilizations 177 (1), 221 (5), 222 (1), (2) first religions 36 (1), 37 (3) Hellenistic world 224 (1), 41 (2) imperial global economy 92 (1) Islam 163 (1), 226 (2), 227 (4), (5), 235 (4) medieval states 187 (5) medieval voyages (1) Mamluks 229 (3), 68 (2) Napoleon 200–201 (1) Ottomans 231 (3), 232–233 (1) Seljuks 228 (1) slave trade 165 (4) the modern world 112 (1), 113 (3), (4) US superpower 138 (1) world religions 226 (1), 49 (4) WWI 233 (2) WWII 104 (1), 210 (1), 211 (4) 20th century 234 (2) 20th-century politics 233 (3), (4), 235 (5) *see also* Aegyptus

and revolution 268 (2) exploration 256 (1) first states 260 (1) medieval states 261 (6), 262–263 (1) Mongols 68–69 (1) trade 267 (3) world religions 49 (3)

ashgar, Khanate of *state* East Asia trade 267 (3)

ashi *Chin.* Kaxgar, K'o-shih, Uigh *see* Varanasi *region/settlement* East Asia (China) early medieval states 244 (2) world religions 242 (2)

ashir *see* Kashgar

ashi/Varanasi *var.* Baranasi; *Eng.* Benares South Asia (India) world religions 243 (4)

ashmir *region/state* South Asia decolonization 251 (4) early medieval states 244–245 (3) empire and revolution 249 (3) exploration 257 (3) Mongols 68–69 (1) Mughal Empire 246 (1) postwar politics 252 (2), 253 (4) Soviet Union 213 (4) trade 267 (3) world religions 243 (4), 49 (3)

ashmira *region* South Asia world religions 242 (2)

asi *mod.* Väränasi, *var.* Kashi South Asia (India) early religions 48 (2)

asi *region/state* South Asia first empires 241 (5) first religions 36 (2)

aska *people* North America cultural groups 123 (3)

askaskia North America (USA) empire and revolution 127 (3)

aspiyskoye More *see* Caspian Sea

aspiy Tengizi *see* Caspian Sea

assa *var.* Kovsice; *Ger.* Kaschau; *mod.* Košice Central Europe (Slovakia) early modern states 193 (4)

assai *see* Kasai

assala East Africa (Sudan) early cultures 161 (4), (5)

assel *prev.* Cassel Central Europe (Germany) early modern states 193 (4)

assites *people* Southwest Asia first civilizations 221 (4)

atagum Central Africa (Nigeria) Islam 167 (3)

ataha East Asia (China) medieval voyages 61 (3)

atak *mod.* Cuttack South Asia (India) Mughal Empire 246 (1) *see also* Cuttack

ataka South Asia (India) early medieval states 244 (2), 244–245 (3)

atanga *region* Central Africa Cold War 109 (1) politics 169 (4)

atarpur South Asia (India) decolonization 250 (1)

atehar *region* South Asia early medieval states 244–245 (3)

atherine Australia colonization 282 (1)

athiawar *state* South Asia Mughal Empire 246 (1)

athio North America (USA) cultural groups 122 (5)

athmandu *prev.* Kantipur South Asia (Nepal) colonialism 248 (1) early medieval states 244–245 (3) early modern states 268 (1) exploration 257 (3) postwar economy 253 (5) postwar politics 252 (1), (2) WWII 251 (3)

atiki, Volcán *mountain* Pacific Ocean early cultures 281 (4)

atima Mullo Southern Africa (Namibia) exploration 157 (4)

atombela *mod.* Catambela Southern Africa (Angola) exploration 157 (4)

atpatuka *see* Cappadocia

atsina Central Africa (Nigeria) economy 168 (2) exploration 157 (4) Islam 163 (1), 167 (3)

atsina state West Africa slave trade 165 (4) trade 164 (2)

attegat *Dan.* Kattegatt *sea waterway* Scandinavia early modern states 197 (3)

attegatt *see* Kattegat

attura South Asia (India) early religions 48 (2)

atruka *archaeological site* East Africa (Tanzania) early cultures 160 (1)

atyn *massacre* Eastern Europe WWII 211 (3)

auen *see* Kaunas, Kovno

aunas *prev.* Rus. Kovno; *Ger.* Kauen, *Pol.* Kowno Eastern Europe (Lithuania) early modern states 195 (3) WWII 211 (3) *see also* Kovno

aupang Scandinavia (Norway) medieval voyages 60–61 (1)

aushambi South Asia (India) first religions 36 (2) world religions 242 (3)

authara Mainland Southeast Asia (Vietnam) ancient India 241 (6)

avalla Greece WWI 207 (6)

avat Central Asia (Turkmenistan) the world in 2500 BCE 22–23

averi *var.* Cauvery *river* South Asia colonialism 247 (3) decolonization 250 (1) early medieval states 244 (2), 244–245 (3), 245 (4) economy 249 (4) first empires 241 (4), (5) first religions 36 (2) Marathas 246 (2) postwar politics 252 (1) world religions 242 (2), 243 (4)

avik North America (USA) cultural groups 123 (3)

avkaz *see* Caucasus

awa East Africa (Sudan) ancient Egypt 159 (5) early cultures 160 (1)

awasaki *bomb target* Japan WWII 273 (3)

awhia New Zealand colonization 283 (4)

awkau *mod.* Songhay *state* West Africa trade 163 (4)

awthule State *see* Kaya

axgar *see* Kashgar, Kashi

aya *Jap.* Mimana East Asia (Korea) medieval states 264 (1)

aya *var.* Kawthule State, Kayin State *state* East Asia medieval states 264 (1)

ayalapatnam *var.* Punneikayal, Kayalpatnam South Asia (India) colonialism 247 (3) world religions 243 (4)

ayankulam South Asia (India) colonialism 247 (3)

ayapo *people* South America early cultures 147 (2)

ayenta *archaeological site* North America (USA) cultural groups 123 (4)

ayes West Africa (Mali) colonization 167 (4)

ayin State *see* Kaya

ayor *state* West Africa trade 164 (2)

ayseri *prev.* Eusebia, Mazacca; *anc.* Caesarea Cappadocae Southwest Asia (Turkey) first civilizations 221 (4) Mongols 68–69 (1) *see also* Caesarea Cappadocae

.azakh Khanate *state* Central Asia trade 267 (3)

.azakhs *people* Central Asia historical geography 275 (5)

.azakhstan *var.* Kazakstan, *Kaz.* Qazaqstan; *Rus.* Kazakhskaya SSR *state* Southwest Asia economy (19th) historical geography 275 (5) Islam 235 (4) postwar economy 214 (2), 275 (5) postwar politics 274 (2) Soviet Union 214–215 (4) the modern world 110–111, 113 (3), (4)

.azakstan *see* Kazakhstan

Kazan' Eastern Europe (Russian Federation) colonialism 269 (3) Soviet Union 208 (2), 214–215 (4) trade 267 (3)

Kazan', Khanate of *state* Eastern Europe/Siberia the world in 1500 74–75

Kazeh *see* Tabora

Kazembe *state* Southern Africa trade 167 (1)

Kazvin *mod.* Qazvin Southwest Asia (Iran) exploration 219 (3) *see also* Qazvin

Kebara *archaeological site* East Africa first humans 12 (1), 13 (2)

Kebbi *see* Kabi

Kedah *region/settlement* Mainland Southeast Asia (Malaysia) colonialism 247 (4) early medieval states 245 (5)

Kedara South Asia (India) world religions 243 (4)

Kediri *state* Maritime Southeast Asia the world in 1200 62–63

Kedungbrubus *archaeological site* Maritime Southeast Asia (Indonesia) first humans 13 (2)

Kefe *see* Kaffa, Theodosia

Keijo *see* Seoul

Keilor Australia exploration 280 (1)

Keishu *see* Kumsong, Kyongju

Kelso North America (USA) cultural groups 122 (5)

Kemp Land *physical region* Antarctica Antarctic Exploration 287 (3)

Kendari Maritime Southeast Asia (Indonesia) WWII 272 (1), 273 (2)

Kenduli South Asia (India) world religions 243 (4)

Kénitra *see* Port Lyautey

Kennesaw Mountain *battle* North America (USA) US Civil War 131 (7)

Kennet and Avon *canal* British Isles economy 204 (1)

Kenniff Cave Australia exploration 280 (1)

Kent *state* British Isles medieval states 183 (3)

Kentucky *state* North America the growth of the US 129 (1) US Civil War 130 (2), (3), (4), (5), 131 (6), (7) US economy 134 (2), 139 (3) US superpower 139 (5)

Kentucky Frontier *region* North America empire and revolution 127 (3)

Kenya *prev.* British East Africa *state* East Africa decolonization 168 (1) economy 168 (2), (3) Islam 235 (4) the modern world 112 (1), 113 (3) WWII 104 (1) Cold War 109 (1) *see also* British East Africa

Kenya, Mount *mod.* Kirinyaga *mountain* East Africa exploration 157 (4)

Kenyérmező Eastern Europe battles 193 (4)

Keppel Island *see* Niuatoputapu

Kerala *region/state* South Asia early religions 48 (2) first empires 241 (5) postwar politics 252 (1), 253 (4) world religions 242 (2)

Keramaikos Cemetery *see* Ceramicus Cemetery

Kerbela *battle* Southwest Asia (Iraq) Islam 226 (2)

Kerch *see* Panticapaeum

Kerguelen *island* Indian Ocean the world in 1800 86–87

Kerikeri New Zealand colonization 283 (4)

Kérkira *see* Corcyra, Corfu

Kerkuk *see* Kirkuk

Kerma East Africa (Sudan) ancient Egypt 159 (4) early cultures 161 (4), (5)

Kernades Islands *island group* New Zealand decolonization 285 (3) early cultures 280–281 (3) medieval voyages 60 (2)

Kerman Southwest Asia (Iran) 20th-century politics 235 (5) early Islam 56–57 (1) economy 234 (1) medieval Persia 231 (4) Ottomans 232–233 (1)

Kerman *region/state* Southwest Asia ancient Persia 225 (6) early Islam 56–57 (1) economy 234 (1) medieval Persia 231 (4)

Kermanshah Southwest Asia (Iran) first civilizations 221 (4), 24 (2) Islam 227 (5) Seljuks 228 (1)

Kernonen *burial mound* France Bronze Age 175 (3)

Kern River *people* North America colonization 125 (4)

Kerulen *river* East Asia exploration 256 (1) first states 260 (1)

Ketu *state* West Africa Islam 167 (3)

Kexholm Eastern Europe (Russian Federation) early modern states 195 (3)

Key Marco North America (USA) cultural groups 122 (5)

Key West Naval Air Station *military base* North America (USA) Cold War 108 (2)

Khabarovsk Siberia (Russian Federation) colonialism 269 (3) economy 275 (4) Soviet Union 208 (2)

Khafajah *see* Tutub

Khairabad South Asia (India) colonialism 247 (3)

Khairpur *state* South Asia colonialism 248 (2)

Khakasia *region* Eastern Europe Soviet Union 214–215 (4)

Khalandriani Greece the world in 2500 BCE 22–23

Khalkha *people* East Asia early modern states 266 (1) trade 267 (3)

Khalkis *see* Chalcis

Khambat, Gulf of *Eng.* Gulf of Cambay *gulf* South Asia first cities 240 (2)

Khami Southern Africa (Zimbabwe) trade 164 (1)

Khanbalik *var.* Khanbaliq; *mod.* Beijing East Asia (China) exploration 256 (1) Mongols 68 (2) *see also* Beijing, Peking

Khandesh *region/state* South Asia early medieval states 244–245 (3) Mughal Empire 246 (1)

Khanka, Lake *var.* Hsing-k'ai Hu, Lake Hanka, *Chin.* Xingkai Hu, *Rus.* Ozero Khanka *lake* East Asia early modern states 265 (5) first states 260 (1) medieval states 264 (1), (2)

Khanka, Ozero *see* Khanka, Lake

Khanty-Mansi *region* Eastern Europe Soviet Union 214–215 (4)

Kharbin *see* Harbin

Kharga Egypt Islam 163 (1)

Kharga *oasis* Egypt ancient Egypt 159 (2), (3), (4), (5)

Kharg Island *var.* Karg; *Per.* Jazireh-ye Khārk *island* Southwest Asia 20th-century politics 235 (5) economy 234 (1)

Khārk, Jazireh-ye *see* Kharg Island

Kharkov Eastern Europe (Ukraine) Soviet Union 208 (2) WWII 211 (3), (4)

Khartoum *var.* El Khartûm, Khartum East Africa (Sudan) colonization 167 (4) economy 168 (2) exploration 157 (5) *see also* Karri

Khasa *region* South Asia early religions 48 (2) world religions 242 (2)

Khasi States *state* South Asia colonialism 248 (2)

Khatanga Siberia (Russian Federation) exploration 287 (2)

Khazar, Daryā-ye *see* Caspian Sea

Khazar Empire *region/state* Central Asia/Eastern Europe early Islam 56–57 (1), 57 (2) Islam 226 (2)

Khe Sanh *battle* Mainland Southeast Asia (Vietnam) 251 (5)

Khios *see* Chios

Khirokitia Southwest Asia (Cyprus) early agriculture 220 (1)

Khitan *state* East Asia medieval states 263 (3)

Khitan *people* East Asia medieval states 262–263 (1)

Khitan Empire *var.* Liao Empire *state* East Asia medieval states 263 (4) the world in 1000 58–59

Khiva *mod.* Khiwa Central Asia (Turkmenistan) colonialism 269 (3) Communism 271 (8) medieval Persia 231 (4) Soviet Union 208 (2) trade 267 (3)

Khiva *var.* Chorasmia, Khwarizm *region/state* Central Asia colonialism 269 (3) medieval Persia 231 (4)

Khiwa *see* Khiva

Khmer *mod.* Cambodia; *prev.* Chenla *state* Mainland Southeast Asia medieval states 262–263 (1), 263 (6) Mongols 68–69 (1) world religions 243 (5) *see also* Cambodia, Chenla, Funan, Kambujadesha

Khocho *Buddhist center* East Asia (China) world religions 49 (3)

Khoisan peoples *people* Southern Africa early cultures 160 (1) economy 163 (2) Islam 163 (1)

Khokand Central Asia (Uzbekistan) trade 267 (3)

Khokand *see* Kokand

Kholm *var.* Cholm, Holm Eastern Europe (Russian Federation) early modern states 195 (3)

Khorasan *see* Khurasan

Khorat *see* Nakhon Ratchasima

Khor Bāhan Egypt ancient Egypt 159 (2)

Khorramabad Southwest Asia (Iran) 20th-century politics 235 (5)

Khorramshahr *var.* Khurramshahr, Muhammerah; *prev.* Mohammerah Southwest Asia (Iran) 20th-century politics 235 (5)

Khorsabad Southwest Asia (Iraq) first civilizations 222 (2)

Khotan *var.* Hotan, Ho-t'ien East Asia (China) ancient trade 44–45 (1) trade 72–73 (1) early medieval states 244 (1) early modern states 268 (1) exploration 256 (1), 257 (3) first empires 241 (4) first states 260 (1) medieval states 262–263 (1) world religions 49 (3)

Khotin Southeast Europe (Moldavia) Ottomans 231 (3)

Khulna South Asia (Bangladesh) postwar politics 252 (3)

Khurasan *region/state* Central Asia ancient Persia 225 (6) early Islam 56–57 (1) Islam 227 (4) medieval Persia 231 (4) Seljuks 228 (1) Timur 229 (4)

Khurja South Asia (India) colonialism 247 (3)

Khurramshahr *see* Khorramshahr

Khúzestán *physical region* Central Asia medieval states 262–263 (1) *see also* Khiva

Khwarizm Shah, Empire of the *state* Southwest Asia early Islam 57 (2) Islam 227 (4) Mongols 68–69 (1) Seljuks 228 (1) the world in 1200 62–63

Kiaka *state* Southern Africa the world in 1800 86–87 the world in 1850 90–91

Kiangmai *see* Chiang Mai

Kiang-ning *see* Jianye, Nanjing

Kiangsi *see* Jiangxi

Kiangsu *see* Jiangsu

Kiatuthiana *archaeological site* North America (USA) cultural groups 123 (4)

Kibi *state* Japan medieval states 264 (1)

Kibris *see* Cyprus

Kibyra *state* Southwest Asia Roman empire 179 (5)

Kichai *people* North America colonization 125 (4)

Kickapoo *people* North America colonization 126 (1)

Kiel Central Europe (Germany) empire and revolution 199 (3) medieval states 189 (3)

Kiet Siel *archaeological site* North America (USA) cultural groups 123 (4)

Kiev *Rus.* Kiyev, *Ukr.* Kyyiv *battle* Eastern Europe (Russian Federation) WWII 105 (3)

Kiev *state* Eastern Europe medieval states 189 (4)

Kievan Rus *state* Eastern Europe medieval states 185 (3) medieval voyages 60–61 (1)

Kifri Southwest Asia (Iraq) 20th-century politics 235 (5)

Kiik-Koba *archaeological site* Eastern Europe (Ukraine) first humans 13 (2)

Kikládhes *see* Cyclades

Kikonja *state* Central Africa the world in 1700 82–83 the world in 1800 86–87 the world in 1850 90–91

Kilimane *see* Quelimane

Kilimanjaro *var.* Uhuru Peak *mountain* East Africa exploration 157 (4), (5)

Killala Bay *bay* British Isles (Ireland) Napoleon 200–201 (1)

Kilmain *see* Quelimane

Kilwa *mod.* Kilwa Kivinje East Africa (Tanzania) economy 163 (2) European expansion 80–81 (1) exploration 156 (3) Islam 163 (1) exploration 68 (2) slave trade 165 (4) trade 230 (2)

Kilwa Kivinje *see* Kilwa

Kimberley Southern Africa (South Africa) colonization 167 (4) economy 168 (2) European imperialism 96 (2)

Kimberley Plateau *plateau* Australia colonization 283 (3) exploration 279 (2)

Kimchaek *prev.* Söngjin East Asia (North Korea) Cold War 109 (4)

Kimmswoi *archaeological site* North America the world in 10,000 BCE 14–15

Kinai *state* Japan medieval states 264 (1)

Kingisepp *see* Yam

Kingman Reef *colonial possession* Pacific Ocean the modern world 110–111 (4)

King's Lynn *var.* Bishop's Lynn, Lynn Regis British Isles (United Kingdom) economy 190 (1)

Kings Mounds North America (USA) cultural groups 122 (5)

King's Table Australia exploration 280 (1)

Kingston West Indies (Jamaica) Cold War 108 (2), 129 (2), 136 (2)

Kingston upon Hull *see* Hull

Kinishba *archaeological site* North America (USA) cultural groups 123 (4)

Kinlichee *archaeological site* North America (USA) cultural groups 123 (4)

Kinneret, Yam *see* Galilee, Sea of

Kinshasa *prev.* Léopoldville Central Africa (Congo (Zaire)) economy 168 (2) *see also* Léopoldville

Kintampo West Africa (Ghana) early agriculture 158 (1)

Kioga, Lake *see* Kyoga, Lake

Kiowa *people* North America colonization 126 (1)

Kirata *state* South Asia first empires 241 (5)

Kirensk Siberia (Russian Federation) exploration 257 (2)

Kirghiz *people* Central Asia historical geography 275 (5) medieval states 262–263 (1) trade 267 (3)

Kirghizia *see* Kyrgyzstan

Kiribati *state/island* Pacific Ocean decolonization 285 (3) early cultures 280–281 (3)

Kirin *var.* Chi-lin, Girin, Ji, Jilin Sheng *province* East Asia Russo-Japanese War 270 (4) *see also* Jilin

Kirinyaga *see* Kenya, Mount

Kiritimati *prev.* Christmas Island *island* Pacific Ocean exploration 278 (1) *see also* Christmas Island

Kirkstall *major cistercian house* British Isles (United Kingdom) medieval states 187 (3)

Kirkuk *var.* Karkük, Kerkuk Southwest Asia (Iraq) 235 (5). economy 234 (1) WWI 233 (2) 20th-century politics 233 (3)

Kirman Southwest Asia (Iran) exploration 219 (3) medieval voyages 61 (3)

Kirov *see* Vologda, Vyatka

Kirte *battle* Southwest Asia (Turkey) WWI 207 (6)

Kisangani *prev.* Stanleyville Central Africa (Congo (Zaire)) economy 168 (2)

Kisese East Africa (Tanzania) prehistoric culture 17 (2)

Kish Southwest Asia (Iraq) early systems 33 (3) first cities 220 (2), 28–29 (1) first civilizations 221 (4), 24 (2), 25 (3)

Kishinev *var.* Chişinău Southeast Europe (Moldava) postwar politics 212 (3) Soviet Union 208 (2) WWI 207 (4)

Kiska *island* North America WWII 272 (1), 273 (2)

Kiso Japan early modern states 265 (5)

Kistna *see* Krishna

Kisumu *prev.* Port Florence East Africa (Kenya) colonization 167 (4)

Kitagiri South Asia (India) world religions 242 (3)

Kitai East Asia (China) ancient trade 44–45 (1)

Kitanosho *battle* Japan early modern states 267 (4)

Kitava *state* South Asia first empires 41 (5)

Kition Cyprus ancient Egypt 159 (5) first civilizations 177 (1)

Kiukiang *see* Jiujiang

Kiungchow *see* Qiongzhou

Kivu, Lac *see* Kivu, Lake

Kivu, Lake *Fr.* Lac Kivu *lake* Central Africa exploration 157 (4), (5) first humans 12 (1)

Kiyev *see* Kiev

Kizil Irmak *river* Southwest Asia first civilizations 24 (2)

Klaipeda Eastern Europe (Lithuania) postwar politics 212 (3)

Klasies River Mouth *archaeological site/settlement* Southern Africa (South Africa) first humans 13 (2)

Klewe *see* Cleves

Klokotnitsa *battle* Greece medieval states 189 (4)

Klondike City North America (Canada) imperial global economy 93 (3)

Klowa New Guinea (Papua New Guinea) exploration 280 (1)

Knight *burial mound* North America (USA) cultural groups 121 (4)

Knights of St. John *state* Malta the world in 1700 82–83

Knights of St. John *state* Greece medieval states 189 (4) Ottomans 230 (1)

Knights of the Cross *see* Teutonic Order

Knin Southeast Europe (Croatia) postwar economy 215 (3)

Knossós *see* Knossos

Knossos *archaeological site/palace/religious site/settlement* Crete ancient Egypt 159 (5) Bronze Age 175 (3) Copper Age 174 (2) early agriculture 174 (1) early systems 223 (3) first cities 28–29 (1) first civilizations 175 (4), 177 (1) first religions 37 (3) Hellenistic world 40–41 (1)

Knoxville North America (USA) the growth of the US 129 (2) US Civil War 131 (6), (7) US society 137 (6)

Kobe *Jap.* Köbe *bomb target/settlement* Japan WWII 273 (3) economy 270 (1), 275 (4)

København *see* Copenhagen

Koblenz Central Europe (Germany) early modern states 197 (5)

Kochi *var.* Köti Japan early modern states 267 (4) economy 270 (1)

Kochi, Ko-chih *see* Cochin

Kodiak Island North America (USA) cultural groups 123 (3)

Kodiak *island* North America imperial global economy 93 (3)

Koepang *see* Kupang

Kofu *Jap.* Köfu *bomb target* Japan WWII 273 (3)

Kofukuji *Buddhist temple army* Japan medieval states 265 (4)

Koguryo *state* East Asia medieval states 264 (1) world religions 49 (4)

Kohat South Asia (India) decolonization 250 (1)

Kohima South Asia (India) postwar politics 252 (1)

Koil South Asia (Estonia) colonialism 247 (3)

Kokala South Asia (Pakistan) Hellenistic world 40–41 (1)

Kokand *var.* Khokand, Qüqon *see* Alexandria Eschate *state* Central Asia the world in 1800 86–87 the world in 1850 90–91 *see also* Khokand

Kokasati *people* North America colonization 125 (4)

Kokchetav *Kaz.* Kökshetaü *archaeological site* Siberia early agriculture 258 (1)

Kokenhausen *mod.* Koknese Eastern Europe (Latvia) medieval states 189 (3)

Koknese *see* Kokenhausen

Kokoli *state* West Africa trade 164 (2)

Koko Nor *lake* East Asia exploration 257 (3) *see also* Qinghai Hu

Kola *region* Eastern Europe Soviet Union 214–215 (4)

Kolam *see* Quilon

Kola Peninsula *Russ.* Kol'skiy Poluostrov *coastal feature* Eastern Europe exploration 257 (2)

Kolberg *mod.* Kołobrzeg Central Europe (Poland) economy 190 (1) medieval states 189 (3)

Kolhapur South Asia (Maharashtra, India) Marathas 246 (2)

Kolkata *see* Calcutta

Kollam *see* Quilon

Kolmar *see* Colmar

Köln *see* Cologne, Colonia Agrippina

Köln-Lindenthal Central Europe (Germany) early agriculture 174 (1)

Ko-lo *state* Mainland Southeast Asia ancient India 241 (6)

Ko-lo Mainland Southeast Asia (Malaysia) ancient India 241 (6)

Kołobrzeg *see* Kolberg

Kololo *people* Africa colonization 166 (2)

Kolomna Eastern Europe (Russian Federation) Mongols 68–69 (1)

Kolomoki North America (USA) cultural groups 122 (5)

Kolozsvár Southeast Europe (Romania) early modern states 193 (4)

Kol'skiy Poluostrov *see* Kola Peninsula

Kolubara *battle* Southeast Europe (Yugoslavia) WWI 207 (6)

Kolyma *river* Siberia exploration 257 (2)

Komandorski Islands *island group* Siberia WWII 272 (1), 273 (2)

Komatipoort Southern Africa (South Africa) European imperialism 96 (2)

Komatsu Japan early modern states 267 (4)

Kom el-Hisn Egypt first cities 28–29 (1)

Komi Eastern Europe Soviet Union 214–215 (4)

Komi-Permyak *region* Eastern Europe Soviet Union 214–215 (4)

Kom Medinet Ghurab Egypt ancient Egypt 159 (5)

Kommos Crete ancient Egypt 159 (5)

Kompong Som Mainland Southeast Asia (Cambodia) postwar politics 251 (5)

Kompong Thom Mainland Southeast Asia (Cambodia) postwar politics 251 (5)

Kondavidu South Asia (India) early medieval states 244–245 (3)

Kondüz *see* Drapsaca, Kunduz

Kong *state* West Africa slave trade 165 (4) trade 167 (1)

Kongju *Jap.* Köshü *var.* Kwangju East Asia (Korea) medieval states 264 (1) *see also* Kwangju

Kongo *state* Central Africa Islam 163 (1) slave trade 165 (4) trade 164 (2), 167 (1)

Kongo *people* Central Africa trade 167 (1)

Konia *see* Iconium, Konya

Konieh *see* Iconium, Konya

Königsberg *battle/rebellion/settlement* Eastern Europe (Russian Federation) crusades 186 (1) early modern states 193 (4), 195 (3) empire and revolution 202 (2) medieval states 189 (3), (4) postwar politics 212 (3) Reformation 194 (2) WWI 207 (4) WWII 105 (3), 210 (1), 211 (4)

Königshofen *Mithraic site* Central Europe (Germany) world religions 48 (1)

Konjic *Mithraic site* Southeast Europe (Bosnia and Herzegovina) world religions 48 (1)

Konkan *region* South Asia colonialism 247 (3)

Konkana *region* South Asia early religions 48 (2)

Konstanz *see* Constance

Kontum *battle* Mainland Southeast Asia (Vietnam) 251 (5)

Konya *var.* Konieh; *prev.* Konia, *anc.* Iconium Southwest Asia (Turkey) crusades 228 (2) early Islam 57 (2) first civilizations 221 (4) Mongols 229 (3) Seljuks 228 (1) Timur 229 (4) *see also* Iconium

Konya, Lake *lake* Southwest Asia historical geography 170–171 (1)

Koobi Fora *archaeological site* East Africa (Kenya) first humans 12 (1), 13 (2)

Koolan Australia the world in 10,000 BCE 14–15

Koolburra *archaeological site* Australia prehistoric culture 17 (5)

Koonalda Cave Australia prehistoric culture 17 (2)

Kopor'ye Eastern Europe (Russian Federation) early modern states 195 (3)

Korat *see* Nakhon Ratchasima

Korčula *It.* Curzola; *anc.* Corcyra Nigra *island* Southeast Europe postwar economy 215 (3)

Korea *region* East Asia ancient trade 44–45 (1) colonialism 269 (3), (4) Communism 271 (8), (3) decolonization 251 (4) early modern states 266 (1), 267 (4), (5), 268 (1) economy 274 (1) empire and revolution 268 (2) first cities 259 (5) first religions 37 (4) first states 260 (1) imperialism 270 (2) medieval states 261 (6) postwar politics 271 (7) Russo-Japanese War 270 (4) Sino-Japanese War 270 (3) Soviet Union 208 (2) trade 267 (3) US superpower 138 (1) world religions 49 (3) WWII 104 (1), 251 (3), 272 (1), 273 (2) Chinese revolution 271 (5) Cold War 109 (1)

Koreans *people* East Asia the world in 750 BCE 30–31 the world in 500 BCE 34–35

Korea Strait *Jap.* Chösen-kaikyö, *Kor.* Taehan-haehyöp *sea waterway* East Asia early modern states 267 (4)

Koriabo *people* South America the world in 1300 66–67

Kórinthos *see* Corinth

Koritsa Southeast Europe (Albania) WWI 207 (6)

Korkai South Asia (India) first empires 241 (4)

Kormarow *battle* Central Europe (Poland) WWI 207 (4)

Korone Greece medieval states 189 (4)

Kororareka *var.* Russell New Zealand colonization 283 (4)

Koroska Egypt exploration 157 (5)

Koryaks *people* Siberia the world in 1700 82–83

Koryo *mod.* Korea *prev.* Koryo; *var.* Choson, Silla; *Jap.* Chösen *var.* Chosen *state* East Asia early modern states 265 (5), (6) Mongols 68–69 (1) *see also* Choson, Korea, Silla

Kosala South Asia (Pakistan) Hellenistic world 40–41 (1)

Koster North America (USA) the world in 5000 BCE 18–19

Kostienki *archaeological site/settlement* Eastern Europe (Russian Federation) prehistoric culture 17 (4)

Kostnitz *see* Constance

Kostroma Eastern Europe (Russian Federation) Soviet Union 208 (2)

Kostromskaya Eastern Europe (Russian Federation) first religions 36 (1)

Köszeg Central Europe (Hungary) Ottomans 195 (4)

Köszeg *see* Güns

Kota Baharu *see* Kota Bharu

Kotabangun Maritime Southeast Asia (Indonesia) world religions 243 (5)

Kota Bharu *var.* Kota Baharu, Kota Bahru Mainland Southeast Asia (Malaysia) WWII 251 (3)

Kot Diji *archaeological site* South Asia (Pakistan) first cities 240 (2)

Köti *see* Kochi

Kotor *see* Cattaro

Kotosh *early ceremonial center/settlement* South America (Peru) early cultures 144 (1), 145 (3)

Kouklia Cyprus ancient Egypt 159 (5)

Kourou *archaeological site* South America (French Guiana) early cultures 145 (3)

Kourounkorokale West Africa (Mali) early agriculture 158 (1)

Kovno *see* Kaunas, Kovno

Kowloon *colonial possession* East Asia (China) empire and revolution 268 (2)

Kow Swamp Australia the world in 10,000 BCE 14–15

Koyahan East Asia (South Korea) medieval states 264 (2)

Koya-san *Buddhist temple army* Japan medieval states 265 (4)

Koya-san *mountain* Japan medieval states 265 (3)

Koyukon *people* North America cultural groups 123 (3)

Kozhikode *see* Calicut, Kalikad, Qalqut

Kragujevac *massacre/settlement* Southeast Europe (Yugoslavia) postwar economy 215 (3) WWII 211 (3)

Kra, Isthmus of *coastal feature* Mainland Southeast Asia European imperialism 97 (3) postwar politics 253 (4)

Krakau *see* Cracow

Krak des Chevaliers *settlement/fort* Southwest Asia (Syria) crusades 228 (2), 65 (3)

Krak des Moabites *fort* Southwest Asia (Jordon) crusades 65 (3)

Kraków *see* Cracow

Kras *see* Karst

Krasnik *battle* Central Europe (Poland) WWI 207 (4)

Krasnoy Eastern Europe (Russian Federation) Napoleon 200–201 (1)

Krasnoyarsk Siberia (Russian Federation) colonialism 269 (3) exploration 257 (2) Soviet Union 208 (2), 213 (4), 214–215 (4)

Kremenets *state* Eastern Europe medieval states 189 (4)

Kreuzberg Central Europe (Germany) postwar politics 212 (2)

Krievija *see* Russia, Russian Empire, Russian Federation, Soviet Union, Union of Soviet Socialist Republics

Krishna *prev.* Kistna *river* South Asia colonialism 247 (3), 248 (2) decolonization 250 (1) early medieval states 244 (1), (2), 244–245 (3), 245 (4) economy 249 (4) first empires 241 (4), (5) first religions 36 (2) Marathas 246 (2) Mughal Empire 246 (1) postwar politics 252 (1) world religions 242 (2), 243 (4)

Kristiania *see* Christiania, Oslo

Kriti *see* Candia, Creta, Crete, Crete

Krivoy Rog Eastern Europe (Ukraine) WWII 211 (4)

Kroatien *see* Croatia

Kromdraai *archaeological site* Southern Africa (South Africa) first humans 12 (1)

Kronstadt *see* Brasov, Brassó

Krung Thep *see* Bangkok

Kruševac Southeast Europe (Yugoslavia) postwar economy 215 (3)

Krym *see* Crimea

Kuachou *see* Guazhou

K'uai Chi Shan *see* Kuaiji Shan

Kuaiji Shan *var.* K'uai Chi Shan *mountain* East Asia first religions 37 (3)

Kuala Lumpur Mainland Southeast Asia (Malaysia) Islam 235 (4) postwar economy 253 (5) WWII 251 (3), 272 (1), 273 (2)

Kuang-chou *see* Canton, Guangzhou

Kuang-tung *see* Guangdong

Kuannei *see* Guannei

Kuaua *archaeological site* North America (USA) cultural groups 123 (4)

Kuba *state* Central Africa slave trade 165 (4) trade 167 (1)

Kubanjug Egypt ancient Egypt 159 (2)

Kucha *var.* Kuqa East Asia (China) first states 260 (1)

Küchek, Rüdkhâneh-ye Zâb-e *see* Little Zab

Kuching *prev.* Sarawak Maritime Southeast Asia (Malaysia) exploration 239 (2) WWII 251 (3)

Kuei-chou *see* Guizhou

Kuei-lin *see* Guilin

Kuei-Yang *see* Guiyang

Kueyang *see* Guiyang

Kufa *var.* Al Küfah Southwest Asia (Iraq) early Islam 56–57 (1)

Kugha *state* West Africa trade 163 (4)

Kuizhou East Asia (China) medieval states 263 (4)

Kuk New Guinea (Papua New Guinea) early cultures 280 (2)

Kuka West Africa (Nigeria) Islam 163 (1) slave trade 165 (4) West Africa (Nigeria) Islam 167 (3)

Ku Klux Klan *movement* North America US politics 135 (6)

Kukura *state* South Asia first empires 241 (5)

Kulam Mali South Asia (India) medieval voyages 61 (3)

Kuldja *var.* Gulja; *Chin.* Yining *Buddhist center/settlement* East Asia (China) ancient trade 44–45 (1) early modern states 268 (1) world religions 49 (3)

Kulm *mod.* Chelmno Central Europe (Poland) medieval states 189 (3)

Kúlna Cave Central Europe (Czech Republic) first humans 13 (2)

Kültepe *var.* Kanesh Southwest Asia (Turkey) first civilizations 24 (2) *see also* Kanesh

Kumasi *prev.* Coomassie West Africa (Ghana) colonization 167 (4) economy 168 (2)

Kumaun *state* South Asia Mughal Empire 246 (1)

Kumillä *see* Comilla

Kumma Egypt ancient Egypt 159 (5)

Kumsong *var.* Kyongju *Jap.* Keishü East Asia (Korea) medieval states 264 (2) *see also* Kyongju

Kumul *see* Hami

Kundagrama South Asia (India) world religions 242 (3)

Kundivrsa *state* South Asia first empires 241 (5)

Kunduz *anc.* Drapsaca; *Per.* Kondüz *state* Central Asia the world in 1800 86–87 the world in 1850 90–91 *see also* Drapsaca

Kungitavik North America (USA) cultural groups 123 (3)

Kungnaesong East Asia (China) medieval states 264 (2)

Kunjakari South Asia (India) world religions 243 (4)

Kunjia North America (Canada) cultural groups 123 (3)

Kunlun Mountains *Chin.* Kunlun Shan *mountain range* Central Asia exploration 256 (1), 257 (3) first states 260 (1) medieval states 261 (6), 262–263 (1) Mongols 68–69 (1)

Kunlun Shan *see* Kunlun Mountains

Kunming *var.* K'un-ming; *prev.* Yunnan East Asia (China) ancient trade 44–45 (1) colonialism 269 (4) postwar economy 274–275 (2), postwar politics 275 (3) WWII 272 (1), 275 (3) *see also* Yunnan

Kunming *people* East Asia medieval states 263 (3)

Kuntala *region/state* South Asia first empires 241 (5) world religions 242 (2)

Kuntur Wasi *archaeological site* South America (Peru) early cultures 145 (3)

Kuocang Shan *var.* K'uo Ts'ang Shan *mountain* East Asia first religions 37 (4)

Kuomintang *movement* East Asia Chinese Civil War 271 (6)

K'uo Ts'ang Shan *see* Kuocang Shan

Kuowu *state* East Asia first cities 259 (4)

Kupang *prev.* Koepang Maritime Southeast Asia (Indonesia) colonialism 247 (4)

Kur *see* Kura, Kucha

Kür *see* Kura

Kura *Az.* Kür, *Geor.* Mtkvari, *Turk.* Kura Nehri *river* Southwest Asia Mongols 68–69 (1)

Kurile Islands *var.* Kuril'skiye Ostrova, *Jap.* Chishima-rettö *island group* Siberia ancient trade 44–45 (1) colonialism 269 (3) early agriculture 258 (1) early modern states 265 (5) imperialism 270 (2) WWII 272 (1), 73 (2)

Kuril'skiye Ostrova *see* Kurile Islands

Kuriyagawa Japan early modern states 265 (5)

Kurkur Egypt ancient Egypt 159 (5)

Kurkur Oasis *oasis* Egypt ancient Egypt 159 (3), (5)

Kurland *see* Courland

Kursk *battle* Eastern Europe (Russian Federation) WWII 105 (3), 211 (4)

Kuru *region* South Asia ancient India 242 (1) early religions 48 (2) world religions 242 (2), (3)

Kurukshetra *battle* South Asia (India) first empires 241 (5)

Kuruman Southern Africa (South Africa) exploration 157 (4)

Kuru-Pancala *see* Kura-Panchala

Kush *var.* Meroe, Cush *settlement/state* East Africa (Sudan) ancient Egypt 159 (4), (5) ancient trade 44–45 (1) early cultures 161 (3), (4) *see also* Meroe

Kushana *state* Central Asia the world in 250 CE 46–47

Kushites *var.* Cushites *people* East Africa ancient trade 44–45 (1) early cultures 160 (1), 161 (5) economy 163 (2) Islam 163 (1)

Kushan Empire *state* Central Asia ancient trade 44–45 (1) early religions 48 (2) medieval states 261 (6)

Kushinara South Asia (India) world religions 242 (3)

Kusinagara South Asia (India) early religions 48 (2) first religions 36 (2)

Kut al Amara Southwest Asia (Iraq) WWI 233 (2)

Kutch *see* Kach

Kutch, Gulf of *see* Kachchh, Gulf of

Kutchin *people* North America cultural groups 123 (3)

Kutch, Rann of *physical region* South Asia economy 249 (4) postwar politics 252 (1)

Kutei *state* Maritime Southeast Asia the world in 1700 82–83 the world in 1800 86–87

Kutná Hora *Ger.* Kuttenberg Central Europe (Czech Republic) economy 190 (1)

Kuttenberg *see* Kutná Hora

Kuvango *see* Cubango

Kuwait *var.* Dawlat al Kuwait, Koweit, Kuweit *colonial possession/state* Southwest Asia (Iraq) 20th-century politics 233 (3), (4), 235 (5) Cold War 109 (1) exploration 219 (4) Islam 235 (4) Ottomans 232–233 (1) the modern world 110–111, 113 (3) US superpower 138 (2) WWI 233 (2) 20th-century politics 233 (3), (4), 235 (5) Cold War 109 (1)

Kuweit *see* Kuwait

Kuybyshev *see* Samara

Kvarby Scandinavia (Sweden) Bronze Age 175 (3)

Kwa *people* West Africa early cultures 160 (1)

Kwajalein *island* Pacific Ocean Cold War 109 (1) US superpower 138 (1) WWII 272 (1), 273 (2)

Kwale *archaeological site* East Africa (Kenya) early cultures 160 (1)

Kwando *see* Cuando

Kwangchow *see* Canton, Guangzhou

Kwangchowwan *see* Guangzhouwan

Kwangchu *see* Konju, Kwangju

Kwangju *var.* Kongju, Kwangju, Kwangchu; *Jap.* Köshü East Asia (South Korea) Cold War 109 (4) *see also* Kongju

Kwangtung *see* Guangdong,

Kwantung *Jap.* Kantö *colonial possession* East Asia imperialism 270 (2)

Kwanza see Cuanza
Kwararafa state West Africa Islam 163 (1)
Kwazulu/Natal see Natal
Kweichow see Guizhou
Kweichu see Guizhou
Kweilin see Guilin
Kweiyang see Guiyang
Kwekwe prev. Que Que Southern Africa (Zimbabwe) economy 168 (2)
Kyoga, Lake var. Lake Kioga lake East Africa exploration 157 (5) first humans 12 (1)
Kyongju var. Kumsong; Jap. Keishū East Asia (Korea) early modern states 265 (5) medieval states 264 (1), (2) see also Kumsong
Kyŏngsŏng see Seoul
Kyoto Jap. Kyōto prev. Heian-kyo Japan early modern states 267 (4), 268 (1) economy 270 (1) medieval states 262–263 (1), 263 (6), 265 (4) trade 267 (3) world religions 49 (4) see also Heiankyo
Kyoto prefecture Japan economy 270 (1)
Kypros see Cyprus
Kyrgyzstan var. Kirghizia state Central Asia historical geography 275 (5) Islam 235 (4) postwar economy 275 (3) postwar politics 274 (2), 275 (5) Soviet Union 214–215 (4) the modern world 113 (3)
Kythera island Greece ancient Greece 177 (2)
Kyushu Jap. Kyūshū island Japan WWII 273 (3) early modern states 265 (5), 267 (4), (5) economy 270 (1) imperialism 270 (2), (3) medieval states 264 (1), (2), 265 (3), (4) Sino-Japanese War 270 (3)
Kyyiv see Kiev

L

Laatokka see Ladoga, Lake
La Banda Oriental see Uruguay
La Baume-Latrone archaeological site France prehistoric culture 17 (3)
Labe see Elbe
Labicana, Via road Italy ancient Rome 181 (2)
Labici var. Labicum Italy early states 178 (1)
Labicum see Labici
La Blanca Central America (Guatemala) first civilizations 121 (2)
Labná Central America (Mexico) first civilizations 123 (2)
Labrada Central America (Mexico) first civilizations 122 (1)
Labrador region North America colonization 126 (1) European expansion 80–81 (1) exploration 118 (1), 119 (2), (3), 129 (2)
Labrador Inuit people North America cultural groups 123 (3)
Labrador Sea sea North America cultural groups 123 (3) exploration 286 (1), 129 (2)
Labuan var. Pulau Labuan island Maritime Southeast Asia the world in 1850 90–91 (1)
Labuan, Pulau see Labuan
Laccadive Islands var. Lakshadweep island group South Asia Mongols 68 (2)
Lacedaemon see Sparta
La Chapelle-aux-Saints archaeological site France first humans 13 (2)
Lachish Southwest Asia (Israel) ancient Egypt 159 (5) first cities 28–29 (1)
Laconia state Greece ancient Greece 179 (4)
La Copa archaeological site South America (Peru) early cultures 145 (3)
La Coruña Iberian Peninsula (Spain) economy 205 (4) interwar 209 (4)
La Couronne France the world in 2500 BCE 22–23
Ladakia mod. Ladakh state South Asia first empires 241 (5) see also Ladakh
Ladakh region South Asia early cultures 145 (3) exploration 257 (3) postwar politics 252 (2)
Ladha region South Asia world religions 242 (3)
Lado vassal state East Africa the world in 1900 94–95
Ladoga, Lake Fin. Laatokka; var. Ladozhskoye, Ozero lake Eastern Europe early modern states 195 (3), economy 205 (4) exploration 172 (1) medieval states 185 (3) Soviet Union 208 (2) WWI 207 (4)
Ladozhskoye, Ozero see Ladoga lake
Lady Franklin Point North America (Canada) cultural groups 123 (3)
Ladysmith Southern Africa (South Africa) European imperialism 96 (2)
Lae New Guinea (Papua New Guinea) WWII 272 (1), 273 (2)
Laetolil archaeological site East Africa (Tanzania) first humans 12 (1), 13 (2)
La Fère-Champenoise battle France Napoleon 200–201 (1)
La Ferrassie archaeological site France prehistoric culture 17 (2)
La Ferté major cistercian house France medieval states 187 (3)
La Florida South America (Peru) the world in 1250 BCE 26–27
La Galgada early ceremonial center/settlement/archaeological site South America (Peru) early cultures 144 (1), 145 (3)
Lagash var. Shirpurla Southwest Asia (Iraq) first cities 220 (2), 28–29 (1) first civilizations 221 (4), 24 (3)
Laghouat North Africa (Algeria) colonization 167 (4)
Lagny France economy 190 (1)
Lagoa Santa archaeological site South America (Brazil) early cultures 145 (2)
Lagos Central Africa (Nigeria) colonization 167 (4) economy 168 (2) European imperialism 96 (1) global immigration 100 (1) Islam 167 (3)
La Gruta archaeological site South America (Venezuela) early cultures 144 (1), 145 (2)
Laguna South America (Brazil) colonization 149 (3)
Laguna de los Cerros Central America (Mexico) first civilizations 121 (2), (3)
La Habana see Havana
La Hoguette France the world in 2500 BCE 22–23
La Honradez Central America (Mexico) first civilizations 123 (2)
Lahontan, Lake North America historical geography 117 (1)
Lahor mod. Lahore South Asia (Pakistan) early medieval states 244–245 (3) Mughal Empire 246 (1) see also Lahore, Lahur
Lahore var. Lahor South Asia (Pakistan) colonialism 247 (3), 248 (1) crusades 65 (1) decolonization 250 (1) early religions 48 (2) economy 249 (4) exploration 257 (3) imperial global economy 93 (5) postwar politics 252 (1)
Lahur see Lahor

Lai East Asia (China) first cities 259 (5)
Laias var. Ayas Southwest Asia (Turkey) exploration 219 (3)
Laibach see Ljubljana
Lai-chou East Asia (China) exploration 256 (1)
Laighin region British Isles medieval states 188 (2)
Lake Mungo Australia the world in 10,000 BCE 14–15
Lake Naoich battle Eastern Europe (Belorussia) WWI 207 (4)
Lakhawar South Asia (India) colonialism 247 (3)
Lakhmids state Southwest Asia the world in 500 CE 50–51
Lakhnau see Lucknow
Lakshadweep see Laccadive Islands
Lalibela Cave archaeological site East Africa (Ethiopia) early agriculture 158 (1) world religions 49 (4)
La Madeleine archaeological site/settlement France prehistoric culture 17 (4)
Lamanai Central America (Mexico) first civilizations 123 (2)
Lamar North America (USA) cultural groups 122 (5)
Lambaesis mod. Tazoult legion headquarters/mithraic site North Africa (Algeria) ancient Rome 180–181 (1) world religions 48 (1)
Lambakannas mod. Sri Lanka; Chin. Hsi-lan; anc. Taprobane state South Asia the world in 250 CE 46–47 the world in 500 CE 50–51 the world in 750 CE 54–55 the world in 1000 58–59 see also Ceylon, Lanka, Simhala, Sri Lanka, Taprobane
Lambayeque river South America early cultures 145 (4), (4)
Lambing Flat goldfield Australia colonization 282 (2)
Lamb Spring North America the world in 10,000 BCE 14–15
La Mosquitia see Mosquito Coast, Mosquito Prefecture
Lampsacus Southwest Asia (Turkey) ancient Greece 177 (3) first civilizations 177 (1)
Lampsacus state Greece ancient Greece 177 (2)
Lamut var. Even people Siberia trade 267 (3)
Lancang Jiang see Mekong
Lancashire admin. region British Isles imperial global economy 93 (4)
Lancaster British Isles (United Kingdom) economy 204 (1)
Lan Chang mod. Louanphabang, Louangphrabang, Luang, Prabang Mainland Southeast Asia (Laos) early medieval states 245 (6)
Lanchow, Lan-chou, Lan-chow see Lanzhou
Langebaan archaeological site Southern Africa (South Africa) first humans 13 (2)
Langkasuka Mainland Southeast Asia (Thailand) ancient India 241 (6)
Lang Son fort Mainland Southeast Asia (Vietnam) 251 (5)
Langtandong archaeological site East Asia (China) first humans 13 (2)
Languedoc region France medieval states 192 (1)
Langweiler Low Countries (Netherlands) early agriculture 174 (1)
Langye Buddhist center East Asia (China) world religions 49 (3)
Langye var. Lang-Yeh region East Asia first religions 37 (4)
Lang-Yeh see Langye
Lanka var. Simhala; see also Ceylon island South Asia first religions 36 (1) world religions 48 (2) see also Lambakannas, Simhala, Sri Lanka, Taprobane
Lanka region South Asia early religions 48 (2)
Lan-Na region Mainland Southeast Asia early medieval states 245 (6)
L'Anse aux Meadows North America (Canada) medieval voyages 60–61 (1)
Lansing North America (USA) the growth of the US 129 (2)
Lantian archaeological site/settlement East Asia (China) first cities 259 (4) first humans 13 (2) first states 260 (1)
Lan-ts'ang Chiang see Mekong
Lanzhou var. Lan-chou, Lanchow, Lan-chow; prev. Kaolan archaeological site/settlement East Asia (China) plague 72–73 (1) early agriculture 258 (2) early modern states 266 (1) economy 274 (1) empire and revolution 268 (2) first states 260 (1) Islam 275 (4) medieval states 261 (6) postwar politics 271 (7), 274 (1)
Lao Cai fort Mainland Southeast Asia postwar politics 251 (5)
Laodicea Southwest Asia (Syria/Turkey) ancient Rome 180–181 (1) world religions 48 (1)
Laodicea ad Mare see Laodicea
Laodicea in Media mod. Nehavend Southwest Asia (Iran) Hellenistic world 41 (2)
Laon battle France Napoleon 200–201 (1)
Laos off. Lao People's Democratic Republic state/vassal state Mainland Southeast Asia Bronze Age 240 (3) Cold War 109 (1) colonialism 269 (4) decolonization 251 (4) early modern states 268 (1) economy 274 (1) European imperialism 97 (3) Islam 275 (4) postwar economy 253 (5), 275, 253 (4), 274 (2)
Laos people Mainland Southeast Asia the world in 1300 66–67
La Paz South America (Mexico) colonization 125 (4)
La Paz var. La Paz de Ayacucho South America (Bolivia) colonization 148 (2) empire and revolution 150 (1), 151 (3) environment 153 (4) Incas 148 (1) narcotics 153 (5) politics 151 (4), 152 (1)
La Paz de Ayacucho see La Paz
La Perouse Strait Jap. Sōya-kaikyō sea waterway East Asia WWII 273 (3)
Lapita archaeological site Pacific Ocean (New Caledonia) early cultures 280–281 (3)
Lapland Fin. Lappi, Swe. Lappland physical region Scandinavia exploration 286 (1)
La Plata South America (Bolivia) colonization 148 (2) exploration 142 (1), 143 (2)
La Plata South America (Argentina) empire and revolution 151 (3)
La Plata see Chuquisaca
La Plata, United Provinces of state South America empire and revolution 150 (1), 88–89 (2)
La Playa South America (Argentina) Incas 147 (3)
Lappland, Lappi see Lapland
Lapps people Scandinavia the world in 1200 62–63 the world in 1300 66–67 the world in 1400 70–71 the world in 1500 74–75

Laptev Sea sea Arctic Ocean exploration 257 (2)
La Puerta battle South America (Venezuela) empire and revolution 150 (1)
Lapurdum see Bayonne
Larache see Lixus
Laredo North America (USA) Mexican Revolution 133 (3)
Larino see Larinum
Larinum mod. Larino Italy early states 178 (1)
La Rioja South America (Argentina) empire and revolution 151 (3)
Larissa Christian archbishopric Greece world religions 48 (1)
La Roche archaeological site France prehistoric culture 17 (4)
La Roche-aux-Moines France medieval states 187 (4)
La Rochelle anc. Rupella France crusades 186 (1) early modern states 197 (5) economy 198 (1) medieval states 192 (1) Reformation 196 (2)
Larsa Southwest Asia (Iraq) first cities 220 (2), 28–29 (1) first civilizations 221 (4)
La-sa see Lhasa
Las Bocas Central America (Mexico) early agriculture 120 (1)
Lascaux archaeological site/settlement France prehistoric culture 17 (3) the world in 10,000 BCE 14–15
La Serena South America (Chile) empire and revolution 151 (3) politics 151 (4)
Las Flores Central America (Mexico) first civilizations 122 (1)
Las Haldas archaeological site/settlement South America (Peru) early cultures 144 (1)
Lashio Mainland Southeast Asia (Burma) WWII 273 (2) WWII 104 (2)
Lashkari Bazar Central Asia (Afghanistan) early Islam 56–57 (1)
Las Limas archaeological site Central America (Mexico) first civilizations 123 (2)
Las Navas de Tolosa battle Iberian Peninsula (Spain) crusades 186 (1) Islam 192 (3)
Las Palomas Iberian Peninsula the world in 10,000 BCE 14–15
Lassa see Lhasa
Las Vegas North America (USA) the growth of the US 129 (2)
Las Vegas South America (Ecuador) early cultures 144 (1) the modern world 113 (4)
Las Victorias Central America (El Salvador) first civilizations 121 (2)
Latacunga South America (Ecuador) Incas 147 (3)
Latakia see Laodicea
Later Kalachuris dynasty South Asia early medieval states 244 (2)
Later Liang dynasty East Asia medieval states 263 (3)
Latina, Via road Italy early states 178 (1) ancient Rome 181 (2)
Latin Cities state Italy the world in 500 BCE 34–35
Latin Empire state Southeast Europe Mongols 68–69 (1)
Latini people East Asia early states 178 (1), (2)
La Tolita South America (Colombia) the world in 250 BCE 38–39
Latome East Africa (Sudan) exploration 157 (4)
La Tranche France early agriculture 174 (1)
Lattaquié see Laodicea
Lattaquié see Laodicea
Latvia Ger. Lettland, Latv. Latvija state Southeast Europe interwar 209 (3), (5) postwar economy 214 (1), (2) postwar politics 212 (3) Soviet Union 208 (2), 213 (4) the modern world 112 (2), 113 (4) WWI 207 (4), 208 (1) WWII 210 (1)
Latvija see Latvia
Laugerie Basse archaeological site France prehistoric culture 17 (3)
Lau Group island group Pacific Ocean early cultures 280–281 (3) medieval voyages 60 (2)
Lauis see Lugano
Launceston Australia colonization 282 (1), (2), 283 (3) exploration 279 (2)
Laurentian Highlands var. Laurentian Mountains, Fr. Les Laurentides plateau North America 129 (2)
Laurentian Mountains see Laurentian Highlands
Laurentide Ice Sheet ice feature North America historical geography 117 (1)
Lausanne It. Losanna Central Europe (Switzerland) early modern states 193 (5)
Lauvak Mainland Southeast Asia 20th-century politics 235 (5)
Lavak oil terminal Southwest Asia (Iran) economy 234 (1)
Lāvān, Jazireh-ye see Lavan
Lavapura mod. Lop Buri Mainland Southeast Asia (Thailand) ancient India 241 (6) see also Lopburi
La Venta Central America (Mexico) first civilizations 121 (2), (3) first religions 36 (1)
La Victoria Central America (Guatemala) first civilizations 121 (2)
Lavo state Mainland Southeast Asia the world in 1300 66–67
Laz people Southwest Asia Ottomans 232–233 (1)
Lazica state Southwest Asia the world in 500 CE 50–51 the world in 750 CE 54–55
Lealui Southern Africa (Zambia) exploration 157 (4)
Lebanon Ar. Al Lubnān, Fr. Liban region/state Southwest Asia exploration 219 (4) Islam 235 (4) Ottomans 232–233 (1) the modern world 113 (3) US economy 138 (2) WWII 210 (1), 211 (4) 20th-century 234 (2) 20th-century politics 235 (5) Cold War 109 (1)
Le Cap var. Cap-Haïtien West Indies (Haiti) empire and revolution 89 (3)
Lechfeld battle Central Europe (Austria) medieval states 185 (3)
L'Écluse see Sluis, Sluys
Le Creusot France economy 205 (4)
Ledo South Asia (India) WWII 251 (3)
Ledro Italy Bronze Age 175 (3)
Leeds British Isles (United Kingdom) economy 204 (1) imperial global economy 93 (4)
Leeds and Liverpool canal British Isles economy 204 (1)
Leer Central Europe (Germany) Reformation 195 (5)
Leeward Islands colonial possession West Indies the world in 1900 94–95 the world in 1925 98–99 the world in 1950 102–103
Lefkosia, Lefkoşa see Nicosia
Lefroy goldfield Australia colonization 282 (2)
Le Gabillou archaeological site France prehistoric culture 17 (3)
Legaceaster see Chester, Deva
Legio VII Gemina legion headquarters Iberian Peninsula (Spain) ancient Rome 180–181 (1)

Legnano battle Italy medieval states 188 (1)
Legnica Ger. Liegnitz Central Europe (Poland) Mongols 68–69 (1) see also Liegnitz
Leh Southwest Asia (India) biological diffusion 72–73 (1) postwar politics 252 (2)
Le Havre var. le Havre-de-Grâce; Eng. Havre France early modern states 197 (5) economy 205 (4) empire and revolution 199 (4) interwar 209 (3)
le Havre-de-Grâce see Le Havre
Leicester Lat. Batae Coritanorum British Isles (United Kingdom) medieval states 204 (1)
Leiden Low Countries (Netherlands) Reformation 195 (5)
Leie see Lys
Leinster region British Isles medieval states 186 (2)
Leipsic see Leipzig
Leipzig anc. Lipsia; hist. Leipsic; Pol. Lipsk Central Europe (Germany) early modern states 193 (4) economy 190 (1), 205 (4) empire and revolution 202 (2) postwar politics 212 (1) Reformation 196 (1)
Leisnig Central Europe (Germany) early modern states 193 (4)
Leli see Tianlin
Leman, le, lac see Geneva lake
Le Mas d'Azil archaeological site France prehistoric culture 17 (3)
Lemberg Pol. Lwów, Rus. L'vov, Ukr. L'viv Eastern Europe (Ukraine) empire and revolution 198 (2) WWI 207 (4) see also L'vov, Lwów
Lemnos island Greece ancient Greece 177 (2), (3), 179 (4) first civilizations 175 (4) WWI 207 (6)
Lemovices see Limoges
Lena river Siberia colonialism 269 (3) early agriculture 20–21 (2), 258 (1) early modern states 268 (1) exploration 257 (2) first humans 13 (2) first states 260 (1) Mongols 68–69 (1) prehistoric culture 16 (1) Soviet Union 208 (2) trade 267 (3)
Leningrad prev. and mod. Sankt-Peterburg, prev. Petrograd; Eng. Saint Petersburg, Rus. Pietari Eastern Europe (Russian Federation) Cold War 108 (3) postwar politics 212 (3) Soviet Union 213 (4) WWII 210 (1), 211 (2), (4) see also Petrograd, St Petersburg
Lens France WWI 206 (2), (3)
Lentia see Linz
Leoben Central Europe (Austria) Napoleon 200–201 (1)
León Central America (Nicaragua) the world in 1900 94–95
León Iberian Peninsula (Spain) Franks 184 (2) interwar 209 (4) Islam 192 (3) medieval states 185 (3)
León state/region Iberian Peninsula crusades 186 (1) Islam 192 (3) medieval states 185 (3) medieval voyages 60–61 (1)
León and Castile state Iberian Peninsula crusades 64–65 (1)
Leopard's Kopje archaeological site Southern Africa (Zimbabwe) early cultures 160 (1)
Ligny/Quatre-Bras var. Ligny Quatre-Bras battle Low Countries (Belgium) Napoleon 200–201 (1)
Léopoldville mod. Kinshasa; Fr. Léopoldville Central Africa (Congo (Zaire)) colonization 167 (4) exploration 157 (4) see also Kinshasa
Lepanto battle Greece Ottomans 231 (3)
Lepenski Vir Southeast Europe the world in 5000 BCE 18–19
Leptis var. Leptis Magna mithraic site/settlement North Africa (Libya) ancient Rome 179 (3), 180–181 (1) ancient trade 44–45 (1) early cultures 160 (1) first civilizations 177 (1) The World in 1975 106–107 world religions 48 (1)
Leptis Magna see Leptis
Lérida settlement/university Iberian Peninsula (Spain) Islam 192 (3) medieval states 187 (4)
Lerma rural Central America first civilizations 121 (2)
Les Bolards mithraic site France world religions 48 (1)
Lesbos island Greece ancient Greece 177 (2), (3), 179 (4) first civilizations 175 (4)
Les Cayes see Cayes
Les Combarelles archaeological site France prehistoric culture 17 (3)
Les Halles France economy 191 (2)
Lesina see Hvar
Les Laurentides see Laurentian Highlands
Lesotho prev. Basutoland state Southern Africa decolonization 168 (1) economy 168 (2), (3) the modern world 113 (3) see also Basutoland
Lespugue archaeological site France prehistoric culture 17 (4)
Lesser Antarctica var. West Antarctica physical region Antarctica Antarctic Exploration 287 (3)
Lesser Antilles island group West Indies colonization 125 (4) exploration 118 (1), 119 (2), (3)
Les Trois Frères archaeological site France prehistoric culture 17 (3)
Lésvos see Lesbos
Le Temple building France economy 191 (2)
Leticia South America (Colombia) politics 152 (1)
Lettland see Latvia
Le Tuc d'Audoubert archaeological site France prehistoric culture 17 (3)
Lëtzebuerg see Luxembourg
Leubingen burial mound/settlement Central Europe (Germany) Bronze Age 175 (3)
Leucas Greece ancient Greece 177 (3)
Leucas island Greece ancient Greece 179 (4)
Leuco-petrae see Luofu Shan
Leucocome Southwest Asia (Saudi Arabia) ancient trade 44–45 (1) early trade 225 (3)
Levant region Southwest Asia Bronze Age 175 (3) first civilizations 24 (2)
Levoča see Locse
Lexington battle/settlement North America (USA) US Civil War 131 (6)
Lexington North America (USA) empire and revolution 127 (3)
Leyte Philippines WWII 251 (3), 273 (2)
Leyte Gulf Philippines WWII 105 (3), 273 (2)
Lezetxiki archaeological site Iberian Peninsula (Spain) first humans 13 (2)
Lhasa var. La-sa, Lassa Central Asia (China) biological diffusion 72–73 (1) colonialism 247 (3), 269 (4) early medieval states 244–245 (3) early modern states 268 (1) exploration 257 (3) Mongols 68–69 (1) world religions 49 (3)
Lhavis see Lindhos, mod.
Lindus var. Lindhos, mod. Lindos Greece ancient Greece 177 (3) first civilizations 177 (1)
Liang state East Asia medieval states 261 (4)
Liangcheng archaeological site East Asia early agriculture 258 (2)
Liang-chou see Liangzhou

Liangzhou var. Liang-chou East Asia (China) early modern states 266 (1) medieval states 262–263 (1) see also Wuwei
Liangzhu archaeological site East Asia (China) early agriculture 258 (1), (2)
Lianyungang East Asia (China) postwar politics 274 (2)
Liao state East Asia early modern states 265 (5)
Liao people East Asia the world in 1200 62–63
Liaodong East Asia (China) early modern states 266 (1)
Liaodong Peninsula coastal feature East Asia Russo-Japanese War 270 (3) Sino-Japanese War 270 (3)
Liao Empire see Khitan Empire
Liaoning province East Asia postwar politics 274 (2)
Liaoxi province East Asia first states 260 (1)
Liaoyang battle East Asia (China) medieval states 263 (3) Russo-Japanese War 270 (3)
Liaoyang province East Asia early modern states 266 (1), (2) medieval states 263 (6)
Liban see Lebanon
Libau see Libava
Libava Ger. Libau Eastern Europe (Latvia) WWI 207 (4)
Liberalitas Julia see Évora
Liberia state West Africa colonization 167 (4) decolonization 168 (1) economy 168 (2) European imperialism 96 (1), Islam 235 (4) the modern world 112 (1), 113 (3) trade 167 (1) WWII 105 (3)
Libreville Central Africa (Gabon) colonization 167 (4) economy 168 (2) exploration 157 (4)
Libya region/state North Africa ancient trade 44 (2) decolonization 168 (1) early Islam 56–57 (1), 57 (2) economy 168 (2) European imperialism 96 (1), 97 (4) Islam 163 (1), 226 (2), 227 (4), (5), 235 (4) Napoleon 200–201 (1) Ottomans 232–233 (1) the modern world 112 (1), 113 (3), (4) world religions 48 (1) WWII 104 (1), (2), 210 (1), 211 (4) Cold War 109 (1)
Lichfield British Isles (United Kingdom) medieval states 183 (3)
Lichtenberg Central Europe (Germany) postwar politics 212 (2)
Lidice massacre Central Europe (Czech Republic) WWII 211 (3)
Liechtenstein state Central Europe early modern states 193 (5) the modern world 112 (2)
Liège Dut. Luik, Ger. Lüttich Low Countries (Belgium) economy 190 (1) Franks 184 (2) Reformation 195 (5) WWI 206 (2)
Liegnitz battle Central Europe (Poland) medieval states 189 (3)
Lietuva see Lithuania
Liger see Loire
Ligny/Quatre-Bras var. Ligny Quatre-Bras battle Low Countries (Belgium) Napoleon 200–201 (1)
Ligure, Mar see Ligurian Sea
Ligurian Republic state Italy the world in 1800 86–87
Ligurians people France/Italy the world in 750 BCE 30–31 the world in 250 BCE 38–39
Ligurian Sea Fr. Mer Ligurienne, It. Mar Ligure sea Italy early states 178 (1)
Ligurienne, Mer see Ligurian Sea
Liivi Laht see Riga, Gulf of
Lille var. l'Isle; prev. Lisle, anc. Insula; Dut. Rijssel, Flem. Ryssel France early modern states 197 (5) economy 190 (1) interwar 209 (3) Reformation 195 (5)
Lilybaeum mod. Marsala Italy ancient Rome 179 (3), 180–181 (1) early cultures 161 (2) first civilizations 177 (1)
Lim river Southeast Europe postwar economy 215 (3)
Lima South America (Peru) colonization 148 (2) early cultures 145 (4) empire and revolution 150 (1), 151 (3) economy 153 (3) European expansion 80–81 (1) exploration 142 (1), 143 (2), (3) global immigration 100 (1) Incas 148 (1) narcotics 153 (5) politics 152 (1)
Lima South America region South America colonization 148 (2)
Lima, Audiencia of region South America colonization 148 (2)
Limassol Southwest Asia (Cyprus) crusades 65 (3)
Limburg province/state Low Countries empire and revolution 202 (1i) Reformation 195 (5)
Limerick Ir. Luimneach British Isles (Ireland) economy 205 (4) medieval states 185 (4) medieval voyages 60–61 (1)
Limin Vathéos see Samos
Limoges anc. Augustoritum Lemovicesium, Lemovices France early modern states 197 (5) medieval states 187 (4)
Limonum see Poitiers
Limpopo var. Crocodile river Southern Africa early cultures 160 (1) European imperialism 96 (2) first humans 12 (1) Islam 163 (1) slave trade 165 (4) trade 164 (1)
Limpurg Central Europe empire and revolution 199 (3)
Lin East Asia (China) first cities 259 (5)
Lin'an var. Hangchou, Hangchow, Hangzhou East Asia (China) medieval states 263 (5) see also Hangzhou
Linceuome Southwest Asia (Saudi Arabia) ancient trade 44–45 (1) early trade 161 (3), (4), (5) early trade 225 (3)
Lincoln anc. Lindum, Lindum Colonia British Isles (United Kingdom) economy 190 (1) medieval states 183 (3) see also Lindum
Lincoln North America (USA) the growth of the US 129 (2)
Lincoln Sea sea Arctic Ocean exploration 287 (2)
Lindhos see Lindus
Lindisfarne religious building/settlement British Isles (United Kingdom) medieval states 183 (3) medieval voyages 60–61 (1)
Lindos see Lindus
Lindsey region British Isles medieval states 183 (3)
Lindum see Lindum Colonia; mod. Lincoln British Isles (United Kingdom) ancient Rome 180–181 (1) see also Lincoln
Lindum Colonia see Lincoln, Lindum
Lindus var. Lindhos; mod. Lindos Greece ancient Greece 177 (3) first civilizations 177 (1)
Lindus state Greece ancient Greece 177 (2)
Liang state East Asia medieval states 261 (4)
Liangcheng archaeological site East Asia early agriculture 258 (2)
Line Islands island group Pacific Ocean colonization 284–285 (1) early cultures 280–285 (3) exploration 279 (3) medieval voyages 60 (2)

Lingen region Central Europe empire and revolution 199 (3)
Lingfang East Asia (China) first states 260 (1)
Lingling province East Asia first states 260 (1)
Lingnan province Central Asia medieval states 262–263 (1)
Lingzhi people East Asia first cities 259 (4)
Linhuai Buddhist center East Asia (China) world religions 49 (3)
Linhuang East Asia (China) the world in 1000 58–59
Linny Egypt ancient Egypt 159 (5)
Lintao East Asia (China) first states 60 (1)
Linyanti Southern Africa (Nambia) exploration 157 (4)
Linz anc. Lentia Central Europe (Austria) economy 190 (1) WWII 210 (1), 211 (2), (3), (4)
Lion Cave Southern Africa (Swaziland) prehistoric culture 17 (2)
Lion, Golfe du; Lion, Gulf of see Lions, Gulf of
Lions, Gulf of Fr. Golfe du Lion; var. Gulf of Lion; anc. Sinus Gallicus gulf France early modern states 197 (5)
Lipan people Central America colonization 126 (1)
Lipan Apache people Central America/North America colonization 125 (4)
Lipari archaeological site Italy Copper Age 174 (2)
Lipsk, Lipsia see Leipzig
Lisan, Lake lake Southwest Asia historical geography 216–217 (1)
Lisboa see Lisbon, Olisipo
Lisbon anc. Felicitas Julia, Olisipo; Port. Lisboa Iberian Peninsula (Portugal) trade 72–73 (1) crusades 186 (1), 64–65 (2) early Islam 56–57 (1) economy 190 (1), 205 (4) empire and revolution 202 (1) European expansion 81 (3), 84–85 (1) exploration 156 (3) Franks 184 (2) interwar 209 (3) medieval states 182 (2), 183 (3), 186 (1), 187 (3), (4), 188 (2) medieval voyages 60–61 (1) Napoleon 200–201 (1), 201 (2), (3) postwar politics 212 (3) Reformation 194 (2) WWI 206 (2), (3), (4), Cold War 108 (3)
Lishi East Asia (China) first cities 259 (5)
Lisieux anc. Noviomagus France Franks 184 (2)
Lisle, l'Isle see Lille
Litauen see Lithuania
Lithuania Ger. Litauen, Lith. Lietuva, Pol. Litwa, Rus. Litva region/state Eastern Europe economy 190 (1) empire and revolution 198 (2) interwar 209 (3), (5) Islam 163 (1) medieval states 189 (3), (4) Ottomans 230 (1) postwar economy 214 (1), (2) postwar politics 212 (3) Soviet Union 208 (2), 213 (4) the modern world 112 (2) WWI 207 (4), 208 (1) WWII 210 (1)
Lithuanians people Eastern Europe crusades 186 (1), 64–65 (2) medieval states 189 (3)
Little Armenia state Southwest Asia economy 190 (1) Mongols 229 (3), 68–69 (1)
Little Big Horn battle North America (USA) the growth of the US 129 (2)
Little Rock North America (USA) the growth of the US 129 (2), 132 (1) US society 137 (6)
Little Salt Spring North America (USA) the world in 10,000 BCE 14–15
Little Wallachia vassal state Eastern Europe Ottomans 197 (4)
Liu Song state East Asia medieval states 261 (4)
Livenza river Italy WWI 207 (5)
Liverpool British Isles (United Kingdom) economy 204 (1), 205 (4) global immigration 100 (1), 101 (3) imperial global economy 93 (4), (5), interwar 209 (3) WWII 210 (1)
Livingstone var. Maramba Southern Africa (Zambia) colonization 167 (4)
Livland see Livonia
Livonia region Central Europe early modern states 195 (3) empire and revolution 198 (2)
Livonians people Eastern Europe medieval states 189 (3)
Lixus mod. Larache North Africa (Morocco) first civilizations 177 (1)
Lizard Mound burial mound North America (USA) first civilizations 121 (4)
Ljubljana anc. Aemona, Emona, Ger. Laibach, It. Lubiana Central Europe (Slovenia) postwar economy 215 (3)
Llano del Jicaro archaeological site Central America (Mexico) first civilizations 121 (3)
Llanos physical region South America early cultures 144 (1), 147 (2) empire and revolution 150 (1), (2) environment 153 (4)
Llanos de Mojos archaeological site South America (Bolivia) early cultures 145 (2)
Loanda see Luanda
Loango Central Africa (Congo) European expansion 84–85 (1) slave trade 165 (4) trade 164 (2)
Loango state Central Africa slave trade 165 (4) trade 164 (2), 167 (1)
Lobito Southern Africa (Angola) Cold War 109 (5) economy 168 (2)
Lob Nor see Lop Nor
Lobo, Cape see St. Mary, Cape
Loburi see Lop Buri
Loch Garman see Wexford
Loc Ninh battle Mainland Southeast Asia (Vietnam) 251 (5)
Locri Italy early states 178 (1), (2) first civilizations 177 (1)
Locri Epizephyrii see Locri
Locse mod. Levoča (hist. Löcse) Central Europe (Slovakia) medieval states 189 (4)
Lodi battle Italy Napoleon 200–201 (1)
Lodi Sultanate of Delhi state South Asia the world in 1500 74–75
Lodz Central Europe (Poland) WWI 207 (4)
Lo Fu Shan see Luofu Shan
Loire var. Liger river France crusades 186 (1), 64–65 (2) early Islam 56–57 (1) early modern states 197 (5) economy 190 (1), 205 (4) empire and revolution 199 (4), 202 (1) exploration 172 (1) Franks 183 (5), (6), 184 (2) medieval states 185 (3), 187 (4), 192 (1), (2) Napoleon 200–201 (1), 201 (2), (3) prehistoric culture 17 (3), (4) WWI

200–201 (1), 201 (2), (3) prehistoric culture 17 (3), (4) WWI 206 (2), (3)
Lokoja West Africa (Nigeria) colonization 167 (4)
Loltun Cave Central America (Mexico) first civilizations 123 (2)
Lombardia see Lombardy
Lombards people Southeast Europe ancient Rome 181 (4), 182 (1) great migrations 53 (2)
Lombardy var. Kingdom of the Lombards; It. Lombardia region/state Italy crusades 64–65 (2) early Islam 56–57 (1) economy 190 (1) empire and revolution 202 (1) Franks 184 (2) Islam 184 (1) medieval states 182 (2), 183 (4), 188 (1)
Lombardy and Venetia, Kingdom of state Italy early modern states 193 (5)
Lombardy-Venetia see Venetia
Lombok island Maritime Southeast Asia early medieval states 245 (5), (6) European imperialism 97 (3) exploration 239 (2)
Lombok Strait battle Maritime Southeast Asia (Indonesia) WWII 272 (1)
Lome West Africa (Togo) colonization 167 (4)
Lomekwi archaeological site East Africa (Kenya) first humans 12 (1)
Lonato battle Italy Napoleon 200–201 (1)
Londinium mod. London; anc. Augusta British Isles (United Kingdom) ancient Rome 180–181 (1), 181 (3) great migrations 52–53 (1) world religions 48 (1) see also London
London North America (Canada) 132 (1)
London anc. Londinium British Isles (United Kingdom) ancient Rome 182 (1) plague 72–73 (1) crusades 186 (1) economy 190 (1), 205 (4) empire and revolution 202 (1) European expansion 84–85 (1) imperial global economy 92 (1), 93 (5) interwar 209 (3) medieval states 182 (2), 183 (3), 186 (1), 187 (3), (4), 188 (2) medieval voyages 60–61 (1) Napoleon 200–201 (1), 201 (2), (3) postwar politics 212 (3) Reformation 194 (2) WWI 206 (2), (3), (4), (5), Cold War 108 (3) see also Londinium
Longaone Italy WWI 207 (5)
Long Island island North America empire and revolution 127 (3)
Longjingcun var. Lungchingtsun East Asia (China) colonialism 269 (4) 270 (2)
Longkou var. Lungkow East Asia (China) colonialism 269 (4)
Longobucco Italy economy 190 (1)
Longreach Australia colonization 282 (1)
Long's Drift East Africa (Kenya) early agriculture 158 (1)
Longwy France early modern states 197 (5)
Longxi province East Asia first states 260 (1)
Longxing East Asia (China) medieval states 263 (4), (5), (6)
Longyu var. Lungyu province Central Asia medieval states 262–263 (1)
Longzhou var. Lungchow East Asia (China) colonialism 269 (4)
Loochoo Islands see Ryukyu Islands
Loos France WWI 206 (2), (3)
Lop Buri var. Loburi Mainland Southeast Asia (Thailand) world religions 243 (5) see also Lavapura
Lopera Iberian Peninsula (Spain) interwar 209 (4)
Lop Nor var. Lob Nor, Lop Nur, Lo-pu Po lake East Asia early agriculture 258 (1) exploration 257 (3) first states 260 (1) Mongols 68–69 (1) world religions 49 (3)
Lop Nur, Lo-pu Po see Lop Nor
Lorca Iberian Peninsula (Spain) Islam 192 (3)
Lorient France early modern states 197 (5)
Lorna Negra South America (Peru) early cultures 145 (4)
Lorraine region France crusades 64–65 (2)
Lorraine, Duchy of state France early modern states 197 (5) Reformation 196 (1)
Los Altos North America (USA) 136 (3)
Los Angeles North America (USA) exploration 119 (3) global immigration 100 (1), 101 (3) the growth of the US 129 (2), 132 (1) the modern world 113 (4) US economy 134 (1), (3), 136 (2) US society 135 (6)
Losanna see Lausanne
Los Gatos North America (USA) 136 (3)
Los Idolos archaeological site Central America (Mexico) first civilizations 121 (3)
Los Millares archaeological site Iberian Peninsula (Spain) Copper Age 174 (2)
Los Naranjos Central America (Honduras) first civilizations 121 (2)
Los Palmos South America (Peru) early cultures 145 (4)
Los Soldados archaeological site Central America (Mexico) first civilizations 121 (3)
Los Toldos archaeological site South America (Argentina) early cultures 144 (1)
Los Tuxtlas Central America (Mexico) first civilizations 122 (1)
Lot river France prehistoric culture 17 (3)
Lothagam archaeological site East Africa (Kenya) first humans 12 (1)
Lothal archaeological site/settlement South Asia (India) first cities 240 (2) first civilizations 24 (2), 25 (3)
Loualaba see Lualaba
Louisbourg North America (Canada) empire and revolution 127 (2) empire and revolution 88 (1)
Louisiana colonial possession/state North America colonization 126 (1) empire and revolution 88 (1) imperial global economy 93 (3) the growth of the US 129 (1), US Civil War 130 (2), (3), (4), (5), 131 (6), (7) US economy 134 (2), 139 (3) US society 137 (6) cotton 139 (3)
Louisville North America (USA) the growth of the US 129 (2), 132 (1) US Civil War 131 (6)
Loulan Buddhist center East Asia (China) world religions 49 (3)
Lourenço Marques mod. Maputo Southern Africa (Mozambique) colonization 166 (2), 167 (4) exploration 156 (3) see also Maputo
Lourenço Marques, Baía de see Delagoa Bay
Louvain Low Countries (Belgium) economy 190 (1)
Louvo region Mainland Southeast Asia early medieval states 245 (5)
Louvre building France economy 191 (2)

M

337

P

European expansion 85 (2) global immigration 100 (1) historical geography 140–141 (1) the growth of the US 133 (4) the modern world 113 (4) US politics 139 (4) Cold War 108 (2), 109 (1)

Puerto San Julián var. San Julián South America (Argentina) European expansion 80–81 (1)

Puket see Phuket

Pulicat var. Pālghāt, Geldria South Asia (India) colonialism 247 (3)

Pulinda region/state South Asia first empires 241 (5) world religions 242 (2)

Pumpo South America (Peru) Incas 147 (3)

Punakha South Asia (Bhutan) colonialism 248 (1)

Puna Pau archaeological site Easter Island early cultures 281 (4)

Pundra South Asia (Bangladesh) first empires 241 (4)

Pundra South Asia (Bangladesh) early religions 48 (2) first empires 241 (5) world religions 242 (2)

Pundravardhana South Asia (Bangladesh) early medieval states 244 (1) world religions 242 (2)

Pune prev. Poona South Asia (India) postwar economy 253 (5) see also Poona

Punjab region/state South Asia colonialism 247 (3), 248 (2) economy 249 (4) empire and revolution 249 (3) postwar politics 252 (2), 253 (4) world religions 243 (4)

Punjab, (East) region South Asia postwar politics 252 (1)

Punjab, (West) region South Asia postwar politics 252 (1)

Punjab States state South Asia colonialism 248 (2)

Punkuri archaeological site South America (Peru) early cultures 145 (3)

Punneikayal see Kayalapattinam

Puno South America (Peru) empire and revolution 150 (1) politics 151 (4)

Punt restoration NE Africa 159 (5)

Punta Arenas prev. Magallanes South America (Chile) empire and revolution 151 (3) environment 153 (4)

Punta de Angamos battle South America (Chile) politics 151 (4)

Puntutjarpa Australia exploration 280 (1)

Pura mod. Iranshahr Southwest Asia (Iran) world religions 48 (2)

Puranadhisthana var. Shrinagara South Asia (India) first empires 241 (4)

Puri South Asia (India) biological diffusion 72–73 (1)

Puritjarra Australia the world in 10,000 BCE 14–15

Purosottama-Puri South Asia (India) world religions 243 (4)

Purus Sp. Rio Purus river South America colonization 149 (3) early cultures 144 (1), 145 (2), 146 (1) environment 153 (4)

Purusapura mod. Peshwar South Asia (Pakistan) Hellenistic world 224 (1)

Purush Khaddum Southwest Asia (Turkey) first civilizations 221 (4)

Purús, Rio see Purus

Pusan var. Busan; Jap. Fusan East Asia (South Korea) early modern states 267 (4) Islam 275 (4) Russo-Japanese War 270 (4) Sino-Japanese War 270 (3) trade 267 (3) Cold War 109 (4)

Pushkar see Puskara

Pushkari archaeological site Eastern Europe (Russian Federation) the world in 10,000 BCE 14–15

Pusilha Central America (Mexico) first civilizations 123 (2)

Puskalavati South Asia (Pakistan) world religions 242 (2)

Puskara mod. Pushkar South Asia (India) early medieval states 244 (1) world religions 243 (4)

Putan Maya state Central America Aztecs 124 (1)

Puteoli Italy ancient Rome 180–181 (1), 181 (3)

Puttalam South Asia (Sri Lanka) colonialism 247 (3)

Putumayo region South America narcotics 153 (5)

Putumayo var. Rio Içá river South America colonization 148 (2) early cultures 145 (4), 146 (1) empire and revolution 150 (2), 151 (3) environment 153 (4) Incas 148 (1)

Puyang East Asia (China) first religions 37 (4)

Puye archaeological site North America (USA) cultural groups 123 (4)

Puyo East Asia (Korea) medieval states 264 (1), (2)

Puzhou var. Pu-chou East Asia (China) Mongols 68–69 (1)

Pydna battle Greece ancient Greece 179 (4)

Pygela state Greece ancient Greece 177 (2)

Pylos Greece ancient Greece 177 (3), 179 (4) Bronze Age 175 (3) early systems 223 (3) first cities 28–29 (1) first civilizations 175 (4)

Pyongyang prev. Luolang; var. P'yŏngyang-si, P'yŏngyang East Asia (North Korea) Cold War 109 (4) early modern states 267 (4) Islam 275 (4) Sino-Japanese War 270 (3) world religions 49 (3) see also Luolang

P'yŏngyang-si see Luolang, Pyongyang

Pyramid Lake battle North America (USA) the growth of the US 129 (2)

Pyrenaei Montes see Pyrenees

Pyrenees Fr. Pyrénées, Sp. Pirineos; anc. Pyrenaei Montes mountain range France/Iberian Peninsula ancient Rome 179 (3), 180–181 (1), 181 (3) Bronze Age 175 (4) crusades 186 (1), 64–65 (2) early agriculture 174 (1) early Islam 56–57 (1), 57 (2) early modern states 197 (5) economy 190 (1), 205 (4) exploration 172 (1) Franks 183 (5), (6), 184 (2) great migrations 52–53 (1) historical geography 170–171 (1) Islam 192 (3) medieval states 185 (3), 192 (1), (2) Napoleon 200–201 (1) prehistoric culture 17 (3), (4) world religions 48 (1) WWII 210 (1), 211 (4)

Pyrrha state Greece ancient Greece 177 (2)

Pyu region/state Mainland Southeast Asia medieval states 262–263 (1) the world in 750 CE 54–55 world religions 49 (3), (4)

Q

Qâbis see Gabès

Qadesh Southwest Asia (Lebanon) first cities 28–29 (1)

Qadisiya battle Southwest Asia (Iraq) early Islam 56–57 (1)

Qafzeh archaeological site Southwest Asia (Israel) first humans 13 (2), 15 (1)

Qaidam Pendi see Tsaidam Basin

Qalat mod. Kalat South Asia (Pakistan) Mughal Empire 246 (1) see also Kalat

Qalat South Asia Mughal Empire 246 (1)

Qalhat see Kalhat

Qalqut var. Kalikod; mod. Calicut, Kozhikode South Asia (India) early medieval states 244–245 (3) see also Calicut, Kalikod

Qānāq see Thule

Qandahar mod. Kandahar South Asia (Pakistan) early medieval states 244–245 (3) Mughal Empire 246 (1) see also Kandahar

Qandahar South Asia Mughal Empire 246 (1)

Qandahar see Kandahar, Qandahar

Qannauj South Asia (India) early medieval states 244–245 (3)

Qaqortoq see Julianehaab

Qarabagh mod. Karabakh region Southwest Asia medieval Persia 231 (4)

Qaraghandy see Karaganda

Qarakhanids var. Karakhanids state Central Asia early Islam 57 (2) see also Karakhanids

Qarmatians dynasty Southwest Asia early Islam 57 (2) Islam 227 (4), (5)

Qarmatis dynasty South Asia the world in 1000 58–59

Qars see Kars

Qatar colonial possession/state Southwest Asia economy 234 (1) Islam 235 (4) the modern world 113 (3) US economy 138 (2) 20th-century politics 233 (4), 235 (5) Cold War 109 (1)

Qatna Southwest Asia (Syria) ancient Egypt 159 (4), (5)

Qaw Egypt ancient Egypt 159 (2)

Qaw el-Kebir Egypt ancient Egypt 159 (4)

Qazaqstan see Kazakhstan

Qazris see Cáceres

Qazvin var. Kazvin Southwest Asia (Iran) early Islam 56–57 (1) Mongols 229 (3), 68–69 (1) 20th-century politics 235 (5) see also Kazvin

Qeshm Southwest Asia (Iran) economy 234 (1)

Qeshm var. Jazireh-ye Qeshm, Qeshm Island island Southwest Asia economy 234 (1)

Qeshm Island see Qeshm

Qeshm, Jazireh-ye see Qeshm

Qi var. Ch'i region/state East Asia first cities 259 (4), (5) first religions 37 (4)

Qiang East Asia (China) first cities 259 (4)

Qiang state East Asia first cities 259 (4)

Qiang people East Asia first cities 259 (4) first states 260 (1), 261 (2) medieval states 261 (4), (6), 262–263 (1)

Qiantang East Asia (China) first states 260 (1)

Qiemo see Cherchen

Qi Empire var. Ch'i state East Asia the world in 500 CE 50–51

Qift Egypt ancient Egypt 159 (4)

Qilian Shan mountain range East Asia early agriculture 258 (1) early modern states 266 (1) first cities 259 (5) first religions 37 (4) first states 260 (1) trade 267 (3)

Qin state East Asia first cities 259 (4), (5) first religions 37 (4)

Qin Empire state East Asia the world in 250 BCE 38–39 see also China

Qing see Qinghai

Qingdao var. Ching-Tao, Ch'ing-tao, Tsingtao, Tsintao; Ger. Tsingtau East Asia (China) economy 274 (1) imperialism 270 (2) Islam 275 (4) postwar politics 274 (2) Russo-Japanese War 270 (4)

Qingdao var. Tsingtao colonial possession East Asia colonialism 269 (4)

Qing Empire mod. China; var. Manchuria, Ch'ing state East Asia colonialism 248 (1), (2), 269 (3), (4) decolonization 250 (2) economy 249 (4) empire and revolution 249 (3), 88–89 (2) European imperialism 97 (3), (4) Russo-Japanese War 270 (4) Sino-Japanese War 270 (3) see also China

Qinghai var. Chinghai, Qing, Tsinghai province/state East Asia Chinese revolution 271 (5) early modern states 266 (1), (2), 268 (1) empire and revolution 268 (2) postwar economy 275 (3)

Qinghai Hu var. Ch'ing Hai, Tsing Hai, Mong. Koko Nor lake East Asia early modern states 266 (1) first states 260 (1)

Qingjiang East Asia (China) medieval states 263 (3)

Qingliangang archaeological site East Asia (China) early agriculture 258 (2)

Qingtang Xiang state East Asia medieval states 263 (3)

Qingyang rebellion East Asia early modern states 266 (2)

Qingzhou prev. Yidu rebellion/settlement East Asia (China) early modern states 266 (2) medieval states 263 (3)

Qinhuangdao var. Chinwangtao East Asia (China) colonialism 269 (4) postwar politics 274 (2)

Qiong see Hainan

Qiongzhou var. Kiungchow East Asia (China) colonialism 269 (4)

Qita Ghazzah see Gaza Strip

Qizhou military base East Asia early modern states 266 (1)

Qom var. Kum, Qum Southwest Asia (Iran) economy 234 (1)

Qomul see Hami

Quadi people Eastern Europe ancient Rome 180–181 (1), 181 (4)

Quang Tri battle Mainland Southeast Asia (Vietnam) 251 (5)

Quanrong state East Asia first cities 259 (3)

Quanzhou East Asia (China) ancient trade 44–45 (1) medieval states 263 (5) Mongols 68 (2), 68–69 (1) trade 267 (3)

Quapaw people North America colonization 126 (1)

Quarai archaeological site North America (USA) cultural groups 123 (4)

Quban Egypt ancient Egypt 159 (4), (5)

Quebec var. Quebéc North America (Canada) colonization 126 (1) empire and revolution 127 (2), (3) empire and revolution 88 (1)European expansion 84–85 (1) exploration 118 (1), 119 (2), (3) global immigration 100 (1), 101 (3) 129 (2), 132 (3) the world in 1800 86–87, 136 (2)

Quebec colonial possession/province North America empire and revolution 127 (3), (2) 129 (2), 132 (1), 136 (2)

Queen Elizabeth Islands see Parry Islands

Queensland region/state Australia colonization 282 (1), (2), 283 (3)

Queenstown New Zealand colonization 283 (5)

Quelimane var. Kilimane, Kilmain, Quilimane Southern Africa (Mozambique) exploration 157 (4) Islam 163 (1) trade 164 (1)

Quelpart Jap. Saishū; Kor. Cheju-do island East Asia Sino-Japanese War 270 (3) see also Cheju-do

Quemoy var. Chinmen Tao, Jinmen Dao island East Asia Cold War 109 (1) postwar economy 275 (3)

Quentovic France medieval states 185 (3)

Que Que see Kwekwe

Quera see Chur, Curia

Querero South America the world in 10,000 BCE 14–15

Queres people North America colonization 126 (1)

Querétaro Central America Mexican Revolution 133 (3) the growth of the US 129 (2)

Quetta South Asia (Pakistan) Hellenistic world 40–41 (1) postwar politics 252 (1)

Quetzaltepec Central America (Mexico) Aztecs 124 (1)

Qufu East Asia (China) first cities 259 (5) first religions 37 (4)

Quiahuac Central America (Mexico) Aztecs 124 (1)

Quiahuitztlan Central America (Mexico) Aztecs 124 (1)

Quiauhteopan state Central America Aztecs 124 (1)

Quiberon Bay battle France empire and revolution 88 (1)

Quierzy France Franks 184 (2)

Quilimane see Quelimane

Quilon var. Kulam, Kollam South Asia (India) biological diffusion 72–73 (1) colonialism 247 (3)

Quimbaya South America the world in 1200 62–63

Quimbaya Chiefdoms state South America early cultures 146 (1)

Quimper anc. Quimper Corentin France Franks 184 (2)

Quimper Corentin see Quimper

Qui Nhon battle Mainland Southeast Asia (Vietnam) postwar politics 251 (5)

Quintana Roo state Central America Mexican Revolution 133 (3)

Quiriguá Central America (Guatemala) first civilizations 122 (1), 122 (2)

Quirinal Hill Lat. Collis Quirinalis hill Italy ancient Rome 181 (2)

Quirinalis Collis see Quirinal Hill

Quito South America (Ecuador) colonization 148 (2) empire and revolution 150 (1), (2), 151 (3) environment 153 (4) exploration 142 (1), 143 (2), (3) Incas 147 (3), 148 (1) politics 152 (1)

Quito, Presidencia of region South America colonization 148 (2)

Quijaling archaeological site East Asia (China) early agriculture 258 (2)

Qum mod. Qom Southwest Asia (Iran) medieval Persia 231 (4) Mongols 229 (3), 68–69 (1) see also Qom

Qumis Southwest Asia (Iran) early Islam 56–57 (1)

Quonset North America (USA) WWII 104 (2)

Qûqon see Kokand

Qurein see Kuwait

Qus var. Assouan, Assuan, Aswân; anc. Syene Egypt crusades 228 (2) see also Aswân, Syene

R

Rabat var. al Dar al Baida North Africa (Morocco) early Islam 56–57 (1) economy 168 (2)

Rabaul military base/settlement New Guinea (Papua New Guinea) WWII 104 (2), 251 (3), 272 (1), 273 (2)

Rabbah Ammon see Amman

Rabbath Ammon see Amman

Rabeh people Central Africa trade 167 (1)

Racibórz see Ratibor

Radom Central Europe (Poland) empire and revolution 198 (2)

Rae Bareli region South Asia decolonization 250 (1)

Raeti people Italy early states 178 (2)

Raetia var. Rhaetia province Central Europe ancient Rome 180–181 (1) Franks 184 (2)

Rafa see Rafah

Rafah var. Rafa, Rafah; Heb. Rafiaḥ, Raphiah Southwest Asia (Gaza Strip) 20th century 234 (2)

Rafiah see Rafah

Ragusa mod. Dubrovnik Southeast Europe (Croatia) early modern states 193 (4) economy 190 (1) medieval states 188 (1), 189 (4) Ottomans 195 (4), 230 (1), 231 (3) Reformation 194 (2) see also Dubrovnik

Ragusa state Southeast Europe early modern states 193 (4), 194 (1) Ottomans 195 (4), 230 (1), 231 (3) Reformation 194 (2)

Rahanagar South Asia (Bangladesh) postwar politics 252 (3)

Rahovec see Orahovac

Rai see Rayy

Rajagriha South Asia (India) first empires 241 (4) first religions 36 (1), (2),36 (2) world religions 242 (3)

Rajamahendri South Asia (India) early medieval states 244–245 (3), 245 (4)

Rajaratha region South Asia first empires 241 (4)

Rajasthan region/state South Asia postwar politics 252 (1) world religions 243 (4)

Rajgir religious site South Asia (India) first religions 36 (2)

Rajputana region South Asia colonialism 247 (3), 248 (1), (2)

Rajputs people South Asia early medieval states 244–245 (3)

Rajput States state South Asia the world in 1500 74–75

Rakhighari West India early city 240 (2)

Rakka see Raqqa

Rakvere see Wesenberg

Raleigh North America (USA) the growth of the US 129 (2), 132 (1) US Civil War 131 (7) US society 137 (6)

Ramagama South Asia (India) world religions 242 (3)

Ramazan state Southwest Asia the world in 1400 70–71 the world in 1500 74–75

Rameshwaram South Asia (India) world religions 243 (4)

Ramhormoz Southwest Asia (Iran) 20th-century politics 235 (5)

Rampur South Asia (India) colonialism 248 (1) economy 249 (4)

Rampur state South Asia colonialism 248 (2)

Ramsay's Mill North America (USA) empire and revolution 127 (3)

Ramsgate British Isles (United Kingdom) WWI 206 (2), (3)

Rana Ghundai archaeological site South Asia (India) first cities 240 (2)

Ranas Central America (Mexico) first civilizations 122 (1)

Ranchillos South America (Argentina) Incas 147 (3)

Rancho la Chua North America (USA) colonization 125 (4)

Rancho Peludo archaeological site South America (Venezuela) early cultures 144 (1), 145 (2)

Rangiroa island Pacific Ocean exploration 278 (1)

Rangoon var. Yangon; anc. Dagon Mainland Southeast Asia (Burma) colonialism 247 (4), 248 (1), 269 (4) economy 249 (4) European expansion 84–85 (1) European imperialism 97 (3) Islam 235 (4) postwar economy 253 (5) US superpower 138 (1) world religions 243 (5) WWII 251 (3), 272 (1), 273 (2)

Rangpur archaeological site/settlement South Asia (Bangladesh) colonialism 247 (3) first cities 240 (2) postwar politics 252 (3)

Rano Kao see Rano Kau

Rano Kau var. Rano Kao volcano Pacific Ocean early cultures 281 (4)

Rano Raraku archaeological site Easter Island early cultures 281 (4)

Rapa Nui var. Isla de Pascua, Easter Island island Pacific Ocean early cultures 280–281 (3), 281 (4) medieval voyages 60 (1) see also Easter Island

Raphiah see Rafah

Raqqa var. Rakka Southwest Asia (Syria) early Islam 56–57 (1)

Raroia island Pacific Ocean exploration 278 (1)

Ra's al Junayz Southwest Asia (Oman) first civilizations 25 (3)

Ras al Khaimah Ar. Ra's al Khaymah Southwest Asia (United Arab Emirates) economy 234 (1)

Ra's al Khaymah see Ras al Khaimah

Ras Dashen mountain East Africa (Ethiopia) exploration 157 (5)

Ras Shamrah see Ugarit

Ras Tannura oil terminal Southwest Asia (Saudi Arabia) economy 234 (1)

Rasulids dynasty Southwest Asia economy 163 (2)

Rataria Christian archbishopric Southeast Europe (Bulgaria) world religions 48 (1)

Ratibor mod. Racibórz Central Europe (Poland) medieval states 189 (4)

Ratisbon anc. Castra Regina, Regimum; hist. Ratisbona; Fr. Ratisbonne, Ger. Regensburg massacre/settlement Central Europe (Germany) crusades 186 (1) early modern states 193 (4) medieval states 189 (4) Napoleon 200–201 (1) see also Castra Regina, Regensburg

Ratisbona see Castra Regina, Ratisbon, Regensburg

Ratisbonne see Castra Regina, Ratisbon, Regensburg

Ratmagiri South Asia (India) exploration 256 (1)

Ratomagus see Rotomagus

Raukawa see Cook Strait

Ravenna Italy ancient Rome 180–181 (1), 181 (4), 182 (1) economy 190 (1) Franks 184 (2) great migrations 52–53 (1) medieval states 182 (2), 183 (4) Ottomans 230 (1) world religions 48 (1) early modern states 194 (1)

Ravenna, Exarchate of state Italy medieval states 183 (4)

Ravensberg region Central Europe empire and revolution 199 (3)

Ravensbrück concentration camp Central Europe WWII 211 (3)

Ravi river South Asia colonialism 247 (3) early medieval states 244 (1), (2), 244–245 (3) economy 249 (4) Marathas 246 (2) Mughal Empire 246 (1)

Rawak Buddhist center East Asia (China) world religions 49 (3)

Rawalpindi South Asia (Pakistan) postwar economy 253 (5)

Rawson South America (Argentina) empire and revolution 151 (3)

Ray see Rayy

Rayigama South Asia (Sri Lanka) early medieval states 244–245 (3)

Raysut Southwest Asia (Oman) early Islam 56–57 (1) medieval voyages 61 (3)

Rayy var. Rai, Ray, Rey; anc. Rhagae Southwest Asia (Iran) biological diffusion 72–73 (1) Islam 227 (5) Mongols 229 (3), 68–69 (1)

Real Alto archaeological site/settlement South America (Ecuador) early cultures 144 (1)

Reao leper colony Pacific Ocean environmentalism 285 (2)

Reate Italy early states 178 (1)

Recife var. Pernambuco; Dut. Mauritsstad South America (Brazil) colonization 149 (3), (4) economy 153 (3) environment 153 (4) exploration 142 (1), 143 (2) politics 152 (1) see also Pernambuco

Recuay South America (Peru) early cultures 145 (4)

Recuay region South America early cultures 145 (4)

Reddis dynasty South Asia the world in 1400 70–71

Red River var. Yuan, Chin. Yuan Jiang, Vtn. Sông Hông Ha river East Asia ancient India 241 (6) Bronze Age 240 (3) colonialism 247 (4), (5) early medieval states 245 (5), (6) postwar politics 251 (5) world religions 243 (5)

Redruth British Isles (United Kingdom) economy 204 (1)

Red Sea anc. Sinus Arabicus sea Africa/Asia ancient Egypt 159 (2), (3), (4), (5) ancient Persia 223 (4) ancient Rome 180–181 (1), 181 (4), 224 (2) ancient trade 44–45 (1), 72–73 (1) crusades 65 (3) early agriculture 158 (1) early Islam 56–57 (1) early medieval states 160 (1), 161 (2), (3), (4), (5) economy 163 (2), (3) exploration 172 (1) first civilizations 24 (2), (3) Islam 226 (2)(s)

Redstone Fort North America (USA) empire and revolution 127 (3)

Reefton see Reef Town

Reef Town mod. Reefton New Zealand colonization 283 (5)

Reged region British Isles medieval states 183 (3)

Regensburg anc. Castra Regina, Regimum; Eng. Ratisbon; hist. Ratisbona; Fr. Ratisbonne Central Europe (Germany) crusades 64–65 (2), 65 (1) economy 190 (1) see also Castra Regina, Ratisbon

Reggio var. Reggio di Calabria; anc Rhegium Italy economy 190 (1) medieval states 188 (1) Ottomans 231 (3) see also Rhegium

Regillus Lacus lake Italy early states 178 (1)

Regina North America (Canada) the growth of the US 129 (2)

Reginum see Castra Regina, Ratisbon, Regensburg

Reichenau Central Europe (Poland) Franks 184 (2)

Reichskommissariat-Ostland region Eastern Europe WWII 211 (3)

Reichskommissariat-Ukraine region Eastern Europe WWII 211 (2)

Reims see Durocortorum, Rheims

Reindeer Lake lake North America the growth of the US 129 (2)

Reine-Élisabeth, Îles de la see Queen Elizabeth Islands

Réunion prev. Bourbon colonial possession/island/state Indian Ocean European expansion 84–85 (1) European imperialism 96 (1) global immigration 101 (3)

Reval Rus. Revel; mod. Tallinn Eastern Europe (Estonia) crusades 186 (1) early modern states 195 (3) economy 190 (1) medieval states 189 (3) see also Revel, Tallinn

Revel Eastern Europe (Estonia) early modern states 197 (3) Soviet Union 208 (2)

Revillagigedo Islands see Revillagigedo, Islas

Revillagigedo, Islas Eng. Revillagigedo Islands island group North America the modern world 110–111

Rewardashur Christian archbishopric Southwest Asia (Iran) world religions 48 (1)

Rey see Rayy

Reykjavik Europe (Iceland) exploration 287 (2) medieval voyages 60–61 (1) WWII 104 (2)

Rezā'īyeh, Daryācheh-ye see Urmia, Lake

Rha river Southwest Asia ancient trade 44 (2)

Rhaetia var. Raetia province/region Central Europe Franks 183 (6) world religions 48 (1) see also Raetia

Rhagae Southwest Asia (Iran) Hellenistic world 40–41 (1)

Rhapta East Africa (Ethiopia) ancient trade 44 (2)

Rhegium var. Reggio; mod. Reggio di Calabria Italy ancient Rome 179 (3), 180–181 (1) early states 178 (1) first civilizations 177 (2) see also Reggio

Rheims France ancient Rome 182 (1) economy 190 (1) Franks 183 (5), (6), 184 (2) medieval states 185 (3), 188 (1), (2), Napoleon 200–201 (1) WWI 206 (2), (3)

Rhein see Rhine

Rhenus see Rhine

Rhin see Rhine

Rhine Dut. Rijn, Fr. Rhin, Ger. Rhein; Lat. Rhenus river Central Europe, Low Countries ancient Rome 180–181 (1), 181 (3), (4) ancient trade 44–45 (1) biological diffusion 72–73 (1) Bronze Age 175 (3) Copper Age 174 (2) crusades 186 (1), 64–65 (2) early agriculture 174 (1), 20–21 (2) early Islam 56–57 (1) early modern states 193 (4), (5) economy 190 (1) empire and revolution 199 (3), (4), 202 (1), (2), (3) exploration 172 (1) first humans 13 (2) great migrations 52–53 (1), 53 (2) medieval states 182 (2), 185 (3), 188 (1), 189 (4) Napoleon 200–201 (1), 201 (2), (3) prehistoric culture 16 (1) Reformation 195 (5), 196 (1) world religions 48 (1) WWI 206 (2), (3) WWII 210 (1), 211 (4)

Rhine, Confederation of the state Central Europe Napoleon 201 (2)

Rhodanus see Rhône

Rhode Iberian Peninsula (Spain) ancient Rome 179 (3)

Rhode Island colonial possession/state North America empire and revolution 127 (2), (3) the growth of the US 129 (1) US Civil War 130 (2), (5) US economy 134 (2)

Rhodes Greece (Rhodes) ancient Greece 177 (3), 179 (4) early Islam 56–57 (1) economy 190 (1) Hellenistic world 40–41 (1) medieval states 187 (5) Ottomans 231 (3) world religions 48 (1) Islam 226 (2)(s)

Rhodes, var. Ródhos Gk. Ródos; Lat. Rhodus, It. Rodi state/island Greece ancient Greece 177 (2), (3), 179 (4) ancient Rome 180–181 (1), 181 (4), (s), 72–73 (1) crusades 65 (3) early agriculture 158 (1) early Islam 56–57 (1), 57 (2) early cultures 160 (1), 161 (2), (3), (4), (5) early Islam 56–57 (1), 57 (2) first civilizations 175 (4), 177 (1), (2), 221 (5) Islam 226 (2) medieval states 187 (5) Ottomans 230 (1) postwar politics 212 (3)

Rhodesia mod. Zimbabwe; prev.

Southern Rhodesia state Southern Africa the world in 1975 106–107 see also Southern Rhodesia, Zimbabwe

Rhodos see Rhodes

Rhodus Greece ancient Rome 180–181 (1)

Rhône Lat. Rhodanus river France ancient Rome 180–181 (1), 181 (3) ancient trade 44–45 (1) biological diffusion 72–73 (1) Bronze Age 175 (3) Copper Age 174 (2) crusades 186 (1), 64–65 (2) early agriculture 174 (1) early Islam 56–57 (1) early modern states 193 (4), (5) economy 190 (1), 205 (4) first civilizations 177 (1) Franks 183 (5), (6), 184 (2) great migrations 52–53 (1), 53 (2) medieval states 185 (3), 188 (1) Napoleon 200–201 (1), 201 (2) postwar politics 212 (3) Reformation 194 (2) Soviet Union 214–215 (4) WWI 207 (4) WWII 211 (4), (3), (4) Cold War 108 (3)

Rialto Bridge bridge Italy economy 191 (3)

Ribe Scandinavia (Denmark) medieval voyages 60–61 (1)

Ribeira Grande var. Concelho de Ribeira Grande island Atlantic Ocean the world in 1500 74–75

Richmond North America (USA) colonization 126 (1) empire and revolution 127 (3) European expansion 84–85 (1) the growth of the US 129 (2), 132 (1) US Civil War 130 (5), 131 (6), (7) US society 137 (6)

Rievaulx major cistercian house British Isles (United Kingdom) medieval states 187 (3)

Rift Valley see Great Rift Valley

Riga Latv. Rīga settlement Eastern Europe (Latvia) biological diffusion 72–73 (1) crusades 186 (1) early modern states 193 (4), 195 (3) economy 190 (1), 205 (4) empire and revolution 198 (2), 202 (1) medieval states 189 (3) Napoleon 200–201 (1), 201 (2) postwar politics 212 (3) Reformation 194 (2) world religions 48 (1), 49 (4) WWII 210 (1), 211 (2), (4) Cold War 108 (2)

Rigaer Bucht see Riga, Gulf of

Riga, Gulf of Est. Liivi Laht, Ger. Rigaer Bucht, Latv. Rīgas Jūras Līcis, Rus. Rizhskiy Zaliv; prev. Est. Riia Laht gulf Eastern Europe WWII 207 (4)

Rīgas Jūras Līcis see Riga, Gulf of

Riia Laht see Riga, Gulf of

Rijeka anc. Tarsatica; Ger. Sankt Veit am Flaum; It. Fiume; Slvn. Reka Southeast Europe (Croatia) postwar economy 215 (3)

Rijn see Rhine

Rijssel see Lille

Rim archaeological site/settlement West Africa (Burkina) early agriculture 158 (1) early cultures 160 (1)

Rimini anc. Ariminum Italy economy 190 (1) medieval states 183 (4), 188 (1) see also Ariminum

Rinaldone Italy the world in 2500 BCE 22–23

Rinan province Mainland Southeast Asia first states 260 (1)

Ringsted Scandinavia (Sweden) medieval voyages 60–61 (1)

Rio see Rio de Janeiro

Riobamba South America (Equador) Incas 147 (3)

Rio Barbate battle Iberian Peninsula (Spain) early Islam 56–57 (1)

Rio Bec Central America (Mexico) first civilizations 123 (2)

Rio Branco South America (Brazil) politics 152 (1)

Rio de Janeiro var. Rio; hist. São Sebastião de Rio de Janeiro South America (Brazil) colonization 149 (3), (4) economy 153 (3) empire and revolution 151 (3) environment 153 (4) European expansion 84–85 (1) exploration 143 (2), (3) global immigration 100 (1) imperial global economy 92 (1) politics 152 (1)

Rio de Janeiro region South America colonization 149 (3)

Rio de la Hacha South America (Columbia) European expansion 85 (2)

Rio de la Plata, Viceroyalty of colonial possession South America colonization 148 (2) empire and revolution 150 (1) European expansion 84–85 (1)

Rio de Oro later Spanish Sahara; mod. Western Sahara state North Africa the world in 1900 94–95 the world in 1925 98–99 see also Spanish Sahara, Western Sahara

Rio Grande var. Rio Grande do Sul; hist. São Pedro de Rio Grande do Sul South America (Brazil) colonization 149 (3) empire and revolution 151 (3) environment 153 (4)

Rio Grande do Sul region South America colonization 149 (3)

Rioni France ancient Rome 182 (1) economy 190 (1) Franks 183 (5), (6), 184 (2) medieval states 185 (3), 188 (1), (2), Napoleon 200–201 (1) WWI 206 (2), (3)

Rio Muni state Central Africa European imperialism 96 (1)

Ripuarian Franks people Central Europe Franks 183 (5)

Riverton settlement/whaling station New Zealand colonization 283 (4), (5)

Rivière au Vase North America (USA) cultural groups 122 (5)

Rivoli var. Rivoli Veronese battle Italy Napoleon 200–201 (1)

Rivoli Veronese see Rivoli

Riyadh Ar. Ar Riyāḍ Southwest Asia (Saudi Arabia) economy 234 (1) exploration 219 (4) 20th-century politics 233 (4), 235 (5)

Rizhskiy Zaliv see Riga, Gulf of

Roanoke river North America empire and revolution 127 (3)

Roazon see Rennes

Roccatrada Italy economy 190 (1)

Roc de Sers archaeological site France prehistoric culture 17 (2)

Rochdale Canal canal British Isles economy 204 (2)

Rochefort France early modern states 197 (5)

Rock Eagle North America (USA) cultural groups 122 (5)

Rockhampton Australia colonization 282 (1), 283 (3)

Rocks Point sealing station New Zealand colonization 283 (4)

Rocky Mountains mountain range North America colonization 125 (4), 126 (1) early agriculture 120 (1), 20–21 (2) exploration 118 (1), 119 (2), (3), 286 (1), 287 (2) prehistoric culture 16 (1) the growth of the US 129 (2)

Rōdhos see Rhodes

Ródos see Rhodes

Rodrigues var. Rodriquez island Indian Ocean the modern world 110–111

Rodriquez see Rodrigues

Roebourne Australia exploration 279 (2)

Roazon see Rennes

Rojadi South Asia (India) first civilizations 24 (2)

Roma var. Rome. Italy ancient trade 44 (2)

Romagna state Italy empire and revolution 202 (3)

Romanelli Southern Europe (Italy)

Roman Empire state Europe/Africa ancient Persia 225 (6) ancient Rome 181 (4), 224 (2), 225 (5) ancient trade 44–45 (1) early cultures 161 (3), (4) early trade 225 (3) great migrations 53 (2) global immigration 226 (1), 49 (4)

Romania Bul. Rumŭniya, Ger. Rumänien, Hung. Románia, Rom. România, SCr. Rumunija, Ukr. Rumuniya; prev. Roumania, Rumania, România state/vassal state Southeast Europe early 20th century 206 (1) economy 205 (4) interwar 209 (3), (5) medieval states 187 (5) Ottomans 202 (4), 232–233 (1) postwar economy 213 (5), 214 (1), (2), 215 (3) postwar politics 212 (3) Soviet Union 208 (2), 213 (4) the modern world 112 (2) WWI 207 (4), (6), 208 (1) WWII 104 (2), 210 (1), 211 (2), (3), (4) Cold War 108 (3), 109 (1)

Rome state Italy the world in 250 BCE 38–39

Rome, Duchy of state Italy medieval states 183 (4)

Rominia see Romania

Roncesvalles battle Iberian Peninsula (Spain) Franks 184 (2)

Rong people East Asia first cities 259 (3)

Ronne Ice Shelf ice feature Antarctica Antarctic Exploration 287 (3)

Roonka Australia exploration 280 (1)

Roque River battle North America (USA) the growth of the US 129 (2)

Rorke's Drift battle Southern Africa (South Africa) European imperialism 96 (2)

Rosario South America (Argentina) empire and revolution 151 (3) environment 153 (4)

Rosario var. Rosario de Tezopaco mine/settlement Central America (Mexico) colonization 125 (4) Mexican Revolution 133 (3)

Rosario de Tezopaco see Rosario

Rosenkrans burial mound North America (USA) first civilizations 121 (4)

Roskilde Scandinavia (Denmark) early modern states 197 (3) medieval states 185 (3)

Ross New Zealand colonization 283 (5)

Ross Ice Shelf ice feature Antarctica Antarctic Exploration 287 (3)

Rossiyskaya Federatsiya see Russia, Russian Empire, Russian Federation, Soviet Union, Union of Socialist Republics

Ross Sea sea Antarctica Antarctic Exploration 287 (3)

Rostock Central Europe (Germany) economy 190 (1), 205 (4) empire and revolution 202 (2) medieval states 189 (3)

Rostov var. Rostov-on-Don Eastern Europe (Russian Federation) biological diffusion 72–73 (1) medieval states 185 (3) Soviet Union 208 (2), 214–215 (4) WWII 210 (1), 211 (4)

Rostov-on-Don see Rostov

Rotomagus var. Ratomagus; mod Rouen Christian archbishopric/settlement France ancient Rome 180–181 (1) world religions 48 (1) see also Rouen

Rotterdam air raid Low Countries WWII 210 (1)

Rottweil Central Europe (Germany) early modern states 193 (5)

Rouad see Aradus

Rouen anc. Ratomagus, Rotomagus France crusades 65 (1) early modern states 197 (5) economy 190 (1) empire and revolution 199 (4) Franks 184 (2) medieval states 185 (3), 186 (2), 187 (4), 192 (1), (2) medieval voyages 60–61 (1) Napoleon 200–201 (1), 201 (2) WWI 206 (2), (3) see also Rotomagus

Roumania see Romania

Roussillon region/state France/Iberian Peninsula early modern states 197 (5) medieval states 192 (2)

Rovereto see Rovreit

Rovine battle Southeast Europe (Romania) medieval states 189 (4)

Rovreit It. Rovereto Italy WWI 207 (5)

Rovuma see Ruvuma

Roxolani people Eastern Europe ancient Rome 180–181 (1)

Royal Military Canal canal British Isles economy 204 (1)

Royal Palace building France economy 191 (2)

Royal Prussia region Central Europe early modern states 193 (4), 195 (3)

Rozwi state Southern Africa slave trade 165 (4) trade 164 (1)

Ruanda see Rwanda

Ruanda-Urundi mod. Burundi, Rwanda state East Africa WWII 104 (1)

Ruaruran var. Ruan East Asia medieval states 261 (4), (6)

Ruapuke Island whaling station New Zealand colonization 283 (4)

Rubuga East Africa (Tanzania) exploration 157 (4)

Rudolf, Lake var. Lake Turkana lake East Africa early agriculture 158 (1) exploration 157 (4), (5) first humans 12 (1) Islam 163 (1) slave trade 165 (4) trade 165 (3)

Rufiji river East Africa exploration 157 (5)

Ruhr region Central Europe empire and revolution 199 (4) WWI 208 (1)

Rum state Southwest Asia economy 190 (1)

Rumania see Romania

343

Szeged *Ger.* Szegedin, *Rom.* Seghedin Central Europe (Hungary) early modern states 193 (4) medieval states 189 (4)

Szegedin *see* Szeged

Székesfehérvár *anc.* Alba Regia; *Ger.* Stuhlweissenberg Central Europe (Hungary) medieval states 188 (1)

Szemao *see* Simao

Szigetvár Central Europe (Hungary) Ottomans 231 (3)

Sziszek *see* Sisak

Szlovákia *see* Slovakia

T

Tabaristan *state* Central Asia early Islam 56–57 (1)

Tabariya, Bahr, Tabariya, Bahrat *see* Galilee, Sea of

Tabasco *state* Central America Mexican Revolution 133 (3) the growth of the US 129 (2)

Tabon Cave Philippines (Philippines) the world in 10,000 BCE 14–15

Tábor Central Europe (Czech Republic) early modern states 193 (4)

Tabora *var.* Unyanyembe, Kazeh East Africa (Tanzania) exploration 157 (4), (5)

Tabriz Southwest Asia (Iran) biological diffusion 72–73 (1) exploration 218 (2), 219 (3) Islam 226 (2), 227 (4), (5) medieval Persia 231 (4) Mongols 68 (2), 68–69 (1) Ottomans 231 (3) Seljuks 228 (1) Soviet Union 208 (2) Timur 229 (4) world religions 226 (1) WWI 233 (2) 20th-century politics 233 (3), 235 (5)

Tabuk Philippines early Islam 56–57 (1)

Tabun *archaeological site* Southwest Asia (Israel) first humans 13 (2)

Tacna South America (Peru) empire and revolution 150 (1), 151 (3) politics 151 (4)

Tacna *region* South America politics 151 (4)

Tacuba Central America (Mexico) Aztecs 124 (2) colonization 125 (5)

Tacubaya Central America (Mexico) Aztecs 124 (2)

Tadmor *var.* Tamar Southwest Asia (Syria) first civilizations 222 (1)

Tadmor *see* Palmyra

Tadmur *see* Palmyra

Tadzhikistan *see* Tajikistan

Taegu East Asia (South Korea) Cold War 109 (4)

Taehan-haehyóp *see* Korea Strait

Taehan Min'guk *see* South Korea

Taejon *Jap.* Taiden East Asia (South Korea) Cold War 109 (4)

Tafahi *island* Pacific Ocean exploration 278 (1)

Taforalt *archaeological site* North Africa (Algeria) first humans 13 (2)

Taga Japan early modern states 265 (5) medieval states 264 (2), 265 (3), (4)

Taghaza West Africa (Mauritania) exploration 156 (3) Islam 163 (1)

Tagish *people* North America cultural groups 123 (3)

Tagliacozzo *battle* Italy medieval states 188 (1)

Tagliamento *river* Italy WWI 207 (5)

Tagus *Port.* Rio Tejo, *Sp.* Rio Tajo *river* Iberian Peninsula ancient Rome 180–181 (1) Bronze Age 175 (3) Copper Age 174 (2) crusades 64–65 (2) early agriculture 174 (1) economy 190 (1), 205 (4) first civilizations 177 (1) Franks 184 (2) great migrations 52–53 (1), 53 (2) interwar 209 (4) Islam 192 (3) Napoleon 200–201 (1), 201 (2) prehistoric culture 17 (3)

Tahert North Africa (Algeria) early Islam 56–57 (1) Islam 163 (1)

Tahirids *dynasty* Central Asia Islam 227 (4)

Tahiti *island* Pacific Ocean colonization 284–285 (1) early cultures 280–281 (3) environmentalism 285 (2) exploration 278 (1), 279 (3) medieval voyages 60 (2)

Tahltan *people* North America cultural groups 123 (3)

Ta'if *Ar.* Al Ta'if Southwest Asia (Saudi Arabia) early Islam 56–57 (1) Islam 226 (3) world religions 226 (1) 20th-century politics 233 (3)

Tai Hu *lake* East Asia early modern states 266 (1) first states 260 (1)

Taiji *var.* Imperial Palace *palace* East Asia (China) medieval states 262 (2)

Taima Taima *archaeological site/settlement* South America (Venezuela) early cultures 144 (1)

Taimyr Peninsula *see* Taymyr, Poluostrov

Taipei East Asia (Taiwan) Islam 275 (4)

Taiping *military campaign* East Asia empire and revolution 88–89 (2)

Taira Japan economy 270 (1)

Tairona *state* South America the world in 1200 62–63

Tairona Chiefdoms *state* South America early cultures 146 (1)

Tai Shan *var.* T'ai Shan *mountain* East Asia first religions 37 (4)

Taiwan *var.* Formosa *prev.* China, Republic of *island/state* East Asia ancient trade 44–45 (1) colonialism 269 (4) decolonization 251 (4), 285 (3) early agriculture 258 (1) early modern states 266 (2), 268 (1) empire and revolution 268 (2) European imperialism 97 (3) first cities 259 (4), (5) first religions 37 (4) first states 260 (1), 261 (2), (3) historical geography 236–237 (1) imperialism 270 (2) Islam 275 (4) medieval states 261 (4), (5), 262–263 (1), 263 (3), (4), (5), (6) Mongols 68–69 (1) postwar economy 253 (5), 275 (3) postwar politics 271 (7) the growth of the US 133 (4) the modern world 113 (4) WWII 251 (3) Communist revolution 274 (1) Cold War 109 (1)

Taiwan *see also* China, Republic of, Formosa

Taiwanese *rebellion* East Asia empire and revolution 268 (2)

Taixicun East Asia early modern states 259 (3)

Taiyuan *prev.* T'ai-yuan, T'ai-yüan, Yangku East Asia (China) biological diffusion 72–73 (1) early modern states 266 (1) economy 274 (1) Islam 275 (4) medieval states 263 (3), (6), 263 (4), (5) postwar politics 271 (7), 274 (2)

Tajikistan *Rus.* Tadzhikistan, *Taj.* Tojikiston *state* Central Asia Islam 235 (4) postwar economy 275 (3) Soviet Union 214–215 (4) the modern world 113 (3)

Tajiks *people* Central Asia historical geography 275 (5)

Tajo, Rio *see* Tagus

Takamatsu *battle* Japan early modern states 267 (4)

Takaoka Japan economy 270 (1)

Takeda *region* Japan early modern states 267 (4)

Takeda West Africa (Mali/Niger) exploration 156 (3)

Ta Kieu Mainland Southeast Asia (Vietnam) ancient India 241 (6)

Takkola Mainland Southeast Asia (Thailand) ancient India 241 (6)

Takla Makan Desert *Chin.* Taklimakan Shamo *desert* East Asia ancient trade 44–45 (1) biological diffusion 72–73 (1) colonialism 269 (4) early agriculture 258 (1) empire and revolution 268 (2) (1) exploration 256 (1), 257 (3) first cities 259 (5) first states 260 (1) medieval states 261 (6), 262–263 (1) Mongols 68–69 (1) trade 267 (3) world religions 49 (3), (4)

Taklimakan Shamo *see* Takla Makan Desert

Takoradi West Africa (Ghana) colonization 167 (4)

Takrur *var.* Toucouleur *state* West Africa Islam 163 (1) trade 163 (4), (6), (7)

Taksashila *var.* Taxila South Asia (Pakistan) early medieval states 244 (1) early empires 241 (4)

Taksashila *see also* Taxila

Takume *island* Pacific Ocean exploration 278 (1)

Takushan *see* Dagushan

Talasea *island* Pacific Ocean early cultures 280–281 (3) medieval voyages 60 (2)

Talas River *battle* Central Asia (Kazakhstan) early Islam 56–57 (1) Islam 226 (2)

Talavera *var.* Talavera de la Reina Iberian Peninsula (Spain) Napoleon 200–201 (1)

Talavera de la Reina *see* Talavera

Talca South America (Chile) empire and revolution 150 (1), 151 (3) environment 153 (4) Incas 147 (3)

Talcahuano *battle* South America (Chile) empire and revolution 150 (1)

Talgai Australia exploration 280 (1)

Ta-lien *see* Dairen, Dalian

Tal-i Ghazir Southwest Asia (Iran) first cities 220 (2)

Tal-i Iblis Southwest Asia (Iran) first civilizations 24 (2)

Tal-i Malyan Southwest Asia (Iran) first cities 220 (2)

Tallahassee *prev.* Muskogean North America (USA) the growth of the US 129 (2) US Civil War 131 (6), (7) US society 137 (6)

Tallasahatchee *battle* North America (USA) the growth of the US 129 (2)

Tallin *see* Reval, Tallinn

Tallinn *Ger.* Reval, *Rus.* Tallin, Revel Eastern Europe (Estonia) postwar politics 212 (1) Soviet Union 214–215 (4)

Tallinn *see also* Reval, Revel

Tall-i Qaleh Southwest Asia (Iran) first civilizations 25 (3)

Taltal South America (Chile) politics 151 (4)

Tamanrasset *var.* Tamenghest North Africa (Algeria) colonization 167 (4)

Tamar *see* Palmyra, Tadmor

Tamar Hat *archaeological site* North Africa (Algeria) prehistoric culture 17 (2)

Tamatsukuri Japan early modern states 265 (5)

Tamaulipas *state* Central America Mexican Revolution 133 (3) the growth of the US 129 (2)

Tamazultec *people* Central America colonization 125 (5)

Tambo Colorado South America (Peru) Incas 147 (3)

Tambora *island* Maritime Southeast Asia European expansion 84–85 (1)

Tambov Eastern Europe (Russian Federation) Soviet Union 208 (2)

Tambo Viejo South America (Peru) early cultures 145 (4)

Tambralinga Mainland Southeast Asia (Thailand) ancient India 241 (6) early medieval states 245 (5)

Tambralinga *region* Mainland Southeast Asia early medieval states 245 (5)

Tame South America (Colombia) empire and revolution 150 (1)

Tamenghest *see* Tamanrasset

Tamil Nadu *region* South Asia postwar politics 252 (1) world religions 243 (4)

Tamluk *religious site/settlement* South Asia (India) ancient trade 44–45 (1) first religions 36 (2)

Tammaulipeco *people* Central America colonization 126 (1)

Tampa North America (USA) Cold War 108 (2)

Tampico Central America (Mexico) colonization 125 (4), 126 (1) exploration 118 (1) Mexican Revolution 133 (3) the growth of the US 129 (2) Cold War 108 (2)

Tamralipti South Asia early medieval states 244 (1) early religions 48 (2) first empires 241 (4) world religions 242 (2), (3)

Tamuin Central America (Mexico) first civilizations 122 (1)

Tamworth British Isles (United Kingdom) medieval states 183 (3)

Tana Eastern Europe (Russian Federation) economy 190 (1) Ottomans 195 (4)

T'ana Häyk' *see* Tana, Lake

Tanais *see* Don

Tana, Lake *var.* T'ana Häyk' *lake* East Asia early cultures 161 (3), (4), (5) early trade 225 (3) exploration 157 (5) first humans 12 (1), 13 (2) trade 165 (3)

Tanana *people* North America cultural groups 123 (3)

Tanana *river* North America imperial global economy 93 (3)

Tanasari Mainland Southeast Asia (Burma) trade 230 (2)

Tanchon East Asia (North Korea) Cold War 109 (4)

Tanchou *see* Tanzhou

Tanegashima *island* Japan early modern states 265 (5) Communism 273 (3)

Tang *vassal state* East Asia first states 259 (3)

Tangana *state* South Asia first empires 241 (5)

Tanganhuato Central America (Mexico) first civilizations 122 (1)

Tanganyika *mod.* Tanzania; *prev.* German East Africa *colonial possession* East Africa WWII 104 (1) Cold War 109 (1)

Tanganyika *see also* German East Africa, Tanzania

Tanganyika, Lake *lake* East Africa early cultures 160 (1) economy 163 (2) European imperialism 96 (1) exploration 156 (3), 157 (4), (5) first humans 12 (1), 13 (2) Islam 163 (1) slave trade 165 (4)

Tang Empire *state* East Asia medieval states 262–263 (1) world religions 49 (4)

Tanggula Shan *see* Tanglha Range

Tangier *var.* Tangiers; *anc.* Tingis; *Fr./Ger.* Tanger, *Sp.* Tánger North Africa (Morocco) early Islam 57 (2) economy 163 (2) European imperialism 96 (1) exploration 156 (3), 157 (4) interwar 209 (4) Islam 163 (1), 192 (3) Mongols 68 (2) Napoleon 200–201 (1), 201 (2) world religions 48 (1)

Tangiers *see* Tangier, Tingis

Tangjin North Africa (South Korea) Sino-Japanese War 270 (2)

Tanglha Range *Chin.* Tanggula Shan *mountain range* East Asia exploration 257 (3)

Tang Protectorate *see* Ferghana

Tanguts *people* East Asia early modern states 266 (1) medieval states 263 (3) trade 267 (3)

Tangxiang *state* East Asia medieval states 263 (3)

Tanis *var.* Avaris Egypt ancient Egypt 159 (5) first civilizations 221 (5)

Tanis *see also* Avaris

Tanjore *var.* Thanjavur South Asia (India) colonialism 248 (1) economy 249 (4) Mughal Empire 246 (1)

Tanjore *region* South Asia (India) colonialism 248 (1) Marathas 246 (2) Mughal Empire 246 (1)

Tanjungpura Maritime Southeast Asia (Indonesia) early medieval states 245 (6) early modern states 239 (1) world religions 243 (5)

Tannenberg *var.* Grunwald *battle* Central Europe (Poland) early modern states 193 (4) WWI 207 (4)

Tannu Tuva *var.* Uriankhai, Uryankhai *region/island* Australia colonization 282 (1), (2), 283 (3) exploration 276–277 (1), 279 (2), (3) medieval voyages 60 (2)

Tan-Tan *state* Mainland Southeast Asia ancient India 241 (6)

Tan-tung *see* Andong, Dandong

Tanzania *prev.* German East Africa, Tanganyika and Zanzibar, *state* East Africa decolonization 168 (1) economy 168 (2), (3), the modern world 112 (1), 113 (3), (4)

Tanzania *see also* German East Africa, Tanganyika, Zanzibar

Tanzhou *var.* Tanchou East Asia (China) medieval states 262–263 (1), 263 (4) first states 259 (3)

Taodeni *Fr.* Taoudenni, Taoudenit West Africa (Mali) Islam 163 (1)

Taos North America (USA) colonization 126 (1) exploration 119 (3)

Taos *people* North America cultural groups 123 (3)

Taos *settlement* see Taodeni, Taoudenni

Taoudenni *var.* Taoudenit, Taodeni West Africa (Mali) colonization 167 (4)

Taoudenni *see also* Taodeni

Taourirt North Africa (Morocco) Islam 163 (1)

Tapajojó *people* South America early cultures 147 (2)

Tapajós *state* South America the world in 1500 74–75

Tapajós *var.* Tapajóz *river* South America colonization 149 (3) early cultures 144 (1), 145 (2) empire and revolution 151 (3) environment 153 (4) exploration 143 (2), 143 (3)

Tapajoz *var.* Santarém *region* South America early cultures 145 (2)

Tapajóz *see* Tapajós

Tapasha *region* South Asia world religions 242 (2)

Taprobane *var.* Sarandib, Saylan, Sri Lanka *island* South Asia ancient trade 44 (2) world religions 49 (3)

Taprobane *see also* Ceylon, Lambakannas, Lanka, Simhala, Sri Lanka

Taquira Tradition *people* South America the world in 1000 58–59

Tara Eastern Europe (Russian Federation) exploration 257 (2)

Ṭarābulus *see* Tripoli, Tripolis

Ṭarābulus al Gharb *see* Oea, Tripoli

Ṭarābulus ash Shām *see* Tripoli, Tripolis

Taradavadi South Asia (India) early medieval states 244 (2)

Tarahumara *people* Central America colonization 125 (4)

Tarahumara *military campaign* Maritime Southeast Asia WWII 273 (2)

Tarakan *island* Maritime Southeast Asia WWII 273 (2)

Tarazona Iberian Peninsula (Spain) medieval states 187 (3)

Tardanizats *rebel faction* France Reformation 196 (2)

Tarentaise France Franks 184 (2)

Tarentum *var.* Tarantum; *mod.* Taranto Italy ancient Rome 179 (3), (5) early states 178 (1), (2) first civilizations 177 (1)

Tarentum *see also* Taranto, Tarentum

Targoviṣte *see* Türgoviṣte

Târgu-Jiu *battle* Southeast Europe (Romania) WWI 207 (6)

Târgușor *prev.* Tîrgușor Southeast Europe (Romania) world religions 48 (1)

Tari South Asia (India) first cities 259 (5)

Tarifa Iberian Peninsula (Spain) Islam 192 (3)

Tarim *river* East Asia exploration 257 (3) first states 260 (1) medieval states 262–263 (1) Mongols 68–69 (1)

Tarkhan Egypt ancient Egypt 159 (2)

Tarma South America (Peru) Incas 147 (3)

Tarnow Central Europe (Poland) WWI 207 (4)

Taroudant *var.* Taroudannt North Africa (Morocco) Islam 163 (1)

Taroudant *see* Taroudannt

Tarquinia *var.* Tarquinii, *hist.* Corneto Italy early states 178 (1), (2) first civilizations 177 (1)

Tarraco *mod.* Tarragona *settlement* Iberian Peninsula (Spain) ancient Rome 179 (3), 180–181 (1), 181 (3), (4), 225 (5) early cultures 161 (2) great migrations 52–53 (1) world religions 48 (1) see also Tarragona

Tarraconensis *province* Iberian peninsula ancient Rome 180–181 (1)

Tarragona Iberian Peninsula (Spain) ancient Rome 182 (1) interwar 209 (4) Islam 192 (3) medieval states 182 (2)

Tarsatica *see* Rijeka

Tarsus *settlement* Southwest Asia (Turkey) ancient Rome 180–181 (1) crusades 228 (2), 65 (3) early Islam 56–57 (1) first civilizations 24 (2), 24 (2) Hellenistic world 40–41 (1) Islam 226 (2), 227 (4) medieval states 185 (3) Mongols 229 (3) world religions 48 (1)

Tartars *see* Tatars

Tartu *see* Dorpat

Taruga *archaeological site/settlement* West Africa (Nigeria) ancient trade 44–45 (1) early agriculture 158 (1) early cultures 160 (1)

Taruma Southwest Asia (Saudi Arabia) first civilizations 24 (3)

Tarut Southwest Asia (Saudi Arabia) first civilizations 24 (3)

Tarvisium *see* Treviso

Tarxien (Malta) the world in 2500 BCE 22–23

Tases *state* Central America Aztecs 124 (1)

Tashauz *see* Dashkhovuz

Tashi Chho Dzong *see* Thimphu

Tashihkiso *see* Dashiqiao

Tashi Lhunpo East Asia (China) exploration 257 (3)

Tashkent *Uzb.* Toshkent Central Asia (Uzbekistan) biological diffusion 72–73 (1) colonialism 269 (3), (4) Communism 271 (8) exploration 256 (1), 257 (3) global imperialism 100 (1) Hellenistic world 40–41 (1) medieval Persia 231 (4) medieval states 261 (6) Mongols 68–69 (1) Ottomans 232–233 (1) Soviet Union 208 (2), 214–215 (4) trade 267 (3)

Tasmania *prev.* Van Diemen's Land *region/island* Australia colonization 282 (1), (2), 283 (3) exploration 276–277 (1), 279 (2), (3) medieval voyages 60 (2)

Tasman Sea *sea* Pacific Ocean colonization 282 (1), 283 (4), (5) environmentalism 285 (2) medieval voyages 60 (2) prehistoric culture 17 (5)

Tatars *var.* Tartars *people* East Asia/Siberia historical geography 275 (5) Mongols 68–69 (1)

Tatarstan *state* Eastern Europe Soviet Union 214–215 (4)

Tatta South Asia (Pakistan) colonialism 248 (1)

Tatta *see* Thatta

Ta-t'ung, Tatung *see* Datong

Tauchira North Africa (Libya) first civilizations 177 (1)

Taung *archaeological site* Southern Africa (South Africa) first humans 12 (1)

Taunton British Isles (United Kingdom) economy 204 (1)

Taupo, Lake *lake* New Zealand colonization 283 (5)

Tauranga New Zealand colonization 283 (5)

Tauroggen *region* Eastern Europe empire and revolution 199 (3)

Taurus Mountains *var.* Toros Dağları *mountain range* Southwest Asia ancient Persia 223 (4), 225 (6) crusades 64–65 (2) early agriculture 220 (1) exploration 218 (1), (2), 219 (3) first cities 220 (2), 28–29 (1) first civilizations 221 (4), (5), 222 (1) Hellenistic world 224 (1) Ottomans 231 (3), 232–233 (1) Seljuks 228 (1) WWI 233 (2)

Tau'u Island *island* Pacific Ocean exploration 278 (1)

Tavascan *see* Michoacan

Tawahi Mainland Southeast Asia (Burma) trade 230 (2)

Tawakoni *people* North America colonization 125 (4)

Taxila Buddhist *center/religious site/settlement* South Asia (India) ancient Persia 225 (6) ancient Rome 224 (2) ancient trade 44 (2), 44–45 (1) exploration 256 (1) first religions 36 (2) Hellenistic world 224 (1), (4) medieval states 262–263 (1) world religions 49 (3), (4)

Taxla Central America (Mexico) first civilizations 121 (2)

Tayasal Central America (Guatemala) Aztecs 124 (1)

Tayloris Battle *battle* North America (USA) the growth of the US 129 (2)

Taymyr, Poluostrov *Eng.* Taimyr Peninsula *headland* Siberia exploration 257 (2)

Tayspun *see* Ctesiphon

Taz *river* Eastern Europe exploration 257 (2)

Tazoult *see* Lambaesis

Tchad Central America (Mexico) first civilizations 123 (2)

Tchad *see* Chad

Tchefuncte Culture *people* North America the world in 250 BCE 38–39

Tchongking *see* Chongqing

Te Anau, Lake *lake* New Zealand colonization 283 (5)

Teano *see* Teanum

Teanum *var.* Teanum Sidicinum; *mod.* Teano Italy early states 178 (1)

Teanum Apulum Italy early states 178 (1)

Teanum Sidicinum *see* Teanum

Tebuk Southwest Asia (Saudi Arabia) 20th-century politics 233 (4)

Tecama Central America (Mexico) Aztecs 124 (1)

Tecklenburg *region* Central Europe empire and revolution 199 (3)

Tecoac Central America (Mexico) colonization 125 (5)

Tecpaltepec *var.* Santo Domingo Tehuantepec Central America (Mexico) first civilizations 122 (1) Mexican Revolution 133 (3)

Tecpan Central America (Mexico) colonization 123 (2)

Tehuantepec, Gulf of *var.* Tehuantepec, Golfo de *gulf* Central America Aztecs 124 (1) Mexican Revolution 133 (3)

Tehuantepec, Isthmus of *var.* Istmo de Tehuantepec *coastal feature* Central America Aztecs 124 (1)

Tehuantepec, Istmo de *see* Tehuantepec, Isthmus of

Tehuelche *people* South America early cultures 147 (2)

Tejo, Rio *see* Tagus

Teke *state* Central Africa the world in 1700 82–83 the world in 1800 86–87 the world in 1850 90–91

Tekesta *people* North America colonization 125 (4), 126 (1)

Telanaipura *see* Jambi

Tel Aviv Southwest Asia (Israel) 20th-century politics 235 (5)

Tel Aviv-Yafo Southwest Asia (Israel) 20th century 234 (2)

Telingana *region/state* South Asia early medieval states 244–245 (3)

Tell Aqrab *var.* Turba Iberian Peninsula (Spain) interwar 209 (4) Islam 192 (3)

Teṡetiċe-Kyjovice Central Europe (Czech Republic) early agriculture 174 (1)

Tell 'Asmar, Tell Asmar *see* Eshnunna

Tell Aswad Southwest Asia (Iraq) first cities 220 (2)

Tell el-Ajjul Southwest Asia (Israel) ancient Egypt 159 (4)

Tell el-Amarna *see* Akhetaten

Tell el 'Ubaid Southwest Asia (Iraq) early agriculture 220 (1) first cities 220 (2)

Tell es Sawwan Southwest Asia (Iraq) first cities 220 (2)

Tell Halaf Southwest Asia (Syria) early agriculture 220 (1)

Tell Ibrahim Awad Egypt ancient Egypt 159 (2)

Tellicherry *var.* Thalassery South Asia (India) colonialism 247 (3)

Telloh Southwest Asia (Iraq) first cities 220 (2)

Tell Sleimeh *var.* Tell as-Suleimeh, Awal Southwest Asia (Iran) first civilizations 24 (3)

Tell 'Uqair *settlement/temple* Southwest Asia (Iraq) first cities 220 (2) first civilizations 221 (4)

Teloapan Central America (Mexico) Aztecs 124 (1)

Telo Martius *see* Toulon

Teluguocadas *state* South Asia Mongols 68–69 (1)

Temacatipan Central America (Mexico) Aztecs 124 (2)

Temesvár *battle* Southeast Europe (Romania) Ottomans 197 (4)

Tempelhof Central Europe (Germany) crusades 186 (1)

Tempelhof *airport* Central Europe (Germany) postwar politics 212 (2)

Tenango Central America (Mexico) Aztecs 124 (1)

Tenanitla Central America (Mexico) Aztecs 124 (3)

Tenasserim *state/colonial possession* Mainland Southeast Asia colonialism 269 (4) European imperialism 97 (3)

Tenayuca Central America (Mexico) Aztecs 124 (3)

Tenerife *battle* South America (Colombia) empire and revolution 150 (1)

Ténès North Africa (Algeria) economy 190 (1)

Teng East Asia (China) first cities 259 (5)

Teng *state* East Asia first states 259 (3)

Tenganapatam *var.* Ft. St. David South Asia (India) colonialism 247 (3)

Tenganapatam *see also* Siam

Teng-chou *see* Dengzhou

Tengchung *see* Dengyue

Tennant Creek Australia exploration 282 (1), 283 (3)

Tennessee *state* North America the growth of the US 129 (1) US Civil War 130 (2), (3), (4), (5), 131 (6), (7) US economy 134 (2), 139 (3) US society 137 (6) US superpower 139 (5)

Tennessee *river* North America cultural groups 122 (5) the growth of the US 129 (2) US Civil War 131 (6)

Tenochtitlán *mod.* Ciudad de Mexico, Mexico, Mexico City *archaeological site/settlement* Central America Aztecs 124 (1), (2), (3) colonization 125 (5) exploration 118 (1) first civilizations 121 (3) see also Mexico, Mexico City

Tenos *mod.* Tinos *island* Greece Ottomans 230 (1)

Teodomiro *state* Iberian Peninsula the world in 750 CE 54–55

Teos *settlement* Greece ancient Greece 177 (2) Greece ancient Greece 179 (4) first civilizations 177 (1)

Teotihuacán *var.* Teotihuacán Central America (Mexico) ancient Rome 180–181 (1)

Teotihuacan *region* Central America (Mexico) first civilizations 121 (2)

Teotitlán Central America (Mexico) Aztecs 124 (1)

Teotitlan del Camino *state* Central America Aztecs 124 (1)

Tepeacac *state* Central America Aztecs 124 (1)

Tepeacac Central America (Mexico) Aztecs 124 (1)

Tepeapulco Central America (Mexico) Aztecs 124 (1)

Tepecano *people* Central America colonization 125 (4)

Tepecuacuilco Central America (Mexico) Aztecs 124 (1)

Tepe Gawra *settlement/temple* Southwest Asia (Iraq) early agriculture 220 (1) first cities 220 (2)

Tepe Giyan Southwest Asia (Iran) early agriculture 220 (1) first civilizations 24 (2)

Tepe Guran Southwest Asia (Iran) early agriculture 220 (1)

Tepe Hissar Southwest Asia (Iran) first civilizations 24 (3)

Tepeleler *see* East Central Europe postwar politics 212 (2)

Tepehuan *people* Central America colonization 125 (4), 126 (1)

Tepe Sabz Southwest Asia (Iran) first civilizations 24 (2)

Tepe Yahya Southwest Asia (Iran) first civilizations 24 (3)

Tepic Central America (Mexico) Mexican Revolution 133 (3)

Tepoatlan Central America (Mexico) Aztecs 124 (1)

Mughal Empire 246 (1) world religions 243 (4)

Thebae *see* Thebes

Thebes Egypt ancient Egypt 159 (3), (4), (5) ancient Persia 223 (4) early cultures 160 (1), 161 (3), (4), (5) Hellenistic world 40–41 (1)

Thebes *settlement* Greece ancient Greece 177 (3), (4), (5) first cities 28–29 (1) first civilizations 175 (4), 222 (2) first religions 37 (1) Hellenistic world 40–41 (1) see also Karnak, Ipet-isut, Luxor

Theiss *see* Tisza

Thenae North Africa (Tunisia) first civilizations 177 (1)

Theodosia *var.* Caffa, Kefe; *mod.* Feodosiya; It. Kaffa Eastern Europe (Ukraine) first civilizations 177 (1) Hellenistic world 40–41 (1) see also Kaffa

Theodosiopolis *see* Erzurum

Thera Greece first civilizations 177 (1), 175 (4) island Greece first civilizations 175 (4)

Theresienstadt *concentration camp* Central Europe WWII (1)

Thermopylae Greece great migrations 52–53 (1) ancient Greece 179 (4) ancient Persia 223 (4)

Thessalonica *mod.* Thessaloniki; *Eng.* Salonica, Salonika, *SCr.* Solun, *Turk.* Selânik Greece ancient Greece 179 (4) ancient Rome 179 (5), 180–181 (1), 181 (4), 182 (1) crusades 64–65 (2) early cultures 161 (2) Hellenistic world 41 (1) world religions 48 (1) see also Salonica

Thessaloniki *see* Salonica, Thessalonica

Thessaly *region* Greece ancient Greece 177 (3), 179 (4) first civilizations 175 (4), 177 (1) first religions 37 (3) Ottomans 202 (4) WWI 207 (6)

Thimbu *see* Thimphu

Thimphu *var.* Thimbu; *prev.* Tashi Chho Dzong South Asia (Bhutan) postwar economy 253 (5)

Thinis Egypt ancient Egypt 159 (3)

Thionville *see* Diedenhofen

Third Cataract *waterfall* Egypt ancient Egypt 159 (4), (5)

Thirteen Colonies *colonial possession* North America empire and revolution 127 (3)

Thiruvanathapuram *see* Trivandrum

Thíva *see* Thebes

Thon Buri Mainland Southeast Asia (Thailand) biological diffusion 72–73 (1)

Thorn *Pol.* Toruń Central Europe (Poland) economy 190 (1) medieval states 188 (1) WWI 207 (4) see also Toruń

Thornton Island *see* Caroline Island

Thospitis *see* Van, Lake

Thovela *state* Southern Africa the world in 1700 82–83

Thrace *anc.* Thracia *region* Greece/Southeast Europe ancient Greece 177 (2), 179 (4) ancient Persia 223 (4) ancient Rome 225 (5) ancient trade 44–45 (1) exploration 218 (1) first civilizations 175 (4), 177 (1) first religions 37 (3) Hellenistic world 224 (1) Ottomans 202 (4), 230 (1) world religions 48 (1) see also Thracia

Thracia *var.* Thrace *province* Southeast Europe ancient Rome 180–181 (1), 181 (4)

Thracians *people* Southeast Europe ancient Rome 179 (5)

Three Kings Islands *island group* Pacific Ocean exploration 278 (1)

Thugga North Africa (Tunisia) ancient Rome 180–181 (1)

Thule *var.* Qânâq North Africa (Greenland) cultural groups 123 (3) exploration 287 (2) the growth of the US 129 (1)

Thule *island* Atlantic Ocean ancient trade 44 (2)

Thuna South Asia (India) world religions 242 (3)

Thurii Italy ancient Rome 179 (3) early states 178 (1)

Thüringen *see* Thuringia

Thuringia *Fr.* Thuringe; *Ger.* Thüringen *region/state* Central Europe empire and revolution 202 (2) Franks 184 (2) medieval states 185 (3), 188 (1)

Thuringian March *region* Central Europe Franks 184 (2)

Thuringians *people* Central Europe ancient Rome 182 (1) Franks 183 (5), (6) great migrations 53 (2) medieval states 182 (2)

Thyatira *mod.* Akhisar *seven churches of asia* Southwest Asia world religions 48 (1)

Thyssus *state* Greece ancient Greece 177 (2)

Tiahuanaco South America (Bolivia) early cultures 146 (1) Incas 147 (3)

Tiahuanaco *state* South America the world in 250 BCE 38–39 the world in 1 CE 42–43 the world in 1000 58–59 the world in 1200 62–63

Tianjin *var.* Tientsin East Asia (China) colonialism 269 (4) empire and revolution 268 (2) Islam 275 (4) postwar politics 274 (2)

Tianjin *province* East Asia postwar politics 274 (2)

Tianjin *battle* East Asia (China) economy 274 (1)

Tianlin *prev.* Leili East Asia (China) medieval states 263 (6)

Tian Shan *see* Tien Shan

Tianshui *var.* T'ien-shui Buddhist *center/sacred monument* East Asia (China) world religions 49 (3)

Tiayo Central America (Mexico) first civilizations 122 (1)

Tiba *see* Chiba

Tibbu Tib *people* East Africa/Central Africa trade 167 (1)

Tiber *river* Italy medieval states 183 (4)

Tiber *var.* Tevere Southwest Asia (Israel) ancient Rome 225 (4)

Tiberias, Lake *lake* Southwest Asia crusades 63 (3)

Tiberis *mod.* Tevere; *Eng.* Tiber *river* Italy ancient Rome 181 (2) early states 178 (1), (2) see also Tevere, Tiber

Tibesti *var.* Tibesti Massif, Ar. Tibisti *mountain range* North Africa ancient trade 44–45 (1) early cultures 160 (1) economy 163 (2) first humans 13 (2) Islam 163 (1)

Tibesti Massif *see* Tibesti

Tibet *var.* Hsi-tsang; *anc.* Xizang; *Chin. prev.* Tufan, Bhota *province/region/state* East Asia colonialism 247 (4), (5), 269 (3), (4) early modern states 266 (1), (2), 268 (1) empire and revolution 249 (3), 268 (2) exploration 257 (3) first states 260 (1) medieval states 261 (6), 262–263 (1), 263 (4), (5), (6) Mongols 68 (2), 68–69 (1) postwar economy 275 (3) postwar politics 252 (1), (2), 271 (7), 274 (2) trade 267 (3) world religions 243 (4), 49 (3) WWII 272 (1), 273 (2) Chinese revolution 271 (5) Cold War 109 (1) Communism 271 (8)

Tibetans *people* East Asia ancient trade 44–45 (1) empire and revolution 268 (2)

Tibet, Plateau of *var.* Xizang Gaoyuan, Qingzang Gaoyuan *plateau* East Asia ancient trade 44–45 (1) biological diffusion 72–73 (1) colonialism 247 (3) early agriculture 258 (1) early religions 48 (2) exploration 256 (1), 257 (3) first humans 13 (2) first religions 37 (4) first states 260 (1) global knowledge 76–77 (1) Marathas 246 (2) medieval states 262–263 (1), 263 (3), (4), (5), (6) Mughal Empire 246 (2) trade 267 (3) world religions 49 (3), (4)

Tibisti *see* Tibesti

Tibur Italy early states 178 (1)

Tiburón, Cabo *headland* South America European expansion 80–81 (1)

Tiburtina vetus, Via *road* Italy ancient Rome 181 (2)

Tiburtina, Via *road* Italy ancient Rome 181 (2) early states 178 (1)

Tichitt West Africa (Mauritania) the world in 2500 BCE 22–23

Ticoman Central America (Mexico) Aztecs 124 (3)

Tidore *var.* Soasiu Maritime Southeast Asia (Indonesia) colonialism 247 (4) colonization 284–285 (1)

Tidore *region* Maritime Southeast Asia colonialism 247 (4) early medieval states 245 (6)

Tien Shan *Chin.* Tian Shan, *Rus.* Tyan'-Shan'; *var.* T'ien Shan *mountain range* East Asia ancient trade 44–45 (1) biological diffusion 72–73 (1) colonialism 269 (4) early agriculture 258 (1) empire and revolution 268 (2) exploration 256 (1), 257 (3) first cities 259 (5) first humans 13 (2) first states 260 (1) historical geography 275 (5) medieval states 261 (6), 262–263 (1) Mongols 68–69 (1) trade 267 (3) world religions 49 (3) the Tianshui

Tien-shui *see* Tianshui

Tientsin *see* Tianjin

Tieoman Central America (Mexico) Aztecs 124 (3)

Tiergarten Central Europe (Germany) postwar politics 212 (2)

Tierra del Fuego *island* South America empire and revolution 151 (3) exploration 142 (1)

Tieum Southwest Asia (Turkey) first civilizations 177 (1)

Tiflis *var.* T'bilisi Southwest Asia (Georgia) early Islam 56–57 (1), 57 (2) Islam 226 (2), 227 (4) medieval Persia 231 (4) Mongols 68–69 (1) Ottomans 195 (4), 231 (3), 232–233 (1) Seljuks 228 (1) Timur 229 (4) world religions 226 (1) *see also* T'bilisi

Tighina *see* Bender

Tigris *Ar.* Dijlah, *Turk.* Dicle *river* Southwest Asia ancient Persia 223 (4), 225 (6) ancient Rome 180–181 (4), 224 (2), 225 (5) ancient trade 44–45 (1), 72–73 (1), 73 (3) crusades 228 (2) early agriculture 174 (1), 20–21 (2), 20 (1) early cultures 161 (3), (4), (5) early Islam 56–57 (1), 57 (2), (3) early systems 223 (3) early trade 225 (3) economy 234 (1) exploration 172 (1), (2), 219 (3), (4) first cities 220 (1), 28–29 (1) first civilizations 221 (4), (5), 222 (2), 25 (3) great religions 36 (1) great migrations 52–53 (1) Hellenistic world 224 (1), 41 (2) Islam 163 (1), 226 (2), 227 (4), (5) medieval Persia 231 (4) medieval states 185 (3) Mongols 229 (3), 68–69 (1) Ottomans 230 (1), 231 (3), 232–233 (1) Seljuks 228 (1) Timur 229 (4) trade 230 (2) world religions 226 (1), 49 (4) WWI 233 (3), (4), 235 (5)

Tih-hua, Tihwa *see* Urumchi, Ürümqi

Tikal Central America (Guatemala) early systems 32 (1), 33 (2), (3) first civilizations 121 (2)

Tikopia *island* Pacific Ocean exploration 278 (1)

Tiksi Siberia (Russian Federation) exploration 287 (2)

Tilanga *region* South Asia world religions 242 (2)

Tilantango Central America (Mexico) first civilizations 122 (1)

Tilcara South America (Argentina) Incas 147 (3)

Tilimsen *see* Tlemcen

Tilio Martius *see* Toulon

Tilsit Eastern Europe (Russian Federation) Napoleon 200–201 (1), 201 (2)

Timaru *settlement/whaling station* New Zealand colonization 283 (4), (5)

Timbuktu *Fr.* Tombouctou West Africa (Mali) ancient trade 44–45 (1) biological diffusion 72–73 (1) colonization 167 (4) crusades 65 (1) economy 163 (2) European expansion 84–85 (1) exploration 156 (3), 157 (4) Islam 163 (1), 167 (3) Mongols 68 (2) trade 163 (5)

Timna Southwest Asia (Jordan) ancient Egypt 159 (5)

Timna Southwest Asia (Yemen) 159 (5) early cultures 161 (3), (5) early trade 225 (3)

Timor *island* Maritime Southeast Asia (Indonesia) colonialism 247 (4) decolonization 251 (4) early medieval states 245 (6) European expansion 81 (3), 84–85 (1) European imperialism 97 (3) exploration 239 (1), (2) WWII 272 (1), 273 (2)

Timor Sea *sea* Maritime Southeast Asia Bronze Age 240 (3) colonialism 247 (4) decolonization 251 (4) early medieval states 245 (6) exploration 239 (1), (2) WWII 272 (1), 273 (2)

Timucua *people* North America colonization 125 (4)

Timur, Empire of *state* Southwest Asia Timur 229 (4)

Timurids *state* Central Asia/Southwest Asia the world in 1500 74–75

Tingis *var.* Tangiers; *Eng.* Tangier, *Fr./Ger.* Tanger, *Sp.* Tánger North Africa (Morocco) ancient Rome 179 (3), 180–181 (1), 181 (3), (4) ancient trade 44–45 (1) *see also* Tangier

Tinian *island* Pacific Ocean WWII 251 (3), 272 (1)

Tinos *see* Tenos

Tin Tellust West Africa (Niger) exploration 157 (4)

Tio *state* Central Africa Islam 163 (1) slave trade 165 (4) trade 167 (1)

Tipecanoe *battle* North America (USA) the growth of the US 129 (2)

Tirana Southeast Europe (Albania) Cold War 108 (3) Ottomans 232–233 (1) postwar politics 212 (3) WWI 207 (6) WWII 210 (1), 211 (2), (4)

Tirangole East Africa (Sudan) exploration 157 (4)

Tirgovişte *mod.* Targovişte Southeast Europe (Bulgaria) Ottomans 195 (4)

Tîrgovişte *var.* Tărguşor Southeast Europe (Romania) world religions 226 (1) *see also* Tărguşor

Tîrnovo *mod.* Veliko Tŭrnovo Southeast Europe (Bulgaria) medieval states 189 (4)

Tiruchchirappalli *see* Trichinopoly

Tiryns *palace/settlement* Greece first cities 28–29 (1) first civilizations 175 (4)

Tisza *Ger.* Theiss *river* Southeast Europe Mongols 68–69 (1) postwar economy 215 (3)

Tiszapolgar *archaeological site* Central Europe (Hungary) Copper Age 174 (2)

Titicaca, Lake *lake* South America colonization 148 (2) early cultures 145 (2), (4), 146 (1), 147 (2) empire and revolution 150 (1) Incas 147 (3), 148 (1)

Titograd *see* Podgorica

Tiwa *people* North America colonization 125 (4)

Tizapán Central America (Mexico) Aztecs 124 (2)

Tizapantzinco Central America (Mexico) colonization 125 (5)

Tizayucan Central America (Mexico) Aztecs 124 (3)

Tjeribon *see* Cheribon

Tlaceteco Central America (Mexico) Aztecs 124 (1)

Tlacho *state* Central America Aztecs 124 (1)

Tlachquiaucho *state* Central America Aztecs 124 (1)

Tlacopan Central America (Mexico) Aztecs 124 (1), (2), (3) colonization 125 (5)

Tlacopaque Central America (Mexico) Aztecs 124 (3)

Tlacquemecan Central America (Mexico) Aztecs 124 (3)

Tlalnepantla Central America (Mexico) Aztecs 124 (2), (3)

Tlaloc, Cerro *mountain range* Central America Aztecs 124 (2)

Tlalpan Central America (Mexico) Aztecs 124 (2)

Tlaltenango Central America (Mexico) Aztecs 124 (3)

Tlapacoya Central America (Mexico) Aztecs 124 (3) first civilizations 121 (2)

Tlapacoyan *state* Central America Aztecs 124 (1)

Tlapan *state* Central America Aztecs 124 (1)

Tlatayan Central America (Mexico) first civilizations 122 (1)

Tlateloco Central America (Mexico) Aztecs 124 (2), (3)

Tlatilco Central America (Mexico) first civilizations 121 (2)

Tlatlauhquitepec *state* Central America Aztecs 124 (1)

Tlaxcala Central America (Mexico) Aztecs 124 (1)

Tlaxcala *state* Central America Mexican Revolution 133 (3) the growth of the US 129 (2)

Tlaxcalan Central America (Mexico) colonization 125 (5)

Tlaxcalan *state* Central America Aztecs 124 (1)

Tlaxcalan *people* Central America colonization 125 (4)

Tlaxialtemalco Central America Aztecs 124 (2)

Tlemcen *var.* Tilimsen, Tlemsen North Africa (Algeria) Islam 163 (1)

Tlemsen *see* Tlemcen

Tlilhuacan Central America (Mexico) Aztecs 124 (3)

Tlingit *region* North America the world in 1700 82–83 the world in 1800 86–87

Tmutarakan Eastern Europe (Russian Federation) medieval states 185 (3)

Toala Island *archaeological site* Central Africa (Chad) early cultures 160 (1)

Toba *var.* Northern Wei; *Chin.* T'o-pa *state* East Asia medieval states 261 (4) the world in 500 CE 50–51

Tobago *island* West Indies empire and revolution 88 (1) European expansion 84–85 (1)

Tobol'sk *var.* Tobolsk Siberia (Russian Federation) colonialism 269 (3) exploration 257 (2) Soviet Union 208 (2)

Tobol'sk *region* Eastern Europe colonialism 269 (3)

Toboso *people* Central America colonization 125 (4), 126 (1)

Tobruk North Africa (Libya) WWII 210 (1), 211 (4)

Tocabaga *fort* North America (USA) colonization 125 (4)

Tocantins *river* South America colonization 149 (3), (4) early cultures 144 (1), 145 (2) environment 153 (4) exploration 142 (1), 143 (2) politics 152 (1)

Tochari *var.* Tocharians *people* East Asia the world in 500 BCE 34–35 ancient trade 44–45 (1)

Tocharian Principalities *state* Central Asia the world in 1 CE 42–43

Tochigi *var.* Totigi *prefecture* Japan economy 270 (1)

Tochpan *state* Central America Aztecs 124 (1)

Tochtepec *state* Central America Aztecs 124 (1)

Tocobaga *jesuit mission* North America (USA) colonization 125 (4)

Tocopilla South America (Chile) empire and revolution 151 (3)

Tocoyanosid *region* South America early cultures 145 (2)

Todaiji Japan medieval states 265 (3)

Todmorden British Isles (United Kingdom) imperial global economy 93 (4)

Toeban *see* Tuban

Togariishi *archaeological site* Japan early agriculture 258 (1)

Togiak North America (USA) cultural groups 123 (3)

Togo *prev.* French Togoland, Togoland *colonial possession/state* West Africa decolonization 168 (1) economy 168 (2) European imperialism 96 (1) Islam 235 (4) the modern world 112 (1), 113 (3) WWII 104 (1)

Togoland *see* Togo

Tohome *people* Central America colonization 125 (4)

Tojikiston *see* Tajikistan

Tokaido *region* Japan medieval states 265 (3)

Tokelau *island group/state* Pacific Ocean colonization 284–285 (1) decolonization 285 (3)

---

environmentalism 285 (2) exploration 279 (3) the modern world 110–111

Tokio *see* Edo, Tokyo

Tokushima Japan early modern states 265 (5)

Tokushima *var.* Tokusima *prefecture* Japan economy 270 (1)

Tokyo *Jap.* Tōkyō; *prev.* Edo Japan Communism 271 (8), 273 (3) imperial globalism 270 (2) imperialism 270 (2) Islam 275 (4) WWII 272 (1), 273 (2) *see also* Edo

Tolan Central America (Mexico) Aztecs 124 (3)

Toledo *anc.* Toletum *settlement* Iberian Peninsula (Spain) ancient Rome 182 (1) crusades 186 (1), 64–65 (2), 65 (1) early Islam 56–57 (1) economy 190 (1) Franks 184 (2) interwar 209 (3), (4) Islam 192 (3), 226 (2) medieval states 182 (2), 185 (3), 192 (1), (2) Napoleon 200–201 (1), 201 (2), 17 (3) Reformation 194 (2) *see also* Toletum

Toletum *mod.* Toledo *Christian archbishopric/settlement* Iberian peninsula (Spain) ancient Rome 180–181 (1) great migrations 52–53 (1) world religions 48 (1) *see also* Toledo

Tolimán Central America (Mexico) first civilizations 122 (1)

Tollantzinco Central America (Mexico) first civilizations 122 (1)

Tollmezzo Italy WWI 207 (5)

Tolosa *mod.* Toulouse France ancient Rome 179 (3), (5), 180–181 (1) ancient trade 44 (2) great migrations 52–53 (1) *see also* Toulouse

Toltec Empire *state* Central America the world in 1000 58–59

Tomar Iberian Peninsula (Portugal) crusades 186 (1)

Tombouctou *see* Timbuktu

Tomebamba South America (Ecuador) Incas 147 (3)

Tomi *mod.* Constanţa Southeast Europe (Romania) ancient Rome 180–181 (1), 181 (4) *see also* Constanţa

Tomóchic Central America (Mexico) Mexican Revolution 133 (3)

Tomsk *region/archaeological site/settlement* Siberia (Russian Federation) colonialism 269 (3) Communism 271 (8) early agriculture 258 (1) exploration 257 (2) Soviet Union 208 (2), 214–215 (4)

Tonalá Central America (Mexico) first civilizations 122 (1), (2)

Tonawa *var.* Friendly Islands *colonial possession/island group/state* Pacific Ocean colonization 284–285 (1) decolonization 285 (3) early cultures 280–281 (3) environmentalism 285 (2) exploration 276–277 (1), 279 (3) medieval voyages 60 (1)

Tongatapu Central America (Mexico) exploration 278 (1)

Tongatapu Group *island group* Pacific Ocean early cultures 280–281 (3) medieval voyages 60 (1)

Tongchuan East Asia (China) medieval states 263 (4)

Tonggou *mod.* Ji'an East Asia (China) medieval states 264 (1) *see also* Ji'an

Tongguan *var.* T'ung-kuan East Asia Mongols 68–69 (1)

Tonghua East Asia (China) Cold War 109 (4)

Tongking *var.* Tonkin *state* Mainland Southeast Asia colonialism 269 (4) European imperialism 97 (3)

Tongking, Gulf of *gulf* Mainland Southeast Asia colonialism 247 (4), 248 (1) decolonization 251 (4) early medieval states 245 (5), (6) early modern states 266 (1) exploration 239 (1) medieval voyages 61 (3) postwar politics 251 (5), 253 (4) WWII 251 (3)

Tongnae East Asia (South Korea) early modern states 267 (4)

Tongzi *archaeological site* East Asia (China) first humans 13 (2)

Tonkawa *people* North America colonization 125 (4), 126 (1)

Tonkin *see* Tongking

Tonle Sap *Eng.* Great Lake *lake* Mainland Southeast Asia postwar politics 251 (5) world religions 243 (5)

Tonto *archaeological site* North America (USA) cultural groups 123 (4)

Toodoloon Mounds *burial mound* North America (USA) first civilizations 121 (4)

Toowoomba Australia colonization 282 (2)

T'o-pa *see* Toba

Topeka North America (USA) the growth of the US 129 (2)

Topoc Maze *archaeological site* North America (USA) cultural groups 123 (4)

Toprakkale Southwest Asia (Turkey) first civilizations 222 (2)

Torgut *people* East Asia early modern states 266 (1)

Torino *see* Augusta, Taurinorum, Turin

Tornacum *see* Tournai

Tornaval South America (Peru) early cultures 145 (4)

Toro Egypt exploration 156 (3)

Toro *state* East Africa the world in 1700 82–83 the world in 1800 86–87 the world in 1850 90–91

Torone Greece first civilizations 177 (1)

Torone *state* Greece ancient Greece 177 (2)

Toropets Eastern Europe (Russian Federation) early modern states 195 (3)

Toros Dağları *see* Taurus Mountains

Torrance North America (USA)

Torreón Central America (Mexico) Mexican Revolution 133 (3)

Torres Strait *sea waterway* Australia exploration 276–277 (1), 279 (2)

Tortoise Islands *see* Galapagos Islands

Tortosa *anc.* Dertosa Iberian Peninsula (Spain) crusades 186 (1) Franks 184 (2) Islam 192 (3) *see also* Dertosa

Tortuga *var.*Tortuga Island; *mod.* Île de la Tortue *island* West Indies empire and revolution 89 (3) European expansion 85 (2)

Toruń *Ger.* Thorn Central Europe (Poland) early modern states 193 (4) medieval states 189 (3) *see also* Thorn

Torwa *state* Southern Africa Islam 163 (1)

Torzhok *var.* Toržok Eastern Europe (Russian Federation) Mongols 68–69 (1)

Toržok *see* Torzhok

Tosando *region* Japan medieval states 265 (3)

Toshka Egypt ancient Egypt 159 (3)

Toshkent *see* Tashkent

Tószeg Southeast Europe (Hungary) Bronze Age 175 (3)

Toterfout *burial mound* Low Countries (Netherlands) Bronze Age 175 (3)

Totigi *see* Tochigi

Totonac *state* Central America Aztecs 124 (1)

Tottori *prefecture* Japan economy 270 (1)

Toucouleur *see* Takrur

Toulon *anc.* Telo Martius, Tilio Martius France early modern states 197 (5) economy 205 (4) empire and revolution 199 (4) European expansion 84–85 (1) Napoleon 200–201 (1) WWII 211 (2)

Toulouse *anc.* Tolosa *settlement* France ancient Rome 182 (1) crusades 186 (1), 64–65 (2) early modern states 197 (5) economy 190 (1), 205 (4) empire and revolution 199 (4) Franks 183 (5), (6), 184 (2) interwar 209 (3) Islam 184 (1), 192 (3), 226 (2) medieval states 187 (3), 192 (1), (2), 17 (3) Napoleon 200–201 (1), 201 (2), 17 (3) Reformation 194 (2) *see also* Tolosa

Toulouse *region* France crusades 64–65 (2) medieval states 187 (4)

Toulouse *battle* France early Islam 184 (1)

Tounany *see* Tournai

Toungoo Mainland Southeast Asia (Burma) early medieval states 245 (6) WWII 251 (3)

Toungoo *state* Mainland Southeast Asia the world in 1400 70–71 the world in 1500 74–75

Tournai *var.* Tournay; *anc.* Tornacum; *Dut.* Doornik Low Countries (Belgium) early modern states 197 (5) economy 190 (1) Franks 183 (5), (6), 184 (2) WWI 206 (2), (3)

Tournay *see* Tournai

Tours *anc.* Caesarodunum, Turoni *settlement* France early modern states 197 (5) Franks 183 (5), 184 (2) medieval states 187 (3), 192 (1), (2) *see also* Caesarodunum, Turoni

Town Creek North America (USA) cultural groups 123 (4)

Townsville Australia colonization 282 (1), 283 (3)

Towosahgy North America (USA) cultural groups 122 (5)

Toyama *prefecture* Japan economy 270 (1)

Toyohashi *var.* Toyohasi Japan economy 270 (1), 275 (4)

Toyohasi *see* Toyohashi

Tŏyohasi *see* Toyohashi

Trâblous *var.* Tarābulus, Ţarābulus ash Shām, Trâblous; *anc.* Tripolis Southwest Asia (Lebanon) crusades 65 (3) medieval states 187 (5) 20th-century politics 233 (3) *see also* Tripolis

Trabzon *see* Trapezus, Trebizond

Trachonitis *state* Southwest Asia ancient Rome 225 (4)

Trafalgar *battle* Iberian Peninsula (Spain) Napoleon 200–201 (1)

Traiana, Aqua *aqueduct* Italy ancient Rome 181 (2)

Traiani, Thermae *see* Trajan, Baths of

Traiectum ad Mosam, Traiectum Tungorum *see* Maastricht

Trajan, Baths of *Lat.* Thermae Traiani *building* Italy ancient Rome 181 (2)

Trajan, Temple of *building* Italy ancient Rome 181 (2)

Trajectum ad Rhenum *see* Utrecht

Trang Mainland Southeast Asia (Thailand) ancient trade 44–45 (1)

Trani *anc.* Turenum Italy economy 190 (1)

Tran Ninh *state* Mainland Southeast Asia the world in 1600 78–79 the world in 1700 82–83 the world in 1800 86–87

Tranquebar *mod.* Tarangambadi South Asia (India) colonialism 247 (3)

Trans-Amazon Highway *road* South America 153 (4)

Transantarctic Mountains *mountain range* Antarctica Antarctic Exploration 287 (3)

Transbaikal *region* Siberia colonialism 269 (3)

Transcaspian *region* Central Asia colonialism 269 (3)

Trans-Gangem *region* South Asia ancient trade 44 (2)

Transilvania *see* Transylvania

Transjordan *mod.* Jordan *region/state* Southwest Asia exploration 219 (4) WWII 104 (1), 211 (4) 20th-century politics 234 (2) *see also* Jordan

Transnistria *state* Eastern Europe WWII 211 (2)

Transoxiana *region/state* Central Asia ancient trade 44–45 (1) early Islam 56–57 (1), 57 (2) Islam 227 (4) medieval Persia 231 (4) medieval states 261 (6), 262–263 (1) Timur 229 (4) world religions 226 (1)

Trans-Siberian Railway *railway* Siberia global immigration 100 (1)

Transvaal *state* Southern Africa European imperialism 96 (2)

Transylvania *Eng.* Ardeal, Transilvania, *Ger.* Siebenbürgen, *Hung.* Erdély *region/state* Southeast Europe medieval states 189 (4) Napoleon 200–201 (1) Ottomans 195 (4), 230 (1) Reformation 194 (2) WWI 208 (1)

Trapani *anc.* Drepanum Italy economy 190 (1)

Trapezus *Eng.* Trebizond, *Turk.* Trabzon *archaeological site/settlement* Southwest Asia (Turkey) ancient Rome 180–181 (1), 181 (3), (4) ancient trade 44–45 (1) early cultures 161 (2) first civilizations 177 (1) Hellenistic world 40–41 (1) world religions 226 (1) *see also* Trebizond

Troyes *anc.* Augustobona Tricassium France crusades 186 (1) early modern states 193 (4) economy 190 (1) medieval states 188 (1), (2) Reformation 194 (2) WWI 206 (2), (3)

Trst *see* Trieste

Trucial Coast *see* Trucial Oman, United Arab Emirates

Trucial Oman *mod.* United Arab Emirates; *prev.* Trucial Coast; *later* Trucial States *colonial possession/state* Southwest Asia 20th-century politics 233 (4) *see also* United Arab Emirates

Trucial States *see* Trucial Oman, United Arab Emirates

Truckee *battle* North America (USA) the growth of the US 129 (2)

Trujillo South America (Venezuela) empire and revolution 150 (1)

Trujillo South America (Peru) colonization 126 (1), 148 (2) empire and revolution 150 (1), 151 (3) exploration 143 (3) politics 152 (1)

Truk *var.* Hogoley Islands, Chuuk *island group* Pacific Ocean WWII 251 (3), 272 (1), 273 (2)

Trundholm Scandinavia (Denmark) the world in 1250 BCE 26–27

Trung Phân *see* Annam

Trung Quôc *see* China

Tsaidam Basin *Chin.* Qaidam Pendi *basin* East Asia exploration 257 (3)

Tsangchou *see* Cangzhou

Tsangpo *see* Brahmaputra

Tsaritsyn *mod.* Volgograd; *prev.* Stalingrad *see* Stalingrad, Volgograd Eastern Europe (Russian Federation) Soviet Union 208 (2)

Tsetsaut *people* North America cultural groups 123 (3)

Tshwane *see* Pretoria

Tsinan *see* Jinan

Tsing Hai, Tsinghai *see* Koko Nor, Qinghai Hu

Tsingtao, Tsingtau, Tsintao *see* Qingdao

Tsou *see* Zou

Tsugaru-kaikyō *see* Tsugaru Strait

Tsugaru Strait *Jap.* Tsugaru-kaikyō *sea waterway* Japan Communism 273 (3)

Tsushima *battle* Japan Russo-Japanese War 270 (4)

Tsushima *var.* Tsushima-tō, Tusima *island group* Japan Cold War 109 (4) early modern states 265 (5), 267 (4) medieval states 264 (2), 265 (3), (4)

Tsushima-kaikyō *see* Tsushima Strait

Tsushima Strait *var.* Tsushima-kaikyō *sea waterway* Japan early modern states 267 (4) medieval states 265 (3)

Tsushima-tō *see* Tsushima

Tu coastal East Asia first cities 259 (3)

Tuadmumu *state* British Isles medieval states 188 (2)

Tuamotu, Archipel des *see* Tuamotu Islands

Tuamotu, Îles *see* Tuamotu Islands

Tuamotu Islands *Fr.* Îles Tuamotu; *var.* Archipel des Tuamotu, Dangerous Archipelago, Tuamotou Archipelago *island group* Pacific Ocean colonization 284–285 (1) early cultures 280–281 (3) exploration 279 (3) medieval voyages 60 (2)

Tuareg *state* West Africa trade 163 (4)

Tuaregs *people* North Africa/West Africa economy 163 (2) Islam 163 (1)

Tuban *prev.* Toeban Maritime Southeast Asia (Indonesia) trade 230 (2)

Tubar *people* Central America colonization 126 (1)

Tubuai, Îles, Tubuai Islands *see* Australes, Îles

Tuchi *see* Duji

Tucson North America (USA) the growth of the US 129 (2), 132 (1)

Tucumán *var.* San Miguel de Tucumán South America (Argentina) empire and revolution 150 (1), 151 (3) politics 151 (4) *see also* San Miguel de Tucumán

Tucumán *battle* South America (Argentina) empire and revolution 88–89 (2)

Tufan *see* Tibet

Tughluq's Empire *state* South Asia the world in 1400 70–71

Tugur *see* Tugursk

Tugursk *mod.* Tugur Siberia (Russian Federation) exploration 257 (2)

Tukela River *river* Southern Africa colonization 166 (2)

Tuktoyaktuk North America (Canada) exploration 287 (2)

Tula Eastern Europe (Russian Federation) Soviet Union 208 (2), 214–215 (4)

Tula *var.* Tula de Allende Central America (Mexico) first civilizations 122 (1) *see also* Tula de Allende

Tula de Allende *see* Tula

Tulpetlac Central America (Mexico) Aztecs 124 (2)

Tulsa *settlement* North America (USA) US economy 134 (1) US politics 135 (6)

Tulucan Central America (Mexico) Aztecs 124 (1)

Tulunids *dynasty* Egypt/Southwest Asia early Islam 57 (2) Islam 227 (4)

Tulyehualco Central America (Mexico) Aztecs 124 (2)

Tumaco South America (Colombia) Incas 148 (1)

Tumbes South America (Peru) colonization 148 (2) empire and revolution 150 (1), 151 (3) Incas 147 (3), 148 (1) *see also* San Juan Bautista

Tumbos East Africa (Sudan) ancient Egypt 159 (5)

Tumet *people* East Asia early modern states 266 (1), trade 267 (3)

Tunes *see* Tunis, Tunisia

T'ung-kuan *see* Tongguan

Tungus *people* Siberia trade 267 (3) *see also* Xianbei, Xianbi

Tunica *people* North America colonization 125 (4), 126 (1)

Tunis *var.* Tunes; *anc.* Tunisia; *anc.* Tunes *region/state* North Africa colonization 167 (4) Napoleon 200–201 (1) slave trade 165 (4) trade 167 (1) *see also* Tunisia

Tunis *settlement* North Africa (Tunisia) WWII 104 (2)

Tunisia *prev.* Tunis, *anc.* Tunes *state* North Africa decolonization 168 (1) early 20th century 206 (1) early Islam 57 (2) economy 168 (2), (3) European imperialism 96 (1), 97 (4) Islam 235 (4) Ottomans 232–233 (1) the modern world 112 (1), 113 (3) WWII 210 (1), 211 (4) *see also* Tunisia

Tunja South America (Colombia) early cultures 146 (1) empire and revolution 150 (1)

Tunjur *state* Central Africa Islam 163 (1)

Tun-Sun *state* Mainland Southeast Asia ancient India 241 (6)

Tupi *people* South America the world in 250 CE 46–47 the world in 500 CE 50–51 the world in 750 CE 54–55 the world in 1500 74–75

Tupi-Guarani *people* South America early cultures 145 (2)

Tupinambá *people* South America early cultures 147 (2)

Tupiza South America (Bolivia) Incas 147 (3)

Turba *see* Teruel

Turenum *see* Trani

Turfan *Buddhist center/settlement* East Asia (China) ancient trade 44–45 (1) early modern states 268 (1) first states 260 (1) medieval states 261 (6), 262–263 (1) trade 267 (3) world religions 49 (3), (4)

Turgay *region* Central Asia colonialism 269 (3)

Turin *It.* Torino; *anc.* Augusta, Taurinorum Italy ancient Rome 182 (1) early modern states 193 (4) economy 205 (4) empire and revolution 202 (2) Franks 184 (2) medieval states 182 (2), 183 (4) Napoleon 200–201 (1)

Turkana, Lake *see* Rudolf, Lake

Turkestan *var.* Sinkiang; Sinking Uighur Autonomous Region; *Chin.* Xin, Sinkiang *region* East Asia colonialism 269 (3) early modern states 268 (1) exploration 257 (3) medieval states 261 (6) trade 267 (3) world religions 49 (3), (4) *see also* Sinkiang, Xinjiang

---

Turkey *Turk.* Türkiye *state* Southwest Asia economy 234 (1) interwar 209 (3) Islam 235 (4) postwar economy 213 (5), 214 (1), (2), postwar politics 212 (3) Soviet Union 208 (2), 213 (4) the modern world 112 (1), (3), (4) US superpower 138 (1) WWI 208 (1) WWII 105 (3), 210 (1), 211 (2), (4) 20th-century politics 233 (3), 235 (5) Cold War 108 (3), 109 (1)

Turkic Peoples *people* Eastern Europe/Siberia the world in 500 CE 50–51 the world in 750 CE 54–55 the world in 1000 58–59 the world in 1200 62–63 the world in 1500 74–75 the world in 1600 78–79

Türkiye *see* Turkey

Turkmenistan *state* Central Asia ancient Rome 224 (2) economy 234 (1) historical geography 275 (5) Islam 235 (4) Soviet Union 214–215 (4) the modern world 113 (3) 20th-century politics 235 (3)

Turkmens *people* Central Asia historical geography 275 (5)

Turku *see* Åbo

Turner *burial mound* North America (USA) first civilizations 121 (4)

Turoni *mod.* Tours France world religions 48 (1) *see also* Caesarodunum, Tours

Turpan *see* Turfan

Turtle Mound North America (USA) cultural groups 122 (5)

Turukhansk Siberia (Russian Federation) exploration 257 (2)

Tus Central Asia (Turkmenistan) early Islam 56–57 (1)

Tusayan *archaeological site* North America (USA) cultural groups 123 (4)

Tuscany *It.* Toscana *region/state* Italy empire and revolution 202 (1), (3), medieval states 188 (1) Napoleon 200–201 (1) Reformation 196 (1), (2)

Tuscarora *people* North America colonization 126 (1)

Tuscia *region* Italy medieval states 183 (4)

Tusculana, Via *road* Italy ancient Rome 181 (2)

Tusculum Italy early states 178 (1)

Tushara *state* Central Asia/South Asia first empires 241 (5) world religions 242 (2)

Tushki Egypt colonization 167 (4)

Tushpa Southwest Asia (Turkey) first civilizations 222 (2)

Tusima *see* Tsushima

Tuskegee *people* North America colonization 125 (4)

Tutchone *people* North America cultural groups 123 (3)

Tutelo *people* North America colonization 125 (4), 126 (1)

Tuticorin South Asia (India) colonialism 247 (3)

Tutishcainyo *archaeological site* South America (Peru) early cultures 144 (1), 145 (2)

Tutub *mod.* Khafajah *settlement/temple* Southwest Asia (Iraq) first cities 220 (2) first civilizations 221 (4), 24 (3)

Tututepec Central America (Mexico) first civilizations 122 (1)

Tuvalu *state/island group* Pacific Ocean decolonization 285 (3) early cultures 280–281 (3) exploration 276–277 (1) Islam 192 (3) medieval voyages 60 (2)

Tuvu *region* Eastern Europe Soviet Union 214–215 (4)

Tuxtepec *var.* San Juan Bautista Tuxtepec Central America (Mexico) first civilizations 122 (1)

Tuyuhun *var.* Tu-yu-hun *state* East Asia the world in 500 CE 50–51

Tuyuhun *people* East Asia medieval states 261 (4)

Tuzigoot *archaeological site* North America (USA) cultural groups 123 (4)

Tuzla Southeast Europe (Bosnia and Herzegovina) postwar economy 215 (3)

Tuz, Lake Southwest Asia WWI 233 (2) 20th-century politics 233 (3)

Tver' *prev.* Kalinin Eastern Europe (Russian Federation) Mongols 68–69 (1) Soviet Union 208 (2)

Two Sicilies, Kingdom of the *state* Italy (Mediterranean Sea) empire and revolution 202 (1), (3)

Tyana Southwest Asia (Turkey) Hellenistic world 40–41 (1)

Tyan'-Shan' *see* Tien Shan

Tylisian Kingdom *state* Southeast Europe the world in 250 BCE 38–39

Tylos *see* Bahrain

Tyne *river* British Isles economy 204 (3) medieval states 186 (2)

Tyras Southeast Europe (Ukraine) Hellenistic world 40–41 (1)

Tyras *see* Dniester

Tyre *var.* Şūr; *anc.* Tyre *var.* Tyrus *settlement* Southwest Asia (Lebanon) ancient Egypt 159 (5) ancient Persia 223 (4) ancient Rome 225 (4), (5) crusades 64–65 (2), 65 (3) early cultures 161 (2), (3), (4), (5) early trade 225 (3) exploration 172 (1) first civilizations 177 (1), 221 (5), 222 (1), (2) Hellenistic world 40–41 (1) medieval states 185 (3) world religions 48 (1) *see also* Tyrus

Tyrol *region/state* Central Europe early modern states 193 (4), 194 (1) medieval states 188 (1) WWI 207 (5)

Tyrrhenian Sea *sea* Italy ancient Rome 179 (3) crusades 64–65 (2) early states 178 (1), (2), economy 190 (1) empire and revolution 202 (3) medieval states 183 (4)

Tyrus *var.* Tyrus; *anc.* Tyre; *Eng.* Tyre Southwest Asia (Lebanon) ancient Rome 180–181 (1), 181 (3) ancient trade 44–45 (1) *see also* Tyre

Tyumen' Eastern Europe (Russian Federation) Soviet Union 208 (2)

Tzauhtlan Central America (Mexico) colonization 125 (5)

Tziccoac *state* Central America Aztecs 124 (1)

Tzilcayoapan Central America (Mexico) first civilizations 122 (1)

Tzintzuntzan Central America (Mexico) Aztecs 124 (1) first civilizations 122 (1)

Tzompantzinco Central America (Mexico) colonization 125 (5)

Tz'u-shan *see* Cishan

U

UAE see United Arab Emirates
Uaxactún Central America (Guatemala) first civilizations 121 (2)
Ubangi Fr. Oubangui river Central Africa early agriculture 158 (1) economy 163 (2) Islam 163 (1) slave trade 165 (4)
Ubangi Shari region Central Africa European imperialism 96 (1)
Ubangi-Shari see Central African Republic
Ucayali river South America colonization 148 (2) early cultures 145 (2), (4), 146 (1) environment 153 (4) exploration 143 (2) Incas 147 (3), 148 (1) narcotics 153 (5) politics 152 (1)
Udabhanda South Asia (Pakistan) early medieval states 244 (2)
Udaiyars state South Asia Mughal Empire 246 (1)
Udichya region South Asia ancient India 242 (1)
Udicya/Uttarapatha region South Asia early religions 48 (2)
Udine Italy WWI 207 (5)
Udmurtia region Eastern Europe Soviet Union 214–215 (4)
Uelen North America (USA) cultural groups 123 (3)
Uesugi region Japan early modern states 267 (4)
Ufa Eastern Europe (Russian Federation) Soviet Union 208 (2), 214–215 (4) trade 267 (3)
Uganda state East Africa Cold War 109 (1) decolonization 168 (1) economy 168 (2), (3) European imperialism 96 (1), 97 (4) the modern world 112 (1), 113 (3) WWII 104 (1)
Ugarit Ar. Ra's Shamrah religious site/settlement Southwest Asia (Syria) ancient Egypt 159 (4), (5) early agriculture 220 (1) first cities 28–29 (1) first civilizations 221 (4), (5) first religions 37 (3)
Ugogi East Africa (Tanzania) exploration 157 (5)
Ugrians people Eastern Europe/Siberia the world in 750 CE 54–55
Uhorshchyna see Hungary
Uhuru Peak see Kilimanjaro
Uige river Carmona, Vila Marechal Carmona Southern Africa (Angola) Cold War 109 (5)
Uighur City States var. Uygur state East Asia the world in 1200 62–63
Uighur Empire state East Asia historical geography 275 (5) medieval states 262–263 (1), 263 (3), (5) trade 267 (3)
Uitenhage Southern Africa (South Africa) colonization 166 (2)
Ujain see Ujjain, Ujjayini
Uji-gawa battle Japan early modern states 265 (5)
Ujiji East Africa (Tanzania) exploration 157 (4), (5)
Ujjain prev. Ujain, Ujjayini South Asia (India) colonialism 248 (1) Marathas 246 (2) see also Ujjayini
Ujjayani see Ujjayini
Ujjayini var. Ujain, Ujjan, Ujjayani settlement South Asia (India) early medieval states 244 (1), (2), 244–245 (3) early religions 48 (2) first empires 241 (4) first religions 36 (2) world religions 242 (2) see also Ujjain
Ujungpandang var. Macassar, Makassar; prev. Makasar Maritime Southeast Asia (Indonesia) postwar economy 253 (5) see also Macassar
Ujung Salang see Phuket
Ukek see Novi Sad
UK see United Kingdom
Ukraina see Ukraine
Ukraine Rus. Ukraina, Ukr. Ukrayina region/state Eastern Europe postwar economy 214 (1), (2) Soviet Union 208 (2), 214–215 (4) the modern world 112 (2) WWI 207 (4) WWII 210 (1)
Ukrayina see Ukraine
Ulaanbaatar see Ulan Bator, Urga
Ulaidh mod. Ulster state British Isles medieval states 188 (2) see also Ulster
Ulan Bator prev. Urga; Mong. Ulaanbaatar East Asia (Mongolia) Communism 271 (8) Islam 275 (4) see also Urga
Ulan-Ude see Verkhneudinsk
Ulenje people Southern Africa trade 164 (1)
Uliassutai East Asia (Mongolia) exploration 256 (1)
Ulithi island Pacific Ocean WWII 251 (3), 272 (1)
Ullung-do island East Asia Cold War 109 (4)
Ulm Central Europe (Germany) early modern states 193 (4) medieval states 188 (1)
Ulsan East Asia (South Korea) early modern states 267 (4)
Ulster region British Isles medieval states 188 (2)
Ulundi battle Southern Africa (South Africa) European imperialism 96 (2)
'Umān, Khalij see Oman, Gulf of
Umataka archaeological site Japan early agriculture 258 (1)
Umayyad Caliphate state Iberian Peninsula/North Africa/Southwest Asia Islam 184 (1)
Umayyads dynasty Iberian Peninsula/North Africa early Islam 57 (2) Islam 227 (4)
Umballa var. Ambala battle South Asia empire and revolution 249 (3)
Umbi people Italy early states 178 (2)
Umbu archaeological site South America (Brazil) early cultures 145 (2)
Umma Southwest Asia (Iraq) first civilizations 24 (3)
Umm an Nar Southwest Asia (United Arab Emirates) first civilizations 24 (2), 25 (3)
Umm Durmān see Omdurman
Umm Said var. Musay'id Southwest Asia (Qatar) economy 234 (1)
Unci see Almería
Undi state Southern Africa slave trade 165 (4) trade 164 (1)
Ungaria, Ungarn see Hungary
Ungava, District of province North America the growth of the US 129 (2)
Ungu region East Asia medieval states 264 (2)
Ungro-Vlachia see Wallachia
Unguja see Zanzibar
Union of Soviet Socialist Republics state Eastern Europe economy 274 (1) interwar 209 (3), (5) postwar economy 213 (5) postwar politics 212 (3), 271 (7) Soviet Union 208 (2), 213 (4) WWI 208 (1) WWII

104 (1), 105 (4), 210 (1), 211 (2), (3), (4), 272 (1), 273 (2) 20th-century politics 233 (3) Cold War 109 (1), (4) Communism 271 (8)
Union Pacific Railroad railway North America the growth of the US 129 (2)
United Arab Emirates abbrev. UAE; prev. Trucial Coast, Trucial States, Trucial Oman state Southwest Asia economy 234 (1) Islam 235 (4) the modern world 113 (3) US economy 138 (2) 20th-century politics 235 (5) see also Trucial Oman
United Arab Republic see Egypt
United Kingdom abbrev. UK state British Isles early 20th century 206 (1) imperial global economy 92 (1) Napoleon 200–201 (1), 201 (2) postwar economy 213 (5), 214 (1) postwar politics 212 (3) Soviet Union 214–215 (4) the modern world 112 (2), 113 (4) Cold War 108 (3), 109 (1) US superpower 138 (1) see also Britain
United Mexican States see Mexico
United Netherlands state Low Countries empire and revolution 202 (1)
United Provinces var. Holland, prev. Batavian Republic, Dutch Republic, United Provinces; Dut. Nederland state Low Countries early modern states 197 (5) Reformation 196 (1), (2) see also Batavian Republic, Netherlands
United States see United States of America
United States of America var. America, The States, prev. United States of North America; abbrev. U.S., USA state North America empire and revolution 127 (3), 88–89 (2) European expansion 84–85 (1) global immigration 101 (2), (3) imperial global economy 92 (1), 93 (5) Mexican Revolution 133 (3) the growth of the US 129 (2), 132 (1), 133 (4) the modern world 112 (1), 113 (4) US economy 138 (2) US politics 139 (4) US superpower 138 (1) WWII 104 (1), 105 (4), 272 (1), 273 (2) Cold War 108 (2), (3)
United States of North America see United States of America
University burial mound North America (USA) first civilizations 121 (4)
Unorganized territory region North America the growth of the US 129 (1) US Civil War 130 (2), (3), (4), (5) US economy 134 (2)
Unterwalden region Central Europe early modern states 193 (5)
Unyanyembe see Tabora
Upper Burma state Mainland Southeast Asia European imperialism 97 (3)
Upper Egypt state Egypt ancient Egypt 159 (5)
Upper Gelderland var. Upper Gelders province/region Central Europe empire and revolution 199 (3) Reformation 195 (5)
Upper Gelders see Upper Gelderland
Upper Lorraine region Central Europe medieval states 185 (3), 188 (1)
Upper Ohio Frontier region North America empire and revolution 127 (3)
Upper Silesia region Central Europe WWI 208 (1)
Upper Swan Australia exploration 280 (1)
Upper Volta state West Africa European imperialism 96 (1)
Uppsala Scandinavia (Sweden) early modern states 197 (3) medieval states 189 (3)
Ur Southwest Asia (Iraq) early systems 223 (3) first cities 28–29 (1) first civilizations 221 (4), (5), 222 (2), 25 (3) first religions 36 (1) first cities 220 (2)
Uraiyur South Asia (India) early medieval states 244 (1) first empires 241 (4) world religions 243 (4)
Ural Kaz. Zayyq river Central Asia/Eastern Europe biological diffusion 72–73 (1) colonialism 269 (3) medieval states 261 (6), 262–263 (1) Mongols 68–69 (1) Ottomans 231 (3)
Ural Mountains Rus. Ural'skiy Khrebet, Ural'skiye Gory mountain range Eastern Europe ancient trade 44–45 (1) biological diffusion 72–73 (1) colonialism 269 (3) early agriculture 174 (1) exploration 172 (1), 257 (2), 286 (1), 287 (2) first humans 13 (2) medieval states 185 (3) Mongols 68–69 (1) Soviet Union 208 (2)
Ural's Kaz. Oral Central Asia (Kazakhstan) Soviet Union 214–215 (4)
Ural's region Central Asia colonialism 269 (3)
Ural'skiye Gory, Ural'skiy Khrebet see Ural Mountains
Urantu mod. Armenia state Southwest Asia first civilizations 222 (2) see also Armenia
Urbino Italy early modern states 193 (4)
Urbino state Italy Ottomans 195 (4) Reformation 194 (2)
Urdunn see Jordan
Uren North America (USA) cultural groups 122 (1)
Ures Central America (Mexico) colonization 125 (4)
Urewe archaeological site East Africa (Kenya) early cultures 160 (1)
Urfa see Edessa
Urga mod. Ulan Bator; Mong. Ulaanbaatar East Asia (Mongolia) colonialism 269 (3) early modern states 268 (1) exploration 256 (1), 257 (3) Soviet Union 208 (2) see also Ulan Bator
Urganch see Urgench
Urgench var. Urganch; prev. Novo-Urgench Central Asia (Uzbekistan) medieval states 261 (6)
Uri Ger. Basel Central Europe early modern states 193 (5)
Uriankhai var. Tannu Tuva, Uryankhai region East Asia medieval states 269 (4)
Uribe South America (Colombia) narcotics 153 (5)
Urmia, Lake var. Matianus, Sha Hi, Urumi Yeh; prev. Daryācheh-ye Reṣā'iyeh lake Southwest Asia ancient Persia 223 (4), 225 (6) early agriculture 220 (1) economy 234 (1) first cities 220 (2) first civilizations 221 (4), (5), 222 (2), 25 (3) Hellenistic world 224 (1) medieval Persia 231 (4) medieval states 185 (3) Mongols 229 (3) Seljuks 228 (1) Timur 229 (4) 20th-century politics 233 (3)
Uruguai, Rio see Uruguay
Uruguay prev. La Banda Oriental state South America Cold War 109 (1) empire and revolution 150 (1), 151 (3), 88–89 (2) environment

153 (4) global immigration 100 (1), 101 (2) imperial global economy 92 (1) politics 152 (1) the modern world 112 (1), 113 (4) US superpower 138 (1) WWII 105 (3)
Uruguay var. Rio Uruguai river South America colonization 148 (2) empire and revolution 151 (3) environment 153 (4) exploration 143 (2) politics 152 (1)
Uruk var. Erech settlement/temple Southwest Asia (Iraq) early agriculture 220 (1) early systems 223 (3) first cities 28–29 (1) first civilizations 221 (4), 222 (2), 25 (3)
Uruk IV Buildings building Southwest Asia (Iraq) first cities 220 (3)
Urumchi var. Tihwa, Urumqi, Urumtsi, Wu-lu-k'o-mu-shi, Wu-lu-mu-ch'i; prev. Ti-hua; mod. Ürümqi early modern states 268 (1) exploration 256 (1), 257 (3) see also Ürümqi
Urumi Yeh see Urmia, Lake
Urumqi see Urumchi, Ürümqi
Ürümqi var. Urumchi, Urumqi, Urumtsi, Tihwa, Wu-lu-k'o-mu-shi, Wu-lu-mu-ch'i; prev. Ti-hua East Asia (China) early modern states 268 (1), 257 (3) see also Urümqi
Urumtsi see Urumchi, Ürümqi
Urundi see Burundi
Uruvela South Asia (India) world religions 242 (2)
Uryankhai var. Tannu Tuva, Uriankhai region East Asia colonialism 269 (3) see also Tannu Tuva, Uriankhai
U.S. see United States of America
U.S.A. see United States of America
Ushinara region South Asia early religions 48 (2)
Üsküb, Üsküp see Scupi, Skopje, Skoplje
Uspanapa river Central America first civilizations 121 (3)
Ussuri region/state Siberia colonialism 269 (3), (4) early modern states 268 (1) postwar economy 275 (3)
Ussuri var. Usuri, Wusuri, Chin. Wusuli Jiang river East Asia first states 260 (1)
Usui East Africa (Tanzania) exploration 157 (4)
Usumacinta river Central America first civilizations 122 (1)
Usumbura mod. Bujumbura East Africa (Burundi) exploration 157 (5)
Usuri see Ussuri
Utah var. Utah Territory state/region North America the growth of the US 129 (1) US Civil War 130 (2), (3), (4), (5) US economy 134 (2)
Utatlán Central America (Guatemala) Aztecs 124 (1) first civilizations 122 (2)
Ute people North America colonization 125 (4), 126 (1)
U Thong Mainland Southeast Asia (Thailand) ancient India 241 (6)
Utica North Africa (Tunisia) ancient Rome 179 (3), 180–181 (1) first civilizations 177 (1)
Utkala region South Asia world religions 242 (2)
Utqiagvik North America (USA) cultural groups 123 (3)
Utrecht Lat. Trajectum ad Rhenum Low Countries (Netherlands) economy 190 (1) empire and revolution 202 (1i) Franks 184 (2) medieval states 188 (1) Reformation 194 (2), 195 (5)
Utrecht province Low Countries Reformation 195 (5)
Utsunomiya Japan early modern states 265 (5)
Uttara Parvat-Asreya region South Asia early religions 48 (2)
Uttarapatha region South Asia first empires 241 (4)
Uttar Pradesh prev. United Provinces, United Provinces of Agra and Oudh region South Asia postwar politics 252 (1)
Utz North America (USA) cultural groups 122 (5)
Uvea island Pacific Ocean early cultures 280–281 (3) medieval voyages 60 (2)
Uvira Central Africa (Congo) exploration 157 (4)
Uvja see Elam
Uxmal Central America (Mexico) first civilizations 123 (2)
Uygur see Uighur City States
Uzbegs see Uzbeks
Uzbek Empire state Central Asia trade 267 (3)
Uzbekistan state Central Asia historical geography 275 (5) Islam 235 (4) Soviet Union 214–215 (4) the modern world 113 (3)
Uzbeks var. Uzbegs dynasty South Asia Mughal Empire 246 (1)
Uzbeks people Central Asia historical geography 275 (5) medieval Persia 231 (4)
Uzhgorod Eastern Europe (Ukraine) postwar politics 212 (3)

V

Vaccaei people Iberian Peninsula ancient Rome 179 (5)
Vadodara prev. Baroda South Asia (India) postwar economy 253 (5) see also Baroda
Vadsø Scandinavia (Norway) exploration 287 (2)
Vagarshapat Christian archbishopric Southwest Asia (Armenia) world religions 48 (1)
Vahavasi South Asia (India) first empires 241 (4)
Vaidisha region South Asia world religions 242 (2)
Vaiaratea island Pacific Ocean exploration 278 (1)
Vaishali mod. Besarh religious site/settlement South Asia (India) early religions 48 (2) first religions 36 (2)
Vaitea physical region Easter Island early cultures 281 (4)
Vajji region South Asia ancient India 242 (1)
Vajji Confederation state South Asia the world in 500 BCE 34–35
Vakatakas dynasty South Asia the world in 500 CE 50–51
Valabhi religious site South Asia (India) first religions 36 (2)
Valachia see Wallachia
Valdivia South America (Chile) colonization 148 (2) empire and revolution 151 (3) exploration 143 (3)
Valdivia archaeological site South America (Ecuador) early cultures 144 (1)
Valence anc. Valentia, Valentia Julia, Ventia France medieval states 192 (1)

Valencia South America (Venezuela) empire and revolution 150 (1), 151 (3) environment 153 (4)
Valencia Iberian Peninsula (Spain) economy 190 (1) Franks 184 (2) interwar 209 (4) Islam 192 (3) Napoleon 200–201 (1), 201 (2)
Valenciennes France early modern states 197 (5)
Valentia mod. Valencia Iberian Peninsula (Spain) ancient Rome 180–181 (1) see also Valencia
Valentia Julia see Valence
Valeria, Via road Italy early states 178 (1)
Valhika var. Bactra; mod. Balkh Central Asia (Afghanistan) early medieval states 244 (1) see also Bactria, Balkh
Valladolid Iberian Peninsula (Spain) economy 190 (1) interwar 209 (4) Islam 192 (3)
Valle de Bravo Central America (Mexico) first civilizations 122 (1)
Vallée d'Andorre see Andorra
Valls d'Andorra see Andorra
Valmiera see Wolmar
Valmy battle France empire and revolution 199 (4)
Valona mod. Vlorë; prev. Vlonë; It. Vlora Southeast Europe (Albania) medieval states 189 (4) WWI 207 (6)
Valparaiso South America (Chile) colonization 148 (2) empire and revolution 150 (1), 151 (3) environment 153 (4) exploration 143 (2), (3) global immigration 100 (1) imperial global economy 92 (1) politics 152 (1)
Valsequillo Central America (Mexico) the world in 10,000 BCE 14–15
Vamsha region South Asia ancient India 242 (1) world religions 242 (2)
Vanavashika region South Asia world religions 242 (2)
Vanavasi South Asia (India) early medieval states 244 (1) world religions 242 (2)
Vanchi South Asia (India) early medieval states 244 (1) first empires 241 (4)
Vancouver North America (Canada) global immigration 100 (1) the growth of the US 129 (2), 132 (1) US economy 136 (2)
Vandals people Eastern Europe ancient Rome 181 (4) great migrations 52–53 (1)
Vandals, Kingdom of state Italy/North Africa ancient Rome 182 (1) early cultures 160 (1) great migrations 53 (2)
Van Diemen's Land mod. Tasmania island Australia exploration 278 (1)
Vanga region South Asia early religions 48 (2) first empires 241 (4) world religions 242 (2)
Van, Lake var. Thospitis salt lake Southwest Asia ancient Persia 223 (4) crusades 228 (2) early agriculture 220 (1) first cities 220 (2) first civilizations 221 (4), (5), 222 (2), 25 (3) great migrations 52–53 (1) Hellenistic world 224 (1) medieval Persia 231 (4) Mongols 229 (3) Ottomans 231 (3) Seljuks 228 (1) Timur 229 (4) WWI 233 (2) 20th-century politics 233 (3)
Vannes anc. Dariorigum France Franks 184 (2) see also Dariorigum
Vanuatu prev. New Hebrides island group/state Pacific Ocean decolonization 285 (3) early cultures 280–281 (3) environmentalism 285 (2) medieval voyages 60 (2)
Vapheio Greece first civilizations 175 (4)
Várad Ger. Grosswardein, Rom. Oradea Southeast Europe (Romania) medieval states 189 (4) Ottomans 195 (4)
Varanasi prev. Banaras, Benares, Baranasi; hist. Kashi South Asia (India) early medieval states 244 (1) postwar economy 253 (5) see also Banaras, Baranasi, Benares
Varaždin Southeast Europe (Croatia) postwar economy 215 (3)
Vardar Gk. Axiós river Southeast Europe economy 215 (3) WWI 207 (6)
Varmans state South Asia early medieval states 244 (2)
Varna state. Stalin; anc. Odessus archaeological site/settlement Southeast Europe (Bulgaria) Copper Age 174 (2) economy 190 (1) Napoleon 200–201 (1) Ottomans 230 (1) WWI 207 (6)
Varshava see Warsaw
Varunadvipa state Maritime Southeast Asia world religions 243 (5)
Vasa Scandinavia (Finland) economy 205 (4)
Vasati state South Asia first empires 241 (5)
Vatapi South Asia (India) early medieval states 244 (1)
Vatapi, Chalukyas of state South Asia early medieval states 244 (1)
Vatican City state Italy the modern world 112 (2)
Vatnajökull glacier Iceland exploration 172 (2)
Vatsa region/state South Asia first empires 241 (5) first religions 36 (2)
Vatsagulma South Asia (India) early medieval states 244 (1)
Vattina Southeast Europe (Romania) Bronze Age 175 (3)
Vauchamps battle France Napoleon 200–201 (1)
Vava'u Group island group Pacific Ocean early cultures 280–281 (3) medieval voyages 60 (2)
Vegkop battle Southern Africa (South Africa) colonization 166 (2)
Veii Italy early states 178 (1), (2) first civilizations 177 (1)
Vela Goa, Velha Goa see Goa, Goa
Velho see Porto Velho
Velia var. Elea Italy early states 178 (1)
Velika Morava var. Glavn'a Morava, March, Morava, Great Morava river Central Europe postwar economy 215 (3)
Velikiye Luki Eastern Europe (Russian Federation) early modern states 195 (3)
Veliko Tŭrnovo see Tirnovo
Veliitrae Italy early states 178 (1)
Velizh Eastern Europe (Russian Federation) early modern states 195 (3)
Vellore South Asia (India) colonialism 247 (3)
Vembar var. Patmadoor South Asia (India) colonialism 247 (3)
Venaissin state France early modern states 197 (5) medieval states 192 (1), (2)
Vendée region France empire and revolution 199 (4)
Venedig see Venice

Veneti people Italy early states 178 (1), (2)
Venetia var. Lombardy-Venetia state Italy empire and revolution 202 (1), (3)
Venetia see Venice
Venetian Republic state Italy/Southwest Europe crusades 186 (1), 64–65 (2) early modern states 193 (4), 194 (1) medieval states 185 (3), 188 (1), 189 (4) Ottomans 195 (4), 231 (3) Reformation 194 (2), 196 (1)
Venezia see Venice
Venezia, Golfo di see Venice, Gulf of
Venezuela state South America economy 153 (3) empire and revolution 150 (1), 151 (3) environment 153 (4) narcotics 153 (5) politics 152 (1) the growth of the US 133 (4) the modern world 112 (1), 113 (4) US politics 139 (4) US superpower 138 (1) WWII 105 (3) Cold War 108 (2), 109 (1)
Venezuela, Gulf of see Venezuela, Gulf of
Venezuela, Gulf of var. Gulf of Maracaibo, Sp. Golfo de Venezuela gulf South America colonization 148 (2) Incas 148 (1)
Vengi South Asia (India) early medieval states 244 (1)
Vengipura South Asia (India) early religions 48 (2)
Vengurla South Asia (India) colonialism 247 (3)
Venice anc. Venetia; Fr. Venise, Ger. Venedig, It. Venezia settlement Italy biological diffusion 72–73 (1) crusades 186 (1), 64–65 (2) early modern states 193 (4) economy 190 (1) empire and revolution 202 (1), (3) European expansion 84–85 (1) Franks 184 (2) Islam 163 (1) medieval states 185 (3), (5), 188 (1) Mongols 68 (2) Napoleon 200–201 (1), 201 (2), (3) Ottomans 195 (4), 231 (3) postwar politics 212 (1), (3) WWI 210 (1), 211 (2), (3), (4) Cold War 108 (3) see also Vindobona
Vienne see Vienna
Viennensis province France ancient Rome 181 (4)
Vientiane Mainland Southeast Asia (Laos) colonialism 247 (4), 248 (1) postwar economy 253 (5) postwar politics 251 (5) world religions 243 (5)
Vientiane state Mainland Southeast Asia the world in 1800 86–87
Vierzon France medieval states 192 (1)
Vietnam state Mainland Southeast Asia Bronze Age 240 (3) colonialism 248 (1) decolonization 251 (4) economy 274 (1) Islam 275 (4) postwar economy 253 (5) postwar politics 251 (5), 253 (4), 274 (2) the modern world 113 (4) US superpower 138 (1) Cold War 109 (1)
Vieux see Viborg, Vyborg
Vijaya mod. Binh Dinh Mainland Southeast Asia (Vietnam) ancient India 241 (6) early medieval states 245 (5), (6)
Vijayanagar state South Asia the world in 1400 70–71 the world in 1500 74–75
Vijayanagara region/settlement South Asia colonialism 247 (3), 245 (4) early medieval states 244–245 (3), 245 (4)
Vijayapura South Asia (India) early medieval states 244 (2)
Vijayapura state Maritime Southeast Asia ancient India 241 (6)
Vijayawada prev. Bezwada South Asia (India) postwar economy 253 (5)
Vijosa, Vijosë see Vjosë
Vikings people Scandinavia medieval states 185 (3)
Vila Artur de Paiva see Cubango
Vila Bela var. Mato Grosso South America (Brazil) colonization 149 (3)
Vila da Ponte see Cubango
Vila do Zumbo see Zumbo
Vilagos mod. Şiria battle Central Europe (Hungary) empire and revolution 88–89 (2)
Vila Henrique de Carvalho see Saurimo
Vila Marechal Carmona see Uige
Vila Serpa Pinto see Menongue
Vilcas South America (Peru) Incas 147 (3)
Vilcas Huamán South America (Peru) Incas 148 (1)
Vilecel see Fellin
Viljandi see Fellin
Villa Alta var. S.I. Villa Alta Central America (Mexico) first civilizations 122 (1)
Villach Central Europe (Austria) WWI 207 (5)
Villa Concepción see Concepción
Villa da Barra see Manãos, Manaus
Villa de la Veracruz Central America (Mexico) colonization 125 (4)
Villa do Forte de Assumpeão see Ceará, Fortaleza
Villahermosa see San Juan Bautista
Villa Montes South America (Bolivia) politics 152 (1)
Villa San Luis Central America (Mexico) colonization 125 (4)
Villefranche-de-Conflent France early modern states 197 (5)
Vilna mod. Vilnius; Ger. Wilna, Pol. Wilno Eastern Europe (Lithuania) early modern states 193 (4), 195 (3) empire and revolution 198 (2) medieval states 189 (3), 190 (1) Napoleon 200–201 (1) WWI 207 (4) see also Vilnius, Wilno
Vilnius prev. Vilna; Ger. Wilna, Pol. Wilno Eastern Europe (Lithuania) postwar politics 212 (3) Soviet Union 214–215 (4) see also Vilna, Wilno
Vilno see Vilna
Vimeiro Iberian Peninsula (Portugal) Napoleon 200–201 (1)
Viminacium legion headquarters Southeast Europe (Yugoslavia) ancient Rome 180–181 (1)
Viminal Hill Lat. Collis Viminalis hill Italy ancient Rome 181 (2)
Viminalis Collis see Viminal Hill
Viña del Mar South America (Chile) empire and revolution 151 (3)
Vinča Southeast Europe (Yugoslavia) early agriculture 174 (1)
Vincennes fort North America (USA) empire and revolution 127 (3)
Vindava Ger. Windau, Lat. Ventspils Eastern Europe (Latvia) WWI 207 (4)
Vindhya Mountains see Vindhya Range
Vindhya-Prstha region South Asia early religions 48 (2)
Vindhya Range var. Vindhya Mountains mountain range South Asia colonialism 247 (3), 248 (1) early medieval states 244 (1), 244–245 (3) first empires 241 (4) Mughal Empire 246 (1)
Vindobona mod. Wien; Eng. Vienna, Hung. Bécs, Slvk. Videň, Slvn. Dunaj legion headquarters Central Europe (Austria) ancient Rome 180–181 (1) see also Vienna
Victoria, Lake var. Victoria Nyanza lake East Africa ancient trade 44–45 (1) early agriculture 158 (1) early cultures 160 (1) economy 163 (2), (3)
Vine Mound burial mound North America (USA) first civilizations 121 (4)
Venedig see Venice

Vinh Thai Lan see Siam, Gulf of; Thailand, Gulf of
Vinh Yen battle Mainland Southeast Asia (Vietnam) postwar politics 251 (5)
Vinjha region South Asia world religions 242 (3)
Vinland region North America medieval voyages 60–61 (1)
Vinot South Asia (Pakistan) world religions 243 (4)
Virginia colonial possession/state North America empire and revolution 127 (2), (3) the growth of the US 129 (1) US Civil War 130 (2), (3), (4), (5), 131 (6), (7) US economy 134 (2), 139 (3) US society 137 (6) US superpower 139 (5)
Virginia Capes battle North America (USA) empire and revolution 127 (3)
Virgin Islands island group West Indies Cold War 108 (1) empire and revolution 88 (1) the growth of the US 133 (4)
Virgin Islands of the United States see American Virgin Islands
Virgo, Aqua aqueduct Italy ancient Rome 181 (2)
Virū river South America early cultures 145 (3)
Virunum Central Europe (Austria) ancient Rome 180–181 (1)
Visakhapatnam South Asia (India) postwar economy 253 (5)
Visby Ger. Wisby Scandinavia (Sweden) economy 190 (1) see also Wisby
Višegrad Southeast Europe (Bosnia and Herzegovina) WWI 207 (6)
Visigoths people Southwest Asia ancient Rome 181 (4) great migrations 52–53 (1)
Visigoths, Kingdom of the state France/Iberian Peninsula ancient Rome 182 (1) early Islam 56–57 (1) Franks 183 (5), (6) great migrations 52–53 (1), 53 (2) medieval states 182 (2)
Vistula Pol. Wisła, Ger. Weichsel river Central Europe Bronze Age 175 (3) Copper Age 174 (2) crusades 64–65 (2) early agriculture 174 (1) early modern states 193 (4) economy 205 (4) empire and revolution 198 (2), 199 (3), 202 (2) exploration 172 (1) great migrations 52–53 (1) medieval states 189 (3), (4) Mongols 68–69 (1) Napoleon 200–201 (1), 201 (2), (3) prehistoric culture 17 (2)
Vitcos South America (Peru) Incas 147 (3)
Vitebsk var. Vitsyebsk Eastern Europe (Belorussia) early modern states 195 (3) economy 190 (1) Soviet Union 208 (2)
Viterbo anc. Vicus Elbii Italy economy 190 (1) medieval states 188 (1)
Vitez Southeast Europe (Bosnia and Herzegovina) postwar economy 215 (3)
Viti Levu island Pacific Ocean early cultures 280–281 (3) medieval voyages 60 (2) US superpower 138 (1)
Vitim river Eastern Europe early modern states 268 (1) first states 260 (1)
Vitoria Iberian Peninsula (Spain) Napoleon 200–201 (1)
Vitória prev. Victoria South America (Brazil) colonization 149 (3) see also Victoria
Vitsyebsk see Vitebsk
Vittorio Veneto Italy WWI 207 (5)
Viye state Southern Africa slave trade 165 (4) trade 167 (1)
Vizagapatam settlement South Asia (India) colonialism 247 (3) decolonization 250 (1) WWII 251 (3), 272 (1)
Vizcaino, Desierto de desert Central America cultural groups 123 (4)
Vjosë var. Vijosa, Vijosë, Gk. Aóos river Southeast Europe WWI 207 (6)
Vladimir var. Volodymyr-Volyns'kyy; Pol. Włodzimierz Eastern Europe (Russian Federation) medieval states 189 (4) Mongols 68–69 (1) see also Włodzimierz
Vladimir state Eastern Europe medieval states 189 (4)
Vladimir-Galich see Galicia-Volhynia
Vladivostok Siberia (Russian Federation) colonialism 269 (3), (4) Communism 271 (8) exploration 257 (2) global immigration 100 (1) imperialism 270 (2) Islam 275 (4) Russo-Japanese War 270 (4) Soviet Union 208 (2), 214–215 (4) Cold War 109 (4)
Vlonë, Vlora, Vlorë see Valona
Vogelherd archaeological site Central Europe (Germany) prehistoric culture 17 (2)
Vojvodina Ger. Wojwodina province Southeast Europe postwar economy 215 (3)
Volaterrae Italy early states 178 (1), (2) first civilizations 177 (1)
Volcae people France ancient Rome 179 (5)
Volci var. Vulci Italy first civilizations 177 (1) see also Vulci
Voldtofte Scandinavia (Denmark) Bronze Age 175 (3)
Volga river Eastern Europe ancient trade 44–45 (1), 72–73 (1) early agriculture 20–21 (2) early Islam 56–57 (1) early modern states 197 (3) economy 205 (4) empire and revolution 202 (1) exploration 172 (1), 218 (2), 219 (3) first humans 13 (2) global immigration 100 (1) great migrations 52–53 (1), 53 (2) Islam 163 (1) medieval voyages 60–61 (1) Mongols 68–69 (1) Ottomans 231 (3), 232–233 (1) prehistoric culture 16 (1), 17 (4) Soviet Union 208 (2) Timur 229 (4) WWII 210 (1), 211 (4)
Volga Bulgaria state Eastern Europe medieval states 185 (3)
Volga Bulgars var. Bulgars, White Bulgars people Eastern Europe Mongols 68–69 (1)
Volga Germans people Eastern Europe Soviet Union 213 (4)
Volgograd prev. Stalingrad, Tsaritsyn Eastern Europe (Russian Federation) Soviet Union 214–215 (4) see also Stalingrad, Tsaritsyn
Vol'mar see Wolmar
Volodymyr-Volyns'kyy see Vladimir
Vologda mod. Kirov Eastern Europe (Russian Federation) Soviet Union 208 (2)
Volsci people Italy early states 178 (2)
Volsiniensis, Lacus lake Italy early states 178 (1)
Volsinii Italy early states 178 (1), (2) first civilizations 177 (1)
Volta river West Africa Islam 163 (1)
Volta, Cape var. Dias Point headland West Africa exploration 156 (3)
Volta, Lake reservoir West Africa economy 168 (2), (3)
Volta Noire see Black Volta
Volterra see Volaterrae

BIBLIOGRAPHY

World history

Atlases:

Atlante Storico De Agostini Novara, 1995

Atlante Storico del Cristianesimo Andrea Dué, Juan Maria Laboa, Milan, 1997

Atlas Historico Universal y de Espagna Santillana Madrid, 1995

Atlas of Ancient Archaeology Jacquetta Hawkes (ed.), London, 1974

Atlas of Atlases: The Map Makers Vision of the World Phillip Allen, New York, 1992

Atlas of Disease Distributions: Analytical Approaches to Epidemiological Data Andrew D. Cliff and Peter Haggett, Oxford, 1988

Atlas of Food Crops J. Bertin (et al.), Paris, 1971

Atlas of Islamic History H.W. Hazard, Princeton, 1952

Atlas of Jewish History Dan Cohen-Sherbok, London and New York, 1996

Atlas of Modern Jewish History (revised from the Hebrew edn.) Evyatar Friesel, Oxford, New York,1990

Atlas of the Christian Church Henry Chadwick and G.R. Evans (eds.), Oxford, 1987

Atlas of the Jewish World Nicholas de Lange, Oxford, 1995

Atlas zur Geschichte V.E.B. Hermann Haack, GDR, 1988

Atlas zur Kirchengeschichte H. Jedin, K.S. Latourette, J. Martin, Freiburg, 1970

Cambridge Illustrated Atlas: Warfare, Renaissance to Revolution 1492–1792 Jeremy Black,Cambridge, 1996

Cambridge Illustrated Atlas: Warfare, The Middle Ages 768–1487 Nicholas Hooper and Matthew Bennett, Cambridge, 1996

Cassell Atlas of World History John Haywood, Brian Catchpole, Simon Hall, Edward Barratt, Oxford, 1997

Chambers Atlas of World History, Edinburgh, 1975

Collins Atlas of Twentieth Century World History Michael Dockrill, 1991

Grand Atlas Historique Georges Duby, Paris,1996

Grosser Atlas zur Weltgeschichte, Braunschweig, 1997

Grosser Historischer Weltatlas (3 vols.) Bayerischer Schulbuch-Verlag, Munich, 1981

Hammond Atlas of World History, Maplewood, New Jersey, 1997

Historical Atlas of Islam William C. Brice (ed.), Leiden, 1981

Historical Atlas of the Muslim Peoples R. Roolvink, London, 1957

Historical Atlas of World Mythology Vol. I: The Way of the Animal Powers J. Campbell, New York, 1984

Historical Atlas of World Mythology Vol. II: The Way of the Seeded Earth, Part I: The Sacrifice Joseph Campbell, New York, 1988

Historical Atlas of the World's Religions, Isma'il Ragi al Faruqi, New York, 1974

New Cambridge Modern History Atlas, H.C. Darby, Harold Fullard (eds.), 1970

Past Worlds: The Times Atlas of Archaeology C. Scarre (ed.) London, 1988

Philip's Atlas of Exploration, London, 1996

Putzger Historische Weltatlas, Berlin, 1997

Rand McNally Atlas of World History 1993 (published in England as **Philip's Atlas of World History**, London, 1992)

Review and Atlas of Palaeovegetation: Preliminary Land Ecosystem Maps of the World Since the last Glacial Maximum J.M. Adams and H. Faure (eds.), Quaternary Environments Network, www.soton.ac.uk/~tjms/adams4.html

Soguatlas, Stockholm, 1992

Társadalom – És Művelődéstörténeti Atlasz Budapest, 1991

The World...its History in Maps W.H. McNeill, M.R. Buske, A.W. Roehm, Chicago, 1969

Times Atlas of Exploration Felipe Fernandez-Armesto (ed.), London, 1991

Times Atlas of the 20th Century Richard Overy (ed.), London, 1996

Times Atlas of the Second World War J. Keegan (ed.), London, 1989

Times Atlas of World History Geoffrey Barraclough (ed.), London, 1993

Times Concise Atlas of World History Geoffrey Barraclough (ed.), London, 1994

Tortenelmi Vilagatlasz, Budapest, 1991

WDTV Atlas zur Weltgeschichte (2 vols.) H. Kinder & W. Hilgemann, Stuttgart, 1964 (Published in English as **The Penguin Atlas of World History** London, 1974 and 1978)

WWF Atlas of the Environment Geoffrey Lean and Don Hinrischsen, Oxford, 1992

West Point Atlas of American Wars: Volume II, 1900-1953 Vincent J. Esposito (chief ed.), New York, 1959

West Point Military History Series: Atlas for the Arab-Israeli War and the Korean War Thomas E. Greiss (series ed.), Wayne, New Jersey,1986

West Point Military History Series: Atlas for the Great War Thomas E. Greiss (series ed.), Wayne New Jersey, 1986

West Point Military History Series: Atlas for the Second World War (vols. I–III) Thomas E. Greiss (series ed.), Wayne, New Jersey,1985

Other works:

A History of Discovery and Exploration: The Search Begins London,1973

A History of Islamic Societies I.M. Lapidus, Cambridge, 1988

A History of World Societies John P. McKay, Bennett D. Hill, John Buckler, Boston, 1997

A Study of History Arnold Toynbee, Oxford, 1972

Asia Before Europe: Economy and Civilization of the Indian Ocean from the Rise of Islam to 1750 K.N. Chauduri, Cambridge, 1991

Before European Hegemony: The World System AD 1250-1350 J.L. Abu-Lughod, Oxford, 1991

Claudius Ptolemy: The Geography Translated and edited by Edward Luther Stevenson, London, 1991

Columbia Lippincott Gazetteer of the World Saul B. Cohen (ed.), New York, 1999

Cross-cultural Trade in World History P.D. Curtin, Cambridge, 1984

Encyclopedia of World History, revised edn. W.L. Langer (ed.), London, 1987

Heck's Pictorial Archive of Military Science, Geography and History J.G. Heck, New York, 1994

Into the Unknown National Geographic Society: Washington, 1987

Maps and History J. Black, New Haven, 1997

Maps and Politics J. Black, London,1997

Maps from the Age of Discovery, Columbus to Mercator Kenneth Nebenzahl, London, 1990

Navies and Nations: Warships, Navies and State Building in Europe and America 1500-1860 J. Glete, Stockholm, 1993

Peoples and Places of the Past National Geographic Society: Washington, 1983

Plagues and Peoples W.H. McNeill, New York, 1992

Portugaliae Monumenta Cartographica Lisbon, 1960

The Atlantic Slave Trade P.D. Curtin, Madison, 1972

The Atlantic Slave Trade: Effects on Economy, Society and Population in Africa, America and Europe J.E. Inikori, S.L. Engerman, Durham, NC 1992

The Discoverers: An Encyclopedia of Explorers and Exploration Helen Delpar (ed.), New York, 1980

The Distribution of Wild Wheats and Barleys J.R. Harlan, D. Zohary, Science, 1966

The Earth and its Peoples: a Global History Richard W. Bulliet, Pamela Kyle, Crossley, Daniel R. Headrick, Steven W. Hirsch, Lyman L. Johnson, David Northrup, Boston, New York, 1997

The Evolution of International Business G. Jones, London, 1996

The First Imperial Age: European Overseas Expansion c. 1400–1715 G.V. Scammel London, 1992

The Geography behind History W.G. East, London, 1965

The History of Cartography (various vols.) J.B. Harley, D. Woodward, Chicago, 1987–

The Hutchinson History of the World, revised edn. J.M. Roberts, London, 1987

The Mapmaker's Art: A History of Cartography John Goss, London, 1993

The Osprey Companion to Military History Robert Cowley and Geoffrey Parker, London, 1996

The Oxford History of the British Empire II, the Eighteenth Century P.J. Marshall (ed.), Oxford, 1998

The Oxford History of the British Empire: The Origins of Empire Nicholas Canny (ed.), Oxford, 1998

The Oxford Illustrated History of Modern War C. Townshend (ed.), Oxford, 1999

The Plants and Animals that Nourish Man J.R. Harlan, Scientific American, 1976

The Revolutionary Age 1760–1791 H. Quebec Neaty, London, 1966

The Rise of Christianity: A Sociologist Reconsiders History R. Stark, Princeton, 1996

The Rise of the West: A History of the Human Community W.H. McNeill, Chicago, 1991

The Rise of Western Christendom: Triumph and Diversity 200–1000 P. Brown, Oxford, 1996

The Story of Archaeology Paul G. Bahn (ed.), London, 1996

The Wealth and Property of Nations D. Landes, London, 1998

The World since 1500: A Global History, 6th edn L.S. Stavrianos, Englewood Cliffs NJ, 1991

The World to 1500: A Global History, 5th edn L.S. Stavrianos, Englewood Cliffs NJ, 1991

The World: an Illustrated History Geoffrey Parker (ed.), London, 1986

The World's Religions Ninian Smart, Cambridge, 1992

War and the World: Military Power and the Fate of Continents 1450–2000 J Black, New Haven, 1998

War in the Early Modern World 1450–1815 J. Black (ed.), London, 1999

Why Wars Happen J. Black, London, 1998

North America

Atlases:

Atlas of American Indian Affairs Francis Paul Prucha, Lincoln, Nebraska, 1990

Atlas of Ancient America Michael Coe, Dean Snow, Elizabeth Benson, Oxford and New York, 1993

Atlas of Early American History L. Cappon (et al), Chicago, 1976

Atlas of Great Lakes Indian History Helen Tanner, Norman, Oklahoma, 1987

Atlas of North American Exploration: from Norse Voyages to the Race to the Pole William H. Goetzmann, Glyndwr Williams, New York, 1992

Atlas of the Civil War James M. McPherson, New York, 1994

Atlas of the North American Indian C. Waldman, M. Braun, New York, 1995

Atlas of Westward Expansion Alan Wexler, Molly Braun, New York, 1995

Civil War Newspaper Maps, a Historical Atlas David Bosse, Baltimore and London, 1993

Historical Atlas of Canada Donald Kerr and Deryck W. Holdsworth (eds.), Toronto, 1990

Historical Atlas of the American West Warren A. Beck and Ynez D. Haase, Norman, Oklahoma, 1989

Historical Atlas of New York E. Homberger, A. Hudson, New York, 1994

Historical Atlas of the United States: Centennial Edition National Geographic Society: Washington, 1988

Mapping America's Past: a Historical Atlas M.C. Carnes, P. Williams, J. A. Garraty, New York, 1997

Our United States...its History in Maps E.B. Wesley, Chicago, 1977

Penguin Historical Atlas of North America Eric Homberger, London,1995

The Settling of North America: the Atlas of the Great Migrations into North America from the Ice Age to the Present Helen Hornbeck Tanner (ed.), New York, 1995)

Other works:

A Guide to the Historical Geography of New Spain Peter Gerhard, Norman, Oklahoma, 1993

America in 1492: the World of the Indian Peoples before the Arrival of Columbus Alvin M. Josephy, New York, 1992

An Introduction to American Archaeology (vols. 1 & 2) Englewood Cliffs, NJ, 1970

Battle Cry of Freedom: the Civil War Era James McPherson, Oxford, 1988

Documents of American History Henry Steele Commager, 1973

European and Native American Warfare 1675–1815 A. Starkey, London, 1998

Encyclopedia of North America Indians Frederick E. Hoxie, Boston, 1996

Handbook of Middle American Indians Austin, Texas, 1964-76

Handbook of North American Indians Smithsonian Institution, Washington, D.C., 1978- (20 volumes projected)

Hispaniola; Caribbean Chiefdoms in the Age of Columbus S. M.Wilson, Tuscaloosa,1990

Native American Time: a Historical Time Line of Native America Lee Francis, New York, 1996

Oxford History of the American West Clyde A. Milner et al., Oxford and New York, 1994

Prehistory of North America, 3rd edn. J.D. Jennings, Mountain View, Calif., 1989

The American Century: the Rise and Decline of the United States as a World Power Donald W. White, New Haven, 1996

The Americans: Their Archaeology and Prehistory D. Snow London, 1976

The Fur Trader and the Indian L.O. Saum London, 1965

The Limits of Liberty Maldwyn A. Jones, Oxford/New York, 1983

The Market Revolution America: Social, Political and Religious Expressions, 1800–1880 M. Stokes, S. Conway, Charlottesville, 1996

The Northern Frontier of New Spain Peter Gerhard, Norman, Oklahoma, 1993

The Slave Trade Hugh Thomas, London/New York, 1997

The Southeast Frontier of New Spain Peter Gerhard, Norman, Oklahoma, 1993

The Spanish Frontier in North America D.J. Weber, New Haven, 1992

The Maya Michael D. Coe, London, 1993

South America

Atlases:

Atlas of Ancient America Michael Coe, Dean Snow, Elizabeth Benson, Oxford and New York, 1993

Latin American History: a Teaching Atlas Cathryn L. Lombardi, John V. Lombardi, Kym L. Stoner, Madison, Wisconsin, 1983

Other works:

A History of Latin America: Empires and Sequels, 1450–1930 Peter John Bakewell, Gainesville, 1997

Anthropological Perspectives A. C. Roosevelt (ed.), Tucson and London, 1994

Ancient Mexico in the British Museum Colin McEwan, London, 1994

Ancient South America K. Bruhns, Cambridge 1994

Archaeology in the Lowland American Tropics P. W. Stahl (ed.), Cambridge, 1994

Cambridge History of Latin America Leslie Bethel (ed.), Cambridge, 1985

Chavin and the Origins of Andean Civilization R. L. Burger, London, 1992

Chiefdoms and Chieftaincy in the Americas E. M. Redmond (ed.), Malden Mass, 1997

Chieftains, Power and Trade: Regional Interaction in the Intermediate Area of the Americas C. H. Langebaek & F. C-Arroyo (eds.), Departamento de Antropologia, Universidad de los Andes: Bogota, Colombia, 1996

Moundbuilders of the Amazon. Geophysical Archaeology on Marajo Island, Brazil A. C. Roosevelt, New York, 1991

Parmana: Prehistoric Maize and Manioc Subsistence along the Amazon and Orinoco A. C. Roosevelt, New York, 1980

Prehistory of the Americas S. J. Fiedel, Cambridge, 1987

The Conquest of the Incas John Hemming, London, 1970

The Discoverie of the Large, Rich and Bewtiful Empire of Guiana by Sir Walter Ralegh N. L. Whitehead (ed.), Exploring Travel Series Vol. 1, Manchester University Press: Manchester, American Exploration and Travel Series Vol. 71, Oklahoma University Press: Norman, 1998

The Incas and Their Ancestors: The Archaeology of Peru M. E. Moseley, New York, 1992

Africa

Atlases:

An Atlas of African History J.D. Fage London, 1958

Atlas of African Affairs Ieuan LL. Griffiths, London and New York, 1994

Atlas of Ancient Egypt John Baines and Jaromir Malek, Oxford, 1996

Cultural Atlas of Africa Jocelyn Murray (ed.), Oxford, 1993

New Atlas of African History G.S.P. Freeman-Grenville, London, 1991

Penguin Historical Atlas of Ancient Egypt Bill Manley, London, 1996

Other works:

A History of West Africa (2 vols.) 3rd edn. J.F.A. Ajaya, M. Crowder, 1985

A Survey of West African History B.A. Ogot (ed.), London, 1974–1976

Africa and Africans in the Formation of the Atlantic World 1400–1680 John Thornton, Cambridge and New York, 1992

Africa and Asia: Mapping Two Continents Natalie Ettinger, Elspeth Huxley, Paul Hamilton, London, 1973

Africa in the Iron Age c.500 BC–AD 1400 R. Oliver, B. Fagan, Cambridge, 1975

Africa since 1800, 3rd edn. R. Oliver, A. Atmore, Cambridge, 1981

African Archaeology, 2nd edn. David W. Phillipson, Cambridge, 1993

An Economic History of Africa From Earliest Times to Partition P.L. Wickins, New York, 1981

Arab Seafaring in the Indian Ocean in Ancient and Medieval Times G.F. Hourani and J.Carswell, Princeton, 1995

Cambridge History of Africa J.D. Fage, R. Oliver (eds.), Cambridge, 1975–

Early Egypt: The Rise of Civilisation in the Nile Valley A.J. Spencer, London, 1993

Economic History of West Africa A.G. Hopkins, London, 1973

General History of Africa II: Ancient Civilizations of Africa G. Mokhtar (ed.), Paris and London, 1981

General History of Africa III: Africa from the Seventh to the Eleventh Century M. Elfasi (ed.), I. Hrbek (asst. ed.), Paris and London, 1981

General History of Africa VII: Africa under Colonial Domination 1880–1935 A.A. Boahen (ed.), Paris and London, 1981

Oxford History of South Africa (vols. 1 & 2) Oxford, 1969, 1971

The African Inheritance Ieuan L.L. Griffiths, London and New York, 1995

The Art and Architecture of Ancient Egypt, revised edn. W.S. Smith, London, 1981

The Changing Geography of Africa and the Middle East Graham P. Chapman and Kathleen M. Baker, London and New York, 1992

Wars and Imperial Conquest in Africa 1830–1914 B. Vandervort, London, 1998

West Africa under Colonial Rule M. Crowder, London, 1968

Europe

Atlases:

Atlas of Medieval Europe Angus Mackay, David Ditchburn (eds.), London, 1997

Atlas of the Classical World A.M. Van der Heydon, H.H. Scullard, London, 1959

Atlas of the Crusades Jonathon Riley-Smith, New York and Oxford, 1991

Atlas of the Greek World Peter Levi, Oxford, 1997

Atlas of the Roman World Tim Cornell, John Matthews, New York, 1982

Atlas Historyczny Polski Warsaw, 1967

Cultural Atlas of France John Ardagh and Colin Jones, Oxford, 1991

Cultural Atlas of Spain and Portugal Mary Vincent and R.A. Stradling, Oxford, 1994

Cultural Atlas of the Viking World J.Graham-Campbell (ed.), Oxford, 1994

Historical Atlas of East Central Europe: Volume I Paul Robert Magosci, Seattle and London, 1993

Penguin Historical Atlas of Ancient Greece Robert Morkot, London, 1996

Penguin Historical Atlas of Ancient Rome Chris Scarre, London, 1995

Penguin Historical Atlas of Russia John Channon with Robert Hudson, London, 1995

Penguin Historical Atlas of the Third Reich Richard Overy, London, 1996

Penguin Historical Atlas of the Vikings John Haywood, London, 1995

Russian History Atlas M. Gilbert, London, 1972

Times Atlas of European History London, 1994

Other works:

A History of Ancient Greece N. Demand, New York, 1996

A History of Business in Medieval Europe 1200–1550 E.H. Hunt and J. Murray, Cambridge, 1999

A Russian Economic History A. Kahan, Chicago, 1991

An Historical Geography of Western Europe before 1800, revised edn. C.T. Smith, London and New York

As the Romans Did: a Sourcebook in Roman Social History, 2nd ed. Jo-Ann Shelton, Oxford, 1997

Britain and Industrial Europe 1750–1870 W.O. Henderson, Liverpool, 1965

Britain as a Military Power 1688–1815 J. Black, London, 1999

Cambridge Economic History of Europe II: Trade and Industry in the Middle Ages, 2nd edn. A. Miller (ed.), Cambridge, 1987

Capetian France 987–1328 E. Hallam, London, 1980

Eighteenth Century Europe 2nd edn. J. Black, London, 1999

Eighteenth Century Europe: Tradition and Progress I. Woloch, London and New York, 1982

Enlightened Absolutism H.M. Scott (ed.), London, 1990

Europe in the Eighteenth Century, 2nd edn J. Black, London, 1999

Europe in the Fourteenth and Fifteenth Centuries D.Hay, London, 1966

Europe under Napoleon, 1799–1815 M.G. Broers, London, 1997

European Warfare 1453–1815 J. Black (ed.), London, 1999

Frederick II. A Medieval Emperor D.Abulafia, London, 1988

From Louis XIV to Napoleon: The Fate of a Great Power J. Black, London, 1999

From Tsar to Soviets C. Read, 1996

Gainful Pursuits: The Making of Industrial Europe 1600–1914 J. Goodman, K. Honeyman, London, 1988

Geography of the Soviet Union J.P. Cole, London, 1984

Germany and the Germans, after Unification John Ardagh, London, 1991

Germany in the Middle Ages 800–1056 T. Reuter, London, 1991

History of the Byzantine State G. Ostrogorsky, Oxford, 1969

History of the National Economy of Russia to the 1917 Revolution P.I. Lyaschenko, New York, 1949

Information USSR Oxford and New York, 1962

Ireland 1912–85 J.J. Lee, 1989

Louis XIV and the French Monarchy A. Lossky, London, 1995

Medieval England: Towns, Commerce and Crafts 1086–1348 E. Miller, J. Hatcher London, 1995

Medieval Trade in the Mediterranean World: Illustrative Documents R.S. Lopez and I.W. Raymond, reprinted New York, 1990

Money and its Use in Medieval Europe P. Spufford, Cambridge, 1988

Moorish Spain R. Fletcher, Phoenix, 1994

Napoleon and the Legacy of the French Revolution M. Lyons, London, 1994

Napoleon's Integration of Europe S.J. Woolf, London, 1991

National States and National Minorities C.A. Macartney, 1968

New Cambridge Medieval History, vol. V, c.1198–c.1300 David Abulafia (ed.), Cambridge, 1999

New Cambridge Medieval History, vol. VI, c.1300–c.1415 Michael Jones (ed.), Cambridge, 1999

New Cambridge Medieval History, vol. VII, c.1415–c.1500 Christopher Allmand Jones (ed.), Cambridge, 1998

Northern Europe in the Early Modern Period: the Baltic World 1492–1772 D. Kirby, London, 1990

Oxford Classical Dictionary, 3rd ed. Simon Hornblower and Antony Spawforth (eds.), Oxford, 1996

Oxford History of the Classical World J. Boardman (ed.), Oxford, 1989

Oxford Illustrated History of the Crusades J. Riley-Smith (ed.), Oxford, 1997

Oxford Illustrated History of the Vikings P. Sawyer (ed.) Oxford, 1997

Oxford Illustrated Prehistory of Europe B. Cunliffe, Oxford, 1994

Poverty and Capitalism in Pre-Industrial Europe C. Lis and H. Soly, Brighton, 1982

Roman Civilization (2 vols) 3rd ed. Naphtali Lewis and Meyer Reinhold (eds.), New York, 1990

Seventeenth-century Europe 1598–1700 T. Munck, London, 1990

Seventeenth–century Europe, 2nd ed. D.H. Pennington, London, 1989

Spain in the Middle Ages: from Frontier to Empire Angus Mackay, London, 1977

Textiles, Towns and Trade J.H. Munro, Aldershot, 1994

The British Revolution: British Politics 1880–1939 Robert Rhodes, London, 1976

The Cambridge Ancient History J.B. Bury, S.A. Cook, F.E. Adcock (eds.), Cambridge, 1923–; 2nd edn 1982–

The Civilization of Europe in the Renaissance J.R.Hale, London, 1993

The Creation of the Roman Frontier S.L. Dyson, Princeton, 1985

The Crusades: a Short History J.Riley-Smith, 1990

The Emergence of the Rus J. Shepherd, S. Franklin, 1996

The European Dynastic States 1494–1660 R. Bonney, Oxford, 1991

The German Hansa P.J. Dollinger, trans. D.S. Ault, S.H. Steinberg, London, 1970

The Habsburg Monarchy, 1618–1815 C. Ingrao, Cambridge, 1994

The Hundred Years War. England and France at War c.1300–c.1450 C.T. Allmand, Cambridge, 1988

The Huns E.A. Thompson, 1996

The Industrialization of Soviet Russia (3 vols.) R.W. Davis, Cambridge, 1989

The Italian City Republics, 3rd edn. D.Waley, London and New York, 1988

The Later Crusades 1274–1580: from Lyons to Alcazar N.Housley, Oxford, 1992

The Legacy of Rome: A New Appraisal Richard Jenkins (ed.) Oxford, 1992

The Making of Europe. Conquest, Colonization and Cultural Change 950–1350 R.Bartlett, London, 1993

The Making of Roman Italy Edward Togo Salmon, Ithaca, NY, 1982

The Mediterranean World in Late Antiquity AD 395–600 A.M. Cameron, London, 1993

The Merovingian Kingdoms 450–758 I.N. Wood, London, 1994

The Old European Order 1660–1800, 2nd ed. W. Doyle, Oxford, 1992

The Origins of the Second World War in Europe P.M.H. Bell, 1986

The Roman Empire, 27 BC–AD 476: A Study in Survival Chester G. Starr, New York, 1982

The State in Early Modern France J.B. Collins, Cambridge, 1995

The Struggle for Mastery in Germany, 1779–1850 B. Simms, London, 1998

The Thirty Years War Geoffrey Parker, London, 1984

The Transformation of the Roman World 400–900 L. Webster, M. Brown, London, 1997

The Two Cities. Medieval Europe 1050–1320 M.Barber, London and New York, 1992

The Wars of Napoleon C.J. Esdaile, London, 1995

The World in Depression 1929–1939 C. Kindleberger, 1973

Venice: A Maritime Republic F.C. Lane, Baltimore, 1973

War and Imperialism in Republican Rome 327–70 BC William V. Harris, Oxford, 1979

War in the Middle Ages P. Contamine, Oxford, 1984

West Asia:

Atlases:

Atlas of the Jewish World Nicholas de Lange, Oxford, 1984

Cultural Atlas of Mesopotamia and the Ancient Near East Michael Roaf, New York and Oxford, 1996

Historical Atlas of Islam William C. Brice (ed.), Leiden, 1981

Historical Atlas of the Middle East G.S.P. Freeman-Grenville, New York, 1993

Times Concise Atlas of the Bible James B. Pritchard (ed.), London, 1991

Other works:

A History of the Arab People A. Hourani, Harvard, 1991

A History of the Ottoman Empire to 1730 M.A. Cook (ed.), Cambridge, 1976

A Popular Dictionary of Islam Ian Richard Netton, Richmond, 1997

An Introduction to Islam David Waites, Cambridge, 1996

Arabia Without Sultans Fred Halliday, London, 1979

Cambridge Encyclopedia of The Middle East and North Africa Cambridge, 1988

Encyclopaedia of Islam (10 vols.) new edn. H.A.R. Gibb et al. (eds.), Leiden, 1960

Histoire de l'Empire Ottoman R. Mantran, Paris, 1989

History of the First World War B.H. Liddell Hart, London, 1979

Lords of Horizons: A History of the Ottoman Empire Jason Goodwin, Henry Hoh and Company, 1999

Middle East Sources: A MELCOM Guide to Middle Eastern and Islamic Books and Materials in the United Kingdom and Irish Libraries Ian Richard Netton, Richmond, 1998

Muhammed, Prophet and Statesman W. Montgomery Watt, London, 1961, 1967

Ottoman Warfare 1500–1600 R Murphy, London, 1999

Palestine and the Arab Israeli conflict C.D. Smith, 1994

The Age of the Crusades. The Near East from the Eleventh Century to 1517 P. M. Holt, London and New York

The Ancient Near East c. 3000–300 BC A.T.L. Kuhrt, London, 1995

The Arabs Peter Mansfield, London , 1997

The Birth of the Palestinian Refugee Problem 1947–1949 Benny Morris, Cambridge, 1988

The Cambridge History of Iran (vol. 3) E Yarshater (ed.) Cambridge, 1983

The Fifty Years War: Israel and the Arabs Ahron Bregman and Jihan el-Jahri, Penguin, London, 1996

The Lessons of Modern War: The Iran-Iraq War Anthony H. Cordesman and Abraham R. Wagner, Boulder and San Francisco, 1990

The Neolithic of the Near East J. Mellaart, London, 1975

The Ottoman Empire: The Classical Age 1300–1600 Halil Inalcik, London, 1994

The Ottoman Turks: an Introductory History to 1923 J. McCarthy, London, 1994

The Prophet and the Age of Caliphates: The Islamic Near East from the Sixth to the Eleventh Century Hugh Kennedy, London and New York, 1986

The Travels of Ibn Battuta AD 1325–1354 (4 vols.) Ibn Battuta trans. by H.A.R. Gibb and C.F. Beckingham, Cambridge, 1958–1984

The Venture of Islam (3 vols.) Marshall G.S. Hodgson, Chicago, 1974

The World of Islam Ernst J. Grube, London, 1966

The World of Islam Bernard Lewis, London, 1976

South and Southeast Asia

Atlases:

Historical Atlas of South Asia, 2nd edn. Joseph E. Schwartzberg, Oxford and New York, 1992

Historical Atlas of South-East Asia Jan M. Pluvier, Leiden, 1995

Historical Atlas of the Indian Peninsula C.C. Davies, London, 1959

Historical Atlas of the Vietnam War Harry G. Summers Jr., Boston and New York, 1995

Macmillan's Atlas of South-East Asia London, 1988

Other works:

A History of India M.A. Edwardes, London, 1961

A History of India Burton Stein, Oxford, 1998

A History of India Romila Thapar, London, 1967

A History of Malaya 1400–1959 J. Kennedy, London, 1967

A History of South-East Asia, 4th edn. D.G.E. Hall London, 1981

A History of Vedic India Z.A. Ragozin, Delhi, 1980

A New History of India S. Wolpert, Oxford, 1993

Cambridge Economic History of India, Vol. 1, c.1200–c.1750 Tapan Raycgaudhuri and Irfan Habib (eds.), Cambridge, 1981

Cambridge Economic History of India, Vol. 2, c.1757–c.1970 Dharma Kumar and Meghnad Desai (eds.), Cambridge, 1983

Early India and Pakistan to Ashoka M. Wheeler, London, 1968

In Search of Southeast Asia, revised edn. David Joel Steinberg, Honolulu, 1987

In Search of the Indo-Europeans: Language, Archaeology and Myth J.P. Mallory, London, 1994

India: A Modern History, new edn. Percival Spear, Ann Arbor, Michigan, 1972

New Cambridge History of India G. Johnson (ed.), Cambridge, 1989

Prehistoric India to 1000 BC S. Piggott, London, 1992

Prehistoric Thailand from Early Settlement to Sukhothai C.F.W. Higham, R. Thosarat, Bangkok, 1999

Prehistory of the Indo-Malay Archipelage P. Bellwood, Ryde, NSW, 1985

South-East Asia C.A. Fisher, London, 1964

Southeast Asia: An Introductory History, 2nd edn. M.E. Osborne

Southeast Asia: History, Culture, People, 5th revised edn. E. Graff, H.E. Hammond, Cambridge, 1980

Thailand: A Short History David Wyatt, New Haven, 1984

The Archaeology of Mainland Southeast Asia Charles Higham, Cambridge, 1989

The Archaeology of Mainland Southeast Asia from 1000 BC to the Fall of Angkor C.F.W. Higham, Cambridge, 1989

The Birth of Indian Civilisation B. and R. Allchin, London, 1968

The History of Post-War Southeast Asia: Independence Problems John F. Cady, Athens, Ohio, 1972

The Indianized states of Southeast Asia Georges Coedes, Honolulu, 1968

The Making of South-East Asia D.J.M. Tate, Kuala Lumpur, 1971

The Stone Age of Indonesia, revised edn. H.R. Van Heekeren, The Hague, 1972

The Traditional Trade of Asia C.F. Simkin, Oxford, 1968

The Vedic Age R.C. Majumdar, Bombay, 1971

The Wonder That Was India (2 vols.) 3rd revised edn. A.L. Basham, London, 1987

Trade and Civilization in the Indian Ocean: An Economic History of the rise of Islam to 1750 K.N. Chauduri, Cambridge, 1985

Vietnam S.C Tucker, London, 1999

War, Culture and Economy in Java 1677–1721 M.C. Ricklefs, The Hague, 1990

North and East Asia

Atlases:

Ajiarekishi chizu Matsui and Mori, Tokyo, 1965

Atlas of China Chiao-min Hsieh, USA, 1973

Cultural Atlas of China, C. Blunden and M. Elvin, Oxford, 1991

Historical and Commercial Atlas of China A. Herrmann, Harvard, 1935

Historical Atlas of China A. Herrmann, Edinburgh, 1966

Cultural Atlas of Japan, M. Collcutt, M. Jansen, Isao Kumakura Oxford, 1991

Nihon rekishi jiten Atlas Tokyo, 1959

Times Atlas of China P.J.M. Geelan D.C. Twitchett (eds.), London, 1974

Tubinger Atlas der Orients (various vols.) Wiesbaden, 1972-

Other works:

A Historical Geography of Russia H.Parker (ed.), London, 1968

A History of the Peoples of Siberia J. Forsyth, Cambridge, 1992

Cambridge Illustrated History of China P. B. Ebrey, Cambridge, 1996

Cambridge History of China D. Twitchett, M. Loewe (eds.), Cambridge, 1979–

China, Korea and Japan: The Rise of Civilization in East Asia, Gina L. Barnes London, 1993

The Early Civilization of China Yong Yap and A. Cotterel, London, 1975

Histoire du Parti Communiste Chinois J. Guillermaz, Paris, 1968, English translation 1972

Inner Asian Frontiers of China O. Lattimore, New York, 1951

An Introduction to Chinese History, B. Wiethoff London, 1975

Le Monde Chinois J. Gernet, Paris, 1969; English translation 1982

The Archaeology of Ancient China, 4th edn. K.C. Chang, New Haven, 1986

The Empire of the Steppes: A History of Central Asia R. Grousset, New Brunswick, NJ, 1970

World Prehistory, G. Clarke, Cambridge, 1977

Australasia and Oceania

Atlases:

Aboriginal Languages and Clans: An Historical Atlas of Western and Central Victoria J.D. Clark, Clayton, South Australia, 1990

Cultural Atlas of Australia New Zealand and the South Pacific Richard Nile and Christian Clerk, Oxford, 1996

Other works:

A Prehistory of Australia, New Guinea, and Sahul J.P. White and J.F. O'Connell, Sydney, 1982

Aboriginal Australians: Black Responses to White Dominance Richard Broome, Sydney, 1982

Australia Unveiled Günter Schilder, Amsterdam, 1976

Australian Civilisation Richard Nile (ed.), Melbourne, 1994

Blood on the Banner: Nationalist Struggles in the South Pacific D.Robie, London, 1989

Convict Workers: Reinterpreting Australian History Stephen Nicholas, Cambridge (UK), 1988

Culture and Democracy in the South Pacific Ron Crocombe et al. (eds.), Suva, Fiji, 1992

Dispossession: Black Australians and White Invaders Henry Reynolds (ed.), Sydney, 1989

Easter Island Studies Steven Roger Fischer (ed.), Oxford, 1993

Ethnicity, Class and Gender in Australia Gill Bottomley and Marie de Lepervanche (eds.), Sydney, 1991

European Vision and the South Pacific Bernard Smith, New Haven, Conn., 1992

Fatal Necessity: British Intervention in New Zealand Peter Adams, Auckland, 1977

Frontier: Aborigines, Settlers and the Land Henry Reynolds, Sydney, 1987

Historical Charts and Maps of New Zealand Peter B. Maling, Auckland, 1996

History of Australia John Malony, Ringwood, Victoria (Australia), 1987

History of New Zealand Keith A. Sinclair, Auckland, 1988

History of the Pacific Islands I.C.Campbell, Berkeley, 1989

Man's Conquest of the Pacific Peter Bellwood, Auckland, 1978

Native Lands: Prehistory and Environmental Usage in Australia and the South-West Pacific J. Dodson (ed.), Melbourne, 1992

New History of Australia Frank Crowley, Melbourne, 1974

New Zealand Politics in Perspective H. Gold, Auckland, 1985

Oxford History of Australia Geoffrey Bolton (ed.), Melbourne, 1994

Oxford History of New Zealand W.H. Oliver and B.R. Williams, Wellington, 1981

Oxford Illustrated History of New Zealand Keith Sinclair (ed.), Auckland, 1990

Pacific Navigation and Voyaging Ben F. Finney (ed.), Wellington, 1976

Social Change in the Pacific Islands A.D. Robillard (ed.), London, 1992

Sunda and Sahul: Prehistoric Studies in Southeast Asia, Melanesia and Australia J. Allen, J. Golson and R. Jones (eds.), London, 1977

The Australian Colonists K.S. Inglis, Melbourne, 1974

The Discovery of the Pacific Islands Andrew Sharp, Oxford, 1960

The Evolution of Highland Papua New Guinea Societies D.K. Feil, Cambridge, 1987

The Exploration of the Pacific J.C. Beaglehole, Stanford, 1966

The Journals of Captain James Cook on his Voyages of Discovery (4 vols.) Beaglehole, J.C. (ed.), Cambridge, 1955–1974

The Maori Population of New Zealand 1769–1971 Ian Pool, Auckland, 1977

The Pacific Islands: Politics, Economics and International Relations Te'o I.J. Fairburn et al., Honolulu, 1991

The Pacific Since Magellan O.H.K. Spate, Canberra, 1988

The People's History of Australia since 1788 Verity Burgman and Jenney Lee (eds.), Melbourne, 1988

The Polynesians Peter Bellwood, London, 1987

The Prehistoric Exploration and Colonisation of the Pacific Geoffrey Irwin, Cambridge, 1992

The Prehistory of Australia D.J. Mulvaney, Ringwood, Victoria (Australia), 1975

The Prehistory of Polynesia Jesse D. Jennings (ed.), Cambridge (USA), 1979

The Quiet Revolution: Turbulence and Transition in Contemporary New Zealand Colin James, Wellington, 1986

The South Pacific: An Introduction Ron Crocombe, Suva, Fiji, 1989 (revised edition)

The World of the First Australians: Aboriginal Traditional Life – Past and Present R.M. and C.H Berndt, Canberra, 1988

We, the Navigators: The Ancient Art of Land-finding in the Pacific David Lewis, Canberra, 1972

Chronologies

Chronology of the Ancient World E.J. Bickermann, London, 1968

Chronology of the Expanding World N. Williams, London, 1969

Chronology of the Modern World N. Williams, London, 1961

Encyclopedia of Dates and Events L.C. Pascoe (ed.), London, 1991

Acknowledgments

The publisher would like to thank the following for their kind permission to reproduce the photographs.

A = Above, b = below, B = Bottom, C = Centre, L = Left, R = Right, T = Top.

1 © 1996 Visual Language.
2/3 © 1996 Visual Language.
5 E.T. Archive: British Library, London TC
10/11 © Michael Holford: British Museum, London.
12 The Natural History Museum, London: TRb, CA, CRA, CB; Science Photo Library: John Reader TL.
13 The Natural History Museum, London: TCL, TR; Science Photo Library: John Reader TCR.
14 DK Picture Library: CL, BCL; Professor Joseph E. Schwartzberg: CR.
15 DK Picture Library: CRA; Ashmolean Museum, Oxford TR; University Museum of Archaeology and Anthropology, Cambridge TL; Eye Ubiquitous: John Miles CRb.
16 CM Dixon: CR; DK Picture Library: CLL, BL, BCR; University Museum of Archaeology and Anthropology, Cambridge TL; Dr David Price Williams: CL.
17 Ancient Art & Architecture Collection: Ronald Sheridan TCR; Coo-ee Historical Picture Library: Ron Ryan BR; DK Picture Library: University Museum of Archaeology and Anthropology, Cambridge TL, CR; © Michael Holford: TCL.
18 Ancient Art & Architecture Collection: Ronald Sheridan TRb; James Mellaart: BR; Scala, Florence: Ancient Art & Architecture, Belgrade CL; The Utah Museum of Natural History, University of Utah: BL.
19 British Museum, London: TCRb; Robert Harding Picture Library: Bildagentur Schuster / Schenk BR; © Michael Holford: Ankara Museum TCL; Catherine Jarrige: Centre de Recherches Archéologiques Indus-Baluchistan, Musée Guimet, Paris CRb.
20 DK Picture Library: CL(round-based shape); British Museum, London TL, CL(flat-based beaker); Museum of London CA.
21 Bridgeman Art Library, London / New York: Photograph: Mrs Sally Greene TL; DK Picture Library: TR, BCL; British Museum, London BC.
22 DK Picture Library: TR; Robert Harding Picture Library: John G Ross BRA; Karachi Museum, Pakistan: Presented by Mrs Alice K Bache, Purchased from James Judge and Eugenia Rodriquez / Photograph: David Heald BL.
23 James Davis Travel Photography: TC; Robert Harding Picture Library: TRb, CR; © Michael Holford: British Museum, London CL.
24 British Museum, London: CLb; DK Picture Library: British Museum, London BL; Werner Forman Archive: Ashmolean Museum, Oxford TR; Hirmer Verlag München: Iraq Museum, Baghdad CbL.
25 Bridgeman Art Library, London / New York: Ashmolean Museum, Oxford BRA; British Museum, London TRb; DK Picture Library: British Museum, London C, CR, BR; University Museum of Archaeology and Anthropology, Cambridge BRA.
26 AKG London / Erich Lessing: BL; Bridgeman Art Library, London / New York: National Archaeological Museum, Athens BL(insert); E.T. Archive: National Museum, Copenhagen TRb; National Museum of the American Indian: Smithsonian Institute / Collected by MR Harrington / Photograph: David Heald CL.
27 AKG London: Archaeological Museum, Heraklion TL; AKG London / Erich Lessing: BCL; © Michael Holford: Musée Cernuschi CRA; DK Picture Library: Musée Cernuschi CRb; The University of Auckland: Department of Anthropology / Excavated by Prof. R.C. Green CRb.
28 Bridgeman Art Library, London / New York: Musée du Louvre, Paris TL; DK Picture Library: British Museum, London BLA; Friedrich-Schiller-Universität Jena / Hilprecht Collection of Near Eastern Antiquities: Prof. Dr. Manfred Krebernik CL; Turkish Information Office, London: BLA.
29 © Michael Holford: BRA; Ashmolean Museum, Oxford BR; The Institute of Archaeology, Beijing: Professor Zheng Zhen Xiang CRA.
30 Werner Forman Archive: Anthropology Museum, Veragruz University, Jalapa TR; South American Pictures: Kathy Jarvis CL.
31 Bridgeman Art Library, London / New York: Royal Albert Memorial Museum, Exeter BCL; DK Picture Library: British Museum, London TCL; E.T. Archive: British Museum, London CRA; Historical Museum of Armenia, Erevn TCR; Robert Harding Picture Library: CRb.
32 Bridgeman Art Library, London / New York: France, Paris TL; DK Picture Library: Peter Willi CLL; DK Picture Library: British Library, London C; British Museum, London TL, TCR, BL, BCL; © Michael Holford: British Museum, London CL; Musée du Louvre, Paris CR.
33 Bridgeman Art Library, London / New York: Ashmolean Museum, Oxford CR(Athenian coin); British Museum, London TLb, CRA; © Michael Holford: British Museum, London TCLb; Robert Harding Picture Library: BCL; AT R.
34 British Museum, London: CL; E.T. Archive: TCR; N.J. Saunders: CLb.
35 DK Picture Library: Ashmolean Museum, Oxford CRb; British Museum, London TLb, CRA; © Michael Holford: British Museum, London TCLb; Robert Harding Picture Library: BCL; AT R.
36 AKG London / Erich Lessing: Iraq Museum, Baghdad TL; E.T. Archive & Architecture Collection: Brian Wilson TCR; Werner Forman Archive: BL.
37 AKG London: BR; The Israel Museum, Jerusalem CRA; AKG London / Erich Lessing: National Museum of Archaeology, Naples CLA; DK Picture Library: British Museum, London TCL; Werner Forman Archive: Musées Royaux du Cinquantenaire, Brussels CbL.
38 E.T. Archive: British Library, London BR; Werner Forman Archive: David Bernstein Collection, New York BL; © Michael Holford: British Museum, London BCR; Tony Stone Images: Robert Everts TCR.
39 E.T. Archive: The Hermitage, Leningrad CRA; National Archaeological Museum, Naples TR; The Art Archive CRb.
40 E.T. Archive: National Archaeological Museum, Naples CL; Robert Harding Picture Library: Archaeological Museum, Istanbul C / Photograph: Christina Gascoigne TL; R Ashworth TCR; Scala, Florence: Museo Capitolini, Rome BL.

41 British Museum, London: CRb; Robert Harding Picture Library: CRA; Réunion des Musées Nationaux Agence Photographique: Musée des Arts Asiatique-Guimet, Paris C; Scala, Florence: Museo di Villa Giulia, Rome TCR; Museo Gregoriano Egizio, Vatican TL.
42 Axiom: Guy Marks TC; Bridgeman Art Library, London / New York: Bridgeman Art Library, London BRA; E.T. Archive: Archaeological Museum, Lima CL; Scala, Florence: Museo della Civilta' Romana, Rome BCL.
43 Axiom: James Morris CR; Robert Harding Picture Library: TRb; Richard Ashworth CRb; Novosti (London): TCL.
44 Bridgeman Art Library, London / New York: British Museum, London TR; CM Dixon: CLb; E.T. Archive: Archaeological Museum of Merida CL; Robert Harding Picture Library: TL, CA.
45 Ancient Art & Architecture Collection: B Crip TR; J Powell: CRA; Chris Scarre: BC.
46 Ancient Art & Architecture Collection: Ronald Sheridan BL; Bridgeman Art Library, London / New York: British Museum, London CL; Fitzwilliam Museum, University of Cambridge TC.
47 Bruce Coleman Ltd: Fred Bruemmer TL; Robert Harding Picture Library: TC; © Michael Holford: British Museum, London TRb; Museo Prenestino CR; Réunion des Musées Nationaux Agence Photographique: Musée des Arts Asiatiques-Guimet, Paris / Photograph: Richard Lambert BR.
48 Bridgeman Art Library, London / New York: British Museum, London TCb; Galleria e Museo Estense, Modena CRb; National Museum of India, New Delhi BCA; British Museum, London: TL.
49 CM Dixon: Victoria & Albert Museum, London BR; Werner Forman Archive: TLb.
50 AKG London / Erich Lessing: Musée Lapidaire, Arles TC; Werner Forman Archive: Private Collection, New York CLb; © Michael Holford: British Museum, London CRb.
51 DK Picture Library: British Museum, London TR; Werner Forman Archive: CRb; Sonia Halliday Photographs: CbL; Chinese Exhibition TCL.
52 Ancient Art & Architecture Collection: Ronald Sheridan BL; Bridgeman Art Library, London / New York: Private Collection TC; © Michael Holford: British Museum, London BC.
53 AKG London / Erich Lessing: National Museum, Budapest CRb; Ancient Art & Architecture Collection: Ronald Sheridan TC; E.T. Archive: Archaeological Museum, Madrid BL.
54 Bridgeman Art Library, London / New York: San Vitale, Ravenna TC; Werner Forman Archive: National Museum of Anthropology, Mexico BR; © Michael Holford: Museum of Mankind, London CbL.
55 Werner Forman Archive: Idemitsu Museum of Arts, Tokyo CR; Robert Harding Picture Library: Bildagentur Schuster / Krauskopf TL; Bridgeman Art Library, London / New York: British Museum, London; Leiden University Library, The Netherlands: (Or. 3101) TCR.
56 Ancient Art & Architecture Collection: Ronald Sheridan TL; Bridgeman Art Library, London / New York: British Library, London (Or.6810 f.27v) CL; Werner Forman Archive: TC.
57 AKG London: Bibliothèque Nationale de France, Paris (Arabe 5847, fol.84) TL; Robert Harding Picture Library: D Kraus TCL.
58 DK Picture Library: British Museum, London CRb; Robert Harding Picture Library: Gavin Hellier TC; Tony Stone Images: Robert Frerck CLb.
59 Bodleian Library: (Ms. Marsh 144 P.167) CR; Bridgeman Art Library, London / New York: British Library, London TL; British Library, London: TC; DK Picture Library: British Museum, London CRb; E.T. Archive: British Museum, London CRb.
60 Bridgeman Art Library, London / New York: Science Museum, London C; Coo-ee Historical Picture Library: BL; Werner Forman Archive: State Historiska Museum, Stockholm TL; © Trustees of the National Museums of Scotland: TCR.
61 AKG London: Bibliothèque Nationale, Paris (Arabe 5847, fol.119) BL.
62 Axiom: Chris Bradley CR; Bodleian Library: Pococke (Ms. fol. 3v-4r) CL; Werner Forman Archive: Maxwell Museum of Anthropology, Albuquerque, New Mexico BL; Robert Harding Picture Library: TCR.
63 Bridgeman Art Library, London / New York: Bibliothèque Nationale de France, Paris (Fr 2630 f.111v) TC; E.T. Archive: National Palace Museum, Taiwan CR; Robert Harding Picture Library: CRb; Hulton Getty: (Ms. Bodleian 264) TL.
64 Bridgeman Art Library, London / New York: Château Roux, Fred Bruemmer CL; British Library, London (Roy 2A XX11 f.220) TL, (Add 42130 f.82) BC.
65 E.T. Archive: Bibliothèque Nationale de France, Paris TLb; Robert Harding Picture Library: C.
66 DK Picture Library: British Library, London BL; Museum of Mankind, London C; Robert Harding Picture Library: Bodleian Library, Oxford TCL.
67 Bridgeman Art Library, London / New York: Bibliothèque Nationale de France, Paris CR; DK Picture Library: National Maritime Museum, London TR; Robert Harding Picture Library: BR; I Van Der Harst BCL; © Michael Holford: British Museum, London TL.
68 Bridgeman Art Library, London / New York: National Palace Museum, Taipei TL; Private Collection TR; DK Picture Library: British Library, London CL.
69 Bridgeman Art Library, London / New York: British Museum, London CR; Victoria & Albert Museum, London BR; Werner Forman Archive: Formerly Gulistan Imperial Library, Teheran CLA.
70 Bridgeman Art Library, London / New York: British Museum, London BL; Werner Forman Archive: University Library, Prague TC.
71 Bridgeman Art Library, London / New York: British Library, London: (Harl.4379, fol.83v) TL; Robert Harding Picture Library: TR; MPH CR; Adam Woolfitt BR.
72 Bridgeman Art Library, London / New York: British Library, London (Harl 4380, f.22) BC; Jean-Loup Charmet: Musée d'Histoire de la Medecine, Lyon CLA; E.T. Archive: National Maritime Museum, London TL; Scala, Florence: State Archive, Lucca BL; Jean-Loup Charmet: Musée du Burghbar BL(insert).
73 Collections: Liz Stares CA; Katz Pictures: The Mansell Collection / Time Inc. BLA; Scala, Florence: Galleria Sabauda, Torino CR.
74 AKG London: BC; E.T. Archive: TR; Tony Stone Images: Jerry Alexander CLb.
75 AKG London: TC; Pinacoteca Vaticana, Rome TL; Ancient Art & Architecture Collection: Ronald Sheridan BLA; E.T. Archive: CRb; Sonia Halliday Photographs: CAR.
76 E.T. Archive: Bibliothèque Nationale de France, Paris TL

77 Bridgeman Art Library, London / New York: Bibliothèque Nationale d France, Paris (Fr 2810 f.188) BCL; E.T. Archive: University Library, Istanbul BL; Library of Congress, Washington, D.C.: (GA 1124 1555 F.8 G&M RR Plate 43) BR.
78 Bridgeman Art Library, London / New York: Kunsthistorisches Museum, Vienna TCR; DK Picture Library: BCL; © Michael Holford: British Museum, London BCR; Peter Newark's Pictures: CL.
79 Bridgeman Art Library, London / New York: Bibliothèque Nationale de France, Paris (Fr 2810, f.84) CRb; DK Picture Library: British Library, London CRb; Sonia Halliday Photographs: Topkapi Palace Museum, Istanbul TL.
80 AKG London: BL; Bridgeman Art Library, London / New York: British Library, London (Sloane 197 f.18) TL; Werner Forman Archive: Art Institute, Chicago BR.
81 Bridgeman Art Library, London / New York: Prado, Madrid / Index BC; British Library, London TC; J Institut Amatller D'Art Hispanic, Barcelona: CR.
82 Bridgeman Art Library, London / New York: Château de Versailles, France / Giraudon TC; Peter Newark's Pictures: CL.
83 E.T. Archive: Musée Guimet Paris TC; Robert Harding Picture Library: BL; M Robertson CRb; © Michael Holford: Science Museum, London TCLb; Royal Geographical Society Picture Library: Cr.
84 Bridgeman Art Library, London / New York: British Library, London BC; DK Picture Library: TL; E.T. Archive: National Maritime Museum, London CAR.
85 AKG London: TL; DK Picture Library: BL; E.T. Archive: Bibliothèque Nationale de France, Paris TCR; Mary Evans Picture Library: Cb; Peter Newark's Pictures: TL.
86 DK Picture Library: National Maritime Museum, London BCL; Peter Newark's Pictures: TC, CL.
87 Bridgeman Art Library, London / New York: Victoria & Albert Museum, London CR; British Museum, London: TC; Werner Forman Archive: British Museum, London BL; National Maritime Museum, London: TL.
88 Bridgeman Art Library, London / New York: Private Collection CA; Hulton Getty: TL; Peter Newark's Pictures: CL.
89 The Granger Collection, New York: TCR; Hulton Getty: BR; Peter Newark's Pictures: BL.
90 Bridgeman Art Library, London / New York: Private Collection CRb; Image Select: Ann Ronan TC; Public Record Office Image Library: BCL; Peter Newark's Pictures: CL.
91 Bridgeman Art Library, London / New York: National Maritime Museum, London TL; Alexander Turnbull Library, National Library of New Zealand, Te Puna Mātauranga o Aotearoa CR; The Stapleton Collection BC; DK Picture Library: TCR.
92 Mary Evans Picture Library: TCR, CL; Hulton Getty: TL; Library of Congress, Washington, D.C.: C.
93 Corbis: Bettmann CA, CRA; Mary Evans Picture Library: CLb.
94 Bridgeman Art Library, London / New York: Historisches Museum der Stadt, Vienna TC; Public Record Office Picture Library: BC; William L Clements Library, University of Michigan CL.
95 AKG London: BC; British Library, London: (Shelfmark No. 2443) TC; Werner Forman Archive: CD Wertheim Collection TL; Peter Newark's Pictures: TR.
96 Jean-Loup Charmet: CLb; Mary Evans Picture Library: TL, TR; Hulton Getty: RAbb.
97 Corbis: BL; Mary Evans Picture Library: TCRb, TRb.
98 Advertising Archives: CL; E.T. Archive: BC; Frank Spooner Pictures: Roger Viollet TCR.
99 AKG London: TL; Jean-Loup Charmet: BC; Jagadeesh: Underwood TL; National Motor Museum, Beaulieu: CR.
100 Corbis: Bettmann BCL; DK Picture Library: National Maritime Museum, London TL; Mary Evans Picture Library: CLA, BL.
101 Corbis: Bettmann CAL; Peter Newark's Pictures: CRb.
102 Corbis: Burs Can TCR; Hulton-Deutsch Collection BR; Hulton Getty: Keystone / Oscar Kersenbaum BC; London Transport Museum: CL.
103 Hulton Getty: TL, TR, BC.
104 Rex Features: TL.
105 – Corbis: UPI / Bettmann BL; Topham Picturepoint: C; Associated Press TLb.
106 Robert Harding Picture Library: David Lomax BC; Frank Imaging CL.
107 DK Picture Library: TC, CR; Hulton Getty: TL; Frank Spooner Pictures: Cilo BC.
108 Corbis: Bettmann / UPI TL; Hulton Getty: BL; Topham Picturepoint: A Young-Joon C.
109 Rex Features: TC; Sipa-Press BL; Topham Picturepoint: A Young-Joon C.
110 Robert Harding Picture Library: R Hanbury-Tenison BC; Rex Features: Sipa-Press TR; Science Photo Library: CNES, 1986 Distribution Spot Image TL.
111 Corbis: Philippe Wojazer / Reuter BC; Rex Features: Setbaun / Sipa-Press TC; Corbis: Jagadeesh Nv / Reuters TCb; Tony Stone Images: Robert Mort CR.
112 Rex Features: TL; Alexandra Boulat BR; Frank Spooner Pictures: Gamma / Tom Kidd CLB; Still Pictures: Jorgen Shytte CLA.
113 Corbis: Reuters TC; Panos Pictures: Chris Stowers CbR; Rex Features: Sipa Press BR.
114/115 © 1996 Visual Language.
116 DK Picture Library: TL.
117 Robert Harding Picture Library: Robert Frerck / Odyssey / Chicago BC; Tony Stone Images: Tom Bean Cb; Jake Rajas CRb.
118 Bibliothèque Nationale de France, Paris: BC; Bridgeman Art Library, London / New York: British Library, London BL; Robert Harding Picture Library: New York Historical Society TL; Musée de L'Homme, Paris TC; Ponsard CLA.
119 DK Picture Library: TL, BL, CRb; Robert Harding Picture Library: TLb.
120 DK Picture Library: TC, CR; E.T. Archive: BL; Werner Forman Archive: Field Museum of Natural History, Chicago CL; Robert Harding Picture Library: Robert Frerck / Odyssey / Chicago TCR.
121 Werner Forman Archive: British Museum, London TC; Ohio State Museum BL.
122 Bridgeman Art Library, London / New York: British Museum, London TL; James Davis Travel Photography: Cb; E.T. Archive: BL; Robert Harding Picture Library: Robert Frerck / Odyssey / Chicago TCR.
123 DK Picture Library: Museum of Mankind, London TL; Werner Forman Archive: Arizona State Museum C; Museum of the American Indian, Heye Foundation, New York CR.
124 Ancient Art & Architecture Collection: Ronald Sheridan TR; E.T. Archive: Antochiw Collection Cb; National Library, Mexico TL; Werner Forman Archive: British Museum, London CA.
125 Ancient Art & Architecture Collection: G Tortoli TL; Robert Harding Picture Library: Mexican Museum of Natural History BR; Peter Newark's Pictures: CRA.
126 E.T. Archive: TC; Peter Newark's Pictures: TL, CR.
127 AKG London: TR; Trinity College, Cambridge BR; Peter Newark's Pictures: CLA, BC.
128 Bridgeman Art Library, London / New York: City of Bristol Museum and Art Gallery TL; Corbis: Bettmann TCR; Peter Newark's Pictures: BCL.
129 Bridgeman Art Library, London / New York: Photograph: D.F. Barry, Dakota TRb; Mary Evans Picture Library: CR; Robert Harding Picture Library: National Gallery of Art, Washington CR.
130 Corbis: Bettmann TR, C; Mary Evans Picture Library: TL.
131 Corbis: Bettmann BC; Mary Evans Picture Library: CRb; Alexander Gardener TC.
132 Bridgeman Art Library, London / New York: Liberty Island, New York TL; Corbis: Bettmann / UPI TCR; Peter Newark's Pictures: TRb, BR.
133 AKG London: Photograph: Agustin Victor Casasola, (1874-1938) TLb; Peter Newark's Pictures: CL.
134 Corbis: CAL, Cb, BL; Bettmann TL; Hulton Getty: TCR.
135 Corbis: TR; Mary Evans Picture Library: CRb; Ronald Grant Archive: CA, © Disney CLA; Peter Newark's Pictures: TL.
136 Corbis: Grant Smith TCR; Robert Harding Picture Library: D Lomax BR; Peter Newark's Pictures: CRb; Frank Spooner Pictures: Hulton Getty Liaison TL.
137 Corbis: CLA; UPI TC, BL; Redferns: Elliot Landy CRb.
138 Corbis: Bettmann / UPI CL; Najlah Feanny C; Rex Features: JFK Library TL.
139 Corbis: Bettmann / UPI TCR; Reuters CR; Sygma TCRb; Rex Features: Sipa-Press TC.
140 Robert Harding Picture Library: Christopher Rennie CLb; N.H.P.A.: M Wendler CR; South American Pictures: Tony Morrison BC.
141 E.T. Archive: Biblioteca Estense, Modena CL; Mary Evans Picture Library: Cartes e Plans, Bibliothèque Nationale de France TC.
142 E.T. Archive: Biblioteca Estense, Modena TLb; Robert Harding Picture Library: TC, CL.
143 Bridgeman Art Library, London / New York: Royal Geographical Society, London BC; Robert Harding Picture Library: National Gallery, East Berlin CRb; Royal Geographical Society Picture Library: TLb.
144 Bridgeman Art Library, London / New York: British Museum, London BR; E.T. Archive: University Museum, Cuzco BL; Robert Harding Picture Library: Robert Frerck / Odyssey / Chicago CRb; South American Pictures: Tony Morrison TL.
145 Ancient Art & Architecture Collection: Mike Andrews BR; Bridgeman Art Library, London / New York: British Museum, London BC; Werner Forman Archive: David Bernstein Fine Art, New York CL.
146 Bridgeman Art Library, London / New York: British Museum, London TL; E.T. Archive: Dumbarton Oaks Research Library and Collections, Washington, D.C.: BC; © Michael Holford: Collection of Señor Mujica Gallo, Lima TL, BL; South American Pictures: Kimball Morrison CbL.
147 Ancient Art & Architecture Collection: Museo Oro del Peru, Lima / Photograph: R Sheridan CbR; E.T. Archive: Museo del Oro, Bogota CL; Werner Forman Archive: Museum fur Volkerkunde, Berlin BCA; Robert Harding Picture Library: BLA; South American Pictures: Tony Morrison TL.
148 Jean-Loup Charmet: TR; E.T. Archive: Archbishop Palace Museum Cuzco TL; Mary Evans Picture Library: BC; Robert Harding Picture Library: British Museum, London Cb; South American Pictures: CL.
149 Bridgeman Art Library, London / New York: Harold Samuel Collection, Corporation of London BC; Jean-Loup Charmet: Bibliothèque des Arts Decoratifs CL; E.T. Archive: BL; Royal Geographical Society Picture Library: TCR.
150 AKG London: TL, CL; DK Picture Library: TCR.
151 Bridgeman Art Library, London / New York: British Museum, London BR; Mary Evans Picture Library: CL; Robert Harding Picture Library: Adam Woolfitt TCR.
152 Rex Features: Sipa-Press / Arias TL; Sygma: A Balaguer TC; Topham Picturepoint: Cb.
153 Panos Pictures: Michael Harvey Cb; Rex Features: Sipa-Press / Patrick Robert TR; Sipa-Press / Poveda TR.
154 Bruce Coleman Ltd: Christer Fredriksson CLb; Tony Stone Images: Hugh Sitton CRb; World Pictures: BC.
155 DK Picture Library: TL; E.T. Archive: British Library, London BR; Katz Pictures: The Mansell Collection / Time Inc. CL.
156 AKG London: TR; Bridgeman Art Library, London / New York: Royal Geographical Society, London CbL; Royal Geographical Society Picture Library: TL; Topham Picturepoint: BR.
157 AKG London: TR; Bridgeman Art Library, London / New York: Egyptian Museum, Berlin, SMPK TL; Robert Estall Photo Library: David Coulson CRA; Dr David Price Williams: TCR.
158 AKG London / Erich Lessing: Egyptian Museum, Berlin, SMPK TL; Bridgeman Art Library, London / New York: Musée du Louvre, Paris / Giraudon TC; Mary Evans Picture Library: BR.
159 Axiom: James Morris CR; Robert Harding Picture Library: Gavin Hellier CL.
160 Werner Forman Archive: Courtesy Entswitle Gallery, London TC; Sonia Halliday Photographs: James Wellard CAR; Dr David Price Williams: CAL.
161 AKG London / Jean-Louis Nou: TR; Ancient Art & Architecture Collection: Ronald Sheridan TC; Werner Forman Archive: Cb.
162 Ashmolean Museum, Oxford: Hebreden Coin Room TL; Werner Forman Archive: TC; Tanzania National Museum, Dar Es Salaam TCb; © Michael Holford: British Museum, London TRB.
163 Musée de l'Homme, Paris: BCL.
164 Bridgeman Art Library, London / New York: British Library, London (Sloane 197 f.225v-6) TCb; British Library, London BR; DK Picture Library: TL.
165 Axiom: Chris Bradley TR; Jean-Loup Charmet: Bibliothèque Nationale, Paris BLA; Robert Hunt Library: BL.
166 Mary Evans Picture Library: TL, CL, CRb; Sonia Halliday Photographs: Africana Library, Durban / Photograph: Jane Taylor BC.

167 Chester Beatty Library, Dublin: (Ms 1599 fols 1v-2r) TCb; Corbis: Bettmann BR.
168 Corbis: Bettmann CAL; UPI Photo TL.
169 PA News Photo Library: EPA Photo / Lusa / Joao Relvas CL; Panos Pictures: Betty Press BR.
170 The J. Allan Cash Photolibrary: BCR; Bruce Coleman Ltd: Dr Eckart Pott Cb; World Pictures: CRb.
171 AKG London: Postmuseum, Berlin BR; DK Picture Library: National Museum CLb(insert); Statens Historika Museum, Stockholm CLb; © Michael Holford: Science Museum, London TL.
172 AKG London: Postmuseum, Berlin TCR; DK Picture Library: National Maritime Museum, London TR; E.T. Archive: Musée Carnavalet, Paris CA.
173 Bridgeman Art Library, London / New York: Hereford Cathedral TC; British Library, London: BL, DC; DK Picture Library: National Maritime Museum, London TR; AKG London / Jean-Louis Nou: BR; Ordnance Survey © Crown Copyright: BR; Royal Geographical Society Picture Library: CLb.
174 Bridgeman Art Library, London / New York: British Museum, London TC, CRb; © Michael Holford: British Museum, London TL; Images Colour Library: The Charles Walker Collection BR.
175 Bridgeman Art Library, London / New York: Archaeological Museum, Iraklion / Lauros-Giraudon BCL; DK Picture Library: Archaeological Museum, Sofia TC.
176 Ancient Art & Architecture Collection: Mike Andrews CL; Dr S Coyne BC; Bridgeman Art Library, London / New York: BL; © Michael Holford: British Museum, London TL.
177 Ancient Art & Architecture Collection: Ronald Sheridan BL; DK Picture Library: British Museum, London TCR; E.T. Archive: National Archaeological Museum, Madrid TL.
178 Robert Harding Picture Library: Robert Frerck / Odyssey / Chicago BC; © Michael Holford: British Museum, London TL; Scala, Florence: Musei Capitolini, Roma TC; Museo di Villa Giulia, Roma Cb.
179 E.T. Archive: CLA(insert); Robert Harding Picture Library: Gascoigne BL; © Michael Holford: CbR; British Museum CLA.
180 Werner Forman Archive: TL; Sonia Halliday Photographs: BL; © Michael Holford: TCRb.
181 Ancient Art & Architecture Collection: Ronald Sheridan BR; DK Picture Library: TL; Sonia Halliday Photographs: The Hatay Museum, Antioch, Turkey BL; © Michael Holford: TC.
182 Ancient Art & Architecture Collection: Ronald Sheridan CbR; DK Picture Library: British Museum, London TL; E.T. Archive: San Apollinare Nuovo, Ravenna CRA; Sonia Halliday Photographs: TR.
183 Bibliothèque Nationale de France, Paris: BC; E.T. Archive: Medieval Museum, Rome TC; © Michael Holford: British Museum, London TLb.
184 AKG London / Erich Lessing: Musée du Louvre, Paris TL; Bridgeman Art Library, London / New York: Musée Goya, Castres (PF 2826, f.106r) / Photograph: Giraudon C; E.T. Archive: Palatine Chapel, Aachen CL.
185 Ancient Art & Architecture Collection: Bridgeman Art Library, London / New York: Musée Conde, Chantilly (PE 7887, Ms. 14) TLb; © Michael Holford: Statens Historiska Museum, Stockholm CRb.
186 AKG London: Biblioteca Apostolica Vaticana, Rome TL; E.T. Archive: Templar Chapel, Cressac CL; © Michael Holford: Musée de Bayeaux C.
187 Bridgeman Art Library, London / New York: Private Collection BLA; E.T. Archive: Bibliothèque de l'Arsenal, Paris CbR; Robert Harding Picture Library: TRb.
188 AKG London: San Benedetto Monastery, Subiaco (Sacro Speco) TCRb; Ancient Art & Architecture Collection: Ronald Sheridan TL; Bridgeman Art Library, London / New York: British Library, London Cb.
189 AKG London: CRb; Robert Harding Picture Library: BC.
190 Archiv der Hansestadt Lübeck: TL; Bridgeman Art Library, London / New York: Bibliothèque Nationale de France, Paris (Fr 12420 f.71) BL.
191 AKG London / Cameraphoto: CRb; E.T. Archive: Bibliothèque Nationale de France, Paris TCRb; Scala, Florence: Museo Correr, Venezia TCLb; Santa Francesco, Prato TCL.
192 Bridgeman Art Library, London / New York: Archives Nationales, Paris / Giraudon TL; Bibliothèque Nationale de France, Paris (Fr 2643 f.165v) TCb; Robert Harding Picture Library: Simon Harris BR.
193 AKG London: Burgerbibliothek, Bern (Ms hist.helv I, 1, fol.70) BL; Robert Harding Picture Library: Wallace Collection, London TL; E.T. Archive: National Gallery of Art, Budapest BR.
194 AKG London: Stadtmuseum, Nordlingen TL; Bridgeman Art Library, London / New York: Musée de Sibiu, Rumania / Giraudon CRb; E.T. Archive: Capodimonte, Naples C.
195 Bridgeman Art Library, London / New York: British Library, London (Add 33733 f.9) C; Nationalmuseet, Copenhagen TL; Mary Evans Picture Library: CR.
196 AKG London: CL; Musée du Louvre, Paris TL; Bridgeman Art Library, London / New York: Private Collection BCR; DK Picture Library: BRA.
197 DK Picture Library: Ashmolean Museum, Oxford BC; Robert Harding Picture Library: Adam Woolfitt CRb; © Michael Holford: National Palace Museum, Taiwan BCL; Rolf Richardson BC.
198 Bridgeman Art Library, London / New York: Private Collection / Giraudon BRA; The Stapleton Collection BCR; Tretyakov Gallery, Moscow TL; By kind permission of the Earl of Leicester and the Trustees of the Holkham Estate: CLA.
199 Bildarchiv Preußischer Kulturbesitz: Kunstbibliothek Preußischer Kulturbesitz, Berlin CR; Bridgeman Art Library, London / New York: Musée Carnavalet, Paris BL.
200 Bridgeman Art Library, London / New York: Bibliothèque Nationale de France, Paris / Lauros-Giraudon TL; Musée du Louvre, Paris / Giraudon CLb; Mary Evans Picture Library: BR.
201 Bridgeman Art Library, London / New York: Musée du Louvre, Paris / Giraudon TC; E.T. Archive: Musée de Versailles CRb; Mary Evans Picture Library: BL.
202 AKG London: TR; Slg. E. Werner, Berlin TL.
203 AKG London: TCLb; E.T. Archive: Palazzo Pubblico, Siena BL; Mary Evans Picture Library: TLb, C.
204 AKG London: BL, BR; DK Picture Library: TL, CR; Corbis: Bettmann CLA; DK Picture Library: TL, CR; E.T. Archive: BR.
205 AKG London: BL, BR; DK Picture Library: TL, CR; The Science Museum, London TR.
206 By kind permission of The Trustees of The Imperial War Museum, London: CLA, CR, CRb; Topham Picturepoint: BR.
207 Corbis: Bettmann TCb; Hulton Getty: TCR; Topham Picturepoint: CRA.
208 Corbis: Bettmann BR; Hulton Getty: CR; Rex Features: Sipa-Press TL.
209 Hulton Getty: CRA; Topham Picturepoint: CLb, BC.
210 Bridgeman Art Library, London / New York: The Stapleton Collection, London BL; Corbis: CLA; Robert Hunt Library: BC.
211 Corbis: UPI / Bettmann CLb; Rex Features: BL.

212 AKG London: TL; Corbis: Jerry Cooke CLb; Hulton Getty: Keystone Munich CRA.
213 Corbis: Bettmann BLA; David King Collection: TLb; Topham Picturepoint: CR.
214 Corbis: Jean-Marc Loos/Reuters CA; Panos Pictures: Jeremy Hartley Cb; Rex Features: TL; Darryn Lyons BL.
215 Rex Features: Sipa-Press / Alexandra Boulat CLA.
216 James Davis Travel Photography: CLb; Robert Harding Picture Library: CRb, BC.
217 DK Picture Library: Danish National Library CLb(insert); Statens Historika Museum, Stockholm CLb; © Michael Holford: Science Museum, London TL.
218 Bridgeman Art Library, London / New York: (Ms Arabe 5847 f.19) BL; Bridgeman Art Library, London / New York: Bibliothèque Nationale de Cartes et Plans, Paris TL; British Library, London: (Maps 856.(6.)) BR.
219 Bridgeman Art Library, London / New York: Bibliothèque Nationale de France, Paris TR; E.T. Archive: Naval Museum, Genoa TCb; Richmond Borough Council BCL; © Koninklijke Bibliotheek, The Hague: (76 F 5: fol. 1r) CR; Royal Geographical Society Picture Library: CRb, BL.
220 Bridgeman Art Library, London / New York: Ashmolean Museum, Oxford TCRb; British Museum, London BR; Mrs James Mellaart: CL; Scala, Florence: The Iraq Museum, Baghdad TL.
221 Caroline Chapman: TRb; Robert Harding Picture Library: CRb; © Michael Holford: British Museum, London CLb.
222 AKG London / Erich Lessing: British Museum, London BR; Musée du Louvre, Paris TCR; Caroline Chapman: TL; Topham Picturepoint: TL.
223 British Museum, London: TCb; Robert Harding Picture Library: CL, CR; © Michael Holford: British Museum, London TL.
224 AKG London: National Museum of Tokyo BL; Ancient Art & Architecture Collection: Ronald Sheridan TCR; E.T. Archive: Ferrer / Wilkinson CRb.
225 Ancient Art & Architecture Collection: Ronald Sheridan TC; Bibliothèque Nationale de France, Paris BL; DK Picture Library: British Museum, London TCb; © Michael Holford: British Museum, London TL.
226 Ancient Art & Architecture Collection: Ronald Sheridan TC; Bridgeman Art Library, London / New York: British Museum, London Cb; Werner Forman Archive: Coptic Museum, Cairo TCb.
227 Bildarchiv Preußischer Kulturbesitz: C; Werner Forman Archive: BR; Robert Harding Picture Library: Ellen Rooney BL.
228 E.T. Archive: Forrester / Wilkinson TL; Victoria & Albert Museum, London BC; Robert Harding Picture Library: TCR; Peter Newark's Pictures: BL.
229 AKG London: CR; Bibliothèque Nationale de France, Paris (Add. 18866, fol.140) CLA; Bildarchiv Preußischer Kulturbesitz: Staatsbibliothek zu Berlin Preußischer Kulturbesitz Orientabteilung (Ms. Diez A.Fol.70) C; Robert Harding Picture Library: CLb.
230 Bridgeman Art Library, London / New York: Victoria & Albert Museum, London BR; Sonia Halliday Photographs: Topkapi Palace Museum, Istanbul (Ms. 3109) TL, (Ms. H1523 p.165A) CL.
231 Werner Forman Archive: CLb; Sonia Halliday Photographs: Topkapi Palace Museum, Istanbul (Ms. H.1523 p.19A) C.
232 AKG London: TL; DK Picture Library: Musée Guimet, Paris BL; Robert Harding Picture Library: BR; Oise / Lauros-Giraudon BC; Jean-Loup Charmet: TCR; By kind permission of The Trustees of The Imperial War Museum, London: BR.
233 Corbis: Bettmann / UPI TR; Hulton Getty: BLA, BCL; Royal Geographical Society Picture Library: Capt. W.I. Shakespear CR.
234 Rex Features: Keystone USA BC; Sipa-Press TL; Reuters: Ali Jasim C.
235 Corbis: Reuters CA; Rex Features: Sipa C, CRB; Frank Spooner Pictures: Eslami Rad TLB.
Frank Spooner Pictures: Eslami Rad TRb; Rex Features: Sipa-Press C, BR; Reuters: TL.
236 Eye Ubiquitous: David Cumming BC; Robert Harding Picture Library: Thomas Laird Cb; Tony Stone Images: Hugh Sitton CLb.
237 Tony Stone Images: Adam Cb, CR; (Egerton 1018 fol.335) BL; E.T. Archive: British Library TCR; Robert Harding Picture Library: C.
238 © Free Gallery of Art Washington BC; The History of Cartography, University of Wisconsin: Bharat Kala Bhavan, Varanasi TL; Professor Joseph E. Schwartzberg: CLb.
239 AKG London: TRb; (Sloane 197, fol.395v-396) CA, CR; Bridgeman Art Library, London / New York: Jim Thompson Collection CRA; Royal Geographical Society Picture Library: CbL, BL, BC.
240 British Museum, London: BR; Robert Harding Picture Library: CLb; HRH Princess Chumbhot Collection BRA; Karachi Museum, Pakistan TL, TC; Scala, Florence: New Delhi Museum, India CRb.
241 Bridgeman Art Library, London / New York: British Library, London BR; Oriental Museum, Durham University CL; Robert Harding Picture Library: BR; Adam Woolfitt TCR.
242 DK Picture Library: Ashmolean Museum, Oxford TL; Robert Harding Picture Library: BRA.
243 British Museum, London: CbL; Werner Forman Archive: Private Collection TRb; Robert Harding Picture Library: BR; Gavin Hellier CR.
244 Robert Harding Picture Library: TL; Nigel Cameron CL; A Kennet TC, C; Adam Woolfitt BC; Hutchison Library: Christine Pemberton BCR.
245 Bridgeman Art Library, London / New York: Robert Harding Picture Library: TR, CA; Bangkok National Museum, Thailand BCL; Rolf Richardson BC.
246 Ancient Art & Architecture Collection: Chebel Sotun Palace, Isfahan / Photograph: Ronald Sheridan BCL; Bridgeman Art Library, London / New York: Metropolitan Museum of Art, New York TL; Private Collection / The Stapleton Collection TCRb; Robert Harding Picture Library: Gavin Hellier CLA.
247 Bridgeman Art Library, London / New York: Private Collection / The Stapleton Collection CR, CLb; British Library, London: BR.
248 Bridgeman Art Library, London / New York: Victoria & Albert Museum, London BC; DK Picture Library: British Library, London TCRb; E.T. Archive: India Office Library BR; Zoological Society of London BL.
249 Bridgeman Art Library, London / New York: British Library, London TLb, (As10 Vol.52 ff.3 4896.cat.201 i-iv) CR; Mary Evans Picture Library: BR.
250 Corbis: UPI BL; Robert Harding Picture Library: Alain Evrard TL; Hulton Getty: CLb.
251 Hulton Getty: CL; Rex Features: Tim Page TCR; Topham Picturepoint: CRA.
252 Hulton Getty: BC; Bert Hardy TL; Frank Spooner Pictures: Gamma CL.
253 Rex Features: Sipa-Press TL; J Bright BL; Pictor International: BCL; Frank Spooner Pictures: Olivier Duffau / Gamma TR; Gamma CRA; Xinhua-Chine / Gamma TC.
254 Rex Features: Sipa-Press TL; Sipa-Press / Patrick Robert Cb, BC; Nigel Blythe CLA.
255 British Library, London: TL, CR, BR; Werner Forman Archive: National Museum, Teheran CRb; Ninnaji Temple, Kyoto: TRb.

257 Fotomas Index: CR; Réunion des Musées Nationaux Agence Photographique: Musée des Arts Asiatiques-Guimet, Paris / Photograph: Arnaudet CLb; Royal Geographical Society Picture Library: Compiled by T.G. Montgomerie from the work of Nain Singh BL.
258 Corbis: Royal Ontario Museum TL; Werner Forman Archive: Art and History Museum, Shanghai BL; Robert Harding Picture Library: Gavin Hellier CRA.
259 Bridgeman Art Library, London / New York: Tomb of Qin Shi Huang Di, Xianyang, China BL; DK Picture Library: British Museum, London C; E.T. Archive: British Museum, London TR.
260 Bridgeman Art Library, London / New York: Private Collection BR; DK Picture Library: British Museum, London TL; E.T. Archive: British Museum, London TC.
261 Corbis: Bonhams, London CR; Werner Forman Archive: Musée Cernuschi Paris C.
262 Ancient Art & Architecture Collection: Ronald Sheridan TR; Werner Forman Archive: Christian Deydier, London BCL; Collection of the National Palace Museum, Taiwan, Republic of China: BL.
263 Ancient Art & Architecture Collection: Kadokawa TLb; Ronald Sheridan CAR, BCR; Fotomas Index: BRA.
264 DK Picture Library: National Museum of Scotland, Edinburgh TL; E.T. Archive: National Museum of Tokyo CL; Robert Harding Picture Library: Nigel Blythe BR.
265 AKG London: National Museum of Tokyo BL; Ancient Art & Architecture Collection: Ronald Sheridan TR; E.T. Archive: Ferrer / Wilkinson CRb.
266 Robert Harding Picture Library: Michael J Howell TC; Collection of the National Palace Museum, Taiwan, Republic of China: TL; Philadelphia Museum of Art, Pennsylvania: Given by John T. Dorrance CR.
267 Bridgeman Art Library, London / New York: National Museum of India, New Delhi CLA; DK Picture Library: British Museum, London BL; Robert Harding Picture Library: Gavin Hellier BL.
268 Christie's Images: TL; E.T. Archive: School of Oriental and African Studies, London Cb; Peter Newark's Pictures: TL.
269 Bridgeman Art Library, London / New York: Taylor Gallery, London BR; Topham Picturepoint: CLA.
270 AKG London: TL; Bridgeman Art Library, London / New York: Archivo Municipal Town, London CL; E.T. Archive: Pratul Museum, Frankfurt Cb; © Michael Holford: Print by Kokyo BC.
271 David King Collection: CR; Smithsonian Institute: Freer Gallery of Art / Arthur M Sackler Gallery Archive / Photograph: Hsun-Ling TC.
272 Robert Hunt Library: TL; Rex Features: Sipa-Press CL; Topham Picturepoint: Associated Press Photos TCR.
273 Robert Hunt Library: BR; Topham Picturepoint: CLb.
274 Corbis: Bettmann / UPI BR; E.T. Archive: TC; David King Collection: CL; Tony Stone Images: TL.
275 Rex Features: Sipa-Press / Photograph: East News BL; Sipa-Press / Photograph: Ben Simmons CbR; Frank Spooner Pictures: Gamma / Photograph: Xinhua TR.
276 Bruce Coleman Ltd: Nicholas de Vore PC; Robert Harding Picture Library: Nick Servian CLb; Planet Earth Pictures: Frank Krahmer Cb.
278 Robert Harding Picture Library: TL; Werner Forman Archive: CL; Mitchell Library, State Library of New South Wales BR; DK Picture Library: Museum of Mankind, London TR; E.T. Archive: National Library, Canberra, Australia TL; Maritiem Museum 'Prins Hendrik', Rotterdam, The Netherlands: BCR.
279 British Library, London: CA; Coo-ee Historical Picture Library: CLb, BL; Mary Evans Picture Library: TL.
280 Bridgeman Art Library, London / New York: British Museum, London TL; Robert Harding Picture Library: Richard Ashworth C; Robert Francis TR; David Holdsworth BL.
281 © Michael Holford: British Museum, London TC; Royal Geographical Society, London CR; Peter Crawford: TRb; Robert Harding Picture Library: Geoff Renner BRA.
282 Coo-ee Historical Picture Library: TL; Corbis: Gleason's Pictorial Drawing-Room Companion BC; State Library of New South Wales: TRb.
283 Panos Pictures: Penny Tweedie TL; Tony Stone Images: Paul Chesley CRb; Topham Picturepoint: CL.
284 Bridgeman Art Library, London / New York: National Library of Australia, Canberra BCL; Robert Harding Picture Library: CLb; Tony Stone Images: Warren Bolster TL.
285 Hutchison Library: C; Science Photo Library: US Department of Energy TRb.
286 Corbis: Bettmann TL; E.T. Archive: BR; British Museum, London CbR.
287 Corbis: Underwood & Underwood CR; Mary Evans Picture Library: TR, BL; Hulton Getty: TL.

Endpapers © 1996 Visual Language.

All other images © Dorling Kindersley.
For further information see
www.dkimages.com

Dorling Kindersley Photography:
David Ashby, Geoff Brighting, Tina Chambers, Andy Crawford, Geoff Dann, Mike Dunning, Lynton Gardiner, Steve Gorton, Peter Hayman, Chas Howson, Ivor Kerslake, Dave King, Andrew McRobb, Gillie Newman, Nick Nicholls, Laurence Pordes, James Stevenson, Linda Whitwam, Peter Wilson, John Woodcock.

Dorling Kindersley would like to thank:
Alice Whitehead at Bridgeman Art Library, Ute Krebs at AKG London, Caroline Haywood and all staff at E.T. Archive, Themis Halvantzi at Werner Forman Archive, Michael Holford, all at Robert Harding Picture Library and Mark Vivian at Mary Evans Picture Library for all their assistance with picture research.